The best and most interesting thesauri are compiled by individuals, not companys like Houghton-Mifflin and Merriam-Webster. First Roget, then Rodale and McCutcheon, and now Meltzer, whose The Thinker's Thesaurus is endlessly readable and wonderfully instructive.

Robert Hartwell Fiske, author of *The Dictionary of Concise Writing*

If you often look up a word in the dictionary and find yourself still browsing in it a half hour later, then this book will lend hours of pleasure -- as well as help you preserve the highest layers of the English vocabulary.

John McWhorter, author of *The Word On The Street: Fact And Fiction About American English*

Generations have resorted to Roget when the right word did not spring to mind. Now we have a better option: a meander through Meltzer is bound to produce a robust result for those times when we cannot come up with the perfect word with conventional thesauruses.

Orin Hargraves, author of *Mighty Fine Words and Smashing Expressions*

The Thinker's Thesaurus

Peter E. Meltzer

The Thinker's Thesaurus

*Sophisticated alternatives
to common words*

Marion Street Press, Inc.
Oak Park, Illinois, USA

Library of Congress Cataloging-in-Publication Data

Meltzer, Peter, 1958-
  The thinker's thesaurus : sophisticated alternatives to
common words / by Peter Meltzer.
     p. cm.
  ISBN 0-9729937-8-9 (hardcover) -- ISBN 0-9729937-9-7
(softcover)
  1. English language--Synonyms and antonyms. I. Title.
  PE1591.M464 2005
  423'.12--dc22

                              2004030759

Cover design by Anne Locascio

ISBN 0-9729937-8-9 (hardcover)
ISBN 0-9729937-9-7 (softcover)

Printed in U.S.A.
Printing 10 9 8 7 6 5 4 3 2 1

Marion Street Press, Inc.
PO Box 2249
Oak Park, IL 60303
866-443-7987
www.marionstreetpress.com

For Thomas and Charlotte:
A father's jewels

Acknowledgments

This book was a lengthy and complex undertaking and to say that I could not have done it by myself, while clichéd, is also true. I had significant amounts of help from many people at all stages of the process on levels tangible — such as providing ideas for words and examples — and intangible — such as providing enthusiasm and moral support (particularly in the early days when people would ingenuously ask me: "Hasn't someone already written a thesaurus?"). While those who chipped in with potential new entries for the book are too numerous to mention, their contributions are known by me and are gratefully remembered.

I must express my gratitude to the incredibly talented lexicographers at the Dictionary Society of North America who were exceedingly generous to me with their time and ideas, especially Erin McKean, the editor of Verbatim, whose influence in the world of books on words and language is pandemic.

I would also like to thank the following:

■ Orin Hargraves, word-master extraordinaire, whose early belief in the need for this book and my ability to create it started the dominoes falling so as to lead to its publication.

■ My sister Lauren Meltzer and her colleagues at The Charles Press, who provided invaluable assistance on many aspects of the book, particularly the Introduction. It is always handy to have someone in the family who is already a book editor.

■ Shilpa Patel who, in addition to spending 100% of her time as an attorney at my firm, has graciously spent another 50% as an editor, consultant and all-around sounding board for the book.

■ Ed Avis, my editor at Marion Street Press, whose insightful judgments shaped every page of the book. He could not have been more helpful to me in the process and I consider myself fortunate to have worked with him.

■ My father, Dr. Lawrence Meltzer, who showed me that it is possible to be an author (in his case many times over) despite having another career.

■ My mother Helga, my sisters Lilly and Zoe, and my brother Konstantin. I am blessed to be in the same family as such wonderful and supportive people.

■ My children Thomas and Charlotte to whom this book is dedicated, and lastly my wife Deirdre whose cheerful tolerance of the immense time spent on this project exceeded all reasonable expectations. I sometimes joke with her about how lucky she is to be married to me, but of course the truth is the other way around.

word (just the right ... or phrase) *n*.: **mot juste** (French) ∎ Paging Mr. Roget — George W. [Bush] appears to have found le **mot juste** to describe everyone from his Cabinet nominees to his closest relatives. On John Ashcroft: "A good man. He's got a good heart." On Colin Powell: "A good friend and a good man." On Donald Rumsfeld: "A good man, an honorable man." On Paul O'Neill: "I look forward to having this good man by my side." On John McCain: "A good man and a fighter." On brother Jeb: "What a good man." (Amanda Bower, *Again & Again*, Time, 01-22-2001, p. 18.)

About this Thesaurus

This book had its genesis in a 1994 discussion with a group of friends and colleagues, all of whom were involved directly or indirectly in the writing profession. The issue of thesauruses arose. To a person, our reactions were virtually identical: while in theory a thesaurus is a marvelous reference aid, the reality tends to be quite different. That "eureka" moment we all hope for when consulting a thesaurus ("That's just the word I need!") occurs far too rarely. Conventional thesauruses present "le mot juste" far less frequently than they should (and never present the term "le mot juste" itself). Moreover, as a vocabulary enhancement tool, a regular thesaurus is almost useless, since the synonyms tend to be just as common as the base words.

I therefore had an ambitious (some might say foolhardy) goal: to create a new kind of thesaurus which is intended to be a genuine improvement over existing versions for the benefit of casual and serious writers alike who want to be able to use just the right word for a given occasion. One may ask: "Isn't that precisely what conventional thesauruses are for?" The answer is yes, but only in theory. The reality is that existing thesauruses suffer from two primary flaws.

The first problem is that one usually finds that no matter how many synonyms an ordinary thesaurus contains, it rarely seems to offer interesting choices. Typically the synonyms offered have already been considered and rejected before even consulting the thesaurus. This is because those synonyms, while numerous, are mostly uninteresting. The mere fact that a person owns a thesaurus means not only that they care enough about words to want to be able to find precisely the right word for the right occasion, but also, because that person cares about words, that his or her basic vocabulary is probably such that any synonyms which are of equal or lesser complexity than the base word given are generally not going to be of much use, because the user will have thought of those synonyms anyway. To address this problem, a thesaurus was needed that would contain interesting, rather than mundane, synonyms.

The second problem is that all thesauruses (other than this one) are set up by starting with only one word — the base word — and then listing a number of synonyms for that one word. In addition, they inevitably compare like word forms — adjective to adjective, noun to noun, and so forth. What if, however, the would-be synonym does not easily lend itself to a one-word base word? This can occur in several different ways.

One example of this is words which involve two distinct concepts. For example "nephew" requires reference to both "son" and to "sister" or "brother"; "claustrophobia" requires reference to both "fear" and "confined spaces." In other words, there is no one-word synonym for "nephew" or "claustrophobia." Another example is where the most logical base word/synonym comparison involves different word forms. Consider the adjective "maternal," in the sense of "maternal grandfather." If this were the synonym, what would be the most logical connecting base word? The answer is obviously "mother," but that word is a noun. Because traditional thesauruses will only list other nouns as synonyms for "mother," there is no way they can lead the user to the synonym "maternal," as simple as that word may be.

Another common problem with the single-base word system is that synonyms are sometimes included for base words in a potentially misleading or incorrect way, because of the complete inability of regular thesauruses to deal with the concept of nuance, since their base words are only one word. Take for example the word "smile." Most thesauruses will include among the synonyms for this word "grin," "smirk," "snicker" and "grimace." Each of these words means something totally different from the others yet they are invariably all listed as synonyms for "smile." Similarly, the most common definition of "elopement" is flight with a lover with the intention of getting married. However, it is obviously not a synonym for "flight" or "marriage" standing alone. Nevertheless, *Roget's International Thesaurus* (6th ed., HarperCollins, 2001), lists "flight" and "wedding" as synonyms for "elopement." "Embezzlement" is stealing something that has been entrusted to one's care. Thus, one does not break into a stranger's house and "embezzle" her belongings. Nevertheless, *Roget's International* lists "embezzle" as being a synonym for "steal" and "misuse."

How can the writers of these thesauruses get away with these types of comparisons? Easy. Because they start with the premise that the user already knows the synonyms. For example, the Foreword to *Webster's New World Thesaurus* states that "the editors asked themselves which bodies of synonymic expressions are sufficiently common so that they belong in a general reference work." Similarly, in recommending one common thesaurus, Will Weng, a former New York Times crossword puzzle editor, stated: "Every so often one finds oneself trying to think of a certain exact word, buried frustratingly in the back of the mind."[1] In other words, the user is familiar with the synonym but has simply forgotten it temporarily, and thus uses the thesaurus to jog his or her memory.

After consulting numerous thesauruses, I realized that there do not appear to be any thesauruses like this one available. On one side are all the traditional thesauruses that tend to avoid inclusion of hard words and which are limited a single base word. On the other side are the numerous word books which delight in presenting the unusual or complex words, but which do not give the user any logical system or means by which to actually find these gems, since these books are inevitably alphabetized by the hard synonym rather than by base word.[2] Thus, these kinds of books are useless as reference tools, since their whole premise is that the reader doesn't know what the synonyms mean in the first place. Presumably one reads these books for amusement only, and not as a thesaurus or any other kind of reference guide, since that would not be possible.

It was therefore my intent to create a thesaurus that would bridge the large gap

---

1. There is actually a word for not being able to remember the word you want, namely "lethologica."

2. Take for example "The Superior Person's Book of Words" (Godine, 2002) which is just one of dozens of such books available. Under the letter "N," the first five entries are "napiform," "natterjack," "naumachia," "naupathia" and "nefandous." If one ever wanted to use any of these words in lieu of some other word (which is unlikely in the first place, given their definitions), the book has no means of guiding the user to those words. A few other examples of many unusual word dictionaries which are alphabetized according to the unusual words include "Weird and Wonderful Words" (Oxford University Press, 2003), "Wordsmanship" (Verbatim, 1991), "Mrs. Byrne's Dictionary of Unusual, Obscure and Preposterous Words" (Citadel Press, 1990), and "The Logodaedalian's Dictionary" (South Carolina Press, 1989). In addition, many of the words in these books are completely obsolete and thus it would be impossible to find an actual example of them, at least to the when relying on sources more recent than the 19th century.

between these two kinds of books and give the user a logical and organized means by which to find (and then actually use) synonyms that are less mundane rather than more; that is, synonyms that users would be unlikely to consider on their own, but which nevertheless are completely legitimate words that are not archaic, obsolete, rare, dialectical, regional, outdated, or which are findable only in the most obscure reference sources. In other words, this thesaurus is *not* designed primarily to help users recall words they already know, but temporarily "buried in the back of the mind." That is the purpose of traditional thesauruses. Rather, it is designed to present words which users may have never heard of in the first place, but that hopefully will meet their exact needs.

To fill the void between conventional thesauruses and rare word books, this thesaurus contains three features, each of which make it unique (and each of which is demonstrated in the example above).

1. Nearly all of the synonyms, while completely legitimate, are harder or more sophisticated words than one would find in a regular thesaurus.

2. Because the synonyms are more interesting and generally more unusual than those found in conventional thesauruses, the entries have actual examples from current books or periodicals. The purposes of providing these examples are numerous:

   a. They demonstrate how the word is properly used.

   b. They to show that these are "real" words in actual current usage by real writers in the real world, and not merely obsolete words which are never used anymore. In other words, besides showing proper usage, the examples serve as an anticipatory rebuttal to those who tend to scoff at harder words and ask rhetorically: "Who ever uses these words anyway? Aren't they obsolete?" (These questions are addressed in more detail below — see "In Defense of the Hard Word."). Moreover, from reading the examples, one can tell that in each instance, the word in question is being used within the natural flow of the passage; i.e., the author is not straining to use the word or artificially forcing it on the reader.

   c. They bring the particular synonym to life and to allow the user to focus on and consider the use of that synonym more strongly than if the word was one among dozens which may be buried in a conventional thesaurus (even putting aside the fact that most of the synonyms herein won't be found in other thesauruses anyway).

   In sum, it is hoped that giving actual examples of the synonyms makes for a more interesting presentation and will make the word easier to remember the next time it might be useful for the user.

3. Finally, I use what I call a "Clarifier" in about 75 percent of the entries herein. This allows for the use of thousands of words as synonyms which either cannot be found at all in other thesauruses, or are used imprecisely. The technique is designed to address the problem with ordinary thesauruses, which are limited to single-word base words. How the Clarifier works is described in Section III below.

Because of the selectivity in the use of synonyms, the average base word in this thesaurus is, by design, not followed by the 10 or 20 (boring) synonyms which accompany base words in most thesauruses. Instead, there are typically only 1 or 2 synonyms for each base word. Let's use a few examples to show how this thesaurus works. There are two kinds of entries contained herein, the single base-word entry and the Clarifier entry.

The Single Base Word Entry

The first type of entry is the use of a single base word to define the synonym. There is no accompanying Clarifier. These entries have the same format as conventional thesauruses, but the synonyms are more interesting than those found in other thesauruses. Take the word "lethargy." Conventional thesauruses suggest synonyms such as "apathy," "idleness," "inactivity," "passivity" and "listlessness." It is likely that if readers were looking for a synonym for "lethargy," they would have already considered those synonyms on their own. Thus, this thesaurus offers the more interesting alternative "hebetude," together with an example.

> **lethargy** *n*.: **hebetude**. ∎ [Bend, Oregon is] a city with a bike rack on every car, a canoe in every garage and a restless heart in every chest. While too many Americans slouch toward a terminal funk of **hebetude** and sloth, Bendians race ahead with toned muscles, wide eyes and brains perpetually wired on adrenaline. (Author not given, *Wild Rides in the Heart of Central Oregon–Bent Out of Shape in Bend*, The Washington Times, 08-11-2001.)

Another word for "cheerful"? Traditional thesauruses offer "gay," "merry," "joyful" and "happy." But how about "eupeptic" as a more interesting alternative?

> **cheerful** *adj*.: **eupeptic**. ∎ [Artist Keith] Haring has little to express beyond a vague pleasantness, a whiff of happiness. Any attempt at true feeling is immediately deflected and thwarted by a blithely **eupeptic** tone that was intrinsic to his art: his AIDS image seems as innocuous as his radiant babies and his barking dogs. (James Gardner, *Radiant Baby*, National Review, 10-27-1997, p. 58.)

Other typical examples follow. Every one has an actual example in the thesaurus to show that these are not archaic words, but rather are words in current usage.

In a traditional thesaurus:
> **basic** *adj*.: **elementary, introductory**

In The Thinker's Thesaurus:
> **basic** *adj*.: **abecedarian**. ∎ [Muhammad Ali] expressed himself in energetic, if **abecedarian**, rhymes. Listen to this excerpt from "Song of Myself": "Yes, the crowd did not dream — When they laid down their money — That they would see — A total eclipse of the Sonny. I am the greatest!" (Keith Mano, *Still the Greatest*, National Review, 11-09-1998, p. 59.)

In a traditional thesaurus:
> **tattle** (on) *v.i.*: **inform, squeal**

In The Thinker's Thesaurus:
> **tattle** (on) *v.i.*: **peach**. ∎ A few days ago a rumor spread like fire through a straw rick that "Deep Throat," world's most famous news source, was [Alexander Haig]. What made this story far-fetched was not that Haig had been a big shot in the Nixon White House in Watergate days, so wouldn't have **peached** on his boss [but rather] on literacy grounds [since] he is utterly incapable of making anything perfectly clear once he starts to talk. (Russell Baker, *Tiresome News Dept.*, The New York Times, 10-07-1989, p. 23.)

In a traditional thesaurus:
> **harmful** *adj.*: **damaging, detrimental**

In The Thinker's Thesaurus:
> **harmful** *adj.*: **nocent**. ▮ [W]ith respect to the disastrous imbalance in trade between the U.S. and the rest of the world, I would urge the administration and Congress to consider alternatives to import limitations. Besides the **nocent** effects on world trade that such limitations would cause, there is the very real threat of imposing exports of capital back to Europe thus completely upsetting the American capital markets. (John Murphy, *Fighting the Trade Imbalance*, The Chicago Tribune, 10-31-1985, p. 26.)

In a traditional thesaurus:
> **laughable** *adj.*: **funny, amusing**

In The Thinker's Thesaurus:
> **laughable** *adj.*: **risible** [As with the word "laughable" itself, this word is sometimes used in the straightforward sense of the word, but is more frequently used pejoratively, as in "his argument was so ridiculous, it was laughable."]. ▮ By endorsing Howard Dean before a single vote has been cast [in the primaries], Al Gore has done Democrats hoping for a victory next November a true disservice. ... [I]t's hard to say what was more **risible** about Gore's remarks: His claim that he respected the prerogative of caucus and primary voters or his suggestion to the other candidates that they should "keep their eyes on the prize" and eschew attacks on the front-runner. (Scott Lehigh, *Gore Hurts Democrats with Premature Nod*, The Boston Globe, 12-12-2003, p. A35.)

In a traditional thesaurus:
> **redundancy** *n.*: **repetition, duplication**

In The Thinker's Thesaurus:
> **redundancy** *n.*: **pleonasm**. ▮ It was, after all, public officials who gave us "safe haven" during the Persian Gulf War. Someone apparently grafted the "safe" from "safe harbor" (not all harbors are safe) onto "haven" (by definition, a safe place). The creation of this obnoxious **pleonasm** ... illustrates the bureaucrat's familiar combination of self-importance, pretension, and ignorance. (John E. McIntyre, *Words That Survive the Test of Time*, The Christian Science Monitor, 12-30-1999, p. 11.)

In a traditional thesaurus:
> **chat** *v.i.*: **talk, converse, discuss**

In The Thinker's Thesaurus:
> **chat** *v.i.*: **confabulate**. ▮ The hotel, on a highway outside Richmond, the state capital of Virginia, braced itself for [boxing promoter Don King's] arrival, as for that of a hurricane. In the lobby his minions **confabulated** in blobs: roly-poly men like waddling molecules, their bangles jangling, their pinky rings glinting, walkie-talkies jutting from their polyester rumps. (Peter Conrad, *The Joy of Slavery*, Independent on Sunday, 03-10-1996, p. 4.)

In short, with regard to the single base word entries, this thesaurus is unique not because other thesauruses won't have the same base words, but because they typically won't have the same synonyms.

The Clarifier Entry

The second type of entry, which is not found in any traditional thesaurus, involves the use of a base word accompanied by a Clarifier. In this case, the base word may not be, by itself, a synonym for the entry, but rather the most likely word the user might be expected to consult to find the synonym. The intent is that the base word, when combined with the Clarifier, will accurately yield the synonym. About 75 percent of the entries herein contain a Clarifier.

The use of the Clarifier is essential to this thesaurus since there are so many wonderful words in the English language which simply do not easily lend themselves to a one-word synonym, and which are not accessible without the Clarifier. In fact, this is one of the primary limitations of even the most compendious standard thesauruses. There are essentially three different occasions in which a Clarifier is necessary, and each of them clearly demonstrates the shortcoming of ordinary thesauruses. These are as follows:

1. The Use of a Clarifier to Provide More Exact Definitions or to Show Nuances in Words

As virtually all thesaurus introductions point out, in a technical sense, there is rarely such a thing as an "exact" synonym. Thus, when using a single word to compare both the base word and the synonym, the base word and the synonym will often not mean the exact same thing. With the Clarifier, however, it is far easier to arrive at a more precise definition for the synonym, since we are no longer limited to a single base word. Let's consider just a few of the numerous examples in this thesaurus to see how this problem is resolved now. The word "malversation" means wrongdoing, but not just any wrongdoing. It means wrongdoing in public office. Let's put aside the fact that "malversation" would rarely appear in a regular thesaurus in the first place, despite being a perfectly legitimate word. Even if it did, that thesaurus could only offer the following: **wrongdoing** *n*.: **malversation**. That comparison would be faulty, however, because unless one is in public office, one cannot commit malversation. The example in this thesaurus is as follows:

> **wrongdoing** (in public office) *n*.: **malversation**. ∎ A third charge is that [President Clinton's first-term national security adviser Anthony] Lake is guilty of **malversation**, the evidence being a token $5,000 fine he was assessed by the Justice Department for failing to sell several stock holdings promptly. (Jacob Heilbrunn, *Dr. Maybe Heads for the CIA*, The New Republic, 03-24-1997.)

The word "neologism" means a word, phrase or expression, but not just any kind. Thus, a regular thesaurus, even if it contained the word in the first place, which it would not, could not properly list it as a synonym for "word," "phrase" or "expression."

> **word** (new ..., phrase or expression) *n*.: **neologism**. ∎ Back during Watergate, the President's men were always having to announce that he had "misspoke himself," an odd **neologism** that made it sound as though Nixon had just wet his pants. Just once it would be nice to hear a White House press secretary say, "The President made a faux pas." (Christopher Buckley, *Hoof In Mouth*, Forbes FYI, 05-04-1998, p. 31)

"Aestivate" (or "estivate") is a synonym for "laze," but one would not "aestivate" by lying in the snow:

> **laze** (around during the summer) *v.i.*: **aestivate** (or **estivate**). ■ Above all, my children **aestivate**. From May to September their life is a langorous stroll from pool to hammock to beach to barbecue. Their biggest challenges are ice creams that melt before the first lick, and fireflies that resist capture in jam jars. (Gerald Baker, *The Long Hot Summer*, Financial Times [London], 07-12-2003.)

One of the definitions of "virago" is a strong and courageous woman. But clearly, it is not a synonym for "woman" or "courageous" standing alone. With the Clarifier, this is not a problem:

> **woman** (who is strong and courageous) *n.*: **virago**. ■ Feminists don't like strong women because too many **viragos** would put them out of business. To prosper they need a steady supply of women who exemplify the other V-word, "victim." (Florence King, *The Misanthrope's Corner, [Female Misogyny]*, National Review, 03-10-1997, p. 64.)[3]

Next, consider the word "nocturne," which means a painting of a night scene. A standard thesaurus would obviously not list the word as a synonym for "painting," because that word would fail to convey the far more specific definition of "nocturne." However, with the help of the Clarifier, we have the following:

> **painting** (dealing with evening or night) *n.*: **nocturne**. ■ Making art outdoors on misty autumn evenings and brisk winter nights has its ups and downs for painter Mike Lynch and photographer Chris Faust, whose serene show of poetic nightscapes opens today at the Minneapolis Institute of Arts. [Faust] had admired Lynch's **nocturnes** for nearly 30 years, having first seen them when he was still in high school. (Mary Abbe, *Night Moves / Photographer Chris Faust and Painter Mike Lynch Do Their Best Work on the Third Shift*, Minneapolis Star Tribune, 12-15-2000, p. 12.)

Finally, the Clarifier is also useful to arrive at a closer match for the synonyms, particularly where the synonym involves a nuance. This can be a particular failing in conventional thesauruses, which may well contain the synonyms, but which can lead the user astray because the nuance is not provided. Indeed, nuances are a completely foreign concept to conventional thesauruses because they necessarily require more than one base word to explain the synonym accurately.[4] Thus, the issue here is not whether the synonyms in question can be found in a regular thesaurus, but whether they can lead to incorrect usage due

---

3. At the risk of stating the obvious, all examples used in this thesaurus were chosen solely for their effectiveness in conveying the meaning of the given word and never for editorial content. Absolutely no opinion is expressed on any of the editorial opinions contained in the examples in this thesaurus, of which there are many.

4. The creators of most thesauruses are well aware of this inherent flaw in their "one word to one word" structure, particularly where the words are not familiar. In their introduction, they always warn the readers to use the thesauruses with caution and to use them in conjunction with a dictionary. As stated in one: "The nature of language and the behavior of words defy precision. ..." And so they do — particularly when one is trying to compare one base word with one synonym. The Clarifier helps to supply that precision.

to a lack of a Clarifier. For example, most thesauruses use the word "fecund" as a synonym for "prolific." While this is not necessarily inaccurate, it does not reflect that the closest synonym for "fecund" is "fertile." Thus, while a person or animal who has given birth to many offspring may be fecund, it would certainly raise an eyebrow to say that Babe Ruth was a "fecund" home run hitter.

> **prolific** (esp. as in fertile) *adj.*: **fecund** (*v.t.*: **fecundate**). ▪ The manatee population continues to grow despite the few that are killed in boating accidents, just as our deer populations continue to thrive despite the deer that are struck on the highways. Manatees are not particularly **fecund** animals, but they have no natural predators. (Frank Sargeant, *Manatees Are Not Endangered Species*, The Tampa Tribune, 09-13-2000, p. 3.)

Consider next the relatively common verb "keen." Virtually every thesaurus will include it as a synonym for "cry," without elaboration. Thus, if one is not familiar with the word, that person may reasonably conclude that a baby who is crying is "keening," but of course this would be an inaccurate use of the word:

> **cry** (in lament for the dead) *v.i.*: **keen**. ▪ When word spread through the convent, recalls one nun, "Everybody rushed to [the Mother Teresa's] room. They were all around her, wailing and hugging the Mother's body." The sisters' **keening** was heard by the communists, whose party headquarters are next door, and they tipped off journalists that Teresa had died. (Tim Mcgirk, *Religion: "Our Mother Is Gone!" In a Lavish Ceremony That Mother Teresa Would Have Scorned, Calcutta and the Rest of the World Bid a Touching Farewell to an Angel of Mercy*, Time International, 09-22-1997, p. 54.)

To have a "sinecure," one must be employed or hold an office, but attempting to make that word a synonym for "occupation" or "office holder" will quickly lead to trouble in most cases. Thus, it is impossible to list "sinecure" as a correct synonym for any single word in a conventional thesaurus.

> **occupation** (requiring little work but paying an income) *n.*: **sinecure**. ▪ [After] nearly ten years in government service, where everything is geared to the lowest common denominator, I find it refreshing to have work that rewards initiative and effort. Certainly I would be happy to have a **sinecure** again, but I am no longer brokenhearted that I left one. (Lars Eighner, *Travels With Lizbeth*, St. Martin's Press [1993], p. 124.)

The verb "peculate" is sometimes listed as a synonym for "steal," yet one would not accuse a child of "peculating" from the cookie jar.

> **steal** (as in embezzle) *v.t., v.i.*: **peculate**. ▪ [The Mazda] Miata gets passersby smiling and talking. ... Other conspicuous cars are costly and imposing and draw hate waves, as they are intended to. Decent householders glare, knowing you couldn't own the thing unless you were a drug dealer or a **peculating** [bureaucrat]. (John Skow, *Living: Miatific Bliss in Five Gears, This is Definitely Not Your Father's Hupmobile*, Time, 10-02-1989, p. 91.)

The adjective "fatuous" is often listed as a synonym for "foolish," yet forgetting one's wallet at home would not be properly termed a "fatuous" mistake.

foolish (in a smug or complacent manner) *adj.*: **fatuous**. ∎ "Jerry Garcia destroyed his life on drugs," Rush Limbaugh fearlessly proclaimed. You don't have to advocate heroin addiction or alcoholism to feel that all this moralistic fury is inanely misdirected. Nothing is more **fatuous** than to indict some performer for his failure to conform to the prescribed virtues of the "role model." Smug, self-satisfied, sanctimonious, this line of thinking fails first of all to acknowledge the true complexities of human existence. (John Taylor, *Live and Let Die: In Praise of Mickey, Jerry, and the Reckless Life [Jerry Garcia and Mickey Mantle]*, Esquire, 12-01-1995, p. 120.)

Sometimes a conventional thesaurus will provide a synonym which, due to its lack of a Clarifier, is nearly the opposite of the base word. For example, a "philosophaster" is one who pretends to be a philosopher but is not truly (or is a bad one). It is a derogatory term which may be used when, for example, an actor or athlete gives his views on the world which, in the view of the writer, are frivolous. And yet, "philosophaster" — if included in a regular thesaurus at all — is generally given as a synonym for "philosopher," as if to suggest to Aristotle was a philosophaster.

philosopher (bad ..., or one who pretends to be a ...) *n.*: **philosophaster**. ∎ Reagan won the 1980 and 1984 debates and elections because he spoke plain sense to the American people. Simple phrases. Common words. Plainstuff. Broken sentences. So what? That's how normal people speak. ... In contrast, Carter and Mondale spoke more in the highfalutin' lingo our professors and other **philosophasters** love. (Author not given, *Silliness About Senility*, The Orange County Register, 12-27-1987, p. G4.)

With words such as "fecund," "keen," "sinecure," and "peculate," the issue is not whether they would be contained in an ordinary thesaurus, but whether the ordinary thesaurus could easily lead the user astray in attempting to use those words correctly, due to their failure to include a Clarifier to explain the nuances in these words.

Finally, to demonstrate more emphatically this particular benefit of the Clarifier, consider just the words "woman" and "women." For synonyms, most thesauruses give us "lady, dame, matron, gentlewoman, maid, spinster, debutante, nymph, virgin, girl, and old woman." While it is unlikely that a user would misuse any of these synonyms, since they are all simple, the lack of a Clarifier again points out one of the flaws of the conventional thesaurus, namely that virtually all of these synonyms have very different meanings, and yet they are all equated to "woman." In contrast, this thesaurus gives 32 different synonyms using "woman" as a base word:

woman (of or like an old ...) *adj.*: **anile**
woman (who is old and ugly) *n.*: **beldam**
woman (with scholarly or literary interests) *n.*: **bluestocking**
woman (hired to do cleaning work) *n.*: **charwoman**
woman (who is charming and seductive) *n.*: **Circe**
woman (old and ugly) *n.*: **crone**
woman (who is married) *n.*: **feme covert**
woman (single ..., whether divorced, widowed or never married) *n.*: **feme sole**
woman (who is coarse and abusive) *n.*: **fishwife**
woman (girl or young ... who is impish or playful) *n.*: **gamine** [French]
woman (regarded as ugly, repulsive or terrifying) *n.*: **gorgon**
woman (French working-class young ...) *n.*: **grisette** [French]

woman (regarded as vicious and scolding) *n.*: **harridan**

woman (beautiful and alluring ...) *n.*: **houri** [French]

woman (young ... who is high-spirited or boisterous) *n.*: **hoyden**

woman (with whom one is in love or has intimate relationship) *n.*: **inamorata**

woman (who is scheming and evil) *n.*: **jezebel**

woman (of a ... who is stately and regal, esp. tending towards voluptuous) *adj.*: **Junoesque**

woman (frenzied or raging ...) *n.*: **maenad**

woman (who is head of a household) *n.*: **materfamilias** [Latin]

woman (who hates men) *n.*: **misandrist**

woman (state of being a ...) *n.*: **muliebrity**

woman (of or relating to a ... who has never given birth) *adj.*: **nulliparous**

woman (who is pregnant for the first time or has had only one child) *n.*: **primipara**

woman (relating to a ... right after childbirth) *adj.*: **puerperal**.

woman (right after childbirth) *n.*: **puerperium**

woman (who is slender and graceful) *n.*: **sylph**

woman (who is a shrew) *n.*: **termagant**

woman (condition of a ... having masculine tendencies) *n.*: **viraginity**

woman (who is strong and courageous) *n.*: **virago**

woman (shrewish ...) *n.*: **vixen**

woman (who is a shrew) *n.*: **Xanthippe**

These examples, and thousands of others in the thesaurus, show how the Clarifier is used to provide more exact synonyms for base words or to show nuances in words in a manner than cannot be duplicated in conventional thesauruses.

2. When the Base Word and Synonym Are Different Word Forms

Ordinarily, thesauruses will always compare identical word forms: verb to verb, adjective to adjective, and so on. But what happens when the best base word for a given synonym is a different word form, as is often the case? Clarifiers are extremely useful for this purpose. For example, suppose the user wanted to use an adjective meaning "like a lion." Because "lion" is a noun, the synonyms in regular thesauruses — though numerous— will also be nouns, since they have no means to allow the switching of word forms. However, in this thesaurus, one will find the following entry:

> **lions** (of, relating to or characteristic of) *adj.*: **leonine**. ∎ [The TV show "Lions" is] nowhere near the scope of the Disney classic The African Lion but includes some intriguing familial disputes — like an episode of a **leonine** soap opera. (Susan Reed, *Picks & Pans: Video*, People, 05-29-1989, p. 20.)

Here the Clarifier allows an adjectival synonym to be listed next to a base word which is a noun, and it also gives the user an easy and logical reference to a useful word which would not be found in most thesauruses.

The same is true for virtually any occasion where the user is looking for an adjective which is "of, relating to, characteristic of, or resembling" a particular noun. A conventional thesaurus is ill-equipped to make these connections because they do not change word forms, even if the synonyms are not necessarily unusual, such as "leonine." Thus, the following types of entries will not and cannot be found in other thesauruses, and for each of them there is an example given:

clay (relating to, resembling or containing) *n.*: **argillaceous**
death (of, relating to or resembling...) *adj.*: **thanatoid**
deer (of, relating to or resembling) *adj.*: **cervine**
dreams (of, relating to or suggestive of) *adj.*: **oneiric**
evening (of, relating to or occurring in) *adj.*: **vespertine**
garlic (characteristic of ... or onion) *adj.*: **alliaceous**
kinds (of all ...) *adj.*: **omnifarious**
lakes (of, or occurring in ... or ponds) *adj.*: **limnetic**
mind (of, relating to, or understood by the ...) *adj.*: **noetic**
mother (of, relating to or derived from name of) *adj.*: **matronymic**
name (of, relating to or explaining a ...) *adj.*: **onomastic**
old age (of or relating to ...) *adj.*: **gerontic**
play (of, relating to, or connoting) *adj.*: **ludic**
wealth (of or relating to the gaining of ...) *adj.*: **chrematistic**
wedding (of or relating to a ...) *adj.*: **hymeneal**
wind (of, relating to, caused by or carried by) *adj.*: **eolian**
wine (of, relating to or made with) *n.*: **vinous**
worms (of, relating to, resembling or caused by) *adj.*: **vermicular**

The Clarifier works equally well when converting from adjectives to nouns. Consider the word "milquetoast," not a particularly unusual word. Although a noun, because it refers to a kind of person, the essence of the word is an adjective, namely "timid" (or similar words such as "meek," "shy" or "unassertive"). Once again, the conventional thesaurus is unable to lead the user to the noun "milquetoast," because it must pass through an adjective to do so. One can look up "shy" and "timid" in a Clarifier-less thesaurus, but those will only yield similar-meaning adjectives. The Clarifier again solves the problem:

> **timid** (and unassertive person) *n.*: **milquetoast**. ∎ [Warren Buffet]: "Mergers will be motivated by very good considerations. There truly are synergies in a great many mergers. But whether there are synergies or not, they are going to keep happening. You don't get to be the CEO of a big company by being a **milquetoast.** You are not devoid of animal spirits." (Brent Schlender, *The Bill & Warren Show — What Do You Get When You Put a Billionaire Buddy Act in Front of 350 Students? $84 Billion of Inspiration*, Fortune, 07-20-1998, p. 48.)

Have you heard of a "bashi-bazouk"? I'm guessing not, legitimate though it is. It's a person (i.e., a noun), but its essence is someone who is undisciplined and uncontrollable (i.e., an adjective). Obviously a regular thesaurus could not put it as a synonym for "undisciplined" (and in fact won't have it as a synonym for any other word either). But in this thesaurus:

> **undisciplined** (and uncontrollable person) *n.*: **bashi-bazouk** [Turkish. Derives from the irregular, undisciplined, mounted mercenary soldiers of the Ottoman army]. ∎ I admit it: I cut through. To get ... to my daughter's school, I drive through residential streets in Homeland. ... This commuter traffic does not please residents of Homeland, to whom apparently, we motorists on our way to school and work are a crowd of **bashi-bazouks** galloping over the hill to plunder their houses and slaughter their cattle. (John McIntyre, *Cruising Through Homeland*, The Baltimore Sun, 01-18-1999, p. 13A.)

Finally, the Clarifier can also be useful to switch a verb to an adjective:

> **persuading** (as in urging someone to take a course of action) *adj.*: **hortatory**.
> ▮ [Writer Meg Greenfield] loved argument and continued a tradition under which [Washington] Post editorials avoided **hortatory** calls to action in favor of making points by marshaling facts. (J.Y. Smith, *Editorial Editor Meg Greenfield Dies; For More Than 30 Years, Opinion Writer Honed Post's Views*, The Washington Post, 05-14-1999, p. A1.)

In short, on almost any occasion when the most likely base word a user would look up to find the right synonym is a different word form from the synonym, the Clarifier makes it possible.

3. The Use of Clarifiers When a Synonym Involves Two Distinct Concepts

Many words in the English language cannot be included in thesauruses that only compare single base words to single synonyms because the synonyms actually involve two distinct concepts that cannot possibly be conveyed with a single base word. Say a person has an abnormal fear of dirt or contamination, which is called "mysophobia." The single base word thesauruses cannot list it under "fear" (because it relates to a specific kind of fear) nor under "dirt" or "contamination" (because it obviously is not a synonym for those words). The Clarifier solves this problem:

> **dirt** (abnormal fear of) *n.*: **mysophobia**. SEE FEAR

> **fear** (of dirt or contamination) *n.*: **mysophobia**. ▮ Dear Ann: My wife has developed an obsession for clean hands and wears cotton gloves constantly, even at mealtimes. She is also afraid to shake hands with anyone or even hold my hand. ... Dear Concerned: Your wife has **mysophobia**, which is an obsessive-compulsive disorder. This condition is not all that rare. (Ann Landers, *Ann Landers*, Newsday, 11-16-1993, p. 80.)

Consider next the word "malinger," again a relatively common verb meaning the faking of a sickness or illness in order to avoid work. But what one base word could be used to come up with this synonym? None. Certainly not "sick" or "ill." The use of the verbs "pretend" or "shirk" get closer, but without the Clarifier, no one could really suggest that those verbs, by themselves, could be considered synonyms for "malinger." The fact is that there is no one word that will do the trick since one needs both the concepts of pretending and being sick to lead to "malinger." In this thesaurus, the user can be lead to "malinger" through both roads:

> **sickness** (pretend to have a ... or other incapacity to avoid work) *v.i.*: **malinger**. SEE SHIRK

> **shirk** (work by pretending to be sick or incapacitated) *v.i.*: **malinger**. ▮ Players are regarded [by team owners] as overpaid louts who greedily want more than they deserve. ... When a player is injured, he is suspected of **malingering** if he doesn't return to action immediately — unless the bone is sticking through the meat. (Ron Mix, *So Little Gain for the Pain: Striking NFL Players Deserve Much, Much More*, Sports Illustrated, 10-19-1987, p. 54.)

How about hatred of women (misogyny) or men (misandry)? By now, the reader gets the point that although words such as "misogyny" are not unusual, there is no way they could be found in a typical thesaurus. For the less common word "misandry," the entries are as follows:

men (hatred of ...) *n.*: **misandry**. SEE HATRED

hatred (of men) *n.*: **misandry**. ▪ I was shocked and horrified by your cover story, not only because of the recent rash of wife and child murders, but also by the strong suggestion that it is in the biological nature of males to be violent and abusive. ... I suppose we can now expect another wave of **misandry** in this country such as the one that followed the Montreal Massacre by Marc Léépine. (Author not given, *Letters: Vikings and Aboriginals*, Maclean's, 08-28-2000, p. 4.)

Combination Words

These are simply words that combine two or all three of the foregoing characteristics of the Clarifier words and include many of the most interesting words, none of which can be approached in an ordinary thesaurus. As always, the actual examples, showing "real world" usages, show that these are legitimate words and not archaic words from some bygone era.

The words range from the serious ...

pessimism (world-weariness or sentimental ... over the world's problems) *adj.*: **Weltschmerz** [German]. ▪ [There appears to be] an unprecedented prevalence of pessimism about the future. The nation appears to be trudging gloomily on its daily round burdened with mental sandwich-boards bearing the doomiest of legends. On cursory inspection, there is little unusual in this nationwide outbreak of **Weltschmerz**: it is the business of polls to point up dissatisfactions and the business of political parties to promise to put them right. (*A Fearful Look to the Future*, The Scotsman, 06-13-1995, p. 10.)

good vs. evil (philosophy which divides the world into ...) *n.*: **manichaeism** (*adj.*: **manichean**). ▪ Lanz and his followers were obsessed by homoerotic notions of a **manichean** struggle between the heroic and creative 'blond' race and a race of predatory 'beast-men' who preyed on the 'blond' women with animal lust and bestial instincts that were corrupting and destroying mankind and its culture. (Kershaw, *Hitler*, Norton [1998], p. 50.)

to the silly ...

nose-picking *n.*: **rhinotillexomania**. ▪ University of Wisconsin-Madison researchers, fighting ignorance, have done a study on **rhinotillexomania**. And not a moment too soon, either. ... [They] gave a questionnaire to 1,200 people, with questions like, "What finger do you use?" and "How often do you find yourself looking at what you have removed?" And thus man's knowledge advances, a booger at a time. (Doug Robarchek, *Alcohol May Cause Brain Damage*, Charlotte Observer [North Carolina], 10-19-2000.)

misunderstanding (of what you think you heard) *n.*: **mondegreen** [derives from Sylvia Wright, who as a child heard the Scottish ballad "The Bonny Earl of Murray" and had believed that one stanza went: "Ye Highlands and Ye Lowlands, Oh where hae you been? They hae slay the Earl of Murray,

And Lady Mondegreen." Wright thought that Lady Mondegreen had been killed, but actually they had slain the Earl of Murray and laid him on the green]. ▪ It's easy to commit a **mondegreen**. You hear Glen Campbell sing, "Rhinestone Cowboy" and you think he's saying "Limestone Cowboy." ... Or you think the song "Guantanamera" is about a "One Ton Tomato.." .. [Or that Paul Simon is singing:] "When I think back on all the crafts [as opposed to crap] I learned in high school." (David Chartrand, *Vote for Me If You Want Red Cologne!* The Kansas City Star, 01-25-2004.)

rear end (having a nicely proportioned ...) *adj.*: **callipygian**. ▪ Are chopped-up celebrities worth more than whole regular people? You betcha. ... **[C]allipygian** singer/actress Jennifer Lopez insured her bodacious back end for a tidy $300,000,000 (and her entire body for $1 billion). (Melissa August, *Notebook: The $400 Million Celebrity*, Time, 12-20-1999, p. 32.)

and everything in between ...

contradiction (in terms or ideas) *n.*: **antilogy**. ▪ "Travel consumer." The juxtaposition of terms rankles. To consume means, variously, "to eat up ... waste or squander ... destroy totally or ravage." If travel ideally is a productive and compassionate activity — nurturing both for individual and for cultures as they meet and mingle — how can we so blithely use such a blatant **antilogy**? (Jim Molnar, *To Consume, or Not to Consume? A Question for Every Traveler*, The Seattle Times, 08-20-1995, p. K1.)

conservatism (as in hatred or fear of anything new or different) *n.*: **misoneism** (person holding this view: **misoneist**). ▪ With predictable corporate **misoneism** ... the [music] industry anointed Jet [as the next hot rock band] not for their singularity, but their overfamiliarity. It's a neat execution of a tried and true formula: a faithful and loving synthesis of classic Stones, AC/DC, the Who and Kinks-era rock, put together by four young guys who love what they're playing, play well and look the part. (Kelsey Munro, *The Formula Works: Humming Along To An Overfamiliar Tune*, Sydney Morning Herald, 07-22-2003.)

leave (hurriedly or secretly) *v.t.*: **absquatulate**. ▪ [Jackie Gleason's] Mother Mae was a rosary addict. Father Herb worked in the death claims department of a small insurance firm, drank like a culvert and **absquatulated** when Jackie was 9, leaving Mae on her uppers. ("He was as good a father," Jackie later quipped, "as I've ever known.") (Brad Darrach, *A Fond Goodbye to the Great One*, People, 07-13-1987, p. 94.)

superficial (knowledge of a subject while pretending to be learned) *n.*: **sciolism**. ▪ [T]alk-show hosts [sit] on their almighty thrones [with their] fingers on the cut-off buttons ready to spring into action at the slightest hint of statements that could expose the hosts' shallowness. ... I feel that if host stations were, by law, forced to allow time for rebuttals by individuals or groups ... unfairly attacked through this medium, most hosts would rapidly seek work elsewhere, unable to face certain exposure of their **sciolism** and hypocrisy. (Jean Paquette [letter writer], *Few Mental Giants?* The Gazette [Montreal, Quebec], 10-11-1996.)

Finally, where I felt that an explanation as to the word's derivation or usage would be helpful or informative, that is included as well.

retort (clever ... that one thinks of after the moment has passed) *n.*: **esprit d'escalier** [French; roughly the "wit of the staircase," as in the thought that comes on the staircase as one is leaving]. ▮ Proselytizing for Jehovah's Witnesses during last Sunday's Vikings game wasn't the smoothest call Prince has ever made. [He knocked on the door of a Jewish woman named Rochelle:] "It was so bizarre, you would have just laughed," she said. The perfect **esprit d'escalier** came to Rochelle after Prince left: "If I showed up at Paisley [Park], would you let me in your front door to talk about Judaism?" (Cheryl Johnson, *I-witness News: Visit from Prince; Proselytizing Pop Star Knocks on Previously Committed Door*, Star Tribune [Minneapolis, MN], 10-12-2003.)

panic *n.*: **Torschlusspanik** [German. This word means literally "gate-closing panic," as in not wanting to be the last one left before the gate closes, or having the feeling that life's opportunities may be passing one by, and is used in a myriad of figurative ways including: (1) for both men and women, a midlife crisis; (2) for women, the sense that one's biological clock is ticking; (3) at an auction, the sense that one must have one of the last pieces of a collection being sold; and (4) in a financial panic, such as when there is a run on a bank. The example used here is somewhat more literal, but the concept is clear.] ▮ The idea for the [Berlin] Wall is credited to Walter Ulbricht, leader of the GDR, who had told a press conference in June 1961: "No one intends building a wall." No one took the hint. But with so many East Germans gripped with **Torschlusspanik** — the rush to escape before the door was finally shut (30,415 arrived in West Berlin in July 1961...) — the authorities had to do something drastic. (Alan Taylor, *The Wall to End All Walls*, Scotland on Sunday, 10-31-1999, p. 14.)

taste (as in personal preference) *n.*: **de gustibus** [Latin, often used as part of the expression "de gustibus non est disputandum," as in "there is no disputing about taste." This phrase is sometimes used pejoratively, as in questioning the taste of others, and sometimes not, as in merely pointing out that everyone has their own opinion.] ▮ Two of the most traditional approaches [determining what goes on TV are paternalism, which] derives its authority from the conviction that culture is all about providing the public with what it needs rather than what it wants [and populism, which] defers meekly to the relativistic assumption that **de gustibus** non est disputandum; it does not so much judge quality as merely rubberstamp the ratings. (Graham McCann, *How to Define the Indefinable: Television*, Financial Times [London], 03-26-2003.)

conformity (marked by insistence on rigid ... to a belief, system or course of action without regard to individual differences) *adj.*: **procrustean** (*n*: **Procrustean bed**) [after Procrutes, a mythical Greek giant who stretched or shortened captives to make them fit his beds]. ▮ Poor [former presidential candidate Al Gore] was abysmally self-satirizing on [Saturday Night Live], ripping the last shreds of dignity from his profile in attempted comedy. ... The chuckles and laughter in his conversation with Lesley Stahl on Sunday night were those of a private person struggling to be free of public life, a man trapped in a **Procrustean bed** built by a father who raised a son to be president. (Suzanne Fields, *It's Sunday Night Live: Gore Should Leave Comedy to the Comics*, The Washington Times, 12-19-2002.)

cautious (tactics, esp. as a means to wear out an opponent) *adj.*: **Fabian** [This adjective derives from Roman general Quinton Fabius Maximus, who, through caution, avoidance of direct confrontation and harassment, defeated Hannibal in the Second Punic War. Today, it has become synonymous with, alternatively, caution or conservativeness, delay or dilatoriness, or guerilla tactics, and is often used in the phrase "Fabian tactics"]. ▪ [After becoming world chess champion in 1960, Mikhail] Tal immediately embarked upon a fresh challenge but at [a tournament in] 1962, instead of the anticipated race between the young lions, Mikhail Tal and Bobby Fischer, the tournament resulted in a narrow victory of attrition for the **Fabian** tactics of the ultra-cautious Armenian Tigran Petrosian. During this tournament Tal's health collapsed and he had to withdraw well before the end. (Author not given, *Mikhail Tal*, The Times [London], 06-30-1992.)

Criteria for Entry in this Thesaurus and Rules Regarding the Examples

The following is a list of the general rules I attempted to abide by for each of the entries in this thesaurus. There may be certain instances where not every rule was followed with respect to every entry, particularly in cases where I felt that a given word was, on balance, a worthy and legitimate inclusion in the thesaurus even if it may not have satisfied every criterion to the letter.

1. All words used are legitimate

What is meant by "legitimate"? A "legitimate" word is any word that appears in one or more recognized major dictionaries and which is not generally described as archaic, rare, obsolete, informal, slang or anything similar. In other words, while less common than what is in one's typical wordhoard, the words are all in actual current use in the English language. The word should appear in one or more standard dictionaries of the entire English language, including the *Oxford English Dictionary*, the 4th Edition of *The American Heritage Dictionary of the English Language*, the 2nd Edition of *The Random House Dictionary of The English Language*, and *Webster's Third International Dictionary*. Foreign words are acceptable if they are included in English dictionaries or are relatively easily found in English language periodicals or books. When a foreign word is used, the language is given as well. Thus, the synonyms in the word base will not ordinarily fall into any of the following categories:

a. Words that appear only in specialized dictionaries such as medical dictionaries, or (with a very few exceptions) slang dictionaries (such as *The Random House Historical Dictionary of American Slang*, by Eric Partridge, *A Dictionary of Slang and Unconventional English*, by Jonathan Green, *The Dictionary of Contemporary Slang* and *Thesaurus of American Slang* by Robert Chapman), dictionaries of regional usage, dialectical words, or nonce words (words coined for a particular occasion).

b. Words that appear only in rare or unusual word books such as *The Superior Person's Book of Words* or *Weird and Wonderful Words*, but are not found in standard dictionaries.

c. Words that appear only in the *Official Scrabble Players Dictionary* or the British equivalent, *Official Scrabble Words*.

d. Words that are specific to the fields of biology, chemistry, physics, botany, zoology, specialized or complex anatomy, or most other medical or scientific specialties.

e. Words that merely constitute specific varieties of a larger category of items. These words would not be considered synonyms for the items themselves. For example, "boudin" is a type of sausage, but is not a synonym for sausage itself.

f. Words that are new or recently coined (known as neologisms), especially computer-related terminology such as "blogger" (from "weblogger"), "google," and "dotcom," and also terms such as "metrosexual," "spin doctor," "infomercial" and the like. The purpose of this thesaurus is to focus on established (albeit not common) words, as opposed to words which have only recently come into vogue.

How is it determined which words go into dictionaries in the first place? Conversely, how is it determined which words that are already in the dictionary have fallen into sufficient disuse to be considered archaic or obsolete?[5] This is clearly a subjective process on both ends. What constitutes a "legitimate word" is ultimately nothing more than a matter of opinion, based on popular vote. When a writer or speaker uses a given word, he is in essence casting a "vote" for the legitimacy of that word, and no one vote counts more or less than any other. As stated by Stefan Fatsis in his book *Word Freak* (Houghton Mifflin, 2001), "dictionaries are as subjective as any other piece of writing. Which words are included in them and which words are removed or ignored are decisions made by lexicographers based on shifting criteria, varying standards and divergent publishing goals."

How are the new words found? Joseph Pickett, executive editor of the Fourth Edition of *The American Heritage Dictionary of the English Language* (Houghton Mifflin, 2000), states that "we have a systematic program for reading publications like TIME, looking for examples of new words and new uses of old words." Based on this review, the people who compile the *American Heritage Dictionary* decided that words like "multitasking," "day trader," "erectile dysfunction," and "shock jocks" were worthy of inclusion in the 4th Edition of *The American Heritage Dictionary*, published in 2000, but not in the 3rd Edition, published in 1992. These words have been "voted for" enough to be considered part of the language. Other words have received some votes through usage, but apparently not enough, such as "stalkerazzi," which did not make the Fourth Edition.

Of course, the reverse process is true as well, which explains how thousands of words become archaic or obsolete: not enough people "voted" for them by using them over the years, so they dropped out of the public vocabulary and hence out of the dictionaries. Of course, this is a subjective process as well. What happens if a dictionary lists a word as "archaic," but it suddenly appears in a current issue of a mainstream publication such as The New York Times or Newsweek or USA Today? Is it no longer archaic? Or was the one "vote" not enough? To take but one example: the word "venery" has two different definitions — sexual intercourse and the sport of hunting. Most dictionaries describe the word as being archaic for both definitions. Yet, the word has popped up in both senses in several different publications over the past 10 years. For example:

> **intercourse** (sexual ...) *n.:* **venery**. ∎ Among the Major government's other recent disasters in the **venery** department have been headlines about (a) the environment minister who was forced to resign for impregnating a local government legislatress established to be not his wife. ... (Daniel Seligman, *Keeping Up: Depravity Among Conservatives,* Fortune, 05-02-1994, p. 129.)

The rule of thumb used here is that if a word appears to be in current usage, it is considered a legitimate word if at least one dictionary does not categorize it as archaic.

---

5. In general, the difference between an obsolete word and an archaic word is that although both have fallen into disuse, an obsolete word has fallen into disuse more recently.

2. The synonym should generally not be found in conventional thesauruses

As discussed above, one of the reasons for the creation of this thesaurus was the premise that conventional thesauruses rarely assist the literate writer because the synonyms they provide are so bland and simple that the synonyms offered were likely considered and rejected by the writer before even opening the thesaurus. On a scale of 1 to 10, the complexity of the synonyms in a conventional thesaurus may range from about 1 to 6. In this thesaurus, the range is from about 6 to 10. Thus, while it would not be accurate to say that there is no overlap between the synonyms in this thesaurus and in a regular thesaurus, there is very little. Even if that overlap does occur, the regular thesaurus, not having the benefit of the Clarifier, can easily lead the user astray. The word is thus included in this thesaurus to protect against the danger of using the synonym the wrong way. In addition, there are some instances where a typical thesaurus may list 20 synonyms for a word and the word in question may be buried down at number 17.

Consider the following two examples: The word "eudemonia" is listed as a synonym for "happiness" in both this thesaurus and in *The Synonym Finder* [Rodale], which is considered a very comprehensive thesaurus. The latter has two paragraphs for the word "happiness" (although not describing how they differ). Under the second sense, the following 16 synonyms for "happiness" are listed:

> paradise, heaven, seventh heaven, Eden, utopia, Elysium, Arcadia, sunshine, halcyon days, beatitude, serenity, peace, eudemonia, gratification, fulfillment, contentment

Thus, while "eudemonia" is there, it's so buried amongst other choices, that it is difficult for the user to really focus on the word and consider its use. The fact that the user probably won't know what the word means anyway merely heightens this probability — not to mention the fact that the absence of the Clarifier will get the user into immediate trouble if he or she thinks that "eudemonia" can be used synonymously with, say, "gratification" or "sunshine." While this thesaurus also lists "eudemonia" as a synonym for "happiness," the presentation is hardly similar:

> **happiness** *n*.: **eudemonia** (or **eudaemonia**) [based on a concept of Aristotle's that the goal of life is happiness, but which is to be achieved through reaching one's full potential, as opposed to through the hedonistic pursuit of pleasure]. ▪ [The] objective is a good life, an Aristotleian **eudemonia**, which embraces a substantial dose of self-interest, but also incorporates concern for others, fulfilment at work, and the respect earned from others by participating in activities, including economic activities, which they value. (John Kay, *Staking a Moral Claim*, New Statesman, 10-11-1996.)

Similarly, both this thesaurus and *The Synonym Finder* list "excrescence" as a synonym for "outgrowth." So is this thesaurus unnecessary with respect to the particular word? The presentation in *The Synonym Finder* is as follows:

> outgrowth *n*.: 1. product, consequence, result, outcome, payoff, effect, aftereffect, aftermath, conclusion, upshot, final issue, eventuation, yield.
> 2. addition, supplement, postscript, sequel.
> 3. excrescence, offshoot, shoot, sprout, bud, burgeon, blossom, flower, fruit, projection, protuberance, bulge, knob, node, nodule, process, caruncle. [6]

---

6. No dictionary seems to support the notion that "excrescence" is synonymous with all the floral-based words in this section, such as sprout, bud, burgeon, blossom, flower, and fruit, but that is another issue.

Compare that presentation of "excresence" with the one in this thesaurus:

> **outgrowth** *n.*: **excrescence** [Note: this word is often used literally, such as
> to describe an abnormal growth on the body or of a bodily part, such as a
> wart, but just as often is used in the sense of being an offshoot or consequence
> of a prior event or circumstance]. ▪ [In *Ceasefire!* author Cathy Young's inten-
> tion] is to unmask the false claims of these "thought police," especially as they
> concern the supposed continued inequality of women in the United States.
> [C]ourt cases involving gender violence and sex crimes, child abuse and
> domestic violence, child custody and school curricula [are] **excrescences** of
> a cultural agenda that has been put in place to support spurious feminist
> claims and provide employment for enforcers. (Elizabeth Powers, *What Our
> Mothers Didn't Tell Us: Why Happiness Eludes the Modern Woman*, Commentary,
> 03-01-1999.)

Even in those rare instances where there is both identity of synonyms between this thesaurus and others and where the use of the word straight out of a conventional thesaurus
is not likely to get the user in trouble (such as it will in the above two examples), the use in
this thesaurus of an example and just one synonym will likely cause the user to focus on
and more seriously consider the use of that synonym than when it is hidden among many
others. Consider the following from *The Synonym Finder*:

enchant (v.): 1. cast a spell upon, spellbind, bewitch, charm, mesmerize, hypnotize,
ensorcell, bind by incantations, hoodoo, hex
2. captivate, allure, delight, enrapture, fascinate, enamor, transport, entice, enthrall,
infatuate, catch, win, lead captive, enchain

Thus, we are given 24 possible synonyms for "enchant." However, it is submitted that
most of these are uninteresting and will already be familiar to the user anyway (with the
exception of "hoodoo" which is an unusual word, but which is presented wrongly in *The
Synonym Finder*, since it is not a synonym for "enchant," but rather "bad luck," and is presented in this thesaurus thereunder). "Ensorsell," on the other hand, is an interesting word
and is correctly listed as a synonym for "enchant." But would the reader really think about
the use of that word, being buried amongst the other 23? Possibly not. This thesaurus presents the word as follows:

> **enchant** *v.t.*: **ensorcell** (or **ensorcel**). ▪ Trying to soften his military image
> and lure more female voters in New Hampshire, Gen. Wesley Clark switched
> from navy suits to argyle sweaters. It's an odd strategy. It's also a little alarm-
> ing that he thinks the way to **ensorcell** women is to swaddle himself in wool-
> ly geometric shapes that conjure up images of Bing Crosby on the links or
> Fred MacMurray at the kitchen table. (Maureen Dowd, *The General Is Sweating
> His Image (Editorial)*, The New York Times, 01-13-2004.)

In any event, for every synonym herein which may be found in a conventional thesaurus, there are dozens of others which are not (and could not or should not be when they
require a Clarifier). Moreover, while some of these words can be found in the unusual word
books, with this thesaurus, the user can actually use the words, since they are alphabetized
according to the base word and not according to the hard synonym, which is the case with
the hard word books.

3. The meaning of the word generally must be understood from the given example alone

Mere correct usage of the word is generally insufficient if the context does not make the definition clear. (There are some exceptions to this rule which are discussed in the following section.) Consider the following example:

> L.L. Cool J. Here's a guy who has fallen in love with the sound of his own voice. All right, that's an occupational hazard for rappers, but rarely has this sort of verbal vanity exerted such a baleful stylistic influence as it does on this young urban **poetaster**. (David Hiltbrand, *Picks & Pans: Song*, People, 09-04-1989, p. 19.)

If the reader did not know the meaning of "poetaster," this particular usage would not be of much use. Consider instead the usage in this thesaurus, in which the meaning of the word is made clear from the rest of the example:

> **poet** (bad ...) *n.*: **poetaster** ∎ And now her first book of poems, *Yesterday I Saw the Sun*, has become a cause for further hiding. Just before the book's publication last month, a New York Post gossip item ridiculed her as a **poetaster**, contributing to her latest headache. "Ally Sheedy from bad to verse," chortled the headline on the item. (Author not given, *Heartbreak–Ally Sheedy Says She Wrote Her Poems to Heal Her Wounds, but Their Publication Has Only Made Them Another Source of Pain*, Entertainment Weekly, 03-29-1991, p. 28.)

This rule has particular applicability where the author may be discussing a certain famous person, television show, movie or book, where the writer assumes familiarity with the subject. If that is not the case, the meaning of the word may not be apparent. This does not of course mean there is anything wrong with the writing or the usage, but simply that the given passage is not appropriate for this thesaurus.

> **midget** *n.*: **homunculus**. ∎ Conceived as a spoof of TV's old amateur hours, [The Gong Show] had all its oddball ingredients in place by episode 1. There was creator and host Chuck Barris, a hyper **homunculus** in a bad tux. (A.J. Jacobs, *Encore: Cool and the 'Gong,'* Entertainment Weekly, 06-11-1999, p. 80.)

Unless one is familiar with Chuck Barris, this example will not help the reader in understanding the meaning of "homunculus," and thus the above example was not used. However, on certain occasions, the word might be used with reference to a particular person, but familiarity with that person may not be necessary if the rest of the example gives context to the word.

> **voluptuous** (woman, often with stately or regal bearing) *adj.*: **Junoesque** [after ancient Italian goddess Juno, wife of Jupiter]. ∎ After rejections from countless modeling agencies, [Anna Nicole Smith was selected to be in Playboy magazine]. Her **Junoesque** appeal led straight to a three-year contract with Guess? "I always wanted to get back to be smaller than I was," she says. "But I just couldn't. Now I feel very good about it, and I wouldn't change my figure for anything." (Author not given, *Anna Nicole Smith Is Livin' Large and Loving it*, People, 09-20-1993, p. 76.)

Even if the reader does not know Ms. Smith, the meaning of the word Junoesque is made clear from the rest of the passage.

4. The word cannot be defined within the example given

Any time the writer uses a word, but then feels compelled to define the word for the reader, that usage is not included. The purpose of giving the examples in the first place is to show that these words are legitimate, non-archaic words which are actually in current usage, and to give the reader a sense of how the words are used in a sentence or passage. However, if the writer defines the word, then, in a sense, both purposes are defeated. Even though the writer may have perfectly legitimate reasons for defining the word, the act of defining it nevertheless means that the word is not being used naturally within the passage. Instead, specific attention is being drawn towards the word, which defeats the second purpose of using the examples. Consider the following:

> **postcards** (collection and study of) *n*.: **deltiology**. ∎ With National Postcard Week on May 6-12, now's a good time to consider expanding your collection, say fans of **deltiology** (a fancy word for postcard collecting). (Penny Walker, *A Passion for Postcards*, The Arizona Republic, 05-05-2001, p. E1.)

Indeed, in theory, any word can be given a "usage" in a sentence simply by stating, for example: "Deltiology means postcard collecting," but this obviously does not further the goal of putting the given word in a context.

Consider next the contrast between the next two examples involving the use of the word "kakistocracy."

> **government** (by the least qualified or least principled people) *n*.: **kakistocracy**
>
> a. No, Matthew. Don Fletcher is right. "**Kakistocracy**. Are you familiar with that word?" Fletcher asked while nursing his coffee at the Bill O' Fare. "It means government by the worst elements.... It doesn't matter whether you vote Republican or Democratic." (Steve Lopez, *Nation/Campaign 2000: Campaign Diary: Is It Over Yet? Gore. No, wait. Bush,* Time, 11-06-2000, p. 69.)
>
> b. Cannon: Well, we couldn't convict [Bill Clinton]. But I think the American people understand what [the Clinton] administration is all about. ... And we have the greatest system on earth, a system strong enough to withstand the assaults over the last six years of this **kakistocracy**. (Sean Hannity, *Ken Starr Investigation,* Hannity & Colmes [Fox News Network], 06-24-1999.)

Of the two usages above, the first merely defines the word, while the second uses it within the flow of the statement. For that reason, it is the second usage which is found in this thesaurus, and the same concept holds true for every usage found herein.

5. Current examples are always used over older examples and archaic words are never used.

Language is always evolving over time, such that not only are new words constantly entering the vocabulary, but old words are constantly leaving. When the usage of the older words has become sufficiently infrequent (but not perhaps extinct altogether), they are designated in dictionaries as "archaic" or "obsolete." None of those words is used here, unless at least one or more current dictionaries does not describe them as outdated. Application of this rule arises frequently with respect to words used by Shakespeare. If the only instances of a particular word usage is found in Shakespeare or other old sources, the example is not used on the assumption that the word has become archaic or rare. However, if the word itself is not described that way in at least one or more current dictionaries, then the word is included if a current example exists.

> **argument** (esp. about a trifling matter) *n.*: **brabble**. AARON: Why, how now, lords! So near the emperor's palace dare you draw, And maintain such a quarrel openly? ... Now, by the gods that warlike Goths adore, This petty **brabble** will undo us all. (William Shakespeare, *Titus Andronicus: Act II, Scene I.*)

The *American Heritage Dictionary* (4th Edition), and others, do not list "brabble" as archaic, (though *Webster's Third* does). Nevertheless, every usage of the word located is from Shakespeare. As for the actual examples used, almost every example is less than 20 years old and most are less than 10 years old.

6. A literal usage of the word is generally used over a figurative usage.

In many instances, a writer will use a word correctly, but in a figurative sense. With some exceptions, discussed below, those usages are avoided here. This is because if a reader trying to learn the word only is presented with figurative examples, this may hinder understanding of the true and correct meaning of the word.

> **murder** (of parent or close relative) *n.*: **parricide**. Sharpton says [Jesse] Jackson, 60, has been his mentor, friend and "surrogate father" but now is an exhausted volcano, viewed by young blacks as "an establishment figure." ... Sharpton compares Jackson to Muhammad Ali: Great once; can't fight anymore. ... **Parricide** isn't pretty. (George F. Will, *Sharpton Eyes the Prize*, The Washington Post, 01-10-2002, p.A19. [AI])

The premise is that when one is trying to understand the appropriate usage of a word, it is easier to expand from the literal to the figurative. Conversely, when one is only familiar with the figurative use of a word, it can be a recipe for trouble. In the above example, Mr. Will used the word "parricide" perfectly appropriately for his purposes. Nevertheless, given his figurative usage of the word, his usage is not the best example for purposes of this thesaurus, because it does not convey the fact that parricide is a literal killing of a parent or relative. Indeed, it could leave a reader who is unfamiliar with the word with the impression that the mere act of disrespecting or criticizing one's parents could be an act of parricide.

One exception to this general rule is those words that are almost always used in their figurative sense and only occasionally in their literal sense. The word "thralldom," meaning "slavery" or "bondage," is used in a figurative sense far more than in a literal sense, and thus this thesaurus gives a figurative usage:

> **bondage** *n.*: **thralldom**. ∎ We Western women, it appears, still have not shucked off male ideas of female beauty; the voluntary mutilation of plastic surgery bears witness to our **thralldom**. (Elizabeth Ward, *The Trouble With Women*, The Washington Post, 05-23-1999, p. 8.)

Similarly, the verb "flagellate" means to "whip" or "flog," but is almost always used in the figurative sense of self-criticism, often as in "self-flagellate." Therefore, a figurative example was again used.

criticize (oneself) *v.t.*: **flagellate** (*n*: **flagellation**) [this word means to whip or flog another, and is properly used in that sense, but is generally used figuratively, esp. as in criticism of oneself, sometimes as in self-flagellation]. ■ Journalists belong to the only profession whose members regularly get together to **flagellate** themselves in public. (Sheryl McCarthy, *Here's How We Cover The Blob*, Newsday, 04-12-1995, p. A17.)

A second exception is where it was felt that the literal meaning of the word was clear, even where the example did not present a literal usage of the word. For example, the word "theanthropic" means to have both human and divine or godlike qualities. The tongue-in-cheek example presented here is as follows:

godlike (having both human and ... attributes) *adj.*: **theanthropic**. ■ [After September 11, 2001,] our government should order the CIA to air drop to the Mullahs and their angry young men millions of pages from the Victoria's Secret catalogues. Anyone familiar with the September 11 atrocities knows that these fellows are sexually repressed. ... Pursuing the **theanthropic** [Victoria's Secret model Laetitia Casta] through Google-space, they will be lured toward the pages of The American Spectator, where they will enjoy the health benefits of cultural diversity. (R. Emmett Tyrell, Jr., *The Continuing Crisis*, The American Spectator, 01-01-2002.)

While Laetitia Casta may indeed be a lovely woman, one presumes that the user will understand that she is not literally a goddess. Just as importantly, however, so long as the writer understands the literal meaning of the word, there is nothing wrong with using it in a figurative sense, as Mr. Tyrell did here and Mr. Will did above.

While literal usages of words are presented in this thesaurus for educational purposes, the use of these words in a figurative or metaphorical sense is encouraged. So long as a writer or speaker knows the actual use of a word, there is nothing wrong with using them in other than their literal sense.

7. The base word must logically lead to the synonym.

The mere fact that a word may be too unusual for a regular thesaurus does not automatically render it appropriate for inclusion in this one. This is because certain words refer to concepts, theories or principles rather than single words. Thus if there is no single word that one might logically connect with a given synonym, that synonym was excluded, no matter how useful the concepts, theories or principles were. For example, the word "meliorism," although a fine word, does not readily lend itself to a one-word base. The same is true for words such as "diglossia," "duopsony," "eponym," "featherbedding," "festschrift," "fideism," "obscurantism," and "prelapsarian." It does no good to include an interesting word if the user is not likely to ever find that word due to an inability to connect it to an appropriate base word. Words such as these may be well suited for the obscure word dictionaries, but not for this thesaurus.

On the opposite end, some synonyms, although unusual, are so close to a common base word that they are not included either, on the theory that they don't add anything to the common base word. For example, most people have probably never heard the word "botheration." However, no surprise that it means the act of bothering or state of being bothered. It is essentially just the noun form of the verb "to bother." Thus, an entry for this word might be as follows:

bother (as in act of bothering or state of being bothered) *n.*: **botheration**. ∎ [F]ew people have stopped to consider: a) why Saddam Hussein has become the perpetual **botheration** of United States foreign policy interests or b) why President Clinton is having so much trouble securing international support for a military strike. (Bonnie Erbe, *U.S. Can't Lead With These Leaders?* Rocky Mountain News, 11-22-1997.)

Similarly, "pefectibilism" is a rare (though perfectly legitimate) synonym for ... guess what? Perfectionism. Words such as "botheration" and "perfectibilism" (of which there are a surprising number) are not included in this thesaurus.

8. A note on the use of "as in."

There are many instances in this thesaurus where the base word is followed by a Clarifier which includes the words "as in." This is done primarily either because the base word may have several different definitions or because the synonym given may not have precisely the same meaning as the base word, but the user may nevertheless be inclined to look up the base word in hopes of finding a similar or related synonym. Thus, in those instances where the connection between the base word and the synonym may be unclear or even appear questionable, that which follows the "as in" construct is intended to explain or fine-tune the connection and hit closer to the mark.

For example, one of the definitions of "fatuous" is "delusional." That word in turn is related to, but not precisely the same as, "imaginary" or "illusory." For example, one might call the tooth fairy imaginary, but not delusional. Nevertheless, there are times when one might look to the word "imaginary" or "illusory" when searching for a good word which is in reality closer to "delusional." This situation, which arises frequently, is addressed in this thesaurus as follows:

> **unreal** (as in delusional) *adj.*: **fatuous**. See DELUSIONAL
> **illusory** (as in delusional) *adj.*: **fatuous**. See DELUSIONAL
> **imaginary** (as in delusional) *adj.*: **fatuous**. See DELUSIONAL

> **delusional** *adj.*: **fatuous**. ∎ After the 1992 election, I wrote [an article] on Bill Clinton. ... I did express high, and in retrospect rather **fatuous**, hopes for the coming Clinton Administration . ... I cherished, for a time, a kind of fresh-start, non-partisan, post-ideological, post-Cold War faith that a new-paradigm Clinton might lead the nation brilliantly toward ... toward, well, the bridge to the twenty-first century! (Lance Morrow, *U.S. v. Clinton*, National Review, 09-28-1998, p. 39.)

In this example, the "as in" is used not only to show that "delusional" is the closest synonym to "fatuous," but also to demonstrate that using "illusory" or "imaginary" as synonyms for "fatuous," while sometimes workable, can also be problematic. The "as in" Clarifier avoids this pitfall. Consider also the following example: The essence of "perspicuous" is something which is understandable. However, in the right context, "clear" and "simple" might be perfectly adequate synonyms for "perspicuous," which is why these words are included among the base words for perspicuous. However, in the wrong context, these words may have no connection whatever. One might call the Caribbean Sea "clear," but not "perspicuous." Once again, the "as in" construct solves this problem.

> **clear** (as in understandable) *adj.*: **perspicuous**. See UNDERSTANDABLE
> **simple** (as in understandable) *adj.*: **perspicuous**. See UNDERSTANDABLE

understandable *adj.*: **perspicuous**. ∎ One [of the "Principles of Mathematics"] was the "theory of descriptions" which purported to solve a problem that Plato had wrestled with, namely how one can think and speak of non-existent things. The theory showed how various tricky propositions could be translated into something more **perspicuous** and less puzzling; it soon came to be seen as a model of how to philosophise. (Author not given, *The Philosophers That Sophie Skipped [Modern Philosophers; Book 'Sophie's World'],* Vol. 341, The Economist, 12-07-1996, p. 79.)

It is a rule of thumb that any word or phrase which follows "as in" as part of a Clarifer is considered the word or phrase which comes closest in meaning to the actual synonym used, and if it seems that a given base word does not appear at first to connect logically to the synonym, then what follows "as in" should provide the logical connection.

9. A note on the use of "see"

As we saw above with the word "perspicuous," many synonyms are arrived at through multiple base words. However, so as to avoid repetition of examples, there is only one example presented for each synonym. The synonym which contains the example will follow the word "see," and is generally considered the synonym which is closest to the base word in question.

Thus, "see understandable" means the example given will be found at "understandable."

10. Notes on the presentation of the examples

a. In presenting the examples, when the author was known, he or she is listed.

b. When there were multiple authors for one passage, only the first author's name is listed.

c. When the author of the piece quoted another person who used the word in question, this is noted, as is when the author was writing a letter to the editor.

d. The titles were occasionally shortened or modified, particularly where there was verbiage in the title which was not relevant to the passage.

e. References to the volume numbers of the periodical were not included.

f. The page on which the passage appeared was provided if known.

g. The source provided may not have been the initial source in which the passage appeared, particularly where the author is a syndicated columnist.

h. Any words in brackets (but not parentheses) are my own words and may represent either (1) an addition to the text without any deletion, often for purposes of clarification or (2) a substitution of fewer words for longer deleted material from the text, which could be of any length. An ellipse (...) obviously represents deletion of material from the text which also could be of any length. In general, the intent was to present as much of the passage as was deemed necessary to give the user a good sense of the word without changing the author's meaning. Small portions of the text were sometimes included as part of the example where it was felt that inclusion of the sentence gave a sense of completeness to the passage. The premise is that if a passage is thought-provoking or if it serves to amuse, intrigue, entertain, or inspire, then the synonym itself might be better remembered than if the example was a mere sentence fragment.

In Defense of the Hard Word

What is a hard word? It is not necessarily a long word. Rather, it is simply a word whose usage is sufficiently infrequent that many English speakers and writers, even the more literate ones, may not be familiar with the word or its definition.[7]

There are many who decry the use of hard words in writing or in speech and who feel we would all be better off if they simply didn't exist. One such person is James Kilpatrick, who has been waging a one-way war against William F. Buckley — or more precisely William F. Buckley's vocabulary — for many years. In article after article, Kilpatrick has railed against what he considers to be Buckley's unnecessary use of "recondite words." These articles include *Each Writer Must Choose to be Erudite or be Clear* in a syndicated column that appeared on February 16, 1997, and a critical book review of Buckley's book *The Right Word*, which appeared in the December 23, 1996 issue of *The National Review*. In addition, while not directly mentioning Buckley, Kilpatrick touched on the same themes in another syndicated column that appeared on November 30, 1997, *Essence of Writing: Have Something to Say and Say it Clearly*.

In each of these pieces and many others, Kilpatrick's theme is the same: write so as to be understood by the widest possible audience and refrain from using words which may not be generally familiar to your readers. To help make his point, Kilpatrick often uses the technique frequently resorted to by him and others who would stand with him on this issue: mockery. Indeed, if one is so inclined, it is easy to try to make fun of those with larger vocabularies by forcing difficult words on the reader in an unnatural fashion, especially by stacking them on top of each other. For example, Kilpatrick opens his review of *The Right Word* as follows:

> If I were to say of Mr. Buckley's latest compendium that it is not at all an anodyne work, I could fairly be indicted for gross meiosis. Even a necessarily truncated review, such as this brief epitome, cannot offer more than a meager adumbration of this kaleidoscopic omnium gatherum. What an epiphany it is, to share his eudaemonia! What a nimiety of logomachical riches have we here! I am quite undone." (James Kilpatrick, *Buckley: The Right Word (Book Reviews)*, National Review, 12-23-1996, p. 48.)

The primary problem with Mr. Kilpatrick's reasoning is that it requires veering away from the dictionary as the standard reference source for what does and does not constitute a "legitimate" English word and instead requires us to draw a completely arbitrary line in the sand as to what words are or are not appropriate. But who sets the standard? Clearly it can't be Mr. Buckley since his standard is evidently too high. Is it then Mr. Kilpatrick himself? Should he be the official word arbiter? But why him? Or, to borrow from the standard set forth by Supreme Court Justice Potter Stewart when deciding what constituted obscene material, should our standard for inappropriately hard words be: "We know them when we

---

7. People often wonder whether there are any one-word synonyms for a hard word or the word "synonym" itself. It is ironic that out of the more than 600,000 words in the English language, the answer appears to be, not really. About the closest we come to a hard word is "sesquepedalian," a noun meaning "long word," or an adjective meaning "given to the use of long words." Also, an "inkhorn" word or term means one which is pedantic or affectedly learned. In addition "recondite" means not easily understood, but this can apply to many concepts and not simply words. Finally, the rare word "polyonymy" (adj.: polyonymous) means the use of various names for one thing. It comes from a Greek word meaning "having many names." As for "thesaurus," a "synonymicon" is a lexicon of synonyms.

see them"?

In attempting to answer these questions, it becomes immediately apparent that any attempt to reach the goal of a universally agreeable standard is a fool's errand. No two people have the same lexicon and thus no one of us can set a standard. Just as certain words in Mr. Buckley's vocabulary are unacceptable to Mr. Kilpatrick, there are undoubtedly words in Mr. Kilpatrick's vocabulary which are unfamiliar to others who may be less literate than he.

Consider a traffic analogy: On a highway where all traffic is moving in the same direction, the left hand lane is for passing. Those who are in the left hand lane should move over to the right hand lane when someone is trying to pass. That is true regardless of the speed of either the front car or the car trying to pass. If the front car is going 80 mph and the car trying to pass is going 90, then the front car should get out of the way. It is not for the driver of the front car to say: "I'm going fast enough; I'll set the standard speed here."

If we were to carry Kilpatrick's argument to its logical conclusion, where would that leave us? It would seem to require that all words that are on the wrong side of an imaginary standard would need to be jettisoned from the language since there would no longer be any need for them (this being an example of reductio ad absurdum, namely disproving an argument by showing the absurdity of its logical conclusion). Thus, just based on his paragraph above, we would likely have to to say goodbye to "anodyne," "meiosis," "adumbration," "omnium gatherum," "epiphany," "nimiety" and "logomachical" as words in the English language, even though other writers have chosen to use all of these words at one time or another. Presumably there are thousands of others which would also become extinct.[8]

Even within Kilpatrick's own teasing of Buckley's word choices, the unsolvable problem of the folly of trying to choose the appropriate standard immediately becomes clear. With words such as "meiosis," "omnium gatherum," "eudaemonia" and "nimety" (all of which are in this thesaurus, incidentally), one knows right away that these are more unfamiliar words. But what about the other words he includes in the same passage, such as "compendium," "truncated," "epitome," "meager" and even "epiphany"? Though none of these words is unusual, it is probably safe to say that they are not necessarily familiar to everyone. But surely Kilpatrick is not suggesting that these words should be included with the rest of his list of words which have no place in the English language? Or should the reader know what those words mean, and thus they should be separated from those words that would be placed on death row?

What are the possible responses one might have in opposing the use of unfamiliar words? Consider the book *Witness*, the biography of Whittaker Chambers by Sam Tanenhaus, which was a Pulitzer Prize finalist in 1998. That book contains the following passages:

A **refulgent** star of the [Communist] movement, as indeed 'the purest Bolshevik writer ever to function in the United States,' Chambers involved himself in various projects.

[Chambers] was an adept linguist, with idiomatic German still Communism's **lingua**

---

8. Mr. Kilpatrick is hardly alone in his views. Indeed, he likely speaks for a majority of people. Virtually any time a book contains more than a handful of less commonly used words, the author is sure to be taken to task by reviewers for the use of words the reviewers did not know. It would seem that Kilpatrick, and many similarly minded people, can be advocating only one possible conclusion, namely that the kinds of words which appear in this thesaurus should never be used and thus should be removed from the dictionary altogether. But isn't that a rather sad result, which simply results in the dumbing down of our collective vocabularies?

franca, and so could easily communicate with agents sent from overseas.

They became a 'tightly knit unit,' bound together by the effort to maintain the household on the **exiguous** sum Jay sent them, eight dollars a week by Vivian's recollection.

Passports were essential for traveling Communist agents and American passports were preferred above all others because anyone, even non-English speakers, could travel on them without arousing suspicion, thanks to the country's vast **polyglot** population, with its many immigrants.

Let us concede, first, that the words in bold are hardly common words known by everyone, and, second, the author could have, but chose not to, used "bright" in place of "refulgent," "common language" in place of "lingua franca," "meager" in place of "exiguous," and "multilingual" in place of "polyglot." So why didn't he? (Indeed, Kilpatrick might pose this very question, because, in his review of *The Right Word*, he asks: "[W]hat is gained in communication by speaking of the politician who tergiversates? The fellow waffles, or flip-flops, or reneges. Why not say so?"). Starting from these premises might yield one of the following responses as to the propriety of their use from one who deplores the use of hard words, the first of which is critical of Tanenhaus and the rest not:

1. Tanenhaus used poor word choices, Pulitzer Prize credentials or not, and it would have been better writing for him to use the simpler synonyms.

2. I personally happen to be familiar with all of his word choices and, because they are within my own lexicon, I have no problem with them even if others might not know their meaning.

3. These words are appropriate because Tanenhaus is writing for a sophisticated and particularly literate audience.

4. This writing is acceptable because the hard words are sporadic and interspersed with easy words; in other words they are not crammed together.

5. Hard words are acceptable if and only if their meanings can be deduced from the context of the passage.

The first response makes no sense unless one is prepared to argue that the authors of virtually every passage in this thesaurus are poor writers because they didn't use the very simplest words at all times. This is obviously a ludicrous argument. The second response again raises the issue of whether we must adopt a hypothetical "reasonable person" standard. But as we have seen, that is impossible. Whose vocabulary do we make the exact dividing line? This too is a silly result.

As to the third response, it is quite true that we often hear it said that authors should "write suitably for their audience." Indeed, Kilpatrick makes this very point himself.[9] If we are talking about differentiating between readers by age, there is certainly merit to this advice. For example, these words would obviously not be appropriate for children. However, once we confine the "audience" to adults, the advice makes far less sense. Indeed, its only possible meaning in that case is that we should differentiate between "smart adults" and "dumb adults" (or, more precisely, "literate adults" and "not-so-literate adults"). It means for example, that a word which might be appropriate in, say, the *National*

---

9. In his review of *The Right Word*, he states: "Every person who writes or speaks for a living must begin his task with certain assumptions. The preacher assumes a certain level of Biblical literacy. The reporter who covers Congress assumes that his readers know what is meant by a partisan vote. ... Fair enough. But in [Buckley's] quotidian columns, he assumes too much." (One wonders why he didn't follow his own practice and use a more mundane word than "quotidian.")

Review or the *Nation*, would not be appropriate in *People* magazine. But isn't that patronizing and doesn't it discourage readers (and, just as important, writers) from ever learning new words?[10] Indeed, based on the fact that so many of the examples herein do in fact come from widely read (shall we say non-snooty?) periodicals such as *People*, *Entertainment Weekly*, *Time*, and *Newsweek*, it would appear that the authors of those articles are implicitly expressing their disagreement with the foes of hard words through their frequent use of excellent but uncommon words, which undoubtedly would fall outside of any mythical and mystical "approved word list."

The fourth response — that the kinds of words used in this thesaurus are perfectly acceptable so long as they are not jammed together, two or three to a sentence, in sentence after sentence — presumes that this is in fact a prevalent problem among writers today. But in fact, who writes like that anyway? Certainly not the authors of any of the examples in this thesaurus. Indeed, virtually the only time one sees the types of sentences written by Kilpatrick above is, ironically, when other writers do exactly what Kilpatrick does, which is to make the multiple hard words the very raison d'être of the sentence for one reason or another, and string them together for humorous effect (often to make fun of writers who use hard words or to salute those who write all of the weird word books). Examples abound.[11] This is in contrast to the authors of the words demonstrated in this thesaurus who are using them only as useful conduits through which to make their points and not as the points themselves. Thus, if the argument is simply against using too many hard words in a row, then those making the argument are simply setting up a straw man so they can blow him down.

As to the final response, if one would approve of the use of all hard words if and only

---

10. Kilpatrick appears to engage in this patronization himself. Returning again to his review of *The Right Word*, he states, as we saw, that in Buckley's "quotidian columns, he assumes too much" and states that "the problem is that Bill writes solely for the discriminating ear and the fastidious eye." He then contrasts this with his own reluctance to use hard words because "my column is aimed at the general readership of the 220 papers that carry it." But what is he really saying here when one reads between the lines? He seems to be saying that his "general readers" may be too illiterate or incurious to deal with hard words which appear in the "quotidian columns" they read. In fact however, virtually every example in this thesaurus comes from a "quotidian column" (or book) which is in fact "aimed at the general readership." The examples are not from specialized sources and certainly are not written "solely for the discriminating ear and the fastidious eye."

11. "I'm sure many of you feel that the English language is already adscititious, and that the nimiety of our lexicon already ascribes words a false equiponderance." Euan Ferguson, *Hang on a minute, isn't there a word for that?* The Observer, 02-02-2003, p. 26.

"In his first formal interview since being dumped as Treasurer, the erudite Mr. Ralph Willis seemingly could find no more eloquent way of expressing his emotion than "I'm very pissed off." [He should have said]: "Well, actually my untimely labefaction has left me feeling somewhat luctiferous and, although I do not intend to indulge in any longanimity, I do admit to a vague sense of lypophrenia. ... And furthermore, I'm not diversivolent, but I feel there was absolutely no nonfeasance or murcidity on my part and I think the whole thing is a real proctalgia." Megan Turner, *Five-Star Words*, Courier-Mail, 03-14-1992.

"Finding the Christmas shopping moliminous? Do you think the whole event is badot, over-promoted by kakistocracy and the gilly-gaupus? Do you drumble down the local High Street feeling nocent about all you haven't done, or are you quite pococurantish in the face of pressure to spend your hard-earned money on finnimbruns?" Author not given, *Present Perfect*, Financial Times, 12-13-2003.

Are these tongue-in-cheek examples truly the kind of writing of Mr. Kilpatrick is fulminating against? Doubtful.

if their meanings can be determined from the context (even if the reader would otherwise have no clue as to its meaning out of context), this only means that those who take this position and I are on the same page, at least in those instances. The use of those specific hard words would need no defense. Even here however, there are problems with this position. First, if the only goal is truly to be clear, then why (one might ask facetiously) even take a chance on an unfamiliar word which forces the reader to guess as to its meaning, a guess which may or may not be accurate? Why not just resort to the simplest possible words? Consider the following example, which is a perfectly appropriate use of the excellent word "sockdolager." In reading it, consider the following two questions: (1) Can you say for certain what it means? (2) Even if the answer is yes, might a simpler word have sufficed?

> The American Council for the Arts [wanted to] show how much the American people love the arts. ... [T]hey retained pollster Lou Harris [who knows that] 99% of a public opinion poll lies in framing the questions to be asked. ... Lou asked them, "How important do you think it is to the quality of life in the community to have such things as museums, theater and concert halls in the community?" That was a **sockdolager** [because 84% said very important or somewhat important.]

A "sockdolager" is a decisive or telling factor, remark or blow, kind of like a knockout punch. It was the perfect word to use in the above passage, in that Harris knew what question to ask that would yield the telling response it did. And yet, might not the author have used a simpler (but less interesting) word of phrase such as "knockout punch" or "telling factor," just to make sure that everyone understood the message? The author could have, but thankfully didn't. And guess who the author was? None other than Mr. Kilpatrick.[12]

Second, we are often on a slippery slope in terms of whether or not the context does the trick. For example, in the passages cited above, wouldn't it have been safer for Tanenhaus to have used simpler terms than "lingua franca" and "polyglot"? Was "refulgent" really necessary? Similarly, at several points in Kilpatrick's article, he is guilty of the very same crime of which he accuses Buckley (as he was in the use of "sockdolager"). At one point, he states that Mr. Buckley's editor "undertook this labor con amore, and all language lovers are in his debt." For those who don't know Italian, why not just say that he did it lovingly? Wouldn't that be simpler? Later, Mr. Kilpatrick states that "my objection, I suppose, is mostly a complaint pro bono publico." Once again, for those who don't know Latin, why not just say that his complaint is for the public good?

There are clearly many instances where the meaning of a hard word is *not* easily ascertainable from the context and yet is the perfect word for the situation. For example, if I were to advise the reader that part of this essay is a "prolepsis," I highly doubt that most readers would know what I meant. And yet, it is the right word. It is a rebuttal by responding to an anticipated objection to an argument before that objection has been made (namely the objection that we should not use hard words because it may impair the understanding of our writing). An example:

> **rebuttal** (as in responding to an anticipated objection to an argument before that objection has been made) *n.:* **prolepsis.** ∎ Stephen Glass' [novel] ... is a **prolepsis**, an extended, creepy one. ... [He] disgraced himself at The New Republic by fabricating interviews. ... [As a result, there was concern that the

---

12. James J. Kilpatrick, *An Artfully Assembled Poll*, St. Petersburg Times (Florida), 04-29-1992, p. 10A.

book wouldn't be reviewed at all or be reviewed poorly.] The problem is that Mr. Glass has pre-empted both [arguments]. ... He brings it up first thing in an author's note: "I was fired in 1998 from my job as a writer at The New Republic." [Presumably, the anticipatory response is not concealing what happened and admitting to it right at the outset.] (Jerome Weeks, *Glass' Repentance Highly Transparent; ex 'New Republic' Writer Seeks Forgiveness in 'The Fabulist,'* The Dallas Morning News, 06-22-2003, p. 11G.)[13]

The word "Luddite" is just the right word in the following passage, but even in context, its meaning is not necessarily clear, not to mention its derivation:

[Al Gore's] role as an enemy of medical progress should come as no surprise. When biotech **Luddite** Jeremy Rifkin wrote Algeny — a diatribe against gene-based drug development in which he implied that the human life span should revert to that enjoyed before the Bronze Age so that mankind could be closer to nature — it was Al Gore who wrote the glowing blurb that Rifkin has given us "an insightful critique of the changing way in which mankind views nature." (Robert Goldberg, *The Luddite: [Al Gore] Invented the Internet?* National Review, 08-14-2000.)[14]

In the following example, the writer uses "aptronym," again a perfect word for the situation, and again one which most readers couldn't define, even in context. Can you figure it out?

Viewers apparently haven't minded that they already knew the ending [to the World Series of Poker]. The well-publicized competition, held in May, was won by Tennessee amateur Chris Moneymaker (talk about **aptronyms**!), whose only previous poker tournaments were on the Internet. (Jack Broom, *A Sure Bet: Poker Is Hot; Televised Games Spur Local Players To Up the Ante*, The Seattle Times, 09-14-2003.)[15]

This same point is especially true with respect to many of the entries which involve phrases rather than single words. Even though the context does not make the phrase clear, it is still le mot juste.

An electioneering budget is an **argumentum ad crumenam**, and most elections in democracies have a strong element of this old argument. It may not be idealistic, but it is the way people vote. (Philip Howard, *Rhetoric and All That Rot*, The Times [London], 04-12-1991.)[16]

---

13. In every situation where the meaning of the word may not be clear from the context, it was the intent that it would be made clear either from the base word itself, the Clarifier, or an explanatory note regarding proper use of the word.

14. traditionalist (spec. a person who is opposed to advancements in technology) n.: Luddite [The word is based on a group of British workers who destroyed laborsaving textile machinery between 1811 and 1816 for fear that the machinery would reduce employment. It is generally, but not always, used disparagingly.]

15. name (of a person well-suited to its owner) n.: aptronym

16. appeal (making an ... to one's monetary self-interest) n: argumentum ad crumenam

A recent article entitled *The Importance of Being Simple*, though being one of the many which supports Kilpatrick's point of view, unwittingly demonstrates its very dilemma. The writer states:

"We must befuddle our readers with at least one rare word in each paragraph, with style and form and with quality of expression — so we tell ourselves. ... *Befuddle*? Isn't this a rare mouthful? Goodness gracious me, I'm not practicing what I'm trying to preach! You're right. There must be simpler words than *befuddle*. How about *baffle* or *confound* then? You think that they're still not simple enough? Well, let's settle for *confuse*. Okay?"[17]

It seems as if the writer is being facetious, but he is not. His viewpoint is apparently that a writer should never use the words "befuddle," "baffle" or "confound," because he or she could just as easily resort to the simplest common denominator, namely "confuse." But isn't this an absurd argument? Can one imagine even Kilpatrick going to this extreme? Where do we ever draw the line? Clearly, if this writer is going to object to "befuddle," "baffle" or "confound," then what would he say about Kilpatrick's choices of "con amore" and "pro bono publico"?

Even if we assume for argument that certain words have an exact simpler synonym, does that mean that the harder word should never be used? For example, an "ecdysiast" is simply a strip tease artist. Even though it is safe to assume that not everyone knows that, the word "ecdysiast" is still used all the time, often with the context providing no assistance as to the word's meaning.[18] Does that mean that we should simply do away with the word because we can insert "stripper" in its place? Or is the use of "ecdysiast" always poor writing unless presented in context?

As Mr. Buckley puts it: "It is a curious thing, this universal assumption . . . that the American people are either unaware of the unusual word or undisposed to hear it and find out what it means, thus broadening not merely their vocabulary — that isn't the important thing — but their conceptual and descriptive powers." In short, even if there is an exact simpler synonym, this thesaurus is useful if a writer does not want to keep using the same word again and again and wants to use a more interesting word choice.[19]

The problem is not only where to draw the line, but the fact that the hard word critics are encouraging us to work towards a lowest common denominator; to shrink our vocabulary as much as possible. Is it not a worthy goal to expand our vocabularies to match the dictionaries as much as possible rather than to prod writers in the opposite direction? The only imaginable response to this is to advocate (once again) a "standard of reason," in deciding which words pass muster and which do not. But that brings us right back to the

---

17. Ang Seng Chai, *The Importance of Being Simple*, New Straits Times, 01-17-2004.

18. "Through the years, disco has lived in the rear Rio Room, which is reliably crammed on weekends with off-duty ecdysiasts and microfiber-clad lunkheads." Mr. Dallas, *Orpheus Descending at the Sellar*, The Dallas Morning News, 04-19-2002, p. 59.

19. While clearly in the minority, Mr. Buckley is not completely alone in his opposition to the dumbing down of our collective vocabulary. Michael Spear, an associate professor of journalism at the University of Richmond has written: "What reporter, after using a word a bit above the level of a high-school dropout, hasn't heard an editor exclaim with a scowl: 'What is this word?' Or, 'Who do you think you are writing for, anyway? We're trying to communicate here.' I'd wonder: 'With whom?...' Unfortunately, the use of multisyllable words still often invites attack, or, at least, eye-rolling. But if we are influenced by this, aren't we relegating ourselves to a rather barren landscape of expression?" See Spear's article, *Lingually Challenged*, in Editor & Publisher, 07-10-2000.

original flaw in the argument: there is no single standard of reason. To many people, portions of Mr. Kilpatrick's own writing ("con amore"? "pro bono publico"?) must come off as abstruse (or would that word be rejected as well?) as Mr. Buckley's do to him. So there can never be a reasonable, let's-all-agree-what-words-are-acceptable-and-what-words-are-not standard. Nor should we even try to set such a standard, for the mere attempt is necessarily an exercise in slicing and dicing perfectly good and legitimate words out of the dictionary, all in the name of dumbing down our vocabulary.

What if, however, one were to disagree with my argument entirely and wholly support Kilpatrick's worldview as to the use of unfamiliar words? Wouldn't it be nice to have a good word to describe the kind of writing that the hard-word critics bemoan? This thesaurus has several. One of them, although technically relating to the use of archaic words rather than merely hard words, is still close, especially if one argues that hard words ought to be treated as if they were archaic anyway, and that using too many of them is a sign of poor writing:

> **writing** (poor ..., esp. characterized by the affected choice of archaic words) *n*.:
> **tushery**. ∎ This novel, set in the last days of Rome in the Eastern Empire, ... tells the story of [a woman] who discovers that she is a born doctor ..., but soon realises that there is no room for her in a society where medicine is the province of men. As a piece of historical romance it is saved from **tushery** by down-to-earth writing and a quite remarkable amount of information about early medicine which proves fascinating in itself. (Robery Nye, *Review of 'The Beacon at Alexandria' by Gillian Bradshaws*, The Guardian [London], 02-06-1987.)

Another word that describes the use of hard words in a derogatory fashion is "lexiphanicism," which means the ostentatious use of obscure words (as opposed to archaic words), with the related adjective being "lexiphanic."

> **writing** (or speech characterized by the affected choice of obscure words) *n*.:
> **lexiphanicism** (*adj*.: **lexiphanic**). ∎ Can a book be both funny and tiresome? It is not the logorrhoea [wordiness] of the narrator, Harry Driscoll, that bothers me, nor his **lexiphanic** prose ... (I love reading with a dictionary to hand). (Debra Adelaide, *In Short*, Sydney Morning Herald, 03-29-2003.)

Can the defense of using unfamiliar words be reconciled with the risk of being lexiphanic? Absolutely. Note that the operative adjective in the definition of both "tushery" and "lexiphanicism" is "affected." That is, pretentious and/or unnatural. Thus, when in the course of just a few sentences Kilpatrick uses "anodyne," "meiosis," "adumbration," "omnium gatherum," "eudaemonia," "nimiety," and "logomachical," he is writing in an "affected" (albeit intentional) fashion. But that kind of writing, in which the hard words are crammed together one right after the other, is a far cry from the examples found in this thesaurus, in which, almost without exception, the hard words are not being used in an affected way, but rather within the natural flow of the text. Indeed, any other conclusion (e.g., that the use of any hard words is automatically lexiphanic) would necessarily lead to the corollary conclusion that virtually every writer quoted in this thesaurus must be a bad writer, which is, of course, absurd.

A recent book by John McWhorter, *Doing Our Own Thing—The Degradation of Language and Music and Why We Should, Like, Care*, (Gotham Books, 2003) contains an excellent discussion of the unfortunate lapse in both quality and formality of written and spoken English in this country over the last 40 years. As evidence of the current mindset in this country towards learning higher vocabulary, he quotes an educator who visited a classroom of 12-year-olds and observed them studying verbal analogies in anticipation of the SAT. "I learned that they spend hours each month ... studying long lists of verbal analogies such as 'untruthful is to mendacious as circumspect is to caution.' The time involved was not aimed at developing the students' reading and writing abilities but rather their test-taking skills." McWhorter stated that "the passage got around in the media, intended to make people shake their heads at such a sad sight," and that:

> "[I]t is telling that it spontaneously struck [the educator] as being so sad, so beside the point of education, that twelve-year-olds were being taught the meaning of written words. ... [He] assumes that this learning of words is unrelated to developing students' reading abilities. ... [H]is discomfort at seeing twelve-year-olds drilled on words like this marks him as a man of our times, for whom learned levels of English are less a main course than a garnish in an education [and that] learning high vocabulary [is] an imposition."

One suspects that those who would object to the use of the words contained in this thesaurus also concur with the notion that the teaching of analogies such as "untruthful is to mendacious as circumspect is to caution" is a waste of time. However, McWhorter notes that this is "hardly self-evident" and quotes an English professor from Rutgers who conducted a study that found "an extraordinarily high correlation" between SAT verbal scores and final grades and a much lower correlation between grades and socio-economic status. In other words, mastering the types of verbal skills tested by the SAT is not an exercise in trivia or one which has no predictive values of future performance in broader academic areas. The same may be said of the synonyms in this thesaurus: learning their use is not an exercise in trivia or becoming lexiphanic.

In a Utopian lexicographical world, the synonyms that appear in this thesaurus will be as familiar and accessible to everyone as the mundane synonyms which now appear in ordinary thesauruses. Perhaps this book is a small step in that direction. However even though none of us can be expected to know every word in the English language, or even

---

20. The word "insouciant" once again points out the flaw with Mr. Kilpatrick's argument. About that word, we may safely assume, first, that Mr. Kilpatrick knows what it means (and has likely used it himself from time to time), second, that he would never equate it with any of Mr. Buckley's word choices which Mr. Kilpatrick mocks, and third, that he would find ludicrous the notion that it should be jettisoned from the language. And yet, despite these assumptions, two things are true: First that the simpler words "nonchalant" or "carefree" could be substituted for "insouciant" just about every time. Second, and more importantly, there are many people who do not know the meaning of "insouciant." But, given our assumptions above, what can Mr. Kilpatrick say to those people? The only thing he could say is that literate people should know that word. Of course, that brings us right back to the problem of setting him up as the standard we would have to consult on every word. One wonders where, for example, would he stand on a less common synonym for "insouciant," such as "dégagé," which is used in this thesaurus? In any event, the point is clear. Of course, it is entirely possible that some words may appear in some dictionaries but not in others. However, this is almost always by virtue of the simple fact that some dictionaries are more comprehensive than others and thus will necessarily contain more words, particularly the kind of which appear in this thesaurus. For example, the number of entries of the typical collegiate dictionary is exceeded by the number of entries in the 4th edition of *The American Heritage Dictionary of the English Language*. This in turn is exceeded by *Webster's Third International Dictionary*, which in turn is exceeded by the *Oxford English Dictionary*.

half of the words, that does not mean that one should be insouciant about ignorance of any particular word or that the writer of the word should be subject to rebuke or mockery.[20] If a writer uses a word I don't know, it is my job to learn the word, to look it up, and I should not be frustrated or critical because some writer has stepped past my own "reasonable person" standard.

Finally, it must be remembered that, as to every entry in this thesaurus which contains a Clarifier (which is most), the point is that either (1) many of those synonyms cannot be accurately contained in ordinary thesauruses since they lack a Clarifier or (2) they are harder words which are not likely to be found in ordinary thesauruses in the first place because they do not lend themselves to one-word base words. (Of course, a great many of the clarifier entries fit both categories — that is, there is no one-word synonym which accurately compares to them and they are too uncommon for an ordinary thesaurus.) Some examples of the benefits of a Clarifer (and the corresponding dangers of the lack of a Clarifier) are discussed above and in fact virtually every Clarifier entry in this thesaurus proves the point. But let's leave two for the road, both of which are apropos to this discussion and which illustrate both of the above situations.

The word "casuistry" is, relatively speaking, a common word which may be found in many ordinary thesauruses as a synonym for "fallacy." Thus, one would suppose that it would be proper to say that the argument that simplest words are always best is a "casuistry." But unfortunately, without a Clarifier, a user would have no way of knowing that such a use of the word for this specific purpose is incorrect (even if the sentiment is correct). The entry in this thesaurus, using a Clarifier to show the precise use of the word, is as follows:

> **fallacy** (as in reasoning which is intended to rationalize or mislead) *n.*: **casuistry**. ▪ [Attorney Alan] Dershowitz continued: "[The jury's finding of liability against O.J. Simpson in his civil trial] doesn't in any way undercut the correctness of the first case at all." Of course not. Simpson did it but Simpson didn't do it, Simpson is guiltless but Simpson is liable. This is the **casuistry** of a man who is correctly worried about his reputation. (Author not given, *"Mr. Guilty Is Liable,"* The New Republic, 02-24-1997.)

Similarly, the word "eristic" has as one of its synonyms "fallacious." This is a much less common word which will not likely be found in a regular thesaurus. It means, specifically, engaging in argument that is specious. For this word, it would be accurate to suggest that the argument that simplest words are always best is, for the reasons discussed herein, eristic.

The bottom line is this: If a word appears in the dictionaries and is not qualified as being archaic or obsolete, it is a legitimate word, entitled to the same respect and holding the same qualifications for use as any other word. We cannot engage in a "hierarchy of legitimacy" with respect to words, since they are equally legitimate — especially the words in this thesaurus, whose validity is proven by examples showing their current usage. The fact that one word may be more familiar to the average person than another does not disqualify the less common word from use, nor should its user be subject to scorn. If a word is not described in the dictionaries as being archaic or obsolete (and at the risk of stating the obvious, that means it is not archaic or obsolete), that means it is considered current and thus legitimate — as legitimate as every other word.

Having defended the hard word, let's go to the synonyms and the examples....

The
Thinker's
Thesaurus

A

abandoned (or deserted baby or child) *n*.: **foundling**. SEE ORPHAN

abandonment (of one's religion, principles or causes) *n*.: **apostasy**. ▪ It was during the 1980s and 1990s that [Barry] Goldwater developed a reputation for **apostasy**. He defended legal abortion and homosexual rights and criticized the religious right, famously arguing that Jerry Falwell deserved "a swift kick in the ass." Some conservatives felt betrayed, while liberals applauded. (Michael Gerson, *Mr. Right*, U.S. News & World Report, 06-08-1998, p. 12.)

(2) abandonment (esp. regarding one's belief, cause or policy) *n*.: **bouleversement** [French]. SEE REVERSAL

(3) abandonment (of one's belief, cause or policy) *n*.: **tergiversation** (*v.i.*: **tergiversate**). SEE CHANGE OF MIND

abate (attempt to ... seriousness of an offense) *v.t.*: **palliate**. ▪ Every civilization needs its self-justifying myths. ... America's great national myth of the settlement and taming of the frontier grew out of the slaughter of indigenous peoples, which it was meant to explain and **palliate**. (James Bowman, *Alien Menace: Lt. Ripley is Hollywood's Mythical Woman - Butch and Ready to Kill*, National Review, 01-26-1998, p. 35.)

abbreviated (something ...) *n*.: **bobtail**. SEE ABRIDGED

abduct (a person, often to perform compulsory service abroad) *v.t.*: **shanghai**. SEE KIDNAP

abhor *v.t.*: **execrate**. SEE HATE
(2) abhor *v.t.*: **misprize**. SEE HATE

abhorrence (develop an ... for, as in dislike) *n*.: **scunner** (esp. as in "take a scunner")[British]. SEE DISLIKE

abhorrent *adj*.: **ugsome**. SEE LOATHSOME

ability (area of ...) *n*.: **métier** [French]. SEE FORTE

ablaze (with intense heat and light) *n*.: **deflagration**. SEE EXPLOSION

able (as in skillful) *adj*.: **habile**. SEE SKILLFUL

abnormal (as in departing from the standard or norm) *adj*.: **heteroclite**. ▪ Their mother was severely authoritarian. It is often from such repressive origins that rebels arise. "You have to assassinate your parents" was Philippe's advice to the young. He did it by running away to join the Foreign Legion. He attended, off and on, a suspiciously **heteroclite** array of schools before graduating with a degree in foreign languages from the Sorbonne. (James Kirkup, *Obituary: Philippe Leotard*, Independent, 08-28-2001, p. 6.)

abolish *v.t.*: **extirpate**. ▪ The argument: that if you are sufficiently fanatical in attempting to **extirpate** all sex discrimination, you will end up abolishing institutions you'd probably prefer to keep, like Wellesley, Hollins and other single-sex women's colleges. (Daniel Seligman, *Keeping Up: A Splash for the Secretary of Energy*, Fortune, 02-05-1996, p. 138.)

(2) abolish (as in put an end to): **quietus** (esp. as in "put the quietus to"). SEE TERMINATE.

abominable *adj*.: **execrable**. ▪ My generation has lots of excuses for our **execrable** parenting. [For example] the economy has forced most women into the workplace. (Dowling, Milwaukee Journal Sentinel, *Parents Can't Duck Blame for Morally Abandoned Kids*, 03-11-96, p. 3.)

abortion *n*.: **feticide**. ▪ [T]he equal-protection clause of the 14th Amendment would seem to require states to extend legal protection to the unborn. [In Roe v. Wade, Justice Harry] Blackmun, however, relying on grossly inaccurate legal history ... concluded that the due-process clause of [the 14th] amendment forbids states from providing any meaningful protection against deliberate **feticide**. (Author not given, *Harry Blackmun, R.I.P.*, National Review, 04-05-1999.)

abound *v.i.*: **pullulate**. SEE TEEM

about (as in concerning or regarding) *prep*.: **anent**. SEE REGARDING

about-face (as in reversal of policy or position) *n*.: **volte-face** [French]. ▪ More than 350 years have passed since Galileo was condemned by the Roman Catholic Church for the correct, if impolitic, declaration that the earth revolved around the sun. Now the church has solemnized its belated **volte-face** on the celestial dispute by mailing an apology [i.e. issuing new stamps commemorating Galileo]. (Author not given, *Chronicles: More than 350 Years Have Passed Since Galileo Was Condemned*, Time International, 06-13-1994, p. 13.)

(2) about-face (as in abandonment of one's religion, principles or causes) *n.*: **apostasy**. SEE ABANDONMENT

(3) about-face (esp. regarding one's beliefs, causes or policies) *n.*: **bouleversement** [French]. SEE CHANGE OF MIND

(4) about-face (regarding one's belief, cause or policy) *n.*: **tergiversation** (*v.i.*: **tergiversate**). SEE CHANGE OF MIND

above (lying ...) *adj.*: **superjacent**. SEE OVERLYING

abridged (something ...) *n.*: **bobtail**. ▪ Senator Trent Lott, the majority leader, said that it would be "a big mistake" for the Senate to vote to dismiss the [impeachment] charges Monday. The Mississippi Republican said it would be a "**bobtail** action of a constitutional process." (Brian Knowlton, *Trial of Clinton Turns Bitter: Democrats 'Appalled' at Sudden Summons of Lewinsky*, International Herald Tribune, 01-25-1999.)

abscond (as in leave hurriedly or secretly) *v.t.*: **absquatulate**. SEE LEAVE

absent (anything better) *adv.*: **faute de mieux** [French]. SEE LACKING

absent-minded (as in distracted, esp. because of worries or fears) *adj.*: **distrait**. SEE DISTRACTED

(2) absent-minded (person, as in an impractical contemplative person with no clear occupation or income) *n.*: **luftmensch** [lit. "man of air"; German, Yiddish]. SEE DREAMER

absolute (esp. when used with "nonsense") *adj.*: **arrant**. SEE TOTAL

(2) absolute (as in inviolable) *adj.*: **infrangible**. SEE INVIOLABLE

(3) absolute (as in complete or unlimited, esp. as in ... power) *adj.*: **plenary**. SEE COMPLETE

absolution (as in place or occasion of humiliation and seeking ...) *n.*: **Canossa**. SEE PENANCE

abstract (as in intangible) *adj.*: **incorporeal**. ▪ As the passage of time removes from the scene more and more of the accused wrongdoers, and more and more of their possible victims, it makes less and less moral or economic sense — and ultimately no sense at all — for the law to exact monetary redress from **incorporeal** institutions such as corporations or governments. (Stuart Taylor Jr., *Legal Affairs: Paying Reparations for Ancient Wrongs Is Not Right*, National Journal, 04-07-2001.)

absurd (as in acting foolishly, esp. in a smug or complacent manner) *adj.*: **fatuous**. SEE FOOLISH

(2) absurd (as in laughable) *adj.*: **gelastic**. SEE LAUGHABLE

(3) absurd (as in laughable) *adj.*: **risible**. SEE LAUGHABLE

absurdity (as in foolishness or stupidity) *n.*: **betise** [French]. SEE STUPIDITY

(2) absurdity *n.*: **folderol** (or **falderal**). SEE NONSENSE

(3) absurdity (statement which contains a logical ..., usually unrealized by the speaker) *n.*: **Irish bull**. SEE INCONGRUITY

(4) absurdity (as in nonsense) *n.*: **piffle**. SEE NONSENSE

(5) absurdity *n.*: **trumpery**. SEE NONSENSE

abundance (illusion of ... when in fact there is little) *adj.*: **Barmecidal** (esp. as in "Barmecidal feast"). SEE ILLUSION

abuse (being subject to ..., esp. public) *n.*: **obloquy**. Despite being the target of so much public **obloquy**, [John D.] Rockefeller seemed fearless. (Ron Chernow, *Titan*, Random House [1998], p. 262.)

abusive (language) *n.*: **billingsgate**. SEE LANGUAGE

(2) abusive (woman who is also vulgar) *n.*: **fishwife**. SEE WOMAN

(3) abusive (language) *n.*: **vituperation** (*adj.*: **vituperative**). SEE INVECTIVE

acceptable (an ..., as in proper or appropriate, thing to do) *n.*: **bon ton** [French]. SEE APPROPRIATE

(2) acceptable (in accord with ... standards) *adj.*: **comme il faut** [French]. SEE PROPER

accepting (of other views and opinions) *adj.*: **latitudinarian**. SEE OPEN-MINDED

accessible (to the general public in terms of comprehension or suitability) *adj.*: **exoteric**. ▪ [Robert Penn Warren] saw nothing contradictory in his esoteric and **exoteric** activities, and wrote with equal facility for magazines such as Life and for those of small circulation. (Daniel Aaron, *A Minor Master*, The New Republic, 10-20-1997.)

accessories (as in finery) *n.*: **caparison**. SEE FINERY

(2) accessories (showy ..., as in finery) *n.*: **frippery**. SEE FINERY

accidental (as in by chance) *adj.*: **adventitious**. SEE CHANCE

acclaim *n.*: **éclat**. ∎ The City of Atlanta held a contest for a slogan that would best illustrate why the City was chosen for the international **éclat** that goes with hosting the 1996 Olympic Games. The winner: "Atlanta - come celebrate our dream." (Nat Hentoff, *Amnesty Focuses Light on Atlanta*, Rocky Mountain News, 07-22-96, p. 27A.)

accompaniment *n.*: **appanage**. SEE ADJUNCT

accompanying (as in incident to) *adj.*: **appurtenant**. SEE PERTAINING

accord (in ...) *adj.*: **consonant**. SEE HARMONY
(2) **accord** (in ..., as in harmonious or compatible) *adj.*: **simpatico**. SEE COMPATIBLE

accouterments (as in trappings) *n.*: **habiliment(s)**. SEE TRAPPINGS

accumulation (confused or jumbled ...) *n.*: **agglomeration**. SEE JUMBLE
(2) **accumulation** (of objects, people or ideas) *n.*: **congeries**. SEE COLLECTION

accurate (as in reflecting reality or truth) *adj.*: **veridical**. SEE REALISTIC AND TRUTHFUL
(2) **accurate** (appearing to be ...) *adj.*: **verisimilar**. SEE REALISTIC

accusation (which is false, defamatory and published for political gain right before an election) *n.*: **roorback**. SEE FALSEHOOD

accuse (an accuser with having committed similar offense) *n.*: **tu quoque** [Latin]. ∎ The Democrats, who still resent Mr. Barbour for raising the money that snatched Congress away from them in 1994, are trying to imply that Mr. Barbour's Republicans are just as sleazy as the Clinton people. ... This **tu quoque** attack on Mr. Barbour begins to look like simple partisanship. (Author not given, *Inside the Belly of the Beast*, The Economist, 07-26-1997.)
(2) **accuse** *v.t.*: **inculpate**. SEE BLAME

accuser (esp. by being an informer) *n.*: **delator**. ∎ The right to file charges against a fellow citizen was not in itself new, but took on a new character when the state began awarding the **delator** a share of the property of the accused; a successful accusation of treason, for example, carried as a prize a quarter of the victim's estate. (Walter Olson, *Tripp Wire: How Informers Ended Up Behind Every Office Potted Plant*, Reason, 04-01-1998, p. 60.)

accustomed *adj.*: **wonted**. SEE CUSTOMARY

acerbic (as in ... remarks) *adj.*: **astringent**. SEE HARSH

acne (tending to produce or aggravate ...) *adj.*: **comedogenic**. ∎ The best skin care in the world isn't going to cure your acne so don't spend a fortune. Always look on labels for **non-comedogenic** products as these won't block follicles. (Author not given, *Health Zone: Tips From the Top Spot of Bother*, The Mirror, 03-21-2002, p. 36.)

acquire (or claim for oneself without right) *v.t.*: **arrogate**. SEE CLAIM
(2) **acquire** (by begging or sponging off of) *v.t.*: **cadge**. SEE BEG
(3) **acquire** (for oneself without permission) *v.t.*: **expropriate**. SEE SEIZE

acquittal (finding ... through testimony of others) *n.*: **compurgation**. ∎ [In medieval times], the ordeal, a form of proof which relied on [torture] to determine the guilt or innocence of the accused [was used] in cases where normal juridical procedures, most notably **compurgation**, the sworn endorsement of friends and neighbors of the accused, were not deemed applicable. (Kathleen Biddick, *Aesthetics, Ethnicity, and the History of Art*, The Art Bulletin, 12-01-1996, p. 594.)

acrimony *n.*: **asperity**. ∎ Mr. Karsh's will assuredly not be the last word. In an exchange last year in Middle East Quarterly, Mr. Shlaim mounted a spirited (and, given the **asperity** of Mr. Karsh's attack, good-natured) defense of his collusion thesis. (Author not given, *The Unchosen People*, The Economist, 07-19-1997.)

across *prep., adv.*: **athwart**. ∎ Dagestan is far more strategically vital than Chechnya: the Russians can build a bypass around Chechnya for Caspian Sea oil; Dagestan, however, lies **athwart** the only Russian route from Baku. (Owen Matthews, *Digging In For Worse to Come*, Newsweek International, 09-20-1999, p. 26.)

action (gracious ...) *n.*: **beau geste**. SEE GESTURE
(2) **action** (as in course of ...) *n.*: **démarche** [French]. SEE COURSE OF ACTION

actions (study of human ...) *n.*: **praxeology**. SEE BEHAVIOR

actors (in a play or story) *n.*: **dramatis personae**. SEE CHARACTERS

actual (as in reflecting reality) *adj.*: **veridical**. SEE REALISTIC

actuality (state of ... as opposed to potentiality) *n.*: **entelechy**. ■ Animals are not only being assimilated to humans; they are being made into the destiny of humans, the **entelechy** of humanity in which it realizes its highest possibility. [Fully social] animals are assumed to have achieved a degree of success as social animals that we ourselves, who invented the idea of society, have not attained, argue the sociobiologists. (Richard Klein, *The Power of Pets: America's Obsession With the Cute and Cuddly*, The New Republic, 07-10-1995, p. 18.)

actualize (as in making an abstract concept seem real) *v.t.*: **reify**. See MATERIALIZE

actually (as in, in fact) *adj., adv.*: **de facto** (as contrasted with *de jure*: legally or by law) [Latin]. See IN FACT

adage *n.*: **apothegm**. See SAYING
 (2) adage (witty or clever ... or line) *n.*: **bon mot**. See LINE
 (3) adage (pithy ...) *n.*: **gnome** (*adj*: **gnomic**). See CATCHPHRASE

adages (given to stating ..., esp. in a moralizing way) *adj.*: **sententious**. See APHORISTIC

addition (as in something which is an accessory to something else) *n.*: **appurtenance**. See APPENDAGE
 (2) addition (as in insertion of something between existing things) *n.*: **intercalation**. See INSERTION

additionally *adv.*: **withal**. See MOREOVER

address (formal ...) *n.*: **allocution**. See SPEECH
 (2) address (a topic, esp. in a long-winded or pompous manner) *v.i.*: **bloviate**. See SPEAK
 (3) address (a subject at length in speech or writing) *v.i.*: **expatiate**. See EXPOUND
 (4) address (lengthy ..., as in speech) *n.*: **peroration**. See MONOLOGUE

adept (as in skillful) *adj.*: **habile**. See SKILLFUL

adhere (together, as with glue) *v.t.*: **agglutinate**. ■ The [rhinoceros] horn is nothing more than **agglutinated** hair with no medicinal value, but is highly coveted — said to contain legendary aphrodisiac properties — in Chinese pharmacopoeia. (Claire Scobie, *Nature Watch*, The Sunday Telegraph, 09-27-1998, p. 21.)
 (2) adhere (closely to a line, rule or principle) *v.i.*: **hew**. See CONFORM

adherent (strong ... of a cause, religion or activity) *n.*: **votary**. See SUPPORTER
 (2) adherent *adj.*: **acolyte**. See FOLLOWER

adjunct *n.*: **appanage**. ■ Some still believe the dream, insisting that [the town of Primorye in eastern Russia] — no longer a pliant **appanage** of Moscow — will unite with the Pacific Rim and arise from its Soviet hangover in a hearty economic rebound. (Andrew Meier, *Europe: Letter From Vladivostok: Surviving on the Edge*, Time International, 02-07-2000, p. 25.)

admiration (as in praise) *n.*: **approbation**. See PRAISE

admirers (group of fawning ...) *n.*: **claque**. On a visit to Time Inc.'s new-media facility, [Bill Gates] answered questions from a collection of magazine editors as if by rote, but on his way out he asked to see the Internet servers and spent 45 minutes grilling the **claque** of awed techies there. (Walter Isaacson, *Business: In Search of the Real Bill Gates*, Time, 01-13-1997, p. 44.)

admission (of sin) *n.*: **peccavi**. See CONFESSION

admit (to one's sins, esp. in church) *v.t., v.i.*: **shrive**. See CONFESS
 (2) admit (as in confide one's thoughts or feelings) *v.t., v.i.*: **unbosom**. See CONFIDE

admonish (sharply) *v.t.*: **keelhaul**. See REBUKE
 (2) admonish *v.t.*: **objurgate**. See CRITICIZE

admonishing (as in criticism) *n.*: **animadversion** (*v.t.*: **animadvert**). See CRITICISM

ado (over a trifling matter) *n.*: **foofaraw**. See FUSS

adoration (as in worship of dead people) *n.*: **necrolatry**. See WORSHIP
 (2) adoration (of women) *n.*: **philogyny**. See WOMEN

adorn (in a showy or excessive manner) *v.t.*: **bedeck**. ■ The best albums preserve not just a show's score but the meaning and joy of the theatrical moment. Sitting at home, you can't see the deliriously gaudy haberdashery that **bedecks** the Guys and Dolls touts. (Richard Corliss, *Reviews Theater: Broadway's Record Year*, Time, 09-14-1992, p. 71.)
 (2) adorn (or dress in a showy or excessive manner) *v.t.*: **bedizen**. ■ Occasionally, I've shown houses out this way, though their owners, fat and **bedizened** as pharaohs, and who should be giddy with

the world's gifts, always seem the least pleasant people in the world. (Richard Ford, *Independence Day*, Knopf [1995], p. 128.)

adornments *n.*: **caparison**. SEE FINERY
(2) adornments (showy ...) *n.*: **frippery**. SEE FINERY

adroit *adj.*: **habile**. SEE SKILLFUL

adulation (one who seeks favor through ..., esp. of one in power) *n.*: **courtier**. SEE FLATTERY

adulterous (man married to ... wife) *n.*: **cuckold** (*v.t.*: to make a ... of). ▪ Married with two children, Don acquired a reputation as an incurable skirt chaser. ... His conquests soon became the stuff of legend. One that is often told but has never been confirmed: A **cuckolded** husband got his revenge by dumping a load of wet cement into Don's convertible. (Kim Clark, *Features: Tough Times for the Chicken King Don Tyson*, Fortune, 10-28-1996, p. 88.)

advance (esp. a military ...) *n.*: **anabasis**. ▪ Federer, carried forward by the momentum from his serve, picked [Andre Agassi's] return out of the air, effortlessly flicking a backhand volley from behind the service line, and continued his **anabasis** toward the net. (L. Jon Wertheim, *That Was as Good as it Gets: So Said a Certain Bald Superstar From Las Vegas About the Play of the Lavishly Talented Roger Federer, Who Elevated the Men's [Tennis] Game in 2003*, Sports Illustrated, 12-29-2003.)

advantage (as in, "to whose ...?") *n.*: **cui bono** [Latin. This phrase is generally posed as a question and usually one to which the writer knows the answer]. ▪ [W]hat if George Bush is a plant ... put here by shadowy somebodies in order to undermine the United States? ... You can ask, **cui bono**? Ah, there's a list: radical Islamicists, international oil cartels, China, the Russian mob, North Korea, Iran, the South American drug cartels, just about anyone who needs a diplomatically inept, chronically weak U.S. administration to consolidate its power. (Jon Carroll, *Daily Datebook*, The San Francisco Chronicle, 06-24-2004.)

adverse (as in harmful) *adj.*: **nocent**. SEE HARMFUL
(2) adverse *adj.*: **oppugnant**. SEE ANTAGONISTIC

advisors (group of ..., often scheming or plotting) *n.*: **camarilla**. ▪ An old-fashioned nationalist, Giesevius had been authorized by Admiral Wilhelm Canaris, the head of German intelligence, to make contact with the Allies on behalf of the German Resistance. He supplied Dulles with tantalizing information on the incessant infighting among Hitler's **camarilla**. (Jacob Heilbrun, *Gentleman Spy: The Life of Allen Dulles*, The New Republic, 03-27-1995, p. 32.)

advocate (or leader, esp. for a political cause) *n.*: **fugleman**. SEE LEADER
(2) advocate (of a cause) *n.*: **paladin**. SEE PROPONENT
(3) advocate (strong ... of a cause, religion or activity) *n.*: **votary**. SEE SUPPORTER

advocating (a particular point of view) *adj.*: **tendentious**. SEE BIASED

affability *n.*: **bonhomie**. ▪ But Peace with Dignity won't come easily [in the Clinton impeachment proceedings]. For all the bipartisan **bonhomie** that has marked the Senate proceedings, Democrats aren't inclined to do much to help Republicans save face with their party's Clinton-loathing right wing. (James Carney, *Nation: Waiting for the Bell*, Time, 02-15-1999, p. 30.)

affair (as in sex outside of marriage) *n.*: **hetaerism**. ▪ Of course, [historically] men still enjoyed conjugal infidelity referred to as **hetaerism**. ... Monogamy was thus only meant for women. (Author not given, *Letters to the Editor*, The Edmonton Sun, 05-07-2000, p. C20.)
(2) affair (love ...) *n.*: **amourette** [French]. SEE LOVE AFFAIR

affected (speech or writing) *adj.*: **fustian**. SEE POMPOUS
(2) affected (of an ..., as in pedantic, word or term) *adj.*: **inkhorn**. SEE PEDANTIC

affectionate (as in amorous) *adj.*: **amative**. SEE AMOROUS

affiliated (with, as in incident to) *adj.*: **appurtenant**. SEE PERTAINING

affinity (as in family ties) *n.*: **propinquity**. SEE KINSHIP

affluence (study of or focus on ..., esp. in artistic works) *n.*: **plutography**. SEE WEALTH

affluent (and/or prominent person) *n.*: **nabob**. SEE BIGWIG
(2) affluent (government by the ...) *n.*: **plutocracy**. SEE GOVERNMENT

affront (an ... to another's dignity) *n*.: **lese majesty**. SEE INSULT

(2) affront (as in insult, delivered while leaving the scene) *n*.: **Parthian shot**. SEE PARTING SHOT

affronted (easily ...) *adj*.: **umbrageous**. SEE OFFENDED

afraid (something that is dreaded, disliked, or to be ... of) *n*.: **bête noire** [French]. SEE DREADED

(2) afraid (as in spineless or indecisive, or such a person) *adj., n*.: **namby-pamby**. SEE SPINELESS

(3) afraid (as in cowardly) *adj*.: **pusillanimous**. SEE COWARDLY

again (as in anew) *adv*.: **afresh**. SEE ANEW

against *adj*.: **oppugnant**. SEE ANTAGONISTIC

against the world *adv., adj*.: **contra mundum** [Latin]. ▮ [Jack Straw said] that negotiations on a new European Constitution could end in failure, with Britain vetoing a deal. ... Prime Minister [Tony Blair] feared the Government would be compared to [John Major and the Tories who] habitually threatened to block EU business unless Britain got its way. [One source said:] "Jack's comments came out as too Majoresque, as if we were saying veto, veto, veto like the Tories. Blair does not want it to be Britain **contra mundum**." (Toby Helm, *Straw in Trouble With Blair For Sounding 'Too Majoresque,' European Constitution*, Daily Telegraph, 11-26-2003.)

aged (of or like an ... woman) *adj*.: **anile**. SEE OLD WOMAN

(2) aged (as in broken down and/or worn out) *adj*.: **raddled**. SEE WORN-OUT

(3) aged (and sick person) *n*.: **Struldbrug**. SEE DECREPIT

agent (as in middleman) *n*.: **comprador**. SEE INTERMEDIARY

aggravation (as in trouble) *n*.: **tsuris** [Yiddish]. SEE TROUBLE

aggregation (of objects, people or ideas) *n*.: **congeries**. SEE COLLECTION

aggressive (as in pugnacious or ready to fight) *adj*.: **bellicose**. SEE BELLIGERENT

aggrieved (easily ..., as in offended) *adj*.: **umbrageous**. SEE OFFENDED

aging *adj*.: **senescent**. ▮ [The literature I received from the] American Association of Retired Persons ... warranted that this organization fought unstintingly for the rights of **senescent** folks everywhere and hinted heavily that even though it already had 27 million members, it could make room for one more if only [I] would put up the highly affordable $5 dues. (Daniel Seligman, *Keeping Up, Staving Off the Old Folks*, Fortune, 12-21-1987, p. 169.)

agitate *v.t*.: **commove**. ▮ Twelve years ago, Fuller founded [Habitat for Humanity to] provide the poor with "simple, decent, affordable housing." ... Fuller, 53, is an Ichabod Crane look-alike who is incessantly joking, cajoling, **commoving**, pressing, pleading for Habitat. (Don Winbush, *American Ideas: Habitat for Humanity a Bootstrap Approach to Low-Cost Housing*, Time, 01-16-1989, p. 12.)

agitated *adj*.: **in a dither**. SEE FLUSTERED

agitation (as in propaganda) *n*.: **agitprop**. SEE PROPAGANDA

(2) agitation (as in a state of tense and nervous ...) *n*. **fantod**. SEE TENSION

(3) agitation (state of ...) *n*.: **swivet** (as in "in a swivet"). SEE DISTRESS

agitator (a political ..., who often believes in violence to attain an end) *n*.: **sans-culotte**. SEE EXTREMIST

agonize (or complain) *v.i*.: **repine**. SEE COMPLAIN

agonizing (journey or experience) *n*.: **via dolorosa**. SEE ORDEAL

agony (as in place or occasion of great suffering, or hell) *n*.: **Gehenna**. SEE HELL

(2) agony (as in occasion or place of great suffering) *n*.: **Gethsemane**. SEE HELL

(3) agony (as in occasion or place of great suffering) *n*.: **Golgotha**. SEE HELL

agreeable (as in pleasing) *adj*.: **prepossessing**. SEE PLEASING

agreement (in ... on the arrangement of parts as part of a whole) *n*.: **concinnity**. SEE HARMONY

(2) agreement (in ...) *adj*.: **consonant**. SEE HARMONY

(3) agreement (temporary ... between opposing parties pending final deal) *n*.: **modus vivendi** [Latin]. SEE TRUCE

(4) agreement (in ..., as in harmonious or compatible) *adj*.: **simpatico**. SEE COMPATIBLE

ahead (of, as in antecedent) *adj*.: **prevenient** (often as in "prevenient grace"). SEE ANTECEDENT

aid (as in, "to whose ...?") *n.*: **cui bono** [Latin]. See ADVANTAGE

aide *n.*: **adjutant**. See ASSISTANT

(2) aide (esp. to organized crime leader) *n.*: **consigliere** [Italian]. See ASSISTANT

(3) aide *n.*: **factotum**. See ASSISTANT

(4) aide (esp. to a scholar or magician) *n.*: **famulous**. See ASSISTANT

(5) aide (who is loyal and unquestioning) *n.*: **myrmidon**. See ASSISTANT

aides (group of ... or advisors, often scheming or plotting) *n.*: **camarilla**. See ADVISORS

ailing (person, esp. one morbidly concerned with his own health) *n., adj.*: **valetudinarian**. See SICKLY

aim (hidden or ulterior ...) *n.*: **arriere-pensee** (or **arrière-pensée**) [French]. See MOTIVE

(2) aim (the ... to achieve a particular goal or desire) *n.*: **nisus**. See GOAL

(3) aim (as in objective) *n.*: **quaesitum**. See OBJECTIVE

(4) aim (directed towards an ...) *adj.*: **telic**. See PURPOSEFUL

(5) aim (esp. of life) *n.*: **telos** [Greek]. See GOAL

(6) aim (which is elusive or not realistically obtainable) *n.*: **will-o'-the-wisp**. See PIPE DREAM

aimless (talk or act in an ... or incoherent fashion) *v.i.*: **maunder**. See RAMBLE

air (as in aura or impalpable emantion) *n.*: **effluvium**. See AURA

(2) air (as in demeanor) *n.*: **mien**. See DEMEANOR

airborne (dancer's seeming ability to stay ...) *n.*: **ballon** [French]. See FLOAT

airheaded (person) *n.*: **flibbertigibbet**. See FLIGHTY

airtight *adj.*: **hermetic**. See SEALED

airy *adj.*: **diaphanous**. See TRANSPARENT

(2) airy *adj.*: **gossamer**. See TRANSPARENT

akin (to, as in related) *adj.*: **cognate**. See RELATED

alarm (bell) *n.*: **tocsin**. ∎ We are now facing a second spate of [Carol] Gilligan-inspired books and articles, this time sounding the **tocsin** about the plight of our nation's isolated, repressed and silenced young males. (Christina Sommers, *The War Against Boys*, Simon & Schuster [2000], p. 137.)

(2) alarm (as in panic) *n.*: **Torschlusspanik** [German]. See PANIC

alcohol (given to or marked by consumption of ...) *adj.*: **bibulous**. See IMBIBING

(2) alcohol (of superior quality) *n.*: **supernaculum**. See WINE

alcoholic *n.*: **dipsomaniac** (*adj.*: **dipsomaniacal**). ∎ A matched pair of **dipsomaniacs**, Caitlin and Dylan [Thomas] led a depraved existence, roaring from pub to pub and brawling over countless infidelities. (David Grogan, *Pages: From Dylan Thomas' Widow, Caitlin, Comes a Portrait of the Poet as a [Mad] Young Dog*, People, 07-06-1987, p. 79.)

alert (as in alarm bell) *n.*: **tocsin**. See ALARM

(2) alert (as in on the ...) *n.*: **on the qui vive** [idiom]. See LOOKOUT

alert (person) *n.*: **Argus**. See WATCHFUL

alertness *n.*: **acuity**. See KEENNESS

(2) alertness (lacking ...) *adj.*: **bovine**. See SLUGGISH

(3) alertness (lacking ...) *adj.*: **logy**. See SLUGGISH

alien (as in foreigner) *n.*: **auslander**. See FOREIGNER

(2) alien (as in foreigner, from another country or place) *n.*: **outlander**. See FOREIGNER

all-around *adj.*: **multifarious**. See VERSATILE

(2) all-around (often used of a performer or artist) *adj.*: **protean**. See VERSATILE

allegation (made without proof or support) *n.*: **ipse dixit** [Latin]. ∎ I have long been convinced that authors of pro-choice literature have no concept of the ideology and philosophy which drive pro-life activities. The January 16 editorial admits that abortion is a deeply divisive, controversial issue, then by **ipse dixit**, declares the pro-choice side to be the right one. (Mary Duhon, *Viewpoints*, The Houston Chronicle, 01-23-1998, p. A33.)

alleged (as in supposed) *adj.*: **putative**. See SUPPOSED

(2) alleged (as in invented or substituted with fraudulent intent) *adj.*: **supposititious**. See SUPPOSED

allegiance *n.*: **fealty**. See LOYALTY

alliance (secret ..., as in conspiracy) *n.*: **cabal**. See PLOT

allocate (proportionately) *v.t.*: **admeasure**. See APPORTION

allot (proportionately) *v.t.*: **admeasure**. See Apportion

allow (as in bestow, by one with higher power) *v.t.*: **vouchsafe**. See Bestow

alluring (and charming woman) *n.*: **Circe**. See Enchantress
(2) alluring (person through magnetism or charm) *n.*: **duende**. See Charisma
(3) alluring (young woman) *n.*: **houri** [French]. See Woman
(4) alluring *adj.*: **piquant**. See Appealing
(5) alluring (as in tempting) *adj.*: **siren**. See Tempting

alone (as in against the world) *adv., adj.*: **contra mundum** [Latin]. See Against the World

aloud (fear of speaking ...) *n.*: **phonophobia**. See Fear

alphabet (one who is learning the ...) *n.*: **abecedarian**. ▪ Why not be **abecedarians** with your family as you discover the sensory delights of spring? You can document spring firsts from A to Z when you make a "Spring ABC Book" together. On each of 26 large index cards, write a letter of the alphabet. (Donna Erickson, *Prime Time With Kids*, St. Louis Post-Dispatch, 03-15-1995, p. 4E.)
(2) alphabet (sentence with every letter of) *n.*: **pangram**. ▪ [Will Shortz:] "It was inspired by a current novel, 'Ella Minnow Pea' by Mark Dunn, which has a number of **pangrams** sprinkled through it ... like 'Pack my box with five dozen liquor jugs.'" (Liane Hansen, *Analysis: Sunday Puzzle*, Weekend Edition - Sunday [NPR], 09-29-2002.)

also (as in moreover) *adv.*: **withal**. See Moreover

alter (esp. in a strange, grotesque or humorous way) *v.t.*: **transmogrify**. See Transform

alteration (complete ...) *n.*: **permutation**. See Transformation

altercation (esp. public) *n.*: **affray**. See Brawl

altruistic *adj.*: **eleemosynary**. See Charitable

always (as in forever) *adv.*: **in aeternum** [Latin]. See Forever

amateur (or dabbler) *n.*: **dilettante** (pl. **dilettanti**). ▪ But [in the world of scavengers or homeless people] eating from dumpsters is what separates the **dilettanti** from the professionals. (Lars Eighner, *Travels With Lizbeth*, St. Martin's Press [1993], p. 112.)

ambiguity (in language) *n.*: **amphibiology**. ▪ Robbe-Grillet wrote some incredibly dull books, if you'll allow me the discourtesy, but also some texts whose undeniable interest resides in what we might call his technical dexterity. For example, *Jealousy*. The title isn't very objective — quite a paradox! — since in French it means both "window blind" and "jealousy," an **amphibiology** that disappears in Spanish (and English). (Mario Vargas Llosa, *Levels of Reality*, The Literary Review, 03-22-2002.)

ambiguous (or obscure) *adj.*: **Delphic** [derives from the oracle of Apollo at Delphi in Greek mythology]. ▪ The star attraction was Colin Powell, and the big issue was whether he would run for president in 1996. And when a member of the audience put the question to him directly, Powell answered with **Delphic** aplomb. "There is no real passion in me to run for office," Powell said. "But I don't want to rule it out." (Robert Shogan, *A Novice, But Maybe a Frontrunner/Powell Leaves Himself on the List as a '96 Presidential Possibility*, Minneapolis Star Tribune, 02-02-1995, p. 4A.)
(2) ambiguous (or obscure speech or writing, esp. deliberately) *adj.*: **elliptical**. See Cryptic
(3) ambiguous (or cryptic or equivocal) *adj.*: **sybilline** (or **sibylline**; often cap.). See Cryptic

ambition (to achieve a particular goal or desire) *n.*: **nisus**. See Goal
(2) ambition (as in energy coupled with a will to succeed) *n.*: **spizzerinctum**. See Energy
(3) ambition (highest ... to be attained, lit. the greatest or highest good) *n.*: **summum bonum** [Latin]. See Ideal

ambivalence (as in the dilemma of being given a choice between two equally appealing alternatives and thus being able to choose neither one) *n.*: **Buridan's ass**. See Paralysis

amend (text or language by removing errors or flaws) *v.t.*: **blue-pencil**. See Edit
(2) amend (text or language by removing errors or flaws) *v.t.*: **emend**. See Edit

amendment (as in correction, esp. in printed material) *n.*: **corrigendum**. See Correction

amends (make ... for) *v.t., v.i.*: **expiate**. See Atone
(2) amends (making ... for) *adj.*: **piacular**. See Atoning

amiability *n.*: **bonhomie**. See AFFABILITY

amnesia (specifically inability to recall meaning of words) *n.*: **paramnesia**. ∎ If you suffer from **paramnesia**, just do what I did: subscribe to the A.Word.A.Day service on the Internet ... and enrich your vocabulary with a plethora of words that will express exactly what you want in the most efficient manner. (Dorothea Helms, *Reining in Rampant Verbosity*, The Toronto Sun, 09-13-2000, p. C6.)

amoral (person) *n.*: **reprobate**. See UNPRINCIPLED

amorous *adj.*: **amative**. ∎ Of course, there's the argument that the baby-boom generation of which the Clintons are a part don't express their **amative** feelings openly, that Hillary Rodham Clinton is a new breed of professional woman with her own political ambitions, or that, quite frankly, the Clintons' personal relationship is their own private business — and not the public's. (Thomas DiBacco, *Will the Real Clinton Stand Up? A Year Later, We're Still Waiting*, Orlando Sentinel, 12-5-1993, p. G3.)

(2) amorous (esp. in the sexual sense) *adj.*: **amatory**. See LOVEMAKING

amuse (oneself in a light, frolicsome manner) *v.t., v.i.*: **disport**. See FROLIC

amused (having an ability or tendency to be ...) *n.*: **risibility**. See LAUGH

amusing (line) *n.*: **bon mot** [French]. See QUIP
(2) amusing (line) *n.*: **epigram**. See QUIP
(3) amusing *adj.*: **gelastic**. See LAUGHABLE
(4) amusing (in a sarcastic or biting way) *adj.*: **mordant**. See SARCASTIC
(5) amusing *adj.*: **risible**. See LAUGHABLE
(6) amusing (as in witty) *adj.*: **waggish**. See WITTY
(7) amusing (person who tries to be ... but is not) *n.*: **witling**. See HUMORLESS

analogous (as in related) *adj.*: **cognate**. See RELATED

analysis (one who is undergoing ...) *n.*: **analysand**. See PSYCHOANALYSIS
(2) analysis (specious ... intended to mislead or rationalize) *n.*: **casuistry**. See FALLACIOUS
(3) analysis (which is complicated and often illogical) *n.*: **choplogic**. See FALLACY
(4) analysis (of a subject, as in survey) *n.*: **conspectus**. See SURVEY
(5) analysis (of a text by adding one's own ideas) *n.*: **eisegesis**. See INTERPRETATION

(6) analysis (esp. of a text) *n.*: **exegesis**. See INTERPRETATION

analytical (as in logical) *adj.*: **ratiocinative**. See LOGICAL

analyze (in minute detail) *v.t.*: **anatomize**. ∎ Few movies attempt to **anatomize** a whole sick society, to dissect the mortal betrayals of country, friend, lover and family; fewer films achieve this goal with such energy and wit. (Richard Corliss, *Cinema: From Failure to Cult Classic*, Time, 03-21-1988, p. 84.)
(2) analyze (logically) *v.i.*: **ratiocinate**. ∎ [Author Steven] Fry talks of his father's "misanthropy and arrogance," his "infuriatingly, cold, precise **ratiocinating** engine of a brain fuelled by a wholly egocentric passion" and says that whenever Fry Senior was in the house, "instantly, fun, freedom and relaxation turned into terrified silence." (Lynn Barber, *Books: But Who Cares About Tishes and Pollies?* The Daily Telegraph, 10-18-1997.)
(3) analyze *v.t.*: **assay**. See EVALUATE
(4) analyze (as in think about) *v.t.*: **cerebrate**. See THINK
(5) analyze (as in think about) *v.t.*: **cogitate**. See THINK

anarchy (movement towards or degree of ... in a system or society) *n.*: **entropy**. See DISORDER
(2) anarchy (as in government by the mob or the masses) *n.*: **mobocracy**. See GOVERNMENT
(3) anarchy (as in government by the mob or the masses) *n.*: **ochlocracy**. See GOVERNMENT

ancestor (of or derived from name of female ...) *adj.*: **matronymic**. See MATERNAL
(2) ancestor (of or derived from name of male ...) *adj.*: **patronymic**. See PATERNAL
(3) ancestor (as in predecessor) *n.*: **progenitor**. See PREDECESSOR

ancestors (excessive reverence for ... or tradition) *n.*: **filiopietistic**. See OLD-FASHIONED

ancient (esp. as in outdated) *adj.*: **antediluvian**. See OUTDATED
(2) ancient *adj.*: **hoary**. See OLD

anecdote (as in example, used to make a point) *n.*: **exemplum**. See EXAMPLE

anemic (from loss or lack of body strength) *adj.*: **asthenic** (*n.*: **asthenia**). See WEAK

anesthetizing (as in sleep-inducing) *adj.*: **soporific**. See SLEEP-INDUCING

anew *adv.*: **afresh**. ▪ But now that the [Internet] mania is over, it's probably time to think **afresh** about the technological revolution, to toss out those wishful fantasies left over from the Romantic era, or the 1960s, and see how these gizmos are really going to change our lives. (David Brooks, *Finding the 'Next' Netheads*, Newsweek International, 08-20-2001, p. 53.)

angelic *adj.*: **beatific** (to make ... *v.t.*: **beatify**). SEE JOYFUL

anger *n.*: **choler** (*adj.*: **choleric**). ▪ [As Richard Marcinko] rages over and over again in [his] book, "Why the hell didn't they let us do what we were trained to do? Even in Vietnam, the system kept me from hunting and killing as many of the enemy as I would have liked." Marcinko's **choler** stems partly from the fact that in 1990 he was convicted of conspiracy to defraud the government. (Elizabeth Gleick, *Pages: Master of Mayhem Richard Marcinko Was Too Loose a Cannon for the U.S. Navy*, People, 05-04-1992, p. 155.)

(2) anger *n.*: **bile**. SEE BITTERNESS

(3) anger *v.t.*: **envenom**. SEE EMBITTER

(4) anger (marked by a sudden or violent ...) *adj.*: **vesuvian** (esp. as in ... temper). SEE TEMPER

angered (easily ..., as in offended) *adj.*: **umbrageous**. SEE OFFENDED

angry (extremely ...) *adj.*: **apoplectic**. ▪ He's not a young man anymore, but John Mellencamp sure is angry. Guys with "suspenders and cigars" piss him off. No-smoking laws make him furious. And record-company execs, well, they make him absolutely **apoplectic**. (Rob Brunner, *Music: Ripe Mellencamp*, Entertainment Weekly, 10-09-1998, p. 83.)

(2) angry *adj.*: **wroth**. ▪ [C]ondescending white liberals have been handing down to the supposedly grateful black man what they're patronizingly confident is good for him. And if an ungrateful black refuses this generous offering, white liberals, seemingly unaware of the racial vanity involved in their assumptions, are **wroth** indeed. But this is nothing compared to how **wroth** are this country's dominant black leaders presently attacking Justice [Clarence] Thomas with rare venom, now that he's assumed a position of real leadership on the Supreme Court. (Richard Grenier, *The Most Courageous Man in America*, The Washington Times, 07-10-1995, p. 29.)

(3) angry (as in surly) *adj.*: **atrabilious**. SEE SURLY

(4) angry *adj.*: **bilious**. SEE SURLY

(5) angry (as in grouchy person) *n.*: **crosspatch**. SEE GROUCH

(6) angry (as in indignant) *n.*: **dudgeon** (often expressed as "in high dudgeon"). SEE INDIGNANT

(7) angry (as in irritable) *adj.*: **liverish**. SEE IRRITABLE

(8) angry (as in irritable) *adj.*: **shirty**. SEE IRRITABLE

(9) angry (as in irritable) *adj.*: **splenetic**. SEE IRRITABLE

anguish (over) *v.t.*: **bewail**. SEE LAMENT

(2) anguish (as in sadness) *n.*: **dolor** (*adj.*: **dolorous**). SEE SADNESS

(3) anguish (expressing ... often regarding something gone) *adj.*: **elegiac**. SEE SORROWFUL

animal (lover) *n.*: **zoophilist**. ▪ Typical of the **zoophilist** who favors life's lower orders over humankind, Robinson Jeffers claimed he'd sooner kill a man than a hawk. (David Yezzi, *J. R. Ackerley, My Dog Tulip* [book review], New Criterion, 11-01-1999.)

(2) animal (that feeds mainly on plants) *n.*: **herbivore** (*adj.*: **herbivorous**). SEE PLANTS

animals (sexual attraction towards ...) *n.*: **zoophilia**. (person attracted: **zoophile**) SEE BESTIALITY

animosity (intense ..., such as towards an enemy) *n.*: **enmity**. SEE HATRED

announce *v.t.*: **annunciate**. ▪ Prior to the summit, U.N. Secretary General Kofi Annan sought to deflect criticism by acknowledging that the agenda was "absurdly ambitious." Mr. Annan saw this as a virtue — that **annunciating** impossibly high-minded aims was nobler and better than pursuing more realistic goals. (Bret Schaefer, *United Nations Nonevent*, The Washington Times, 09-23-2000, p. A11.)

(2) announce (as in assert) *v.t.*: **asseverate**. SEE DECLARE

announcement (of forthcoming marriage, esp. in a church) *n.*: **banns**. SEE MARRIAGE

(2) announcement (as in decree) *n.*: **diktat**. SEE DECREE

(3) announcement (made without proof or support) *n.*: **ipse dixit** [Latin]. SEE ALLEGATION

annoy *v.t.*: **chivvy**. SEE PESTER

(2) annoy (as in bother or inconvenience) *v.t.*: **discommode**. SEE INCONVENIENCE

(3) annoy (as in bother or inconvenience) *v.t.*: **incommode**. SEE INCONVENIENCE

annoyance (as in trouble) *n.*: **tsuris** [Yiddish]. SEE TROUBLE

annoyed (as in irritable) *adj.*: **splenetic**. SEE IRRITABLE

(2) annoyed (easily ..., as in offended) *adj.*: **umbrageous**. SEE OFFENDED

annoying (as in repellent) *adj.*: **rebarbative**. SEE REPELLENT

anomalous (as in departing from the standard or norm) *adj.*: **heteroclite**. SEE ABNORMAL

anonymous *adj.*: **innominate**. ∎ Situated in an otherwise **innominate** strip mall on Olive Boulevard in the heart of University City, Kelly's Golf Repair and Club Makers Center is a working man's laboratory of golf club fitting and construction. (Dan O'Neill, *Clubs That Don't Fit May Cause Bad Habits*, St. Louis Post-Dispatch, 05-09-1998, p. T8.)

answer (clever ... that one thinks of after the moment has passed) *n.*: **esprit d'escalier** [French]. SEE RETORT

(2) answer (as in responding to an anticipated objection to an argument before that objection has been made) *n.*: **prolepsis**. SEE REBUTTAL

(3) answer (charging accuser with similar offense) *n.*: **tu quoque** [Latin]. SEE ACCUSE

antagonism (event which causes or provokes war, literally or figuratively) *n.*: **casus belli** [Latin; occasion of war]. SEE PROVOCATION

antagonistic *adj.*: **oppugnant**. ∎ [I]f city officials [who are] **oppugnant** to the [monorail initiative which was enacted into law by the voters] had expended half of the energy of their opposition ... in respectfully fulfilling the mandate and spirit of the law, we'd be well on our way to riding above the increasing gridlock. (Laurence Ballard, *Monorail — Effort to Repeal Vote — Disrespects Citizens' Decision and Needs*, Seattle Times, 06-23-2000, p. B7.)

antecedent *adj.*: **prevenient** (often as in "prevenient grace"). ∎ The symbolism behind Catholic doctrines of Mary is lost on most Protestants. The doctrine of the immaculate conception, for example, symbolizes **prevenient** grace — the grace that "comes before" faith in Christ, the grace that moves us to place our faith in Christ. It has nothing to do with Mary's virginity or with the virgin birth of Jesus. (James Gaughan, *Protestants Embrace New Vision of Mary*, Minneapolis Star Tribune, 11-13-1999, p. 8B.)

anthology (as in collection of writings by an author) *n.*: **chrestomathy**. ∎ *Readings: Essays and Literary Entertainments*, by Michael Dirda. Book World readers need no introduction to the author of this collection. ... *Readings* is an assortment of perambulations and reflections on literary, cultural and autobiographical themes reprinted from the author's monthly columns bearing the same name. It is, in other words, a **chrestomathy** of all things Dirda. (Author not given, *In Brief*, The Washington Post, 11-05-2000.)

antic *n.*: **dido**. SEE PRANK

anti-change (as in hatred or fear of anything new or different) *n.*: **misoneism** (person holding this view: **misoneist**). SEE CONSERVATISM

anticipation (nervously excited with ...) *adj.*: **atwitter**. SEE EXCITED

(2) anticipation (that something is going to occur) *n.*: **presentiment**. SEE PREMONITION

(3) anticipation (spec. acting as if or threatening that a future event [usually unwanted] has already occurred by reference to an event that precedes it, for example "if you look at my diary, you're dead") *n.*: **prolepsis**. SEE PREDICTION

anticipatory *adj.*: **prevenient**. ∎ Organizations set up to tell us about how to educate or otherwise raise our children usually have some ax to grind. Often they are driven by some ideological demon. ... [Thus], what aroused my hackles when I saw the news reports on the Academy's [of Pediatrics] findings [that young people should not specialize in one sport] was the **prevenient** sense that here again was another propaganda statement. But no, it is common sense based on research. (R. Emmett Tyrrell Jr., *Sporting Chance for the Young*, The Washington Times, 07-07-2000, p. A14.)

anticlimax *n.*: **bathos**. ∎ [Watching a film about outer space on a giant IMAX screen] is a dizzy mixture of true grandeur and sudden **bathos**. ... When an image is this large in scope as well as in area on the screen, it squeezes a silent gasp out of you. ... On the other hand, when the IMAX is displaying things that aren't intrinsically giant, the size of the image registers as a grotesque inflation, and anticlimax swiftly follows. (Francis Spufford, *Essay: The Outerspace Documentary as Big as the Ritz*, Independent on Sunday, 05-30-1999, p. 2.)

antiquated *adj.*: **antediluvian**. SEE OUTDATED

ants (of or relating to) *adj.*: **formic**. ■ Woody Allen voices worker ant Z-4195 ("the middle child in 5 million"), who becomes an accidental war hero in the **formic** army's battle against the termites. (Stuart Price, *Preview: Film - Christmas Films*, Independent on Sunday, 12-23-2001, p. 27.)

(2) ants (study of) *n.*: **myrmecology**. ■ Most kids are **myrmecologists** at one time or another. That's the great thing about **myrmecology**: no matter where you are or who you are, and no matter what resources you arrive with, ants are there too, awaiting study. (Bill Roorbach, *King of the Anthill*, Newsday, 11-13-1994, p. 38.)

anxiety *n.*: **inquietude**. ■ [In a survey], people felt the world has become unsafe and expressed a belief that real change is not in sight. It is true that similar statements of dissatisfaction and **inquietude** might have been elicited during any decade in U.S. history. Now, however, one obtains responses of exasperation and desperation from all parts of the population about all types of events, communicating an urgency. (Ralph Hyatt, *American Hearts Have Hardened*, USA Today [Magazine], 03-01-1994.)

(2) anxiety (as part of depressed state) *n.*: **dysphoria**. See DEPRESSION

(3) anxiety (in a state of ...) *idiom*: **swivet** (*inf.*: as in "in a swivet"). See DISTRESS

(4) anxiety (in a state of ...) *idiom*: [on] **tenterhooks**. See SUSPENSE

anyway (as in nevertheless) *adv.*: **withal**. See NEVERTHELESS

apathetic *adj.*: **pococurante**. ■ The only child of an interminably famous literary theorist, and now **pococurante** chair of the English Department, Hank published one critically acclaimed novel — "Off the Road" — 20 years ago. ... [His] fate [is] a middle-aged, middle-class guy trapped by his successes. ... [T]he faculty meetings and search committees that footnote his daily existence [are not gratifying]. ... Is this middle age, he thinks, the cruel punch line of prostate trouble visited on an irreverent man? (Gail Caldwell, *College Bound; Richard Russo's Comic/Sad Novel of Learning and Campus Politics*, The Boston Globe, 07-13-1997, P. N20.)

(2) apathetic (as in sluggish or lethargic) *adj.*: **torpid**. See LETHARGIC

apathy (sometimes in matters spiritual, and sometimes leading to depression) *n.*: **acedia**. ■ What makes our situation today different from previous periods in American history — and fundamentally more serious — is the "de-moralization" of much of middle- and upper-middle-class life. The causes are varied and complicated — my list would include ... modernity itself, affluence, spiritual **acedia**, intellectual trends, movies and television, advertising, and flawed government programs. (William Bennett, *Moral Corruption in America*, Commentary, 11-01-1995, p. 29.)

(2) apathy (as in lethargy) *n.*: **hebetude**. See LETHARGY

(3) apathy (esp. on matters of politics or religion) *n.*: **Laodiceanism**. See INDIFFERENCE

(4) apathy (as in lethargy) *n.*: **torpor**. See LETHARGY

ape (of, relating to, or resembling) *adj.*: **anthropoid**. ■ One limb [of the evolutionary tree] led to the prosimians, or lower primates, such as lemurs and bush babies, and the other to the **anthropoids**, or higher primates, such as monkeys, apes and humans. (Alice Park, *Linking Man to a Monkey: New Fossils Point to a Tiny, Tree-dwelling Ancestor*, Time, 03-27-2000.)

(2) ape (of, relating to, or resembling) *adj.*: **simian**. To the Flikshteins ... Cookie Flikshtein is a beloved — albeit **simian** — member of the family. She may be a monkey, they say, but she has adjusted enough to the human condition to spend most evenings eating rocky road ice cream and watching the nightly news. (Alan Feuer, *Family Not Ready to Give Up Pet Monkey: State Wants to Put Rare Creature in Zoo*, The Dallas Morning News, 07-23-2000, p. 14A.)

apex *n.*: **apogee**. See HEIGHT

aphorism *n.*: **apothegm**. See SAYING

(2) aphorism (witty or clever ... or line) *n.*: **bon mot**. See LINE

(3) aphorism (pithy ...) *n.*: **gnome** (*adj*: **gnomic**). See CATCHPHRASE

aphoristic (as in given to stating aphorisms, esp. in a moralizing way) *adj.*: **sententious**. ■ [Rockefeller] delivered brief sermons along with the coins, exhorting children to work hard and be frugal if they wanted a fortune; the coins were for saving, not indulgence. ... He informed children that the nickel represented a year's interest on a dollar. For someone of Rockefeller's **sententious** nature, this was a very comfortable persona to adopt. (Ron Chernow, *Titan*, Random House [1998], p. 614.)

aphrodisiac *n.*: **philter**. See POTION

aplomb (esp. under pressure or trying circumstances) *n.*: **sang-froid** [French]. See COMPOSURE

apology (which is formal, full and genuine) *n*.: **amende honorable** [French]. ∎ [A]ppeasement fuels the appetite of the moral blackmailer. ... Visiting the Yad Vashem memorial, [Pope John Paul II] expressed regret for historical antipathies "that led to the deaths of Jews by Christians at any time and in any place." That comprehensive **amende honorable** was immediately denounced as inadequate, because it did not condemn the Pope's predecessor, Pius XII, for alleged complicity in the Nazi murder of the Jews. (Gerald Warner, *Sorry Is the Most Dangerous Word for the Church in Crisis,* Scotland on Sunday, 03-26-2000, p. 18.)

(2) apology (as in place or occasion to offer ... and to seek forgiveness) *n*.: **Canossa**. SEE PENANCE

apparel *n*.: **raiment**. SEE CLOTHING

apparition *n*.: **phantasm**. ∎ In 1993 he brought out "The Ghosts of Virginia," a much larger compilation of his stories. "I thought I was finished," he says, "but people from all over started writing me and calling me." That resulted in three more volumes on Old Dominion **phantasms**, each about 400 pages long. (Rick Britton, *Ghosts; Colonial Past Haunts Williamsburg,* The Washington Times, 10-28-1999, p. M4.)

(2) apparition *n*.: **wraith**. ∎ We sat for hours in our crude tumbleweed blind. I can't remember if we heard the golden eagle or saw it first, but suddenly it was there, slipping through the fog like a **wraith**. (Larry Rice, *Nature's Wild Gifts: Abrupt and Fleeting Encounters with Animals Leave Impressions That Last Forever,* Backpacker, 05-01-1998, p. 118.)

appeal (to earnestly) *v.t.*: **adjure**. SEE PLEAD

(2) appeal (of an ... to one's sense of pity or compassion) *adv., adj.*: **ad misericordium**. SEE ARGUMENT

(3) appeal (making an ... to one's monetary self-interest) *n*.: **argumentum ad crumenam** [Latin]. SEE ARGUMENT

(4) appeal (as in plea) *n*.: **cri de coeur** [French; lit. cry of the heart]. SEE PLEA

appealing *adj.*: **piquant**. ∎ Philip Malbone, his anti-hero, is a puzzling mix of bad and good, of mal and bon. "There was for him something **piquant** in being ... neither innocent nor guilty," Higginson writes, "but always on some delicious middle ground." (Caleb Crain, *The Monarch of Dreams,* The New Republic, 05-28-2001.)

(2) appealing (person through magnetism or charm) *n*.: **duende**. SEE CHARISMA

(3) appealing *adj.*: **prepossessing**. SEE PLEASING

(4) appealing (physically ...) *n*.: **pulchritude**. SEE BEAUTY

appear (as in emerge or materialize) *v.i.*: **debouch**. SEE EMERGE

appearance (of plenty when in fact there is little) *adj.*: **Barmecidal** (esp. as in "Barmecidal feast"). SEE ILLUSION

(2) appearance (as in demeanor) *n*.: **mien**. SEE DEMEANOR

(3) appearance (facial ...) *n*.: **physiognomy**. SEE FACIAL FEATURES

(4) appearance (of knowledge which is actually superficial) *n*.: **sciolism**. SEE SUPERFICIAL

appease *v.t.*: **dulcify**. ∎ One of Pakistan's most notorious homegrown terrorists was elected to parliament — from prison. ... His pro-Taliban, pro-al Qaeda outlawed party, Sipah-e-Sahaba (Guardians of the Friends of the Prophet), was one of five extremist groups banned by President Pervez Musharraf last January as he tried to **dulcify** U.S. concerns. (Arnaud de Borchgrave, *A Triumph for Taliban's Tutors* [Commentary], The Washington Times, 11-12-2002.)

(2) appease *v.t.*: **propitiate**. SEE PLACATE

appeasing (as in peacemaking) *adj.*: **irenic**. SEE PEACEMAKING

appendage *n*.: **appurtenance**. ∎ To Baron, a firearm is an unpleasant, even repulsive **appurtenance** of life in L.A. — he would gladly throw his away, he says, if he ever moved back to New York. (Justin Davidson, *Guns In America,* Newsday, 12-18-2000, p. B6.)

appetite (abnormally increased ... for food) *n*.: **hyperphagia**. ∎ It also is the time of year when all bears are going into "**hyperphagia**," a phase in which they are almost crazed by hunger and must try to put on two or three times their body weight in fat before winter. They feel like they are starving — they are ravenous — and it just doesn't seem like there is enough food. (Michael Babcock, *Tough Time of Year for Black Bears,* Gannett News Service, 09-06-2001.)

(2) appetite (excessive ...) *n*.: **polyphagia**. ∎ Beginning in the 1950s, obesity shifted to being considered a condition best dealt with through medical intervention. ... Even the language changed to reflect the new perspective. ... Instead of engaging in gluttonous or gorging behavior, [fat people] were considered victims of ... "**polyphagia**." (Mike Powers, *In the Eye of the Beholder*, Human Ecology Forum, 09-01-1996, p. 16.)

(3) appetite (loss resulting from chronic disease) *n.*: **cachexia**. SEE WASTING

(4) appetite (having a strong ..., esp. sexual) *adj.*: **concupiscent** (*n.*: **concupiscence**). SEE LUST-FUL

(5) appetite (excessive ...) *n.*: **gulosity**. SEE GLUT-TONY

(6) appetite (condition involving ... for eating non-food items) *n.*: **pica**. SEE CRAVING

appetizing *adj.*: **sapid**. SEE TASTY

(2) appetizing *adj.*: **toothsome**. SEE TASTY

applaud (persons hired to ... at a performance) *n.*: **claque**. ■ [New York Mayor Rudy Giuliani] brought a **claque** of 40 to 50 supporters and City Hall employees to envelop him as he walked in the Lesbian and Gay Pride March. Their job: to cheer and applaud the mayor whenever any of the specta-tors along the route booed him. (Sydney H. Schanberg, *Giuliani on Parade — With a Human Heat Shield*, Newsday, 06-27-1995, p. A21.)

applause (as in praise) *n.*: **approbation**. SEE PRAISE

apples (of, relating to or derived) *adj.*: **pomaceous**. ■ Many apples are biennial, which in practise means they alternate between good and bad crops. Some fruit will be scabby and others have bitterpit, and the earwigs and wasps and moths will have their day. But that is an important part of their **pomaceous** charm. (Monty Don, *Life & Soul: Gardens: Apple of His Eye*, The Observer, 10-29-2000, p. 82.)

appoint (as in delegate, authority or duties to anoth-er) *v.t.*: **depute**. SEE DELEGATE

appointment (esp. for illicit sexual relations) *n.*: **assignation**. ■ The next scene takes place two years earlier, in a flat that Jerry and Emma have been renting for years to accommodate their afternoon trysts. Only there's no trysting on this bleak winter's day. Neither has time for midday **assignations** any longer, nor are they willing to upend their lives by dumping their respective spouses. (Steve Parks, *The Genesis of a "Betrayal,"* Newsday, 03-20-1998.)

apportion *v.t.*: **admeasure**. ■ The Admiral, David Robinson, the admirable Tim Duncan and the **admeasuring** [i.e. ball distributing] point guard Avery Johnson will make the Spurs the favorites [in the NBA finals], on and off the court, whether they

host the Knicks or the Pacers. (John Walters, *SI View: The Week in TV Sports*, Sports Illustrated, 06-14-1999, p. 19.)

appreciation (as in perception or awareness) *n.*: **ken**. SEE PERCEPTION

apprehend (based on past experience) *v.t.*: **apper-ceive**. SEE COMPREHEND

(2) apprehend (through the senses) *adj.*: **sensate**. SEE FEEL

apprehension (that something is going to occur) *n.*: **presentiment**. SEE PREMONITION

apprentice (as in beginner) *n.*: **abecedarian**. SEE BEGINNER

appropriate (an ... thing to do) *n.*: **bon ton** [French]. ■ But what remains very similar after all these years is the sense of elitism and the sentiment of "we are better than them" which still unabashedly pervades Labor ranks. ... [Labor leader Tiki Dayan] thought it **bon ton** to haughtily intimate that Likud support-ers are unthinking low-class trash — definitely not as good as us. (Sarah Honig, *Barak's Delayed Reaction: Will it Help Netanyahu?* Jerusalem Post, 05-03-1999, p. 2.)

(2) appropriate *adj.*: **felicitous**. ■ [B]aseball never had it so good as it did in the era immediately after World War II. ... But pivotal is the more **felicitous** expression for this period. ... These, after all, were the years of Jackie Robinson, of the gestation of a players' union that would eventually topple the despised reserve clause, [and] of middle-class flight to the suburbs (which drastically altered the game's demographics). (Ron Fimrite, *Scorecard/Books: Those Were The Days*, Sports Illustrated, 04-19-1999, p. R26)

(3) appropriate (as in usurp) *v.t.*: **accroach**. SEE USURP

(4) appropriate (as in relevant) *adj.*: **apposite**. SEE RELEVANT

(5) appropriate (for oneself without right) *v.t.*: **arrogate**. SEE CLAIM

(6) appropriate *adj.*: **comme il faut** [French]. SEE PROPER

(7) appropriate (esp. in reference to a punishment) *adj.*: **condign**. SEE DESERVED

approval (as in praise) *n.*: **approbation**. SEE PRAISE

approve (officially) *v.t.*: **approbate**. SEE AUTHORIZE

apt (as in relevant) *adj.*: **apposite**. SEE RELEVANT

arch (slightly) *v.t., v.i.*: **camber**. SEE CURVE

archconservative (in beliefs and often stuffy, pompous and/or elderly) *adj., n.*: **Colonel Blimp**. SEE CONSERVATIVE

archer *n.*: **toxophilite**. ∎ Sir — Your reporter rather disparagingly refers to Robin Hood as having used "a makeshift wooden bow." ... As a former keen **toxophilite**, I would point out that the longbow demands a higher degree of skill in use than the modern bow with all its hi-tech gadgetry. (Marcus Wells [letter writer], *Longbows [Letters]*, Western Mail [Cardiff, Wales], 9-10-2001.)

Arctic (of or relating to the ... region) *adj.*: **hyperborean** [Note: this word also means very cold and in the following example, both meanings would be appropriate]. ∎ [If there were drilling in the Arctic National Wildlife Refuge,] how many drilling rigs, it's fair to ask, would cause postpartum psychosis among caribou? ... Would oil pipes and pumps in just 2,000 acres of the 9 million-acre refuge seriously harm animals and migrating birds? And if it does, is that the overriding consideration? Certainly no tourist jobs are at stake in that desolate, **hyperborean** plain. (Edwin A. Roberts, Jr., *Ruminations On Oil And Its Origins*, The Tampa Tribune, 11-18-2001.)

ardent *adj.*: **perfervid**. SEE IMPASSIONED

arduous (task, esp. of cleaning up or remedying bad situations) *n.*: **Augean task**. SEE HERCULEAN
(2) arduous *adj.*: **operose**. SEE LABORIOUS
(3) arduous (as in difficult or painful, journey or experience) *n.*: **via dolorosa**. SEE ORDEAL

area (as in sphere or realm) *n.*: **ambit**. SEE REALM
(2) area (surrounding ... served by an institution, such as a school or hospital) *n.*: **catchment area**. SEE DISTRICT
(3) area (populated by persons from many countries or backgrounds) *n.*: **cosmopolis**. SEE DIVERSITY
(4) area (esp. small, between things or events) *n.*: **interstice**. SEE GAP
(5) area (densely populated ...) *n.*: **megalopolis**. SEE CROWDED
(6) area *n.*: **purlieu**. SEE VICINITY
(7) area (physical ...) *n.*: **vicinage**. SEE VICINITY

areas (as in vicinity or environs) *n., pl.*: **purlieus**. SEE OUTSKIRTS

arguable (as in controversial opinion or person who holds one) *n.*: **polemic**. SEE CONTROVERSY

argue (against) *v.t.*: **expostulate**. SEE OBJECT

(2) argue (against a statement, opinion or action) *v.t.*: **oppugn**. SEE OPPOSE
(3) argue (about petty matters) *v.i.*: **pettifog**. SEE QUIBBLE

argument (of an ... appealing to one's emotions or designed for crowd-pleasing) *adj., adv.*: **ad captandum** (or **ad captandum vulgus**)[Latin]. ∎ [Prime Minister Blair] spent much of Monday trying to corner the market in opinions on the row [after a soccer coach made controversial comments about disabled people]. First, **ad captandum vulgus**, he took the role of prosecutor ..., announcing that it would be "very difficult" for Mr. Hoddle to stay. Then, having failed to secure plaudits from the tabloids, he telephoned the England coach to make his peace. (Author not given, *The Correct Way Forward*, The Daily Telegraph, 02-03-1999.)

(2) argument (appealing to one's purse) *n.*: **argumentum ad crumenam** [Latin for "to the purse"]. ∎ An electioneering budget is an **argumentum ad crumenam**, and most elections in democracies have a strong element of this old argument. It may not be idealistic, but it is the way people vote. (Philip Howard, *Rhetoric and All That Rot*, The Times [London], 04-12-1991.)

(3) argument (of an ... appealing to pity or compassion) *adv., adj.*: **argumentum ad misericordium** [Latin]. ∎ I empathize absolutely with Kit Marx, who has "qualms about 'taking' private lands."... Every one of us [has seen] heart-wringing stories about elderly couples, standing on their land and dolefully declaring, "This swamp was our retirement." There surely are injustices, and Kit Marx is not the only "radical preservationist" who is swayed by the endless resorts to **argumentum ad misericordium**. (Harvey Manning [letter writer], *'The Taking Myth' — Land Preservationists Should Be Better Educated on Laws of State*, The Seattle Times, 08-13-1992, p. A11.)

(4) argument (that silence from an opposing side or absence of evidence is itself indicative that the person making the argument must be correct) *n.*: **argumentum ex silentio** [Latin. This is generally, though not always, considered to be a fallacious argument.] ∎ Sir — Your report ... quoted Prof Sean Freyne as claiming that "Ireland has one of Europe's oldest Jewish communities." This is plainly fallacious. ... The earliest indication of a resident Jewish community in Ireland does not occur before the 1230s ... although [I recognize that] this is an **argument[um] ex silentio**. (Anthony Gandon [letter writer], *Jewish History In Ireland*, The Irish Times, 11-19-1997, p. 15.)

(5) argument (suggesting the use of force to settle an issue) *n.*: **argumentum ad baculum** [Latin]. SEE THREAT

(6) argument (specious ... intended to mislead or rationalize) *n.*: **casuistry**. SEE FALLACIOUS

(7) argument (which is complicated and often illogical) *n.*: **choplogic**. SEE FALLACY

(8) argument (given to ... which may be specious or one who is so given) *adj., n.*: **eristic**. SEE SPECIOUS AND DEBATE

(10) argument (characterized by internal ...) *adj.*: **factious**. SEE DISPUTE

(11) argument (about words) *n.*: **logomachy**. SEE WORDS

(12) argument (person who hates rational ... or enlightenment) *n.*: **misologist**. SEE CLOSED-MINDED

(13) argument (about a philosophical or theological issue) *n.*: **quodlibet**. SEE DEBATE

(14) argument (as in heated disagreement or friction between groups) *n.*: **ruction**. SEE DISSENSION

argumentative *adj., n.*: **eristic**. SEE DEBATE

(2) argumentative *adj.*: **querulous**. SEE PEEVISH

arid (of or adapted to an ... habitat) *adj.*: **xeric**. SEE DRY

aristocracy (as in fashionable society) *n.*: **beau monde** [French]. SEE HIGH SOCIETY

(2) aristocracy (as in fashionable society) *n.*: **bon ton** [French]. SEE HIGH SOCIETY

arithmetic (difficulty with or inability to do ...) *n.*: **acalculia; dyscalculia**. SEE MATH

(2) arithmetic (having ability with ... and math generally) *adj.*: **numerate**. SEE MATHEMATICAL

armistice (temporary ... between opposing parties pending final deal) *n.*: **modus vivendi** [Latin]. SEE TRUCE

armor *n.*: **cuirass**. ▪ [T]he difference [between dancing just topless and totally nude] is huge psychologically. ... When you're completely naked, you're out there, sans **cuirass**. (Lily Burana, *Strip City*, Talk Miramax Books [2001], p. 170.)

armpit *n.*: **axilla**. ▪ [In the] Old Spice Red Zone poll of the 50 sweatiest cities in the United States, St. Louis finished 15th — 15th! We didn't even make the Top 10. Any St. Louis resident who has been up to the **axillas** in permanent 'pit rings and a sweaty back stuck to vinyl car seats may be surprised by the

results. According to the poll, San Antonio is the sweatiest city. (Joe Holleman, *We're No. 15? Local Sweathogs Are Up in [Under]arms at City's Ranking*, St. Louis Post-Dispatch, 07-11-2002, p. F1.)

arms (move by swinging with ..., like a monkey) *v.i.*: **brachiate**. SEE SWING

army (of, relating to or suggesting) *adj.*: **martial**. SEE WARLIKE

arrange (close together, side-by-side or in proper order) *v.t.*: **collocate**. SEE PLACE

arrangement (temporary ... between opposing parties pending final deal) *n.*: **modus vivendi** [Latin]. SEE TRUCE

array (as in assortment) *n.*: **farrago**. SEE ASSORTMENT

(2) array (as in assortment) *n.*: **gallimaufry**. SEE ASSORTMENT

(3) array (as in assortment) *n.*: **olla podrida** [Spanish]. SEE ASSORTMENT

(4) array (as in assortment) *n.*: **omnium-gatherum** [Latin]. SEE ASSORTMENT

(5) array (as in assortment) *n.*: **salmagundi**. SEE ASSORTMENT

arrogance *adj.*: **hubris**. ▪ Like any Greek tragic hero, Clinton is also guilty of **hubris**: He indulged himself most of all when things were going well and he thought that his office, good polls and the election results made him invulnerable to his enemies and free to defy Congress. (Morton Kondracke, Roll Call, *Impeachment Fight a Tragedy for All*, The Arizona Republic, 12-20-1998, p. E1.)

(2) arrogance (in behavior or speech) *n.*: **contumely**. SEE CONTEMPT

(3) arrogance (as in boastful behavior) *n.*: **rodomontade**. SEE BLUSTER

arrogant (as in pushy and assertive) *adj.*: **bumptious**. SEE PUSHY

(2) arrogant (as in condescending) *adj., adv.*: **de haut en bas** [French]. SEE CONDESCENDING

(3) arrogant (as in pompous) *adj.*: **flatulent**. SEE POMPOUS

(4) arrogant (as in pompous or haughty) *adj.*: **hoity-toity**. SEE POMPOUS

(5) arrogant (and shameless person) *n.*: **jackanapes**. SEE CONCEITED

arrows (one who makes ...) *n.*: **fletcher**. ▪ Kingmaker is a similar set-up at the castle, where children can watch the **fletcher** construct traditional bows and arrows. (Katie Bowman, *Ye Complete Guide to Ye Olde England*, Independent, 12-15-2001, p. 2.)

art (sale of ... by a museum to purchase more) *v.t.*: **deaccession**. SEE SELL

(2) **art** (or writings created in the artist's or author's youth) *n.*: **juvenilia**. SEE COMPOSITIONS

(3) **art** (work of ... dealing with evening or night) *n.*: **nocturne**. SEE PAINTING

arthritis (or joint pain) *n.*: **arthralgia**. ▪ Cave divers face the near certainty of [high-pressure nervous syndrome] on deep descents. The syndrome often hits in combination with a condition called compression **arthralgia**, known to Navy divers as "no joint juice" because it feels as if their knees, elbows and wrists have suddenly rusted solid. (Michael Ray Taylor, *Scuba Diving*, Sports Illustrated, 10-03-1994, p. 5.)

artificial *adj.*: **factitious**. ▪ Moguls in a mythic land [i.e. Hollywood, Louis B. Mayer and Samuel Goldwyn] lived extravagantly, inventing a **factitious** world peopled by gorgeous chorus girls and chaste heroines and handsome leading men. (Walter Guzzardi, *Laurels: The National Business Hall of Fame*, Fortune, 03-12-1990, p. 118.)

artistic (piece imitating previous pieces) *n.*: **pastiche**. SEE IMITATION

artwork (which looks like a photograph or something real) *n.*: **trompe l'oeil** [French]. SEE ILLUSION

ascending *adj.*: **assurgent**. SEE RISING

(2) **ascending** (esp. too high for safety) *adj.*: **Icarian**. SEE SOARING

ascent (as in upward slope) *n.*: **acclivity** (*adj.*: **acclivitous**). SEE INCLINE

ashen (as in pale or corpselike) *adj.*: **cadaverous**. SEE CORPSELIKE

aside (as in digression) *n.*: **excursus**. SEE DIGRESSION

(2) **aside** (as in, as an ...) *n.*: **obiter dictum** [Latin]. SEE PASSING COMMENT

asinine (in a smug or complacent manner) *adj.*: **fatuous**. SEE FOOLISH

ask (as in plead to earnestly) *v.t.*: **adjure**. SEE PLEAD

(2) **ask** (for by begging or sponging off of) *v.t.*: **cadge**. SEE BEG

(3) **ask** *v.t.*: **catechize**. SEE QUESTION

aspect (as in demeanor) *n.*: **mien**. SEE DEMEANOR

ass (having a nicely proportioned ...) *adj.*: **callipygian**. SEE REAR END

(2) **ass** (having a hairy ...) *adj.*: **dasypygal**. SEE REAR END

(3) **ass** (as in buttocks) *n., pl.*: **nates**. SEE BUTTOCKS

(4) **ass** (a fat ...) *n.*: **steatopygia** (having a fat ... *adj.*: **steatopygic**). SEE REAR END

assail *v.t.*: **flay**. SEE CRITICIZE

(2) **assail** *v.t.*: **oppugn**. SEE OPPOSE

assault (surprise ...) *n.*: **coup de main** [French; attack by hand]. SEE ATTACK

(2) **assault** (as in attack in writing) *n.*: **coup de plume** [French; attack by pen]. SEE ATTACK

assemble (clumsily, roughly or hastily) *v.t.*: **cobble**. ▪ The next day I pored over my manuscripts and **cobbled** together a couple of short stories from various scraps. (Lars Eighner, *Travels With Lizbeth*, St. Martin's Press [1993], p. 101.)

(2) **assemble** (cheaply and flimsily) *v.t.*: **jerry-build**. SEE BUILD

assembly (as in group) *n.*: **gaggle**. SEE GROUP

assert *v.t.*: **asseverate**. SEE DECLARE

assertion (made without proof or support) *n.*: **ipse dixit** [Latin]. SEE ALLEGATION

assertive (in an obnoxious or loud way) *adj.*: **bumptious**. SEE PUSHY

assess *v.t.*: **assay**. SEE EVALUATE

(2) **assess** (under a new standard, esp. one which differs from conventional norms) *v.t.*: **transvaluate**. SEE EVALUATE

assiduous (in effort or application) *adj.*: **sedulous**. SEE DILIGENT

assign (authority or duties to another) *v.t.*: **depute**. SEE DELEGATE

assistant *n.*: **adjutant**. ▪ For 17 seasons as an assistant coach, Craig Esherick sat quietly and nondescriptly next to John Thompson on Georgetown's bench. [Thus, when Thompson resigned, it] was natural for the rest of the world to wonder whether this faceless, voiceless **adjutant** was up to the job he had unexpectedly inherited. (Seth Davis, *Inside College Basketball*, Sports Illustrated, 01-22-2001, p. 80.)

(2) assistant (esp. to organized crime leader) *n*.: **consigliere** [Italian]. ∎ Forbes.com rustled through [Mafia boss John] Gotti's wit and wisdom, as captured by FBI wiretaps, and put together these useful tips: ... On caring for subordinates: "Chrissake, I love you (speaking to Gambino family **consigliere** Frank Locascio) more than I love myself. ... I'm worried about you going to jail. I don't give two (bleeps) about my going to jail." (Michael Precker, *Working World*, The Dallas Morning News, 06-18-2002, p. 1C.)

(3) assistant (esp. to a scholar or magician) *n*.: **famulous**. ∎ [T]elevision is trying to coolify magic by ridding it of its associations with slimeballs in sequined suits, assisted by a mute **famulus** bedecked in feathers, mascara, and an inane grin, together partaking in a mindless ritual of sawing, stabbing, and vanishing. (Victor Lewis-Smith, *Don't Shoot, This Is Live* ..., The Evening Standard [London, England], 10-06-2003.)

(4) assistant *n*.: **factotum**. ∎ At the time of Annie [Sullivan's] death in 1936, Polly Thompson, who was five years younger than Helen, had been with the household for twenty-two years as a secretary and general **factotum**. (Dorothy Herrmann, *Helen Keller*, Knopf [1998], p. 266.)

(5) assistant (who is loyal and unquestioning) *n*.: **myrmidon**. ∎ Judge Wright concluded, "the record demonstrates by clear and convincing evidence that [President Clinton] responded to plaintiff [Paula Jones's] questions by giving false, misleading, and evasive answers that were designed to obstruct the judicial process." (How many times did the president's **myrmidons** tell us he equivocated to spare his family embarrassment?) (Bruce Fein, *A Protracted List of Discredits*, The Washington Times, 04-20-1999, p. A17.)

assistants (group of ... or advisors, often scheming or plotting) *n*.: **camarilla**. SEE ADVISORS

associate *n*.: **confrere**. SEE COLLEAGUE
  (2) associate (as in comrade) *n*.: **tovarich** [Russian]. SEE COMRADE

associated (with, as in incident to) *adj*.: **appurtenant**. SEE PERTAINING

assortment *n*.: **farrago**. ∎ Though tickets cost only $25 and the dress code was casual, a fair number of attendees wore tuxedos and party gowns anyway. The band offered some '70s guitar-rock, and once it started playing, the wood-tile floor in front of the stage became a strange tangle of disparate body rhythms and dance styles, a **farrago** of denim, taffeta and tulle. (Romesh Ratnesar, *Lefties Left Out*, The New Republic, 02-10-1997.)

(2) assortment *n*.: **gallimaufry**. Old South Africa [journalists] have lived for decades with a **gallimaufry** of some 100 press restrictions. It has long been an offense to quote locally or transmit abroad the words of "listed" or "banned" activists. (Ezra Bowen, *Press: Whiteout on the Bad News*, Time, 06-30-1986, p. 62.)

(3) assortment *n*.: **olla podrida** [Spanish]. ∎ The trouble is, Petronius is so infernally readable, and his **olla podrida** of conmanship, bitchy lit. crit., absurd gastronomy, bed-bouncing, murder and anecdotes (werewolves, susceptible widows) is so enticing that we tend to forget the horrendous social implications of what we're reading. (Peter Green, *The Satyricon (book reviews)*, The New Republic, 10-28-1996, p. 42A.)

(4) assortment *n*.: **omnium-gatherum** [Latin]. ∎ A kind of cyclonic **omnium-gatherum**, [the book] *The Tornado* packs in science and superstition [about tornados], lore and personal narratives, safety tips, forecasting breakthroughs, snapshots of famous storm chasers and their quarry, common myths ..., tons of statistics ... and all sorts of odd facts and findings. (David Laskin, *Ill Wind*, The Washington Post, 04-22-2001, p. T7.)

(5) assortment *n*.: **salmagundi**. ∎ [Paraguay] is a place where dreamers, dictators, fugitives and fantasists have gone to find peace. Among these are conquistadors, Jesuits, Nazis, Mennonites, Australian socialists, Japenese utopians, German vegetarians, White Russians [etc.] There are no misfits in Paraguay because in this particular **salmagundi** of a place, everyone fits, more or less. (Ben Macintyre, *You Don't Want to Live There*, New York Times Book Review, 02-29-2004, p. 18.)

(6) assortment (as in diversity) *n*.: **heterogeneity** (*adj*: **heterogenous**). SEE DIVERSITY

assuage (as in appease) *v.t*.: **dulcify**. SEE APPEASE
(2) assuage *v.t*.: **propitiate**. SEE PLACATE

assurance (as in self-..., and poise) *n*.: **aplomb**. SEE SELF-CONFIDENCE

astute *adj*.: **perspicacious**. ∎ The companies below occupy market niches, have strong brand-name franchises or provide special services in a way that inspires long-term loyalty from a small number of **perspicacious** stock pickers. (Marguerite T. Smith, *Wall Street: Smart-money Stocks: Homely Companies That Leading Pros Are Swooning Over*, Money, 05-01-1990, p. 57.)

(2) astute (as in having a penetrating quality) *adj.*: **gimlet** (esp. as in "gimlet eye"). SEE PENETRATING

(3) astute *adj.*: **trenchant**. SEE INCISIVE

atheist (as in one with no faith or religion) *n., adj.*: **nullifidian**. SEE NONBELIEVER

atmosphere (distinctive ... or spirit of a place) *n.*: **genius loci** [Latin]. SEE SPIRIT

(2) atmosphere (which is thick and vaporous or noxious) *n.*: **miasma**. SEE NOXIOUS

(3) atmosphere (as in setting or physical environment) *n.*: **mise en scène** [French; lit. putting on stage]. SEE SETTING

atone (for) *v.t., v.i.*: **expiate**. ▪ In recent years the American press has written countless stories about South Africa's efforts to **expiate** its racist past — about the Truth and Reconciliation Commission; about the renaming of streets, airports, and government buildings; about the conversion of Nelson Mandela's prison into a museum. (Author not given, *TRB From Washington*, The New Republic, 09-17-2001.)

atoning *adj.*: **piacular**. ▪ [T]his high-ranking Greek guy actually came around to 1009 after Saturday's supper to assure me that ragged-necked Lebanese heads were even at that moment rolling down various corridors in **piacular** recompense for my having had to carry my own bag. (Wallace, *Shipping Out: On the Nearly Lethal Comforts of a Luxury Cruise*, Harpers Magazine, 01-01-1996, p. 33.)

atrocious *adj.*: **execrable**. SEE ABOMINABLE

attack (surprise ...) *n.*: **coup de main** [French; lit. attack by hand]. ▪ When Coca-Cola cajoled Venezuela's only bottler to defect from Pepsi and join its own ranks, it exploited the strategic lessons of one of history's most successful covert ops, the Israeli attack on Entebbe. That **coup de main** was marked by minutely detailed planning, lightning-fast execution, a shroud of secrecy, superb intelligence and the use of elite shock troops. (Dennis Laurie, *In War and in Business, Strategy Brings Success*, The Washington Times, 08-20-2001.)

(2) attack (in writing) *n.*: **coup de plume** [French; lit. attack by pen]. ▪ [I] understand Premier Parizeau's bigoted remarks about "les ethniques" on Quebec referendum night. ... What offends me is that Mr. Rheaume chose to attack Mr. Richler rather than Mr. Parizeau's antagonistic speech itself. ... Mr. Rheaume's awkward **coup de plume** serves to embarrass him while focusing an even brighter spot-light on the masterful "sleight of pen" of the literate Mr. Richler. (Elizabeth Irving [letter writer], *Rheaume Should Have Attacked Jacques Parizeau*, The Gazette [Montreal, Quebec], 07-21-1996, p. A6.)

(3) attack (initiate an ..., fighting or violence) *v.i.*: **aggress**. SEE FIGHT

(4) attack (esp. as in military advance) *n.*: **anabasis**. SEE ADVANCE

(5) attack (as in criticize) *v.t.*: **flay**. SEE CRITICIZE

(6) attack (harshly, as in criticize) *v.t.*: **fustigate**. SEE CRITICIZE

(7) attack (as in complaint) *n.*: **jeremiad**. SEE COMPLAINT

(8) attack (as in insult another's dignity) *n.*: **lese majesty**. SEE INSULT

(9) attack (being subject to verbal ..., esp. public) *n.*: **obloquy**. SEE ABUSE

(10) attack (of or relating to being under ... or siege) *adj.*: **obsidional**. SEE BESEIGED

(11) attack (a statement, opinion or action) *v.t.*: **oppugn**. SEE OPPOSE

attempt (the ... to achieve a particular goal or desire) *n.*: **nisus**. SEE GOAL

attendant (esp. to a scholar or magician) *n.*: **famulous**. SEE ASSISTANT

(2) attendant (who is loyal and unquestioning) *n.*: **myrmidon**. SEE ASSISTANT

attendants (line or train of ... as for an important person) *n.*: **cortege**. SEE PROCESSION

attention (treat another with excessive ...) *n., v.t.*: **wet-nurse**. SEE CODDLE

attentive (as in watchful person) *n.*: **Argus**. SEE WATCHFUL

attic (or loft or room on top floor) *n.*: **garret**. SEE LOFT

attire (showy article of ...) *n.*: **froufrou**. SEE CLOTHING

(2) attire (as in clothes) *n.*: **habiliment(s)**. SEE CLOTHING

(3) attire (as in clothes) *n.*: **raiment**. SEE CLOTHING

attired (being partially, carelessly or casually ...) *n.*: **dishabille** [French]. ▪ The average college football player is about as fashionably attired as a hotel guest fleeing an early-morning fire. Surely no one with any pride in his appearance would wish to be caught in such a state of **dishabille**. (Ron Fimrite, *Point After: Because My Own Taste in Men's Apparel Has Not Changed Appreciably*, Sports Illustrated, 05-17-1993, p. 85.)

attitude (as in demeanor) *n.*: **mien**. See demeanor

(2) **attitude** (preconceived or biased ... on an issue) *n.*: **parti pris** [French]. See preconception

(3) **attitude** (of an era) *n.*: **zeitgeist**. See spirit

attorney (who may be petty, dishonest or disreputable) *n.*: **pettifogger**. See lawyer

attract (power to ... through magnetism or charm) *n.*: **duende**. See charisma

attraction (sexual ... towards the elderly) *n.*: **gerontophilia**. See lust

(2) **attraction** (as in lure or temptation) *n.*: **Lorelei call**. See lure

(3) **attraction** (sexual ... towards animals) *n.*: **zoophilia** (person attracted: **zoophile**). See bestiality

attractive (as in pleasing) *adj.*: **prepossessing**. See pleasing

(2) **attractive** (esp. sexually) *adj.*: **toothsome**. See sexy

attractiveness (physical ...) *n.*: **pulchritude**. See beauty

atypical (holding ... opinions or having an ... perspective) *adj.*: **heterodox** (*n.*: **heterodoxy**). See unconventional

(2) **atypical** (as in unusual or rare) *adj.*: **recherché** [French]. See rare

auction (act of bidding or selling at) *n.*: **licitation**. ■ Brazil: Small players can be benefitted in auction. ... The **licitation** to explore oil and natural gas areas ... can benefit small players of the sector. Specialists believe the major companies already acquired their areas in 1999 and 2000. (Author not given, *Brazil: Small Players Can Be Benefitted in Auction*, South American Business Information, 06-12-2001.)

(2) **auction** (or sale by a museum of items in order to purchase more) *v.t.*: **deaccession**. See sell

audacity *n.*: **hardihood**. See gall

augur *v.t.*: **adumbrate**. See foreshadow

aura *n.*: **effluvium**. ■ To record his return to [surfing] greatness, Harmon recruits down-and-out surf-mag photographer Jack Fletcher, who also needs another chance. Along with a couple of younger guys dripping with Southern California **effluvium**, they head for a place that may or may not exist, Heart Attacks, where the waves are said to be 30 feet or higher. (Ken Wisneski, *Adventure/Northern California Setting Rounds Out an Eerie Thriller*, Minneapolis Star Tribune, 04-27-1997, p. 21F.)

(2) **aura** (having an ... through magnetism or charm) *n.*: **duende**. See charisma

austere (as in strictly disciplined or regimented) *adj.*: **monastic**. See strict

austerity (as in person who practices extreme..., esp. for spiritual improvement) *n., adj.* **ascetic**. ■ Always an **ascetic**, [Austrian philosopher Ludwig Wittgenstien] gave away his inheritance, relying on the generosity of his Cambridge champions, Russell and John Maynard Keynes, to secure academic employment for him, living frugally and in later life being cared for by his disciples. (Daniel Dennett, *Time 100: Philosopher Ludwig Wittgenstein*, Time, 03-29-1999, p. 88.)

(2) **austerity** (as in marked by simplicity, frugality, self-discipline and/or self-restraint) *adj.*: **Lacedaemoninan**. See spartan

authentic *adj.*: **pukka**. See genuine

(2) **authentic** (appearing to be ... or accurate) *adj.*: **verisimilar**. See realistic

author (of, by or pertaining to) *adj.*: **auctorial**. ■ [In the bookstore, I found] a dozen or so issues of a typewritten fanzine from the 1980s called, shamelessly, Books Are Everything! ... I bought all the issues — as who would not? — and doled them out to myself over the next few weeks. ... Of course, having duly secured such ... **auctorial** largesse, I could hardly stop myself from poking around the bookstore a while longer. (Michael Dirda, *Pulp Fiction, Critical Journals and Other Ephemeral Pleasures*, The Washington Post, 02-25-2001, p. T15.)

(2) **author** (professional ...) *n.*: **wordmonger**. Jonathan Franzen ... won the National Book Award for fiction here tonight for his novel "The Corrections," about the breakdown of an American family. ... The 52nd [National Book] awards drew 800 or so dolled-up denizens of the publishing world — down 20 percent from last year — to the Marriott Marquis Hotel. In the grand ballroom, **wordmongers** supped on red meat, mushroom bisque and New York State apple pie. (Linton Weeks, *Oprah-Pick Franzen Wins National Book Award*, The Washington Post, 11-15-2001.)

(3) **author** (of fiction, esp. who writes in quantity) *n.*: **fictioneer**. See novelist

(4) **author** (as in compose or write) *v.t.*: **indite**. See compose

authoritative (as in influential person, esp. in intellectual or literary circles) *n.*: **mandarin**. SEE INFLUENTIAL

authority (as in a person's area of expertise) *n.*: **bailiwick**. SEE EXPERTISE

(2) **authority** *n.*: **cognoscente**. SEE CONNOISSEUR

(3) **authority** (of one political state over others) *n.*: **hegemony**. SEE DOMINANCE

authorize (officially) *v.t.*: **approbate**. ▪ [National Security Advisor] Sandy Berger said there is a widespread consensus, and he mentioned a number of states more or less **approbating** the use of force against Iraq in support of U.S. action. (Author not given, *Iraqi Deputy Foreign Minister Holds News Conference*, Washington Transcript Service, 02-13-1998.)

(2) **authorize** (authority or duties to another) *v.t.*: **depute**. SEE DELEGATE

autograph (collecting) *n.*: **philography**. ▪ The fourth annual Houston Celebrity/Autograph Collector's Show, sponsored by Focus on **Philography**, will be 10 a.m.-5 p.m. Saturday. (Author not given, *Around Houston*, The Houston Chronicle, 01-30-2000.)

automatic (as in trained to show a conditioned response) *adj.*: **Pavlovian**. SEE CONDITIONED

(2) **automatic** (reaction, as in reflex) *n.*: **tropism**. SEE REFLEX

avail (as in, "to whose ...?") *n.*: **cui bono** [Latin]. SEE ADVANTAGE

avarice *n.*: **cupidity**. SEE GREED

aver *v.t.*: **asseverate**. SEE DECLARE

aversion (develop a strong ... to) *n.*: **scunner** (esp. as in "take a scunner")[British]. SEE DISLIKE

avert *v.t.*: **forfend**. ▪ [The New York Times] had repeatedly demanded that Governor Cuomo forgo a scheduled state tax-rate reduction while also allowing the city to raise income-tax rates. ... It suggested that for Mario to resist this course "smacked of national ambition." **Forfending** further charges of smackery, the governor has now set aside the state income-tax reduction for the second year in a row. (Daniel Seligman, *Incredible Shrinking Humans, a King's Troubles, Mario Cuomo's Ambition, and Other Matters*, Fortune, 09-23-1991, p. 215.)

avocation (as in favorite topic or activity) *n.*: **cheval de bataille** [French for "battle-horse"]. SEE HOBBY

avoid (as in avert or ward off) *v.t.*: **forfend**. SEE AVERT

(2) **avoid** (a straight answer) *v.t.*: **tergiversate**. SEE EVADE

avoidance (engaging in ... tactics, esp. as a means to wear out an opponent or avoid confrontation) *adj.*: **Fabian**. SEE DILATORY, GUERILLA AND CAUTION

avoided (something that is dreaded, disliked or to be ...) *n.*: **bête noire** [French]. SEE DREADED

avow *v.t.*: **asseverate**. SEE DECLARE

awakened (as in revived) *adj.*: **redivivus**. SEE REVIVED

aware (as in watchful person) *n.*: **Argus**. SEE WATCHFUL

(2) **aware** (self-proclaimed ..., as in enlightened, people) *pl.*, *n.*: **illuminati**. SEE ENLIGHTENED

(3) **aware** (as in consciously perceiving) *adj.*: **sentient**. SEE CONSCIOUS

awareness (moment of ..., often the point in the plot at which the protagonist recognizes his or her or some other character's true identity or discovers the true nature of his or her own situation) *n.*: **anagnorisis**. SEE RECOGNITION

(2) **awareness** (sudden ...) *n.*: **epiphany**. SEE REALIZATION

(3) **awareness** *n.*: **ken**. SEE PERCEPTION

awash *adj.*, *adv.*: **aslosh**. ▪ Half the fun of the New Year clearance sales is the fossicking about, but the temptation to buy simply because the price has been slashed can leave unwanted omelette on your face and your limited cellar space **aslosh** with wine you rather wished you hadn't bought. (Anthony Rose, *Bargain Bottles*, Independent, 01-20-1996, p. 40.)

awful (person) *n.*: **caitiff**. SEE DESPICABLE

(2) **awful** *adj.*: **execrable**. SEE ABOMINABLE

(3) **awful** *adj.*: **ugsome**. SEE LOATHSOME

awkward (to make one feel ..., as in disconcert) *v.t.*: **discomfit**. SEE DISCONCERT

(2) **awkward** (and clumsy boy) *n.*: **hobbledehoy**. SEE CLUMSY

(3) **awkward** (as in clumsy) *adj.*: **lumpish**. SEE CLUMSY

(4) **awkward** (habitually ..., as in bumbling person) *n.*: **schlemiel** [Yiddish]. SEE BUMBLER

awkwardness (resulting from an inopportune occurrence) *n.*: **contretemps**. SEE MISHAP

ax *v.t.*: **hew.** ∎ [There are a] host of private Christmas-tree farms to sate your appetite for axing. And there is an appetite: As many as 10,000 Forest Service trees in Colorado will be **hewn** and trimmed for the holidays. (James B. Meadow, **Hew** *it Yourself Forest Service Sites, Tree Farms Ensure a Merry Ax-mas for All*, Denver Rocky Mountain News, 11-29-1997, p. 3D.)

B

babble (as in meaningless talk or nonsense) *n.*: **galimatias.** SEE GIBBERISH
(2) babble *v.i.*: **maunder.** SEE RAMBLE

babbler (as in one who often talks foolishness) *adj.*: **blatherskite.** ∎ When [Governor Christine Todd Whitman's] campaign consultant, a Washington **blatherskite**, regaled reporters after the election with tales of money used to suppress the black turnout, Whitman's reaction — fury leavened by disdain — stamped her as an exception to the rule that in politics as in professional wrestling, there is no role for authentic passion. (George Will, *A Governor Who Makes Waves*, St. Louis Post-Dispatch, 04-06-1994, p. 7B.)

baby (who is deserted or abandoned) *n.*: **foundling.** SEE ORPHAN
(2) baby (collection of clothing and equipment for newborn ...) *n.*: **layette.** SEE NEWBORN
(3) baby (newborn ..., esp. less than 4 weeks old) *n.*: **neonate.** SEE NEWBORN
(4) baby (as in wimp or sissy) *n.*: **pantywaist.** SEE SISSY

back (in or towards the ...) *adv.*: **astern.** ∎ Yet an estate car was, originally, exactly that: a car to cart the gentry around their country estates, hunting, shooting and fishing gear stowed **astern**. (John Simister, *Loaded With Style*, Independent, 01-25-1997, p. 21.)
(2) back (of, toward or near the ... of a person or an organ or body part of a person or animal) *adj.*: **dorsal.** ∎ Tattoo, reportedly the world's largest-selling tattoo magazine, is probably the best-written of the bunch. (And that's still not saying a lot.) ... But, in the end, who wants to actually read any of these campy, trashy magazines when there are such distracting photos as the one of a **dorsal** homage to the rockers KISS or of a smiling, rotund Buddha image on an equally rotund tummy? (Author not given, *Tattoo*

Mags Get to the Needle-Sharp Point, The Toronto Star, 08-26-2000.)

back away *v.i.*: **resile.** SEE RECOIL

backbreaking (task, esp. of cleaning up or remedying bad situations) *n.*: **Augean task.** SEE HERCULEAN

backer (esp. who supports or protects a political leader) *n.*: **Janissary.** SEE SUPPORTER

backward (or stagnant place or situation) *n.*: **backwater.** SEE STAGNANT
(2) backward (as in intellectually or morally unenlightened) *adj.*: **benighted.** SEE UNENLIGHTENED

bacon *n.*: **flitch.** ∎ Uncle Charles, my mother's favourite brother, had a gift for curing bacon, using a secret recipe that he never even told her about. It produced **flitches** as stiff as boards, which, when the brine had done its work, hung from huge hooks set in the dairy ceiling. The bacon smelled sweet and dry. (Anna Pavord, *Border Crossings: How to Save Your Own Bacon*, Independent, 10-27-2001, p. 15.)

bad (as in mischiveous) *adj.*: **elfin.** SEE MISCHIEVOUS
(2) bad (very ..., as in abominable) *adj.*: **execrable.** SEE ABOMINABLE
(3) bad (as in evil or wicked) *adj.*: **iniquitous.** SEE WICKED
(4) bad (as in evil or wicked) *adj.*: **malefic.** SEE EVIL
(5) bad (as in evil or wicked) *adj.*: **malevolent.** SEE EVIL

bad faith (with or in ...) *adv., adj.*: **mala fide** [Latin]. ∎ The inescapable conclusion, from the Indian point of view, is that either U.S. intentions in India are **mala fide**, or, even worse, India is so low on Clinton's list of priorities that it does not merit a serious policy. (K.V. Bapa Rao, *Clinton's India Policy*, India Currents, 04-30-1994.)

bad dream (or episode having the quality of a ...) *n.*: **Walpurgis Night.** SEE NIGHTMARE

bad luck *n., adj.*: **hoodoo** [sometimes as in "a hoodoo" when used in the sense of a curse or jinx; also used as an adjective as in "hoodoo team"]. ∎ Mo Vaughn had no idea what he was stepping into April 6 when he plunged feet-first into the visitor's dugout during the first inning of his first game as an Anaheim Angel. Eighty million bucks [Vaughn's salary] might keep you toasty at night, but no truckload of cash covers ... four decades of **hoodoo**. Vaughn dismissed the opening-day misstep as a freak accident. (Chris Dufresne, *The Hex Files; Angels Have Been Foiled by Something for Almost Four Decades*, Los Angeles Times, 05-27-1999, p. D1.)

bad temper *n.*: **bile**. SEE BITTERNESS

(2) bad temper *n.*: **choler** (*adj.*: **choleric**). SEE ANGER

bad-tempered (as in surly) *adj.*: **atrabilious**. SEE SURLY

(2) bad-tempered (as in surly) *adj.*: **bilious**. SEE SURLY

(3) bad-tempered *adj.*: **choleric**. SEE ANGRY

(4) bad-tempered (as in grouchy person) *n.*: **crosspatch**. SEE GROUCH

(5) bad-tempered (as in irritable) *adj.*: **liverish**. SEE IRRITABLE

(6) bad-tempered (as in irritable) *adj.*: **shirty**. SEE IRRITABLE

badger *v.t.*: **hector**. SEE BULLY

(2) badger *v.t.*: **chivvy**. SEE PESTER

bag (women's drawstring ...) *n.*: **reticule**. SEE HANDBAG

bagpipes (high, shrill sound of ...) *n.*: **skirl**. ∎ With eyes dried and hearts lifted — thanks to the **skirl** of bagpipes played by kilt-wearing pipers coming up the hill — Grant, Gill and the wedding guests arrived at Grant's rented home. (Karen S. Schneider, *Weddings: Perfect Harmony*, People, 03-27-2000, p. 57.)

balance (as in equilibrium) *n.*: **equipoise**. SEE EQUILIBRIUM

bald (or hairless) *adj.*: **glabrous**. ∎ In the Brazilian rainforests Dutch scientists have located the world's tiniest species of monkey. ... Too small to eat or even to perform with an organ grinder, the diminutive monkey might be used as a hairpiece, and if these Dutch scientists are as bald as most middle-aged Dutchmen, they may return to Holland as saviors of their **glabrous** race. (Author not given, *The Continuing Crisis: Scrabbled Brains*, The American Spectator, 10-01-1997.)

(2) bald (headed man) *n.*: **pilgarlic**. ∎ Moving from pogonotrophy to **pilgarlics**, many politicians perceive that the voters won't go for a bald-headed candidate, according to John T. Capps, III of (where else?), Moorehead City, North Carolina, President and Founder of Bald-Headed Men of America. (*Eye on Long Island*, Newsday, 03-12-95.)

(3) bald (become ... by shaving one's head) *v.t.*; *n.*: **tonsure**. SEE SHAVE

baldness *n.*: **alopecia**. ∎ Coming on the eve of the muckraking era, Rockefeller's **alopecia** had a devastating effect on his image: It made him look like a hairless ogre, stripped of all youth, warmth and attractiveness, and this played powerfully on his mother's imaginations. (Ron Chernow, *Titan*, Random House [1998], p. 408.)

ball (formal ... esp. for debutantes) *n.*: **cotillion**. ∎ [He is] one of six blacks in a Catholic school of 1,200 males wearing blazers to class each day. ... He's at a **cotillion**. He's very quiet. Perfectly mannerly. But he's making one debutante's mother nervous. She asks what his family name is. "Wilkens," he replies. She asks what his father's profession is. "My father's dead." (Gary Smith, *Bonus Piece*, Sports Illustrated, 12-05-1994, p. 68.)

ballet (admirer or fan of ...) *n.*: **balletomane**. ∎ Although he would go on to dance with more than 40 companies, [Rudolf] Nureyev's most successful relationship was with England's Royal Ballet, partnering Margot Fonteyn. In the body-conscious 1960s, his athletic, pantherlike approach enraptured audiences and created a whole new generation of **balletomanes**. (Eileen Clarke, *The Final Curtain— Eight Years Ago, Groundbreaking Dancer Rudolf Nureyev Succumbed to AIDS*, Entertainment Weekly, 01-11-2002, p. 76.)

balls (as in testicles; surgical removal of one or both ...) *n.*: **orchiectomy**. SEE TESTICLES

balm (or lotion which is soothing) *n.*: **demulcent**. SEE SOOTHING

bamboozle *v.t.*: **hornswoggle**. SEE DECEIVE

banal (as in insipid, intellectual nourishment, like baby food) *n.*: **pabulum** (also **pablum**). SEE INSIPID

(2) banal (remark or statement) *n.*: **platitude**. SEE CLICHE

banality (in speech or writing) *n.*: **pablum**. SEE TRITENESS

banditry *n.*: **brigandage** (**bandit** *n.*: **brigand**). SEE ROBBERY

bank (of or relating to a ... of water) *adj.*: **riparian**. SEE WATER BANK

banner (suspended from a crossbar, as opposed to on a flagstaff) *n.*: **gonfalon**. ∎ [The New York] Rangers, who went 54 years between [Stanley] Cups, have ...

ascended to the championship throne ... as the **gonfalon** was hoisted in New York. (Austin Murphy, *Hockey: It Was the Kind of Gaudy Excess That New York Does Best*, Sports Illustrated, 01-30-1995, p. 24.)

(2) banner (an inspiring ...) *n.*: **oriflamme**. ∎ Nobody has raised an **oriflamme** — the scarlet banner to which scattered troops may repair — to rally all people to a great cause, saying, "This is an epic in which we all have a role. This is something we will be proud to bequeath to our children." (Jon Cypher, *Lights! Camera! Action! It's Time to Script a New Show for NASA*, Omni, 07-01-1994, p. 4.)

bannister (and supports for) *n.*: **balustrade**. See HANDRAIL

banter *n.*: **badinage**. ∎ Front runners can stumble, but the mayor exudes confidence. In the middle of a formal Transport for London Board meeting, a white-haired woman got up to denounce him. Instead of having her ejected, Mr Livingstone engaged in a lively debate, calling her "darling." After five minutes of **badinage**, the woman sat down, apparently content. Few ministers could have handled her so deftly. (Author not given, *Britain: A Shoo-in; London's Mayor*, The Economist, 02-23-2002, p. 33.)

(2) banter *v.t., v.i., n.*: **chaff**. See TEASING

(3) banter (one skilled at dinner ...) *n.*: **deipnosophist**. See CONVERSATION

(4) banter *n.*: **persiflage**. See CHITCHAT

(5) banter (as in good-natured teasing) *n.*: **raillery**. See TEASING

barb (as in insult, delivered while leaving the scene) *n.*: **Parthian shot**. See PARTING SHOT

barbarian (as in boor) *n.*: **grobian**. See BOOR

(2) barbarian (as in indifferent or antagonistic to artistic or cultural values) *adj.*: **philistine**. See UNCULTURED

(3) barbarian *n.*: **troglodyte**. See NEANDERTHAL

(4) barbarian (as in crude or uncouth person) *n.*: **yahoo**. See BOOR

barbaric *adj.*: **gothic**. ∎ "I am opposed to Asiatics being brought here," said the [Congressman in 1870]. But "while they are here it is our duty to protect them [from] barbarous and cruel laws that place upon them unjust and cruel burdens." Over the past 100 years, California has passed a **gothic** variety of laws discriminating against aliens; but the Court has balked only when some aliens were discriminated against more than others. (Jeffrey Rosen, *The War on Immigrants: Why the Courts Can't Save Us*, The New Republic, 01-30-1995, p. 22.)

barren *adj.*: **acarpous**. See STERILE

barricade *n.*: **bulwark**. See PROTECTION

base *adj.*: **ignoble**. See MEAN

(2) base (on which something is built) *n.*: **warp and woof**. See FOUNDATION

baseless (and/or illogical argument) *n.*: **choplogic**. See FALLACY

bashful (esp. from lack of self-confidence) *adj.*: **diffident**. See TIMID

(2) bashful (and unassertive person) *n.*: **Milquetoast**. See UNASSERTIVE

basic *adj.*: **abecedarian**. ∎ [Muhammad Ali] expressed himself in energetic, if **abecedarian**, rhymes. Listen to this excerpt from "Song of Myself": "Yes, the crowd did not dream — When they laid down their money — That they would see — A total eclipse of the Sonny. I am the greatest!" (Keith Mano, *Still the Greatest*, National Review, 11-09-1998, p. 59.)

(2) basic (as in essential) *adj.*: **constitutive**. See ESSENTIAL

basis (initial ... as in prime mover) *n.*: **primum mobile** [Latin]. See PRIME MOVER

(2) basis (on which something is built) *n.*: **warp and woof**. See FOUNDATION

(3) basis (principal ... or source) *n.*: **wellhead**. See SOURCE

basket (often one of a pair, on either side of a bike or animal) *n.*: **pannier**. ∎ In Vietnam the unemployed not only get on their bikes, they load them up with saleable goods. The contents of whole supermarkets are available from the **panniers** of trusty Flying Pigeon bicycles. (Stanley Stewart, *Travel: Oh What a Lovely Peace; The Vietnam War Helped Save Old Hanoi*, The Daily Telegraph, 11-15-1997, p. 20.)

bat (one's eyes) *v.i.*: **nictitate**. See BLINK

batch (confused or jumbled ...) *n.*: **agglomeration**. See JUMBLE

baths (of or relating to ... or bathing) *adj.*: **balneal**. ∎ When ... boats are bobbing and becking on the blue water, Jayne Ikard likes nothing better than to draw a bath in her forest green bathroom and soak herself as she surveys the scene spread before her. ... "You might call Jayne a sort of assistant harbormaster," said one friend of Ikard's **balneal** supervision of the boats. (William MacKaye, *Edgartown Harbor From the Second-floor Bath*, The Washington Post, 05-04-1996, p. 27.)

battered (as in decrepit) *adj.*: **spavined**. SEE DECREPIT

battle (as in brawl, esp. public) *n.*: **affray**. SEE BRAWL
(2) battle (act or event which causes or provokes ...) *n.*: **casus belli** [Latin; occasion of war]. SEE PROVOCATION
(3) battle (over an idea or principle) *n.*: **jihad**. SEE CRUSADE
(4) battle (people who ... as if to the death) *n.*: **Kilkenny cats** (esp. as in "fight like Kilkenny cats"). SEE FIGHT
(5) battle (of or about words) *n.*: **logomachy**. SEE WORDS
(6) battle (or conflict among the gods) *n.*: **theomachy**. SEE GODS

bauble (as in trinket) *n.*: **bibelot**. SEE TRINKET
(2) bauble (as in trinket) *n.*: **bijou**. SEE TRINKET
(3) bauble (as in trinket) *n.*: **gewgaw**. SEE TRINKET

bay window *n.*: **oriel**. ▮ The newer Renaissance section [of the Rothenburg town hall], built in 1572, replaced the portion destroyed in the fire. It's decorated with intricate friezes, an **oriel** extending the building's full height, and a large stone portico opening onto the square. (Author not given, *Germany: The Romantic Road*, Frommer's Europe, 01-01-1998.)

beaming (as in shining brightly) *adj.*: **effulgent**. SEE BRIGHT
(2) beaming (as in shining brightly) *adj.*: **fulgurant**. SEE BRIGHT
(3) beaming (as in shining brightly) *adj.*: **refulgent**. SEE BRIGHT

bear (of, resembling or relating to) *adj.*: **ursine**. ▮ The worm of doubt that really eats at market watchers taurine and **ursine** [e.g. bull and bear] is the high price/earnings multiple, recently about 24.4 for the S&P 500. (Terence P. Pare, *Investment Strategy & Vehicles*, Fortune, 10-26-1992, p. 16.)

beard (having a ...) *adj.*: **barbate**. ▮ It took the Western pioneers to make woolly faces fashionable again, and it took Abraham Lincoln in 1861 to bring a **barbate** visage to the White House. (David Wharton, *Face to Face With Hairy Situations*, The Los Angeles Times, 08-06-1991, p. E1-5.)

bearing *n.*: **mien**. SEE DEMEANOR

beat (repeatedly, often used figuratively) *v.t.*: **buffet**. SEE HIT
(2) beat (with a club) *v.t.*: **cudgel**. SEE CLUB
(3) beat (as in whip, generally used figuratively) *v.t.*: **larrup**. SEE WHIP

beat up (sometimes in jest) *v.t.*: **spiflicate** [British slang]. ▮ My wife and daughter-in-law will **spiflicate** me for saying so, but I find the invitation to Annika Sorenstam to play in a men's pro golf tournament laughable. There would be a huge hue and cry if Tiger Woods played in a girls' rich tournament and won by 20 strokes, playing left-handed. (Terry Tuckey [letter writer], *Midweek Status Suits Women Down To A Tee*, Sydney Morning Herald, 05-22-2003, p. 12.)
(2) beat up (as in broken down and/or worn out) *adj.*: **raddled**. SEE WORN-OUT
(3) beat-up (as in decrepit) *adj.*: **spavined**. SEE DECREPIT

beaten (capable of being ...) *n.*: **vincible**. ▮ Probably the worst thing the Yankees did in playing barely .500 ball for the last month is give heart to the players they'll meet later this month and in October. The invincible team has been distinctly **vincible**. (Steve Jacobson, *The Playoffs — Just Win, Baby*, Newsday, 09-29-1998, p. D8.)

beau (as in boyfriend) *n.*: **inamorato**. SEE BOYFRIEND

beautiful (young woman) *n.*: **houri** [French]. SEE WOMAN
(2) beautiful (of a ... and stately woman, esp. tending towards voluptuous) *adj.*: **Junoesque**. SEE VOLUPTUOUS
(3) beautiful (esp. sexually) *adj.*: **toothsome**. SEE SEXY

beautiful people (as in fashionable society) *n.*: **beau monde** [French]. SEE HIGH SOCIETY
(2) beautiful people (as in fashionable society) *n.*: **bon ton** [French]. SEE HIGH SOCIETY

beauty (highest ..., esp. moral ..., as conceived by Aristotle) *n.*: **kalon** [Greek]. ▮ The "great-souled man" had a character of such undiluted integrity, inspiration and achievement in the real world that his life expressed, for Aristotle, the **kalon**, moral beauty. Ronald Reagan was a morally beautiful human being. (Jack Wheeler, *The 'Great-souled Man'; Reagan Was a Classic*, The Washington Times, 06-08-2004.)

(2) beauty (physical ...) *n*.: **pulchritude**. ▪ [Baseball player Mike] Piazza has hit the mother lode of visual **pulchritude**. His girlfriend is Darlene Bernaola. He has her initials tattooed on his ankle. Bernaola and her twin sister are Playboy's playmates of the Millennium. (Richard Deitsch, *The Fans: Knowwhatimsayin'? Fuggedabowdit!* Sports Illustrated, 11-01-2000, p. 82.)

bed (mattress filled with straw) *n*.: **palliasse**. See MATTRESS

bed-wetting *n*.: **nocturnal enuresis**. ▪ Severe "**nocturnal enuresis**," characterized by three or more bed-wetting episodes per week in children older than age seven, affects some 7 percent of the population. (Josie Glausiusz, *Strange Genes*, Discover Magazine, 01-01-1996, p. 33.)

bedlam (and confusion, esp. from simultaneous voices) *n*.: **babel**. See NOISE

(2) bedlam (as in commotion) *n*.: **maelstrom**. See COMMOTION

(3) bedlam (as in chaos) *n*.: **tohubuhu**. See CHAOS

beehive *n*.: **skep**. ▪ Back on the ground, I turned the **skep** upside-down, with the bottom open, and propped up so that stragglers could rejoin the main tribe. Inward migration confirmed that the queen [bee] was inside, but it took nearly an hour for all to be gathered in. (Duff Hart-Davis, *Country: 'I'm Not Going Near Them,' Said Mr. X*, Independent, 06-15-1996, p. 8.)

beer-bellied *adj*.: **abdominous**. ▪ We chaps also know what it's like to be grossly **abdominous**, and if my byline photo were full length and in profile, you'd realise that I've been 14 months pregnant for the past five years. (Victor Lewis-Smith, *Womb for Improvement*, The Evening Standard [London, England], 08-09-2001.)

befog (over one's vision) *v.t*.: **obnubilate**. See OBSCURE

before (a meal, esp. dinner) *adj*.: **preprandial**. See MEAL

(2) before (coming ...) *adj*.: **prevenient** (often as in "prevenient grace"). See ANTECEDENT

befuddled (esp. used of a person, as in ... and stupid) *adj*.: **addlepated**. See CONFUSED

beg (from or sponge off of) *v.t*.: **cadge**. ▪ None of the adulation, though, quieted a deep insecurity that Nicholas Gage, author of Greek Fire, a new biogra-phy of Callas and Onassis, says began with an unstable mother who alternately criticized Callas and **cadged** money from her. A fed-up Callas finally told her mother to get a job or, failing that, "jump out of the window or drown yourself," TIME once reported. (Christina Cheakalos, *Auction: Diva's Delight*, People, 12-04-2000, p. 131.)

(2) beg (as in plead) *v.t*.: **adjure**. See PLEAD

beggar *n*.: **mendicant**. ▪ In [Graham Greene's] 1940 novel, The Power And The Glory, he created a character who was a street **mendicant**, and observed, "He had the grudging independence you find in countries where it is the right of a poor man to beg." (Philip Marchand, *Hed Goes Here*, The Toronto Star, 07-18-1998.)

begging the question (as in assuming in the premise that which is to be proved) *n*.: **petitio principii** [Latin. A common misusage of the phrase "begging the question" is in the sense of "raising or inviting a further question." However its correct usage requires a conclusion which restates the premise. For example: "Affirmative Action can never be just because you cannot remedy one injustice by committing another." Here the premise is that affirmative action is unjust and that premise is used as the basis for the exact same conclusion.] ▪ It has been objected, from Gassendi downward, that to say [as Descartes did], "I think, therefore I am," is a begging of the question; since existence has to be proved identical with thought. Certainly, if Descartes had intended to prove his own existence by reasoning, he would have been guilty of the **petitio principii** Gassendi attributes to him. (George Henry Lewes, *Birth of Modern Scientific Methods, Bacon and Descartes*, History of the World, 01-01-1992.)

beginner *n*.: **abecedarian**. ▪ Apprentice alphabetarians are **abecedarians** (as are apprentice anythings). [But] Richard A. Firmage's entertaining and eclectic book ... is chiefly aimed at more advanced readers who are fascinated by language and how letters are formed and used. (Andrew McKie, *Books: Nothing Simple about A, B, C*, The Daily Telegraph, 04-08-2000, p. 5.) See BASIC

(2) beginner *n*.: **catechumen**. ▪ Sonny appears to be the only child of Jake and Lily Cantrell. Jake raises gamecocks as proprietor of the Snake Nation Cock Farm. ... Sonny is an eager **catechumen** in his father's cockfighting religion. (Jonathan Taylor, *The Small Press/Journey to Manhood*, Newsday, 03-15-1998, p. B14.)

(3) beginner (as in amateur) *n*.: **dilettante**. See AMATEUR

beginning (from the ...) *adv.*: **ab initio** [Latin]. ▪ In contrast with "regular" wars where most nations agree to operate within certain rules, terrorism is characterized by the fact that its perpetrators permit themselves **ab initio** any means and any target. (Yigal Carmon, *A Very Costly Naivete*, Jerusalem Post, 07-30-1996, p. 6.)

(2) beginning (from the ...) *adv.*: **ab ovo** [Latin]. ▪ To describe this project's gestation, **ab ovo**, I need to take you back to 1990, when Penguin published my comic-book version of The Waste Land. (Martin Rowson, *Books*, Independent on Sunday, 09-01-1996, p. 29.)

(3) beginning (existing from the ..., as in innate) *adj.*: **connate**. See INNATE

(4) beginning (often of a speech or writing) *n.*: **exordium**. See INTRODUCTION

(5) beginning (as in establishment, of something) *n.*: **instauration**. See ESTABLISHMENT

(6) beginning (as in coming into being) *adj.*: **nascent**. See EMERGING

beginning and end *n.*: **alpha and omega**. ▪ From my room at the Holiday Inn [in Sarajevo], the **alpha and omega** of the war lay before me. [To the left, in 1979, a woman] took a sniper's bullet and so became the first of 10,615 of the city's residents to die. ... The last fatality occurred not 75 yards to the right. (Alexander Wolff, *Big Game, Small World*, Warner Books [2002], p. 109.)

beguile *v.t.*: **ensorcell** (or **ensorcel**). See ENCHANT

beguiling (as in tempting) *adj.*: **siren**. See TEMPTING

behavior (study of human ...) *n.*: **praxeology**. ▪ [In the black church,] they talk about what Jesus did. Yes they will say what he did, but they won't do it themselves. The difference between what is being said in church (doctrine) and what action is being taken (**praxeology**), confuses people in and outside the church. (H. Dwight Sterling, *Black Church Must Act With Words And Deeds*, Oakland Post, 06-12-1994.)

(2) behavior (appropriate ...) *n.*: **correctitude**. See PROPRIETY

behind (as in towards the back) *adv.*: **astern**. See BACK

(2) behind (having a nicely proportioned ...) *adj.*: **callipygian**. See REAR END

(3) behind (having a hairy ...) *adj.*: **dasypygal**. See REAR END

(4) behind (as in buttocks) *n., pl.*: **nates**. See BUTTOCKS

(5) behind (a fat ...) *n.*: **steatopygia** (having a fat ...) *(adj.)*: **steatopygic**). See REAR END

being (while coming into ...) *adv.*: **aborning**. See BORN

belaboring (as in repeating a particular act over and over, often after initial stimulus has ceased) *n.*: **perseveration** (*v.i.*: **perseverate**). See REPEATING

belch *v.t., v.i.*: **eruct**. ▪ Scientists have been telling us for decades that the greatest contributors to smog, the greenhouse effect and global warming are automobiles. In response, we've choked our cities with spaghetti strands of interstates on which stalled, snorting tank cars **eruct** their fetid air. (Gary Corseri, *Letters: In My Opinion: The Enemy on Four Wheels*, The Atlanta Journal and Constitution, 06-26-2000, p. 9A.)

belief (which is odd, stubborn or whimsical) *n.*: **crotchet**. See NOTION

(2) belief (as in reliance on ... alone [as in faith] rather than reason, esp. in philosophical or religious matters) *n.*: **fideism**. See FAITH

(3) belief *n.*: **shibboleth**. See PRINCIPLE

believable (as in appearing to be true or accurate) *adj.*: **verisimilar**. See PLAUSIBLE

belittle (oneself) *v.t.*: **self-flagellate** (*n.*: **self-flagellation**). See CRITICIZE

(2) belittle *v.t.*: **vilipend**. See DISPARAGE

belittlement (as in disdain) *n.*: **misprision** (*v.t.*: **misprize**). See DISDAIN

belittling (another, often by being insulting or humiliating) *adj.*: **contumelious**. See CONTEMPTUOUS

bell ringing (art of ...) *n.*: **campanology**. ▪ Writer Christopher Russell set his story in the enclosed and slightly mysterious world of **campanology**. Bellringers are a little like many wicket keepers, goalies or steeplejacks — lonely, obsessive figures devoted to ancient rules and customs. (Peter Paterson, *It Always Rings a Bell...*, The Daily Mail, 09-16-2002.)

belligerent *adj.*: **bellicose**. ▪ Ever since they split in a civil war 50 years ago, China has been a very real danger to Taiwan. The People's Republic has menaced the island with missile tests and **bellicose** threats of invasion. (Mahlon Meyer, *Risky Business*, Newsweek International, 08-14-2000, p. 36.)

bells (ringing or sounding of) *n*.: **tintinnabulation**. ▪ [Beauty and The Beast's] dancing clocks and singing teacups will blend marvelously with the **tintinnabulation** of bells this holiday season. (Mark Goodman, *Picks & Pans*, People, 11-18-1991, p. 21.)

belonging (as in associated with or incident to) *adj*.: **appurtenant**. See PERTAINING

beloved (as in darling) *n*.: **acushla** [Irish]. See DARLING

(2) beloved (my ...) *n*.: **Mavoureen** [Irish]. See DARLING

bend (slightly) *v.t., v.i*.: **camber**. See CURVE
(2) bend (in and out) *v.i*.: **sinuate**. See WIND

bendable *adj*.: **ductile**. See PLIABLE

benediction *n*.: **benison**. See BLESSING

benefactor (generous ..., esp. of the arts) *n*.: **Maecenas** [after Gaius Maecenas, a Roman statesman, who was a patron of Horace and Virgil.] ▪ Christie's star [auction] was the sale of 14 works from the collection of Paul Mellon, the octogenarian **Maecenas**, who must be considered America's premier collector; his father founded Washington's National Gallery and he has given literally hundreds of works to institutions. (Geraldine Norman, *Blue Period for High Prices*, The Independent, 11-25-1989, p. 43.)

beneficial (as in having the power to cure or heal) *adj*.: **sanative**. See HEALTHFUL

benefit (as in, "to whose ...?") *n*.: **cui bono** [Latin]. See ADVANTAGE
(2) benefit (extra or unexpected ..., sometimes given as thanks for a purchase) *n*.: **lagniappe**. See GIFT

benevolent *adj*.: **eleemosynary**. See CHARITABLE

berate *v.t*.: **flay**. See CRITICIZE
(2) berate *v.t*.: **objurgate**. See CRITICIZE

berating (as in criticism) *n*.: **animadversion** (*v.t*.: **animadvert**). See CRITICISM
(2) berating (being subject to ..., esp. public) *n*.: **obloquy**. See ABUSE

bereft *adj*.: **lorn**. See FORLORN

beseech (as in plead) *v.t*.: **adjure**. See PLEAD
(2) beseech (as in begging for or sponging off of) *v.t*.: **cadge**. See BEG

besides *adv*.: **withal**. See MOREOVER

besieged *adj*.: **obsidional**. ▪ The observation of the historian Michel Winock that in late-nineteenth-century France one sector of public opinion embraced — as if the country were under siege — a nationalism "whose mission was to defend the cohesive social organism against modernity" — could equally have been made about France in the 1920s. That "**obsidional**" nationalism, he continues, oriented itself toward the interior and the past. (Frederick Brown, *Perfumed Rot*, The New Republic, 06-26-2000.)

best (as in first-class) *adj*.: **pukka**. See FIRST-CLASS
(2) best (the ..., lit. the greatest or highest good) *n*.: **summum bonum**. [Latin]. See IDEAL

bestiality (as in sexual attraction towards animals) *n*.: **zoophilia** (person attracted: **zoophile**). ▪ Zoophiles say they favour companionship with animals that can include unforced sexual contact. Woods said her patient told her that **zoophilia** today was where homosexuality was 20 years ago and before long could be considered normal, accepted behaviour. (Michael Conlon, *Web Skews Sex Education, U.S. Psychiatrist Warns*, Reuters, 05-16-2000.)

bestow (by one with higher power) *v.t*.: **vouchsafe**. ▪ Robin Cook ... [the Foreign Secretary] has become dismayed. There is too much regulation, he observes. The [European Union in Brussels is] too remote from the electors of Europe, he complains, with the air of a man who believes he has been **vouchsafed** a unique insight. (Author not given, *Look, But Don't Touch*, The Daily Telegraph, 08-14-1998.)

betray (oneself by selling one's soul to the devil) *adj*.: **Mephistophelean**. See SELLOUT
(2) betray (as in tattle) *v.i*.: **peach**. See TATTLE

betrayer (esp. under guise of friendship) *n*.: **Judas**. ▪ [Russian President Boris] Yeltsin has more than enough enemies. To fanatical nationalists he is the **Judas** who sold his country to the West for 30 silver dollars. (John Kohan, *Moscow, Russia: Looking for Mr. Good Czar*, Time, 04-05-1993, p. 24.)
(2) betrayer (esp. who aids an invading enemy) *n*.: **quisling**. See TRAITOR

betrayers (as in traitors or group of ... working within a country to support an enemy and who may engage in espionage, sabotage or other subversive activities) *n*.: **fifth column**. See TRAITORS

betrothed (to be ...) *v.t.*: **affianced**. SEE MARRIAGE

better (state of being ...) *n.*: **meliority**. SEE SUPERIORITY

bewitch *v.t.*: **ensorcell** (or **ensorcel**). SEE ENCHANT

bewitching (as in tempting) *adj.*: **siren**. SEE TEMPTING

bias (preconceived ... on an issue) *n.*: **parti pris** [French]. SEE PRECONCEPTION

(2) bias (develop a strong ... against) *n.*: **scunner** (esp. as in "take a scunner")[British]. SEE DISLIKE

biased (toward a particular point of view) *adj.*: **tendentious**. ▪ This **tendentious** and unpleasant [and unflattering biography of New York mayor Rudy Giuliani] also reads like the revenge of a jilted lover, which is no coincidence. ... [To the author, Giuliani] evidently personifies Evil. (Michael Grunwald, *Rudolph Giuliani's Means and Ends*, The New Republic, 01-15-2001.)

Bible (worshiper) *n.*: **bibliolater**. ▪ There is a form of heart disease defined, not by clogged arteries, but by blockage of the spirit. ... There is no magical elixir here and no "quick fix," despite what many spiritual gurus proclaim. But, let me recommend one tried-and-true source of bracing tonic for a despairing, confused or starving spirit. Regular readers know that I am no **bibliolater**. But the remedy I'm talking about is from the Bible. It's the collection of poetry known as the Psalms. (Tom Harpur, *The Psalms Are Healing Tonic for an Ailing Spirit*, The Toronto Star, 07-14-1996, p. B7.)

(2) Bible (excessive adherence to literal interpretation of ...) *n.*: **bibliotary**. ▪ Christians who have a high view of Scripture — of its divine inspiration, infallibility and authority — are sometimes accused of **bibliolatry**. (Author not given, *Religion; Spirited Media*, The Dallas Morning News, p. 6G.)

(3) Bible (seller) *n.*: **colporteur**. ▪ Named after the **colporteurs** who on horseback sold Bibles and other "edifying" books door-to-door, Moody's Colportage Library was a series of 10-cent reprints of sermons and tracts that sold well enough to establish his publisher, the Fleming H. Revell Co., as the largest publisher of religion books by the turn of the century. (John D. Spalding, *Stirring the Waters of Reflection: How the Anguish of the 1960s Transformed the Role of Religious Publishing*, Publishers Weekly, 07-01-1997.)

bid (the ... to achieve a particular goal or desire) *n.*: **nisus**. SEE GOAL

bidding (act of ... at an auction) *n.*: **licitation**. SEE AUCTION

big (very ...) *adj.*: **brobdingnagian** (often cap.). SEE HUGE

(2) big (very ...) *adj.*: **Bunyanesque**. SEE ENORMOUS

(3) big (like an elephant) *adj.*: **elephantine**. SEE ENORMOUS

(4) big (very ... object) *n.*: **leviathan**. SEE HUGE

(5) big (like an elephant) *adj.*: **pachydermatous**. SEE ELEPHANT

(6) big (very ...) *adj.*: **Pantagruelian**. SEE GIGANTIC

(7) big (very ...) *adj.*: **pythonic**. SEE HUGE

big toe *n.*: **hallux**. ▪ Left undiagnosed and untreated, turf toe can develop into a career-ending arthritic condition known as **hallux** rigidus. When this happens, the injured big toe stiffens and the player can no longer push off on the affected foot, thereby losing most of his mobility, a critical commodity in today's speed-dominated pro game. (Jill Lieber, *Medicine: Turf Toe: The NFL's Most Pesky Agony of Da Feet*, Sports Illustrated, 12-12-1988, p. 8.)

bigot (as in one who clings to an opinion or belief even after being shown that it is wrong) *n.* **mumpsimus**. SEE STUBBORN

bigwig (often arrogant or self-important) *n.*: **high muck-a-muck**. ▪ Landing at Teterboro [Airport] also allows corporate fliers to avoid having to mingle with the perspiring masses — people who happen not to be **high muck-a-mucks**; people like you and the guy who lives across the street — they would encounter at Newark, Kennedy, and LaGuardia. (Jeffrey Page, *Fat Cats Are Left Cooling Their Jets*, The Record [Bergen County, NJ], 02-06-2004.)

(2) bigwig *n.*: **nabob**. ▪ "People look at Washington," said George W. [Bush] last week, "and they don't like what they see." Oh? Mr. Outsider went to a Washington, D.C., ballroom jammed with 2,000 entrenched political **nabobs**, mostly lobbyists and lawyers who wrote checks for more than $2 million. George W. liked what he saw. (Author not given, *Fireworks Lid Inflicts Undue Pain on Vendors*, The Columbian, 07-06-1999.)

(3) bigwig *n.*: **panjandrum**. ▪ Still, for reasons known only to the preposterous **panjandrums** who run college athletics, we can watch 13 hours of New Year's Day bowl games and come away with only a suggestion as to the identity of the national college football champion. (Dave Kindred, *Here's a Super Bowl Solution*, The Sporting News, 01-10-1994, p. 6.)

(4) bigwig *n.*: **wallah**. SEE NOTABLE

bilingual *adj.*: **diglot**. ▪ A pocket size edition of the Constitution of India in **diglot** form is in the final stage of publication. It will be in the twin languages of English and Hindi. (Author not given, *Indian Government: Pocket Size Edition of Constitution of India*, M2 PressWire, 09-29-1999.)

bind (together) *v.t.*: **colligate**. SEE UNITE

(2) bind (a person by holding down their arms) *v.t.*: **pinion**. SEE IMMOBILIZE

binding (act of ... or tying up or together) *n.*: **ligature**. SEE TYING

biographer (as in one who, out of admiration or friendship, records the deeds and words of another) *n.*: **Boswell** [after James Boswell (1740-1795), the biographer of Samuel Johnson]. ▪ From the beginning, [Katherine] Hepburn knew that in Berg she had found not only a companion but her **Boswell**. Over the years, he kept notes on their many meetings. He knew that eventually he would do her bidding and write her story. ... Throughout the 370-page reminiscence, Berg sets aside his biographer's independence and takes his cues from one of America's greatest movie stars. (Linton Weeks, *Hepburn And Her* **Boswell***; A. Scott Berg's Memoir Caps a 20-Year Friendship With the Legend*, The Washington Post, 07-12-2003.)

biography (which is worshipful or idealizing) *n.*: **hagiography** (*adj*: **hagiographic**). ▪ Nella hoped to write [Helen Keller's] biography. It would be similar to the one she had written of Annie Sullivan wherein she had painted a **hagiographic** portrait of Teacher as a true heroine and master teacher. (Dorothy Herrmann, *Helen Keller*, Knopf [1998], p. 269.)

(2) biography (esp. in relation to other people or within a specific historical, social, or literary context) *n.*: **prosopography**. ▪ [U]ntil now, we have known surprisingly little about most of the men who ran [London between 1890 and 1914]. Youssef Cassis, in this pioneering study full of telling detail and perceptive analysis, does much to change that. The engine of his book is a sample of 460 leading bankers active in these years, in effect a collective biography of the City. ... [T]his is **prosopography** on the grand scale. (David Kynaston, *Heyday of the*

Banking Purple [sic], Financial Times [London], 03-30-1995.)

bird dung (esp. that of sea birds) *n.*: **guano**. ▪ [Hucks Gibbs's] family had made much of their money from working the vast deposits of **guano** in Peru. (Doggerel of the day referred, not unkindly, to 'The House of Gibbs that made their Dibs by selling Turds of Foreign Birds'). (Simon Winchester, *The Meaning of Everything*, Oxford [2003], p. 129.)

birdhouse *n.*: **aviary**. ▪ The bald eagle has a good buddy in Dolly Parton. At her Dollywood theme park in Tennessee, the country star will break ground next month for an **aviary** to house the U.S.'s largest collection of bald eagles unable to survive in the wild. (Emily Mitchell, *People: Best Little Birdhouse*, Time, 07-30-1990, p. 71.)

birds (of, relating to or characteristic of) *adj.*: **avian**. ▪ Frank X. Ogasawara, one of the world's leading poultry scientists whose pioneer studies in **avian** reproduction helped create the plumper, meatier turkeys that grace U.S. tables on Thanksgiving, died June 8. He was 88. (Dennis McLellan, *Obituaries/Frank X. Ogasawara, Poultry Science Pioneer*, Newsday, 06-21-2002, p. A65.)

(2) birds (of, relating to or characteristic of) *adj.*: **ornithic**. ▪ But Johnson has other problems ... of an **ornithic** nature. Pedro Borbon, the 48-year-old (he says) replacement pitcher cut by the Reds last week, sold Johnson two parrots for $500 each. At midnight Friday, Johnson had to take one of the parrots to a hospital in Lakeland, Fla., with some sort of infection. (Rick Hummel, *Reds Boss Bonds Better With Birds Than Replacements*, St. Louis Post-Dispatch, 03-26-1995, p. 9F.)

birth (before ...) *adj.*: **antenatal**. ▪ When I say I've no way of knowing [the sex of the unborn child] because I'm not having any **antenatal** tests — no, not even ultrasound scans — people are generally flabbergasted. Isn't ultrasound a routine part of **antenatal** care in this day and age? Doesn't everyone have to have a scan? The answer is no, and no again. (Joanna Moorhead, *Health: Ultrasound? I Don't Want to Know*, Independent, 10-03-2001, p. 8.)

(2) birth (having given ... one or more times) *n.*: **parous**. ▪ Women who have already had a child tend to be more likely than those who have not to recognize their pregnancy early; however, when there are significant differences in prenatal behavior, **parous** women are less likely to follow their provider's recommendations. (Kathryn Kost,

*Predicting Maternal Behaviors During Pregnancy —
Does Intention Status Matter?* Family Planning
Perspectives, 03-01-1998, p. 85.)

(3) birth *n.*: **parturition**. ∎ He cannot forget that he
was born a mere six months after his parents were
married at a time when people counted the months
between wedding and **parturition**. (Arnold
Beichman, *A Rascal Looks Back on Life*, The
Washington Times, 02-15-1998, p. 25.)

(4) birth (giving ... to, esp. a dog) *v.t., v.i.*: **whelp**. ∎ It
was a block from her veterinarian's office, where she
was going since she was **whelped**. (Lars Eighner,
Travels With Lizbeth, St. Martin's Press [1993], p. 95)

(5) birth *n.*: **accouchement**. SEE CHILDBIRTH

(6) birth (period before giving ...) *n.*: **antepartum**
[Latin]. SEE PREGNANCY

(7) birth (existing from ..., as in innate) *adj.*: **connate**. SEE INNATE

(8) birth (of or relating to giving ...) *adj.*: **parturient**.
SEE CHILDBIRTH

(9) birth (woman who has given ... only once or is
pregnant for the first time) *n.*: **primipara**. SEE
PREGNANT

(10) birth (attitude or policy which encourages giving ...) *n.*: **pronatalism**. SEE CHILDBEARING

(11) birth (relating to a woman during or right after
...) *adj.*: **puerperal**. SEE POSTPARTUM

(12) birth (woman right after ...) *n.*: **puerperium**.
SEE POSTPARTUM

bisexual (as in one having characteristics or reproductive organs of each gender) *n.*: **hermaphrodite**. ∎ For example, [James] Callendar ... once
described [John] Adams as a "hideous **hermaphroditical** character which has neither the force and
firmness of a man, nor the gentleness and sensibility
of a woman." (Ambrose, *Undaunted Courage*, Simon
& Schuster [1996], p. 65.)

bistro (or café) *n.*: **estaminet** [French]. ∎ Wander into
an **estaminet** and ask for a cognac on the wrong
day of the week, or order a black coffee when that
was the only sort available in a French cafe, and you
were instantly identifiable as a Limey. (Christopher
Silvester, *The Spying Game*, The Sunday Times
[London], p. 35.)

bit (as in trace or small amount of) *n.*: **tincture**. SEE
TRACE

bitchy (woman) *n.*: **harridan**. SEE SHREW
(2) bitchy (woman) *n.*: **termagant**. SEE SHREW
(3) bitchy (woman) *n.*: **virago**. SEE SHREW
(4) bitchy (woman) *n.*: **vixen**. SEE SHREW

(5) bitchy (woman) *n.*: **Xanthippe**. SEE SHREW

biting *adj.*: **acidulous**. SEE TART
(2) biting (as in ... remarks) *adj.*: **astringent**. SEE
HARSH
(3) biting (as in sarcastic) *adj.*: **mordant** (or **mordacious**). SEE SARCASTIC

bits and pieces *n.*: **flinders**. ∎ However ... the one
woman [Prince Charles] desperately wanted to wed
— was Anna Wallace, a sexy Scottish lass with a rip-roaring sense of humor. Alas, Anna also had a fiery
temper ... and one night at a palace ball it blew their
affair to **flinders**. The prince carelessly ignored his
ladylove for several hours, and when at last he went
looking for her she was gone — forever. (Brad
Darrach, *Prince Charles — A Dangerous Age*, People,
10-31-1988, p. 96.)

bitter (to the taste or smell) *adj.*: **acrid**. SEE PUNGENT
(2) bitter (to make ...) *v.t.*: **envenom**. SEE EMBITTER

bitterness *n.*: **bile**. ∎ But in the wake of the feminist
movement, some men are beginning to pipe up. In
the intimacy of locker rooms and the glare of large
men's groups, they are spilling their **bile** at the
incessant criticism, much of it justified, from women
about their inadequacies as husbands, lovers,
fathers. (Sam Allis, *The Changing Family: Essay —
What Do Men Really Want?* Time, 11-08-1990, p. 80.)

(2) bitterness (as in acrimony) *n.*: **asperity**. SEE
ACRIMONY
(3) bitterness *n.*: **choler** (*adj.*: **choleric**). SEE
ANGER

bizarre (as in unconventional) *adj.*: **outré** [French].
SEE UNCONVENTIONAL

black (admirer of ... persons) *n.*: **negrophile**. ∎
[*Negrophilia* by Petrine Archer-Shaw] reveals that the
Parisian obsession with black culture in the 1920s
went far beyond the exuberant Josephine Baker. ...
Archer-Straw concludes that the **negrophile's**
embrace of blacks was "a very difficult relationship." (Emma Hagestadt, *Books: Paperbacks*,
Independent, 09-30-2000, p. 11.)

(2) black (one who fears or dislikes ... persons) *n.*:
negrophobe. ∎ [Lincoln's] death [was] at the
hands of John Wilkes Booth, a **negrophobe** and
white supremacist who was enraged at Lincoln's
endorsement of black civil equality. (Allen Guelzo,
*Proclamation Takes Some Hits: 'How Abe Lincoln Lost
the Black Vote,'* The Washington Times, 05-11-2002.)

(3) black (person who is 1/4th ...) *n.*: **quadroon**. ∎
The racial calculus employed by both print and tele-

vision media to describe [golfer Tiger] Woods is a throwback to the racial classifications used in the Old South. People were classified as mulatto if they were half white and half black, **quadroon** if they were a quarter black, octoroon if an eighth and so on. (Henry Yu, *The Profit in Counting Tiger's Stripes*, Newsday, 12-05-1996, p. A53.)

black and white (as in colorless) *adj.*: **achromatic**. SEE COLORLESS

(2) black and white (spotted) *adj.*: **piebald**. SEE SPOTTED

black magic *n.*: **necromancy**. ∎ Scattered around Meszaros's den are the paraphernalia of **necromancy**: a desiccated frog, a glass-encased tarantula, a lead crystal ball and two skulls, one with nails through the cranium. ... The bookshelves sag under the weight of tomes detailing spells, voodooism, the formation of covens, the enactment of jinxes and other black lore. (Julius Strauss, *International: Taxman Casts Spell on Witches*, The Sunday Telegraph, 01-11-1998.)

blackness (or tending towards ...) *n.*: **nigrescense**. ∎ The second major perspective of Black racial identity development consists of the **nigrescence** [model which is] the developmental process through which one "becomes Black" (Helms, 1990). Here, Black does not refer to complexion, but the manner in which African Americans evaluate themselves and their reference group (Helms, 1990). (Reginald Alston, *Racial Identity and African Americans with Disabilities*, The Journal of Rehabilitation, 04-15-1996, p. 11.)

blackout *n.* **syncope**. SEE FAINTING

blame *v.t.*: **inculpate**. ∎ There is a [proposed bill that] would make it illegal for any state law enforcement agency to maintain gun ownership records. This means the next time police recover a gun used in a felony, the trail of clues would begin and end with the gun. ... [T]his outrageous bill would eliminate access to crucial forensic information — information that is often as likely to exonerate the innocent as **inculpate** the guilty. (Christopher D. Brown, *Taking Gun-Ownership Records From Police Is 'Pandering Legislation,'* The Miami Herald, 12-23-2003, p. A17.)

(2) blame (oneself) *v.t.*: **self-flagellate** (*n.*: **self-flagellation**). SEE CRITICIZE

bland *adj.*: **anodyne**. ∎ [John] McEnroe seemed to save his snittiest behaviour for No. 1: perhaps he found the acoustics more effective there than on Centre Court. It says something about the **anodyne** nature of contemporary tennis that the sight of McEnroe in full flood tugs so at the heart-strings. (Andrew Baker, *Emotional Farewell to Home of the Tantrum*, Independent on Sunday, 06-16-1996, p. 22.)

blank slate *n.*: **tabula rasa**. ∎ The dominant picture of mind since the Renaissance — it is common to classical empiricism, which embraced consciousness, and modern behaviorism, which eschewed it — is the **tabula rasa**: the blank ledger upon which the environment leaves its trace as the mind is given whatever structure and content it finally possesses. (Colin McGinn, *The Know-It-All*, The New Republic, 02-23-1998.)

blasé *adj.*: **pococurante**. SEE APATHETIC

blaze (with intense heat and light) *v.t.*, *v.i.*: **deflagrate** (*n.*: **deflagration**). SEE EXPLOSION

bleak *adj.*: **Cimmerian**. SEE GLOOMY

blemished (or **impure**) *adj.*, *v.t.*: **maculate**. SEE IMPURE

blend *v.t.*, *v.i.*: **inosculate**. ∎ After recombination [of districts], New Foshan will be the third largest city in Guangdong. ... According to CCTV, experts stated that New Foshan must solve the problems of disordered city planning, overlapping layout and economic structure duplication. Some experts even suggest to build a super-administrative organization ..., just like Tokyo Area, and to further **inosculate** with Hong Kong, Macau and Taiwan. (Author not given, *New Foshan Government Starts to Function*, AsiaInfo Services, 01-13-2003.)

(2) blend (esp. involving dissimilar elements) *adj.*: **admixture**. SEE MIXTURE

(3) blend *v.t.*: **amalgamate**. SEE COMBINE

(4) blend (as in bring together) *v.t.*: **conflate**. SEE COMBINE

blended (as in composed of a mixture of items) *adj.*: **farraginous**. SEE MIXED

(2) blended (of things that cannot be ...) *adj.*: **immiscible**. SEE INCOMPATIBLE

blessing *n.*: **benison**. ∎ [Bill Gates] looked upon cable this week and saw that it was good and sprinkled $1 billion of his spare $9 billion or so over the industry, in an investment in Comcast, America's fourth-largest cable-television operator. Barely had the **benison** arrived from [Gates] when the nearest thing in the cable companies' lives to Lucifer — Rupert Murdoch — turned out to be an angel after all. (Author not given, *Cable Television: Enter God, With $1 Billion*, The Economist, 06-14-1997.)

(2) blessing (as in praise) *n.*: **approbation**. See PRAISE

blind (almost, but not quite ...) *adj.*: **purblind**. ∎ At birth he was sightless in one eye and **purblind** in the other, so his father, a craftsman who made tatamis (straw mats), sent him at age six to the city of Kumamoto, where he could attend a subsidized school for the blind. (James Walsh, *Shoko Asahara: The Making of a Messiah*, Time, 04-03-1995, p. 30.)

(2) blind (window ... with adjustable horizontal slats) *n.*: **jalousie**. See WINDOW BLIND

blind spot *n.*: **scotoma**. ∎ [A] short-sighted driver could be much more dangerous than an elderly chap who can compensate for a small **scotoma** in his field of vision by keeping his head and eyes moving (as a good driver should). (Honest John, *Motoring: Not Seeing Eye to Eye with Authority*, The Daily Telegraph, 08-09-1997.)

blindly (as in, in a disorderly and hasty manner) *adv.*: **pell-mell**. See DISORDERLY

blindness *n.*: **amaurosis**. ∎ Still, Pernice's professional heartaches [as a golfer] were no match for what he felt in 1995, when his daughter, Brooke, was born with a retinal disorder, Leber's **amaurosis**, so severe that she was legally blind. (L. Jon Wertheim, *Golf Plus*, Sports Illustrated, 08-31-1998, p. G10.*)*

(2) blindness (at night) *n.*: **nyctalopia**. ∎ Medical science now recognizes a pathological condition called Carsonogeneous Monocular **Nyctalopia**: temporary blindness in one eye caused by watching the [Late Show With Johnny Carson] with one visual organ buried in the pillow and the other on the box. (Author not given, *Top 25 Stars: Johnny Carson H-e-e-e-r-r-e's TV's Top*, People, 05-04-1989, p. 20.) See NIGHT BLINDNESS

blink (one's eyes) *v.i.*: **nictitate**. ∎ Thanks to thick fur and loose skin, a badger can turn around with amazing ease in a tight burrow. And a **nictitating** membrane protects its beady eyes from flying dirt. Oh does the dirt fly! (Les Line, *The Benefits of Badgers*, National Wildlife, 12-10-1995, p. 18.)

blinking (spasmodic ... of the eyes) *n.*: **blepharospasm**. ∎ It is an unsightly affliction. Victims of **blepharospasm** suffer from continual eyelid muscle spasms that clamp the lids closed for seconds to minutes. In effect, sufferers are left blind. (Author not given, *Medicine: Eye Misery Insurance Loss Halts Drug Test*, Time, 10-27-1986, p. 71.)

bliss *n.*: **beatitude**. ∎ When he gets to talking about his stewardship of the 49ers' offense, [quarterback] Steve Young often lapses into a dreamlike state usually associated with religious rapture. His eyes glaze over with a kind of gauzy joy. ... [But the 49ers' poor showing on offense recently is] enough to shatter Young's **beatitude** like a concrete pie to the face. (John Crumpacker, *Sharing the Load*, Denver Rocky Mountain News, 11-23-1997, p. 28C.)

(2) bliss *n.*: **felicity**. See HAPPINESS

blissful *adj.*: **Elysian**. ∎ [In one TV makeover show, a man] and his partner supposedly turned their run-down garden into an **Elysian** vision in the space of a weekend, using only a spade and elbow grease. He never did work out how the director managed to keep two-dozen navvies, a gang of landscape gardeners and the heavy-duty diggers permanently out of shot. (Greg Wood, *Sweet Science*, Independent on Sunday, 01-07-2001, p. 14.)

(2) blissful *adj.*: **beatific**; (to make ...) *v.t.*: **beatify**. See JOYFUL

blissfulness (causing or tending to produce ...) *adj.*: **felicific**. See HAPPINESS

blisters (producing or tending to produce ... or an agent which does so) *adj., n.*: **vesicant**. ∎ Vesicants such as Lewisite and sulfur mustard can cause irritation to the mouth and skin with terrible blistering, and death is possible within 12 to 24 hours after exposure. (Thomas Inglesby, *The Germs of War; How Biological Weapons Could Threaten Civilian Populations*, The Washington Post, 12-09-1998, p. H1.)

bloated (or disheveled in appearance) *adj.*: **blowsy** (or **blowzy**). See DISHEVELED

(2) bloated (as in pompous or bombastic) *adj.*: **flatulent**. See POMPOUS

(3) bloated (as in pompous or bombastic) *adj.*: **tumid**. See BOMBASTIC AND SWOLLEN

block (up) *v.t.*: **occlude**. ∎ It has clearly been shown that there is a higher incidence of Sudden Infant Death Syndrome when infants are put to sleep on their stomachs. Also, pillows should not be used in an infant bed because of the possibility of **occluding** the airway. (Author not given, *Letters from the People*, St. Louis Post-Dispatch, 01-24-1996, p. 6C.)

blockhead *n.*: **jobbernowl** [British]. See IDIOT

(2) blockhead *n.*: **mooncalf**. See fool

blood (of, relating to or tinged with) *adj.*: **sanguino-lent**. [A German magazine] tried to bring the violence done to women in war right into 520,000 readers' homes. American artist Jenny Holzer used blood donated by eight German and Yugoslav women volunteers in her design for the cover, a black page with a white card glued to it carrying the **sanguinolent** message: "Anywhere women are dying, I am wide awake." (Author not given, *Chronicles: Talk of the Streets*, Time, 11-29-1993, p. 12.)

(2) blood (to cover or stain with ...) *v.t.*: **ensan-guine**. See stain

blood-red *adj.*: **incarnadine**. See crimson

bloodletting *n.*: **phlebotomy**. ▪ About 1.3 million Americans have a disorder called hemochromatosis, an ailment in which the body improperly metabolizes iron. There is an effective treatment, though: old-fashioned bloodletting. Each year, more than 100,000 Americans get regular "therapeutic **phle-botomies**." (Dana Hawkins, *Throwing Out Good Blood*, U.S. News & World Report, 09-01-1997, p. 26.)

bloody *adj.*: **sanguinary**. ▪ [In] "The Patriot," a sadistic British colonel and his soldiers provoke the peace-minded Mel Gibson into a bloody bout of reprisals. ... The film performs a service by reminding us that this war was a good deal more **san-guinary** than most think — per capita, it took more American lives than any but the Civil War. (Author not given, *The Fourth of July*, The Washington Post, 07-04-2000, p. A18.)

(2) bloody *adj.*: **sanguineous**. ▪ [The movie] "Quills" ... is obviously not for the squeamish or the high-minded. The film opens with a victim's-eye-view of an oversize (by 10 feet) guillotine and a basketful of severed heads, as spectators cheer on the **sanguineous** spectacle. (Glenn Lovell, *Idolizing Iconoclasts*, San Jose Mercury News, 12-16-2000, p. 1E.)

(3) bloody (to make ...) *v.t.*: **ensanguine**. See stain

bloom (as in burgeon or expand; lit.: bear fruit) *v.i.*: **fructify**. See burgeon

blooming *n.*: **efflorescence**. ▪ Almost two decades later, black writers and artists, musicians, dancers and actors find themselves in an era of creativity unrivaled in American history. The current **efflo-rescence** may have begun with the literature and criticism by black women published in the early '80s, especially the works of Ntozake Shange,

Michele Wallace, Alice Walker and Toni Morrison. (Henry Louis Gates Jr., *Black Creativity: On the Cutting Edge*, Time, 10-10-1994, p. 74.)

(2) blooming *n.*: **florescence**. ▪ Today's [fireworks] displays unfold in time [like flowers]. It is not surprising that the similes are floral. Not only is their blossom short-lived; as in nature, these chemical **florescences** are designed, but not down to the last detail. Their beauty lies, as so often, in the conjunction of perfection and imperfection. (Hugh Aldersey-Williams, *A Flaming Liberty, [Fireworks Business]*, New Statesman, 10-30-1998.)

blooper (as in a transposition of letters or sounds, which creates a comic effect, usually unintentionally) *n.*: **spoonerism** [after William Spooner, a British cleric, whose first recorded Spoonerism was when he said to a groom at the end of a ceremony: "It is now kisstomary to cuss the bride."]. ▪ My vote for the prince of **spoonerisms** goes to a young announcer I helped break in to broadcasting. ... [The copy read:] Good evening, ladies and gentlemen. This is your invitation to join the gay groups at the beautiful Park Lane cocktail lounge." [Instead he said:] "Good ladies, evening and gentlemen. This is your invitation to join the gray goops at the Park Tail cocklane lounge." (Gene Amole, *Spoonerisms Can Bangle Words Beyond Melief*, Denver Rocky Mountain News, 12-21-2000.)

(2) blooper (such as a slip of the tongue or malapropism) *n.*: **parapraxis**. See blunder

blossoming *n.*: **efflorescence**. See blooming
(2) blossoming *n.*: **florescence**. See blooming

blotched (or impure) *adj., v.t.*: **maculate**. See impure

blue (sky-...) *adj.*: **cerulean**. ▪ In contrast, Bryant, blessed with a much larger canvas, produces vibrant watercolors of summer green, golden wheat, and **cerulean** blue that recall the visual sweetness of a technicolor movie. (Terri Heard, *Reflections of a Black Cowboy*, Philadelphia Tribune, 01-27-1995.)

blue-collar (class of people) *adj.*: **plebian**. See common

blues (having the ..., as in being depressed) *n.*: **cafard** [French]. See depression
(2) blues (having the ..., as in being depressed) *n.*: **megrims** (plural of **megrim**) (also means migraine headache). See headache

bluff *v.t.*: **four-flush** (*n.*: **four-flusher**). ▪ [I]f the [job applicant] obviously doesn't fit the slot you're looking for, give him a "half-pitch" on the shop and ask for a resume. Don't waste a lot of time, but don't **four-flush** him, either. You may need someone with his lack of qualifications in the future. (Author not given, *Uncle Paul: My Reality Check Bounced*, Dealernews, 09-01-1999, p. 66.)

blunder (verbal ... such as a slip of the tongue or malapropism) *n.*: **parapraxis**. ∎ In this construction, TV news in the Soviet Union becomes a tableau in which the journalist is cowering beneath the fist of the state. ... More than one **parapraxis** while reading the glad tidings about the leader's health, and the newsreaders (news bimbskis employed for their looks) could lose their jobs. (Andrew Billen, *"And Here Is Today's News of the World...,"* New Statesman, 06-27-1997, p. 42.)

blunt (as in to dull or deaden) *v.t.*: **narcotize**. SEE DEADEN

(2) blunt *v.t.*: **obtund**. SEE DEADEN

blur (one's vision as if by clouds, fog or vapor) *v.t.*: **obnubilate**. SEE OBSCURE

bluster (as in boastful behavior) *n.*: **rodomontade**. ∎ The best those commentators could do [to support President Clinton's claim that radio was being used to spread hatred] was to quote an imprudent remark by Gordon Liddy, but what he said — that if any official came to his house to requisition his pistol, he'd better shoot straight — was more **rodomontade** than a call to arms or hatred. (William F. Buckley, *What Does Clinton Have in Mind?* National Review, 05-29-1995, p. 70.)

(2) bluster (full of ... and vanity) *adj.*: **vainglorious**. SEE BOASTFUL

blusterer (who often talks foolishness) *adj.*: **blatherskite**. SEE BABBLER

blustering (behavior) *n.*: **fanfaronade**. SEE BRAVADO

boast (esp. about the accomplishments of a relative) *v.t.*; *n.*: **kvell** [Yiddish]. ∎ Our visit to Yale was highlighted by the admissions officer informing [my son] Michael that he had been accepted for the fall term, and then genially turning to congratulate me and shake my hand. Now, as a Jewish mother, I can **kvell** with the best of them, but this was truly my son's moment in the sun, not mine. (Esther Berger, *One Family's Perspective, [College Admissions]*, Town & Country, 07-01-2000.)

boaster (who often talks foolishness) *adj.*: **blatherskite**. SEE BABBLER

boastful *adj.*: **thrasonical**. ∎ In his earlier days, Roald Dahl [author of *Charlie and the Chocolate Factory* and *James and the Giant Peach*] was a **thrasonical** bully. (Gerald Windsor, *Portrait of Another Malodorous Old Fart*, Sydney Morning Herald, 05-07-1994.)

(2) boastful (and vain) *adj.*: **vainglorious**. ∎ The 1935 trial of Bruno Hauptmann, arrested for the kidnapping and murder of Charles Lindbergh's infant son, featured [columnist] Walter Winchell at his most **vainglorious**. ... When the jury found Hauptmann guilty, Winchell reportedly leaped to his feet and shouted to the press pack: "I predicted he'd be guilty! Oh, that's another big one for me!" (Walter Shapiro, *Arts & Media*, Time, 10-10-1994, p. 86.)

(3) boastful (being in a state of ... exultation or elation) *adj.*: **cock-a-hoop**. SEE ELATED

(4) boastful (talk or person) *n.*: **cockalorum**. SEE EGOTISTIC

(5) boastful (and vain person) *n.*: **coxcomb**. SEE CONCEITED

(6) boastful (behavior, as in bravado) *n.*: **fanfaronade**. SEE BRAVADO

(7) boastful (person) *n.*: **Gascon** (act of being ... *n.*: **Gasconade**). SEE BRAGGART

(8) boastful (as in vain, person) *n.*: **popinjay**. SEE VAIN

(9) boastful (behavior) *n.*: **rodomontade**. SEE BLUSTER

bodies (repository for dead ...) *n.*: **charnel**. SEE REPOSITORY

(2) bodies (fascination with or erotic attraction to dead ...) *n.*: **necrophilia**. SEE CORPSES

body build (esp. as relating to tendency to develop disease) *n.*: **habitus**. SEE PHYSIQUE

body (of or relating to the ...) *adj.*: **corporeal**. ∎ What the two [dance] works share is an almost forensic interest in the **corporeal**; in what happens when you push limbs beyond beauty and pain. In the age of virtual reality, the [dance] company focuses on what Obarzanek calls "the vulnerable human body that's vicious and beautiful and ugly and sweating." (Michael Fitzgerald, *The Arts/Dance*, Time International, 09-13-1999, p. 69.)

body odor (from foul-smelling sweat) *n.*: **bromidrosis**. SEE SWEAT

bog *n.*: **fen**. SEE SWAMP

boil down (the flavor or essence of something) *v.t.*: **decoct**. ∎ "Shopping is a form of entertainment," as Riggio phrases it. ... [Consumers shop] to mingle with others in a prosperous-feeling crowd, to see what's new, to enjoy the theatrical dazzle of the display, to treat themselves to something interesting or unexpected. So Riggio learned to craft stores that **decoct** the pure elixir of the shopping experience. In 1989, he began to perfect the formula: a high-visibility, upscale, usually suburban location to draw the crowds where they live. (Myron Magnet, *Let's Go For Growth [Profiles of Six Companies]*, Fortune, 03-07-1994.)

boisterous (girl) *n., adj.*: **hoyden**. SEE TOMBOY

(2) boisterous (to engage in ... revelry or merrymaking) *v.i.*: **roister**. SEE REVEL

(3) boisterous *adj.*: **strepitous**. SEE LOUD

bold (offensively ... and conceited person) *n.*: **jackanapes**. SEE CONCEITED

(2) bold (or courageous while under the influence of alcohol) *adj.*: **potvaliant**. SEE COURAGEOUS

boldness (and daring) *n.*: **hardihood**. SEE COURAGE

bombastic *adj.*: **tumid**. ∎ Nothing is easier than for educated persons to mock "I move the reference back," "I must consult my executive" and the rest of it [as used by the Shadow Cabinet of the British Labour Party]. But the **tumid** phrases and tedious procedures have a long and honourable history, going back to the artisans' societies of the early 19th century. (Alan Watkins, *Shadow Cabinet Hokey-Cokey: Right Leg In, Left Leg Out*, Independent on Sunday, 07-14-1996, p. 19.)

(2) bombastic (style) *n.*: **ampollosity**. SEE POMPOUSNESS

(3) bombastic *adj.*: **flatulent**. SEE POMPOUS

(4) bombastic (of speech or writing which is ...) *adj.*: **fustian**. SEE POMPOUS

(5) bombastic (speech or writing) *n.*: **grandiloquence**. SEE POMPOSITY

(6) bombastic *adj.*: **magniloquent**. SEE POMPOUS

(7) bombastic (esp. regarding speaking or writing style) *adj.*: **orotund**. SEE POMPOUS

(8) bombastic (behavior) *n.*: **rodomontade**. SEE BLUSTER

(9) bombastic *adj.*: **turgid**. SEE POMPOUS

bond (together, as with glue) *v.t.*: **agglutinate**. SEE ADHERE

(2) bond (as in chain or link) *n.*: **catenation** (*v.t.*: **catenate**). SEE CHAIN

bondage *n.*: **thralldom**. ∎ We Western women, it appears, still have not shucked off male ideas of female beauty; the voluntary mutilation of plastic surgery bears witness to our **thralldom**. (Elizabeth Ward, *The Trouble With Women*, The Washington Post, 05-23-1999, p. 8.)

(2) bondage (free from ...) *v.t.*: **manumit**. SEE EMANCIPATE

bone (composed of, relating to, or resembling) *adj.*: **osseous**. ∎ If you want to get ahead — or get down to the bare bones of the matter — you could do very much worse than meet the interactive skeleton. It's a fascinating new multimedia construct developed by University College of London's department of medical physics and bioengineering. ... For student and interested amateurs, a fascinating insight into all things **osseous**. (Joe Donnelly, *Shake, Rattle and Scroll*, The Herald [Glasgow], 08-31-1996, p. 42.)

(2) bone (or tooth decay) *n.*: **caries**. SEE DECAY

bones (repository for ... of the dead) *n.*: **charnel**. SEE REPOSITORY

bonkers *adj.*: **doolally**. SEE CRAZY

bonus (as in extra or unexpected gift or benefit, sometimes as thanks for a purchase) *n.*: **lagniappe**. SEE GIFT

bony (composed of, relating to, or resembling) *adj.*: **osseous**. SEE BONE

book (worshiper) *n.*: **bibliolater**. ∎ The disorderly bins outside a secondhand bookshop are like a potter's field. ... Their uniform token price — ANY BOOK THIS BOX $1 — signifies their all-but-worthlessness. It was in just such a **bibliolater's** boneyard that I happened upon Scarne on Teeko. (Blake Eskin, *Cards and Gambling Authority John Scarne Claimed to Have Invented One of the Greatest Board Games of All Time*, The Washington Post, 07-15-2001, p. W18.)

(2) book (for ready reference like a guidebook) *n.*: **vade mecum**. SEE GUIDEBOOK

books (one who steals ...) *n.*: **biblioklept**. ∎ The author was — and, he implies, may still be — a compulsive **biblioklept**. The first book he stole as a schoolboy was "Dracula"; but it was at Cambridge, in the vast, irresistible canyons of Heffer's bookshop, that Mr. Rayner's literary thievery began in earnest. (Ben Macintyre, *A Gentleman, a Scholar, a Thief*, The New York Times, 10-22-1995, p. 14.)

(2) books (extreme desire to own or collect ...) *n.*:

bibliomania. ∎ There are detailed lists of his reading, which ranged voraciously from the most arcane corners of medieval German literature and philosophy to every new Simenon mystery ... and not least importantly, unflagging reports on his **bibliomania** and latest acquisitions. (David Stern, *Profane Illumination*, The New Republic, 04-10-1995, p. 31.)

(3) books (lover or collector of ...) *n.*: **bibliophile.** ∎ "I've always been a bit of a **bibliophile**," says Arthur Ashe, the former Wimbledon and U.S. Open champion who, in the 1960s, started collecting books written by and about African-Americans. (Daphne Hurford, *Books*, Sports Illustrated, 11-04-1991, p. 88.)

(4) books (aversion to or fear of ...) *n.*: **bibliophobia**. ∎ *Reading Contemporary Fiction*, by Elizabeth Dipple (Routledge, Pounds 25). Elizabeth Dipple is anxious to dispel readers' fears about contemporary texts. Perfect for sufferers from Nabokov-angst, Beckett-fear, Borges-terror, and general undirected **bibliophobia**. (Author not given, *New Books*, The Times [London], 04-07-1988.)

(5) books (people who read too many ...) *n.*: **bibliobibuli**. See READ

(6) books (or artistic works created in the author's or artist's youth) *n.*: **juvenilia**. See COMPOSITIONS

bookworm *n.*: **bibliophage** [This word, like bookworm itself, can have both a literal meaning, as in a worm that eats through the paste in book bindings, or a figurative meaning, namely one who is an ardent reader.] ∎ Bookstores in urban cores across America have been exiled to the suburbs or extinction by onslaughts from the Internet, the big chains, and huge spikes in downtown commercial rents. ... Even New York has been savaged. **Bibliophages** consider Manhattan a lunar landscape today compared to what it offered five years ago. (Sam Allis, *Bookstores' Demise a Sad Chapter*, The Boston Globe, 05-23-1999, p. A1.)

boor *n.*: **grobian**. ∎ Me, I like melted cheese on my hot dogs. And more often than not I slap plenty of hot sauce on my morning ration of scrambled eggs. Factor in the notion that I'm basically a loud-mouth **grobian** who'd rather guffaw than grimace, and there's little reason why I shouldn't be on the right side of [the band] Sex Mob and their second opus de squawk. (Jim Macnie, *Solid Sender [Review]*, Down Beat, 05-01-2000.)

(2) boor *n.*: **yahoo**. ∎ The Dallas Cowboys showed up at their hotel in Santa Monica and there were more guys with yellow Event Staff jackets on than there were **yahoos**. An NFL event staff guy who

ordinarily likes to flex some crowd-control muscle was thoroughly disappointed. "This is America's Team?" he said, disgusted, looking for a **yahoo** to wrestle to the ground. (Richard Hoffer, *Super Bowl XXVII: Dear Phoenix*, Sports Illustrated, 02-08-1993, p. 14.)

boorish (or dull or ignorant or obtuse or stupid) *adj.*: **Boeotian**. See DULL

(2) boorish (person with respect to artistic or cultural values) *adj.*: **philistine**. See UNCULTURED

boost (as in stimulus) *n.*: **fillip**. See STIMULUS

bootlicker *n.*: **lickspittle**. See SYCOPHANT

(2) bootlicker (esp. someone who seeks to associate with or flatter persons of rank or high social status) *n.*: **tuft-hunter**. See HANGER-ON

border *n.*: **selvage**. See EDGE

bored *adj.*: **pococurante**. See APATHETIC

boredom (sometimes in matters spiritual, and sometimes leading to depression) *n.*: **acedia**. See APATHY

boring (writer or speaker) *n.*: **dryasdust**. ∎ [The Congressional Budget Office's] recent study Long-Term Budgetary Pressures and Policy Options describes the economic future our children and grandchildren are likely to face. The report is written in the CBO's **dryasdust** style, but for anyone with a tolerance for numbers and an interest in policy, it is as scary as a Stephen King novel. (N. Gregory Mankiw, *Government Debt: A Horror Story*, Fortune, 08-03-1998, p. 52.)

(2) boring *adj.*: **anodyne**. See BLAND

(3) boring (as in uninteresting) *adj.*: **jejune**. See UNINTERESTING

(4) boring (passage or section in a book or work of performing art) *n.*: **longueur**. See TEDIOUS

(5) boring (as in insipid, intellectual nourishment, like baby food) *n.*: **pabulum** (also **pablum**). See INSIPID

(5) boring (lit. sleep-inducing) *adj.*: **soporific**. See SLEEP-INDUCING

born (while being ...) *adv.*: **aborning**. ∎ One idea, briefly debated, was to merge Olds, GM's oldest and weakest franchise, with Saturn, its youngest and strongest, so that Oldsmobiles would become step-up vehicles from Saturns. The idea died **aborning**, but it had merit; today Saturn outsells Olds. (Alex Taylor III, *Giants of the Fortune 5 Hundred*, Fortune, 04-28-1997, p. 94.)

(2) born (being ..., as in coming into being) *adj.*: **nascent**. SEE EMERGING

(3) born (being ..., esp. a dog) *v.t., v.i.*: **whelp**. SEE BIRTH

borrow (from without real intent to repay, as in sponging off of) *v.t.*: **cadge**. SEE BEG

bosoms (overly large ...) *n.*: **macromastia**. SEE BREASTS

bosomy *adj.*: **bathycolpian**. SEE BUSTY

boss *n.*: **padrone** [Italian]. ▪ [E]rmando Rosa [is an] Italian small-business man who lives for his company and his family and often melds the two. [He and his family] help run his eponymous machine-tool company, an arrangement that typifies the triangular relationship linking the **padrone**, the business and the family that is an enormous source of strength in the Italian economy. (John Wyles, *Italy: Being Small Is Best*, Time International, 07-11-1994, p. 43.)

(2) boss (as in manager or overseer) *n.*: **gerent**. SEE MANAGER

(3) boss (brutal ..., as in taskmaster) *n.*: **Simon Legree**. SEE TASKMASTER

botch (esp. a golf shot) *v.t., n.*: **foozle**. ▪ I am not any good at golf. At all. I have played for years, but that has only increased the variety of skulls, yips and **foozles** I can produce. When I started, for example, I hit everything on a low banana slice to the right. Today, I have improved to the point where I have no idea where the ball will go. (C.W. Nevius, *It's Time for the Truth About Golf — It's a Game, Not a Sport*, The San Francisco Chronicle, 04-28-2002, p. E1.)

bother *v.t.*: **incommode**. ▪ [G]iven that the National Gallery's "Johannes Vermeer" show had scarcely opened on Nov. 12 before it was shut down — first by budget politics, then by weather — none of the art pilgrims on the train felt at all **incommoded** by the cost or effort of the journey. (Sylviane Gold, *On Track to Vermeer*, Newsday, 01-22-1996, p. B2.)

(2) bother *v.t.*: **chivvy**. SEE PESTER

(3) bother *v.t.*: **discommode**. SEE INCONVENIENCE

(4) bother (as in fuss, over a trifling matter) *n.*: **foofaraw**. SEE FUSS

(5) bother (as in bully or browbeat) *v.t.*: **hector**. SEE BULLY

(6) bother (as in trouble) *n.*: **tsuris** [Yiddish]. SEE TROUBLE

bothered *adj.*: **in a dither**. SEE FLUSTERED

(2) bothered (as if by a witch or by unfounded fears) *adj.*: **hagridden**. SEE TORMENTED

bothersome (as in repellent) *adj.*: **rebarbative**. SEE REPELLENT

bottom (having a nicely proportioned ...) *adj.*: **callipygian**. SEE REAR END

(2) bottom (having a hairy ...) *adj.*: **dasypygal**. SEE REAR END

(3) bottom (as in buttocks) *n., pl.*: **nates**. SEE BUTTOCKS

(4) bottom (a fat ...) *n.*: **steatopygia** (having a fat ... *adj.*: **steatopygic**). SEE REAR END

bound (together by a close relationship) *adj.*: **affined**. SEE CONNECTED

(2) bound (as in set the boundaries of) *v.t.*: **delimit**. SEE DEMARCATE

boundary (as in sphere or realm) *n.*: **ambit**. SEE REALM

bouquet *n.*: **nosegay**. ▪ Corsages are history — something from the '50s that should stay there. If you want the mother of the bride or the grandmother to have flowers, give her a two-inch **nosegay**. (Heidi K. Schiller, *T&C's Guide to the Perfect Wedding*, Town & Country Monthly, 02-01-1998, p. 141.)

bourgeois (esp. one indifferent or antagonistic to artistic or cultural values) *adj.*: **philistine**. SEE UNCULTURED

bow (down, often in a servile manner) *v.i.*: **genuflect**. SEE KNEEL

bowl (shallow ... or cup with a handle) *n.*: **porringer**. ▪ We had a pewter **porringer** with a lid in the shape of a mountain that was a trophy my brother had won before the war. The German soldier was holding the bowl and trying to open the lid, but he couldn't. (Sarah Ballard, *Skiing*, Sports Illustrated, 12-02-1991, p. 14.)

boxing (against a shadow or imaginary foe) *n.*: **sciamachy**. SEE SHADOW-BOXING

boy (who has sexual relations with a man) *n.*: **catamite**. SEE SEX

(2) boy (who is awkward and clumsy) *n.*: **hobbledehoy**. SEE CLUMSY

(3) boy (man who has sexual relations with a ...) *n.*: **pederast**. SEE SODOMIZER

boyfriend (of a married woman) *n.*: **cicisbeo**. ▪

Walpole, meanwhile, attached himself to the young and beautiful (and married) Elisabetta Grifoni. These were bloodless infidelities condoned in Florence. Walpole became Elisabetta's **cicisbeo**. (Richard Edmonds, *All Poetic Roads Lead to Florence; A Golden Ring, By Charles Hobday*, The Birmingham Post, 05-02-1998.)

(2) boyfriend (or man with whom one is in love or has intimate relationship with) *n.*: **inamorato**. ▪ Instead of his usual manic intensity, Jack Nicholson acts his reined-in, middle-aged mafioso with little more than a stiff upper lip to give his patient, expressionless face character. Kathleen Turner plays his lover, a classy California professional woman, thunderstruck with vibrant passion for her Brooklyn-born **inamorato**. (Author not given, *Prizzi's Honor*, Magill's Survey of Cinema, 06-15-1995.)

bra (narrow ...) *n.*: **bandeau**. ▪ The best new bras feel good — and look sexy — thanks to extra-soft microfiber, smooth styling, and sophisticated colors. Our favorites: Three in One Convertible straps let you wear this **bandeau** as shown, crisscrossed, or even strapless. (Tina McIntyre, *Beauty & Style: Is Your Bra the Right Size?* Parenting, 09-01-2000, p. 63.)

brag (esp. about the accomplishments of a relative) *v.t., n.*: **kvell** [Yiddish]. SEE BOAST

braggart *n.*: **Gascon** (act of bragging *n.*: **Gasconade**) [based on stereotype of people from Gascon, France as being braggarts]. ▪ Italian journalist Luigi Barzin ... cites Edmond Rostand's fictional Cyrano as the quintessence of French character, at least as outsiders exaggerate it: the boastful, cocksure **Gascon** whose fellow provincials are defined in Rostand's play as "free fighters, free lovers, free spenders, defenders of old homes, old names and old splendors ... bragging of crests and pedigrees." (James Walsh, *If Geography Is Destiny ...*, Time International, 07-15-1991, p. 8.)

(2) braggart (who often talks foolishness) *adj.*: **blatherskite**. SEE BABBLER

bragging (talk or person) *n.*: **cockalorum**. SEE EGOTISTIC

(2) bragging (behavior) *n.*: **rodomontade**. SEE BLUSTER

(3) bragging *adj.*: **thrasonical**. SEE BOASTFUL

(4) bragging (and vain) *adj.*: **vainglorious**. SEE BOASTFUL

brain (congenital absence of) *n.*: **anencephaly**. ▪ **Anencephaly** occurs in the very early stages of pregnancy, when the neural tube — an embryonic structure that normally develops into the brain and spinal cord — fails to close. (David Grogan, *Scene: The Baby Killer*, People, 09-27-1993, p. 86.)

brainstorming (spec. a final effort made by architectural students to complete a solution to a problem within an allotted time, but sometimes is used to refer to any kind of ... or workshop session) *n.*: **charette** (or **charrette**). SEE WORKSHOP

brainwashing *n.*: **menticide**. ▪ An African-centered curriculum is also essential to repair the **menticide** afflicting our [African-American] youth through racism, cultural aggression and the imposition of a Eurocentric education on our children in the schools. (Ron Daniels, *Vantage Point: Redefining The Role Of Schools In The African-American*, New Pittsburgh Courier, 04-23-1994.)

brashness *n.*: **impudicity**. ▪ What needs to be emphasized is that [stealing a bust of Edgar Allan Poe from a bank] is not the sort of shenanigan that would occur to just anyone. The notion would come only to one of unique sensibility — playful and rash, with a dash of **impudicity**. (Jack Matthews, *The Raven Caper and the Writing Curse [Theft of Bust of Edgar Allan Poe]*, The Antioch Review, 01-01-1994, p. 157.)

brassiere (narrow ...) *n.*: **bandeau**. SEE BRA

bravado *n.*: **fanfaronade**. ▪ Here's some other [adult education] courses that could capture the public imagination: ... [Stripping]. **Fanfaronade** will take you through the steps necessary to become a confident exotic dancer. Each participant is expected to have partially completed a semester each of Tassel Making, Cracking Walnuts with Your Own Buttocks on Stage and Booking the Light Entertainment Circuit. (Author not given, *One Bourbon, One Scotch and One Gin*, Sydney Morning Herald, 07-01-2000, p. 2.)

(2) bravado (person with ...) *n.*: **Gascon** (act of being a person with ... *n.*: **Gasconade**). SEE BRAGGART

(3) bravado *n.*: **rodomontade**. SEE BLUSTER

brave *adj.*: **doughty**. ▪ Well, finally — the president we deserve, a morally square peg in the Oval Office. ... He is also, as it turns out, physically brave and uncannily resourceful under life-threatening pressure. And he looks a lot like the reliably **doughty** Harrison Ford. (Richard Schickel, *The Arts/Cinema*, Time, 07-28-1997, p. 69.)

(2) brave (and strong woman) *n.*: **virago**. See WOMAN

bravery *n.*: **hardihood**. See COURAGE

brawl (esp. public) *n.*: **affray**. ∎ [John] Lewis added to his own reputation for bravery when, after being invited to join the Congress of Racial Equality's (CORE) Freedom Ride bus demonstration, in May 1961, he led the group into its first **affray**, entering the "Whites Only" waiting room in the Rock Hill, South Carolina, bus terminal and getting knocked down and bloodied by a band of local toughs. (Sean Wilentz, *The Last Integrationist: John Lewis' American Odyssey*, The New Republic, 07-01-1996, p. 19.)

brawny (having a ... body build) *adj.*: **mesomorphic**. See MUSCULAR

brazenness *n.*: **impudicity**. See BRASHNESS

break (as in pause) *n.*: **caesura**. See PAUSE

break apart (tending to ... or disintegrate) *adj.*: **fissiparous**. See BREAK UP

break in (suddenly or forcibly) *v.i.*: **irrupt**. See BURST IN

break up (tending to ... or disintegrate) *adj.*: **fissiparous**. ∎ But however novel, when Elizabeth II was crowned, the idea [that a royal family should be an ideal family] was a powerful one. It didn't last: with her sister and three of her four children divorced, the queen's clan is even more **fissiparous** than most modern families. (Author not given, *Britain: Twenty-five Out of Fifty; Queen Elizabeth II*, The Economist, 06-01-2002, p. 31.)

(2) break up (or apart, into component parts) *v.i*: **disaggregate**. See SEPARATE

breakable *adj.*: **frangible**. ∎ The red-gray, meringuelike substance ices some of the cave's surfaces and ledges like cake frosting, from a millimeter to several inches thick, and is so **frangible** you could cut it with a butter knife. (Peter Nelson, *The Cave That Holds Clues to Life on Mars*, National Wildlife, 08-18-1996, p. 36.) See FRAGILE

breakdown (of a group or social structure as a result of lack of standards or values) *n.*: **anomie**. ∎ "All of a sudden," said drummer Jerry Carrigan, "nobody cared [about how the Elvis Presley recording session was going]. We all felt, What can we do to get this over with? He'd settle for anything." In keeping with the spirit of general **anomie**, Carrigan failed to show up at all the second day. (Guralnick, *Careless Love: The Unmaking of Elvis Presley*, Little Brown [1999], p. 437.)

(2) breakdown (violent or turbulent ... of a society or regime) *n.*: **götterdämmerung** [German]. See COLLAPSE

breaking (act of ... up into parts) *n.*: **fission**. See SPLITTING

breasts (overly large ...) *n.*: **macromastia**. ∎ Breast reduction improves symptoms of **macromastia** and has a long-lasting effect. (Claudette Heddens, *Breast Reduction for the Older Woman*, Plastic Surgical Nursing, 09-22-2000.)

breathe *v.t.*: **aspirate**. See INHALE

breathing (temporary absence or cessation of) *n.*: **apnea** (*adj.*: **apneic**). ∎ They have a potentially life-threatening health condition even they have trouble describing, since it affects them only when they're deeply asleep. It's called sleep **apnea**, and it means that every night after they doze off, they go through regular periods in which they completely stop breathing. (Donovan Webster, *Dead Tired*, Men's Health, 03-01-2002, p. 119.)

(2) breathing (characterized by loud snoring or ... sounds) *adj.*: **stertorous**. See SNORING

(3) breathing (heavily) *adj.*: **suspirious** (*v.t.*: **suspire**). See PANTING

breathing space (as in adequate space for living) *n.*: **lebensraum** [German; sometimes cap.]. ∎ Even the most gung-ho frontier boosters admit that Alaska is no longer the kind of wild and woolly place it was when the gold miners rushed in 100 years ago. ... On the other hand, even if it is not the frontier it once was, it still has space, space, space, residents said, and that **lebensraum** is stamped on the state's psyche. (Carey Goldberg, *Has the Modern Age Overtaken 'The Last Frontier'?* Minneapolis Star Tribune, 08-15-1997, p. 15A.)

breeze (gentle ...) *n.*: **zephyr**. ∎ From the south, there was a warm wind blowing, gentle **zephyrs** that barely rippled the surface of Long Island Sound. (Nick Karas, *Outdoors — Striped Bass Fishing On an Ideal Evening*, Newsday, 10-13-1992, p. 114.)

breezy (as in relaxed and easygoing) *adj.*: **dégagé** [French]. See EASYGOING

bribe-taker *n.*: **boodler**. See GRAFTER

bribery (open to ...) *adj.*: **venal**. See CORRUPTIBLE

bribes (one who accepts ...) *n.*: **boodler**. SEE CORRUPT

bric-a-brac (esp. trivial or worthless) *n.*: **trumpery**. SEE JUNK

bride (personal possessions of) *n.*: **trousseau**. ■ Crown Prince Naruhito of Japan & Masako Owada [were married on] June 9, 1993, [in] the Imperial Palace, Tokyo. The dress ... reportedly cost $300,000. ... [M]emorable detail: In the bride's **trousseau** was a small sword. Tradition dictates that it be used for self-defense or, in the case of dishonor such as adultery, suicide. (Hilary Sterne, *The Royals: The Princess Brides*, In Style, 06-01-1999, p. 143.)

bridge (situated across a ...) *adj.*: **transpontine**. ■ The galleries of the Royal Academy of Arts have been transformed into a watery Lilliput by "Living Bridges," a celebration of the inhabited bridge. Visitors peer down at 20-odd immaculate models of bridges ancient and modern, extant and imagined, all of which have higher ambitions than the mere facilitation of **transpontine** traffic. (Author not given, *The Weasel*, The Independent [London], 11-23-1996.)

brief (speech or writing being very ..., as in terse) *adj.*: **elliptical**. SEE TERSE

(2) brief (as in transient or fleeting) *adj.*: **evanescent**. SEE TRANSIENT

(3) brief (saying) *n.*: **gnome** (*adj*: **gnomic**). SEE CATCHPHRASE

bright (as in shining ...) *adj.*: **effulgent**. ■ It's a glorious afternoon of **effulgent** sunshine and fresh western breezes. (John Brant, *Formula for Success*, Runner's World, 11-01-1995, p. 78.)

(2) bright (as in shining ..., like lightning) *adj.*: **fulgurant**. ■ The more we know about Hitler, the more enigmatic he — or rather, his **fulgurant** success — becomes. Here was a man without character, or with a most uninspiring personality. He had no vices; he did not drink or smoke, and he did not really care for women. ... "Outside politics," Kershaw writes, "Hitler's life was largely a void." (Istvan Deak, *The Making of a Monster*, The New Republic, 04-12-1999.)

(3) bright (as in shining ...) *adj.*: **refulgent**. ■ As a **refulgent** star of the [Communist] movement — as indeed the "purest Bolshevik writer ever to function in the United States" — Chambers involved himself in various projects. (Sam Tanenhaus, *Whittaker Chambers*, Random House [1997], p. 73.)

(4) bright (as in emitting flashes of light) *adj.*: **coruscant**. SEE GLITTERING

(5) bright (as in happy and cheerful) *adj.*: **eupeptic**. SEE CHEERFUL

(6) bright (esp. as to talent, wit or ability) *adj.*: **lambent**. SEE BRILLIANT

(7) bright (softly ...) *adj.*: **lambent**. SEE SHIMMERING

(8) bright (as in radiant or glowing) *adj.*: **lucent**. SEE GLOWING

brilliance (of performance or achievement) *n.*: **eclat**. SEE SUCCESS

brilliant (esp. as to talent, wit or ability) *adj.*: **lambent**. ■ TV is about to become home to a pair of unusual British detectives. First, the medieval. On PBS, Sir Derek Jacobi (I, Claudius) portrays Brother Cadfael, the 12th-century Benedictine monk and hero of a popular series of mysteries by Ellis Peters (the nom de plume of Edith Pargeter). This [show] is a sort of Murder, He Scribed, illuminated by Jacobi's **lambent** talent. (David Hiltbrand, *Picks & Pans*, People, 01-16-1995, p. 13.)

(2) brilliant (as in shining brightly) *adj.*: **effulgent**. SEE BRIGHT

(3) brilliant (as in shining brightly) *adj.*: **fulgurant**. SEE BRIGHT

(4) brilliant (as in shining brightly) *adj.*: **refulgent**. SEE BRIGHT

bring (together) *v.t.*: **colligate**. SEE UNITE

British (exaggerated fondness for ... manners, customs, styles etc.) *n.*: **Anglomania**. ■ Within a relatively short time dandyism swept across the Channel to capture French fashion in a wave of **Anglomania**. While the British wore fitted jackets, the French made waists so tight they could barely breathe. English shirt collars reached up to the cheekbone; French collars almost obscured the vision. (G. Bruce Boyer, *The Return of Dandyism*, Forbes Magazine, 03-09-1998, p. 248.)

(2) British (admiration of ... manners, customs, styles etc.) *n.*: **Anglophilia**. ■ [Y]ou would expect George herself to be as British as high tea at Brown's Hotel. Not so. Born in Ohio, she grew up in northern California and now lives outside L.A., just a mile from the Pacific. Yet her rampant **Anglophilia**, which she says took root during a summer in England at age 16, has resulted in six Brit-based novels. (Marjorie Rosen, *Pages: No True Brit*, People, 08-23-1993, p. 59.)

(3) British (fear, distrust or disliking of ... manners, customs, styles, etc.) *n.*: **Anglophobia**. ■ The experience [of traveling around Europe] bred in the Colonel a lifelong love for the plainness of the

American Midwest and an undying distaste for the Old World, particularly for England. His **Anglophobia** was world-class, though it never extended to his wardrobe, which was pure Savile Row, or his preference in athletics, which was polo. (Andrew Ferguson, *Books in Review*, The American Spectator, 09-01-1997.)

brittle (as in breakable) *adj.*: **frangible**. SEE BREAK-ABLE

broad (in scope or applicability) *adj.*: **ecumenical**. SEE UNIVERSAL

(2) **broad** (as in widespread) *adj.*: **pandemic**. SEE WIDESPREAD

(3) **broad** (as in widespread) *adj.*: **regnant**. SEE WIDESPREAD

broad-minded *adj.*: **latitudinarian**. SEE OPEN-MINDED

broaden (in scope) *v.t.*: **aggrandize**. SEE EXPAND

broken down (and/or worn out) *adj.*: **raddled**. SEE WORN-OUT

(2) **broken down** (as in decrepit) *adj.*: **spavined**. SEE DECREPIT

brook (small) *n.*: **rivulet**. SEE STREAM

broom (esp. made of twigs) *n.*: **besom**. ∎ The hit Harry Potter movie has sparked a magical spin-off for a Golden Bay man who has almost sold out of brooms. ... Mr Greer said even though he had not promoted his **besom** business in conjunction with the movie, parents have been buying the smaller ones for children. (Loney Kelly, *Wizardry Sparks Busy Spell*, The Nelson Mail [Nelson, New Zealand], 01-16-2002, p. 1.)

brothel *n.*: **bagnio**. ∎ Minna [Everleigh] and her older sister, Ada, opened what would become the best little bordello in Chicago and, for a time, one of the best known in the world. ... Raised in a prosperous Southern family, the sisters fled bad marriages to become touring actresses and ended up in Chicago after running a **bagnio** in Omaha during the Trans-Mississippi Exposition. (Louise Kiernan, *Events That Shaped Chicago*, The Chicago Tribune, 04-01-1997, p. 2.)

browbeat *v.t.*: **hector**. SEE BULLY

brown-nose *v.t.*: **bootlick**. SEE KOWTOW

brown-noser *n.*: **lickspittle**. SEE SYCOPHANT

(2) **brown-noser** (esp. someone who seeks to asso-ciate with or flatter persons of rank or high social status) *n.*: **tuft-hunter**. SEE HANGER-ON

brownish-red *adj.*: **ferruginous**. SEE RUST

brush (as mass of bushes or shrubs) *n.*: **boscage**. SEE BUSHES

brutal (in the manner of an oppressive and despotic organization) *adj.*: **jackbooted**. SEE OPPRESSIVE

(2) **brutal** (spectacle in which shame, degradation or harm is inflicted on a person, often for the enjoyment of onlookers) *n.*: **Roman holiday**. SEE SPECTACLE

bucolic (as in a place which is ..., rustic and simple) *adj.*: **Arcadian**. SEE PASTORAL

budding (as in coming into being) *adj.*: **nascent**. SEE EMERGING

buffalo (of, relating to or resembling) *adj., n.*: **bovine**. ∎ [In filming the movie Dances With Wolves,] the live, hoofed extras used in the hunt — some 2,300 buffalo from the herd of South Dakota rancher Roy Houck — were unpredictable. Wranglers worked for six hours to round up the fidgety, cantankerous, 1,600-lb. **bovines** and get them charging. (Author not given, *Dances with Buffaloids*, People, 03-27-1991, p. 100.)

buffoon (who is sometimes boastful) *n.*: **Scaramouch**. ∎ Q - I can't seem to get a straight answer. Where will the Dow Jones averages be one year from now? A - ... Because your question commands a "yes, but and if" answer, only a **Scaramouch** or a blind dog would venture an opinion in the market's direction. (Malcom Berko, *Bears Make Headlines, But ... Likelihood That Dow Will Make New Highs Continues to Rise*, The Chicago Tribune, 08-20-1993, p. 11.)

(2) **buffoon** (one who resembles a short, fat ..., as in clown) *n.*: **Punchinello**. SEE CLOWN

bug *v.t.*: **chivvy**. SEE PESTER

bug-eyed *adj.*: **exopthalmic**. ∎ And then the conversation turns to condoms. McIlvenna hates condoms. They're antisex. They're stupid, and bad medicine. Suddenly, he is furious. Up go the lids. The eyes are practically **exophthalmic**: "The hell with condoms!" he spews. "I don't have faith in condoms!" (Rene Chun, *The Goo That Saved the World*, Esquire, 01-01-1998.)

bugs (feeding on ...) *adj.*: **entomophagous**. ∎ That's right, bugs are good food. At least that's the thrust behind the Eatbug.com Web site. Run by a 17-year-old girl, it's a two-year-old online guide for insect eaters. From raising and slaughtering, to cooking and eating, this site has everything you never wanted to know about the gentle art of being **entomophagous**. (Edward Mazza, *Weird Wide Web*, The New York Daily News, 05-28-2000, p. 9.)

(2) bugs (study of ...) *n.:* **entomology**. See INSECTS

(3) bugs (sensation that ... are crawling on you) *n.:* **formication**. See INSECTS

build (cheaply and flimsily) *v.t.:* **jerrybuild**. ■ In truth, Britt is a sort of pioneer: His home, however, is a **jerrybuilt** wigwam on state-owned land near Boston's Chestnut Hill — a haute community of $500,000 mansions and country club sensibilities. (Cable Neuhaus, *Main Street: Facing Eviction From His Boston Hovel, Hermit Bill Britt Pleads There's No Place Like Home*, People, 04-13-1987, p. 61.)

(2) build (as in assemble, clumsily, roughly or hastily) *v.t.:* **cobble**. See ASSEMBLE

builder (of houses, spec. a carptenter) *n.:* **housewright**. See CARPENTER

building (art of ..., esp. large buildings) *n.:* **tectonics**. See CONSTRUCTION

built-in *adj.:* **immanent**. See INHERENT

(2) built-in (as in innate) *adj.:* **connate**. See INNATE

bulb-shaped (or rounded) *adj.:* **bulbous**. ■ Like the coupe, its styling is reminiscent of the **bulbous** Porsche ragtops of the late 1950s and early '60s, with rounded contours and an industrial-strength high-tech interior. (Frank Aukofer, *Audi Gets TT Roadster Right*, The Washington Times, 05-19-2000, p. E17.)

bulging (marked by ... eyes) *adj.:* **exopthalmic**. See BUG-EYED

(2) bulging (used often of body parts such as the penis) *adj.:* **tumescent**. See SWOLLEN

(3) bulging (as in swollen or distended) *adj.:* **tumid**. See SWOLLEN

bull (of or resembling) *adj.:* **taurine**. ■ The worm of doubt that really eats at market watchers **taurine** and ursine [e.g. bull and bear] is the high price/earnings multiple, recently about 24.4 for the S&P 500. (Terence P. Pare, *Finding Buys When Stocks Are High*, Fortune, 10-26-1992, p. 16.)

bullfight *n.:* **corrida**. ■ The bulls were in a corral, swishing their tails to ward off hordes of flies. They came in a variety of colors — black, brown, gray and even chestnut — and weighed about 900 pounds each. ... They seemed calm, but that would change the instant the **corrida** started. (Bill Barich, *Bullfighting*, Sports Illustrated, 05-15-2000, p. R28)

bullfighting (of or relating to) *adj.:* **tauromachy**. ■ Animal rights activists are trying to close America's only bullfighting school — where, instead of facing a raging bull, students armed with wooden swords fight an instructor waving a pair of horns and snorting loudly. The Humane Society claims that although the California Academy of **Tauromachy**, in San Diego, does not use real bulls, it nevertheless desensitizes people to the "cruelty actually suffered by a bull in a ring." (Tunku Varadarajan, *Matador School a Red Rag to Activists*, The Times [London], 09-15-1997.)

bullish (as in one habitually expecting an upturn in one's fortunes, sometimes without justification) *adj.:* **Micawberish** (*n.:* **Micawber**). See OPTIMISTIC

(2) bullish (esp. blindly or naively) *adj.:* **Panglossian**. See OPTIMISTIC

bully *v.t.:* **hector**. ■ I don't know about you but I'm getting mighty sick of Wilfred Brimley **hectoring** me about Quaker Oats [in the TV commercial]. (Tony Kornheiser, *Pumping Irony*, Times Books [1995], p. 216.)

bully (as in intimidate) *v.t.:* **Bogart**. See INTIMIDATE

bum (off of) *v.t.:* **cadge**. See BEG

(2) bum *n.:* **clochard** [French]. See VAGRANT

bumbler (habitual ...) *n.:* **schlemiel** [Yiddish. The counterpart to this word is "schlimazel," a perpetually unlucky person. Thus, the schlemiel will spill his soup and it will land on the schlimazel]. ■ Excited by the applause and growing confident, Avner seems to improvise ways to entertain the audience, finding and balancing a ladder on his chin, and walking across a rope. ... [B]y the end of the show, Avner has transformed himself from an inept bumbler into a confident, occasionally competent performer. ... "I want the audience to care about this poor **schlemiel** who is trying to do something beyond his capabilities because he wants to please the audience." (Patricia Lerner, *Lil' Avner*, Los Angeles Times, 02-10-1991.)

bunch (of riders in a bike race) *n.:* **peloton** [French]. See CLUSTER

bundle (of objects, people or ideas) *n.:* **congeries**. See COLLECTION

(2) bundle (as in group) *n.*: **gaggle**. SEE GROUP

bungle (esp. a golf shot) *v.t., n.*: **foozle**. SEE BOTCH

bungler (habitual ...) *n.*: **schlemiel** [Yiddish]. SEE BUMBLER

buoyancy (as in dancer's seeming ability to float) *n.*: **ballon** [French]. SEE FLOAT

burden (which is oppressive) *n.*: **incubus**. The essays range over other topics, including attempts by some German historians in the 1980s to liberate Germans from the **incubus** of the Holocaust by placing it within the broader context of other mass murders of the twentieth century, especially those in Stalin's Soviet Union. (Daniel E. Rogers, *Murder in Our Midst*, National Forum, 01-01-1997, p. 44.)

(2) burden *v.t., v.i., n.*: **cark**. SEE WORRY

bureaucracy (as in actions of government officials who are pompous but inefficient) *n.*: **bumbledom** [after a character in *Oliver Twist* by Dickens]. ∎ Congress [has created a new job] to help a city with severe managerial and operational problems [i.e. Washington D.C. The appointee] will be responsible for ... making sweeping changes in no less than 80 percent of the government. It's a tall order for someone new to Washington and to that unresponsive bureaucratic **bumbledom** known locally as the District government. (Author not given, *The CMO's Challenge*, The Washington Post, 12-24-1997, p. A12.)

burgeon (lit.: bear fruit) *v.i.*: **fructify**. ∎ What distinguishes her work is an ability, if not need, to write with her senses as well as her intellect. The sights and sounds of what she calls Hong Kong's "**fructifying** untidiness" are abundant and enthusiastically conveyed. (R.Z. Sheppard, *Books: Wind and Water*, Time, 01-16-1989, p. 72.)

burial (ground) *n.*: **necropolis**. SEE GRAVEYARD

burly (having a ... body build) *adj.*: **mesomorphic**. SEE MUSCULAR

burn (with intense heat and light) *v.t., v.i.*: **deflagrate** (*n.*: **deflagration**). SEE EXPLOSION

burning (of, relating to or resulting from) *adj.*: **pyric**. ∎ Still, most of us will sometimes long for a fire — for sociability, to grill a trout, to bake bread, or simply to avoid technology. So when the **pyric** urge does strike, first think habitat. (Ted Kerasote, *How to Build a Fire in 1996*, Sports Afield, 03-01-1996, p. 18.)

(2) burning (of heretics at the stake) *n.*: **auto-da-fe**. SEE EXECUTION

(3) burning (as in of or relating to dog days of summer) *adj.*: **canicular**. SEE DOG DAYS

(4) burning (or prickling sensation on skin) *n.*: **paresthesia**. SEE PRICKLING

burp (as in belch) *v.t., v.i.*: **eruct**. SEE BELCH

burst in (suddenly or forcibly) *v.i.*: **irrupt**. ∎ The Summer House (Samuel Goldwyn) proves again that even if you can't teach an old dog new tricks, the old tricks can still be amusing when neatly done. This film is one more go-round with the gimmick of the colorful stranger **irrupting** into some colorless lives and improving them. (Stanley Kauffmann, *The Summer House*, The New Republic, 01-10-1994, p. 31.)

bushes (mass of ...) *n.*: **boscage**. ∎ He also views the Allied nighttime drop of the 82nd and 101st Airborne in the **boscage** country ... a mistake and believes it would have been better to have landed them at first light. He faults Allied intelligence for not recognizing the difficulty of fighting in the hedgerows, thick bushes [that] enclosed every Normandy field and farm and provided natural defenses for the Germans. (Leah Rawls Atkins, *Book Reviews*, National Forum, 09-01-1994, p. 45.)

busty *adj.*: **bathycolpian**. ∎ [The Duchess of York] has ordered 12 new outfits from the London couturier Isabell Kristensen. [Kristensen] was unwilling to comment on the duchess's style, other than to say that her influences for this season's collections have been twofold: the **bathycolpian** cartoon character Jessica Rabbit and reed-slender Audrey Hepburn. "One of my great specialities is the corset," she says. "And they are padded for both bust and hips." (Author not given, *Haught Couture*, The Times [London], 06-01-1995.)

busybody *n.*: **quidnunc**. ∎ To become enriched by the information that Beethoven might have had syphilis is of great moment to the **quidnunc**, but to do a forensic analysis of Beethoven's harmonics might give insight into what went on under his scalp and benefit us all. (Author not given, *Letters*, Time, 07-01-1996, p. 5.)

(2) busybody (as in officious meddler who frustrates the success of a plan by stupidly getting in the way) *n.*: **marplot**. SEE MEDDLER

butchery (as in slaughterhouse) *n.*: **abattoir**. SEE SLAUGHTERHOUSE

butler *n.*: **major-domo**. ∎ Mr. Roberts believes his

previous jobs have prepared him for a life as a **major-domo** and considers his personality well suited to service. These days butlers are not so much man-servants a la Jeeves, as managers and administrators who may be responsible for 20 or 30 staff. (Barrie Clement, *Servants Back in Below-Stairs Britain*, Independent, 07-01-1996, p. 3.)

butt (having a nicely proportioned ...) *adj.*: **callipygian**. See REAR END

(2) **butt** (having a hairy ...) *adj.*: **dasypygal**. See REAR END

(3) **butt** (as in buttocks) *n., pl.*: **nates**. See BUTTOCKS

(4) **butt** (a fat ...) *n.*: **steatopygia** (having a fat ... *adj.*: **steatopygic**). See REAR END

butterfly (or, relating to or resembling) *adj.*: **lepidopterous**. ∎ At the end of winter, as the weather warms up, the monarch [butterflies] mate in what can only be described as an orgy. "Everybody mates with everybody else. It is quite a fantastic sight, I assure you," says University of California, Davis, entomologist Arthur Shapiro, who has witnessed this spectacle of **lepidopterous** lechery. (Author not given, *Fluttering Peril — Are Bred Monarchs a Menace in the Wild?* Sacramento Bee, 01-12-2002, p. B6.)

buttocks *n., pl.*: **nates**. ∎ This is followed by a fashion show, during which Andrea ... delicately shriek[s] as a bare-chested, chocolate-colored young chap saunters up and down the runway. "Is it hot in here," says Andrea, fanning her face with her Kwanza program and eyeing the lad's strutting, splendidly molded young **nates**, "or is it just me?" (E. Jean Carroll, *The Return of the White Negro*, Esquire, 06-01-1994, p. 100.)

buxom *adj.*: **bathycolpian**. See BUSTY

buying (mania for ... things) *n.*: **oniomania**. See SHOPPING

buzzing (a ... and droning hum) *n.*: **bombilation**. ∎ The treatment of Darryl Strawberry at Shea Stadium this past season stands out in my mind, although Phil Simms and the entire Knick squad have also played to the **bombilations** of hometown booing. (Author not given, *Boos or Cheers?* The New York Times, 01-11-1987, p. 11.)

(2) **buzzing** (or ringing sound in one's ears) *n.*: **tinnitus**. See RINGING

buzzword *n.*: **shibboleth**. See CATCHPHRASE

by the book *idiom*: **according to Hoyle** [after Edmond Hoyle, c. 1672-1769, British writer on games and their rules]. ∎ [Saddam Hussein's use of] civilians as human shields "is not a military strategy." It is "a violation of the laws of armed conflict," [stated Defense Secretary Donald Rumsfeld]. Since the premise ... is that Hussein is evil and ruthless, which is certainly true, it would be remarkable if he played the game of war **according to Hoyle**. Why should he? It's not going to improve his reputation and will do nothing for his life expectancy either. (Michael Kinsley, *Problems of International Law*, The Washington Post, 03-03-2003.)

C

cabaret (as in nightclub) *n.*: **boîte** [French]. See NIGHTCLUB

cable (operated or moved by ...) *adj., n.*: **funicular**. ∎ Last Saturday the weather was particularly fine, and the 9 a.m. **funicular** train to one of the country's most popular high-altitude ski resorts ... was filled to capacity. As many as 180 people, including dozens of youngsters, were in the cable-driven car when it headed into a 3,200 m tunnel burrowed through the side of the mountain. Eight people would make it out alive. (Andrew Purvis, *Alpine Nightmare: A Fire in a Funicular Train Kills at Least 150 People at a Popular High-Altitude Ski Resort in Austria*, Time International, 11-20-2000.)

cackle (as in guffaw) *v.i.*: **cachinnate** (*n*: **cachinnation**). See LAUGH

cacophonous *adj.*: **scrannel**. ∎ There are burnings and beatings, there are feces and mud, there is animal torture and incestuous rape, and soaring above the cacophony in this pious Catholic village, where every nose is bulbous and every jaw undershot, are the screeches and **scrannel** note of the church organ which is, naturally, untuned. (Peter Walker, *Nasty, Brutish, Grimm*, Independent on Sunday, 03-23-1997, p. 34.)

cadavers (fascination with or erotic attraction to ...) *n.*: **necrophilia**. See CORPSES

(2) **cadavers** (abnormal fear of ... or dead people) *n.*: **necrophobia**. See FEAR

café *n.*: **estaminet** [French]. See BISTRO

cajolery (to win over or obtain by ...) *v.t.*: **inveigle**. See LURE

cajoling (by flattery) *n.*: **blandishment** (*v.t.*: **blandish**). See FLATTERY

calamity (one who is always predicting ...) *n.*: **catastrophist**. SEE PESSIMIST

(2) **calamity** (as in episode having the quality of a nightmare) *n.*: **Walpurgis Night**. SEE NIGHTMARE

calculating (act or process of ..., as in measuring) *n.*: **mensuration**. SEE MEASURING

callous (as in thick-skinned) *adj.*: **pachydermatous**. SEE THICK-SKINNED

calm *adj.*: **equable**. SEE SERENE

(2) **calm** (esp. with respect to the wind) *adj.*: **favonian**. SEE MILD

(3) **calm** (as in unemotional or even-tempered) *adj.*: **phlegmatic**. SEE EVEN-TEMPERED

(4) **calm** *v.t.*: **propitiate**. SEE PLACATE

calmness *n.*: **ataraxy** (or **ataraxia**). ∎ [I made an obscene gesture and he marched up to me nose-to-nose and shouted:] "You've got something to say to me?" ... "No, I don't think so," I responded with a calm that would have earned me full marks from several schools of philosophy. Raw **ataraxy**. (Tabor Fischer, *The Thought Gang*, The New Press [1994], p. 219.)

(2) **calmness** (as in peace of mind) *n.*: **heartsease**. SEE PEACE OF MIND

(3) **calmness** (in the face of adversity or suffering) *n.*: **longaminity**. SEE PATIENCE

(4) **calmness** (as in gentleness) *n.*: **mansuetude**. SEE GENTLENESS

(5) **calmness** (as in tranquility) *n.*: **quietude**. SEE TRANQUILITY

(6) **calmness** (esp. under pressure or trying circumstances) *n.*: **sang-froid** [French]. SEE COMPOSURE

can't-miss (esp. with respect to a plan, deal or investment that can be trusted completely because it is supposedly safe and sure to succeed) *adj.*: **copper-bottomed** [British]. SEE SURE-FIRE

cane (instrument such as a ... for punishing children) *n.*: **ferule**. SEE PADDLE

cannibalistic *adj.*: **anthropophagous**. ∎ There seems to be an ingrained taboo, a knee-jerk response that simultaneously combines repulsion from, and fascination with, the **anthropophagous** act. From earliest times, cannibalism has been depicted as the ultimate horror. (Thomas Hodgkinson, *The Essay: Cannibalism: A Potted History*, The Independent [London], 03-17-2001.)

capable (as in skillful) *adj.*: **habile**. SEE SKILLFUL

caper (as in prank) *n.*: **dido**. SEE PRANK

capital letter *n.*: **majuscule**. ∎ A had its bomb, B its movie, C its section and D its day. Now E is having its era. ... You must have seen its amazing breakthrough performance in e-mail. Soon there were E-Stamps, Etrade, eToys.com, e-etc. Now, E's got capital status; as we like to say, E is "E-biquitous!" ... What versions does E come in? You can get E in a manly, three-pronged **majuscule** or a dainty, curly [lower case] that almost looks like a smiley face! (Jesse Green, *E-nough Already*, The Washington Post, 11-21-1999.)

caprice (as in whim) *n.*: **boutade** [French]. SEE WHIM

captivate *v.t.*: **ensorcell** (or **ensorcel**). SEE ENCHANT

captivating *adj.*: **piquant**. SEE APPEALING

captivity (as in bondage) *n.*: **thralldom**. SEE BONDAGE

care (treat another with excessive ...) *n., v.t.*: **wet-nurse**. SEE CODDLE

carefree *adj.*: **dégagé** [French]. SEE EASYGOING

careless (and irresponsible) *adj.*: **feckless**. SEE IRRESPONSIBLE

(2) **careless** (as in irresponsible or reckless) *adj.*: **harum-scarum**. SEE RECKLESS

carelessly (as in, in a disorderly and hasty manner) *adv.*: **pell-mell**. SEE DISORDERLY

caress *v.i.*: **canoodle** (often as in "canoodle with"). ∎ Really, it would probably be worth aging into a saggy, babbling hack — as [John Phillips and Denny Doherty of the Mamas and the Papas] both now seem to be — if one could have spent a few nights **canoodling** with Michelle [Phillips] in her swivel-hippied prime. (Ken Tucker, *Television: Hard Rock*, Entertainment Weekly, 02-05-1999, p. 51.)

carnal (relating to or exhibiting ... behavior in many forms) *adj.*: **pansexual**. SEE SEXUAL

carouse (noisily) *v.i.*: **roister**. SEE REVEL

carpenter (who builds houses) *n.*: **housewright**. ∎ A 1754 white colonial with dark red shutters ... built by a wealthy **housewright** for himself, still possessing original floorboards and a few original windowpanes. (Suzanne Berne, *A Perfect Arrangement*, Algonquin Books of Chapel Hill [2001], p. 19.)

carry (a person or group from one place to another against their will, whether literally or figuratively) *v.t.*: **frogmarch**. See MARCH

case (as in example) *n.*: **exemplum**. See EXAMPLE

cast (of characters in a play or story) *n.*: **dramatis personae**. See CHARACTERS

castle (master of ...) *n.*: **chatelain** (mistress: **chatelaine**). ▪ By virtue of their wealthy owners, many castles are graced by lovely gardens. In the days of the Tudor royal visits, a topiary garden or maze was a way to impress important guests, while Victorian **chatelains** sought to cultivate rare plants brought from exotic travels. (Allison Culliford, *The Complete Guide to British Castles*, The Independent, 05-04-2002, p. 6.)

castrate *v.t.*: **geld**. ▪ Percy's problems, experts say, started when he was fed from a bottle soon after birth. Then the llama's handlers failed to castrate him. So it came as no surprise ... that Percy pounced on an amusement park attendant on Friday. ... While several llama authorities denounced the Weeki Wachee attraction for failing to **geld** Percy, the attraction said it had done nothing wrong. (Justin Blum, *Llama Attacks Park Attendant*, St. Petersburg Times, 07-09-1995, p. 7.)

castration *n.*: **orchidectomy**. ▪ [O]ne of the rare surviving examples of a castrato singing [is] a 1903 recording of Alessandro Moreschi, the last singer to be subjected to **orchidectomy** to preserve his unbroken voice. (Brian Morton, *Suffering For Your Art Is One Thing But Counter-Tenor Beats Castrato*, Scotland on Sunday, 11-12-1995.)

casual (as in relaxed and easygoing) *adj.*: **dégagé** [French]. See EASYGOING

casualness (appearance of ...) *n.*: **sprezzatura** [Italian]. See EFFORTLESSNESS

cat hater *n.*: **ailurophobe**. ▪ Q: I received a modest inheritance from an aunt and wished to give some portion of it to charity. Did I have a moral obligation to donate to causes she specifically believed in? A: Once it passed into your hands, it became yours to do with as you wished. Even had your aunt been, say, a militant **ailurophobe**, you could have contributed honourably to a home for recalcitrant cats. (Author not given, *Tapping the Tourists for 20's*, The Toronto Star, 02-17-2002.)

cat lover *n.*: **ailurophile**. ▪ An animal decked out in peasant garb is one thing, but — holy cat! — Herbert has tails peeking out from monks' robes and halos perched on furry heads. Judging from their pious expressions, though, these kitties mean no disrespect. And what **ailurophile** could resist a cat in a wimple? (Marlene McCampbell, *Picks & Pans: Pages*, People, 04-10-1995, p. 25.)

catalyst *n.*: **fillip**. See STIMULUS
(2) catalyst (as in creative inspiration) *n.*: **afflatus**. See INSPIRATION

catastrophe (as in episode having the quality of a nightmare) *n.*: **Walpurgis Night**. See NIGHTMARE

catchphrase (pithy ...) *n.*: **gnome** (*adj*: **gnomic**). ▪ [Frank Yablans] had gotten a lot of credit for *Love Story*, with its **gnomic**, but effective tag line: "Love means never having to say you're sorry." (Peter Biskind, *Easy Riders, Raging Bulls*, Simon & Schuster [1998], p. 145.)
(2) catchphrase (or catchword) *n.*: **shibboleth**. ▪ The word self-esteem has become one of the obstructive **shibboleths** of education. Why do black children need Afrocentrist education? Because, its promoters say, it will create self-esteem. (Robert Hughes, *Essay: The Fraying Of America*, Time, 02-03-1992, p. 44.)

caught (in the act, esp. of committing an offense or a sexual act) *adv.*: **in flagrante delicto**. See IN THE ACT

cause (as in event which is ... of war, literally or figuratively) *n.*: **casus belli** [Latin]. See PROVOCATION
(2) cause (as in prime mover) *n.*: **primum mobile** [Latin]. See PRIME MOVER

causes (study of ..., esp. relating to medical conditions) *n.*: **etiology**. ▪ An essential component of the initial assessment is a detailed and accurate history of the event in order to determine **etiology**. The causes of seizures vary with age, and knowledge of these age-related causes can also help establish the diagnosis. (Genell Hilton, *Seizure Disorders in Adults*, The Nurse Practitioner, 09-01-1997, p. 42.)

caustic *adj.*: **acidulous**. See TART
(2) caustic (as in ... remarks) *adj.*: **astringent**. See HARSH
(3) caustic *adj.*: **mordant**. See SARCASTIC

cautious (tactics, esp. as a means to wear out an opponent) *adj.*: **Fabian** [This adjective derives from Roman general Quinton Fabius Maximus, who, through caution, avoidance of direct confrontation, and harassment, defeated Hannibal in the Second Punic War. Today, it has become synonymous with, alternatively, caution or conservativeness, delay or dilatoriness, or guerilla tactics, and is often used in the phrase "Fabian tactics"]. ∎ [After becoming world chess champion in 1960, Mikhail] Tal immediately embarked upon a fresh challenge but at [a tournament in] 1962, instead of the anticipated race between the young lions, Mikhail Tal and Bobby Fischer, the tournament resulted in a narrow victory of attrition for the **Fabian tactics** of the ultra-cautious Armenian Tigran Petrosian. During this tournament Tal's health collapsed and he had to withdraw well before the end. (Author not given, *Mikhail Tal*, The Times [London], 06-30-1992.)

cave dweller *n.*: **troglodyte** SEE NEANDERTHAL

cavort *v.t.*, *v.i.*: **disport**. SEE FROLIC
(2) cavort *v.i.*: **gambol**. SEE FROLIC

ceasefire (temporary ... between opposing parties pending final deal) *n.*: **modus vivendi** [Latin]. SEE TRUCE

cede (esp. responsibility or duty) *v.t.*: **abnegate**. SEE RENOUNCE
(2) cede (as in give back, often property or territory) *v.i.*: **retrocede**. SEE RETURN

celebrate (with boisterous public demonstrations) *v.i.*: **maffick** [British] [This word derives from celebrating in England after a British military success during the Boer War on May 17, 1900 in Mafeking, South Africa]. ∎ Currently, on the southern shore of the Thames, from the archetypal working-class districts ..., a large percentage of locals are preparing for **mafficking** on a scale not seen for decades; all subject to the dreamy prospect of Millwall beating Manchester United in this afternoon's FA Cup final. (Michael Collins, *Millwall: The Island That Time Forgot; Its Footballers Stand on the Brink of Sporting Glory*, The Independent [London], 05-22-2004.)
(2) celebrate (or boast, esp. about the accomplishments of a relative) *v.t.*, *n.*: **kvell** [Yiddish]. SEE BOAST

celebration (riotous ...) *n.*, *adj.*: **bacchanal**. SEE REVELRY

celebratory (and social) *adj.*: **Anacreontic**. SEE CONVIVIAL

celebrity *n.*: **réclame** [French]. SEE PUBLICITY

celestial *adj.*: **empyreal**. SEE LOFTY
(2) celestial *adj.*: **ethereal**. SEE HEAVENLY

cemeteries (one who loves ...) *n.*: **taphophile**. ∎ [Before] he died in 1994, [horror movie star Peter] Cushing, fearing that any tangible memorial would become a shrine for cinematic **taphophiles**, arranged for [his remains to be buried] at an undisclosed location. (Matthew Sweet, *Film: Why Do the Press Only Call Me a Horror Actor?* The Independent [London], 02-25-2001.)

cemetery *n.*: **necropolis**. SEE GRAVEYARD

censor (a book or a writing in a prudish manner) *v.t.*: **bowdlerize**. SEE EDIT

censorship (of arts, theater or literature) *n.*: **Comstockery**. [Named for Anthony Comstock (1844-1915), secretary of the New York Society for the Suppression of Vice, who helped destroy 160 tons of literature and pictures that he deemed immoral]. ∎ The [Communication Decency Act says], in effect, that if you display "indecent" or "patently offensive" material on the Internet, "in a manner available to a person under 18 years of age," you are a criminal. ... The best argument for upholding this electronic **Comstockery** can be summed up in a single world: zoning. (Jeffrey Rosen, *Can the Government Stop Cyberporn?* The New Republic, 03-31-1997.)

censure (as in criticism) *n.*: **animadversion** (*v.t.*: **animadvert**). SEE CRITICISM
(2) censure (as in criticize) *v.t.*: **flay**. SEE CRITICIZE
(3) censure (harshly) *v.t.*: **fustigate**. SEE CRITICIZE
(4) censure (being subject to ..., esp. public) *n.*: **obloquy**. SEE ABUSE

center (moving, directed or pulled towards) *adj.*: **centripetal**. ∎ Sometimes wildly diverse interests may be a better bet. Keep in mind, one of the big threats to wedded bliss is **centripetal** force, the tendency for a marriage to ... collapse in on itself. If both peas are from the same pod, it can get claustrophobic in there. (Hugh O'Neill, *Have You Met Your Match? Get a Wife!* Men's Health, 06-01-2001, p. 126.)

center of attention *n.*: **cynosure**. ∎ **Cynosure** on the court though he was, [basketball star Bill] Russell never enjoyed being the celebrity alone. ... Maybe that's one reason the team mattered so to him; it hugged him back. (Frank Deford, *The 20th Century: The Ring Leader*, Sports Illustrated, 05-10-1999, p. 96.)

ceremony (or ritual which is pretentious) *n.*: **mummery**. ▪ [In the London courtroom, Barrister] Richard Rampton, who wears a short gray-blond wig and the silk robes of a Queen's Counsel, and his black-robed junior Heather Rogers, whose wig partially covers her own gray hair, add yet a further note of **mummery** to the proceedings. (D.D. Guttenplan, *The Holocaust on Trial*, Norton [2001], p. 19.)

certain (as in sure-fire, esp. with respect to a plan, deal or investment that can be trusted completely because it is supposedly safe and sure to succeed) *adj.*: **copper-bottomed** [British]. SEE SURE-FIRE

(2) certain (as in unavoidable) *adj.*: **ineluctable**. SEE UNAVOIDABLE

chafe *v.t.*: **abrade**. ▪ [If one uses chewing tobacco, the] gums may recede, the teeth loosen, biting surfaces are **abraded**, and tough, white patches called leukoplakia may appear on the gums and cheeks. After several years the mouth can be devastated. (Claudia Wallis, *Medicine*, Time, 07-15-1985, p. 68.)

chagrin (resulting from an inopportune occurrence) *n.*: **contretemps**. SEE MISHAP

chain *n.*: **catenation** (*v.t.*: **catenate**). ▪ The subject we're on is adultery. ... Tonight [Sondra] will be Joan's fictitious sick aunt or her friend in dire need of a babysitter. Her alibi. This arrangement is ongoing, a round-robin [with 2 other women], a quid pro quo. Yet despite, or perhaps because of, this seamless **catenation** of adultery, these New York City women consider themselves very happily married. (Binnie Kirshenbaum, *The Cheaters' Club*, Harper's Bazaar, 10-01-1995, p. 138.)

challenge (a statement, opinion or action) *v.t.*: **oppugn**. SEE OPPOSE

(2) challenge (as in hostile meeting) *n.*: **rencontre** [French]. SEE DUEL

champion (of a cause) *n.*: **paladin**. SEE PROPONENT

chance (by ...) *adj.*: **adventitious**. ▪ [F]or depth of experience, breadth of repertory, theatrical understanding and a touch of old-school maestro bossiness — not to mention the **adventitious** advantage of his British nationality — my vote for music director of the Royal Opera would go to Mark Elder any day. (Rupert Christiansen, *The Arts*, The Daily Telegraph, 02-11-1999, p. 29.)

(2) chance (pertaining to or dependent upon ...) *adj.*: **aleatory**. SEE UNPREDICTABLE

change (sudden ... of events, often in a literary work) *n.*: **peripeteia**. SEE TURNAROUND

(2) change (complete ...) *n.*: **permutation**. SEE TRANSFORMATION

(3) change (esp. in a strange, grotesque, or humorous way) *v.t.*: **transmogrify**. SEE TRANSFORM

change of mind (esp. regarding one's beliefs, causes or policies) *n.*: **bouleversement** [French]. ▪ The timing of this week's **bouleversement** [by British Prime Minister Tony Blair] in Brussels was rotten. It is less than a month since [Blair] decided to break cover, ... launch his "national changeover plan," and make it plain to anyone who had ever doubted it that he really did intend to lead Britain into the promised land of the euro, the single European currency. (Author not given, *Moses Blair and His Promised Euroland*, The Economist, 03-20-1999.) SEE REVERSAL

(2) change of mind (esp. regarding one's beliefs, causes or policies) *n.*: **tergiversation** (*v.i.*: **tergiversate**). ▪ [Rudolph Giuliani] had himself changed positions over the years, having been pro-life and then pro-choice, and he knew the pain and punishment of **tergiversation**. But, after all, he was elected mayor, and like so many others, concluded that to oppose abortion is politically more dangerous than to tolerate it. (William F. Buckley, Buffalo News, *Temporizing on the Abortion Issue*, 08-03-94, p. 3.)

(3) change of mind (as in abandonment, from one's religion, principles or causes) *n.*: **apostasy**. SEE ABANDONMENT

(4) change of mind (as in reversal of policy or position) *n.*: **volte-face** [French]. SEE ABOUT-FACE

changeable *adj.*: **labile**. ▪ The beautiful show of Guercino drawings ... reminds you, moreover, how **labile** reputation can be. Guercino was one of those 17th century Italian artists who sank under the weight of an earlier age's revival [i.e. the Renaissance]. (Robert Hughes, *Reviews Art: Exhibit: Guercino*, Time International, 07-13-1992, p. 49.)

(2) changeable (one that is ... or varies with trends) *n.*: **weathercock**. SEE FICKLE

chanting (responsive ... or singing) *n.*: **antiphony**. ▪ I left the church to the soft **antiphony** of monks chanting the liturgy. (Nancy Shute, *Into and Out of the Mystic*, U.S. News & World Report, 04-19-1999, p. 86.)

chaos *n.*: **tohubuhu** [derives from the Hebrew "tohu wa-bhohu" in the second verse of Genesis, translated in the King James Version in 1611 as "And the earth was without form, and void"]. ▮ Brother of Sleep [by Robert Schneider includes] a meditation on the wiles, the vulnerabilities and the potential for mishap of the human body. ... Time and again ... Elias tunes in to the "mad **tohubohu**" of the body noises of his neighbours "an incredible noise of swallowing, gurgling, snorting, and belching, a churning of gall-like stomach juices, a quiet splash of urine." (Valentine Cunningham, *The Week in Reviews: Books: Who Needs Enemas...*, The Observer, 11-24-1996, p. 16.)

(2) chaos (movement towards or degree of ... in a system or society) *n.*: **entropy**. SEE DISORDER

(3) chaos (and confusion) *n., adj.*: **hugger-mugger**. SEE CONFUSION

(4) chaos (as in commotion) *n.*: **maelstrom**. SEE COMMOTION

character (of a person, people or culture) *n.*: **ethos**. ▮ Copyright ... involves the exclusive use of private property. And it often appears in conflict with the computer world, which values usable and immediate public access. "The **ethos** of the Internet," says Marci Hamilton ... "is that anything online may be downloaded, cut, copied, and sent along to others." (Daniel Grant, *Copyright Law Faces Sea Change*, The Christian Science Monitor, 02-25-1999, p. 16.)

(2) character (showing an idea without words, e.g., $, or Chinese or Japanese symbols) *n.*: **ideogram**. SEE SYMBOL

(3) character (lit. "humanity," often used in the sense of decency) *n.*: **menschlichkeit** [German, Yiddish]. SEE DECENCY

characterize (as in describe, by painting or writing) *v.t.*: **limn**. SEE DESCRIBE

characters (in a play or story) *n.*: **dramatis personae**. ▮ Jenkins just finished a second romance novel, due out this fall. (The setting: Michigan, 1876; the **dramatis personae**: a black woman doctor from California and a Civil War veteran.) (Betsy Israel, *Pages: Heat in Another Color*, People, 02-13-1995, p. 153.)

charge (as in order or direct) *v.t.*: **adjure**. SEE ORDER

(2) charge (an accuser with having committed similar offense) *n.*: **tu quoque** [Latin]. SEE ANSWER

charisma *n.*: **duende**. ▮ [There is] a quality called **duende**. Fred Astaire had it, he said, Gene Kelly didn't, Joe DiMaggio did, Stan Musial didn't. Willie Mays had it, but not Henry Aaron. Ken Griffey Jr.

has **duende** whether he gets sixty homers this season or not. He will always have it. ... There is just something about him. A spark. A smile. A flair. (Mike Lupica, *Roger and Him [Baseball Player Ken Griffey Jr.]*, Esquire, 09-01-1994, p. 96.)

charitable *adj.*: **caritative**. ▮ This should appear, for instance, in the form of responsibility and consideration [by the nurse] and, above all, as reverence for the suffering patient. This also can be seen as an expression of an unconditional **caritative** ethic, involving responsibility and a desire to do good. (Dahly Matilainen, *Patterns of Ideas in the Professional Life and Writings of Karin Neuman-Rahn*, Advances in Nursing Science, 09-01-1999, p. 78.)

(2) charitable *adj.*: **eleemosynary**. ▮ Nevertheless, paying the chief executive less than an underling often makes sense — and many good chief executives know it. ... "I'm not **eleemosynary**, mind you," says [Bally's] Chairman Robert E. Mullane, who pulled down $592,222 himself. "[Paying certain Bally's employees more than I make] is what's best for the company. I live very nicely. I like my job." (John Paul Newport Jr., *Managing: How to Outearn the Boss and Keep Your Job*, Fortune, 05-27-1985, p. 73.)

charlatan (esp. who sells quack medicines) *n.*: **mountebank**. SEE HUCKSTER

charm (power to ...) *n.*: **duende**. SEE CHARISMA

(2) charm *v.t.*: **ensorcell** (or **ensorcel**). SEE ENCHANT

charming (and seductive woman) *n.*: **Circe**. SEE ENCHANTRESS

(2) charming *adj.*: **piquant**. SEE APPEALING

chaste *adj.*: **vestal**. ▮ [The bride] has the advantage that her dress is so distinct that nobody could mistake her for anyone else. She is not even to be confused with her bridesmaids, for although they too are "clothed in white samite, mystic, wonderful," they lack that supreme symbol of **vestal** virginity, the veil. Their time will come. (Nigel Nicolson, *Review Features: Marriage, Magic and Memories*, The Sunday Telegraph, 08-15-1999, p. 3.)

chasten *v.t.*: **objurgate**. SEE CRITICIZE

chat (informal ...) *n.*: **causerie**. ▮ "[W]hile it is true that the people Mr. Terkel interviews are all old, and that sometimes he so far forgets himself as to ask some of them about death and the irreversible canter of time, this is not a gentle **causerie** with greying America. It is a defiant tribute to an 'other America' that may indeed be dying." (Author not given, *Coming of Age: The Story of Our Century By Those Who've Lived It*, The Economist, 10-07-1995, p. 100.)

(2) chat *n.*: **chinwag** [slang]. ∎ Recently Republican presidential hopeful George W. Bush decided he wanted CNN's schmoozy Larry King and NBC's somewhat tougher Tim Russert ("Meet the Press") to mediate two of his three potential TV appearances with Democratic rival Al Gore. ... If George and Al opt for the King style of TV **chinwag**, they will place personality, vibes and image over issues and information. (Kinney Littlefield, *As Bush Pushes to Control Debates, Fragmentation of Viewership Continues*, The Orange County Register, 09-08-2000.)

(3) chat *v.i.*: **confabulate**. ∎ The hotel, on a highway outside Richmond, the state capital of Virginia, braced itself for [boxing promoter Don King's] arrival, as for that of a hurricane. In the lobby his minions **confabulated** in blobs: roly-poly men like waddling molecules, their bangles jangling, their pinky rings glinting, walkie-talkies jutting from their polyester rumps. (Peter Conrad, *The Joy of Slavery*, Independent on Sunday, 03-10-1996, p. 4.)

(4) chat (light or playful ...) *n.*: **badinage**. SEE BANTER

(5) chat (esp. about art or literature) *n.*: **conversazione** [Italian]. SEE CONVERSATION

(6) chat *n.*: **interlocution**. SEE DISCUSSION

(7) chat (idle ...) *n.*: **palaver**. SEE SMALL TALK

chatter *n.*: **bavardage**. SEE CHITCHAT

(2) chatter *n.*: **persiflage**. SEE CHITCHAT

chatting (one skilled at dinner ...) *n.*: **deipnosophist**. SEE CONVERSATION

chatty (and flighty person) *n.*: **flibbertigibbet**. SEE FLIGHTY

cheap (and showy, or such an object) *adj., n.*: **brummagem**. SEE SHOWY

(2) cheap (as in made without regard to quality) *adj.*: **catchpenny**. SEE INFERIOR

(3) cheap (as in stingy) *adj.*: **costive**. SEE STINGY

(4) cheap (and tasteless or showy, or such an object) *adj., n.*: **gimcrack**. SEE SHOWY

(5) cheap (as in stingy) *adj.*: **mingy**. SEE STINGY

(6) cheap (as in stingy) *adj.*: **niggardly**. SEE STINGY

(7) cheap (as in stingy) *adj.*: **penurious**. SEE STINGY

cheapskate *n.*: **lickpenny**. SEE MISER

cheat *v.t.*: **euchre**. ∎ Peepgass knew then, if not before, that whatever he could do to **euchre** PlannersBanc out of Croker's [assets] was justified. (Tom Wolfe, *A Man in Full*, Farrar, Straus & Giroux [1998], p. 606.)

(2) cheat (as in swindle) *v.t.*: **bunco**. SEE SWINDLE

(3) cheat (as in deceive or defraud) *v.t., v.i.*: **cozen**. SEE DEFRAUD

(4) cheat (as in deceive or defraud) *v.t.*: **hornswoggle**. SEE DECEIVE

checkered *adj.*: **tessellated**. ∎ Price: More than $400,000. Address: 1 Dunkley Ave. Type: Six-bedroom return-veranda sandstone villa, three bathrooms. All three bathrooms have black and white **tessellated** floors. (Author not given, *Graceful Family Home With History*, The Advertiser, 07-07-2001.)

cheek (of or pertaining to) *adj.*: **buccal**. ∎ Eli Lilly is developing a **buccal** inhaler that delivers insulin by mouth, to be absorbed through the walls of the inner cheeks. (Laura Common, *Medicine 2010 - Custom-Tailored Medicines Coming of Age*, Medical Post, 05-22-2001.)

cheekbone (of or relating to) *adj.*: **malar**. ∎ Just because the **malar** fat pads, which started out over your cheekbones, have slipped an inch or two and are dragging down the corners of your mouth, should you have to go around looking like a perpetual sourpuss? (Patricia McLaughlin, *Face It: Forces of Gravity Are Beginning to Show in the Mirror*, St. Louis Post-Dispatch, 08-04-1994, p. 9.)

cheer (persons hired to ... at a performance) *n.*: **claque**. SEE APPLAUD

cheerful *adj.*: **eupeptic**. ∎ [Artist Keith] Haring has little to express beyond a vague pleasantness, a whiff of happiness. Any attempt at true feeling is immediately deflected and thwarted by a blithely **eupeptic** tone that was intrinsic to his art: his AIDS image seems as innocuous as his radiant babies and his barking dogs. (James Gardner, *Radiant Baby*, National Review, 10-27-1997, p. 58.)

(2) cheerful *adj.*: **riant** [This word comes the French and is sometimes defined (in both French and English) as "cheerful" and sometimes as "laughing." Since those words are often not exactly synonymous, it is open to question whether it applies to a cheerful person who is not laughing, although based on the (few) examples found of the word, it is my view that the word does encompass the broader concept of cheerfulness, and not only the narrower concept of laughing.] ∎ My wife was enjoying the article by John van Tiggelen on Noel Pearson in the Good Weekend until she encountered the phrase "the **riant** Peter Costello."... I nodded understandingly. "Probably give him a good laugh when he reads it," I said. "He looks a cheerful bloke in the photo." (Paul Roberts [letter writer], *Worth a Laugh*, Sydney Morning Herald, 02-18-1994.)

(3) cheerful *adj.*: **Falstaffian**. See JOVIAL

(4) cheerful (as in rosy) *adj.*: **roseate**

cheerfulness (causing or tending to produce ...) *adj.*: **felicific**. See HAPPINESS

cheerless (as in person who never laughs) *n.*: **agelast**. See HUMORLESS

cheese (of or resembling) *adj.*: **caseous**. ∎ A square of rare Tibetan [very old] cheese has [sold at Sotheby's auction]. ... This cheese — don't snicker — has been named "Eye of the Tiger." Hence, the price that Simon Perry paid was stiff. However, **caseous** allure ripens with age. (Author not given, *Listener Letters Address Guns, Power Lines and Cheese*, All Things Considered [NPR], 02-11-1993.)

cherished (household items) *n.*, *pl.*: **lares and penates**. See TREASURES

chew *v.t.*, *v.i.*: **masticate**. ∎ In its most pristine presentation, the best Kava is produced not with a grinder or a pestle, but **masticated** by young, chaste girls. The girls work the root chunk around in their mouths until the cuds become the consistency of Pablum. Then they spit it out on to a leaf. (Author not given, *Chugga Cuppa Kava - the Drink That Bites Back*, The Toronto Star, 12-22-1999.)

chewing (practice of very thorough ...) *n.*: **Fletcherism**. ∎ Then there was Horace Fletcher, called the "Great Masticator" or the "chew-chew man," for his devotion to the act of chewing. ... [I]n his book "The AB-Z of Our Nutrition," written in 1903, ... he took chewing to a new level. **Fletcherism** eventually fell out of favor, and diets, of course, are still subject to fashion. (Michael Stroh, *Some Diets Gain or Lose Weight Over Time*, The Baltimore Sun, 07-15-2002, p. 2A.)

chic (and wealthy young people) *n.*: **jeunesse dorée** [French]. See FASHIONABLE

(2) chic *adj.*: **nobby** [British]. See ELEGANT

chicken (as in coward) *n.*: **poltroon**. See COWARD

chide *v.t.*: **objurgate**. See CRITICIZE

chiding (as in criticism) *n.*: **animadversion** (*v.t.*: **animadvert**). See CRITICISM

chief (of a party, school of thought or group of persons) *n.*: **coryphaeus**. See LEADER

(2) chief *n.*: **duce** (Italian). See COMMANDER

child *n.*: **bairn** [Scottish]. ∎ The scan shows that there are four, possible five babies. I can't believe it. I didn't think I could carry that amount of **bairns**. (Anna Smith, *I Can't Believe it ... My Scan Shows Five Little Babies*, Daily Record, 12-22-2000, p. 34.)

(2) child *n.*: **moppet**. ∎ The Wiggles, Australia's most popular music group for **moppets**, are fast winning fans in the U.S. via live tours, clips on the Disney Channel and videos. ... [They are] often billed [in Australia] as the "Fab Four for the under 5s." (Don Groves, *Top Gaffney Property Wiggles Way Into U.S. Moppet Market*, Variety, 05-06-2002.)

(3) child (of or relating to) *adj.*: **filial**. See OFFSPRING

(4) child (esp. infant, who is deserted or abandoned) *n.*: **foundling**. See ORPHAN

childbearing (attitude or policy which encourages) *n.*: **pronatalism**. ∎ Lafayette ... calls [her ChildFree Network] "an alternative voice in this wilderness of **pronatalism**." She remembers, "When I started the ChildFree Network, no one was giving women a chance to think through their options. It seemed taboo to even bring it up." Lafayette has become the lone, brave Betty Friedan for the voluntarily childless. (Cynthia Kling, *Childless by Choice*, Harper's Bazaar, 06-01-1996, p. 134.)

childbirth *n.*: **accouchement**. ∎ Born on the island of Kiribat, [Millie] slid into the world on Jan. 1, 2000 at 12:00:01 a.m. ... Millie didn't just happen to be born on Kiribati. [Her] parents moved there a few months before the **accouchement** because the island sits along the international date line and, as such, it would be the first place on the planet to welcome the new year. (Elvira Cordileone, *The Frenzy of Baby Day*, The Toronto Star, 04-09-1999.)

(2) childbirth (slow or difficult ...) *n.*: **dystocia**. ∎ Significantly higher rates of virtually every complication of pregnancy [for women over 40], with the "most striking" differences in malpresentation and **dystocia**. (Author not given, *First-time Mothers Over 40 Can Have Healthy Babies, But Largest Study to Date Shows Higher Complication Rates*, Medical Post, 02-09-1999, p. 8.)

(3) childbirth (of or relating to) *adj.*: **parturient**. ∎

But hormones aside, the stimulating role of motherhood itself would seem to play a role. When the investigators gave ... rats [who had never given birth] another mother's pups to raise, the ... foster moms did almost as well in tests as their truly **parturient** counterparts. (Author not given, *Does Mothering Make Females Smarter?* Medical Post, 02-09-1999, p. 37.)

(4) childbirth (before ...) *adj.*: **antenatal**. SEE BIRTH

(5) childbirth (period before ...) *n.*: **antepartum** [Latin]. SEE PREGNANCY

(6) childbirth *n.*: **parturition**. SEE BIRTH

(7) childbirth (relating to a woman right after ...) *adj.*: **puerperal**. SEE POSTPARTUM

(8) childbirth (woman right after ...) *n.*: **puerperium**. SEE POSTPARTUM

childish *adj.*: **jejune**. SEE JUVENILE

(2) childish *adj.*: **puerile**. SEE JUVENILE

childless (of or relating to a ... female) *adj.*: **nulliparous**. ▪ But hormones aside, the stimulating role of motherhood itself would seem to play a role. When the investigators gave **nulliparous** rats another mother's pups to raise, the ... foster moms did almost as well in tests as their ... counterparts [who had given birth]. (Author not given, *Does Mothering Make Females Smarter?* Medical Post, 02-09-1999, p. 37.)

childlike (false showing of innocent or ... behavior) *adj.*: **faux-naif** [French]. SEE DISINGENUOUS

children (hatred of ...) *n.*: **misopedia**. SEE HATRED

(2) children (of or relating to a woman who has never had ...) *adj.*: **nulliparous**. SEE CHILDLESS

(3) children (having had one or more ...) *n.*: **parous**. SEE BIRTH

(4) children (attitude or policy which encourages having ...) *n.*: **pronatalism**. SEE CHILDBEARING

chilliness (often in relations between people) *n.*: **froideur** [French]. ▪ I used to run into [fellow teacher] Sue Hodges quite a lot. [But] there was something of a **froideur** between us, dating from an occasion a few years earlier when Sue had caught me sniggering over one of her class work sheets entitled "Dem Bones: The Cultural Roots of the Negro Spiritual." (Zoë Heller, *What Was She Thinking?* Henry Holt [2003], p. 35.)

chilling (as in causing coldness) *adj.*: **frigorific**. SEE COLDNESS

chills (from having a cold or fever) *n.*: **ague**. ▪ When

Moses finds me later, my head is throbbing, and my teeth chatter like the spoons Papa used to play. ... I know what this is: fever and **ague**. And no Mama to cure me this time. (Liza Ketchum, *Orphan Journey Home; Chapter 15: Stop the Boat!* The Washington Post, 05-04-2000, p. J2)

chilly *adj.*: **algid**. SEE COLD

chimpanzee (of or relating to, or resembling) *adj.*: **anthropoid**. SEE APE

Chinese (object reflecting ... artistic influence) *n.*: **chinoiserie**. ▪ Four years ago, she lavished $22,000 on a bed built for a decorator show house using Chinese-style parasols as the canopy. ... Mandarins and parasols are classic images of **chinoiserie**, the style that took Europe by storm in the 17th and 18th centuries. (Linda Hales, *The China Syndrome; Decorator Charlotte Moss Takes On a Tall Order*, The Washington Post, 04-17-1999, p. C4.)

(2) Chinese (custom or trait peculiar to the ...) *n.*: **Sinicism**. ▪ The Europeans were a different matter, and by 1900 it was clear that things must change radically — in a way that would break the old molds that had not been affected for several millenia. But what then? Could China acquire technology and awareness while keeping its inner **Sinicism**? (Joseph Losos, *Weaving the Long Strands of Chinese History*, St. Louis Post-Dispatch, 04-15-1990, p. 5C.)

chinks (full of ...) *adj.*: **rimose**. SEE CRACKS

chirp (like a bird) *v.i.*: **chitter**. ▪ In Arlington [National Cemetery], the lens peered down the slope, over the row of clipped bushes and into the granite bowl that Jackie had helped design as President Kennedy's gravesite. The granite bowl is a haunted place, but it isn't quiet. Birds **chitter** loudly and full of life in the nearby magnolia trees. (Charlotte Grimes, *Once More, a Service in Arlington: Mrs. Onassis Laid to Rest Beside the Eternal Flame*, St. Louis Post-Dispatch, 05-24-1994, p. 5C.)

chitchat *n.*: **bavardage**. ▪ [The cookhouse is] small to the point of intimate. ... It is a warm, bouncy, friendly, neighbourhood place. There is an appreciable volume of **bavardage** among people who know the place, if not each other, well, and that makes for an off-with-the-jacket-and-tie-roll-up-the-sleeves-and-pour-out-a-glass atmosphere. (Matthew Fort, *Food & Drink: Rhapsody in Blue*, The Guardian [London], 06-28-1997.)

(2) chitchat *n.*: **persiflage**. ▪ Well-coiffed

American women say, "You look just like a little leprechaun, I could put you in my pocket and take you home." Of course, that's not the prime ambition of a male. ... But I've always evoked indulgence, if not admiration, from women. It's good to have a capacity for **persiflage**. If you can't dazzle people with looks, at least fall back on some nifty bullshit. (Robert Marks, *Look On the Bright Side*, Independent, 09-09-2000, p. 6.)

(3) chitchat (light or playful ...) *n.*: **badinage**. SEE BANTER

(4) chitchat (one skilled at dinner ...) *n.*: **deipnosophist**. SEE CONVERSATION

(5) chitchat (idle ...) *n.*: **palaver**. SEE SMALL TALK

choice (as in personal preference) *n.*: **de gustibus** [Latin]. SEE TASTE

(2) choice (as in select or excellent) *adj.*: **eximious**. SEE EXCELLENT

(3) choice (of taking what is offered or nothing; i.e. no real choice at all) *n.*: **Hobson's choice**. SEE PREDICAMENT

(4) choice (as in first-class) *adj.*: **pukka**. SEE FIRST-CLASS

(5) choice (bad ..., as in the situation of having to make a move where any move made will weaken the position) *n.*: **zugzwang** [German]. SEE PREDICAMENT

choke (as in strangle) *v.t.*: **garrote**. SEE STRANGLE

(2) choke (as in strangle) *v.t.*: **jugulate**. SEE STRANGLE

chop (with an ax) *v.t.*: **hew**. SEE AX

chorus girl *n.*: **chorine**. ▮ [Pre-censorship code] musicals tell audiences how great it is to be young. *Roman Sandals* was just such a production, with all of the vital ingredients on hand: a comic star, comelly **chorines**, a few melodies, and a happy ending to take the public mind away from the Depression for an hour and a half. (Stefan Kanfer, *Ball of Fire*, Knopf [2003], p. 40.)

Christ (depiction of ... wearing crown of thorns) *n.*: **ecce homo**. SEE JESUS

Christianity (teacher of) *n.*: **catechist**. ▮ The murders of six Jesuit priests, their housekeeper and her daughter in El Salvador in 1989 are among the higher profile killings. Haugen said a church he visited had written special music and had a plaque listing the names of the disappeared. A number were **catechists** who'd taught people to read and write as they taught them the gospel. (Susan Hogan,

Otherworldly Unplugged, Minneapolis Star Tribune, 12-12-1998, p. 7B.)

(2) Christianity (one who is taught principles of ... before baptism) *n.*: **catechumen**. ▮ "Orthodox Christians are not going to tell people they are lost and going to hell. There is never any pressure to join." And a convert's required year-long, weekly tutoring in the faith, in the **catechumen** tradition of first-century Christians, puts off some "church shoppers" seeking lively weekday activities, new music and entertaining worship styles, Schaeffer said. (Patricia Rice, *Converts Help Fuel Pan-Orthodox Efforts*, St. Louis Post-Dispatch, 02-23-2002, p. 16.)

chubby (condition of having a ... physique) *n.*: **embonpoint**. SEE PLUMP

(2) chubby (person, esp. with a large abdomen) *n.*: **endomorph** (*adj.*: **endomorphic**). SEE POT-BELLIED

(3) chubby (having a short ... physique) *adj.*: **pyknic**. SEE STOCKY

(4) chubby (woman) *adj.*: **zaftig** [Yiddish]. SEE FULL-FIGURED

chunky (condition of having a ... physique) *n.*: **embonpoint**. SEE PLUMP

(2) chunky (having a short ... physique) *adj.*: **pyknic**. SEE STOCKY

church (of or relating to) *adj.*: **ecclesiastical**. ▮ A Catholic annulment is an **ecclesiastical** finding that, due to some impediment under Church law, a true marriage never existed. (Susan Jacoby, *A Kennedy Wife Says No*, Newsday, 05-11-1997, p. G12.)

churches (concerned with establishing unity among ...) *adj.*: **ecumenical**. ▮ [D]espite the signs of **ecumenical** progress, Christian splintering remains the dominant trend. Last year, according to the World Christian Encyclopedia, the number of denominations throughout the world surpassed 33,800, with an average of 10 new ones organized each week. (Jeffery L. Sheler, *In a Time of Division, an Urge to Merge*, U.S. News & World Report, 01-15-2001, p. 46.)

circle (around) *v.t.*: **girdle**. SEE SURROUND

circular (or spiraling motion an ocean current) *n.*: **gyre**. SEE SPIRALING

(2) circular (argument, as in begging the question) *n.*: **petitio principii** [Latin]. SEE BEGGING THE QUESTION

circulate (as in to spread news or a rumor about) *v.t.*: **bruit**. SEE RUMOR

circulating (as in surrounding) *adj.*: **ambient**. SEE SURROUNDING

circumstance (which is difficult or complex) *n.*: **nodus**. SEE COMPLICATION

(2) circumstance (occurring necessarily by force of ...) *adv.*: **perforce**. SEE NECESSARILY

citizen (of a town) *n.*: **burgher**. SEE RESIDENT

city (as in urban region) *n.*: **conurbation**. SEE METROPOLIS

(2) city (populated by persons from many countries or backgrounds) *n.*: **cosmopolis**. SEE DIVERSITY

(3) city (densely populated ... or region) *n.*: **megalopolis**. SEE CROWDED

Civil War (period prior to) *adj.*: **ante-bellum** [Latin]. ▮ Williamsburg itself is probably the most important historic town in the US, and was one of the last Confederate towns to fall during the Civil War. It has perfectly preserved **ante-bellum** buildings — dating from the 18th-Century. (Doc Holiday, *Mirror Travel: How to Roll Up in Olden Virginia*, The Mirror, 11-25-2000, p. 46.)

civilities (relating to ..., where the purpose is to establish a mood of sociability rather than to communicate information or ideas, such as "have a nice day") *adj.*: **phatic**. SEE PLEASANTRIES

claim (or take for oneself without right) *v.t.*: **arrogate**. ▮ Where the Olympic Charter goes astray is [where the International Olympic Committee] **arrogates** for itself Supreme Authority. When you're eight years old and have broken the antique crystal decanter, your mother is the supreme authority. So too are the deities in various, but not all, religions. Men in blazers, who have become powerful and imperious as a result of the Olympics, don't qualify. (Paul A. Witteman, *Essay: Less Wretched Excess, Please*, Time, 08-17-1992, p. 72.)

(2) claim (as in assert) *v.t.*: **asseverate** SEE DECLARE

(3) claim (or take for oneself without permission) *v.t.*: **expropriate**. SEE SEIZE

clairvoyant *adj.*: **fey**. ▮ Crow is particularly **fey** when it comes to the economic future. He even knows precisely how much the Phoenix metropolitan area needs to invest to capture the next big thing for ourselves: $500 million to $600 million a year in fundamental science expenditures, at least half of it on biological endeavors. (Robert Robb, *Let's Keep Arizona's Economy 'Cool' — Not Chase It*, The Arizona Republic, 11-11-2001, p. V5.)

clamor (and confusion, esp. from simultaneous voices) *n.*: **babel**. SEE NOISE

(2) clamor *n.*: **bruit**. SEE DIN

clamorous *adj.*: **strepitous**. SEE LOUD

clandestine (activity) *n.*: **hugger-mugger**. SEE SECRECY

(2) clandestine (as in, of or relating to a court, legislative body or other group that meets in private, and often makes decisions which are harsh or arbitrary) *adj.*: **star chamber**. SEE CLOSED-DOOR

clap (persons hired to ... at a performance) *n.*: **claque**. SEE APPLAUD

clarification *n.*: **éclaircissement** [French] ▮ It is the scope of the tale to recapture some, if not all, of the lost memories of an architect named Jorn. ... Early on in the text the starting point for Jorn's gradual **éclaircissement** is described. ... After the war and during Jorn's adolescence his insights and experiences increase, but there is never a linear progression of his development. (Franz P. Haberl, *Der Fehlende Rest*, World Literature Today, 09-22-1997, p. 777.)

class (lowest ... of society) *n.*: **lumpenproletariat**. SEE UNDERCLASS

classy *adj.*: **nobby** [British]. SEE ELEGANT

clay (relating to, resembling or containing) *adj.*: **argillaceous**. ▮ Next day brother and I had to go further than the last row of peach trees in the orchard to fetch some potter's clay. My uncle came with us and, touching the **argillaceous** earth, pinching it with his agile fingers, he said, "This must be the best clay in the world," and I knew he would make a vase of this clay. (Ana Doina, *Village* [Poem], The North American Review, 01-01-2001.)

clean slate *n.*: **tabula rasa**. SEE BLANK SLATE

clean up (a book or a writing in a prudish manner) *v.t.*: **bowdlerize**. SEE EDIT

cleaning woman *n.*: **charwoman**. SEE MAID

cleaning (material or device) *n.*: **abstergent**. ▮ Regarding **abstergents**, I was glad to learn that medievals used hay balls and sticks to clean themselves [of human excrement which got on the body while using it as fertilizer], while Rabelais' Gargantua employed a live goose to do his dirty work. (Adam Bresnick, *Baedeker for the Bowels*, Los Angeles Times, 11-14-1999, p. 8.)

cleanse *v.t., v.i.*: **depurate**. ∎ It wasn't long ago when the bay's surface was covered with an oily sheen and Ed Dumont was as likely to haul up a bottle as a clam. Now, the clammers can see clear to the bay floor. Over the winter, they were allowed to clam a section of the Navesink River without having to **depurate** the clams. (Debra Lynn Vial, *Tide Turns for Clammers*, The Record, 05-27-1997, p. A1.)

cleansing (of the body) *n.*: **ablution**. ∎ In my little down-Maine coastal growing-up town (the date would be 1918) ... we had the town water piped in. However, there were times that the bathtub faucet delivered a rich, chocolate-brown fluid that was a bit too brisk for tidy **ablutions**. (John Gould, *How Baby Joe's Bath Made the Town Come Clean*, The Christian Science Monitor, 08-07-1998, p. 13.)

(2) cleansing (like detergent) *v.t.*: **detersive**. ∎ Anionic surfactants are very effective detergents, and while they may be well suited for "clarifying" products, their **detersive** action may be too harsh in other systems, completely stripping the hair of its natural oils and lipids, and leaving the hair dull and brittle. (Marianne P. Berthiaume, *Formulation of Conditioning Shampoos*, Drug & Cosmetic Industry, 05-01-1997, p. 54.)

clear (in thought or expression) *adj.*: **pellucid**. ∎ Mr. Richardson, author of the magnificent "A Life of Picasso," two volumes of which have appeared, is a shrewd judge of character. He's also the master of a **pellucid** prose that makes his portraits all the more powerful. (Author not given, *Larger Than Life, 20th-Century Standouts, Both the Very Good and the Marvelously Bad*, The Washington Times, 12-16-2001.)

(2) clear (like glass) *adj.*: **hyaline**. SEE GLASSY

(3) clear (as in understandable) *adj.*: **limpid**. SEE UNDERSTANDABLE

(4) clear (as in understandable) *adj.*: **perspicuous**. SEE UNDERSTANDABLE

(5) clear (as in unambiguous) *adj.*: **univocal**. SEE UNAMBIGUOUS

clearing up (as in clarification) *n.*: **éclaircissement** [French]. SEE CLARIFICATION

clenching (or grinding of teeth during sleep) *n.*: **bruxism**. SEE GRINDING

clergy (government by ...) *n.*: **hierocracy**. SEE GOVERNMENT

clergyman (replacement ...) *n.*: **locum tenens**. SEE TEMPORARY

clever (line) *n.*: **bon mot** [French]. SEE QUIP

(2) clever (as in resourceful, person) *n.*: **debrouillard** (or **débrouillard**) [French]. SEE RESOURCEFUL

cliché *n.*: **bromide**. ∎ [In *Authentically Black: Essays for the Black Silent Majority*, John McWhorter] attacks "so-called black leaders" and scheming "white leftists" who peddle the **bromide** of black "victimization" over the balm of personal responsibility. "Since the late 1960s," McWhorter writes, "blacks have been taught that presenting ourselves and our people as victims when whites are watching is the essence of being 'authentically black.'" (Brian Palmer, *Black Like Who?* Newsday, 02-21-2003.)

(2) cliché *n.*: **platitude**. ∎ The night of that bowling date, we're sitting on a couch at Rebecca's house. The air is electric, fed by our percolating hormones. I seize the moment with a question: "What's going on here?" "Well, Brian. I love you." The L-word? Twice in one day? Since running from the room isn't an option, I stutter out a **platitude**. "Love is a big step, you know." (Joshua Mooney, *What I Learned From My Sex Coach*, Men's Health, 04-01-1998, p. 130.)

cliff (steep ...) *n.*: **escarpment**. ∎ "We're gonna have to walk from here," Mr. Hayes tells me as he parks the truck at the bottom of an **escarpment** that — to my middle-aged legs and lungs — seems to shoot straight up. This is a harsh and desolate yet colorful environment: a rocky, sun-scorched palette of gray cliffs and brick-red buttes. (Tom Verde, *Indian Cliff-Dwelling Ruins Still Impressive, Mysterious*, The Washington Times, 02-19-2000, p. E3.)

climbing (esp. too high for safety) *adj.*: **Icarian**. SEE SOARING

clinging *adj.*: **osculant**. SEE HUGGING

clocks (science of making ... or watches) *n.*: **horology**. SEE TIME

clomp (as in move heavily or clumsily) *v.i.*: **galumph**. SEE TROMP

close (up) *v.t.*: **occlude**. SEE BLOCK

closed-door (of or relating to a court, legislative body or other group that meets in private, and often makes decisions which are harsh or arbitrary) *adj.*: **star chamber** [This term derives from a courtroom in England that existed until 1641, which sat in closed session and which had stars on its ceiling]. ∎ [A] national problem [is that] colleges and universities are secretly "adjudicating" and hiding crimes as serious as sexual assault. Colleges hide crimes using **star chamber**-type proceedings to protect their enrollment and alumni donations from bad publicity. Unfortunately, they are accountable to nobody. They leave victims without justice and the student body at large at undue risk. (Author not given, *Crimes on Campus*, The Washington Post, 03-11-2002.)

closed-minded (person who hates reasoning or enlightenment) *n.:* **misologist**. ∎ The typical rationalist's antipathy toward religion, like the **misologist's** resentment of intellectualism, is born of a misconception based on models and definitions that have given an incomplete picture at best or have been caricatures and travesties. (Larry A. Gray, *To Bind Again [Humanist Ideals in Religious Thought and Doctrines]*, The Humanist, 03-01-2001.)

(2) closed-minded *adj.:* **hidebound**. SEE NARROW-MINDED

(3) closed-minded (as in one who clings to an opinion or belief even after being shown that it is wrong) *n.:* **mumpsimus**. SEE STUBBORN

closeness (in place, time or relation) *n.:* **propinquity**. ∎ He marched up for nose-to-nose contact, and in spite or our **propinquity**, shouted: "You've got something to say to me?" (Tabor Fischer, *The Thought Gang*, The New Press [1994], p. 219.)

clothe (as in outfit or equip) *v.t.:* **accouter**. SEE OUTFIT

(2) clothe (or adorn in a showy or excessive manner) *v.t.:* **bedizen**. SEE ADORN

clothed (being partially, carelessly or casually ...) *n.:* **dishabille** [French]. SEE ATTIRED

clothes *n.:* **habiliment(s)**. SEE CLOTHING

clothier (for men) *n.:* **haberdasher**. ∎ The outlook for menswear retailers is, in fact, bright, insisted Len Kubas, president of Kubas Consultants, in Toronto. [One] reason for **haberdashers** to be optimistic [is that] the casual clothing sector is seeing yet another wave of U.S. retailers coming to Canada. (Steven Theobald, *Menswear Ripe for Consolidation*, The Toronto Star, 12-29-2000.)

clothing (showy article of ...) *n.:* **froufrou**. ∎ The color-splashed cartoon couture of French fashion sensation Christian Lacroix may be fine for playful Parisiennes, but what's a working woman to do? Impress a client by turning up in a bustle? Show up for a board meeting wearing a **froufrou**? (Mary Vespa, *Style*, People, 11-23-1987, p. 149.)

(2) clothing *n.:* **habiliment(s)**. ∎ Any one coming to London for the first time would be shocked at the extraordinary departure from the regulation black **habiliments** of an old-time Londoner's wardrobe to the wildest extravagances based on the time-honored elements of the rainbow and developed into half-holiday superlatives of a color mixer's dreams. (Author not given, *In Our Pages: 100, 75 and 50 Years Ago: 1897: Wild Fashion*, International Herald Tribune, 07-12-1997.)

(3) clothing *n.:* **raiment**. ∎ The All England Clubbies [at the Wimbledon Tennis Club] were quaking, remembering the 1972 contretemps over little Rosie Casals' nifty little dress adorned with violet squiggles. The frocked-up Casals was ordered to leave Court One and change to the prescribed "predominantly white" **raiment** forthwith. Presumably, the offending gown was sent to the Tower to be drawn-and-quartered. (Bud Collins, *Wimbledon 2001: Agassi at Peak of Arrogant Artistry*, Independent, 06-25-2001, p. 6.)

(4) clothing (richly ornamented) *n.:* **caparison**. SEE FINERY

(5) clothing (and equipment for newborn baby) *n.:* **layette**. SEE NEWBORN

cloud (type of ... which is dense, white and fluffy) *n.:* **cumulus**. ∎ Humidity in the air condenses to form puffy, **cumulus** clouds, which can grow to produce showers or even thunderstorms. (Bill Leonard, *Clouds Often Mark Seabreeze Front*, USA Today, 07-07-1994, p. 12.)

(2) cloud (low dark gray ... which precedes rain) *n.:* **nimbostratus**. ∎ **Nimbostratus** clouds follow next, bringing with them a gray day. Rain tends to be widespread, coming steadily or in long showers alternating with drizzle. (Eliot Tozer, *An Eye to the Sky*, Horticulture, The Art of American Gardening, 03-01-1998, p. 58.)

(3) cloud (over one's vision) *v.t.:* **obnubilate**. SEE OBSCURE

clouds (used of ... which are luminous at night) *adj.:* **noctilucent**. ∎ The clouds are called **noctilucent** because they are visible long after dusk. They float 50 miles up, Thomas said, reflecting sunlight during the long twilight hours of summer months in polar regions. (Robert Cooke, *A Lovely Glow in Sky Signals Ugly Warning*, Newsday, 05-31-1994, p. B29.)

clown (one who resembles a short, fat ...) *n.:* **Punchinello**. ∎ The ringmaster, a hunchbacked **Punchinello** with bright red coat and bright red hair, is only one performer among many. (John Gross, *The Arts: Incredible Feats Amid the Flames*, The Sunday Telegraph, 01-11-1998.)

(2) clown (as in buffoon, who is sometimes boastful) *n.*: **Scaramouch**. SEE BUFFOON

club (as in to beat with a ...) *v.t.*: **cudgel**. ∎ They were **cudgeling** people who could barely raise an arm in self-protection. (Daniel Goldhagen, *Hitler's Willing Executioners*, Knopf [1996], p. 357.)

(2) club (as in nightclub or cabaret) *n.*: **boîte** [French]. SEE NIGHTCLUB

clue (to solving a puzzle or deciphering a code which has not previously been solved or deciphered) *n.*: **Rosetta stone** [derives from a tablet found in 1799 in Rosetta, Egypt which furnished the first clues to deciphering Egyptian hieroglyphics]. ∎ Cancer researchers say they've discovered a tumor-control gene which, when abnormal, leads to several types of cancer. ... "They've hit upon the **Rosetta stone** of cancer study," said Marston Linehan of the National Cancer Institute. ... "We are already tremendously impressed and excited to hear about it." (Author not given, *Rosetta Stone of Cancer Study*, Newsday, 02-24-1996.)

clueless (as in intellectually or morally unenlightened) *adj.*: **benighted**. SEE UNENLIGHTENED

(2) clueless (as in ignorant) *adj.*: **nescient** (*n.*: **nescience**). SEE IGNORANT

clumsy (like an elephant) *adj.*: **elephantine**. ∎ The bureaucracy in a company that employs 526,000 people [Sears] is **elephantine**, out of touch with the consumer, and too unwieldy to coordinate change. (Patricia Sellers, *Selling: Why Bigger Is Badder at Sears*, Fortune, 12-05-1988, p. 79.)

(2) clumsy (and awkward boy) *n.*: **hobbledehoy**. ∎ To hear Republicans tell it, however, Clinton remains a **hobbledehoy**, stuck in the immature foreign policy of what might be called his first term, the period from 1992 to 1994. (Jacob Heilbrun, *Univisionary [Bill Clinton's Foreign Policy]*, The New Republic, 11-11-1996, p. 6.)

(3) clumsy *adj.*: **lumpish**. ∎ Farley may make people feel better, but his character, Tommy Callahan, just makes them nervous. Ever since he was a kid, the **lumpish** youth has been walking into glass doors and making a shambles of his life and furniture. (John Anderson, *Farley and Spade's "SNL" Skit Gone Long*, Newsday, 03-31-1995, p. B2.)

(4) clumsy (habitually ... person) *n.*: **schlemiel** [Yiddish]. SEE BUMBLER

cluster (of riders in a bike race) *n.*: **peloton** [French]. ∎ [Bicycle racer Greg LeMond] conquers the hills. He conquers the flat-out sprints. He conquers the piranhas of the **peloton**, the grand mass of 197 riders that surrounds him. (Leigh Montville, *Triumph*, Sports Illustrated, 07-30-1990, p. 16.)

(2) cluster (of objects, people or ideas) *n.*: **congeries**. SEE COLLECTION

(3) cluster (as in group) *n.*: **gaggle**. SEE GROUP

clutching (adapted for ..., esp. a tail) *adj.*: **prehensile**. SEE GRASPING

clutter (as in confusion) *n., adj.*: **hugger-mugger**. SEE CONFUSION

co-worker (as in colleague) *n.*: **confrere**. SEE COLLEAGUE

coach *v.t.*: **catechize**. SEE TEACH

(2) coach (as in teacher) *n.*: **pedagogue**. SEE TEACHER

coarse (language) *n.*: **billingsgate**. SEE LANGUAGE

(2) coarse (woman who is also abusive) *n.*: **fishwife**. SEE WOMAN

(3) coarse (or poorly put together, esp. with respect to a writing or speech) *adj.*: **incondite**. SEE CRUDE

coastline *n.*: (of or on a ...) *adj.*: **littoral**. SEE SHORE

coaxing (by flattery) *n.*: **blandishment** (*v.t.*: **blandish**). SEE FLATTERY

(2) coaxing (to win over or obtain by ...) *v.t.*: **inveigle**. SEE LURE

cocky (and vain) *adj.*: **vainglorious**. SEE BOASTFUL

coddle *n., v.t.*: **wet-nurse**. ∎ [Tennis coach Nick Bollettieri on deciding to stop coaching Mary Pierce:] "It's been coming for quite a while now. Mary has to get her own coach. She needs somebody. I refuse to go on baby-sitting for Mary Pierce; I am not going to **wet-nurse** her. She has to commit herself all over again to her career." (Author not given, *Old Hand Woodforde Advances to Quarterfinals*, USA Today, 01-21-1996.)

(2) coddle *v.t.*: **cosset**. SEE PAMPER

(3) coddle (in an overprotective way or indulge) *v.t.*: **mollycoddle**. SEE OVERPROTECT

code (as in figure of speech, where a part is used to stand for the whole or vice versa) *n.*: **synecdoche**. SEE FIGURE OF SPEECH

code name *n.*: **cryptonym**. ∎ [There was] a decade-long effort [by U.S. intelligence] to encourage a military coup in Iraq. For much of that time, the secret coup plot was known within the CIA by the **cryptonym** "DBACHILLES." Now, with Saddam Hussein's regime deposed, U.S. and Iraqi sources have provided a detailed account of a coup strategy that never delivered. (David Ignatius, *The CIA and the Coup That Wasn't*, The Washington Post, 05-16-2003.)

code words (spec. words conveying an innocent meaning to an outsider but with a concealed meaning to an informed person, often to avoid censorship or punishment) *n.*: **Aesopian language** ∎ Previously [in the Soviet Union], students and teachers were forced to follow patently false and hypocritical programs of history and social thought. Any opposition was forced into covert speech in **Aesopian language**. Extraordinarily sharp political jokes and anecdotes abounded — the dark humor of suffering. (Irwin Weil, *The USSR's Creative Democrats Refused to Be Cowed*, Chicago Tribune, 08-23-1991.)

codes (secret ... hidden in various forms of communication) *n.*: **steganography**. ∎ [Some] who monitor terrorism decry **steganography** as a threat, it's also a liberating tool for people in countries like China, where Internet blocks, or "firewalls," prevent citizens from learning anything that is not advantageous to the regime. "For every Al Qaeda member who's using **steganography** to hide something, there's someone else using it to aid the democratic process," argues Diebert. (Olivia Ward, *Global Terror Battle Moves to Net*, The Toronto Star, 09-07-2003, p. A14.)

coerce (to act, esp. by violent measures or threats) *v.t.*: **dragoon**. ∎ If the men and women using and **dragooning** slave laborers are included (over 7.6 million in the German Reich in August 1944), then the numbers of Germans who perpetrated grievous crimes might run into the millions. (Daniel Goldhagen, *Hitler's Willing Executioners*, Knopf [1996], p. 166.)

(2) coerce (or trick someone into doing something, esp. by fraud) *v.t.*: **shanghai** (person who does so, *n.*: **shanghaier**.) ∎ They live apart and she can't remember the date they got married. But Carmen Electra wants the world to know that she is very definitely Mrs. Dennis Rodman and that she's not a gold-digging, NBA-star **shanghaier**. "We are legally married," the actress and singer said yesterday. "We love each other very much and we're doing

great." (Claire Bickley, *Together, Whatever; Marriage to Rodman's Real, Though Bizarre, Electra Says*, The Edmonton Sun, 01-08-1999, p. WE22.)

(3) coerce (a person or group to go from one place to another, whether literally or figuratively) *v.t.*: **frogmarch**. SEE MARCH

cognizant (as in consciously perceiving) *adj.*: **sentient**. SEE CONSCIOUS

cohabitation (as in marriage or sexual relations involving people of different races) *n.*: **miscegenation**. SEE SEX

coincidence (as in discovering fortunate things by accident) *n.*: **serendipity** (*adj.*: **serendipitous**). SEE FORTUITOUS

coins (of or relating to ..., including collecting) *adj.*: **numismatic**. ∎ [T]here are some very legitimate **numismatic** collectibles being promoted. For instance, the U.S. Mint regularly advertises highly polished mirror proof and uncirculated American coins — real coins that collectors eagerly snap up. (Peter Rexford, *How to Tell if Coin is a Good Investment*, St. Louis Post-Dispatch, 09-21-1995, p. 3G.)

cold *adj.*: **algid**. ∎ Anyone who has read Paul Theroux's *Riding the Iron Rooster, By Train Through China* will know of the wonders of Harbin, the **algid** Chinese city where remarkable ice sculptures remain all winter long. (William Furney, *N'ice and Easy Does it at Ice Carving Contest*, The Jakarta Post, 07-09-2000.)

(2) cold (of or relating to very ... temperatures) *adj.*: **cryogenic**. ∎ To deal with the outlaws [in the movie Demolition Man set in 2032], Cocteau frees a killer named Simon Phoenix (Wesley Snipes) from **cryogenic** prison (they took to deep-freezing criminals as early as 1996, during the last convulsive phase of urban warfare). (Richard Schickel, *The Arts*, Time International, 11-01-1993, p. 47.)

(3) cold (causing or producing) *adj.*: **frigorific**. ∎ Boston is ill-equipped for [a Mardi Gras-type celebration]. Picture it: people exposing sensitive body parts in the **frigorific** breezes. It just wouldn't happen, and if it did, these raucous individuals would be picked up for indecent exposure or end up at [the hospital]. Generally with painful and unusual cases of frostbite. (Christopher Muther, *Go! Tuesday*, The Boston Globe, 02-12-2002, p. E2.)

(4) cold (very ...) *adj.*: **gelid**. ∎ It's evening [in December]. I begin to walk across the parking lot toward my hotel. My exhalations are steamy in the **gelid** air. Suddenly, my feet slide out from under me on a sheer patch of ice. (Mark Leyner, *Xmas in Newark*, Esquire, 12-01-1997, p. 52.)

(5) cold (as in of, like or occurring in winter) *adj.*: **brumal**. SEE WINTER

(6) cold (very ...) *adj.*: **hyperborean**. SEE FREEZING

cold-blooded *adj.*: **ectothermic** ∎ The assumption that dinosaurs were **ectothermic** — cold-blooded — was originally based on a simple argument. Reptiles are **ectothermic** — they can't regulate their body heat. If they get too hot, they die. If they get too cold, they get sluggish. Dinosaurs were closely related to reptiles. End of argument. (Michael D. Lemonick, *Science: Rewriting the Book on Dinosaurs*, Time, 04-26-1993, p. 42.)

coldness (often in relations between people) *n.*: **froideur** [French]. SEE CHILLINESS

collapse (violent or turbulent ... of a society or regime) *n.*: **götterdämmerung** [German]. ∎ What did happen to Hitler in the **Gotterdammerung** of the Third Reich? The widely accepted version ... is that on April 30, 1945, Hitler committed suicide in his command bunker in Berlin and that his body was burned in the garden just outside, as he had expressly ordered. (Julie K. Dam, Time International, 05-08-1995, p. 45.)

(2) collapse (of a group or social structure as a result of lack of standards or values) *n.*: **anomie**. SEE BREAKDOWN

(3) collapse (as in downfall, esp. from a position of strength or condition) *n.*: **dégringolade** [French]. SEE DOWNFALL

colleague *n.*: **confrere**. ∎ [Lamar Alexander] defends the environmental legislation that his congressional **confreres** are trying to gut, arguing that Republicans "should be the champions of the great outdoors ... of clean air, clean water, an open space to walk in. Our party is doing a poor job on conservation." (Ruth Shalit, *Sinking, Shining Tennessean: On the Road with Lamar Alexander*, The New Republic, 02-26-1996, p. 18.)

(2) colleague (faithful ..., as in companion) *n.*: **Achates**. SEE COMPANION

(3) colleague (as in comrade) *n.*: **tovarich** [Russian]. SEE COMRADE

collect (as in assemble, clumsily, roughly or hastily) *v.t.*: **cobble** SEE ASSEMBLE

collected (as in unemotional or even-tempered) *adj.*: **phlegmatic**. SEE EVEN-TEMPERED

collection (of objects, people or ideas) *n.*: **congeries**. ∎ Unlike touch or taste, pain is not a simple sensation. It involves a complex **congeries** of senses, memories, attitudes, and emotions that affect how people perceive pain and how their bodies respond to it. (Gene Bylinsky, *Health: New Gains in the Fight Against Pain*, Fortune, 03-22-1993, p. 107.)

(2) collection (confused or jumbled ...) *n.*: **agglomeration**. SEE JUMBLE

(3) collection (of writings by an author) *n.*: **chrestomathy**. SEE ANTHOLOGY

collision (spec. the act of one object striking a stationary object, usually applied to ships) *n.*: **allision**. ∎ The analysis said more than 300 collisions and "**allisions**," which involve a moving vessel striking a stationary object, have occurred in the Port of New Orleans in the last 10 years. (George F. W. Tefler, *Casinos in New Orleans Port Increase Risks, Report Says*, Journal of Commerce, 11-11-1994, p. 1B.)

colloquial (language of the people) *n.*: **vulgate**. SEE VERNACULAR

color (relating to ... or colors) *adj.*: **chromatic**. ∎ New York designers have wiped the slate clean of all that is dark, drab and dreary. Whether such colourful optimism is authentic or wishful thinking, this funky, **chromatic** vibration embraces spring's sleek, sexy clothing with lightness and brightness. (Sylvi Capelaci, *Colour Report*, The Ottawa Sun, 02-15-2000, p. 28.)

(2) color (having only one ...) *adj.*: **monochromatic**. ∎ Turns out, quiz-show host Regis Philbin, a newly minted menswear purveyor, is the one legislating this summer's hot new look: a men's cotton dress shirt with a glossy necktie in the same color — solid black, tan, blue or green. [Several designers] have sent the **monochromatic** look down the runways. (Francine Parnes, *"Millionaire's" Philbin Sets the Style*, The Washington Times, 07-26-2000, p. C8.)

colorblindness (total ...) *n.*: **achromatopsia**. ∎ Olof Sundin, an assistant professor of ophthalmology at Johns Hopkins and a co-investigator of the **achromatopsia** study, said the condition results from the lack of a protein required for color detection and optimal daytime sight. (Delthia Ricks, *Origins of Our Diversity*, Newsday, 06-27-2000, p. D13.)

colorful (esp. in an iridescent way) *adj.*: **opalescent**. SEE IRIDESCENT

coloring (of or relating to ..., as in dyeing) *adj.:* **tinctorial**. SEE DYEING

colorless *adj.:* **achromatic**. ∎ Men also typically dream in black and white. ... **Achromatic** dreaming probably reflects the fact that men have more rigid boundaries — between thoughts and emotions, right and wrong, sanity and madness — than women do. (Michael Segell, *Dreams: His and Hers*, Esquire, 02-01-1996, p. 42.)

colors (use of many ..., esp. in paintings, statues and works of art) *n.:* **polychromy**. ∎ Riemenschneider was one of the first to abandon **polychromy**, relying on wood transfigured by his own virtuosic technique to boost religious devotion. ... Avoiding color was a way to make his sculptures more safely abstract, distancing them from the accusations of idolatry that the Reformation continuously hurled at religious art. (Ariella Budick, *Sculpting an Enduring Name for a Gothic Great*, Newsday, 02-10-2000, p. B35.)

(2) colors (having many ...) *n.:* **polychromatic**. SEE MULTICOLORED

combat (act or event which causes or provokes ...) *n.:* **casus belli** [Latin; occasion of war]. SEE PROVOCATION

combative *adj.:* **agonistic**. ∎ Within weeks, the two had begun a complex, occasionally adulterous, often **agonistic** but enduringly loving relationship. (George W. Stocking, Jr., *The Forest Person*, The New York Times, 12-10-2000.)

(2) combative *adj.:* **bellicose**. SEE BELLIGERENT

combine *v.t.:* **amalgamate**. ∎ A key part of the program's ideology is to have special-needs children mix with other Jewish day-school pupils as much as possible [which] allows them "to see themselves more as normal children." Moreover, Leberman believes that **amalgamating** classes also helps the community as a whole. (Author not given, *A Light Unto the Schools*, Jewish Exponent, 03-18-1999, p. 1.)

(2) combine (as in bring together) *v.t.:* **conflate**. ∎ The women who passed through [Jerry Lewis'] life are cast by his words as mothers, not sex partners [Lewis often claimed that "they wanted to burp me"]. ... It would be cheap Freudianism to suggest that he slept around because his mother hadn't shown him sufficient love, but he was the one who repeatedly **conflated** extramarital sex with the care and feeding of an infant. (Shawn Levy, *The King of Comedy*, St. Martin's Press [1996], p. 95.)

(3) combine (in a series or chain) *v.t., adj.:* **concatenate** (*n.:* **concatenation**). SEE CONNECT

(4) combine *v.t., v.i.:* **inosculate**. SEE BLEND

combined (closely ...) *adj.:* **coadunate**. SEE JOINED

(2) combined (of things that cannot be ...) *adj.:* **immiscible**. SEE INCOMPATIBLE

come in (suddenly or forcibly, as in burst in) *v.i.:* **irrupt**. SEE BURST IN

come to pass (as in happen or occur) *v.t.:* **betide**. SEE HAPPEN

come up with (an idea, plan, theory or explanation after careful thought) *v.t.:* **excogitate**. SEE DEVISE

comeback (of something after a period of dormancy or inactivity) *n.:* **recrudescence** (*v.i.:* **recrudesce**). SEE REAPPEARANCE

(2) comeback (clever ... that one thinks of after the moment has passed) *n.:* **esprit d'escalier** [French]. SEE RETORT

comedown (as in anticlimax) *n.:* **bathos**. SEE ANTICLIMAX

comeliness *n.:* **pulchritude**. SEE BEAUTY

comes back (one who ... after lengthy absence or death) *n.:* **revenant**. SEE RETURNS

comfort (as in placate) *v.t.:* **propitiate**. SEE PLACATE

comfortable (as in warm and cozy) *adj.:* **gemütlich** [German]. SEE COZY

comforting (agent) *n.:* **anodyne**. SEE PAIN-RELIEVER AND SOOTHING

(2) comforting (lotion or balm) *n.:* **demulcent**. SEE SOOTHING

comical *adj.:* **gelastic**. SEE LAUGHABLE

(2) comical *adj.:* **risible**. SEE LAUGHABLE

coming-of-age (spec. a novel which follows the development of its main character over time) *n.:* **bildungsroman** [German]. ∎ Taken as a whole, the trilogy is a **bildungsroman** about Patrick Melrose — a damaged 5-year-old in the first novel, a 22-year-old junkie in the second and, in the third, a drug-free 30-year-old trying to put the past behind him. (Leo Carey, *A Bag of Heroin and a Crisp White Shirt*, The New York Times, 01-04-2004.)

command (as in order or direct) *v.t.:* **adjure**. SEE ORDER

commander *n.*: **duce** [Italian]. ■ [In Bosnia and Kosovo, Serbian leader] Slobodan Milosevic unleashed a violent campaign of terror against an ethnicity that represents a challenge to the legitimacy of his rule and its fascist, racialist foundations. Once again it took a particular bloodbath to concentrate the minds of Washington, New York, and Brussels on the policies of the **duce** of Serbia. (Author not given, *The Villain*, The New Republic, 10-26-1998.)

(2) commander (or ruler, esp. hereditary) *n.*: **dynast**. SEE RULER

commendation *n.*: **approbation**. SEE PRAISE

comment (as in insight or observation) *n.*: **aperçu** [French]. SEE INSIGHT

(2) comment (in which one references an issue by saying that they will not discuss it; e.g. "I'm not even going to get into the character issue") *n.*: **apophasis**. SEE FIGURE OF SPEECH

(3) comment (or expression or phrase which is elegant, concise, witty and/or well-put) *n.*: **atticism**. SEE EXPRESSION

(4) comment (on a topic, esp. in a long-winded or pompous manner) *v.i.*: **bloviate**. SEE SPEAK

(5) comment (upon, esp. at length) *v.i., n.*: **descant**. SEE TALK

(6) comment (or line which is witty) *n.*: **epigram**. SEE QUIP

(7) comment (on in a scholarly manner, often used in a derogatory fashion) *v.i.*: **lucubrate**. SEE DISCOURSE

commingled (of things that cannot be ...) *adj.*: **immiscible**. SEE INCOMPATIBLE

common (of or relating to the ... people) *adj.*: **plebian**. ■ [Queen] Victoria worked on two levels: She liked **plebian** pleasures, such as those offered by the showman P.T. Barnum and his midget Tom Thumb [but she also liked art,] ballet and the opera. (Stanley Weintraub, *In His Own Words: Victorian in Name Only, the Queen Was Amused in the Bedroom and Elsewhere*, People, 06-22-1987, p. 58.)

(2) common (the ... people, as in the masses) *n.*: **canaille**. SEE MASSES

(3) common (pertaining to the ... people) *adj.*: **demotic**. SEE MASSES

(4) common (in tastes and ideas and culture) *adj.*: **philistine**. SEE UNCULTURED

(5) common (as in mundane; everyday) *adj.*: **sublunary**. SEE EARTHLY

(6) common (language of the people) *n.*: **vulgate**. SEE VERNACULAR

commoners *n.*: **hoi polloi**. ■ Fame has style, glamour, money, attention; ignites the sudden light of recognition in strangers' eyes, commands the comic deference of headwaiters as they sweep you past the serfs and **hoi polloi** to the best table. (Lance Morrow, *Fame Offers Delights and Burdens, Boredom And — Especially — Menace*, Time, 09-15-1997, p. 76.)

commonplace *adj.*: **quotidian**. SEE MUNDANE

common sense (person who hates ... or enlightenment) *n.*: **misologist**. See CLOSED-MINDED

commotion *n.*: **maelstrom**. ■ Monica Lewinsky — The former White House intern is at the center of the **maelstrom**, alleged to have had an extended sexual liaison with [President] Clinton. (Linda Feldmann, *The Stakes Suddenly Rise for Clinton*, The Christian Science Monitor, 01-23-1998, p. 1)

(2) commotion *n.*: **pother**. ■ Australia's arts community is in a colossal **pother**. On March 7 it was revealed that the supposedly Aboriginal painter Mr. Eddie Burrup, whose daubings have recently been the wow of Australian museum curators and gallery owners, is no Aborigine at all. Mr. Burrup is actually an 82-year-old woman of Irish descent, Miss Elizabeth Durack. (Author not given, *The Continuing Crisis: Al Gets Chinese, the Danes Get Wild*, The American Spectator, 05-01-1997.)

(3) commotion (and confusion, esp. from simultaneous voices) *n.*: **babel**. SEE NOISE

(4) commotion (over a trifling matter) *n.*: **foofaraw**. SEE FUSS

companion (faithful ...) *n.*: **Achates** (often as in "fidus Achates," "fidus" being Latin for "faithful") [derives from Achates, who was a close companion of Aeneas in Virgil's Aeneid]. ■ In my teens, [Tony Mulligan] was the first in our little backwater who was "cool." ... I cultivated him like a hothouse plant. And then I noticed the second advantage to being his fidus **Achates** — girls. He was exceptionally popular with girls — all of the good-looking, clean and clever ones that nobody else could get near. (Dennis O'Donnell, *Words of Wisdom: An Open-Sesame to the World of Romance*, The Scotsman, 11-13-1998, p. 20.)

communicate (as in send a signal) *v.t., v.i.*: **semaphore**. SEE SIGNAL

communication (medium of ... between people of

different languages) *n.*: **lingua franca**. See LAN-GUAGE

(2) communication (with the dead or their spirits) *n.*: **necromancy**. See DIVINATION

community (Spanish-speaking) *n.*: **barrio**. See SPANISH

compacted (something ..., as in abridged) *n.*: **bobtail**. See ABRIDGED

companion (as in comrade) *n.*: **tovarich** [Russian]. See COMRADE

compare (by way of setting in contrast) *adv.*: **per contra**. See CONTRAST

(2) compare (by way of setting in contrast) *v.t.*: **counterpose**. See CONTRAST

compassion (relating to an argument appealing to one's sense of ...) *adv., adj.*: **ad misericordium** [Latin]. See ARGUMENT

compatibility (in the arrangement of parts as part of a whole) *n.*: **concinnity**. See HARMONY

compatible *adj.*: **simpatico**. ▪ Hundt voices the "new Democrat" themes of economic expansion and job growth. "He's very **simpatico** with the Clinton economic principles," Allard says. (Del Jones, *FCC Chief Doesn't Take His Role Lightly*, USA Today, 02-25-1994, p. 2.)

(2) compatible *adj.*: **consonant**. See HARMONY

compatriot *n.*: **paisano**. See COUNTRYMAN

compel (to act, esp. by violent measures or threats) *v.t.*: **dragoon**. See COERCE

(2) compel (a person or group to go from one place to another, whether literally or figuratively) *v.t.*: **frogmarch**. See MARCH

(3) compel (or trick someone into doing something, esp. by fraud or coercion) *v.t.*: **shanghai** (person who does so *n.*: **shanghier**). See COERCE

compelling (as in urgent) *adj.*: **necessitous**. See URGENT

compensation (as in payment or wages) *n.*: **emolument**. See WAGES

compensation (awarded for injured feelings, as opposed to financial loss or physical suffering) *n.*: **solatium**. ▪ Japan intends to review the way **solatium** payments are made to South Korean women who were forced into sexual slavery by Japanese soldiers before and during World War II,

Chief Cabinet Secretary Hiromu Nonaka indicated Monday. (Author not given, *Kyodo News Summary*, Kyodo World News Service, 05-10-1999.)

competitive *adj.*: **agonistic**. ▪ But the Greeks were a wildly **agonistic** people, which means they were keenly competitive at everything. It didn't take long before play and recreational fitness were formatted into local contests, then inter-municipal meets. (Rosie DiManno, *But If, My Heart, You Wish to Sing of Contests, Look No Further For Any Star Warmer Than the Sun*, The Toronto Star, 09-14-2000.)

complain (or fret) *v.i.*: **repine**. ▪ [Jess and her husband took] up the burden of the three aged relatives living with them, [including her] mother-in-law ... a spiteful Presbyterian. ... Not that she noticed [but Jess] was an object of pious admiration among those who did, because of her strength and selflessness and refusal to **repine**. God had a stiffer test of her character in store, though: her husband disappeared without warning, and Jess feared he had gone into the river to escape his ghastly mother. (Thomas Sutcliffe, *The Weekend's Television: Hellishly Stiff Tests of Character*, The Independent [London], 09-13-2004.)

(2) complain (as in raise trivial objections) *v.t.*: **cavil**. See QUIBBLE

(3) complain (against) *v.t.*: **expostulate**. See OBJECT

(4) complain (in a whiny or whimpering way) *v.i.*: **girn** (Scottish). See WHINE

(5) complain (about petty matters) *v.i.*: **pettifog**. See QUIBBLE

(6) complain (in a whiny or whimpering way) *v.i.*: **pule**. See WHIMPER

complaining *adj.*: **querulous**. See PEEVISH

complaint (mournful or bitter ...) *n.*: **jeremiad**. ▪ So far Perot has trained most of his fire on the Republicans. And his **jeremiads** against "mean-spirited campaigning" could make it harder for Dole to chip away at Clinton on the "character issue." (John B. Judis, *The Third Rail — Ross Perot: America's Charles de Gaulle?* The New Republic, 05-20-1996, p. 22.)

complementary (as in compatible) *adj.*: **simpatico**. See COMPATIBLE

complete (esp. as in ... power) *adj.*: **plenary**. ▪ In 1976 the [Supreme Court] held that Congress's **plenary** control over immigration gives it broad discretion to discriminate against aliens, and therefore it could restrict Medicare benefits to legal aliens who had lived in the United States for five years. "Citizens," the Court announced deferentially, "may reasonably be presumed to have a greater affinity with the United States." (Jeffrey Rosen, *The War on Immigrants: Why the Courts Can't Save Us*, The New Republic, 01-30-1995, p. 22.)

(2) complete (esp. when used with "nonsense") *adj.*: **arrant**. SEE TOTAL

completely (as in, in the entirety) *adv.*: **in extenso** [Latin]. SEE ENTIRETY

complex *adj.*: **byzantine**. SEE COMPLICATED

complex (as in difficult to understand, sometimes due to being obscure) *adj.*: **abstruse**. SEE DIFFICULT

(2) complex (in design or function, as in intricate) *adj.*: **daedal**. SEE INTRICATE

(3) complex (situation or problem) *n.*: **nodus**. SEE COMPLICATION

(4) complex (as in difficult to understand) *adj.*: **recondite**. SEE COMPLICATED

compliance (as in marked by insistence on rigid conformity to a belief, system or course of action without regard to individual differences) *adj.*: **procrustean** (*n*: **Procrustean bed**). SEE CONFORMITY

compliant *adj.*: **biddable**. SEE OBEDIENT

complicated *adj.*: **byzantine**. ∎ Political life in Reed's day was dominated by powerful "bosses," and riddled with corruption. But Reed believed profoundly in representative government. Elected speaker in 1890, he launched a frontal assault on the **byzantine** system of House rules, an intricate maze "calculated better than anything else to obstruct legislation" and frustrate the will of the majority. (Katherine Kersten, *For Integrity in Politics, Take a Lesson From Tom Reed*, Minneapolis Star Tribune, 03-12-1997, p. 17A.)

(2) complicated (as in difficult to understand) *adj.*: **recondite**. ∎ Paul Hoffman not only gives us a sympathetic and beautifully observed account of [mathematician Paul] Erdos's strange life, he also helps us to appreciate the appeal of this most **recondite** of human activities [i.e. pure mathematics]. *The Man Who Loved Only Numbers* is one of the most accessible and engaging introductions to the world of pure mathematics you are ever likely to come across. (Graham Farmelo, *Books: The Prime Numbers of Mr. Paul Erdos*, The Sunday Telegraph, 07-19-1998.)

(3) complicated (as in difficult to understand, sometimes due to being obscure) *adj.*: **abstruse**. SEE DIFFICULT

(4) complicated (situation or problem) *n.*: **nodus**. SEE COMPLICATION

complication (or difficult situation) *n.*: **nodus**. ∎ The status of Jerusalem has been the most difficult issue in the peace talks between the two sides, as Israel ... and the Palestinians [have both claimed rights to the City]. ... Meanwhile, the Knesset endorsed a bill on the return of Palestinian refugees, another **nodus** in the Israeli-Palestinian talks, in the first reading with a vote of 90 in favor and nine against. (Author not given, *Israeli Parliament Adopts Bills on Jerusalem, Palestinian Refugees*, Xinhua [China], 11-27-2000.)

compliment (as in giving praise or ...) *n.*: **encomium** (one who delivers praise or ... *n.*: **encomiast**). SEE PRAISE

(2) compliment (as in tribute) *n.*: **panegyric** (one who does so *n.*: **panegyrist**). SEE TRIBUTE

complimenting (insincerely ...) *adj.*: **fulsome**. SEE INSINCERE

comportment *n.*: **mien**. SEE DEMEANOR

compose *v.t.*: **indite**. ∎ Second on my bill of rights would be a non-write clause. It would bar forever the **inditing** of letters to the editor by those of the frail facade. Women seem to dip their pens in their visceral fluids, eschewing the black ink of logic or the green ink of pure venom. (Christine Bertelson, *Old Curmudgeon at His Very Best*, St. Louis Post-Dispatch, 07-09-1996, p. 1B.)

composed *adj.*: **equable**. SEE SERENE

(2) composed *adj.*: **phlegmatic**. SEE EVEN-TEMPERED

compositions (or artistic works created in the artist's or author's youth) *n.*: **juvenilia**. ∎ Like fox-hunting and badger-baiting, tracking down the "juvenile" works of writers and artists is a traditional British sport. Biography has never been so popular — the more revisionist the better. And **juvenilia** is one of biography's purest raw materials. (Adrian Turpin, *Drawing on Inexperience*, Independent on Sunday, 11-19-2000, p. 25.)

composure (esp. under pressure or trying circumstances) *n.*: **sang-froid** [French]. ∎ The message conveyed by [Kurt Waldheim's] demeanor [appearing with Ted Koppel on "*Nightline*"] was that he'd dealt with even ruder people than we, and that nothing could interfere with his **sang-froid**. (Ted Koppel, *Nightline*, Times Books [1996], p. 165.)

(2) composure *n.*: **ataraxy** (or **ataraxia**). SEE CALMNESS

(3) composure (in the face of adversity or suffering) *n.*: **longaminity**. SEE PATIENCE

comprehend (based on past experience) *v.t.*: **apperceive**. ▪ Here, then, is [diet book author] Allen Carr's great strength: he understands. He's been there, done that, bought the stretchy cardigan and outsize trousers. Serial slimmers, like smokers, are not so much lacking in will as they are willful. No one, after all, likes to be told what to do. This Carr has clearly **apperceived**. (Rose Shepherd, *Slim Chance*, Independent, 01-11-1997, p. 15.)

(2) comprehend (inability to ... spoken or written words due to brain injury) *n.*: **aphasia**. SEE UNCOMPREHENDING

(3) comprehend (difficult to ...) *adj.*: **recondite**. SEE COMPLICATED

comprehensible (to the general public) *adj.*: **exoteric**. SEE ACCESSIBLE

(2) comprehensible *adj.*: **limpid**. SEE UNDERSTANDABLE

(3) comprehensible (in thought or expression) *adj.*: **pellucid**. SEE CLEAR

(4) comprehensible *adj.*: **perspicuous**. SEE UNDERSTANDABLE

comprehension (sudden ...) *n.*: **epiphany**. SEE REALIZATION

(2) comprehension (as in perception or awareness) *n.*: **ken**. SEE PERCEPTION

comprehensive (in scope or applicability) *adj.*: **ecumenical**. SEE UNIVERSAL

compulsion (irresistible ...) *n.*: **cacoëthes**. ▪ [My girlfriend has asked me what I want for my birthday] so many times I've been this close to replying, "Well, I heard that [attractive actress] Sean Young is selling her [underwear] on her website." It's a **cacoëthes**, the words itch under my tongue — somewhere in the delusional, crumbling corridors of my mind, I picture her replying, "Yeah, okay, then. I admire the quirkiness of that request." (Mil Millington, *Relationships: Things My Girlfriend and I Argue About*, The Guardian, 10-06-2001, p. 85.)

compulsion (to shop) *n.*: **oniomania**. SEE SHOPPING

compulsive (about work) *n.*: **Stakhanovite**. SEE WORKAHOLIC

computing (act or process of ..., as in measuring) *n.*: **mensuration**. SEE MEASURING

comrade *n.*: **tovarich** [Russian]. ▪ Canadian company enters joint venture with Russian company. ... Russian partner tells Canadian partner, "We want to buy you out, **tovarich**." Canadian company [says no. They send someone to check out the project and he is shot.] As soon as he hits the deck, a fax arrives at the Canadian company's headquarters, basically saying, "What are you gonna do now?" (Doug Beazley, *In Lawless, Corrupt Russia, Guns Do the Talking*, The Edmonton Sun, 07-11-2001, p. 7.)

con (as in deceive) *v.t.*: **hornswoggle**. SEE DECEIVE

(2) con (as in deceive) *v.t.*: **humbug**. SEE DECEIVE

concealed *adj.*: **delitescent**. SEE HIDDEN

(2) concealed (as in state of being absent from view, lost to notice or ...) *n.*: **occultation**. SEE DISAPPEARANCE

concealment (in ...) *adv.*: **doggo** (esp. as in "lying doggo"; slang). ▪ Even as his parents prepare to brag on their family values and family, First Son Neil Bush has been conspicuously absent, even though he now lives in Houston. In the wake of the Silverado Savings and Loan scandal, Mr. Bush has been lying **doggo**, and is expected to surface only when the Bush children appear on stage for Barbara Bush's speech on Wednesday night. (Maureen Dowd, *Republicans in Houston: The Houston Thing*, The New York Times, 08-17-1992, p. A7.)

(2) concealment *n.*: **hugger-mugger**. SEE SECRECY

(3) concealment (deliberate ... or misrepresentation of facts to gain an advantage) *n.*: **subreption**. SEE MISREPRESENTATION

conceit *adj.*: **hubris**. SEE ARROGANCE

conceited (and vain person) *n.*: **coxcomb**. ▪ [I]t sounds as if Vain Tours, a travel agency on Jerusalem's King George Street, specializes in making arrangements for these **coxcombs** to attend international conferences for the uncommonly conceited. (Alex Berlyne, *Circumstances Alter Faces*, Jerusalem Post, 12-11-1998, p. 31.)

(2) conceited (and shameless person) *n.*: **jackanapes**. ▪ [Actor Jim Carrey] is such a conceited, mugging lout that he makes us glum. If this **jackanapes** can attract large audiences, maybe we should worry a little less about the survival of the human race. (Stanley Kauffmann, *Stanley Kauffmann on Films*, The New Republic, 04-28-1997.)

(3) conceited (talk or person) *n.*: **cockalorum**. SEE EGOTISTIC

(4) conceited (as in vain person) *n.*: **fop**. SEE VAIN

(5) conceited (person) *n.*: **Gascon** (act of being ... *n.*: **Gasconade**). SEE BRAGGART

(6) conceited (as in vain person) *n.*: **popinjay**. SEE VAIN

(7) conceited (and vain) *adj.*: **vainglorious**. SEE BOASTFUL

conceivable (as in appearing to be true or accurate) *adj.*: **verisimilar**. SEE PLAUSIBLE

conceivably *adv.*: **perchance**. SEE POSSIBLY

conceive (of, or form an image of) *v.t.*: **ideate**. SEE VISUALIZE

concentrate (emotional energy on) *v.t.*: **cathect**. SEE FOCUS

(2) concentrate (the flavor or essence of something, as if by boiling down) *v.t.*: **decoct**. SEE BOIL DOWN

concentration (of emotional energy on an object or idea) *n.*: **cathexis**. SEE FOCUS

concept (or idea which can be expressed in one word) *n.*: **holophrasis** (*adj.*: **holophrastic**). SEE IDEA

(2) concept (about which one is obsessed) *n.*: **idée fixe** [French]. SEE OBSESSION

conception (to form a ... of) *v.t.*: **ideate**. SEE VISUALIZE

concern (as in worry) *v.t., v.i., n.*: **cark**. SEE WORRY

(2) concern (in a state of ...) *idiom*: [on] **tenterhooks**. SEE SUSPENSE

(3) concern (treat another with excessive ...) *n., v.t.*: **wet-nurse**. SEE CODDLE

concerned (as if by a witch or without reason) *adj.*: **hagridden**. SEE TORMENTED

concerning *prep.*: **anent**. ▮ SEE REGARDING

conciliate *v.t.*: **propitiate**. SEE PLACATE

conciliatory (as in peacemaking) *adj.*: **irenic**. SEE PEACEMAKING

concise (speech or writing being very ...) *adj.*: **elliptical**. SEE TERSE

conclusion (as in inference) *n.*: **illation**. SEE INFERENCE

conclusive (necessarily or demonstrably ...) *adj.*: **apodictic**. SEE INCONTROVERTIBLE

(2) conclusive (as in indisputable or unquestionable) *adj.*: **irrefragable**. SEE UNQUESTIONABLE

(3) conclusive (remark, blow or factor) *n.*: **sockdolager**. SEE DECISIVE

(4) conclusive (as in unambiguous) *adj.*: **univocal**. SEE UNAMBIGUOUS

concoct (an idea, plan, theory or explanation after careful thought) *v.t.*: **excogitate**. SEE DEVISE

concubine *n.*: **odalisque**. ▮ "I was living his life, not mine. All the choices, plans, goals were his and would remain so. ... What I saw in the mirror was a finely dressed business and pleasure. Here I was, this liberated woman, and I was actually an **odalisque** out of la belle epoque." (Betty Fussell, *The Century's Almost Over ... and You're Still Living Through a Man?* Cosmopolitan, 06-01-1996, p. 200.)

condemn *v.t.*: **execrate**. SEE HATE

(2) condemn (as in criticize) *v.t.*: **flay**. SEE CRITICIZE

(3) condemn (as in scold or rebuke) *v.t.*: **objurgate**. SEE CRITICIZE

condemnation (as in criticism) *n.*: **animadversion** (*v.t.*: **animadvert**). SEE CRITICISM

(2) condemnation (as in damnation) *n.*: **perdition**. SEE DAMNATION

(3) condemnation (in speech) *n.*: **philippic**. SEE TIRADE

condemning (of convicted persons, spec. burning of heretics at the stake) *n.*: **auto-da-fe**. SEE EXECUTION

condense (the flavor or essence of something, as if by boiling down) *v.t.*: **decoct**. SEE BOIL DOWN

(2) condense (as in thicken) *v.t., v.i.*: **inspissate**. SEE THICKEN

condensed (something ..., as in abridged) *n.*: **bobtail**. SEE ABRIDGED

condescend (as in bestow, by one with higher power) *v.t.*: **vouchsafe**. SEE BESTOW

condescending *adj., adv.*: **de haut en bas** [French; lit. from high to low]. ▮ Love it or hate it, everyone instantly acknowledges that the [New York Review of Books] is saturated with fashionable left-wing politics. ... From its very first issue in 1963, the Review has epitomized the snotty **[de] haut-en-bas** leftism of the academy. ... [They believe that] their view of the world is not a political view but simply an accurate transcription of the way the world appears to any right-thinking (i.e., left-lean-ing) person. (Author not given, *Notes & Comments: September 2003*, New Criterion, 09-01-2003.)

condition *n.*: **fettle**. ∎ Given the importance of the bank's financial condition, it's possible for two borrowers in the same town, in similar financial **fettle**, to face drastically different loan prospects depending on where they bank. (Gary Hector, *The Economy: Victims of the Credit Crunch*, Fortune, 01-27-1992, p. 100.)

conditioned (as in trained to show a ... response) *adj.*: **Pavlovian** [based on Russian physiologist Ivan P. Pavlov (1849-1936), who trained dogs to respond instantly to various stimuli]. ∎ President Clinton's final, and longest, State of the Union address evoked a **Pavlovian** partisan response. Republicans denounced, in the words of their shaky heir apparent, George W. Bush, the "litany of spending." Democrats lined up to praise a speech that stroked every tender party cause from education to hate crimes. (Author not given, *Two States of the Union [Bill Clinton's Budget Plans]*, The Nation, 02-21-2000.)

conduct (appropriate ..., as in propriety) *n.*: **correctitude**. SEE PROPRIETY

(2) conduct (as in demeanor) *n.*: **mien**. SEE DEMEANOR

(3) conduct (study of human ...) *n.*: **praxeology**. SEE BEHAVIOR

conference (as in dialogue in which neither side hears or understands or pays attention to the other) *n.*: **dialogue des sourds** [French]. SEE DIALOGUE

(2) conference (esp. with an enemy or adversary) *n., v.t.*: **parley** SEE DISCUSSION

confess (one's sins, esp. in church) *v.t., v.i.*: **shrive**. ∎ [Worldcom CEO Bernie Ebbers] made his first public comments about the fraud allegations to a Baptist church in Brookhaven, Miss. Churches are perfect places to **shrive** and be forgiven, but Ebbers was unapologetic, denying any knowledge of fraud. It's hard to imagine that a multibillion-dollar gaffe could slip by Ebbers undetected. (Ed Gubbins, *Scandalism [Worldcom]*, Telephony, 07-08-2002.)

(2) confess (one's thoughts or feelings) *v.t., v.i.*: **unbosom**. SEE CONFIDE

confession (of sin) *n.*: **peccavi**. ∎ Clinton performed miserably in his first public ceremonies of repentance [over the Monica Lewinsky affair], but then last Friday, at the White House prayer breakfast, delivered at last a persuasive **peccavi**, mea culpa. (Lance Morrow, *Essay: That Old Familiar Uncharted*

Territory: Clinton's Survival May Depend on a Combination of Forgiveness and Boredom, Time, 09-21-1998, p. 120.)

confide (one's thoughts or feelings) *v.t., v.i.*: **unbosom**. ∎ The President had received a copy of the page proofs and, in response, now confessed to Wattenberg that in his first two years in office he had "lost the language" of values, and thereby "let Democrats down." ... Clinton's **unbosoming** certainly helped, however briefly, to call attention to this book, and to Wattenberg's cause. (Richard Brookhiser, *Values Matter Most [Book Reviews]*, Commentary, 04-01-1996, p. 62.)

confidence (and poise) *n.*: **aplomb**. ∎ Obviously, style wasn't my native tongue. I got style more or less the way I got French, through a combination of study and osmosis. It was a long time before I had the nerve, the experience or the **aplomb** necessary to hold forth. (Judith Thurman, *Features: The Search for Style*, In Style, 10-15-1998, p. 81.)

(2) confidence (excess ...) *adj.*: **hubris**. SEE ARROGANCE

confident (behavior, as in bravado) *n.*: **fanfaronade**. SEE BRAVADO

(2) confident (as in one habitually expecting an upturn in one's fortunes, sometimes without justification) *adj.*: **Micawberish** (*n.*: **Micawber**). SEE OPTIMISTIC

(3) confident (esp. blindly or naively ..., as in optimistic) *adj.*: **Panglossian**. SEE OPTIMISTIC

confidential (as in secret activity) *n.*: **huggermugger**. SEE SECRECY

(2) confidential (as in, of or relating to a court, legislative body or other group that meets in private, and often makes decisions which are harsh or arbitrary) *adj.*: **star chamber**. SEE CLOSED-DOOR

confine *v.t.*: **immure**. ∎ In 1793, the 8-year-old son of the guillotined monarchs, King Louis XVI and Queen Marie Antoinette, was flung into Paris' Temple prison. Then, according to competing legends, one of two things happened: [He] was **immured** in a windowless dungeon, ignored, barely fed and left alone in his own filth. (Author not given, *The DNA Test That Solved a Royal Puzzle*, Minneapolis Star Tribune, 04-26-2000, p. 19A.)

(2) confine (a person's movement by holding down his arms) *v.t.*: **pinion**. SEE IMMOBILIZE

confined (by not affording enough space) *adj.*: **incommodious**. SEE CRAMPED

confinement (as in imprisonment) *n*.: **durance** (often as in "in durance vile"). SEE JAIL

confiscate (property to compel payment of debts) *v.t.*: **distrain**. ▪ Mr. Yeltsin went on television to assure investors that Russia would weather the storm, but he made clear that it needs increased tax revenue to do so. ... He also signed a decree giving tax police powers to **distrain** tax dodgers' property. (Genine Babakian, *International: Tax Chief is Victim as Yeltsin Shields Rouble*, The Daily Telegraph, 05-30-1998.)

conflict (in literature) *n*.: **agon**. ▪ Bloom's view of literature as a ceaseless **agon** between challengers and titleholders is interesting and, in some instances, true. (Paul Gray, *Ideas: Hurrah for Dead White Males!* Time, 10-10-1994, p. 62.)

(2) conflict (between laws, rules, or principles) *n*.: **antinomy**. ▪ [In Florida, people under 21 cannot go to dance clubs or juice bars, because they are supposed to lack the necessary judgment. Despite that,] a 13-year-old boy arrested in a school shooting in Lake Worth was found to be vested with plenty enough judgment and maturity to stand trial as an adult on first-degree murder charges. This qualifies, perhaps, as an **antinomy** or a contradiction. (Fred Grimm, *Geezers' Revenge: Ban the Brats*, The Miami Herald, 06-04-2000.)

(3) conflict (in terms or ideas) *n*.: **antilogy**. SEE CONTRADICTION

(4) conflict (act or event which causes or provokes ...) *n*.: **casus belli** [Latin; occasion of war]. SEE PROVOCATION

(5) conflict (characterized by internal ...) *adj*.: **factious**. SEE DISPUTE

(6) conflict (of or relating to ... within a group or country) *adj*.: **internecine**. SEE DISSENSION

(7) conflict (in the soul between good vs. evil) *n*.: **psychomachia**. SEE GOOD VS. EVIL

(8) conflict (as in heated disagreement or friction between groups) *n*.: **ruction**. SEE DISSENSION

(9) conflict (or battle among the gods) *n*.: **theomachy**. SEE GODS

conflicting (as in things which do not mix together) *adj*.: **immiscible**. SEE INCOMPATIBLE

conform (closely to a line, rule, or principle) *v.i.*: **hew** ▪ But during his three decades in Congress, the upstate New Yorker [Samuel Stratton] **hewed** to the orthodox liberal line on many issues, supporting school busing and economic sanctions against South Africa. (Author not given, *Milestones*, Time, 09-24-1990, p. 97.)

conforming (do things in a ... manner, as in "by the book") *idiom*: **according to Hoyle**. SEE BY THE BOOK

conformity (marked by insistence on rigid ... to a belief, system or course of action without regard to individual differences) *adj*.: **Procrustean** (*n*: **Procrustean bed**) [after Procrustes, a mythical Greek giant who stretched or shortened captives to make them fit his beds]. ▪ Poor [former presidential candidate Al Gore] was abysmally self-satirizing on [Saturday Night Live], ripping the last shreds of dignity from his profile in attempted comedy. ... The chuckles and laughter in his conversation with Lesley Stahl on Sunday night were those of a private person struggling to be free of public life, a man trapped in a **Procrustean bed** built by a father who raised a son to be president. (Suzanne Fields, *It's Sunday Night Live: Gore Should Leave Comedy to the Comics*, The Washington Times, 12-19-2002.)

(2) conformity (precise ... with formalities or etiquette) *n*.: **punctilio**. SEE ETIQUETTE

confrontation (event which causes or provokes ...) *n*.: **casus belli** [Latin; occasion of war]. SEE PROVOCATION

confuse *v.t.*: **befog**. SEE MUDDLE

confused (esp. used of a person, as in ... and stupid) *adj*.: **addlepated**. ▪ *Bias: A CBS Insider Explains How the Media Distort the News* by Bernard Goldberg, is making a splash in the very media that are its target. ... Some of the response to "Bias" has been more vitriolic than polemical. ... [T]elevision critic Tom Shales dismisses Goldberg as an "**addlepated** windbag who is trying to make a second career out of trashing his former employer." (Cathy Young, *Skewed News: Fair and Balanced Coverage Requires Diversity of Opinion*, The Boston Globe, 02-04-2002.)

confusion (disorderly ...) *n., adj*.: **hugger-mugger**. ▪ If this all sounds complicated, it is: The first hour of The Last of the Mohicans plays like a convoluted history lesson. ... When the English are defeated and skulk away, only to be massacred, it feels like a cheat: All that historical **hugger-mugger** just to get Hawkeye, the colonel's daughter, and her younger sister (Jodhi May) stranded in the wilderness. (Owen Gleiberman, *Native Son Michael Mann's the Last of the Mohicans Is a Powerfully Realistic Adventure Saga*, Entertainment Weekly, 09-25-1992, p. 38.)

(2) confusion (of one's memory with actual fact) *n*.: **paramnesia**. SEE MISREMEMBER

(3) confusion (as in chaos) *n.*: **tohubuhu**. SEE CHAOS

(4) confusion (as in disarrayed mass) *n.*: **welter**. SEE JUMBLE

congenital (as in innate) *adj.*: **connate**. SEE INNATE

conglomeration (as in assortment) *n.*: **farrago**. SEE ASSORTMENT

(2) conglomeration (as in assortment) *n.*: **gallimaufry**. SEE ASSORTMENT

(3) conglomeration (as in assortment) *n.*: **olla podrida** [Spanish]. SEE ASSORTMENT

(4) conglomeration (as in assortment) *n.*: **omnium-gatherum** [Latin]. SEE ASSORTMENT

(5) conglomeration (as in assortment) *n.*: **salmagundi**. SEE ASSORTMENT

congratulate *v.t.*: **felicitate**. ■ President Soeharto of Indonesia has also **felicitated** President Negasso Gidada and Prime Minister Meles Zenawi [in connection with the 6th anniversary of May 28, the day on which the Ethiopian people ousted the dictatorial Derg regime], who also received a congratulatory message sent from Mr. Ahmed Ouyahia, head of state of Algeria. (Author not given, *Clinton and Other Leaders Welcome Ethiopia's Achievements*, Africa News Service, 05-29-1997.)

congregation (at church) *n.*: **ecclesia**. ■ These changes reflect changes in theology of worship and our understanding of the **ecclesia** — the Christian community meeting in worship. Today there is a preference for seats in a semi-circle round a nave altar; rather than worshipping a God out there, we feel it better to worship a God in the midst of us. (Alan D. Skyes, *Letter: Redesigned Churches*, Independent, 11-19-1997, p. 22.)

(2) congregation (at church) *n.*: **laity**. SEE PARISH

connect (in a series or chain) *v.t., adj.*: **concatenate** (*n.*: **concatenation**). ■ [A]s anyone involved in the criminal trade will affirm (although I didn't know this at the time), the phrase "I don't know anything about it" is employed almost exclusively by those, paradoxically, who do know all about it; that this **concatenation** of words is a code, a slang, a camoflouged way of saying: prove it. (Tabor Fischer, *The Thought Gang*, The New Press [1994], p. 4.)

(2) connect (as in bring together) *v.t.*: **conflate**. SEE COMBINE

(3) connect (as in blend) *v.t., v.i.*: **inosculate**. SEE BLEND

connected (by a close relationship) *adj.*: **affined**. ■ When Reinette says that next year she wants to go to art school in Paris, Mirabelle invites her to share her apartment since her present roommate is leaving. The matter is not immediately settled, because the two, the city sophisticate and the country enthusiast, are not completely **affined**. Next morning they experience the [beautiful hour before dawn] together. The moment is so lovely that it unites them. (Stanley Kauffman, *Four Adventures of Reinette and Mirabelle*, The New Republic, 08-28-1989.)

(2) connected (closely ...) *adj.*: **coadunate**. SEE JOINED

(3) connected (of things that cannot be ...) *adj.*: **immiscible**. SEE INCOMPATIBLE

connection *n.*: **catenation** (*v.t.*: **catenate**). SEE CHAIN

conniving (and evil or shameless woman) *n.*: **jezebel** (sometimes cap.). SEE WOMAN

connoisseur *n.*: **cognoscente**. ■ Become an art **cognoscente**. ArtNet Magazine, a new trade publication for the visual arts world, offers columns, auction reports and photos. (Sam Vincent Meddis, *Net: New and Notable*, USA Today, 05-30-1996, p. 6D.)

(2) connoisseur (of good food and drink) *n.*: **epicure**. SEE GOURMET

(3) connoisseur (of good food and drink) *n.*: **gastronome**. SEE GOURMET

conscientious (in effort or application) *adj.*: **sedulous**. SEE DILIGENT

conscious *adj.*: **sentient**. ■ Could a mechanical device ever duplicate human intelligence — the ultimate test being whether it could cause a real human to fall in love with it? And if such a machine could be built, would it actually be conscious? Would dismantling it be the snuffing out of a **sentient** being[?] (Steven Pinker, *Can a Computer Be Conscious?* U.S. News & World Report, 08-25-1997, p. 63.)

consciousness (as in soul) *n.*: **anima**. SEE SOUL

consequence (as in outgrowth) *n.*: **excrescence**. SEE OUTGROWTH

conservatism (as in hatred or fear of anything new or different) *n.*: **misoneism** (person holding this view: **misoneist**). ■ With predictable corporate **misoneism** ... the [music] industry anointed Jet [as the next hot rock band] not for their singularity, but their overfamiliarity. It's a neat execution of a tried and true formula: a faithful and loving synthesis of classic Stones, AC/DC, the Who and Kinks-era rock, put together by four young guys who love what they're playing, play well and look the part. (Kelsey Munro, *The Formula Works: Humming Along To An Overfamiliar Tune*, Sydney Morning Herald, 07-22-2003.)

conservative (very ... in beliefs and often stuffy or pompous) *adj., n.*: **Colonel Blimp** [after a British cartoon character having these qualities]. ▪ [The campaign by those supporting a conversion of Britain's monetary system from the pound to the Eurodollar (i.e. the Yes campaign) is based in part on the] assumption is that they will be able to portray the No campaign as a bunch of right-wing loonies: **Colonel Blimp** types desperately clinging to a vision of a long-forgotten Britain. (Author not given, *Murdoch Seals E1.5bn Italy Pay-TV Deal With Vivendi*, Sunday Business [London], 06-09-2002.)

(2) conservative (tactics, esp. as a means to wear out an opponent) *adj.*: **Fabian**. See CAUTIOUS

(3) conservative (person, spec. a person who is opposed to advancements in technology) *n.*: **Luddite**. See TRADITIONALIST

consider (something, often used as a directive, as in "Consider this:") *v.t.*: **perpend**. ▪ Former Oxford teacher Bernard Richards says the first-year exams of the [Language and Literature students at Oxford] show an "alarming" decline in spelling skills over the past 10 years. **Perpend**: They misspelled gnats as "knats," unpalatable as "unpalletable," expressed as "escpressed," paddle as "padel," angry as "angery," vehicle as "vehicule," and so on. (Chris Floyd, *Global Eye*, The Moscow Times, 01-24-1998.)

(2) consider (as in think about) *v.t.*: **cerebrate**. See THINK

(3) consider (as in think about) *v.t.*: **cogitate**. See THINK

(4) consider (logically) *v.i.*: **ratiocinate**. See ANALYZE

consistent (as in harmonious or compatible) *adj.*: **simpatico**. See COMPATIBLE

consolidate *v.t.*: **amalgamate**. See COMBINE

conspiracy *n.*: **cabal**. See PLOT

constant (as in unvarying) *adj.*: **equable**. See UNVARYING

(2) constant (in rhythm or tempo) *adj.*: **metronomic**. See STEADY

(3) constant (as in everlasting) *adj.*: **sempiternal**. See EVERLASTING

constantly (as in forever) *adv.*: **in aeternum** [Latin]. See FOREVER

constellation *n.*: **asterism**. See STARS

constellations (of or relating to) *adj.*: **sidereal**. See STARS

constipated *adj.*: **costive**. ▪ "Buzzed" [is a] guide to the most used and abused drugs. ... With typical cool, the good doctors quote an expert who decided that "if you didn't mind being impotent and constipated, opiate addiction really wasn't too bad." No wanly romantic early demise, but 20 or 30 years of flabby, **costive** desperation. Glamorous, or what? (Boyd Tonkin, *Books*, Independent, 04-25-1998, p. 11.)

constrain (as in confine) *v.t.*: **immure**. See CONFINE

constricted (by not affording enough space) *adj.*: **incommodious**. See CRAMPED

construct (cheaply and flimsily) *v.t.*: **jerrybuild**. See BUILD

constructed (finely or skillfully ..., as in intricate) *adj.*: **daedal**. See INTRICATE

construction (art of ..., esp. of large buildings) *n.*: **tectonics**. ▪ The dangerous, shattering glass of I.M. Pei's controversial John Hancock Mutual Life Insurance Company Tower in Boston in the 1970s is a famous and graphic example of faulty **tectonics** as faulty publicity. There, problems with the skyscraper's glass curtain walls took months to repair at great expense. (Scott Berman, *Public Buildings as Public Relations*, Public Relations Quarterly, 04-15-1999.)

consumable *adj.*: **esculent**. See EDIBLE

consume (greedily) *v.t.*: **guttle**. See DEVOUR

(2) consume (as in ingest) *v.t.*: **incept**. See INGEST

consuming (act or process of ..., as in swallowing) *n.*: **deglutition**. See SWALLOWING

consummation (as opposed to potentiality) *n.*: **entelechy**. See ACTUALITY

contaminated (morally ...) *v.t.*: **cankered**. See CORRUPTED

contamination (abnormal fear of ...) *n.*: **mysophobia**. See FEAR

contemplate (on something, often used as a directive, as in "Consider this:") *v.t.*: **perpend**. See CONSIDER

contemplation (staring at one's belly-button as an aid to ...) *n.*: **omphaloskepsis**. SEE MEDITATION

contemporaneous (as in over the same period) *adj.*: **coetaneous**. ∎ This course was created to examine institutionalized prejudice in the field of psychology. Psychology, as a discipline, has been an arena for examining the structure and etiology of prejudice. ... **Coetaneously**, psychology has been rife with institutionalized prejudice in terms of theories, especially Freud's theory. (Mary Ballard, *The Politics of Prejudice in Psychology: A Syllabus and Bibliography*, Contemporary Women's Issues Database, 03-01-1995, p. 16.)

contemporary (as in of the same era) *adj., n.*: **coeval**. ∎ Go ahead, baby. Wail. You're due. It sure is nice to hear [singer Gladys Knight] tear into some material with spirit in its soul. After more than 35 years, she still boasts one of the most assured and moving voices in the business. ... Unlike her **coeval**, that big, bad wolf Patti LaBelle, Knight doesn't huff and puff and try to blow the roof off the sucker every time out of the box. (David Hiltbrand, *Picks & Pans: Song*, People, 02-22-1988, p. 13.)

contempt (in behavior or speech) *n.*: **contumely**. ∎ And now Madeleine Albright addresses Benjamin Netanyahu approximately as she addresses Slobodan Milosevic, as though he merited **contumely** rather than respect, as though he were the head of a hostile power rather than an ally. (Author not given, *A Crisis of Partnership*, The New Republic, 06-01-1998.)
(2) contempt (treat with ...) *v.t.*: **contemn**. SEE SCORN
(3) contempt *n.*: **misprision** (*v.t.*: **misprize**). SEE DISDAIN
(4) contempt (develop a ... for) *n.*: **scunner** (esp. as in "take a scunner")[British]. SEE DISLIKE

contemptible (person) *n.*: **caitiff**. SEE DESPICABLE
(2) contemptible *adj.*: **ugsome**. SEE LOATHSOME

contemptuous (of another, often by being insulting or humiliating) *adj.*: **contumelious**. ∎ I worked for part of a summer in a hellish Texarkanan carnival as the **contumelious** clown you get to drop into a tank of water after he calls you pencil-dick. (Michael Chabon, *Wonder Boys*, Villard [1995], p. 18.)
(2) contemptuous *adj.*: **opprobrious** (*n.*: **opprobrium**). ∎ While the label "fiscal conservative" might seem **opprobrious** to [Jesse] Jackson, it is a compliment in many places, including California,

the cradle of the 1970s tax revolt. (Laurence I. Barrett, *Nation: The Grail of the Golden State*, Time, 06-06-1988, p. 19.)
(3) contemptuousness (as in disdain) *n.*: **misprision** (*v.t.*: **misprize**). SEE DISDAIN

contend (as in assert) *v.t.*: **asseverate**. SEE DECLARE

contention (made without proof or support) *n.*: **ipse dixit** [Latin]. SEE ALLEGATION
(2) contention (as in heated disagreement or friction between groups) *n.*: **ruction**. SEE DISSENSION

contentious (as in pugnacious; ready to fight) *adj.*: **bellicose**. SEE BELLIGERENT
(2) contentious (as in controversial opinion or person holding one) *n.*: **polemic**. SEE CONTROVERSY

contentment *n.*: **eudemonia** (or **eudaemonia**). SEE HAPPINESS
(2) contentment (delusive or illusory ...) *n.*: **fool's paradise**. SEE ILLUSION
(3) contentment (as in peace of mind) *n.*: **heartsease**. SEE PEACE OF MIND
(4) contentment (as in well-being) *n.*: **weal** (usu. as in *weal or woe* or *weal and woe*). SEE WELL-BEING

contest (a statement, opinion or action) *v.t.*: **oppugn**. SEE OPPOSE
(2) contest (as in hostile meeting) *n.*: **rencontre** [French]. SEE DUEL

contortion (gaping ... of the face due to pain or disgust) *n.*: **rictus**. SEE GRIMACE

contour (distinctive ... or outline, often of a face) *adj.*: **lineament** (often **lineaments**). ∎ There's another low building behind the park: painted blue, almost lost in the weak light of evening. It's neglected-looking, the asphalt shingles of its roof patchy and stained. I pull into the parking lot before this building and its **lineaments** are unmistakable. At the center of America, an abandoned motel. (Mark Baechtel, *Dead Center America*, The Washington Post, 01-16-2000, p. E1.)

contradict (as in oppose a statement, opinion or action) *v.t.*: **oppugn**. SEE OPPOSE

contradiction (in terms or ideas) *n.*: **antilogy**. ∎ "Travel consumer." The juxtaposition of terms rankles. To consume means, variously, "to eat up ... waste or squander ... destroy totally or ravage." If travel ideally is a productive and compassionate activity — nurturing both for individual and for cultures as they meet and mingle — how can we so blithely use such a blatant **antilogy**? (Jim Molnar, *To Consume, or Not to Consume? A Question for Every Traveler*, The Seattle Times, 08-20-1995, p. K1.)

(2) contradiction (as in conflict between laws, rules, or principles) *n.*: **antinomy**. SEE CONFLICT

(3) contradiction (statement which contains a logical ..., usually unrealized by the speaker) *n.*: **Irish bull**. SEE INCONGRUITY

contradictory (having ... ideas or qualities) *adj.*: **bipolar**. SEE OPPOSITE

(2) contradictory (as in things which do not mix together) *adj.*: **immiscible**. SEE INCOMPATIBLE

contrary (stubbornly ... or disobedient) *adj.*: **froward**. ▪ "The pigeons hang out on the light fixtures and the droppings get on the sidewalk right in front of the front door," said Assistant City Manager George Brown. For the past year, city maintenance crews have frequently pressure-cleaned the sidewalks, but the birds have been relentless. Tired of cleaning, the city decided to go on the offensive against the **froward** fowl. (John Murawski, *Pigeons Foil Boca Efforts to Evict Them*, The Palm Beach Post, 11-25-2000, p. 1B.)

(2) contrary (on the ...) *adv.*: **per contra**. SEE CONTRAST

(3) contrary (as in peevish) *adj.*: **querulous**. SEE PEEVISH

contrast (to set in ...) *v.t.*: **counterpose**. ▪ A British appeals court ruled Friday that six-week-old conjoined twins will have to be separated, even though the operation will almost certainly mean the death of one of them. The desperate parents fought unsuccessfully against the surgery. [The question is, what should the government do] when medical science and the religion-based wishes of the parents are **counterposed**? (William Raspberry, *The Ultimate Sacrifice*, The Washington Post, 09-25-2000, p. A21.)

(2) contrast (by way of ...) *adv.*: **per contra**. ▪ The Israelis believe God gave them Israel in perpetuity. ... The Palestinians, **per contra**, believe equally firmly that the land is theirs, and that it was simply seized in the late 1940s by an influx of Jewish refugees from Europe. (William Rusher, *Camp David Designs*, The Washington Times, 07-19-2000, p. A17.)

contribution (which is all one can afford) *n.*: **widow's mite**. SEE DONATION

contrition (as in place or occasion to express ... and to seek forgiveness) *n.*: **Canossa**. SEE PENANCE

contrived (as in artificial) *adj.*: **factitious**. SEE ARTIFICIAL

control (as in dominate) *v.t.*: **bestride**. SEE DOMINATE

(2) control (as in marked by simplicity, frugality, self-discipline and/or ...) *adj.*: **Lacedaemoninan**. SEE SPARTAN

(3) control (as in domination, of a nation or group over another) *n.*: **suzerainty**. SEE DOMINATION

controversy (point of view which is the subject of ..., or person who holds one) *n.*: **polemic**. ▪ In "The Coming Collapse of China," Gordon G. Chang launches directly into his controversial argument that the country's many woes add up to a terminal illness. [After describing a familiar litany of problems, Chang] takes his startling **polemic** one step further: He says that ... the Communist Party will soon collapse — possibly within 5 years. (Roberts, *Books: Pessimism on a Grand Scale*, Business Week, 08-27-2001.)

(2) controversy (given to argument or ... which may be specious) *adj., n.*: **eristic**. SEE SPECIOUS AND DEBATE

(3) controversy (of or relating to ... within a group or country) *adj.*: **internecine**. SEE DISSENSION

convention (as in habit or custom) *n.*: **praxis**. SEE CUSTOM

conventionality (intolerant insistence on ...) *n.*: **Grundyism**. SEE PURITANICAL

conversation (esp. about art or literature) *n.*: **conversazione** [Italian] (*pl.* **conversazioni**). ▪ At times, in the corner of my eye, I think I can still see a skinny streak of mottled fur and hear a tiny, bossy [meow], demanding to be let in, [or] to be let out. ... Perhaps she's summoning my husband and me, in her usual highhanded She-Who-Must-Be-Obeyed manner, for one of her elegant drawing-room **conversazioni** on great themes in art and literature. (Ann Leslie, *Farewell Posy, Most Magnificent of [Cats]*, The Daily Mail [London], 09-07-2001.)

(2) conversation (between two people) *n.*: **duologue**. ▪ The unlikely ice partners — tiny francophone Isabelle Brasseur and giant anglophone Lloyd Eisler — won Olympic bronze twice and the Worlds once. They share their lives on and off the ice in an interesting **duologue**. (Gina Mallet, *Various Positions*, Chatelaine, 12-01-1996, p. 16.)

(3) conversation (between three people) *n.*: **trialogue**. ▪ Greenberg was in Jakarta yesterday attending the International Scholars Annual **Trialogue**, a meeting of Christian, Muslim and Jewish scholars. (Jacqueline Trescott, *N.Y. Rabbi To Chair Holocaust Museum; Irving Greenberg Seen As Bridge Builder*, The Washington Post, 02-16-2000.)

(4) conversation (light or playful back and forth ...) *n.*: **badinage**. SEE BANTER

(5) conversation (casual ..., as in chitchat) *n.*: **bavardage**. SEE CHITCHAT

(6) conversation (informal ...) *n.*: **causerie**. SEE CHAT

(7) conversation (in which neither side hears or understands or pays attention to the other): *n.*: **dialogue des sourds** [French]. SEE DIALOGUE

(8) conversation *n.*: **interlocution**. SEE DISCUSSION

(9) conversation (idle ...) *n.*: **palaver**. SEE SMALL TALK

(10) conversation (casual ..., discussion of a subject, as in chitchat) *n.*: **persiflage**. SEE CHITCHAT

conversationalist (skilled dinner ...) *n.*: **deipnosophist**. ∎ At the age of six his future as a **deipnosophist** seemed certain. Guzzling filched apples he loved to prattle. Hogging the pie he invariably piped up and rattled on. (MacDonald Daly, *Malice Aforethought: The Fictions of Ellis Sharp*, Critique: Studies in Contemporary Fiction, 01-01-1998, p. 139.)

converse (esp. in a long-winded or pompous manner) *v.i.*: **bloviate**. SEE SPEAK

(2) converse (casually) *n.*: **chinwag** [slang]. SEE CHAT

(3) converse (casually) *v.i.*: **confabulate**. SEE CHAT

convert (recent ... to a belief) *n.*: **neophyte**. ∎ For the story of the small but steadily expanding number of Westerners who are converting to the religion of Mohammed has something to say to us all. ... The majority of **neophytes** are between 35 and 55, said Batool al-Toma, an Irishwoman who was once called Mary. (Paul Vallely, *The New Muslims*, Independent, 11-03-1998, p. 1.)

(2) convert (esp. in a strange, grotesque, or humorous way) *v.t.*: **transmogrify**. SEE TRANSFORM

convey (as in send a signal) *v.t., v.i.*: **semaphore**. SEE SIGNAL

convict *n.*: **malefactor**. SEE WRONGDOER

convivial *adj.*: **Anacreontic**. ∎ The less-than-glorious origin of our national anthem was indeed a drinking song, To Anacreon in Heaven, the theme song of the **Anacreontic** Club of London. The melody, published in England around 1780, is attributed to [two] members of the club, a group of wealthy men who liked to celebrate music, food and drink. The club took its name from Anacreon, a sixth-century-B.C. Greek lyric poet who also celebrated, well, celebrating. (Mike Rudeen, Rocky Mountain News, 03-01-2003, p. 9D)

(2) convivial *adj.*: **Falstaffian**. SEE JOVIAL

convulsions (during or after pregnancy) *n.*: **eclampsia**. ∎ Doctors try to keep pre-eclampsia from progressing to convulsions, a condition known as **eclampsia** that can be very harmful to mother and unborn child. (*Gene Found That Links High Blood Pressure, Pregnancy*, Newsday, 05-11-1993, p. 63.)

cool *adj.*: **algid**. SEE COLD

(2) cool (as in unemotional or even-tempered) *adj.*: **phlegmatic**. SEE EVEN-TEMPERED

coolness (esp. under pressure or trying circumstances) *n.*: **sang-froid** [French]. SEE COMPOSURE

coop up (as in confine) *v.t.*: **immure**. SEE CONFINE

coordination (loss of ...) *n.*: **apraxia**. ∎ Most [Rett Syndrome] victims suffer from **apraxia**, in which the body can't do what the brain tells it to, such as moving and talking. (Judy Siegel-Itzkovich, *Autism or Cerebral Palsy? No, It's Rett*, The Jerusalem Post, 07-08-2001, p. 17.)

copier (inferior ..., often of an artist, writer or entertainer) *n.*: **epigone**. SEE IMITATOR

copulation *n.*: **houghmagandy** [Scottish]. SEE INTERCOURSE

(2) copulation *n.*: **venery**. SEE INTERCOURSE

copy (of a previous artistic, musical or literary piece) *n.*: **pastiche**. SEE IMITATION

copying (pathological or uncontrollable or a child's ... of another's words) *n.*: **echolalia**. SEE REPEATING

(2) copying (pathological or uncontrollable ... of another's actions) *n.*: **echopraxia**. SEE REPEATING

(3) copying (of the real world in art or literature) *n.*: **mimesis**. SEE IMITATION

coquettish (as in flirtatious glance) *n.*: **oeillade** [French]. SEE GLANCE

cordiality *n.*: **empressement** [French]. ∎ In an atmosphere of international excitement, the mentors fretted about whether Albert was enough of a flirt. He had, Leopold's doctor friend Baron Stockmar ruefully acknowledged, "more success with men than with women," in whose company he showed, alas, "too little **empressement**." (Ben Pimlott, *A Bit Too Good to Be True? Independent on Sunday*, 05-04-1997, p. 31.)

(2) cordiality *n*.: **bonhomie**. See affability

core (of a matter, as in the essence) *n*.: **quiddity**. See essence

corpselike (appearing ... or pale) *adj*.: **cadaverous**. ▮ Jordan, for his part, felt [Ann] Rice's casting suggestions [to play the Vampire Lestat] all were too old and too predictable. He wanted to avoid the same cliched, **cadaverous**-looking actors familiar to audiences from Max Schreck and Bela Lugosi Dracula flicks. (Jennet Conant, *Lestat, C'est Moi*, Esquire, 03-01-1994, p. 70.)

corpses (fascination with or erotic attraction to ...) *n*.: **necrophilia**. ▮ Jeffrey Dahmer stood before a Milwaukee court last week, finally adding his voice to the tales of mutilation, cannibalism and **necrophilia** that had held the country in a macabre thrall since his crimes were discovered last July. ... [He] had the presence of mind to wear a protective condom when having sex with corpses. (Karen S. Schneider, *Up Front: Day of Reckoning*, People, 03-02-1992, p. 38.)

(2) corpses (abnormal fear of ... or dead people) *n*.: **necrophobia**. See fear

correct (text or language by removing errors or flaws) *v.t.*: **blue-pencil**. See edit

(2) correct (as in proper or suitable) *adj*.: **comme il faut** [French]. See proper

(3) correct (text or language by removing errors or flaws) *v.t.*: **emend**. See edit

correcting (as in atoning for) *adj*.: **piacular**. See atoning

correction (esp. of printed material) *n*.: **corrigendum**. ▮ [Delly Bonsange, editor of the daily newspaper *Alerte Plus*] was sentenced to six months on 6 September by a Kinshasa court for publishing a report that Democratic Republic of the Congo Security Minister Mwenze Kongolo had been poisoned. Next day, Alerte Plus had published a **corrigendum** stating that the information was false. (Author not given, *Media Watchdog Decries Poor Health of Jailed Journalist*, Africa News Service, 10-01-2002.)

correctly (as in "by the book") *idiom*: **according to Hoyle**. See by the book

correctness (precise observance of ..., as in etiquette) *n*.: **punctilio**. See etiquette

correspondence (of or relating to ..., as in letters) *adj*.: **epistolary**. See letters

corridor (spec. the ... in a stadium which connects the outer concourse to the interior of the stadium itself) *n*.: **vomitory**. ▮ Yankees tradition will be personified at the new park, from a replica of the monuments at Yankee Stadium, which will be located outside the park, to the signs identifying rows and seats at the six **vomitories** entering Legends Field. (Bill Chastain, *To Honor Tradition, Yanks' Spring Park Called Legends Field*, The Tampa Tribune, 12-16-1995.)

corrugated (as in grooved) *adj*.: **striated**. See grooved

corrupt (person, spec. one who accepts bribes) *n*.: **boodler**. ▮ [Bill Clinton] knew exactly what he was doing [when he pardoned Marc Rich], which returns us to the original point: Does anyone believe Denise Rich didn't pay for the pardon? Isn't this exactly what it seems to be: An unclad case of bribery? ... Defending Clinton is hard for anyone with a conscience. He's a fraud, a **boodler**, a coward and a thief. (R. Cort Kirkwood, The Ottawa Sun, 02-18-2001, p. C7.)

(2) corrupt (politician) *n*.: **highbinder**. ▮ The theory that animated the term limits vogue (which is now clearly subsiding) is a populist one: These here **highbinders** get themselves into their cushy [jobs] and stay on forever, lining their pockets and their cronies' pockets with honest graft (or doing some other undesirable things), until in extreme old age they're carted off drooling. (Dan Polsby [interviewee], *Q&A on Gerrymandering with Dan Polsby*, United Press International, 09-25-2002.)

(3) corrupt (group of ... politicians) *n*.: **plunderbund**. ▮ In 1952, the Chicago Daily News reported that Big Joe [Dan Rostenkowski's father] had three no-show employees on his committee payroll. ... The next year, in an anti-corruption editorial, the Sun-Times called ... Big Joe and a couple of other aldermen "the council's worst specimens." In 1955, the same paper termed Big Joe "an undeviating member of the **plunderbund** that now controls the council." (Peter Carlson, *Dan Rostenkowski Goes Down In History*, The Washington Post, 10-17-1993.)

(4) corrupt (as in unscrupulous) *adj*.: **jackleg**. See unscrupulous and grafter

(5) corrupt (government by ... persons) *n.*: **kleptocracy**. SEE GOVERNMENT

corrupted (morally ...) *v.t.*: **cankered**. ❚ [SS officer Blobel] testified to the difficulty his men faced [in perpetrating mass killings] — testimony **cankered** by his continued belittling of the victims: Blobel: "Our men ... suffered more from nervous exhaustion than those who had to be shot." [Judge:] "In other words, your pity was more for the men who had to shoot than the victims?" Blobel: "Our men had to be cared for." (Richard Rhodes, *Masters of Death*, Knopf [2003], p. 162.)

(2) corrupted (morally ...) *adj.*: **scrofulous**. SEE DEPRAVED

corruptible *adj.*: **venal**. ❚ In 1988 he took on Democrat Jim Wright, launching a yearlong ethics probe that ultimately brought Wright down. Gingrich's weapon of choice was always charges of corruption: by showing that the people who ran the system were **venal**, he could undermine the entire Democratic edifice. (Nancy Gibbs, *Man of the Year: Master of the House*, Time, 12-25-1995, p. 54.)

corruption (place of ... and filth) *n.*: **Augean stable** [after Augeas, a legendary Greek king who did not clean out his stable for 30 years, until it was cleaned by Hercules]. ❚ A federal judge ruled Thursday that the nearly-bankrupt International Brotherhood of Teamsters (IBT) must absorb at least $6 million of the estimated $7.4 million cost of its rerun election scheduled for this spring. Last week, U.S. District Judge David Edelstein ruled, "The time has come when the IBT must bear its own costs of cleansing its **Augean stable**. ... In plainer words, [the Teamsters] made the mess. It is their job to clean it up at any price." (Author not given, *The Teamsters' Augean Stables*, The Washington Times, 12-22-1997.)

(2) corruption *n.*: **knavery**. ❚ Woodrow Wilson warned of the **knavery** that results when the uninitiated gain public office. **Knavery** characterizes all of the Nigerian military government's actions, from its human rights record to foreign policy formulations. Journalists languish in prison; publishing houses are shut down at will; daring publishers appear on the hit lists of government agents. (Yereba Yemmy Kina, *The Tragic Misrule of Nigeria*, St. Louis Post-Dispatch, 11-11-1996, p. 7B.)

cosmetics *n.*: **maquillage** [French]. SEE MAKEUP

cough (of, relating to or caused by) *adj.*: **tussive**. ❚ And then there was the coughing. Believe me, I know all about coughing. When it comes to **tussive** endeavour, I've put in the hours. When they come to write the annals of the great expectorators, I'll get an embossed first paragraph. (John Walsh, *The Worst Bout of Flu Ever, the Worst Poetry Reading*, Independent, 01-30-1997, p. 17.)

counterattack (esp. to recover lost territory or political standing) *n.*: **revanche** [French]. SEE REVENGE

counterclockwise *adv.*: **widdershins**. ❚ More spiral stairs. Along with labyrinthine passages and skull-crushing door lintels, they seem to sprout from every turret in Fordell. Some wind clockwise, some go **widdershins**. This helps with navigation, but if you wind up in the wrong bedroom, at least you have a good excuse. (Tom Kidd, *Property: A Tower That Mary Queen of Scots Was Pleased to Sleep In*, The Daily Telegraph, 08-14-1999, p. 5.)

counterfeit *adj.*: **pinchbeck** [after Christopher Pinchbeck (1670-1732), a London watchmaker, who invented an alloy of five parts copper and one part zinc, which looked a bit like gold, and was used in making cheap jewelry. Now used more generally to refer to something counterfeit.] ❚ Lying comes easy in "Dreams of Dead Women's Handbags" [a collection of short stories by Shena Mackay]. In "The Blue Orchestra," a woman has reinvented herself as The Contessa, after "so many glass tiaras, aliases, false campaign ribbons, **pinchbeck** baubles, forged checks." Her scam is working until she's vacationing in the tropics and runs into a vagrant who turns out to be a girlfriend from school days. (Emily White, *Outside the Curve*, Newsday [New York], 11-27-1994, p. 36.)

counterpart (ghostly ... or twin of a living person) *n.*: **doppelganger**. SEE TWIN

countryman *n.*: **paisano** [Spanish]. ❚ [Mexicans were abuzz because] Oklahoma star Eduardo Náájera became the first Mexican ever to be drafted to an NBA team. As one [Mexican] cab driver [said] "Presidents come and go, but placing a **paisano** in the NBA is not so common." (Author not given, *Today's Story Line*, The Christian Science Monitor, 06-30-2000, p. 6.)

countryside (of or relating to) *adj.*: **bucolic**. SEE RUSTIC

coup (sudden attempt at a ...) *n.*: **putsch**. ❚ "But as the economic crisis worsens, active discontent is growing." ... [Boris] Yeltsin sternly rejects any possibility of a **putsch**. But, in a new poll, 46 percent of his countrymen said they think a coup is possible; only 30 percent rule it out. (Robin Knight, *A Creeping Coup in Russia?* U.S. News & World Report, 07-20-1992, p. 40.)

coup de grace *n.*: **quietus** (esp. as in "put the quietus to"). SEE TERMINATE

couple (as in pair of two people) *n.*: **duumvirate**. SEE DUO

(2) couple (two individuals or units regarded as a ...): **dyad**. SEE PAIR

(3) couple (arranged in or forming a ...) *adj.*: **jugate**. SEE PAIR

courage *n.*: **hardihood**. ■ Gentle reader, this is the truth, and you know it. Water is wet, the sky is blue, men fight wars, women don't — here are basic truths about the natural order. Sexual politics can't alter or amend such truths. ... None of this is to depreciate the valor and **hardihood** of women: traits demonstrated so many times as to require no proof. (William Murchison, *Unisex Military Works Poorly*, The Dallas Morning News, 11-20-1996, p. 25A.)

courageous (or bold while under the influence of alcohol) *adj.*: **potvaliant**. ■ While many music lovers will be at this weekend's non-alcoholic Irish festival, we'll be celebrating a different kind of Celtic culture — the 20-ounce variety, if you know what we mean. Call us old-fashioned lushes or **potvaliant** know-it-alls ..., but we believe St. Paddy's Day is best celebrated with a 39- to 45-degree Guinness, properly poured in an imperial pint glass and lovingly delivered with a shamrock on top. (Author not given, *For a Stout Pour, Take it to New Max's, [St. Patrick's Day Calls for the Perfect Pint of Guinness, but Not at Those Faux Irish Pubs]*, The Register-Guard [Eugene, OR], 03-12-2004.)

(2) courageous *adj.*: **doughty**. SEE BRAVE

(3) courageous (and strong woman) *n.*: **virago**. SEE WOMAN

course of action *n.*: **démarche** [French]. ■ The decision by ... the regulator of British Gas, to enforce a new round of price restrictions ... produced vitriol from the company, which accused her of a "smash and grab raid." ... Although British Gas's reaction to the week's **demarche** was exaggerated, it does have a point about the volatility and subjectivity of regulatory action over the years. (Author not given, *All Gas and Downsizing*, New Statesman & Society, 05-17-1996, p. 5.)

cover (a surface in a scattered way) *v.t.*: **bestrew**. ■ She was wearing a baby-blue cotton print summer dress which showed off her slender figure and exposed the constellation of freckles **bestrewing** her shoulders. (Erik Tarloff, *The Man Who Wrote the Book*, Crown [2000], p. 7)

covering (protective ..., like a turtle shell) *n.*: **carapace**. SEE SHELL

covert (activity) *n.*: **hugger-mugger**. SEE SECRECY

covetous (as in lustful) *adj.*: **lickerish**. SEE LUSTFUL

covetousness (esp. for wealth) *n.*: **cupidity**. SEE GREED

cow (of, relating to or resembling) *adj., n.*: **bovine**. ■ So far, cow theft hasn't been a problem, say police, but maybe that's because the fiberglass creatures weigh almost 600 pounds with their concrete bases. There have been a few incidents of vandalism, however. The worst case occurred at Oak Street Beach when thugs tried hauling away "Wow Cow" but dropped the abstract-design **bovine** and ran when they were spotted. (Lisa Newman, *Chicago's Udder Delight: Whimsical Herd of Sculptures Creates a Bull Market in Tourism*, The Washington Post, 08-11-1999, p. C1.)

coward *n.*: **poltroon**. ■ And the problem isn't even all these poor politiclones, either. It's us. We listen to them. We tolerate their existence. We vote for them. If we had a leader with moral character, we'd get rid of her in the blink of an eye. We demand **poltroons** and panderers. (Crispin Sartwell, *Nearly All U.S. Political Leaders Are Frauds*, The Arizona Republic, 10-21-1998, p. B7.)

cowardly *adj.*: **pusillanimous**. ■ Until now, the European countries have hesitated to back Washington fully [in the war against Iraq], even though they depend more on Middle East oil than the U.S. does. Last week's spurt of resolve came just in time to save continental governments from appearing totally **pusillanimous** not only in the eyes of Washington but also in European public opinion. (Lisa Beyer, *The Gulf: The Center Holds — For Now*, Time, 09-03-1990, p. 34.)

cower *v.i.*: **blench**. SEE FLINCH

(2) cower *v.i.*: **resile**. SEE RECOIL

(3) cower *v.i.*: **truckle**. SEE KOWTOW

coy (as in flirtatious, glance) *n.*: **oeillade** [French]. SEE GLANCE

cozy (or warm or friendly) *adj.*: **gemütlich** [German] ∎ The public rooms give testimony to the Danish gift for interior design, for mixing the old with the modern, creating a cozy atmosphere without ever lapsing into cuteness. [W]hitewashed brick and ancient, wonderfully irregular oak timber ... are combined here to create a mood of warm, familiar, unostentatious well-being. The bedrooms are no less **gemütlich**. (Michel Arnaud, *A Great Little Dane*, Town & Country Monthly, 10-01-1995, p. 118.)

crabby *adj.*: **atrabilious**. SEE SURLY

(2) **crabby** *adj.*: **bilious**. SEE SURLY

(3) **crabby** (person) *n.*: **crosspatch**. SEE GROUCH

(4) **crabby** *adj.*: **liverish**. SEE IRRITABLE

(5) **crabby** *adj.*: **shirty**. SEE IRRITABLE

(6) **crabby** *adj.*: **splenetic**. SEE IRRITABLE

crack (open) *v.t., v.i., n.*: **fissure**. ∎ The steeple-shattering light was followed by quakes of thunder as violent as any shift in the San Andreas. The sky **fissured** and rain fell. (Dean Koontz, *Intensity*, Knopf [1995], p. 99.)

crackle *v.i.*: **crepitate**. ∎ The Sixties People are rapidly getting past it. Their knees are going, their hips **crepitate** as they walk, gravity is doing what gravity does, their juices are drying up, liberal relativism and pot-smoking have extinguished their inner spark, they're all going deaf, and soon all that will be left is the contemplation of past glories. (Michael Bywater, *Porn With a Silver Spoon in its Mouth*, Independent on Sunday, 03-15-1998, p. 34.)

cracks (full of ...) *adj.*: **rimose**. ∎ Sir — As one (of the many) who have been delivered from the grip of substance abuse, I can understand the reasoning of the pro-cannabis clique. However, I am bemused at the willingness of The Press to give it some credence by publishing (Soapbox, July 28) their shallow sophistry, and their **rimose** ruminations. (Author not given, *Marijuana Law*, The Press [Canterbury, New Zealand], 08-10-2001, p. 4.)

crafty (behavior) *n.*: **knavery**. SEE CORRUPTION

(2) **crafty** (characterized by ... and cunning conduct) *adj.*: **Machiavellian**. SEE DECEITFUL

(3) **crafty** (conduct) *n.*: **skullduggery**. SEE DECEITFULNESS

cramped (by not affording enough space) *adj.*: **incommodious**. ∎ Trading a 67,200-sq.-ft. house (the White one) for a not-**incommodious** 5,232-sq.-ft. Dutch Colonial, Hillary Rodham Clinton, 52, spent the first night at her new home in Chappaqua, N.Y, on Jan. 5, as part of her bid to establish residency in the state and run for the senate. (David Cobb Craig, *Passages*, People, 01-24-2000, p. 95.)

cranky *adj.*: **atrabilious**. SEE SURLY

(2) **cranky** *adj.*: **bilious**. SEE SURLY

(3) **cranky** (person) *n.*: **crosspatch**. SEE GROUCH

(4) **cranky** *adj.*: **liverish**. SEE IRRITABLE

(5) **cranky** *adj.*: **querulous**. SEE PEEVISH

(6) **cranky** *adj.*: **shirty**. SEE IRRITABLE

(7) **cranky** *adj.*: **splenetic**. SEE IRRITABLE

(8) **cranky** *adj.*: **tetchy**. SEE GROUCHY

crash (spec. the act of one object striking a stationary object, usually applied to ships) *n.*: **allision**. SEE COLLISION

craving *n.*: **appetence**. ∎ Male sexual **appetence**, monotonous and warlike, can be enough to make any unprepared young wife major in menstruation for life. Resort people know that. They set out to mitigate and feminize sexuality. (Keith D. Mano, *Honeymoon Hotels in the Pocono Mountains*, Playboy, 02-1989, p. 118.)

(2) **craving** (strong ...) *n.*: **avidity**. ∎ [The movie "Crouching Tiger, Hidden Dragon"] concerns the theft of a sword, the Green Destiny. [Jen] arrives, and everything tips off-balance. The wiser, more cautious adults are both drawn to and upset by Jen's beauty and vagrant energy. They sense Jen's **avidity** for rare toys like the Green Destiny. (Richard Corliss, *The Arts/Cinema: Martial Masterpiece*, Time International, 07-10-2000, p. 44.)

(3) **craving** (condition involving ... to eat nonfood items) *n.*: **pica**. ∎ **Pica**, which is normally observed in children and is thought to result from iron deficiencies or lead exposure, causes cravings for clay, sand, dirt, plaster and paint. (Jamie Talan, *New Research Zeros In On the Lead Question*, Newsday, 11-25-1993, p. 61.)

(4) **craving** *adj.*: **athirst**. SEE EAGER

crawl (as in teem or swarm) *v.i.*: **pullulate**. SEE TEEM

craze (as in irresistible compulsion) *n.*: **cacoëthes**. SEE COMPULSION

(2) **craze** (the latest ...) *n.*: **dernier cri** [French]. SEE TREND

crazy (informal, as in daffy or loony) *adj.*: **doolally** [British; often as in "going doolally." This word is an alteration of *Deolali*, a town near Bombay in India where British soldiers awaited their return home and where sickness and boredom caused some to break down.] ∎ I see why big names feature in a [list of worst songs] of all time. It's hard not to remember the shock of a great artist going **doolally**. David Bowie (who does not feature in the list) must have had his reasons for recording "The Little Drummer Boy" with Bing Crosby, and one day he might tell them to a therapist. (David Lister, *Even the Biggest Stars Can Hit the Wrong Note*, The Independent [London], 04-24-2004, p. 43.)

(2) crazy (appearing ... as if under a spell) *adj.*: **fey**. ▪ [O]ur host, now full of wine, failed to spot an approaching roundabout in the dark and drove straight up the central grassy mound and stopped on top. ... [He] said genially: "Sorry about that, but I swear that roundabout came a good 200 yards earlier than usual." ... That is an example of what Claud Cockburn once called the kind of **fey** logic peculiar to the Irish. (Miles Kington, *It's Enough to Drive You to Nuits-St-Georges*, Independent, 06-05-1997, p. 20.)

(3) crazy (slightly mentally ..., often used humorously) *adj.*: **tetched**. ▪ A long, empty coffin sits on the rag rug, its lid propped open. ... I shrug, as if I'm used to seeing empty coffins in parlors. "Who died?" I manage to ask. "No one." He laughs. "Mr. Cottland built it for himself. He's crazy; **tetched** in the head, as my mama would say. Keeps a jug of whiskey in there, 'case he gets thirsty on the way to heaven." (Liza Ketchum, *Orphan Journey Home*, The Dallas Morning News, 11-04-1998, p. 6C.)

(4) crazy (person) *n.*: **bedlamite**. See LUNATIC

(5) crazy (as in frenzied) *adj.*: **corybantic**. See FRENZIED

(6) crazy (as in not of sound mind) *adj.*: **non compos mentis** [Latin]. See INSANE

crease (or wrinkle) *n.*, *v.t.*: **rimple**. See WRINKLE

creased (very ..., as in wrinkled) *adj.*: **rugose**. See WRINKLED

create (an idea, plan, theory or explanation after careful thought) *v.t.*: **excogitate**. See DEVISE

creation (as in establishment, of something) *n.*: **instauration**. See ESTABLISHMENT

creative (as in resourceful person) *n.*: **debrouillard** (or **débrouillard**) [French]. See RESOURCEFUL

creativity (source of ..., as in inspiration) *n.*: **Pierian spring**. See INSPIRATION

credulous (person) *n.*: **gobemouche** [French]. See GULLIBLE

creeky (as in decrepit) *adj.*: **spavined**. See DECREPIT

crestfallen *adj.*: **chapfallen**. See DEJECTED

crevices (full of ...) *adj.*: **rimose**. See CRACKS

crime (as in wrongdoing in public office) *n.*: **malversation**. See WRONGDOING

criminal (spec. an adult who instructs children how to steal) *n.*: **Fagin** [based on character on Dickens novel *Oliver Twist*, who teaches children to be pickpockets]. See THIEF

(2) criminal *n.*: **malefactor**. See WRONGDOER

crimson *adj.*: **incarnadine**. ▪ [In] The Tale of the Body Thief, the fourth entry in Anne Rice's enormously successful series, The Vampire Chronicles ... [she writes] prose that is not so much purple as **incarnadine**. "Blood is warm, cherie. Come with me, and drink blood, as you and I know how to do." (Author not given, *Print Source: Gene Lyons: A Fang Too Far, the Tale of the Body Thief by Anne Rice*, Entertainment Weekly, 11-06-1992, p. 60.)

cringe *v.i.*: **blench**. See FLINCH

(2) cringe *v.i.*: **resile**. See RECOIL

crinkle *n.*, *v.t.*: **rimple**. See WRINKLE

cripple (as in deprive of strength) *v.t.*: **enervate**. See DEBILITATE

(2) cripple (as in deprive of strength) *v.t.*: **geld**. See WEAKEN

crisis (stage or period) *n.*, *adj.*: **climacteric**. See CRITICAL

(2) crisis *n.*: **Torschlusspanik** [German]. See PANIC

critic (severe ...) *n.*: **aristarch**. ▪ [T.K. Chidambaranatha Mudaliar] was fond of saying that poetry must be rescued from the pundits, and that it was rarer to come across a genuine rasika than a good poet. [But] know that his ruthless trouncing of the spurious is in direct proportion to his passion for poetry. He was no grim **aristarch** out to censure, but [one who] identified himself with the creative mind in the niceties and nuances of expression. (Gowri Ramnarayan, *The Price of a Poet*, The Hindu, 04-08-01.)

(2) critic (who is inferior or incompetent) *n.*: **criticaster**. ▪ [S]ince [book] awards are always with us, it is better to have writers, practitioners, people who ply the trade, taking a hand in the decisions made. The alternatives are clear and ghastly [i.e. those with no literary skill]. ... In some distant studio sits the familiar panel [of judges] from hell: the rumpled iconoclast, the seething bard, and the pert **criticaster**. (Christopher Hope, *Bloomsday Schoomsday*, New Statesman [1996], 06-21-1996, p. 12.)

critical (stage or period) *n., adj.*: **climacteric**. ▪ During the autumn of 1932, the state crisis of the Weimar Republic deepened. No resolution was in sight. In the first months of the winter of 1932-3, it entered its **climacteric** phase. (Ian Kershaw, *Hitler*, Norton [1998], p. 379.)

(2) critical (as in faultfinding) *adj.*: **captious**. SEE FAULTFINDING

(3) critical (as in urgent) *adj.*: **necessitous**. See URGENT

(4) critical (as in faultfinding, person) *n.*: **smellfungus**. SEE FAULTFINDER

(5) critical (as in decisive remark, blow or factor) *n.*: **sockdolager**. SEE DECISIVE

criticism (hostile ...) *n.*: **animadversion** (*v.t.*: **animadvert**.) ▪ One of the most pressing challenges for the secretary of defense ... is the proliferation of nuclear weaponry to North Korea; but here is the secretary of defense-designate [Bobby Ray Inman] fleeing government, and citing as a cause of his flight the **animadversions** of [journalist] Ellen Goodman. ... A man who will not stand up to Ellen Goodman will not stand up to Kim Il Sung. (Leon Wieseltier, *Remembering Bobby*, The New Republic, 02-07-1994, p. 4.)

(2) criticism (delivered while leaving the scene) *n.*: **Parthian shot**. SEE PARTING SHOT

criticize (oneself) *v.t.*: **flagellate** (*n*: **flagellation**) [this word means to whip or flog another, and is properly used in that sense, but is generally used figuratively, esp. as in criticism of oneself, sometimes as in self-flagellation]. ▪ Journalists belong to the only profession whose members regularly get together to **flagellate** themselves in public. (Sheryl McCarthy, *Here's How We Cover The Blob*, Newsday, 04-12-1995, p. A17.)

(2) criticize (harshly) *v.t.*: **flay**. ▪ These young [tennis players] today. They are a favorite target for Jimmy Connors; he doesn't like their high-octane game, their monochromatic personalities, the fact that they're not ... well, like him. ... With soaring TV ratings to boost his case, Connors **flayed** the younger men mercilessly. (S.I. Price, *Tennis*, Sports Illustrated, 05-26-1997, p. 92.)

(3) criticize (harshly) *v.t.*: **fustigate**. ▪ France is at peace, prosperous, economically and socially dynamic after years of stagnation, firmly committed to the European Union in which it is perhaps the

major player. ... How paradoxical then that in this summer of 2000, a book that **fustigates** the French for their frenetic pursuit of a vague ideal of happiness and sharply criticizes French society and its values would be a runaway bestseller. (Thomas Bishop, *Notebook/France in Pursuit of Happiness*, Newsday, 09-24-2000, p. B4.)

(4) criticize (or scold or rebuke) *v.t.*: **objurgate**. ▪ The act about to be **objurgated** here calls on the Food and Drug Administration to oversee a broad revision of food labeling. ... The agency must also Solomonically settle the age-old question of how large is a "serving," which Congress has unhelpfully defined as "an amount customarily consumed." ... Who needs all this? Aside from the silliness the law will generate, the nutritional information has a cost. (Daniel Seligman, *Keeping Up*, Fortune, 07-01-1991, p. 94.)

(5) criticize (as in raise trivial objections) *v.t.*: **cavil**. SEE QUIBBLE

(6) criticize (by making false or malicious statements) *v.t.*: **calumniate**. SEE MALIGN

(7) criticize (or attack in writing) *n.*: **coup de plume** [French; attack by pen]. SEE ATTACK

(8) criticize (sharply) *v.t.*: **keelhaul**. SEE REBUKE

(9) criticize (a statement, opinion or action) *v.t.*: **oppugn**. SEE OPPOSE

(10) criticize (in a false way so as to humiliate or disgrace) *v.t.*: **traduce**. SEE MALIGN

(11) criticize (as in disparage) *v.t.*: **vilipend**. SEE DISPARAGE

critique *v.t.*: **assay**. SEE EVALUATE

crook (as in thief) *n.*: **gonif** or **ganef** or **goniff** [Yiddish]. SEE THIEF

crooked (politician) *n.*: **highbinder**. SEE CORRUPT

(2) crooked (as in unscrupulous) *adj.*: **jackleg**. SEE UNSCRUPULOUS

(3) crooked (behavior) *n.*: **knavery**. See CORRUPTION

(4) crooked (group of ... politicians) *n.*: **plunderbund**. SEE CORRUPT

cross (a body of water, esp, in a shallow part) *v.t.*: **ford**. ▪ "In some places the lagoon is no more than 2 meters high," Sarunis had said. "Sabonis could walk across it!" By this he meant that a 7-footer could **ford** the lagoon, not literally walk across it. (Alexander Wolff, *Big Game, Small World*, Warner Books [2002], p. 24.)

(2) cross (as in surly) *adj.*: **atrabilious**. SEE SURLY

(3) cross (as in surly) *adj.*: **bilious**. SEE SURLY

(4) cross (as in grouchy, person) *n.*: **crosspatch**. SEE GROUCH

(5) cross (as in irritable) *adj.*: **liverish**. SEE IRRITABLE

(6) cross (as in cranky or testy) *adj.*: **querulous**. SEE PEEVISH

(7) cross (as in irritable) *adj.*: **shirty**. SEE IRRITABLE

(8) cross *adj.*: **splenetic**. SEE IRRITABLE

(9) cross *adj.*: **tetchy**. SEE GROUCHY

crosswise *prep., adv.*: **athwart**. SEE ACROSS

crossword puzzles (one who enjoys solving or creating ...) *n.*: **cruciverbalist**. ▪ Despite the fact that thousands of people across the nation are hooked on crosswords and their seductive siblings, acrostics, no 12-step program has been developed to treat it. ... In high school, I was a closet **cruciverbalist** [because] working crosswords seemed so uncool. (Kristin Tillotson, *The Life and Times of a Crossword Addict*, Minneapolis Star Tribune, 03-13-1995, p. 10.)

crow (hoarse, raucous sound of) *n.*: **caw**. ▪ [T]ens of thousands of crows ... inexplicably flock to the treetops above downtown buildings and parks about this time every year. The birds call incessantly, with loud, grating, monotonous **caws**. (Susan Levine, *City Hopes Crows Respond to Distress Signal*, The Dallas Morning News, 12-22-1996, p. 16A.)

(2) crow (of, resembling or characteristic of) *adj.*: **corvine**. ▪ Periodic calls for the stoning of the crows [due to overpopulation] are not new to Moscow, whose **corvine** population pre-dates Ivan the Terrible. (Phil Reeves, *Something to Crow About Amid Another False Spring*, Independent, 03-08-1996, p. 12.)

crowd (of people as in multitude or throng) *n.*: **ruck**. SEE MULTITUDE

crowd-pleasing (of an argument designed for ...) *adj., adv.*: **ad captandum** (or **ad captandum vulgus**) [Latin]. SEE ARGUMENT

crowded (heavily ... region or city) *n.*: **megalopolis**. ▪ Deng's plan envisions the **megalopolis** of 13 million inhabitants [Shanghai, China] as a booster engine, towing the country's midriff and north into the 21st century. (James Walsh, *Nothing in Wang Hon Gwen's Life Belittled Him So Much As ...*, Time International, 10-05-1992, p. 18.)

(2) crowded (together, esp. in rows) *adj.*: **serried**. ▪ The crowd went wild at Hitler's entrance, standing on chairs and benches, waving, shouting "Heil," stamping their feet. Around 200 stormtroopers in **serried** ranks with banners filed past Hitler, greet-ing him with the fascist salute. (Ian Kershaw, *Hitler*, Norton [1998], p. 292.)

(3) crowded (with) *adj.*: **aswarm**. SEE TEEMING

crucial (stage or period) *n., adj.*: **climacteric**. SEE CRITICAL

(2) crucial (as in urgent) *adj.*: **necessitous**. SEE URGENT

crude *n.*: **artless**. ▪ [For George Bush and Al Gore in campaign ads], clever is dangerous. You can inadvertently alienate important sectors of the electorate (for instance, the stupid) or come off as slick and dishonest. Since Watergate, ads have been much more straightforward — and **artless**. [With all the] ugly, blaring ads, perhaps every ad, regardless of its content, becomes a negative one. (James Poniewozik, *Nation/Campaign 2000: Campaign Ad Nauseam*, Time, 11-13-2000, p. 40.)

(2) crude (or poorly put together, esp. with respect to a writing or speech) *adj.*: **incondite**. ▪ Suddenly I'm tired, despite the java fix, and resigned to the fact that come Monday, I'll have about enough free time — between diaper origami and learning the baby language of the day and getting the turkey loaf done before my wife comes home — to write an **incondite** self-pitying limerick: "There was an old pop in Seattle/Who was stuck between bottle and rattle." (R. W. Lucky, *What I Want to Be After My Child Grows Up*, The Seattle Times, 03-27-1994, p. L5.)

(3) crude (person) *n.*: **grobian**. SEE BOOR

(4) crude (as in rough) *adj.*: **scabrous**. SEE ROUGH

(5) crude (person) *n.*: **yahoo**. SEE BOOR

cruel (in the manner of an oppressive and despotic organization) *adj.*: **jackbooted**. SEE OPPRESSIVE

crumbly *adj.*: **friable**. ▪ But there is a much easier way to make these crumb-crowned desserts. You can make a pastry base and a crumbly topping from one mixture, instead of preparing two separate doughs. Simply blend the ingredients for a sweet dough in the food processor until it forms a **friable** mixture. (Faye Levy, *Crumb-Topped Treats*, Jerusalem Post, 02-24-1995.)

(2) crumbly *adj.*: **pulverulent**. SEE POWDERY

crumple (or wrinkle) *n., v.t.*: **rimple**. SEE WRINKLE

(2) crumple *n., v.t.*: **rimple**. SEE WRINKLE

crusade (for an idea or principle) *n.*: **jihad**. ▪ Mr. Withey was convinced that electromagnetic fields cause cancer. And, at the time he was waging his courtroom **jihad** against Big Electric, he had at least two widely reported scientific papers to support his conclusion — to give him real hope that, one day, he just might extract an asbestoslike or breast-implant-like settlement from the nation's deep-pocket utilities. (Joseph Perkins, *Payoffs for Junk Science*, The Washington Times, 08-03-1999, p. A17.)

crush (as in reduce to powder) *v.t.*: **comminute**. SEE PULVERIZE

crux (of a matter, as in the essence) *n.*: **quiddity**. SEE ESSENCE

cry (in lament for the dead) *v.i.*: **keen**. ∎ When word spread through the convent, recalls one nun, "Everybody rushed to [the Mother Teresa's] room. They were all around her, wailing and hugging the Mother's body." The sisters' **keening** was heard by the communists, whose party headquarters are next door, and they tipped off journalists that Teresa had died. (Tim Mcgirk, *Religion: "Our Mother Is Gone!" In a Lavish Ceremony That Mother Teresa Would Have Scorned, Calcutta and the Rest of the World Bid a Touching Farewell to an Angel of Mercy*, Time International, 09-22-1997, p. 54.)

(2) cry (over, as in lament) *v.t.*: **bewail**. SEE LAMENT

(3) cry (as in screech, like a cat in heat) *v.i.*: **caterwaul**. SEE SCREECH

(4) cry (as in plea) *n.*: **cri de coeur** [French, lit. cry of the heart]. SEE PLEA

(5) cry (weakly) *v.i.*: **mewl**. SEE WHIMPER

(6) cry (in a whiny or whimpering way) *v.i.*: **pule**. SEE WHIMPER

(7) cry (as in wail) *v.i.*: **ululate**. SEE WAIL

crying (of or relating to) *adj.*: **lachrymal**. SEE TEARS

(2) crying *adj.*: **lachrymose**. SEE TEARFUL

crypt (esp. under a church) *n.*: **undercroft**. ∎ There are also distortions that are simply silly. "Every Christmas night the entire population squeezes into the **undercroft** to hear read the passages of the Gospel of St. Luke," ... he writes. It is not only ridiculous to imagine the entire population of 12,000 crowding into one little crypt on Christmas Eve; it is silly to expect all the Christians of Beit Sahour to attend any service together. (David Bar-Illan, *Fiction Which Passes as "Respectable" Reportage*, Jerusalem Post, 01-20-1995.)

cryptic (or obscure speech or writing, esp. deliberately) *adj.*: **elliptical**. ∎ "We're thinking of building out here — we'll have to if we're going to have kids," [Melanie Griffith] says offhandedly. "Excuse me?" Griffith's smile is as ambiguous as the Mona Lisa's. ... Is she **elliptically** trying to confirm a persistent

tabloid report? Not this day. (Peter Chandler, *Features: Melanie in Love*, In Style, 03-01-1996, p. 80.)

(2) cryptic (or ambiguous or equivocal) *adj.*: **sybilline** (or **sibylline**; often cap.) [This word derives from Sybil (or Sibyl), one of a number of women regarded as prophets by the ancient Greeks. It also means "prophetic".] ∎ It was crucial, [Federal Reserve Board chairman Alan] Greenspan added, that the US continue to keep inflation in check. Although there were "some reasons for concern, at least with regard to the nearer term," prospects for achieving this were "fundamentally good." This typically **sybilline**, central bankerly language does nothing to reduce the likelihood that the policy-setting Federal Open Market Committee will raise rates at its meeting next Tuesday. (Rupert Cornwall, *Fed Chief Hints Any Interest Rate Rise Will Be Small*, The Independent [London], 01-26-1995, p. 33.)

(2) cryptic (or obscure) *adj.*: **Delphic**. SEE AMBIGUOUS

cryptography *n.*: **steganography**. SEE CODES

cuddle (as in caress or fondle) *v.i.*: **canoodle** (often "canoodle with"). SEE CARESS

cultivated (person) *n.*: **bel esprit**. ∎ Momigliano [showed] that the "antiquarians" of the sixteenth and seventeenth centuries were neither maniacal collectors nor narrow specialists, but strong and disciplined minds, philosophically well-equipped scholars [and] Gibbon, who detested the **bel esprit** side of the Enlightenment, was the heir of these scholars, and he knew it. (Marc Fumaroli, *The Antiquarian as Hero*, The New Republic, 05-28-2001.)

cultivation (fit for ...) *adj.*: **arable**. SEE FARMING

cultural (moral and/or intellectual spirit of an era) *n.*: **zeitgeist**. SEE SPIRIT

culture (modification of one's ... through living in another culture) *n.*: **acculturation**. ∎ He describes acculturatic as the process of exchange by which immigrants modify their attitudes, cultural norms and behaviors as a result of interaction within the United States culture. "**Acculturation** produces changes in sexual attitudes and behavior," Sabogal says. (Sandra Varner, *Demographics Help Explain Hispanic Sexual Behavior*, Oakland Post, 10-29-1995.)

culture wars *n.*: **Kulturkampf** [German]. ∎ Amid all the hubbub surrounding the defections of [two African-American studies professors] from Harvard to Princeton recently, it went unmentioned that only thirty years ago, African-American studies as we know it today didn't even exist. Although the **Kulturkampf** of the 1960s touched many academic disciplines, it was the creation of black studies programs that led to the most rancorous debates on American campuses. (John McMillan, *Black Unlike Me [White Boy: A Memoir by Mark D. Naison]*, The Nation, 07-15-2002.)

cumbersome (and clumsy like an elephant) *adj.*: **elephantine**. SEE CLUMSY

cunning (characterized by ... conduct) *adj.*: **Machiavellian**. SEE DECEITFUL
  (2) **cunning** (conduct) *n.*: **skullduggery**. SEE DECEITFULNESS

cup (shallow ... or bowl with a handle) *n.*: **porringer**. SEE BOWL

curative (as in having the power to cure or heal) *adj.*: **sanative**. SEE HEALTHFUL

cure (alleged ... which is untested or unproved) *n.*: **nostrum**. SEE REMEDY

cure-all *n.*: **catholicon**. SEE REMEDY

currency (of or relating to ..., including collecting) *adj.*: **numismatic**. SEE COINS

curse (as in put a ... upon) *v.t.*: **imprecate**. ▪ [Chinese Premier Li Peng] has a gift for remorselessness. He has gone out of his way not merely to trounce human rights and crush democracy, but to do so in a way calculated to insult and to taunt the U.S. government. He is convinced, not without reason, that Washington will never do anything more than **imprecate**. Trade, he is sure, certainly will never become an instrument of American pressure. (Michael Kelly, *A Toast [Al Gore's Shameful Salute to Chinese Premier Li Peng]*, The New Republic, 04-14-1997.)
  (2) **curse** *n.*: **malediction**. ▪ Almost everyone knows about Irish blessings: May the wind always be at your back, and may you be in heaven half an hour before the Devil knows you're dead. But there's a darker side to the coin: The Irish curse. The **malediction** is as Irish as cable-knit sweaters, soda bread and Guinness Stout. (Bill Marvel, *The Good Auld Curse: In the Spirit of St. Patrick's Day, We Look to the Art Form of the True Irish Curse*, The Dallas Morning News, 03-17-2000, p. 1C.)
  (3) **curse** (as in detest) *v.t.*: **execrate**. SEE HATE
  (4) **curse** *n., adj.*: **hoodoo**. SEE BAD LUCK

cursed (perpetually ... , as in unlucky person) *n.*: **schlimazel** [Yiddish]. SEE SUPERFICIAL

cursing (excessive, esp. involuntarily when mentally ill) *n.*: **coprolalia**. ▪ "I've always said that 15 percent of the people with Tourette's have **coprolalia**, but 100 percent of jazz musicians have it," Wolff jokes. "So I definitely swear, but not because of Tourette's." (Brett Anderson, *Playing It Backward; Musician's Medical Disorder May Be a Grace Note*, The Washington Post, 06-08-2001, p. C1.)

cursory (as in superficial knowledge of a subject while pretending to be learned) *n.*: **sciolism**. SEE SUPERFICIAL

curtailed (something ..., as in abridged) *n.*: **bobtail**. SEE ABRIDGED

curve (slightly) *v.t., v.i.*: **camber**. ▪ Favourably **cambered** bends are great. Bikers love them, because they instill confidence and allow faster cornering. Off-**cambered** bends are horrible; they give less ground clearance and your bike can easily slide away from you, especially in the wet. (Olly Duke, *Motoring: Going Round the Bend*, The Daily Telegraph, 08-22-1998.)
  (2) **curve** (in and out) *v.i.*: **sinuate**. SEE WIND
  (3) **curve** (away from a course or intended path) *v.t.*: **yaw**. SEE VEER

custom (as in habit or practice) *n.*: **praxis**. ▪ Pot for the nausea and the heaviness of heart, vitamin C for cell structure, sugar for the depleted blood, caffiene to burn off the moral fog — the whole **praxis** of alcoholism and reckless living. (Michael Chabon, *Wonder Boys*, Villard [1995], p. 132.)
  (2) **custom** (excessive reverence for ... or forebears) *n.*: **filiopietistic**. SEE OLD-FASHIONED
  (3) **custom** (precise observance of ...) *n.*: **punctilio**. SEE ETIQUETTE

customary *adj.*: **wonted**. Of course, the [CIA], with its **wonted** high-handedness, was trying to find a substitute for the democratically elected president, Jean-Bertrand Aristide, whom it slandered in one of its famous "psychological profiles." The CIA seems to feel that democracy is all very well and good, but it can be overdone. (Mary McGrory, *Resources Wasted on Costly CIA*, St. Louis Post-Dispatch, 10-21-1994, p. 15D.)

customer (regular ... of a place, esp. a place of entertainment) *n.*: **habitué** [French]. SEE REGULAR

customs (of a person, people or culture) *n.*: **ethos**. SEE CHARACTER

cut down (with an ax) *v.t.*: **hew**. SEE AX

cut off (as in consider separately) *v.t.*: **prescind** (generally as in "prescind from"). SEE ISOLATE

cutting (as in ... remarks) *adj.*: **astringent**. SEE HARSH

cynic *n.*: **crepehanger**. SEE PESSIMIST

cynical (as in skeptical) *adj.*: **zetetic**. SEE SKEPTICAL

D

dabbler (as in amateur) *n.*: **dilettante**. SEE AMATEUR

daffy (informal as in daffy or loony) *adj.*: **doolally**. SEE CRAZY

daily *adj.*: **diurnal**. ∎ Wilt [Chamberlain] remains the most nocturnal of men; often, he will not call it a day before the sun comes up. Apart from the hours he sets aside for his exercise, there is no pattern to his existence. He does not even live a **diurnal** life as we know it. He will, for example, go on a complete fast, eat nothing at all for three days, and then suddenly, at 4:30 in the morning, devour five greasy pork chops. ... He is as independent as anyone in the world. (Frank Deford, *Doing Just Fine, My Man*, Sports Illustrated, 08-18-1986.)

dainty (in an affected manner) *adj.*: **niminy-piminy**. ∎ "Jo does use such slang words," observed Amy, with a reproving look at the long figure stretched on the rug. ... "Don't, Jo; it's so boyish." "That's why I do it," [said Jo]. "I detest rude, unlady-like girls," [said Amy]. "I hate affected, **niminy-piminy** chits," [said Jo]. (Polly Frost, *The Woman in Winona*, Harper's Bazaar, 12-01-1994, p. 162.)

damages (awarded for injured feelings, as opposed to financial loss or physical suffering) *n.*: **solatium**. SEE COMPENSATION

damaging (mutually ... to both sides) *adj.*: **internecine**. SEE DESTRUCTIVE

(2) damaging *adj.*: **nocent**. SEE HARMFUL

(3) damaging (as in harmful) *adj.*: **nocuous**. SEE HARMFUL

damnation (as in loss of the soul) *n.*: **perdition**. ∎

The question is whether expanding the definition of marriage to include same-sex couples launches us on the path to **perdition** or merely heralds the shedding of another irrational prejudice. (William Raspberry, *Why Not Encourage Monogamy?* The Washington Post, 05-01-2000, p. A25.)

dampen (flax to separate fibers) *v.t.*: **ret**. SEE MOISTEN

dance (in a leaping or frolicking manner) *v.i.*: **curvet**. ∎ [The Fiesta] is about to begin. ... On a terrace above us looms Zozobra, a forty-foot-high, white-skirted monster. ... Long white arms and hands flail helplessly at his sides as two high-crowned dancers leap and **curvet** up a stone stairway to the foot of the scaffold, brandishing torches. (Herb Greer, *American Shangri-la*, The World & I, 09-01-1995, p. 122.)

(2) dance (uncontrollable urge to ...) *n.*: **tarantism**. ∎ [In the 15th to 17th century, in Italy, people] would react to the bite of the [tarantula] spider by developing uncontrollable urges to dance ... until the victim died of poison or exhaustion. [L]ater medical historians ... regarded **tarantism** as a mental disease, in other words, mass hysteria. (Simon Wessely, *Laughs on the Way to Salvation*, The Times, 06-28-1994.)

(3) dance (formal ... esp. for debutantes) *n.*: **cotillion**. SEE BALL

dance hall (in France) *n.*: **bal musette**. ∎ At first, while the audience is settling into its ad hoc cabaret in the chapel of Mount Vernon College on Friday, the "Encore Paris" show seems to be a dance program. A striking couple is putting old 78s on a phonograph and behaving as though the chapel were a Parisian **bal musette**. (Author not given, *Performing Arts*, The Washington Post, 05-02-2000, p. C8.)

dancing (act of ..., sometimes with leaping about) *n.*: **saltation**. ∎ Yes, folks, it's [the] sultan of sexy Broadway **saltation**. ... Welcome back, Bob Fosse! You may have been in hoofer heaven/hell for 11 years now, but your snazzy steps are alive and kicking — and prancing and slithering and popping too. Not just in the hit revival of "Chicago," but now in "Fosse: A Celebration in Song and Dance." (Jan Breslauer, *Theater Review; Paying Homage the Best Way Hoofers Can*, The Los Angeles Times, 10-23-1998, p. F1.)

(2) dancing (of or related to) *adj.*: **terpischorean**. ∎ The real scandal in my working as a stripper is that I can't dance. It's just not a talent I've ever possessed. ... But lacking **terpischorean** skills never hurt me that much. (Lily Burana, *Strip City*, Talk Miramax Books [2001], p. 33.)

dandruff (covered with ...) *adj.*: **scurfy**. ■ Q: I have a 10-year-old cat who has never been outside. ... The only problem I see is that her fur has dandruff at the back. I groom her regularly and the fur on her paws and face is fine. Mrs. Ann Lyons, Glasgow. A: A dry and **scurfy** coat is not an uncommon problem in animals that live indoors. (Author not given, *Can My Moggie Shake Off Her Dandruff Problem?* Sunday Mail, 10-01-2000, p. 35.)

dandy *n.*: **fop**. SEE VAIN

dangerous (journey or passage, with dangers on both sides) *idiom*: **between Scylla and Charybdis**. SEE PRECARIOUS

(2) dangerous (very ..., as in causing or portending death) *adj.*: **funest**. SEE DEADLY

(3) dangerous (as in irresponsible or reckless) *adj.*: **harum-scarum**. SEE RECKLESS

(4) dangerous (or harmful) *adj.*: **noisome**. SEE HARMFUL

(5) dangerous (as in perilous) *adj.*: **parlous**. SEE PERILOUS

(6) dangerous (potentially ... place or situation) *n.*: **tinderbox**. SEE EXPLOSIVE

dank (as in musty) *adj.*: **fusty**. SEE MUSTY

daring *n.*: **hardihood**. SEE COURAGE

(2) daring (as in gall or temerity) *n.*: **hardihood**. SEE GALL

(3) daring (overly ...) *adj.*: **Icarian**. SEE OVERAMBITIOUS

(4) daring (or bold while under the influence of alcohol) *adj.*: **potvaliant**. SEE COURAGEOUS

dark (esp. as to the ocean) *adj.*: **aphotic**. ■ The depths [of the ocean] can be divided into three realms — sunlit, twilight and midnight where there is no light at all and temperatures are near freezing. The midnight zone, called the **aphotic** zone by oceanographers, makes up 90 percent of the ocean. It is the home of little-known creatures and blind fish that will never see day, never venture even into the twilight. (Linton Weeks, *Cosmic Relief*, The Washington Post, 01-02-2000, p. F4.)

(2) dark (and misty and gloomy) *adj.*: **caliginous**. ■ But the ... pervasive creepiness [of the television show "the X-Files"] is not for everyone. Even the look of the show is **caliginous** — much of the action takes place in the dark, with the agents' trademark flashlights beaming through the mist. (M.S. Mason, *Decoding 'X-Files': the Movie*, The Christian Science Monitor, 06-19-1998.)

(3) dark *adj.* (*adv.*: in the ...): **darkling**. ■ Not every competitive field has been surrendered to foreigners. Bright spots on the **darkling** plain include the computer industry, which 28% of bosses think is America's best world competitor. (Terence P. Pare, *CEO Poll/Cover Stories: Why Some Do it the Wrong Way*, Fortune, 05-21-1990, p. 75.)

(4) dark (literary style which is ..., gloomy, remote and/or grotesque) *adj.*: **gothic**. ■ Steeped in creepy **gothic** gloom, the narrative provides a series of mazes within mazes, dead ends and sudden tantalizing glimpses of a logical solution. It's pleasant enough entertainment for the sort of reader who likes spooky thrills mixed with serious edification. (Francine Prose, *Picks & Pans: Pages*, People, 05-12-1997, p. 28.)

(5) dark (and gloomy) *adj.*: **acherontic**. SEE GLOOMY

(6) dark (and gloomy) *adj.*: **Cimmerian**. SEE GLOOMY

(7) dark (and gloomy, as in suggestive of a funeral) *adj.*: **sepulchral**. SEE FUNEREAL

(8) dark (and gloomy) *adj.*: **tenebrous**. SEE GLOOMY

darling *n.*: **acushla** (my ...) [Irish]. ■ When St. Patrick offered to allow [the women to propose marriage] every seven years, St. Bridget threw her arms round his neck and said: "Arrah, Patrick, jewel, I daurn't go back to the girls wid such a proposal. Make it one year in four." St. Patrick replied: "Bridget, **acushla**, squeeze me that way agin, an' I'll give ye leap-year, the longest of the lot." (William Hartston, *Numbers a Giant Leap in Time*, Independent, 02-29-1996, p. 26.)

(2) darling (my ...) *n.*: **Mavoureen** [Irish]. ■ "Come back to Erin, **Mavoureen**, **Mavoureen**, come back aroon to the land of my birth, come with the shamrock in the springtime, **Mavoureen**." And [President Kennedy] continued, "This is not the land of my birth, but it is the land for which I hold the greatest affection, and I will certainly come back in the springtime." (Edythe Preet, *Presidents & First Ladies Of Irish Ancestry*, Irish America, 08-31-1994.)

dash (as in small amount) *n.*: **soupçon** [French]. SEE TRACE

date (as in appointment, esp. for illicit sexual relations) *n.*: **assignation**. SEE APPOINTMENT

dated (as in out of style) *adj.*: **démodé** [French]. SEE OUTMODED

daughter (of or relating to a son or ...) *adj.*: **filial**. SEE OFFSPRING

dawdle (as in idle or waste time) *v.i.*: **footle** (usu. as in "footle around"). ∎ [Hillman says] you can't use accidents as a measure of danger. ... Name the safest form of transport, he commands. You **footle** around until he comes up with the answer, which is a heavy [truck], because if you're driving one you're unlikely to be killed in a crash. Now name the most dangerous. Answer: again a heavy [truck], because if one hits you, you're pretty sure to be killed. (Anne Karpf, *A Chain Reaction: For 30 Years Mayer Hillman Has Been Busily Turning Conventional Political Thinking on its Head*, The Guardian [London], 11-02-2002.)

(2) dawdle (due to indecision) *v.i.*: **dither**. SEE PROCRASTINATE

(3) dawdle (as in procrastinate or hesitate to act) *v.i.*: **shilly-shally**. SEE PROCRASTINATE

dawdler (as in one who strolls through city streets idly) *n.*: **flâneur** [French]; (**dawdling** *n.*: **flânerie**). SEE IDLER

dawn (of or relating to ... or dusk, as in twilight) *adj.*: **crepuscular**. SEE TWILIGHT

(2) dawn (of or relating to ... or morning) *adj.*: **matutinal**. SEE MORNING

daybreak (of or relating to ...) *adj.*: **matinal**. SEE MORNING

(2) daybreak (of or relating to ...) *adj.*: **matutinal**. SEE MORNING

daydreamer (as in an impractical contemplative person with no clear occupation or income) *n.*: **luftmensch** [lit. "man of air"; German, Yiddish]. SEE DREAMER

daze *v.t.*: **benumb**. ∎ The main flaw, though, is that he **benumbs** the reader with too many useless facts. At times, for instance, he seems more taken with minutiae about the yacht than with the passion of Callas and Onassis. And that sinks the story. (Linnea Lannon, *Picks & Pans: Pages*, People, 11-20-2000, p. 57.)

dazzling (in effect) *adj.*: **foudroyant** [French]. ∎ Heavy on elan and the damper pedal, pianists such as Simon, Earl Wild, Jorge Bolet and Byron Janis wow you with **foudroyant** playing. (Andrew Druckenbrod, *Pianist Abbey Simon Mixes Flashiness*, Substance, Minneapolis Star Tribune, 07-07-1999, p. 4B.)

(2) dazzling (as in shining brightly) *adj.*: **effulgent**. SEE BRIGHT

(3) dazzling (as in shining brightly) *adj.*: **fulgurant**. SEE BRIGHT

(4) dazzling (as in shining brightly) *adj.*: **refulgent**. SEE BRIGHT

dead (repository for bones or bodies of the ...) *n.*: **charnel**. SEE REPOSITORY

(2) dead (worship of ... people) *n.*: **necrolatry**. SEE WORSHIP

(3) dead (fascination with or erotic attraction to ... people) *n.*: **necrophilia**. SEE CORPSES

(4) dead (list of recently ... persons) *n.*: **necrology**. SEE OBITUARY

(5) dead (abnormal fear of ... people) *n.*: **necrophobia**. SEE FEAR

deaden *v.t.*: **narcotize**. ∎ Imagine being locked in a room with [Ontario's Premier Mike Harris]. How long do you think you could stay awake? Five minutes? ... Harris was helped by the **narcotizing** drone of his voice and the way he walked as though someone had shot novocaine into both shoulders. (Paul Wells, *Canada/Election 2000*, Time International, 11-20-2000, p. 64.)

(2) deaden *v.t.*: **obtund**. ∎ [He hoped he] would recover in time for their proposed [naval] action upon Boxing Day, or weather not permitting, upon the New Year's day. It seemed wise to attack when the better part of their foes, complacent with garrison duty, would be **obtunded** from holiday celebrations. (S.N. Dyer, *Resolve and Resistance*, Omni, 04-01-1995, p. 66.)

deadly (as in causing or portending death) *adj.*: **funest**. ∎ Something that regularly clangs painfully on my ears is abuse of the word "fun" [as in:] "It's the funest thing I've ever done." That means the opposite of what is intended. If you take advantage of a deal and pay only $1 to to bungee jump on a system designed and built by 12-year-olds, it could be the [most] **funest** thing you ever did. (Dave Brown, *Case of the Disappearing Canadian Corpses Has Been Resolved*, Ottawa Citizen, 11-21-2002, p. B5.)

dealer (esp. a person who sells quack medicines) *n.*: **mountebank**. SEE HUCKSTER

dear (as in darling) *n.*: **acushla** [Irish]. SEE DARLING

(2) dear (my ...) *n.*: **Mavoureen** [Irish]. SEE DARLING

death (of, relating to or resembling...) *adj.*: **thanatoid**. ∎ The Marquess of Bristol had been dying in public for many years [from drug abuse]. At first his audience was amused — they gathered in Deauville for grand house parties held at his expense. **Thanatoid** flamboyance commanded morbid respect until it became apparent that to be a member of Bristol's entourage was to experience the throes of his disorders. (Jessica Berens, *Obituary: The Marquess of Bristol*, Independent, 01-12-1999, p. 6.)

(2) death (fascination with ...) *n.*: **thanatophilia**. ∎ A worker in a palliative care unit in Paris, [Marie De Hennezzel's book] is filled with honeyed words, New Age gimcrackery, and a fair amount of Mary Worth-style common sense, as is usual in self-help books. When she holds the dying or listens to their life-narratives, she can't help a bit of self-congratulatory preening. The clinical name for her malady might be **thanatophilia**. (Jon Newlin, *Death Prattle*, Times-Picayune [New Orleans, LA], 07-13-1997, p. D7.)

(3) death (object which reminds one of ...) *n.*: **memento mori** [Latin]. See MORTALITY

(4) death (notice of ...) *n.*: **necrology**. See OBITUARY

(5) death (fascination with or erotic attraction to ...) *n.*: **necrophilia**. See CORPSES

(6) death (abnormal fear of ...) *n.*: **necrophobia**. See FEAR

(7) death (blow, as in put an end to) *n.*: **quietus** (esp. as in "put the quietus to"). See TERMINATE

deathly (as in pale or corpselike) *adj.*: **cadaverous**. See CORPSELIKE

death sentence (for convicted persons, spec. burning of heretics at the stake) *n.*: **auto-da-fe**. See EXECUTION

debased (morally ...) *v.t.*: **cankered**. See CORRUPTED

debatable (as in controversial opinion or person who holds one) *n.*: **polemic**. See CONTROVERSY

debate (given to argument or ...) *adj., n.*: **eristic**. ∎ Within the war room [of General Motors' strategy board], the atmosphere is informal, spirited, irreverent, **eristic** — and often openly critical of GM's past practices. (Author not given, *Inside GM's War Room*, Time, 12-13-1993, p. 70.)

(2) debate (about a philosophical or theological issue) *n.*: **quodlibet** [see also the use of this word at "subtlety"]. ∎ Sir: Your [article] supporting the ordination of women, like other exponents of this bias, has its argument flawed by one simple fact. For the Christian, this **quodlibet** is not to be solved by worldly conjecture or current trends but by informed examination of biblical doctrine. The Bible

is the basic text and first book of reference on Christianity and to depart from it when formulating doctrine will be eventually harmful to the Christian church. (Colin Poyner [letter writer], *Biblical Doctrine vs. Modern Ideology*, Sydney Morning Herald, 01-03-1992.)

(3) debate (as in dialogue, in which neither side hears or understands or pays attention to the other) *n.*: **dialogue des sourds** [French]. See DIALOGUE

(4) debate (person who hates rational ... or enlightenment) *n.*: **misologist**. See CLOSED-MINDED

debauched *adj.*: **scrofulous**. See DEPRAVED

debilitate (as in deprive of strength) *v.t.*: **enervate**. ∎ To some the [extension of credit to ex-slaves] was worse than crooked. It resembled an old-fashioned dole, a series of **enervating** handouts, although the tenants had earned their money through backbreaking work. (David Oshinsky, *Worse Than Slavery*, The Free Press [1996], p. 118.)

debilitated (from loss or lack of body strength) *adj.*: **asthenic** (*n.*: **asthenia**). See WEAK

debonair (as in refined or elegant) *adj.*: **raffiné** (or **raffine**) [French]. See REFINED

debris *n.*: **detritus**. ∎ Either these beachgoers were unusually tidy or the French comb this beach regularly, because there was very little interesting **detritus**. (Katharine Weber, *Objects in Mirror Are Closer Than They Appear*, Crown [1995], p. 35.)

debutantes (formal ball for) *n.*: **cotillion**. See BALL

decade *n.*: **decennium**. ∎ We'll call this the **decennium**-plus-five list. It's a compendium wrought from 15 years of covering state government and politics. Contemplating this list of Ohio's political bests and worsts since 1985 is bound to make you ... listless. (Joe Hallett, *Best, Worst, Whatever: This List Tops Off 15 Years of Coverage*, The Columbus Dispatch, 12-26-1999, p. 3C.)

decadent (excessively ..., esp. in a sensuous way) *adj.*: **sybaritic**. See LUXURIOUS

decay (of bone or teeth) *n.*: **caries** (*adj.* **carious**). ∎ What are we to make of the success of the water fluoridation program? Initiated and endlessly encouraged by the U.S. Public Health Service and many local agencies, the program has dramatically reduced dental **caries**, just as its proponents predicted four decades ago. ... Fifty years ago, 90% of American kids had some form of tooth decay. Today the country is close to eliminating decay. (Daniel Seligman, *Keeping Up: The Terrible News About Teeth*, Fortune, 10-10-1988, p. 175.)

deceit *n.*: **legerdemain**. SEE TRICKERY

deceitful (characterized by ... and cunning conduct) *adj.*: **Machiavellian**. ▮ Every drafting system leaves room for some **Machiavellian** stacking ploy. In leagues where managers rate their own players, several managers say one trick (which they've never tried themselves, of course) is to rate a good player lower than he deserves. That way other managers will leave the kid alone long enough for the same manager to draft him again. (Patrick Boyle, *Choosing Sides/Today's Little League Coaches Put Together Teams Through a Mix of Skill, Luck and, Sometimes, a Little Cunning*, Newsday, 04-13-1997, p. E8.)

(2) deceitful (as in unscrupulous) *adj.*: **jackleg**. SEE UNSCRUPULOUS

(3) deceitful (as in hypocritical) *adj.*: **Janus-faced**. SEE TWO-FACED

(4) deceitful (scheming or trickery) *n.*: **jiggery-pokery**. SEE TRICKERY

(5) deceitful (behavior) *n.*: **knavery**. SEE CORRUPTION

(6) deceitful *adj.*: **mendacious**. SEE DISHONEST

deceitfulness *n.*: **skullduggery**. ▮ Although no one knows exactly how much money is lost to financial planner fraud each year, a 30-state survey ... estimated it totaled $400 million in 1988. ... "Investments are the perfect vehicle for **skullduggery** because you don't expect to get a return for months or years. By the time you discover the fraud, the money is long gone." (Christine Dugas, *Fraud Warnings — You Can't Protect Yourself From Bad Advice Unless You Keep Some Control Over Your Money*, Newsday, 05-07-1995, p. 3.)

deceive *v.t.*: **hornswoggle**. ▮ The JCC Holding Corp. says its Canal Street casino is "poised to do well in the future," and so many people believe it that the share price, though still modest, came close to doubling in the last few weeks. But experience tells us that it is not difficult to **hornswoggle** stock market investors, and that it is not wise to rely on the veracity of any pronouncement from the casino. (James Gill, *Jackpot for Harrah's? Don't Bet on it*, The Times-Picayune, 03-24-2002, p. 7.)

(2) deceive *v.t.*: **humbug**. ▮ [A] speechwriter for Dan Quayle declared that for the past decade and a half, the American people have been hypocrites, wanting smaller government, lower taxes and all the benefits of the welfare state, all at the same time. And that is the truth. Our people wanted to be **humbugged**, which is the reason they liked Ronald Reagan so much. He was a master at equivocation and hypocrisy. (William Brown [letter writer], *Americans Want it All*, Pittsburgh Post-Gazette, 01-27-1997.)

(3) deceive (as in swindle) *v.t.*: **bunco**. SEE SWINDLE

(4) deceive (specious reasoning intended to ... or rationalize) *n.*: **casuistry**. SEE FALLACIOUS

(5) deceive (and defraud in the process) *v.t., v.i.*: **cozen**. SEE DEFRAUD

(6) deceive (as in trick or cheat) *v.t.*: **euchre**. SEE CHEAT

(7) deceive (as in bluff) *v.t.*: **four-flush** (*n.*: **four-flusher**). SEE BLUFF

(8) deceive (or force someone into doing something, esp. by fraud or coercion) *v.t.*: **shanghai** (person who does so *n.* **shanghier**). SEE COERCE

deceiving (something which is ..., as in delusion) *n.*: **ignis fatuus**. SEE DELUSION

decency (lit. humanity) *n.*: **menschlichkeit** [German, Yiddish]. ▮ [John Paul II] is a selfless figure in a me-first world. [When traveling, not once] did the pope ever ask where he was going to sleep, what he would eat or wear, or what his creature comforts would be. ... A person may be liberal or conservative, avant garde or traditional, but let him or her be decent, and most of the time that's enough. This realm of **menschlichkeit**, authentic humanity is where John Paul's appeal comes from. (John L. Allen, Jr., *Twenty-Five Years: In His Long, Polarizing Pontificate, John Paul II Has Defied Categorization*, National Catholic Reporter, 10-10-2003.)

deception *n.*: **legerdemain**. SEE TRICKERY

deceptive (words or language) *n.*: **flummery**. ▮ A lot of the yammering about welfare "reform" is pure **flummery**. Politicians know there is a pent-up urge to drastically cut welfare and are calling their intention to try to do so "reform." (Linda Chavez, *The Welfare-Reform Fantasy*, USA Today, 01-25-1995.)

(2) deceptive (something which is ..., as in delusion) *n.*: **ignis fatuus**. SEE DELUSION

decision-making (based on faith alone rather than reason, esp. in philosophical or religious matters) *n.*: **fideism**. SEE FAITH

decisive (remark, blow, or factor) *n.*: **sockdolager**. ▮ The American Council for the Arts [wanted to] show how much the American people love the arts. ... [T]hey retained pollster Lou Harris [who knows that] 99% of a public opinion poll lies in framing the questions to be asked. ... Lou asked them, "How important do you think it is to the quality of life in the community to have such things as museums, theater and concert halls in the community?" That was a **sockdolager**. [84% said very important or somewhat important.] (James J. Kilpatrick, *An Artfully Assembled Poll?* St. Petersburg Times [Florida], 04-29-1992, p. 10A.)

declaration (made without proof or support) *n.*: **ipse dixit** [Latin]. SEE ALLEGATION

declare *v.t.*: **asseverate**. ◼ Nowhere do you even try to show why, under the U.S. Constitution, [the right of privacy] leads to [the right of abortion]. Instead, you simply **asseverate**: "This right of privacy ... is broad enough to encompass a woman's decision whether or not to terminate her pregnancy." Harry [Blackmun], be reasonable. Your job is to prove it, not just say it. (Daniel Seligman, *Keeping Up: Big Applesauce,* Fortune, 08-27-1990, p. 111.)

(2) declare *v.t.*: **annunciate**. SEE ANNOUNCE

decline *n.*: **declension**. ◼ "When Richard Nixon got into trouble, the cliché was that there was something Shakespearean about his crisis, and his fall, if it lacked Shakespearean poetry, had a Shakespearean subject: the slow **declension** of ambition into crime, and of crime into evil. But nobody would call Clinton's troubles Shakespearean; they're more bourgeois than that. (Author not given, *Culture, et Cetera,* The Washington Times, 11-18-1998, p. A2, [quoting from Adam Gopnik, writing on "American Studies" in the September 28, 1998 issue of New Yorker magazine.])

(2) decline (as in downward slope) *n.*: **declivity** (*adj.*: **declivitous**). ◼ People have been building houses and hotels atop ravines and steep slopes for years. ... Environmental law actually forbids building on ravines with a certain **declivity**. But which official was up to upholding the law during the New Order regime? (Putu Wirata, *Digging of Steep Slopes Spells Disaster for Many,* The Jakarta Post, 03-02-1999.)

(3) decline (esp. extending down from a fortification) *n.*: **glacis**. ◼ Those who fought their way across the deadly **glacis** of Normandy's beaches had little time to reflect on the justice of their cause or the morality of their mission. (Christopher Redman, *Special Report/D-Day,* Time International, 06-06-1994, p. 39.)

(4) decline (esp. from a position of strength or condition) *n.*: **dégringolade** [French]. SEE DOWNFALL

(5) decline (esp. of moral principles or civil order) *n.*: **labefaction**. SEE WEAKENING

declining (as in worsening) *adj.*: **ingravescent**. SEE WORSENING

decorate (or dress in a showy or excessive manner) *v.t.*: **bedeck**. SEE ADORN

(2) decorate (or dress in a showy or excessive manner) *v.t.*: **bedizen**. SEE ADORN

(3) decorate (as in spruce up) *v.t.*: **titivate**. SEE SPRUCE UP

decoration *n.*: **garniture**. ◼ Q. I would like to know more about my pair of vases that I inherited from my grandparents. They're made of pink glass with painted flowers. ... A. ... Art glass vases such as these were purely decorative and often used as mantle **garniture**. (Jay Moore, *Hand-Blown Glass Vases Were Purely Decorative,* The Tampa Tribune, 08-31-2002.)

decorum (precise observance of ... or etiquette) *n.*: **punctilio**. SEE ETIQUETTE

decrease *n.*: **declension**. SEE DECLINE

decree *n.*: **diktat**. ◼ When [Coppolla] brought up Brando's name [to play the lead in The Godfather], Stanley Jaffe ... slammed his fist on the table, and announced that the actor would never play the Don as long as he was head of Paramount Pictures. Whereupon [Coppolla] appeared to have an epileptic fit, and dramatically collapsed in a heap on the floor, as if rendered senseless by the stupidity of Jaffe's **diktat**. (Peter Biskind, *Easy Riders, Raging Bulls,* Simon & Schuster [1998], p. 153.)

(2) decree *n.*: **ukase**. ◼ Florida Secretary of State ... Katherine Harris announced preemptively that she wouldn't honor any hand recounts in the [2000] presidential contest in Florida, no matter what they showed. ... "For Bush's own sake, he should be more open to a recount," said Rep. Peter King (R-N.Y.), who spoke in an interview before Harris issued her **ukase**. (E. J. Dionne Jr., *Back To '84,* The Washington Post, 11-17-2000, p. A45.)

decrepit *adj.*: **spavined**. ◼ I have patellar tendinitis in each knee ... a "degenerative disk" ... a chronically stiff neck ... a budding hernia [etc.] ... Here's the problem: I didn't play basketball yesterday. Nor the day before that. I played three days ago. When I was 25, I could play from sunup to sundown and feel nothing. And now 72 hours go by and I am still

spavined and weak. Is this how God taps you on the shoulder, before he slaps you silly? (Michael Segell, *Over the Hill, My Ass! [Middle-Aged Basketball Players]*, Esquire, 03-01-1997.)

(2) decrepit (and sick elderly person) *n.*: **Struldbrug** [This is based on a group of characters in Swift's *Gulliver's Travels* who never die, but who, as they age, become ever sicker, more decrepit and live on wretchedly at the state's expense. The term is sometimes applied in connection with the challenges imposed on governments and society when people have outlived their actuarial tables.] ∎ In the end, all one can say to the food fascists is to leave well enough alone. For the government to reduce the joy of life that comes with eating and imbibing [by constantly publishing dietary guidelines] is not a good deal. Sometimes, it seems as if our social planners wish to make **Struldbrugs** of us all — those decrepit, shuffling human beings Gulliver met who could never die. (Barbara Amiel, *Food Police Cook Up More Nonsense*, The Toronto Sun, 08-21-1994, p. M15.)

(3) decrepit (as in broken down or worn out) *adj.*: **raddled**. See WORN-OUT

deduce (as in analyze, logically) *v.i.*: **ratiocinate**. See ANALYZE

deduction (as in inference) *n.*: **illation**. See INFERENCE

deductive (as in logical) *adj.*: **ratiocinative**. See LOGICAL

deep (as in difficult to understand) *adj.*: **recondite**. See COMPLICATED

deep-rooted (as in innate) *adj.*: **connate**. See INNATE

deer (of, relating to or resembling) *adj.*: **cervine**. ∎ Deer and elk, especially, rely on this place, ... to sustain them through the long and often brutal Colorado winters. ... [But as a result of developing the land] come the next killer winter (and come it will), this place, this wildlife "refuge," will become a place of suffering and horror, a **cervine** dying field. (David Petersen, *Searching for Common Ground*, Backpacker, 12-01-1995, p. 46.)

defame *v.t.*: **asperse**. ∎ The inquiry ... has alleged that the military was either directly or indirectly involved in violence in East Timor. ... "We have lost the territory (East Timor), lost our best sons, caused many to become orphans and widows, ... and now we are still being **aspersed** with these groundless

accusations," [the military officer] said. (Author not given, *Military Men Deplore Comments Made by Rights Commission*, The Jakarta Post, 12-11-1999.)

(2) defame (by making false or malicious statements) *v.t.*: **calumniate**. See MALIGN

(3) defame (so as to humiliate or disgrace) *v.t.*: **traduce**. See MALIGN

defeated (capable of being ...) *n.*: **vincible**. See BEATEN

defeatist *n.*: **crepehanger**. See PESSIMIST

defect (tragic ..., esp. in a literary character) *n.*: **hamartia**. See FLAW

defection (from one's religion, principles or causes) *n.*: **apostasy**. See ABANDONMENT

defend (intended to ... against evil) *adj.*: **apotropaic**. See PROTECT

(2) defend *v.t.*: **forfend**. See PROTECT

(3) defend (attempt to ... seriousness of an offense) *v.t.*: **palliate**. See DOWNPLAY

defender (of a cause) *n.*: **paladin**. See PROPONENT

defense (line of ... which is thought to be effective, but is not in reality) *n.*: **Maginot Line** [after André Maginot, French Minister of War, who set up a line of defense along France's border with Germany prior to World War II, which proved ineffective when the Germans attacked through Belgium instead]. ∎ I am dismayed by the Bush administration's decision to scrap the Antiballistic Missile Treaty with Russia. The antimissile system for which President Bush would destroy this treaty will give us a false sense of security while draining our resources away from wiser defense measures. It will be a **Maginot Line** in space: an extraordinarily expensive and cumbersome system that cannot possibly work. (Richard Mullen [letter writer], *Is ABM Treaty Our Best Defense?* The New York Times, 12-14-2001, p. A38.)

(2) defense (formal ... of one's acts or beliefs) *n.*: **apologia**. See JUSTIFICATION

(3) defense (against attack or danger) *n.*: **bulwark**. See PROTECTION

(4) defense (spec. a piece of armor) *n.*: **cuirass**. See ARMOR

defenseless (when born) *adj.*: **altricial**. See HELPLESS

defer (esp. a session of Parliament) *v.t.*: **prorogue**. See DISCONTINUE

deference (not necessarily sincere or unforced) *n.*: **obeisance**. SEE HOMAGE

deferential *adj.*: **biddable**. SEE OBEDIENT
 (2) deferential (to behave towards in a ... manner) *v.t.*: **bootlick**. SEE KOWTOW

defiant *adj.*: **contumacious**. SEE OBSTINATE
 (2) defiant (as in unrepentant) *adj.*: **impenitent**. SEE UNREPENTANT

deficiency (tragic ..., esp. in a literary character) *n.*: **hamartia**. SEE FLAW

deficient (psychiatric diagnosis for one who is mentally ..., as in retarded) *adj.*: **oligophrenic**. SEE RETARDED

defining (as in distinctive, shape or outline, often of a face) *adj.*: **lineament** (often **lineaments**). SEE CONTOUR

definite (necessarily or demonstrably ..., as in incontrovertible) *adj.*: **apodictic**. SEE INCONTROVERTIBLE
 (2) definite (as in sure-fire, esp. with respect to a plan, deal, or investment that can be trusted completely because it is supposedly safe and sure to succeed) *adj.*: **copper-bottomed** [British]. SEE SURE-FIRE

definition (as in the word or phrase which is being defined in a dictionary or elsewhere) *n.*: **definiendum**. ▪ Still, it is noteworthy that this clause [i.e. the definition of "sub-standard or secondary cases of punishment" in the textbook being analyzed] includes a puzzling circularity: The very term "punishment" is included in the **definiendum** of substandard or secondary cases of punishment. (Douglas Husak, *Philosophical Analysis and the Limits of the Substantive Criminal Law*, Criminal Justice Ethics, 06-22-1999.)
 (2) definition (of word or phrase in a dictionary or elsewhere) *n.*: **definiens**. ▪ By "evaluative" I assume he means a definition that includes in the **definiens** at least one term that either is or implies a normative concept. (Leon Rosenstein, *The End of Art Theory*, Humanitas, 03-22-2002.)
 (3) definition (using a ... of a word other than in its customary sense) *adj.*: **Pickwickian** [derives from the odd sense given to common words by certain characters in The Pickwick Papers, by Charles Dickens]. ▪ Only by using the word in its most **Pickwickian** sense would I ever call myself a "young" theologian. Indeed, I belong, at least chronologically, to that post-fifty generation — so

effectively dissected by Christopher Ruddy in his article "Young Theologians." (Edward T. Oakes, *Continuing the Conversation*, Commonweal, 06-02-2000.)
 (4) definition (inability to recall ... of words or using them incorrectly) *n.*: **paramnesia**. SEE AMNESIA
 (5) definition (having more than one ...) *adj.*: **polysemous** (or **polysemic**). SEE MEANING

definitive (as in unambiguous) *adj.*: **univocal**. SEE UNAMBIGUOUS

defraud *v.t., v.i.*: **cozen**. ▪ Slack enforcement spells opportunity for crooks. Institutional Treasury Management, a registered investment advisory outfit in Irvine, California, managed to **cozen** investors out of $174 million in the late Eighties and early Nineties. Instead of putting his clients' money in conservative investments as he promised, ITM's owner, Steven D. Wymer, speculated in derivatives and used his customer's cash to buy toys for himself, including a Ferrari, a pair of Mercedes-Benzes, and a couple of boats. (Terence P. Pare, *Money & Markets: How to Find a Financial Planner: It's Easy to Spend Good Money on Bad Advice*, Fortune, 05-16-1994, p. 103.)
 (2) defraud (as in deceive) *v.t.*: **hornswoggle**. SEE DECEIVE
 (3) defraud (as in embezzle) *v.t., v.i.*: **peculate**. SEE EMBEZZLE
 (4) defraud (or force someone into doing something) *v.t.*: **shanghai**. (person who does so *n.* **shanghier**). SEE COERCE

degenerate *n., v.i.*: **atrophy**. SEE WITHER
 (2) degenerate (morally ...) *adj.*: **scrofulous**. SEE DEPRAVED

degenerating (as in worsening) *adj.*: **ingravescent**. SEE WORSENING

degradation (of a religious, national or racial group) *n.*: **helotism** (*v.t.*: **helotize**). SEE OPPRESSION

deification *n.*: **apotheosis** (*v.t.*: **apotheosize**). SEE EXALTATION

deign (as in bestow, by one with higher power) *v.t.*: **vouchsafe**. SEE BESTOW

deity (belief in one ... without denying others) *n.*: **henotheism**. ▪ On the empirical side, Lind thinks he sees an accelerating pattern of religious indifferentism in this country; Americans, he argues, have adopted the **henotheism** of "one God and many equally true religions." (George Weigel, *The Next

American Nation: The New Nationalism and the Fourth American Revolution, Commentary, 07-01-1995, p. 62.)

(2) deity (belief there is only one ...) *n.*: **monotheism**. ∎ This myth — the belief in one God, creator of the heavens and the earth — constitutes "a system in which identity depends upon rejection of the Other and subjection of the Self." Sometimes Schwartz goes so far as to suggest that **monotheism** lies at the root of evil in the Western world. (Peter Berkowitz, *Thou Shalt Not Kill*, The New Republic, 06-23-1997.)

(3) deity (worship of or belief in more than one ...) *n.*: **polytheism**. ∎ The Vikings believed in gods and goddesses, led by Odin, Frey and Thor. ... With their tradition of **polytheism**, adding Jesus to the list was no problem. (Sharon Begley, *The Ancient Mariners*, Newsweek, 04-03-2000, p. 48.)

(4) deity (guardian ... of a place) *n.*: **genius loci** [Latin]. SEE SPIRIT

déjà vu (false ..., as in confusion of remembrance with actual fact) *n.*: **paramnesia**. SEE MISREMEMBER

dejected *adj.*: **chapfallen**. ∎ Under the headline "Wielders of mass deception?" on the cover of this week's Economist, President Bush sits, stroking his chin, mouth covered by his right hand, his brow furrowed, with ... a melancholy look that seems to say, "Now what?" Seated next to him is a **chapfallen** British Prime Minister Tony Blair, weary head propped up by his left hand, whose unspoken thought could easily be, "I'm not his poodle, but no one believes me." (Arnaud de Borchgrave, *Loony Lucubrations*, The Washington Times, 10-10-2003.)

(2) dejected (chronically ..., as in depressed) *adj., n.*: **dysthymic**. SEE DEPRESSED

dejection (as in inability to experience pleasure or happiness) *n.*: **anhedonia**. SEE UNHAPPINESS

(2) dejection (as in depression) *n.*: **cafard** [French]. SEE DEPRESSION

(3) dejection (general feeling of ..., as form of depression) *n.*: **dysphoria**. SEE DEPRESSION

(4) dejection (as in depression) *n.*: **megrims** (plural of megrim) (also means migraine headache). SEE HEADACHE

(5) dejection (to fret or complain, including as a result of ...) *v.i.*: **repine**. SEE COMPLAIN

delay (intentional ... or procrastination) *n.*: **cunctation**. ∎ Vansittart advocated a policy of **cunctation**: delay a confrontation with Nazi Germany, buy time for rearmament, and keep Germany guessing about British policy while being ready to negotiate.

(Michael Carley, *Churchill* [book reviews], Canadian Journal of History, 08-01-1995.)

(2) delay (as in hesitate to act due to indecision) *v.i.*: **dither**. SEE PROCRASTINATE

(3) delay (engaging in ... tactics, esp. as a means to wear out an opponent or avoid confrontation) *adj.*: **Fabian**. SEE DILATORY

(4) delay (as in procrastinate or hesitate to act) *v.i.*: **shilly-shally**. SEE PROCRASTINATE

delectable *adj.*: **sapid**. SEE TASTY

(2) delectable *adj.*: **toothsome**. SEE TASTY

delegate (authority or duties to another) *v.t.*: **depute**. ∎ After a long eight years, the residents of Dhaka ... will cast their vote today to choose their mayors and ward commissioners. Large contingents of army ... have been deployed to maintain law and order so that the electorate can exercise their franchise freely without any fear or intimidation. ... The Canadian High Commission in Dhaka has also **deputed** one observer to monitor the polls. (Author not given, *All Set for Battle of Ballot in Three Cities*, The Independent, 04-25-2002.)

deleterious *adj.*: **nocent**. SEE HARMFUL

delicacy *n.*: **bonne bouche** [French]. ∎ Janine, who spent five years of her life in the lobster Valhalla that is Maine, USA, wondered for a moment if it was over-buttered, then decided it was the best she'd ever had in London. The portion she grudgingly allowed me to taste seemed the last word in succulent bliss, the kind of **bonne bouche** you imagine forking into Kim Basinger's blindfolded face, should they ever plan a sequel to *9-1/2 Weeks*. (John Walsh, *Rock Stars Wow a Sole Man*, The Independent, 09-23-1994.)

delicate (as in sheer or transparent) *adj.*: **diaphanous**. SEE TRANSPARENT

(2) delicate (as in fragile) *adj.*: **frangible**. SEE FRAGILE

(3) delicate (as in sheer or transparent) *adj.*: **gossamer**. SEE TRANSPARENT

(4) delicate (in an affected manner) *adj.*: **niminy-piminy**. SEE DAINTY

delicious *adj.*: **sapid**. SEE TASTY

(2) delicious *adj.*: **toothsome**. SEE TASTY

delight *n.*: **beatitude**. SEE BLISS

(2) delight *n.*: **delectation**. SEE PLEASURE

(3) delight (causing or tending to produce ...) *adj.*: **felicific**. SEE HAPPINESS

(4) delight *n.:* **felicity**. SEE HAPPINESS

delighted (often in a boastful way) *adj.:* **cock-a-hoop**. SEE ELATED

delightful *adj.:* **Elysian**. SEE BLISSFUL

(2) delightful *adj.:* **frabjous** (often as in "Oh frabjous day!"). SEE WONDERFUL

(3) delightful *adj.:* **galluptious** [slang]. SEE WONDERFUL

delineate (as in describe, by painting or writing) *v.t.:* **limn**. SEE DESCRIBE

deliver (from slavery, servitude or bondage) *v.t.:* **manumit**. SEE EMANCIPATE

delivery (slow or difficult ... of a baby) *n.:* **dystocia**. SEE CHILDBIRTH

(2) delivery (of or relating to ... of a baby) *adj.:* **parturient**. SEE CHILDBIRTH

delude (as in deceive) *v.t.:* **humbug**. SEE DECEIVE

deluge *n.:* **cataract**. SEE DOWNPOUR

delusion (held by two closely associated persons) *n.:* **folie à deux** [French]. ∎ Yet the [fire] ants were real enough or else [my dog] Lizbeth had become my partner in a **folie à deux**. (Lars Eighner, *Travels With Lizbeth*, St. Martin's Press [1993], p. 127.)

(2) delusion *n.:* **ignis fatuus**. ∎ A trans-Atlantic labor charter, if not likely, is at least possible, unlike the **ignis fatuus** of a global labor-law regime. (Michael Lind, *A Plea for a New Global Strategy: Looking Past NATO*, The New Leader, 06-30-1997, p. 9.)

(3) delusion (living in a world of ..., with a glorified or romanticized conception of oneself, as a result of boredom in one's life) *n.:* **Bovarism**. SEE SELF-DELUSION

delusional *adj.:* **fatuous**. ∎ After the 1992 election, I wrote [an article] on Bill Clinton. ... I did express high, and in retrospect rather **fatuous**, hopes for the coming Clinton Administration. ... I cherished, for a time, a kind of fresh-start, non-partisan, post-ideological, post-Cold War faith that a new-paradigm Clinton might lead the nation brilliantly toward ... toward, well, the bridge to the twenty-first century! (Lance Morrow, *U.S. v. Clinton*, National Review, 09-28-1998, p. 39.)

(2) delusional (having ... fantasies about having power, fame, omnipotence, etc.) *n.:* **megalomania**. ∎ After that, [David] Koresh took over [the Branch Davidian cult]. His **megalomania**, say for-mer followers, quickly became evident. ... One of his teachings was that he was the "Lamb," or the son of God — something most of his followers grew to accept without question. (Joe Treen, *On His Road to Armageddon, Would-be Messiah David Koresh Seduced His Followers Into a Life of Paranoia, Violence and Sexual Abuse*, People, 03-15-1993, p. 38.)

delusionary (hope or goal which is not realistically obtainable) *n.:* **will-o'-the-wisp**. SEE PIPE DREAM

demanding (attention) *adj.:* **clamant**. SEE URGENT

(2) demanding (as in difficult situation or problem) *n.:* **nodus**. SEE COMPLICATION

demarcate (as in set the boundaries of) *v.t.:* **delimit**. ∎ When viewed from above, some state boundaries make sense — they follow rivers, declivities, chain of hills — but the straight lines defining Wyoming are purely notional and basically **delimit** a mammoth sandbox. (Walter Kirn, *Up in the Air*, Doubleday [2001], p. 202.)

demean *v.t.:* **vilipend**. SEE DISPARAGE

demeanor *n.:* **mien**. ∎ When Roosevelt addressed [George Marshall] as "George," [Marshall] frowned. The president, who thereafter always called him "General," was taken aback at first by this plain-spoken soldier of serious **mien**. But in the end he concluded that Marshall was an anchorage of honesty in a sea of flattery and guile. (Gerald Parshall, *The Strategists of War*, U.S. News & World Report, 03-16-1998, p. 50.)

demented (slightly ..., often used humorously) *adj.:* **tetched**. SEE CRAZY

demon (who has sex with sleeping women) *n.:* **incubus**. ∎ Here's some good marketing advice: Never name women's footwear after a demon who in medieval lore had sex with sleeping women. Common sense? Well, Reebok International found out that it had done just that with its line of women's running shoes named after the mythically infamous **incubus**. (Betsy Streisand, *Whoops! Did the Devil Make Them Do It?* U.S. News & World Report, 03-03-1997, p. 59.)

(2) demon (female ... who has sex with sleeping men) *n.:* **succubus**. ∎ Q: My best friend — who is a guy — told me that when his girlfriend went to see her parents over the holidays, he had a dream that he had sex with a ghost. ... Dr. Judy: ... Folklore would say he was visited by a **succubus** who seduces men in their sleep to take their spirit, or that a witch put a spell on him to make him succumb to her. (*Fitness File/Sex Q&A*, Newsday, 01-11-1999, p. B13.)

demure (as in prudish) *adj.*: **missish**. SEE PRUDE

denigrate (by making false or malicious statements) *v.t.*: **calumniate**. SEE MALIGN
(2) denigrate (oneself) *v.t.*: **flagellate** (*n.*: **flagellation**). SEE CRITICIZE
(3) denigrate (so as to humiliate or disgrace) *v.t.*: **traduce**. SEE MALIGN

denouement (as in moment of recognition, often the point in the plot at which the protagonist recognizes his or her or some other character's true identity or discovers the true nature of his or her own situation) *n.*: **anagnorisis**. SEE RECOGNITION

denounce *v.t.*: **execrate**. SEE HATE
(2) denounce *v.t.*: **flay**. SEE CRITICIZE
(3) denounce (harshly) *v.t.*: **fustigate**. SEE CRITICIZE
(4) denounce *v.t.*: **objurgate**. SEE CRITICIZE

dense (as in region or city with ... population) *n.*: **megalopolis**. SEE CROWDED
(2) dense (as in slow to understand or perceive) *adj.*: **purblind**. SEE OBTUSE

denunciation (as in criticism) *n.*: **animadversion** (*v.t.*: **animadvert***). SEE CRITICISM
(2) denunciation (being subject to ..., esp. public) *n.*: **obloquy**. SEE ABUSE
(3) denunciation *n.*: **philippic**. SEE TIRADE

denunciatory (language) *n.*: **vituperation** (*adj.*: **vituperative**). SEE INVECTIVE

deny (as in disavow or recant) *v.t.*: **abjure**. SEE DISAVOW
(2) deny (esp. responsibility or duty) *v.t.*: **abnegate**. SEE RENOUNCE

depart (hurriedly or secretly) *v.t.*: **absquatulate**. SEE LEAVE
(2) depart (hurriedly or secretly) *v.t.*: **decamp**. SEE LEAVE

departure (which is unannounced, abrupt, secret or unceremonious) *n.*: **French Leave** [derives from 18th century French custom of leaving a party without saying goodbye to the host or hostess]. [The New England Patriots training camp] hasn't even been in session for two weeks yet, but [coach] Belichick had already endured the ... unauthorized defection of linebacker Andy Katzenmoyer. A day after Panos retired, Katzenmoyer took **French Leave**. ("I don't think he was kidnapped, but I don't know," Belichick cracked in reporting Katzenmoyer's absence.) (Boston Herald, 08-08-2001.)
(2) departure (act of ... as in abandonment, from one's religion, principles or causes) *n.*: **apostasy**. SEE ABANDONMENT

dependence (on faith alone rather than reason, esp. in philosophical or religious matters) *n.*: **fideism**. SEE FAITH

dependent (as in acting subservient as opposed to leading) *adj.*: **sequacious**. SEE SUBSERVIENT

depict (as in describe, by painting or writing) *v.t.*: **limn**. SEE DESCRIBE

deplete (of strength) *v.t.*: **enervate**. SEE DEBILITATE

deplorable (as in abominable) *adj.*: **execrable**. SEE ABOMINABLE

deportment (appropriate ..., as in propriety) *n.*: **correctitude**. SEE PROPRIETY
(2) deportment *n.*: **mien**. SEE DEMEANOR

deposit (of mud or sand on a riverbank) *n.*: **alluvium**. SEE MUD

depraved (morally ...) *adj.*: **scrofulous**. ▪ In my opinion, we are not unlike those confused, **scrofulous** hippies of the late 1960s who finally showed up at the doors of the free clinics in Haight-Ashbury to get their dose of traditional medicine [after getting bizarre diseases resulting from not bathing]. ... We need to take an active stand against the divisive unlearning that is corrupting the integrity of our society. (Christina Hoff Sommers, *Are We Living in a Moral Stone Age?* USA Today Magazine, 03-01-1999.)
(2) depraved (preference for ... or unusual sexual practices) *n.*: **paraphilia**. SEE DEVIANT

depravity (place of ..., as in corruption) *n.*: **Augean stable**. SEE CORRUPTION

depressant (as in something which induces forgetfulness or oblivion of pain, suffering or sorrow) *n.*: **nepenthe**. SEE NARCOTIC

depressed (chronically ...) *adj., n.*: **dysthymic**. ▪ "Before taking Prozac," recalls a middle-aged woman with **dysthymic** symptoms, "my first thought on waking up would be, 'Oh God, when can I go back to bed.' I felt ugly and stupid. I'd change my clothes fifty times before a party and then decide not to go because nobody would notice or care whether I was there." (Kathleen McAuliffe, *Prozac: What's in it For You*? Cosmopolitan, 03-01-1995, p. 208.)

(2) depressed *adj.*: **chapfallen**. See DEJECTED

depressing *adj.*: **tristful** See SAD

depression *n.* **cafard** [French]. ∎ This January was apparently the most light-starved since records began, preceded by the tenth coldest December this century and the chilliest February for two decades. All of which has a demoralising impact on the human psyche. The weather produced record levels of winter depression. Arctic countries have long had terms for the **cafard** of winter: "Cabin fever" and "Lapp sickness." (Andrew Brown, *After the Gloom, a Lighter Outlook*, The Independent [London], 04-01-1996, p. 19.)

(2) depression (general feeling of ...) *n.*: **dysphoria**. ∎ Let me be more detailed about those mood swings, because they bear directly on the question of whether Myrna was depressed when she killed herself. ... In euphoria she never thought of suicide; in **dysphoria** she was wholly involved in fretting over relative trivia. In euphoria she was rash and impulsive. In **dysphoria** she could not make a decision and could not act. (Jamie Talan, *Deathbed Suicide — The Depression Factor*, Newsday, 05-21-1996, p. B21.)

(3) depression (sometimes resulting from spiritual apathy) *n.*: **acedia**. See APATHY

(4) depression (as in inability to experience pleasure or happiness) *n.*: **anhedonia** See UNHAPPINESS

(5) depression *n.*: **megrims** (plural of megrim) (also means migraine headache). See HEADACHE

(6) depression (as in world-weariness or sentimental pessimism over the world's problems) *adj.*: **Weltschmerz** [German]. See PESSIMISM

deprive (of strength) *v.t.*: **enervate**. See DEBILITATE

deprived (of something, as in bereft or forlorn) *adj.*: **lorn**. See FORLORN

depth (measurement of ... of bodies of water) *n.*: **bathymetry**. ∎ The only way to obtain precise depths in the open ocean is with traditional **bathymetry**, in which a ship measures the distance to the ocean floor by bouncing sound waves off the bottom. Unfortunately, a ship can take soundings only in a narrow strip. (Dana Mackenzie, *Earth Science: Ocean Floor Is Laid Bare by New Satellite Data*, Science, 09-26-1997.)

deranged (person) *n.*: **bedlamite**. See LUNATIC

(2) deranged (informal as in daffy or loony) *adj.*: **doolally**. See CRAZY

(3) deranged (slightly ..., often used humorously) *adj.*: **tetched**. See CRAZY

deride (esp. through the use of satire) *v.t.*: **pasquinade**. See SATIRIZE

derivation (principal ... or source) *n.*: **wellhead**. See SOURCE

derogatory (as in faultfinding) *adj.*: **captious**. See FAULTFINDING

(2) derogatory (as in faultfinding person) *n.*: **smellfungus**. See FAULTFINDER

derrière (having nicely proportioned ...) *adj.*: **callipygian**. See REAR END

(2) derrière (having a hairy ...) *adj.*: **dasypygal**. See REAR END

(3) derrière (as in buttocks) *n., pl.*: **nates**. See BUTTOCKS

(4) derrière (a fat ...) *n.*: **steatopygia** (having a fat ... *adj.*: **steatopygic**). See REAR END

descent (esp., in Greek mythology, into the underworld) *n.*: **katabasis** [the word also means a military retreat]. ∎ Like Western civilization itself, as his friend and chief critical promoter Harold Rosenberg sardonically remarked, De Kooning was always in decline. This **katabasis** is supposed to have begun in the early '50s, with the Women series. (Robert Hughes, *Seeing the Face in the Fire* [Painting: Willem De Kooning: National Gallery, Washington, D.C.], Time, 05-30-1994.)

(2) descent *n.*: **declension**. See DECLINE

(3) descent (as in downward slope) *n.*: **declivity** (*adj.*: **declivitous**). See DECLINE

(4) descent (esp. from a position of strength or condition) *n.*: **dégringolade** [French]. See DOWNFALL

(5) descent (esp. extending down from a fortification) *n.*: **glacis**. See DECLINE

(6) descent (a ... down an incline such a snowy mountain) *n.*: **glissade**. See SLIDE

describe (by painting or writing) *v.t.*: **limn**. ∎ A few weeks ago, Newsweek ran a cover story on what it called "the new male dilemma," as **limned** by writer Susan Faludi in amusingly overcooked prose: "As the nation wobbled toward the millennium, its pulse-takers all seemed to agree that a domestic apocalypse was underway: American manhood was under siege." (William Powers, *Media: She-Male Nation*, National Journal, 10-02-1999.)

(2) describe (in a sketchy or incomplete way) *v.t.*: **adumbrate**. SEE OUTLINE

(3) describe (as in set the boundaries of) *v.t.*: **delimit**. SEE DEMARCATE

description (as in brief summary) *n.*: **precis** [French]. SEE SUMMARY

desensitize *v.t.*: **hyposensitize**. ▮ Allergy shots can **hyposensitize** your pet, making it less sensitive to whatever is causing the itchiness. (Author not given, *Pet Talk / Allergy May Cause Dog to Pull Out Hair*, Minneapolis Star Tribune, 07-16-1995, p. 6E.)

(2) desensitize *v.t.*: **narcotize**. SEE DEADEN

deserted (or abandoned baby) *n.*: **foundling**. SEE ORPHAN

desertion (from one's religion, principles or causes) *n.*: **apostasy**. SEE ABANDONMENT

deserved (esp. in reference to a punishment) *adj.*: **condign**. ▮ Those who had seen the Standard Oil dissolution as **condign** punishment for Rockefeller were in for a sad surprise: It proved to be the luckiest stroke of his career. (Ron Chernow, *Titan*, Random House [1998], p. 556.)

designer (of women's fashions) *n.*: **modiste**. ▮ Trendsetting **modiste** Clare Potter, one of the designers credited with inventing American sportswear, died on Jan. 5 in Fort Ann, N.Y. She was 95. Her unconventional notions in the 1930s and '40s helped make trousers on women, for example, standard wear today. (David Cobb Craig, *Passages*, People, 01-25-1999, p. 81.)

desire *n.*: **appetence**. SEE CRAVING

(2) desire (hidden or ulterior ...) *n.*: **arriere-pensee** (or **arrière-pensée**) [French]. SEE MOTIVE

(3) desire (strong ...) *n.*: **avidity**. SEE CRAVING

(4) desire (as in irresistible compulsion) *n.*: **cacoëthes**. SEE COMPULSION

(5) desire (mental process marked by ... to do something) *n.*: **conation**. SEE DETERMINATION

(6) desire (having a strong ..., esp. sexual) *adj.*: **concupiscent** (*n.*: **concupiscence**). SEE LUSTFUL

(7) desire (excessive ... for wealth) *n.*: **cupidity**. SEE GREED

(8) desire (as in hope for or want) *v.t.*: **desiderate**. SEE WANT

(9) desire (sexual ... for the elderly) *n.*: **gerontophilia**. SEE LUST

(10) desire (condition involving ... to eat nonfood items) *n.*: **pica**. SEE CRAVING

(11) desire (excessive sexual ... by a man) *n.*: **satyriasis**. SEE HORNINESS

(12) desire (slight or faint ...) *n.*: **velleity**. SEE HOPE

(13) desire (which is delusive or not realistically obtainable) *n.*: **will-o'-the-wisp**. SEE PIPE DREAM

desirous *adj.*: **athirst**. SEE EAGER

(2) desirous (as in lustful) *adj.*: **lickerish**. SEE LUSTFUL

desk *n.*: **escritoire**. ▮ Each room is furnished differently with high-quality reproduction antiques in boudoir settings (a soft-blue "queen single," for instance, invites correspondence at a lovely **escritoire**). (Author not given, *Three Faces of NYC*, USA Today, 05-23-1997, p. 4D.)

despair (as in inability to experience pleasure or happiness) *n.*: **anhedonia**. SEE UNHAPPINESS

(2) despair (over) *v.t.*: **bewail**. SEE LAMENT

(3) despair (as in depression) *n.*: **cafard** [French]. SEE DEPRESSION

(4) despair *n.*: **dolor** (*adj.*: **dolorous**). SEE SADNESS

(5) despair (general feeling of ... as form of depression) *n.*: **dysphoria**. SEE DEPRESSION

(6) despair *n.*: **megrims** (plural of megrim) (also means migraine headache). SEE HEADACHE

(7) despair (to fret or complain, including as a result of ...) *v.i.*: **repine**. SEE COMPLAIN

despicable (person) *n.*: **caitiff**. ▮ [The purpose of the Black Liberation Army] was indiscriminate slaughter of whites to provoke a revolution and race war. Jacob John Dougan and four of his [fellow members] cruised Jacksonville searching for potential victims and decided on an 18-year-old hitchhiker. The gang of **caitiffs** stabbed the youth repeatedly, and the rebarbative Dougan ended the ordeal by shooting him in the chest and in the ear amid pleas for mercy. (Bruce Fein, *Justice's Views May Set Back War on Crime*, Insight on the News, 11-22-1993.)

(2) despicable *adj.*: **ugsome**. SEE LOATHSOME

despise (as in treat with contempt) *v.t.*: **contemn**. SEE SCORN

(2) despise *v.t.*: **execrate**. SEE HATE

(3) despise *v.t.*: **misprize**. SEE HATE

despite (that) *adv.*: **withal**. SEE NEVERTHELESS

despondency (general feeling of ... as form of depression) *n.*: **dysphoria**. SEE DEPRESSION

despondent (chronically ..., as in depressed) *adj., n.*: **dysthymic**. SEE DEPRESSED

despotic (ruthlessly and violently ...) *adj.*: **jackbooted**. See OPPRESSIVE

destination (as in final point) *n.*: **terminus**. See END

destiny *n.*: **kismet**. See FATE

destitute *adj.*: **impecunious**. See POOR
 (2) **destitute** *adj.*: **necessitous**. See POOR

destitution *n.*: **penury**. See POVERTY

destroy *v.t.*: **extirpate**. See ABOLISH

destruction (of ecology or environment by mankind) *n.*: **ecocide**. See ENVIRONMENT

destructive (mutually ... to both sides) *adj.*: **internecine**. ▪ What such worries suggest is that even if the airlines manage to avoid their usual **internecine** struggles over ticket prices, they will have to move gingerly in their effort to raise prices. Any sizable across-the-board increase would also bring squawks from business travelers, who account for about 60% of the industry's revenues. (Kenneth Labich, *Competition: What Will Save The U.S. Airlines*, Fortune, 06-14-1993, p. 98.)
 (2) **destructive** (as in harmful) *adj.*: **nocent**. See HARMFUL

detach (as in consider separately) *v.t.*: **prescind** (generally as in "prescind from"). See ISOLATE

detached (as in unemotional or even-tempered) *adj.*: **phlegmatic**. See EVEN-TEMPERED

details (precise observance of ... or etiquette) *n.*: **punctilio**. See ETIQUETTE

detect (by careful observation or scrutiny) *v.t.*: **descry**. See PERCEIVE

deter *v.t.*: **forfend**. See AVERT

deteriorated (as in broken down and/or worn out) *adj.*: **raddled**. See WORN-OUT

deteriorating (as in worsening) *adj.*: **ingravescent**. See WORSENING

deterioration (of a group or social structure as a result of lack of standards or values) *n.*: **anomie**. See BREAKDOWN
 (2) **deterioration** *n., v.i.*: **atrophy**. See WITHER
 (3) **deterioration** *n.*: **declension**. See DECLINE
 (4) **deterioration** (esp. from a position of strength or condition) *n.*: **dégringolade** [French]. See DOWNFALL

(5) deterioration (movement towards or degree of ... or disorder in a system or society) *n.*: **entropy**. See DISORDER

(6) deterioration (esp. of moral principles or civil order) *n.*: **labefaction**. See WEAKENING

determination (mental process marked by ... to do something) *n.*: **conation**. ▪ [Bill Clinton] is unique as an instance of pure **conation**. He will do whatever is required to hold himself together. No principles or ideals or moral scruples are allowed to get in the way of this self-protective impulse. (Loren Lomasky, *Piling on the Prez*, Reason, 12-01-1998.)
 (2) **determination** (as in decree) *n.*: **diktat**. See DECREE
 (3) **determination** *n.*: **hardihood**. See COURAGE

determinative (remark, blow or factor) *n.*: **sockdolager**. See DECISIVE

determined (but obstinate) *adj.*: **contumacious**. See OBSTINATE

detest *v.t.*: **execrate**. See HATE
 (2) **detest** *v.t.*: **misprize**. See HATE

detrimental (mutually ... to both sides) *adj.*: **internecine**. See DESTRUCTIVE
 (2) **detrimental** *adj.*: **nocent**. See HARMFUL
 (3) **detrimental** (as in harmful) *adj.*: **nocuous**. See HARMFUL

developing (as in coming into being) *adj.*: **nascent**. See EMERGING

deviant (preference for ... sexual practices) *n.*: **paraphilia**. ▪ There are many **paraphilias**, ranging from frotteurism (compulsively rubbing up against strangers) to acrotomophilia (an attraction to amputees). Their most striking feature is that they are an almost exclusively male phenomenon. (Michael Segell, *Meet the Kinks*, [Fetishism], Esquire, 05-01-1996, p. 40.)

deviate (from the subject) *v.i.*: **divagate**. See DIGRESS
 (2) **deviate** (from a course or intended path) *v.t.*: **yaw**. See VEER

deviation (as in digression) *n.*: **excursus**. See DIGRESSION
 (2) **deviation** (as in passing comment) *n.*: **obiter dictum** [Latin]. See PASSING COMMENT

devil *n.*: **Beelzebub**. See SATAN
 (2) **devil** (who has sex with sleeping women) *n.*: **incubus**. See DEMON

(3) devil (as in scoundrel or unprincipled person) *n.*: **blackguard**. SEE SCOUNDREL

(4) devil (female ... who has sex with sleeping men) *n.*: **succubus**. SEE DEMON

(5) devil (as in scoundrel or rascal) *n.*: **scapegrace**. SEE SCOUNDREL

devious (scheming or trickery) *n.*: **jiggery-pokery**. SEE TRICKERY

(2) devious (behavior) *n.*: **knavery**. SEE CORRUPTION

(3) devious (characterized by ... and cunning conduct) *adj.*: **Machiavellian**. SEE DECEITFUL

(4) devious (conduct) *n.*: **skullduggery**. SEE DECEITFULNESS

devise (an idea, plan, theory or explanation after careful thought) *v.t.*: **excogitate**. ∎ You have agreed and the majority and minority have agreed to several changes that have, in my judgment, greatly improved the [anti-terrorism] bill, left it a very effective law enforcement effort. ... And we have been able to do that by working together between Thursday and today. Another week would make it do even better. It's no criticism of your work product to note that no one can **excogitate** the perfect [anti-terrorism] bill here, and working together helped. (Rep. Barney Frank (speaker), *Media Coverage of Activities Regarding Government Response to Terrorism*, Talk of the Nation (NPR), 09-24-2001.)

devitalize (as in deprive of strength) *v.t.*: **geld**. SEE WEAKEN

devoted (and unquestioning assistant) *n.*: **myrmidon**. SEE ASSISTANT

(2) devoted (overly ... or submissive to one's wife) *adj.*: **uxorious**. SEE DOTING

devotee (of a place, esp. a place of entertainment) *n.*: **habitué** [French]. SEE REGULAR

(2) devotee (strong ... of a cause, religion or activity) *n.*: **votary**. SEE SUPPORTER

devotion (as in loyalty) *n.*: **fealty** SEE LOYALTY

devour (food like a glutton) *v.t.*: **gormandize**. ∎ The problem is that matzo — unless it's of the whole-wheat variety — has little fiber and often is eaten to excess [on Passover]. ... "People say, 'I love matzo,' and it's addictive. It's like trying to eat one potato chip," said Harriet Roth. ... "They look forward to this all year and when Passover comes they **gormandize** and they overindulge." (Author not given, *Jews Share Joys of Passover, Pain of 'Matzo*

Stomach,' The Arlington Morning News, 04-18-1998, p. 6A.)

(2) devour *v.t.*: **guttle**. ∎ Best of all, gastronomes have the option of lounging at a barstool bolted elegantly to a raised green cement podium or taking advantage of generous car parking facilities to **guttle** foot-long hotdogs without leaving the comfort of their shaggin' wagons. (Emma Tom, *Here's A Tip For All You Food Lovers*, Sydney Morning Herald, 06-27-1998.)

(3) devour (greedily) *v.t.*: **englut**. SEE SWALLOW

(4) devour (as in ingest) *v.t.*: **incept**. SEE INGEST

devouring *adj.*: **edacious**. SEE VORACIOUS

diabolic *adj.*: **iniquitous**. SEE WICKED

(2) diabolic *adj.*: **malefic**. SEE EVIL

(3) diabolic *adj.*: **malevolent**. SEE EVIL

dialect (regional ...) *n.*: **patois**. ∎ George Broomfield, a Hempstead resident who grew up speaking a lilting **patois** in his native Jamaica, said he knows from experience how hard it can be for black children to learn the tongue of white America. (Martin C. Evans, *Locally, Few Favor Movement*, Newsday, 01-13-1997, p. A5.)

dialogue (in which neither side hears or understands or pays attention to the other) *n.*: **dialogue des sourds** [French; dialogue of the deaf]. ∎ The transatlantic debate on muliculturalism has many aspects of a **dialogue des sourds**. Both sides end up sounding like right wingers to the other. ... When some French intellectuals hear "multiculturalism," they think ... "globalization" and "threat to the Republic." When US multiculturalists hear French anti-multiculturalism, it sounds to them like the discredited "color blind" and "integrationist" discourse of 1950s white liberals. (Ella Shohat, *French Intellectuals and the U.S. Culture Wars*, Black Renaissance/Renaissance Noire, 03-22-2001.)

(2) dialogue (informal ..., as in chat or discussion) *n.*: **causerie**. SEE CHAT

(3) dialogue (one skilled at dinner ...) *n.*: **deipnosophist**. SEE CONVERSATION

(4) dialogue (between two people) *n.*: **duologue**. SEE CONVERSATION

(5) dialogue *n.*: **interlocution**. SEE DISCUSSION

diatribe *n.*: **jeremiad**. SEE COMPLAINT

(2) diatribe *n.*: **philippic**. SEE TIRADE

dictate (as in order or direct) *v.t.*: **adjure**. SEE ORDER

dictation (one who takes ...) *n.*: **amanuensis**. SEE SECRETARY

dictator (esp. in Spanish-speaking countries) *n.*: **caudillo**. ▪ [Mexican Presidential candidate Vicente Fox] speaks of himself in the third person, seems to have all the answers and sometimes sounds messianic. It is not impossible that he would be tempted to overstep the limits of a democratic presidency and follow the traditional Mexican role of the populist **caudillo**, the strongman who ... imposes his personal decisions by fiat. (Enrique Krauze, *Latin America: The Psychology Of Power*, Time International, 05-29-2000, p. 20.)

dictionary (process of writing or compiling) *n.*: **lexicography**. ▪ Even the **lexicographers** in their rarified world are aware of the pressures of an increasingly cut-throat market [to sell dictionaries]. Judy Pearsall, who compiles for Oxford University Press, says research shows that clarity of entries is of pivotal importance. (Kathy Marks, *Dictionaries Try Every Trick in the Book as They Battle For Sales*, Independent, 08-14-1998, p. 10.)

(2) dictionary *n.*: **lexicon**. ▪ Though Noah Webster produced his first American dictionary in 1806, his name never appeared in the title of his editions until after his death. Webster's has since passed into generic usage, and any publisher can slap the word into the titles of its own **lexicons**. (Jesse Birnbaum, *Language: Defining Womyn [and Others] — Random House's New Dictionary Is Gender Neutral, Politically Correct — and an English-Lover's Disappointment*, Time, 06-24-1991, p. 51.)

(3) dictionary (entry which defines a word or phrase) *n.*: **definiendum**. SEE DEFINITION

(4) dictionary (or word list) *n.*: **onomasticon**. SEE WORD LIST

difference (as in that quality which makes one thing different from any other) *n.*: **haeccity**. SEE INDIVIDUALITY

(2) difference (as in diversity) *n.*: **variegation** *v.t.*: **variegate**. SEE DIVERSITY

different (state or quality of being ... from others) *n.*: **alterity**. ▪ [The novel 'Le Divorce'] wants to appeal to our latent Francophobia [i.e. fear or dislike of France]. The French eat vile things. They are still very much into fur and hide. They are ridiculously involved with their cheese and wine, their old plates and antique chairs. They retain a formidable **alterity**. (Neil Schmitz, *The Toast of France Meets the White Bread of American Women*, Buffalo News, 02-09-1997.)

(2) different (as in not homogenous) *adj.*: **heterogeneous** (*n.*: **heterogeneity**). SEE DISSIMILAR

(3) different (holding ... opinions or having a ... perspective) *adj.*: **heterodox** (*n.*: **heterodoxy**). SEE UNCONVENTIONAL

(4) different (love of or enthusiasm for anything new and ...) *n.*: **neophilia**. SEE NOVELTY

differentiate (as in separate) *v.i.*: **disaggregate**. SEE SEPARATE

differentiating *adj.*: **diacritical**. SEE DISTINGUISHING

differentiation (as in diversity) *n.*: **variegation** (*v.t.*: **variegate**). SEE DIVERSITY

differing (esp. from majority view) *adj.*: **dissentient**. SEE DISSENTIENT

difficult (to understand, sometimes due to being obscure) *adj.*: **abstruse**. ▪ Roger Penrose is hardly the sort of man who would normally excite much popular interest, let alone controversy. The shy, somewhat rumpled and unfailingly polite Oxford professor, 58, has spent most of his career spinning theories in the most **abstruse** areas of mathematics and physics. (Michael D. Lemonick, *Ideas: Those Computers Are Dummies*, Time, 06-25-1990, p. 74.)

(2) difficult (situation or problem) *n.*: **nodus**. SEE COMPLICATION

(3) difficult (to understand) *adj.*: **recondite**. SEE COMPLICATED

(4) difficult (as in painful journey or experience) *n.*: **via dolorosa**. SEE ORDEAL

diffusion (as in diversity) *n.*: **variegation**. SEE DIVERSITY

dig (as in insult, delivered while leaving the scene) *n.*: **Parthian shot**. SEE PARTING SHOT

digest (as in brief summary) *n.*: **precis** [French]. SEE SUMMARY

digestion (of or relating to) *adj.*: **peptic**. ▪ Dear Reader: Air in the stomach often has a fetid odor when it is mixed with stomach contents and digested food, and expelled through the mouth. This perception suggests the possibility of **peptic** disease or a common condition called reflux, when stomach contents with or without air are inappropriately released and travel upward into the esophagus. (Dr. Peter Gott, *Jaw Pain Could Be Angina Sign*, The Ottawa Sun, 09-23-2000, p. 30.)

dignity (beneath one's ...) *adj.*: **infra dig**. SEE UNDIGNIFIED

(2) dignity (personal ...) *n.*: **izzat** [Hindi]. See HONOR

(3) dignity (an insult to another's ...) *n.*: **lese majesty**. See INSULT

digress *v.i.*: **divagate**. ■ The story **divagates**, exfoliates, crumbles and reconstitutes itself. It can move simultaneously in two or three different time frames, so that we get someone recounting a story in which someone recounts another story. (Richard Eder, *An Act of Omission*, Newsday, 02-12-1995, p. 33.)

digression *n.*: **excursus**. ■ [Pragmatism is] in its bare bones, the view that the meaning of ideas is simply to be found in terms of their consequences. ... The pragmatists were only interested in results. It was their distinctive feature and their proudest boast. That, therefore, is how they must be judged. To do so in detail here would require an unwarranted **excursus**. (Robin Harris, *Post-Civil War Thought; Four American Thinkers Who Made America Modern*, The Washington Times, 05-27-2001, p. B8.)

(2) digression (as in passing comment) *n.*: **obiter dictum** [Latin]. See PASSING COMMENT

digressive *adj.*: **discursive**. See RAMBLING

dilapidated (and worn-out) *adj.*: **raddled**. See WORN-OUT

(2) dilapidated *adj.*: **tatterdemalion**. See RAGGED

dilatory (engaging in ... tactics, esp. as a means to wear out an opponent or avoid confrontation) *adj.*: **Fabian** [This adjective derives from Roman general Quinton Fabius Maximus, who, through caution, avoidance of direct confrontation and harassment, defeated Hannibal in the Second Punic War. Today, it has become synonymous with caution or conservativeness, delay or dilatoriness, or guerilla warfare, and is often used in the phrase "Fabian tactics"]. ■ Last Thursday, Senate Judiciary Committee Chairman Patrick Leahy, Vermont Democrat, and Subcommittee Chairman Charles Schumer, New York Democrat ... ardently defended the committee's **Fabian** tactics (i.e, refusing hearings or committee votes) to thwart a bevy of President George Bush's glittering judicial nominees. (Bruce Fein, *Confirmation Equivocations*, The Washington Times, 05-14-2002.)

dilemma (which is difficult to solve) *n.*: **Gordian knot** [This term derives from an exceedingly complicated knot tied by King Gordius of Phrygia, with the promise that whoever could undo it would be the next ruler of Asia. The problem was solved by Alexander the Great, who cut through it with his sword, thus leading to the expression "cutting the Gordian knot."]. ■ [The first sign came with the collapse of Digital Entertainment Network], considered an early pioneer in the convergence of Hollywood and the Internet. ... The company blithely burned through $3 million a month [and filed for bankruptcy]. ... Despite this object lesson, other Internet companies in Hollywood hoped to cut the **Gordian knot** — finding ways to make money from free Web entertainment. (Sharon Waxman, *The Film Industry's Dot-Combustion*, The Washington Post, 09-17-2000, p. G14.)

(2) dilemma (resulting from an inopportune occurrence) *n.*: **contretemps**. See MISHAP

(3) dilemma (as in choice of taking what is offered or nothing; i.e. no real choice at all) *n.*: **Hobson's choice**. See PREDICAMENT

(4) dilemma (as in dangers on both sides) *idiom*: **between Scylla and Charybdis**. See PRECARIOUS

(5) dilemma (as in the situation of having to make a move where any move made will weaken the position) *n.*: **zugzwang** [German]. See PREDICAMENT

diligent (in effort or application) *adj.*: **sedulous**. ■ Much of the public worries about school names [renaming a school in honor of Congresswoman Barbara Jordan instead of Jefferson Davis] because, for ease and convenience, it beats worrying about, or doing anything about, academic standards and achievement. And here is what we should find truly sad: That same portion of the public pretends this **sedulous** attention is for the sake of low-income kids, largely black and Hispanic. (William Murchison, *School Names Irrelevant to Real Problem*, The Dallas Morning News, 06-30-1999, p. 19A.)

(2) diligent (appearing ... only when the boss is watching) *n.*: **eyeservice**. See WORK

dilute (as in deprive of strength) *v.t.*: **geld**. See WEAKEN

dim (as in dark, mist or gloomy) *adj.*: **caliginous**. See DARK

(2) dim *adj.* (in the ... *adv.*): **darkling**. See DARK

dim-witted (esp. used of a person, as in ... and confused) *adj.*: **addlepated**. See CONFUSED

(2) dim-witted *adj.*: **gormless** [British]. See UNINTELLIGENT

(3) dim-witted (as in slow to understand or perceive) *adj.*: **purblind**. See OBTUSE

diminish (as in deprive of strength) *v.t.*: **geld**. See WEAKEN

diminutive *adj.*: **bantam**. SEE TINY

(2) diminutive (person) *n.*: **hop-o'-my-thumb**. SEE MIDGET

(3) diminutive (person) *n.*: **homunculus**. SEE MIDGET

(4) diminutive *adj., n.*: **Lilliputian**. SEE TINY

din *n.*: **bruit**. ∎ I believe that, to many, noise exaggerates — and, sadly, heightens — the experience of dining. ... Thought is impossible. We are, as it were, poleaxed by the **bruit**. (It's the roar of the lion, remember, that freezes its victim.) (Alexander Theroux, *The Din of Dining Out*, Cosmopolitan, 06-01-1996, p. 36.)

(2) din (and confusion, esp. from simultaneous voices) *n.*: **babel**. SEE NOISE

dining (science of ...) *n.*: **aristology**. ∎ At a glance, [the cookbook written by former baseball pitcher Catfish Hunter] wouldn't get him inducted into the Hot Stove League, but everybody's doing it these days, so why not a nice old pitcher? Way to go, Cat. ... It does not pretend to be history, sociology, literature or, even, **aristology**. ... He says he likes to eat and these are his favorite dishes. (Robert Sherill, *An Unsavory South / These Cookbooks Offer a Sadly "Nonexpert" View of Southern Food*, St. Petersburg Times [Florida], 10-11-1987, p. 7D.)

(2) dining (of or relating to ... with others) *adj.*: **commensal**. ∎ A close examination of our everyday lives will reveal that they are permeated with rituals ... such as how we greet each other, how we make introductions, how we conduct ourselves at **commensal** gatherings, and the like. ... The structures of a shared meal can simultaneously be expressing sociologic, psychologic, and religious functions. (Joseph Keenan, *The Japanese Tea Ceremony and Stress Management*, Holistic Nursing Practice, 01-01-1996, p. 30.)

(3) dining (art or science of good ...) *n.*: **gastronomy**. SEE EATING

dire (as in causing or portending death) *adj.*: **funest**. SEE DEADLY

direct (as in give an order to) *v.t.*: **adjure**. SEE ORDER

directive (as in decree) *n.*: **diktat**. SEE DECREE

director (as in manager or overseer) *n.*: **gerent**. SEE MANAGER

dirge *n.*: **threnody**. SEE REQUIEM

dirt (abnormal fear of) *n.*: **mysophobia**. SEE FEAR

dirty (to make ...) *v.t.*: **begrime**. ∎ All told, diesel emissions — from tailpipes, at ground level — expose New Yorkers to the risks of lung cancer, pneumonia, pleurisy, asthma, bronchitis, chronic coughs and mutant genes. Plus they smell bad and **begrime** the city's buildings. (Joanna D. Underwood, *New York Forum About Transit — The TA's Route To Pollution*, Newsday, 08-06-1993, p. 48.)

(2) dirty (to make ...) *v.t.*: **besmirch**. SEE TARNISH

(3) dirty (as in unkempt or slovenly) *adj.*: **frowzy**. SEE MESSY

(4) dirty (as in sooty) *adj.*: **fuliginous**. SEE SOOTY

(5) dirty (or impure) *adj., v.t.*: **maculate**. SEE IMPURE

disabled (as in out of action) *adj., adv.*: **hors de combat** [French]. ∎ [Fashion designer] Oscar de la Renta was **hors de combat** for a moment there after a model accidentally stabbed him with her 5-foot stiletto heel on a fashion runway. Ah, the perils of haute couture! (Liz Smith, *How Oscar Partied*, Newsday, 03-26-1998, p. A15.)

disaffirmance (as in retraction) *n.*: **palinode**. SEE RETRACTION

disagree (with, as in oppose, a statement, opinion or action) *v.t.*: **oppugn**. SEE OPPOSE

disagreeable (as in surly) *adj.*: **atrabilious**. SEE SURLY

(2) disagreeable (as in surly) *adj.*: **bilious**. SEE SURLY

(3) disagreeable (as in grouchy person) *n.*: **crosspatch**. SEE GROUCH

(4) disagreeable (as in irritable) *adj.*: **liverish**. SEE IRRITABLE

(5) disagreeable (as in repellent or irritating) *adj.*: **rebarbative**. SEE REPELLENT

(6) disagreeable (as in irritable) *adj.*: **shirty**. SEE IRRITABLE

disagreeing (esp. with majority view) *adj.*: **dissentient**. SEE DISSENTIENT

disagreement (characterized by internal ...) *adj.*: **factious**. SEE DISPUTE

(2) disagreement (heated ... or friction between groups) *n.*: **ruction**. SEE DISSENSION

disappear *v.t.*: **evanesce**. ∎ It used to be that people had to be famous for a reasonably long time before anyone would want to read a book by them. But in the go-go '90s, the period between appearing on TV and getting a fat book deal is **evanescing**. (Belinda Luscombe, *People*, Time, 02-10-1997, p. 85.)

(2) disappear (as if by melting away) *v.i.*: **deliquesce**. SEE MELT

(3) disappear (as in a departure which is unannounced, abrupt, secret or unceremonious) *n.*: **French Leave**. SEE DEPARTURE

disappearance (as in state of being absent from view, lost to notice or concealed) *n.*: **occultation**. ∎ Is there, moreover, a single underlying viewpoint in [the biblical texts of] Genesis and Samuel [?] [I]n the former God walks the earth and looks like a man, whereas in the latter He is almost entirely absent from the human stage. Friedman invokes his thesis of the progressive **occultation** of God ... to explain the disparity, but it seems a bit implausible that a single author would have shifted grounds so drastically. (Robert Alter, *The Genius of J*, The New York Times, 11-15-1998.)

disappearing (as in lasting only briefly) *adj.*: **evanescent**. SEE TRANSIENT

disappointed (as in dejected) *adj.*: **chapfallen**. SEE DEJECTED

disappointment *n.*: **Dead Sea fruit** [derives from a fruit described by ancient writers as externally appealing but which dissolves into smoke and ashes when plucked; also referred to as "Apples of Sodom".] ∎ Harold Macmillan, whose elevation [to British Prime Minister] was achieved by a brutality, cunning and greed for power normally met only in conclaves of Mafia capi, said, after he had climbed the greasy pole and pushed all his rivals off ... that the whole thing was **Dead Sea fruit**. Even he, who had revelled in the post more than any other prime minister since Disraeli, found that the glittering prizes were made not of diamonds, nor even convincing paste, but glass. (Bernard Levin, *Frittering Away Their Lives for a Little Sham Authority*, The Times [London], 11-20-1990.)

(2) disappointment (as in anticlimax) *n.*: **bathos**. SEE ANTICLIMAX

disapproval (as in criticism) *n.*: **animadversion** (*v.t.*: **animadvert**). SEE CRITICISM

(2) disapproval (develop a strong ... of) *n.*: **scunner** (esp. as in "take a scunner")[British]. SEE DISLIKE

disapprove (of, as in scold or rebuke) *v.t.*: **objurgate**. SEE CRITICIZE

disapproving (as in faultfinding) *adj.*: **captious**. SEE FAULTFINDING

(2) disapproving (as in faultfinding, person) *n.*: **smellfungus**. SEE FAULTFINDER

disarray *n., adj.*: **hugger-mugger**. SEE CONFUSION

disaster (one who is always predicting ...) *n.*: **catastrophist**. SEE PESSIMIST

(2) disaster (as in episode having the quality of a nightmare) *n.*: **Walpurgis Night**. SEE NIGHTMARE

disastrous (as in causing or portending death) *adj.*: **funest**. SEE DEADLY

disavow *v.t.*: **abjure**. SEE RENOUNCE

(2) disavow (esp. responsibility or duty) *v.t.*: **abnegate**. SEE RENOUNCE

disavowal (as in retraction) *n.*: **palinode**. SEE RETRACTION

disbeliever (as in one with no faith or religion) *n., adj.*: **nullifidian**. SEE NONBELIEVER

discern *v.t.*: **descry**. SEE PERCEIVE

discernible (barely ...) *adj.*: **liminal**. SEE INVISIBLE

discerning (as in having a penetrating quality) *adj.*: **gimlet** (esp. as in "gimlet eye"). SEE PENETRATING

(2) discerning *adj.*: **perspicacious**. SEE ASTUTE

(3) discerning (as in wise) *adj.*: **sapient**. SEE WISE

discernment *n.*: **aperçu** [French]. SEE INSIGHT

discharge (waste from the body) *v.t.*: **egest**. SEE EXCRETE

disciple *adj.*: **acolyte**. SEE FOLLOWER

(2) disciple (strong ... of a cause, religion or activity) *n.*: **votary**. SEE SUPPORTER

disciplinarian (strict ...) *n.*: **martinet**. ∎ Certainly, Wolfgang Schmidt did not fit the mold of the model East German sports hero — sober, stoic, obedient. In recent years he had sometimes seemed to go out of his way to irritate the **martinets** and party hardliners who ran [the East German athletic governing body]. He had flouted the rules that forbade him to befriend athletes from the West. (William Oscar Johnson, *Wolfgang Schmidt, the Discus Thrower*, Sports Illustrated, 01-21-1991, p. 50.)

discipline (as in marked by simplicity, frugality, self-restraint and/or ...) *adj.*: **Lacedaemoninan**. SEE SPARTAN

disciplined (strictly ...) *adj.*: **monastic**. SEE STRICT

disclaim *v.t.*: **abjure**. SEE RENOUNCE

(2) disclaim (esp. responsibility or duty) *v.t.*: **abnegate**. SEE RENOUNCE

disclose *v.t.*: **disinter**. ∎ Most mortifying of all to Rockefeller, [reporter Ida] Tarbell **disinterred** his oldest and deepest shame: [his father] Big Bill's rape indictment in Moravia in the late 1840's. (Ron Chernow, *Titan*, Random House [1998], p. 459.)

(2) disclose (one's thoughts or feelings) *v.t.*, *v.i.*: **unbosom**. SEE CONFIDE

discomfort (as in bother or inconvenience) *v.t.*: **incommode**. SEE BOTHER

disconcert *v.t.*: **discomfit**. ∎ The agonies he must have suffered in those terrible asylum nights have granted us all a benefit. He was mad, and for that, we have reason to be glad. A truly savage irony, on which it is **discomfiting** to dwell. (Simon Winchester, *The Professor and the Madman*, Harper Collins [1998], p. 214.)

disconnected (talk or act in a ... or incoherent fashion) *v.i.*: **maunder**. SEE RAMBLE

disconnection (into two parts, esp. by tearing apart or violent separation) *n.*: **diremption**. SEE SEPARATION

(2) disconnection (as in a fallacious argument where one proves or disproves a point which is not at issue) *n.*: **ignoratio elenchi** [Latin]. SEE IRRELEVANCY

discontent (to fret or complain, including as a result of ...) *v.i.*: **repine**. SEE COMPLAIN

discontentment (as in disappointment) *n.*: **Dead Sea fruit**. SEE DISSAPPOINTMENT

discontinuance (state of inactivity or ...) *n.*: **desuetude**. SEE DISUSE

discontinue (temporarily ... esp. a session of Parliament) *v.t.*: **prorogue**. ∎ While the government introduced an Ontarians with Disabilities Act last November, the proposed legislation died on the order paper in December, when the Legislature **prorogued**. ... Citizenship Minister Isabel Bassett has promised to reintroduce the act when the Legislature resumes this spring. (Caroline Mallan, *Group Seeks Barrier-Free Election Polls*, The Toronto Star, 04-15-1999.)

discord (of or relating to ... within a group or country) *adj.*: **internecine**. SEE DISSENSION

(2) discord (as in heated disagreement or friction between groups) *n.*: **ruction**. SEE DISSENSION

discordant (sounds) *adj.*: **scrannel**. SEE CACOPHONOUS

discouraged (as in dejected) *adj.*: **chapfallen**. SEE DEJECTED

(2) discouraged (chronically ..., as in depressed) *adj.*, *n.*: **dysthymic**. SEE DEPRESSED

discourse (about in a scholarly manner, often used in a derogatory fashion) *v.i.*: **lucubrate** [Occasionally defined as limited to writing only, but in actual usage it is used to refer to writing or speech]. ∎ The Westminster world endlessly **lucubrates** on the horrors of a politics without vision, of a leader without a streak of grandeur, of the mesmerising bitterness at large in the Conservative Party. But even in politics, talk can sometimes be taken for what it is: no more than talk. (Hugo Young, *Commentary: It Will Be Surprising If John Major Doesn't Face a Leadership Challenge After Three Years*, The Guardian, 04-08-1993, p. 22.)

(2) discourse *v.i.*, *n.*: **descant**. SEE TALK

discover (by careful observation or scrutiny) *v.t.*: **descry**. SEE PERCEIVE

discovery (moment of ..., often the point in the plot at which the protagonist recognizes his or her or some other character's true identity or discovers the true nature of his or her own situation) *n.*: **anagnorisis**. SEE RECOGNITION

(2) discovery (of fortunate things by accident) *n.*: **serendipity** (*adj.*: **serendipitous**). SEE FORTUITOUS

(3) discovery (lucky ...) *n.*: **trouvaille** [French]. SEE FIND

discredit (by making false or malicious statements) *v.t.*: **calumniate**. SEE MALIGN

(2) discredit (being subject to ..., esp. public) *n.*: **obloquy**. SEE ABUSE

(3) discredit (by making false statements) *v.t.*: **traduce**. SEE MALIGN

discrepancy (in terms or ideas) *n.*: **antilogy**. SEE CONTRADICTION

discriminating (as in discerning and astute) *adj.*: **perspicacious**. SEE ASTUTE

discrimination (against homosexuals) *n.*: **heterosexism**. SEE HOMOSEXUALS

discriminatory (unjustly ... in matters of distinguishing between groups) *adj*.: **invidious**. ▪ Of course only a lunatic would believe that the predominance of black males on NBA rosters was a product of **invidious** discrimination against white males, let alone against, say, Asian females. (Paul Campos, *The Lies We Tell About Diversity*, Denver Rocky Mountain News, 10-24-2000, p. 29A.)

discuss (esp. in a long-winded or pompous manner) *v.i.*: **bloviate**. SEE SPEAK

(2) discuss (casually) *n*.: **chinwag** [slang]. SEE CHAT

(3) discuss (casually) *v.i.*: **confabulate**. SEE CHAT

(4) discuss (esp. at length) *v.i., n*.: **descant**. SEE TALK

(5) discuss (a subject at length in speech or writing) *v.i.*: **expatiate**. SEE EXPOUND

(6) discuss (in a scholarly manner, often used in a derogatory fashion) *v.i.*: **lucubrate**. SEE DISCOURSE

discussion *n*.: **interlocution**. ▪ [The movie "Chasing Amy" is] a boy-meets-lesbian, boy-loses-lesbian romantic comedy loaded with wit, charm, and unbelievably filthy dialogue, including an epic **interlocution** on the perils of oral sex. (Benjamin Svetkey, *News & Notes/Behind the Scenes: Getting the Girl: 'Clerks' Creator Kevin Smith Comes Out From Behind the Counter with 'Amy,'* Entertainment Weekly, 04-11-1997, p. 25.)

(2) discussion (esp. with an enemy or adversary) *n., v.t.*: **parley**. ▪ America cannot deal with [its potential enemies] all on its own ... especially as new threats — cyberwar, biological war, economic instability, cults and disease — now jostle with the more familiar ones of ethnic hatred and religious rivalry. [The instruments to deal with such threats] range from diplomatic **parley** through economic sanctions to military support to armed attack. (Author not given, *Dubya's World [Editorial]*, Seattle Post-Intelligencer, 01-11-2001.)

(3) discussion (esp. at the start of negotiations) *n*.: **pourparler** [French]. ▪ [The Swiss publishers trying to sign up French authors] calculated how they could undercut the Parisian publishers by shaving costs and profits and then set out to steal the best authors. ... They entered into **pourparlers** with d'Alembert, Raynal, Beaumarchais, Mably, Marmontel, and Morellet. They even approached Benjamin Franklin with a scheme to peddle French books in the New World. (Robert Darnton, *The Forgotten Middlemen, [The Perils of Publishing, Part 4]*, The New Republic, 09-15-1986.)

(4) discussion (light or playful back and forth ...) *n*.: **badinage**. SEE BANTER

(5) discussion (informal ...) *n*.: **causerie**. SEE CHAT

(6) discussion (spec. a final effort made by architectural students to complete a solution to a problem within an allotted time, but sometimes is used to refer to any kind of workshop or brainstorming session) *n*.: **charette** (or **charrette**). SEE WORKSHOP

(7) discussion (esp. about art or literature) *n*.: **conversazione** [Italian]. SEE CONVERSATION

(8) discussion (one skilled at dinner ...) *n*.: **deipnosophist**. SEE CONVERSATION

(9) discussion (in which neither side hears or understands or pays attention to the other) *n*.: **dialogue des sourds** [French]. SEE DIALOGUE

(10) discussion (between two people) *n*.: **duologue**. SEE CONVERSATION

(11) discussion (idle ...) *n*.: **palaver**. SEE SMALL TALK

(12) discussion (of a subject in a light-hearted way, as in chitchat) *n*.: **persiflage**. SEE CHITCHAT

(13) discussion (about a philosophical or theological issue) *n*.: **quodlibet**. SEE DEBATE

(14) discussion (between three people) *n*.: **trialogue**. SEE CONVERSATION

disdain *n*.: **misprision** (*v.t.*: **misprize**). ▪ The Government does, of course, support the countryside in theory. [Prime Minister Blair has said that] there is a great "tourism industry" (sic) out there that needs our support. That, however, is at the root of Labour's **misprision** of rural matters. To them, it is a theme park, where "their people" play at weekends. What they fail to understand is that the theme park is only kept open by the people who farm it and the millions who live in it and sustain it. (Simon Heffer, *This Election Is Between Town and Country: Simon Heffer Says That Labour's Ignorance of Rural Affairs Has Split Britain*, Sunday Telegraph [London], 05-06-2001, p. 18.)

disdain *v.t.*: **contemn**. SEE SCORN

disdainful (towards another, often by being insulting or humiliating) *adj*.: **contumelious**. SEE CONTEMPTUOUS

disease (showing no evidence of) *n*.: **asympomatic**. ▪ Some HIV-positive people have remained **asymptomatic** for extensive periods. Moreover, several studies indicate that exercise and diet can help an individual remain **asymptomatic**. (Jack McCallum, *There He Stood, 24 Feet From the Basket*, Sports Illustrated, 02-17-1992, p. 18.)

(2) disease (caused by a physician) *adj.:* **iatrogenic**. ∎ While medical technology and knowledge of diseases have leapt forward over the past two decades, the rate of **iatrogenic** diseases has remained the same — especially from prescribed drugs. (Author not given, *Hospital Deaths Linked to Drug Errors [French Study]*, Medical Post, 02-09-1999, p. 8.)

(3) disease (which is widespread) *n.:* **pandemic**. ∎ Our world has been swept by three influenza **pandemics** in this century. The most devastating by far was the so-called Spanish flu in 1918: virtually every person on Earth was infected, and an estimated 30 million died, many more than those killed in World War I. (Patricia Gadsby, *There Was a Fear of Flu*, Discover Magazine, 01-01-1999.)

(4) disease (causing) *adj.:* **pathogenic**. ∎ There is growing evidence that preventing diseases in infancy may be a mixed blessing. Can intervening in an illness sometimes be worse than doing nothing at all? ... It is, of course, well known that preventing or treating an infectious disease can have profound effects on the **pathogenic** organism that causes it. (Author not given, *Plagued by Cures*, The Economist, 11-22-1997.)

(5) disease (carrier) *n.:* **vector**. ∎ Having a pesky new mosquito is bad enough, but the real danger lies in the tiger mosquito's ability to carry some truly awful viral diseases, including dengue and yellow fever. "The tiger mosquito is a competent **vector** for both viruses," as well as others. (Robert Cooke, *A Plague on All Our Houses [Infectious Diseases]*, Popular Science, 01-01-1996, p. 50.)

(6) disease (of a ... which has no known cause) *adj.:* **idiopathic** (*n.:* **idiopathy**). SEE ILLNESS

(7) disease (early sign of ...) *n.:* **prodrome**. SEE SYMPTOM

disgrace (to one's reputation) *n.:* **blot (or stain) on one's escutcheon** *idiom*. SEE DISHONOR

(2) disgrace (being subject to ..., esp. public) *n.:* **obloquy**. SEE ABUSE

(3) disgrace (by making false statements) *v.t.:* **traduce**. SEE MALIGN

disgraceful *adj.:* **opprobrious** (*n.:* **opprobrium**). SEE CONTEMPTUOUS

disguise (or mask) *n., v.t.:* **vizard**. ∎ In the old days it was the baddies who hid their faces. Now it's just as likely to be the good guys in disguise. But why this need for anonymity? And why do celebrities such as [Jacqueline Onassis and Princess Diana] feel the need to cover up? Henry Porter [writes] on the transformation of the **vizard**, from executioner's helm to badge of courage to fashion accessory. (Author not given, *Going Behind The Mask*, The Guardian [London], 06-10-1996, p. T2.)

(2) disguise (as in something which is impressive-looking on the outside but which hides or covers up undesirable conditions or facts) *n.:* **Potemkin village**. SEE FACADE

disgust (develop a ... about) *n.:* **scunner** (esp. as in "take a scunner")[British]. SEE DISLIKE

disgusting *adj.:* **ugsome**. SEE LOATHSOME

disheartened *adj.:* **chapfallen**. SEE DEJECTED

disheveled (or bloated in appearance) *adj.:* **blowsy** (or **blowzy**). "I'd rather stay home and watch the soaps," a big, **blowsy** woman in curlers said, and they all laughed. (Joe Klein, *Primary Colors*, Random House [1996], p. 160.)

(2) disheveled *adj.:* **frowzy**. SEE MESSY

dishonest *adj.:* **mendacious**. ∎ Clinton continues to injure himself with optional nonsense like his bragging about his agricultural knowledge. Voters know nonsense when they hear it. And they may be concluding that although Clinton is not consciously **mendacious** when he says things such as he said in Iowa, he thinks that whatever makes him feel good when he blurts it out must be true. (George Will, *Clinton Attempts to Reap Farm Vote*, St. Louis Post-Dispatch, 05-04-1995, p. 7B.)

(2) dishonest (person or scoundrel) *n.:* **blackguard**. SEE SCOUNDREL

(3) dishonest (person, spec. one who accepts bribes) *n.:* **boodler**. SEE CORRUPT

(4) dishonest (politician) *n.:* **highbinder**. SEE corrupt

(5) dishonest (as in unscrupulous) *adj.:* **jackleg**. SEE UNSCRUPULOUS

(6) dishonest (scheming or trickery) *n.:* **jiggery-pokery**. SEE TRICKERY

(7) dishonest (characterized by ... and cunning conduct) *adj.:* **Machiavellian**. SEE DECEITFUL

(8) dishonest (group of ... politicians) *n.:* **plunderbund**. SEE CORRUPT

(9) dishonest (conduct) *n.:* **skullduggery**. SEE DECEITFULNESS

dishonesty *n.:* **knavery**. SEE CORRUPTION

dishonor (to one's reputation) *n.:* **blot (or stain) on (one's) escutcheon** *idiom*. ∎ Women fleeing bondage to fathers, husbands, or male relatives are denied eligibility for asylum in the United States despite the moral abomination that their plights present. This **stain on** the nation's **escutcheon** should be removed. Holding females in servitude is every bit as morally repugnant as are the outrages that qualify for asylum. (Watson, *A Stain on Our Asylum Law?* The Washington Times, 06-08-2003.)

(2) dishonor (as in insult another's dignity) *n.*: **lese majesty**. SEE INSULT

dishonorable (as in shameful) *adj.*: **opprobrious** (*n.*: **opprobrium**). SEE CONTEMPTUOUS

(2) dishonorable (and unprincipled person) *n.*: **reprobate**. SEE UNPRINCIPLED

disillusionment (as in disappointment) *n.*: **Dead Sea fruit**. SEE DISSAPOINTMENT

disinclination *n.*: **nolition**. SEE UNWILLINGNESS

disingenuous (as in false showing of naive or simplistic behavior) *adj.*: **faux-naif** [French]. ∎ Much of the fault of *The Language of Life* lies with [Bill] Moyers' decision to "go soft" — to play the genial, wide-eyed interviewer who encounters a revelation at every turn. He's fond of **faux-naif** questions (at least one hopes the faux is genuine) such as, "So politics is not only a matter of revolution?" (Brad Leithauser, *The Arts & Media/Television: "I'm Ed, and I'm a Poet"; In His Earnest Series The Language of Life, Bill Moyers Turns Poetry into a Mixture of Therapy Session and A.A. Meeting*, Time, 07-03-1995, p. 54.)

(2) disingenuous (as in hypocritical) *adj.*: **Janus-faced**. SEE TWO-FACED

disintegrate (tending to ... or break up) *adj.*: **fissiparous**. SEE BREAK UP

disinterestedness (esp. on matters or politics or religion) *n.*: **Laodiceanism**. SEE INDIFFERENCE

disjunction (into two parts, esp. by tearing apart or violent separation) *n.*: **diremption**. SEE SEPARATION

dislike (strong ...) *n.*: **scunner** (esp. as in "take a scunner")[British]. ∎ [M]ost recent evidence suggests that the great British public has at last taken a **scunner** [to the proposed British lottery]. For although most people are happy enough to have a flutter on the Lottery, they don't like the scale of the profits being made by the contractors who run it, and have been disappointed by how little of their ticket money is reaching charities. (Ian Aitken, *Chocolate-*

Bar Politics [Housing Policy of UK Government], New Statesman & Society, 06-09-1995, p. 12.)

(2) dislike (intense ..., such as towards an enemy) *n.*: **enmity**. SEE HATRED

(3) dislike (strongly ...) *v.t.*: **execrate**. SEE HATE

(4) dislike (person who has ... for all people) *n.*: **misanthrope**. SEE HATRED

(5) dislike (strongly) *v.t.*: **misprize**. SEE HATE

(6) dislike (of strangers or foreigners) *n.*: **xenophobia**. SEE DISTRUST

disliked (something that is ..., dreaded, or to be avoided) *n.*: **bête noire** [French]. SEE DREADED

disloyal (man married to ... wife) *n.*: **cuckold** (*v.t.*: to make a ... of). SEE ADULTEROUS

(2) disloyal *adj.*: **perfidious**. SEE UNFAITHFUL

(3) disloyal (to a belief, duty or cause) *adj.*: **recreant**. SEE UNFAITHFUL

dismal (as in dark and gloomy) *adj.*: **acherontic**. SEE GLOOMY

disobedient *adj.*: **contumacious**. SEE OBSTINATE

(2) disobedient (or contrary in a stubborn way) *adj.*: **froward**. SEE CONTRARY

(3) disobedient (as in resistant to control or authority) *adj.*: **refractory**. SEE STUBBORN

disorder (movement towards or degree of ... in a system or society) *n.*: **entropy**. ∎ This basic tenet of modern physics, you may recall, maintains that the universe tends to move from order to disorder. But if this [new theory of] emerging science is right, then **entropy** may not be the final answer. (Suneel Ratan, *Books & Ideas: It's Not That Simple*, Fortune, 03-08-1993, p. 137.)

(2) disorder (and confusion) *n., adj.*: **hugger-mugger**. SEE CONFUSION

(3) disorder (as in commotion) *n.*: **maelstrom**. SEE COMMOTION

(4) disorder (as in chaos) *n.*: **tohubuhu**. SEE CHAOS

(5) disorder (as in confused or disarrayed mess) *n.*: **welter**. SEE JUMBLE

disorderly (in a ... and hasty manner) *adv.*: **pell-mell**. ∎ [L]ike many of her neighbors, she has heard City Hall's promises of renewal before. They worry that the city has rushed **pell-mell** into demolition [of abandoned buildings in Philadelphia] without knowing what will rise upon the rubble. (Michael Powell, *Raze of Sunshine in Philadelphia? City Pins Renewal Hopes on Clearing Vast Areas of Blight, Seeking Development*, The Washington Post, 03-19-2002, p. A3.)

(2) disorderly (as in unruly) *adj.*: **indocile**. SEE UNRULY

disorganization (of a person or group as a result of lack of standards or values) *n.*: **anomie**. SEE BREAKDOWN

(2) disorganization (and confusion) *n., adj.*: **hugger-mugger**. SEE CONFUSION

disorganized (talk or act in a ... or incoherent fashion) *v.i.*: **maunder**. SEE RAMBLE

disparage *v.t.*: **vilipend**. ∎ He began by yelling [at the mules] in a coarse, strident voice, "Arre! arre!" (Get up!) [He then] proceeded to **vilipend** the galloping beasts separately, beginning with the leader. He informed him, still in this wild, jerking scream, that he was a dog, that his mother's character was far from that of Caesar's wife. (John Hay, *Castilian Days: A Castle In The Air*, History of the World, 01-01-1992.)

(2) disparage (by making false or malicious statements) *v.t.*: **calumniate**. SEE MALIGN

(3) disparage (in a false way so as to humiliate or disgrace) *v.t.*: **traduce**. SEE MALIGN

disparaging (as in faultfinding) *adj.*: **captious**. SEE FAULTFINDING

(2) disparaging (another, often by being insulting or humiliating) *adj.*: **contumelious**. SEE CONTEMPTUOUS

(3) disparaging (as in faultfinding, person) *n.*: **smellfungus**. SEE FAULTFINDER

(4) disparaging (language) *n.*: **vituperation** (*adj.*: **vituperative**). SEE INVECTIVE

disparagement (as in disdain) *n.*: **misprision** (*v.t.*: **misprize**). SEE DISDAIN

disparate (as in not homogenous) *adj.*: **heterogeneous** (*n.*: **heterogeneity**). SEE DISSIMILAR

(2) disparate (as in things which do not mix together) *adj.*: **immiscible**. SEE INCOMPATIBLE

disperse (able to ... freely in a given environment; used of species) *adj.*: **vagile**. SEE MOVE

dispersion (as in diversity) *n.*: **variegation** (*v.t.*: **variegate**). SEE DIVERSITY

dispirited *adj.*: **chapfallen**. SEE DEJECTED

displace (esp. from one's accustomed environment) *v.t.*: **deracinate**. SEE UPROOT

displaced (of ... people having lost class status) *adj.*:

lumpen. ∎ The University of Phoenix is a for-profit [on-line] enterprise. ... [A typical] faculty member is part time and earns only $2,000 a course, teaching from a standardized curriculum. Is Phoenix then an academic sweatshop where underpaid **lumpen** intellectuals slave for a pittance? No way. ... Most of the profs hold down full-time jobs in the professions they teach. (Lisa Gubernick, *I Got My Degree Through E-mail*, Forbes Magazine, 06-16-1997, p. 84.)

display (violent ... in which shame, degradation or harm is inflicted on a person, often for the enjoyment of onlookers) *n.*: **Roman holiday**. SEE SPECTACLE

(2) display (glass ... case) *n.*: **vitrine**. SEE SHOWCASE

disposition (of a person, people or culture) *n.*: **ethos**. SEE CHARACTER

dispossessed (of ... people having lost class status) *adj.*: **lumpen**. SEE DISPLACED

disputable (as in controversial, opinion or person who holds one) *n.*: **polemic**. SEE CONTROVERSY

disputatious *adj., n.*: **eristic**. SEE DEBATE

dispute (characterized by internal ...) *adj.*: **factious**. ∎ Before this switch from anti-government to pro-government, the most conspicuous feature of Democratic conventions was divisiveness. In the 1800s, for example, the Democrats were notoriously **factious** because their roots were Southern. ... These factions made resolution of the slavery issue difficult and ultimately led to the party's division in 1860. (Thomas V. DiBacco, *Nothing Conventional About Democrats' History*, The Washington Times, 08-13-2000, p. C6.)

(2) dispute (engaging in frequent and possibly specious ...) *adj., n.*: **eristic**. SEE SPECIOUS AND DEBATE

(3) dispute (about words) *n.*: **logomachy**. SEE WORDS

(4) dispute (a statement, opinion or action) *v.t.*: **oppugn**. SEE OPPOSE

disputing (esp. majority view) *adj.*: **dissentient**. SEE DISSENTING

disregard (intentionally) *v.t.*: **pretermit**. SEE OMIT

disregarding (or omitting or passing over) *n.*: **preterition**. SEE OMITTING

disrespect (religious ...) *n.*: **impiety** (*adj.* **impious**). SEE IRREVERENCE

dissatisfaction (as in disappointment) *n.*: **Dead Sea fruit**. SEE DISSAPPOINTMENT

dissect (as in analyze closely) *v.t.*: **anatomize**. SEE ANALYZE

dissension (of or relating to ... within a group or country) *adj.*: **internecine**. ∎ In a dangerous new trend in the Muslim world — one that has already blossomed into brutal **internecine** violence — the most militant among these groups also look down on more moderate Islamic groups, such as the 70-year-old Muslim Brotherhood, that seek power through the ballot box. (Susan Sachs, *Roots of the Jihad*, Newsday, 09-24-1996, p. A5.)

(2) dissension (as in heated disagreement or friction between groups) *n.*: **ruction**. ∎ The OSP [Office of Special Plans] is the brainchild of Defense Secretary Donald Rumsfeld [to show] that the CIA had overlooked the threat posed [by Saddam Hussein and Iraq]. But its rise has caused massive **ructions** in the normally secretive world of intelligence gathering. ... Former CIA officials are caustic about the OSP. Unreliable and politically motivated, they say it has undermined decades of work by the CIA's trained spies. (Paul Harris, *Iraq after Saddam: US Rivals Turn on Each Other as Weapons Search Draws a Blank*, The Observer, 05-11-2003.)

dissent (characterized by internal ...) *adj.*: **factious**. SEE DISPUTE

(2) dissent (from, as in oppose a statement, opinion or action) *v.t.*: **oppugn**. SEE OPPOSE

dissenter (orig. Catholics who did not follow Church of England) *n.*: **recusant**. ∎ Rehnquist, in his book, also expressed doubts about the validity of most of the articles of impeachment against [Republican President Andrew] Johnson. ... The "**recusant** Republican senators" who defied their party and "tipped the balance in favor of Johnson" won praise from Rehnquist for putting principle above politics. (Gaylord Shaw, *Portrait of a Trial*, Newsday, 01-05-1999, p. B6.)

dissenting (esp. from majority view) *adj.*: **dissentient**. ∎ For younger composers [in Great Britain], exile or isolation still loom as certainties. Politicised by chronic underfunding, they can be dangerously critical of the status quo, so much so that serious contemporary music is often classified as **dissentient**. (Marc Bridle, *Unacknowledged Notation*, New Statesman & Society, 04-12-1996, p. 32.)

dissident (as in rebel) *n.*: **frondeur** [French]. SEE REBEL

dissimilar (as in not homogenous) *adj.*: **heterogeneous** (*n.*: **heterogeneity**). ∎ [T]he starting point for [the change to the Eurodollar] is that Europe currently has **heterogeneous** customers who largely buy **heterogeneous** products with different ingredients, labels and packages. Much else will need to converge before prices do. (Author not given, *Survey: Borders and Barriers*, The Economist, 12-01-2001, p. 18.)

(2) dissimilar (state or quality of being ... from others) *n.*: **alterity**. SEE DIFFERENT

dissolute (morally ...) *adj.*: **scrofulous**. SEE DEPRAVED

dissolve (by melting away) *v.i.*: **deliquesce**. SEE MELT

dissuade (as in argue against) *v.t.*: **expostulate**. SEE OBJECT

distant (or remote destination or goal) *n.*: **ultima Thule** [Latin; derives from Thule, thought by ancient geographers to be the northernmost point of the habitable world.] ∎ High in those mountains [of the Provencal Alps], Meailles, a remote, deserted and windblown depot, was the **ultima Thule** of my journey — about as far in style and spirit as you can get from the modern station at Paris' Charles de Gaulle Airport, where our trip had begun last March. (Karl Zimmerman, *France; Two Rail Ways, Swift and Scenic*, Los Angeles Times, 06-23-2002, p. L11.)

distaste (develop a strong ... for) *n.*: **scunner** (esp. as in "take a scunner")[British]. SEE DISLIKE

distasteful (as in unpalatable) *adj.*: **brackish**. SEE UNPALATABLE

(2) distasteful (as in repellent) *adj.*: **rebarbative**. SEE REPELLENT

distended (as in swollen, used often of body parts such as the penis) *adj.*: **tumescent**. SEE SWOLLEN

(2) distended *adj.*: **tumid**. SEE SWOLLEN

distinct (state or quality of being ... from others) *n.*: **alterity**. SEE DIFFERENT

distinction (marking a ...) *adj.*: **diacritical**. SEE DISTINGUISHING

distinctive (shape or outline, often of a face) *adj.*: **lineament** (often **lineaments**). SEE CONTOUR

distinctness (as in that quality which makes one thing different from any other) *n*.: **haeccity**. SEE INDIVIDUALITY

distinguished (as in select or excellent) *adj*.: **eximious**. SEE EXCELLENT

distinguishing (between) *adj*.: **diacritical**. ∎ My husband's Eastern European surname ["Ode," pronounced "OH-dee"] is consistently mispronounced. Our sixth-grader no longer wants to call attention to himself by correcting people, while our third-grader has taken matters in the opposite direction by reverting to the Old World pronunciation, complete with **diacritical** embellishments. (Kim Ode, *You Can Call Me Anything, But ... // ... Don't Ever Think That a Name Doesn't Influence Who We Are, How We Got There*, Minneapolis Star Tribune, 05-21-2000, p. 5E.)

(2) distinguishing (shape or outline, often of a face) *adj*.: **lineament** (often **lineaments**). SEE CONTOUR

distortion (of words or of language) *n*.: **verbicide**. ∎ One manager, Rep. Steve Buyer of Indiana, said the president [Clinton] really is guilty of **verbicide** for his linguistic gymnastics and personal definitions. "He murdered the plain-spoken English language," Mr. Buyer said. (Frank J. Murray, *Prosecutors Demand Removal, Not Censure; Managers End Round of Arguments*, The Washington Times, 01-17-1999, p. A1.)

distracted (esp. because of worries or fears) *adj*.: **distrait**. ∎ As it looks to the start of the 21st century [France] is **distrait** and irresolute. At home, the nation is racked by a 12.3% unemployment rate; a growing gap between rich and poor; festering urban problems; and a tide of social unrest that has seen tens of thousands of protesting students, workers, homeless and aids activists take to the streets over the past few weeks. (Thomas Sancton, *France: If at First You Don't Succeed; Jacques Chirac Has Come From Behind to Lead the Race for the Presidency; But Polls Suggest it Will Be a Fight to the Finish*, Time International, 04-24-1995, p. 46.)

distress (state of extreme ...) *n*.: **swivet** (as in "in a swivet") *inf*. ∎ Gosh, silly us, getting **in a swivet** over war and peace. The president is on vacation! He's giving interviews to Runner's World, not Meet the Press. ... We don't have to worry, so party hearty, and try not to make a big deal out of the fact that the Bush's lawyers are now claiming he can launch an attack on Iraq without congressional approval. (Molly Ivins, *Can Bush Look Himself in Either of His Faces?* Rocky Mountain News, 08-28-2002.)

(2) distress (experience of intense ..., as in suffering) *n*.: **Calvary** [based on hill near Jerusalem where Jesus was crucified]. SEE SUFFERING

(3) distress (as in worry) *v.t., v.i., n*.: **cark**. SEE WORRY

(4) distress (as in a state of nervous tension) *n*.: **fantod**. SEE TENSION

(5) distress (as in trouble) *n*.: **tsuris** [Yiddish]. SEE TROUBLE

distressed (as if by a witch or by unfounded fears) *adj*.: **hagridden**. SEE TORMENTED

distribute (proportionately) *v.t*.: **admeasure**. SEE APPORTION

district (surrounding ... served by an institution, such as a school or hospital) *n*.: **catchment area**. ∎ The periodic eruption of unruly, and even criminal behavior in our student body would seem to be a fact of school life for the forseeable future. Given the socioeconomic profile of our **catchment area**, only a fool would imagine otherwise. (Zoë Heller, *What Was She Thinking?* Henry Holt [2003], p. 63.)

(2) district (Spanish-speaking ...) *n*.: **barrio**. SEE SPANISH

distrust (of strangers or foreigners) *n*.: **xenophobia**. ∎ It is widely known that the word for enemy and stranger are often the same in many cultures. **Xenophobia** is tearing our country apart. There are a lot of black people that have never had a white friend and vice versa. (Author not given, *State of the Union / Sample of Readers' Opinions on the State of the Union*, Minneapolis Star Tribune, 02-05-1997, p. 14A.)

(2) distrust (person who has ... for humankind) *n*.: **misanthrope**. SEE MISTRUST

disturb (as in agitate) *v.t*.: **commove**. SEE AGITATE

(2) disturb (as in bother or inconvenience) *v.t*.: **discommode**. SEE INCONVENIENCE

(3) disturb (as in bother or inconvenience) *v.t*.: **incommode**. SEE BOTHER

disturbance (over a trifling matter) *n*.: **foofaraw**. SEE FUSS

(2) disturbance (as in commotion) *n*.: **maelstrom**. SEE COMMOTION

(3) disturbance (as in commotion) *n*.: **pother**. SEE COMMOTION

disuse (state of inactivity or ...) *n*.: **desuetude**. ∎

Since Vietnam, members of Congress have tried to prevent administrations from sneaking the country into a war. The first effort, the War Powers Act, fell into **desuetude**. It was designed to give Congress a mechanism for disapproving incremental escalations, but Congress hesitated to invoke it when troops were in peril. (Michael Barone, *A Question of Going to War*, U.S. News & World Report, 11-01-1993, p. 49.)

diver *n.*: **urinator**. ■ It's a safe bet that Aristotle, an advocate of reason and moderation, would not have become a **urinator** for all the tea in China. To go underwater simply defies the natural order. [W]ater is a hostile element where the most basic life-fuel, air, cannot be guaranteed. (Stuart Wavell, *Artists of the Floating World*, Sunday Times [London], 08-05-2001.)

diverge (from a course or intended path) *v.t.*: **yaw**. SEE VEER

diverse *adj.*: **multifarious**. SEE VERSATILE
(2) diverse (often used of a performer or artist) *adj.*: **protean**. SEE VERSATILE

diversion (as in digression) *n.*: **excursus**. SEE DIGRESSION

diversity (as in region populated by people from a ... of countries or backgrounds) *n.*: **cosmopolis**. ■ The subway, I find, is also oddly liberating. It takes you not only to your destination, but along the way to another world. ... Your fellow riders are a jostling microcosm of a teeming **cosmopolis**: men, women and children from every stratum of society, of every imaginable color, sporting all kinds of dress (or undress) and chattering in most of the languages of the planet. (Shashi Tharoor, *Letter From America: Notes From The Underground*, Newsweek International, 08-27-2001, p. 41.)
(2) diversity *n.*: **heterogeneity** (*adj*: **heterogenous**). ■ His growing **heterogeneity** of interests ... could, with hindsight, be seen as the first overt signs of a growing alienation from convention and society that would later evolve into a radical sense of separateness and disconnection. (Sylvia Nasar, *A Beautiful Mind*, Simon & Schuster [1998], p. 143.)
(3) diversity *n.*: **variegation** (*v.t.*: **variegate**). ■ A typical sentence as heard coming out of our TV set might be: "Mah fellow Ah Mare Cuns. This country is in whore-bull shape. ... " [But] we ought to rejoice that in an age dominated by trite, homogenized media English, so much heterogeneity of speech sur-

vives, even thrives. The great diversity of tongues in America ... give texture and **variegation** to our common nationhood. It would be whore-bull if we all talked alike. (Robert Reno, *Reno at Large, Just Whose English Do We Declare Our Official Language?* Newsday, 09-27-1995, p. A43.)

divert (oneself in a light, frolicsome manner) *v.t.*, *v.i.*: **disport**. SEE FROLIC

divide (proportionately) *v.t.*: **admeasure**. SEE APPORTION
(2) divide (into thin layers) *v.i.*: **delaminate**. SEE SEPARATE
(3) divide (into parts) *v.i.*: **disaggregate**. SEE SEPARATE
(4) divide (from others, as in isolate) *v.t.*: **enisle**. SEE ISOLATE
(5) divide (tending to ... into parts or break up) *adj.*: **fissiparous**. SEE BREAK UP

divided *adj.*: **cloven**. SEE SPLIT

dividing (act of ... into parts) *n.*: **fission**. SEE SPLITTING

divination (by picking random Bible passages) *n.*: **bibliomancy**. ■ We sat cross-legged on the floor in front of her modest library of religious books. ... [S]he gave advice over the phone on questions concerning religious precepts and a suitable marriage alliance. She also ... performed a **bibliomancy** for the husband of a member of her gatherings concerning whether he should embark on a new business venture. (Azam Torab, *Piety as Gendered Agency*, Journal of the Royal Anthropological Institute, 06-01-1996.)
(2) divination (by communing with the dead) *n.*: **necromancy**. ■ The great escapologist, Houdini, was briefly obsessed with **necromancy** and set out to disprove that the dead could communicate with the living. (Patrick Gale, *Books: Final Escape — Into Death*, The Daily Telegraph, 03-27-1999.)
(3) divination (by touching or proximity to an object) *n.*: **psychometry**. ■ The **Psychometry** Test. Anita: "This is where I hold a personal object belonging to you [that] can tell me other things about you and your past." (Jane hands over a Russian wedding ring and Anita twists it around her finger). "It takes a couple of seconds for me to tune into it." ... Anita: "I'm also getting something else. ... Do you drive?" Jane: "Yes!" Anita: "But you failed your test the first time you took it." Jane: "Yes!" (Author not given, *So What's on the Cards for Leanne?* The People [London], 01-16-2000.)

(4) divination (by fire) *n.*: **pyromancy**. ▮ [A]n Abenaqui female shaman, a convert to Christianity, explaining to her mission priest why she continued to practice **pyromancy**: "Listen, God has given men different gifts. To the Frenchmen, he has given the Scriptures by which you learn the things that take place far from you as if they were in front of you; to us he has given the art of knowing, by fire, things remote in time or place." (Gordon Sayre, *Native Signification and Communication*, Early American Literature, 09-22-2003.)

divine (having both human and ... [as in godlike] attributes) *adj.*: **theanthropic**. SEE GODLIKE

diviner (by using lightning or animal innards) *n.*: **haruspex**. SEE FORTUNETELLER

division (into two parts, esp. by tearing apart or violent separation) *n.*: **diremption**. SEE SEPARATION
(2) division (often from or within a group or union) *n.*: **scission**. SEE SPLIT

divulge *v.t.*: **disinter**. SEE DISCLOSE
(2) divulge (one's thoughts or feelings) *v.t.*, *v.i.*: **unbosom**. SEE CONFIDE

dizzy *adj.*: **vertiginous**. ▮ More than anything, however, I felt positively giddy — that sort of **vertiginous** wooziness which I usually associate with the third Martini or the second bottle of Champagne. But it wasn't just the high altitude — and the hyper-pure mountain air — that was making me feel more than a little light headed. (Douglas Kennedy, *The Essay: A Walking Miracle*, Independent, 09-15-2001, p. 35.)

docile *adj.*: **biddable**. SEE OBEDIENT

doctor (equipment, including supplies and instruments, used by a ...) *n.*: **armamentarium**. ▮ In the Latin phrases that get tossed about by physicians, "primum non nocere" ("first, do no harm") ... is a Hippocratic albatross that today's physicians have come to understand subconsciously in its appropriate context. Every weapon in the physician's **armamentarium** is double-edged; every cure has a potential harm. (Kenneth LeCroy, [letter writer], *The Lie of Primum Non Nocere ["First, Do No Harm"]*, American Family Physician, 12-15-2001.)
(2) doctor (disease caused by a ...) *adj.*: **iatrogenic**. SEE DISEASE
(3) doctor (replacement ...) *n.*: **locum tenens**. SEE TEMPORARY

doctrine *n.*: **shibboleth**. SEE PRINCIPLE

dodge (as in avoid a straight answer) *v.t.*: **tergiversate**. SEE EVADE

dog days (of or relating to ... of summer) *adj.*: **canicular**. ▮ What happens in Venice, Rome, Positano, and San Gimignano [in the movie *Only You*] is appalling: witless, crudely contrived, blatantly preposterous, and desperately sweaty under the collar — and I am not referring to the **canicular** Italian climate. (John Simon, *Only You*, [Movie Reviews], National Review, 11-07-1994.)

dogged (in holding to a belief or opinion) *adj.*: **pertinacious**. SEE STUBBORN
(2) dogged (in effort or application) *adj.*: **sedulous**. SEE DILIGENT

doldrums (as in depression) *n.*: **cafard** [French]. SEE DEPRESSION

dole out (proportionately) *v.t.*: **admeasure**. SEE APPORTION

dolt *n.*: **jobbernowl** [British]. SEE IDIOT
(2) dolt *n.*: **mooncalf**. SEE FOOL

domain (as in area of activity or interest) *n.*: **purlieu**. ▮ In fact, [Stanley] Dance regarded Swing as the **purlieu** of white musicians like Benny Goodman and Artie Shaw. Mainstream was to encompass the work of black musicians including Duke Ellington, Earl Hines, Count Basie, Coleman Hawkins and Buck Clayton. (Steve Voce, *Obituary: Stanley Dance*, Independent, 03-02-1999, p. 6.)

dominance (of one political state over others) *n.*: **hegemony**. ▮ Now, however, the United States has claimed authority to hold sovereign nations accountable, in American courts, for failing to honor American laws in their dealings with Cuba. Even for the United States, that's carrying **hegemony** too far. (Author not given, *Cuba / The United States is Out of Step*, Minneapolis Star Tribune, 10-16-1998, p. 24A.)
(2) dominance (as in superiority or state of being better) *n.*: **meliority**. SEE SUPERIORITY

dominant *adj.*: **regnant**. SEE PREDOMINANT

dominate *v.t.*: **bestride** (past tense: **bestrode**). ▮ Napoleon III ruled France as emperor during the American Civil War. ... Yet the specter of another Napoleon, the first, haunted Civil War battlefields. Bonaparte died at St. Helena about 40 years before the war, but his figure **bestrode** the 19th century. In art and legend, he incarnated martial glory. In military theory, he was celebrated as the model genius of the times. (Tom O'Brien, *Napoleon's Shadow Over American Warriors*, The Washington Times, 09-09-2000.)

domination (of a nation or group over another) *n.*: **suzerainty**. ∎ No doubt, not everyone in the German leadership saw their **suzerainty** over so many Jews purely in terms of "opportunity," for the disposal of so many Jews posed enormous practical problems and created day-to-day difficulties for those charged with Jewish affairs. (Daniel Goldhagen, *Hitler's Willing Executioners*, Knopf [1996], p. 144.)

(2) domination (of a religious, national or racial group) *n.*: **helotism** (*v.t.*: **helotize**). SEE OPPRESSION

domineering (woman who is overbearing and ...) *n.*: **virago**. SEE SHREW

donation (which is all one can afford) *n.*: **widow's mite**. ∎ "The true measure of philanthropy lies in giving, even when it hurts. And then a **widow's mite** trumps the rich man's might." Owen Willis, Tantallon, N.S. (Author not given, *Letters*, Time, 08-14-2000, p. 9.)

(2) donation (as in offering) *n.*: **oblation**. SEE OFFERING

donor (generous ..., esp. to the arts) *n.*: **Maecenas**. SEE BENEFACTOR

doom (as in damnation) *n.*: **perdition**. SEE DAMNATION

doomsayer *n.*: **catastrophist**. SEE PESSIMIST
(2) doomsayer *n.*: **crepehanger**. SEE PESSIMIST

doomsday (branch of theology concerned with) *n.*: **eschatology**. SEE JUDGMENT DAY

dope *n.*: **jobbernowl** [British]. SEE IDIOT
(2) dope *n.*: **mooncalf**. SEE FOOL

dormant (as in inanimate) *adj.*: **insensate**. SEE INANIMATE
(2) dormant (as in not moving or temporarily inactive) *adj.*: **quiescent**. SEE INACTIVE
(3) dormant *adj.*: **torpid**. SEE LETHARGIC

dote (on, as in treat with excessive concern) *n., v.t.*: **wet-nurse**. SEE CODDLE

doting (overly ... or submissive to one's wife) *adj.*: **uxorious**. ∎ [Jay Leno's wife Mavis] was an aspiring writer who read far more than she wrote; she still devours 10 books a week. "I don't make wife jokes," Leno points out. He may be the first comedian since George Burns who could be described as **uxorious**. (Richard Stengel, *Jay Leno, Succeeding Johnny Carson as Late-Night Host to Millions, Has Already Won the Office of Most Popular Regular Guy in America*, Time, 03-16-1992, p. 58.)

dotted (with a darker color) *adj.*: **brindled**. SEE SPOTTED

double (ghostly ... of a living person) *n.*: **doppelganger**. SEE TWIN

double meaning (in language) *n.*: **amphibiology**. SEE AMBIGUITY

double negative (as a means of understatement, as in "He's not bad.") *n.*: **litotes**. SEE UNDERSTATEMENT

double-crossers (as in traitors or group of ... working within a country to support an enemy and who may engage in espionage, sabotage or other subversive activities) *n.*: **fifth column**. SEE TRAITORS
(2) double-crosser (esp. who betrays under guise of friendship) *n.*: **Judas**. SEE BETRAYER
(3) double-crosser (esp. who aids an invading enemy) *n.*: **quisling**. SEE TRAITOR

double-sided *adj.*: **Janus-faced**. SEE TWO-FACED

doubt (expression of ... as to one's opinion on an issue, esp. arising from awareness of an opposing viewpoint) *n.*: **aporia**. ∎ [Several scenes in the movie *Do the Right Thing*] all suggest that [director Spike] Lee advocates violence. Or is there an honest uncertainty, a true **aporia**, expressed in the two quotations Lee appends to the film: one from Dr. King, decrying violence as a solution, followed by another from Malcolm X, saying that it is stupid not to resort to violence in "self-defense," i.e., in righting social inequity. (James Gardner, *A Star is Reborn*, National Review, 08-04-1989.)

(2) doubt (esp. as in "beyond ...") *n.*: **peradventure**. ∎ According to an NBC/Wall Street Journal survey, the lying cheating hound [President Clinton] has risen in his job approval ratings from 64 per cent to 67 per cent. Prove to the American people beyond **peradventure** that he's a Grade A philanderer and fraud — and they conclude that he's even better at doing his job! (Boris Johnson, *How Clinton Gets Off*:

Reach Out and Touch, The Daily Telegraph, 09-15-1998.)

(3) doubt (as in oppose, a statement, opinion or action) *v.t.*: **oppugn**. SEE OPPOSE

doubter *n.*: **crepehanger**. SEE PESSIMIST

doubtful (morality or taste) *adj.*: **louche**. SEE QUESTIONABLE

(2) doubtful (as in skeptical) *adj.*: **zetetic**. SEE SKEPTICAL

doubtfulness *n.*: **dubiety**. ■ Republicans now calling for revival of the [independent counsel] law are ignoring its constitutional **dubiety**. But today the word "Watergate" still serves as an argument for the law. That is absurd. (George Will, *Let the Voters be the Judge*, Newsday, 01-09-1994, p. 32.)

(2) doubtfulness (statement of ..., as in unlikelihood, expressed in the form of an exaggerated comparison with a more obvious impossibility; for example "the sky will fall before I get married.") *n.*: **adynaton**. SEE UNLIKELIHOOD

dour (as in person who never laughs) *n.*: **agelast**. SEE HUMORLESS

(2) dour (as in dark and gloomy) *adj.*: **acherontic**. SEE GLOOMY

(3) dour (as in sullen or morose) *adj.*: **saturnine**. SEE SULLEN

douse (as in soak) *v.t.*: **imbrue**. SEE SOAK

downcast *adj.*: **chapfallen**. SEE DEJECTED

(2) downcast (as in sullen or morose) *adj.*: **saturnine**. SEE SULLEN

downfall (esp. from a position of strength or condition) *n.*: **dégringolade** [French]. ■ TIME [magazine's] greatest influence was exerted in forming the nation's attitudes, its political opinions and social conscience — especially in the decades after World War II. In the '60s, during Vietnam, TIME was caught in a general American **dégringolade**, a deconstruction of established authority from the President on down. (Lance Morrow, *The Time of Our Lives*, Time, 03-09-1998.)

(2) downfall (violent or turbulent ... of a society or regime) *n.*: **götterdämmerung** [German]. SEE COLLAPSE

(3) downfall (esp. of moral principles or civil order) *n.*: **labefaction**. SEE WEAKENING

downplay (attempt to ... seriousness of an offense) *v.t.*: **palliate**. ■ Every civilization needs its self-justifying myths. ... America's great national myth of the settlement and taming of the frontier grew out of the slaughter of indigenous peoples, which it was meant to explain and **palliate**. (James Bowman, *Alien Menace: Lt. Ripley is Hollywood's Mythical Woman — Butch and Ready to Kill*, National Review, 01-26-1998, p. 35.)

downpour *n.*: **cataract**. ■ It takes a bit more than a downpour to ruffle his demeanour. Let there be a deluge of Biblical proportions, let the winds crack their cheeks and **cataracts** and hurricanes spout on the Wimbledon Park Road and Des would glance out of the window, raise an eyebrow and murmur: "Nasty out." (Andrew Baker, *Wimbledon 1997: Golden Days Brighten the Grey Afternoons*, Independent on Sunday, 06-29-1997, p. 22.)

downright (esp. when used with "nonsense") *adj.*: **arrant**. SEE TOTAL

downturn *n.*: **declension**. SEE DECLINE

downward (slope) *n.*: **declivity** (*adj.*: **declivitous**). SEE DECLINE

(2) downward (slope, esp. extending down from a fortification) *n.*: **glacis**. SEE DECLINE

draft (as in compose or write) *v.t.*: **indite**. SEE COMPOSE

drag (a person or group from one place to another, whether literally or figuratively) *v.t.*: **frogmarch**. SEE MARCH

drain (of strength) *v.t.*: **enervate**. SEE DEBILITATE

dramatic (overly ... behavior) *n., adj.*: **operatics**. SEE MELODRAMATIC

(2) dramatic (or artistic piece imitating previous picces) *n.*: **pastiche**. SEE IMITATION

draw (as in describe, by painting or writing) *v.t.*: **limn**. SEE DESCRIBE

drawing (dealing with evening or night) *n.*: **nocturne**. SEE PAINTING

(2) drawing (which looks like a photograph or something real) *n.*: **trompe l'oeil** [French]. SEE ILLUSION

dread (source or object of ... or fear) *n.*: **hobgoblin**. SEE FEAR

(2) dread (as in panic) *n.*: **Torschlusspanik** [German]. SEE PANIC

dreaded (something that is ..., disliked or to be avoided) *n.*: **bête noire** [French]. ■ Line drives [hit back at the pitcher] are the **bête noire** of this glittering season. And as the season moves into its final month, come-backers are an unpredictable "X" factor nobody wants to think about. If, say, Padres ace [pitcher] Kevin Brown went down, San Diego's World Series dreams virtually would vanish. (Steve Marantz, *Duck! [Increased Amount of Dangerous Line Drives Hit Back at the Pitchers]*, The Sporting News, 08-31-1998, p. 14.)

dream (bad ..., or episode having the quality of one) *n.*: **Walpurgis Night**. See NIGHTMARE

dreamer *n.*: **fantast**. ∎ In his dreams, Boris Yeltsin believes he is president of Russia. Similarly, Ryutaro Hashimoto likes to imagine he is the actual leader of Japan. The two **fantasts** got together on April 18th in Kawana, a resort south-west of Tokyo, for a weekend of mutual make-believe. (Author not given, *Dreams Among the Cherry Blossom*, The Economist, 04-25-1998.)

(2) dreamer (as in an impractical contemplative person with no clear occupation or income) *n.*: **luftmensch** [lit. "man of air"; German, Yiddish]. ∎ Humor analysts trying to explain [Seinfeld's] popularity have overlooked the Jewish connection ...: George is the "schlemiel," the born loser; Elaine plays the lovable "yenta." Kramer is the proverbial "**luftmensch**." His head in the clouds; he is forever involved in impractical schemes to make money. And Jerry Seinfeld? He's the rabbi, of course. (Robert Menchin, *"Seinfeld" Explained*, Chicago Tribune, 01-02-1998.)

dreamland (living in a ..., with a glorified or romanticized conception of oneself, as a result of boredom in one's life) *n.*: **Bovarism**. See SELF-DELUSION

dreams (of, relating to or suggestive of) *adj.*: **oneiric**. ∎ I bet Stanley Kubrick never had a nightmare while shooting a movie. Oh, I'm sure he had budgetary and logistic nightmares as any filmmaker must, but no **oneiric**, forehead-dampening visitations. (Richard Alleva, *Stanley Kubrick*, Commonweal, 04-23-1999.)

dreamworld (as in place of extreme luxury and ease where physical comforts and pleasures are always at hand) *n.*: **Cockaigne**. See PARADISE

(2) dreamworld (spec. a place of fabulous wealth or opportunity) *n.*: **El Dorado**. See PARADISE

(3) dreamworld (as in paradise) *n.*: **Xanadu**. See PARADISE

drench (as in soak) *v.t.*: **imbrue**. See SOAK

dress (as in outfit or equip) *v.t.*: **accouter**. See OUTFIT

(2) dress (in a showy or excessive manner) *v.t.*: **bedeck**. See ADORN

(3) dress (or adorn in a showy or excessive manner) *v.t.*: **bedizen**. See ADORN

(4) dress (showy article of ...) *n.*: **frippery**. See FINERY

(5) dress (showy article of ...) *n.*: **froufrou**. See CLOTHING

(6) dress (as in clothes) *n.*: **habiliment(s)**. See CLOTHING

dressed (being partially, carelessly or casually ...) *n.*: **dishabille** [French]. See ATTIRED

drift (from the subject) *v.i.*: **divagate**. See DIGRESS

(2) drift (aimlessly) *v.i.*: **maunder**. See ROAM

drifter *n.*: **clochard** [French]. See VAGRANT

drill *v.t.*: **catechize**. See TEACH

drink (final ... before leaving) *n.*: **doch-an-dorris** See NIGHTCAP

drinking (of or related to) *adj.*: **potatory**. ∎ [You] arrive in Upper Woodford for a thirst-quenching pint at The Bridge. Beyond the pub, turn right down a track and back to the river. Follow the track beside the river and up again, cross the road and down through the woods opposite. ... [T]his is a good place for a post-**potatory** snooze. (Author not given, *Time Off: Romancing the Stones*, The Guardian [London], 06-20-1996.)

(2) drinking (or eating in moderation) *adj.*: **abstemious**. See RESTRAINED

(3) drinking (as in given to or marked by consumption of alcohol) *adj.*: **bibulous**. See IMBIBING

drip (as in light splash) *n.*: **plash**. See SPLASH

drive (as in energy coupled with a will to succeed) *n.*: **spizzerinctum**. See ENERGY

drivel (as in nonsense) *n.*: **folderol** (or **falderal**). See NONSENSE

(2) drivel (as in meaningless talk or nonsense) *n.*: **galimatias**. See GIBBERISH

(3) drivel (as in nonsense) *n.*: **piffle**. See NONSENSE

(4) drivel (as in nonsense) *n.*: **trumpery**. See NONSENSE

drone (as in speaker or writer who is dull and boring) *n.*: **dryasdust**. See BORING

droning (a ... hum) *n*.: **bombilation**. See buzzing

drool *v.i., n*.: **slaver**. ∎ OK, I admit it. When the rhino stuck her head in the van and drooled on my lap — I flat-out flinched. I also fumbled the apple I was supposed to feed her. ... The rhinoceros **slavered**, blinked and dropped her lower lip farther open; it looked like a wet, fleshy trapdoor the size of a shoe box. (Catherine Watson, *Going Wild in San Diego/ Braving Rhino Slobber*, Minneapolis Star Tribune, 09-27-1998, p. 1G.)

drop (as in downward slope) *n*.: **declivity** (*adj*.: **declivitous**). See decline

(2) drop (to the bottom of the ocean) *v.i*.: **go to Davy Jones's locker**. See ocean

(3) drop (as in light splash) *n*.: **plash**. See splash

drops (having or resembling) *adj*.: **guttate**. ∎ Yet fully a third of psoriasis patients encounter it in the first two decades of life. Your daughter seems to have the **guttate** form, marked by small raindrop — like lesions amid the familiar white-scaled red patches. (Dr. Paul Donohue, *There Are Several Heartburn Options: Choose From Medical or Surgical*, St. Louis Post-Dispatch, 01-03-1996, p. 2E.)

drowning (mass ...) *n*.: **noyade**. ∎ The ghastly events [of the French Revolution] prove Dostoyevsky's words: "If there is no God, everything is permitted."... Equally hideous were the **noyades**, the drownings in the Loire ... of naked men and women coupled and fettered in pairs. (Erik von Kuehnelt-Leddihn, *Reflections on the Terror [French Revolution]*, National Review, 07-14-1989.)

drowsiness (relating to period of ... just before falling asleep) *adj*.: **hypnagogic**. ∎ Sometimes, between sleeping and waking, I suddenly glimpse the shadowy forms [standing nearby]. ... As the **hypnagogic** state deepens into sleep, they merge into the background of panelled wall and moulded ceiling and are lost to view. (Peter Simple, *Hypnagogic Days*, Daily Telegraph, 08-02-2002.)

drowsy (as in sluggish or lethargic) *adj*.: **torpid**. See lethargic

drudge *v.i*.: **moil**. See toil

drug (as in something which induces forgetfulness or oblivion of pain, suffering or sorrow) *n*.: **nepenthe**. See narcotic

drum (relating to or resembling) *adj*.: **tympanic**. ∎ The hammering of her compressed heart against her breastbone echoed **tympanically** within her, and it seemed to fill the claustrophobic confines of her hiding place to such an extent that the intruder was certain to hear. (Dean Koontz, *Intensity*, Knopf [1995], p. 20.)

drum roll *n*.: **paradiddle**. ∎ I never wanted to be a guitar hero. When I was 8, I wanted to play drums like my best friend John Priestley, but a few klutzy **paradiddles** set me straight about that. (Ty Burr, *Rock & Roll Fantasy*, Entertainment Weekly, 02-03-1995, p. 57.)

drumbeat (or other repeating noise such as machine-gun fire or hoofs of a galloping horse) *n*.: **rataplan**. See noise

drunk (as in given to or marked by consumption of alcohol) *adj*.: **bibulous**. See imbibing

drunkard *n*.: **dipsomaniac** (*adj*: **diposmaniacal**). See alcoholic

dry (out thoroughly) *v.t., v.i*.: **desiccate**. ∎ With summertime temperatures in the shade — if you can find any — exceeding [120 degrees], **desiccating** winds and no water, surviving a day in the Arabian desert is hot work. (Author not given, *How to Be Cool in the Desert*, The Economist, 12-18-1999.)

(2) dry (of or adapted to a very ... habitat) *adj*.: **xeric**. ∎ In 1886, he was asked to design the campus for a university to be built in Palo Alto, California. Here the landscaping challenge was to convince Leland Stanford to forgo his dream of lush lawns and trees — characteristic of New England — in favor of a drought-resistant **xeric** landscape more suited to the western climate. (Norma Jane Langford, *A Place to Unbend*, The World & I, 03-01-1995.)

(3) dry (as in uninteresting) *adj*.: **jejune**. See uninteresting

dry humping (between two women) *n*.: **tribadism**. See intercourse

dry up (and shrivel) *v.i*.: **wizen**. See shrivel

dubious (as in skeptical) *adj*.: **zetetic**. See skeptical

duel (as in hostile meeting) *n*.: **rencontre** [French]. ∎ [A] young Frenchman named Georges d'Anthès started paying increasingly indiscreet attention to Pushkin's beautiful wife. Rumors, probably untrue, began to circulate. Then one day Pushkin received an anonymous note enrolling him in a society of cuckolds [i.e. husbands whose wives are cheating on them]. He immediately issued a challenge to d'Anthès, but their **rencontre** was averted through the machinations of friends. (Michael Dirda, *Russia's Greatest Poet Was Also a Rake, a Gambler and a Hot-tempered Aristocrat*, The Washington Post, 11-16-2003, p. T15.)

dull (or ignorant, stupid, obtuse or uncultured) *adj.*: **Boeotian** [derives from ancient Greek region of Boeotia, noted for the dullness and stupidity of its inhabitants]. ▪ [As a writer,] Violeta is no Garcia Marquez [who won the Nobel Prize for Literature in 1982]. She refers to herself as a writer [but] left alone, she writes lines like, "I am ever vigilant about feelings that alight on my subconscious carrying a concealed pain." No wonder the C.I.A. ghosted her Op-Ed. ... [This is a] repetitive, fuddled, **Boeotian** and dispiriting autobiography. (H. Aram Vesser, *Dreams of the Heart: The Autobiography of President Violeta Barrios De Chamorro of Nicaragua (Book Reviews)*, The Nation, 09-30-1996.)

(2) dull *adj.*: **anodyne**. SEE BLAND

(3) dull (as in daze) *v.t.*: **benumb**. SEE DAZE

(4) dull (as in sluggish) *adj.*: **bovine**. SEE SLUGGISH

(5) dull (writer or speaker) *n.*: **dryasdust**. SEE BORING

(6) dull (as in desensitize) *v.t.*: **hyposensitize**. SEE DESENSITIZE

(7) dull *adj.*: **jejune**. SEE UNINTERESTING

(8) dull (passage or section in a book or work of performing art) *n.*: **longueur**. SEE TEDIOUS

(9) dull *v.t.*: **narcotize**. SEE DEADEN

(10) dull (to make ..., as in deaden) *v.t.*: **obtund**. SEE DEADEN

(11) dull (as in insipid, intellectual nourishment, like baby food) *n.*: **pabulum** (also **pablum**). SEE INSIPID

dull-witted (as in slow to understand or perceive) *adj.*: **purblind**. SEE OBTUSE

dullness (as in lethargy) *n.*: **hebetude**. SEE LETHARGY

dumb (esp. used of a person, as in ... and confused) *adj.*: **addlepated**. SEE CONFUSED

(2) dumb (or dull or ignorant or obtuse or uncultured) *adj.*: **Boeotian**. SEE DULL

(3) dumb (class of people regarded as ... or unenlightened) *n.*: **booboisie**. SEE UNSOPHISTICATED

(4) dumb (person) *n.*: **dummkopf** [German]. SEE STUPID

(5) dumb *adj.*: **gormless** [British]. SEE UNINTELLIGENT

(6) dumb (as in slow to understand or perceive) *adj.*: **purblind**. SEE OBTUSE

dunce *n.*: **jobbernowl** [British]. SEE IDIOT

(2) dunce *n.*: **mooncalf**. SEE FOOL

dung (obsession with) *n.*: **coprology**. SEE EXCREMENT

(2) dung (feeding on) *n.*: **coprophagous**. SEE EXCREMENT

(3) dung (interest in ..., often sexual) *n.*: **coprophilia**. SEE EXCREMENT

(4) dung *n.*: **egesta**. SEE EXCREMENT

(5) dung (esp. that of sea birds) *n.*: **guano**. SEE BIRD DUNG

(6) dung (study of or obsession with) *n.*: **scatology**. SEE EXCREMENT

(7) dung (eating) *adj.*: **scatophagous**. SEE EXCREMENT

(8) dung (of or relating to) *adj.*: **stercoraceous**. SEE EXCREMENT

duo *n.*: **duumvirate**. ▪ [Abstract painter Cy] Twombly ... is the Third Man, a shadowy figure, beside that vivid **duumvirate** of his friends Jasper Johns and Robert Rauschenberg. (Robert Hughes, *Arts & Media: The Grafitti of Loss in Nuanced Abstractions*, Time, 10-17-1994, p. 72.)

(2) duo (two individuals or units regarded as a ...): **dyad**. SEE PAIR

(3) duo (arranged in or forming a ...) *adj.*: **jugate**. SEE PAIR

dupe (as in one easily deceived) *n.*: **gudgeon**. SEE SUCKER

duplicate (ghostly ... of a living person) *n.*: **doppelganger**. SEE TWIN

duplicating (a particular act over and over, often after initial stimulus has ceased) *n.*: **perseveration** (*v.i.*: **perseverate**). SEE REPEATING

duplicitous (characterized by ... and cunning conduct) *adj.*: **Machiavellian**. SEE DECEITFUL

(2) duplicitous (conduct) *n.*: **skullduggery**. SEE DECEITFULNESS

duration (of or over the same ... period) *adj.*: **coetaneous**. SEE CONTEMPORANEOUS

dusk (of or relating to ... or dawn, as in twilight) *adj.*: **crepuscular**. SEE TWILIGHT

(2) dusk *n.*: **gloaming**. SEE TWILIGHT

(3) dusk (of, relating to or occurring in ... or evening) *adj.*: **vespertine**. SEE EVENING

dust storm (esp. in Arabia and Africa) *n.*: **haboob**. SEE SANDSTORM

dwarf *n.*: **homunculus**. SEE MIDGET

(2) dwarf *n.*: **hop-o'-my-thumb**. SEE MIDGET

(3) dwarf (like a ...) *n., adj.*: **Lilliputian**. SEE TINY

dwell on (as in repeating, a particular act over and over, often after initial stimulus has ceased) *n.*: **perseveration** (*v.i.*: **perseverate**). SEE REPEATING

dwelling (on a height) *n.*: **aerie**. ▪ For six years [the couple] had a million-dollar view of Atlanta's skyline. ... Their 22nd floor **aerie** at Buckhead's posh Park Place was far above the din. But slowly the din has come up to meet them and other residents on the south side of the 40-floor condominium complex, whose most famous resident is rock star Elton John. (Tinah Saunders, *Buckhead Condo Now More Noisy, Less Scenic*, The Atlanta Constitution, 10-19-2001, p. F3.)

dyeing (of or relating to) *adj.*: **tinctorial**. ▪ Pantone adheres to rigorous standards in producing the swatches in a miniature dye pilot plant. It analyzes each batch of reactive dye for purity and **tinctorial** value. (Edward J Elliott, *Chemical Treatment & Finishing: How Textiles Is Perfecting Color*, Textile World, 01-01-2000.)

E

eager *adj.*: **athirst**. ▪ From its inception the Whitney was obviously an artist-oriented institution, in contrast with the major art museums of the time, which addressed aesthetic consumers **athirst** for the beauty and spiritual meaning attributed to the fine arts. (Arthur C. Danto, *Books & The Arts: Of Time and the Artist*, The Nation, 06-07-1999, p. 27.)

(2) eager (extremely ...) *adj.*: **perfervid**. SEE IMPASSIONED

eagerness *n.*: **avidity**. SEE CRAVING

eagle (pertaining to or similar to) *adj.*: **aquiline** (esp. as in aquiline nose). ▪ This 53-year-old CEO, who with a bald head and **aquiline** nose looks himself a bit like an eagle, sets back-breaking standards and raises them methodically each year. (Brian Dumaine, *Managing: Those Highflying Pepsico Managers*, Fortune, 04-10-1989, p. 78.)

ear (pleasing to the ...) *adj.*: **dulcet**. SEE MELODIOUS

(2) ear (of a sound which is pleasing to the ...) *adj.*: **euphonious** (*n.*: **euphony**). SEE MELODIOUS

earlier (as in antecedent) *adj.*: **prevenient** (often as in "prevenient grace"). SEE ANTECEDENT

early *adv.*: **betimes**. ▪ It would be hard to say who was more excited — us or the [Finnish sleigh] dogs. ... The younger huskies had been so keen to get going that they'd whined and barked at the imperturbable older dogs who headed the team and placidly prevented them from setting off **betimes**. (Danuta Brooke, *Santa Really Does Wear a Red Coat*, Independent on Sunday, 11-16-1997, p. 2.)

(2) early (as in relating to morning) *adj.*: **matutinal**. SEE MORNING

earnest (but in a smug or false manner) *adj.*: **oleaginous**. SEE UNCTUOUS

earnings (as in payment or wages) *n.*: **emolument**. SEE WAGES

Earth (of, relating to or inhabiting) *adj.*: **tellurian** [also used as a noun for earthling]. ▪ Thus, the once integrated earthly being, whose relationship with both **tellurian** and heavenly realms had been fluid and balanced, was transformed into a strictly celestial force. (Bettina Knapp, *The Archetypal Woman Fulfilled*, Symposium, 03-01-1996, p. 28.)

earthly *adj.*: **sublunary**. [This word literally means "beneath the moon" and is sometimes used in the more literal sense of "of the earth" and sometimes in the sense of "mundane." The example used here conveys both senses of the word.] ▪ Can it really be two decades since Neil Armstrong set foot on the moon? It seems like only last summer. ... The moment was genuinely unique, absolutely unrepeatable. Its symbolism dwarfed the landings of Columbus and Lindbergh: for the first time, man had walked on a heavenly body other than this one. The nation returned to its **sublunary** concerns refreshed, inspired, somehow strengthened. (Author not given, *Getting High, [20th Anniversary of Moon Landing]*, National Review, 08-18-1989.)

earthquake *n.*: **temblor**. ▪ Registering 6.6 on the moment-magnitude scale, a measure of earthquake energy that among scientists has largely replaced the Richter scale, the Northridge **temblor** didn't qualify as a Big One. (J. Madeleine Nash, *The Next Big One*, Time, 01-31-1994, p. 45.)

easy (as in elementary or basic) *adj.*: **abecedarian**. See BASIC

easygoing *adj.*: **dégagé** [French]. ■ Rather than emphasize her feminine fragility, Katharine Hepburn preferred to play up her "one of the boys" personality with turtleneck sweaters, fluid men's trousers and sneakers. ... Whether on-duty at state dinners or off-duty and swimming in Long Island Sound, [women like Katherine Hepburn] had a wonderful **dégagé** attitude toward dressing, as if they just ran out the door. (Jennifer Alfano, *The Best of American Fashion*, Harper's Bazaar, 05-01-2003.)

eat (like a glutton) *v.i.*: **gormandize**. See DEVOUR

(2) eat (greedily) *v.t.*: **guttle**. See DEVOUR

(3) eat (as in ingest) *v.t.*: **incept**. See INGEST

(4) eat (excessive desire to ...) *n.*: **polyphagia**. See APPETITE

eater (hearty ...) *n.*: **trencherman**. See GLUTTON

eating (art or science of good ...) *n.*: **gastronomy**. You'd think that moving into the premises of Gordon — one of Chicago's most beloved and sorely missed dining rooms — would anger the gods of **gastronomy**, but the spirits have been smiling on Naha [restaurant] and chef Carrie Nahabedian. (John Mariani, *The Best New Restaurants [2001]*, Esquire, 12-01-2001, p. 90.)

(2) eating (or drinking in moderation) *adj.*: **abstemious**. See RESTRAINED

(3) eating (science of ..., spec. dining) *n.*: **aristology**. See DINING

(4) eating (of or relating to ... with others) *adj.*: **commensal**. See DINING

eccentric *adj.*: **pixilated**. ■ In a bizarre encounter with a man seeking employment, [Steve] Jobs demands to know if the guy is "a virgin" and then insults him before stomping off in a huff and a half. ... "I need artists!" he screams in regard to his **pixilated** personnel practices, denouncing employees who are "clock-punching losers." (Tom Shales, *TNT's 'Pirates': The Geek Tycoons; Tale of Computer Icons Gates & Jobs a Net Loss*, The Washington Post, 06-20-1999, p. G1.)

(2) eccentric (as in unconventional) *adj.*: **outré** [French]. See UNCONVENTIONAL

echo (mindlessly ideas which have been drilled into the speaker or repeat things which reflect the opinions of the powers-that-be) *v.t., v.i., n.*: **duckspeak**. See RECITE

echoing (pathological or uncontrollable or a child's ... of another's words) *n.*: **echolalia**. See REPEATING

eclipse (of a star or planet by the moon) *n.*: **occultation**. ■ On Dec. 7, the crescent moon passes in front of the planet Jupiter between 3:50 and 5 a.m. in a rare **occultation** of the planet by the moon. (Tom Burns, *Another Total Lunar Eclipse Awaits Astronomer's Telescope*, Columbus Dispatch [Ohio], 01-20-2004.)

economical (speech or writing being very ...) *adj.*: **elliptical**. See TERSE

ecstatic (often in a boastful way) *adj.*: **cock-a-hoop**. See ELATED

edge *n.*: **selvage**. ■ One Midtown Kitchen. Located on a ragged **selvage** of Piedmont Park, this restaurant is all about buzz, ... commerce and its own sure vision of comfort chic. (John Kessler, 2003 *Guide Book: Dining: Dig In: You'll Find All Kinds of Tastes*, The Atlanta Journal-Constitution, 07-24-2003.)

edible *adj.*: **esculent**. ■ America's Founding Fathers, Washington, Jefferson, Madison and Monroe, had long urged Congress to "collect, cultivate and distribute the various vegetable productions of this and other countries, whether medicinal, **esculent**, or for the promotion of arts and manufactures." (Suzanne Richardson, *Lush Growth at the New Botanic Garden*, The Washington Post, 12-21-2001, p. T64.)

edict *n.*: **diktat**. See DECREE

(2) edict *n.*: **ukase**. See DECREE

edification *n.*: **éclaircissement** [French]. See CLARIFICATION

edit (text or language by removing errors or flaws) *v.t.*: **blue-pencil**. ■ [S]he went looking for a magazine job — but ended up as an editor at Random House, where she has **blue-penciled** the prose of Julia Phillips, David Mamet, and Sandra Cisneros for the Turtle Bay Books division. (Author not given, *Features That Deal With More Than One Media*, Entertainment Weekly, 02-26-1993, p. 26.)

(2) edit (a book or a writing in a prudish manner) *v.t.*: **bowdlerize** [after Thomas Bowdler (1754-1825), who published a sanitized edition of Shakespeare in 1818]. ■ Today the robust words [of the Marseillaise], which ... enjoin the children of revolutionary France to "drench our fields" with the "tainted blood" of the enemy, are under siege by those who feel the piece smacks of political incorrectness. The idea of **bowdlerizing** the ferocious lyrics ... first surfaced three years ago. (Kevin Fedarko, *France Meddling With the Marseillaise; A Proposal to Bowdlerize France's Barn-burning Anthem Provokes an Indignant Mon Dieu! From Traditionalists*, Time, 03-16-1992, p. 42.)

(3) edit (text or language by removing errors or flaws) *v.t.*: **emend**. ∎ As it turned out, the opinion written by Justice Anthony Kennedy showed considerable understanding of how speech is translated into print. Kennedy condoned the widespread journalistic practice of **emending** quotations in the areas of grammar and syntax. (Paul Gray, *Press: Justice Comes in Quotes: Journalists Can Tinker With the Words of Interview Subjects — But Reckless Falsity Can Be Libelous*, Time, 07-01-1991, p. 68.)

educate *v.t.*: **catechize**. See TEACH

educated (people as a group) *n.*: **clerisy**. ∎ Adorno was ... heir to a German romantic tradition, according to which intellectuals form a secular **clerisy** guarding the moral and intellectual health of the nation. (Ian Buruma, *Real Wounds, Unreal Wounds*, The New Republic, 02-12-2001.)

(2) educated (person, as in lover of learning) *n.*: **philomath**. See SCHOLAR

(3) educated (person who is very ..., as in knowledgeable, in many areas) *n.*: **polyhistor**. See KNOWLEDGEABLE

(4) educated (person who is very ..., as in knowledgeable, in many areas) *n.*: **polymath**. See SCHOLAR

education (excess striving for or preoccupation with ..., as in knowledge) *n.*: **epistemophilia**. See KNOWLEDGE

(2) education (universal ..., as in knowledge) *n.*: **pansophy** (*adj.*: **pansophic**). See KNOWLEDGE

educator *n.*: **pedagogue**. See TEACHER

eerie *adj.*: **eldritch**. ∎ Many things go into the making of a movie classic, but Alfred Hitchcock's timeless thriller is inseparable in our memory from Bernard Hermann's **eldritch**, bump-in-the-night score [in the movie Psycho]. (Michael Walsh, *The Arts & Media/Music*, Time, 09-11-1995, p. 77.)

effect (as in outgrowth) *n.*: **excrescence**. See OUTGROWTH

effeminate *adj.*: **epicene**. ∎ The world will be poorer without Quentin Crisp. He stood apart from the rest of us, not so much because of his lilac hair and **epicene** manners as because of his genuine individualism. Homosexuality, like other alternative life-

styles, can impose a conformity of its own; but Mr. Crisp was having none of it. (Author not given, *Leading Article: Crisp and Courteous*, The Daily Telegraph, 11-22-1999.)

(2) effeminate (person) *n.*: **pantywaist**. See SISSY

effort (mental process marked by ... to do something) *n.*: **conation**. See DETERMINATION

(2) effort (the ... to achieve a particular goal or desire) *n.*: **nisus**. See GOAL

(3) effort (which is laborious but futile) *adj.*: **Sisyphean**. See FUTILE

effortlessness (appearance of ...) *n.*: **sprezzatura** [Italian. Taken from a 1528 book by Baldassare Castiglione, who stated: "Practice in all things a certain sprezzatura ... so as to conceal art, and make whatever is done or said appear to be without effort and almost without any thought about it."] ∎ Anthony Blunt, when principal of the Courtauld — where [National Museum Director Neil] MacGregor trained after giving up on the law — called him "the most brilliant student I ever had." His tutor, Anita Brookner, said: "He was brilliant then and he's brilliant now." He epitomises the Renaissance ideal of **sprezzatura** — the studied nonchalance that makes achievement seem effortless. (Alice Thomson, *Britain's Paintings*, The Daily Telegraph [London], 02-01-2002.)

effrontery *n.*: **hardihood**. See GALL

effusive (as in characterized by a ready and easy flow of words) *adj.*: **voluble**. See TALKATIVE

egg (shaped) *adj.*: **ovoid**. [I]n the corner [was a] wooden egg shaped like Boris Yeltsin that holds successively tinier **ovoid** representations of the leaders of the Soviet Union, from Lenin to Gorbachev. (Stanley Bing, *While You Were Out...*, Fortune, 07-19-1999, p. 49.)

ego (as in self-esteem) *n.*: **amour-propre** [French]. See SELF-ESTEEM

egotist (esp. a little man) *n.*: **cockalorum**. ∎ Murray Lachlan Young, the expensive young man who writes the sort of poetry that one finds on the walls of public lavatories, is, I can reveal, getting married today to his girlfriend of two years. ... It is rather charming to discover that Lachlan Young, a true **cockalorum**, has been reduced to a quivering wreck about the whole event. (Simon Davies, *Peterborough: What Rhymes With Quivering Wreck, My Love?* The Daily Telegraph, 05-01-1998.)

egotistical (and vain person) *n.*: **coxcomb**. See CONCEITED

(2) egotistical (person) *n.*: **Gascon** (act of being ... *n.*: **Gasconade**). See BRAGGART

(3) egotistical (and vain) *adj.*: **vainglorious**. See BOASTFUL

elaborate (on a subject at length in speech or writing) *v.i.*: **expatiate**. See EXPOUND

(2) elaborate *adj.*: **rococo**. See ORNATE

elated (often in a boastful way) *adj.*: **cock-a-hoop**. ∎ Forced onto the [auction] market by death duties, [the collection of paintings] was exactly the sort of property that would once have gone to Christies' as a matter of course, and Sotheby's was **cock-a-hoop** that their competitive commission cuts had secured such prestigious business so soon after their move. (Robert Lacey, *Sotheby's — Bidding For Class*, Little Brown [1998], p. 68.)

elderliness *n.*: **senectitude**. ∎ British fiction has been besieged by a heaving regiment of late-adolescent thirty somethings, visibly clinging to their youth. ... With his second novel James Hawes is the first to break away from this ... and admit his age. ... Hawes' comfortable submersion into **senectitude** is daring in its honesty. But this initial bravery is about the only thing he deserves credit for. (Ra Page, *Rancid Aluminiu [book reviews]*, New Statesman [1996], 08-08-1997, p. 52.)

elderly (of or relating to ... people, esp. women) *adj.*: **blue-rinse**. ∎ As for elderly drivers, sorry, but [my thesis is] that slow drivers cause accidents. From my observation, and here I will anger the **blue-rinse** crowd, if I have a problem with a driver, it's often a small, elderly woman who appears to be observing the road through her steering wheel. (John Downing, *Life in the Slow Lane; Speed Limits Don't Make Us Safer, Just More Regulated*, The Toronto Sun, 08-13-2003, p. 15.)

(2) elderly (branch of science dealing with) *adj.*: **gerontology**. ∎ To Dr. Barbara Stancil, age was nothing but a number, one that should not be ignored, but celebrated. As founder and longtime director of the **Gerontology** Center at Georgia State University, a nationally recognized research center, Dr. Stancil devoted her professional life to studying older Americans and advocating on their behalf. (Stephania H. Davis, *Obituaries: Dr. Barbara Stancil, 81, an Advocate for Elderly*, The Atlanta Constitution, 07-23-2001, p. C4.)

(3) elderly (of or like an ... woman) *adj.*: **anile**. See OLD WOMAN

(4) elderly (of or relating to the ...) *adj.*: **gerontic**. See OLD AGE

(5) elderly (government by the ...) *adj.*: **gerontocracy**. See GOVERNMENT

(6) elderly (sexual attraction towards the ...) *n.*: **gerontophilia**. See LUST

(7) elderly (growing ...) *adj.*: **senescent**. See AGING

(8) elderly (and sick person) *n.*: **Struldbrug**. See DECREPIT

eldest (child) *n.*: **primogeniture**. See FIRSTBORN

election (direct ... where electorate exercises right of self-determination) *n.*: **plebiscite**. ∎ It is precisely because direct democracy is such a manipulatable sham that every two-bit Mussolini adopts it as his own. Pomp and **plebiscites**. The Duce and the people. No need for the messy stuff in between. Not for nothing did the Founders abhor direct democracy. They knew it to be a highway to tyranny. (Charles Krauthammer, *Essay: Ross Perot and the Call-In Presidency*, Time, 07-13-1992, p. 84.)

elections (study of) *n.*: **psephology**. ∎ Pippa Norris ... surveys what has been found out about voters and their motivations in Britain since 1945, and in particular since David Butler and Donald Stokes, doyens of **psephology** in Britain and in America respectively, published their first numerical analyses of political change in the 1960s. (Author not given, *British Political Books: Division Time*, The Economist, 03-22-1997.)

elegant *adj.*: **nobby** [British]. ∎ According to a recent survey by the slightly oxymoronic British Hospitality Association, increasing numbers of three- and four-star hotels are insisting on dress codes. A few **nobby** five-star joints tried to give the impression that they were above such vulgar requirements, but my experience suggests that they're just as bad. (Author not given, *The Weasel*, Independent, 10-05-1996, p. 9.)

(2) elegant *adj.*: **soigné** [French]. ∎ A description was provided, suggesting that ... the Baron had survived his prison experience without obvious damage to his **soigné** airs: "Always well-dressed. Has a distinguished appearance because of his polished manners. Speaks very courteously. Always stays at the best hotels." (Ben Macintyre, *The Napoleon of Crime*, Farrar, Straus and Giroux [1997], p. 204.)

(3) elegant (and stately, as befitting a baron) *adj.*: **baronial**. See STATELY

(4) elegant *adj.*: **raffiné** (or **raffine**) [French]. See REFINED

elegy *n*.: **threnody**. SEE REQUIEM

elemental (as in essential) *adj*.: **constitutive**. SEE ESSENTIAL

elementary *adj*.: **abecedarian**. SEE BASIC

elephant (of, relating to or resembling; sometimes as in big like an ...) *adj*.: **pachydermatous**. ∎ The agenda [for a demolition derby] was — and is — breathtakingly basic: a mess of very big, very old cars slam into one another until just one, the winner, is still running. "Boys must wreck cars," summarized Tommy Walkowiak, 24, a boiler repairman who brought a **pachydermatous** Ford, a 1976 Country Squire station wagon, to Riverhead Raceway here this Saturday night. (Douglas Martin, *It Destroys, It Brings Chaos And It Just Won't Die*, The New York Times, 09-13-1996, p. B1.)

elevated (as in lofty) *adj*.: **empyreal**. SEE LOFTY

eliminate *v.t.*: **extirpate**. SEE ABOLISH

(2) **eliminate** (something that serves to ...) *n*.: **quietus** (esp. as in "put the quietus to"). SEE TERMINATE

elite (person, esp. in intellectual or literary circles) *n*.: **mandarin**. SEE INFLUENTIAL

elixir *n*.: **catholicon**. SEE REMEDY

(2) **elixir** (supposed ... which is untested or unproved) *n*.: **nostrum**. SEE REMEDY

elsewhere (as in originating from ...; not endemic) *adj*.: **ecdemic**. SEE FOREIGN

elusive (lit. soapy) *adj*.: **saponaceous**. SEE SLIPPERY

emaciated (esp. in a pale or corpselike way) *adj*.: **cadaverous**. SEE CORPSELIKE

emaciation (due to chronic disease) *n*.: **cachexia**. SEE WASTING

emanation *n*.: **effluence**. ∎ Look at her. She has the same lizard-lidded eyes, the same cute little dropseat mouth that marred and made her daddy's famous face. Like her old man, Lisa Marie Presley exudes a none-too-subtle **effluence** of brat and sings, it's said, with instinctive ease and wooing charm. (Author not given, *The 25 Most Intriguing People: Lisa Marie Presley*, People, 12-26-1988, p. 59.)

(2) **emanation** (impalpable ... as in aura) *n*.: **effluvium**. SEE AURA

(3) **emanation** (which is thick and vaporous or noxious) *n*.: **miasma**. SEE NOXIOUS

emancipate (from slavery, servitude or bondage) *v.t.*: **manumit**. ∎ As President, Lincoln tried for years to exclude slavery from his war aims, and actually reimposed slavery after two of his generals **manumitted** slaves in Southern areas they held. (Garry Wills, *Dishonest Abe — America's Most Revered Politician Dissembled, Waffled, Told Racist Stories and Consorted With Corrupt Politicians*, Time, 10-05-1992, p. 41.)

emasculate *v.t.*: **geld**. SEE CASTRATE

embarrass (to ..., as in disconcert) *v.t.*: **discomfit**. SEE DISCONCERT

(2) **embarrass** (by making false statements) *v.t.*: **traduce**. SEE MALIGN

embarrassing (as in inappropriate or tasteless comments) *n*.: **dontopedalogy**. SEE FOOT-IN-MOUTH

embarrassment (as in dishonor to one's reputation) *n*.: **blot (or stain) on one's escutcheon** *idiom*. SEE DISHONOR

(2) **embarrassment** (resulting from an inopportune occurrence) *n*.: **contretemps**. SEE MISHAP

embellish (as in exaggerate) *v.t.*: **aggrandize**. SEE EXAGGERATE

embellishment (abnormal propensity towards ...) *n*.: **mythomania**. ∎ [Victor Hugo's conception] took place in a forest 3,000 ft. up on the flank of Mount Donon, overlooking the Rhineland, in May 1801, though it's typical of Hugo's own **mythomania** that in adult life he claimed it happened 3,000 ft. higher still, and on Mont Blanc. (Robert Hughes, *The Arts/Art: Sublime Windbag Writer, Lover, National Hero, Victor Hugo Was Also a Brilliant Draftsman of the Unconscious*, Time, 04-27-1998, p. 71.)

embezzle *v.i.*: **defalcate**. ∎ According to local reports, some government institutions and non-governmental organizations (NGO) **defalcate** special funds donated by foreign countries, draining precious resources from the fight on AIDS. (Cheng Zhiliang, *Roundup: HIV/AIDS Keeps on Spreading in Africa*, Xinhua News Agency, 09-20-2003.)

(2) **embezzle** *v.t.*, *v.i.*: **peculate**. ∎ [The Mazda] Miata gets passersby smiling and talking. ... Other conspicuous cars are costly and imposing and draw hate waves, as they are intended to. Decent householders glare, knowing you couldn't own the thing unless you were a drug dealer or a **peculating** [bureaucrat]. (John Skow, *Living: Miatific Bliss in Five Gears, This is Definitely Not Your Father's Hupmobile*, Time, 10-02-1989, p. 91.)

embitter *v.t.*: **envenom**. ▪ The idea is to convince both sides [in the Arab-Israeli peace talks] that neither is a demon and that however **envenomed** the territorial disputes become, they can still reach accommodation on other issues. (George J. Church, *World: Middle East–Must We Talk? Now?* Time, 10-21-1991, p. 67.)

embodiment *n.*: **avatar**. ▪ Today, [Susan Sarandon] is a certified member of Hollywood's coveted A-list, and the **avatar** of a maturing era of cinematic sex women who are intelligent, self-assured, sensual, and gasp, in their 40s. (Hilary de Vries, *Late Bloomer Susan Sarandon's Career Didn't Really Catch Fire Until "Bull Durham,"* Newsday, 02-23-1993.)

embody (as in making an abstract concept seem real) *v.t.*: **reify**. SEE MATERIALIZE

embrace (as in caress or fondle) *v.i.*: **canoodle** (often "canoodle with"). SEE CARESS

embracing *adj.*: **osculant**. SEE HUGGING

embryo (of or relating to malformations in) *adj.*: **teratogenic**. SEE FETUS

emerge *v.i.*: **debouch**. ▪ [In 1914,] Princeton played many of its [hockey] games in big-city arenas, notably the St. Nicholas in Manhattan, where the socially prominent **debouched** in evening finery from limousines and carriages as if attending a cotillion. (Ron Fimrite, *Bonus Piece*, Sports Illustrated, 03-18-1991, p. 78.)

emergency (as in critical, stage or period) *n., adj.*: **climacteric**. SEE CRITICAL

emerging (as in coming into being) *adj.*: **nascent**. ▪ Out of a thousand **nascent** business plans, maybe 100 will have enough merit to justify a few hundred thousand dollars of angel investment. (Gary Hamel, *Innovation's New Math*, Fortune, 07-09-2001, p. 130.)

emitting (out or forth) *n.*: **effluence**. SEE EMANATION

emoting (behavior) *n., adj.*: **operatics**. SEE MELODRAMATIC

emotional (overly ... and sentimental) *adj.*: **mawkish**. SEE SENTIMENTAL

employee (as in aide or assistant) *n.*: **factotum**. SEE ASSISTANT

employer (as in boss or owner) *n.*: **padrone**. SEE BOSS

employment (requiring little work but paying an income) *n.*: **sinecure**. SEE OCCUPATION

empty (or discharge waste from the body) *v.t.*: **egest**. SEE EXCRETE

encapsulate (the flavor or essence of something, as if by boiling down) *v.t.*: **decoct**. SEE BOIL DOWN

enchant *v.t.*: **ensorcell** (or **ensorcel**). ▪ Trying to soften his military image and lure more female voters in New Hampshire, Gen. Wesley Clark switched from navy suits to argyle sweaters. It's an odd strategy. It's also a little alarming that he thinks the way to **ensorcell** women is to swaddle himself in woolly geometric shapes that conjure up images of Bing Crosby on the links or Fred MacMurray at the kitchen table. (Maureen Dowd, *The General Is Sweating His Image* [Editorial], The New York Times, 01-13-2004.)

enchantress *n.*: **Circe** [based on a goddess in Greek mythology who turns men into swine]. ▪ Having honed her characterization of Morticia [Addams] to larger-than-large eyes, a curl of a mouth, and a whisper of a voice, [Angelica] Huston floats through the scenes, underplaying remarkably. ... Whether delighting in her labor pains, consoling her husband, or commiserating with Debbie's unhappy childhood, Morticia is "the serene center of the film ... almost mythical," a **Circe** without the attitude problem, according to the Baltimore Sun. (Author not given, *Addams Family Values*, Magill's Survey of Cinema, 06-15-1995.)

encircle (often protectively) *v.t.*: **embosom**. SEE SURROUND

(2) **encircle** *v.t.*: **girdle**. SEE SURROUND

encircling (as in surrounding) *adj.*: **ambient**. SEE SURROUNDING

(2) **encircling** (as in surrounding) *adj.*: **circumambient**. SEE SURROUNDING

enclose (as in surround, often protectively) *v.t.*: **embosom**. SEE SURROUND

(2) **enclose** (as in confine) *v.t.*: **immure**. SEE CONFINE

enclosed (completely ..., as in sealed) *adj.*: **hermetic**. SEE SEALED

encompass (as in surround, often protectively) *v.t.*: **embosom**. SEE SURROUND

(2) **encompass** (as in surround) *v.t.*: **girdle**. SEE SURROUND

encompassing (as in surrounding) *adj.*: **ambient**. See surrounding

(2) encompassing (as in surrounding) *adj.*: **circumambient**. See surrounding

encounter (as in hostile meeting) *n.*: **rencontre** [French]. See duel

encountering (fortunate things by accident) *n.*: **serendipity** (*adj.*: **serendipitous**). See fortuitous

encouragement (as in stimulus) *n.*: **fillip**. See stimulus

encouraging (as in urging someone to take a course of action) *adj.*: **hortatory**. See urging

encyclopedic (person with ... knowledge) *n.*: **polyhistor**. See knowledgeable

(2) encyclopedic (person with ... knowledge) *n.*: **polymath**. See scholar

end (point or destination) *n.*: **terminus**. ∎ Michalak's attitude was understandable, given that his baseball life had been an eight-season, five-organization odyssey, but now his traveling days may be over ... after his 2000 season at Albuquerque (the **terminus** of that cross-country haul), where he went 11-3 with a 4.26 ERA. (Daniel G. Habib, *The Truck Stops Here*, Sports Illustrated, 06-04-2001, p. 94.)

(2) end (as in objective) *n.*: **quaesitum**. See objective

(3) end (something that serves to put an ... to) *n.*: **quietus** (esp. as in "put the quietus to"). See terminate

end of the world (branch of theology concerned with) *n.*: **eschatology**. See Judgment Day

endangered (journey or passage, with dangers on both sides) *idiom*: **between Scylla and Charybdis**. See precarious

endeavor (which is fruitless or hopeless) *n.*: **fool's errand**. See hopeless

(2) endeavor (the ... to achieve a particular goal or desire) *n.*: **nisus**. See goal

end of the world (branch of theology concerned with) *n.*: **eschatology**. See Judgment Day

endemic (as in indigenous) *adj.*: **authochthonous**. See indigenous

ending (violent or turbulent ... to a society or regime) *n.*: **götterdämmerung** [German]. See collapse

endless *adj., adv.* (endlessly): **ad infinitum**. See forever

(2) endless *adj.*: **aeonian** (or **eonian**). See eternal

(3) endless (as in everlasting) *adj.*: **sempiternal**. See everlasting

endlessly *adv.*: **in aeternum** [Latin]. See forever

enduring (forever) *adj.*: **sempiternal**. See everlasting

enema *n.*: **clyster**. ∎ I had imagined liposuction as a slow, precise, dignified art; it isn't. A huge needle, the diameter of a turkey baster or **clyster** pipe, is shoved around blind inside the patient's body like roughly vacuum-cleaning the inside of a cushion cover while in a pre-menstrual bad mood; meanwhile, at the end of a tube, blood and yellow fat splash into a jar. (Lynne Truss, *Vanity Galore, Almost Enough for a Bonfire*, The Times [London], 10-21-1994.)

energetic (not ...) *adj.*: **bovine**. See sluggish

(2) energetic (not ...) *adj.*: **logy**. See sluggish

energize (as in enliven) *v.t.*: **vivify**. See enliven

energy (full of ...) *n.*: **brio**. ∎ What [Woody Allen and his band] communicate is a rowdy, loose, primitive sensibility that has less to do with re-creating Dixieland jazz and more to do with projecting a modern Manhattan form of New Orleans jazz (the rhythm is more Times Square than Congo Square), played with emotional **brio**. (Norman Weinstein, *Woody Allen Takes Manhattan*, The Christian Science Monitor, 02-20-1998.)

(2) energy (coupled with a will to succeed) *n.*: **spizzerinctum**. ∎ [In the 1950's,] super-salesman mayor, M.E. Sensenbrenner, laid the foundation for Columbus to become one of the nation's largest cities in area. [After losing the mayoral election in 1959,] Sensenbrenner came back to win in 1963 and again in 1967, enlivening the city with his trademark **spizzerinctum** — an optimistic, slogan-filled brand of politicking and governing. (Michael Curtin, *In Politics, a Century of Reform Corruption Abates*, Columbus Dispatch [Ohio], 10-31-1999.)

(3) energy (lacking ...) *adj.*: **bovine**. See sluggish

(4) energy *n.*: **élan** [French]. See spirit

(5) energy (lack of ... from having no energy or nourishment) *n.*: **inanition**. See exhaustion

(6) energy (lacking ...) *adj.*: **logy**. See sluggish

enfeeble (as in deprive of strength) *v.t.*: **enervate**. See debilitate

(2) enfeeble (as in deprive of strength) *v.t.*: **geld**. SEE WEAKEN

enfeebled *adj.*: **etiolated**. SEE WEAKENED

engaged (to be ...) *v.t.*: **affianced**. SEE MARRIAGE

engagement (as in appointment, esp. for illicit sexual relations) *n.*: **assignation**. SEE APPOINTMENT

engaging *adj.*: **piquant**. SEE APPEALING

English (exaggerated fondness for ... manners, customs, styles, etc.) *n.*: **Anglomania**. SEE BRITISH

(2) English (admiration of ... manners, customs, styles, etc.) *n.*: **Anglophilia**. SEE BRITISH

(3) English (fear, distrust or disliking of ... manners, customs, styles, etc.) *n.*: **Anglophobia**. SEE BRITISH

enigmatic (as in cryptic or ambiguous) *adj.*: **Delphic**. SEE AMBIGUOUS

(2) enigmatic (as in cryptic or obscure speech or writing, esp.deliberately) *adj.*: **elliptical**. SEE CRYPTIC

enjoy (the taste of) *v.t.*: **degust**. SEE SAVOR

enjoyment (as in pleasure) *n.*: **delectation**. SEE PLEASURE

(2) enjoyment (from witnessing other's misfortunes) *n.*: **Roman holiday**. SEE SADISM

(3) enjoyment (from other's misfortunes) *n.*: **schadenfreude** [German]. SEE SADISM

(4) enjoyment (as in well-being) *n.*: **weal** (usu. as in *weal or woe* or *weal and woe*). SEE WELL-BEING

enlarge (in scope) *v.t.*: **aggrandize**. SEE EXPAND

enlarged (as in swollen, used often of body parts such as the penis) *adj.*: **tumescent**. SEE SWOLLEN

(2) enlarged (as in swollen or distended) *adj.*: **tumid**. SEE SWOLLEN

enlargement (abnormal ... of the bones, hands or feet) *n.*: **acromegaly**. ∎ I knew hGH was expensive, but I'd read in a muscle magazine that it was safer than steroids, and I wanted to believe that. I also knew that hGH could cause **acromegaly** — the enlargement of the brow, hands and feet that's sometimes called "Frankenstein's syndrome." (Tommy Chaikin, *Bonus Piece: The Nightmare of Steroids*, Sports Illustrated, 10-24-1988, p. 82.)

enlightened (self-proclaimed ... people) *pl., n.*: **illuminati**. ∎ [The premise of contemporary liberals] is that most Americans, particularly African-Americans, are pathologically incapable of controlling atavistic urges to gratify their every sexual desire. Among these self-proclaimed **illuminati**, it is considered unfashionable to suggest that this basic instinct would best be channeled toward the goal of creating long-term, loving relationships between men and women in a traditional family mode. (Gerald Ortbals, *Who Lost America?* St. Louis Post-Dispatch, 06-16-1992, p. 3B.)

enlightenment (as in clarification or clearing up) *n.*: **éclaircissement** [French]. SEE CLARIFICATION

(2) enlightenment (person who hates ... or reasoning) *n.*: **misologist**. SEE CLOSED-MINDED

enliven *v.t.*: **vivify**. ∎ [In "Tidal Wave — How Women Changed America At Century's End" by Sara M. Evans,] her depictions of a broad spectrum of activity in the 1970s and '80s — countercultural music festivals, Emily's List, campaigns against forced sterilization, feminist-inspired labor organizing — **vivify**, as no generalizations could, the extraordinary creative reach of the movement. (Christine Stansell, *After the Revolution*, The Washington Post, 03-23-2003.)

ennui (sometimes in matters spiritual, and sometimes leading to depression) *n.*: **acedia**. SEE APATHY

enormous *adj.*: **Bunyanesque**. ∎ Clamping a bear hug on the appliance, the 6-ft. 3-in, 286-lb. Russian hoisted it off the floor. "It was a huge fridge," he recalls, "and I carried it to my apartment up eight flights of stairs." ... This **Bunyanesque** figure is a husband and the father of three children, including a daughter who was born this year. (John Greenwald, *The Summer Olympics/The Ones To Beat: Alexander Kareli*, Time, 09-11-2000, p. 80.)

(2) enormous (like an elephant) *adj.*: **elephantine**. ∎ My crusade started when I turned 13. A chubbette-size five-foot-two-inch preadolescent tipping the scales at more than 160, I was determined not to spend my teen years feeling **elephantine**. (Paula M. Siegel, *How I Lost 45 Pounds ... And Never Gained Them Back*, Redbook, 08-01-1996, p. 53.)

(3) enormous *adj.*: **brobdingnagian** (often cap.). SEE HUGE

(4) enormous (object) *n.*: **leviathan**. SEE HUGE

(5) enormous (like an elephant) *adj.*: **pachydermatous**. SEE ELEPHANT

(6) enormous *adj.*: **Pantagruelian**. SEE GIGANTIC

(7) enormous *adj.*: **pythonic**. SEE HUGE

enraged *adj.*: **apoplectic**. SEE ANGRY

(2) enraged *adj.*: **wroth**. SEE ANGRY

enslavement *n.*: **thralldom**. SEE BONDAGE

ensue (as in happen or occur) *v.t.*: **betide**. SEE HAPPEN

enter (suddenly or forcibly, as in burst in) *v.i.*: **irrupt**. SEE BURST IN

entertain (oneself in a light, frolicsome manner) *v.t., v.i.*: **disport**. SEE FROLIC

entertainer (street ...) *n.*: **busker**. SEE PERFORMER

entertainment (as in pleasure) *n.*: **delectation**. SEE PLEASURE

enthusiasm (as in full of energy) *n.*: **brio**. SEE ENERGY

(2) **enthusiasm** *n.*: **élan** [French]. SEE SPIRIT

(3) **enthusiasm** (undue ... for one subject or idea) *n.*: **monomania**. SEE OBSESSION

enthusiast (strong ... for a cause, religion or activity) *n.*: **votary**. SEE SUPPORTER

enthusiast (as in fanatic) *n.*: **energumen**. SEE FANATIC

enthusiastic (speech or writing) *n.*: **dithyramb**. ▪ Your correspondent has not pinpointed the recent epiphanic moment when he suddenly got it all together in his head about yuppies and realized that he was feeling quite affirmative about them. And has had it up to Ronald Reagan's keister with yuppie-bashing. Warning: You are about to read a **dithyramb**, or at least a few kind words, about the controversial species in question. (Daniel Seligman, *Keeping Up; Hurray for Yuppies*, Fortune, 08-13-1990, p. 119.)

entice (as in bewitch or enchant) *v.t.*: **ensorcell** (or **ensorcel**). SEE ENCHANT

(2) **entice** *v.t.*: **inveigle**. SEE LURE

enticement (by flattery) *n.*: **blandishment** (*v.t.*: **blandish**). SEE FLATTERY

(2) **enticement** (as in incentive) *n.*: **fillip**. SEE INCENTIVE

(3) **enticement** (as in lure or temptation) *n.*: **Lorelei call**. SEE LURE

enticing (as in tempting) *adj.*: **siren**. SEE TEMPTING

entire (as in complete or unlimited, esp as in ... power) *adj.*: **plenary**. SEE COMPLETE

entirety (in the ...) *adv.*: **in extenso** [Latin]. ▪ Oddly, [Soviet spy Kim] Philby's comments on world politics and on his colorful past seem wan and trite. It is almost as if this supermole wanted to demystify his own legend, making double agentry seem as banal as bartending. The impression of ordinariness is reinforced by his chatty letters to Knightley, which are cited **in extenso**. (John Elson, *Books: Supermole*, Time, 04-24-1989, p. 86.)

entrance (as in bewitch or enchant) *v.t.*: **ensorcell** (or **ensorcel**). SEE ENCHANT

(2) **entrance** (spec. the corridor in a stadium which connects the outer concourse to the interior of the stadium itself) *n.*: **vomitory**. SEE CORRIDOR

entrancing *adj.*: **piquant**. SEE APPEALING

entreat (earnestly) *v.t.*: **adjure**. SEE PLEAD

entreating (someone to take a course of action) *adj.*: **hortatory**. SEE URGING

entrust (authority or duties to another) *v.t.*: **depute**. SEE DELEGATE

envelop (as in surround, often protectively) *v.t.*: **embosom**. SEE SURROUND

enveloping (as in surrounding) *adj.*: **ambient**. SEE SURROUNDING

(2) **enveloping** (as in surrounding) *adj.*: **circumambient**. SEE SURROUNDING

environment (destruction of ... by mankind) *n.*: **ecocide**. ▪ [I]n their new book, "**Ecocide** in the U.S.S.R." (Basic Books, $24) [the authors contend that] no other great industrial civilization so systematically and so long poisoned its air, land, water and people. (Douglas Stanglin, *Toxic Wasteland*, U.S. News & World Report, 04-13-1992.)

(2) **environment** (physical ... or setting) *n.*: **mise en scène** [French; putting on stage]. SEE SETTING

environs *n., pl.*: **purlieus**. SEE OUTSKIRTS

envision (as in to conceive of or form an image of) *v.t.*: **ideate**. SEE VISUALIZE

ephemeral *adj.*: **fugacious**. SEE FLEETING

epidemic *adj.*: **pandemic**. SEE WIDESPREAD

equal (in strength, power or effectiveness) *adj.*: **equipollent**. ▪ We should live in a world of **equipollent** continents. African civilisation would have contended on equal terms with those of Eurasia and the Americas. White abuse of black slavery would have been impossible, modem racism unthinkable. (Felipe Fernandez-Armesto, *What if the Armada Had Landed ...?* New Statesman, 12-20-1999.)

(2) equal (person or thing without ...) *n.*: **nonesuch**. SEE PARAGON

equanimity (esp. under pressure or trying circumstances) *n.*: **sang-froid** [French]. SEE COMPOSURE

equestrian *n.*: **caballero**. ▮ He was raised riding horses, learning at the knee of his **caballero** grandfather. (William Nack, *Only Way That Horses Will Win is if You Sit There and Spend Time ...*, Sports Illustrated, 06-10-1991, p. 66.)

equilibrium *n.*: **equipoise**. ▮ "Peace," insists this book again and again, "does not keep itself," but must be maintained both by substantial forces in being and a credited willingness to use them. Take the Peloponnesian War, which broke out in a bipolar world like that of the Cold War. Sea-power Athens and its empire were in uneasy **equipoise** with land-power Sparta and its allies. (Donald Lyons, *On the Origins of War and the Preservation of Peace (book reviews)*, National Review, 03-06-1995, p. 65.)

equip (as in outfit or clothe) *v.t.*: **accouter**. SEE OUTFIT

equitable (uncompromisingly ..., as in just) *n.*: **Rhadamanthine**. SEE JUST

equivalent (in strength, power or effectiveness) *adj.*: **equipollent**. SEE EQUAL

equivocal (or cryptic or ambiguous) *adj.*: **sybilline** (or **sibylline**; often cap.). SEE CRYPTIC

equivocate (as in avoid a straight answer) *v.i.*: **tergiversate**. SEE EVADE

era (of or over the same ...) *adj.*: **coetaneous**. SEE CONTEMPORANEOUS

(2) era (of the same ...; contemporary) *adj., n.*: **coeval**. SEE CONTEMPORARY

eradicate (as in abolish) *v.t.*: **extirpate**. SEE ABOLISH

erase (as in abolish) *v.t.*: **extirpate**. SEE ABOLISH

erect (having an ... penis) *adj.*: **ithyphallic**. SEE PENIS

(2) erect (having a persistently ... penis) *adj.*: **priapic**. SEE PHALLIC

erection (loss of ...) *n.*: **detumescence**. SEE SHRINKAGE

erode *v.t.*: **abrade**. SEE CHAFE

erogenous (relating to or exhibiting ... behavior in many forms) *adj.*: **pansexual**. SEE SEXUAL

erotic (as in sexual lovemaking) *adj.*: **amatory**. SEE LOVEMAKING

(2) erotic (as in lustful) *adj.*: **concupiscent** (*n.*: **concupiscence**). SEE LUSTFUL

(3) erotic (relating to or exhibiting ... behavior in many forms) *adj.*: **pansexual**. SEE SEXUAL

(4) erotic (desire to look at ... scenes or images) *n.*: **scopophilia**. SEE VOYEURISM

(5) erotic (attraction to animals) *n.*: **zoophilia** (person attracted: **zoophile**). SEE BESTIALITY

erring (as in sinful) *adj.*: **peccant**. SEE SINFUL

erroneous (reasoning intended to mislead or rationalize) *n.*: **casuistry**. SEE FALLACIOUS

(2) erroneous (and/or illogical argument) *n.*: **choplogic**. SEE FALLACY

(3) erroneous (engaging in argument which may be ..., as in specious) *adj., n.*: **eristic**. SEE SPECIOUS

error (correction of ..., esp. in printed material) *n.*: **corrigendum**. SEE CORRECTION

(2) error (tragic ..., as in flaw, esp. by a literary character) *n.*: **hamartia**. SEE FLAW

(3) error (in writing) *n.*: **lapsus calami** [Latin]. SEE SLIP OF THE PEN

(4) error (in speech) *n.*: **lapsus linguae** [Latin]. SEE SLIP OF THE TONGUE

(5) error (verbal ... such as a slip of the tongue or malapropism) *n.*: **parapraxis**. SEE BLUNDER

(6) error (small or trifling ...) *n.*: **peccadillo**. SEE INFRACTION

(7) error (confession of ..., as in sin) *n.*: **peccavi**. SEE CONFESSION

(8) error (in grammar) *n.*: **solecism**. SEE MISUSE

eruption (of emotion, feeling or action) *n.*: **paroxysm**. SEE OUTBURST

(2) eruption (volcanic ...) *adj.*: **pelean** (or **Pelean**). SEE VOLCANIC

escape (from danger) *n.*: **hegira**. ▮ The Lindberghs rose early on December 31, 1935, in Liverpool's harbor [having fled to England to escape from the pressures of living in America and because of threats on their lives]. It suddenly seemed as though this **hegira** might be for naught, as a frenzied gauntlet of photographers gathered at the gangplank. (Scott Berg, *Lindbergh*, Putnam [1998], p. 346.)

(2) escape (desperate ..., as in retreat) *n.*: **Dunkirk**. SEE RETREAT

(3) escape (as in a departure which is unannounced, abrupt, secret or unceremonious) *n.*: **French Leave**. SEE DEPARTURE

esoteric (as in difficult to understand) *adj.*: **recondite**. SEE COMPLICATED

essence *n.*: **quiddity**. ∎ Baker reminds us that the entire microfilm process is thoroughly riven with shoddiness. Whole pages might be skipped, images darkened to invisibility, text rendered blurry and illegible, the film itself liable to chemical degradation and, not least, the historical **quiddity** of the original book or periodical utterly lost — in the case of unique items, irrevocably so. (Author not given, *Double Fold*, The Washington Post, 04-15-2001, p. T15.)

(2) essence (as in embodiment) *n.*: **avatar**. SEE EMBODIMENT

essential *adj.*: **constitutive**. ∎ [Homophobia] brings together into a new configuration beliefs and attitudes that evolved at different times and in different contexts. Fone chronicles the successive appearance, in Western philosophy, literature, theology and law, of the **constitutive** elements of homophobia as we know it. (Laurent Cartayrade, *With Prejudice*, The Washington Post, 10-08-2000, p. 10.)

(2) essential (element or condition) *n.*: **sine qua non** [Latin]. SEE INDISPENSABLE

establishment (of something) *n.*: **instauration**. ∎ The anti-colonial struggles in the Third World were emancipatory too, but have not resulted in the **instauration** of the liberal order in Asia, Africa or the Caribbean. (Author not given, *A Disquisition on Civil Society*, Social Research, 06-1994.)

estate (grounds belonging to an ...) *n.*: **demesne**. ∎ The two houses I own, side by side, are on a quiet, well-treed street in the established black neighborhood known as Wallace Hill, snugged in between our small [Central Business District] and the richer white **demesnes** on the west side, more or less behind the hospital. (Richard Ford, *Independence Day*, Knopf [1995], p. 24.)

esteem (as in homage, not necessarily sincere or unforced) *n.*: **obeisance**. SEE HOMAGE

eternal *adj.*: **aeonian** (or **eonian**). ∎ During **aeonian** stretches of oppressive silence, interspersed with "All of our customer service representatives are currently ...," my ear got that familiar numb sensation against the receiver. (Anne R. Lawrence, *Voting Virgin: An Ardent Alien's Confounding Quest for Citizenship*, The World & I, 09-01-2001, p. 282.)

(2) eternal (as in everlasting or immortal) *adj.*: **amaranthine**. SEE IMMORTAL

(3) eternal *adj.*: **sempiternal**. SEE EVERLASTING

eternity (for...) *adv.*: **in aeternum** [Latin]. SEE FOREVER

ethics (deciding right and wrong by applying ...) *n.*: **casuistry** ∎ P. is particularly critical of **casuistry** and the traditional moral manuals, asserting that together they misled the whole discipline of Christian ethics into an improper preoccupation with law and obligation, rather than centering reflection on the moral life in terms of beatitude and the virtues. (James T. Bretzke, *The Sources of Christian Ethics [book reviews]*, Theological Studies, 06-01-1996, p. 371.)

(2) ethics (study of) *n.*: **deontology**. ∎ Deontology concentrates on the righteousness of the human action itself, while teleology focuses on the rightness of the consequences of that action (Hunt and Vitell, 1986). (Author not given, *Spousal Ethical Justifications of Casino Gambling: A Psychometric Analysis*, Journal of Consumer Affairs, 06-1991.)

etiquette (precise observance of ...) *n.*: **punctilio**. ∎ Have you ever wondered whether you should invite the boss home for dinner, or what to say when you're late to an important business meeting? If you have, you may need help from Miss Manners [the] high priestess of **punctilio**. (Judith Martin [Miss Manners], *Executive Life: Miss Manners on Office Etiquette*, Fortune, 11-06-1989, p. 155.)

(2) etiquette (appropriate ..., as in propriety) *n.*: **correctitude**. SEE PROPRIETY

eulogy (as in giving praise or tribute) *n.*: **encomium** (one who delivers praise or tribute *n.*: **encomiast**). SEE PRAISE AND TRIBUTE

euphemism (opposite of ...) *n.*: **dysphemism**. ∎ Most of us know euphemism, substitution of a kinder, gentler word for one that might be thought harsh. Have you run in to its antonym, **dysphemism**? Examples include shrink for psychiatrist; pencil pusher for superbly skilled print-media communicator. (Alden Wood, *Lawyerly Phrase of "Counsel" Finds Itself Hitched to a Hip New Communicause*, Communication World, 12-01-1997, p. 43.)

evade (a straight answer) *v.t.*: **tergiversate**. ∎ The proceedings were short, confusing and often hilarious, as Worth **tergiversated** [on the witness stand], trying to throw [the prosecutor] off with a combination of charm, equivocation, calculated self-incrimination, and straightforward perjury. (Ben Macintyre, *The Napoleon of Crime*, Farrar, Straus and Giroux [1997], p. 195.)

(2) evade (as in avert or ward off) *v.t.*: **forfend**. SEE AVERT

evaluate *v.t.*: **assay**. ∎ "Right now Jackie Robinson doesn't shape up as a first baseman," wrote Pat Lynch of the New York Journal American. "His weak hitting is something the shrewd **assayers** of baseball talent have been on to all along." (*William Nack, Baseball: The Breakthrough Fifty Years Ago*, Sports Illustrated, 05-05-1997, p. 56.)

(2) evaluate (under a new standard, esp. one which differs from conventional norms) *v.t.*: **transvaluate**. ∎ After all, in the **transvaluated** world of Germany during the Nazi period, ordinary Germans deemed the killing of Jews to be a beneficent act for humanity. (Daniel Goldhagen, *Hitler's Willing Executioners*, Knopf [1996], p. 452.)

evaluating (act or process of ..., as in measuring) *n.*: **mensuration**. SEE MEASURING

evaporate (as in vanish or disappear) *v.t.*: **evanesce**. SEE DISAPPEAR

evasive (engaging in ... tactics, esp. as a means to wear out an opponent or avoid confrontation) *adj.*: **Fabian**. SEE DILATORY, GUERILLA AND CAUTIOUS

evasiveness (in speech or writing) *n.*: **circumlocution**. ∎ To do that — to break the memoir curse — a full treatment of [Bill Clinton's] mistakes should include at least: ... 5) His failure in using preposterous **circumlocutions** and flimsy legalisms to try to escape the consequences of his affair with Monica Lewinsky. (Jonathan Alter, *Writing the Book of Bill*, Newsweek, 08-20-2001, p. 22.)

even-tempered *adj.*: **phlegmatic**. ∎ Outwardly, [Vancouver Grizzlies' coach Brian] Winters has remained composed; volcanic eruptions are not his style. "Really, what would be the point?" he says. However, at halftime of the Grizzlies' 86-75 defeat on March 26 in Detroit, the **phlegmatic** Winters threw what for him is a tantrum. (Austin Murphy, *Pro Basketball: Down ... But Not Out as Their NBA-Record Losing Streak Hits 22*, Sports Illustrated, 04-08-1996, p. 54.)

evening (of, relating to or occurring in) *adj.*: **vespertine**. ∎ For television sets should be like theatres, concert halls, owls, bats and vampires: they are **vespertine** creatures, and may properly emerge only in the evening from their daytime slumbers. It upsets television's natural biorhythms to be hauling it out of its bed and bestirring it to work at dawn. (Kevin Myers, *Comment: Breakfast TV is a Dog's Dinner*, The Sunday Telegraph, 10-11-1998.)

(2) evening (as in twilight) *n.*: **gloaming**. SEE TWILIGHT

event (secondary ... which accompanies or results from another) *n.*: **epiphenomenon**. (*adj.*: **epiphenomenal**) SEE PHENOMENON

everlasting *adj.*: **sempiternal**. ∎ [Will] private colleges will be utterly priced out of the market[?] That's unlikely for the really high-priced institutions. Princeton is nowhere near setting a "market clearing price" (the price that is so high that it exhausts the number of potential buyers). This is a **sempiternal** truth for institutions of high prestige. Someone will pay (almost) anything for Ivy-ish credentials. (Dennis O'Brien, *A "Necessary" of Modern Life? A Very Expensive College Education*, Commonweal, 03-28-1997, p. 9.)

(2) everlasting *adj.*: **aeonian** (or **eonian**). SEE ETERNAL

(3) everlasting *adj.*: **amaranthine**. SEE IMMORTAL

everlastingly *adv.*: **in aeternum** [Latin]. SEE FOREVER

everyday (as in routine or mechanical) *adj.*: **banausic**. SEE ROUTINE

(2) everyday (people, as in the masses) *n.*: **canaille**. SEE MASSES

(3) everyday (people, as in the masses) *n.*: **hoi polloi**. SEE COMMONERS

(4) everyday (of or relating to the ... people) *adj.*: **plebian**. SEE COMMON

(5) everyday *adj.*: **quotidian**. SEE MUNDANE

(6) everyday (as in mundane) *adj.*: **sublunary**. SEE EARTHLY

evidence (early ... of disease) *n.*: **prodrome**. SEE SYMPTOM

evil *adj.*: **malefic**. ∎ It is not remarkable that celluloid Russians would change from villains to heroes and back over time. Yet, I never expected them to prove so volatile, or to move so consistently with fluctuations in U.S. policy toward the Soviets. Nor could I have conceived how overly angelic would be the good Russians and how utterly **malefic** the bad ones. (Michael J. Strada, *Politics and the Movies: Art Anticipating Life*, USA Today Magazine, 11-01-1998.)

(2) evil *adj.*: **malevolent**. ∎ The [tobacco] companies' threat is simple. Without their agreement, it may be hard to get rid of advertising to kids. When Bill

Clinton heard they were walking, he asked disparagingly, "What are they going to do? Say, we're going to go back to advertising to children?" Well, bless their **malevolent** hearts, yes. (Ellen Goodman, *The Bluster and Bluff of Big Tobacco*, St. Louis Post-Dispatch, 04-15-1998, p. B7.)

(3) evil (intended to ward off ...) *adj.*: **apotropaic**. SEE PROTECT

(4) evil (portending ...) *adj.*: **baleful**. SEE SINISTER

(6) evil (person) *n.*: **caitiff**. SEE DESPICABLE

(7) evil *adj.*: **facinorous**. SEE WICKED

(8) evil (as in wicked) *adj.*: **flagitious**. SEE WICKED

(9) evil (spirit who has sex with sleeping women) *n.*: **incubus**. SEE DEMON

(10) evil *adj.*: **iniquitous**. SEE WICKED

(11) evil (and scheming woman) *n.*: **jezebel** (sometimes cap.). SEE WOMAN

(12) evil (female spirit who has sex with sleeping men) *n.*: **succubus**. SEE DEMON

evildoer *n.*: **malefactor**. SEE WRONGDOER

(2) evildoer *n.*: **miscreant**. SEE WRONGDOER

evil vs. good (philosophy which divides the world into ...) *n.*: **manichaeism** (*adj.*: **manichean**). SEE GOOD VS. EVIL

(2) evil vs. good (conflict in the soul between ...) *n.*: **psychomachia**. SEE GOOD VS. EVIL

exacting (overly ...) *adj.*: **persnickety**. SEE PICKY

exaggerate *v.t.*: **aggrandize**. ∎ It is hardly an act of heroism to reject neo-Nazism. Hasselbach exaggerates the importance of his former life so as to **aggrandize** the importance of his present life. Though no longer a fascist, he is still peddling the fascination of fascism. (Noah Isenberg, *Fuhrer-Ex: Memoirs of a Former Neo-Nazi [book reviews]*, The New Republic, 04-08-1996, p. 28.)

exaggerated (behavior) *n., adj.*: **operatics**. SEE MELODRAMATIC

exaggeration (abnormal propensity towards ...) *n.*: **mythomania**. SEE EMBELLISHMENT

exaltation (to divine rank or stature) *n.*: **apotheosis** (*v.t.*: **apotheosize**). ∎ Mother [Theresa] would probably have recoiled at the extravagance. A state funeral televised around the world. A military guard bearing her coffin to a ceremony attended by the powerful and the famous. Billboards proclaiming her **apotheosis**. (Author not given, *World: For the Poor, an Immortal*, Time, 09-22-1997, p. 42.)

exalted *adj.*: **empyreal**. SEE LOFTY

examination (of a subject, as in survey) *n.*: **conspectus**. SEE SURVEY

examine (as in analyze closely) *v.t.*: **anatomize**. SEE ANALYZE

(2) examine (closely) *v.t.*: **catechize**. SEE QUESTION

(3) examine (as in touch, esp. for medical reasons) *v.t.*: **palpate**. SEE TOUCH

examiner (as in observer) *n.*: **scrutator**. SEE OBSERVER

example *n.*: **exemplum**. ∎ His thesis ... was that white male America was praising Asians as the "ideal minority." He made use of revisionist history by citing examples from the 19th century, when white planters in Mississippi brought in Chinese workers as an **exemplum** for the black sharecroppers, thereby driving home his propaganda that Asians and blacks are at odds because of whites. (W.J. Reeves, *Will Zealots Spell the Doom of Great Literature?* USA Today Magazine, 09-01-1996.)

(2) example (original ...) *n.*: **archetype**. SEE MODEL

(3) example (which serves as a pattern or model) *n.*: **paradigm**. SEE MODEL

exceed (the limits, resources or capabilities of) *v.t.*: **beggar**. SEE SURPASS

excellence (as in superiority or state of being better) *n.*: **meliority**. SEE SUPERIORITY

excellent (generally used in the sense of select, choice or distinguished) *adj.*: **eximious** [sometimes considered obscure, but recent uses are not uncommon]. ∎ One claim not to be made for Edouard Vuillard is that he is "one of the great modern masters of his generation." ... That [such a claim is] made by the President of the Royal Academy in a foreword to the catalogue of that **eximious** institution's latest exhibition is, however, excusable in that it is his duty to whip us in to see it, and the lash of hyperbole is far more ready and at his hand than the carrot of simple truth. (Brian Sewell, *The Minor Master of Domestic Detail*, The Evening Standard [London], 01-30-2004.)

(2) excellent *adj.*: **galumptious** [slang]. ∎ [The] Ford F-150 pickup moves with lightning speed and scares the devil out of anyone who gets in its way. It's a big, muscular truck with a 240-horsepower V-8 that'll thump lesser vehicles. ... Add 17-inch cast-aluminum wheels, performance shock absorbers and that **galumptious** V-8, and you've got something that really hauls ... fast. (Warren Brown, *Lightning Hot Rod*, The Washington Post, 12-02-1994, p. N74.)

(3) excellent *adj.*: **palmary**. ∎ This [the Middle Ages] is the very age of Universities; it is the classical period of the schoolmen; it is the splendid and **palmary** instance of the wise policy and large liberality of the Church, as regards philosophical inquiry. When was there ever a more curious, more meddling, bolder, keener, more penetrating, more rationalistic exercise of the reason than at that time? (William Hoye, *The Religious Roots of Academic Freedom*, Theological Studies, 09-01-1997, p. 409.)

(4) excellent *adj.*: **skookum**. ∎ Yes, the boys of Alien Ant Farm are cheekier than Adam Ant in red leather pants, but we admire their foolhardy spirit and infamous reverse mohawks. On Sunday night, the band that took on the king of pop with a **skookum** cover of "smooth criminal" stops by Axis at 8; $10. (Christopher Muther, *Go! Weekend*, The Boston Globe, 07-25-1993, p. C3.)

(5) excellent (as in of the highest quality) *n.*: **first water** (usu. as in "of the first water"). SEE QUALITY

(6) excellent *adj.*: **frabjous** (often as in "Oh frabjous day!"). SEE WONDERFUL

(7) excellent (as in first-class) *adj.*: **pukka**. SEE FIRST-CLASS

excess *n.*: **nimiety**. ∎ Just as daily life contains all the comforts of what one owns, there is also a natural shedding or forgetting and a natural dulling, otherwise one becomes burdened with a sense of **nimiety**, a sense (as Kenneth Clark put it in his autobiography) of the "too-muchness" of life. Of course, this **nimiety** is also just tiredness, to be expected in an old man, and Prince registers that on seeing the Caravaggios: "By this time I have been/too long on my feet,/seen too much and am tiring." (Nicholas Poburko, *Poetry, Past and Present: F. T. Prince's Walks in Rome*, Renascence: Essays on Values in Literature, 01-01-1999.)

excessive *adj.*: **de trop** [French]. ∎ [The CEO of Starbucks Coffee] is the perfect spokesman for an era when "decaf latte" has entered the upper-middle-class lexicon as shorthand for a little self-indulgence. Indulgence? Once, we knew the true meaning of that word. Indulgences should be decadent, degenerate, altogether **de trop**. They should not be decaffeinated. (Andrew Stuttaford, *Food & Drink: Mug's Game*, National Review, 12-07-1998, p. 71.)

exchange (as in dialogue, in which neither side hears or understands or pays attention to the other) *n.*: **dialogue des sourds** [French]. SEE DIALOGUE

excited (nervously ...) *adj.*: **atwitter**. ∎ Left, right, left, right ... forward, backward ... hop, hop, hop. Pardon me, but I'm in training for the 2000 Olympics. In case you missed the big news that has set the Olympic world **atwitter**, on April 3 the International Olympic Committee granted provisional recognition to ballroom dancing and surfing. (E.M. Swift, *Point After: Calling Arthur Murray: Ballroom Dancing Has as Much Right to Be in the Olympics As, Say, Rhythmic Gymnastics*, Sports Illustrated, 04-24-1995, p. 72.)

(2) excited (or enthusiastic speech or writing) *n.*: **dithyramb**. SEE ENTHUSIASTIC

excitement (moment of intense ...) *n.*: **frisson** [French]. SEE SHUDDER

(2) excitement (sexual ... from rubbing against something or someone) *n.*: **frottage**. SEE RUBBING

exciting (wildly ... as in frenzied) *adj.*: **corybantic**. SEE FRENZIED

exclude (as in consider separately) *v.t.*: **prescind** (generally as in "prescind from"). SEE ISOLATE

(2) exclude (as in omit intentionally) *v.t.*: **pretermit**. SEE OMIT

exclusive (person, esp. in intellectual or literary circles) *n.*: **mandarin**. SEE INFLUENTIAL

excrement (obsession with) *n.*: **coprology**. ∎ TMP: How did your interest in fecal matter develop? Lewin: I noted differences in the shape and size of various kinds of deer pellets and wondered what made them so different. ... That led me in turn to consider the wider subject of what we might call comparative **coprology** in general, and begin this survey of what seems to be a fascinating if neglected topic. (Elaine McNinch, *Merde!* Medical Post, 10-12-1999.)

(2) excrement (feeding on) *adj.*: **coprophagous**. ∎ Some dogs are **coprophagous**, says Gerba. That means they eat feces. When Scruffy laps your face, he can transmit E. coli, salmonella, or Pasteurella multocida, possibly giving you the trots. (Tom Zoellner, *Where the Germs Are*, Men's Health, 09-01-1999, p. 119.)

(3) excrement (interest in ..., often sexual) *n.*: **coprophilia**. ∎ My "Ugh" column really struck a nerve. So many of you sent me examples of offensive ads and clippings that I must now be in possession of the largest collection of pictures of toilets outside the ranks of the National Association for the Advancement of **Coprophilia**. (Florence King, *The*

Misanthrope's Corner [Distasteful Advertising], National Review, 08-12-2002.)

(4) excrement *n*.: **egesta**. ∎ [The novel] *Bridget Jones's Diary* has a lot to answer for. It's not just literary diarrhea, it's the thin bowel water which tells you that your session of diarrhea is at an end, and (although PR hype has turned this diluted **egesta** into an international bestseller) we all know that a series of fragmented testimonials does not a novel make. (Victor Lewis-Smith, *The World of Hump it And Hop it*, The Evening Standard, 02-04-1999, p. 35.)

(5) excrement (study of or obsession with) *n*.: **scatology**. ∎ Eliminated matter is something of a theme for Frewer. ... Ask him about proposing to Amanda, 32: "... I almost stepped in a pile of dog poo," he says. "And instead of going 'Whooa!' I said, 'Will you marry me?' I can actually thank a dog with bowel problems for my being married." Psychiatrists would have to listen for hours to find an explanation for Frewer's **scatology**. (Margot Dougherty, *Tube: With Max Headroom Behind Him, Matt Frewer Mad-libs Through Doctor, Doctor and a Smash Film*, People, 07-17-1989, p. 111.)

(6) excrement (eating) *adj*.: **scatophagous**. ∎ [In India], I ordered a local fish dish with an unfamiliar name. William, a fellow traveler, leaned across the table to tell me, "That fish is called **Scatophagous** Argos, the keen-eyed shit-eater." I took a mouthful; it tasted divine. (Colin Barraclough, *Oil and Herbs Blend Well With Sun and Sea Breeze*, Insight on the News, 09-30-1996.)

(7) excrement (of or relating to) *adj*.: **stercoraceous**. ∎ [In the movie *Goldmember*,] there are ... more than a few shit jokes, and I don't mean jokes that aren't funny. Indeed, there are times in Goldmember when Myers's vision is hilariously ... **stercoraceous**. ... It's tasteless and vulgar, offensive and utterly puerile. I loved every minute of it. (Philip Kerr, *Hitting the Base Notes: [Goldmember] [Movie Review]*, New Statesman, 08-05-2002.)

(8) excrement (esp. that of sea birds) *n*.: **guano**. SEE BIRD DUNG

excrete (or discharge waste from the body) *v.t*.: **egest**. ∎ The correlation between [fossilized excrement] dimensions and animal size is not absolute, however. Although the quantity of **egested** waste is proportional to body size, the entire fecal mass may not be recovered because of the fragmentary nature of fecal material. (Karen Chin, *On the Elusive Trail of Fossil Dung [Digging Dinosaurs]*, National Forum, 06-22-1998, p. 36.)

excusable *adj*.: **venial**. SEE FORGIVABLE

excuse (formal ..., as in justification, for one's acts or beliefs) *n*.: **apologia**. SEE JUSTIFICATION

(2) excuse (attempt to ... an offense or crime) *v.t*.: **palliate**. SEE DOWNPLAY

execute (by strangling or cutting the throat) *v.t*.: **garrote**. SEE STRANGLE

execution (of convicted persons, spec. burning of heretics at the stake) *n*.: **auto-da-fe**. ∎ In theory, Bill Clinton should have been nervous. It had been nearly a year since he'd held a full-scale press conference — a year in which he'd been exposed, impeached, humiliated and nearly convicted for lying under oath. The networks were going live for the **auto-da-fe**. (Howard Fineman, *In The Line of Fire*, Newsweek, 03-29-1999, p. 28.)

exemplary *adj*.: **palmary**. SEE EXCELLENT

exhaust (as in deprive of strength) *v.t*.: **geld**. SEE WEAKEN

exhausted (as in weakened) *adj*.: **etiolated**. SEE WEAKENED

exhausting (as in laborious) *adj*.: **operose**. SEE LABORIOUS

exhaustion (from lack of energy or nourishment) *n*.: **inanition**. ∎ But why should we assume that divorce is always preceded by open conflict? Some marriages die a quiet death, preceded by boredom, silent contempt, or sheer **inanition**. (Joseph Adelson, *Splitting Up [Research on Harmful Effects of Divorce]*, Commentary, 09-01-1996, p. 63.)

exhilarated (often in a boastful way) *adj*.: **cock-a-hoop**. SEE ELATED

exhorting (strong attempt, as in ... someone to take a course of action) *adj*.: **hortatory**. SEE URGING

exiled (as in against the world) *adv., adj*.: **contra mundum** [Latin]. SEE AGAINST THE WORLD

existence (while coming into ...) *adv*.: **aborning**. SEE BORN

exit (hurriedly or secretly) *v.t*.: **absquatulate**. SEE LEAVE

(2) exit (hurriedly or secretly) *v.t*.: **decamp**. SEE LEAVE

(3) exit (as in a departure which is unannounced, abrupt, secret or unceremonious) *n*.: **French Leave**. SEE DEPARTURE

exodus (from danger) *n.*: **hegira**. SEE ESCAPE

exoneration (obtaining ... through testimony of others) *n.*: **compurgation**. SEE ACQUITTAL

exotic (as in unusual or rare) *adj.*: **recherché** [French]. SEE RARE

expand (in scope) *v.t.*: **aggrandize**. ▪ Thus, where the old history took place primarily in the political arena, the new history focuses on the home, family, community, workplace — in short, on civil society. The effect of the new history has been not only to depoliticize history but to de-**aggrandize** it as well, to shift attention from great, public, historic events and personages to the daily lives of the "anonymous masses." (Gertrude Himmelfarb, *For the Love of Country [Importance of Patriotism]*, Commentary, 05-01-1997, p. 34.)

(2) expand (as in burgeon; lit.: bear fruit) *v.i.*: **fructify**. SEE BURGEON

expectant (nervously ... and excited) *adj.*: **atwitter**. SEE EXCITED

(2) expectant *adj.*: **prevenient**. SEE ANTICIPATORY

expectation (that something is going to occur) *n.*: **presentiment**. SEE PREMONITION

expecting (as in pregnant) *adj.*: **enceinte** [French]. SEE PREGNANT

(2) expecting (as in pregnant) *adj.*: **gravid**. SEE PREGNANT

expedition (to a sacred place or shrine, esp. to Mecca) *n.*: **hadj**. SEE PILGRIMAGE

experience (difficult or painful ...) *n.*: **via dolorosa**. SEE ORDEAL

experiment (with) *v.t.*: **assay**. ▪ Jazz and blues have been inseparable since the birth of the former; indeed, the dividing line between some barrelhouse piano and jazz keyboard pyrotechnics can be hard to find. And virtually every jazz personage has **assayed** the blues at least once. (Author not given, *New CDs Prove the Significance of Blues*, Philadelphia Tribune, 01-08-1999, p. 5E.)

expert *n.*: **cognoscente**. SEE CONNOISSEUR

expertise (area of ...) *n.*: **bailiwick**. ▪ The law, after all, can do very little to prevent espionage — or even the score. Such a task would seem to be the **bailiwick** of the CIA, which ... could in theory spy on foreign corporations and steal their secrets. (Jamie

Malanowski, *Features: Silicon Bond Looking to Become a Superspy?* Time, 06-01-1997, p. 36.)

(2) expertise (area of ...) *n.*: **métier** [French]. SEE FORTE

expiatory *adj.*: **piacular**. SEE ATONING

explain (a subject at length in speech or writing) *v.i.*: **expatiate**. SEE EXPOUND

(2) explain (attempt to ... an offense with excuses) *v.t.*: **palliate**. SEE DOWNPLAY

explanation (formal ... of one's acts or beliefs) *n.*: **apologia**. SEE JUSTIFICATION

(2) explanation (of a text by adding one's own ideas) *n.*: **eisegesis**. SEE INTERPRETATION

(3) explanation (esp. of a text) *n.*: **exegesis**. SEE INTERPRETATION

explanatory (as in interpretative, often regarding a document or text, such as scripture) *n.*: **hermeneutic**. SEE INTERPRETATION

exploitation (of a religious, national or racial group) *n.*: **helotism** (*v.t.*: **helotize**). SEE OPPRESSION

exploration (of a subject, as in survey) *n.*: **conspectus**. SEE SURVEY

explosion (causing intense heat and light) *n.*: **deflagration**. ▪ Grove claims that the Bismarck's shell ignited the 100 tons of cordite propellant in the aft magazines [of HMS Hood], which created "a massive **deflagration** that burnt its way like a blowlamp through the ship." (Simon Crerar, *The Riddle of the Hood*, Sunday Times [London], 12-16-01.)

explosive (potentially ... or volatile place or situation) *n.*: **tinderbox**. ▪ The Serbian province of Kosovo is a **tinderbox** that poses the biggest threat to Europe and the Balkan region since the Bosnian war ended in 1995. (Lee Michael Katz, *Kosovo Has the Potential to be Another Bosnia*, USA Today, 03-10-1998, p. 8A.)

expose (as in disclose) *v.t.*: **disinter**. SEE DISCLOSE

expound (on a subject at length in speech or writing) *v.i.*: **expatiate**. ▪ In interviews, [French President Francois Mitterand] **expatiated** on his attitude [about] death. He paraded a highly intellectual agnosticism, logically not able to believe in a God but emotionally unable to embrace atheism. (Mary Dejevsky, *A Long Dying Ends With a Vicious Irony*, Independent, 01-09-1996, p. 8.)

(2) expound *v.i., n.*: **descant**. SEE TALK

express (as in send a signal) *v.t., v.i.*: **semaphore**. SEE SIGNAL

expressed (not capable of being) *adj.*: **ineffable**. SEE INDESCRIBABLE

expression (or phrase or comment which is elegant, concise, witty and/or well-put) *n.*: **atticism**. ∎ Can a former adviser to [former British Prime Minster Margaret] Thatcher, an establishmentarian and literary grandee make you laugh? Step forward Ferdinand Mount, in whose confident, brilliant comedy *Of Love and Asthma* witty **atticisms** flop like cream oozing from a sponge cake. (Brendan O'Keefe, *Books: Fostering Love out of Failure*, The Observer, 09-15-1991, p. 62.)

(2) expression (in which one references an issue by saying that they will not discuss it; e.g.: "I'm not even going to get into the character issue.") *n.*: **apophasis**. SEE FIGURE OF SPEECH

(2) expression (as in manner of speaking) *n.*: **façon de parler** [French]. SEE WAY OF SPEAKING

(3) expression (pithy ...) *n.*: **gnome** (*adj.*: **gnomic**). SEE CATCHPHRASE

(4) expression (written ... which is concise, precise or refined; lit. "as if engraved in a precious stone") *adj.*: **lapidary**. SEE WRITING

(5) expression *n.*: **locution**. SEE PHRASE

(6) expression (as in using one word or phrase in ... for something with which it is usually associated, such as using "city hall" to refer to city government) *n.*: **metonymy**

(7) expression (as in demeanor) *n.*: **mien**. SEE DEMEANOR

(8) expression (just the right ... or word) *n.*: **mot juste** [French]. SEE WORD

(9) expression (new ..., phrase or word) *n.*: **neologism**. SEE WORD

(10) expression (in which one makes only passing mention of something in order to emphasize rhetorically the significance of what is being omitted; often preceded by the phrase "not to mention") *n.*: **paraleipsis**. SEE FIGURE OF SPEECH

(11) expression (facial ... in the form of a grimace due to pain or disgust) *n.*: **rictus**. SEE GRIMACE

(12) expression (as in figure of speech) *n.*: **trope**. SEE FIGURE OF SPEECH

expunge (a book or a writing in a prudish manner) *v.t.*: **bowdlerize**. SEE EDIT

expurgate (a book or a writing in a prudish manner) *v.t.*: **bowdlerize**. SEE EDIT

extensive (as in widespread) *adj.*: **pandemic**. SEE WIDESPREAD

extenuate (as in attempt to minimize seriousness of an offense) *v.t.*: **palliate**. SEE DOWNPLAY

exterminate *v.t.*: **extirpate**. SEE ABOLISH

(2) exterminate (as in put an end to): **quietus** (esp. as in "put the quietus to"). SEE TERMINATE

externally *adv.*: **ab extra** [Latin]. ∎ Surely ... the two Tory finance ministers on the bridge during fiscal 1992-93 did not sit with their pencils in hand working out their very own budget estimates. In fact, the estimates would come from the best minds in the treasury department, aided by those at the bank and abetted **ab extra** by some of [the 200 economists which Finance Minster Paul Martin convened to meet]. (Dalton Camp, *We Need Good Forecasting, Not Ottawa Gamesmanship*, The Toronto Star, 12-12-1993, p. E3.)

extortion *n.*: **chantage** [French]. ∎ [A woman hired a witch doctor to put a hex on another woman having an affair with her husband. She said:] "Soon after [that, the witch doctor] started blackmailing me. It was **chantage**, I tell you. **Chantage**." "What could she blackmail you with?" ... [S]he said if I did not give her what she wanted, she would take away the hex." (Manfred Wolf, *The Two Witch Doctors*, The Literary Review, 03-22-2001.)

extra (or unexpected gift or benefit, sometimes as thanks for a purchase) *n.*: **lagniappe**. SEE GIFT

extract (the flavor or essence of something, as if by boiling down) *v.t.*: **decoct**. SEE BOIL DOWN

extramarital (sex or relations) *n.*: **hetaerism**. SEE AFFAIR

extraneous (as in argument where one proves or disproves a point which is not at issue) *n.*: **ignoratio elenchi** [Latin]. SEE IRRELEVANCY

(2) extraneous (words) *n.*: **macrology**. SEE VERBOSITY

(3) extraneous (word or phrase) *n.*: **pleonasm**. SEE REDUNDANCY

extraordinary (state of being ..., as in superior or state of being better) *n.*: **meliority**. SEE SUPERIORITY

(2) extraordinary (as in supernatural) *adj.*: **preternatural**. SEE SUPERNATURAL

extravagant (as in lavish) *adj.*: **Lucullan**. SEE LAVISH

extreme (to the ...) *adv.*: **à l'outrance** [French]. SEE UTMOST

extremism (esp. in political matters) *n.*: **ultraism**. ∎ In the final week of the last general election, [Scottish National Party head] Alex Salmond posed awkwardly for one last photo-call. The slogan [he was] advertising proclaimed that no-one ever celebrated devolution day. It was the height of SNP **ultraism**, the "independence, nothing less" approach. [The issue was whether Scotland should become independent of the United Kingdom with devolution being the alternate choice.] (Author not given, *Salmond Still Pushing for Power Over Purity*, The Scotsman, 09-25-1995, p. 4.)

extremist (a political ..., who often believes in violence to attain an end) *n.*: **sans-culotte** [French; derives from name given in the first French revolution to members of the extreme republican party, who rejected breeches as an emblem peculiar to the upper classes or aristocracy]. ∎ The second revolutionary redistribution of Russian property in this century [which created a new upper and middle class] now seems likely to last [as a result of Yeltsin's victory]. Yet, while Russia's **sans-culotte** did not storm the red walls of the Kremlin, they did register a powerful protest that the nation's triumphant masters will ignore at their peril. Nearly 40 million Russians backed Yeltsin, but more than 29 million supported his Communist rival. (Chrystia Freeland, *A Foothold for Democracy; Yeltsin's Election Indicates Russia Is on Track, But Now it Needs to Share the Wealth*, Rocky Mountain News, 07-07-1996.)

extrovert (someone who is halfway between an ... and an introvert) *n.*: **ambivert**. ∎ [Bob] Woodward affords us a glimpse behind the veil. Here, a recurring image is [of Fed Chairman Alan] Greenspan as the borderline **ambivert** — inherently a shy man, he feasts on the politicking of Beltway parties, but only as an anthology of intimate *téte a tétes*, not as a gather-round-the-piano stage show. (David Guo, *Greenspan Bio Gives Readers Their Money's Worth*, Pittsburgh Post-Gazette, 01-07-2001, p. G8.)

exult (in, or boast, esp. about the accomplishments of a relative) *v.t., n.*: **kvell** [Yiddish]. SEE BOAST

(2) **exult** (with boisterous public demonstrations) *v.i.*: **maffick** [British]. SEE CELEBRATE

exultant (often in a boastful way) *adj.*: **cock-a-hoop**. SEE ELATED

eye (of or relating to) *adj.*: **ocular** ∎ With the National Hockey League (NHL) season in full swing, *Ophthalmology Times* continues its ongoing series on sports-related eye injuries. In interviews with team eyecare physicians throughout the league, OT found that serious **ocular** injuries — while they do happen — are few and far between. (Sheryl Stevenson, *Ophthalmologists Help Put NHL Eye Injuries on Ice*, Ophthalmology Times, 11-15-1997, p. 1.)

eye for an eye *n.*: **lex talionis** [Latin]. ∎ The Golden Rule ["do unto others as you would have them do unto you"] was not submitted to systematic analysis until Albrecht Dihle's classic work in 1962. Dihle rooted it in the oldest norm of human conduct, the principle of retribution. ... The most severe form of this principle, found in primitive law and primitive morality, was the **lex talionis**. (John Topel, *The Tarnished Golden Rule (Luke 6:31): The Inescapable Radicalness Of Christian Ethics*, Theological Studies, 09-01-1998, p. 475.)

eyebrows (smooth area between ... and above the nose) *n.*: **glabella**. ∎ Injecting Botox into the **glabella**, the area between the brows, releases the vertical lines and lifts the outer brow. The result: You appear more relaxed and less angry. Makes a nice gift for Charles Bronson. (Lucinda Chriss, *Looks: The End of the Lines*, Men's Health, 10-01-1999, p. 94.)

eyeglasses (with a short handle like opera glasses) *n.*: **lorgnette**. ∎ David McVicar's new production of Massenet's opera at the London Coliseum is in the style of a modern thing in old clothes. The company, bepowdered and bewigged, eye the audience critically through **lorgnettes** as we take our seats. (Dermot Clinch, *Manon [Opera Reviews]*, New Statesman [1996], 05-22-1998, p. 51.)

(2) **eyeglasses** (clipped to the bridge of the nose) *n.*: **pince-nez**. ∎ Tammany Hall Democrats, however, weren't swooning [over Frankin Roosevelt]. They noted the freshman's habit of tossing his head back and peering down his nose (on which he wore **pince-nez** like Theodore Roosevelt, a fifth cousin) and read in it a squire's disdain for grubby city boys. (Gerald Parshall, *A Monumental Man*, U.S. News & World Report, 04-28-1997, p. 59.)

eyelids (spasmodic blinking of) *n.*: **blepharospasm**. SEE BLINKING

eyes (having watery ...) *adj.*: **rheumy**. SEE WATERY

eyesight (loss of) *n.*: **amaurosis**. SEE BLINDNESS

(2) **eyesight** (having poor ..., as in nearly blind) *adj.*: **purblind**. SEE BLIND

F

fable (moral ...) *n.*: **apologue**. ▪ [D]espite a known history of mental illness and suicide attempts ... repeated requests for anti-psychotic medication by the inmate and a social worker were ignored, and he was soon found hanging in his cell, "cold to the touch." The report describing this incident reads like a series of all-too-truthful **apologues** illustrating how detainees with mental illnesses slip through the cracks, wither, and die behind bars. (Spencer P. M. Harrington, *New Bedlam: Jails — Not Psychiatric Hospitals — Now Care for the Indigent Mentally Ill*, The Humanist, 05-01-1999, p. 9.)

fabrication (which is defamatory and published for political gain right before an election) *n.*: **roorback**. See FALSEHOOD

(2) fabrication (petty or minor ...) *n.*: **taradiddle** (or **tarradiddle**). See LIE

facade (as in something which is impressive-looking on the outside but which hides or covers up undesirable conditions or facts) *n.*: **Potemkin village** [derives from Grigori Potemkin, a Russian statesman, who had impressive fake villages erected along the route that Catherine the Great was to travel.] ▪ [M]any people thought the show of diversity [at the 2000 Republican Convention] was too over-the-top to be taken as sincere. ... Alan Brinkley [stated:] "The level of artificiality in this is so palpable that it's hard to imagine that many people believe this is the true Republican Party on display. It's a **Potemkin village**." In fact, he said, Republicans have not attracted sizeable number of black voters in many decades. (Nita Lelyveld, *Skepticism Remains on GOP Efforts to Woo Minorities*, Knight Ridder/Tribune News Service, 08-04-2000.)

face (appearance of ...) *n.*: **physiognomy**. See FACIAL FEATURES

facial (expression in the form of a grimace due to pain or disgust) *n.*: **rictus**. See GRIMACE

facial features *n.*: **physiognomy**. ▪ The realistic depictions of the ancestors' countenances don't merely show the influence of European draftsmanship, however. ... Chinese tradition held that character and destiny were revealed by **physiognomy**, so the contours of an individual's face told a story that shouldn't be ignored. (Mark Jenkins, *Haunting,*

Hallowed Portraits, The Washington Post, 06-29-2001, p. T54.)

facility (as in appearance of effortlessness) *n.*: **sprezzatura** [Italian]. See EFFORTLESSNESS

fact (in ...) *adj., adv.*: **de facto** (as contrasted with de jure: legally or by law) [Latin]. See IN FACT

(2) fact (invented ... believed true due to repetition) *n.*: **factoid**. See INACCURACY

factions (tending to break into ... or disintegrate) *adj.*: **fissiparous**. See BREAK UP

factual (necessarily ...) *adj.*: **apodictic**. See INCONTROVERTIBLE

(2) factual (as in reflecting reality) *adj.*: **veridical**. See REALISTIC

fad (the latest ...) *n.*: **dernier cri** [French]. See TREND

fade (as in vanish or disappear) *v.t.*: **evanesce**. See DISAPPEAR

fading (away quickly) *adj.*: **fugacious**. See FLEETING

failed (as in unsuccessful) *adj.*: **abortive**. See UNSUCCESSFUL

faint (as in lightheaded or dizzy) *adj.*: **vertiginous**. See DIZZY

fainthearted *adj.*: **pusillanimous**. See COWARDLY

fainting *n.*: **syncope**. ▪ Her pulse was close to stopping. Was it the drugs she was taking? ... She had been sent from her cardiologist's office, the first stop after a fainting episode at home. His note read, "67 y.o. with **syncope** and bradycardia." ... [T]his is the United States in the late 1990s, where bradycardia is more likely to be inflicted by a doctor than nature. (Tony Dajer, *When Pills Kill*, Discover, 08-01-1999.)

fair (uncompromisingly ...) *n.*: **Rhadamanthine**. See JUST

fairylike (as in otherwordly) *adj.*: **fey**. See OTHERWORDLY

faith (reliance on ... alone rather than reason, esp. in philosophical or religious matters) *n.*: **fideism**. ▪ In the middle is Father Sirico, who warns against two predominant and equally wrongheaded decision-making tendencies: to rely purely on reason on the one hand and **fideism** on the other, which he calls the "I'm just trusting on the Lord and I'm not going to think about it" approach. He suggests depending on reason but recognizing that reason alone doesn't explain all the mysteries of life. (Steven Greenhut, *Decisions, Decisions; Here's How to Think About How to Make Up Your Mind,* The Orange County Register [California], 06-20-1999.)

faithful (and unquestioning assistant) *n.:* **myrmidon**. See ASSISTANT

faithfulness *n.:* **fealty**. See LOYALTY

faithless (man married to ... wife) *n.:* **cuckold** (*v.t.:* to make a ... of). See ADULTEROUS

(2) faithless *adj.:* **perfidious**. See UNFAITHFUL

(3) faithless (to a belief, duty or cause) *adj.:* **recreant**. See UNFAITHFUL

fake (as in artificial) *adj.:* **factitious**. See ARTIFICIAL

(2) fake (out, as in bluff) *v.t.:* **four-flush** (*n.:* **four-flusher**). See BLUFF

(3) fake (sickness or other incapacity to avoid work) *v.i.:* **malinger**. See SHIRK

(4) fake (esp. a person who sells quack medicines) *n.:* **mountebank**. See HUCKSTER

(5) fake *adj.:* **pinchbeck**. See COUNTERFEIT

(6) fake (as in invented or substituted with fraudulent intent) *adj.:* **supposititious**. See SUPPOSED

fake front (as in something which is impressive-looking on the outside but which hides or covers up undesirable conditions or facts) *n.:* **Potemkin village**. See FACADE

faker (as in hypocrite, esp. one who affects religious peity) *n.:* **Tartuffe** (or **tartuffe**). See HYPOCRITE

(2) faker (as in hypocrite, esp. one who acts humbly) *n.:* **Uriah Heep**. See HYPOCRITE

fall (downward ...) *n.:* **declension**. See DECLINE

(2) fall (esp. from a position of strength or condition) *n.:* **dégringolade** [French]. See DOWNFALL

(3) fall (to the bottom of the ocean) *v.i.:* **go to Davy Jones' locker**. See OCEAN

fallacious (engaging in argument which may be ..., as in specious) *adj., n.:* **eristic**. See SPECIOUS

(2) fallacious (argument where one proves or disproves a point which is not at issue) *n.:* **ignoratio elenchi** [Latin]. See IRRELEVANCY

(3) fallacious (argument, where one begs the question) *n.:* **petitio principii** [Latin]. See BEGGING THE QUESTION

fallacy (as in reasoning which is intended to rationalize or mislead) *n.:* **casuistry**. ▪ [Attorney Alan] Dershowitz continued: "[The jury's finding of liability against O.J. Simpson in his civil trial] doesn't in any way undercut the correctness of the first case at all." Of course not. Simpson did it but Simpson didn't do it, Simpson is guiltless but Simpson is liable. This is the **casuistry** of a man who is correctly worried about his reputation. (Author not given, *Mr. Guilty Is Liable,* The New Republic, 02-24-1997.)

(2) fallacy (and/or illogical argument) *n.:* **choplogic**. ▪ Anything that makes Quebec's separatists so mad can't be all bad. So, yes, partition does have something to be said for it. ... They have had it all their own way far too long. Now, their lies about painless secession are being challenged. The puck has been shot into their end for a change, and the separatists are getting tangled in their own **choplogic**. Good. (Norman Webster, *If Quebec Is Divisible, So Is Federalism,* Maclean's, 03-11-1996, p. 64.)

(3) fallacy (or illogical argument) *n.:* **paralogism** (*adj.:* **paralogical**). ▪ Yes, it is silly to bring up, as though they had a bearing on one another, increased executive salaries and diminished work forces. But that **paralogism** doesn't authorize scornful inattention to the implications of preposterous salaries. (William F. Buckley, Jr., *Rich-Baiting Time [Exorbitant Salaries of American CEOs],* National Review, 05-06-1996, p. 62.)

(4) fallacy (accepted as fact due to repetition in print) *n.:* **factoid**. See INACCURACY

falling apart (of a group or social structure as a result of lack of standards or values) *n.:* **anomie**. See BREAKDOWN

false (make ... or malicious statements about) *v.t.:* **calumniate** (*n.:* **calumny**). See MALIGN

(2) false (story, report or rumor, often deliberately) *n.:* **canard**. See HOAX

(3) false (reasoning intended to ... rationalize or mislead) *n.:* **casuistry**. See FALLACIOUS

(4) false (and/or illogical argument) *n.:* **choplogic**. See FALLACY

(5) false (as in artificial) *adj.:* **factitious**. See ARTIFICIAL

(6) false (as in untruthful or dishonest) *adj.:* **mendacious**. See DISHONEST

(7) false (make ... statements about, so as to humiliate or disgrace) *v.t.:* **traduce**. See MALIGN

false front (as in something which is impressive-looking on the outside but which hides or covers up undesirable conditions or facts) *n.:* **Potemkin village**. See FACADE

falsehood (which is defamatory and published for

political gain right before an election) *n.*: **roorback** [derives from an incident in the election of 1844, when backers of Whig Party candidate Henry Clay circulated a false report by a fictional "Baron Roorback" claiming that Democratic candidate James K. Polk branded slaves with an iron. Polk won anyway]. ∎ For the next day or so, [don't] believe everything you read. Especially if it's about politics [and] if it's in a campaign brochure. ... Because there's a good chance it might be a **roorback**. ... [For example,] fliers with a grainy black-and-white photo of a candidate standing behind superimposed jail bars, under a headline that screams, "Candidate Bob Schmedlap Guilty of Drunk Driving!" (Gordon Dillow, *Beware the Wily Ghost of Roorback*, Orange County Register [California], 11-01-1998, p. B1.)

(2) falsehood (as in lie) *n.*: **fabulation** (one who does so: **fabulist**). SEE LIE

(3) falsehood (accepted as fact due to repetition in print) *n.*: **factoid**. SEE INACCURACY

(4) falsehood (petty or minor ...) *n.*: **taradiddle** (or **tarradiddle**). SEE LIE

falsification (deliberate ... or concealment of facts to gain an advantage) *n.*: **subreption**. SEE MISREPRESENTATION

falter (as in hesitate to act, due to indecision) *v.i.*: **dither**. SEE PROCRASTINATE

(2) falter (as in hesitate to act) *v.i.*: **shilly-shally**. SEE PROCRASTINATE

fame *n.*: **réclame** [French]. SEE PUBLICITY

(2) fame (one obsessed with one's own greatness or ...) *n.*: **megalomania**. SEE OBSESSION

family *n., pl.*: **kith and kin**. SEE RELATIVES

family ties *n.*: **propinquity**. SEE KINSHIP

famished *adj.*: **esurient**. SEE HUNGRY

fanatic *n.*: **energumen**. ∎ So Pat Buchanan comes along and argues that Great Britain would have been better off, in 1939, letting Hitler take Poland — and go on to take Moscow. Critics are justified in disagreeing, but it hardly follows from the conjecture that Buchanan is moved by the anti-Semitic **energumen**. (William F. Buckley, Jr., *On the Right*, National Review, 10-25-1999.)

fanciful *adj.*: **chimerical**. SEE UNREALISTIC

(2) fanciful (as in idealistic but likely impractical or unrealistic) *adj.*: **quixotic**. SEE IDEALISTIC

fancy *adj.*: **nobby** [British]. SEE ELEGANT

(2) fancy (as in ornate) *adj.*: **rococo**. SEE ORNATE

fanfare *n.*: **eclat**. SEE ACCLAIM

fans (group of ..., as in fawning admirers) *n.*: **claque**. SEE ADMIRERS

fantasies (having delusional ... about power, fame, omnipotence, etc.) *n.*: **megalomania**. SEE DELUSIONAL

fantasized (or glorified conception of oneself, as a result of boredom in one's life) *n.*: **Bovarism**. SEE SELF-DELUSION

fantastic *adj.*: **frabjous** (often as in "Oh frabjous day!"). SEE WONDERFUL

(2) fantastic *adj.*: **galluptious** [slang]. SEE WONDERFUL

(3) fantastic *adj.*: **palmary**. SEE EXCELLENT

(4) fantastic *adj.*: **skookum**. SEE EXCELLENT

fantasy (living in a world of ..., with a glorified or romanticized conception of oneself, as a result of boredom in one's life) *n.*: **Bovarism**. SEE SELF-DELUSION

(2) fantasy (as in delusion held by two closely associated persons) *n.*: **folie à deux** [French] SEE DELUSION

(3) fantasy (as in delusion) *n.*: **ignis fatuus**. SEE DELUSION

(4) fantasy (as in hope or goal which is not realistically obtainable) *n.*: **will-o'-the-wisp**. SEE PIPE DREAM

farewell (act of bidding ...) *n.*: **valediction**. ∎ And yet, how many times had I flown into Newark International Airport (EWR) and heard that hoary **valediction** from the flight attendant, "If Newark is your final destination, we hope your stay is a pleasant one," without realizing its profound implications. One can chuckle at the comic dimension of the line — the number of fliers who consider Newark their destination is few indeed. (Mark Leyner, *Xmas in Newark [Perspectives on Little Moments That Make up Life]*, Esquire, 12-01-1997, p. 52.)

farming (fit for ...) *adj.*: **arable**. ∎ Since Asia will be nine times as densely populated per acre of **arable** land, farm exports from the Western Hemisphere should be the salvation of that continent's already scarce environmental resources. (Dennis Avery, *What Does the Future Hold for Agriculture?* USA Today Magazine, 05-01-1995.)

farsightedness (as in unable to see close objects) *n.*:

presbyopia. ∎ There's even a surgical solution in the works for **presbyopia**, or aging-eye syndrome — the affliction that drives nearly all middle-aged people into reading glasses. "Bad vision no longer has to be a disability," says Soloway. "It can be fixed, permanently." (Mary Murray, *Features/Laser Eye Surgery: Should You Have Your Eyes Lasered?* Fortune, 09-27-1999, p. 194.)

farthest (as in most distant, or remote, destination or goal) *n.*: **ultima Thule**. SEE DISTANT

farting (of or relating to reducing ...) *adj.*: **carminative**. ∎ Good for treating bad breath and digestive problems, parsley has diuretic properties that help the body get rid of excessive water. It is also a **carminative**, easing flatulence and colic. (Batsheva Mink, *A Bouquet of Herbs*, Jerusalem Post, 08-15-2001, p. 11.)

(2) farting (of or relating to) *adj.*: **borborygmic**. SEE PASSING GAS

fascinate (as in bewitch or enchant) *v.t.*: **ensorcell** (or **ensorcel**). SEE ENCHANT

fashion (out of ...) *adj.*: **démodé** [French]. SEE OUTMODED

(2) fashion (the latest ...) *n.*: **dernier cri** [French]. SEE TREND

fashionable (and wealthy young people) *n.*: **jeunesse dorée** [French]. ∎ One of the most popular topics of conversation among the **jeunesse dorée** of Plettenberg Bay this past vacation season was who had brought their maids down from Johannesburg for the holidays. One blond, bejeweled young mother had worried about taking her "girl" so far from home. "But she's having a super time," she chirped. "She's just yakking away with all her other little friends," that is, the other Johannesburg maids. (Richard Stengel, *Whites [Crime and Race in South Africa]*, The New Republic, 04-22-1996, p. 13.)

(2) fashionable (society) *n.*: **beau monde** [French]. SEE HIGH SOCIETY

(3) fashionable (society) *n.*: **bon ton** [French]. SEE HIGH SOCIETY

(4) fashionable *adj.*: **nobby** [British]. SEE ELEGANT

(5) fashionable *adj.*: **soigné** [French]. SEE ELEGANT

fast *adj.*: **velocious**. ∎ Fasten your seatbelt. Select your course; day or night, novice or expert. Will it be manual or automatic? Get ready. ... Five, four, three, two, one GO!! The car begins to vibrate, humming and jerking, whipping your body around at a **velocious** pace. ... Welcome to GameWorks; computer simulated games at its best. (Author not given, *GameWorks*, Yolk, 09-30-1998, p. 28.)

(2) fast (as in hasty) *adj.*: **festinate**. SEE HASTY

(3) fast (as in at top speed) *adv.*: **tanivy**. SEE TOP SPEED

(4) fast (very ..., as in, in an instant) *n.*: **trice** (as in, in a trice). SEE QUICKLY

fastidious *adj.*: **governessy**. ∎ [M]aria and Christina were **governessy** types whose interior lives were a good deal more intense than their buttoned-up appearance would suggest. (Kathryn Hughes, *Christina Rossetti [Book Reviews]*, New Statesman & Society, 01-06-1995, p. 40.)

(2) fastidious (overly ...) *adj.*: **persnickety**. SEE PICKY

fat *adj.*: **adipose**. ∎ Bank shot Fast Eddie Felson is back and director Martin Scorsese's got him. Fast Eddie, of course, is the pool shark played by Paul Newman in 1961's The Hustler. Jackie Gleason played his **adipose** rival Minnesota Fats. (Author not given, *Screen Preview*, People, 09-01-1986, p. 101.)

(2) fat *adj.*: **Pickwickian** [after the heavy-set Samuel Pickwick in Dickens' 1870 novel *The Pickwick Papers*]. ∎ Appearances did not greatly help. No one, least of all Mr. Pitt, ever doubted his intelligence and erudition. But regulators should have a lean and hungry look. The rotund Mr. Pitt has a **Pickwickian** air. Hard worker though he is, he more easily imagined departing Le Cirque restaurant in New York after a decent lunch than drafting lawsuits against transgressors. (Robert Cornwell, *Business Analysis: How the Pendulum Finally Swung Against [Harvey] Pitt after Series of Gaffes; Heavyweight SEC Chairman Undone by Controversial Hiring of Accounting Watchdog*, The Independent [London], 11-07-2002.)

(3) fat (as in beer-bellied) *adj.*: **abdominous**. SEE BEER-BELLIED

(4) fat (state of being ...) *n.*: **avoirdupois**. SEE WEIGHT

(5) fat (branch of medicine concerning ... people) *n.*: **bariatrics**. SEE OBESITY

(6) fat (condition of being) *n.*: **embonpoint**. SEE PLUMP

(7) fat (person, esp. with a large abdomen) *n.*: **endomorph** (*adj.*: **endomorphic**). SEE POT-BELLIED

(8) fat (and squat) *adj.*: **fubsy**. SEE SQUAT

(9) fat (having a short, ... physique) *adj.*: **pyknic**. SEE STOCKY

(10) fat (woman, as in plump or full-figured) *adj.*: **zaftig** [Yiddish]. SEE FULL-FIGURED

fat ass *n.:* **steatopygia** (having a fat ...) *adj.:* **steatopygic**. SEE REAR END

fatal (as in causing or portending death) *adj.:* **funest**. SEE DEADLY

fate *n.:* **kismet** ∎ Edley ... thought it **kismet** when he won his first U.S. [Scrabble] championship in 1980, but the suspicion that he was nothing but a tool for fate left him depressed — "like a higher power was leading me, and I didn't have much to do with it," Edley says. (S.I. Price, *Scrabble: Your Words Against Mine*, Sports Illustrated, 12-18-1995, p. 106.)

father (biological ... or mother) *n.:* **genitor**. SEE PARENT

(2) father (of a family) *n.:* **paterfamilias**. SEE HEAD OF HOUSEHOLD

(3) father (of, relating to or derived from name of) *adj.:* **patronymic**. SEE PATERNAL

fathom (difficult to ...) *adj.:* **recondite**. SEE COMPLICATED

fatigue (in the muscles) *n.:* **myasthenia** (or **myasthenia gravis**). ∎ In **myasthenia**, the immune system barricades muscle receptors with antibodies, preventing acetylcholine attachment. That results in a feeble muscle contraction. The cardinal symptom of **myasthenia**, therefore, is muscle weakness. (Dr. Paul Donohue, *Advice — Dr. Paul Donohue*, St. Louis Post-Dispatch, 08-20-2001, p. E6.)

(2) fatigue (from lack of energy or nourishment) *n.:* **inanition**. SEE EXHAUSTION

fatigued (as in weakened) *adj.:* **etiolated**. SEE WEAKENED

fault (find ... with on trivial grounds) *v.t.:* **cavil**. SEE QUIBBLE

(2) fault (oneself) *v.t.:* **flagellate** (*n.:* **flagellation**). SEE CRITICIZE

(3) fault (tragic..., esp. in a literary character) *n.:* **hamartia**. SEE FLAW

(4) fault (small or trifling ...) *n.:* **peccadillo**. SEE INFRACTION

faultfinder *n.:* **smellfungus** [derives from Smellfungus, a hypercritical traveler in the Laurence Sterne novel, *A Sentimental Journey Through France and Italy* (1768)]. ∎ The players used [the resignation of Denver Nuggets coach Dan Issel] as a convenient excuse for their own overweening, underachieving ineptitude. "Issel quit on us," the players wailed and whined when they weren't sucking on their thumbs.

And a ... **smellfungus** from the [Rocky Mountain News] carped that Issel chose to jump when the schedule reached its toughest stretch. (Woody Paige, *Issel Is the Wrong Scapegoat in Nuggets' Mess*, The Denver Post, 02-13-1995, p. 2D.)

faultfinding *adj.:* **captious**. ∎ [E]very time Cal [Ripken's] hitting went south, those hard workin' airwaves were filled with **captious** comment. People said Cal ought to sit down. Take a rest. Stop acting like Superman. Stop putting his own streak ahead of the team! (Richard Ben Cramer, *Baseball: A Native Son's Thoughts [Many of Them Heretical] About Baltimore [Which Isn't What It Used To Be]*, Sports Illustrated, 09-11-1995, p. 56.)

(2) faultfinding (as in criticism) *n.:* **animadversion** (*v.t.:* **animadvert**). SEE CRITICISM

faulty (reasoning intended to rationalize or mislead) *n.:* **casuistry**. SEE FALLACIOUS

(2) faulty (and/or illogical argument) *n.:* **choplogic**. SEE FALLACY

(3) faulty (as in fallacious or illogical argument) *n.:* **paralogism** (*adj.:* **paralogical**). SEE FALLACY

favoring (a particular point of view) *adj.:* **tendentious**. SEE BIASED

fawn *v.i.:* **truckle**. SEE KOWTOW

fawner (esp. someone who seeks to associate with or flatter persons of rank or high social status) *n.:* **tufthunter**. SEE HANGER-ON

(2) fawner *n.:* **lickspittle**. SEE SYCOPHANT

fawning (to behave towards in a ... manner) *v.t.:* **bootlick**. SEE KOWTOW

(2) fawning (admirers) *n.:* **claque**. SEE ADMIRERS

(3) fawning (one who seeks favor through ..., esp. of one in power) *n.:* **courtier**. SEE FLATTERY

(4) fawning (as in sycophantic) *adj.:* **gnathonic**. SEE SYCOPHANTIC

(5) fawning (or worshipful biography) *n.:* **hagiography** (*adj:* **hagiographic**). SEE BIOGRAPHY

fear (of heights) *n.:* **acrophobia**. ∎ As someone who had **acrophobia**, I understand how a person can be afraid of things that most others don't find threatening. I beat my **acrophobia** by riding on roller coasters and going to the top of the Eiffel Tower. (Author not given, *Letters*, Time, 04-23-2001, p. 14.)

(2) fear (of air or drafts or flying) *n.:* **aerophobia**. ∎ The horrific terrorist attacks [on the World Trade Center] in New York have meant that even those who were quite happy to fly before are now developing "**aerophobia**." (Caroline Green, *Health: How to Beat Your Fear of Flying*, The Mirror, 11-03-2001, p. 32.)

(3) fear (of open spaces or public places) *n.*: **agora-phobia**. ▪ [S]he suffered a bout of **agoraphobia** in college. It happened during her sophomore year as a drama major at Rutgers University. ... [She] returned home — and spent most of the next eight months on a couch in the den watching TV. The thought of venturing almost anywhere else, she says, would provoke panic attacks that took the form of severe stomachaches. (Michael A. Lipton, *Tube: Phobic No More: Once Overwhelmed by Fear, Leila Kenzle Lets Loose on Mad About You*, People, 12-11-1995, p. 107.)

(4) fear (source or object of ... or dread) *n.*: **hobgoblin**. ▪ Global warming may turn out to be a reality, but right now there are enough reasons to conclude that what is masquerading as the most serious of environmental threats may be just another **hobgoblin** being used to advance agendas that can't survive on their own merits. (William F. O'Keefe, *It's Time to Reconsider Global Climate Change Policy*, USA Today Magazine, 03-01-1997.)

(5) fear (of water) *n.*: **hydrophobia**. ▪ It takes Truman until his thirties to overcome his **hydrophobia** and cross the road-bridge to the mainland. (Matthew Sweet, *Cinema: The Truman Doctrine*, Independent on Sunday, 10-11-1998, p. 5.)

(6) fear (of dirt or contamination) *n.*: **mysophobia**. ▪ Dear Ann: My wife has developed an obsession for clean hands and wears cotton gloves constantly, even at mealtimes. She is also afraid to shake hands with anyone or even hold my hand. ... Dear Concerned: Your wife has **mysophobia**, which is an obsessive-compulsive disorder. This condition is not all that rare. (Ann Landers, *Ann Landers*, Newsday, 11-16-1993, p. 80.)

(7) fear (abnormal ... of death or corpses) *n.*: **necrophobia**. ▪ The Governor, who favors [building a stadium], recently told the people of Minnesota, who do not, that without major league sports the Twin Cities would be like Des Moines, "absolutely dead," which caused some consternation in Iowa and not much in Minnesota, where the fear of being like Des Moines, or **necrophobia**, is not so potent, except in Minneapolis, of course. (Garrison Keillor, *Essay: Sweet Home, Minnesota*, Time, 03-24-1997, p. 108.)

(8) fear (of noises, voices or speaking aloud) *n.*: **phonophobia**. ▪ [K]amau's auditory reception is also marked by a love/hate relationship toward the voice, which can turn abruptly from phonomania to

phonophobia. (Ulrich Schonherr, *Topophony of Fascism: On Marcel Beyer's The Karnau Tapes*, The Germanic Review, 09-22-1998, p. 328.)

(9) fear (abnormal ... of or sensitivity to light) *adj.*: **photophobic**. ▪ Unlike largemouths or sunnies, smallmouths are difficult to keep. Simply turning on the aquarium lights can frighten them because they are **photophobic** and avoid light whenever possible. (Robert H. Boyle, *First Person: I Forget Why I Overimbibed One Night Some 14 Years Ago*, Sports Illustrated, 04-22-1991, p. 102.)

(10) fear (of being buried alive) *n.*: **taphephobia**. ▪ [My mother had] bosoms so large she brought about my **taphephobia** every time we embraced. (Cornelious Biggins, *My Thoughts*, Internet Website www.aledrjones.me.uk/blog_biggins/, 05-17-03.)

(11) fear (as in worry) *v.t., v.i., n.*: **cark**. SEE WORRY

(12) fear (as in anxiety or worry) *n.*: **inquietude**. SEE ANXIETY

(13) fear (that something is going to occur) *n.*: **presentiment**. SEE PREMONITION

(14) fear (of God or God's wrath) *n.*: **theophobia**. SEE GOD

(15) fear (as in panic) *n.*: **Torschlusspanik** [German]. SEE PANIC

(16) fear (or distrust of strangers or foreigners) *n.*: **xenophobia**. SEE DISTRUST

feared (something that is ..., disliked, or to be avoided) *n.*: **bête noire** [French]. SEE DREADED

fearful *adj.*: **tremulous**. ▪ The Gaullist tradition from which Mr. Chirac springs still makes him nervous of the market and **tremulous** at the word "globalisation." ... But ducking the challenge facing France is not the way to recovery. Mr. Chirac and his friends need to win the election — and then find the courage to succeed in a brave new world. (Author not given, *The Chance for France*, The Economist, 05-24-1997.)

(2) fearful (as if by a witch or without reason) *adj.*: **hagridden**. SEE TORMENTED

(3) fearful (as in cowardly) *adj.*: **pusillanimous**. SEE COWARDLY

fearless *adj.*: **doughty**. SEE BRAVE

fearlessness *n.*: **hardihood**. SEE COURAGE

feasible (as in appearing to be true or accurate) *adj.*: **verisimilar**. SEE PLAUSIBLE

February 29 (of or relating to) *adj.*: **bisextile**. SEE LEAP YEAR

fecal (full of ... matter) *adj.*: **feculent**. ▪ The Hon. Joe

Knollenberg, Michigan Republican, is moving to repeal the hateful toilet law passed before the Revolution of 1994 that limits toilets to using 1.6 gallons of water, about half the amount used previously. The Hon. Knollenberg has noted that the new toilets are becoming **feculent** swamps. (Author not given, *The Continuing Crisis: The Big Sleep; Soho Dog Show; Gorby Fails Detector Test*, The American Spectator, 06-01-1997.)

feces (obsession with) *n.*: **coprology**. SEE EXCREMENT

(2) feces (interest in ..., often sexual) *n.*: **coprophilia**. SEE EXCREMENT

(3) feces (feeding on) *n.*: **coprophagous**. SEE EXCREMENT

(4) feces *n.*: **egesta**. SEE EXCREMENT

(5) feces (study of or obsession with) *n.*: **scatology**. SEE EXCREMENT

(6) feces (eating) *adj.*: **scatophagous**. SEE EXCREMENT

(7) feces (of or relating to) *adj.*: **stercoraceous**. SEE EXCREMENT

feeble (as in weakened) *adj.*: **etiolated**. SEE WEAKENED

(2) feeble (and ineffective) *adj.*: **feckless**. SEE INEFFECTIVE

(3) feeble (as in powerless) *adj.*: **impuissant**. SEE POWERLESS

(4) feeble (as in decrepit) *adj.*: **spavined**. SEE DECREPIT

(5) feeble (elderly person) *n.*: **Struldbrug**. SEE DECREPIT

feeble-minded (psychiatric diagnosis for one who is ..., as in retarded) *adj.*: **oligophrenic**. SEE RETARDED

feebleness (that comes with old age) *n.*: **caducity**. SEE OLD AGE

feed (excessive desire to ... oneself) *n.*: **polyphagia**. SEE APPETITE

feel (having ... through the senses) *adj.*: **sensate**. ∎ [The candidate] was running on sheer willpower now; he was not entirely **sensate**, and the ceremonies of the stump — meeting, greeting, talking, walking — were performed reflexively. (Joe Klein, *Primary Colors*, Random House [1996], p. 167.)

(2) feel (around with one's hands) *v.i.*: **grabble**. SEE GROPE

(3) feel (as in of or relating to sense of touch) *adj.*: **haptic**. SEE TOUCH

(4) feel (as in touch, esp. for medical reasons) *v.t.*: **palpate**. SEE TOUCH

feeling (as in aura or impalpable emantion) *n.*: **effluvium**. SEE AURA

(2) feeling (medical examination by ... the body) *n.*: **palpation**. SEE TOUCHING

(3) feeling (that something is going to occur) *n.*: **presentiment**. SEE PREMONITION

feet (having two ...) *adj.*: **biped**. ∎ I blame my plight [being short] on my ancestors. Protoancestors, to be precise. If they hadn't risen to the challenge of evolution, abandoned their tails, and stood upright on two feet, I wouldn't be so downcast. Within an eon or two, nature seemed to favor the fastest, strongest, and tallest **bipeds**. (Melissa Rossi, *A Shorty Speaks Up*, Cosmopolitan, 08-01-1994, p. 106.)

feign (sickness or other incapacity to avoid work) *v.i.*: **malinger**. SEE SHIRK

fell (with an ax) *v.t.*: **hew**. SEE AX

felon *n.*: **malefactor**. SEE WRONGDOER

female SEE WOMAN

femininity *n.*: **muliebrity**. ∎ Even more than shunning make-up, women felt that (in the U.S. at least) hair on our legs, under our arms, and on our face indisputably affronts the narrow boundaries of patriarchally-constructed **muliebrity**. Only one of us could recall an instance in which the mainstream media has featured a woman with body hair (Susan Sarandon in White Palace). (Author not given, *Exploration of Issues-Women's Bodies*, Contemporary Women's Issues Database, 01-01-1992.)

ferret (out) *v.t.*: **fossick** [Australian]. SEE RUMMAGE

fertile *adj.*: **fecund**. ∎ The manatee population continues to grow despite the few that are killed in boating accidents, just as our deer populations continue to thrive despite the deer that are struck on the highways. Manatees are not particularly **fecund** animals, but they have no natural predators. (Frank Sargeant, *Manatees Are Not Endangered Species*, The Tampa Tribune, 09-13-2000, p. 3.)

(2) fertile (in producing offspring) *adj.*: **philoprogenitive**. ∎ Vavasour was supposed to be an illegitimate son of the late **philoprogenitive** Sir Thomas, and thus Francis Tresham's half-brother. (Antonia Fraser, *Faith & Treason*, Doubleday [1996], p. 200.)

festive (and social) *adj.*: **Anacreontic**. SEE CON-VIVIAL

fetus (of or relating to malformations in) *adj.*: **teratogenic**. ■ [M]cBride noticed that a disturbing number of women who had been taking the anti-morning-sickness drug thalidomide gave birth to children with terrible limb deformities. After he outlined his concerns in a 1961 letter to the British medical journal The Lancet, the drug's **teratogenic** effects were confirmed and it was withdrawn from sale. (Lisa Clausen, *Time 100: Pioneers Of Medicine*, Time International, 10-25-1999, p. 65.)

(2) fetus (destruction of) *n.*: **feticide**. SEE ABORTION

fever (reducing) *adj.*: **antipyretic**. ■ Fever, however, makes people feel awful. So, it's all right to use **antipyretics** for comfort during ubiquitous illnesses, such as colds and flu. (Dr. Peter Gott, *Let Body's Defenses Kick In*, The Ottawa Sun, 10-30-2001, p. 36.)

(2) fever (alternating with chills) *n.*: **ague**. SEE CHILLS

feverish *adj.*: **febrile**. ■ My mind is like a fly; it buzzes around in a ... **febrile** fashion, and when it alights on some crumb or fragment of an idea, it's off again before I can apprehend a thing. (Will Self, *Inclusion [Short Story]*, Esquire, 02-01-1995, p. 108.)

fib *n.*: **fabulation** (one who does so: **fabulist**). SEE LIE

(2) fib (petty or minor ...) *n.*: **taradiddle** (or **tarradiddle**). SEE LIE

fickle (one that is ... or varies with trends) *n.*: **weathercock**. ■ Far from being a unifier, Mr. Chirac is seen increasingly as a man of few convictions or ideas; power alone is his compass. Indeed, he looks like one of the great **weathercocks** of French politics. Once an outright Europhobe, now a lukewarm "pro-European." (Author not given, *Jacques Chirac, Out of Steam*, The Economist, 07-31-1999.)

(2) fickle *adj.*: **labile**. SEE CHANGABLE

fiction (work of ... published in installments) *n.*: **feuilleton** [French]. SEE NOVEL

(2) fiction (which is dark, gloomy, remote and/or grotesque) *adj.*: **gothic**. SEE DARK

fidelity (as in loyalty) *n.*: **fealty** SEE LOYALTY

fidgeting (as in a state of nervous tension, often with irritability) *n.*: **fantod**. SEE TENSION

field (as in area of activity or interest) *n.*: **purlieu**. SEE DOMAIN

fierce (as in wild or untamed) *adj.*: **farouche** [French]. SEE UNTAMED

fiery (and infernal) *adj.*: **sulfurous** (or **sulphurous**). SEE INFERNAL

fifty (years or a person who is ... or in his fifties) *n., adj.*: **quinquagenarian**. ■ DiMaggio was lucky to garner a [single] or better in 56 straight games in 1941, a feat you will be hearing a lot about in the **quinquagenarian** year of this astounding feat. (Daniel Seligman, *Keeping Up: Luck in the Batter's Box*, Fortune, 05-06-1991, p. 115.)

fight (initiate a ... or violence) *v.i.*: **aggress**. ■ There are some, such as Joshua Andrews, who need special help in learning not to **aggress**. By the time Joshua had reached the age of 2, says his mother, Susan Andrews, he ... kicked and head-butted relatives and friends. He poked the family hamster with a pencil and tried to strangle it. (Constance Holden, *The Violence of the Lambs*, Science, 07-28-2000.)

(2) fight (people who ... as if to the death) *n.*: **Kilkenny cats** (esp. as in "fight like Kilkenny cats") [British; after an 1846 cartoon entitled "Kilkenny cats." The caption reads "Oh, leave them alone, They'll fight to the bone, And leave naught but their tails behind 'em."]. ■ While many Liberals [in the Australian Labor Party] talk of a "union bloc," many unions are in different and opposing factions. They agree on some issues, but often disagree and **fight like Kilkenny cats** — particularly when they are competing for members. (Mark Skulley, *Battle Of The Networks*, Australian Financial Review, 09-27-2002.)

(3) fight (esp. public) *n.*: **affray**. SEE BRAWL

(4) fight (ready to ... or pugnacious) *adj.*: **bellicose**. SEE BELLIGERENT

(5) fight (for an idea or principle) *n.*: **jihad**. SEE CRUSADE

(6) fight (as in hostile meeting) *n.*: **rencontre** [French]. SEE DUEL

(7) fight (as in heated disagreement or friction between groups) *n.*: **ruction**. SEE DISSENSION

fighting (with a shadow or imaginary foe) *n.*: **sciamachy**. SEE SHADOW-BOXING

(2) fighting (or conflict among the gods) *n.*: **theomachy**. SEE GODS

figure of speech (in which one references an issue by saying that he will not discuss it; e.g. "I'm not even going to get into the character issue.") *n.*: **apophasis**. ■ [A friend told me that] Bush used ...

apophasis [in his debate with Michael Dukakis]. ... Mr. Bush began a rebuttal with "There's so many things [to challenge] there I don't quite know where to begin," that disarming pretense of being at a loss for words. [Safire's friend's use of this word in this context is correct if we assume that Bush did not in fact start challenging whatever he found wrong with Dukakis's statement and had no intention of doing so.] (William Safire, *On Language* [*Debatesmanship*], The New York Times, 10-09-1988.)

(2) figure of speech (as in using one word or phrase in place of something with which it is usually associated, such as using "city hall" to refer to city government) *n.*: **metonymy**. ∎ You thank Defense Secretary Donald H. Rumsfeld for scolding reporters who repeatedly say "The White House says" and pointing out that "White Houses do not talk ... buildings can't speak." Not to be overly pedantic, but aren't reporters merely engaging in the time-honored use of **metonymy**? (Tim Toner [letter writer], *He's the Secretary of Stating the Obvious*, Chicago Sun-Times, 02-10-2002, p. 10.)

(3) figure of speech (in which one makes only passing mention of something in order to emphasize rhetorically the significance of what is being omitted; often preceded by the phrase "not to mention") *n.*: **paraleipsis**. ∎ The trick in playing the [blame game] is to play to win by denouncing the playing of it by the other side, thus associating oneself with a voter's self-deluding self-image as a reasonable and nonpartisan person who hates bickering. The astute player of the blame game thereby avoids the easily seen-through **paraleipsis** of "I refuse to get down in the gutter with my opponent by reminding you of his prior convictions — " etc. (William Safire, *The Blame Game*, The New York Times, 06-02-2002.)

(4) figure of speech (where a part is used to stand for the whole or vice versa) *n.*: **synecdoche**. ∎ Auschwitz has indeed come to serve as a **synecdoche** for the Nazis' deliberate, systematic destruction of the European Jews. (D.D. Guttenplan, *The Holocaust on Trial*, Norton [2001], p. 21.)

(5) figure of speech *n.*: **trope**. ∎ In the most general terms, a key **trope** has been Thabo Mbeki's evocation of the "African Renaissance" to describe the moment, continental and national, that he and his [African National Congress] now embrace. (John S. Saul, *Cry for the Beloved Country: The Post-Apartheid Denouement*, Monthly Review, 01-01-2001, p. 1.)

(6) figure of speech *n.*: **façon de parler** [French]. SEE WAY OF SPEAKING

fill (to the point of excess, esp. with things sweet) *v.t.*: **cloy**. SEE SATIATE

filled (with) *adj.*: **aswarm**. SEE TEEMING

filler (words such as *um, uh, you know*, etc.) *n.*: **embolalia** (or **embololalia**). SEE STAMMERING

film (lover) *n.*: **cineaste**. SEE MOVIE

(2) film (lover) *n.*: **cinephile**. SEE MOVIE

filth (place of ..., as in corruption) *n.*: **Augean stable**. SEE CORRUPTION

(2) filth (abnormal fear of) *n.*: **mysophobia**. SEE FEAR

filthy (full of ... matter, such as feces) *adj.*: **feculent**. SEE FECAL

final (stroke or blow) *n.*: **quietus** (esp. as in "put the quietus to"). SEE TERMINATE

(2) final (as in decisive remark, blow or factor) *n.*: **sockdolager**. SEE DECISIVE

(3) final (point or destination) *n.*: **terminus**. SEE END

final resort *n.*: **pis aller** [French]. SEE LAST RESORT

financial *adj.*: **pecuniary**. SEE MONETARY

find (lucky ...) *n.*: **trouvaille** [French]. ∎ Currin lives on the western edge of SoHo. ... To enter his apartment, which occupies a space that previously belonged to a dry cleaner, you knock on a window. The place is furnished casually with thrift-shop **trouvailles** and shag rugs. (Deborah Solomon, *Mr. Bodacious*, The New York Times, 11-16-2003.)

finding (fortunate things by accident) *n.*: **serendipity** (*adj.*: **serendipitous**). SEE FORTUITOUS

fine (impose a monetary ...) *v.t.*: **amerce**. ∎ On December 15, 2003, Tianjin Municipality announced that [it] would start banning any company or individual from making, selling, and using undegraded super thin plastic bags. Otherwise law enforcement officials will **amerce** a lawbreaking seller [$3,625]. (Author not given, *Tianjin to Stop Using Undegraded Plastic Bags*, AsiaInfo Services, 12-23-2003.)

(2) fine (very ...) *adj.*: **frabjous** (often as in "Oh frabjous day!"). SEE WONDERFUL

(3) fine (very ...) *adj.*: **galumptious**. SEE EXCELLENT

(4) fine (as in penalty) *n., v.t.*: **mulct**. SEE PENALIZE

(5) fine (as in first-class) *adj.*: **pukka**. SEE FIRST-CLASS

(6) fine (very ...) *adj.*: **skookum**. SEE EXCELLENT

fine points (precise observance of ... of etiquette) *n.*: **punctilio**. SEE ETIQUETTE

finery *n.*: **caparison**. ∎ There are art lovers, after all, who are mainly in it for a touch of the high life, elegance, opulence, pageantry. Pisanello is certainly their man. His work shows a keen delight in costumes, accessories and ornaments, regalia and **caparisons**. (Tom Lubbock, *The Case of the Missing Master*, Independent, 10-23-2001, p. 10.)

(2) finery (showy article of ...) *n.*: **frippery**. ∎ [Designer Vera Wang] first forged her reputation with bridal dresses that banished the lacy **fripperies** adorning wedding-cake dolls in favor of the glowing sheen of modern romance. (Hal Rubenstein, *The Look: The Look Of Vera Wang*, In Style, 12-01-2000, p. 142.)

(3) finery (showy article of ... or attire) *n.*: **froufrou**. SEE CLOTHING

fingers (having more than normal number of ... or toes) *adj.*: **polydactyl**. SEE TOES

finicky (overly ...) *adj.*: **persnickety**. SEE PICKY

finisher (as in decisive remark, blow or factor) *n.*: **sockdolager**. SEE DECISIVE

finishing (stroke or blow) *n.*: **quietus** (esp. as in "put the quietus to"). SEE TERMINATE

fireball (meteoric ...) *n.*: **bolide**. ∎ Once scientists had used the Apollo trove to learn the geological signature of meteorite impacts on the moon, Spudis said, they were then able to recognize signs of similar events on Earth — notably the Yucatan imprint of the huge **bolide** that wiped out the dinosaurs 65 million years ago. (Kathy Sawyer, *After Apollo 11; What's Happened Since*, The Washington Post, 07-14-1999, p. H8.)

firm (in holding to a belief or opinion) *adj.*: **pertinacious**. SEE STUBBORN

first (in sequence or time) *adj.*: **primordial**. ∎ The [Indian] rishis believed that, just as each animal has its signature call, the universe also generates a unique "sound" that changes every eight hours in a lunar cycle. At the time of your birth, the universe had a particular sound — this is your **primordial** mantra. (Rita Silvan, *Roots Music*, Flare: Canada's Fashion Magazine, 04-01-2000, p. 88.)

(2) first (among equals) *n.*: **primus inter pares** [Latin]. ∎ Sudarsono is one of many who think that the void after Suharto will initially be filled by the armed forces. There is simply no one else with enough clout. What is likely to take over, he expects, is a "military collective" from which a new leader will emerge as **primus inter pares**, much as Suharto did 30 years ago. (Author not given, *The*

Army Can Control the Political Opposition, But May Itself be Divided, The Economist, 07-26-1997.)

first-class *adj.*: **pukka**. ∎ The one I drink is Lille Blanc. Buy a bottle for around pounds 9.50 if you can find it at Threshers, or at superior independents such as La Vigneronne (0171 589 6113) and **pukka** outlets such as Selfridges and Harrods. (Richard Ehrlich, *Richard Ehrlich's Beverage Report: Rebranding for Britain*, Independent on Sunday, 08-30-1998, p. 30.)

first-rate (as in of the highest quality) *n.*: **first water** (usu. as in "of the first water"). SEE QUALITY

(2) first-rate *adj.*: **galumptious**. SEE EXCELLENT

(3) first-rate *adj.*: **pukka**. SEE FIRST-CLASS

(4) first-rate *adj.*: **palmary**. SEE EXCELLENT

(5) first-rate *adj.*: **skookum**. SEE EXCELLENT

firstborn (child) *n.*: **primogeniture**. ∎ Nepotism rules at Brown-Forman, a meritocratic sort of nepotism for the most part, but one that still allows **primogeniture** to determine who becomes CEO. (Brett Duval Fromson, *Dynasties: Keeping it All in the Family*, Fortune, 09-25-1989, p. 86.)

fish (study of) *n.*: **ichthyology**. [T]he group was playing the biggest trivia game in America — "Showdown" on the National Trivia Network (NTN). Questions rolled up with multiple choice answers. Players scrambled to log in the right one in a matter of seconds: ... "Which fish can grow over 500 pounds?" "The striped marlin!" chimed several who knew their **ichthyology**. (Walt Belcher, *Bar Wars*, The Tampa Tribune, 08-31-2001, p. 20.)

(2) fish (eating or feeding on) *adj.*: **ichthyophagous**. ∎ Though most often seen fishing, the great blue [heron] is not entirely **ichthyophagous**. It also eats frogs, snakes, insects, and small mammals. In fact, it will even eat small birds. (Ian de Silva, *A Feathered Friend Stands Tall*, The World & I, 04-01-1996, p. 192.)

(3) fish (of or relating to) *adj.*: **piscatorial**. ∎ Host of the syndicated TV show Good Fishing, which appears in 89 markets, Babe is America's hottest video angler. Each week some 2 to 3 million armchair anglers tune in for 30 minutes of easy-to-follow advice from the perfect master of things **piscatorial**. (Jack Friedman, *Jocks: Playing All the Anglers, TV's Babe Winkelman Hooks a Huge Piscatorial Audience*, People, 09-11-1989, p. 132.)

(4) fish (of or relating to) *adj.*: **piscine**. ∎ [At Le Bernardin], the late Gilbert Le Coze revolutionized seafood cookery and forever changed the way we eat it. ... Le Coze's influence is reflected in the growing number of superb chefs ... who have developed their own distinctive styles. Le Bernardin may still reign as the great **piscine** paragon, but these chefs aren't just pretenders to the throne; they're its legitimate heirs. (John Mariani, *Who's the Biggest Fish Now?[Seafood Restaurants]*, Esquire, 09-01-1997, p. 146.)

(5) fish (eating or feeding on) *adj.*: **piscivorous**. ▪ Unlike the entrepreneurs who took American fast food to Europe and Canada, Fujita had to induce his customers [in Japan] to try a new diet [McDonald's food]. Had he failed, the Japanese might still be a **piscivorous** people; he argues that eating fish leaves people looking "pale-faced and undignified." (Frederick Hiroshi Katayama, *Profile: Japan's Big Ma — In the Land of Sushi, Den Fujita Operates McDonald's Biggest Overseas Venture*, Fortune, 09-15-1986, p. 114.)

(6) fish (with a net) *v.t., v.i.*: **seine**. ▪ His hands were raised in front of him, stretched as high as he could reach [for the spider], and his fingers languorously combed the air. ... His **seining** fingers, stained with blood, looked crushingly strong. (Dean Koontz, *Intensity*, Knopf [1995], p. 32.)

fishing (of or related to ...) *adj.*: **halieutic**. ▪ In two volumes — A History of Flyfishing (1992) and The Dry Fly [1996] — he evoked with relish and gentle erudition the deep pleasure he found in the origins and traditions of his passionate pursuit, and his pages were free of that claptrap and mumbo-jumbo from which much **halieutic** prose frequently suffers. (Tam Dalyell, *Obituary: Conrad Voss Bark*, The Independent [London], 11-28-2000.)

fit (as in temper tantrum) *n.*: **boutade** [French]. See TEMPER TANTRUM

(2) fit (of emotion, feeling or action) *n.*: **paroxysm**. See OUTBURST

fit out (as in outfit or equip) *v.t.*: **accouter**. See OUTFIT

fitting *adj.*: **apposite**. See RELEVANT

(2) fitting (as in appropriate) *adj.*: **comme il faut** [French]. See PROPER

(3) fitting (esp. in reference to a punishment) *adj.*: **condign**. See DESERVED

(4) fitting (as in appropriate) *adj.*: **felicitous**. See APPROPRIATE

five (group of) *n.*: **pentad**. Rigsbee says the success of partnering is based on the partnering **pentad**, the five key areas of every business. (Author not given, *Building A Better Business Through Partnering*, Trailer/Body Builders, 01-01-1998.)

(2) five (occurring once every ... years) *n.*: **quinquennial**. ▪ In this study we investigate male and female age-specific suicide rates in Quebec for every five-year interval from 1931 to 1986. Five- year intervals are observed because many of the data in this analysis are derived from the **quinquennial** censuses of Canada and the provinces, including Quebec. (Catherine Krull, *The Quiet Revolution and the Sex Differential in Quebec's Suicide Rates: 1931-1986*, Social Forces, 06-01-1994, p. 1121.)

fix (text or language by removing errors or flaws) *v.t.*: **blue-pencil**. See EDIT

(2) fix (text or language by removing errors or flaws) *v.t.*: **emend**. See EDIT

(3) fix (up, as in spruce up) *v.t.*: **titivate**. See SPRUCE UP

fixation (on an idea or concept) *n.*: **idée fixe** [French]. See OBSESSION

(2) fixation (undue ... on one subject or idea) *n.*: **monomania**. See OBSESSION

(3) fixation (with shopping) *n.*: **oniomania**. See SHOPPING

fixing (as in atoning for) *adj.*: **piacular**. See ATONING

flag (suspended from a crossbar, as opposed to on a flagstaff) *n.*: **gonfalon**. See BANNER

(2) flag (an inspiring ...) *n.*: **oriflamme**. See BANNER

flagrant (as in infamous, esp. as to a crime or evil deed) *adj.*: **flagitious**. See SCANDALOUS

flags (study of ...) *n.*: **vexillology**. ▪ Artist Dread Scott's work, "What is the Proper Way to Display the U.S. Flag?" involves placing the flag on the floor and inviting visitors to walk over it to sign the artist's book. ... Despite the furor, college officials said there are no plans to remove the Exhibit, "**Vexillology**: The American Symbol in Art," which features a dozen artists' work scheduled to run through Oct. 1 at the college. (Olivia Winslow, *Flag Art Exhibit Raises Objections/Despite Furor, College Has No Plans to Remove Work*, Newsday, 09-11-2003.)

flair (having ... as magnetism or charm) *n.*: **duende**. See CHARISMA

flamboyant (as in ornate) *adj.*: **baroque**. See ORNATE

(2) flamboyant (as in ornate) *adj.*: **florid**. See ORNATE

flap (on airplane wing) *n.*: **aileron**. ∎ Ideally, rubber de-icer boots expand and contract to break off ice as it forms on leading edge. Air flows smoothly over the wing, maintaining pressure over the **aileron**. (Stephen J. Hedges, *Fear of Flying: One Plane's Story*, U.S. News & World Report, 03-06-1995, p. 40.)

flash-forward (spec. acting as if or threatening that a future event [usually unwanted] has already occurred by reference to an event that precedes it, for example "if you look at my diary, you're dead") *n.*: **prolepsis**. SEE PREDICTION

flashing (as in emitting flashes of light) *adj.*: **coruscant**. SEE GLITTERING

flashy (as in ornate) *adj.*: **baroque**. SEE ORNATE
(2) flashy (but cheap, or such an object) *adj., n.*: **brummagem**. SEE SHOWY
(3) flashy (as in ornate) *adj.*: **florid**. SEE ORNATE
(4) flashy (but cheap or tasteless, or such an object) *adj., n.*: **gimcrack**. SEE SHOWY
(5) flashy (in a gaudy way) *adj.*: **meretricious**. SEE GAUDY

flatterer *n.*: **lickspittle**. SEE SYCOPHANT
(2) flatterer (esp. someone who seeks to associate with or flatter persons of rank or high social status) *n.*: **tuft-hunter**. SEE HANGER-ON

flattering (insincerely ...) *adj.*: **fulsome**. SEE INSINCERE
(2) flattering (as in sycophantic) *adj.*: **gnathonic**. SEE SYCOPHANTIC

flattery (coaxing by ...) *n.*: **blandishment** (*v.t.*: **blandish**). ∎ But why would a woman mature enough to vote, have an abortion, or pilot a nuclear bomber be too fragile to resist the **blandishments** of a male, however "powerful"? In Lewinsky's case it isn't even a question of **blandishments**; she made the first move, on her own story. (George Jonas, *Bill and the Big Lie*, The Toronto Sun, 12-17-1998, p. 17.)
(2) flattery (one who seeks favor through ..., esp. of one in power) *n.*: **courtier**. ∎ Sometimes it is a sense that pomposity or flattery cries out to be pricked. Even Louis XIV, not famous for his humility, felt that a **courtier** had gone too far when he compared, "not the king to God, but God to the king." "Too much, monsieur," was the monarch's murmured rebuke, "is always too much." (Godfrey Hodgson, *Moments of Truth*, Independent, 03-09-1996, p. 6.)
(3) flattery (to win over or obtain by ... or coaxing) *v.t.*: **inveigle**. SEE LURE
(4) flattery *n.*: **palaver**. SEE sweet TALK

flatulence (of or relating to reducing ...) *adj.*: **carminative**. SEE FARTING

flavor (which is delicious) *n.*: **ambrosia** (*adj.*: **ambrosial**). ∎ Tropical Shrimp Salad — For a refreshing lunch on a steamy summer day, try this **ambrosial** mix of coconut milk, orange juice, and jalapeno pepper sauce splashed over cooked shrimp, Boston lettuce, and Texmati rice. (Author not given, *Salads That Really Satisfy*, Redbook, 08-01-1996, p. 123.)

flavorful *adj.*: **sapid**. SEE TASTY

flaw (tragic ..., esp. in a literary character) *n.*: **hamartia**. ∎ [For director Oliver Stone] Nixon [was] undercut by his strict puritanical upbringing, his lack of charm especially vis-a-vis Kennedy, and his not having the right school tie and social background. These minuses [in the movie "Nixon"] are meant to add up to the **hamartia**, the tragic flaw in Nixon's potentially heroic stature. (John Simon, *Nixon [Movie Reviews]*, National Review, 02-12-1996, p. 57.)

flawed *adj.*: **peccable**. ∎ "I understand the politics of this country better than anyone else in it," Hawke thundered. "My judgment on major political events has been impeccable." Most Australians, however, consider him **peccable** indeed. In the face of a deepening recession and a 10.5% unemployment rate, Hawke's approval rating in opinion polls has sunk to its lowest level ever. (Damien Murphy, *Asia/Pacific*, Time International, 12-23-1991, p. 22.)
(2) flawed (reasoning intended to rationalize or mislead) *n.*: **casuistry**. SEE FALLACIOUS
(3) flawed (and/or illogical argument) *n.*: **choplogic**. SEE FALLACY
(4) flawed (engaging in argument which may be ..., as in specious) *adj., n.*: **eristic**. SEE SPECIOUS
(5) flawed (as in fallacious or illogical, argument) *n.*: **paralogism** (*adj.*: **paralogical**). SEE FALLACY

flecked (with a darker color) *adj.*: **brindled**. SEE SPOTTED

flee (as in a departure which is unannounced, abrupt, secret or unceremonious) *n.*: **French Leave**. SEE DEPARTURE

fleece (as in deceive) *v.t.*: **hornswoggle**. SEE DECEIVE

fleeing (desperate ..., as in retreat) *n.*: **Dunkirk**. SEE RETREAT

fleeting *adj.*: **fugacious**. ∎ On Sunday mornings I

get up early and [go to a] café, ... nurse a doppio espresso and consider my options. Between making a living, barely, and parenting, an occupation that keeps me fully employed in an emotional economy with its own recessions and surges, considering my options is a luxury, **fugacious** though it is. (R.W. Lucky, *What I Want to Be After My Child Grows Up*, The Seattle Times, 03-27-1994, p. L5.)

(2) fleeting *adj.*: **evanescent**. SEE TRANSIENT

fleshy (condition of having a ... physique) *n.*: **embonpoint**. SEE PLUMP

(2) fleshy (person, esp. with a large abdomen) *n.*: **endomorph** (*adj.*: **endomorphic**). SEE POT-BEL-LIED

flexible (as in pliable) *adj.*: **ductile**. SEE PLIABLE

flickering (light ... softly over a surface) *adj.*: **lambent**. SEE SHIMMERING

flight (desperate ..., as in retreat) *n.*: **Dunkirk**. SEE RETREAT

(2) flight (from danger) *n.*: **hegira**. SEE ESCAPE

flighty (person) *n.*: **flibbertigibbet**. ▪ Ultimately, Siggins concludes, a plethora of such triumphs must signal the end of "those demoralizing and demeaning stereotypes that have shadowed women like an ugly, black cloud since time immemorial ... the ridiculous point of view that posits women as morally weak, intellectually inferior, the **flibbertigibbets** of the ages, is finally being exposed for what it is: a lie." (Elizabeth Abbott, *A Class Act*, The Toronto Star, 04-23-2000.)

flimsy (as in sheer or transparent) *adj.*: **diaphanous**. SEE TRANSPARENT

(2) flimsy (as in sheer or transparent) *adj.*: **gossamer**. SEE TRANSPARENT AND TENUOUS

flinch (as in draw back from or shy away from) *v.i.*: **blench**. ▪ [Russian] strongman Alexander Lebed ... hawks law and order in a way that would make any redneck sheriff **blench**. (Josef Joffe, *Viewpoint: Embracing Mr. Wonderful: The West's Problems with Russia Haven't Been Resolved by Yeltsin's Victory*, Time International, 07-15-1996, p. 26.)

(2) flinch *v.i.*: **resile**. SEE RECOIL

fling (as in love affair) *n.*: **amourette** [French]. SEE LOVE AFFAIR

flirtatious (glance) *n.*: **oeillade** [French]. SEE GLANCE

float (dancer's seeming ability to ...) *n.*: **ballon** [French]. ▪ An impossible consummation may be the definition of all ballet: the great dancer's yearning to become totally airborne and never to touch ground. Ballet is **ballon** writ large: the defeat of the force of gravity. (John Simon, *The Master and the Muse*, [Choreographer George Balanchine and Dancer Suzanne Farrell], The New Leader, 02-10-1997, p. 21.)

(2) float (along swiftly and easily, used esp. of clouds) *v.i.*: **scud**. SEE MOVE

flock (of geese) *n.*: **gaggle** (generally as in ... of geese). SEE GEESE

(2) flock (as in parish or congregation) *n.*: **laity**. SEE PARISH

flog (oneself) *v.t.*: **flagellate** (*n.*: **flagellation**). SEE CRITICIZE

(2) flog (generally used figuratively) *v.t.*: **larrup**. SEE WHIP

flood (of, relating to or produced by) *adj.*: **diluvial**. ▪ A storm broke out as we entered Tetema in late afternoon. **Diluvial** rain clattered on corrugated zinc roofs and cascaded into buckets. (Victor Englebert, *A Joyful Funeral: Ghana's Rite of Eternal Rest*, The World & I, 05-01-2000, p. 198.)

floral (arrangement) *n.*: **nosegay**. SEE BOUQUET

flounce (so as to attract attention) *v.i.*: **tittup**. SEE STRUT

flounder (around with one's hands) *v.i.*: **grabble**. SEE GROPE

flourish (often at another's expense) *v.i.*: **batten**. SEE THRIVE

flower (cluster) *n.*: **inflorescence**. ▪ The most aggressive of the male bushes is Skimmia japonica "Rubella." Its flowers may be tiny, but they are produced in huge conical heads, several hundreds packed tightly together in one **inflorescence** that can be 9 in. tall and 3-4 in. across at the base. (Fred Whitsey, *Gardening: Fortune's Favourite Skimmia Sex Wars*, The Daily Telegraph, 02-05-2000.)

(2) flower (petals of a ... taken separately or as a whole) *n.*: **corolla**. SEE PETALS

flowering (as in blooming) *n.*: **efflorescence**. SEE BLOOMING

(2) flowering (as in blooming) *n.*: **florescence**. SEE BLOOMING

flowers (bearing ...) *adj.*: **floriferous**. ▪ In February

2002 garden centres will be full of hebe "Pink Pixie" — a very disease-resistant variety. A good compact shrub, it's hugely **floriferous** and is better than hebe "Rosie." (Howard Drury, *Living: All Change!* Sunday Mercury, 09-16-2001, p. 38.)

(2) flowers (bunch of ...) *n*.: **nosegay**. See bouquet

flowery (as in ornate) *adj*.: **florid**. See ornate

flowing (out or forth) *n*.: **effluence**. See emanation
(2) flowing (of, relating to or living in ... water systems, such as rivers and streams) *adj*.: **lotic**. See water

fluffy (having a ... appearance) *adj*.: **flocculent**. ▪ Today, however, the glass (which is populated by cherubs, a celestial mother figure, a harp or two, ethereal blue sky and sunlit, **flocculent** clouds) isn't restored so much as reborn. (James B. Meadow, *Great Panes Restoring, Creating Stained Glass Is Precision Work*, Denver Rocky Mountain News, 10-10-1998, p. 3D.)

flustered *adj*.: **in a dither**. ▪ She had never been away from her puppyhood home and the separation from me and the presence of all the other dogs left her **in a dither**. (Lars Eighner, *Travels With Lizbeth*, St. Martin's Press [1993], p. 10.)

flutter (one's eyes) *v.i.*: **nictitate**. See blink

flying (fear of ...) *n*.: **aerophobia**. See fear
(2) flying (esp. too high for safety) *adj*.: **Icarian**. See soaring

focal point (of attention) *n*.: **cynosure**. See center of attention

focus (emotional energy on an object, idea or person) *v.t.*: **cathect** (*n*.: **cathexis**). ▪ The real problem, in other words, is that there is no strong male within the prison with whom Marie Allen, the protagonist, can **cathect**. She is thus thrown to the mercy of "the boys" who run a shoplifting syndicate, which eventually recruits her for a life of continued crime. (Anne Morey, *"The Judge Called Me an Accessory,"* [Women's Prison Films], Journal of Popular Film and Television, 06-01-1995, p. 80.)
(2) focus (of attention) *n*.: **cynosure**. See center of attention
(3) focus (undue ... on one subject or idea) *n*.: **monomania**. See obsession

fog *n*.: **brume**. ▪ Whiteness: the perfect whiteness of an enveloping fog. Muted sounds: voices, the creak of sails and rigging. Very slowly, the outlines of a 19th century sailing ship begin to take shape through the **brume**. (Richard Schickel, *Cinema: Hail the Epic-Size Hero*, Time, 01-02-1989, p. 94.)
(2) fog (over one's vision) *v.t.*: **obnubilate**. See obscure

foil (as in person who serves as a ... to another) *n*.: **deuteragonist**. See secondary

fold (of loose skin hanging from neck, esp. of cattle, but also of people) *n*.: **dewlap**. See jowl
(2) fold (or wrinkle) *n., v.t.*: **rimple**. See wrinkle

follow (slowly) *v.i.*: **draggle**. ▪ A year ago, when Carolina Herrera showed bustles and a few other [dress] designers showed trains, it seemed like a joke. Then trains **draggled** across the stage after several movie stars at the Oscars. (Patricia McLaughlin, *The Train Chugs Into the Future*, St. Louis Post-Dispatch, 10-13-1994, p. 8.)
(2) follow (as in happen or occur) *v.t.*: **betide**. See happen
(3) follow (closely to a line, rule, or principle) *v.i.*: **hew**. See conform
(4) follow (apt to ... as opposed to leading) *adj*.: **sequacious**. See subservient

follower (devoted) *adj*.: **acolyte**. ▪ Observes Kristol, a senior Bush Administration official: "Newt [Gingrich is] a complicated man; there's a lot of ego there, and there's a little bit of susceptibility to grandiose promises. He can sort of invent this giant scheme for the future, and his **acolytes** tell him that it's great." (Julie Johnson, *Congress: In the Eyes of Newt — The Minority Whip Has His Sights on a G.O.P. Takeover of the House*, Time, 10-10-1994, p. 35.)
(2) follower (who is loyal and unquestioning) *n*.: **myrmidon**. See assistant
(3) follower (devout ... of a cause, religion or activity) *n*.: **votary**. See supporter

following (a meal, esp. dinner) *adj*.: **postprandial**. See meal

folly *n*.: **betise** [French]. See stupidity

fondle *v.i.*: **canoodle** (often "canoodle with"). See caress

food (lover of good ...) *n*.: **gourmandise**. ▪ During his first winter in Virginia, Captain John Smith, known more for his love life than his **gourmandise**, extolled the virtues of native American foods introduced to him by the Powhatan Indians. (Annette Stramesi, *Final Take [Pumpkin]*, Colonial Homes, 11-01-1997, p. 112.)

(2) food (item of) *n.*: **viand**. ∎ The chic Chicagoan now turns his eye on what can be done with exotic as well as more familiar **viands** with "Charlie Trotter's Meat and Game" (Oct., $50) by Charlie Trotter. (Author not given, *Ten Speed Press, [Cookbook Publishing]*, Publishers Weekly, 07-23-2001.)

(3) food (item of) *n.*: **victual**. ∎ Tables inside his studio hold a variable smorgasbord of [fake] **victuals**, enough fake baked hams, plum puddings, cookies, cakes, plump walnuts, boiled beef, artichokes and pastry-topped stews to make a hungry reporter weep. (Melissa Stoeltje, *Fee Fi Faux Fare: Herni Gadbois Is a Giant in the Field of Fake Food*, The Houston Chronicle, 12-23-1994, p. 1.)

(4) food (as in nourishment) *n.*: **alimentation**. SEE NOURISHMENT

(5) food (lover of good ...) *n.*: **epicure**. SEE GOURMET

(6) food (lover of good ...) *n.*: **gastronome**. SEE GOURMET

(7) food (abnormally increased appetite for) *n.*: **hyperphagia**. SEE APPETITE

(8) food (esp. insipid, like baby food) *n.*: **pabulum** (also **pablum**). SEE INSIPID

(9) food (excessive desire or craving for) *n.*: **polyphagia**. SEE APPETITE

fool *n.*: **mooncalf**. ∎ The Buckley vs. Valeo case, decided in 1976, says that money is equal to speech. As a result, any limits on how much politicians collect or spend is a violation of free speech rights under the Constitution. Any **mooncalf** knows money is not equal to speech. If a man standing next to me has a million dollars to donate to a senator, I can yell as loudly as he can, but he'll get a meeting with the senator to discuss his legislative needs a lot more quickly than will I. (Bonnie Erbe, *It Looks Hopeless on the Reform Front [Editorial]*, Rocky Mountain News [Denver], 10-18-1997.)

(2) fool (as in swindle) *v.t.*: **bunco**. SEE SWINDLE

(3) fool *v.t.*: **hornswoggle**. SEE DECEIVE

(4) fool (as in deceive) *v.t.*: **humbug**. SEE DECEIVE

(5) fool *n.*: **jobbernowl** [British]. SEE IDIOT

(6) fool (as in buffoon, who is sometimes boastful) *n.*: **Scaramouch**. SEE BUFFOON

(7) fool (or force someone into doing something, esp. by fraud or coercion) *v.t.*: **shanghai** (person who does so *n.*: **shanghier**). SEE COERCE

fool around (as in idle or waste time) *v.i.*: **footle** (usu. as in "footle around"). SEE DAWDLE

foolhardy (as in irresponsible or reckless) *adj.*: **harum-scarum**. SEE RECKLESS

(2) foolhardy *adj.*: **Icarian**. SEE OVERAMBITIOUS

foolish (in a smug or complacent manner) *adj.*: **fatuous**. ∎ "Jerry Garcia destroyed his life on drugs," Rush Limbaugh fearlessly proclaimed. You don't have to advocate heroin addiction or alcoholism to feel that all this moralistic fury is inanely misdirected. Nothing is more **fatuous** than to indict some performer for his failure to conform to the prescribed virtues of the "role model." Smug, self-satisfied, sanctimonious, this line of thinking fails first of all to acknowledge the true complexities of human existence. (John Taylor, *Live and Let Die: In Praise of Mickey, Jerry, and the Reckless Life [Jerry Garcia and Mickey Mantle]*, Esquire, 12-01-1995, p. 120.)

foolishness *n.*: **betise** [French]. SEE STUPIDITY

(2) foolishness *n.*: **folderol** (or **falderal**). SEE NONSENSE

(3) foolishness (or talk ...) *v.i., n.*: **piffle**. SEE NONSENSE

(4) foolishness *n.*: **trumpery**. SEE NONSENSE

foot-in-mouth (disease) *n.*: **dontopedalogy** [This word was coined by Prince Philip to describe his own frequent tendency in this regard, and in this example is being applied to him]. ∎ Brickbats — For chronic **dontopedalogy**, to Prince Philip. The prince has often suffered from foot-in-mouth disease and last week he displayed serious symptoms . ... Speaking on BBC radio [about a school shooting, he said that], handguns are no more lethal than ... cricket bats [and that "if somebody] decided to go into a school and batter a lot of people to death with a cricket bat ... I mean, are you going to ban cricket bats?" (Author not given, *Bouquets & Brickbats*, The Gazette [Montreal, Quebec], 12 -21-1996, p. B4.)

for want of (anything better) *adv.*: **faute de mieux** [French]. SEE LACKING

forage (about or through) *v.t.*: **fossick** [Australian]. SEE RUMMAGE

forbearance (in the face of adversity) *n.*: **longanimity**. SEE PATIENCE

force (to act, esp. by violent measures or threats) *v.t.*: **dragoon**. SEE COERCE

(2) force (a person or group to go from one place to another, whether literally or figuratively) *v.t.*: **frogmarch**. SEE MARCH

(3) force (initial ... as in prime mover) *n.*: **primum mobile** [Latin]. SEE PRIME MOVER

(4) force (as in power or might) *n.*: **puissance**. SEE POWER

(5) force (or trick someone into doing something, esp. by fraud or coercion) *v.t.*: **shanghai** (person who does so *n.*: **shanghier**). SEE COERCE

forebears (excessive reverence for ... or tradition) *n.*: **filiopietistic**. SEE OLD-FASHIONED

foreboding (that something is going to occur) *n.*: **presentiment**. SEE PREMONITION

forecaster (as in one who makes correct predictions of misfortune which are ignored) *n.*: **Cassandra**. SEE PREDICTOR

forefathers (excessive reverence for ... or tradition) *n.*: **filiopietistic**. SEE OLD-FASHIONED

foreign (as in originating from elsewhere; not endemic) *adj.*: **ecdemic**. ∎ In recent years, while Shanghai was trying to fetch in foreign capital, they drew up a system of favorable policy to attract **ecdemic** investment. ... The favorable policy included special service of industrial and commercial registration, non-retesting of registration capital. Until now, over 1500 **ecdemic** enterprises have settled in Shanghai. (Author not given, *Domestic Investors Think Highly of Shanghai*, AsiaInfo Services, 08-31-02001.)

(2) foreign (person who appreciates ... customs and manners) *n.*: **xenophile**. ∎ Today's global society demands that we become **xenophiles**, respecting and appreciating people, things, and customs from cultures other than our own. Nursing and health care are culturally defined, so you need to understand the systems and beliefs important to patients from other cultures. (Edwina McConnell, *26 Words Toward a Successful Nursing Career [Enhancing Nurses' Self-Esteem]*, Nursing, 06-01-1997, p. 41.)

foreigner *n.*: **auslander**. ∎ The result is that more and more U.S. managers are learning what it's like to have a boss from abroad. While the experience varies from employer to employer, veterans say a few lessons should be borne in mind by anyone thinking of working for an **auslander**. First, be sure your prospective employer knows what it's doing in coming to America. (Faye Rice, *Executive Life: Should You Work for a Foreigner?* Fortune, 08-01-1988, p. 123.)

(2) foreigner (in Japan) *n.*: **gaijin**. ∎ But over the last decade, that facade of virtue [in the Japanese sport of sumo wrestling] has crumbled in the face of new temptations — dope, fast cars, girls — as much as from the **gaijin** invasion [into the sport]. In 1986, baseball replaced sumo as the most popular sport on Japanese television. (Velisarios Kattoulas, *Selling Sumo*, Newsweek International, 06-21-1999, p. 84.)

(3) foreigner (from another country or place) *n.*: **outlander**. ∎ The Middle American Dream, circa the mid-1950s and `60s, a time when Washington became what Manhattan had been a generation before: a magnet for young **outlanders** with yearning sensations to go East and make a mark for themselves. (Victor Gold, *Fitzwater's Wit and Charm Come Out in "Call the Briefing,"* The Washington Times, 11-06-1995, p. 24.)

foreigners (fear or distrust of) *n.*: **xenophobia**. SEE DISTRUST

forerunner *n.*: **progenitor**. SEE PREDECESSOR

foreshadow *v.t.*: **adumbrate**. ∎ Some America Firsters [argued that the Nuremburg trials] were inevitably tainted by the involvement of the Soviets, who were "just as bad [as the Nazis]." In this, the old right isolationists **adumbrated** Buchanan's own later fixation [on the Justice Department's pursuit of Nazi war criminals which he believed] was delegitimated by its reliance on Soviet sources. (Charles Lane, *Daddy's Boy: The Roots of Pat Buchanan's Authoritarianism*, The New Republic, 01-22-1996, p. 15.)

(2) foreshadow *v.t.*: **betoken**. SEE PORTEND

foreshadowing *adj.*: **fatidic**. SEE PROPHETIC

forest (of or relating to woods or ..., or having many trees) *adj.*: **bosky**. SEE TREES

forestall (as in avert or ward off) *v.t.*: **forfend**. SEE AVERT

foretell *v.t.*: **adumbrate**. SEE FORESHADOW

(2) foretell *v.t.*: **betoken**. SEE PORTEND

(3) foretell (as in one who makes correct predictions of misfortune which are ignored): *n.*: **Cassandra**. SEE PREDICTOR

(4) foretell *v.t.*: **vaticinate**. SEE PREDICT

foretelling *adj.*: **fatidic**. SEE PROPHETIC

forever *adj., adv.*: **ad infinitum**. ∎ Too bad the play can't be extended **ad infinitum** so everybody in town could see it. (Wendell Brock, *A Stunning Evening With Life's Big Issues*, The Atlanta Constitution, 04-14-2000, p. D1.)

(2) forever *adv.*: **in aeternum** [Latin]. ∎ "The Brady Bunch," which ran from 1969 to 1974, but which will live in syndication **in aeternum**, may be one of the worst sitcoms of all times. (Author not given, *Generation X Digs Their Story; Brady Bunch Film Is a Surprise Hit*, Washington Times, 03-13-95.)

(3) forever (lasting ...) *adj.*: **aeonian** (or **eonian**). SEE ETERNAL

(4) forever (lasting ...) *adj.*: **sempiternal**. SEE EVERLASTING

forget (to ... the meaning of words or to use them incorrectly) *n.*: **paramnesia**. SEE AMNESIA

forgetfulness (as in oblivion) *n.*: **Lethe**. SEE OBLIVION

forgivable *adj.*: **venial**. ∎ Many Americans regard the denial of a sexual affair as a **venial** sin. Most people have lied about their sex lives at one time or another. You lie to protect yourself, your spouse, your lover, your children. (Arthur Schlesinger, Jr., *Starr Pursues Clinton as Ahab Did the Whale*, Minneapolis Star Tribune, 08-10-1998, p. 9A.)

forgiveness (as in place or occasion of humiliation and seeking ...) *n.*: **Canossa**. SEE PENANCE

forlorn *adj.*: **lorn**. ∎ If every melodrama needs a poor, **lorn** widow, cheated by a scheming cad, then Mrs. Backus perfectly fitted Tarbell's description of Rockefeller. (Ron Chernow, *Titan*, Random House [1998], p. 445.)

form (take ... as in making an abstract concept seem real) *v.t.*: **reify**. SEE MATERIALIZE

formalities (precise observance of ... or etiquette) *n.*: **punctilio**. SEE ETIQUETTE

formality (one who demands adherence to ...) *n.*: **martinet**. SEE DISCIPLINARIAN

former *adj.*: **ci-devant** [French]. ∎ Having read so much about recession-torn New Hampshire, I half expected, at the border crossing from Vermont near Lebanon, to encounter scenes reminiscent of the **ci-devant** Soviet Union: throngs clamoring for bread, [etc.] (Alexander Cockburn, *Sex, Clinton and Contras*, The Nation, 02-10-1992.)

(2) former *adj.*: **quondam**. ∎ The most extraordinary detail at Nell's is its ever-present namesake, Nell Campbell. A **quondam** actress whose best credit is her role as the tap-dancing groupie Columbia in The Rocky Horror Picture Show, Nell, 33, presides over the club as if it were "my own drawing room." (Michael Small, *Host: If You Want to Lounge on a Love Seat in New York's Hippest Club, You'll Have to Get Nell Campbell's Okay*, People, 02-02-1987, p. 117.)

formulate (an idea, plan, theory or explanation after careful thought) *v.t.*: **excogitate**. SEE DEVISE

fornication *n.*: **houghmagandy** (Scottish). SEE INTERCOURSE

(2) fornication *n.*: **venery**. SEE INTERCOURSE

forsake (esp. responsibility or duty) *v.t.*: **abnegate**. SEE RENOUNCE

forsaken (as in forlorn) *adj.*: **lorn**. SEE FORLORN

forswear *v.t.*: **abjure**. SEE RENOUNCE

forte *n.*: **métier** [French]. ∎ Within a few years of his arrival at Paramount, [Hal Wallis] signed Kirk Douglas, Burt Lancaster, Anna Magnani, Lizabeth Scott and Charlton Heston. As his résumé indicates, comedy wasn't Wallis' **métier**. (Shawn Levy, *The King of Comedy*, St. Martin's Press [1996], p. 89.)

(2) forte (as in favorite topic or activity) *n.*: **cheval de bataille** [French for "battle-horse"]. SEE HOBBY

fortification *n.*: **barbican**. ∎ These magnificent 13th- and 14th-century walls surround the city centre in a three-mile circuit. ... It costs nothing to climb these sentinel towers with their commanding gates, ... and **barbicans** — they provide good reference points for lost tourists looking for the "big church." (Anna Melville-James, *Between You, Me and the Gatehouse*, Sunday Telegraph, 12-17-2000.)

(2) fortification *n.*: **bulwark**. SEE PROTECTION

fortitude *n.*: **hardihood**. SEE COURAGE

fortuitous (occurrence) *n.*: **serendipity** (*adj.*: **serendipitous**). ∎ Then **serendipity** struck again. ... [I] read a story that caught my eye. It was about a bear incident in Anchorage. There were no injuries, but I recognized the name of the Fish and Game trooper who was quoted. I'd roomed with him for a year during college. I hadn't heard from him in a decade, so I called him up, and we arranged to meet. (Jim Buchta, *In Alaska, Only Thing Predictable Is its Unpredictability*, Minneapolis Star Tribune, 03-10-1996, p. 10G.)

fortunate (discovering ... things by accident) *n.*: **serendipity** (*adj.*: **serendipitous**). SEE FORTUITOUS

fortune (as in destiny or fate) *n.*: **kismet**. SEE FATE

(2) fortune (devotion to the pursuit of ..., as in wealth) *n.*: **mammonism**. SEE WEALTH

fortuneteller (by using lightning or animal innards) *n.*: **haruspex**. ∎ The **haruspex** who cast Rome's future from the examination of sheep entrails was no less a scientist than those of us who scour for significant portent in the results of the Iowa straw poll. (Murray Kempton, *GOP Is Showing Democrat-Like Fissures*, Newsday, 08-23-1995, p. A34.)

fortunetelling (by picking random Biblical passages) *n.*: **bibliomancy**. SEE DIVINATION

(2) fortunetelling (by reading palms) *n.*: **chiromancy**. SEE PALM-READING

(3) fortunetelling (by touching or proximity to an object) *n.*: **psychometry**. SEE DIVINATION

(4) fortunetelling (by fire) *n.*: **pyromancy**. SEE DIVINATION

forward (as in assertive, in an obnoxious or loud way) *adj.*: **bumptious**. SEE PUSHY

foul (language) *n.*: **billingsgate**. SEE LANGUAGE

(2) foul (full of ... matter, such as feces) *adj.*: **feculent**. SEE FECAL

(3) foul (odor) *adj.*: **fetid**. SEE SMELLY

(4) foul (odor) *adj.*: **mephitic** (*n.*: **mephitis**). SEE SMELLY

(5) foul (odor) *adj.*: **noisome**. SEE SMELLY

foul up (esp. a golf shot) *v.t., n.*: **foozle**. SEE BOTCH

foundation (on which something is built) *n.*: **warp and woof**. ▮ Corporations will have to decide whether and how to use the [Internet] in manufacturing, distributing, advertising, and recruiting — whether to make it part of the **warp and woof** of American business. (Andrew Kupfer, *Fortune's Information Technology: 4 Forces That Will Shape the Internet*, Fortune, 07-06-1998, p. 92.)

four (year period) *n.*: **quadrennium**. ▮ Of the [United States Olympic Committee's] operating budget of $149.9 million for the current (1985-88) **quadrennium**, only $2.2 million has gone directly to prospective Olympians, via a program called Operation Gold. (E.M. Swift, *An Olympian Quagmire*, Sports Illustrated, 09-12-1988, p. 38.)

fowl (of or relating to the domestic ..., esp. if used for food or hunted as game) *adj.*: **gallinaceous**. ▮ Chickens are **gallinaceous** birds like pheasants and quail — and their young hatch out able to walk, feed, and drink for themselves. (Buff Orpingtons, *Save the Chickens!* Mother Earth News, 12-10-1996, p. 26.)

fox (of, relating to or characteristic of) *adj.*: **vulpine**. ▮ Eli Broad has all the appearances of a fox. His **vulpine** cunning is evident in everything he does, from becoming one of the luminaries of Los Angeles'

high society to accumulating one of the world's best collections of modern art. (Author not given, *The Cunning of the Hedgehog*, The Economist, 09-27-1997.)

fracas (esp. public) *n.*: **affray**. SEE BRAWL

fraction (as in portion) *n.*: **moiety**. SEE PORTION

fragile *adj.*: **frangible**. ▮ As with so many two-night "miniseries," its soul is thin as March ice and just as **frangible**. But the movie's zeal for unearthing an obscure fragment of American history [escorting Jewish refugees from Europe to America in 1944] partly counteracts the poetical shortcomings, and within its fragile framework lie some striking performances. (Author not given, *Big Names in Small Roles Ultimately Save "Haven"* [Television Review], Seattle Post-Intelligencer, 02-09-2001.) SEE BREAKABLE

fragments *n.*: **flinders**. SEE BITS AND PIECES

frail (from loss or lack of body strength) *adj.*: **asthenic** (*n.*: **asthenia**). SEE WEAK

(2) frail (as in powerless) *adj.*: **impuissant**. SEE POWERLESS

(3) frail (and sickly person, esp. one morbidly concerned with his own health) *n., adj.*: **valetudinarian**. SEE SICKLY

frailty (that comes with old age) *n.*: **caducity**. SEE OLD AGE

France (one who is fond of ... or its people) *n.*: **Francophile**. ▮ Most [home] buyers are die-hard **Francophiles** who love the slow pace and country comforts — hearty cuisine and cheap and plentiful wine — of rural France. (Thomas K. Grose, *Once More Onto the Beach!* U.S. News & World Report, 01-12-1998, p. 10.)

(2) France (one who dislikes ... or its people) *n.*: **Francophobe**. ▮ If business in Germany is hard work, it is even tougher in France: across Europe, French companies came top of the list of those with whom their fellow Europeans think it is hardest to do business. The Dutch were most **Francophobe**: 59% put French firms top of the list. (Author not given, *There Was a German, a Belgian and a Spaniard ...*, The Economist, 01-23-1999.)

frantic (as in frenzied) *adj.*: **corybantic**. SEE FRENZIED

(2) frantic (and frenzied woman) *n.*: **maenad**. SEE WOMAN

fraud (esp. a person who sells quack medicines) *n.*: **mountebank**. SEE HUCKSTER

(2) fraud (as in deliberate misrepresentation of facts to gain an advantage) *n.*: **subreption**. SEE MISREPRESENTATION

(3) fraud (as in hypocrite, esp. one who affects religious peity) *n.*: **Tartuffe** (or **tartuffe**). SEE HYPOCRITE

(4) fraud (as in hypocrite, esp. one who acts humbly) *n.*: **Uriah Heep**. SEE HYPOCRITE

fraudulent (as in invented or substituted with ... intent) *adj.*: **supposititious**. SEE SUPPOSED

frayed (in appearance) *adj.*: **tatterdemalion**. SEE RAGGED

freckled *adj.*: **lentinginous**. ▪ My own addiction [to makeup] started young, when I realised that my freckly Celtic complexion wasn't a curse I had to endure for life, and my offensively **lentiginous** skin could be smoothed into picture-perfect ivory. (Simon Price, *Slap-happy: Cover-up, Powder and Eyeliner*, The Guardian [London], 12-14-2002, p. 6.)

free (from slavery, servitude or bondage) *v.t.*: **manumit**. SEE EMANCIPATE

free speech *n.*: **parrhesia**. ▪ [O]ne of the functions of poetry is, to tell the truth, to exercise **parrhesia**, to engage in frank and plain speech about a very delicate and difficult situation [i.e. the war in Iraq]. (Cornel West, *Analysis: War Poems*, The Tavis Smiley Show [NPR], 02-26-2003.)

free-thinker (esp. on matters of morals and religion) *n.*: **libertine**. ▪ Henri urges the driver to return to his senses, to be "reasonable." He reasserts the most conventional sort of orderliness in the Western tradition. ... The driver ... accuses Henri of being "only the most banal and predictable of poets. No **libertine**, no man of vision and hence suffering, but a banal moralist." The driver's disregard for order as safe-haven is easily surpassed by his contempt for the pretensions, the presumptions that the orderly man displays. (Joseph M. Conte, *"Design and Debris": John Hawkes's "Travesty," Chaos Theory, and the Swerve*, Critique: Studies in Contemporary Fiction, 01-01-1996, p. 120.)

freewheeling (as in uninhibited, in exhibiting emotion or celebration) *adj.*: **saturnalian**. ▪ The young New Yorker perceived that the Hijra, lower in caste even than the Untouchable dung-cleaners, somehow cut to the heart of the paradox of India. They were clownish and **saturnalian** in spirit: "I thought of them almost like Shakespearian fools, being given permission to comment on society and speak their mind in the way that no one else could." (Author not given, *Caste Aside*, Independent, 07-29-1997, p. 6.)

(2) freewheeling (and reckless person) *n.*: **rantipole**. SEE WILD

freeze *v.t.*: **glaciate**. ▪ Schwarzenegger, meanwhile, masticates freeze-dried one-liners, from "the Iceman cometh" to "Let's kick some ice." He plays a scientist who has caught a permanent chill while trying to cryogenically preserve his wife. Wearing refrigerated armor, he is a Teutonic Tin Man, crashing around with giant guns that **glaciate** all comers. (Brian D. Johnson, *Films: A Bat out of Hell: The Latest Batman Movie is an Infernal Mess*, Maclean's, 07-01-1997, p. 106.)

freezing (and storing of deceased body) *n.*: **cryonics**. ▪ Two Southern California **cryonics** companies have shut down in recent years, and a third is said to be seeking alternative storage facilities for a dozen "patients" still on ice. (Davis Lazarus, San Francisco Chronicle, *Cryonics Suffers From Freezer Burn*, The Arizona Republic, 08-26-2001, p. D4.)

(2) freezing *adj.*: **hyperborean** [Note: this word also means the Arctic or far north region, and in the following example, both meanings would be appropriate]. ▪ [If there were drilling in the Arctic National Wildlife Refuge,] how many drilling rigs, it's fair to ask, would cause postpartum psychosis among caribou? ... Would oil pipes and pumps in just 2,000 acres of the 9 million-acre refuge seriously harm animals and migrating birds? And if it does, is that the overriding consideration? Certainly no tourist jobs are at stake in that desolate, **hyperborean** plain. (Edwin A. Roberts, Jr., *Ruminations On Oil And Its Origins*, The Tampa Tribune, 11-18-2001.)

(3) freezing *adj.*: **algid**. SEE COLD

(4) freezing (as in of, like or occurring in winter) *adj.*: **brumal**. SEE WINTER

(5) freezing (of or relating to ... temperatures) *adj.*: **cryogenic**. SEE COLD

(6) freezing *adj.*: **gelid**. SEE COLD

French *adj.*: **Gallic**. ▪ On a hot summer evening, dozens of limousines and SUVs ferrying the cream of Parisian society pull up in front of the Pompidou Center, the city's contemporary art complex. ... The luminaries are gathered to applaud Jean-Marie Messier as he accepts that most **Gallic** of awards, the insignia of the Chevalier of the Legion of Honor. (Devin Leonard, *Mr. Messier Is Ready For His Close-Up*, Fortune, 09-03-2001, p. 136.)

(2) French (become ... in character or custom) *v.t.*, *v.i.*: **Gallicize**. ▪ Tunisia was occupied by France in

1881 and remained a French protectorate for 75 years. The French impact on Tunisia was profound, imposing French institutions, leaving the imprint of French culture and technology, and creating a **gallicized** elite to whom leadership passed when the protectorate was ended in 1956. (Robert Rinehart, *Tunisia: Chapter 1A. Historical Setting*, Countries of the World, 01-01-1991.)

(3) French (word, phrase or idiom used in another language) *n.*: **Gallicism**. ∎ I am not a native French speaker, but do speak the language and learned some French words directly in context without being sure of the English. I've sat under many more Francophone pergolas than Anglophone pergolas, and would have said "trellis," not being sure of the English term and fearing that "pergola" was a **Gallicism**. (Author not given, *Letters*, The Washington Post, 07-19-2001, p. H2.)

frenzied *adj.*: **corybantic**. ∎ Activision's Quake II, a first-person shooter for the Macintosh, was worth the wait and is one of the best multiplayer games ever developed. [The game provides] provide fast, **corybantic**, and brutal game action. The single player version consists of many levels of gothic corridors, hideous villains, and destructive weapons. Fighting is furious and bloody, and the gamer gets to wield many revamped Quake I weapons. (Rick Sanchez, *Quake II*, SoftBase, 09-30-2001.)

(2) frenzied (woman) *n.*: **maenad**. See WOMAN

frenzy (of emotion, feeling or action) *n.*: **paroxysm**. See OUTBURST

(2) frenzy (in a ..., as in distress) *n.*: **swivet** (as in "in a swivet") *inf.* See DISTRESS

(3) frenzy (as in panic) *n.*: **Torschlusspanik** [German]. See PANIC

frequenter (of a place, esp. a place of entertainment) *n.*: **habitué** [French]. See REGULAR

fresh (love of or enthusiasm for anything ...) *n.*: **neophilia**. See NOVELTY

fret *v.t., v.i., n.*: **cark**. See WORRY

(2) fret (or complain) *v.i.*: **repine**. See COMPLAIN

fretting (as in a state of nervous tension, often with irritability) *n.*: **fantod**. See TENSION

friction (of or relating to ... within a group or country) *adj.*: **internecine**. See DISSENSION

(2) friction (as in heated disagreement or ... between groups) *n.*: **ruction**. See DISSENSION

friend (faithful ..., as in companion) *n.*: **Achates**. See COMPANION

(2) friend (as in comrade) *n.*: **tovarich** [Russian]. See COMRADE

friendliness (as in affability) *n.*: **bonhomie**. See AFFABILITY

(2) friendliness (as in cordiality) *n.*: **empressement** [French]. See CORDIALITY

fright (as in panic) *n.*: **Torschlusspanik** [German]. See PANIC

frighten *v.t.*: **affright**. See SCARE

frightened *adj.*: **tremulous**. See FEARFUL

frigid *adj.*: **algid**. See COLD

(2) frigid *adj.*: **hyperborean**. See FREEZING

fringe benefit (sometimes as thanks for a purchase) *n.*: **lagniappe**. See GIFT

fritter (something away) *v.t.*: **fribble**. See SQUANDER

frivolous (and flighty person) *n.*: **flibbertigibbet**. See FLIGHTY

(2) frivolous (as in trivial) *adj.*: **nugacious**. See TRIVIAL

frog (of, relating to or resembling) *adj.*: **ranine**. ∎ [I] began writing for newspapers in the Far East. ... [E]very night [while writing] a large frog came and called "Waah!" so loudly that I could not concentrate. After periods of deep breathing I would explode, racing out to the jungle's edge to hurl rocks and anti-**ranine** abuse. The frog would fall politely silent, allow my breathing to recover, allow me to reseat myself and return to the story. Then he would start again. "Waaah!" (Kevin Rushby, *Small is Beautiful*, The Guardian [London], 10-26-2002.)

frolic *v.t., v.i.*: **disport**. ∎ Late in the ballet, [Tinkerbell's] fairy cohorts add to the merriment, stumbling across stage tipsy from revels, preening goofily and in general **disporting** themselves as a wild parody of every classical ballet fairy who ever bourreed gracefully. (Margaret Putnam, *Flight of Fancy: FWDB's 'Peter Pan' Swoops in and Soars*, The Dallas Morning News, 04-22-2000, p. 33A.)

(2) frolic *v.i.*: **gambol**. ∎ Soon [the lions and cubs] walked off, leaping, pouncing on each other, wrestling, dancing, seemingly as benign as Disney lions. ... Suddenly the **gamboling** ceased and the pride swung into single file and turned into the bush, making not a sound, not even that of a breaking twig. (R.W. Apple, Jr., *Rebirth of a Nation [The Physical Beauty of South Africa]*, Town & Country Monthly, 05-01-1996, p. 92.)

(3) frolic *v.i.*: **curvet**. SEE DANCE

frolicsome (as in playful) *adj.*: **gamesome**. SEE PLAYFUL

frostbite (or inflamation of skin due to exposure to cold) *n.*: **chilblains**. SEE INFLAMMATION

frosty *adj.*: **gelid**. SEE COLD

frown (as in pout) *n.*: **moue** [French]. SEE POUT

frowner (as in person who never laughs) *n.*: **agelast**. SEE HUMORLESS

frugal (excessively) *adj.*: **costive**. SEE STINGY

(2) frugal (excessively) *adj.*: **niggardly**. SEE STINGY

(3) frugal (excessively) *adj.*: **penurious**. SEE STINGY

frugality (person who practices extreme ..., esp. for spiritual improvement) *n., adj.*: **ascetic**. SEE AUSTERITY

(2) frugality (as in marked by simplicity, self-discipline, self-restraint and/or ...) *adj.*: **Lacedaemoninan**. SEE SPARTAN

fruit (with one stone, such as peach, plum or cherry) *n.*: **drupe**. ▪ Plums are more varied in size, color, flavor, and texture than other stone, or **drupe**, fruits, including apricots and peaches. (Lucy Wing, *A Passion for Plums*, Country Living, 07-01-1995, p. 120.)

(2) fruit (bearing ...) *adj.*: **fructiferous**. ▪ A 401(k) contribution invested in assets earning 9% a year will return a whopping 63.5% annually, after tax benefits and a 50% company match are taken into account. ... So be thankful for the **fructiferous** 401(k), but water it well. (Elizabeth Fenner, *Retirement Planning: How to Grow a Lush 401[k]*, Money, 11-01-1992, p. 92.)

(3) fruit (eating) *adj.*: **frugivorous**. ▪ The Society for the Protection of Nature in Israel is trying to help local authorities cope with a problem that is driving some people batty. **Frugivorous** bat season is here again, the time of year when the little nocturnal flying mammals are particularly drawn to the fruit ripening on trees with very little respect to the fact that they might be fouling private property. (Liat Collins, *SPNI Offers Advice for Battling Seasonal Invaders*, Jerusalem Post, 04-12-2001.)

(4) fruit (study of ...) *n.*: **pomology**. ▪ I'll [think I'll] try a lecture on **pomology** aimed at the state of

Washington, whence come these beautiful but tasteless Red Delicious apples. (Author not given, *A Thing or Two About Apples*, The Christian Science Monitor, 02-02-2001.)

fruitful (make ...) *v.i.*: **fructify**. ▪ Sex, associated with procreation, had always been recognized as the principle of life; but for these liberators, the orgiastic energy of the sexual act takes precedence over the fate of the seed, whether **fructified** or wasted. (Ruth Wisse, *Sabbath's Theater [Book Reviews]*, Commentary, 12-01-1995, p. 61.)

(2) fruitful (esp. as in fertile) *adj.*: **fecund**. SEE FERTILE

fruition (while coming into ...) *adj.*: **aborning**. SEE BORN

fruitless (as in unsuccessful) *adj.*: **abortive**. SEE UNSUCCESSFUL

(2) fruitless (mission or project) *n.*: **fool's errand**. SEE HOPELESS

fruits (mixture of ... and/or vegetables) *n.*: **macédoine** [French]. SEE MIXTURE

frustrated (in realizing one's goals) *adj.*: **manque** (esp. as in "artist ..."). ▪ Scowling from a sofa, Martin Amis declares that: "Any biographer is likely to be some sort of artist **manque**. It's second or third best to what you want to be." (Peter Parker, *Literary Lifers: The Good, the Bad and the Nosey*, Independent, 03-09-1996, p. 9.)

frustration (as in disappointment) *n.*: **Dead Sea fruit**. SEE DISAPPOINTMENT

full (sound or voice) *adj.*: **orotund**. SEE SONOROUS

(2) full (as in complete or unlimited, esp as in ... power) *adj.*: **plenary**. SEE COMPLETE

full length (at ...) *adv.*: **in extenso** [Latin]. SEE ENTIRETY

full speed (at ...) *adv.*: **tanivy**. SEE TOP SPEED

full-bosomed *adj.*: **bathycolpian**. SEE BUSTY

full-figured (woman) *adj.*: **zaftig** [Yiddish]. ▪ Amber soon finds she has a **zaftig** rival: Tracy Turnblad (Ricki Lake), who is plump, perky and, pound for bouffanted pound, the snappiest Caucasian dancer in town. (Richard Corliss, *Cinema: Buxom Belles in Baltimore Hairspray*, Time, 02-29-1988, p. 101.)

fumble (around with one's hands) *v.i.*: **grabble**. SEE GROPE

fumes (malodorous ... from waste or decayed matter) *n.*: **effluvium**. SEE ODOR

fun (as in playful) *adj.*: **ludic**. SEE PLAYFUL

fun-loving (as in playful) *adj.*: **gamesome**. SEE PLAYFUL

(2) fun-loving (as in lazy person devoted to seeking pleasure and luxury) *n.*: **lotus-eater**. SEE HEDONIST

functional *adj.*: **utile**. SEE USEFUL

fundamental (as in essential) *adj.*: **constitutive**. SEE ESSENTIAL

funeral (rite or ceremony) *n.*: **obsequy** (often pl.). ∎ In all the words spent on Strom Thurmond's life and times since his death, I saw no acknowledgment of the most interesting of his sundry racial legacies. She is Essie Mae Washington Williams, a widowed former school teacher in her 70s, living in Los Angeles. Presumably she did not show up for any of the **obsequies** even though Strom Thurmond was almost certainly her father. Williams is black. (Diane McWhorter, *Strom's Race Against His Past*, Philadelphia Daily News, 12-27-2003, p. 15.)

(2) funeral (procession at a ...) *n.*: **cortege**. SEE PROCESSION

funereal *adj.*: **sepulchral**. ∎ In a David Fincher movie a house is never a home. Take a peek inside the dank Gothic asylum of Alien 3, the **sepulchral** gloom of apartment ... forbidding, underlit and about as friendly as a funeral parlour. You wouldn't want to live there. Bela Lugosi wouldn't want to live there. (Anthony Quinn, *Film: They Know Where You Live*, Independent, 05-03-2002, p. 10.)

funny (line) *n.*: **bon mot** [French]. SEE QUIP

(2) funny (line) *n.*: **epigram**. SEE QUIP

(3) funny *adj.*: **gelastic**. SEE LAUGHABLE

(4) funny (in a sarcastic or biting way) *adj.*: **mordant**. SEE SARCASTIC

(5) funny *adj.*: **risible**. SEE LAUGHABLE

(6) funny (finding things ..., as in ability or tendency to laugh) *n.*: **risibility**. SEE LAUGH

(7) funny (as in witty) *adj.*: **waggish**. SEE WITTY

(8) funny (person who tries to be ... but is not) *n.*: **witling**. SEE HUMORLESS

fur (of a rabbit) *n.*: **lapin** [French]. SEE RABBIT FUR

furious *adj.*: **apoplectic**. SEE ANGRY

(2) furious *adj.*: **vesuvian** (esp. as in ...temper). SEE TEMPER

(3) furious *adj.*: **wroth**. SEE ANGRY

furnish (as in outfit or equip) *v.t.*: **accouter**. SEE OUTFIT

furnishings (as in trappings) *n.*: **habiliment(s)**. SEE TRAPPINGS

furrowed (as in grooved) *adj.*: **striated**. SEE GROOVED

furthermore *adv.*: **withal**. SEE MOREOVER

furthest (as in most distant, or remote, destination or goal) *n.*: **ultima Thule**. SEE DISTANT

fuse (as in bring together) *v.t.*: **conflate**. SEE COMBINE

fused (of things that cannot be ...) *adj.*: **immiscible**. SEE INCOMPATIBLE

fuss (over a trifling matter) *n.*: **foofaraw**. ∎ As political plums go, it was not particularly juicy: the establishment of a minor international agency with 30 jobs attached. Even so, Environment Minister Sheila Copps managed to turn what should have been a straightforward decision and a routine announcement last week into a familiar Canadian **foofaraw**. At issue was Copps's choice of Montreal over 24 other Canadian cities in competition for a $5-million-a-year environmental watchdog agency. (E. Kaye Fulton, *The Sound and the Fury: a Regional Dogfight Explodes after a NAFTA Agency Goes to Montreal*, Maclean's, 04-11-1994, p. 16.)

(2) fuss (as in commotion) *n.*: **maelstrom**. SEE COMMOTION

(3) fuss (about petty matters) *v.i.*: **pettifog**. SEE QUIBBLE

(4) fuss (as in commotion) *n.*: **pother**. SEE COMMOTION

(5) fuss (as in fret or complain) *v.i.*: **repine**. SEE COMPLAIN

(6) fuss (in a state of ..., as in distress) *n.*: **swivet** (as in "in a swivet") *inf.* SEE DISTRESS

fussy (overly ...) *adj.*: **persnickety**. SEE PICKY

futile *adj.*: **bootless**. ∎ A subpoena to Mr. Clinton to testify would not be a **bootless** exercise, even if he declined by asserting his Fifth Amendment privilege. An impeachment trial is a non-criminal proceeding. In such cases, the Supreme Court held in Baxter vs. Palmigiano (1976), the trier of fact may consider as evidence of wrongdoing a party's Fifth Amendment silence. (Bruce Fein, *The Power, But Not* *the Will?* The Washington Times, 01-19-1999, p. A17.)

(2) futile (relating to the view that all human striving and aspiration is ..., or people who hold such a view) *adj., n.*: **futilitarian**. ▮ Some medical ethicists and health care cost utilitarians uphold the belief that it is unethical for a hopelessly ill person to demand for any medical intervention just to gain extra few weeks of life. ... Welcome to the surrealistic world of biomedical ethics, where **futilitarians** are actively redefining the role of doctors, the ethics of health care, the perceived moral worth of sick and disabled people, and the power of patients over their own bodies. (Wesley J. Smith, *The Discardable People [Rights of Terminally and Hopelessly Ill Individuals]*, The Human Life Review, 06-22-1998.)

(3) futile (efforts which are laborious but ...) *adj.*: **Sisyphean**. ▮ Medical studies and painful individual experiences have shown dieting is too often a **Sisyphean** nightmare. At least two-thirds of people who shed weight will gain back the lost pounds — and often more — in a few years. (Anastasia Toufexis, *Health: Forget About Losing Those Last 10 Pounds: The Pursuit of Sylphlike Thinness Is Not Only Futile for Most Men and Women, it Can Be Downright Unhealthy*, Time, 07-08-1991, p. 50.)

(4) futile (as in unsuccessful) *adj.*: **abortive**. See UNSUCCESSFUL

(5) futile (mission or project) *n.*: **fool's errand**. See HOPELESS

(6) futile *adj.*: **nugatory**. See WORTHLESS

(7) futile *adj.*: **otiose**. See USELESS

G

gabby (and flighty or scatterbrained person) *n.*: **flibbertigibbet**. See FLIGHTY

gain (as in, "to whose ...?") *n.*: **cui bono** [Latin]. See ADVANTAGE

gall *n.*: **hardihood**. ▮ [Louis Marshall stated: "Henry Ford] had the **hardihood** to say to me through his agents that he knew nothing of the [anti-Semitic] articles published in his paper." (Neil Baldwin, *Henry Ford and the Jews,* Public Affairs [2001], p. 236.)

galloping (as in at top speed) *adv.*: **tanivy**. See TOP SPEED

gambling (pertaining to ...) *adj.*: **aleatory**. ▮ Las Vegas, Nevada, the fastest growing city in the U.S. ... (Wagers are available on everything from the Big Game's winner to whether Dennis Rodman's combined points and rebounds will number higher than Denver's points.) To the casual visitor, it's a good time. To the addicted sports bettor, it's **aleatory** bliss. (Ken Kurson, *Las Vegas Rules: Sports Betting Isn't Like the Market, It Is the Market*, Esquire, 04-01-1998, p. 138.)

gap (between teeth) *n.*: **diastema**. ▮ Brown just beams when he looks at his [sculpture of former mayor Sharon Sayles Belton]. He was not receptive to any critiques. I didn't think the sculpture's **diastema** was wide enough. "I don't want any big gap in her teeth," Brown said. I wasn't proposing a Dave Letterman gap. (Cheryl Johnson, *Sculptor Brown Proud of Bust of Ex-Mayor*, Star Tribune [Minneapolis, MN], 07-14-2002, p. 4B.)

(2) gap (esp. small ... between things or events) *n.*: **interstice**. ▮ I subscribe to the belief that we live most fully in the **interstices** — en route, in between, on hiatus. My whole desperate life has been an effort to find some kind of perpetual interstice to inhabit, however paradoxical and ultimately futile that may be. (Mark Leyner, *Xmas in Newark, [Perspectives on Little Moments That Make up Life]*, Esquire, 12-01-1997, p. 52.)

(3) gap *n.*: **lacuna**. ▮ For the biographer of John D. Rockefeller, the most exasperating **lacuna** in his story is [his wife] Cettie's transformation from a bright, witty girl into a rather humorless woman, prone to a rather nunlike religiosity. (Ron Chernow, *Titan*, Random House [1998], p. 233.)

(4) gap (in continuity, esp. between the end of a sovereign's reign and the ascension of a successor) *n.*: **interregnum**. See INTERVAL

garb (as in clothes) *n.*: **habiliment(s)**. See CLOTHING

garbage (study of a culture by examining its ...) *n.*: **garbology**. ▮ During a recent speech to the Society of Forensic Toxicologists, Rathje said, "Every bag of garbage tells a story. If archaeologists learn important things about ancient societies by looking at old garbage, then we should be able to learn important things about ourselves by looking at fresh garbage." Rathje pioneered **garbology**. (Lee Siegel, *Trash Talks to Top Garbologist*, Denver Rocky Mountain News, 11-03-1997, p. 4D.)

(2) garbage (as in printed material which is trivial) *n.*: **bumf** [British]. See JUNK

(3) garbage *n.*: **dross**. See TRASH

(4) garbage (accumulation of ..., esp. prehistoric) *n.*: **midden**. See TRASH

(5) garbage *n.*: **offal**. See TRASH

garish *adj.*: **meretricious**. See GAUDY

garland (for the head) *n.*: **chaplet**. ∎ In the middle of it were three poles decorated with coils of cloth, a sort of maypole arrangement around which women wearing **chaplets** of limes and fantastic, heavy jewellery were dancing to drums. (Harriet O'Brien, *New Year's Day of the Dead*, Independent, 12-27-1997, p. 1.)

garlic (characteristic of ... or onion) *adj.*: **alliaceous**. See ONION

garment *n.*: **raiment**. See CLOTHING

gas (of or relating to reducing passing ...) *adj.*: **carminative**. See FARTING

gatekeeper (as in watchdog) *n.*: **Cerebus**. See WATCHDOG

gather (clumsily, roughly or hastily) *v.t.*: **cobble**. See ASSEMBLE

gaudy *adj.*: **meretricious**. ∎ Working for wealthy clients in Europe and America, he managed to take large and imposing sites and bestow on them a design that was typically balanced, matching the majesty of the property without becoming **meretricious**. (Adrian Higgins, *Expert's Picks: Gardening*, The Washington Post, 05-02-1999, p. X6.)

gaunt (esp. in a pale or corpselike way) *adj.*: **cadaverous**. See CORPSELIKE

gawky (and clumsy boy) *n.*: **hobbledehoy**. See CLUMSY

gay (as in merry and social) *adj.*: **Anacreontic**. See CONVIVIAL

(2) gay (discrimination against ... people) *n.*: **heterosexism**. See HOMOSEXUALS

(3) gay (person or one concerned with gay rights) *n., adj.*: **homophile**. See HOMOSEXUAL

(4) gay (as in cheerful) *adj.*: **riant**. See CHEERFUL

(5) gay (as in lesbian) *adj.*: **sapphic**. See LESBIAN

(6) gay (as in lesbian) *n.*: **tribade**. See LESBIAN

geese (flock of) *n.*: **gaggle** (generally as in ... of geese). ∎ Geese toting M-16s? Well, not quite, but after a successful trial run, **gaggles** of geese will soon begin guard duty at American military installations in West Germany. (Author not given, *World Notes — West Germany: Enter the Goose Patrol*, Time, 05-26-1986, p. 42.)

gel (esp. used to groom hair) *n.*: **pomade**. See HAIR GEL

gem (which is highly polished and unfaceted) *n.*: **cabochon**. See JEWEL

gems (one who cuts and polishes ...) *n.*: **lapidary**. See JEWELER

gender (one having characteristics or reproductive organs of each ...) *n.*: **hermaphrodite**. See BISEXUAL

general (in scope or applicability) *adj.*: **ecumenical**. See UNIVERSAL

(2) general (as in widespread) *adj.*: **pandemic**. See WIDESPREAD

(3) general (as in widespread) *adj.*: **regnant**. See WIDESPREAD

generous (as in charitable) *adj.*: **caritative**. See CHARITABLE

geniality *n.*: **bonhomie**. See AFFABILITY

(2) geniality *n.*: **empressement** [French]. See CORDIALITY

genitalia (male ...) *n.*: **virilia**. ∎ In this memoir, Nigel Slater recalls ... his dad in the greenhouse with his penis looking larger than it did in the bath; a jolly gardener who was sportingly unashamed of showing his **virilia** to a young boy. (Murrough O'Brien, *Paperbacks*, Independent on Sunday [London], 05-23-2004, p. 32.)

gentle (esp. with respect to the wind) *adj.*: **favonian**. See MILD

gentleness *n.*: **mansuetude**. ∎ Jem wisely surrounds the lovely sadness of her voice with buoyant beats and chipper melodies, and it's this contrast that fuels her music. And while her voice may have an air of **mansuetude**, she proved that she could easily cut above the din of the boys in her band, particularly when she launched into a vibrant interpretation of "They." (Christopher Muther, *Vibrant Jem Proves a Cut Above*, The Boston Globe, 06-24-2004.)

genuine *adj.*: **pukka**. ∎ A quasiparticle is, as its name suggests, not exactly real. But it is real enough to be detectable — it is a stable excitation state of some of the atoms in the helium that behaves enough like a **pukka** particle to be detected like one. (Author not given, *Hearts of Darkness; Artificial Black Holes*, The Economist, 01-26-2002, p. 83.)

(2) genuine (appearing to be ... or accurate) *adj.*: **verisimilar**. See REALISTIC

gesture (gracious ...) *n.*: **beau geste**. ∎ [After the fire, company owner Aaron Feuerstein] made a stunning announcement to several hundred employees: Not only would he rebuild his factory, he would also continue paying their salaries and benefits for at least another month — at a cost of $1.5 million a week. ... Feuerstein's **beau geste** made him America's newest overnight folk hero. (Richard Jerome, *Angels: Holding the Line After Fire Wrecked His Mill, Aaron Feuerstein Didn't Let His Workers Down*, People, 02-05-1996, p. 122.)

(2) gesture (esp. while speaking) *v.t., v.i.*: **gesticulate**. ∎ [A] driver and a female passenger were **gesticulating** heatedly, indicating a marital-type disagreement. (Carl Hiaasen, *Stormy Weather*, Knopf [1995], p. 254.)

get (by begging or sponging off of) *v.t.*: **cadge**. SEE BEG

getaway (desperate ..., as in retreat) *n.*: **Dunkirk**. SEE RETREAT

(2) getaway (as in a departure which is unannounced, abrupt, secret or unceremonious) *n.*: **French Leave**. SEE DEPARTURE

ghetto (esp. in Brazil) *n.*: **favela**. SEE SLUM

ghost (that manifests itself by making various noises) *n.*: **poltergeist**. ∎ We are stopped, yet the can of Mountain Dew in the cup holder is doing the watusi. The windows are closed, yet my hair is doing a scene from Twister. The truck roof is bouncing up and down like popcorn in a pan. **Poltergeist**? No, just Shaquille O'Neal turning up the 3,700-watt stereo system in his blue Ford Expedition. (Rick Reilly, *Pro Basketball*, Sports Illustrated, 04-21-1997, p. 82.)

(2) ghost *n.*: **phantasm**. SEE APPARITION

(3) ghost *n.*: **wraith**. SEE APPARITION

ghostly (as in pale or corpselike) *adj.*: **cadaverous**. SEE CORPSELIKE

(2) ghostly (as in pale, as from absence of sunlight) *adj.*: **etiolated**. SEE PALE

giant *adj.*: **brobdingnagian** (often cap.). SEE HUGE

(2) giant *adj.*: **Bunyanesque**. SEE ENORMOUS

(3) giant (like an elephant) *adj.*: **elephantine**. SEE ENORMOUS

(4) giant *n.*: **leviathan**. SEE HUGE

(5) giant (like an elephant) *adj.*: **pachydermatous**. SEE ELEPHANT

(6) giant *adj.*: **Pantagruelian**. SEE GIGANTIC

(7) giant *adj.*: **pythonic**. SEE HUGE

gibberish *n.*: **galimatias**. ∎ [M]ost of the television I've reviewed this year has struck me as utter cack. I can't recall — off hand — a single documentary that's taught me anything much. ... I think that many documentaries would be considerably more informative, for me, if I had a pre-frontal lobotomy. [The new documentary,] Position Impossible [is] a peculiar example of televisual **galimatias**. (Will Self, *Television: Bad Enough to Make Your Lingam Shrivel Up*, Independent on Sunday, 02-18-2001, p. 12.)

giddy (as in lightheaded or dizzy) *adj.*: **vertiginous**. SEE DIZZY

gift (extra or unexpected ... sometimes given with customer's purchase) *n.*: **lagniappe**. ∎ Forbes FYI is the magazine that GQ and Esquire want to be. Under the editorship of Christopher Buckley, the magazine is consistently humorous, crisply written and slightly, but not obnoxiously, tongue in cheek. ... Unfortunately, you can't find the magazine on newsstands. It's the quarterly **lagniappe** sent to devoted subscribers of Forbes magazine. (Cathy Hainer, *Dreaming of a Martha Stewart Christmas — "Forbes FYI" Gives the Funny Bone a Good Workout*, USA Today, 11-29-1994, p. 10.)

(2) gift (as in blessing) *n.*: **benison**. SEE BLESSING

(3) gift (such as flowers, to a wife from a guilty husband) *n.*: **drachenfutter** [German; lit. dragon-fodder]. SEE PEACE-OFFERING

(4) gift (as in offering) *n.*: **oblation**. SEE OFFERING

(5) gift (as in donation, which is all one can afford) *n.*: **widow's mite**. SEE DONATION

gigantic *adj.*: **Pantagruelian** [This word is generally defined as "marked by coarse satire," a definition with which this example does not match. However, the word derives from Pantagruel, the gigantic son of Gargantua in Rebelais's 1533 novel *Pantagruel*, and this sense of "gigantic" is the far more commonly used sense of the word]. ∎ [At Voila! restaurant,] portions are sensible, not **Pantagruelian**. (Patricia Brooks, *Dining Out*, The New York Times, 01-11-1998.)

(2) gigantic *adj.*: **brobdingnagian** (often cap.). SEE HUGE

(3) gigantic *adj.*: **Bunyanesque**. SEE ENORMOUS

(4) gigantic (like an elephant) *adj.*: **elephantine**. SEE ENORMOUS

(5) gigantic (object) *n.*: **leviathan**. SEE HUGE

(6) gigantic *adj.*: **pythonic**. SEE HUGE

G.I. Joe (British equivalent of ...) *n*.: **Tommy Atkins**. See soldier

gilded (as in golden) *adj*.: **aureate**. See golden

girl (who is playful or impish) *n*.: **gamine** [French]. ∎ Though just 4 ft. 6 1/2 in. and a slight 72 lbs, [gymnast Dominique] Moceanu is a fetching **gamine** who can ignite an arena with her Audrey Hepburn-like looks and contagious ebullience. (Jill Smolowe, *Altius: Flexible Flyer: Big Things Are Expected From the Small Package of Teenybopper Dominique Moceanu*, Time, 06-28-1996, p. 64.)

(2) girl (French working-class ...) *n*.: **grisette** [French]. ∎ Some [women who eventually became prostitutes] were upper-class girls, down on their luck, who chose to service rich men rather than serve as governesses to their children. ... Many more were born into a life of poverty, earning paltry livings as **grisettes**, or seamstresses, before emerging like glittering butterflies from the grey muslin dresses that gave them their name. (Lucy Moore, *How to Get Ahead in Bed*, The Sunday Times [London], 02-24-2002.)

(3) girl (who is high-spirited and boisterous) *n*.: **hoyden**. See tomboy

girlfriend (or woman with whom one is in love or has intimate relationship) *n*.: **inamorata**. ∎ One of the few people who was close to both of the Waleses, Hoare invited [Prince] Charles and his **inamorata** Camilla Parker Bowles to discreet dinners at his home and served as an ad hoc counselor for [Princess Diana]. (Michelle Green, *A Princess in Peril — Accused of Harassing a Married Friend With Silent Phone Calls, a Troubled Diana Seems to Be Spinning Out of Control*, People, 09-05-1994, p. 70.)

gist (of a matter, as in the essence) *n*.: **quiddity**. See essence

give back (often a territory) *v.t*.: **retrocede**. See return

give up (as in renounce or disavow) *v.t*.: **abjure**. See renounce

(2) give up (esp. responsibility or duty) *v.t*.: **abnegate**. See renounce

glad *adj*.: **eupeptic**. See cheerful

gladness (causing or tending to produce ...) *adj*.: **felicific**. See happiness

glamorized (or romanticized conception of oneself, as a result of boredom in one's life) *n*.: **Bovarism**. See self-delusion

glance (with a sideways ...) *adv*.: **asquint**. ∎ Over a weakish chin, [the baseball pitcher] sports a sparse salt-and-pepper beard that appears to be fashioned after Yasir Arafat's. Peering in for the sign with mild eyes **asquint** and lips parted slightly, he could not cow a Cub Scout. (Scott Raab, *The Face of Baseball [Cleveland Indians Pitcher Paul Assenmacher]*, Esquire, 05-01-1998, p. 108.)

(2) glance (quick ...) *n*.: **coup d'oeil** [French]. ∎ "Remember that ... it is only at length that I can hope to please, and then only if there is in those who regard me a grain of indulgence; but for the passer-by, the **coup d'oeil** is too hasty, he sees only the surface, he who does not have the time, moves on." [Written by French painter Camille Pissarro to his son in 1883]. (Rachael Ziady DeLue, *Pissarro, Landscape, Vision, and Tradition*, The Art Bulletin, 12-01-1998, p. 718.)

(3) glance *n*.: **dekko** [British inf.]. ∎ Alas, eBay is the too-perfect distraction for a writer stuck at home. Here I am, just now, finishing this, and it occurs to me that my wastepaper basket is falling apart. Let's just take a quick **dekko** at rattan baskets. Hmm, here's a Chinese reed basket, supposedly Qing dynasty. (Kate Jennings, *Something For Kate*, Australian Financial Review, 12-12-2003.)

(4) glance (which is flirtatious) *n*.: **oeillade** [French]. ∎ [In the movie "Witness," Captain Book] exchang[es] loving glances with Rachel ... especially during a barn raising at which he carpenters and she waits on the communal tables. The two swap so many **oeillades** that it is a miracle the milk doesn't end up in a Lapp's lap, and Book's finger nailed to the roof beam. (John Simon, *Witness [Movie Reviews]*, National Review, 04-05-1985.)

glass (of, relating to, or resembling ...) *adj*.: **hyaline**. See glassy

(2) glass (display case) *n*.: **vitrine**. See showcase

glasses (with a short handle like opera ...) *n*.: **lorgnette**. See eyeglasses

(2) glasses (clipped to the bridge of the nose) *n*.: **pince-nez**. See eyeglasses

glassy *adj*.: **hyaline**. ∎ Graham and Rorem also share the ability to balance elegantly on the rim of sentimentality. "Early in the Morning," a deceptively simple setting of a genuinely simple poem by Robert Hillyer, captures the **hyaline** clarity that comes from mixing memories of Paris and youth. (Justin Davidson, *On the Record/Classical Music*, Newsday, 04-28-2000, p. D26.)

gleaming *adj.*: **coruscant**. SEE GLITTERING

(2) gleaming *adj.*: **effulgent**. SEE BRIGHT

(3) gleaming *adj.*: **fulgurant**. SEE BRIGHT

(4) gleaming *adj.*: **refulgent**. SEE BRIGHT

glee (from witnessing other's misfortunes) *n.*: **Roman holiday**. SEE SADISM

(2) glee (from other's misfortunes) *n.*: **schadenfreude** [German]. SEE SADISM

gleeful *adj.*: **Falstaffian**. SEE JOVIAL

glimmer (as in trace or small amount of) *n.*: **tincture**. SEE TRACE

glimpse (with a sideways ...) *adv.*: **asquint**. SEE GLANCE

(2) glimpse (quick ...) *n.*: **coup d'oeil** [French]. SEE GLANCE

(3) glimpse *n.*: **dekko** [British inf.]. SEE GLANCE

glittering *adj.*: **coruscant**. ▌ Not since Joan Sutherland used to dazzle us from the Met's stage with the bravura of "Ah! Non giunge" from La sonnambula has a Met audience heard quite such **coruscant** pyrotechnics [as from Italian mezzo-soprano Cecilia Bartoli in La Cenerentola]. (John Ardoin, *Love Match: In "Cenerentola," Glitter is More Bartoli Than Glass*, The Dallas Morning News, 11-13-1997, p. 39A.)

(2) glittering *adj.*: **refulgent**. SEE BRIGHT

global (in scope or applicability) *adj.*: **ecumenical**. SEE UNIVERSAL

gloominess (as in depression) *n.*: **cafard** [French]. SEE DEPRESSION

(2) gloominess (as in world-weariness or sentimental pessimism over the world's problems) *adj.*: **Weltschmerz** [German]. SEE PESSIMISM

gloomy *adj.*: **acherontic**. ▌ Bob Dole ... can deliver a dry one-liner. But the brand of wit that comes naturally to him does not play well in prime time; it can be sharp, even, gad!, mean-spirited. So the man is trying his darndest to be nice. [Despite that, his demeanor] is, yes, doleful, the image verges on the **acherontic**, the look of souls confronting hell. Never mind. If he should actually win the nomination and the election, he will probably cheer up. (Walter Goodman, *Never Mind His Politics, Is the Man Telegenic?* The New York Times, 02-20-1996, p. C18.)

(2) gloomy *adj.*: **Cimmerian**. ▌ There is still the semblance of an independent judiciary [in Zimbabwe], though probably not for long. ... And a free press still operates under heroic circumstances, although journalists in Harare see a **Cimmerian** darkness descending on them. (Tony Leon, *South Africa's Defining Moment — Why Mbeki Should Offer Zimbabwe More Sticks and Fewer Carrots*, Time International, 04-23-2001, p. 48.)

(3) gloomy (and dark) *adj.*: **tenebrous**. ▌ [In 1944, Alfred Kazin wrote an article] that will live long in the annals of that **tenebrous** time [i.e. the era of Nazi Germany]. "In Every Voice, in Every Ban" was a cry of outrage at the suicide of Shmuel Ziegelboim, the representative of the Bund who killed himself in London to protest the world's indifference to the extermination of the Jews. (Author not given, *Alfred Kazin*, The New Republic, 06-29-1998.)

(4) gloomy (and dark and misty) *adj.*: **caliginous**. SEE DARK

(5) gloomy (as in sullen or morose) *adj.*: **saturnine**. SEE SULLEN

(6) gloomy (as in suggestive of a funeral) *adj.*: **sepulchral**. SEE FUNEREAL

(7) gloomy (as in hellish) *adj.*: **Stygian**. SEE HELLISH

(8) gloomy (as in sad or melancholy) *adj.*: **tristful**. SEE SAD

glorification *n.*: **apotheosis** (*v.t.*: **apotheosize**). SEE EXALTATION

glorified (or romanticized conception of oneself, as a result of boredom in one's life) *n.*: **Bovarism**. SEE SELF-DELUSION

glory (in, or boast, esp. about the accomplishments of a relative) *v.t.*, *n.*: **kvell** [Yiddish]. SEE BOAST

gloss (over, as in make pleasant or less harsh) *v.t.*: **edulcorate**. SEE SWEETEN

gloss over (try to ... an offense with excuses) *v.t.*: **palliate**. SEE DOWNPLAY

glowing *adj.*: **lucent**. ▌ The Postman, however, is strangely rib-tickling and heart-melting, strange even in what went on behind the scenes, which, in this case, is not irrelevant, and further irradiates an already **lucent** movie. (John Simon, *The Postman* [*Movie Reviews*], National Review, 07-31-1995, p. 64.)

(2) glowing *adj.*: **effulgent**. SEE BRIGHT

(3) glowing *adj.*: **fulgurant**. SEE BRIGHT

(4) glowing (softly ...) *adj.*: **lambent**. SEE SHIMMERING

(5) glowing *adj.*: **refulgent**. SEE BRIGHT

glue (or bond together) *v.t.*: **agglutinate**. SEE ADHERE

gluey *adj.*: **viscid**. SEE STICKY

glum (as in sullen or morose) *adj.*: **saturnine**. SEE SULLEN

glutton *n.*: **trencherman**. ❚ "Deeelicious!" says [Tommy Lasorda], the 59-year-old manager of the Los Angeles Dodgers, an epic **trencherman** who claims that he "never met a meal I didn't like." In fact he carries a spare fork in his back pocket, just in case he runs into a dish he can't resist. (Todd Gold, *Host: Next to His Family and His Beloved Dodger Blue, Tommy Lasorda Lives for Food — and His Restaurant*, People, 07-13-1987, p. 103.)

(2) glutton (to eat like a ...) *v.t.*: **gormandize**. SEE DEVOUR

gluttony *n.*: **gulosity**. ❚ But humans, especially Americans, scarf up whatever's shoved in their face. ... The result of my holiday **gulosity** impacted upon me one night at a Santa Monica restaurant called Rix. The owner had stopped by to chat and was discussing a live jellyfish he planned on placing in a tank as part of the restaurant's decor. I was in a comatose state and when I heard jellyfish I said, "Sure, I'll try it, just a small bite." (Al Martinez, *Eat, Eat, Eat, Drink, Eat, Chat, Drink, Eat, Eat*, Los Angeles Times, 12-22-1999, p. B1.)

gnashing (of teeth during sleep) *n.*: **bruxism**. SEE GRINDING

go beyond (or exceed the limits, resources or capabilities of) *v.t.*: **beggar**. SEE SURPASS

go-between *n.*: **comprador**. SEE INTERMEDIARY

goal *n.*: **nisus**. ❚ [Review of *Scufflin* by Magic Slim & the Teardrops:] "Shufflin' " is more like it. However Morris "Magic Slim" Holt wishes to title his latest effort, his **nisus** is shuffling the blues along a well-worn path, inviting you to stomp your feet and clap your hands. (Paul Hampel, *Music/Album Reviews*, St. Louis Post-Dispatch, 02-06-1997, p. 8.)

(2) goal (esp. of life) *n.*: **telos** [Greek; derives from Aristotle's inquiry into our goal and purpose in life; our reason for being.] ❚ [The preamble to the constitution to the European Union] presents a picture of Europe's past in terms that suggest the EU is the ... Aristotelian **telos**, toward which Europe has been enthusiastically striving over thousands of years. ... The implication is that the European constitution represents the consummation of this dream. (Peter Jones, *Perverted View of History in EU Preamble: Bureaucrat-Written Constitution Says a Lot About EU's*

Mentality, The Gazette [Montreal, Quebec], 01-11-2004.)

(3) goal (hidden or ulterior ...) *n.*: **arriere-pensee** (or **arrière-pensée**) [French]. SEE MOTIVE

(4) goal (as in objective) *n.*: **quaesitum**. SEE OBJECTIVE

(5) goal (highest ... to be attained, lit. the greatest or highest good) *n.*: **summum bonum** [Latin]. SEE IDEAL

(6) goal (directed towards a ...) *adj.*: **telic**. SEE PURPOSEFUL

(7) goal (which is delusive or not realistically obtainable) *n.*: **will-o'-the-wisp**. SEE PIPE DREAM

goat (of or relating to, esp. as to smell) *adj.*: **hircine**. ❚ Did I do something to deserve to be called a goat? Was I employing the best of conflict resolution skills by bellowing in reply, "No, pal, you're the goat"? Yet after some thought, I have a clear conscience about my near fisticuffs last Friday. There are times when one must take a stand, even at the risk of being outed as an ill-tempered **hircine** ruminant. I fought my fight for my own self-respect as a man among Russian men. (Author not given, *Sorry, Pal, You're the Goat!* The Moscow Times [Russia], 04-23-2001.)

gobble (food like a glutton) *v.t.*: **gormandize**. SEE DEVOUR

gobbledygook *n.*: **galimatias**. SEE GIBBERISH

god (belief in one ... without denying others) *n.*: **henotheism**. SEE DEITY

(2) god (worship of or belief in more than one ...) *n.*: **polytheism**. SEE DEITY

God (belief in the existence of ..., esp. one ...) *n.*: **theism**. ❚ "Abortion is a matter between a woman, her doctor and God." — Premier Ralph Klein of Alberta. ... By referring to such an entity he has at least taken a stand for **theism**. Whether atheists like it or not, he says, "God" is a factor in the abortion question. (Virginia Ted-Byfield, *What Exactly Does Ralph Klein Mean When He Brings "God" into the Abortion Issue?* Alberta Report/Western Report, 10-16-1995, p. 41.)

(2) God (centering on ... as the primary concern) *adj.*: **theocentric**. ❚ The concept that "man is the measure of all things," as Protagoras put it, confronted the church's **theocentric** portrait of the universe. (John Elson, *Looking Back: The Millennium of Discovery*, Time, 10-15-1992, p. 16.)

(3) God (having an animal form) *adj.*: **theriomorphic**. ❚ In the myth Yeluri personifies evil. ... With the help of several **theriomorphic** goddesses such as the hedgehog goddess, the rat goddess, and the eagle goddess, to mention only the most important ones, the good goddesses finally succeed in beating back the attacks of the demon Yeluri and ban him to live under the surface of the earth. (Georg Heyne, *Mandschurische Gottinnen Und Iranische Teufel [book review]*, Asian Folklore Studies, 06-01-2001.)

(4) God (vindication of the justice of ..., esp. in permitting or ordaining natural or moral evil) *n.*: **theodicy**. ▪ [The novel *Hey Nostradamus!* by Douglas Coupland chronicles the aftermath of a shooting spree at a Vancouver high school in 1988. It contains] a more serious (if glancingly handled) treatment of **theodicy**: If you believe in God, how do you answer the question "Why does God allow these horrific things to happen?" (Meghan O'Rourke, *Ambitious Novel Leaves Unanswered Questions*, Chicago Sun-Times, 08-17-2003.)

(5) God (controlled or governed by ...) *n.*: **theonomous**. ▪ Cinema, especially in mythic form, is concerned with the depth dimension of the human situation. It is concerned with ultimates, which most people call God. God is in us, closer to us than we are to ourselves. Yet God flows beyond us in every way. This means that the human situation is **theonomous**. In its depths, it can be transparent to the God who lives there. (Ellwood Keiser, *Why I Make Movies*, National Catholic Reporter, 04-09-1999.)

(6) God (appearance of ... to a person) *n.*: **theophany**. ▪ Leaders can hope to influence, not by majestic miracles and thunderous **theophanies**, but rather by silent sensitivity and loving outreach. (Shlomo Riskin, *Judaism's Silent Thunder*, The Jerusalem Post, 03-12-2004, p. 32.)

(7) God (fear of ... or God's wrath) *n.*: **theophobia**. ▪ School officials at a public high school in Hampton, Va., have ordered a student Christian club to eliminate "Easter" from the title of an annual canned food drive because it may offend students of other faiths. ... "This sets a terrible precedent," said [the students' lawyer]. "This smacks of **theophobia** where now the schools are nitpicking at names. This is simply a result of being overzealous and being overly cautious on the issue of the separation of church and state." (Ellen Sorokin, *School Tells Club "Easter" Must Be Off Food-Drive Title; Christians Told Use "Spring" Instead*, The Washington Times, 03-14-2002.)

(8) God (belief there is only one ...) *n.*: **monotheism**. See DEITY

(9) God (government by ... or a divine being) *n.*: **theocracy**. See GOVERNMENT

godlike (having both human and ... attributes) *adj.*: **theanthropic**. ▪ [After September 11, 2001,] our government should order the CIA to air drop to the Mullahs and their angry young men millions of pages from the Victoria's Secret catalogues. Anyone familiar with the September 11 atrocities knows that these fellows are sexually repressed. ... Pursuing the **theanthropic** [Victoria's Secret model Laetitia Casta] through Google-space, they will be lured toward the pages of The American Spectator, where they will enjoy the health benefits of cultural diversity. (R. Emmett Tyrell, Jr., *The Continuing Crisis*, The American Spectator, 01-01-2002.)

gods (battle or conflict among ...) *n.*: **theomachy**. ▪ Kuhn's thesis is that ... science is all theoretical talk and negotiation, which never really establishes anything. ... [His theory] is also an instance of the enduring appeal of **theomachy**, [namely] what was previously thought to be a continuous and uninteresting succession of random events is discovered to be a conflict of a finite number of hidden gods (classes, complexes, paradigms, as the case may be), who manipulate the flux of appearances to their own advantage. (James Franklin, *Thomas Kuhn's Irrationalism [Book Review]*, New Criterion, 06-01-2000.)

gold (of, pertaining to or containing) *adj.*: **auric**. ▪ [From the movie *Goldfinger*:] **Auric** Goldfinger: This is gold, Mr. Bond. All my life I've been in love with its color, its brilliance, its divine heaviness. I welcome any enterprise that will increase my stock, which is considerable. [James Bond:] I think you've made your point, Goldfinger. Thank you for the demonstration. (Scott Simon, *Interview: Professor James Chapman, Film Historian, Discusses the James Bond Movie Series*, Weekend Edition — Saturday [NPR], 09-09-2000.)

golden *adj.*: **aureate**. ▪ In the second quarter of '86, he lost $100 million. "We took too much risk. I should have been fired," he says. Suddenly First Boston's California golden boy wasn't looking so **aureate**. (Andy Serwer, *Features: The Hidden Beauty Of Bonds*, Fortune, 03-19-2001, p. 118.)

gondolier (song of) *n.*: **barcarole**. See SONG

good (very ..., as in excellent) *adj.*: **galumptious**. See EXCELLENT

(2) good (very ...) *adj.*: **palmary**. See EXCELLENT

(3) good (greatest or highest ...) *n.*: **summum bonum**. [Latin]. See IDEAL

good vs. evil (philosophy which divides the world into ...) *n.*: **manichaeism** (*adj.*: **manichean**). ∎ Lanz and his followers were obsessed by homoerotic notions of a **manichean** struggle between the heroic and creative "blond" race and a race of predatory "beast-men" who preyed on the "blond" women with animal lust and bestial instincts that were corrupting and destroying mankind and its culture. (Kershaw, *Hitler*, Norton [1998], p. 50.)

(2) good vs. evil (conflict in the soul between ...) *n.*: **psychomachia**. ∎ [Boxer Sonny] Liston was seen, by black as well as white, as the Bad Nigger. Of course, if the NAACP had any faith that the Good Nigger [Floyd Patterson] had a shot in hell at vanquishing the Bad Nigger, they would have supported the fight. ... How had boxing become **psychomachia**? (Nick Tosches, *The Devil and Sonny Liston*, Little Brown [2000], p. 160.)

good-looking (esp. sexually) *adj.*: **toothsome**. SEE SEXY

good-naturedness *n.*: **bonhomie**. SEE AFFABILITY

goodbye (act of saying ...) *n.*: **valediction**. SEE FAREWELL

goodness (lit. "humanity," often used in the sense of decency) *n.*: **menschlichkeit** [German, Yiddish]. SEE DECENCY

(2) goodness (as in virtue or integrity) *n.*: **probity**. SEE INTEGRITY

goody-goody (like a prudish ...) *adj.*: **missish**. SEE PRUDE

gooey *adj.*: **viscid**. SEE STICKY

goof-off *n.*: **wastrel**. SEE SLACKER

goose (of, relating to or resembling) *adj.*: **anserine**. ∎ Brian was aiming to expand the circle of my **anserine** acquaintances and he was given the chance when he discovered six White-fronted geese in a flock of 30 Greylags at the tail-end of the year. (James O'Hagan, *Wind and Sun Cook Watcher's Goose Country Diary*, The Scotsman [Edinburgh, Scotland], 01-09-1999.)

goose bumps (get ... from fear, anxiety or cold) *v.t.*: **horripilate** (*n.*: **horripilation**). ∎ Tessa [a flirtatious attractive student] extricated herself from the seat-and-desk contraption she was in and came over to [the professor]. He felt himself **horripliating**. What was expected of him now? (Erik Tarloff, *The Man Who Wrote the Book*, Crown [2000], p. 137.)

gorge (to the point of excess, esp. things sweet) *v.t.*: **cloy**. SEE SATIATE

(2) gorge (on food) *v.i.*: **gormandize**. SEE DEVOUR

gorilla (of or relating to, or resembling) *adj.*: **anthropoid**. SEE APE

gory (as in bloody) *adj.*: **sanguinary**. SEE BLOODY

gossip (as in spread news or a rumor about) *v.t.*: **bruit**. SEE RUMOR

(2) gossip (idle ..., as in small talk) *n.*: **palaver**. SEE SMALL TALK

(3) gossip (person who is a ...) *n.*: **quidnunc**. SEE BUSYBODY

gourmet *n.*: **epicure**. ∎ In my last column, I reviewed the best new entrants on London's revived restaurant scene, but it would be a shame to overlook some of the city's long-established gems — restaurants that have been seducing international **epicures** for many years. (James Villas, *London's Classics, Updated: Our Critic Discovers That Britain's Grand Old Restaurants Haven't Lost Their Savor*, Town & Country Monthly, 08-01-1996, p. 54.)

(2) gourmet *n.*: **gastronome**. ∎ The growing diversity of foods available in the US. is enough to make even the most picky **gastronome** swoon. (James Villas, *The Genuine Article [Foods That Are Best Eaten in Their Native Regions]*, Town & Country Monthly, 02-01-1996, p. 56.)

government (or political dominance of men) *n.*: **androcracy**. ∎ All the varieties of Christianity in Africa are riddled with androcentrism and misogyny. For women to be at home in Christianity, they suspend belief that it is **androcracy** that dominates them and not the will of God or their own special innate sinfulness arising out of being women. (Mercy Amba Oduyoye, *Christianity and African Culture*, International Review of Mission, 01-01-1995.)

(2) government (by old people) *n.*: **gerontocracy**. ∎ Ezra Taft Benson [was] the supreme authority of the Mormon Church until his death last week at the age of 94. [His successor may be 86-year-old Howard Hunter] who had open-heart surgery eight years ago and a gall-bladder operation last year. ... In spite of this **gerontocracy**, the Church of Jesus Christ of Latter-day Saints remains vibrant. (Sophfronia Scott Gregory, *Religion: Saints Preserve Us — The Mormons Are Likely to Choose Another Aged, Ailing Leader, but Nevertheless Their Church is Thriving*, Time, 06-13-1994, p. 65.)

(3) government (by women) *n*.: **gynarchy**. ∎ By far the philosopher's most-favoured correspondent was his mother, Maude, for whom he confessed "an Oedipal complex the size of a house." She appears in these letters as a formidable matriarch in the family tradition of strong females, which her approval-seeking son called "the **gynarchy**." (Chris Champion, *And Now, the Real George Grant Emerges*, Alberta Report/Western Report, 11-18-1996, p. 45.)

(4) government (by women or political or social dominance by women) *n*.: **gynocracy**. ∎ All my working life, there have been women. This newspaper is edited by a woman; I send in this column to a woman. The publisher I am down here writing a book for is a woman. Most of my editors have been women. The odd thing is that working, as I do, in a delightful, intelligent, staunch, humane **gynocracy** is an experience that simply wasn't available to this house's founder. (Michael Bywater, *It's a Man's Man's Man's World*, Independent on Sunday, 03-16-1997, p. 38.)

(5) government (by clergy) *n*.: **hierocracy**. ∎ When asked which existing regime most closely approximates an ideal Islamic order, fundamentalists most often cite the governments of the Sudan or Iran — the first a military regime, the second a **hierocracy** ruled by an increasingly autocratic cleric, and both first-order violators of human rights. (Martin Kramer, *Islam vs. Democracy [Future of Islamic Fundamentalism]*, Commentary, 01-01-1993.)

(6) government (by the least qualified or least principled people) *n*.: **kakistocracy**. ∎ CANNON: Well, we couldn't convict [Bill Clinton]. But I think the American people understand what [the Clinton] administration is all about. ... And we have the greatest system on earth, a system strong enough to withstand the assaults over the last six years of this **kakistocracy**. (Sean Hannity, Alan Colmes, *Ken Starr Investigation*, Hannity & Colmes [Fox News Network], 06-24-1999.)

(7) government (characterized by greed and corruption) *n*.: **kleptocracy**. ∎ Conversely, when narrow elites establish a chokehold on foreign trade, and also steal most of the foreign aid and foreign loans coming into the country, then the country will become even poorer — just what's happening in sub-Saharan Africa, where almost every government is a **kleptocracy**. (Dave Kopel, *Police Shootings Need Closer Look*, Denver Rocky Mountain News, 07-29-2001, p. 7E.)

(8) government (by the mob or the masses) *n*.: **mobocracy**. ∎ The spasm of communal violence [by Hindu militants] has almost brought down the 11-month-old government of Prime Minister V.P. Singh. ... Said [one politician]: "The country is at a crossroads. We have to choose between secularism and religious fundamentalism, between democracy and **mobocracy**, between unity and disintegration." (Guy D. Garcia, *India: The Awesome Wrath of Rama Religious Nationalism Threatens to Bring Down the Government and Splinter the Country*, Time, 11-12-1990, p. 47.)

(9) government (by the mob or the masses) *n*.: **ochlocracy**. ∎ [There are] ominous signs of how unrest is taking hold all across the U.S.S.R. ... Discontent is everywhere. ... "Intellectuals have mostly withdrawn to their homes, and it is **ochlocracy** that now reigns in the streets in the absence of either a strong hand or democracy," [said one journalist]. (Yuri Zarakhovich Tbilisi, *Europe: It Was Just What the Other Republics Fear*, Time International, 01-29-1990, p. 13.)

(10) government (by a few persons or factions) *n*.: **oligarchy**. ∎ Atlanta in 1964 was run by an **oligarchy** of conservative white businessmen and lawyers, most of whom hung around the crusty old Piedmont Driving Club or the Capital City Club, and virtually all of whom had no use for the civil rights movement. (John Huey, *The Atlanta Game Against All Odds: This Sunbelt Hustler Snagged the Olympics by Selling Itself as a Third World City; The Biggest Lie it Ever Told Turns Out to Be True*, Fortune, 07-22-1996, p. 42.)

(11) government (utopian ... where everyone rules equally) *n*.: **pantisocracy**. ∎ Utopia has never existed. ... [W]henever it fails, there is always someone around to tell you the wrong reasons for it and propose another model, which in turn proves equally unworkable. This is as true of nutty little proposals by discontented geniuses — like the idea of communalist, rural "**pantisocracy**" put forward by Shelley, Coleridge and others in their youth. (Robert Hughes, *The Arts/Ideas: The Phantom of Utopia Geniuses*, Time, 11-06-2000, p. 120.)

(12) government (industry owned or partly controlled by ...) *adj*.: **parastatal**. ∎ Nigeria's **parastatal** organisations illustrate the point nicely. Set up to run everything from telephones to electricity, insurance and paper-making, these state enterprises now number over 1,000, their board members over 4,000. The grants and write-offs they receive each year from the government are bigger than the rest of the national budget. (Author not given, *Nigeria in Civvy Street*, The Economist, 06-19-1999.)

(13) government (by the wealthy) *n*.: **plutocracy**. ∎ One of the biggest problems of modern US politics, he said, is wealthy individuals from the business world bumping veterans who've worked their way up. "You don't want a **plutocracy** running your government," he said. (Tim Cornwell, *Wealth Talks Loudest in Race for California Governor*, Independent, 02-16-1998, p. 10.)

(14) government (by God or a divine being) *n.*: **theocracy**. ▮ The essay, "God as a Running Mate," reminded readers that the Constitution decrees the separation of church and state, and worried — scornfully — that Republican and Democratic presidential candidates have been making speeches in which they "sound as if they would not be uncomfortable in an evangelical **theocracy**." (Michael Joseph Gross, *Books & the Arts: Mourning and America*, The Nation, 11-01-1999, p. 29.)

(15) government (in proportion to wealth or property ownership) *n.*: **timocracy**. ▮ The battle for Seattle over the World Trade Organization's meetings was the embryonic stage of the struggle against global "**timocracy**," ... Aristotle's idea of a state in which political power is in direct proportion to property ownership. To the uninitiated in the globalism phenomenon, **timocracy** appears to be rearing its ugly head. The three executives at the top of the Microsoft ladder are now worth more than 170 million Americans. (Arnaud De Borchgrave, *Warm-up for the Long Haul [Commentary]*, The Washington Times, 12-06-1999.)

(16) government (by three entities) *n.*: **triarchy**. ▮ For international financial negotiations, Grant suggests a new G8. This would consist of the US, Russia, China, Euroland, Canada, Brazil, India, and Japan, and he sees the world economy as being dominated by a **triarchy** — the US, the enlarged EU, and a new East Asian grouping, including China, Japan, Korea, and the ASEAN countries. (Leonard Dick, *Eye on the EU [Predictions of European Union's Future]*, Europe, 11-01-2000.)

(17) government (actions of pompous but inefficient ... officials) *n.*: **bumbledom**. See BUREAUCRACY

grab (property to compel payment of debts) *v.t.*: **distrain**. See CONFISCATE

grabbing (adapted for ..., esp. a tail) *adj.*: **prehensile**. See GRASPING

graceful (and slender woman) *n.*: **sylph**. See WOMAN

graceless (as in clumsy) *adj.*: **lumpish**. See CLUMSY

grafter *n.*: **boodler**. ▮ You'd think we might catch a break from the **boodlers** and influence peddlers, if only out of a wartime sense of patriotic duty. Won't happen. [Chicago] can continue to revel in the stink of its corruption and greed. Just when we need it, along comes the news that we still are in the boodle playoffs. Through it all, Chicago still is Chicago. (Dennis Byrne, *Disgraceful Behavior Not a Problem*, Chicago Tribune, 10-29-2001, p. N17.)

grammarian (who is petty or pedantic) *n.*: **grammaticaster**. See PEDANATIC

grand (and stately, as befitting a baron) *adj.*: **baronial**. See STATELY

grandeur (having a delusional fantasy that one has ...) *n.*: **megalomania**. See DELUSIONAL

grandiose (esp. regarding speaking or writing style) *adj.*: **magniloquent**. See POMPOUS

(2) grandiose (esp. regarding speaking or writing style) *adj.*: **orotund**. See POMPOUS

grant (as in bestow, by one with higher power) *v.t.*: **vouchsafe**. See BESTOW

grasping (adapted for ..., esp. a tail) *adj.*: **prehensile**. ▮ Kinkajous and spider monkeys grasp branches with wraparound **prehensile** tails. (Mary Roach, *Aliens in the Treetops*, International Wildlife, 11-01-1994, p. 4.)

grass-eating *adj.*: **graminivorous**. ▮ If a computer program were asked to define a "horse," it would respond with an updated, animated version of Mr. Gradgrind's answer in Hard Times — "Quadruped. **Graminivorous**. Forty teeth," etc. (James Fallows, *The Cult of Information: The Folklore of Computers and the True Art of Thinking, [Book Reviews]*, The New Republic, 07-14-1986.)

gratification (sexual ... from rubbing against something or someone) *n.*: **frottage**. See RUBBING

gratified (often in a boastful way) *adj.*: **cock-a-hoop**. See ELATED

grating (on the ears) *adj.*: **scrannel**. See CACOPHONOUS

gratuity (in Near Eastern countries, esp. to expedite service) *n.*: **baksheesh**. ▮ **Baksheesh** is to Egypt as oil is to engines: It makes things work. It probably greased the palms of the process that built the pyramids. (Catherine Watson, *In Egypt, the Extended Palm* *is Found Almost Everywhere*, Minneapolis Star Tribune, 03-09-1997, p. 1G.)

(2) gratuity *n.*: **pourboire** [French]. ■ Simply uncorking the bottle early is practically useless. It will expose an amount of wine in the neck of the bottle equal to the size of the bottom of the cork. In other words, almost no wine at all. Mostly it gives the waiter or wine steward a bit of stage business to help inflate the **pourboire**. (Frank J. Prial, *Liquid Assets / Wine Has to Breathe, You Say? Put a Cork in it*, Minneapolis Star Tribune, 12-02-1999, p. 5T.)

(3) gratuity (as in extra or unexpected gift or benefit, sometimes as thanks for a purchase) *n.*: **lagniappe**. SEE GIFT

grave (suggestive of a ..., as in a funeral) *adj.*: **sepulchral**. SEE FUNEREAL

graveyard *n.*: **necropolis**. ■ French researchers ... were called in to examine a stash of mummies unearthed by the Egyptians in a **necropolis** at Ain Labakha, a village within the oasis inhabited by 500 to 1,000 people around the time of Christ. Because working-class graves are of little interest to treasure hunters, the mummies were virtually undisturbed. (Michael D. Lemonick, *Archaeology: Working Stiffs Mummies From a Rural Oasis Provide a Rare Window Onto the Brief, Backbreaking Lives of Ordinary Egyptians 2,000 Years Ago*, Time, 04-06-1998, p. 60.)

graveyards (one who loves ...) *n.*: **taphophile**. SEE CEMETERIES

gray (covered with ... or white hair as if with age) *adj.*: **hoary**. ■ We live in an age where old age is scorned; rather than honoring a **hoary** head, we lock it away behind closed doors in an institution commonly called a nursing home. (Rabbi Shlomo Riskin, *Beauty That Lasts*, Jerusalem Post, 09-24-1999, p. 9B.)

greasy (as in slippery) *adj.*: **lubricious**. SEE SLIPPERY

great (as in of the highest quality) *n.*: **first water** (usu. as in "of the first water"). SEE QUALITY

(2) great (as in wonderful) *adj.*: **frabjous** (often as in "Oh frabjous day!"). SEE WONDERFUL

(3) great (as in wonderful) *adj.*: **galluptious** [slang]. SEE WONDERFUL

(4) great (as in excellent) *adj.*: **galumptious**. SEE EXCELLENT

(5) great (as in excellent) *adj.*: **palmary**. SEE EXCELLENT

(6) great *adj.*: **skookum**. SEE EXCELLENT

greatest (good) *n.*: **summum bonum**. [Latin]. SEE IDEAL

greatness (having a delusional fantasy that one has ...) *n.*: **megalomania**. SEE DELUSIONAL AND OBSESSION

Greece (one who admires or is interested in) *n.*: **philhellene**. ■ Much of Mr. Hanson's book will definitely please the **philhellene**. As the military might of ancient civilizations ebbed and flowed, the emergence of the Greek polis permanently changed the geopolitical balance of power. ... In every Western victory, Mr. Hanson sees a road leading back to classical Greece. (Author not given, *2,500 Years of Military Supremacy?* The Washington Times, 09-16-2001.)

greed (esp. for wealth) *n.*: **cupidity**. ■ Europe's past keeps sending awful bonbons to its present. In recent months, we have learned that Swiss banks piled up millions of dollars in assets stolen from Jewish victims of the Nazis. ... No one would argue that German evil absolves Swiss **cupidity** or French collaboration. (John Marks, *Swiss Cupidity, But German Evil*, U.S. News & World Report, 12-15-1997.)

greedy (person; lit. a large, fish-eating sea bird) *n.*: **cormorant**. ■ Bleeding from the most savage political bites in its twenty-five-year history, the National Endowment for the Arts — that profoundly underfunded government agency devoted to the development of culture and the needs of artists — is now foundering in the water with its belly up for all the **cormorants** to feed on [including various pressure groups and constituencies]. (Robert Brustein, *The NEA Belly Up*, The New Republic, 06-18-1990.)

(2) greedy *adj.*: **banausic**. SEE MATERIALISTIC

greeting (relating to a ... or other speech where the purpose is to establish a mood of sociability rather than to communicate information or ideas, such as "have a nice day") *adj.*: **phatic**. SEE PLEASANTRIES

gregarious (and social) *adj.*: **Anacreontic**. SEE CONVIVIAL

grief *n.*: **dolor** (*adj.*: **dolorous**). SEE SADNESS

(2) grief (expressing ... often regarding something gone) *adj.*: **elegiac**. SEE SORROWFUL

(3) grief (as in world-weariness or sentimental pessimism over the world's problems) *adj.*: **Weltschmerz** [German]. SEE PESSIMISM

grieve (over) *v.t.*: **bewail**. SEE LAMENT

grieved (easily ..., as in offended) *adj.*: **umbrageous**. SEE OFFENDED

grimace (gaping ...) *n*.: **rictus**. ▮ [After a horse-racing accident,] the flesh of his leg had been ripped away, exposing the bone. Pollard's face was a **rictus** of agony, his lips peeled back over his teeth, and gusts of pain were rolling through his body. (Laura Hillenbrand, *Seabiscuit*, Random House [2001], p. 218.)

grime (abnormal fear of) *n*.: **mysophobia**. SEE FEAR

grin (in a silly, self-conscious or affected manner, or to say something in such a fashion) *v.i., n*.: **simper**. SEE SMIRK

grind (as in crush or reduce to powder) *v.t*.: **comminute**. SEE PULVERIZE
(2) grind (as in toil) *v.i*.: **moil**. SEE TOIL

grinding (of teeth during sleep) *n*.: **bruxism**. ▮ The findings suggest that **bruxism** is not only a serious medical condition but also extremely common. About 8% of those surveyed reported grinding their teeth at least once a week, suggesting that 27 million Americans may be afflicted. (Mitch Nelin, *Developments to Watch: Bad News for Teeth Grinders*, Business Week, 02-12-2001, p. 97.)

gripe (as in fret or complain) *v.i*.: **repine**. SEE COMPLAIN

grogginess (relating to period of ... just before falling asleep) *adj*.: **hypnagogic**. SEE DROWSINESS

grooved *adj*.: **striated**. ▮ You have to spend the whole day outside in this miserable, steamy summer heat surrounded by people with **striated** fat rolls that look like Hostess Ho-Hos. (Tony Kornheiser, *Pumping Irony*, Times Books [1995], p. 37.)

grope *v.i*.: **grabble**. ▮ The concept is simple: breaking down divisions between formal eating and informal drinking. But blaring bar music and a steady traipse of drinkers wobbling past to the loo, as you **grabble** with your lobster crackers, isn't conducive to a restful evening out. (Adrian Turpin, *Food & Drink: Eating Out — As Time Goes By*, Independent on Sunday, 06-10-2001, p. 41.)
(2) grope (literally, fish with a net) *v.t., v.i*.: **seine**. SEE FISH

grouch *n*.: **crosspatch**. ▮ This collection of [Charlie] LeDuff's journalism and street vignettes for *The New York Times* portrays a city of a thousand faltering dreams, hard work and that special camaraderie at the Yankee Tavern, where old-timers deride the postponement of opening day and where sits

"Paulie Peterson, the 75-year-old **crosspatch** who lives alone and is delighted when he is able to tell somebody, anybody, to go to hell." (Tyler D. Johnson, *Work and Other Sins — Life in New York City and Thereabouts*, The New York Times, 03-28-2004.)

grouchy *adj*.: **tetchy**. ▮ He estimated that the first volume of the dictionary would be available to the world within two years. "And were it not for the dilatoriness of many contributors," he wrote, clearly in a **tetchy** mood, "I should not hesitate to name an earlier period." (Simon Winchester, *The Professor and the Madman*, Harper Collins [1998], p. 108.)
(2) grouchy *adj*.: **atrabilious**. SEE SURLY
(3) grouchy *adj*.: **bilious**. SEE SURLY
(4) grouchy *adj*.: **liverish**. SEE IRRITABLE
(5) grouchy *adj*.: **querulous**. SEE PEEVISH
(6) grouchy *adj*.: **shirty**. SEE IRRITABLE
(7) grouchy *adj*.: **splenetic**. SEE IRRITABLE

groundless (and/or illogical argument) *n*.: **choplogic**. SEE FALLACY

group *n*.: **gaggle**. ▮ On most Saturday nights Barry Bowman and a **gaggle** of his Southwestern Louisiana teammates gather around a television set to watch American Gladiators. (Tim Crothers, *Inside College Basketball*, Sports Illustrated, 01-23-1995, p. 87.)
(2) group (together) *v.t*.: **colligate**. SEE UNITE
(3) group (of objects, people or ideas) *n*.: **congeries**. SEE COLLECTION
(4) group (of riders in a bike race) *n*.: **peloton** [French]. SEE CLUSTER

grovel *v.i*.: **genuflect**. SEE KNEEL
(2) grovel *v.i*.: **truckle**. SEE KOWTOW

groveling (to behave towards in a ... manner) *v.t*.: **bootlick**. SEE KOWTOW
(2) groveling (person) *n*.: **lickspittle**. SEE SYCOPHANT

grow (as in burgeon or expand; lit.: bear fruit) *v.i*.: **fructify**. SEE BURGEON

growth (as in outgrowth) *n*.: **excrescence**. SEE OUTGROWTH

grueling (as in difficult or painful, journey or experience) *n*.: **via dolorosa**. SEE ORDEAL

grumble (as in fret or complain) *v.i*.: **repine**. SEE COMPLAIN

grumbling (as in complaining) *adj*.: **querulous**. SEE ORDEAL

grumpy (person) *n.*: **crosspatch**. See GROUCH

(2) grumpy *adj.*: **splenetic**. See IRRITABLE

(3) grumpy *adj.*: **tetchy**. See GROUCHY

guaranteed (esp. with respect to a plan, deal or investment that can be trusted completely because it is supposedly safe and sure to succeed) *adj.*: **copper-bottomed** [British]. See SURE-FIRE

guardian (as in watchdog) *n.*: **Cerebus**. See WATCHDOG

(2) guardian (of a place) *n.*: **genius loci** [Latin]. See SPIRIT

guerilla (warfare or tactics, esp. as a means to wear out an opponent) *adj.*: **Fabian** [This adjective derives from Roman general Quinton Fabius Maximus, who, through caution, avoidance of direct confrontation and harassment, defeated Hannibal in the Second Punic War. Today, it has become synonymous with, alternatively, caution or conservativeness, delay or dilatoriness, or guerilla tactics, and is often used in the phrase "Fabian tactics"]. ■ **Fabian tactics** also were employed by the Confederacy at times. ... The South sometimes resorted to such strategy because it did not have the manpower or the industrial might of the North and could ill afford the head-on clashes that sapped its strength much more quickly than its enemy's. But guerrilla tactics and avoidance of battle were not congenial to the Southern temperament. (Edward Colimore, *Could South Have Won With Other Strategy?* Charlotte Observer [North Carolina], 07-09-2001, p. 11A.)

guffaw *v.i.*: **cachinnate** (*n.*: **cachinnation**). See LAUGH

guide (for tourists) *n.*: **cicerone**. ■ At the end of this 500-page account readers are left with the grateful feeling that they have been led through the labyrinth of Russian names, events and cataclysms by a charming and witty guide, not an odious, mercenary **cicerone**. (Tatyana Tolstaya, *Lenin's Tomb: The Last Days of the Soviet Empire [book reviews]*, The New Republic, 04-11-1994, p. 29.)

(2) guide (and interpreter for travelers, esp. where Arabic, Turkish or Persian is spoken) *n.*: **dragoman**. ■ Sometimes during our journey across eastern Afghanistan, the threat of violence has been more obvious. A group of bandits fired shots in the general direction of our two vehicles as we drove through a river valley. It was their way of showing they wanted a lift. Our Afghan **dragoman**, a delightfully piratical character, ran over to head

them off. (John Simpson, *International: How I Was Robbed by Afghan Bandits*, The Sunday Telegraph, 10-05-1997.)

guidebook (to a country) *n.*: **Baedeker** (or **baedeker**). ■ This income, supplemented by royalties from his books on Italian painting (carried by superior tourists along with their **Baedekers**), allowed him gradually to form his own exquisite collection, still to be seen in the villa. (William Weaver, *The Renaissance of I Tatti*, Town & Country Monthly, 08-01-1994, p. 94.)

(2) guidebook *n.*: **vade mecum**. ■ Since, unlike most curators, the writers [of the program accompanying the Edward Hopper exhibit at the Whitney Museum] can write, one can read this **vade mecum** with pleasure after the show. (Robert Hughes, *The Arts & Media/Art: Under the Crack of Reality — Edward Hopper Saw an America That No Other Painter Had Got Right*, Time, 07-17-1995, p. 54.)

(3) guidebook *n.*: **enchiridion**. See HANDBOOK

guileless *n.*: **artless**. ■ [H]e presents a Cleopatra who likes to put on an artfully **artless** show of guileless girlishness. ... (In the all-male production of Cleopatra) Rylance skips about barefoot, like some innocent heroine from pastoral. (Paul Taylor, *Theatre: Everything but the Girl*, Independent, 08-03-1999, p. 9.)

guilt (caused by murder or bloodshed) *n.*: **bloodguilt**. ■ The Roman triumph served three crucial purposes. First, and most venerable, the ceremony not only acknowledged military success but also purified the city of Rome and its soldiers contaminated by the **bloodguilt** of war. (Peter Holliday, *Roman Triumphal Painting: Its Function, Development, and Reception*, The Art Bulletin, 03-01-1997, p. 130.)

guilty (as in sinful) *adj.*: **peccant**. See SINFUL

gullible (person) *n.*: **gobemouch** [French]. A "gobemouche" is "one who believes everything he hears." This word derives from the French gober, "to swallow," and mouche, "a fly." (Howard Richler, *English is Rich in Rare But Useful Words*, The Gazette [Montreal, Quebec] 03-13-1999, p. J2.)

(2) gullible (person) *n.*: **gudgeon**. See SUCKER

gulp (down greedily) *v.t.*: **englut**. See SWALLOW

(2) gulp (as in guzzle) *v.t., v.i.*: **ingurgitate**. See GUZZLE

gummy *adj.*: **glutinous**. See STICKY

(2) gummy (as in sticky) *adj.*: **mucilaginous**. See STICKY

gunfire (directed along a sweeping target) *n.*: **enfilade**. ∎ For more than a year, White and fellow Seattle-area freshman, Randy Tate, have been subjected to an **enfilade** of ads from the AFL-CIO and other liberal groups that has been continuous, massive, and damaging. (Rich Lowry, *Surviving in Seattle?[Washington State Politics and 1996 Presidential and Congressional Elections]*, National Review, 11-11-1996, p. 21.)

gurgle *v.t.*: **plash**. ∎ They burble, they babble, they **plash**. ... No matter how you describe the calm-down sound of water trickling over polished stones into a serene pool, Zen-inspired tabletop relaxation fountains — now available just about everywhere — are making a big splash this holiday shopping season. (Don Oldenburg, *Focus: A Cash Niagara From Desktop Waterfalls*, The Washington Post, 12-21-1999, p. C4.)

gush (as in speak quickly and excitedly) *v.t.*: **burble**. ∎ On Tuesday night, ... a host of celebrities worshipped at the altar of Michael Flatley, self-annointed Lord of the Dance. By Wednesday, we were down to the more humble disciples but their faith was absolute. "Ooh look: 'Video available October,'" **burbled** the folk behind me excitedly as they devoured their souvenir programme — and they hadn't even seen the show yet. (Louise Levene, *Lord of the Dance — Coliseum, London*, Independent, 07-26-1996, p. 7.)

(2) gush (as in excessive or contrived sentimentality) *n.*: **bathos**. SEE SENTIMENTALITY

(3) gush (of emotion, feeling or action) *n.*: **paroxysm**. SEE OUTBURST

gushiness (as in excessive or contrived sentimentality) *adj.*: **bathetic**. SEE SENTIMENTAL

gushy (as in overly sentimental) *adj.*: **mawkish**. SEE SENTIMENTAL

gust (sudden violent ... of wind) *n.*: **williwaw**. ∎ With the bad weather approaching, Phil and Linda rowed the short distance across to Fallado from where Windora was anchored in a calm spot on the island's western coast. In the time it took to look at the "chart," the sea had become choppy and **williwaws** had begun slamming into the bay from the hilltops above. (Tracy Neal, *Storm Story*, The Nelson Mail [New Zealand], 05-05-2004, p. 17.)

gutless (as in cowardly) *adj.*: **pusillanimous**. SEE COWARDLY

guts *n.*: **hardihood**. SEE COURAGE

gutsy (or bold while under the influence of alcohol) *adj.*: **potvaliant**. SEE COURAGEOUS

guzzle *v.t., v.i.*: **ingurgitate**. ∎ [T]he French cling patriotically to their contrariness, buoyed no doubt by their recent defiance of all Western, Eastern and alternative medicine in being the one country that can laugh at heart disease as its people **ingurgitate** the red wine, triple-cream cheeses and foie gras that kill everyone else. (Jonathan Reynolds, *The Death of French Food*, The New York Times, 07-23-2000.)

gymnastics (club) *n.*: **turnverein** [German]. ∎ [Lou] Gehrig loved all sports: football, baseball, soccer, swimming, ice skating, gymnastics (his father used to take him to the local German **turnverein**, or gym club). (Robert W. Creamer, *Lou Gehrig: The Original Iron Man*, Sports Illustrated, 09-15-1995, p. 24.)

H

habit (or custom) *n.*: **praxis**. SEE CUSTOM

habitual (frequenter of a place, esp. a place of entertainment) *n.*: **habitué**. SEE REGULAR

hackneyed (remark or statement) *n.*: **platitude**. SEE CLICHE

hag *n.*: **beldam**. ∎ Re: Police say man near airport was practicing satanic ritual, Jan. 17. We see by the papers that a witch has been arrested by police in Tampa, who suspect him of practicing a religion. Mr. Richard Lee Mullins, who is an unusual witch in that he carries no broom and is not the ordinary **beldam** one associates with the faith, has been charged with trespassing on Aviation Authority land. (Earl Irey [letter writer], *Letters to the Editor*, St. Petersburg Times [Florida], 01-28-1989.)

(2) hag *n.*: **crone**. ∎ As Magda, the over-tanned **crone** who kisses her dog with a touch too much enthusiasm, Shaye had a central role in the gross-out comedy of 1998 [There's Something About Mary]. In one spectacularly tasteless scene, Shaye undresses in front of a window, revealing what appears to be her leather-skinned, over-tanned, sagging and cronish bosom. (Liz Braun, *Shaye it Ain't So: "Mary" Actor Real Ugly Hag at Times*, The Ottawa Sun, 12-24-1998, p. 33.)

haggardly (of or like a ... old woman) *adj.*: **anile**. See OLD WOMAN

hair (remove one's own ... from the head or body) *v.t.*: **auto-depilatation**. ∎ A computer could quickly examine all of these graphs, but most people would tear their hair out long before finishing. With the help of a little logic, such **auto-depilitation** can be avoided. (Bruce Schecter, *My Brain is Open*, Simon & Schuster [1998], p. 84.)

(2) hair (of, relating to or covered with) *adj.*: **capillary**. ∎ Embracing research that fortifies the **capillary** with nutrients like a soy protein known as guar, Erilia offers a range of hair products that nourish the keratin fibers, thereby leaving hair healthier and easier to maintain. (Amy Barone, *Hair Care in Italy: Untapped Potential*, Drug & Cosmetic Industry, 04-01-1997, p. 12.)

(3) hair (head of ...) *n.*: **chevelure**. ∎ [T]he current show has to do with the social and psychological meaning of hair. ... In one giant image, the lines [of hair] flail like snakes, perhaps on the unseen head of Medusa. The viewer does not turn to stone, but the unruly **chevelure**, unframed and held only by pins, could at any minute break loose. (Henry Lehmann, *Good Hair, Bad Hair Days at the Saidye Bronfman Centre*, The Gazette [Montreal], 03-15-1997, p. I6.)

(4) hair (desire to pull out one's ...) *n.*: **trichotillomania**. ∎ Thank you for printing the letter from the woman whose daughter has **trichotillomania**. I, too, pull my hair out compulsively and didn't even know there was a name for it. (Joseph & Teresa Graedon, *The People's Pharmacy/Does Alcohol Increase Risk of Breast Cancer?* Newsday, 06-11-2001, p. C4.)

(5) hair (covered with ...) *adj.*: **pilose**. See HAIR

hair gel (esp. used to groom hair) *n.*: **pomade**. ∎ The antifrizz product is the hottest hair item of the nineties, and there are literally hundreds to choose from. ... Dan Sharp, a hairstylist to Marisa Tomei ... adds a generous amount of **pomade** to sopping-wet hair, then combs it through from root to ends. (Rachael Combe, *Beauty Report: Frizzies, Split Ends, Bad Bangs, Creeping Gray? Hair Masters Reveal 30 Great Fixes for the Trickiest Problems*, In Style, 10-01-1998, p. 244.)

hairless *n.*: **alopecia**. See BALDNESS
(2) hairless *adj.*: **glabrous**. See BALD

hairpiece (esp. worn by men in 17th and 18th centuries) *n.*: **peruke**. See WIG

hairstyle (with deep waves made by a curling iron) *n.*: **marcel**. ∎ Style secret: Barnard created thirties-era **marcels** using a curling iron and hairpins. (Joseph V. Amodio, *Beauty Report: Sheared Perfection*, In Style, 08-01-2000, p. 194.)

hairy *adj.*: **pilose**. ∎ So, who is this year's hair apparent? According to the Hair Club for Men, a company that knows a thing or two about the importance of a **pilose** head, it's [George W.] Bush — with his fluffier, let's-touch-it-and-see kind of hair. In contrast, Gore's bald spot, or "sandtrap" as some have taken to calling it, almost gleams when lighted from the back. (Saeed Ahmed, *Hair Vote Goes to Bush; Height Favors Gore: Creative Ways to Pick Winner Abound Campaign 2000*, The Atlanta Constitution, 11-07-2000, p. A7.)

half *n.*: **moiety**. See PORTION

half-truth (considered true due to printed repetition) *n.*: **factoid**. See INACCURACY

hallway (spec. the hallway in a stadium that connects the outer concourse to the interior of the stadium itself) *n.*: **vomitory**. See CORRIDOR

halo *n.*: **aureole**. ∎ There are five versions of Christ on the Sea of Galilee in the Philadelphia show, in two of which Christ's sleeping head is surrounded by an **aureole**. (Arthur C. Danto, *Books & the Arts: Art: The Late Works of Delacroix*, The Nation, 11-09-1998, p. 30.)

handbag (women's drawstring ...) *n.*: **reticule**. ∎ But there is an actual **reticule** also associated with Iago. In the opening lines of the play Roderigo says, "I take it much unkindly that thou, Iago, who hast had my purse, as though the strings were thine, shouldst know of this." From the beginning, then, Shakespeare represents Iago as the one who holds the purse strings. (Author not given, *"Prophetic Fury": Othello and the Economy of Shakespearian Reception*, Studies in the Literary Imagination, 04-1993.)

handbook *n.*: **enchiridion**. ∎ The writer-director, Alan Rudolph, has learned only one thing in the 15 films he has churned out: how to make each worse than the one before. ... [His movie] *Afterglow* is an **enchiridion** of every known literary and cinematic cliche. (John Simon, *The Sweet Hereafter*, National Review, 02-09-1998, p. 59.)

(2) handbook (for ready reference like a guidebook) *n.*: **vade mecum**. See GUIDEBOOK

handkerchief *n.*: **mouchoir** [French]. ∎ She is interviewed about her abstinence [and] declares with a **mouchoir** held to her deep tragic eyes that she only drank because her heart broke when Hartley Manners passed away, however she will have a little medicinal triple Scotch if the reporter can get the waiter fast enough because she is so emotionally upset now over the possibility of Hartley's coming to life again. (Tim Page, *Letters by Dawn Powell to Edmund Wilson*, New Criterion, 09-01-1999.)

handrail (and supports for) *n.*: **balustrade**. ∎ Descending the staircase — its **balustrade** laced with ivy and white orchids — she tossed handfuls of red rose petals from a basket. (Jill Smolowe, *Kilt By Association — Amid Tears, Tiaras and Scottish Tartan, Madonna and Guy Ritchie Baptize Baby Rocco and Tie the Knot*, People, 01-08-2001, p. 44.)

hands (requiring or using both ...) *adj*: **bimanual**. ∎ The **bimanual** examination comes next. In this procedure, the doctor inserts one or two lubricated fingers into your vagina and uses the other hand to press down on your abdomen. This helps detect abnormalities of the internal organs, such as the ovaries and the uterus. (Author not given, *10 Ways to Take Charge of Your Health*, Good Housekeeping, 03-01-1995, p. 173.)

handsome (or pretty) *adj.*: **toothsome**. SEE SEXY

handwriting (study of ..., esp. to study character) *n.*: **graphology**. ∎ Because everyone's handwriting, like DNA, is different, and because your loops and squiggles are the windows to your identity, **graphology** is even being used by companies to screen out potential crooks and incompetents. (Nadia Lerner, *Handwriting Reveals Your Soul, Expert Says*, The Dallas Morning News, 02-03-1999, p. 4C.)

handwritten (document entirely ... by signatory) *n.*: **holograph**. ∎ Abraham Lincoln **holographs** appearing on the auction block these days are likely to be routine memos from the 16th President — a postmaster's appointment or some such. Much rarer is a Lincoln paper in his own hand on a key political issue. (Author not given, *Society: A $500,000 Fragment: Part of Lincoln's Pivotal "House Divided" Speech Will be Auctioned*, Time, 08-31-1992, p. 20.)

hanger-on (esp. someone who seeks to associate with or flatter persons of rank or high social status) *n.*: **tuft-hunter** [Tuft-hunters often flatter those with whom they are trying to curry favor, and thus, *sycophant*, *flatterer* and their synonyms are, in most instances, perfectly proper synonyms for this word.

However, to be precise, the essence of the word is in the first instance simply the attempt to associate with those persons, which may well (and in the example given here, does) include acting like a sycophant, but not always.]. ∎ [Attorney General Janet] Reno has demonstrated pretty convincingly that she is no fawning courtier who hovers nearby eagerly waiting to clean up the messes that [President Clinton] leaves behind. [S]he possesses the quality that is indispensable in the nation's premier law enforcement officer: integrity. And if her critics attempt to paint her as a pliant **tuft-hunter** trying to ingratiate herself with the man who appointed her, they will disgrace themselves. (Ross Baker, *A Commendable Woman in Unenviable Job*, The Los Angeles Times, 12-8-1997, p. B5.)

hangout (as in a place one frequents) *n.*: **purlieu**. ∎ The gym of the Holy Family Boxing Club, their former **purlieu**, has been converted into a community center; group photos of young boxers, now scattered or killed, incongruously bedeck the walls. (John Simon, *The Boxer [Book Reviews]*, National Review, 03-09-1998, p. 67.)

hangover *n.*: **katzenjammer**. ∎ Peebles, in his rejoinder, compared the intense activity in cosmology over the last few years to "a really good party." But he also listed open questions that, he said, left him with an "uneasy feeling" — a kind of cosmic **katzenjammer** — about whether the concordance will survive new and more precise tests. (James Glanz, *Cosmology: Does Science Know the Vital Statistics of the Cosmos?* Science, 11-13-1998.)

(2) hangover (or eating too much) *n.*: **crapulence**. SEE INDULGENCE

hapless (perpetually ..., as in unlucky, person) *n.*: **schlimazel** [Yiddish]. SEE UNLUCKY

happen *v.t.*: **betide**. Whatever **Betides**, Think Stocks. (Forbes Magazine, 07-06-1998, p. 282.)

happening (secondary ... which accompanies or results from another) *n.*: **epiphenomenon** (*adj.*: **epiphenomenal**). SEE PHENOMENON

happenstance (as in by chance) *adj.*: **adventitious**. SEE CHANCE

happiness *n.*: **eudemonia** (or **eudaemonia**) [Based on a concept of Aristotle that the goal of life is happiness, but which is to be achieved through reaching one's full potential, as opposed to through the hedonistic pursuit of pleasure]. ∎ [The] objective is a good life, an Aristotleian **eudemonia**, which embraces a substantial dose of self-interest, but also incorporates concern for others, fulfillment at work, and the respect earned from others by participating in activities, including economic activities, which they value. (John Kay, *Staking a Moral Claim*, New Statesman, 10-11-1996.)

(2) happiness *n.*: **felicity** (causing or tending to produce ...) *adj.*: **felicific**. ▪ If the only purpose of a marriage is for two persons to make each other happy, then that marriage is bound to fail. First of all, no one can give happiness as a gift to another, and no couple can experience unending and uninterrupted **felicity**. (Michael Medved, *Skip the Honeymoon, Save Your Marriage*, The Washington Times, 06-09-1996, p. 31.) ▪ The hedonistic argument that [the poet John] Donne will be found a better **felicific** investment than Agatha Christie is often used dishonestly by teachers, I think. The number of those for whom it is true must be small, and many people read Agatha Christie over and over again with the greatest of pleasure. (A.D. Nuttall, *Why Scholarship Matters*, The Wilson Quarterly, 09-22-2003.)

(3) happiness (supreme ...) *n.*: **beatitude**. SEE BLISS

(4) happiness (as in pleasure) *n.*: **delectation**. SEE PLEASURE

(5) happiness (delusive or illusory ...) *n.*: **fool's paradise**. SEE ILLUSION

(6) happiness (from witnessing other's misfortunes) *n.*: **Roman holiday**. SEE SADISM

(7) happiness (from other's misfortunes) *n.*: **schadenfreude** [German]. SEE SADISM

(8) happiness *n.*: **weal** (usu. as in *weal or woe* or *weal and woe*). SEE WELL-BEING

happy (blissfully ...) *adj.*: **beatific** (to make ... *v.t.*: **beatify**). SEE JOYFUL

(2) happy (very ... often in a boastful way) *adj.*: **cock-a-hoop**. SEE ELATED

(3) happy (as in delightful or blissful) *adj.*: **Elysian**. SEE BLISSFUL

(4) happy *adj.*: **eupeptic**. SEE CHEERFUL

(5) happy *adj.*: **riant**. SEE CHEERFUL

happy medium *n.*: **juste milieu** [French]. ▪ [T]here is a sneaking suspicion that maybe the French have got it right, that they have located the **juste milieu**, and that their particular blend of artistic modishness and cultural conservatism, of welfare-statism and intense individualism, of clear-eyed realism and sappy romanticism — that these proportions are

wise, time-tested and as indisputable as they are subtle. (Jeff Baker [quoting Edmund White in *The Flaneur*], *Lucky Novelists Wander Through Paris, Sydney and Florence*, The Sunday Oregonian, 06-23-2002, p. D7.)

harangue *n.*: **philippic**. SEE TIRADE

harass *v.t.*: **chivvy**. SEE PESTER

(2) harass *v.t.*: **hector**. SEE BULLY

harassed (as if by a witch or by unfounded fears) *adj.*: **hagridden**. SEE TORMENTED

hard-working (appearing ... only when the boss is watching) *n.*: **eyeservice**. SEE WORK

harden *v.t., adj.*: **indurate**. ▪ Years of adroit propaganda by the religious right have convinced many [in Congress] that a vote for preserving the [National Endowment for the Arts] in any form is a vote for sodomy, blasphemy and child abuse. This has become a matter of **indurated** faith, resistant to any insert of mere fact. (Robert Hughes, *The Arts & Media: Pulling the Fuse on Culture — The Conservatives' All-out Assault on Federal Funding Is Unenlightened, Uneconomic and Undemocratic*, Time, 08-07-1995, p. 60.)

(2) harden *v.t.*: **anneal**. SEE STRENGTHEN

hardship (as in burden) *n.*: **incubus**. SEE BURDEN

hardworking *n.*: **Stakhanovite**. SEE WORKAHOLIC

hare (of or relating to) *adj.*: **leporine**. SEE RABBIT

harem *n.*: **seraglio**. ▪ The title [of the movie *8 1/2 Women*], at least, is precise. A financier, rich and recently widowed, transforms his stately country home into a **seraglio** for eight-point-five mistresses. The fraction is a mute, legless Japanese woman. Cute touch. (Leah Rozen, *Picks & Pans: Screen*, People, 06-12-2000, p. 39.)

harm (portending ...) *adj.*: **baleful**. SEE SINISTER

harmful *adj.*: **nocent**. ▪ [W]ith respect to the disastrous imbalance in trade between the U.S. and the rest of the world, I would urge the administration and Congress to consider alternatives to import limitations. Besides the **nocent** effects on world trade that such limitations would cause, there is the very real threat of imposing exports of capital back to Europe, thus completely upsetting the American capital markets. (John Murphy, *Fighting the Trade Imbalance*, The Chicago Tribune, 10-31-1985, p. 26.)

(2) harmful *adj.*: **nocuous**. ▪ Since late April, the city's authorities have made four large-scale inspections to crack down on the crimes of making counterfeit and poor quality food. ... The inspections were aimed at checking for **nocuous** chemicals and heavy-metal additives in food. (Author not given, *Tianjin Destroys Counterfeit Food*, Xinhua News Agency, 06-22-2001.)

(3) harmful (or dangerous) *adj.:* **noisome**. ∎ The [2000 summer] Olympics that Americans ignored in large numbers ... was nothing less than sensational. The food in Sydney was fine, the weather mostly fine, the hosts the finest. Even a **noisome** appearance by that menace of modern Olympics, performance-enhancing drugs, couldn't spoil this party. (Author not given, *Field Of Dreams: Did Americans Just Sleep Through the Most Dazzling Olympic Games in Decades? Time, 10-09-2000.)

(4) harmful (mutually ... to both sides) *adj.:* **internecine**. See DESTRUCTIVE

(5) harmful (in matters of discrimination between groups) *adj.:* **invidious**. See DISCRIMINATORY

(6) harmful (atmosphere or influence) *n.:* **miasma**. See NOXIOUS

harmonious (sound) *adj.:* **euphonious** (*n.:* **euphony**). See MELODIOUS

(2) harmonious (voice or sound) *adj.:* **mellifluous**. See MELODIOUS

(3) harmonious *adj.:* **simpatico**. See COMPATIBLE

harmonizing (a statement ... conflicting ideas, esp. to make peace) *n.:* **eirenicon**. See PEACE-OFFERING

harmony (in the arrangement of parts with respect to a whole) *n.:* **concinnity**. ∎ [A]n amendment that would absolutely forbid abortions has the same chance an amendment to abolish slavery would have had in 1850. [Senator Dole] knows this [and thus his] contribution to Republican **concinnity** was his idea that the platform should also profess "tolerance" for positions different from the Pro-Life position. (William F. Buckley, Jr., *Tolerate Dole? [Presidential Candidate Bob Dole and the Abortion Plank]*, National Review, 07-15-1996, p. 58.)

(2) harmony (in ...) *adj.:* **consonant**. ∎ "The early work [of photographer Ansel Adams] is more **consonant** with his experience of being in those woods alone; it's quieter and more private. The later work is more public and declamatory," says Szarkowski, director emeritus of the New York Museum of Modern Art's photography department. (Marco R. della Cava, *"Ansel Adams at 100" Refocuses Artist's Legacy*, USA Today, 08-27-2001, p. 5D.)

(3) harmony (concerned with establishing ... among churches or religions) *adj.:* **ecumenical**. See CHURCHES

harp on (as in repeating a particular act over and over, often after initial stimulus has ceased) *n.:* **perseveration** (*v.i.:* **perseverate**). See REPEATING

harsh (as in ... remarks) *adj.:* **astringent**. ∎ [S]ome of his most **astringent** remarks are directed at figures such as Ronald Reagan, whose "macho talk around the White House" concerning aid to the Nicaraguan contras prompts Jacobs to observe: "President Reagan, though sometimes confused about it, spent World War II in California making training films for the government and regular ones (with pretty ladies) for himself." (Scott Sherman, *Politics*, The Washington Post, 11-21-1999, p. 13.)

(2) harsh (as in sharp or bitter to taste or smell) *adj.:* **acrid**. See PUNGENT

(3) harsh (as in rough) *adj.:* **scabrous**. See ROUGH

(4) harsh (on the ears) *adj.:* **scrannel**. See CACOPHONOUS

harshness *n.:* **asperity**. See ACRIMONY

haste *n.:* **celerity**. See SPEED

hasty *adj.:* **festinate**. ∎ In October 1997, Eric Schmidt told us he was giving himself two to three years to turn Novell around. ... Even [Novell's] successes like GroupWise, ManageWise and ZENworks are vestiges of 1990s thinking. They may halt a **festinate** death, but you don't build a company around them. (Fritz Nelson, *Faith or Wraith?[Novell]*, Network Computing, 08-21-2000.)

(2) hasty (as in impetuous) *adj.:* **gadarene**. See IMPETUOUS

hat (bell-shaped woman's ...) *n.:* **cloche**. ∎ Cloche hats, named after the French word for "bell" because of their distinctive shape, have become a staple this season for women who want to shut out unpleasant weather or unwanted stares. (Julie K.L. Dam, *Style Watch: Cloche Encounters*, People, 03-29-1999, p. 127.)

hate *v.t.:* **execrate**. ∎ [June O'Leary states:] "I **execrate** and loathe the way TV stations speed up and obliterate the credits and cast list at the end of movies or previews." (George Gamestar, *Cell Phone Abusers Belong in a Cell*, Toronto Star, 11-11-96, p. A4.)

(2) hate *v.t.:* **misprize**. Like jaded millionaires, we [Floridians] see all our water wealth as a damnable nuisance. Cloudbursts slow our suntans, cut short our golf games, ruin our picnics, rot our citrus crops, back up our drains, mildew our bathroom tiles and spawn algae in our swimming pools. We cannot wait for the rain to stop. We **misprize** every drop. ... Then, once the water is gone [we want it back], for showers, dishwashers, Jacuzzis and miniature golf waterfalls. (Michael Browning, *Whatever Happened to Florida's Water?* The Miami Herald, 05-24-1998, p. 1A.)

(3) hate (as in treat with contempt) *v.t.*: **contemn**. SEE SCORN

(4) hate (person who has ... for reason and logic) *n.*: **misologist**. SEE CLOSED-MINDED

hateful *adj.*: **ugsome**. SEE LOATHSOME

hatred (towards an enemy) *n.*: **enmity**. ∎ Dr. Baruch Goldstein was so blinded by **enmity** toward Arabs as to seem "batty" even to some of his fellow ultra-nationalist, fervently religious neighbors in the Jewish settlement of Kiryat Arba, near Hebron in the West Bank. (George J. Church, *Middle East*, Time International, 03-07-1994, p. 16.)

(2) hatred (of men) *n.*: **misandry** (one who hates men *n.*: **misandrist**.). ∎ I was shocked and horrified by your cover story, not only because of the recent rash of wife and child murders, but also by the strong suggestion that it is in the biological nature of males to be violent and abusive. ... I suppose we can now expect another wave of **misandry** in this country such as the one that followed the Montreal Massacre by Marc Léépine. (Author not given, *Letters: Vikings and Aboriginals*, Maclean's, 08-28-2000, p. 4.)

(3) hatred (person who feels ... towards all people) *n.*: **misanthrope**. ∎ Thomas Bernhard — dramatist, novelist, warped genius and **misanthrope** — despised his fellow Austrians with such ferocious thoroughness that, when he died of a heart attack in 1989, he left a will expressly forbidding the performance of any of his plays there. (Paul Taylor, *Fear and Loathing*, Independent, 08-20-1997, p. 4.)

(4) hatred (man who has ... towards women) *n.*: **misogynist**. ∎ Q [to the author]: In your novel *Less Than Zero*, a 12-year-old girl is raped. In *The Rules of Attraction*, a college girl has a violent sexual experience. Do you see yourself as a completely demented **misogynist**? A. Yes. Yes I am. I am a completely demented **misogynist**. (Roger Friedman, *Bret Speaks*, Entertainment Weekly, 03-08-1991, p. 33.)

(5) hatred (of children) *n.*: **misopedia**. ∎ [T]he subject of the meeting — to ensure that America's 15 million young people have access to resources "that can help them lead healthy, fulfilling and productive lives" — might not appeal to [W.C.] Fields, who was infamous for his ... **misopedia** (as in, "Children should neither be seen nor heard from — ever again"). (Author not given, *Volunteering / Do it For Your Own Sake, Too*, Minneapolis Star Tribune, 04-16-1997, p. 14A.)

(6) hatred (develop a ... for) *n.*: **scunner** (esp. as in "take a scunner") [British]. SEE DISLIKE

haughty *adj.*: **orgulous**. ∎ Long may Gill and Michael Winner ... prosecute their quest to deride and deflate the **orgulous** arrogance of that most pretentious, patronising and pompous person — The Celebrity (sic) Cook. (Ian Liversedge, *Gill Gets Kebabed*, Sunday Times [London], 10-25-1998.)

(2) haughty (as in condescending) *adj., adv.*: **de haut en bas** [French]. SEE CONDESCENDING

(3) haughty *adj.*: **hoity-toity**. SEE POMPOUS

haunt (as in place one frequents) *n.*: **purlieu**. SEE HANGOUT

haunted (as if by a witch or by unfounded fears) *adj.*: **hagridden**. SEE TORMENTED

hawk (with long tail) *n.*: **accipiter**. ∎ An **accipiter**, the Cooper [hawk's] short, powerful, rounded wings and long tail are designed for quick pursuit of medium-sized forest mammals and birds. (George Harrison, *A Raptor's Return: The Increasingly Common Cooper's Hawk Is No Chicken*, Sports Afield, 11-01-1997, p. 28.)

hawker (esp. who sells quack medicines) *n.*: **mountebank**. SEE HUCKSTER

haze (over one's vision) *v.t.*: **obnubilate**. SEE OBSCURE

head (of, relating to, located on, in or near) *adj.*: **cephalic**. ∎ The British in 1901 decided that Hafeez's forefathers fit into the category of Arab or Pathan conquerors, not local converts. They reached the conclusion by applying the **Cephalic** index: measuring the proportion of the breadth of the head to its length, as well as of the breadth of the nose to its length. (Parthasarathi Swami, *Asia: Viewpoint: Serving God and Mammon — India's Religious Crisis Has More to Do With Economics Than Faith*, Time International, 02-15-1999, p. 19.)

(2) head (abnormally small ...) *n.*: **microcephaly**. ∎ Other parents, though, feel certain that the Gulf War somehow left their children deformed. One-year-old Amanda Miedona of Chicago Ridge, Ill., suffers from **microcephaly**. Her head, which measures about 12 1/4 inches in circumference, is about one-third smaller than normal. (Richard Jerome, *An Enemy Within — Gulf War Vets Face a Medical Mystery: The Birth Defects Threatening Many of Their Children*, People, 01-30-1995, p. 32.)

(3) head (back of the ...) *n.*: **occiput**. ▪ All you have to do is watch TV commercials to know that real people have headaches. Real people are intimate with Excedrin, Tylenol, Advil, Aleve and Alka-Seltzer. Real people have felt that jackhammer in the temples, the stiletto stab in the **occiput**. (Mary Schmich, *Headache-free People Are Alien Even to the Pros*, Chicago Tribune, 09-12-2003, p. C1.)

(4) head (of a party, school of thought or group of persons) *n.*: **coryphaeus**. SEE LEADER

(5) head (male ... of a household) *n.*: **paterfamilias**. SEE HEAD OF HOUSEHOLD

(6) head (study of shape of) *n.*: **phrenology**. SEE SKULL

head of household (female ...) *n.*: **materfamilias** [Latin]. ▪ As one physician noted in 1884: The time has passed when paterfamilias can complacently congratulate himself upon having disinfected his house with a bottle of carbolic acid, which he has brought in his vest pocket from the corner drug store. Indeed, it was now time for **materfamilias** to take charge. The democratization of the indoor toilet brought the responsibility of scrubbing the bowls to ever greater numbers of women. (Janet Golden, *Germ Warfare*, Women's Review of Books, 10-01-1998, p. 9.)

(2) head of household (male) *n.*: **paterfamilias**. ▪ Another traveling companion remembered the Rockefellers sitting at a private dining room in a Roman hotel as the **paterfamilias** [John D. Rockefeller] dissected the weekly bill, trying to ascertain whether they had really consumed two whole chickens, as these slippery foreigners alleged. (Ron Chernow, *Titan*, Random House [1998], p. 236.)

head-in-the sand (as in complacent person who ignores any unpleasant facts) *n.*: **Podsnap** (*adj.*: **Podsnappian**). SEE OSTRICH

headache (as in migraine) *n.*: **megrims** (plural of megrim). ▪ Barich ages another 25 years and his marriage takes sick, as the state suffers severe economic **megrims** and rattles with real earthquakes, not toy ones, and realists among its population head for Oregon, where they are cordially requested to go away. (John Skow, *Arts & Media/Books: Lotus Land No More*, Time, 07-04-1994, p. 74.)

(2) headache (as in hangover) *n.*: **katzenjammer**. SEE HANGOVER

(3) headache (as in trouble) *n.*: **tsuris** [Yiddish]. SEE TROUBLE

headless *n.*: **acephalous** [lit. without a head, but often used in the sense of leaderless]. SEE LEADERLESS

headlong (as in impetuous) *adj.*: **gadarene**. SEE IMPETUOUS

(2) headlong *adv.*: **pell-mell**. SEE DISORDERLY

(3) headlong (as in at top speed) *adv.*: **tanivy**. SEE TOP SPEED

headstrong *adj.*: **contumacious**. SEE OBSTINATE

(2) headstrong (as in one who clings to an opinion or belief even after being shown that it is wrong) *n.*: **mumpsimus**. SEE STUBBORN

(3) headstrong (in holding to a belief or opinion) *adj.*: **pertinacious**. SEE STUBBORN

healing (used often of a medicinal treatment) *adj.*: **balsamic**. SEE SOOTHING

health (as in condition) *n.*: **fettle**. SEE CONDITION

healthful (as in having the power to cure or heal) *adj.*: **sanative**. ▪ Americans sometimes think the benefits from this relationship flow only one direction — toward Tokyo. But that's short-sighted. [T]he challenge Japanese economic strength poses may turn out to be more **sanative** than harmful. The Japanese example has helped force issues like the low American savings rate to the fore. Japanese management theories have sparked useful reform in American industry. (Author not given, *Ties to Tokyo*, Christian Science Monitor, 10-31-1989, p. 20.)

heap *n.*: **cumulus**. ▪ Oceanaire is the only restaurant I've been to where a waiter has volunteered to "break down" my Key lime pie (hidden under a **cumulus** of whipped cream, the wedge is served with a steak knife). (Tom Sietsema, *Big Fish; Bigger Fish*, The Washington Post, 11-19-2000, p. W21.)

(2) heap (confused or jumbled ...) *n.*: **agglomeration**. SEE JUMBLE

hearing (of or pertaining to sense of ...) *adj.*: **auricular**. ▪ **Auricularly**, after thirty, you gradually lose sensitivity to high-frequency noises as sound-receptor cells in the inner ear decrease. (Michael Segell, *How Your Body Ages*, Cosmopolitan, 04-01-1994, p. 172.)

(2) hearing (act of ..., often with a stethoscope) *n.*: **auscultation**. SEE LISTENING

hearsay (as in paraphrase) *n.*: **oratio obliqua** [Latin for "indirect speech"]. SEE PARAPHRASE

heart (of a matter, as in the essence) *n*.: **quiddity**. SEE ESSENCE

heartbeat (abnormally slow ...) *n*.: **bradycardia**. ▪ Arrhythmias may develop because of abnormalities in how impulses are conducted. Delays in the spreading of impulses can occur anywhere in the conduction system. When the transmission of impulses is blocked intermittently or completely, **bradycardia** may result. (Author not given, *Arrhythmias*, USA Today Magazine, 02-01-1997.)

heat (releasing) *adj*.: **exothermic**. ▪ Washington is by nature **exothermic**. Let us take you to the hot zones. You want hot? Fine. Try stem cells. See if that heats ya up. Stem cell research is the hottest science going. It's so hot, President Bush interrupted his month-long vacation in Texas (where, we might note, it's hot) on Thursday night to tell the nation his policy on stem cell funding. (Frank Ahrens, *Sizzling City; Even When the Temperature Cools, You Can Feel the Heat*, The Washington Post, 08-11-2001.)

(2) heat (subject person or thing to intense ..., often to create sweat) *v.t*.: **parboil**. ▪ He also dreamed up a particularly foul-smelling recipe for self-**parboiling** that required [jockeys] to steep for up to 35 minutes ... in piping-hot water mixed with 3 to 5 pounds of Epsom salts, one quart white vinegar, 2 ounces of household ammonia and a mystery lather he called Hawley's cream. (Laura Hillenbrand, *Seabiscuit*, Random House [2001], p. 68.)

(3) heat (as in of or relating to dog days of summer) *adj*.: **canicular**. SEE DOG DAYS

heave (as in making an effort to vomit) *v.i*.: **keck**. SEE VOMIT

heaven *n*.: **Abraham's bosom**. ▪ An exception to this rule is his chilling parable of Lazarus and Dives: The rich master, consigned to hell, lifts up his eyes to the beggar, who has been "carried by angels into **Abraham's bosom**," requesting that Lazarus dip a finger in some water to cool him. (David Van Biema, *Religion: Does Heaven Exist? It Used to Be That the Hereafter Was Virtually Palpable, But American Religion Now Seems Almost Allergic to Imagining It*, Time, 03-24-1997, p. 70.)

(2) heaven (highest reaches of ...) *n*.: **empyrean**. ▪ The celestial being who would become Satan had many names in heaven. Most of Western tradition identifies him as Lucifer, the Morning Star, the most brilliant of all the denizens of the **empyrean**. (Howard Chua-Eoan, *Angels Among Us*, Time, 12-27-1993.)

(3) heaven (as in place of extreme luxury and ease where physical comforts and pleasures are always at hand) *n*.: **Cockaigne**. SEE PARADISE

(4) heaven (spec. a place of fabulous wealth or opportunity) *n*.: **El Dorado**. SEE PARADISE

(5) heaven (as in paradise) *n*.: **Xanadu**. SEE PARADISE

heavenly (as in celestial) *adj*.: **ethereal**. ▪ Anyone who has ever wondered what a heavenly chorus might sound like need only listen to the opening track, "Love Letters from Old Mexico," on this performing debut by one of Nashville's most successful songwriters. On that lovely tune, Emmylou Harris and Alison Krauss provide backing vocals, helping Satcher create an angelic, **ethereal** sound. (Nick Charles, *Song*, People, 04-16-2001, p. 41.)

(2) heavenly *adj*.: **empyreal**. SEE LOFTY

heavens (the ...) *n*.: **welkin**. ▪ Liza Gennaro's choreography is entry-level but diverting, Bruce Coughlin's deft orchestrations make the **welkin** ring. (Stefan Kanfer, *Once Upon A Mattress [Broadhurst Theater, New York, NY] [Theater Reviews]*, The New Leader, 01-13-1997, p. 22.)

heaviness (as in being overweight) *n*.: **avoirdupois**. SEE WEIGHT

heavy (as in beer-bellied) *adj*.: **abdominous**. SEE BEER-BELLIED

(2) heavy (as in fat) *adj*.: **adipose**. SEE FAT

(3) heavy (person, esp. with a large abdomen) *n*.: **endomorph** (*adj*.: **endomorphic**). SEE POT-BELLIED

(4) heavy (as in overweight, and squat) *adj*.: **fubsy**. SEE SQUAT

(5) heavy *adj*.: **Pickwickian**. SEE FAT

hedge (as in avoid a straight answer) *v.t*.: **tergiversate**. SEE EVADE

hedonist (as in lazy person devoted to seeking pleasure and luxury) *n*.: **lotus-eater** [derives from the Lotophagi, a group of people described in Homer's *Odyssey* who eat lotuses and live in a state of lazy contentment]. ▪ All the ingredients are here: the innocent/not-so-innocent celebration of sensual pleasure; the mix of locals with wannabe locals from Europe and Latin America [and the] sense that just about any law can be ignored or manipulated. The South Beach cocktail. I've been here for less than 24 hours and part of me is already seduced, like a **lotus-eater**, by the manifold pleasures of this place.

(Don George, *Travel Essay/South Beach's Manifold Pleasures*, Newsday, 01-26-2001.)

hedonistic *adj., n.*: **libertine**. See promiscuous

heedless (as in impetuous) *adj.*: **gadarene**. See impetuous

(2) heedless *adj.*: **harum-scarum**. See reckless

height (as in "the ... of") *n.*: **apogee**. ▪ Is animation a market that will always expand? Or was the Simba spectacular [i.e., Disney's The Lion King] the **apogee** of a trend? Or a glorious fluke? (Richard Corliss, *The Arts/Cinema: There's Tumult in Toon Town — For 60 Years, the Animated Feature Was a Disney Monopoly; Now Rival Studios Are Muscling In, Led by Fox With a Winsome Anastasia*, Time, 11-17-1997, p. 88.)

(2) height (fear of ...) *n.*: **acrophobia**. See fear

(3) height (the ..., lit. the greatest or highest good) *n.*: **summum bonum** [Latin]. See ideal

hell (as in opposite of utopia) *n.*: **dystopia**. ▪ In this optimistic season, two thoughtful writers warn that we are stumbling toward **dystopia**. ... In this **dystopia**, the affluent would most likely live as they do in Latin America — behind walls topped with shards of glass and with riflemen patrolling their lawns. And the great mass of people would live as many of our poorest citizens do today — in a society where violent males kill other men and abuse women. (Michael Barone, *Slouching Toward Dystopia*, U.S. News & World Report, 12-20-1993.)

(2) hell *n.*: **Gehenna**. ▪ There has been little pretense in [Russian President] Boris Yeltsin's war against the Chechens. ... "We have been told to fire and fire again. There are no other choices," said a brigade commander. Grozny was a free-fire zone. For the moment, however, the tides of war may have shifted. Hundreds of Russian soldiers have been killed, trapped in the **Gehenna** of their burning tanks. (Author not given, *The Chechen Adventure [US Relations With Russia]*, The New Republic, 01-23-1995, p. 7.)

(3) hell (as in place or occasion of great suffering) *n.*: **Gethsemane** [derived from garden east of Jerusalem on the Mount of Olives where Jesus was arrested]. ▪ The Japanese suffered most, of course [at Okinawa in 1945]. About 76,000 perished, as did 24,000 Okinawan conscripts. But the GIs and Marines lost 7,631 killed ... and 39,000 wounded. ... For all the gore, the Japanese saw dead GIs and Marines as a mere bonus. Their true target was the American fleet — and off Okinawa, the United States Navy would endure its own **Gethsemane**. (Harry Levins, *Hell and Glory in the Pacific — Japanese Exact Bloody Toll in Fierce Battles for Iwo Jima and Okinawa*, St. Louis Post-Dispatch, 02-19-1995, p. 4B.)

(4) hell (as in place or occasion of great suffering) *n.*: **Golgotha** [derives from hill near Jerusalem where Jesus was crucified]. ▪ Auschwitz is a place that was once described as "having scared God," and which Pope John Paul has called "the **Golgotha** of our century." (Stephen C. Feinstein, *A Chilling Story of Extreme Manifestation of Evil / Brilliant Work Puts Auschwitz Into Context of Romanticism, Political Defeat, Racism That Led to Resettlement, Genocide*, Minneapolis Star Tribune, 02-09-1997, p. 18F.)

(5) hell (as in damnation, as in loss of the soul) *n.*: **perdition**. See damnation

hellish *adj.*: **Stygian**. ▪ Meanwhile, older and older fossils have all but proved that life did not evolve at the leisurely pace Darwin envisioned. Perhaps most intriguing of all, the discovery of organisms living in oceanic hot springs has provided a **Stygian** alternative to Darwin's peaceful picture. Life ... may not have formed in a nice, warm pond, but in "a hot pressure cooker." (Madeleine Nash, *Science: How Did Life Begin? In Bubbles? On Comets? Along Ocean Vents? Scientists Find Some Surprising Answers to the Greatest Mystery on Earth*, Time, 10-11-1993, p. 68.)

(2) hellish *adj.*: **sulfurous** (or **sulphurous**). See infernal

helper *n.*: **adjutant**. See assistant

(2) helper (as in aide or assistant) *n.*: **factotum**. See assistant

(3) helper (as in assistant, esp. to a scholar or magician) *n.*: **famulous**. See assistant

(4) helper (who is loyal and unquestioning) *n.*: **myrmidon**. See assistant

helpless (when born) *adj.*: **altricial**. ▪ Those bare-naked, helpless-type babies, and they include all the songbirds, are **altricial**. The other kind — ducks, geese, Easter chicks, killdeers and so on — are precocial. Think of "precocious." It is as if human children arrived asking to borrow the car. (Joey Slinger, *Birding for Cynics [Excerpts from Joey Slinger's Book "Down & Dirty Birding"]*, Maclean's, 05-20-1996, p. 58.)

(2) helpless (as in powerless) *adj.*: **impuissant**. See powerless

helpmate *n.*: **helpmeet**. [It would be difficult not to list *helpmate* as the closest synonym to *helpmeet*, and in fact a helpmeet can be male or female. However, the word is very frequently used as a synonym for *wife*, and specifically a traditional wife who may, for example, stay at home and raise the children, as in the example used here]. ∎ Maureen Dowd writes that "[Presidential candidate Howard Dean's wife] Judith Steinberg has shunned the role of **help-meet**." Reporters who itch to ride campaign roller coasters do not approve that a spouse would prefer to keep the home fires burning and tend her own business. (Annlinn Grossman [letter writer], *To Love, Honor And Campaign For?* The New York Times, 01-16-2004, p. A20.)

helter-skelter *adv.*: **pell-mell**. SEE DISORDERLY

Herculean (task, esp. of cleaning up or remedying bad situations) *n.*: **Augean task** [after Augeas, a legendary Greek king who did not clean out his stable for 30 years, until it was cleaned by Hercules]. ∎ Gorbachev came to realize several years ago that the apparatus of Soviet power both at home and abroad was expensive, wasteful, cumbersome, distracting and provocative. ... All those missiles in their silos, all those troops in foreign lands, all those rubles and cheap oil flowing to Cuba, represented resources that he desperately needed for the **Augean task** of cleaning up the mess that stretches from Vilnius to Vladivostok. (Strobe Talbott, *Goodfellas: How Mikhail Gorbachev and George Bush Developed One of the Most Extraordinary Yet Subtle Collaborations in History*, Time, 08-05-1991.)

heretic (orig. Catholics who did not follow Church of England) *n.*: **recusant**. SEE DISSENTER

hermit (as in recluse, esp. for religious reasons) *n.*: **anchorite**. SEE RECLUSE

(2) hermit (as in recluse, esp. for religious reasons) *n.*: **eremite**. SEE RECLUSE

heroic (task, esp. of cleaning up or remedying bad situations) *n.*: **Augean task**. SEE HERCULEAN

hesitancy (as in indecisiveness) *n.*: **abulia**. SEE INDECISIVENESS

(2) hesitancy (as in the dilemma of being given a choice between two equally appealing alternatives and thus being able to choose neither one) *n.*: **Buridan's ass**. SEE PARALYSIS

(3) hesitancy (as in unwillingness) *n.*: **nolition**. SEE UNWILLINGNESS

hesitant (as in spineless or indecisive, or such a person) *adj., n.*: **namby-pamby**. SEE SPINELESS

hesitate (to act due to indecision) *v.i.*: **dither**. SEE PROCRASTINATE

(2) hesitate (as in vacillate) *v.i.*: **shilly-shally**. SEE VACILLATE AND PROCRASTINATE

hesitation (words such as *um, uh, you know*, etc.) *n.*: **embolalia** (or **embololalia**). SEE STAMMERING

hex *n.*: **malediction**. SEE CURSE

(2) hex (as in put a ... upon) *v.t.*: **imprecate**. SEE CURSE

hibernate (in the summertime, esp. used of animals) *v.t.*: **aestivate** (or **estivate**). ∎ Snails are remarkable in that they are extremely resistant to climatic conditions. They can hibernate, that is become dormant in winter. ... They can also **estivate** in summer, sealing themselves in their shells with a sort of glue that keeps their vital fluids inside, and only wakening when the rains come and the moisture dissolves their gluey seal. (D'vora Ben Shaul, *Creatures Close to the Ground*, Jerusalem Post, 08-11-1995.)

hibernating (as in dormant or motionless) *adj.*: **torpid**. SEE LETHARGIC

hidden *adj.*: **delitescent**. ∎ [The TV hostess, Marla] had just begun to chat it up with Brevard Commissioner Sue Schmitt. Well, sort of. ... Commissioner Sue was nowhere to be seen. Not on my screen anyway. [Marla] was looking off toward someone or some mystery thing the rest of us could not see. ... The hostess kept referring to this **delitescent** entity as "Sue" or "Commissioner." I tell you, it was eerie. (Allen Rose, *Unseen TV Guest Pulls Off Interview*, The Orlando Sentinel, 01-15-1994, p. C1.)

(2) hidden (as in state of being ... from view, lost to notice or concealed) *n.*: **occultation**. SEE DISAPPEARANCE

hiding (as in, in concealment) *adv.*: **doggo** (esp. as in "lying doggo"; slang). SEE CONCEALMENT

(2) hiding *n.*: **hugger-mugger**. SEE SECRECY

(3) hiding (social ...) *n.*: **purdah**. SEE SECLUSION

(4) hiding (deliberate ... or misrepresentation of facts to gain an advantage) *n.*: **subreption**. SEE MISREPRESENTATION

hiding place (esp. for valuables or goods) *n.*: **cache**. ∎ Days after a Freemen militia sympathizer was seriously injured in an explosion at his home, a powerful **cache** of explosives was seized at the motor home of two of his associates. (Associated Press, *Friends of Injured Freemen Sympathizer Are*

Arrested; Cache of Explosives Found, Denver Rocky Mountain News, 05-02-1997, p. 56A.)

high society *n.*: **beau monde** [French]. ▪ New York's **beau monde** is currently up in arms about a ghastly new threat to its continued well-being: stealth paparazzi. These are apparently normal kids who frequent Manhattan's trendy nightspots and fashionable parties armed with hidden video cameras. (To Young, *New York Confidential: Titanic Sequel Sinks Without a Trace*, Independent, 07-03-1998, p. 8.)

(2) high society *n.*: **bon ton** [French]. ▪ Nick Truelocke can't wait to see it happen — to see the champagne corks popping, the love affairs blossoming, the song and dance and romance. And he need wait only a few hours now, because tomorrow night the doors of his club, the Cafe de Paris, will open once more, to admit the **bon ton** of the Nineties. (James Style, *Come to the Cafe: Chill out in Style*, Independent, 10-02-1996, p. 4.)

high wire (walker, or one who balances on things) *n.*: **equilibrist**. SEE TIGHTROPE

high-class *adj.*: **nobby** [British]. SEE ELEGANT

high-pitched (sound made by bagpipes) *n.*: **skirl**. SEE BAGPIPES

high-spirited (as in jolly) *adj.*: **Falstaffian**. SEE JOVIAL

(2) high-spirited (girl) *n., adj.*: **hoyden**. SEE TOMBOY

(3) high-spirited *adj.*: **mettlesome**. SEE SPIRITED

highest (point) *n.*: **apogee**. SEE HEIGHT

hill (as in upward slope) *n.*: **acclivity** (*adj.*: **acclivitous**). SEE INCLINE

hint (as in clue to solving a puzzle or deciphering a code which has not previously been solved or deciphered) *n.*: **Rosetta stone**. SEE CLUE

(2) hint (as in small amount) *n.*: **soupçon** [French]. SEE TRACE

(3) hint (as in trace or small amount of) *n.*: **tincture**. SEE TRACE

hissing (pronounce with ... sounds) *v.t.*: **assibilate**. ▪ In fact, some American gay men do pronounce sibilants (s, z, sh, and so on) distinctively, but not with a lisp. They hiss — adding more sibilation — a phenomenon phonologists call assibilation. Gay men are not the only group prone to **assibilate**. (Author not given, *Boy George, I Think He's Got It*, [Speech Differences Among Gay and Straight Men], The Economist, 07-15-1995, p. 63.)

historic (of an event or period which is ...) *adj.*: **epochal**. SEE MOMENTOUS

histrionic (behavior) *n., adj.*: **operatics**. SEE MELODRAMATIC

hit (repeatedly, often used figuratively) *v.t.*: **buffet**. ▪ The administration acknowledged this week that Ickes improperly used a White House fax machine, telephone and possibly a computer in communicating with an intermediary about the donation. Ickes' actions could pose a more serious problem for the White House, already **buffeted** by the widening fund-raising furor. (Author not given, *Agency Opens Inquiry Into Claims of Illegal Fund-raising by Ickes*, Minneapolis Star Tribune, 02-06-1997, p. 4A.)

(2) hit (with a club) *v.t.*: **cudgel**. SEE CLUB

(3) hit (with the critics but not the public) *n.*: **succes d'estime** [French]. SEE SUCCESS

hoarseness (causing inability to speak) *n.*: **dysphonia**. ▪ It may seem like a case of laryngitis you just can't shake. Your voice remains hoarse and sounds weak, even after you clear your throat. ... "Chronic **dysphonia** can occur in people such as teachers who use their voices a lot, and in people who have experienced trauma or surgery that affects the larynx," says Nicolas E. Maragos, M.D. (The Mayo Clinic Health Letter, *Finding Your Voice: New Procedure Offers Hope to Chronically Hoarse*, St. Louis Post-Dispatch, 05-02-1993, p. 21.)

hoax (as in false story, often deliberately) *n.*: **canard**. ▪ [Christina Hoff Sommers] exposes a number of influential hoaxes, meticulously tracking the way they have been mindlessly repeated by the media until they have been come to seem part of received wisdom. These include the Super Bowl **canard** holding that wife beating increases 40 percent during the game (utterly baseless, but TV stations ran ads urging men to remain calm). (Tama Starr, *Who Stole Feminism: How Women Have Betrayed Women* [Book Reviews], Reason, 10-01-1994, p. 62.)

hobbling (as in limping, from lack of blood flow to leg muscles) *n.*: **claudication**. SEE LIMPING

hobby (as in favorite topic or activity) *n.*: **cheval de bataille** [French for "battle-horse"] ▪ "Though I studied everything [said Podles], Rossini was my **cheval de bataille**. I would finish every exam with some Rossini, and later a Rossini aria would be my finale in every competition." Nevertheless, while Rossini arias were her staple, she had yet to tackle complete roles. (Barrymore Laurence Scherer, *Alto*

Rhapsody, [Poland's Ewa Podles, Contralto], Opera News, 06-01-1997.)

hobo *n.*: **clochard** [French]. SEE VAGRANT

hodgepodge (composed of a ... of items) *adj.*: **farraginous**. SEE MIXED

(2) hodgepodge (as in assortment) *n.*: **farrago**. SEE ASSORTMENT

(3) hodgepodge (as in assortment) *n.*: **gallimaufry**. SEE ASSORTMENT

(4) hodgepodge (as in assortment) *n.*: **olla podrida** [Spanish]. SEE ASSORTMENT

(5) hodgepodge (as in assortment) *n.*: **omnium-gatherum** [Latin]. SEE ASSORTMENT

(6) hodgepodge (as in assortment) *n.*: **salmagundi**. SEE ASSORTMENT

(7) hodgepodge (as in assortment) *n.*: **welter**. SEE JUMBLE

hog (as in hearty eater) *n.*: **trencherman**. SEE GLUTTON

hogs (give birth to a litter of ...) *v.t.*: **farrow**. SEE PIGS
(2) hogs (of or relating to) *adj.*: **porcine**. SEE PIGS

hold (closely to a line, rule, or principle) *v.i.*: **hew**. SEE CONFORM

holding (adapted for ..., esp. a tail) *adj.*: **prehensile**. SEE GRASPING

hole (as in gap) *n.*: **lacuna**. SEE GAP

holes (full of ..., as in cracks) *adj.*: **rimose**. SEE CRACKS

holier-than-thou *adj.*: **Pecksniffian**. SEE SELF-RIGHTEOUS

(2) holier-than-thou (in a hypocritical way) *adj.*: **Pharisaical**. SEE SELF-RIGHTEOUS

holy (having both human and ... [as in godlike] attributes) *adj.*: **theanthropic**. SEE GODLIKE

holy oil (often used at baptisms and confirmations) *n.*: **chrism**. ∎ [On Joe DiMaggio Day in 1998, he rode around the warning track and he] held both hands above his head — half a wave, half a blessing, like the Pope does. He'd part his hands, throw them open towards the crowd, both at once, [so that] a whiff of his **chrism**, some glint of his godhood would fly from him back top the crowd. (Richard Ben Cramer, *Joe DiMaggio: The Hero's Life*, Simon & Schuster [2001], p. v.)

holy place (or sanctum) *n.*: **adytum**. SEE SANCTUM

holy water (sprinkle with ...) *v.t.*: **asperse** SEE SPRINKLE

homage (not necessarily sincere) *n.*: **obeisance**. ∎ Given that throughout history those who did not find their culture's gods credible have suffered for it, simple self-preservation explains [why people pretend to have religious beliefs]. The early Christians (along with everyone else) were required to give token **obeisance** to the Roman gods once a year. ... Those who refused even that option were considered unpatriotic and punished. (Author not given, *Letter from Reader*, Minneapolis Star Tribune, 10-30-1999, p. 6B.)

(2) homage (as in tribute) *n.*: **panegyric** (one who does so *n.*: **panegyrist**). SEE TRIBUTE

home (on a height) *n.*: **aerie**. SEE DWELLING

homebuilder (spec. a carpenter) *n.*: **housewright**. SEE CARPENTER

homeless (child who roams the streets) *n.*: **gamine** (or **gamin** for masculine) [French]. ∎ In Cali, ragged-looking Black youth between six and 14-years-old form protective bands that roam city blocks in search of food and shelter. The **gamines** (street urchins) live on the streets and face constant harassment from police and businesses. (Michael J. Franklin, *Colombian Blacks Face Heart-Wrenching Racism: State Denies They Even Exist*, Chicago Citizen, 02-13-1994.)

homogenous (of things that cannot be made ...) *adj.*: **immiscible**. SEE INCOMPATIBLE

homosexual (person or one concerned with gay rights) *n., adj.*: **homophile**. ∎ In 1971, Hislop co-founded one of the earliest gay support groups in the country, the Community **Homophile** Association of Toronto. (Scott Steele, *Coming Out: The State is Out of the Bedroom, But After 25 Years, Old Attitudes Still Linger*, Maclean's, 05-16-1994, p. 40.)

(2) homosexual (as in lesbian) *adj.*: **sapphic**. SEE LESBIAN

homosexuals (discrimination against ...) *n.*: **heterosexism**. ∎ Growing acceptance of gays is part of a movement more concerned with democratic integration and individual rights than with nationalistic separatism and collective responsibilities, he writes. As this consensus gains power, legal discrimination and cultural **heterosexism** wither. (Wayne Hoffman, *Book World: The Gay Israelis*, The Washington Post, 07-26-2000, p. C9.)

honest (as in truthful) *adj.*: **veridical**. SEE TRUTHFUL

honesty (as in integrity) *n.*: **probity**. SEE INTEGRITY

honeyed (voice or sound) *adj.*: **mellifluous**. SEE MELODIOUS

honor (personal ...) *n.*: **izzat** [Hindi]. ∎ Mateen's life is not easy. He wants to donate sufficient funds to the building of a new mosque to keep his dignity and his family's **izzat**, but he has little money to spare. (Sushil Jain, *The Song of the Loom [Book Reviews]*, World Literature Today, 03-22-1997, p. 454.)

(2) honor (to pay ... to, not necessarily sincere or unforced) *n.*: **obeisance**. SEE HOMAGE

(3) honor (as in tribute) *n.*: **panegyric** (one who does so *n.*: **panegyrist**). SEE TRIBUTE

(4) honor (as in integrity) *n.*: **probity**. SEE INTEGRITY

hood (woolen ... which covers head and neck) *n.*: **balaclava**. ∎ The **balaclava** fits tight around my face and extends well into my turtleneck undershirt to prevent air leaks. (Ed Pavelka, *Dress for Duress: Toasty Tips for Safe and Comfortable Winter Cycling*, Bicycling, 02-01-1995, p. 86.)

hoofs (an animal having ...) *n., adj.*: **ungulate**. ∎ It takes clout to be a good elk tracker. Sorry, the pun was irresistible. Clout is the name of half a cloven hoof, one toe, if you will, of a deer, elk, moose or any other two-toed **ungulate**. (Ed Dentry, *Tracking Video Turns Hunters Into Sleuths*, Rocky Mountain News, 10-27-1999.)

hooker *n.*: **bawd**. SEE PROSTITUTE

(2) hooker *n.*: **demimondaine**. SEE PROSTITUTE

(3) hooker *n.*: **doxy**. SEE PROSTITUTE

(4) hooker *n.*: **trollop**. SEE PROSTITUTE

hookers (as a group) *n.*: **bawd**. SEE PROSTITUTES

hope (slight or faint ...) *n.*: **velleity**. ∎ "Out of the Depths" contains private, not communal, women's prayers, more than half of which pertain (as if they were indeed one lifelong prayer) to childbirth: from a woman's first pre-conception **velleity** through (many months or years later) her last post-delivery beatitude. (Susan Schnur, *Out of the Depths I Call You: A Book of Prayers for the Married*, Lilith, 04-30-1993.)

(2) hope (for) *v.t.*: **desiderate**. SEE WANT

(3) hope (as in reliance on ... alone [as in faith] rather than reason, esp. in philosophical or religious matters) *n.*: **fideism**. SEE FAITH

(4) hope (which is delusive or not realistically obtainable) *n.*: **will-o'-the-wisp**. SEE PIPE DREAM

hopeful (as in one habitually expecting an upturn in one's fortunes, sometimes without justification) *adj.*: **Micawberish** (*n.*: **Micawber**). SEE OPTIMISTIC

(2) hopeful (esp. blindly or naively ...) *adj.*: **Panglossian**. SEE OPTIMISTIC

(3) hopeful (excessively or unrealistically ... person) *n.*: **Pollyanna**. SEE OPTIMISTIC

hopeless (mission or project) *n.*: **fool's errand**. ∎ Just how likely is it that the United States will sustain an attack with biological weapons? In one sense ... the quest for a clear threat assessment is essentially a **fool's errand**. No attack has ever been registered in the United States, and accordingly there is no way to assign degrees of probability. (Helle Bering, *A Plague of Chad? It Could Be Biological Terrorism*, The Washington Times, 11-29-2000, p. A19.)

(2) hopeless (esp. as to poverty) *adj.*: **abject**. SEE WRETCHED

(3) hopeless (as in unrealistic) *adj.*: **chimerical**. SEE UNREALISTIC

(4) hopeless (relating to the view that all human striving and aspiration is ..., or people who hold such a view) *adj., n.*: **futilitarian**. SEE FUTILE

hopelessness (as in world-weariness or sentimental pessimism over the world's problems) *adj.*: **Weltschmerz** [German]. SEE PESSIMISM

horniness (male ...) *n.*: **satyriasis**. ∎ [T]hose who are angry over the Clinton scene are angry not with [Hillary] but with [Bill]. They might be tangentially angry with her for putting up with his **satyriasis**, but almost certainly not in critical numbers. (William F. Buckley, Jr., *Senator Hillary?* National Review, 01-25-1999.)

horny *adj.*: **ithyphallic**. SEE LUSTFUL

horrible (person) *n.*: **caitiff**. SEE DESPICABLE

(2) horrible *adj.*: **ugsome**. SEE LOATHSOME

horseman *n.*: **caballero**. SEE EQUESTRIAN

hostile *adj.*: **bellicose**. SEE BELLIGERENT

(2) hostile *adj.*: **oppugnant**. SEE ANTAGONISTIC

hostility (initiate ... or violence) *v.i.*: **aggress**. SEE FIGHT

(2) hostility (intense ..., such as towards an enemy) *n.*: **enmity**. SEE HATRED

(3) hostility (develop a strong ... towards) *n.*: **scunner** (esp. as in "take a scunner") [British]. SEE DISLIKE

hot (white-...) *adj*.: **candescent**. See white-hot

(2) hot (as in of or relating to dog days of summer) *adj*.: **canicular**. See dog days

hot water (of or relating to ...) *adj*.: **hydrothermal**. ∎ Very hot (greater than 400 degrees C) water is still found today in underground geothermal and undersea **hydrothermal** areas, where the pressure is supplied by the overlying rock or water. (Gary Olsen, *Origins of Life*, National Forum, 01-01-1996, p. 20.)

hotel (proprietor or innkeeper) *n*.: **boniface**. See innkeeper

(2) hotel (actually an inn, but generally used as synonym for ... as well) *n*.: **caravansary**. See inn

house (on a height) *n*.: **aerie**. See dwelling

(2) house (very large ...) *n*.: **manse**. See mansion

housekeeper (in India and Orient, often serving as a wet nurse) *n*.: **amah**. See maid

(2) housekeeper (hired to do cleaning work) *n*.: **charwoman**. See maid

howl (like a cat in heat) *v.i.*: **caterwaul**. See screech

(2) howl (as in wail) *v.i.*: **ululate**. See wail

hub (person or object which is the focal point of ...) *n*.: **cynosure**. See center of attention

hubbub (and confusion, esp. from simultaneous voices) *n*.: **babel**. See noise

huckster (esp. who sells quack medicines) *n*.: **mountebank**. ∎ As a traveling **mountebank**, selling dubious cures to credulous rural folk, [John D. Rockefeller's father] Bill took a dim view of people's intelligence and didn't hesitate to exploit their naive trust. (Ron Chernow, *Titan*, Random House [1998], p. 25.)

hue *n*.: **tincture**. ∎ The morning light had broadened, gained greater depth, and lay in a clean sheet across the bay, giving it a silver **tincture**. (Guterson, *Snow Falling From Cedars*, Harcourt, Brace [1994], p. 12.)

(2) hue (having only one ...) *adj*.: **monochromatic**. See color

hug (as in caress or fondle) *v.i.*: **canoodle** (often "canoodle with"). See caress

huge *adj*.: **brobdingnagian** (often cap.) [derives from Brobdingnag, an imaginary land inhabited by giants in Jonathan Swift's *Gulliver's Travels* (1745)]. ∎ Target isn't Wal-Mart, the giant that wooed suburbia with its acres of guns and gummy bears. And it def-

initely isn't Kmart, which still seems downscale despite its Martha Stewart tea-towel sets. [Target] may have been founded in 1962, the same year as those other **Brobdingnagian** outlets, but it has developed its own distinct interpretation of the big-box format. (Shelly Branch, *Features/Retailing: How Target Got Hot Hip: Goods and Hipper Ads Are Luring the MTV and BMW Crowds Into the Big Box*, Fortune, 05-24-1999, p. 169.)

(2) huge (object) *n*.: **leviathan**. ∎ One of the largest industrial machines in existence, [papermaking machine] No. 35 took two years to build and cost $395 million. It is higher than a five-story building and a third longer than a football field. ... Every 60 seconds, this **leviathan** generates a stream of office paper more than half a mile long and 29 feet wide. (Alex Taylor III, *Competition: Why an Industry That Was Up a Tree is On a Big Roll — Everything is Monumental in the Paper Game*, Fortune, 04-17-1995, p. 134.)

(3) huge *adj*.: **pythonic**. ∎ There are more than 120 courses [near Myrtle Beach, SC], with more being added all the time, and I suspect that as America turns into the world's largest amusement park, with fairways replacing wetlands, the entire Carolina coast will become one **pythonic** links with 25,000 holes. ... A lunatic golfer may one day be able to play almost continuously from Wilmington to Hilton Head Island, S.C. (William Nack, *Shoving Off ... On an Unscripted Golfing Adventure*, Sports Illustrated, 03-23-2004.)

(4) huge *adj*.: **Bunyanesque**. See enormous

(5) huge (like an elephant) *adj*.: **elephantine**. See enormous

(6) huge (like an elephant) *adj*.: **pachydermatous**. See elephant

(7) huge *adj*.: **Pantagruelian**. See gigantic

hugging *adj*.: **osculant**. ∎ Timkul and Chung remove each other's filmy, linen nightshirts and kiss each other's bodies. Then they pour it on — warm, succulent, **osculant**, shadowy love. (Stephen Short, *Pride & Passion Director Nonzee Nimibutr Makes Movies That Set Thailand's Box-office Alight*, Time International, 04-16-2001, p. 54.)

human (resembling or characteristic of ... being) *n*.: **anthropoid**. ∎ So far, Hawass's team has explored four tombs, with a total of 105 mummies laid on top of one another in neat stacks. All told, the remains were interred in four distinct ways. One type was ... placed in so-called **anthropoid** coffins — pottery sarcophagi with human faces — and a few were only wrapped in linen. (Andrea Dorfman, *Archaeology: Valley of the Lost Tombs — A Cache of Pristine Mummies Offers a Look at Egyptian Life and Death Around the Time of Jesus*, Time, 09-06-1999, p. 62.)

(2) human (ascribe ... characteristics to) *v.t.*: **anthropomorphize**. ▪ [To make the movie "Cats and Dogs"] the canine and feline stars had to take on the facial expressions, emotions and eccentricities of humans, but still look as if they were exhibiting natural animal behavior. **Anthropomorphizing** the animals, though cute and cuddly, was no walk in the park. (Claudia Puig, *"Cats & Dogs" Unleashes a Host of Effects Treats — Painstaking Movements Took Time*, USA Today, 07-09-2001, p. 5D.)

(3) human (resembling a ... being) *adj.*: **hominoid**. ▪ Human evolution comes alive — or nearly so — in a permanent exhibition at the American Museum of Natural History that is one of the city's most popular current attractions. ... [T]he display traces human history from early **hominoids** to "Lucy," who lived in Ethiopia 3.2 million years ago, to 15,000-year-old Cro-Magnon fossils found in France. (Jeffery C. Rubin, *Traveler's Advisory: North America*, Time International, 05-10-1993, p. 6.)

(4) human (having both godlike and ... attributes) *adj.*: **theanthropic**. See GODLIKE

humanity (lit. meaning, often used in the sense of decency) *n.*: **menschlichkeit** [German, Yiddish]. See DECENCY

humble (condition of being ...) *n.*: **pudency**. See MODESTY

humid (as in of or relating to dog days of summer) *adj.*: **canicular**. See DOG DAYS

humiliate (by making false statements) *v.t.*: **traduce**. See MALIGN

humiliating (or insulting another) *adj.*: **contumelious**. See CONTEMPTUOUS

humiliation (as in place or occasion of ... and seeking forgiveness) *n.*: **Canossa**. See PENANCE

humility *n.*: **pudency**. See MODESTY

humming (and droning sound) *n.*: **bombilation**. See BUZZING

humor (having a sense of ..., as in ability or tendency to laugh) *n.*: **risibility**. See LAUGH

humorless (as in person who never laughs) *n.*: **agelast**. ▪ [Comedian Sandi Toksvig has to go off] to do her bit for the literary festival, which, it turns out, is less a book plug, more an hour of stand-up, which the audience absolutely loves. I don't spot a single **agelast**. (Deborah Ross, *For a National Treasure, the Comedian and Author Sandi Toksvig is Not Terribly Conventional*, The Independent, 07-16-2001.)

(2) humorless (as in person who tries to be funny but is not) *n.*: **witling**. The Woman Author on the Market: "'She is an authoress!' has long been the sneering remark among ignorant **witlings**, of both sexes," the Ladies Magazine observed. ... [In the 19th century,] women's authorship was still the exception ..., and certainly no American woman could dream of sustaining a living from her pen. The author was male. (Michael J. Everton, *The Courtesies of Authorship: Hannah Adams and Authorial Ethics in the Early Republic*, Legacy: A Journal of American Women Writers, 01-01-2003.)

humorous *adj.*: **gelastic**. See LAUGHABLE
(2) humorous *adj.*: **risible**. See LAUGHABLE

hunch (that something is going to occur) *n.*: **presentiment**. See PREMONITION

hunger (as in craving) *n.*: **appetence**. See CRAVING
(2) hunger (as in craving) *n.*: **avidity**. See CRAVING
(3) hunger (condition involving ... for nonfood items) *n.*: **pica**. See CRAVING
(4) hunger (excessive or pathological ...) *n.*: **polyphagia**. See APPETITE

hungry *adj.*: **esurient**. ▪ These new censors, the deconstructionists, take the most luscious and delicious apple and show it to a hungry person. They then seal the fruit with plastic wrap and demand that the **esurient** victim enjoy its flavour. (Michael Coren, *Behold the Deconstructionist, Who Liberates Literature by Confining it to a Cult*, Alberta Report/Western Report, 04-10-1995, p. 36.)

(2) hungry (as in voracious) *adj.*: **edacious**. See VORACIOUS

hunt (about or through) *v.t.*: **fossick** [Australian]. See RUMMAGE

hunter *n.*: **nimrod** [based on a hunter in the Book of Genesis]. ▪ [If my readers want their trophy photos published in the paper,] I will give preferential treatment to firearms hunters who have the good sense to wear a hunter orange hat, coat or vest for photographic purposes. State research shows the wearing of hunter orange dramatically reduces a person's chances of being involved in a hunting accident, and

[sets] a good example for young **nimrods**. (J. Michael Kelly, *Hunters Should Think Safety First*, The Post-Standard [Syracuse, NY], 11-18-2001.)

hunting (of or relating to ...) *adj.*: **cynegetic**. ∎ The best summation of [the relationship a hunter has to his prey] is to be found in the title of author Paul Shepard's 1973 **cynegetic** classic, The Tender Carnivore and the Sacred Game. (Thomas McIntyre, *The Most Serious Act of All [A Hunter's View]*, Sports Afield, 10-01-1994, p. 13.)

(2) hunting (act of ...) *n.*: **venery**. ∎ His lawyers argued that, as owner of 900 acres in Wyoming, he had a preferential right to hunt wildlife on it without state interference. ... This legal concept, called the "right of **venery**," is more appropriate to medieval Europe than to the twentieth-century American West. (Author not given, *How NWF is Defending Our Natural Heritage*, National Wildlife, 10-20-1995, p. 50.)

hurl (something or someone out of a window) *v.t.*: **defenestrate** (*n.*: **defenestration**). SEE THROW

hurried (as in hasty) *adj.*: **festinate**. SEE HASTY

hurriedly (as in, in a disorderly and hasty manner) *adv.*: **pell-mell**. SEE DISORDERLY

hurry (as in, in a ..., as in very shortly) *n.*: **trice** (as in, in a trice). SEE QUICKLY

hurt (as in bother or inconvenience) *v.t.*: **discommode**. SEE INCONVENIENCE

(2) hurt (as in bother or inconvenience) *v.t.*: **incommode**. SEE BOTHER

hurtful (as in harmful) *adj.*: **nocent**. SEE HARMFUL

husband (having more than one ... at a time) *n.*: **polyandry**. ∎ In Bhutan, many women practice **polyandry** because in the poor valleys of the Himalayas a lone husband cannot support a family. (Sharon Begley, *Sex and the Single Fly*, Newsweek, 08-14-2000, p. 44.)

(2) husband (overly devoted to or submissive to one's ...) *adj.*: **uxorious**. SEE DOTING

hushed (said in ... tones, not to be overheard) *adv., adj.*: **sotto voce**. SEE WHISPERED

husky (having a ... body build) *adj.*: **mesomorphic**. SEE MUSCULAR

hyperbole (abnormal propensity towards ...) *n.*: **mythomania**. SEE EMBELLISHMENT

hypercritical *adj.*: **captious**. SEE FAULTFINDING

(2) hypercritical (person) *n.*: **smellfungus**. SEE FAULTFINDER

hypnotize (as in bewitch or enchant) *v.t.*: **ensorcell** (or **ensorcel**). SEE ENCHANT

hypocrite (esp. one who affects religious piety) *n.*: **Tartuffe** (or **tartuffe**) [after the protagonist in the play *Tartuffe* by Molière]. ∎ Add to this melange the pathetic figure of Al Gore's nominee for Vice-President, Senator Joe Lieberman. He is the American **Tartuffe**, the consummate hypocrite. Lieberman, an orthodox Jew, suddenly discovered on his way to wooing black votes that he had a great deal of respect for American black Muslim leader Louis Farrakhan, author of some of America's nastiest anti-Semitic quotes. (Barbara Amiel, *The Empty-Headed Myths That America's Voters Laid to Rest*, Daily Telegraph [London], 12-18-2000.)

(2) hypocrite (esp. one who acts humbly) *n.*: **Uriah Heep** [based on the villainous character of the same name from the Charles Dickens novel, *David Copperfield*, who always effected false humility] ∎ More than any presidential campaign in memory, [Senator John] Edwards's crusade against "special interests" is beholden to an interest group — his fellow trial lawyers — whose lucrative rapacity depends on thwarting reforms from Washington. He uses their millions to advertise his hardscrabble origins and oneness with the masses. His **Uriah Heep** candidacy should pay royalties to Charles Dickens. (George F. Will, *The Politics of Manliness*, The Washington Post, 01-29-2004.)

hypocritical (or sanctimonious, pious and/or insincere speech) *n.*: **cant**. SEE PIOUS

(2) hypocritical *adj.*: **Janus-faced**. SEE TWO-FACED

(3) hypocritical (in a self-righteous or sanctimonious way) *adj.*: **Pecksniffian**. SEE SELF-RIGHTEOUS

hysterical *adj.*: **gelastic**. SEE LAUGHABLE
(2) hysterical (woman) *n.*: **maenad**. SEE WOMAN
(3) hysterical *adj.*: **risible**. SEE LAUGHABLE

I

ice (coating of ...) *n.*: **rime**. ∎ Even the ... ice storm [in the movie The Ice Storm] is made to look preposterous, what with **rime** covering everything in bluish-silvery splendor, like a Disney wonderland. (John Simon, *The Ice Storm [Movie Reviews]*, National Review, 11-24-1997, p. 61.)

(2) ice (from a storm or floating ... chunks) *n.*: **tiddledies**. ∎ Dear Sharon: I can't seem to ever be warm when the temperature dips. No matter what I wear, I'm always the one who's chilled to the bone. What can I do to avoid my death of cold? — Fashion Freeze-out. Dear Fashion Freeze-out: Brrrr, those jarring Siberian blues. But, my glacial princess, besides a case of the sniffles and surfing the **tiddledies** of an ice storm, there are real dangers of hypothermia and frostbite when the mercury plummets below the freezing level. (Sharon Haver, *Potions Leave No Excuse for Damaged Skin*, Rocky Mountain News, 01-22-1998.)

(3) ice (thin coating of ..., as on a rock) *n.*: **verglas**. ∎ The scene was magnificent — [there was] pure white [snow] across the loch and, above us, tiny figures moved in and out of the mist on the ridge. My, we felt smug, even when it became clear that the obvious way back up [the ski mountain] consisted of nasty shiny **verglas**! (Donald Shiach, *Tour Party*, The Scotsman, 03-06-1999.)

iciness (often in relations between people) *n.*: **froideur** [French]. SEE CHILLINESS

iconoclast (orig. Catholics who did not follow Church of England) *n.*: **recusant**. SEE DISSENTER

icy (as in of, like or occurring in winter) *adj.*: **brumal**. SEE WINTER

(2) icy *adj.*: **gelid**. SEE COLD

(3) icy *adj.*: **hyperborean**. SEE FREEZING

idea (or concept which can be expressed in one word) *n.*: **holophrasis** (*adj.*: **holophrastic**). ∎ [We] looked at the term *Thomson*, as the market leader [in the London travel agent business]. Where was its magic? They might have called themselves Lord Thomson, but self-effacingly stayed plain Thomson, like the bloke next door. ... Thomson ... has hardly any subtext. Despite this mild heritage, Thomson sells [travel] packages easy as shooting fish in a barrel. Thomson is **holophrastic**. (Trader Horn, *Travel: Agents of Change*, The Guardian [London], 09-17-1994.)

(2) idea (as in creative inspiration) *n.*: **afflatus**. SEE INSPIRATION

(3) idea (which is odd, stubborn or whimsical) *n.*: **crotchet**. SEE NOTION

(4) idea (to form an ... of or about) *v.t.*: **ideate**. SEE VISUALIZE

(5) idea (about which one is obsessed) *n.*: **idée fixe** [French]. SEE OBSESSION

(6) idea (which is controversial or person who holds one) *n.*: **polemic**. SEE CONTROVERSY

ideal (the ..., lit. greatest or highest good) *n.*: **summum bonum** [Latin]. ∎ Over and over, I hear parents complain that their kids don't like to read, that the boys are obsessed with sports and the girls are already superconscious — at 8 — of their looks and their weight and their clothes. But where do children get a different message about what's important? In Hercules, being strong and destructive is the **summum bonum** for all the men and, being beautiful, thin and sexy is the basic requirement for all the female characters. (Katha Pollitt, *Get Thee Behind Me, Disney [Boycott of Walt Disney Co. Productions]*, The Nation, 07-21-1997.)

idealist (as in dreamer) *n.*: **fantast**. SEE DREAMER

idealistic (but likely impractical or unrealistic) *adj.*: **quixotic**. ∎ Few serious candidates are **quixotic** enough to refuse to descend to the level of their opponents' demeaning and deceptive attacks. The best hope remains the classic free-market solution: a voter rebellion against candidates whose [negative campaigning] tactics are an embarrassment to democracy. (Walter Shapiro, *Ethics: Voters vs. The Negative Nineties — What to Do When Campaigns Are as Nasty as a David Lynch Film*, Time, 10-15-1990, p. 98.)

(2) idealistic (person, as in an impractical contemplative person with no clear occupation or income) *n.*: **luftmensch** [lit. "man of air"; German, Yiddish]. SEE DREAMER

(3) idealistic (as in one habitually expecting an upturn in one's fortunes, sometimes without justification) *adj.*: **Micawberish** (*n.*: **Micawber**). SEE OPTIMISTIC

(4) idealistic (esp. blindly or naively ..., as in optimistic) *adj.*: **Panglossian**. SEE OPTIMISTIC

idealized (or romanticized conception of oneself, as a result of boredom in one's life) *n.*: **Bovarism**. SEE SELF-DELUSION

(2) idealized (or worshipful biography) *n.*: **hagiography** (*adj*: **hagiographic**). SEE BIOGRAPHY

ideas (source of ..., as in inspiration) *n.*: **Pierian spring**. SEE INSPIRATION

identical (in strength, power or effectiveness) *adj.*: **equipollent**. SEE EQUAL

identity (as in self-identity) *n.*: **ipseity**. SEE SELF-IDENTITY

idiom (as in phrase or expression) *n.*: **locution**. SEE PHRASE

idiot *n.*: **jobbernowl** [British]. ∎ There's no point beating a dead horse, or commenting sensibly on a **jobbernowl**, and in his defense I should say this about [Reagan's Secretary of the Interior James Watt]: there is no asinine statement he can make that would surprise a single soul. (Henry Mitchell, *Of Being Born Dumb And Standing Fast*, The Washington Post, 04-08-1983, p. B1.)
(2) idiot (as in one mentally deficient from birth) *n.*: **ament**. SEE MORON
(3) idiot *n.*: **mooncalf**. SEE FOOL

idle (... during the summer) *v.i.*: **aestivate** (or **estivate**). SEE LAZE
(2) idle (as in lazy) *adj.*: **fainéant** [French]. SEE LAZY
(3) idle (to waste time) *v.i.*: **footle** (usu. as in "footle around"). SEE DAWDLE
(4) idle (as in not moving or temporarily inactive) *adj.*: **quiescent**. SEE INACTIVE
(5) idle (person, who stays in bed out of laziness) *n.*: **slugabed**. SEE LAZY

idleness (as in disuse) *n.*: **desuetude**. SEE DISUSE
(2) idleness (as in lethargy) *n.*: **hebetude**. SEE LETHARGY
(3) idleness *n.*: **torpor**. SEE LETHARGY

idler (as in one who strolls through city streets idly) *n.*: **flâneur** [French] (idling *n.*: **flânerie**). ∎ All that is missing from a footloose, fanciful exhibit in Bonn of nearly 1,000 shoes is Cinderella's glass slipper and a donation from the Imelda Marcos collection. ... "My ideal viewer," [said the show's creator], "is a **flâneur**, a Charles Baudelaire sauntering down a boulevard, enjoying its glamour." (Emily Mitchell, *Sightings: Dance/United States*, Time International, 01-03-1994, p. 55.)
(2) idler (as in work avoider) *n.*: **embusque** [French]. SEE SLACKER
(3) idler *n.*: **wastrel**. SEE SLACKER

idyllic (as in a place which is rustic, peaceful and simple) *adj.*: **Arcadian**. SEE PASTORAL

iffy (as in tenuous) *adj.*: **gossamer**. SEE TENUOUS
(2) iffy (morality or taste) *adj.*: **louche**. SEE QUESTIONABLE

ignominious *adj.*: **opprobrious** (*n.*: **opprobrium**). SEE CONTEMPTUOUS

ignorant *adj.*: **nescient** (*n.*: **nescience**). ∎ Occasionally, I am invited to share my thoughts about my life as a lesbian with college classes — Alternative Lifestyles 101. After being asked the **nescient**, yet well-meaning, question, "When did you know you were a lesbian?" I'm usually asked, "How do you know you're a lesbian?" Oh, seekers of knowledge, let me count the ways. (Amy Adams, *Too Much Emphasis on Sex*, St. Louis Post-Dispatch, 06-09-1998, p. B7.)
(2) ignorant (intellectually or morally ...) *adj.*: **benighted**. SEE UNENLIGHTENED
(3) ignorant (or dull, stupid, obtuse or uncultured) *adj.*: **Boeotian**. SEE DULL
(4) ignorant (class of people regarded as ..., as in unsophisticated) *n.*: **booboisie**. SEE UNSOPHISTICATED
(5) ignorant (person with respect to artistic or cultural values) *adj.*: **philistine**. SEE UNCULTURED

ill (and sickly person, esp. one morbidly concerned with his own health) *n., adj.*: **valetudinarian**. SEE SICKLY

ill temper (as in acrimony) *n.*: **asperity**. SEE ACRIMONY
(2) ill temper *n.*: **bile**. SEE BITTERNESS
(3) ill temper *n.*: **choler** (*adj.*: **choleric**). SEE ANGER

ill-bred (person) *n.*: **grobian**. SEE BOOR

ill-tempered *adj.*: **atrabilious**. SEE SURLY
(2) ill-tempered *adj.*: **bilious**. SEE SURLY
(3) ill-tempered (as in grouchy, person) *n.*: **crosspatch**. SEE GROUCH
(4) ill-tempered (as in irritable) *adj.*: **liverish**. SEE IRRITABLE
(5) ill-tempered *adj.*: **querulous**. SEE PEEVISH
(6) ill-tempered (as in irritable) *adj.*: **shirty**. SEE IRRITABLE
(7) ill-tempered *adj.*: **splenetic**. SEE IRRITABLE

illiterate *adj.*: **analphabetic**. ∎ It is not so surprising when one reflects that all cultures possess a literature. In an **analphabetic** culture, the literature will be an oral one. (Scott Herring, *Du Bois and the Minstrels*, [W.E.B. du Bois], Melus, 06-22-1997, p. 3.)

illness (of an ... or disease which has no known cause) *adj.*: **idiopathic** (*n.*: **idiopathy**). ∎ The male reproductive system has so many mysterious foes, the cause of infertility is often listed as **idiopathic** — unknown. (Michael Krantz, *Dealing With Male Infertility*, Cosmopolitan, 01-01-1996, p. 102.)

(2) illness (caused by a physician) *adj.*: **iatrogenic**. SEE DISEASE

(3) illness (pretend to have an ... or other incapacity to avoid work) *v.i.*: **malinger**. SEE SHIRK

illogical (something which is ...) *n.*: **alogism**. ▪ Concurrent works [in the show] dubbed "alogic compositions," or "**alogisms**," depict illogical combinations of unrelated elements such as a bar of music, a serpentine ladder and a cone or trapezoid. (Janet Kutner, *Exhibit Expands Our Understanding of Kazimir Malevich's Spare Vision*, The Dallas Morning News, 12-31-2003.)

(2) illogical (... or fallacious argument) *n.*: **choplogic**. SEE FALLACY

(3) illogical (argument where one proves or disproves a point which is not at issue) *n.*: **ignoratio elenchi** [Latin]. SEE IRRELEVANCY

(4) illogical (statement which is ..., as in logically impossible, usually unrealized by the speaker) *n.*: **Irish bull**. SEE INCONGRUITY

(5) illogical (... or fallacious argument) *n.*: **paralogism** (*adj.*: **paralogical**). SEE FALLACY

(6) illogical (... argument, where one begs the question) *n.*: **petitio principii** [Latin]. SEE BEGGING THE QUESTION

illusion (of plenty when in fact there is little) *adj.*: **Barmecidal** (esp. as in "Barmecidal feast") [after Barmecide, a character in *The Arabian Nights*, who served an imaginary feast to a beggar]. ▪ Here is an English manor house with a rather unusual staff. Alan Bates is the butler, Helen Mirren the housekeeper, and Eileen Atkins the head cook. ... [Upstairs] too, are unusual folk: Michael Gambon, the manorial master, Kristin Scott Thomas, his wife, and such guests as Maggie Smith, a countess . ... What a promising feast. But it turns out to be **Barmecidal**. Gosford Park runs 137 minutes and spends two-thirds of that time introducing the many characters. (Stanley Kauffman, *On Films — Promises, Promises [Gosford Park Movie Review]*, The New Republic, 12-31-2001.)

(2) illusion (of contentment or happiness) *n.*: **fool's paradise**. ▪ No one denies that the upsurge in energy prices is causing pain. It clearly is. But we have been living in something of a **fool's paradise** over much of the past 10 to 12 years, counting on cheap energy supplies as though they would last forever. (Author not given, *Cutting Fuel Taxes Panders to Gas Guzzlers*, The Toronto Star, 09-21-2000.)

(3) illusion (painting or drawing which gives ... of being a photograph or something real) *n.*: **trompe l'oeil** [French; deceive the eye]. ▪ "Of course it's a hoax!" says Melamid later in the van. "But, you see, all art is a hoax. C'mon! Like the idea of three-dimensionality in paintings, the creation of illusion." He assumes the voice of an amazed museum-goer looking at, say, Flemish **trompe l'oeil**: "It's a window! No, it's a painting! Oh my God, what a master!" (David Eggers, *Portrait of Artist with Trunk [Teaching Elephants to Paint]*, Esquire, 12-01-1998, p. 65.)

(4) illusion (as in delusion) *n.*: **ignis fatuus**. SEE DELUSION

(5) illusion (as in something which is impressive-looking on the outside but which hides or covers up undesirable conditions or facts) *n.*: **Potemkin village**. SEE FACADE

(6) illusion (as in hope or goal which is not realistically obtainable) *n.*: **will-o'-the-wisp**. SEE PIPE DREAM

illusory (as in unrealistic) *adj.*: **chimerical**. SEE UNREALISTIC

(2) illusory (as in delusional) *adj.*: **fatuous**. SEE DELUSIONAL

(3) illusory (as in idealistic but likely impractical or unrealistic) *adj.*: **quixotic**. SEE IDEALISTIC

image (as in representation) *n.*: **simulacrum**. SEE REPRESENTATION

imaginary (as in unrealistic) *adj.*: **chimerical**. SEE UNREALISTIC

(2) imaginary (as in delusional) *adj.*: **fatuous**. SEE DELUSIONAL

(3) imaginary (as in invented or substituted with fraudulent intent) *adj.*: **supposititious**. SEE SUPPOSED

imagination (source of ..., as in inspiration) *n.*: **Pierian spring**. SEE INSPIRATION

imagine *v.t.*: **ideate**. SEE VISUALIZE

imaginative (as in resourceful, person) *n.*: **debrouillard** (or **débrouillard**) [French]. SEE RESOURCEFUL

imbecile (as in one mentally deficient from birth) *n.*: **ament**. SEE MORON

(2) imbecile *n.*: **jobbernowl** [British]. SEE IDIOT

(3) imbecile *n.*: **mooncalf**. SEE FOOL

imbibing (as in given to or marked by consumption of alcohol) *adj.*: **bibulous**. ▪ Sometimes the course of history is dictated by obscure forces at work beneath the surface. One theory, for example, suggests that Rome declined and fell because the lead content in the wine cups of the **bibulous** power elite made them weak and stupid. (Lance Morrow, *Essay: Guerrillas in Our Midst*, Time, 03-18-1996, p. 102.)

imitation (of the real world in art or literature) *n.*: **mimesis**. ∎ Still, the fact is I *would* like to see more marital equity in the pages of our fiction. And I'd be willing to honor the principle of **mimesis** and settle for a straight 50 percent success/failure rate. (Penny Kaganoff, *Women on Divorce*, Harcourt, Brace [1995].)

(2) imitation (of a previous artistic, musical or literary piece) *n.*: **pastiche**. ∎ [P]astiches can be more attractive than authentic works. Those who make them have only one goal: to seduce viewers. For that reason, they tend to exaggerate an already forceful manner, or to sweeten an already gentle style. In the case of the Milkmaid, I believe the work can only be understood as by the hand of a follower of Goya. (Juliet Wilson-Bareau, *Letter: Doubt About Goyas*, Independent, 04-14-2001, p. 2.)

(3) imitation (as in counterfeit) *adj.*: **pinchbeck**. SEE COUNTERFEIT

imitator (inferior ... of artist, writer or painter) *n.*: **epigone**. ∎ [L]ike Japan itself, [Takeshi] has grown into a bloated, entertainment superpower, still funny, still possessing formidable hidden powers, but an **epigone** of what he once was and, in many ways, the embodiment of the rigid patriarchy he used to despise. (Tim Larimer, *The Arts/Cinema: The Beat Goes On*, Time International, 02-12-2001, p. 46.)

immaterial *adj.*: **nugatory**. SEE UNIMPORTANT
(2) immaterial *adj.*: **picayune**. SEE TRIVIAL
(3) immaterial *adj.*: **piffling**. SEE TRIVIAL

immateriality (as in argument where one proves or disproves a point which is not at issue) *n.*: **ignoratio elenchi** [Latin]. SEE IRRELEVANCY

immature *adj.*: **jejune**. SEE JUVENILE
(2) immature *adj.*: **puerile**. SEE JUVENILE

immense *adj.*: **brobdingnagian** (often cap.). SEE HUGE
(2) immense *adj.*: **Bunyanesque**. SEE ENORMOUS
(3) immense (like an elephant) *adj.*: **elephantine**. SEE ENORMOUS
(4) immense (object) *n.*: **leviathan**. SEE HUGE
(5) immense *adj.*: **Pantagruelian**. SEE GIGANTIC
(6) immense *adj.*: **pythonic**. SEE HUGE

immerse *v.t.*: **imbrue**. SEE SOAK

immigration (of Jews into Israel) *n.*: **aliyah**. ∎ Making **aliyah** is made possible by the "Law of Return," passed by the Israeli parliament in 1950. It grants the right to Israeli citizenship to anyone with a Jewish grandparent. ... Over the last half-century, Jews from around the world have taken advantage of the law to go to Israel. American Jews who make **aliyah** can also keep their U.S. citizenship. (Miranda Leitsinger, *Move to Israel Stirs Fear of Violence; Jewish Couple's Friends, Relatives Cite Dangers in "Aliyah,"* The Washington Times, 06-16-2001, p. C12.)

immobilize (a person by holding down his arms) *v.t.*: **pinion**. ∎ [The Tibetan king wanted to build a temple] but the site he chose was directly over the heart of a demoness who was reputed to sleep deep beneath Tibet. In order to keep the demoness at rest, [he] built 12 other temples at vast distances to **pinion** her arms, feet and hips. Only when these were complete could construction on the main temple begin. (Thomas Dunn, *Detour*, Time International, 02-19-2001, p. 8.)

immoral (government by the most ... people) *n.*: **kakistocracy**. SEE GOVERNMENT
(2) immoral (as in of questionable morality) *adj.*: **louche**. SEE QUESTIONABLE
(3) immoral (person) *n.*: **reprobate**. SEE UNPRINCIPLED

immorality (place of ..., as in corruption) *n.*: **Augean stable**. SEE CORRUPTION

immortal (or everlasting) *adj.*: **amaranthine**. ∎ The novel [Quicksilver] begins in 1713, with the apparently **amaranthine** Enoch Root (a mysterious figure who appears also in the twentieth-century world of Cryptonomicon). (Deborah Friedell, *Tap Tap Tap*, The New Republic, 10-27-2003.)
(2) immortal (having a delusional fantasy that one is ...) *n.*: **megalomania**. SEE DELUSIONAL
(3) immortal (as in everlasting) *adj.*: **sempiternal**. SEE EVERLASTING

immortality (one obsessed with one's own greatness, fame or ...) *n.*: **megalomania**. SEE OBSESSION

immune (as in thick-skinned) *adj.*: **pachydermatous**. SEE THICK-SKINNED

impairment (esp. of moral principles or civil order) *n.*: **labefaction**. SEE WEAKENING

impart (as in send a signal) *v.t., v.i.*: **semaphore**. SEE SIGNAL

impartial (uncompromisingly ..., as in just) *n.*: **Rhadamanthine**. SEE JUST

impassioned *adj.*: **perfervid**. ■ It is spring, always a time when an NFL general manager's fancy turns to quarterbacks. But in this first season of true free agency, the courting has been especially **perfervid**. (Peter King, *Pro Football*, Sports Illustrated, 04-25-1994, p. 26.)
(2) impassioned (or enthusiastic speech or writing) *n.*: **dithyramb**. SEE ENTHUSIASTIC

impassive (as in unemotional or even-tempered) *adj.*: **phlegmatic**. SEE EVEN-TEMPERED

impede (as in block up) *v.t.*: **occlude**. SEE BLOCK

impenetrable (as in difficult to fathom through investigation or scrutiny) *adj.*: **inscrutable**. SEE MYSTERIOUS

imperative *adj.*: **clamant**. SEE URGENT
(2) imperative (as in urgent) *adj.*: **necessitous**. SEE URGENT

imperceptive (as in slow to understand or perceive) *adj.*: **purblind**. SEE OBTUSE

imperfect (or impure) *adj.*: **maculate**. SEE IMPURE
(2) imperfect *adj.*: **peccable**. SEE FLAWED

imperiled (journey or passage, with dangers on both sides) *idiom*: **between Scylla and Charybdis**. SEE VULNERABLE

impermanent *adj.*: **evanescent**. SEE TRANSIENT

imperturbability *n.*: **ataraxy** (or **ataraxia**). SEE CALMNESS
(2) imperturbability (esp. under pressure or trying circumstances) *n.*: **sang-froid** [French]. SEE COMPOSURE

imperturbable (as in unemotional or even-tempered) *adj.*: **phlegmatic**. SEE EVEN-TEMPERED

impervious (to outside influences) *adj.*: **hermetic**. SEE SEALED

impetuous *adj.*: **gadarene** [often cap.; derives from the Gadarene swine (Matthew 8:28) who rushed into the sea and drowned after Jesus sent into them demons exorcised from a demoniac person.] ■ [Quoting] Ross Mackenzie of the *Richmond* (Va.) *Times-Dispatch*: [Why did George Bush win the election? Partly because voters] fear the culture is tracking in the wrong direction — perhaps even has reached the chasm's edge. They draw their fears from today's horrific tugs at the young. They fear the drift — the **gadarene** rush — aided by Hollywood, television, and rock "artists"; they fear a corresponding collapse of education. (Jane Pope, *Observations*, Charlotte Observer [NC], 11-14-2004, p. 1P.)

impetuously (as in, in a disorderly and hasty manner) *adv.*: **pell-mell**. SEE DISORDERLY

impetus *n.*: **fillip**. SEE STIMULUS

impish (and magical) *adj.*: **elfin**. SEE SPRIGHTLY
(2) impish (girl with ... or playful appeal) *n.*: **gamine** [French]. SEE GIRL
(3) impish (or playful young woman) *n.*: **hoyden**. SEE TOMBOY

implication (as in inference) *n.*: **illation**. SEE INFERENCE

implicit *adj.*: **immanent**. SEE INHERENT

implore *v.t.*: **adjure**. SEE PLEAD

impolite (or tasteless comments) *n.*: **dontopedalogy**. SEE FOOT-IN-MOUTH
(2) impolite (comment which seems to be offering sympathy but instead makes the person feel worse, either intentionally or unintentionally) *n.*: **Job's comforter**. SEE TACTLESS

impoliteness (in behavior or speech due to arrogance or contempt) *n.*: **contumely**. SEE CONTEMPT

importance (of equal ...) *n.*: **equiponderance**. ■ Such linkages go far toward explaining both the sheer abundance of apparent musical digression in the opera and its strange **equiponderance** with the terse main line of the action. They are not digressions at all — or only digressions at first hearing. (Richard Toruskin, *Another World: Why the Queen of Spades is the Great Symbolist Opera*, Opera News, 12-23-1995.)

important (as in critical stage or period) *n., adj.*: **climacteric**. SEE CRITICAL
(2) important (of an event or period which is ...) *adj.*: **epochal**. SEE MOMENTOUS
(3) important (or self-important person or official) *n.*: **high muck-a-muck**. SEE BIGWIG
(4) important (person, esp. in intellectual or literary circles) *n.*: **mandarin**. SEE INFLUENTIAL
(5) important (or self-important person or official) *n.*: **panjandrum**. SEE BIGWIG
(6) important (person in a field or organization) *n.*: **wallah**. SEE NOTABLE

impossibility (statement of ..., as in unlikelihood, expressed in the form of an exaggerated comparison with a more obvious impossibility; for example "the sky will fall before I get married.") *n.*: **adynaton**. SEE UNLIKELIHOOD

(2) impossibility (statement which contains a logical ..., usually unrealized by the speaker) *n.*: **Irish bull**. SEE INCONGRUITY

imposter (esp. one who sells quack medicines) *n.*: **mountebank**. SEE HUCKSTER

(2) imposter (as in hypocrite, esp. one who acts humbly) *n.*: **Uriah Heep**. SEE HYPOCRITE

impostor (as in hypocrite, esp. one who affects religious peity) *n.*: **Tartuffe** (or **tartuffe**). SEE HYPOCRITE

impotent (as in ineffective) *adj.*: **feckless**. SEE INEFFECTIVE

(2) impotent (as in powerless) *adj.*: **impuissant**. SEE POWERLESS

impoverished *adj.*: **impecunious**. SEE POOR
(2) impoverished *adj.*: **necessitous**. SEE POOR

impractical (and contemplative person with no clear occupation or income) *n.*: **luftmensch** [lit. "man of air"; German, Yiddish]. SEE DREAMER

(2) impractical (as in idealistic but likely unrealistic or ...) *adj.*: **quixotic**. SEE IDEALISTIC

impregnate *v.t.*: **fecundate**. ∎ China now has about 1,000 giant pandas, including 70 artificially **fecundated** ones, according to a national survey recently. (Author not given, *Survey: China Has about 1,000 Pandas*, Xinhua News Agency, 04-22-2001.)

impressing (favorably) *adj.*: **prepossessing**. SEE PLEASING

impressive (very ... in effect, as in dazzling) *adj.*: **foudroyant** [French]. SEE DAZZLING

imprison (as in confine) *v.t.*: **immure**. SEE CONFINE

imprisonment *n.*: **durance** (often as in "in durance vile"). SEE JAIL

improbability (statement of ..., expressed in the form of an exaggerated comparison with a more obvious impossibility; for example "the sky will fall before I get married.") *n.*: **adynaton**. SEE UNLIKELIHOOD

improbable (as in unrealistic) *adj.*: **chimerical**. SEE UNREALISTIC

(2) improbable (as in idealistic but likely impractical or unrealistic) *adj.*: **quixotic**. SEE IDEALISTIC

improper (as in inappropriate, comments) *n.*: **dontopedalogy**. SEE FOOT-IN-MOUTH

(2) improper (as in inappropriate or out-of-place) *adj.*: **malapropos**. SEE INAPPROPRIATE

impropriety (in public office) *n.*: **malversation**. SEE WRONGDOING

improve (text or language by removing errors or flaws) *v.t.*: **blue-pencil**. SEE EDIT

(2) improve (text or language by removing errors or flaws) *v.t.*: **emend**. SEE EDIT

impudence *n.*: **hardihood**. SEE GALL

impudent (and conceited person) *n.*: **jackanapes**. SEE CONCEITED

impugn (by making false or malicious statements) *v.t.*: **calumniate**. SEE MALIGN

(2) impugn (so as to humiliate or disgrace) *v.t.*: **traduce**. SEE MALIGN

impulse (as in creative inspiration) *n.*: **afflatus**. SEE INSPIRATION

(2) impulse (mental process marked by ... to do something) *n.*: **conation**. SEE DETERMINATION

impulsive (as in impetuous) *adj.*: **gadarene**. SEE IMPETUOUS

(2) impulsive (as in irresponsible or reckless) *adj.*: **harum-scarum**. SEE RECKLESS

impure *adj.*: **maculate**. ∎ Rabbi Halivni endeavors to show that a Jew can accept, along with the Bible's critics, that the Torah is a **maculate** text, full of "bumps and fissures" and still remain an observant, believing Jew. (Author not given, *When Perfect Faith Meets Imperfect Text*, Forward, 06-26-1998, p. 13.)

in the act (esp. of committing an offense or a sexual act) *adv.*: **in flagrante delicto**. ∎ Of Worth's inner circle, Ned Wynert ... had suffered the traditional adulterer's fate, gunned down **in flagrante delicto** by an enraged husband. (Ben Macintyre, *The Napoleon of Crime*, Farrar, Straus & Giroux [1997], p. 175.)

in fact *adj., adv.*: **de facto** (as contrasted with *de jure*: legally or by law) [Latin]. ∎ While ultra-Orthodox leaders [in Israel] regularly bluster against the courts, they comply with court rulings. Even more telling, they regularly turn to the courts when they think that doing so will protect their interests. The ultra-Orthodox oppose the courts de jure, but they do not **de facto**. (Noah Efron, *Real Jews*, Basic Books [2003], p. 218.)

inability (statement of ... to do something) *n*.: **non possumus** [Latin]. ∎ [French President Jacques Chirac stated:] "[O]ur ambitions [to form a constitution for the European Union] have been reduced on tax and social questions. ... The '**non possumus**' clearly and strongly put forward by the United Kingdom" — in essence, a plea of inability by Britain's government to cede any power to Brussels on these questions in the face of fierce opposition among voters at home. (Thomas Fuller, *EU Waters Down Charter to Save it*, International Herald Tribune, 06-18-2004.)

inaccuracy (accepted as fact due to repetition in print) *n*.: **factoid**. ∎ What better time [than now] to dispose of some of the persistent myths that impede sound public policy? 1. "Guns in the home are 43 times more likely to kill a family member or friend than an intruder." Ellen Goodman wrote that in 1993, but let's not pick on her. This **factoid** is endlessly repeated by congressmen, by Handgun Control, Inc. by TV crime shows, and even sitcoms. (Ramesh Ponnuru, *The New Myths [Myths in Public Life]*, National Review, 11-09-1998, p. 42.)

inactive (temporarily ...) *adj*.: **quiescent**. ∎ The People Power revolution that brought down Philippine dictator Ferdinand Marcos in 1986 wrote a script almost too perfect: a nation **quiescent** for more than a decade would rise and, relatively peacefully, replace their leader with his assassinated rival's widow. (Nisid Hajari, *Time 100: Asians Of The Century — A Combination of Towering Individuals and Societies That Played Down Individualism Helped Liberate, Ravage and Resurrect the Vast Protean Region*, Time International, 08-23-1999, p. 32.)

(2) inactive (as in lazy) *adj*.: **fainéant** [French]. See LAZY

(3) inactive *adj*.: **torpid**. See LETHARGIC

inactivity (spend the summer in a state of relative ...) *v.i.*: **aestivate** (or **estivate**). See LAZE

(2) inactivity (as in disuse) *n*.: **desuetude**. See DISUSE

(3) inactivity *n*.: **torpor**. See LETHARGY

inadequate (as in meager) *n*.: **exiguous**. See MEAGER

inalienable (as in inviolable) *adj*.: **infrangible**. See INVIOLABLE

inane (in a smug or complacent manner) *adj*.: **fatuous**. See FOOLISH

inanimate *adj*.: **insensate**. ∎ When the guys who wrote the Bible made lust one of the seven deadly sins, they were talking about bad lust. You know, the kind that hoots at and objectifies women, that stupid, grunting, hubba-hubba kind of lust. I'm talking about good lust, the kind that might even be described as zest or vitality. ... A man without good lust is an **insensate** mass, a lump. (Hugh O'Neill, *Your Honey or Your Wife, [Staying Faithful to Your Wife]*, Men's Health, 01-11-1996, p. 72.)

inapplicabilty (as in argument where one proves or disproves a point which is not at issue) *n*.: **ignoratio elenchi** [Latin]. See IRRELEVANCY

inappropriate *adj*.: **malapropos**. ∎ After Lot's wife turns back to look at the destruction of Sodom and Gomorrah and is transformed into a pillar of salt as a result, Lot tells Noah, "She always said she was the salt of the earth, and suddenly, she was." Such **malapropos** wise cracks are driven home with a relentlessly upbeat soundtrack which serenades scenes of human tragedy with bouncy, Disneyesque melodies. (Steve Rabey, *"Noah's Ark" Hits Bottom: Miniseries Suffers From Lack of Accuracy*, The Arlington Morning News, 05-02-1999, p. 1B.)

(2) inappropriate (comments) *n*.: **dontopedalogy**. See FOOT-IN-MOUTH

(3) inappropriate (comment which seems to be offering sympathy but instead makes the person feel worse, either intentionally or unintentionally) *n*.: **Job's comforter**. See TACTLESS

inapt (as in inappropriate or out-of-place) *adj*.: **malapropos**. See INAPPROPRIATE

inattentive (or preoccupied, esp. because of worries or fears) *adj*.: **distrait**. See DISTRACTED

inborn (as in innate) *adj*.: **connate**. See INNATE

(2) inborn *adj*.: **immanent**. See INHERENT

inbred (as in innate) *adj*.: **connate**. See INNATE

incapable (as in powerless) *adj*.: **impuissant**. See POWERLESS

incapacitated (as in out of action) *adj., adv*.: **hors de combat** [French]. See DISABLED

(2) incapacitated (pretend to be ... to avoid work) *v.i.*: **malinger**. See SHIRK

incarcerate (as in confine) *v.t.*: **immure**. See CONFINE

incarceration *n*.: **durance** (often as in "in durance vile"). See JAIL

incensed (as in indignant) *n.*: **dudgeon** (often expressed as "in high dudgeon"). SEE INDIGNANT

(2) incensed *adj.*: **wroth**. SEE ANGRY

incentive (as in stimulus) *n.*: **fillip**. SEE STIMULUS

incident (to) *adj.*: **appurtenant**. SEE PERTAINING

incidental (as in by chance) *adj.*: **adventitious**. SEE CHANCE

incisive *adj.*: **trenchant**. ▪ [In] this rewarding six-hour documentary series [about Australia] writer-host Robert Hughes ... provides the TV reviewer with enough witty, **trenchant** observations to fill three notebooks. (Terry Kelleher, *Picks & Pans: Tube*, People, 09-04-2000, p. 39.)

incisiveness *n.*: **acuity**. SEE KEENNESS

incivility (in behavior or speech, due to arrogance or contempt) *n.*: **contumely**. SEE CONTEMPT

inclination (mental process marked by ... to do something) *n.*: **conation**. SEE DETERMINATION

(2) inclination (slight or faint ...) *n.*: **velleity**. SEE HOPE

incline (as in upward slope) *n.*: **acclivity** (*adj.*: **acclivitous**). ▪ Nearby is Mummy Mountain, where every Saturday at sunrise a large pack heads out for runs of 10 to 20 miles over paved, rolling terrain — with a few monster **acclivities** — through some of Phoenix's poshest neighborhoods. (Doug Rennie, *Phoenix and Scottsdale [Resources for Runners]*, Runner's World, 08-01-1994, p. 40.)

(2) incline (downward ..., esp. extending down from a fortification) *n.*: **glacis**. SEE DECLINE

inclusion (as in insertion, of something between existing things) *n.*: **intercalation**. SEE INSERTION

incoherent (speech, esp. heard in certain Christian congregations) *n.*: **glossolalia**. SEE UNINTELLIGIBLE

(2) incoherent (talk or act in an aimless or ... fashion) *v.i.*: **maunder**. SEE RAMBLE

incomparable (state of being ..., as in superior or state of being better) *n.*: **meliority**. SEE SUPERIORITY

incompatible (as in things which do not mix together) *adj.*: **immiscible**. ▪ [T]o put it in high-tech terms, the Israelis and the Palestinians seem like different computer systems — say, IBM and Apple. Each system makes elaborate and perfect sense within its own universe, but ... is utterly incapable of communicating with the other. ... The two sides seem **immiscible** systems of culture and thought and history. (Lance Morrow, *World: Israel — At 40, the Dream Confronts Palestinian Fury and a Crisis of Identity*, Time, 04-04-1988, p. 36.)

incompetent (as in ineffective) *adj.*: **feckless**. SEE INEFFECTIVE

(2) incompetent (mentally ...) *adj.*: **non compos mentis** [Latin]. SEE INSANE

incomprehensible (speech, esp. heard in certain Christian congregations) *n.*: **glossolalia**. SEE UNINTELLIGIBLE

(2) incomprehensible (as in difficult to fathom through investigation or scrutiny) *adj.*: **inscrutable**. SEE MYSTERIOUS

incongruity (statement which contains an ... or is logically impossible, usually unrealized by the speaker) *n.*: **Irish bull**. ▪ "After the stewardess made the announcement," he told us, "nobody said a word! We just kept right on talking." [For another] **Irish Bull** ... I'm indebted to my wife. At dinner, while cautioning one of the children about stuffing his mouth, she said, "Don't you put another thing in your mouth until you've swallowed it first." (Will Stanton, *Watch out for the Wollypops*, Saturday Evening Post, 05-01-1991.)

incongruous (as in things which do not mix together) *adj.*: **immiscible**. SEE INCOMPATIBLE

inconsequential (as in unimportant or insignificant) *adj.*: **nugatory**. SEE UNIMPORTANT AND WORTHLESS

(2) inconsequential *adj.*: **picayune**. SEE TRIVIAL

(3) inconsequential (as in unimportant or trivial) *adj.*: **piffling**. SEE TRIVIAL

inconsiderate (comment which seems to be offering sympathy but instead makes the person feel worse, either intentionally or unintentionally) *n.*: **Job's comforter**. SEE TACTLESS

inconsistency (in terms or ideas) *n.*: **antilogy**. SEE CONTRADICTION

(2) inconsistency (statement which contains a logical ..., usually unrealized by the speaker) *n.*: **Irish bull**. SEE INCONGRUITY

inconsistent (as in hypocritical) *adj.*: **Janus-faced**. SEE TWO-FACED

incontestable (necessarily or demonstrably ...) *adj.*: **apodictic**. SEE INCONTROVERTIBLE

(2) incontestable *adj.*: **irrefragable**. SEE UNQUESTIONABLE

incontrovertible (as in an ... truth) *adj.*: **apodictic** [In the precise use of the term, for something to be apodictic it must necessarily be true, such as a mathematical equation. However, it is frequently used as a rhetorical device, such as in expressing a matter of opinion that something must be true in the opinion of the writer, or sarcastically, such as accusing another of treating something as being apodictic, when it obviously is not.] ▪ A number of letters in response to your excellent June 27 editorial "The Disaster of Failed Policy" reveal that many still do not accept the **apodictic** fact that Hussein had no hand in the 9/11 outrage. Bush's "great courage" was perfectly justified in the invasion of Afghanistan but totally served a personal vendetta ... in the case of the war and occupation of Iraq. (Paul McCaig [letter writer], *Surveying Iraq With Allawi at the Helm*, Los Angeles Times, 07-02-2004, p. B12.)

(2) incontrovertible *adj.*: **irrefragable**. SEE UNQUESTIONABLE

inconvenience *v.t.*: **discommode**. ▪ You kept quiet when they made air bags compulsory. When they passed laws to keep adults from owning guns. When they tried to censor the Internet. Yes, all of these eroded Americans' freedom to make decisions for themselves. ... But none of them **discommoded** you personally, so you didn't see any reason to speak out. (Jeff Jacoby, *Posse Poised to Ambush Junk Food*, The Washington Times, 11-27-1998, p. A53.)

(2) inconvenience *v.t.*: **incommode**. SEE BOTHER

incorrigible (person) *n.*: **scapegrace**. SEE SCOUNDREL

increase (as in burgeon or expand; lit.: bear fruit) *v.i.*: **fructify**. SEE BURGEON

incriminate *v.t.*: **inculpate**. SEE BLAME

incumbent (and in reigning) *adj.*: **regnant**. SEE REIGNING

indecent (compulsive ... behavior) *n.*: **corpropraxia**. SEE OBSCENE

(2) indecent (as in lewd or obscene) *adj.*: **fescennine**. SEE OBSCENE

(3) indecent (as in vulgar) *adj.*: **meretricious**. SEE VULGAR

indecision (as in doubt) *n.*: **peradventure**. SEE DOUBT

(2) indecision *adj.*, *v.i.*; *n.*: **shilly-shally**. SEE VACILLATE

indecisive (or such a person) *adj.*, *n.*: **namby-pamby**. SEE SPINELESS

(2) indecisive (to be ...) *v.i.*: **dither**. SEE PROCRASTINATE

indecisiveness *n.*: **abulia**. ▪ When the rebellion came, in his first engagement as commander of the U.S. Army [in the Civil War, General Grant] lost 17,000 men by nightfall. The survivors, accustomed to McClellan's chronic **abulia** at such moments, assumed he would call retreat. But after a night during which he is said to have wept, Grant gave the signal for pursuit. A soldier wrote: "For the first time, we felt the boss had arrived." (Matthew Scully, *Memoirs [book reviews]*, National Review, 12-17-1990.)

(2) indecisiveness (as in the dilemma of being given a choice between two equally appealing alternatives and thus being able to choose neither one) *n.*: **Buridan's ass**. SEE PARALYSIS

indecorous (as in inappropriate or out-of-place) *adj.*: **malapropos**. SEE INAPPROPRIATE

indefensible (as in unpardonable) *adj.*: **irremissible**. SEE UNPARDONABLE

indefinitely *adv.*: **sine die** [Latin; generally used with respect to an adjournment of a meeting or of a political session]. ▪ Both chambers adjourned **sine die** Sunday, ending the Legislature's third special session of the year. (Peggy Fikac, *Legislature OKs New Map*, San Antonio Express-News [Texas], 10-13-2003, p. 1A.)

independent (thinker, esp. on matters of morals and religion) *n.*: **libertine**. SEE FREE-THINKER

indescribable *adj.*: **ineffable**. ▪ There's no question that Charles Schulz' characters tap into an **ineffable** quality of the human spirit. (Mary Voboril, *Importance of "Peanuts,"* Newsday, 12-29-1999, p. B6.)

indeterminate (in depth, meaning or significance) *adj.*: **unplumbable**. SEE UNEXPLORABLE

indicate *v.t.*: **adumbrate**. SEE FORESHADOW

(2) indicate *v.t.*: **betoken**. SEE PORTEND

(3) indicate (as in send a signal) *v.t.*, *v.i.*: **semaphore**. SEE SIGNAL

indication (early ... of disease) *n.*: **prodrome**. SEE SYMPTOM

indifference (esp. on matters or politics or religion)

n.: **Laodiceanism**. ∎ As Kevin Myers wrote in *The Irish Times* in 1991 [describing bishop] Walton Empey: the accent is broad, the manner genial, the figure ample, the laughter ready, and most important of all, the opinion strong and free and forthright. All the political timidity, the [pretense] at **Laodiceanism** lest opinion on all but traffic accidents and dog licences be taken as disloyalty to Ireland, ... all are absent from Walton Empey. (Patsy McGarry, *Archbishop Walton Empey to Retire in July*, The Irish Times, 05-01-2002, p. 5.)

(2) indifference (sometimes in matters spiritual, and sometimes leading to depression) *n.*: **acedia**. SEE APATHY

indifferent (esp. neither right nor wrong, beneficial nor harmful) *adj.*: **adiaphorous**. SEE NEUTRAL
(2) indifferent *adj.*: **pococurante**. SEE APATHETIC

indigence *n.*: **penury**. SEE POVERTY

indigenous *adj.*: **authochthonous**. ∎ Just as the Japanese can adjust to being the world leaders in information technology without ceasing to be Japanese, so the Inuit can adjust to the snowmobile and the rifle without losing touch with whatever it is that binds them together. For cultures are not monoliths. They are fragmentary, patchworks of **autochthonous** and foreign elements. (Anthony Pagden, *Culture Wars*, The New Republic, 11-16-1998.)
(2) indigenous *adj.*: **aboriginal**. SEE NATIVE

indigent *adj.*: **impecunious**. SEE POOR
(2) indigent *adj.*: **necessitous**. SEE POOR

indigestion *n.*: **dyspepsia** (*adj.*: **dyspeptic**). ∎ Now that she was so close to what she wanted all her life [a high tennis ranking], Willy's stomach didn't yowl with appetite, but clenched in clammy, **dyspeptic** fear. (Lionel Shriver, *Double Fault*, Doubleday [1997], p. 162.)

indignant (mood) *n.*: **dudgeon** (often expressed as "in high dudgeon"). ∎ The American College of Obstetricians and Gynecologists was in high **dudgeon** last week over the difference some private health insurers see between Viagra, the new impotency pill, and birth control pills. Some insurers will pay for Viagra prescriptions but will not cover prescription birth control. That, the doctors said, constitutes a clear case of gender discrimination. (Author not given, *Viagra & the Pill / A Silly Attempt to Find Gender Bias*, Minneapolis Star Tribune, 05-18-1998, p. 8A.)

indignity (being subject to ..., esp. public) *n.*: **obloquy**. SEE ABUSE

indispensable (element or condition) *n.*: **sine qua non** [Latin]. ∎ A lean physique is a **sine qua non** of physical attractiveness in girls and women alike. In the words of a Bloomingdale's ad, the current ideal womanly shape is "being lean, slender as the night, narrow as an arrow, pencil thin," get the point? (Debra Lynn Stephens, *The Beauty Myth and Female Consumers: The Controversial Role of Advertising*, Journal of Consumer Affairs, 06-22-1994, p. 137.)

indisputable (necessarily or demonstrably ...) *adj.*: **apodictic**. SEE INCONTROVERTIBLE
(2) indisputable *adj.*: **irrefragable**. SEE UNQUESTIONABLE

individual (as in specific to one person or thing; e.g. languages which use symbols or pictures instead of words) *adj.*: **idiographic**. SEE UNIQUE

individualist (esp. on matters of morals and religion) *n.*: **libertine**. SEE FREE-THINKER

individuality (as in that quality which makes one thing different from any other) *n.*: **haeccity**. ∎ [Author Nicholson Baker has] an ability to evoke the sensual **haecceity** of ordinary things. [He] notices a Franklin Library edition of [John Updike's] "*Rabbit, Run,*" which he pulls from the shelf: "The padded, bright red binding was somewhat more reminiscent of a comfortable corner booth at an all-night, all-vinyl coffee shop than one might have thought fitting for so aggressively 'classic' an enterprise." (Michael Dirda, *Book World; Rabbit Pursuit: A Passion For Updike*, The Washington Post, 05-06-1991, p. B3.)
(2) individuality (as in self-identity) *n.*: **ipseity**. SEE SELF-IDENTITY

indivisible (or unbreakable) *adj.*: **infrangible**. SEE UNBREAKABLE

indolent (as in lazy) *adj.*: **fainéant** [French]. SEE LAZY

inducement (as in stimulus) *n.*: **fillip**. SEE STIMULUS

indulge *v.t.*: **cosset**. SEE PAMPER
(2) indulge (in a pampering or overprotective way) *v.t.*: **mollycoddle**. SEE OVERPROTECT
(3) indulge (as in placate) *v.t.*: **propitiate**. SEE PLACATE
(4) indulge (as in treat with excessive concern) *n.*, *v.t.*: **wet-nurse**. SEE CODDLE

indulgence (excessive ... esp. by eating or drinking

too much) *n.*: **crapulence**. ■ What better way is there to shrug off your Yuletide **crapulence** than by slumping on the sofa and ogling at a game of darts? The world championships have arrived. ... Some participants will no doubt look like they, too, have been overdoing the grub and grog, but the game is trying determinedly to rid itself of a slovenly image. (Travers, *Botham and Lloyd: A Partnership Founded on Expertise*, Scotland on Sunday, 12-26-1999.)

(2) indulgence (in the face of adversity) *n.*: **longanimity**. See PATIENCE

indulgent (in exhibiting emotion or celebration) *adj.*: **saturnalian**. See UNINHIBITED

industrious *n.*: **Stakhanovite**. See WORKAHOLIC

ineffective *adj.*: **feckless**. ■ The Rangers, often defensively **feckless** during a season in which they finished with 86 points — 18 fewer than the Devils — have been airtight since the start of the playoffs, yielding 15 goals in 10 games. Why hadn't they played this way all season? (Austin Murphy, *NHL Playoffs: Crunch Time — The Pursuit of the Stanley Cup Raises the Level of Intensity*, Sports Illustrated, 05-19-1997, p. 36.)

(2) ineffective (as in powerless) *adj.*: **impuissant**. See POWERLESS

(3) ineffective *adj.*: **inutile**. See USELESS

(4) ineffective *adj.*: **otiose**. See USELESS

(5) ineffective (as in vain or worthless) *adj.*: **nugatory**. See WORTHLESS

(6) ineffective (efforts which are laborious but ...) *adj.*: **Sisyphean**. See FUTILE

inefficient (actions of pompous but ... government officials) *n.*: **bumbledom**. See BUREAUCRACY

inept (actions of pompous but ... government officials) *n.*: **bumbledom**. See BUREAUCRACY

(2) inept (habitually ... person) *n.*: **schlemiel** [Yiddish]. See BUMBLER

inescapable *adj.*: **ineluctable**. See UNAVOIDABLE

inevitable (as in unavoidable) *adj.*: **ineluctable**. See UNAVOIDABLE

inexcusable (as in unpardonable) *adj.*: **irremissible** See UNPARDONABLE

inexpressible *adj.*: **ineffable**. See INDESCRIBABLE

infallibility *n.*: **inerrancy**. ■ "A wife is to submit graciously to the servant leadership of her husband, even as the church willingly submits to the headship of Christ." — New 18th Article of the Baptist Faith and Message. The Southern Baptists, who have always believed in biblical **inerrancy**, set off an uproar this week when they lifted their language on family life straight into the headlines. (Cathy Lynn Grossman, *Baptists Explain the Moral Tone*, USA Today, 06-11-1998.)

infallible (necessarily or demonstrably ..., as in indisputable) *adj.*: **apodictic**. See INCONTROVERTIBLE

infamous *adj.*: **flagitious**. See SCANDALOUS

infant (who is deserted or abandoned) *n.*: **foundling**. See ORPHAN

(2) infant (collection of clothing and equipment for newborn ...) *n.*: **layette**. See NEWBORN

(3) infant (newborn ..., esp. less than 4 weeks old) *n.*: **neonate**. See NEWBORN

infantile *adj.*: **jejune**. See JUVENILE

(2) infantile *adj.*: **puerile**. See JUVENILE

infected (morally ...) *v.t.*: **cankered**. See CORRUPTED

inference *n.*: **illation**. ■ Pat Swindall is in prison in Atlanta where it is costing the taxpayers over $25,000. He is no threat to society. And, his family is [missing a] godly father. I didn't know Pat personally in the days when he got into trouble with the law, but I can assure you that the **illation** [that he is] even remotely involved with drugs or drug money, as several local and national papers infer, is pernicious and unfounded. (James Keffer, *Gwinnett Voices: Readers' Letters, Tell Us What You Think, The Real Tragedy Behind Officer's Death*, The Atlanta Journal and Constitution, 04-21-1994, p. J4.)

inferior (as in made without regard to quality) *adj.*: **catchpenny**. ■ Nothing in *Gladiator* or *The Patriot* proved as engrossing as Mike Figgis' *Time Code*, a split-screen, real-time movie that applied *Blair Witch* economics to a grown-up storyline. This, not the **catchpenny** *Blair Witch 2*, was the true sequel to last year's most striking cinematic invention [i.e. the original "Blair Witch Project"]. (Thomas Sutcliffe, *Review Of The Year: Arts — Cultural Overview*, Independent, 12-29-2000, p. 14.)

(2) inferior (as in acting subservient as opposed to leading) *adj.*: **sequacious**. See SUBSERVIENT

(3) inferior (rank, esp. in the military) *n.*: **subaltern**. See SUBORDINATE

infernal (and fiery) *adj.*: **sulfurous** (or **sul-**

phurous). ■ Any man who becomes Senate majority leader [like Trent Lott is] someone who instinctively knows that opening his raincoat to flash a little nostalgia for the segregation era — the obvious interpretation of his testimonial to Mr. Thurmond's segregationist presidential candidacy — will induce sudden political death, not to mention a **sulfurous** afterlife. How could Mr. Lott have meant what he seemed to say? It had to be a dopey mistake. ... (Diana West, *The Lott Parable: America Must Be Colorblind,* The Washington Times, 12-20-2002.)

(2) infernal (as in dark and gloomy) *adj.*: **acherontic**. See GLOOMY

(3) infernal (relating to gods and spirits of the ... regions) *adj.*: **chthonic**. See UNDERWORLD

(4) infernal *adj.*: **Stygian**. See HELLISH

infinite (as in everlasting) *adj.*: **sempiternal**. See EVERLASTING

infinitely *adv.*: **in aeternum** [Latin].

infirm (elderly person) *n.*: **Struldbrug**. See DECREPIT

(2) infirm (and sickly person, esp. one morbidly concerned with his own health) *n., adj.*: **valetudinarian**. See SICKLY

inflamation (of skin due to exposure to cold) *n.*: **chilblains**. ■ Metropolitan smokers are a forlorn lot these days. As more cities ban cigarettes in public places, smokers are altering every daily habit but the one they most crave. ... Shivering in shirtsleeves outside their office complexes, they increase the risk that they will succumb not to emphysema but to **chilblains**. (Richard Corliss, *Marketing: Chuff Chuff, Puff Puff All Aboard the Marlboro Unlimited, a High-tech Train Where You Can Smoke in Nearly Every Car,* Time, 01-08-1996, p. 51.)

inflated (as in pompous) *adj.*: **flatulent**. See POMPOUS

(2) inflated (as in swollen, used often of body parts such as the penis) *adj.*: **tumescent**. See SWOLLEN

(3) inflated (as in swollen or distended) *adj.*: **tumid**. See SWOLLEN AND BOMBASTIC

(4) inflated (as in pompous) *adj.*: **turgid**. See POMPOUS

inflexible (and stern) *adj.*: **flinty**. See STERN

(2) inflexible (as in narrow-minded) *adj.*: **hidebound**. See NARROW-MINDED

(3) inflexible (to make or become ...) *v.t., adj.*: **indurate**. See HARDEN

(4) inflexible (as in one who clings to an opinion or belief even after being shown that it is wrong) *n.*: **mumpsimus**. See STUBBORN

(5) inflexible (in holding to a belief or opinion) *adj.*: **pertinacious**. See STUBBORN

influence (of one political state over others) *n.*: **hegemony**. See DOMINANCE

influential (person, esp. in intellectual or literary circles) *n.*: **mandarin**. ■ [New York Post reporter Murray] Kempton was a **mandarin** among the street columnists, schooled in subjects as various as Etruscan mosaics and the internal politics of the Five Families. (David Remnick, *King of the World,* Random House [1999], p. 45.)

inform (on, as in tattle) *v.i.*: **peach**. See TATTLE

informal (language of the people) *n.*: **vulgate**. See VERNACULAR

information (false ... accepted as fact due to repetition in print) *n.*: **factoid**. See INACCURACY

informed (self-proclaimed ... people) *pl. n.*: **illuminati**. See ENLIGHTENED

(2) informed (person who is very ... in many areas) *n.*: **polyhistor**. See KNOWLEDGEABLE

(3) informed (person who is very ... in many areas) *n.*: **polymath**. See SCHOLAR

informer *n.*: **delator**. See ACCUSER

(2) informer (esp. who betrays under guise of friendship) *n.*: **Judas**. See BETRAYER

infraction (small or trifling ...) *n.*: **peccadillo**. ■ They got their baseball uniforms dirty, chugged booze, chased women, ate slabs of red meat, smoked unfiltered cigarettes and busted up the Copacabana night club every now and then. And the sports heroes never had to say they were sorry, because the newspapers godded them up and never told us about their **peccadilloes**. (Bernie Miklasz, *Life in a Bottle Over, The Mick Has New Fight,* St. Louis Post-Dispatch, 06-09-1995, p. 1D.)

ingenious (as in resourceful, person) *n.*: **debrouillard** (or **débrouillard**) [French]. See RESOURCEFUL

ingenuous (as in guileless) *n.*: **artless**. See GUILELESS

(2) ingenuous (false showing of ... behavior) *adj.*: **faux-naif** [French]. See DISINGENUOUS

ingest *v.t.*: **incept**. ■ With the improvement of living level and the change of meal structure that means people **incept** more fat than ever, the obesity patients are more and more in China, which will introduce easily many kinds of diseases, especially the cardiovascular diseases. (Author not given, *Weight Loss/Diet Products Industry Assessments [China]*, Chinese Markets for Weight Control/Loss Products, 01-01-2003.)

ingesting (act or process of) *n.*: **deglutition**. SEE SWALLOWING

ingratiating (in a smug or false manner) *adj.*: **oleaginous**. SEE UNCTUOUS

inhabitant (of a town) *n.*: **burgher**. SEE RESIDENT

inhale *v.t.*: **aspirate**. ▌ Dr. Austin went on to explain that my mother might need the help of a respirator. Already, he said, he had contacted the intensive care unit (ICU) on the assumption that she had pneumonia, a typical result of **aspirating** foreign matter into the lung. (Leslie Goerner, *You Do Understand About DNR? Don't You? Don't You? [Do-Not-Resuscitate Order by Patients Regarding Artificial Life Support]*, Commonweal, 11-21-1997, p. 20.)

inherent *adj.*: **immanent**. ▌ For the first time in my young life, I glimpsed something [i.e. Sophia Loren] sublime and preternatural and irrevocable and everlasting — at once an aura, a presence, an **immanent** beauty and elegance, a luminous charisma of sensuality and serenity, maternal light and darkest passion — that imbues certain women. (Jimmy Breslin, *Women We Love: The Definitive Selection, 1994*, Esquire, 08-01-1994, p. 58.)

(2) inherent (as in innate) *adj.*: **connate**. SEE INNATE

(3) inherent (as in inviolable) *adj.*: **infrangible**. SEE INVIOLABLE

initial (in sequence or time) *adj.*: **primordial**. SEE FIRST

initiation (as in establishment, of something) *n.*: **instauration**. SEE ESTABLISHMENT

initiative (as in energy coupled with a will to succeed) *n.*: **spizzerinctum**. SEE ENERGY

injection (as in insertion, of something between existing things) *n.*: **intercalation**. SEE INSERTION

injudicious (comments) *n.*: **dontopedalogy**. SEE FOOT-IN-MOUTH

injured (as in out of action) *adj., adv.*: **hors de combat** [French]. SEE DISABLED

injurious (mutually ... to both sides) *adj.*: **internecine**. SEE DESTRUCTIVE

(2) injurious *adj.*: **nocent**. SEE HARMFUL

(3) injurious *adj.*: **nocuous**. SEE HARMFUL

inn (large ...) *n.*: **caravansary**. ▌ Because L. A. is the endless-summer beach city, you might as well enjoy a room with a view, an ocean view, especially since the pink grande dame, the Beverly Hills Hotel, has been closed for a three-year renovation. The **caravansary** of the moment is Shutters on the Beach. (William Stadiem, *L.A. When it Settles, [What to Do in Los Angeles, California]*, Esquire, 03-01-1994, p. 37.)

innate *adj.*: **connate**. ▌ Was this the first time these two members of the Palestinian Army showed any propensity for blowing themselves up in the vicinity of Jews? ... If there was a conspiracy, did their superiors know about it? ... These and similar questions would be easy to pose to Yasser Arafat, but his **connate** predilection for lying would probably prevent our getting any serious answers. (Yehiel Leiter, *Cost & Consequence*, Jerusalem Post, 04-04-1997, p. 5.)

(2) innate *adj.*: **immanent**. SEE INHERENT

(3) innate (reaction, as in reflex) *n.*: **tropism**. SEE REFLEX

inner circle (as in advisors, often scheming or plotting) *n.*: **camarilla**. SEE ADVISORS

inner-self (as in soul) *n.*: **anima**. SEE SOUL

innermost (as in secret parts, thoughts or places) *n.*: **penetralia**. SEE SECRET

innkeeper *n.*: **boniface**. ▌ Else Barth's Seventh Inn in the Seven Trails subdivision is marking its 30th anniversary. The Copenhagen-born **boniface** recently visited her hometown and caught song stylist Clinton Gallagher at that city's premiere hotel lounge. (Jerry Berger, *Newspaper Recalls "Gentlemen's Agreement" That Casts Mizzou in Bad Light*, St. Louis Post-Dispatch, 05-06-2001, p. A2.)

innocence (determining ... or determination of ... through testimony of others) *n.*: **compurgation**. SEE ACQUITTAL

innocent (as in guileless) *n.*: **artless**. SEE GUILELESS

(2) innocent (false showing of childlike or ... behavior) *adj.*: **faux-naif** [French]. SEE DISINGENUOUS

innovative (love of or enthusiasm for anything ...) *n.*: **neophilia**. SEE NOVELTY

inopportune (occurrence, leading to an awkward or

embarrassing situation) *n*.: **contretemps**. See MISHAP

inquire (closely) *v.t.*: **catechize**. See QUESTION
(2) inquire (formally about governmental policy or action) *v.t.*: **interpellate**. See INTERROGATE

inquirer (of an astrologer) *n*.: **querent**. See QUESTIONER
(2) inquirer *n*.: **querist**. See QUESTIONER

insane (as in not of sound mind) *adj*.: **non compos mentis** [Latin]. ∎ Three years ago, when Spargur, a retired Indianapolis beautician, attended the tap-dance recital of one of her 11 great-great-grandchildren, she declared her intention to sign up for lessons. Hearing the news, her family wanted to have her declared **non compos mentis**. (Author not given, *On the Move: When Octogenarian Dance Queen Ruth Spargur First Put on Taps Three Years Ago, Something Clicked*, People, 06-20-1988, p. 75.)
(2) insane (person) *n*.: **bedlamite**. See LUNATIC
(3) insane (informal as in daffy or loony) *adj*.: **doolally**. See CRAZY
(4) insane (slightly ..., often used humorously) *adj*.: **tetched**. See CRAZY

insatiable *adj*.: **edacious**. See VORACIOUS

insects (study of) *n*.: **entomology**. ∎ "We have 450,000 bugs and spiders that all have to go to the new building intact, so we'll hand-carry the specimen drawers," said Virginia Scott, manager of the museum's **entomology** collection. (Jim Erickson, *Bugging Out: 450,000 Fragile Insects Being Packed up for Trip to New Lodgings in CU's Natural History Museum*, Denver Rocky Mountain News, 05-14-2001, p. 4A.)
(2) insects (sensation that ... are crawling on you) *n*.: **formication**. ∎ Ants produce and will exude — when they are crushed, for example — formic acid, a pungent, acrid substance. One school of thought holds that crows roll in ants in order to smear themselves with this acid, which may act as a repellant to body parasites. ... About anting crows, Quammen has written in his book Natural Acts: "They revel in **formication**." (Bil Gilbert, *Goodbye, Hell — The Common Crow Is an Uncommonly Charming Bird, Says a Man Who Knows His Fine Feathered Friends*, Sports Illustrated, 12-19-1988, p. 108.)
(3) insects (feeding on) *adj*.: **entomophagous**. See BUGS

inseminate *v.t.*: **fecundate**. See IMPREGNATE

insensitive (as in thick-skinned) *adj*.: **pachydermatous**. See THICK-SKINNED

inseparable (or unbreakable) *adj*.: **infrangible**. See UNBREAKABLE

insertion (of something between existing things) *n*.: **intercalation**. ∎ [In the employment process for low-wage jobs, there is no bargaining stage for the employee because] first you are an applicant and then suddenly you are an orientee. ... The **intercalation** of the drug test between application and hiring tilts the playing filed even further, establishing that you, and not the employer, are the one who has something to prove. (Barbara Ehrenreich, *Nickel & Dimed*, Metropolitan Books [2001], p. 149.)
(2) insertion (esp. of penis into vagina) *n*.: **intromission** (*v.t.*: **intromit**). See PENETRATION

insight *n*.: **aperçu** [French]. ∎ He lights another cigarette and gives me another **aperçu**: "You don't drink and drive in Russia, and you don't pick a fight. They're all in the military. They like Schwarzenegger. They love Chuck Norris. They like to kill." (Patric Kuh, *Comrade, Your Table Is Ready [Restaurants in Moscow, Russia]*, Esquire, 03-01-1997, p. 96.)
(2) insight (sudden ...) *n*.: **epiphany**. See REALIZATION

insightful *adj*.: **trenchant**. See INCISIVE

insignificant (thing or matter) *n*.: **bagatelle**. See TRIFLING
(2) insignificant (or worthless matter) *n*.: **dross**. See WORTHLESS
(3) insignificant *adj*.: **footling** [chiefly British]. See UNIMPORTANT
(4) insignificant *adj*.: **nugacious**. See TRIVIAL
(5) insignificant *adj*.: **nugatory**. See UNIMPORTANT
(6) insignificant *adj*.: **picayune**. See TRIVIAL
(7) insignificant *adj*.: **piffling**. See TRIVIAL
(8) insignificant (as in excusable fault, offense or sin) *adj*.: **venial**. See FORGIVABLE

insincere (esp. praise or flattery) *adj*.: **fulsome**. ∎ One of the Chicago Cubs, third baseman Tyler Houston, had reached first. ... "Tell you what," Houston said [to the opposing Phillies first baseman]. "You guys got a good club." The numbers the game produces are ruthlessly truthful, but baseball conversation is often false or **fulsome**. What is honest stands out, and Houston was telling the truth. (Michael Bamberger, *Baseball: No Sitting Still:*

Throwing an Impressive Combination of Pitching and Muscle at the Hapless Cubs, the Phillies Showed Why They Might Soon Blossom Into a Contender, Sports Illustrated, 07-12-1999, p. 42.)

(2) insincere (as in excessive or contrived sentimentality) *adj.*: **bathetic**. (*n.*: **bathos**.) SEE SENTIMENTAL

(3) insincere (or hypocritical, sanctimonious and/or pious speech) *n.*: **cant**. SEE PIOUS

(4) insincere *adj.*: **oleaginous**.

insipid (intellectual nourishment, like baby food) *n.*: **pabulum** (also **pablum**). ◼ Idealist or Egotist? The only infraction that Greco-Roman silver medalist Matt Ghaffari is guilty of is accepting all the invitations extended to him and not having an agent to spoon-feed him noble **pabulum** to regurgitate for the media. (Author not given, *Letters*, Sports Illustrated, 10-21-1996, p. 8.)

(2) insipid *adj.*: **anodyne**. SEE BLAND

(3) insipid (as in uninteresting or dull) *adj.*: **jejune**. SEE UNINTERESTING

insistent (as in one who clings to an opinion or belief even after being shown that it is wrong) *n.*: **mumpsimus**. SEE STUBBORN

(2) insistent (but obstinate) *adj.*: **contumacious**. SEE OBSTINATE

(3) insistent (in holding to a belief or opinion) *adj.*: **pertinacious**. SEE STUBBORN

insolence (in behavior or speech) *n.*: **contumely**. SEE CONTEMPT

(2) insolence *n.*: **hardihood**. SEE GALL

inspiration (creative ...) *n.*: **afflatus**. ◼ As for the world of high intellect, that is where my doubts about the claims for the genome begin. There are all kinds of intellect. Some types of intellect, for instance the artistic, are distinguished by aesthetic **afflatus**. Only a person far gone on the scientific method would believe an artist's genius can be explained by genes. (R. Emmett Tyrrell Jr., *Miracles ... and Misgivings*, The Washington Times, 06-30-2000, p. A20.)

(2) inspiration (source of ...) *n.*: **Pierian spring** [drives from spring in Macedonia which was sacred to the Muses in Greek mythology]. ◼ By 1918, aged 30, [Giorgio] de Chirico was already past his peak and about to spend the next 60 years in deliberate decline, but ... no old enthusiast should neglect this opportunity, sad though it is, to witness his flawed genius unfulfilled. He took too shallow a [drink] of the **Pierian spring**. (Brian Sewell, *Flawed Genius and*

a Haunting Obsession; His Work Influenced Ernst, Dali and Magritte. Now a Brave New Show Celebrates the Best — and Worst — of Giorgio De Chirico [Review], The Evening Standard [London], 01-24-2003.)

instance (as in example) *n.*: **exemplum**. SEE EXAMPLE

instant (as in, in an ...) *n.*: **trice** (as in, in a trice). SEE QUICKLY

instigation (as in event which causes or provokes war, literally or figuratively) *n.*: **casus belli** [Latin; occasion of war]. SEE PROVOCATION

instinctive (reaction, as in reflex) *n.*: **tropism**. SEE REFLEX

institution (as in establishment of something) *n.*: **instauration**. SEE ESTABLISHMENT

instruct *v.t.*: **catechize**. SEE TEACH

instruction (providing introductory ...) *n.*, *adj.*: **propaedeutic**. SEE INTRODUCTION

instruction book *n.*: **enchiridion**. SEE HANDBOOK

instructor *n.*: **pedagogue**. SEE TEACHER

insubordinate *adj.*: **contumacious**. SEE OBSTINATE

insubstantial *adj.*: **diaphanous**. SEE TRANSPARENT

(2) insubstantial (as in tenuous) *adj.*: **gossamer**. SEE TENUOUS and TRANSPARENT

insult (an ... on another's dignity) *n.*: **lese majesty**. ◼ Mr. Clinton is an honorable man, at least as honorable as Brutus and Cassius in Shakespeare's "Julius Caesar." To suggest that he might economize on the truth would smack of **lese majesty**. (Bruce Fein, *Vintage Clinton*, The Washington Times, 12-28-1999, p. A16.)

(2) insult (delivered while leaving the scene) *n.*: **Parthian shot**. SEE PARTING SHOT

insulted (easily ..., as in offended) *adj.*: **umbrageous**. SEE OFFENDED

insulting (or humiliating another) *adj.*: **contumelious**. SEE CONTEMPTUOUS

(2) insulting (in behavior or speech due to arrogance or contempt) *n.*: **contumely**. SEE CONTEMPT

insurgent (as in rebel) *n.*: **frondeur** [French]. SEE REBEL

insurrection *n.*: **émeute** [French]. SEE REBELLION

intangible *adj.*: **incorporeal**. ∎ As the passage of time removes from the scene more and more of the accused wrongdoers, and more and more of their possible victims, it makes less and less moral or economic sense — and ultimately no sense at all — for the law to exact monetary redress from **incorporeal** institutions such as corporations or governments. (Stuart Taylor Jr., *Legal Affairs: Paying Reparations for Ancient Wrongs Is Not Right*, National Journal, 04-07-2001.)

integral (as in innate) *adj.*: **connate**. SEE INNATE
(2) integral (as in essential) *adj.*: **constitutive**. SEE ESSENTIAL

integrity *n.*: **probity**. ∎ [Special prosecutor Kenneth] Starr's indifference to polls is a facet of the **probity** that makes him unintelligible to Clinton, and surely there are Democrats of **probity** who are unwilling to ratify by passivity any more of his defining political deviancy down. (George Will, *Moments of Truth — a Half-Century Apart — Over Issues Great and Small*, St. Louis Post-Dispatch, 08-06-1998, p. B7.)
(2) integrity (personal ..., as in honor) *n.*: **izzat** [Hindi]. SEE HONOR

intellect (of, relating to, or understood by the ...) *adj.*: **noetic**. ∎ The mental ego, according to Wilber, is "the first structure that can not only think about the world but think about thinking; hence, it is the first structure that is clearly self-reflexive and introspective. ... It is also the first structure capable of ... propositional reasoning ('if a, then b'), which allows it to apprehend higher or purely **noetic** relationships." (Sean M. Kelly, *Revisioning the Mandala of Consciousness*, ReVision, 04-01-1996, p. 19.)

intellectual (people as a group) *n.*: **clerisy**. SEE EDUCATED
(2) intellectual (pertaining to knowledge of ... or spritual things) *adj.*: **gnostic**. SEE SPIRITUAL
(3) intellectual (self-proclaimed ..., as in enlightened, people) *pl. n.*: **illuminati**. SEE ENLIGHTENED
(4) intellectual (person who is prominent in ... or literary circles) *n.*: **mandarin**. SEE INFLUENTIAL
(5) intellectual (moral and/or cultural spirit of an era) *n.*: **zeitgeist**. SEE SPIRIT

intelligent (person who is cultivated) *n.*: **bel esprit**. SEE CULTIVATED
(2) intelligent (as in wise) *adj.*: **sapient**. SEE WISE

intelligible *adj.*: **limpid**. SEE UNDERSTANDABLE
(2) intelligible (as in clear, in thought or expression) *adj.*: **pellucid**. SEE CLEAR

(3) intelligible *adj.*: **perspicuous**. SEE UNDERSTANDABLE

intense *adj.*: **perfervid**. SEE IMPASSIONED

intent (hidden or ulterior ...) *n.*: **arriere-pensee** (or **arrière-pensée**) [French]. SEE MOTIVE
(2) intent (to achieve a particular goal or desire) *n.*: **nisus**. SEE GOAL
(3) intent (as in goal, esp. of life) *n.*: **telos** [Greek]. SEE GOAL

intercourse (sexual ...) *n.*: **houghmagandy** [Scottish]. ∎ [A Penn State University] major study of sexual activity involving 10,000 Americans has just been completed. [It showed that those] with doctorates manage less **houghmagandy** than those with first degrees only, jazz enthusiasts more than rock music lovers, Catholics a weeny bit more than Protestants but 20 per cent less than agnostics or Jews. (David Aaronovitch, *If Only I Were a Hard-Working, Hard-Drinking Jewish Agnostic*, Independent, 01-17-1998, p. 19.)
(2) intercourse (simulated ... between two women) *n.*: **tribadism**. ∎ [T]he romantic comedy Rescuing Desire comes out against penetration, although more subtly. Middle-aged, baby dyke Toni is counseled by her more experienced lesbian friend that she doesn't need her recently purchased dildo and other toys for lesbian sex. Sex scenes clearly signify **tribadism** ... and oral sex, but penetration seems left out of the performance. (Mary Conway, *Inhabiting the Phallus-Reading Safe is Desire*, Contemporary Women's Issues Database, 05-01-1996.)
(3) intercourse (sexual ...) *n.*: **venery**. ∎ Among the Major government's other recent disasters in the **venery** department have been headlines about (a) the environment minister who was forced to resign for impregnating a local government legislatress established to be not his wife. (Daniel Seligman, *Keeping Up: Depravity Among Conservatives*, Fortune, 05-02-1994, p. 129.)
(4) intercourse (sexual ..., spec. insertion of penis into vagina) *n.*: **intromission** (*v.t.* **intromit**). SEE PENETRATION

interest (undue ... over one subject or idea) *n.*: **monomania**. SEE OBSESSION

interesting (as in lively or stimulating) *adj.*: **piquant**. SEE STIMULATING AND PROVOCATIVE

interferer (officious ... who frustrates the success of a plan by stupidly getting in the way) *n.*: **marplot**. SEE MEDDLER

interim (esp. short ... between things or events) *n.*: **interstice**. SEE GAP

interim (esp. between the end of a sovereign's reign and the ascension of a successor) *n.*: **interregnum**. SEE INTERVAL

interlude (esp. short ... between things or events) *n.*: **interstice**. SEE GAP

intermeddler (officious ... who frustrates the success of a plan by stupidly getting in the way) *n.*: **marplot**. SEE MEDDLER

intermediary *n.*: **comprador**. ∎ Foreigners doing business in Asia have long relied on middlemen — **compradors**, as they are known in the region — to cut through red tape, hook up with the right people, get deals done, and occasionally take a small piece of the action. (Louis Kraar, *Global: Need a Friend in Asia? Try the Singapore Connection*, Fortune, 03-04-1996, p. 172.)

interpretation (of a text by adding one's own ideas) *n.*: **eisegesis**. ∎ "In this approach, you place yourself in the text and basically use your imagination to decide what the text says," Pfizenmaier said. ... "Now people want to understand scripture by **eisegesis** — putting themselves into Scripture," he said. (Patricia Rice, *Presbyterians Here Discuss Question of Ordaining Gays, Lesbians: Regional Legislatures Will Vote on Whether to Allow Such Ordinations*, St. Louis Post-Dispatch, 06-18-2001, p. A1.)
(2) interpretation (esp. of a text) *n.*: **exegesis**. ∎ For nearly 40 years, Bob Dylan has tantalized us with inscrutable images. Most have been of the verbal variety — phrases such as "the geometry of innocence," "darkness at the break of noon," "the ghost of electricity," and hundreds of others that continue to pique our collective id and defy easy **exegesis**. (Tom Sinclair, *His Back Pages — The Times May Have Changed, but Early Dylan ... Revisits His Evolution From a Dusty Young Folkie to a Plugged-in Rock & Roller*, Entertainment Weekly, 10-22-1999, p. 44.)
(3) interpretation (having more than one ...) *adj.*: **polysemous** (or **polysemic**). SEE MEANING

interpretative (often regarding a document or text, such as scripture) *n.*: **hermeneutic**. ∎ Longerich quickly demonstrates that he is ... perfectly at ease with **hermeneutic** considerations. ... "What a historian has to do ... is look at each document and look at the context and then try to reconstruct from the context what actually the meaning of this passage might be." (D.D. Guttenplan, *The Holocaust on Trial*, Norton [2001], p. 236.)

interpreter (and guide for travelers, esp. where Arabic, Turkish or Persian is spoken) *n.*: **dragoman**. SEE GUIDE

interrogate (as in question formally about governmental policy or action) *v.t.*: **interpellate**. ∎ [At the upcoming meeting of political parties] opposition parties plan to **interpellate** the government on the alleged bribery case involving former Construction Minister Eiichi Nakao and on other issues such as the bankruptcy of major department store operator Sogo Co. (Author not given, *Opposition Parties Set to Grill Coalition*, The Daily Yomiuri [Tokyo], 07-28-2000, p. 3.)
(2) interrogate (closely) *v.t.*: **catechize**. SEE QUESTION

interruption (as in pause) *n.*: **caesura**. SEE PAUSE

interval (in continuity, esp. between the end of a sovereign's reign and the ascension of a successor) *n.*: **interregnum**. ∎ During the **interregnum** between [Jack] Parr and [Johnny] Carson, various guest hosts were used to keep "The Tonight Show" in the public eye. (Shawn Levy, *The King of Comedy*, St. Martin's Press [1996], p. 278.)
(2) interval (esp. short ... between things or events) *n.*: **interstice**. SEE GAP

intimidate *v.t.*: **Bogart** [slang, after roles played by Humphrey Bogart]. ∎ Here are some tips to help avoid getting drawn into a road-rage situation. ... Do not glare at other drivers, or try to "**Bogart**" — i.e., intimidate them with scowls, frowns, and rude gestures, such as giving the "bird." You have no way of knowing whether the other motorist you're making faces at is near the end of his rope on this particular day and just looking for someone to go off on. (Eric Peters, *Dealing with "Road Rage" Safely and Effectively*, Consumers' Research Magazine, 05-01-2003.)

intimidation (as in suggesting the use of force to settle an issue or argument) *n.*: **argumentum ad baculum** [Latin]. SEE THREAT

intolerable (as in unpardonable) *adj.*: **irremissible**. SEE UNPARDONABLE

intolerant (insistence on conventionality) *n.*: **Grundyism**. SEE PURITANICAL
(2) intolerant (as in narrow-minded) *adj.*: **hidebound**. SEE NARROW-MINDED

intoxicated (as in given to or marked by consumption of alcohol) *adj.*: **bibulous**. SEE IMBIBING

intrepid *adj.*: **doughty**. SEE BRAVE

intricate (or skillful in design or function) *adj.*: **daedal**. ■ He gathered toward the end of his life a very extensive collection of illustrated books and illuminated manuscripts, and took heightened pleasure in their **daedal** patterns as his own strength declined. (Florence Boos, *The Collected Letters of William Morris, [book reviews]*, Victorian Studies, 06-22-1997, p. 730.)
(2) intricate (as in complicated) *adj.*: **byzantine**. SEE COMPLICATED

intriguing *adj.*: **piquant**. SEE PROVOCATIVE

intrinsic (as in innate) *adj.*: **connate**. SEE INNATE
(2) intrinsic *adj.*: **immanent**. SEE INHERENT

introduction (often to a speech or writing) *n.*: **exordium**. ■ Women who successfully conceive [after age 40] know, of course, that giving birth isn't the end of the story. It's really a new beginning, an **exordium** to the challenges and rewards of midlife motherhood. (Leslie Laurence, *Pregnancy After Forty*, Town & Country Monthly, 08-01-1995, p. 86.)
(2) introduction (to a lengthy or complex work) *n.*: **prolegomenon**. ■ All this, however, is by way of a **prolegomenon** to the book's real work, which is to show what feminist thought has to contribute to bioethics. (Hilde Lindemann Nelson, *Feminist Approaches to Bioethics: Theoretical Reflections and Practical Applications [Review]*, Hypatia, 09-22-1998, p. 112.)
(3) introduction *n., adj.*: **propaedeutic**. ■ A 50-page **propaedeutic** locates Schelling in his cultural, philosophical, and religious times, while a lengthy retrospect discusses the meaning and value of this philosophy of religion for today. (Thomas F. O'Meara, *Schelling's Philosophy of Mythology and Revelation [book reviews]*, Theological Studies, 03-01-1997, p. 192.)
(4) introduction (as in insertion of something between existing things) *n.*: **intercalation**. SEE INSERTION
(5) introduction *n.*: **proem**. SEE PREFACE

introductory (as in basic) *adj.*: **abecedarian**. SEE BASIC

introvert (someone who is halfway between an ... and extrovert) *n.*: **ambivert**. SEE EXTROVERT

intrude (as in burst in, suddenly or forcibly) *v.i.*: **irrupt**. SEE BURST IN

intuition (as in premonition, that something is going to occur) *n.*: **presentiment**. SEE PREMONITION

invade (as in burst in, suddenly or forcibly) *v.i.*: **irrupt**. SEE BURST IN

invective *n.*: **vituperation** (*adj.*: **vituperative**). ■ And when the wave [of antisemitic expression] subsides, the diminution of antisemitic **vituperation** is understood to have been caused by a decrease in, or the passing of, antisemitic belief and writing. This account of antisemitism is wrong. (Daniel Goldhagen, *Hitler's Willing Executioners*, Knopf [1996], p. 43.)

invent (an idea, plan, theory or explanation after careful thought) *v.t.*: **excogitate**. SEE DEVISE

invented (or substituted with fraudulent intent) *adj.*: **supposititious**. SEE SUPPOSED

inventive (as in resourceful, person) *n.*: **debrouillard** (or **débrouillard**) [French]. SEE RESOURCEFUL
(2) inventive (love of or enthusiasm for anything ...) *n.*: **neophilia**. SEE NOVELTY

investigate (through formal questioning about governmental policy or action) *v.t.*: **interpellate**. SEE INTERROGATE

invigorate (as in enliven) *v.t.*: **vivify**. SEE ENLIVEN

inviolable *adj.*: **infrangible**. ■ Like banks, marbled and colonnaded to instill confidence in their investors, orchestras have only approximate control over the stuff they deal with every day. Consequently, opening night at the New York Philharmonic arrives every year with certain **infrangible** guarantees: a marquee soloist, a pair of blue-chip scores and plenty of vigorous applause. (Justin Davidson, *Routine Opener With a Special Flair*, Newsday, 09-25-1999, p. B9.)

invisible (nearly ...) *adj.*: **liminal**. ■ [David Shipler's book *The Working Poor* shows] that even those who hold steady, minimum-wage jobs in the sweatshops, bakeries, canning factories, and other unseen venues that make our economy run are not saints. Shipler clearly humanizes this **liminal** army of workers who clean up our tables, stitch our clothes, and care for our elderly. (Dalton Conley, *Labor Intensive*, The Boston Globe, 04-04-2004, p. D8.)
(2) invisible (as in hidden) *adj.*: **delitescent**. SEE HIDDEN

inviting (as in warm and cozy) *adj.*: **gemütlich** [German]. SEE COZY

(2) inviting (as in tempting) *adj.*: **siren**. SEE TEMPT-ING

irate *adj.*: **apoplectic**. SEE ANGRY
(2) irate (as in indignant) *n.*: **dudgeon** (often expressed as "in high dudgeon"). SEE INDIGNANT
(3) irate *adj.*: **vesuvian** (esp. as in ... temper). SEE TEMPER
(4) irate *adj.*: **wroth**. SEE ANGRY

ire *n.*: **bile**. SEE BITTERNESS
(2) ire *n.*: **choler** (*adj.*: **choleric**). SEE ANGER

iridescent (like a pearl) *adj.*: **nacreous**. ∎ Asked to name their personal favorites in the [pearl] show, the curators bristle, as if required to choose a favorite child. However, Mr. Landman concedes that he feels particularly fond of the "fossil pearls from 40 million years ago, which still retain their **nacreous** luster. ... [I]t is important to recognize that pearls have been around probably as long as mollusks have, some 530 million years." (Benjamin Ivy, *The Luster of "Pearls" is Focus of New Exhibition: Two Museums String Together a Dazzling Story*, The Christian Science Monitor, 10-19-2001.)
(2) iridescent *adj.*: **opalescent**. ∎ The future of cosmetics is glossy and bright. Vibrant hues of pink, coral, orange, purple, lime, aqua and gold are key players in spring and summer beauty palettes. ... [M]ost new products are sheer and **opalescent**, giving a translucent, glowing finish. Sheer formulas allow women of all ages to experiment with brighter looks and shimmery eye, lip and cheek colours. (Heather Toskan, *Sheer & Shimmery/Colour Is Key, With Co-ordinated Eyes, Cheeks, Lips and Nails the Order of the Day*, The London Free Press, 05-08-2001, p. C1.)

Irish (of or relating to Ireland or the ...) *adj.*: **Hibernian**. ∎ "Notre Dame has nothing to do with the rest of Indiana," I argued [to my son who was resisting considering it because it is in Indiana]. ... "Notre Dame is the mystical cradle of the Irish-American dream, the repository of our Celtic hopes, the spawning ground of our **Hibernian** reveries, the incubator of our most fiercely beloved stereotypes." (Joe Queenan, *Endpaper, The Age of Reasons*, The New York Times, 11-09-2003.)

irony (spec. the use of a word of phrase which is contrary to its normal meaning, such as "a 7-foot midget") *n.*: **antiphrasis**. ∎ Then there are the titles that work by irony or "**antiphrasis**." *Far From the Madding Crowd* is about passion and violence, not

rural calm. *Ulysses* does not have any epic hero. (John Mullan, *What's in a Name? John Mullan on a Compendium of Titles*, The Guardian [London], 01-11-2003, p. 15.)

irrational (something which is ..., as in illogical) *n.*: **alogism**. SEE ILLOGICAL
(2) irrational (as in not of sound mind) *adj.*: **non compos mentis** [Latin]. SEE INSANE

irrefutable (necessarily or demonstrably ...) *adj.*: **apodictic**. SEE INCONTROVERTIBLE
(2) irrefutable *adj.*: **irrefragable**. SEE UNQUESTIONABLE

irregular (as in departing from the standard or norm) *adj.*: **heteroclite**. SEE ABNORMAL

irrelevancy (as in a fallacious argument where one proves or disproves a point which is not at issue) *n.*: **ignoratio elenchi** [Latin]. ∎ [In his argument in favor of immigration, Julian Simon] will occasionally indulge in the logical fallacy of **ignoratio elenchi**, more popularly known as creating a straw man. Thus, to counter the valid claim that many of our immigrants are ill-educated and low-skilled, he argues that they are more educated than the natives on average. This is interesting, but it is not the issue. (Jagdish Bhagwati, *The Economic Consequences of Immigration [Book Reviews]*, The New Republic, 05-14-1990.)

irresolute *adj.*, *v.i.*, *n.*: **shilly-shally**. SEE VACILLATE

irresponsible *adj.*: **feckless**. ∎ We hear an awful lot about teenagers these days. According to the tabloids, they are lazy, **feckless** and ignorant. According to just about everyone, including the Office of National Statistics, they are having too much sex. (Maureen Freely, *"They Never Tell Us the Things We Really Want to Know,"* The Independent [London], 11-01-1999, p. 8.)
(2) irresponsible *adj.*: **harum-scarum**. SEE RECKLESS

irreverence (religious ...) *n.*: **impiety** (*adj.*: **impious**). ∎ Jewish **impiety**, unlike the impiety of other non-Christians, was understood by John Chrysostom and those who thought as he did to be not just mere **impiety**, born of ignorance or the inability to recognize the true path, but a sort of madness. (Daniel Goldhagen. *Hitler's Willing Executioners*, Knopf [1996], p. 51.)

irreversibility *n.*: **Rubicon** (esp. as in "cross the

Rubicon") [derives from name of a river in Italy which Julius Caesar crossed in 49 B.C. to start a civil war, stating en route, "The die is cast."]. ∎ The growing fear [is that] North Korea has already made the fundamental decision to develop a nuclear arsenal and no longer intends to treat its nuclear program as a bargaining chip to be bartered away in exchange for money and pacts. "It's possible North Korea has **crossed the Rubicon**," says Prof. Ashton Carter of Harvard University. "The regime may now believe it has to have nuclear weapons for its own security." (B.J. Lee, *Driving a Hard Bargain*, Newsweek International, 04-21-2003.)

irrevocability *n.*: **Rubicon**. SEE IRREVERSIBILITY

irritability (as in acrimony) *n.*: **asperity**. SEE ACRIMONY

(2) irritability *n.*: **bile**. SEE BITTERNESS

(3) irritability *n.*: **choler** (*adj.*: **choleric**). SEE ANGER

(4) irritability (as in a state of tense and nervous ...) *n.*: **fantod**. SEE TENSION

irritable *adj.*: **liverish**. ∎ Oh, shut up: Actor Jason Patric sounds a bit **liverish** about the movies he saw this summer: "Take Angelina Jolie. It doesn't matter that everyone hates Tomb Raider II," he told the British Glamour magazine. "She looks great and so everyone says how wonderful it is. It's like Charlie's Angels — everyone pretending it's empowering. It's pure crap." (Doug Camilli, *Diaz's Nose Out of Joint: Surfing Accident Has Her "Bummed Out*," The Gazette [Montreal, Quebec], 09-04-2003, p. D4.)

(2) irritable *adj.*: **shirty**. ∎ At a press conference, an American reporter asked French President Jacques Chirac a question in French, and Bush got all **shirty**. "Very good," he snapped sarcastically. "The [reporter] memorizes four words and he plays like he's intercontinental. I'm impressed. Que bueno. Now I'm literate in two languages." (Patt Morrison, *In Plain English, the Big Enchilada Got French Fried*, Los Angeles Times, 06-19-2002.)

(3) irritable *adj.*: **splenetic**. ∎ "I'd like to see us piss people off occasionally," said Gatehouse. "I think a lot of people out there think they know the kind of thing they are going to read in Maclean's. I think it's time to throw them some curves. I think we can be grumpier, argumentative, even **splenetic** sometimes. That's where I fit in." (Murray Whyte, *Can Maclean's Leave it to Beaver to Survive?* The Toronto Star, 8-22-2002.)

(4) irritable *adj.*: **querulous**. SEE PEEVISH

(5) irritable *adj.*: **tetchy**. SEE GROUCHY

irritate *v.t.*: **chivvy**. SEE PESTER

irritating (as in repellent) *adj.*: **rebarbative**. SEE REPELLENT

isolate (from others) *v.t.*: **enisle**. ∎ Meryle Secrest, the biographer of the fraudulent art connoisseur Bernard Berenson, records that, when depressed, he referred to himself as feeling **enisled** in the sea of life. (Christopher Hawtree, *Words*, The Independent [London], 09-22-1998.)

(2) isolate (as in consider separately) *v.t.*: **prescind** (generally as in "prescind from"). ∎ The Internet is fast becoming a ... universal library of books in print. Millions of books are available almost immediately, through a simple click of the mouse. But even if we **prescind** from the conservative complaint that books aren't as good as they used to be, it's still statistically improbable that the best books in any given field will happen to be the most recent ones. That's why it's so important that worthy old titles be restored to print. (Mike Potemra, *Book Shelf [Review]*, National Review, 10-09-2000.)

isolated (and stagnant or backward place or situation) *n.*: **backwater**. SEE STAGNANT

(2) isolated (as in against the world) *adv., adj.*: **contra mundum** [Latin]. SEE AGAINST THE WORLD

(3) isolated (from outside influences) *adj.*: **hermetic**. SEE SEALED

isolation (social ...) *n.*: **purdah**. SEE SECLUSION

itch (as in irresistible compulsion) *n.*: **cacoëthes**. SEE COMPULSION

itching (of skin with prickling sensation) *n.*: **paresthesia**. SEE PRICKLING

J

jail *n.*: **durance** (often as in "in durance vile"). ∎ We know quite definitely that Mr. Clinton did lie to a grand jury, and then to the electorate, and then to Congress. For an ordinary citizen the first of the lies on that list is a clearly indictable offense for which you can be landed **in durance vile** and/or heavily fined. (Herb Greer, *Bill Clinton and John Profumo*, The Washington Times, 12-29-1998, p. A19.)

(2) jail *n.*: **bastille**. SEE PRISON

(3) jail (as in confine) *v.t.*: **immure**. SEE CONFINE

(4) jail (where a guard can see all prisoners) *n.*: **panopticon**. SEE PRISON

(5) jail (study of ... management) *n.*: **penology**. See PRISON

jammed (together, esp. in rows) *adj.*: **serried**. See CROWDED

jargon (regional ...) *n.*: **patois**. See DIALECT

jaunt (a slow, leisurely ...) *n.*: **paseo**. See STROLL

javelin (or spear) *n.*: **assegai**. See SPEAR

jaw (protruding lower ...) *n.*: **lantern jaw**. ■ [Coach Bill Cowher] takes no notice of a copy of Steeler Digest with his face on the cover, that pronounced **lantern jaw** jutting out from the surface of the coffee table in the living room. ... [H]e has the jawbone of a blue whale. (Tim Crothers, *The Face: Bill Cowher's Mug — like His Steelers — Is Beloved in Pittsburgh*, Sports Illustrated, 01-09-1995, p. 52.)

(2) jaw (having a prominent ...) *adj.*: **prognathous**. ■ Bolt, though, was a cartoon. Tall (5'11"), with Marine Corps-erect posture, he had a swagger. He stood with his head cocked, which accentuated his **prognathous** jaw. (Al Barkow, *All the Rage With the U.S. Open: Returning to the Scene of His Greatest Win, Terrible Tommy Bolt is Suddenly Hot Again*, Sports Illustrated, 05-21-2001, p. G15)

jawbone (lower) *n.*: **mandible**. ■ [Poem by George Foreman's trainer Archie Moore before Foreman fight against Muhammad Ali in 1974:] Foreman's left will make you dance; Turkey in the straw; When his right connects with your **mandible**; Goodbye jaw! (George Plimpton, *Scorecard*, Sports Illustrated, 12-21-1998, p. 29.)

jaws (or mouth or stomach of a carniverous animal) *n.*: **maw**. See MOUTH

Jell-O (as in relating to or resembling gelatin) *adj.*: **gelatinous**. ■ In her mind's athletic eye, she was trotting the length of the corridors, shoving open every door that was ajar, calling [out for her missing son] in a clear, Doris Day voice, welcoming him. In fact, her legs were **gelatinous**, she could not stand. (Jacqueline Mitchard, *The Deep End of the Ocean*, Viking [1996], p. 30.)

jellyfish (a ..., or relating to or resembling a ...) *n., adj.*: **medusoid**. ■ "Almost no one [here] would ever consider eating a jellyfish," the Darien News reported two years ago. "It has certainly never been on any local restaurant's menu." Yet [Yao-Wen Huang, a seafood expert at the University of Georgia] feels duty-bound to introduce the maligned **medusoid** to the palates of the American public. (Dan Chapman, *Georgia Shrimpers Cash in on Asian Delicacy: Jellyfish*, The Atlanta Journal and Constitution, 02-26-2003.)

jest *v.i., n.*: **jape**. See JOKE

Jesus (depiction of ... wearing crown of thorns) *n.*: **ecce homo**. ■ Taxi drivers still reminisce fondly about Mark Wallinger's statue for the Fourth Plinth in Trafalgar Square. They know what they like, and even if they don't know the artist's name, they loved **Ecce Homo**, the life-size figure of a diminutive Christ wearing a crown of thorns that topped the vacant plinth last year. (Rose Aidin, *Profile: Mark Wallinger — Race, Class and Sex*, Independent, 06-02-2001, p. 5.)

jet set *n.*: **beau monde** [French]. See HIGH SOCIETY

(2) jet set *n.*: **bon ton** [French]. See HIGH SOCIETY

jewel (which is highly polished and unfaceted) *n.*: **cabochon**. ■ Terms of Adornment: ... Retro: 1935-1950; big and bold American, often in 14K gold; stones are both **cabochon** and faceted. (Jennifer Jackson, *Treasure Map, [Recommended Antique Jewelry Stores in the U.S.]*, Harper's Bazaar, 12-01-1996, p. 60.)

(2) jewel (or trinket) *n.*: **bijou**. See TRINKET

jeweler (or jewels) *n.*: **lapidary**. ■ Of the town's 38,000 inhabitants ... there are some 600 **lapidary** workshops, studios, and factories, which purvey to gem buyers, collectors, and wholesale and retail jewelers around the globe. (John Dornberg, *Idar-Oberstein: The Gemstone Capital*, German Life, 11-30-1995.)

jiffy (as in, in a ...) *n.*: **trice** (as in, in a trice). See QUICKLY

jingling (of bells) *n.*: **tintinnabulation**. See RINGING

jinx *n., adj.*: **hoodoo**. See BAD LUCK

(2) jinx (as in put a ... upon) *v.t.*: **imprecate**. See CURSE

jinxed (perpetually ... , as in unlucky, person) *n.*: **schlimazel** [Yiddish]. See UNLUCKY

job (as in profession) *n.*: **métier** [French]. See PROFESSION

(2) job (requiring little work but paying an income) *n.*: **sinecure**. See OCCUPATION

join (together, as with glue) *v.t.*: **agglutinate**. See ADHERE

(2) join (together) *v.t.*: **colligate**. SEE UNITE

(3) join (in a series or chain) *v.t., adj.*: **concatenate** (*n.*: **concatenation**). SEE CONNECT

(4) join (as in bring together) *v.t.*: **conflate**. SEE COMBINE

(5) join (as in blend) *v.t., v.i.*: **inosculate**. SEE BLEND

joined (closely ...) *adj.*: **coadunate**. ▪ [Samuel Coleridge] shows a consistent desire to see the many diverse parts of a scene in relationship to the whole of the scene. In projecting his **coadunating** imagination into nature, he follows his own basic principle of the reconciliation of the many into one, the establishing of unity in the presence of variety. (Author not given, *Works of Samuel T. Coleridge: Interpretation: The Main Theme Of "Kubla Khan,"* Monarch Notes, 01-01-1963.)

(2) joined (by a close relationship) *adj.*: **affined**. SEE CONNECTED

(3) joined (of things that cannot be ...) *adj.*: **immiscible**. SEE INCOMPATIBLE

joints (pain in ...) *n.*: **arthralgia**. SEE ARTHRITIS

joke *v.i., n.*: **jape**. ▪ Posing as "Tweeds" Bush (a take-off on Tammany Hall's Boss Tweed) in a top hat and shades, [George W. Bush while in high school] could get 800 sullen teenage boys laughing and roaring with his **japes** and riffs. (Evan Thomas, *A Son's Restless Journey*, Newsweek, 08-07-2000, p. 32.)

(2) joke (as in quip) *n.*: **bon mot** [French]. SEE QUIP

(3) joke (as in quip) *n.*: **epigram**. SEE QUIP

joker (as in buffoon, who is sometimes boastful) *n.*: **Scaramouch**. SEE BUFFOON

joking (as in good-natured teasing) *n.*: **raillery**. SEE TEASING

jolly *adj.*: **eupeptic**. SEE CHEERFUL

(2) jolly *adj.*: **Falstaffian**. SEE JOVIAL

(3) jolly *adj.*: **riant**. SEE CHEERFUL

josh (playfully) *v.t., v.i., n.*: **chaff**. SEE TEASING

journey (to a sacred place or shrine, esp. to Mecca) *n.*: **hadj**. SEE PILGRIMAGE

(2) journey (from danger) *n.*: **hegira**. SEE ESCAPE

(3) journey (about, esp. on foot, and esp. as in roam or wander) *v.t., v.i.*: **perambulate**. SEE ROAM

(4) journey (about, esp. on foot and esp. as in roam or wander) *v.t., v.i.*: **peregrinate**. SEE ROAM

(5) journey (difficult or painful ...) *n.*: **via dolorosa**. SEE ORDEAL

jovial *adj.*: **Falstaffian** [based on John Falstaff, a character in Henry IV and Merry Wives of Windsor by William Shakespeare]. ▪ From the time [Don King] arrived full-bore on the boxing landscape as the promoter of the "Rumble in the Jungle" between Muhammad Ali and George Foreman in Zaire in 1974, followed a year later by the epic "Thrilla in Manila" between Ali and Joe Frazier, King has manipulated the pieces of his sport with **Falstaffian** flamboyance. (Leigh Montville, *He Is a Storm on the Horizon as He Approaches*, Sports Illustrated, 09-19-1994, p. 136.)

(2) jovial (and social) *adj.*: **Anacreontic**. SEE CONVIVIAL

(3) jovial *adj.*: **riant**. SEE CHEERFUL

jowl (esp. of cattle, but also of people) *n.*: **dewlap**. ▪ "You have to wonder" said Nels Gudmundsson, and he began to massage his throat again and pull at the **dewlaps** of skin there. (Guterson, *Snow Falling From Cedars*, Harcourt, Brace [1994], p. 17.)

joy *n.*: **beatitude**. SEE BLISS

(2) joy (as in pleasure) *n.*: **delectation**. SEE PLEASURE

(3) joy (causing or tending to produce ...) *adj.*: **felicific**. SEE HAPPINESS

(4) joy *n.*: **felicity**. SEE HAPPINESS

joyful *adj.*: **beatific** (to make ... *v.t.*: **beatify**). ▪ Six months later I was signing books at a Barnes & Noble, half a continent away from my office. A lovely woman dressed in bright purple-and-blue silk floated up to me like Glinda the Good Witch, her face transformed by a **beatific** smile. (Martha Beck, *How to Find Your Happiest Self*, Redbook, 04-01-2001, p. 96.)

(2) joyful *adj.*: **eupeptic**. SEE CHEERFUL

(3) joyful *adj.*: **riant**. SEE CHEERFUL

jubilant (often in a boastful way) *adj.*: **cock-a-hoop**. SEE ELATED

judge *v.t.*: **assay**. SEE EVALUATE

(2) judge (under a new standard, esp. one which differs from conventional norms) *v.t.*: **transvaluate**. SEE EVALUATE

Judgment Day (branch of theology concerned with) *n.*: **eschatology**. ▪ The Jews, the central demonic figures in Nazi **eschatolgy**, inevitably fared badly when Germans gave free rein to their eliminationist sensibilities, to their dreams of reconstructing the social landscape and "human substance" of Europe, and to their "problem"-solving inventiveness.

(Daniel Goldhagen, *Hitler's Willing Executioners*, Knopf [1996], p. 144.)

jumble *n*.: **agglomeration**. ▮ "Ranting Mophead" [1995] presents a mop and a rant. The mop stands upright beside a lectern. Attached to its handle is a mechanized **agglomeration** of valves, pipes, clothes pins, screw-top plastic water bottles, garbage bag twist-ties, gears and paper clips, which, when operating properly, babbles. It says: "I am a blabbermouth." And "Ow Ow Ow Wow." And "I am a man." (Paul Richard, *Bodily Charm; Tim Hawkinson Really Puts Himself Into His Art, Truly*, The Washington Post, 04-15-2001, p. G1.)

(2) jumble (as in confused or disarrayed mass) *n*.: **welter**. ▮ Now, as [Japan's ruling Liberal Democratic Party] crumbles — 57 members of parliament already have resigned — and a **welter** of splinter parties and reform groups pop up promising change, Japanese voters have a real choice for the first time in a generation. (Steven Butler, *Peddling a New Line*, U.S. News & World Report, 07-12-1993, p. 35.)

(3) jumble (as in assortment) *n*.: **farrago**. SEE ASSORTMENT

(4) jumble (as in assortment) *n*.: **gallimaufry**. SEE ASSORTMENT

(5) jumble (and confusion) *n., adj*.: **hugger-mugger**. SEE CONFUSION

(6) jumble (as in assortment) *n*.: **olla podrida** [Spanish]. SEE ASSORTMENT

(7) jumble (as in assortment) *n*.: **omnium-gatherum** [Latin]. SEE ASSORTMENT

(8) jumble (as in assortment) *n*.: **salmagundi**. SEE ASSORTMENT

jump (esp. by a horse) *n*.: **capriole**. ▮ And the **capriole**, in which the horse leaps into the air and kicks out its hind legs, could be used to extricate horse and rider from nasty combat situations. (Susan Davis, *Equestrian: Operation Cowboy — In 1945 a Group of U.S. Soldiers Liberated 375 Lipizzans From Nazi Captivity*, Sports Illustrated, 10-16-1995, p. R4.)

junior (rank, esp. in the military) *n*.: **subaltern**. SEE SUBORDINATE

junk (as in printed material which is trivial) *n*.: **bumf** [British]. ▮ Teachers these days are used to receiving a barrage of official **bumf** telling them how to do their jobs. Never before, however, have they been given a step-by-step guide on how to eat carrots. ... Teachers yesterday said the guidelines were patronising and "bureaucracy gone mad." (Laura Clark,

How to Eat a Carrot; Munch from the Bottom and Discard the Top, the Health Police Tell Primary School Pupils, The Daily Mail, 09-25-2003.)

(2) junk *n*.: **trumpery**. ▮ Trump's **Trumpery**. A Mar-a-Lago garage sale was held in West Palm Beach Tuesday. About 100 treasure hunters picked through truckloads of Trump junk purchased by a salvage dealer who emptied out the garage and pump house at the famed estate in Florida. Among the trashy treasures, an arched window that went for $90 and a 3 1/2-foot plastic Santa Claus that sold for $110. (Tom Collins, *You Can't Make This Stuff Up*, Newsday [New York], 04-20-1995, p. A29.)

juror *n*.: **venireman**. ▮ [In one case, a woman was sentenced to life in prison] in the shooting death of her allegedly abusive husband. The defendant unsuccessfully sought to have her conviction overturned because she had not been allowed to strike one white male juror, who she said was "smirking" during [jury selection]. ... The judge rejected [this argument] because he did not see the **venireman** smirk. (Susan Hightower, *Sex and the Peremptory Strike: An Empirical Analysis*, Stanford Law Review, 04-01-2000.)

just (uncompromisingly ..., as in fair) *n*.: **Rhadamanthine** [after Rhadamanthus, son of Zeus and Europa, who, in reward for his exemplary justice, was made one of the judges of the souls of the underworld]. ▮ A governor must behave with ... **Rhadamanthine** impartiality. Even overtly political appointees have been able to do so. ... By contrast, when governors or governors-general descend into the political fray, they forgo their nonpartisan position, they demean the office and undermine our system. (Janet Albrechtson, *Butler's Duty to Serve the People, Not to Play Politics*, The Australian, 08-27-1993, p. 11.)

(2) just (as in deserved, esp. in reference to a punishment) *adj*.: **condign**. SEE DESERVED

justification (formal ... of one's acts or beliefs) *n*.: **apologia**. ▮ In October, The Washington Post ... tried to explain why the belief is widely held in black neighborhoods that the CIA was behind the crack epidemic in the inner city of Los Angeles. "Conspiracy theories can often ring true; history feeds blacks' mistrust," read the Post's headline. This **apologia** for African American credulity ran alongside a story that proved that the allegation about the CIA and crack was utterly unfounded. (Jeffrey Rosen, *The Bloods and the Crips: O.J. Simpson, Critical Race Theory, the Law, and the Triumph of Color in America*, The New Republic, 12-09-1996, p. 27.)

justify (attempt to ... an offense with excuses) *v.t.*: **palliate**. SEE DOWNPLAY

juvenile (as in childish) *adj.*: **jejune**. ∎ [The TV show] Mad TV has turned out to be a formidable opponent [to Saturday Night Live]. ... It has also developed a following among teenagers who can be readily found on the Internet proclaiming its superiority with appropriately **jejune** postings like "Mad TV blows SNL away." (Ginia Bellafante, *The Battle for Saturday Night Comedy Isn't Pretty, and SNL Is Losing its Outrageous Edge to a Hot New Rival on Fox*, Time, 02-12-1996, p. 70.)

(2) juvenile (as in childish) *adj.*: **puerile**. ∎ [In the TV comedy "Arli$$"] a session with another owner ... ends when [a sports agent's] client (a pitcher demanding $2 million a year after a one-win season) emits an impossibly powerful stream of urine across the owner's desk. Not all the humor is that **puerile**, though neither is it exactly highbrow. (Richard O'Brien, *Scorecard: Medalists Hit the Talk Shows*, Sports Illustrated, 08-19-1996, p. 31.)

K

keen (as in having a penetrating quality) *adj.*: **gimlet** (esp. as in "gimlet eye"). SEE PENETRATING

(2) keen (as in incisive or perceptive) *adj.*: **trenchant**. SEE INCISIVE

keenness *n.*: **acuity**. ∎ [T]here has always been a nagging suspicion that the subtle changes in personality and lapses in mental **acuity** that are sometimes seen after bypass surgery might be the result of brain damage caused by the operation itself. (Christine Gorman, *Medicine: Hearts and Minds*, Time, 02-19-2001, p. 58.)

key (to solving a puzzle or deciphering a code which has not previously been solved or deciphered) *n.*: **Rosetta stone**. SEE CLUE

kid (playfully) *v.t.*, *v.i.*, *n.*: **chaff**. SEE TEASING

(2) kid (as in young child) *n.*: **moppet**. SEE CHILD

kidding (as in good-natured teasing) *n.*: **raillery**. SEE TEASING

kidnap (often to perform compulsory service abroad) *v.t.*: **shanghai**. ∎ Chinese cooking obviously isn't an American franchise. But what about fate, encapsulated in that bivalved wafer known as the Chinese fortune cookie? Made in U.S.A. Legend suggests it was invented in San Francisco by coolies **shanghaied** to build the first transcontinental railroads. (Adam Piore, *The Meaning of Life*, Newsweek International, 07-08-2002, p. 37.)

kids (hatred of) *n.*: **misopedia**. SEE HATRED

kill (by strangling or cutting the throat) *v.t.*: **garrote**. SEE STRANGLE

(2) kill (oneself by fire) *v.t.*: **immolate**. SEE SUICIDE AND SACRIFICE

(3) kill (by strangling or cutting the throat) *v.t.*: **jugulate**. SEE STRANGLE

(4) kill (figuratively, as in to put an end to) *n.*: **quietus** (esp. as in "put the quietus to"). SEE TERMINATE

kill time (as in idle or waste time) *v.i.*: **footle** (usu. as in "footle around"). SEE DAWDLE

killer (of one wife after another) *n.*: **bluebeard** (or **Bluebeard**). SEE MURDERER

killing (mass ... of unresisting persons) *n.*: **battue** [French]. ∎ Historians agree that police fired into the crowd at a mid-afternoon football match in Dublin, killing about a dozen people. ... The plan really was to stop the match and search the crowd. Once they reached the Park, however, the police began shooting without provocation. There were no rebel gunmen outside the park, and there was no return fire from the crowd. The Croke Park massacre was a **battue**, not a battle. (David Leeson, *Death in the Afternoon: The Croke Park Massacre, 21 November 1920 [Controversial Event of the Irish War of Independence]*, Canadian Journal of History, 04-01-2003.)

(2) killing (of one's mother) *n.*: **matricide**. ∎ A Brooklyn man accused of **matricide** told detectives he has multiple personalities and claimed one of his alter egos stabbed his mother to death Friday morning, according to police sources. (Sean Gardiner, *Cops: Man Admits Killing His Mother*, Newsday, 04-14-2001, p. A14.)

(3) killing (of parent or close relative) *n.*: **parricide**. ∎ Pierson is one of the 300 or so children each year across the U.S. who murder one or both of their parents. ... Says Paul Mones, a Los Angeles attorney and **parricide** expert: "Courts are finally waking up to the problem. Kids just don't take these actions unless something is very, very wrong." (Jon D. Hull, *Behavior: Brutal Treatment, Vicious Deeds*, Time, 10-19-1987, p. 68.)

(4) killing (of one's father) *n.*: **patricide**. ∎ By the time he was sixteen, however, John [D. Rockefeller] was sufficiently embittered against his father to commit metaphorical **patricide**. ... He would publicly deny his father's existence for thirty years. (Jackson Lears, *Capitalism, Corrected and Uncorrected: The Lobster and the Squid*, The New Republic, 02-15-1999.)

(5) killing (of a king) *n.*: **regicide**. ∎ An unidentified man in a mask severs the royal head; another waves it aloft: the scene ... might have been expressly designed to drive home to those who witnessed it the enormity of the act of **regicide**. Any nation that separates the head of its lawful king from his body had better be sure that it did so with good cause. (Author not given, *Bagehot: The End of the King — and Kings: 1649*, The Economist, 12-31-1999.)

(6) killing (of wife by her husband) *adj.*: **uxoricide**. ∎ We can think badly enough of O.J. Simpson if we recognize that he misgoverned himself by the logical standards of the wife beater, and wait to find out whether he finally compounded his infamies with **uxoricide** plus stranger murder. The puzzle of why this man beat this woman is quite tough enough as it is. (Murray Kempton, *A Wife-Beater Starts Small*, Newsday, 06-26-1994, p. A35.)

(7) killing (of one's brother or sister) *n.*: **fratricide**. SEE MURDER

(8) killing (large-scale ... or sacrifice) *n.*: **hecatomb**. SEE SLAUGHTER

killjoy *n.*: **crepehanger**. SEE PESSIMIST

kind (original ... or example) *n.*: **archetype**. SEE MODEL

kinds (of all ...) *adj.*: **omnifarious**. SEE VARIED

king (or other ruler who holds great power or sway) *n.*: **potentate**. SEE RULER

(2) king (killing of ...) *n.*: **regicide**. SEE KILLING

kinship *n.*: **propinquity**. ∎ For individuals, kin ties through one's parents and by marriage to a wide range of persons define rights, obligations, and opportunities. ... But kinship rights and obligations are not immutably fixed: an individual often has a choice as to which links he will seek to shore up or, looked at in another way, take advantage of. Sometimes this will be governed by **propinquity**. (Margarita Dobert, *Tanzania: Chapter 3B, Ethnic Groups*, Countries of the World, 01-01-1991.)

kiss *v.t.*: **osculate**. To judge from the kiss, they like wedded bliss. In fact Charles and Diana were **osculating** all over the British tabloids last week. (Guy D. Garcia, *People*, Time, 07-15-1985, p. 67.)

klutzy *adj.*: **lumpish**. SEE CLUMSY

(2) klutzy (habitually ... person) *n.*: **schlemiel** [Yiddish]. SEE BUMBLER

kneel (in worship, often in a servile manner) *v.i.*: **genuflect**. ∎ "Why do people want to be on TV?" asks author Neal Gabler. ... Because of the fame, the power, the money, the glory, the women, everything. We live in a society that absolutely extols and worships and **genuflects** before celebrity." (Verne Gay, *Look at Me! I'm on TV!/Who Wants to Be on Television? Maybe You Should Ask Who Doesn't*, Newsday, 06-30-2000, p. D6.)

knickknack *n.*: **gewgaw**. SEE TRINKET

(2) knickknack *n.*: **bibelot**. SEE TRINKET

knockout (blow, as in put an end to) *n.*: **quietus** (esp. as in "put the quietus to"). SEE TERMINATE

knotty (situation or problem) *n.*: **nodus**. SEE COMPLICATION

know-it-all (as in one who clings to an opinion or belief even after being shown that it is wrong) *n.*: **mumpsimus**. SEE STUBBORN

(2) know-it-all (as in smart aleck or wise guy) *n.*: **wisenheimer**. SEE SMART ALECK

knowledgable (person who is very ... in many areas) *n.*: **polyhistor**. ∎ At the weekly salon [Srenus] Zeitblom encounters Dr. Chaim Breisacher. A Jew, he was also [according to Zeitblom] "a **polyhistor**, who could talk about anything and everything, a philosopher of culture, whose opinions, however, were directed against culture insofar as he affected to see all of history as nothing but a process of decline." (Stephen Goode, *The Conscience of a Composer, and a Nation*, [Books], The Washington Times, 04-05-1998.)

knowledge (excess striving for or preoccupation with ...) *n.*: **epistemophilia**. ∎ [Sigmund Freud] hinted at the ease with which scholarship can spill over into psychosis. ... Nowhere is this state of what he termed "**epistemophilia**" more in evidence than in the spectral silence of the public library. In its peculiar role of providing open access to private worlds, it both allows and denies us possession of those mysteries that feed our pathology. Libraries make us consumers who lack the power of purchase, bibliophiles doomed to eternal browsing. (Graham Caveney, *Books: When Too Much Learning Can Be a Fatally Dangerous Thing*, The Independent, 03-23-2002.)

(2) knowledge (universal ...) *n.*: **pansophy** (*adj*: **pansophic**). ∎ Comenius was most famous for his **pansophic** plan to universalize knowledge, holding that if an educational idea or method was good for one group of people in one place, it must be good for all people in all places. (Dederik C. D. De Jong, *Krcek: Jan Amos Comenius [Symphony 3]*, American Record Guide, 05-01-1997.)

(3) knowledge (pertaining to ... of spiritual or intellectual things) *adj.*: **gnostic**. See SPIRITUAL

(4) knowledge (as in perception or awareness) *n.*: **ken**. See PERCEPTION

(5) knowledge (of a subject which is superficial while pretending to be learned) *n.*: **sciolism**. See SUPERFICIAL

knowledgeable (person who is very ... in many areas) *n.*: **polymath**. See SCHOLAR

kowtow *v.t.*: **bootlick**. A risk for humorists brought into close contact with their prey is that they'll get an attack of politeness. But Maher doesn't observe the prevailing TV conventions about what you can't say to guests; he doesn't **bootlick** "important" panelists as (the otherwise contemptuous) Letterman and (the always jovial) Leno tend to do. (Scott Shuger, *Comic Relief*, U.S. News & World Report, 01-20-1997.)

(2) kowtow *v.i.*: **truckle**. ∎ Missouri is the nation's second-biggest auto-producing state, but [Senator John] Danforth doesn't **truckle** to the carmakers. He calls the industry's seat-belt proposals a sham and wants to require air bags in all new U.S. cars by 1989. (Craig C. Carter, *Politics & Policy: Voice of Commerce Committee — Chairman Danforth Makes Himself Heard on Issues From Autos to Beer Ads*, Fortune, 06-24-1985, p. 87.)

kowtower (esp. someone who seeks to associate with or flatter persons of rank or high social status) *n.*: **tuft-hunter**. See HANGER-ON

L

labor (forced ... for little or no pay) *n.*: **corvee**. See SERVITUDE

(2) labor (slow or difficult ... [regarding a pregnancy]) *n.*: **dystocia**. See CHILDBIRTH

(3) labor (avoider) *n.*: **embusque** [French]. See SLACKER

(4) labor (doing ... only when the boss is watching) *n.*: **eyeservice**. See WORK

(5) labor (as in toil) *v.i.*: **moil**. See TOIL

(6) labor (of or relating to ... before childbirth) *adj.*: **parturient**. See CHILDBIRTH

laborer (Mexican ... allowed to work in U.S.) *n.*: **bracero**. ∎ For two decades until 1964, the United States had such an arrangement, the **bracero** program, which brought seasonal farmworkers from Mexico to California. While on paper "guestworkers" are guaranteed labor rights, they depend on a job's continuation to remain in the country. (David Bacon, *INS Declares War on Labor*, The Nation, 10-25-1999.)

laborious *adj.*: **operose**. ∎ Computers and the Internet offer unprecedented access to a world of information. Rather than becoming obsolete, basic skills such as spelling, referencing source material and typing are vital in maneuvering one's way efficiently through the electronic multimedia landscape. With three splendiferous CD-ROMs, users can complete these **operose** tasks expediently and efficiently. (Donald Liebenson, *Fact Finders: With These Reference Works, a World of Knowledge Is Only a Few Keystrokes Away*, The Chicago Tribune, 05-08-1997, p. 8.)

(2) laborious (task, esp. of cleaning up or remedying bad situations) *n.*: **Augean task**. See HERCULEAN

(3) laborious *n.*: **Stakhanovite**. See WORKAHOLIC

lacking (anything better) *adv.*: **faute de mieux** [French]. ∎ [T]here is probably no alternative to Mr. Buchanan [as the Reform Party candidate], unless [Jesse] Ventura changes his mind and agrees to run himself. The governor of Minnesota seems unprepared to stand in his way. ... So if Mr. Buchanan [decides to] leave the Republican Party, he stands a good chance of winning the Reform Party nomination, **faute de mieux**. (Author not given, *Pat Buchanan's Reforming Moment*, The Economist, 09-18-1999.)

ladies' man (as in man who seduces women) *n.*: **Lothario**. See PLAYBOY

(2) ladies' man *n.*: **roué** [French]. See PLAYBOY

lake (of or relating to) *adj.*: **lacustrine**. ∎ When Cortes and his men entered the Valley of Mexico almost 500 years ago they found mostly water: a vast lake, actually five interlocking lakes, stretched across the basin. ... For years this final outpost of a **lacustrine** empire seemed destined for landfill. (Michael Ybarra, *Cruising on an Aztec Lake*, The New York Times, 05-12-1996.)

lakes (of, or occurring in ... or ponds) *adj.*: **limnetic**. SEE WATERS

lamb (of, relating to or characteristic of sheep or ...) *adj.*: **ovine**. SEE SHEEP

lame (as in limping, from lack of blood flow to leg muscles) *n.*: **claudication**. SEE LIMPING

(2) lame (as in decrepit) *adj.*: **spavined**. SEE DECREPIT

lament (over) *v.t.*: **bewail**. ∎ Hamed Essafi, the U.N. disaster-relief coordinator, could only **bewail** the extent to which lifesaving measures fell short in Bangladesh. (James Walsh, *And No Bells Tolled*, Time International, 05-20-1991, p. 56.)

(2) lament (expressing ... often regarding something gone) *adj.*: **elegiac**. SEE SORROWFUL

(3) lament (esp. bitter ...) *n.*: **jeremiad**. SEE COMPLAINT

(4) lament (wail in ... for the dead) *v.i.*: **keen**. SEE WAIL

(5) lament (poem or song of ..., esp. for a dead person) *n.*: **threnody**. SEE REQUIEM

(6) lament (as in wail) *v.i.*: **ululate**. SEE WAIL

lampoon (esp. by ridiculing or making fun of someone) *n., v.t.*: **pasquinade**. SEE SATIRIZE

lance (or spear) *n.*: **assegai**. SEE SPEAR

land (of, relating to, containing or possessing ...) *adj.*: **praedial**. ∎ Norma believes she was born to be a farmer, smelling the soil. She recognizes the problems of **praedial** larceny but says that [while] much depends on what you have on your farms, goats are prime targets for thieves. (Marie Gregory, *Problems of Jamaican Women Farmers*, Caribbean Today, 11-30-1994.)

(2) land (consisting of ... and water) *adj.*: **terraqueous**. ∎ I'm certain that in recent days Bill Esrey and Bernie Ebbers, the chief players in the proposed merger of Sprint and MCI WorldCom, have felt at times that they could cup-cushion this entire **terraqueous** globe in the palms of their hands. (George Gurley, *The Sprint Deal Proves That No Matter How Big You Get, There's Always Room to Get a Little Bigger*, The Kansas City Star, 10-31-1999, p. 34.)

land of opportunity (spec. a place of fabulous wealth or opportunity) *n.*: **El Dorado**. SEE PARADISE

landslide (from mudslide or a volcano) *n.*: **lahar**. ∎ "If you have a big eruption, you're going to have a long lead time. Mount St. Helens was rumbling and shaking for almost a year" before it erupted in May 1980, Finn said. "But with small eruptions, you don't get that much lead time, and that's the thing you have to worry about with these **lahars**," she said. "They're dangerous because they travel pretty fast." (Jim Erickson, *Scientists Peer into Heart of Giant*, Denver Rocky Mountain News, 02-01-2001, p. 12A.)

language (coarse, offensive or abusive ...) *n.*: **billingsgate**. ∎ The remarks were what I later came to know as anti-Semitic cliches: about money, noses, ambition, slyness, and all the rest. The tone of this suburban **billingsgate** was chummy, almost chortling, as if passwords or signs of mutual recognition were being exchanged. (Herb Greer, *An Amateur Jew*, Commentary, 03-01-1995, p. 52.)

(2) language (common ... spoken between people of different languages) *n.*: **lingua franca**. ∎ [Chambers] was an adept linguist, with idiomatic German — still communism's **lingua franca** — and so could easily communicate with agents sent from overseas. (Sam Tanenhaus, *Whittaker Chambers*, Random House [1997], p. 80.)

(3) language (person who knows only one ...) *n.*: **monoglot**. ∎ [M]odern English-speakers [have] a taste for foreign writers — Colombian, Japanese, German, as well as Latin and Greek. But, since English-speakers themselves are notoriously **monoglot**, they rely on translation to import into the language the international output of books. (Author not given, *Back to the Basics*, The Economist, 05-18-1996, p. 85.)

(4) language (specialized ... or speech used by a particular group) *n.*: **argot**. SEE VERNACULAR

(5) language (used by members of the underworld or a particular group) *n.*: **cant**. SEE VERNACULAR

(6) language (which is meaningless or deceptive) *n.*: **flummery**. SEE DECEPTIVE

(7) language (pattern which is unique to each person) *n.*: **idiolect**. SEE SPEECH

(8) language (as in vocabulary) *n.*: **lexicon**. SEE VOCABULARY

(9) language (one who studies ... and words) *n.*: **philologist**. SEE LINGUIST

(10) language (distortion or destruction of sense of ...) *n.*: **verbicide**. SEE DISTORTION

(11) language (common ... of the people) *n.*: **vulgate**. SEE VERNACULAR

languages (mixture of two or more ...) *adj.*: **macaronic**. ∎ Mikhalkov charges in. ... He gives Mastroianni a hearty hug, then shouts, "Hokay!"

and dashes about the pseudo-stage like a Cossack, interpreting nine roles at once with magical expressiveness — but in Russian, which his aide, Alla Garrubba, translates into Italian. It's a **macaronic** ramble-scramble but it works. (Brad Darrach, *Bio: Marcello Mastroianni: He Lives for Art, He Lives for Love — at 63, He's the Old Wild King of the Movies*, People, 12-07-1987, p. 98.)

(2) languages (speaking or writing in many different ...) *adj.*: **polyglot**. SEE MULTILINGUAL

large (very ...) *adj.*: **brobdingnagian** (often cap.). SEE HUGE

(2) large (very ...) *adj.*: **Bunyanesque**. SEE ENORMOUS

(3) large (very ..., like an elephant) *adj.*: **elephantine**. SEE ENORMOUS

(4) large (very ... object) *n.*: **leviathan**. SEE HUGE

(5) large (like an elephant) *adj.*: **pachydermatous**. SEE ELEPHANT

(6) large (very ...) *adj.*: **Pantagruelian**. SEE GIGANTIC

(7) large (very ...) *adj.*: **pythonic**. SEE HUGE

large-chested *adj.*: **bathycolpian**. SEE BUSTY

laryngitis (as in loss of voice due to disease, injury or psychological causes) *n.*: **aphonia**. ∎ So strong was Schnitzler's faith in hypnosis, in fact, that in the conclusion of his article on **aphonia** he proposed that hypnosis might be used to treat the more general neurotic conditions responsible for loss of voice. (Laura Otis, *The Language of Infection: Disease and Identity in Schnitzler's "Reigen,"* The Germanic Review, 03-01-1995, p. 65.)

lascivious *adj.*: **fescennine**. SEE OBSCENE

(2) lascivious *adj.*: **ithyphallic**. SEE LUSTFUL

(3) lascivious *adj.*: **lickerish**. SEE LUSTFUL

(4) lascivious *adj.*: **lubricious**. SEE LEWD

(5) lascivious (man or playboy) *n.*: **roué** [French]. SEE PLAYBOY

lash (generally at oneself) *v.t.*: **flagellate** (*n.*: **flagellation**). SEE CRITICIZE

(2) lash (generally used figuratively) *v.t.*: **larrup**. SEE WHIP

Last Judgment (branch of theology concerned with) *n.*: **eschatology**. SEE JUDGMENT DAY

last resort *n.*: **pis aller** [French]. ∎ Like Warhol and Harvey, Rodchenko was a commercial as well as a fine artist. Unlike Warhol, he began as fine, but unlike Harvey, his downshift into visual rhetoric was not a **pis aller** — a matter of having to make a living. (Arthur C. Danto, *Books & the Arts: "Art Into Life": Rodchenko*, The Nation, 09-21-1998.)

last stop *n.*: **terminus**. SEE END

lasting (forever or immortal) *adj.*: **amaranthine**. SEE IMMORTAL

(2) lasting (only a brief time) *adj.*: **fugacious**. SEE FLEETING

(3) lasting (forever) *adj.*: **sempiternal**. SEE EVERLASTING

latent (as in temporarily inactive) *adj.*: **quiescent**. SEE INACTIVE

latest (the ... thing) *n.*: **dernier cri** [French]. SEE TREND

latrine *n.*: **cloaca**. ∎ "Pecunia non olet," replied the Emperor Vespasian when it was suggested to him that it might be unseemly to put a tax on public toilets. A piece of gold, after all, can emerge even from a **cloaca**. (Richard Klein, *Get a Whiff of This: Breaking the Smell Barrier*, The New Republic, 02-06-1995, p. 18.)

lauding (insincerely ...) *adj.*: **fulsome**. SEE INSINCERE

laugh (loud and hard) *v.i.*: **cachinnate** (*n.*: **cachinnation**). ∎ In "The Animal Ridens: Laughter as Metaphor in Modern American Literature," Del Kehl contrasts [Nathaniel] Hawthorne's "sharp, dry **cachinnation**" and [Mark] Twain's laughter that can "blow the colossal humbug to rags and atoms at a blast" with [Saul] Bellow's "animal ridens, the laughing creature, forever rising up." (Don Nilsen, *Humorous Contemporary Jewish-American Authors: An Overview of the Criticism*, Melus, 12-01-1996, p. 71.)

(2) laugh (having an ability or tendency to ...) *n.*: **risibility**. ∎ In the early '60s, hiding a TV camera was a fresh idea, and Allen Funt's sly use of hidden cameras touched the nation's **risibility**. "Smile," his befuddled victims were told, "you're on Candid Camera." Funt died last week. The humor predeceased him by years. Today, few public spaces are without a camera. Surveillance cameras, both hidden and obvious, are ubiquitous — and unfunny. (Author not given, *Editorial/It's No Longer Funny to Be Caught on Camera*, Newsday, 09-13-1999.)

laughable *adj.*: **gelastic** [This word is synonymous with "risible" (see next entry) but is not used nearly as frequently. In fact, its most common usage is when referring to the medical condition "gelastic epilepsy," which is a form of epilepsy producing uncontrollable laughter. Thus, while "gelastic," like "laughable" and "risible," could presumably be used in both a straightforward sense and pejoratively (see the example accompanying "risible"), its usage does not appear sufficiently frequently to show examples of the word being used in the pejorative sense.]. ▮ [In the TV show Men Behaving Badly], curiously, the word "lager" is considered hilarious, and the drinking of it to excess positively **gelastic**. Supplementing this, tonight's episode also relies on telegraphed sight gags and a well-rehearsed studio audience with the lowest laugh threshold in the northern hemisphere. (Mike Harris, *Tube*, The Australian, 10-31-1996.)

(2) laughable *adj.*: **risible** [As with the word "laughable" itself, this word is sometimes used in the straightforward sense of the word, but is more frequently used pejoratively, as in "his argument was so ridiculous, it was laughable."]. ▮ By endorsing Howard Dean before a single vote has been cast [in the primaries], Al Gore has done Democrats hoping for a victory next November a true disservice. ... [I]t's hard to say what was more **risible** about Gore's remarks: His claim that he respected the prerogative of caucus and primary voters or his suggestion to the other candidates that they should "keep their eyes on the prize" and eschew attacks on the front-runner. (Scott Lehigh, *Gore Hurts Democrats With Premature Nod*, The Boston Globe, 12-12-2003, p. A35.)

laughing *adj.*: **riant**. SEE CHEERFUL

lavish *adj.*: **Lucullan**. ▮ Whited, a ... psychic experimenter [swears that she has been getting recipes from the late noted chef James Beard]. ... [A]nybody could lose weight following the recipes Whited says Beard has been dictating to her. Far from the **Lucullan** feasts for which he was renowned, they include such prim nibbles as tofu pudding pie, rye sesame sticks and carob cookies. (Mary Huzinec, *The New Soup-to-Nuts Cookbook: A Channeler Says She's Getting Recipes From the Late James Beard, [Christina Whited]*, People Weekly, 03-07-1988.)

(2) lavish (excessively ..., esp. in a sensuous way) *adj.*: **sybaritic**. SEE LUXURIOUS

law (as a matter of ...) *adj., adv.*: **de jure** (lit. by law, as contrasted with de facto: in reality or in fact) [Latin]. SEE LEGALLY

lawbreaker *n.*: **malefactor**. SEE WRONGDOER

lawful *adj.*: **licit**. SEE LEGAL

lawless (as in unruly) *adj.*: **indocile**. SEE UNRULY

lawlessness (as in government by the mob or the masses) *n.*: **mobocracy**. SEE GOVERNMENT

(2) lawlessness (as in government by the mob or the masses) *n.*: **ochlocracy**. SEE GOVERNMENT

lawsuits (persistent instigation of ..., esp. groundless ones) *n.*: **barratry**. ▮ Why is jurisprudence suddenly the hot new pop read? ... [T]his year lawyers, next year civil engineers or professional bowlers. ... In any case, the entire, ever wistful publishing industry now chases riches through **barratry**, the offense of excessive litigation. There is a cranked-out feel to most legal thrillers. (John Skow, *Reviews — Books: Burden of Turow*, Time, 01-11-1993, p. 51.)

lawyer (who may be petty, dishonest or disreputable) *n.*: **pettifogger**. ▮ For 27 years, Nolo has thrived on unrestrained hostility to **pettifoggers**. The desks of some Nolo executives contain treats of shark-shaped gummy lawyers, and the company's award-winning Web site features a running list of lawyer jokes classified in 20 categories ranging from "Outrageous Fees" to "Lawyers as Crooks, Cheats and Felons." (Doreen Carvajal, *Legal Publisher Under Fire: Texas Lawyers Challenge Firm's Do-it-Yourself Guides*, The Atlanta Journal, 08-26-1998, p. F10.)

laying down *adj.*: **decumbent**. SEE LYING DOWN

laying low (as in, in concealment) *adv.*: **doggo** (esp. as in "lying doggo"; slang). SEE CONCEALMENT

laypersons (as in parish or congregation) *n.*: **laity**. SEE PARISH

laze (around during the summer) *v.i.*: **aestivate** (or **estivate**). ▮ Above all, my children **aestivate**. From May to September their life is a langorous stroll from pool to hammock to beach to barbecue. Their biggest challenges are ice creams that melt before the first lick, and fireflies that resist capture in jam jars. (Gerald Baker, *The Long Hot Summer*, Financial Times [London], 07-12-2003.)

laziness (as in lethargy) *n.*: **hebetude**. SEE LETHARGY

lazy *adj.*: **fainéant** [French]. ▮ [I]f nonhunters ever knew how many properly dressed, entirely palatable big-game carcasses wind up in dumpsters because someone was simply too **fainéant** to butcher and cook and eat an animal he could find the time and energy to shoot and kill, hunting would be in even greater jeopardy than it is today. (Thomas

McIntyre, *The Meaning of Meat [A Hunter's View]*, Sports Afield, 08-01-1997, p. 18.)

(2) lazy (person, who stays in bed out of laziness) *n.*: **slugabed**. ∎ If the Patriots win the Super Bowl, Bill Parcells will finally get a good night's sleep. It seems the least the franchise could do for him. "I was up at 3:30 and my mind started racing with all the things I had to do," Parcells said the morning after New England's 20-6 win over Jacksonville in the AFC Championship game. It's a safe bet the coach hasn't been a **slugabed** since that morning, either. (Michael Gee, *10 Reasons the New England Patriots Should Win the Super Bowl; Reason 2; It's a Great Farewell Present for Bill Parcells*, The Boston Herald, 01-22-1997.)

(3) lazy (person, as in work avoider) *n.*: **embusque** [French]. See SLACKER

(4) lazy (person devoted to seeking pleasure and luxury) *n.*: **lotus-eater**. See HEDONIST

(5) lazy (person) *n.*: **wastrel**. See SLACKER

leader (of a party, school of thought or group of persons) *n.*: **coryphaeus**. ∎ The official titles for Stalin used in Pravda and the official histories: Leader and Teacher of the Workers of the World, Father of the Peoples, Wise and Intelligent Chief of the Soviet People, the Greatest Genius of All Times and Peoples, the Greatest Military Leader of All Times and Peoples, **Coryphaeus** of the Sciences, Faithful Comrade-In-Arms of Lenin, Devoted Continuer of Lenin's Cause, the Lenin of Today, the Mountain Eagle and Best Friend of All Children. (David Remnick, *Standing by Stalin; In the Glasnot Era, a Cadre of Loyalists Stuck in Time*, The Washington Post, 11-15-89, p. B1.)

(2) leader (or spokesman esp. for a political cause) *n.:* **fugleman**. ∎ [Arthur Schlesinger Jr.:] "The battles of the Thirties shaped my politics. ... I remain to this day a New Dealer, unreconstructed and unrepentant." ... In that context it is interesting to learn that the "particular hero" of this **fugleman** for the New Deal was H.L. Mencken ... for whom he retains affection and admiration even in the face of Mencken's "virulent attacks on Franklin D. Roosevelt and the New Deal" and the "mean-spirited" tone of his posthumously published diaries. (Jonathan Yardley, *A Life in the 20th Century [Book Review]*, The Washington Post, 11-12-2000.)

(3) leader (political ...) *n.*: **sachem**. ∎ The Republican presidential field has something for everyone (and comedy tonight?). But no matchup of the contenders provides a more vivid contrast than social conservative **sachem** Gary Bauer and "capi-

talist tool" Steve Forbes. (Don Feder, *OP-ED; Bauer & Forbes: Main St. vs. Wall St.*, The Boston Herald, 04-07-1999.)

(4) leader (as in dictator, esp. in Spanish-speaking countries) *n.*: **caudillo**. See DICTATOR

(5) leader *n.*: **duce** [Italian]. See COMMANDER

(6) leader (esp. hereditary) *n.*: **dynast**. See RULER

(7) leader (or proponent of a cause) *n.*: **paladin**. See PROPONENT

(8) leader (or ruler who holds great power or sway) *n.*: **potentate**. See RULER

leaderless *n.*: **acephalous** (lit. without a head). ∎ Since the Umuofians are **acephalous**, their central political power is invested in the ndichie, council of elders, and in the egwu-gwu, masked spirits of the ancestors who come to sit in judgement over civil and criminal disputes. (Ato Quayson, *Realism, Criticism, and the Disguises of Both: A Reading of Chinua Achebe's "Things Fall Apart" with an Evaluation of the Criticism Relating to It*, Research in African Literatures, 12-22-1994, p. 117.)

leaf (of or relating to a ...) *adj.*: **foliar**. ∎ Thirty years ago, Smith was assigned to work with and breed red clover. His success is evident in the breeding he performed to make red clover plants resistant to root rots such as Fusarium and to **foliar** diseases such as anthracnose ... — a disease that causes plants to lose their leaves, weaken, and die. (Linda Cooke, *New Red Clover Puts Pastures in the Pink*, Agricultural Research, 12-01-1996, p. 9.)

leafy *adj.*: **frondescent**. ∎ *White Interior* (1932) [by Pierre Bonnard greets] the viewer upon arrival. ... A fiery sky peeks in over the Mediterranean Sea and above a coastal town, through a cluster of **frondescent** trees, through a window and its windowpane, shimmering in reflection. (James Panero, *Bonnard's "Butterflies,"* New Criterion, 12-01-2002.)

lean (body type) *adj.*: **ectomorphic**. ∎ Tina Gaudoin writes in the July issue of *Bazaar* that the magazine has received "stacks and stacks of angry letters, newspaper articles and phone calls decrying our use of 'stick figure, prepubescent, anorexic-looking models who represent an unattainable ideal for most females.'" Yet she goes on to say, "This is an **ectomorphic** body type. It's in fashion. You'll be seeing more of it." (Anne Tumlinson, *Strong Women Are Not in Fashion*, St. Louis Post-Dispatch, 09-17-1993, p. 7E.)

leap (esp. by a horse) *n.*: **capriole**. See JUMP

leap year (of or relating to) *adj*.: **bisextile**. ■ Officially called "**bisextile**" year because of its placement in the Julian calendar, it became known as "leap" year because English courts did not recognize Feb. 29, so it was "leapt" over. (Author not given, *Four Million People Worldwide Celebrate Leap Year Birthdays*, PR Newswire, 04-07-2000.)

learned (people as a group) *n*.: **clerisy**. See EDUCATED

(2) learned (of a ..., but pedantic, word or term) *adj*.: **inkhorn**. See PEDANTIC

(3) learned (person, as in lover of learning) *n*.: **philomath**. See SCHOLAR

(4) learned (person who is very ... in many areas) *n*.: **polyhistor**. See KNOWLEDGEABLE

(5) learned (person who is very ... in many areas) *n*.: **polymath**. See SCHOLAR

learning (excess striving for or preoccupation with ...) *n*.: **epistemophilia**. See KNOWLEDGE

(2) learning (pertaining to ... of spiritual or intellectual things) *adj*.: **gnostic**. See SPIRITUAL

(3) learning (universal ...) *n*.: **pansophy** (*adj*: **pansophic**). See KNOWLEDGE

(4) learning (on a subject which is superficial while pretending to be learned) *n*.: **sciolism**. See SUPERFICIAL

leave (hurriedly or secretly) *v.t*.: **absquatulate**. ■ [Jackie Gleason's] Mother Mae was a rosary addict. Father Herb worked in the death claims department of a small insurance firm, drank like a culvert and **absquatulated** when Jackie was 9, leaving Mae on her uppers. ("He was as good a father," Jackie later quipped, "as I've ever known.") (Brad Darrach, *A Fond Goodbye to The Great One*, People, 07-13-1987, p. 94.)

(2) leave (hurriedly or secretly) *v.t*.: **decamp**. ■ She had deliberately packed for only four days, so she would have an excuse for a short visit. When her clothes ran out, she would have to go home. ... She was glad that she had had the foresight to arrange an unbreakable excuse for **decamping** soon. She had no intention of getting stuck in a very small town. (Aaron Latham, *The Ballad of Gussie & Clyde: A True Story of True Love*, Good Housekeeping, 08-01-1997, p. 149.)

leave out (intentionally) *v.t*.: **pretermit**. See OMIT

leaves (of or relating to ...) *adj*.: **foliar**. See LEAF

(2) leaves (having many ...) *adj*.: **frondescent**. See LEAFY

leaving (as in a departure which is unannounced, abrupt, secret or unceremonious) *n*.: **French Leave**. See DEPARTURE

leaving out (or omitting or passing over) *n*.: **preterition**. See OMITTING

lecherous *adj*.: **concupiscent** (*n*.: **concupiscence**). See LUSTFUL

(2) lecherous *adj*.: **ithyphallic**. See LUSTFUL

(3) lecherous *adj*.: **lickerish**. See LUSTFUL

(4) lecherous *adj*.: **lubricious**. See LEWD

(5) lecherous (man or playboy) *n*.: **roué** [French]. See PLAYBOY

lecture (on a topic, esp. in a long-winded or pompous manner) *v.i*.: **bloviate**. See SPEAK

(2) lecture (pompously, loudly, or theatrically) *v.i*.: **declaim**. See PROCLAIM

(3) lecture (about, esp. at length) *v.i., n*.: **descant**. See TALK

(4) lecture (very enthusiastic or excited ... or writing) *n*.: **dithyramb**. See ENTHUSIASTIC

(5) lecture (as in complaint) *n*.: **jeremiad**. See COMPLAINT

(6) lecture (at length) *v.i*.: **perorate** (*n*.: **peroration**). See MONOLOGUE

(7) lecture (scolding ...) *n*.: **philippic**. See TIRADE

left (on the ... side or left-handed) *adj*.: **sinistral**. See LEFT-HANDED

left-handed *adj*.: **sinistral**. ■ The model predicts that today everyone has genes which confer a basic predisposition of 78% to be right-handed. How children actually turn out, however, can be influenced by whether their parents are dextral [right-handed] or **sinistral**. (Author not given, *Sinister Evolution: Population Genetics*, The Economist, 08-26-1995, p. 69.)

leftover (as in warmed over, food or old material) *n., adj*.: **rechauffé** [French]. See WARMED OVER

legal *adj*.: **licit**. ■ Diane's liaison with "The Weasel," as her cyber-Romeo signed his E-mail, may not meet the legal definition of adultery — which implies physical, not virtual, coupling. But there's no doubt that cyberromances, whether **licit** or not, generate genuine feelings. (Anastasia Toufexis, *Behavior: Romancing the Computer: The First Cyberadultery Suit Shows the Risks of Looking for Love Online*, Time, 02-19-1996, p. 53.)

legally *adj., adv*.: **de jure** (lit. by law, as contrasted with de facto: in reality or in fact) [Latin]. ∎ While ultra-Orthodox leaders [in Israel] regularly bluster against the courts, they comply with court rulings. Even more telling, they regularly turn to the courts when they think that doing so will protect their interests. The ultra-Orthodox oppose the courts **de jure**, but they do not de facto. (Noah Efron, *Real Jews*, Basic Books [2003], p. 218.)

lender (who charges high interest) *n.*: **shylock**. ∎ Chili — so named for his infinite cool — has spent the past dozen or so years as the laid-back enforcer for a mob-connected loan-sharking operation in Miami. ... He quickly masters the latest Hollywood jargon. ("There were a lot of terms you had to learn, as opposed to the **shylock** business where all you had to know how to say was 'Give me the f*** money.'") (Josh Rubins, *Get Shorty by Elmore Leonard*, Entertainment Weekly, 08-17-1990, p. 24.)

lengthy (as in rambling) *adj.*: **discursive**. SEE RAMBLING

lesbian *adj.*: **sapphic**. ∎ Sheba and I were a bit *too* fond of one another, she told people; a bit *too* close. The implication was that Sheba and I were involved in some sort of **sapphic** love affair. ... I am quite accustomed to [this] by now. Vulgar speculation about sexual proclivity would seem to be an occupational hazard for a single woman like myself [i.e. in her 60's], particularly one who insists on maintaining a certain discretion about her private life. (Zoë Heller, *What Was She Thinking?* Henry Holt [2003], p. 147.)

(2) lesbian *n.*: **tribade**. ∎ The tough "queer-core" [girl] band Tribe 8 — the name plays on **tribade** — is not for the timid. (Margaret Saraco, *Where Feminism Rocks*, On the Issues, 03-01-1996, p. 26.)

lessen (in value, amount or degree) *v.t.*: **attenuate**. ∎ We must ... sometimes **attenuate** perfect freedom so as to ensure safety and security for all. To reasonably ensure the safety of jurors so as further to provide a fair and evenhanded trial for [Timothy] McVeigh, the trial judge is correct in modestly curtailing the right of open court to the public. (Peter J. Riga, *Judge Right to Close Trial*, USA Today, 04-24-1997, p. 12A.)

lesson (used to make a point) *n.*: **exemplum**. SEE EXAMPLE

let (as in bestow, by one with higher power) *v.t.*: **vouchsafe**. SEE BESTOW

letdown (as in anticlimax) *n.*: **bathos**. SEE ANTICLIMAX

(2) letdown (as in disappointment) *n.*: **Dead Sea fruit**. SEE DISAPPOINTMENT

lethal (as in causing or portending death) *adj.*: **funest**. SEE DEADLY

lethargic *adj.*: **torpid**. ∎ One reason nerds are nerds is that parents don't make them play sports. They wile away the hours at Dungeons and Dragons while other boys are outside playing sports. They park in front of video games, gobble potato chips and Cokes, and pretend to wreak retribution on the world. Yet for all their electronic bravado, they are fat, soft, **torpid** and complacent. Whose fault is that? (R. Cort Kirkwood, *Blame Isn't Sporting*, The Ottawa Sun, 05-09-1999, p. C4.)

(2) lethargic *adj.*: **bovine**. SEE SLUGGISH

(3) lethargic *adj.*: **logy**. SEE SLUGGISH

lethargy *n.*: **hebetude**. ∎ [Bend, Oregon is] a city with a bike rack on every car, a canoe in every garage and a restless heart in every chest. While too many Americans slouch toward a terminal funk of **hebetude** and sloth, Bendians race ahead with toned muscles, wide eyes and brains perpetually wired on adrenaline. (Author not given, *Wild Rides in the Heart of Central Oregon — Bent out of Shape in Bend*, The Washington Times, 08-11-2001.)

(2) lethargy *n.*: **torpor**. ∎ Eliza Mowry ... awoke many atheists from ineffectual complaining and **torpor** to become an effective force against the social evils they observed resulting from organized religion. Unfortunately, today we find much the same sluggishness and inactivity among freethinkers that Eliza found in her day. Groups meet only to complain about religion. (Carole Gray, *Atheism and Activism: The Life and Work of Eliza Mowry Bliven*, The Humanist, 01-11-1996, p. 18.)

(3) lethargy (sometimes in matters spiritual, and sometimes leading to depression) *n.*: **acedia**. SEE APATHY

letter (love ...) *n.*: **billet-doux** [French]. SEE LOVE LETTER

(2) letter (capital ...) *n.*: **majuscule**. SEE CAPITAL LETTER

(3) letter (lowercase ...) *n.*: **minuscule**. SEE LOWERCASE

letters (of or relating to ... or the writing of ...) *adj.*: **epistolary**. ∎ [I received a letter from Sanjay Krishnaswamy who was aware] that I was a big fan of Elvis Costello and was wondering if I might have in my possession an extremely rare recording [by] Costello. ... Mr. Krishnaswamy would soon find out that his **epistolary** endeavors were to pay off in spades [because I found the recording and mailed it to him.] (Joe Queenan, *My Goodness*, Hyperion [2000], p. 64.)

(2) letters (one who is learning the ... of the alphabet) *n*.: **abecedarian**. SEE ALPHABET

lewd *adj*.: **lubricious**. ■ On some of the desert visits, police allege, [coach] Pearson took along two boys and played a **lubricious** game with them. Everyone would flip a quarter simultaneously, after which, depending on how the coins landed, the players would either have to touch Pearson's genitals or let him touch theirs. (William Nack, *Every Parent's Nightmare*, Sports Illustrated, 09-13-1999, p. 40.)

(2) lewd (compulsive ... behavior) *n*.: **corpropraxia**. SEE OBSCENE

(3) lewd *adj*.: **fescennine**. SEE OBSCENE

(4) lewd (as in lustful) *adj*.: **ithyphallic**. SEE LUSTFUL

(5) lewd *adj*.: **lickerish**. SEE LUSTFUL

lexicon (or word list) *n*.: **onomasticon**. SEE WORD LIST

liar *n*.: **Ananias** [based on an early Christian, who, according to Acts, dropped dead when he lied to the Apostle Peter]. ■ [Twelve women] are subjects of Claudia Roth Pierpont's "Passionate Minds." ... [T]he consummate liar Anais Nin (whose name, perhaps, should have been **Ananias**) [emerges] as the most loathsome. Although trenchant in her criticisms, Pierpont shows sympathy for all her subjects. (Only Nin's pathological dishonesty and narcissism seem to exhaust her tolerance.) (Merle Rubin, *Essays Take Critical Look at Female Icons*, The Los Angeles Times, 03-27-2000.)

libel (which is published for political gain right before an election) *n*.: **roorback**. SEE FALSEHOOD

liberal (person in beliefs and conduct) *n*.: **latitudinarian**. SEE OPEN-MINDED

liberate (from slavery, servitude or bondage) *v.t*.: **manumit**. SEE EMANCIPATE

library *n*.: **athenaeum**. ■ Whole wings of libraries could be built around the literature of loss. A person dies, and if a novelist is nearby there's a pretty good chance a book will be born. ... *The Summer After June*, Ashley Warlick's second novel, belongs in that vast annex of the **athenaeum** reserved solely for stories

of mourning. (Chris Bohjalian, *Starting Over*, The Washington Post, 04-02-2000, p. X07.)

licentious *adj*.: **fescennine**. SEE OBSCENE

(2) licentious *adj*.: **lickerish**. SEE LUSTFUL

(3) licentious *adj*.: **lubricious**. SEE LEWD

lie *n*.: **fabulation** (one who does so: **fabulist**). ■ Given that no one had witnessed their altercation, [the defendant] was clearly at liberty to give any answer he wished. ... [He] could have asserted [self-defense] or, at the very least, that [the victim] threatened his life. These would have been the obvious **fabulations** of a defendant seeking sympathy, a savvy criminal trying to confect a safe story. (Graham Burnett, *A Trial By Jury*, Knopf [2001], p. 144.)

(2) lie (petty or minor ...) *n*.: **taradiddle** (or **tarradiddle**). ■ The Bosnian war has produced its own crop of nonsense. [Two Serbs] uncloak[ed] Bosnia's president as a closet Muslim fundamentalist, with a pre-war membership video put out by his party to prove it. Alas, the pair also rashly offered a translation, which proved exactly the opposite. ... That sort of **taradiddle** is old stuff, though. (Author not given, *The Injuries of War*, The Economist, 07-29-1995, p. 64.)

(3) lie (as in a false story, often deliberately told) *n*.: **canard**. SEE HOAX

(4) lie (accepted as fact due to repetition in print) *n*.: **factoid**. SEE INACCURACY

(5) lie (as in something which is impressive-looking on the outside but which hides or covers up undesirable conditions or facts) *n*.: **Potemkin village**. SEE FACADE

(6) lie (which is defamatory and published for political gain right before an election) *n*.: **roorback**. SEE FALSEHOOD

lies (abnormal propensity towards telling ..., esp. by embellishing) *n*.: **mythomania**. SEE EMBELLISHMENT

life (as in soul or inner self) *n*.: **anima**. SEE SOUL

lifeless (as in sluggish) *adj*.: **bovine**. SEE SLUGGISH

(2) lifeless (as in sluggish) *adj*.: **logy**. SEE SLUGGISH

(3) lifeless (as in sluggish or lethargic) *adj*.: **torpid**. SEE LETHARGIC

lifestyle *n*.: **modus vivendi** [Latin]. ■ Under normal conditions they would grow to hate each other, but their strange **modus vivendi** inadvertently keeps the dew on the rose. Claude lives with Maggie in

Brooklyn during the cold months and takes off as soon as the weather turns warm. She doesn't know where he goes but he always comes back, and when he does it's like a honeymoon again. (Florence King, *The Joys of Re-reading*, National Review, 12-23-1996, p. 52.)

light (interplay of ... and shadows, often in a pictorial representation) *n*.: **chiaroscuro**. ∎ The clearing he emerged into was a **chiaroscuro** of torchlight and strangely elongated shadows. (Val McDermid, *A Place of Execution*, St. Martin's Press [2000], p. 36.)

(2) light (without ..., esp. as to the ocean) *adj*.: **aphotic**. See DARK

(3) light (and delicate, sheer or transparent) *adj*.: **diaphanous**. See TRANSPARENT

(4) light (and delicate, sheer or transparent) *adj*.: **gossamer**. See TRANSPARENT

(5) light (abnormal fear of or sensitivity to) *adj*.: **photophobic**. See FEAR

light-hearted (as in playful) *adj*.: **ludic**. See PLAYFUL
(2) light-hearted (discussion of a subject, as in chitchat) *n*.: **persiflage**. See CHITCHAT

lightheaded *adj*.: **vertiginous**. See DIZZY

like-minded *adj*.: **simpatico**. See COMPATIBLE

likely (as in appearing to be true or accurate) *adj*.: **verisimilar**. See PLAUSIBLE

likeness (of sounds to each other) *n*.: **assonance**. See SIMILARITY
(2) likeness (as in representation) *n*.: **simulacrum**. See REPRESENTATION

likes (as in personal preference) *n*.: **de gustibus** [Latin]. See TASTE

limelight *n*.: **réclame** [French]. See PUBLICITY

limit (as in set the boundaries of) *v.t*.: **delimit**. See DEMARCATE

limitless *adj., adv*.: (limitlessly): **ad infinitum**. See FOREVER

limping (from lack of blood flow to leg muscles) *n*.: **claudication**. ∎ [T]he 53-year-old couldn't walk more than 100 yards without some pain; he was unable to prowl the mall or go on strolls with his wife. Specialists had told him he'd just have to live with it. The little pills changed all that. "Now I can walk as much as I want," he says happily. Yet intermittent **claudication** is often linked to bad habits

— smoking, lack of exercise, obesity. (Scott Woolley, *The Quest for Youth*, Forbes Magazine, 05-03-1999, p. 146.)

line (witty or clever ...) *n*.: **bon mot**. ∎ Here are some of Mae West's most memorable **bon mots**: "It's not the men in my life that counts — it's the life in my men." "A man in the house is worth two in the street." "Too much of a good thing can be wonderful." "He who hesitates is last." (Kevin Thomas, *Mae West–She Helped Make Sex Into a Laughing Matter*, St. Louis Post-Dispatch, 08-15-1993, p. 4C.)

linen (household ..., esp. table ..., such as napkins) *n*.: **napery**. ∎ On Aug. 30, the last night she had fended off those advances, Diana sat with Dodi inside Paris's Ritz Hotel. Amid the starched **napery** of L'Espadon restaurant, the 36-year-old princess ... seemed happy. (J.D. Reed, *Goodbye England's Rose*, People, 09-01-1997, p. 78.)

linguist *n*.: **philologist**. ∎ American wordsmiths are a quiet bunch, rarely shaking the beehive of lexicography. But not the late Frederic Cassidy. He broke out his **philologist** shovel and set to work unearthing the buried gems of American regional English. (Lane Hartill, *Let's Hit the "Flang Dang" and "Honeyfuggle" the Chaperones*, The Christian Science Monitor, 04-17-2001, p. 14.)

link *n*.: **catenation** (*v.t*.: **catenate**). See CHAIN
(2) link (in a series or chain) *v.t., adj*.: **concatenate** (*n*.: **concatenation**). See CONNECT

linked (by a close relationship) *adj*.: **affined**. See CONNECTED

lions (of, relating to or characteristic of) *adj*.: **leonine**. ∎ [The TV show "Lions" is] nowhere near the scope of the Disney classic The African Lion but includes some intriguing familial disputes ! — like an episode of a **leonine** soap opera. (Susan Reed, *Picks & Pans: Video*, People, 05-29-1989, p. 20.)

lips (of or relating to both ...) *adj*.: **bilabial**. ∎ The raspberry — that goofy noise created by vibrating upper and lower lips and tongue — is what phoneticians call **bilabial** trills. (Laura Flynn McCarthy, *Infants: Why Babies Do What They Do*, Parenting, 03-01-1998, p. 88.)

liquor (given to or marked by consumption of ...) *adj*.: **bibulous**. See IMBIBING
(2) liquor (one having an insatiable craving for ...) *n*.: **dipsomaniac** (*adj*: **dipsomaniacal**). See ALCOHOLIC

listening (act of ..., often with a stethoscope) *n.*: **auscultation**. ∎ Auscultation requires extremely focused listening and counting of each fetal heart beat as it is heard. (Linda Goodwin, *Intermittent Auscultation of the Fetal Heart Rate: A Review of General Principles*, Journal of Perinatal & Neonatal Nursing, 12-01-2000, p. 53.)

listless *adj.*: **bovine**. SEE SLUGGISH

(2) **listless** (as in weakened) *adj.*: **etiolated**. SEE WEAKENED

(3) **listless** *adj.*: **logy**. SEE SLUGGISH

(4) **listless** (as in sluggish or lethargic) *adj.*: **torpid**. SEE LETHARGIC

listlessness (as in lethargy) *n.*: **hebetude**. SEE LETHARGY

literary (woman with ... or scholarly interests) *n.*: **bluestocking**. SEE WOMAN

(2) **literary** (style which is dark, gloomy, remote and/or grotesque) *adj.*: **gothic**. SEE DARK

(3) **literary** (piece imitating previous pieces) *n.*: **pastiche**. SEE IMITATION

literate (people as a group) *n.*: **clerisy**. SEE EDUCATED

litigation (persistent instigation of ..., esp. groundless suits) *n.*: **barratry**. SEE LAWSUITS

litter *n.*: **detritus**. SEE DEBRIS

(2) **litter** *n.*: **offal**. SEE TRASH

little (very ...) *adj.*: **bantam**. SEE TINY

(2) **little** (person) *n.*: **homunculus**. SEE MIDGET

(3) **little** (person) *n.*: **hop-o'-my-thumb**. SEE MIDGET

(4) **little** (very ...) *adj.*, *n.*: **Lilliputian**. SEE TINY

liveliness *n.*: **brio**. SEE ENERGY

(2) **liveliness** *n.*: **élan** [French]. SEE SPIRIT

lively (as in stimulating) *adj.*: **piquant**. SEE STIMULATING

living (way of ...) *n.*: **modus vivendi** [Latin]. SEE LIFESTYLE

lizard (of, relating to or resembling) *adj.*: **lacertilian**. ∎ Lizards are the real-world inspiration for the dragons of medieval fantasies, for reasons that will become obvious to readers of Lizards: Windows to the Evolution of Diversity. ... This engaging, well-researched volume depicts an amazing variety of **lacertilian** beasts in its lavish illustrations and deft-ly examines their bizarre lifestyles and behaviors. (Michael Szpir, *Slithy Toves [Lizards: Windows to the Evolution of Diversity]*, American Scientist, 11-01-2003.)

loaf (around during the summer) *v.i.*: **aestivate** (or **estivate**). SEE LAZE

(2) **loaf** (or waste time) *v.i.*: **footle** (usu. as in "footle around"). SEE DAWDLE

(3) **loaf** (by pretending to be sick or incapacitated) *v.i.*: **malinger**. SEE SHIRK

loafer (as in work avoider) *n.*: **embusque** [French]. SEE SLACKER

(2) **loafer** (as in one who strolls through city streets idly) *n.*: **flâneur** [French]; (**loafing** *n.*: **flânerie**). SEE IDLER

(3) **loafer** (as in one who avoids work or assigned duties) *n.*, *v.i.*: **goldbrick**. SEE GOLDBRICK

(4) **loafer** *n.*: **wastrel**. SEE SLACKER

loathe *v.t.*: **execrate**. SEE HATE

(2) **loathe** *v.t.*: **misprize**. SEE HATE

loathsome *adj.*: **ugsome**. ∎ War makes deep and longstanding hatred and prejudices temporarily dissolve. During World War II, for example, the United States transformed the **ugsome** Josef Stalin, co-villain with Adolf Hitler in the Ribbentrop-Molotov pact, into a fetching "Uncle Joe" after an alliance was struck with the Soviet Union to defeat the Third Reich. (Author not given, *Looming Afghan Shipwreck*, The Washington Times, 01-01-2002.)

(2) **loathsome** (person) *n.*: **caitiff**. SEE DESPICABLE

(3) **loathesome** (as in repellent) *adj.*: **rebarbative**. SEE REPELLENT

local (as in parochial) *adj.*: **parish pump** [British]. SEE PAROCHIAL

location (surrounding ... served by an institution, such as a school or hospital) *n.*: **catchment area**. SEE DISTRICT

(2) **location** (as in condition of being located in a particular place) *n.*: **ubiety**. SEE PLACE

lock up (as in confine) *v.t.*: **immure**. SEE CONFINE

loft (or attic or room on top floor) *n.*: **garret**. ∎ Two years ago I sought out Levy to see what was happening to the embattled species [i.e. the inventor] in its natural habitat: the **garret**. As it happens, Levy's is the top floor of an old three-story house in Cambridge, Mass. Clumping up to his cluttered loft from time to time, I've had a chance to observe the magic of intellectual property aborning. (David Stipp, *Inventor*, Fortune, 03-29-1999, p. 104.)

lofty *adj.*: **empyreal**. ▪ The sold-out production by the acclaimed Steppenwolf Theater Company is lifted to **empyreal** heights by the presence of Ladysmith Black Mambazo, the South African a cappella group. (Emily Mitchell, *Sightings: Theater*, Time International, 05-04-1992, p. 66.)

logic (which is complicated and often illogical) *n.*: **choplogic**. SEE FALLACY
(2) logic (person who hates ... or enlightenment) *n.*: **misologist**. SEE CLOSED-MINDED

logical *adj.*: **ratiocinative**. ▪ "What do you say to folks who play with snakes in church?" Lester asked. "You can't appeal to their **ratiocinative** capacities." His reference to playing with snakes in church alluded to a bizarre form of Christian worship practiced by certain Pentecostal congregations, where the handling of poisonous serpents is, like speaking in tongues, regarded as a sign of salvation. (Darcy O'Brien, *Crime and Politics in Appalachia*, The World & I, 01-01-1995, p. 300.)

logrolling *n.*: **birling**. ▪ Her legs are corded with muscles, and she **birls** like a bucking horse, in spasms of bobs, reverses, runs and kicks. "I'm a total powerhouse," says Salzman, who is 5'6" and weighs 148 pounds. "The other women hang on [to the log] for dear life." (Michael Finkel, **Birling**: *The World Logrolling Championships Make a Splash Every Summer in Wisconsin*, Sports Illustrated, 11-27-1995, p. R2.)

loner (as in recluse, esp. for religious reasons) *n.*: **anchorite**. SEE RECLUSE
(2) loner (as in recluse, esp. for religious reasons) *n.*: **eremite**. SEE RECLUSE

long (for) *v.t.*: **desiderate**. SEE WANT

long shot (statement of being a ..., expressed in the form of an exaggerated comparison with a more obvious impossibility; for example "the sky will fall before I get married.") *n.*: **adynaton**. SEE UNLIKELIHOOD

long-winded (as in rambling) *adj.*: **discursive**. SEE RAMBLING
(2) long-winded (as in characterized by a ready and easy flow of words) *adj.*: **voluble**. SEE TALKATIVE

longing *n.*: **avidity**. SEE CRAVING

look (with a sideways ...) *adv.*: **asquint**. SEE GLANCE

(2) look (quick ..., as in glance) *n.*: **coup d'oeil** [French]. SEE GLANCE
(3) look (as in glance) *n.*: **dekko** [British inf.]. SEE GLANCE
(4) look (as in demeanor) *n.*: **mien**. SEE DEMEANOR

lookout (on the ...) *n.*: **on the qui vive** *idiom*. ▪ It was [Desi Arnaz] who saw dollar signs upon reading *The Untouchables* by retired G-man Eliot Ness. ... Warner Brothers had taken an option on the book, but never got around to developing it. Desi ordered his legal department to stay **on the qui vive**: the day Warner dropped its option they were to grab the project for Desilu. (Stefan Kanfer, *Ball of Fire*, Knopf [2003], p. 192.)

loony *adj.*: **doolally**. SEE CRAZY
(2) loony (slightly ..., often used humorously) *adj.*: **tetched**. SEE CRAZY

loose (sexually) *adj., n.*: **libertine**. SEE PROMISCUOUS
(2) loose (as in of questionable morality) *adj.*: **louche**. SEE QUESTIONABLE

loot (as in plunder) *v.t., v.i.*: **depredate** (*n.*: **depredation**). SEE PLUNDER

looting *n.*: **rapine**. ▪ This being the age of image enhancement, descendants of the Vikings would like it understood that their fierce, sea-scouring, village-slaughtering, monastery-looting, town-burning ancestors also had a kinder, gentler side. ... Obscured by all this **rapine** and slaughter, the show's 15 curators note, is the earth-girdling significance of the Vikings' westward voyaging. (Hank Burchard, *The Civilized Side of Viking Life*, The Washington Post, 07-14-2000, p. N49.)

losing (capable of ...) *n.*: **vincible**. SEE BEATEN

lot (as in destiny or fate) *n.*: **kismet**. SEE FATE

lotion (or balm which is soothing) *n.*: **demulcent**. SEE SOOTHING

loud *adj.*: **clamant**. ▪ [Patrick] Buchanan has been the most **clamant** anti-war voice of the 1990s; he is also the only prominent politician of either party who addresses the appalling maldistribution of wealth in our erstwhile republic — all of which makes him the nation's leading leftist. (Bill Kauffman, *The Americans Who Won't Be Celebrating NATO's 50th*, Independent on Sunday, 04-25-1999, p. 24.)
(2) loud *adj.*: **clangorous**. ▪ My freedom [living in a Swiss apartment in the 1970's was very limited.] Often, no showers are permitted between 10 P.M.

and 7 A.M. No toilets may be flushed during those hours, either. When relieving themselves, men are expected to sit. (Is it the likelihood of an errant drop that so offends? Or the **clangorous** tinkle?) (Alexander Wolff, *Big Game, Small World*, Warner Books [2002], p. 54.)

(3) loud (and boisterous) *adj.*: **strepitous**. ▪ From shortly after noon to six o'clock [Londoners] filled Drury Lane with a riot of enthusiasm, a torrent of emotion, a hurly-burly of hysteria, and sang "Auld Lang Syne" in chorus, not without tears. For in our experience we have seen nothing quite like [it], nothing so crowded with hearty and demonstrative citizens, nothing so "rich and varied," nothing so lengthy, and nothing so **strepitous**. (Author not given, *Ellen Terry Celebration*, The Times [London], 06-13-1991.)

(4) loud (as in gaudy) *adj.*: **meretricious**. SEE GAUDY

loudmouth (who often talks foolishness) *adj.*: **blatherskite**. SEE BABBLER

lout (person) *n.*: **grobian**. SEE BOOR

love (pertaining to ..., esp. in the sexual sense) *adj.*: **amatory**. SEE LOVEMAKING

(2) love (of or relating to illicit ...) *adj.*: **paphian** (or **Paphian**). SEE SEXUAL

(3) love (of women) *n.*: **philogyny**. SEE WOMEN

love affair *n.*: **amourette** [French]. ▪ [A sociology professor] is trying to test the notion that the baby boom generation, the cohort that began "the sexual revolution," came into adulthood with different cultural and moral values from their parents'. Using data from other studies and some 300 interviews she plans to conduct, she hopes to chart the details of baby boom love, sex and marriage, including extramarital **amourettes**. (Michael Norman, *Getting Serious About Adultery; Who Does It And Why They Risk It*, The New York Times, 07-04-1998, p. B7.)

love letter *n.*: **billet-doux** [French]. ▪ Hyped as a treasury of tidbits from the 120 **billets-doux** [Princess] Diana had sent [Major James Hewitt] during their five-year affair, Hewitt's *Love and War* in fact reveals little: Copyright laws prevented him from quoting the princess's letters. (Kim Hubbard, *Royals: A Cad's Lament*, People, 11-01-1999, p. 163.)

love potion *n.*: **philter**. SEE POTION

loveliness (physical) *n.*: **pulchritude**. SEE BEAUTY

lovemaking *adj.*: **amatory**. ▪ Harris's List of Covent-Garden Ladies [was] an annual publication that made "frequent use of nautical expressions in describing the physical accomplishments of some of the [prostitutes]," among them Miss Devonshire of Queen Anne Street; this being a family newspaper, we cannot quote Harris's delicious account of Miss Devonshire's **amatory** skills. (Jonathan Yardley, *Women Sailors and Sailors' Women*, The Washington Post, 03-04-2001, p. T2.)

(2) lovemaking *n.*: **houghmagandy** (Scottish). SEE INTERCOURSE

(3) lovemaking *n.*: **venery**. SEE INTERCOURSE

lover (male ... of a married woman) *n.*: **cicisbeo**. SEE BOYFRIEND

(2) lover (female) *n.*: **inamorata**. SEE GIRLFRIEND

(3) lover (male ...) *n.*: **inamorato**. SEE BOYFRIEND

loving (as in amorous) *adj.*: **amative**. SEE AMOROUS

lower (rank, esp. in the military) *n.*: **subaltern**. SEE SUBORDINATE

lowercase letter *n.*: **minuscule**. ▪ A had its bomb, B its movie, C its section and D its day. Now E is having its era. ... You must have seen its amazing breakthrough performance in e-mail. Soon there were E-Stamps, Etrade, eToys.com, e-etc. Now, E's got capital status; as we like to say, E is "E-biquitous!"... What versions does E come in? You can get E in a manly, three-pronged [capital letter] or a dainty, curly **minuscule** that almost looks like a smiley face! (Jesse Green, *E-nough Already*, The Washington Post, 11-21-1999.)

loyal (subordinate, esp. of a political leader) *n.*: **apparatchik**. SEE UNDERLING

(2) loyal (and unquestioning assistant) *n.*: **myrmidon**. SEE ASSISTANT

loyalist (esp. who supports or protects a political leader) *n.*: **Janissary**. SEE SUPPORTER

(2) loyalist (strong ... for a cause, religion or activity) *n.*: **votary**. SEE SUPPORTER

loyalty *n.*: **fealty**. ▪ The revenues from black crude — which reached a high of $113 billion in 1981 and this year are expected to top $60 billion — have enabled the House of Saud to create a modern state almost overnight and, in the process, buy the continued **fealty** of its subjects. (Lisa Beyer, *The Gulf: Lifting The Veil*, Time, 09-24-1990, p. 38.)

lucid *adj.*: **limpid**. SEE UNDERSTANDABLE

(2) lucid *adj.*: **perspicuous**. SEE UNDERSTANDABLE

luck (as in unpredictable outcome) *adj.*: **aleatory**. SEE UNPREDICTABLE

(2) luck (bad ...) *n., adj.*: **hoodoo**. SEE BAD LUCK

(3) luck (of finding good things by accident) *n.*: **serendipity** (*adj.*: **serendipitous**). SEE FORTUITOUS

luckless (perpetually ... person) *n.*: **schlimazel** [Yiddish]. SEE UNLUCKY

ludicrous (as in laughable) *adj.*: **gelastic**. SEE LAUGHABLE

(2) ludicrous (as in laughable) *adj.*: **risible**. SEE LAUGHABLE

lull (as in pause) *n.*: **caesura**. SEE PAUSE

luminous (softly ...) *adj.*: **lambent**. SEE SHIMMERING

(2) luminous *adj.*: **lucent**. SEE GLOWING

lunatic *n.*: **bedlamite**. ∎ Night is theater. ... No wonder it's "Hallowe'en" and not "Hallowmornin'." The nighttime is the right time to dress up like somebody else, to laugh like a **bedlamite** and be scared half to death by your own shadow. (David Kirby, *Books: Searching Souls Find Each Other in This "Night,"* The Atlanta Journal and Constitution, 04-15-2001, p. G2.)

lure *n.*: **Lorelei call** [derived from Lorelei, who was a siren of Germanic legend]. ∎ As media scholar Richard D. Heffner said: I don't like [cameras in the courts]. ... [I believe] that what happens in the view of courtroom cameras will inevitably and increasingly be molded by trial participants' awareness of what will "play" on the 6 or the 11 o'clock news! Can we realistically expect that they alone in American life will resist the **Lorelei call** of mass media? (Christo Lassiter, *TV or Not TV — That Is the Question*, Journal of Criminal Law and Criminology, 03-22-1996.)

(2) lure *v.t.*: **inveigle**. ∎ Forty-three-inch-tall Eddie Gaedel, who was **inveigled** by Bill Veeck into stepping to the plate in a major league game with the promise of baseball immortality, would probably have given the shirt off his back to be ensconced in the Baseball Hall of Fame. [Now his jersey is.] (John Walters, *Scorecard: Forty-three-inch-tall Eddie Gaedel*, Sports Illustrated, 07-15-1991, p. 17.)

(3) lure (as in bewitch or enchant) *v.t.*: **ensorcell** (or **ensorcel**). SEE ENCHANT

luring (by flattery) *n.*: **blandishment** (*v.t.*: **blandish**). SEE FLATTERY

luscious *adj.*: **toothsome**. SEE TASTY

lush *n.*: **dipsomaniac** (*adj*: **diposmaniacal**). SEE ALCOHOLIC

lust (sexual ... for the elderly) *n.*: **gerontophilia**. ∎ The reader must also be warned that this reviewer is subject to a passion many might consider warped or queer, what Havelock Ellis might have called **gerontophilia** rosacea. That is, I have this thing for old unrepentant Reds. There is something about that handful of octogenarian men and women I cannot resist. (John Mage, *Unrepentant Leftist: A Lawyer's Memoir [book reviews]*, Monthly Review, 11-01-1996, p. 43.)

(2) lust (excessive ... for wealth) *n.*: **cupidity**. SEE GREED

lustful *adj.*: **concupiscent** (*n.*: **concupiscence**). ∎ The name is Klein and the subject is underwear. But it's the designer's wife, Kelly, who's behind *Underworld*, published by Knopf, and hers is a curatorial rather than **concupiscent** approach to the subject. So keep your pants on. (E. Jean Carroll, *How Not to Buy a Woman Lingerie*, Esquire, 12-01-1995, p. 54.)

(2) lustful *adj.*: **ithyphallic**. ∎ [T]he women testifying to the **ithyphallic** social ways of President Clinton brought fact and collateral details with them. Each came forward, some with dates and corroborating witnesses, to divulge a steamy encounter with Bill Clinton. ... Ultimately their revelations contributed to a composite profile of a sex maniac, our forty-second president, a deviant in need of therapy. (R. Emmett Tyrell, Jr., *The Worst Book of the Year; Prof. Dr. Anita Hill Undistinguishes Herself Again*, The American Spectator, 06-1998.)

(3) lustful *adj.*: **lickerish**. ∎ In [Richardson's] professedly moral work there is more descriptive lubricity by far than one finds in Fielding. When Pamela is brought to bed between Mrs. Jewkes and Mr. B_____, for example, Richardson's superficial horror cannot conceal a certain **lickerish** interest in physical detail. (Author not given, *Works of Henry Fielding: Character Analyses*, Monarch Notes, 01-01-1963.)

(4) lustful *adj.*: **lubricious**. SEE LEWD

(5) lustful (man or playboy) *n.*: **roué** [French]. SEE PLAYBOY

lustrous (like a pearl) *adj.*: **nacreous**. SEE IRIDESCENT

luxurious (excessively ..., esp. in a sensuous way) *adj.*:

sybaritic. ▪ When [Peter Guber] entertained a visitor for lunch in his private dining room, he served low-fat cuisine but extolled the **sybaritic** pleasures of lolling in his new at-home flotation tank — which included a television screen on which he could watch films. (Griffin and Masters, *Hit and Run*, Simon & Schuster [1996], p. 389.)

(2) luxurious *adj.*: **Lucullan**. See LAVISH

lying *adj.*: **mendacious**. See DISHONEST

(2) lying (abnormal propensity towards ..., esp. by embellishing) *n.*: **mythomania**. See EMBELLISHMENT

(3) lying (above) *adj.*: **superjacent**. See OVERLYING

lying down *adj.*: **decumbent**. ▪ With much satisfaction, [William Least Heat-Moon] reports it was Thomas Jefferson who directed that all of the nation except the already mapped East be ruled into grids, never mind natural or political borders. "Chase County [Kansas] sleeps north-south or east-west ..., the **decumbent** folk like an accountant's figures neatly between ruled lines, their slumber neatly compartmentalized in Tom's grand grid." (John Skow, *PrairyErth* [sic] *[book reviews]*, Time 10-21-1991.)

M

machine (having the form or qualities of a ...) *adj.*: **mechanomorphic**. ▪ The young [William] Roberts drew his subject matter largely from clubs, pubs and music halls, painting dancers and their audiences as if they were the idols of some primitive cult; or abstracting them into **mechanomorphic** shapes with pumping pistons for limbs; or depicting them like shards of some crystalline material. (Author not given, *Caveman's Last Relic; Art [Review]*, Sunday Telegraph [London], 05-02-2004.)

(2) machine (self-operating ...) *n.*: **automaton**. See ROBOT

mad (informal as in daffy or loony) *adj.*: **doolally**. See CRAZY

(2) mad (as in indignant) *n.*: **dudgeon** (often expressed as "in high dudgeon"). See INDIGNANT

(3) mad (slightly ..., as in deranged, often used humorously) *adj.*: **tetched**. See CRAZY

madam (as in prostitute) *n.*: **bawd**. See PROSTITUTE

made (finely or skillfully ..., as in intricate) *adj.*: **daedal**. See INTRICATE

made-up (as in invented or substituted with fraudulent intent) *adj.*: **supposititious**. See SUPPOSED

madman *n.*: **bedlamite**. See LUNATIC

magic *n.*: **necromancy**. ▪ But no one factors into the bizarre arrangement the measure of Tita's heartbreak, the power of her love and, more to the point, the extent of her culinary **necromancy** — a talent that is the catalyst for much of the novel's [*Like Water For Chocolate*] drama. (Joanne Kaufman, *Picks & Pans: Pages*, People, 11-16-1992, p. 39.) See BLACK MAGIC

(2) magic (feat of ..., sometimes in a deceitful way) *n.*: **legerdemain**. See TRICKERY

(3) magic (as in supernatural) *adj.*: **numinous**. See SUPERNATURAL

(4) magic (as in sleight of hand) *n.*: **prestidigitation**. See SLEIGHT-OF-HAND

magic potion (or love potion) *n.*: **philter**. See POTION

magical *adj.*: **fey**. ▪ As Sallie Tisdale writes in "A Weight That Women Carry," "The first **fey** days of a new diet would be colored with a sense of control — organization and planning, power over the self." But after those first few days (or hours or minutes) "the basic futile misery took over." (Leora Tanenbaum, *Mirror, Mirror on the Wall* ..., Women's Review of Books, 11-01-1994, p. 14.)

(2) magical (having a ... and sprightly quality) *adj.*: **elfin**. See SPRIGHTLY

magician *n.*: **thaumaturgist**. See MIRACLE WORKER

magnetism (personal ...) *n.*: **duende**. See CHARISMA

maid (in India and Orient, often serving as a wet nurse) *n.*: **amah**. ▪ Sadly, my father died when I was just four. My mother had scarce means and almost no education. To survive, she took a job as a live-in **amah** for a wealthy Chinese family. (Emily Lau, *Reflections: A Passion for Politics*, Time International, 05-15-1997, p. 36.)

(2) maid (esp. woman hired to do cleaning) *n.*: **charwoman**. ▪ Mrs. Arris Goes to Paris (CBS, Sun, Dec. 27, 9 P.M. ET) is a charming little fantasy in which Angela Lansbury plays a dowdy London **charwoman** whose dream is to have a Dior gown created just for her. (David Hiltbrand, *Picks & Pans: Tube*, People, 12-21-1992, p. 13.)

majestic (and stately, as befitting a baron) *adj*.: **baronial**. SEE STATELY

make (as in devise an idea, plan, theory or explanation after careful thought) *v.t.*: **excogitate**. SEE DEVISE
(2) make (cheaply and flimsily) *v.t.*: **jerrybuild**. SEE BUILD

make known (as in send a signal) *v.t., v.i.*: **semaphore**. SEE SIGNAL

make up for *v.t., v.i.*: **expiate**. SEE ATONE

makeup (cosmetic or theatrical) *n.*: **maquillage** [French]. ∎ The world is learning what [the top models] already know about makeup artist Kevyn Aucoin. Wearing black boots and black Levi's, chains around his wrist and neck, a striped vest, a goatee, and a Caesar haircut, Kevyn Aucoin, 31, the Michelangelo of **maquillage**, stares intently at his canvas, brush in hand. The canvas is the delicate face of Kate Moss. (James Servin, *The Face Maker, [Makeup Artist Kevyn Aucoin]*, Harper's Bazaar, 01-01-1994, p. 30.)

malaise (general feeling of ... as form of depression) *n.*: **dysphoria**. SEE DEPRESSION

malcontent *n.*: **crepehanger**. SEE PESSIMIST
(2) malcontent (as in rebel) *n.*: **frondeur** [French]. SEE REBEL

male (centered on point of view of a ...) *adj.*: **androcentric**. ∎ Amy Agigian denies that [the use of "him or her"] is cumbersome ...: "The charges of awkwardness are usually a thinly veiled cover for hostility toward treating women as equals. This is a pseudo-issue where those who are benefitting from male privilege and from an **androcentric** world try to accuse those who want change of frivolity [and] nitpicking. (Daniel Seligman, *Keeping Up: Where Henry Fonda Went Wrong*, Fortune, 04-01-1996, p. 163.)
(2) male (lover of a married woman) *n.*: **cicisbeo**. SEE BOYFRIEND
(3) male (one having characteristics or reproductive organs of both ... and female genders) *n.*: **hermaphrodite** SEE BISEXUAL
(4) male (with whom one is in love) *n.*: **inamorato**. SEE BOYFRIEND
(5) male (of or derived from name of ... ancestor) *adj.*: **patronymic**. SEE PATERNAL

males (government by or political dominance of ...) *n.*: **androcracy**. SEE GOVERNMENT

malfeasance (in public office) *n.*: **malversation**. SEE WRONGDOING
(2) malfeasance (confession of ...) *n.*: **peccavi**. SEE CONFESSION

malicious *adj.*: **flagitious**. SEE WICKED
(2) malicious (comment which seems to be offering sympathy but instead makes the person feel worse, either intentionally or unintentionally) *n.*: **Job's comforter**. SEE TACTLESS
(3) malicious *adj.*: **malefic**. SEE EVIL
(4) malicious *adj.*: **malevolent**. SEE EVIL

malign (by making false or malicious statements) *v.t.*: **calumniate**. ∎ [C]learly, the time has come for some argumentative character to utter a kind word about poor old trickle-down economics (hereafter TDE). Bill Clinton and Al Gore have combined to **calumniate** TDE 17 times in this year's titanic debates, and neither George Bush nor Dan Quayle has attempted to defend it. (Daniel Seligman, *Keeping Up, Tricklism*, Fortune, 11-16-1992, p. 199.)
(2) malign (so as to humiliate or disgrace) *v.t.*: **traduce**. ∎ [S]ome [Britons] request that if their reputation is to be besmirched, the movie [The Patriot] should at least be worth seeing. "Failure to entertain is the supreme crime of [this] movie," chides Adam Mars-Jones. ... "If you're going to **traduce** my ancestors — blacken their names — then at least give me a better time when you do it." (Kim Campbell, *Brits Take Brunt as Hollywood Rewrites History*, The Christian Science Monitor, 07-14-2000, p. 1.)

malleable (as in pliable) *adj.*: **ductile**. SEE PLIABLE

malnourishment (condition of ... of a child) *n.*: **marasmus**. ∎ The UN team reached a shocking conclusion. Child mortality had risen fivefold since 1990. Diseases of malnutrition, like kwashshiorkor and **marasmus**, which had been virtually unknown in Iraq, were rampant. ... Studies have shown that half a million Iraqi children have died because of the sanctions and 30% of the survivors are permanently maimed or stunted by malnutrition. (Deidre Griswold, *A Silent War: The Children Are Dying; The Impact Of Sanctions On Iraq*, Atlanta Inquirer, 06-22-1996.)

man (centered on point of view of a ...) *adj.*: **androcentric**. SEE MALE
(2) man (who is a lover of a married woman) *n.*: **cicisbeo**. SEE BOYFRIEND
(3) man (with whom one is in love or has intimate relationship) *n.*: **inamorato**. SEE BOYFRIEND

(4) man (who seduces women) *n.*: **Lothario**. SEE PLAYBOY

(5) man (who hates women) *n.*: **misogynist**. SEE HATRED

(6) man (who has sexual relations with a boy) *n.*: **pederast**. SEE SODOMIZER

man-eating *adj.*: **anthropophagous**. SEE CANNIBALISTIC

man-made (as in artificial) *adj.*: **factitious**. SEE ARTIFICIAL

manager *n.*: **gerent**. ▌ [Henry VIII] appointed himself "supreme governor" of the English church. His chief minister, Thomas Cromwell, became "vice-**gerent**," overseeing it on his behalf. (Author not given, *Church and State: Monastic Error: 1539*, The Economist, 12-31-1999.)

(2) manager (as in boss or owner) *n.*: **padrone**. SEE BOSS

mandate (as in decree) *n.*: **diktat**. SEE DECREE

maneuver (as in course of action) *n.*: **démarche** [French]. SEE COURSE OF ACTION

mania (as in irresistible compulsion) *n.*: **cacoëthes**. SEE COMPULSION

(2) mania (for shopping) *n.*: **oniomania**. SEE SHOPPING

manic (as in frenzied) *adj.*: **corybantic**. SEE FRENZIED

manifestation (early ... of disease) *n.*: **prodrome**. SEE SYMPTOM

manly (relating to or concerned with being ...) *adj.*: **priapic**. ▌ Anthropologist Matthew Gutmann ... wanted to find out how the realities of Mexican men's lives compared to the popular image of Mexican men as violent, hard-drinking, **priapic** machos. (Michael Schwalbe, *The Meanings of Macho: Being a Man in Mexico City* [book reviews], Social Forces, 06-01-1997, p. 1488.)

(2) manly (condition of a woman having ... tendencies) *n.*: **viraginity** (*adj.*: **viraginous**). SEE MASCULINE

manner (as in demeanor) *n.*: **mien**. SEE DEMEANOR

manner of speaking *n.*: **façon de parler** [French]. SEE WAY OF SPEAKING

manners (appropriate ..., as in propriety) *n.*: **correctitude**. SEE PROPRIETY

(2) manners (precise observance of ...) *n.*: **punctilio**. SEE ETIQUETTE

manor (grounds belonging to a ...) *n.*: **demesne**. SEE ESTATE

mansion *n.*: **manse**. ▌ [Michael Medavoy] and Patricia built a massive vanilla-colored house in Coldwater Canyon, which was displayed in a full-color spread in the November, 1992 issue of W magazine. ... Patricia complained that decorating the **manse** had actually given her chronic fatigue syndrome. (Griffin and Masters, *Hit and Run*, Simon & Schuster [1996], p. 355.)

(2) mansion (grounds belonging to a ...) *n.*: **demesne**. SEE ESTATE

manual *n.*: **enchiridion**. SEE HANDBOOK

manufacture (cheaply and flimsily) *v.t.*: **jerrybuild**. SEE BUILD

many (and varied) *adj.*: **manifold**. SEE NUMEROUS

marble (of, relating to or resembling) *adj.*: **marmoreal**. ▌ She, Bruce and Teddy hit the road together and drive to a Palladian dream-house in search of a sixth-century BC fragment of marble statuary, featuring the hips and bottom of a nameless Greek athlete. After a long wait, Bruce appears, his arms wrapped around the **marmoreal** bum, which he manhandles into his car — en route, not to Sotheby's, but to his own London flat. (Author not given, *The Books Interview: Hopes and Anchors*, Independent, 04-17-1999, p. 12.)

march (a person or group from one place to another against their will) *v.t.*: **frogmarch** [spec. carrying a resisting prisoner face down by the arms and legs, but more generally used in the sense of forcing a person or group from one place to another, whether literally or figuratively; chiefly British]. ▌ [O]h, the pleasure it gives to meet and greet children and hear the same old excuses I've made on behalf of my children being repeated back to me: "It's because he's not on his home turf,"..."She's just exhausted, aren't you darling?" ... And then my favourite ... when one traditionally grips a child by the shoulders and **frogmarches** her up to the hostess to "say goodbye." (Rachel Johnson, *The Mummy Diaries — Negotiating the Maze of Modern Motherhood*, The Daily Telegraph [London], 05-03-2003.)

marionettes (or employing ...) `*n., pl.*: **fantoccini** [Italian]. ▌ Dennis Silk, [author of] William the

Wonder-Kid: Plays, Puppet Plays and Theater Writings [is] like a traveling hurdygurdy player and **fantoccini** man. ... [His book] is a collection of plays for puppets and actors, some of which have been performed successfully in Israel and will now reach a wider public of performers and spectators. (Zvi Jagendorf, *The Thing's the Play*, Jerusalem Post, 03-20-1997.)

marriage (pledge of ...) *v.t.*: **affiance**. ∎ "It's the [sexual] tension that makes it interesting for an audience." Then it may be lucky that the **affianced** Catherine Zeta-Jones and Michael Douglas share no screen time in December's "Traffic." "Once people are married, it's like, eh," says marketing analyst Tony Angellotti. "Married people know there's no more sexual tension when people are married — you're not going to fool them." (Gillian Flynn, *News & Notes: Love is a Battlefield*, Entertainment Weekly, 10-06-2000, p. 10.)

(2) marriage (announcement of forthcoming ..., esp. in a church) *n.*: **banns**. ∎ In a renewed attempt to circumvent laws that bar gay marriages, two same-sex couples exchanged wedding vows in a Toronto church after following the tradition of publishing marriage **banns** announcing their intention to wed. (Author not given, *Notebook/World Watch*, Time International, 01-29-2001, p. 12.)

(3) marriage (within a group based on applicable custom) *n.*: **endogamy**. ∎ Thirty years ago, Jews were considered the most **endogamous** ethnic group in the United States; in the early 1960s, less than 11 percent of Jews who married chose non-Jewish spouses. (Rachel Altman, *The New Minority: Jews Who Choose Jews*, Lilith, 06-30-1994.)

(4) marriage (outside the clan or other social unit) *n.*: **exogamy**. ∎ Not only was the ancient rabbinic standard [as to who was Jewish] universally accepted, the barriers to intermarriage created by internal Jewish taboos as well as by Gentile hostility saw to it that the standard was fairly easily maintained. But with today's massive increase in **exogamy**, some have been prompted to reconsider traditional definitions. (Jack Wertheimer, *Judaism Without Limits*, Commentary, 07-01-1997, p. 24.)

(5) marriage (to one of lower social status) *n.*: **mesalliance** [French]. ∎ Grand Duke Kirill married a divorcee, and was accordingly banished from Russia. ... Grand Duke [Paul was] banished for marrying a divorced commoner. ... But until at least 1907 Nicholas believed the succession still to be more or less safe. ... [H]is brother, Grand Duke Michael, had yet to follow his cousins down the road of **mesal-**

liance and disgrace. (Anne Applebaum, *Michael and Natasha: The Life and Love of the Last Tsar of Russia* [book reviews], New Statesman, 10-17-1997, p. 54.)

(6) marriage (hatred of ...) *n.*: **misogamy**. ∎ In Jeremiah Johnson, Bear Claw says that his former Cheyenne wife of 10 years was "the meanest bitch that ever balled for beads." Such bleak hatred illuminates the misogyny and **misogamy** harbored by mountain veterans who prefer being alone or exclusively in the company of men. (Patrick McCarthy, *Westers, Not Westerns: Exteriorizing the "Wild Man Within,"* Journal of Popular Film and Television, 09-01-1995, p. 116.)

(7) marriage (of or relating to a ... to a person of inferior rank where the rank of the inferior partner remains unchanged and children of the marriage do not succeed to the titles of the parent of higher rank) *adj.*: **morganatic**. ∎ Public opinion may forever stand in the way of Camilla Parker Bowles being crowned Queen, but couldn't she and Prince Charles enter into a "**morganatic** marriage"? ... A **morganatic** marriage was also suggested as a way of solving Britain's abdication crisis in 1936, when Edward VIII chose to give up his throne rather than the woman he loved, twice-divorced Wallis Simpson. (Author not given, *There Is a Way They Could Marry*, The Birmingham Post [England], 01-29-1999.)

(8) marriage (as in absence, nonrecognition or non-regulation of ...) *n.*: **agamy**. See UNMARRIED

(9) marriage (of or relating to ...) *adj.*: **hymeneal**. See WEDDING

(10) marriage (or sexual relations involving persons of different races) *n.*: **miscegenation**. See SEX

married (happily ... elderly couple seldom seen apart) *n.*: **Darby and Joan** [British]. ∎ "It didn't cross my mind that something which is so old [i.e. having an affair with a married man who she later married herself] could become an issue," she says. "I mean it all happened 20 or 30 years ago. Desmond and I thought we had turned into **Darby and Joan** and I didn't expect it to become a priority." (Diane Parkes, *The Big Interview: Esther Rantzen*, Evening Mail, 03-17-2001, p. 18.)

(2) married (woman) *n.*: **feme covert**. [French] ∎ If, as J. Paul Hunter suggests, "novels are an easy place ... to sort out the ways of the world, to crack the code of adulthood and social expectation," then what might have the young woman reader of [Mary Davys's 1724 novel *The Reform'd Coquet*] sorted out? Certainly a grim portent of what it means to be a **feme covert**, for whom a husband thinks, speaks, and acts. (Natasha Saje, *The Assurance to Write*, Essays in Literature, 09-22-1996, p. 165.)

marsh *n.*: **fen**. SEE SWAMP

marshy *adj.*: **paludal**. SEE SWAMPY

marvelous (as in of the highest quality) *n.*: **first water** (usu. as in "of the first water"). SEE QUALITY

(2) marvelous *adj.*: **frabjous** (often as in "Oh frabjous day!"). SEE WONDERFUL

(3) marvelous *adj.*: **galumptious**. SEE EXCELLENT

(4) marvelous *adj.*: **galluptious** [slang]. SEE WONDERFUL

(5) marvelous *adj.*: **palmary**. SEE EXCELLENT

(6) marvelous *adj.*: **skookum**. SEE EXCELLENT

masculine (condition of a woman having ... tendencies) *n.*: **viraginity** (*adj.*: **viraginous**). ∎ Krafft-Ebing ... did equate the most degenerate forms of lesbianism with an inverted gender style. ... In describing **viraginity**, Krafft-Ebing focuses on the women's tomboyish childhood; their preference for playing with soldiers; and their inclination for male garments, science, smoking, drinking, and imagining themselves men in relation to women. (Cheshire Calhoun, *The Gender Closet: Lesbian Disappearance Under the Sign "Women,"* Feminist Studies, 03-22-1995.)

(2) masculine (relating to or concerned with being ...) *adj.*: **priapic**. SEE MANLY

mask (or disguise) *n., v.t.*: **vizard**. SEE DISGUISE

masochism *n.*: **algolagnia** [this word includes both ends of the pain spectrum, i.e. pleasure from receiving pain and from giving it]. ∎ The French, and indeed almost all the rest of the world, have been amazed for centuries by the English habit, begun at school but continuing for ever, of hitting one another with sticks and suchlike; statistics must inevitably be difficult or impossible to acquire, but I would bet a lot that the English would demonstrate an addiction to **algolagnia** far greater than in any other country. (Bernard Levin, *Oh, to Slap the Jailer in the Jug*, The Times [London], 12-14-1989.)

mass (confused or jumbled ...) *n.*: **agglomeration**. SEE JUMBLE

(2) mass (of people) *n.*: **ruck**. SEE MULTITUDE

massacre (of unresisting persons) *n.*: **battue** [French]. SEE KILLING

masses (of common people) *n.*: **canaille**. ∎ "How I loved the game [of golf]," [P.G. Wodehouse] wrote in

1973. "I have sometimes wondered if we of the **canaille** don't get more pleasure out of it than the top-notchers. (Robert Sullivan, *Golf: Bard of the Links*, Sports Illustrated, 05-29-1995, p. R10.)

(2) masses (pertaining to the ...) *n.*: **demotic**. ∎ Unlike Jefferson, however, [Supreme Court Justice John] Marshall never acquired the cultivated elegance of his Randolph forebears. He never shed the rough but genial manners of his frontier father. He had simple tastes and a **demotic** temperament that Jefferson lacked, a common touch that Jefferson snidely attributed to "his lax lounging manners." (Gordon S. Wood, *The Father of the Court*, The New Republic, 02-17-1997.)

(3) masses (suitable for or comprehensible by the ...) *adj.*: **exoteric**. SEE ACCESSIBLE

(4) masses (as in the common people) *n.*: **hoi polloi**. SEE COMMONERS

(5) masses (government by the ...) *n.*: **mobocracy**. SEE GOVERNMENT

(6) masses (government by the ...) *n.*: **ochlocracy**. SEE GOVERNMENT

master (as in boss or owner) *n.*: **padrone**. SEE BOSS

(2) master (or ruler who holds great power or sway) *n.*: **potentate**. SEE RULER

masterpiece (esp. in art or literature) *n.*: **chef-d'oeuvre** [French]. ∎ So, welcome to the High Museum's [art exhibition]. Only three paintings, but what stellar canvases they are, starring van Gogh's **chef d'oeuvre** and one of his most famous works, "The Starry Night." (Catherine Fox, *Fans to Get Starry-Eyed View of Van Gogh Classic*, The Atlanta Journal and Constitution, 09-01-2000, p. E1.)

masturbation *n.*: **autoerotism**. ∎ More-recent studies indicate that the number of women who masturbate has risen to about half (15 percent do it "quite often"), while the proportion of men who do remains about the same. Unmarried women and college-educated women are more likely to indulge in **autoeroticism** than others. (Michael Segell, *Sexual Performance: A Hard Look at the Primal Urge*, Esquire, 03-01-1994, p. 119.)

(2) masturbation *n.*: **onanism**. ∎ Although sexual self-satisfaction is as old as the Bible ... males have begun to rely on it heavily. The reason: As they get on with the great project of letting vanity rule every aspect of their lives, they become less attractive as bed partners to women. The result is a burgeoning **onanism** industry, with the "Body Electric" masturbation school for men in Oakland. (Guy Martin, *The*

Encyclopedia of Male Vanity, Esquire, 03-01-1997, p. 82.)

matchless (person or thing) *n.*: **nonesuch**. See PARAGON

matchmaker (Jewish ...) *n.*: **shadchan** [Yiddish]. ▪ Matchmaking is an ancient tradition, especially among small, isolated communities like those of the Eastern European shtetl, where the key to survival was tight social cohesion. In many ways, Hakimian is the modern-day inheritor of the generations-old role of the **shadchan**. (Jonathan Krashinsky, *Bringing People Together*, Jerusalem Post, 02-02-2001, p. 9.)

materialistic *adj.*: **banausic**. ▪ Those [studying Latin will be asked,] "What on earth are you going to do with that?" The question is often intended to be merely rhetorical, because the assumption is that no justification could possibly exist. ... Students of Latin typically subscribe to a different view, one in which people do not assume that everything must have a **banausic** purpose. (Author not given, *Finding Beauty and Meaning in Latin Despite Modern History of Rejection*, The Washington Times, 07-29-2001.)

(2) materialistic *adj.*: **bourgeois**. ▪ And what happened to romance? I grew up on images of struggling artists shacking up in Bohemian apartments, surviving mostly on love and thumbing their noses at shallow **bourgeois** values. The people I knew dreamed of passion and poetry rather than rocks on ring fingers or maid service. (Rekha Basu, *"Multimillionaire" Show Pitted Marriage Values Against Money*, Gannett News Service, 02-24-2000.)

materialize (as in making an abstract concept seem real) *v.t.*: **reify**. ▪ [Ron Haskins] says that in returning over and over to the human stories, DeParle made a "constant attempt to **reify** the abstract principles of welfare reform. You could see what it meant to have a work requirement, when you have a mom in Milwaukee with six kids, and she has to get up at 6 in the morning to catch a bus or whatever." (William Powers, *Welfare: The Trickster*, National Journal, 03-10-2001.)

(2) materialize (as in emerge) *v.i.*: **debouch**. See EMERGE

maternal (of or relating to name of ... ancestor) *adj.*: **matronymic**. ▪ Although there are numerous variations, Spanish surnames usually consist of two parts: the patronymic name followed by the **matronymic**. In the case of President Luis Alberto Monge Alvarez, for example, Monge is his father's name; Alvarez, his mother's name. (Harold D. Nelson, *Costa Rica: Front Matter*, Countries of the World, 01-01-1991.)

math (difficulty with or inability to do ...) *n.*: **acalculia** (or **dyscalculia**) ▪ Whatever the reason for the lack of popularity of this kind of research, the topic of learning disabilities in mathematics requires serious attention. Many children receive diagnoses of mathematics learning disability, or the related **dyscalculia** and **acalculia**. (Herbert P. Ginsburg, *Mathematics Learning Disabilities: A View From Developmental Psychology*, Journal of Learning Disabilities, 01-01-1997.)

mathematical (having ... ability) *adj.*: **numerate**. ▪ Some of the most prominent chief executives, presidents, entrepreneurs, and inventors in the world are graduates of IIT, India's elite institution of higher learning. Its impossibly high standards, compelling the mostly male student body to average fewer than five hours of sleep a night, produce **numerate** graduates who are masters at problem-solving. (Manjeet Kripalani, *Management: Whiz Kids*, Business Week, 12-07-1998.)

matrimony (of or relating to ...) *adj.*: **hymeneal**. See WEDDING

mattress (straw-filled ...) *n.*: **palliasse**. ▪ After lights out, on their beds of lumpy **palliasses** on wooden planks, [military] recruits moaned about their lot, their fag-ends glowing like agitated fireflies, but all shared the companionship of the temporarily oppressed; the enforced community living often leading to lasting friendships. (Albert Morris, *Last Post Sounds for the Barracks Dorm*, The Scotsman [Edinburgh, Scotland], 03-17-2001.)

maudlin *adj.*: **bathetic**. See SENTIMENTAL

maverick (orig. Catholics who did not follow Church of England) *n.*: **recusant**. See DISSENTER

mawkish (as in excessive or contrived sentimentality) *adj.*: **bathetic**. See SENTIMENTAL

mawkishess (as in excessive or contrived sentimentality) *n.*: **bathos**. See SENTIMENTALITY

maxim *n.*: **apothegm**. See SAYING

(2) maxim (witty or clever ... or line) *n.*: **bon mot**. See LINE

(3) maxim (pithy ...) *n.*: **gnome** (*adj:* **gnomic**). See CATCHPHRASE

maxims (given to stating ..., esp. in a moralizing way) *adj.*: **sententious**. SEE APHORISTIC

maximum (to the ...) *adv.*: **à l'outrance** [French]. SEE UTMOST

maybe *adv.*: **perchance**. SEE POSSIBLY

meager *n.*: **exiguous**. ∎ They became a "tightly knit unit," bound together by the effort to maintain the household on the **exiguous** sum Jay sent them — eight dollars a week by Vivian's recollection. (Sam Tanenhaus, *Whittaker Chambers*, Random House [1997], p. 7.)
(2) meager *adj.*: **mingy**. [This is likely a blended word — also known as a portmanteau word — which combines "mean" and "stingy." However, in actual usage, it is generally used as a synonym for "stingy" or for the less pejorative "meager."] ∎ While overall retail sales — excluding the highly volatile auto sales — edged up a **mingy** 0.2 percent in February, sales in the nation's furniture and home furnishings outlets jumped up by 1.4 percent over January levels. (Don Hogsett, *Home Outpaces Overall Retail Sales*, Home Textiles Today, 03-25-2002.)

meal (following a ..., esp. dinner) *adj.*: **postprandial**. ∎ Even [Rockefeller's] daily breaks — the midmorning snack of crackers and milk and the **postprandial** nap — were designed to conserve energy and strike the ideal balance between the physical and mental forces. (Ron Chernow, *Titan*, Random House [1998], p. 174.)
(2) meal (before a ..., esp. dinner) *adj.*: **preprandial**. ∎ Any fellow dinner guest reading [my dull resumé] could have been forgiven for sneaking up to the table for a quick squint during the **preprandial** stage and doing a quick shuffle of the placement cards. (Tony Rennell, *Why I Hate Dinner Parties Now*, New Statesman, 06-28-1999.)

mealy *adj.*: **farinaceous**. SEE STARCHY

mean *adj.*: **ignoble**. ∎ We are, sadly, living in a rude, **ignoble** age in this country, and professional sports have become the living, seething proof. Our kids see pro athletes trash-talking, brawling, spitting, taunting, and retaliating — and being rewarded and admired for behavior that used to be the opposite of the American ideal of sportsmanship. (John Kehe, *Remember When Playing Kids' Sports Was Actually Fun?* The Christian Science Monitor, 07-19-2000, p. 14.)
(2) mean (as in portend) *v.t.*: **betoken**. SEE PORTEND

(3) mean (as in despicable, person) *n.*: **caitiff**. SEE DESPICABLE
(4) mean *adj.*: **flagitious**. SEE WICKED

meander (as in talk or act in an aimless or incohcrent fashion) *v.i.*: **maunder**. SEE RAMBLE

meaning (having more than one ...) *adj.*: **polysemous** (or **polysemic**) [This word can refer to a word having literally more than one meaning, as in the example given, or can mean a word that means different things to different people. For example, one writer stated: "We cannot control the meaning of such a slippery and **polysemic** concept as 'multi-culturalism.'"]. ∎ There is nothing like a game of Scrabble with non-native speakers to heighten your appreciation for your own native tongue. ... Just take the word run: You can run up a bill, or you can run up a hill. You can be on the run — as in dodging the law — or you can have the runs. How versatile three little letters can be. (Genine Babakian, *Coming To Grips With* **Polysemous** *Vocabulary*, The St. Petersburg Times [Russia], 07-25-2000.)
(2) meaning (inability to recall ... of words or using them incorrectly) *n.*: **paramnesia**. SEE AMNESIA
(3) meaning (using a ... of a word other than in its customary sense) *adj.*: **Pickwickian**. SEE DEFINITION

meaningless (words or language) *n.*: **flummery**. SEE DECEPTIVE

measly *n.*: **exiguous**. SEE MEAGER
(2) measly (as in meager) *adj.*: **mingy**. SEE MEAGER

measuring (act or process of ...) *n.*: **mensuration**. ∎ Yet [the issue of which is the world's tallest building is] hotly contested. One Randall Krause, for example ... is lord of the International Superstructure **Mensuration** Alliance, the master of its Website, and something of a rebel among the edifice-measurement set. He's the one out there asking the hard questions. ("What is the meaning of high? How does it differ from tall?") (Author not given, *Features/The World's Tallest Buildings: Too Big To Lose*, Fortune, 05-24-1999, p. 232.)

mechanical (as in routine) *adj.*: **banausic**. SEE ROUTINE
(2) mechanical (as in having the form or qualities of a machine) *adj.*: **mechanomorphic**. SEE MACHINE

meddle (one who would ... into other's affairs) *n.*: **quidnunc**. SEE BUSYBODY

meddler (officious ... who frustrates the success of a plan by stupidly getting in the way) *n*.: **marplot** [after Marplot, a character in The Busy Body, a play by Susanna Centlivre (1669-1723)]. ∎ For Thanksgiving, [several George W. Bush supporters have] given a big fat turkey of an issue to Sen. John McCain in his campaign for the GOP presidential nomination [by allegedly] spreading rumors that McCain's imprisonment as a POW in Vietnam made him unstable, mentally unfit for the presidency. ... [T]he chief **marplot** [is Senator Trent Lott, who denies the charge]. (Guy Friddell, *Rumors Rile Ex-POW McCain and His Supporters*, The Virginian Pilot, 11-25-1999.)

medication (which is untested or unproved) *n*.: **nostrum**. SEE REMEDY

medicine (which relieves pain) *n*.: **anodyne**. SEE PAIN-RELIEVER

mediocre (as in made without regard to quality) *adj*.: **catchpenny**. SEE INFERIOR

meditate (on something, often used as a directive, as in "Consider this:") *v.t.*: **perpend**. SEE CONSIDER

meditation (staring at one's belly-button as an aid to ...) *n*.: **omphaloskepsis**. ∎ The point [of Paul Goodman's philosophy], as near as I can make it out, is to achieve a kind of perpetual **omphaloskepsis**, repeatedly examining yourself and your motives and connections with the world around, and thus achieving health, or at least avoiding neurosis, by putting forth, as much and continuously as possible, the authentic self. (Talk about the examined life!). (Kirkpatrick Sale, *Crazy Hope and Finite Experience: Final Essays of Paul Goodman [book reviews]*, The Nation, 4-10-1995.)

medley (as in mixture) *n*.: **farrago**. SEE ASSORTMENT
(2) medley (as in assortment) *n*.: **gallimaufry**. SEE ASSORTMENT
(3) medley (esp. of fruits and vegetables) *n*.: **macédoine** [French]. SEE MIXTURE
(4) medley (as in assortment) *n*.: **olla podrida** [Spanish]. SEE ASSORTMENT
(5) medley (as in assortment) *n*.: **omnium-gatherum** [Latin]. SEE ASSORTMENT
(6) medley (as in assortment) *n*.: **salmagundi**. SEE ASSORTMENT

meek (esp. from lack of self-confidence) *adj*.: **diffident**. SEE TIMID
(2) meek (and unassertive person) *n*.: **milquetoast**. SEE UNASSERTIVE

(3) meek (as in timid person) *n*.: **nebbish** [Yiddish]. SEE TIMID
(4) meek (as in cowardly) *adj*.: **pusillanimous**. SEE COWARDLY

meeting (esp. for illicit sexual relations) *n*.: **assignation**. SEE APPOINTMENT
(2) meeting (spec. a final effort made by architectural students to complete a solution to a problem within an allotted time, but sometimes is used to refer to any kind of workshop or brainstorming session) *n*.: **charette** (or **charrette**). SEE WORKSHOP
(3) meeting (esp. with an enemy or adversary) *n., v.t.*: **parley** SEE DISCUSSION

melancholy (as in depression) *n*.: **cafard** [French]. SEE DEPRESSION
(2) melancholy (as in sullen or morose) *adj*.: **saturnine**. SEE SULLEN
(3) melancholy *adj*.: **tristful**. SEE SAD
(4) melancholy (as in world-weariness or sentimental pessimism over the world's problems) *adj*.: **Weltschmerz** [German]. SEE PESSIMISM

melange (as in assortment) *n*.: **farrago**. SEE ASSORTMENT
(2) melange (as in assortment) *n*.: **gallimaufry**. SEE ASSORTMENT
(3) melange (of fruits or vegetables) *n*.: **macédoine** [French]. SEE MIXTURE
(4) melange (as in assortment) *n*.: **olla podrida** [Spanish]. SEE ASSORTMENT
(5) melange (as in assortment) *n*.: **omnium-gatherum** [Latin]. SEE ASSORTMENT

meld (as in bring together) *v.t.*: **conflate**. SEE COMBINE
(2) meld (as in blend) *v.t., v.i.*: **inosculate**. SEE BLEND

melee *n*.: **affray**. SEE BRAWL

mellifluous (sound) *adj*.: **euphonious** (*n.*: **euphony**). SEE MELODIOUS

melodious (to the ear) *adj*.: **dulcet**. ∎ In the quirky world of National Public Radio, **dulcet**-toned commentators provide long, thoughtful analyses of issues both momentous and amusing, their reports bookended by tinkling music. (Elizabeth Gleick, *Nation: Static on Public Radio*, Time, 04-07-1997, p. 55.)
(2) melodious (voice or sound) *adj*.: **euphonious** (*n.*: **euphony**). ∎ Moments after his death was disclosed Thursday night, Sinatra's silvery tone flowed into every communication channel, reclaiming the

airwaves with a **euphony** and honesty that never goes out of fashion. (Edna Gundersen, *A Silvery Tone for a Lifetime, Sinatra Forever an Inspiration*, USA Today, 05-18-1998, p. 3D.)

(3) melodious (voice or sound) *adj.*: **mellifluous.** ■ Silence also puts us in tune with the extraordinary world around. ... It is in silence that we often hear soothing, healing sounds: the **mellifluous** song of a bird, a gentle wind whispering through leaves, the scampering of a squirrel up the trunk of a tree or the voice of God. (Dayle Allen Shockley, *We Should Cherish the Sound of Silence*, The Dallas Morning News, 07-18-1999, p. 7J.)

melodrama (as in excessive or contrived sentimentality) *n.*: **bathos.** SEE SENTIMENTALITY

melodramatic (behavior) *n., adj.*: **operatics.** ■ The conventional melodrama provides Fassbinder with his most powerful techniques for constructing his narrative. The earliest street melodramas were silent and depended on exaggerated posturings and prolonged stares. ... Fassbinder also revives the theatrical, **operatic** posturings of the early melodramas. (Author not given, *Fox and His Friends; Faustrecht Der Freiheit; Fist-right of Freedom; Fox*, Magill's Survey of Cinema, 06-15-1995.)

(2) melodramatic (as in excessive or contrived sentimentality) *adj.*: **bathetic.** SEE SENTIMENTAL

melt *v.i.*: **deliquesce.** ■ [Sugar Ray] Robinson was hitting Maxim at will for 11 rounds, winning easily on all cards and about to take his third world title before **deliquescing** in the 104 degree heat. (William Nack, *The 20th Century*, Sports Illustrated, 06-07-1999, p. 100.)

memorandum (which contains outline or summary of diplomatic negotiations) *n.*: **aide-mémoire** [French]. ■ Russia is pulling out of a 1995 arms agreement signed by Vice President Al Gore after portions of the pact were disclosed in The Washington Times, U.S. officials said yesterday. ... The Times published sections of the **aide-mémoire** on Oct. 17. The agreement [was] signed by Mr. Gore and then-Russian Prime Minister Viktor Chernomyrdin. ... The Gore campaign said the disclosures were politically motivated. (Bill Gertz, *Russia Will Not Honor Gore's Secret Arms Deal*, The Washington Times, 11-23-2000.)

memory (an aid to ..., such as a mnemonic device) *n.*: **aide-mémoire.** ■ Can't remember the name of a bird between *shrike* and *tern*? In [a 1558 vocabulary book by John Withals], there is *swallow* and *swift* —

and at a stroke, his book becomes, if little else, an **aide-mémoire.** (Simon Winchester, *The Meaning of Everything*, Oxford University Press [2003], p. 20.)

(2) memory (having detailed ... of visual images) *adj.*: **eidetic.** ■ His mind was **eidetic** — that is to say, it could hold and retrieve images with photographic accuracy, be they mid-game positions in chess, crossword puzzles or encoded German naval signals — and he was working with his eyes closed. (Robert Harris, *Enigma*, Random House [1995], p. 57.)

(3) memory (having an exact or vivid ...) *n.*: **hypermnesia.** ■ The story resembles the natural but morbid tendency for **hypermnesia** touched off when we know that we are about to die. Our memory plays out the details of important scenes from our lives. (Anthony Wall, *Chatter, Memory, and Mysticism in Louis-Rene Des Forets*, The Romanic Review, 05-01-1993.)

(4) memory (recalling to ...) *n.*: **anamnesis.** SEE REMEMBRANCE

(5) memory (confusion of one's ... with actual fact) *n.*: **paramnesia** SEE MISREMEMBER

men (government by or political dominance of ...) *n.*: **androcracy.** SEE GOVERNMENT

(2) men (hatred of ...) *n.*: **misandry.** SEE HATRED

menacing *adj.*: **minatory.** Allied forces must win big enough to change Iraq's politics. It is not sufficient to drive Saddam from Kuwait, waggle a **minatory** finger at him, and say, "Be a good boy and don't ever do that again." (Thomas A. Stewart, *War/Cover Stories: Winning the Peace*, Fortune, 02-25-1991, p. 28.)

(2) menacing *adj.*: **baleful.** SEE SINISTER

menopause (period culminating in ...) *n., adj.*: **climacteric** (usu. as in "the ..."). ■ Menopause is actually not a single event but a transition period during which a woman experiences changes in menstruation leading to the **climacteric.** (Dianne Kieren, *Women's Choicemaking About Menopause: Issues and Directions for Action*, Contemporary Women's Issues Database, 09-01-1995, p. 143.)

menstruation (suppression of or absence of ...) *n.*: **amenorrhea.** ■ Women who train intensely — and who don't eat enough to keep up with the demands of that training — may stop having their periods. That, in and of itself, is not harmful, but the estrogen deficiency that causes **amenorrhea** also can cause bone loss and osteoporosis. (Bill Stump, *Don't Ignore These Symptoms*, Runner's World, 06-01-1999, p. 66.)

(2) menstruation (woman's first ...) *n*.: **menarche**. ∎ Full bosomed and womanly by her early teens, she obviously had started **menarche** at a young age. (Dorothy Herrmann, *Helen Keller*, Knopf [1998], p. 107.)

mental (having ... balance) *adj*.: **compos mentis**. SEE SANE
(2) mental (activity) *n*.: **mentation**. SEE THINKING

mentally ill (person) *n*.: **bedlamite**. SEE LUNATIC

mere (as in meager) *adj*.: **mingy**. SEE MEAGER

merged (of things that cannot be ...) *adj*.: **immiscible**. SEE INCOMPATIBLE

merited (esp. in reference to a punishment) *adj*.: **condign**. SEE DESERVED

merry (and social) *adj*.: **Anacreontic**. SEE CONVIVIAL
(2) merry *adj*.: **eupeptic**. SEE CHEERFUL
(3) merry *adj*.: **Falstaffian**. SEE JOVIAL
(4) merry *adj*.: **riant**. SEE CHEERFUL

mesmerize (as in bewitch or enchant) *v.t.*: **ensorcell** (or **ensorcel**). SEE ENCHANT

mess (as in disorderly confusion) *n., adj.*: **huggermugger**. SEE CONFUSION

mess around (as in idle or waste time) *v.i.*: **footle** (usu. as in "footle around"). SEE DAWDLE

mess up (esp. a golf shot) *v.t., n.*: **foozle**. SEE BOTCH

messy (as in unkempt or slovenly) *adj*.: **frowzy**. ∎ Beethoven's bad hair just got worse. Scientists analyzed eight strands of the composer's **frowzy** mane and found lead at more than 100 times the norm. Lead poisoning could explain his constant abdominal distress, irritability, and depression and may have led to his death. The lock behind it all is profiled in a new book, Beethoven's Hair. (Author not given, *Transitions*, U.S. News & World Report, 10-30-2000.)
(2) messy (as in disheveled) *adj*.: **blowsy** (or **blowzy**). SEE DISHEVELED

metamorphosis (complete ...) *n*.: **permutation**. SEE TRANSFORMATION

metaphor (misuse or strained use of a word, phrase or ..., sometimes deliberate) *n*.: **catachresis**. SEE MISUSE
(2) metaphor (or figure of speech) *n*.: **trope**. SEE FIGURE OF SPEECH

meteor (exploding ...) *n*.: **bolide**. SEE FIREBALL

methodical (as in logical) *adj*.: **ratiocinative**. SEE LOGICAL

meticulous (as in fastidious) *adj*.: **governessy**. SEE FASTIDIOUS
(2) meticulous (overly ...) *adj*.: **persnickety**. SEE PICKY

metropolis *n*.: **conurbation**. ∎ London, said to be the largest city in Europe, was [in the early 1600's] a vast, sprawling **conurbation** of teeming tenements and slums, as well as palaces and mansions. (Antonia Fraser, *Faith & Treason*, Doubleday [1996], p. 100.)

mettle *n*.: **hardihood**. SEE COURAGE

mezzanine *n*.: **entresol** [French]. ∎ Defining characteristics of this example of Creole-American style include the second-floor balcony with iron railing, and the **entresol**, a half-floor or mezzanine between the first and second floors, usually used for storage. (David Maurer, *Good for What Ails You [New Orleans Pharmacy Museum]*, Colonial Homes, 04-01-1997, p. 76.)

mice (of or relating to ... or rats) *adj*.: **murine**. SEE RODENTS

middle (moving, directed or pulled towards the ...) *adj*.: **centripetal**. SEE CENTER

middle ground *n*.: **tertium quid** [Latin for "third thing"]. ∎ If you want to increase support for a tyrant, bomb his people. It's no skin off his nose. Something must be done about this genocide [in the Balkans]. But Cook and Blair have expressed a false opposition between non-intervention on the one hand, and the "bombing for peace" of a sovereign state on the other, as if there were no **tertium quid**. (Chris Maslanka, *Puzzle Master*, The Independent [London], 03-27-1999.)
(2) middle ground (appropriate ..., as in happy medium) *n*.: **juste milieu** [French]. SEE HAPPY MEDIUM

middle-class (as a group, who is smug, narrow-minded and conformist; also a group who recognizes material success but not artistic values) *n*.: **Babbitry**. ∎ We know no spectacle so ridiculous as the arts establishment in one of its periodic fits of immorality. It sets out boldly to shock the bourgeoisie, but when the bourgeoisie is shocked, [the arts establishment] starts back nervously and babbles about **Babbitry**. ... For years now the arts establishment has repeated mantra-like that the purpose of art is to shock, to disturb, to challenge. (John O'Sullivan, *Philistines at the Gate, [Controversy Over National Endowment for the Arts Funding of Art With Erotic Content]*, National Review, 06-11-1990.)

middleman *n.*: **comprador**. SEE INTERMEDIARY

midget *n.*: **homunculus**. ∎ How irredeemably bad is this latest version of the H. G. Wells novel [The Island of Dr. Moreau]? Start with the scene where Marlon Brando wears an ice bucket on his head for no discernible reason. Move on to the blender-size **homunculus** who accompanies him everywhere. (Ty Burr, *Best & Worst/Video*, Entertainment Weekly, 12-26-1997, p. 164.)

(2) midget *n.*: **hop-o'-my-thumb**. ∎ Joseph and the Amazing Technicolour Dreamcoat — Stephen Gately is [a television personality]. I had only the vaguest idea who this little **hop-o'-my-thumb** was, but ... I found him quite beguiling. ... Gately posed in a variety of shiny outfits and gold pants and looked understandably terrified when Mrs. Potiphar, a giantess, flung one of her great gams over his shoulder. (Author not given, *Theatre: Opening this Week, [Features]*, The Independent Sunday [London], 03-16-2003.)

(3) midget (like a ...) *adj., n.*: **Lilliputian**. SEE TINY

midlife crisis *n.*: **Torschlusspanik** [German]. SEE PANIC

might (as in power) *n.*: **puissance**. SEE POWER

migraine *n.*: **megrims** (plural of **megrim**). SEE HEADACHE

mild (esp. with respect to the wind) *adj.*: **favonian**. ∎ Go! is feeling about as ornery as Donald Rumsfeld as we wait for spring to make a glorious return. After a week of **favonian** breezes, we're having a hard time enduring any air mass under 70 degrees. (Christopher Muther, *Go! Wednesday; Got to Be Real*, The Boston Globe, 04-02-2003.)

mildew (smelling of ...) *adj.*: **fusty**. SEE MUSTY

mildness *n.*: **mansuetude**. SEE GENTLENESS

milieu (as in setting or physical environment) *n.*: **mise en scène** [French; putting on stage]. SEE SETTING

military (or, relating to or suggesting ... life) *adj.*: **martial**. SEE WARLIKE

milk (producing, secreting or conveying) *adj.*: **lactiferous**. ∎ If you're nursing, examine yourself immediately following a feeding, since it's easier to detect lumps when the breasts are empty. Be aware, though, that clogged **lactiferous** ducts can cause masses that feel suspicious, but are nothing to be alarmed about. (Daryn Eller, *Your Health: Your Health*, Parenting, 08-01-1998, p. 45.)

(2) milk (giving ...) *adj.*: **milch** [German]. ∎ He even turned his stylish official colonial residence in New Delhi into the crude dwelling of a prosperous farmer from his home state of Haryana, complete with a string of **milch** cows. ... Irrespective of the hour it was mandatory for anyone visiting [him], including journalists, to drink enormous glasses of milk, thick with cream, in an acknowledgement of his hospitality. (Kuldip Singh, *Obituary: Devi Lal*, Independent, 04-28-2001, p. 7.)

millenium *n.*: **chiliad**. ∎ In a sense, the millennium is Bill Clinton's larger theater; for him there is a balm in the **chiliad**. ... The millennium is a sort of hallucination — the calendar's neverland. ... For three years after this week's Inauguration, Clinton will play variations on the great-expectations theme inherent (however artificially) in time's odometer, the rolling toward three zeroes. (Lance Morrow, *Will the Crescendo Toward 2000 Help Clinton Beat the Second-Term Jinx?* Time, 01-27-1997.)

mimicking (pathological, uncontrollable or a child's ... of another's words) *n.*: **echolalia**. SEE REPEATING

(2) mimicking (pathological or uncontrollable ... of another's actions) *n.*: **echopraxia**. SEE REPEATING

mimicry (of the real world in art or literature) *n.*: **mimesis**. SEE IMITATION

mincing *adj.*: **niminy-piminy**. SEE DAINTY

mind (taking place entirely within the ...) *adj.*: **immanent**. SEE SUBJECTIVE

(2) mind (of, relating to, or understood by the ...) *adj.*: **noetic**. SEE INTELLECT

(3) mind (as a blank before receiving outside information) *n.*: **tabula rasa**. SEE BLANK SLATE

mindless (repetition of ideas which have been drilled into the speaker or which reflect the opinions of the powers-that-be) *v.t., v.i., n.*: **duckspeak**. SEE RECITE

miniature *adj.*: **bantam**. SEE TINY

(2) miniature *adj., n.*: **Lilliputian**. SEE TINY

minimize (attempt to ... seriousness of an offense) *v.t.*: **palliate**. See DOWNPLAY

minister (government by a ... or other clergy members) *n.*: **hierocracy**. See GOVERNMENT

minor (a fuss over a ... matter) *n.*: **foofaraw**. See FUSS
 (2) minor *adj.*: **picayune**. See TRIVIAL
 (3) minor (as in excusable fault, offense or sin) *adj.*: **venial**. See FORGIVABLE

minute (in a ...) *adv.*: **anon**. See MOMENTARILY
 (2) minute (as in, in a ..., as in very shortly) *n.*: **trice** (as in, in a trice). See QUICKLY

miracle (worker) *n.*: **thaumaturgist**. ∎ George Malley is a nice, smiling auto mechanic [who], amid mysterious circumstances, is visited with genius. This has the crowd-pleasing aspects of enabling him to make objects move without touching them. ... This offensive concoction [the movie "Phenomenon"] is well acted ... but it would take a greater **thaumaturgist** than George Malley to make me stomach it. (John Simon, *Lone Star [movie reviews]*, National Review, 07-29-1996, p. 49.)

miracles (study of ...) *n.*: **thaumatology**. ∎ Already built is a half-scale replica of the Eiffel Tower [where you can] look out on the skyline of New York City. Yes, that's a replica of the Statue of Liberty. ... In clear view: pirate ships fighting, multistory lions watching and a pyramid sending a beam which can be seen in outer space. It's enough to prompt you to enroll in a course on **thaumatology**. (Jack Williams, *Forget it, Florida, and Hello, Vegas!* The Boston Herald, 04-16-1999.)

mirror image *n.*: **enantiomorph**. ∎ The d- and l-tartaric acids are **enantiomorphs**; each molecule is asymmetrical and is the mirror image of the other. (Author not given, *Isomer*, The Columbia Encyclopedia, Fifth Edition, 01-01-1993.)

mirthful *adj.*: **eupeptic**. See CHEERFUL
 (2) mirthful *adj.*: **riant**. See CHEERFUL

mirthless (as in person who never laughs) *n.*: **agelast**. See HUMORLESS

misappropriate (as in embezzle) *v.t., v.i.*: **peculate**. See EMBEZZLE

miscellaneous (composed of a group of ... items) *adj.*: **farraginous**. See MIXED

miscellany (as in assortment) *n.*: **farrago**. See ASSORTMENT

(2) miscellany (as in assortment) *n.*: **gallimaufry**. See ASSORTMENT

(3) miscellany (as in assortment) *n.*: **olla podrida** [Spanish]. See ASSORTMENT

(4) miscellany (as in assortment) *n.*: **omnium-gatherum** [Latin]. See ASSORTMENT

(5) miscellany (as in assortment) *n.*: **salmagundi**. See ASSORTMENT

mischief *n.*: **doggery** [i.e. doglike behavior]. ∎ [Jerry Springer] is the closest I've ever seen to a male feminist. No matter what he does after the show (it is rumoured he frequently liaises with guests, especially if they are busty strippers), he is a man absolutely intent on depicting men in all their **doggery**. Especially himself. [When] asked if any of the guests were fake. "No," replied Jerry sadly. "They're all real. I'm the fake." (Emma Forrest, *Iconography: So His Show's Sleazy, But He is a Feminist*, The Guardian [London], 04-06-1998.)
 (2) mischief (as in prank) *n.*: **dido**. See PRANK

mischief-maker *n.*: **scapegrace**. See SCOUNDREL

mischievous *adj.*: **elfin**. ∎ [Filmmaker Ken Russell] and Shirley [his first wife] were this sly, mischievous, way off-centre pair; hippy before hippies, maverick before mavericks. They were **elfin**, the two of them, very much a little republic. (Isabel Lloyd, *How We Met: Melvyn Bragg & Ken Russell*, Independent on Sunday, 01-28-2001, p. 62.)
 (2) mischievous (girl who is high-spirited or boisterous) *n.*: **hoyden**. See TOMBOY

misconception (accepted as fact due to repetition in print) *n.*: **factoid**. See INACCURACY
 (2) misconception (as in delusion held by two closely associated persons) *n.*: **folie à deux** [French]. See DELUSION

misconduct (in public office) *n.*: **malversation**. See WRONGDOING
 (2) misconduct (confession of ...) *n.*: **peccavi**. See CONFESSION

misconstruing (of what you think you heard) *n.*: **mondegreen**. See MISUNDERSTANDING

miser *n.*: **lickpenny**. ∎ In our politically correct, "caring is sharing" times, it takes bravery to be a cheapskate. These daring souls care not about "suggested donation" prices, aren't deterred by indignant looks, and completely ignore righteous huffing. So, you remorse-free **lickpennies**, test drive your miserly ways at these places. (Melanie McFarland, *Hey,*

Cheapskate, Not Even a Donation? The Seattle Times, 06-03-1999, p. G5.)

miserable (esp. as to poverty) *adj.*: **abject**. SEE WRETCHED

miserly *adj.*: **costive**. SEE STINGY
(2) miserly *adj.*: **mingy**. SEE STINGY
(3) miserly *adj.*: **niggardly**. SEE STINGY
(4) miserly *adj.*: **penurious**. SEE STINGY

misery (as in inability to experience pleasure or happiness) *n.*: **anhedonia**. SEE UNHAPPINESS
(2) misery (experience of intense ... , as in suffering) *n.*: **Calvary**. SEE SUFFERING
(3) misery (as in place, condition or society filled with ...; spec., opposite of utopia) *n.*: **dystopia**. SEE HELL
(4) misery (as in place or occasion of great suffering, or hell) *n.*: **Gehenna**. SEE HELL
(5) misery (as in occasion or place of great suffering) *n.*: **Gethsemane**. SEE HELL
(6) misery (as in occasion or place of great suffering) *n.*: **Golgotha**. SEE HELL

misfortune (esp. involving an awkward or embarrassing situation) *n.*: **contretemps**. SEE MISHAP
(2) misfortune *n., adj.*: **hoodoo**. SEE BAD LUCK

mishap (esp. involving an awkward or embarrassing situation) *n.*: **contretemps**. ∎ Another diplomatic **contretemps** flared up when U.S. troops briefly invaded the residence of Nicaragua's Ambassador to Panama Antenor Ferrey, apparently to search for a cache of weapons. They turned up five rifles, which were later returned with an apology. (George J. Church, *Panama — No Place to Run; With Noriega Cornered But Not Caught, Was the Pain of Invasion Worth the Gain?* Time, 01-08-1990, p. 38.)

mishearing (of what you think you heard) *n.*: **mondegreen**. SEE MISUNDERSTANDING

mishmash (as in assortment) *n.*: **farrago**. SEE ASSORTMENT
(2) mishmash (as in assortment) *n.*: **gallimaufry**. SEE ASSORTMENT
(3) mishmash (as in assortment) *n.*: **olla podrida** [Spanish]. SEE ASSORTMENT
(4) mishmash (as in assortment) *n.*: **omnium-gatherum** [Latin]. SEE ASSORTMENT
(5) mishmash (as in assortment) *n.*: **salmagundi**. SEE ASSORTMENT
(6) mishmash (as in assortment) *n.*: **welter**. SEE JUMBLE

misinterpretation (of what you think you heard) *n.*: **mondegreen**. SEE MISUNDERSTANDING

mislead (specious reasoning intended to ... or rationalize) *n.*: **casuistry**. SEE FALLACIOUS
(2) mislead (as in deceive or defraud in the process) *v.t., v.i.*: **cozen**. SEE DEFRAUD
(3) mislead (as in bluff) *v.t.*: **four-flush** (*n.*: **four-flusher**). SEE BLUFF
(4) mislead (as in deceive) *v.t.*: **humbug**. SEE DECEIVE

misleading (appearance of plenty when in fact there is little) *adj.*: **Barmecidal** (esp. as in "Barmecidal feast"). SEE ILLUSION
(2) misleading (story, report or rumor, often deliberately) *n.*: **canard**. SEE HOAX
(3) misleading (speech or writing which is ..., as in evasive) *n.*: **circumlocution**. SEE EVASIVENESS

misremember (as in confusion of one's memory with actual fact) *n.*: **paramnesia**. ∎ What causes déjà vu? Sixteen centuries ago Saint Augustine called this phenomenon false memory. It has also been called **paramnesia**, double perception, and false recognition. Charles Dickens's character David Copperfield called it "the strange feeling to which no one is quite a stranger." (Kaylan Pickford, *I Lost My Daughters to a Cult*, Redbook, 03-01-1995, p. 54.)

misrepresent (as in exaggerate) *v.t.*: **aggrandize**. SEE EXAGGERATE
(2) misrepresent (as in bluff) *v.t.*: **four-flush** (*n.*: **four-flusher**). SEE BLUFF

misrepresentation (deliberate ... or concealment of facts to gain an advantage) *n.*: **subreption**. ∎ [In *Farewell the Peaceful Kingdom: The Seduction and Rape of Canada*, author Joe C.W. Armstrong states:] "Most of our prime ministers have been elected by **subreption** — they gain the job by concealing their true ambitions. ... The citizens continue to be de-democratized by an entrenched autocracy. ... Regardless of which party is in power, change however limited is out of the question." (Barry Eastwood, *Analyzing 30 Years of National Destruction*, Alberta Report/Western Report, 08-14-1995.)

mission (which is fruitless or hopeless) *n.*: **fool's errand**. SEE HOPELESS
(2) mission (to achieve a particular goal or desire) *n.*: **nisus**. SEE GOAL

misspeak (as in a transposition of letters or sounds, which creates a comic effect, usually unintentionally) *n.*: **spoonerism**. SEE BLOOPER

misspelling (use of ... to represent either an uneducated speaker or dialectical or colloquial speech, such as "sez" for "says") *n.*: **eye dialect.** ▪ "Gotcha is not slang," insists Jesse Sheidlower, a senior editor in the reference division of Random House and a slang specialist. "The **eye-dialect** spelling suggests informality, but it's actually standard usage, and wouldn't be entered in any of the slang thesauri." (So how come, Jesse, you can find it in the Random House Historical Dictionary of American Slang? Gotcha!) (William Safire, *On Language; Gotcha, Hobbes,* The New York Times, 04-13-1997.)

mist *n.*: **brume.** SEE FOG

mistake (tragic ..., as in flaw, esp. by a literary character) *n.*: **hamartia.** SEE FLAW

(2) mistake (in writing) *n.*: **lapsus calami** [Latin]. SEE SLIP OF THE PEN

(3) mistake (in speech) *n.*: **lapsus linguae** [Latin]. SEE SLIP OF THE TONGUE

(4) mistake (verbal ... such as a slip of the tongue or malapropism) *n.*: **parapraxis.** SEE BLUNDER

(5) mistake (small or trifling ...) *n.*: **peccadillo.** SEE INFRACTION

(6) mistake (in grammar) *n.*: **solecism.** SEE MISUSE

mistranslation (of what you think you heard) *n.*: **mondegreen.** SEE MISUNDERSTANDING

mistrust (person who has ... for humankind) *n.*: **misanthrope.** ▪ Lofton and Nelson agree with Mancini that mistrust is a fundamental part of [baseball player Albert] Belle's personality. It wasn't always. Growing up in a middle-class section of Shreveport, Belle gave no signs of becoming the public **misanthrope** he is today. (Michael Bamberger, *Baseball: He Thrives on Anger,* Sports Illustrated, 05-06-1996, p. 72.)

misty (and dark and gloomy) *adj.*: **caliginous.** SEE DARK

misunderstanding *n.*: **malentendu** [French]. ▪ [In the movie *Eurotrip*, Scotty] and his friend Cooper ... head to Germany because of an amusing **malentendu.** It seems that Scotty has been e-mailing a German pen pal for years in the belief the pal was a boy named Mike. It turns out that it is someone named Mieke, which is (get this) a German girl's name! (Jay Stone, *Stupid, Vulgar and Proud of It: This Teen Sex Comedy Glories in Bad Taste, Cultural Bigotry and, of Course, Gratuitous Nudity,* Ottawa Citizen, 02-20-2004.)

(2) misunderstanding (of what you think you

heard) *n.*: **mondegreen** [derives from Sylvia Wright, who as a child heard the Scottish ballad "The Bonny Earl of Murray" and had believed that one stanza went: "Ye Highlands and Ye Lowlands, Oh where hae you been? They hae slay the Earl of Murray, And Lady Mondegreen." Wright thought that Lady Mondegreen had been killed, but actually they slayed the Earl of Murray and "laid him on the green"]. ▪ It's easy to commit a **mondegreen.** You hear Glen Campbell sing, "Rhinestone Cowboy" and you think he's saying "Limestone Cowboy." ... Or you think the song "Guantanamera" is about a "One Ton Tomato."... [Or that Paul Simon is singing:] "When I think back on all the crafts [as opposed to crap] I learned in high school." (David Chartrand, *Vote for Me If You Want Red Cologne!* The Kansas City Star, 01-25-2004.)

misuse (or strained use of words or phrases, sometimes deliberate) *n.*: **catachresis.** ▪ Cat scan: They call their party The Furball. And leading the band is a lady called Lily Wilde. This might lure a lesser columnist into wordplay, but — not willing to risk an outbreak of **catachresis** — I'm just going to say that the Feral Cat Coalition of Oregon will be feline groovy June 4 at the World Forestry Center. (Jonathan Nicholas, *Californians, Catastrophes and the Most Musselcular Man in Portland,* The Oregonian, 05-10-1999, p. E1.)

(2) misuse (of word or phrase in grammar) *n.*: **solecism.** ▪ "If we pass this all-encompassing tax-reform bill," he says, "it will be the hallmark of my career." He probably means to say capstone. **Solecisms** and malapropisms are a hallmark of Rostenkowski's 28 years in Congress. (Montgomery Brower, *Illinois Rep. Dan Rostenkowski Cut the Deals in Congress That May Cut Your Taxes,* People, 09-01-1986, p. 38.)

(3) misuse (as in embezzle) *v.i.*: **defalcate.** SEE EMBEZZLE

(4) misuse (as in embezzle) *v.t., v.i.*: **peculate.** SEE EMBEZZLE

(5) misuse (of words or of language) *n.*: **verbicide.** SEE DISTORTION

mix *v.t.*: **amalgamate.** SEE COMBINE

(2) mix (as in bring together) *v.t.*: **conflate.** SEE COMBINE

(3) mix (as in blend) *v.t., v.i.*: **inosculate.** SEE BLEND

mixed (composed of a ... group of items) *adj.*: **farraginous.** ▪ [The] linguine alla grana (whole wheat pasta) was a disaster, a **farraginous** mound with bits of filet mignon and mushrooms in a fatty brown sauce. (M.H. Reed, *Dining Out; Where the Appetizers Take Center Stage*, The New York Times, 11-05-1995, p. 19.)

(2) mixed (of things that cannot be ...) *adj.*: **immiscible**. SEE INCOMPATIBLE

mixed-up (esp. used of a person, as in ... and stupid) *adj.*: **addlepated**. SEE CONFUSED

mixture (esp. involving dissimilar elements) *adj.*: **admixture**. ∎ The keys to certain attributes of [George W. Bush's] character — his irreverence, his disdain for "arrogant liberal intellectuals," his complex **admixture** of superficiality and self-discipline — lie half-hidden in Bush's formative years, in his schooling and especially in his loving but demanding relationship with his parents. (Evan Thomas, *A Son's Restless Journey*, Newsweek, 08-07-2000, p. 32.)

(2) mixture (of fruits or vegetables) *n.*: **macédoine** [French]. ∎ At Chef Allen's in North Miami Beach, Allen Susser's most popular dishes include rock-shrimp hash topped by a mustardy sabayon sauce, followed perhaps by seared citrus-crusted yellowfin tuna with a **macédoine** of papaya, mango and yellow pepper. (Cathy Booth, *Food: A Taste of Miami's New Vice*, Time, 08-19-1991, p. 60.)

(3) mixture (as in assortment) *n.*: **farrago**. SEE ASSORTMENT

(4) mixture *n.*: **gallimaufry**. SEE ASSORTMENT

(5) mixture (of two or more languages) *adj.*: **macaronic**. SEE LANGUAGES

(6) mixture *n.*: **olla podrida** [Spanish]. SEE ASSORTMENT

(7) mixture *n.*: **omnium-gatherum** [Latin]. SEE ASSORTMENT

(8) mixture (as in assortment) *n.*: **salmagundi**. SEE ASSORTMENT

mob (government by the ...) *n.*: **mobocracy**. SEE GOVERNMENT

(2) mob (government by the ...) *n.*: **ochlocracy**. SEE GOVERNMENT

mock (esp. through the use of satire) *v.t.*: **pasquinade**. SEE SATIRIZE

model (original ... or example) *n.*: **archetype**. ∎ Slow and stagy, the [1993 remake of the movie "Frankenstein"] also suffers the fate that greets singers interpreting Beatles tunes: The original version with Boris Karloff is such an indelible **archetype** that any imitation is doomed. (David Hiltbrand, *Picks & Pans: Tube*, People, 06-14-1993, p. 13.)

(2) model (of an intended larger work such as a building) *n.*: **maquette**. ∎ Before Graham started on [his 24-foot bronze sculpture called "Monument to Joe Louis"], he submitted a **maquette**, a two-foot-high model of the larger work, for approval. (Donald J. Barr, *From the Publisher*, Sports Illustrated, 10-27-1986, p. 4.)

(3) model (example which serves as a ...) *n.*: **paradigm**. ∎ "School-to-Work" is bureaucratic jargon for imposing a new **paradigm** on public schools that de-emphasizes traditional academic studies and replaces them with vocational-technical (vo-tech) courses for all students. (Phyllis Schlafly, *Education Policy Competition*, The Washington Times, 12-22-2000, p. A20.)

(4) model (as in example) *n.*: **exemplum**. SEE EXAMPLE

moderate (as in not indulgent) *adj.*: **abstemious**. SEE RESTRAINED

moderation *n.*: **sophrosyne**. ∎ [In ancient Greece, the artists and the state] were bound together by a common mythology and shared archetypes, a sense of belonging. While they honored the individual, they also saw the value of holding individualism in some kind of check. Their watchword was **sophrosyne**: moderation in all things. (J. Carter Brown [interviewee], *The Arts and Liberation*, U.S. News & World Report, 11-30-1992.)

(2) moderation (appropriate ..., as in happy medium) *n.*: **juste milieu** [French]. SEE HAPPY MEDIUM

modern (as in of recent origin) *adj.*: **neoteric**. SEE RECENT

modernization (of an organization to meet contemporary conditions, esp. as proposed by Pope John XXIII with respect to the Catholic church after Vatican II) *n.*: **aggiornamento** [Italian]. SEE UPDATING

modesty *n.*: **pudency**. ∎ "The most important thing is the ship, and the ship needed someone at the helm who knew better about the operational aspects of getting a business to grow than me," says Fields with typical **pudency**. (Melanie Warner, *The New Black Power/Companies: A Singular Visionary: After Bumping Heads With One of the Software Industry's Bad Boys, Michael Fields Explored His Options — $1 Million of Them — and Scored*, Fortune, 08-04-1997, p. 59.)

moisten (flax to separate fibers) *v.t.*: **ret**. ∎ Water **retting**, primarily used by the Belgians and Irish, **rets** the fibers by leaving them in running water and produces a classic, pale-yellow linen. (Tracy A. Keegan, *Flaxen Fantasy: The History of Linen*, Colonial Homes, 08-01-1996, p. 62.)

moistener *n., adj.*: **humectant**. ▪ Tropical Fruit Masque/Smooths wrinkles, refreshes your skin. ... Each [piece of fruit] contains a natural enzyme (bromelain in pineapple and papain in papaya) that sloughs off dead skin cells. When combined with honey, a natural **humectant** that hydrates your skin, the result is a soft, luminescent complexion. (Paula Hunt, *Look Younger Naturally!* Prevention, 06-01-1999, p. 128.)

mold (of body part often used in criminal investigation or disaster relief) *n.*: **moulange**. ▪ In some cases a husband would punish his wife for even suspected infidelities by slicing off her nose. ... [My father was a plastic surgeon who cared for these victims.] Sometimes, using clay, he molded a nose directly on a woman's face, to see what shape might look good on her, or he made a mold of her face. Once, he tried a plastic **moulage** on my brother before applying it to a patient. (Mary Blocksma, *My Father and Other Good Guys: Plastic Surgeons Abroad [Practice in Third World Countries]*, Saturday Evening Post, 03-01-1986.)

molded (capable of being ..., such as with plastic, clay or earth) *adj.*: **fictile**. ▪ Qahtan Al Amin's work is another creative approach towards artistic expression. He has used **fictile** material to form dimensional shapes where he carved various drawings and symbols as a manifestation of the pastoral life in Iraq. (Rasheed Al Roussan, *"Mercury 20" — The Quest for Identity*, The Star [Jordan], 03-04-1999.)

moldy (as in musty) *adj.*: **fusty**. SEE MUSTY

mollify *v.t.*: **dulcify**. SEE APPEASE
(2) **mollify** (as in placate) *v.t.*: **propitiate**. SEE PLACATE

mollifying (as in peacemaking) *adj.*: **irenic**. SEE PEACEMAKING

moment (as in, in a ..., as in very shortly) *n.*: **trice** (as in, in a trice). SEE QUICKLY

momentarily *adv.*: **anon**. ▪ Most campuses are awash with talk about things racial (and sexual, and other categories indispensable for the practice of identity politics, more about which **anon**). (George F. Will, *Focus on Race Distracts Nation From Real Problem*, Minneapolis Star Tribune, 06-20-1997, p. 23A.)

momentary *adj.*: **fugacious**. SEE FLEETING

momentous (of an event or period which is ...) *adj.*: **epochal**. ▪ Is the hunger for "Star Wars" so insatiable that the audience won't notice that this **epochal** event [Star Wars: Episode I, The Phantom Menace] is actually a little ... dull? (David Ansen, *Star Wars: The Phantom Movie*, Newsweek, 05-17-1999, p. 56.)

monarch (who holds great power or sway) *n.*: **potentate**. SEE RULER

monetary (of or relating to ... gain) *adj.*: **chrematistic**. ▪ Work is still seen as productive transformation of nature, but with the conceptual divorce of production and consumption, all work is seen as **chrematistic** accumulation. (John Dupre, *A Brief History of Work*, Journal of Economic Issues, 06-01-1996, p. 553.)

(2) **monetary** *adj.*: **pecuniary**. ▪ Obits. Write your own! Tony O'Brien did: ... Preceded in death by most of the people who have ever lived. Known far and wide as a charitable man, Mr. O'Brien made his **pecuniary** contributions mainly to obscure organizations such as the IRS, of Washington, D.C, and Guido's Sports Parlor, located in the Graft Exchange Building in northeast Minneapolis. (James Lileks, *Change Isn't in the Wind — It's in the Pants / Those Coins Jingling in Men's Pockets Are All Part of a Long, Silly Tradition*, Minneapolis Star Tribune, 09-28-1997, p. 3B.)

money (source of ...) *n.*: **Golconda**. SEE WEALTH
(2) **money** (devotion to the pursuit of ...) *n.*: **mammonism**. SEE WEALTH
(3) **money** (as in wealth) *n.*: **pelf**. SEE WEALTH

moneylender (who charges high interest) *n.*: **shylock**. SEE LENDER

monk (person who lives as if a ..., esp. for spiritual improvement) *n., adj.*: **ascetic**. SEE AUSTERITY

monkey (move by swinging with arms, like a ...) *v.i.*: **brachiate**. SEE SWING
(2) **monkey** (of, relating to, or resembling) *adj.*: **simian**. SEE APE

monologue (as in lengthy speech) *n.*: **peroration**. ▪ The monologues went on and on, taking on a form, or formlessness, of their own, sometimes almost crowding out the music. On the last night he delivered what amounted to a kind of extended **peroration**, with Priscilla and Lisa Marie sitting with Sheila in the booth. (Peter Guralnick, *Careless Love: The Unmaking of Elvis Presley*, Little Brown [1999], p. 541.)

monotonous (speaker or writer, as in one who is dull and boring) *n*.: **dryasdust**. SEE BORING
(2) monotonous (as in uninteresting or dull) *adj*.: **jejune**. SEE UNINTERESTING

monument (honoring a dead person buried elsewhere) *n*.: **cenotaph**. ∎ Congressional Cemetery also features great diversity in stone styles. Its name, incidentally, comes from the **cenotaphs**, sandstone monuments erected to memorialize senators and members of Congress buried elsewhere. (Lisa Rauschart, *Now the Memorials are in Neighborhoods*, The Washington Times, 05-25-2001, p. G2.)

mood (of an era) *n*.: **zeitgeist**. SEE SPIRIT

moody (as in sullen or morose) *adj*.: **saturnine**. SEE SULLEN

mope (as in pout) *n*.: **moue** [French]. SEE POUT

moral (intellectual and/or cultural spirit of an era) *n*.: **zeitgeist**. SEE SPIRIT

moralistic (hypocritically ...) *adj*.: **Pecksniffian**. SEE SELF-RIGHTEOUS
(2) moralistic (and self-righteous) *adj*.: **Pharisaical**. SEE SELF-RIGHTEOUS

morality (of questionable ...) *adj*.: **louche**. SEE QUESTIONABLE
(2) morality (as in integrity) *n*.: **probity**. SEE INTEGRITY

moralizing (giving to ..., by using aphorisms and maxims) *adj*.: **sententious**. SEE APHORISTIC

morals (deciding right and wrong by applying ...) *n*.: **casuistry**. SEE ETHICS
(2) morals (study of) *n*.: **deontology**. SEE ETHICS

moreover *adv*.: **withal**. ∎ [Joe DiMaggio] excelled and continued to excel, against injury and age, against the mounting "natural" odds. He exceeded, **withal**, the cruelest expectations: He was expected to lead and to win — and he did. (Richard Ben Cramer, *The DiMaggio Nobody Knew*, Newsweek, 03-22-1999, p. 52.)

morning (of or relating to ...) *adj*.: **matinal**. ∎ [As a gesture of goodwill, I decided to deliver Krispy Kreme doughnuts to protesters in Lafayette Square.] The person I found protesting in Lafayette Square shortly after daybreak was a relatively handsome bearded man. ... "How do you feel about some Krispy Kremes this morning?" I asked. ... The beneficiary of my **matinal** munificence now identified himself as Troy. (Joe Queenan, *My Goodness*, Hyperion [2000], p. 108.)
(2) morning (of or relating to ...) *adj*.: **matutinal**. ∎ Margaret Roythorne's **matutinal** stroll through her local park in Hastings turned to nightmare when her tiny Cairn terrier Flynn dashed out from some bushes and was sucked up and killed by a mobile "pooper-scooper." (Paul Sieveking, *It Was a Very Bad Year...*, Independent, 12-31-1994, p. 38.)

moron (as in one mentally deficient from birth) *n*.: **ament**. [Note: the writer of the example uses an adjectival version of the word ("amentic") which does not appear in dictionaries (and in fact was unnecessary for the writer's purpose anyway), although the meaning is clear. However the adjectival form of "moron" and its synonyms "imbecile" and "idiot" do end in "ic."] ∎ In Ottawa, Canada, a close aide of Prime Minister Jean Chretien, Francoise Ducros, paid dearly for her ... abusiveness: her job. When President Bush called on member states to increase defense spending at the NATO summit in Prague, Francoise muttered within earshot of reporters: "What a moron." [She] should have said ... "**amentic**" instead. (Author not given, *Casualties in the War on Terror [Opinion & Editorial]*, Manila Bulletin, 12-16-2002.)
(2) moron *n*.: **jobbernowl** [British]. SEE IDIOT
(3) moron *n*.: **mooncalf**. SEE FOOL

morose (as in person who never laughs) *n*.: **agelast**. SEE HUMORLESS
(2) morose *adj*.: **saturnine**. SEE SULLEN

mortality (object[s] which remind[s] of our ...) *n*.: **memento mori** [Latin]. ∎ [T]he show [of Paul Cezanne's work] includes dozens of lesser-known works in less familiar genres: portraits, interiors, tableaux of card players, and perhaps most unexpected, several paintings of skulls, **memento mori** that he composed in the decade preceding his own death, in 1906. (Jim Lewis, *Cezanne*, Harper's Bazaar, 03-01-1996, p. 334.)

mother (biological ... or father) *n*.: **genitor**. SEE PARENT
(2) mother (who is head of a household) *n*.: **mater familias** [Latin]. SEE HEAD OF HOUSEHOLD
(3) mother (of or derived from name of ... or maternal ancestor) *adj*.: **matronymic**. SEE MATERNAL
(4) mother (attitude or policy which encourages becoming a ...) *n*.: **pronatalism**. SEE CHILDBEARING

motion (of, relating to or produced by) *adj.*: **kinetic**. ∎ The **kinetic** art movement ... began around 1914 — when artists felt the urge to incorporate the illusion, and ultimately the reality, of motion into their work. (Author not given, *The Biology of Art*, The Economist, 04-03-1999.)

motionless (as in not moving or temporarily inactive) *adj.*: **quiescent**. SEE INACTIVE

(2) motionless *adj.*: **torpid**. SEE LETHARGIC

motivation (mental process marked by ... to do something) *n.*: **conation**. SEE DETERMINATION

motive (hidden or ulterior ...) *n.*: **arriere-pensee** (or **arrière-pensée**) [French. This derives from the French for "behind" (or back) plus "thought." It is sometimes used in the sense of having mental reservations about something and sometimes in the sense of having a hidden or ulterior motive, as in the example given here.] ∎ The vast majority of French men and women, including the less viscerally anti-American, supported President Jacques Chirac's opposition to the Iraq war. But so did [Tour de France favorite, American Lance] Armstrong. ... "I'm no fan of war," he said. ... It would be unkind to suspect any **arriere-pensee** — but he might have had an inkling that his fifth appearance on the winner's podium would be sticky enough this year without any Stars-and-Stripes triumphalism. (Geoffrey Wheatcroft, *Lance Armstrong: The Texan Rider's Four Consecutive Victories Against All Odds in the Tour De France: [But] He Still Has to Capture the Hearts of the French*, Financial Times [London], 07-26-2003, p. 13.)

mottled *adj.*: **dappled**. SEE SPOTTED

motto (at the start of a literary piece setting forth a theme or message) *n.*: **epigraph**. SEE QUOTATION

(2) motto (pithy ...) *n.*: **gnome** (*adj*: **gnomic**). SEE CATCHPHRASE

(3) motto *n.*: **shibboleth**. SEE CATCHWORD

mound *n.*: **cumulus**. SEE HEAP

mountain (as in heap or pile) *n.*: **cumulus**. SEE HEAP

mournful (sounds) *adj.*: **plangent**. ∎ Her songs catalog every sin a man can commit, every pain a woman can bear. If you turn on the radio and hear a strong heart breaking, chances are it's the one in that **plangent** [Patty] Loveless voice. (Richard Corliss, *The Arts/Music: She Can Handle the Truth: In Her Gorgeous, Pulverizing New Album, Country Torch*

Artist Patty Loveless Sings About the Aftershock of Betrayal, Time, 03-11-1996, p. 71.)

(2) mournful (often regarding something gone) *adj.*: **elegiac**. SEE SORROWFUL

(3) mournful *adj.*: **tristful**. SEE SAD

mournfulness *n.*: **dolor** (*adj.*: **dolorous**). SEE SADNESS

mourning (poem or song of ... esp. for a dead person) *n.*: **threnody**. SEE REQUIEM

mouth (or jaws or stomach of a carniverous animal) *n.*: **maw**. ∎ All in a day's work for the most famous alligator wrestler in America. Kenny Cypress likes being famous, even if it came at the expense of half his head of hair, a trip to the hospital, a fractured jaw and 30 unpleasant seconds with his head stuck in the **maw** of one of the creatures he regularly plays with. (Mike Williams, *Crazy About Gators: Wrestlemania*, The Atlanta Journal and Constitution, 03-22-1998, p. M3.)

move (swiftly and easily, used esp. of clouds) *v.i.*: **scud**. ∎ It was windy. Thunderclouds **scudded** by overhead, and hawks swooped and circled. (Ellen Ficklen, *An Unexpected Kind of Family Foresight*, Newsweek, 03-25-2002.)

(2) move (able to ... freely in a given environment; used of species) *adj.*: **vagile**. ∎ [Two experts] propose that most families of birds common to the two continents arrived in South America by long-distance dispersal. According to [two other experts], less **vagile** mammals, such as primates and caviomorph rodents, likewise arrived considerably after the separation, in these cases via island hopping. (Robert A. Voeks, *Biological Relationships Between Africa and South America*, The Geographical Review, 01-01-1995, p. 115.)

(3) move (as in course of action) *n.*: **démarche** [French]. SEE COURSE OF ACTION

(4) move (heavily or clumsily) *v.i.*: **galumph**. SEE TROMP

movement (for an idea or principle) *n.*: **jihad**. SEE CRUSADE

(2) movement (of, relating to or produced by) *adj.*: **kinetic**. SEE MOTION

movie (lover) *n.*: **cineaste**. ∎ Quinlan's updated guide to the stars is a treasure chest for anyone who loves movies — the experienced viewer and the budding **cineaste** alike. (Dan Kincaid, *Starring Lineup: "Ultimate" Bios for Movie Lovers*, The Arizona Republic, 01-21-2001, p. J4.)

(2) movie (lover) *n.*: **cinephile**. ∎ A quiet **cinephile** meets a smart-mouthed party girl in a genial comic valentine from Ireland. ... The introverted hero of "When Brendan Met Trudy" is not merely an obsessive movie nerd, he seems particularly enamored of films, such as "Sunset Boulevard" and "Breathless," whose chief reference point are other movies. (Jan Stuart, *This Time, Reel Love Conquers All*, Newsday, 03-08-2001, p. B6.)

moving (about) *adj.*: **ambulant** (*v.i.*: **ambulate**, *adj.*: **ambulatory**). ∎ Thinly clad **ambulant** hospital patients shelter under scant eaves in winter on a rainy day [to smoke]. (Author not given, *Tunnel Vision*, Waikato Times [New Zealand], 05-25-2000, p. 6.)

(2) moving (with soles of feet entirely on the ground, as humans and bears do) *adj.*: **plantigrade**. SEE WALKING

moving force *n.*: **primum mobile** [Latin]. SEE PRIME MOVER

much (too ..., as in excessive) *adj.*: **de trop** [French]. SEE EXCESSIVE

mud (deposited from flowing water on a riverbank) *n.*: **alluvium**. ∎ The resulting tidal drop, at times approaching 25 feet, exposes hundreds of acres of mud flats: the foreshore of the Thames. In that unassuming mud lies treasure. ... **Alluvium** beachcombers, whether dedicated scholars or afternoon idlers, are called "mudlarks" — persons who grub in the mud. (John J. Ronan, *Down & Dirty: When the Tide's Away, Treasure Hunters Scour Thames Banks at London*, The Dallas Morning News, 01-09-2000, p. 1G.)

(2) mud (soil with or cause to sink into ...) *v.t.*: **bemire**. ∎ On the 4th of July, seas started to moderate and by 6 July they were calm, but the heavens were not. "The second week of occupation brought torrential downpours that **bemired** virtually all mobile equipment, rendering doubly difficult the task of unloading the landing craft as they beached." (George C. Dyer, *The Amphibians Came to Conquer*, U.S. History, 09-01-1990.)

(3) mud (prepared for therapeutic purposes) *n.*: **peloid**. ∎ A number of thermal muds can offer therapeutic benefits ... but only the **peloid** variety employ the particular ripening process which allows them to be used in home treatments. (Dr. Pierfrancesco Morganti, *Glorious Mud [Therapeutic Use of Thermal Muds]*, Soap Perfumery & Cosmetics, 06-01-1998, p. 56.)

muddle *v.t.*: **befog**. ∎ And it is clear that [the debate over tax cuts] is going to be politics of a broader band than we are accustomed to, which will help clarify things, which is good. Without such clarification, the tax debate gets **befogged** by claims about lock boxes, the reliability of 10-year forecasts, [and] goody-two-shoes bidding wars about who is more "fiscally responsible." (Ben J. Wattenberg, *Defining the Stakes*, The Washington Times, 03-01-2001, p. A16.)

(2) muddle (as in disorderly confusion) *n., adj.*: **hugger-mugger**. SEE CONFUSION

muddled (esp. used of a person, as in ... and stupid) *adj.*: **addlepated**. SEE CONFUSED

muddy *adj.*: **turbid**. ∎ The influx of sediment from rain or swollen streams can make water so **turbid** you can't see your lure, even if it's just inches below the surface. (Homer Circle, *Muddy Waters*, Sports Afield, 04-01-1995, p. 53.)

(2) muddy (as in swampy) *adj.*: **paludal**. SEE SWAMPY

mudslide (or landslide from a volcano) *n.*: **lahar**. SEE LANDSLIDE AND VOLCANO

mull (over something, often used as a directive, as in "Consider this.") *v.t.*: **perpend**. SEE CONSIDER

multicolored *n.*: **polychromatic**. ∎ Here are some of the more glaring design problems: ... Too many colors, or colors that clash. Like an excess of materials, too many colors can spoil the look of a house. ... Making a house monochromatic may not be desirable, but making it overly **polychromatic** is equally undesirable. (Roger K. Lewis, *Blossoming Trees Can Hide a Multitude of "Grammatical Errors" in Design*, The Washington Post, 04-07-2001, p. H1.)

(2) multicolored (esp. in an iridescent way) *adj.*: **opalescent**. SEE IRIDESCENT

multifaceted (as in two-faced) *adj.*: **Janus-faced**. SEE TWO-FACED

(2) multifacted *adj.*: **multifarious**. SEE VERSATILE

(3) multifaceted (often used of a performer or artist) *adj.*: **protean**. SEE VERSATILE

multilingual (as in speaking or writing in many different languages) *adj.*: **polyglot**. ∎ Passports were essential for traveling Communist agents and American passports were preferred above all others because anyone, even non-English speakers, could travel on them without arousing suspicion, thanks to the country's vast **polyglot** population, with its many immigrants. (Sam Tanenhaus, *Whittaker Chambers*, Random House [1997], p. 99.)

multiple (and varied) *adj.*: **manifold**. SEE NUMEROUS

multitude (of people) *n.*: **ruck**. ∎ He might have watched a game show on television, read a couple of chapters in a romance novel by Robert James Waller, and skimmed an issue of "People" to remind himself of those things that the desperate **ruck** of humanity uses to anesthetize itself against the awareness of its true animal nature and the inevitability of death. (Dean Koontz, *Intensity*, Knopf [1995], p. 207.)

mundane *adj.*: **quotidian**. ∎ Fed up with special effects, mega-stars and simulation, audiences seem to have turned to so-called reality. Why are we so fascinated by this phenomenon that alternately, and sometimes even simultaneously, exposes the tediously **quotidian** and threatens the sanctity of privacy? (Marshall Blonsky, *"Real" Has Appeal But It's Not Reality; What We See in Voyeur TV*, The Washington Post, 07-30-2000, p. B4.)
(2) mundane (as in routine or mechanical) *adj.*: **banausic**. SEE ROUTINE
(3) mundane (as in uninteresting or dull) *adj.*: **jejune**. SEE UNINTERESTING
(4) mundane *adj.*: **sublunary**. SEE EARTHLY

murder (of one's brother or sister) *n.*: **fratricide**. ∎ [T]he filmed-in-Hamilton drama profiles the turbulent lives of Jim and Artie Mitchell, the San Francisco siblings who shot the breakthrough XXX-rated classic Behind the Green Door in 1971. The Mitchells' quick wealth and subsequent descent into a world of drugs, sex and booze ended in **fratricide**. (Author not given, *Entertainment Buzz*, The London Free Press, 06-29-2000, p. C2.)
(2) murder (mass ... of unresisting persons) *n.*: **battue** [French]. SEE KILLING
(3) murder (by strangling or cutting the throat) *v.t.*: **garrote**. SEE STRANGLE
(4) murder (large-scale ... or sacrifice) *n.*: **hecatomb**. SEE SLAUGHTER
(5) murder (by strangling or cutting the throat) *v.t.*: **jugulate**. SEE STRANGLE
(6) murder (of one's mother) *n.*: **matricide**. SEE KILLING
(7) murder (of parent or close relative) *n.*: **parricide**. SEE KILLING
(8) murder (of one's father) *n.*: **patricide**. SEE KILLING
(9) murder (of a king) *n.*: **regicide**. SEE KILLING

(10) murder (of wife by her husband) *adj.*: **uxoricide**. SEE KILLING

murderer (of one wife after another) *n.*: **bluebeard** (or **Bluebeard**). ∎ Henri Verdoux is a contemporary **Bluebeard** who makes a career out of marrying wealthy women and then murdering them for their fortunes. Monsieur Verdoux is Chaplin's most controversial film, as well as one of his personal favorites. (Author not given, *Monsieur Verdoux*, Magill's Survey of Cinema, 06-15-1995.)

murmured (said in ... tones, not to be overheard) *adv.*, *adj.*: **sotto voce**. SEE WHISPERED

murmuring (as in to make a soft rustling sound) *v.i.*: **soughing**. SEE RUSTLING
(2) murmuring (or whispering sound) *n.*: **susurrous**. SEE WHISPERING

muscle (loss resulting from chronic disease) *n.*: **cachexia**. SEE WASTING

muscle tone (loss of ... due to extreme emotional stimulus) *n.*: **cataplexy**. ∎ "The patient with this symptom may fall face forward into his soup," McCutcheon said. "This is something over which he has little control. **Cataplexy** is very disabling and very embarrassing." (Madelyn Birdzell, *New Clue, New Treatment for Narcolepsy; Chronic Sleep Disorder Can Be Terrifying and Dangerous*, The Washington Post, 08-31-1999, p. Z06.)

muscles (loss of coordination of) *n.*: **ataxia**. ∎ She was diagnosed with a form of hereditary **ataxia**, a neuromuscular disease. By her mid-20s, she no longer had enough control over her throat muscles to continue singing. (Heidi Mulik, *An Essay on Familial Discovery; Winner Learns Mom's History*, The Washington Times, 03-03-2001, p. B1.)
(2) muscles (weakness or fatigue in) *n.*: **myasthenia** (or **myasthenia gravis**). SEE FATIGUE

muscular (having a ... body build) *adj.*: **mesomorphic**. ∎ The cartoonist, as is so often the case, captured the point of India testing its nuclear bomb. Ann Telnaes, published in Newsday last week, depicted a bespectacled Indian with atomic biceps and **mesomorphic** upper body attached to a frail torso and scrawny legs. (Les Payne, *From the Begging Bowl to the Big Time*, Newsday, 05-17-1998, p. B6.)

mush (as in excessive or contrived sentimentality) *n.*: **bathos**. SEE SENTIMENTALITY

mushy *adj.*: **bathetic**. SEE SENTIMENTAL

(2) musty *adj.*: **fusty**. ∎ Like a homeowner airing out a **fusty** basement, Huntington officials recently made a deliberate effort to open the town's timid, slow and dilatory planning procedures to new ideas and outside advice. (Author not given, *Editorial/Lesson for Huntington and LI: Fight NIMBYitis*, Newsday, 06-09-1998, p. A32.)

mute (lit. loss of voice due to disease, injury or psychological causes) *n.*: **aphonia**. See LARYNGITIS

muttered (said in ... tones, not to be overheard) *adv.*, *adj.*: **sotto voce**. See WHISPERED

mysterious (as in difficult to fathom through investigation or scrutiny) *adj.*: **inscrutable**. ∎ A lifeguard sat on his chair, surveying the bathers **inscrutably** from behind his dark glasses. (Anne Tyler, *Ladder of Years*, Knopf [1995], p. 75.)

(2) mysterious (as in eerie) *adj.*: **eldritch**. See EERIE

mysterious (or cryptic or ambiguous) *adj.*: **sybilline** (or **sibylline**; often cap.). See CRYPTIC

mystical (as in supernatural) *adj.*: **numinous**. See SUPERNATURAL

N

nabbed (as in ... in the act, esp. of committing an offense or a sexual act) *adv.*: **in flagrante delicto**. See IN THE ACT

nag *v.t.*: **chivvy**. See PESTER

(2) nag (female ..., as in shrew) *n.*: **harridan**. See SHREW

(3) nag (female ..., as in shrew) *n.*: **termagant**. See SHREW

(4) nag (female ..., as in shrew) *n.*: **virago**. See SHREW

(5) nag (female ..., as in shrew) *n.*: **vixen**. See SHREW

(6) nag (as in shrew) *n.*: **Xanthippe**. See SHREW

naive (as in guileless) *n.*: **artless**. See GUILELESS

(2) naive (false showing of ... behavior) *adj.*: **faux-naif** [French]. See DISINGENUOUS

name (of a person well-suited to its owner) *n.*: **aptronym**. ∎ Viewers apparently haven't minded that they already knew the ending [to the World Series of Poker]. The well-publicized competition, held in May, was won by Tennessee amateur Chris Moneymaker (talk about **aptronyms**!), whose only previous poker tournaments were on the Internet. (Jack Broom, *A Sure Bet: Poker Is Hot, Televised Games Spur Local Players to Up the Ante*, The Seattle Times, 09-14-2003.)

(2) name (having the same ..., or same sounding ...) *adj.*: **homonymous**. ∎ Their **homonymous** designs to the contrary, Ralph Lauren, Gloria Vanderbilt and Calvin Klein aren't Dr. Ruth Kavenoff's competition. They make jeans; she makes genes. Well, sort of. [She makes clothing] decorated with stunning copies of magnified pictures of chromosomes, genes and RNA and DNA molecules from the common intestinal bacteria called E. coli. (Author not given, *Style: Ruth Kavenoff Liked What She Saw in Her Microscope, So She's Putting Genes and Germs on Her T-shirts*, People, 11-09-1987, p. 133.)

(3) name (of a ... or term consisting of one word) *adj.*: **monomial**. ∎ The attractive cast also includes the **monomial** Polish actress Tess, as a ski-patrol exchange student. (Ralph Novak, *Ski Patrol [Movie Reviews]*, People Weekly, 02-05-1990.)

(4) name (or term consisting of one word) *n.*: **mononym**. ▪ No one else projects romantic anguish amid such lush upholstery as Seal. Like Sade, another celebrated English **mononym**, he has become a global soul-soother by evoking not ache's desolation but its multi-hued cornucopia of emotion, its limitless swank. (Steve Dollar, *Weekend at Home: Music: Mini Reviews*, The Atlanta Constitution, 11-19-1998.)

(5) name (of, relating to or explaining a ...) *adj.*: **onomastic**. ▪ The greengage's **onomastic** originator was Sir William Gage, who in 1725 gave his name to a newly imported yellow-green plum. He also marketed the blue gage and the purple gage, but those names did not survive. (Christopher Howse, *Comment: Nice Name, Pity About the Image*, The Sunday Telegraph, 09-05-1999, p. 31.)

(6) name (last ...) *n.*: **cognomen**. SEE SURNAME

nameless (as in anonymous) *adj.*: **innominate**. SEE ANONYMOUS

namely *adv.*: **scilicet**. ▪ ["Millenium"] was the M-word, that was. Y1K has gone. Let her go. I do not care if this year I have to read "millennium" as often as the word occurs in the Bible. **Scilicet**, NEVER. (Philip Howard, *Philip Howard Column*, The Times [London], 01-07-2000.)

(2) namely *adv.*: **videlicet**. ▪ PRIVATE PROPERTY. No skateboarding. No bicycling. No loitering. There is a certain kind of person to which a sign like that is directed, **videlicet**, [14 year-old] Cliff Howard, who is mounted on a $1,300 blue BMX bicycle and who passes the sign going maybe 25 mph. His bike is not equipped with brakes, nor is his skull with a helmet, and he is a few moments away from a crash. (*Skidding on the Edge of Injury and Trouble*, Milwaukee Journal Sentinel, 05-10-2002, p. 2B.)

napkins (linen ...) *n.*: **napery**. SEE LINEN

narcotic (as in something which induces forgetfulness or oblivion of pain, suffering or sorrow) *n.*: **nepenthe**. ▪ "If suffering has no value, Jesus wasted all his pain and agony," wrote Gerald W. Potkay, suggesting that Dr. Jack Kevorkian by assisting suicides is depriving sufferers of their heavenly reward. ... Potkay wrote that self-inflicted death may bring an even more unpleasant suffering from which there is never hope of escape. Perhaps so. But if my death entails prolonged terminal agony, I wonder which person I would like to find at my biside — Potkay

with his dire alternative, or Kevorkian with his **nepenthe**? (Lou Houston, *If Agony Has Value, Why Did Jesus Relieve It?* The News & Record, 01-03-1997.)

narrow-minded *adj.*: **hidebound**. ▪ [The right to watch the trial of accused Sept. 11 terrorist-conspirator Zacarias Moussaoui on television will not] be extended to ... Americans who watched in horror as 110-story buildings collapsed and the nation's defense headquarters burned. Thanks to the outdated policies of the federal judiciary, the televising of federal trials is forbidden. That **hidebound** attitude will be challenged at a hearing Wednesday before the judge who will preside over the trial. (Author not given, *Televise Terrorist Trial; War Effort Will Benefit [Editorial]*, USA Today, 01-07-2002.)

nasal *adj.*: **adenoidal**. ▪ B-Real, the lead rapper for L.A.'s Cypress Hill, has an **adenoidal** squall that makes him sound as if he has overdosed on helium, but his cartoonish delivery has served him well. (Billy Altman, *Picks: Song*, People, 08-30-1993, p. 20.)

native *adj.*: **aboriginal**. ▪ If Ottawa had any hope **aboriginal** people would register their guns in droves, that was dashed by an Alberta chief and Alberta's Indian Association head. Neither of them are complying with the legislation. (Rachel Evans, *Natives Won't Register Guns/Chiefs Say They Oppose Idea*, The Edmonton Sun, 04-13-2001, p. 6.)

(2) native (as in indigenous) *adj.*: **authochthonous**. SEE INDIGENOUS

nature (of a person, people or culture) *n.*: **ethos**. SEE CHARACTER

(2) nature (true ... of something, as in its essence) *n.*: **quiddity**. SEE ESSENCE

naughty (behavior, as in mischief) *n.*: **doggery** [i.e. doglike behavior]. SEE MISCHIEF

(2) naughty (as in mischiveous) *adj.*: **elfin**. SEE MISCHIEVOUS

(3) naughty (as in scandalous) *adj.*: **scabrous**. SEE SCANDALOUS

nauseating (as in overly sentimental) *adj.*: **mawkish**. SEE SENTIMENTAL

naval (supremacy) *n.*: **thalassocracy**. SEE SUPREMACY

ne'er-do-well (as in scoundrel or unprincipled person) *n.*: **blackguard**. SEE SCOUNDREL

(2) ne'er-do-well *n.*: **scapegrace**. SEE SCOUNDREL

neanderthal *n.*: **troglodyte**. ▪ Most [executive recruiters] try to keep the identity of their client secret in the early stages, but they still want to know how computer-literate you are. Expect questions like "How do you write your letters and memos?" One **troglodyte** killed his chances forever by replying, "I call my gal in to dictate." (Marshall Loeb, *What to do if a Headhunter Calls*, Fortune, 08-07-1995, p. 266.)

nearness (in place, time or relation) *n.*: **propinquity**. SEE CLOSENESS

necessarily (due to force of circumstance) *adv.*: **perforce**. ▪ [In defending his decision to speak to the media about the Microsoft antitrust case where he was the judge, District Judge Thomas stated:] "The ostensible reason [there should be no public commentary about a case] is that anything said informally, but publicly, about a case must **perforce** detract from the court's 'appearance of impartiality.'" (James Grimaldi, *Microsoft Judge Takes His Case to the Public*, The Washington Post, 10-07-2002.)

necessary (element or condition) *n.*: **sine qua non** [Latin]. SEE INDISPENSABLE

necessity (as in irresistible compulsion) *n.*: **cacoëthes**. SEE COMPULSION

neck (twisted or sprained ...) *n.*: **torticollis**. ▪ In 1984, one of my patients attended a chiropractor for the treatment of headaches, was given neck manipulation, and developed painful **torticollis** which persisted for several months. (Author not given, *Letters to the Editor: "Don't Let Them Touch Your Neck,"* Medical Post, 02-16-2000.)
(2) neck (as in kiss) *v.t.*: **osculate**. SEE KISS

need (as in irresistible compulsion) *n.*: **cacoëthes**. SEE COMPULSION
(2) need (mental process marked by ... to do something) *n.*: **conation**. SEE DETERMINATION

needless (words) *n.*: **macrology**. SEE VERBOSITY
(2) needless (word or phrase) *n.*: **pleonasm**. SEE REDUNDANCY

needy (as in poor) *adj.*: **impecunious**. SEE POOR
(2) needy (as in poor) *adj.*: **necessitous**. SEE POOR

negative (as in faultfinding) *adj.*: **captious**. SEE FAULTFINDING
(2) negative (as in faultfinding person) *n.*: **smell-fungus**. SEE FAULTFINDER

negativity (as in criticism) *n.*: **animadversion** (*v.t.*: **animadvert**). SEE CRITICISM

neglect (intentionally) *v.t.*: **pretermit**. SEE OMIT

neglecting (or omitting or passing over) *n.*: **preterition**. SEE OMITTING

negligible *adj.*: **nugatory**. SEE UNIMPORTANT
(2) negligible *adj.*: **picayune**. SEE TRIVIAL
(3) negligible *adj.*: **piffling**. SEE TRIVIAL

negotiation (the start of ...) *n.*: **pourparler** [French]. SEE DISCUSSION

Negro (admirer of ... persons) *n.*: **Negrophile**. SEE BLACK
(2) Negro (one who fears or dislikes black persons) *n.*: **Negrophobe**. SEE BLACK
(3) Negro (person who is 1/8th ...) *n.*: **octoroon**. SEE BLACK
(4) Negro (person who is 1/4 ...) *n.*: **quadroon**. SEE BLACK

neighborhood (Spanish-speaking) *n.*: **barrio**. SEE SPANISH
(2) neighborhood *n.*: **purlieu**. SEE VICINITY
(3) neighborhood (physical ..., as in vicinity) *n.*: **vicinage**. SEE VICINITY

neighborhoods (as in outskirts) *n., pl.*: **purlieus**. SEE OUTSKIRTS

neophyte *n.*: **dilettante**. SEE AMATEUR

nerve (as in gall or temerity) *n.*: **hardihood**. SEE GALL

nervous (excitement) *adj.*: **atwitter**. SEE EXCITED

nervousness (as in a state of tense ..., often with irritability) *n.*: **fantod**. SEE TENSION
(2) nervousness (as in panic) *n.*: **Torschlusspanik** [German]. SEE PANIC

nest (esp. in a high place) *n.*: **aerie**. ▪ [In] the Snake River Canyon ... cliffs drop 700 feet to the narrow canyon floor; ledges, cracks, and crevices along the cliff walls provide shelter for birds to nest and raise their young. Some eagle **aeries** — thick fortresses of interwoven branches and twigs — weigh 2,000 pounds and measure seven feet across. (Guy Hand, *Sagebrush and Time: Wide-eyed in the Idaho Desert* [Hiking Narrative], Sierra, 03-13-1998, p. 24.)

neutral (esp. neither right or wrong, beneficial or harmful) *adj.*: **adiaphorous**. ▪ Much thanks for the marvelous profile on the great US radio talk host, Larry Elder. Unlike the anemic, **adiaphorous**, lightweight, thumb-suckingly dull and crude "shock jocks" on air in this country, Larry Elder is brilliant in using the genre for telling not the story of the day, but the "real" story of the day. (Chuck Brooks [letter writer], *Letters to the Editor*, The Australian, 01-20-2003, p. 14.)

nevertheless *adv.*: **withal**. ▪ [T]raffic is considerably less in Havana than in U.S. cities its size (approximately 2 million people). This may be due to a shortage of petroleum, only a portion of which is produced by the island itself. **Withal**, life seems to move on, in many ways normally, despite politics and shortages. (Benjamin P. Tyree, *Calling on Communist Cuba*, The Washington Times, 03-09-2001, p. A17.)

new (love of or enthusiasm for anything ...) *n.*: **neophilia**. SEE NOVELTY

(2) new (as in of recent origin) *adj.*: **neoteric**. SEE RECENT

newborn (collection of clothing and equipment for the ...) *n.*: **layette**. ▪ If you know someone who is expecting a baby, chances are you've been browsing baby shops for the perfect little gift to welcome home both Mom and child. While anything to add to the **layette** or to outfit the nursery is sure to be appreciated, there's really nothing like a gift you make, assemble or dream up on your own. (Martha Stewart, *Homemade Presents For Baby — And The Parents*, Newsday, 03-27-2002, p. B21.)

(2) newborn (baby, esp. less than 4 weeks old) *n.*: **neonate**. ▪ Systems should be in place so that nurses respond quickly and appropriately when a fetus or **neonate** is in jeopardy. (Camille D. DiCostanzo, *Legal Issues in Neonatal Nursing*, Journal of Perinatal & Neonatal Nursing, 12-01-1996, p. 47.)

newest (the ... thing) *n.*: **dernier cri** [French]. SEE TREND

next-to-last *adj.*: **penultimate**. ▪ Level with Woods and Flesch after 16 holes, Els ... went to the top of the leaderboard when he knocked a drive and six-iron to three feet at the **penultimate** hole. (Lewine Mair, *Sport: Golf: Open Championship: Els Steals in on Wind to Snatch Lead*, The Daily Telegraph, 07-21-2000, p. 22.)

nice (as in pleasing) *adj.*: **prepossessing**. SEE PLEASING

nickname (as a term of endearment) *n.*: **hypocorism** (*adj.*: **hypocoristic**). ▪ The nicknames occurring in the sagas [in Icelandic literature], rude and demeaning beyond description, were, as far as we can judge, not looked upon as offensive. ... Finnur Jonsson ... explained about everything there was to collect in Icelandic literature: ... **hypocoristic** names [such] as fiss (weak farter) and Pambarskelfir (belly shaker). (Anatoly Liberman, *Gone With the Wind: More Thoughts on Medieval Farting*, Scandinavian Studies, 01-01-1996.)

(2) nickname *n.*: **sobriquet**. ▪ The [Connecticut womens' basketball freshmen] arrived in the summer of 1998 with high expectations and a slick **sobriquet**. Dubbed the T.A.S.S.K. Force, the quintet of high school All-Americas included [Tamika Williams, Asjha Jones, Swin Cash, Sue Bird, and Keirsten Walters]. (Richard Deitsch, *Big East Tournament: Up To The T.A.S.S.K.*, Sports Illustrated, 04-19-2000, p. 40.)

niggle *v.i.*: **pettifog**. SEE QUIBBLE

night blindness *n.*: **nyctalopia**. ▪ Medical science now recognizes a pathological condition called Carsonoge-neous Monocular **Nyctalopia**: temporary blindness in one eye caused by watching the Carson show with one visual organ buried in the pillow and the other on the box. (Author not given, *Top 25 Stars: Johnny Carson: H-e-e-e-r-r-e's TV's Top Gun*, People, 05-04-1989, p. 20.)

nightcap *n.*: **doch-an-dorris** [Scottish Gaelic] ▪ [W]hen the boozed, kilted MacBryde leads a halting Court audience in a chorus of "Just a wee **doch-an-dorris**," Byrne encourages the music-hall notion that the Scots are a race of drunken comics. (Michael Billington, *Theatre: Shrouded in Scotch Myths; Michael Billington on John Byrne's Sorry Parade of Stereotypes at the Royal Court*, The Guardian [London], 09-24-1992, p. 27.)

nightclub *n.*: **boîte** [French]. ▪ The Dynasty *Nightclub* had been open for only a week, but the tables in the rooftop **boîte** were packed with affluent customers drinking imported beer and applauding the performance of a sultry chanteuse. (Richard Hornik Rangoon, *Burma*, Time International, 11-09-1992, p. 20.)

nightfall (as in twilight) *n.*: **gloaming**. SEE TWILIGHT

(2) nightfall (of or relating to) *adj.*: **vespertine**. SEE EVENING

nightmare (or episode having the quality of a ...) *n.*: **Walpurgis Night** [derives from the evening before May Day, believed during medieval times to be the night that witches celebrate Sabbath. The German word "Walpurgisnacht" is sometimes used instead.] ∎ I love New York ... but I have thoroughly lost patience with the self-congratulatory myth, trumpeted ad nauseam since the recent blackout, that New York is a changed city since 9/11. ... The latest piece of "evidence" offered on behalf of the city's transformation is the near-absence of looting in comparison to the 1977 blackout — a **Walpurgis Night** that produced more than 3,700 arrests, 1,600 ransacked stores and 1,000 fires. (Susan Jacoby, *I Want to Wake Up in the City That Can Get Over Itself*, The Washington Post, 08-24-2003, p. B5.)

nine (group or set of ...) *n.*: **ennead**. ∎ [At Disney's Animal Kingdom] an **ennead** of gorillas — four bachelors on one side of a waterfall, a family of five safely on the other — scuff their knuckles as they proudly prowl. (Richard Corliss, *The Arts/Leisure: Beauty and the Beasts*, Time, 04-20-1998, p. 66.)

nitpick *v.t.*: **cavil**. SEE QUIBBLE

(2) nitpick *v.i.*: **pettifog**. SEE QUIBBLE

nitpicker (on issues of grammar) *n.*: **grammaticaster**. SEE PEDANATIC

noise (and confusion, esp. from simultaneous voices) *n.*: **babel**. ∎ Homer Explosion — Hot Bats, Hot Air — At times it seems everyone but Jim Garrison has chimed in with reasons for baseball's offensive explosion. But might the **babel** emanating from purists and conspiracy theorists be drowning out the reasoned voice of science? (Richard Hoffer, *Scorecard*, Sports Illustrated, 05-15-2000, p. 31.)

(2) noise (which is harsh and unpleasant) *n.*: **cacophony**. ∎ As dusk settles in over Melbourne's majestic Royal Botanical Gardens, winged black silhouettes fill the sky, accompanied by a **cacophony** of shrill barks. The bats are out. (Laurie Garrett, *Bat-Borne Viruses*, Newsday, 07-20-1999, p. C6.)

(3) noise (which is repeating such as a drumbeat, machine-gun fire or hooves of a galloping horse) *n.*: **rataplan**. ∎ Gore accused Dukakis of being "absurdly timid" in criticizing [Jesse] Jackson, declared that "we're not choosing a preacher, we're choosing a president," and finally, after garnering what he thought was the coveted endorsement of Ed Koch, stood by as the irascible mayor delivered a **rataplan** of one-liners about [Jackson]. (Ellen Nakashima, *13 Ways of Looking at Al Gore and Race*, The Washington Post, 04-23-2000, p. W6.)

(4) noise *n.*: **bruit**. SEE DIN

(5) noise (which is unpleasant or incongruous) *n.*: **dissonance**. SEE SOUND

(6) noise (which is pleasant) *adj.*: **euphonious** (*n.*:

euphony). SEE MELODIOUS

(7) noise (fear of) *n.*: **phonophobia**. SEE FEAR

noisy *adj.*: **clangorous** (*n.*: **clangor**). ∎ My freedom [living in a Swiss apartment in the 1970's was very limited.] Often, no showers are permitted between 10 P.M. and 7 A.M. No toilets may be flushed during those hours, either. When relieving themselves, men are expected to sit. (Is it the likelihood of an errant drop that so offends? Or the **clangorous** tinkle?) (Alexander Wolff, *Big Game, Small World*, Warner Books [2002], p. 54.)

(2) noisy *adj.*: **clamant**. SEE LOUD

(3) noisy *adj.*: **strepitous**. SEE LOUD

non-reliance (on imports or economic aid) *n.*: **autarky**. SEE SELF-SUFFICIENT

nonbeliever (as in one with no faith or religion) *n.*, *adj.*: **nullifidian**. ∎ Down with the infidels of multi-culturalism ... condoms for kiddies ... [and] two mommies. ... Religion arms the faithful with a comprehensive strategy for living; denying religion leaves the **nullifidians** in a personal void, which they try to fill with the litany of their moral confusion, composed in the cords of dissonance. (Paul Heusinger [letter writer], *Down With the PC Crowd and its Multiculturalism*, Sun-Sentinel [Fort Lauderdale, FL], 01-14-1994.)

nonchalance (esp. on matters or politics or religion) *n.*: **Laodiceanism**. SEE INDIFFERENCE

(2) nonchalance (as in appearance of effortlessness) *n.*: **sprezzatura** [Italian]. SEE EFFORTLESSNESS

nonchalant *adj.*: **dégagé** [French]. SEE EASYGOING

nonconformist (orig. Catholics who did not follow Church of England) *n.*: **recusant**. SEE DISSENTER

nonessential (as in superfluous) *adj.*: **supererogatory**. SEE SUPERFLUOUS

nonetheless *adv.*: **withal**. SEE NEVERTHELESS

nonpariel (person or thing) *n.*: **nonesuch**. SEE PARAGON

nonsense *n.*: **folderol** (or **falderal**). ∎ The conservative **folderol** that legalizing drugs will tell impressionable youngsters it's OK to snort up is foolishness so perfect that even liberals should be impressed. (Thomas W. Hazlett, *Guns, Drugs, and Rock 'N' Roll: Weeding out the Root Causes of Violence*, Reason, 03-01-1994, p. 66.)

(2) nonsense (or talk ...) *v.i.*, *n.*: **piffle**. ∎ [British

Prime Minister Tony] Blair denied he was seeking to impose a candidate and insisted it was up to the party in Wales to elect its candidate for the leadership of the Welsh Assembly. But, he said, it was "nonsense" and "**piffle**" that the leadership contest was a fight between Wales and London. (Auslan Cramb, *Scots and Welsh Inflict Double Misery on Blair*, The Daily Telegraph, 11-28-1998.)

(3) nonsense *n.*: **trumpery**. ▮ We have been told since the moment bin Laden's name was mentioned in connection with the horrible events of Sept. 11 that America's military would face dire consequences and overwhelming difficulty in any action taken in Afghanistan. This **trumpery** is fed to us [by the same] ninnies who told us the "elite" Republican Guard in Iraq was a well-trained, well-supplied force that was to be feared by the U.S. military. (Robert Stewart, *Why the United States Can Succeed in Afghanistan*, Buffalo News, 11-11-2001, p. H1.)

(4) nonsense (as in meaningless talk) *n.*: **galimatias**. SEE GIBBERISH

nonsensical (as in fallacious or illogical argument) *n.*: **paralogism** (*adj.*: **paralogical**). SEE FALLACY

nonviolence (Hindu doctrine of) *n.*: **ahimsa**. ▮ In a century marked by brutality, Gandhi perfected a different method of bringing about change, one that would turn out (surprisingly) to have more lasting impact. The words he used to describe it do not translate readily into English: ... **ahimsa** (the love that remains when all thoughts of violence are dispelled). (Walter Isaacson, *Person Of The Century: Who Mattered And Why*, Time, 12-31-1999, p. 48.)

normal (as in usual or customary) *adj.*: **wonted**. SEE CUSTOMARY

north (of or pertaining to) *adj.*: **boreal**. ▮ There is reason, but not rhyme, to the travels of **boreal** seed-eaters. Contrary to popular belief, hard winters do not drive the birds south. ... Immune to winter's worst, then, immense flocks of **boreal** birds wander the Canadian forest year-round. (Les Line, *Staying the Winter [Migration of Birds]*, National Wildlife, 02-12-1995, p. 52.)

(2) north (of or relating to the far ...) *adj.*: **hyperborean**. SEE ARCTIC

northern lights *n.*: **aurora borealis**. ▮ Scientists find space catalyst for **aurora borealis**. ... The Northern Lights will be just as mystical the next time you see them, but slightly less mysterious. (Peter Calamai, *Weird Waves Help Light Night Sky*, The Toronto Star, 03-29-2001.)

nose (within the ...) *adj.*: **intranasal**. ▮ What is jammed up nostrils, supposedly provides a jolt, and isn't cocaine? Presenting Ener-B, an **intranasal** gel loaded with vitamin B12 and sold in health stores for $12 a twelve-dose box. (Author not given, *Health & Fitness: New Nostril Nostrum*, Time, 03-30-1987, p. 74.)

(2) nose (which is turned up) *adj.*: **retroussé** [French. Although the word is an adjective meaning "turned up," it is almost always used in reference to a nose]. ▮ He just looked so undistinguished. Medium height. Medium build. Medium-brown hair — a small nose, positively **retrousse** — the photo had been a very flattering one. What a dud, I thought. (Tiffany Trott, *The Back Page: "Did Any of the 11 Men I Met Last Night Ask for My Number?" Dating Diary*, The Daily Telegraph, 09-27-1997.)

(3) nose (having a runny ... or watery eyes) *adj.*: **rheumy**. SEE WATERY

nose job *n.*: **rhinoplasty**. ▮ During Andrea's consultation, Dr. Glasgold suggested not only a nose job but an implant to improve her receding chin. ... According to Glasgold, 25 percent of all **rhinoplasty** patients also have receding chins. (Marjorie Rosen, *New Face, New Body, New Self — Five Teens Talk About the Trials and Triumphs of Plastic Surgery*, People, 04-26-1993, p. 88.)

nose-picking *n.*: **rhinotillexomania**. ▮ Advancing science: University of Wisconsin-Madison researchers, fighting ignorance, have done a study on **rhinotillexomania**. And not a moment too soon, either. ... [They] gave a questionnaire to 1,200 people, with questions like, "What finger do you use?" and "How often do you find yourself looking at what you have removed?" And thus man's knowledge advances, a booger at a time. (Doug Robarchek, *Alcohol May Cause Brain Damage*, Charlotte Observer [North Carolina], 10-19-2000.)

nosy (person) *n.*: **quidnunc**. SEE BUSYBODY

notable (person in a field or organization) *n.*: **wallah** ▮ Shaw got a computer science Ph.D. from Stanford in 1980. ... He wasn't the only **wallah**-in-training at Stanford in those days. Leonard Bosack and Andreas Bechtolsheim, co-founders of Cisco Systems and Sun Microsystems, respectively, and Jim Clark, founder of Silicon Graphics and now chairman of Netscape — all were either faculty members or fellow students. (James Aley, *Extreme Investing: Wall Street's King Quant David Shaw's Secret Formulas Pile Up Money; Now He Wants a Piece of the Net*, Fortune, 02-05-1996, p. 108.)

(2) notable (of an event or period which is ...) *adj.*: **epochal**. SEE MOMENTOUS

nothing (from or out of ...) *adj., adv.*: **ex nihilo** [Latin]. ∎ Planning a city **ex nihilo** is an awesome undertaking, but it is easier to build roads, homes and schools than to create the ineffable feeling of community one finds in the best towns. (Noah Efron, *Real Jews*, Basic Books [2003], p. 115.)

noticable (barely ...) *adj.*: **liminal**. SEE INVISIBLE

notice (something which may be difficult to discern) *v.t.*: **descry**. SEE PERCEIVE

notion (which is odd, stubborn or whimsical) *n.*: **crotchet**. ∎ But [Presidential candidate Pat] Buchanan's **crotchets** — Wall Street bankers, immigration (legal as well as illegal), trade and the New World Order (whatever that is) — are idiosyncratic enough to keep his following to a minority. (Mona Charen, *Republicans Need Candidate Who Can Lead on Moral Issues*, St. Louis Post-Dispatch, 10-16-1995, p. 7B.)

(2) notion (about which one is obsessed) *n.*: **idée fixe** [French]. SEE OBSESSION

notorious *adj.*: **flagitious**. SEE SCANDALOUS

notwithstanding (that) *adv.*: **withal**. SEE NEVERTHELESS

nourishment *n.*: **alimentation**. ∎ Aside from computer management designed to select out the most productive cows, Mr. Blumstein hopes to implement new **alimentation** methods and erect an Israeli-engineered payload that requires fewer workers and provides detailed milk-related data on each cow. (Masha Leon, *Israeli Milkman Mooooving Into New Territory*, Forward, 11-04-1994.)

(2) nourishment (esp. insipid, like baby food) *n.*: **pabulum** (also **pablum**). SEE INSIPID

nouveau riche *n.*: **parvenu**. SEE UPSTART

novel (published in installments) *n.*: **feuilleton** [French]. ∎ Policarpo Quaresma, who gives name to the third book in the list, is a tragicomic ultranationalist hero. Lima Barreto (1881-1922) initially published the story in 1911 in installments in Rio's Jornal do Commercio, as a **feuilleton**. The book would only appear four years later. (Author not given, *Literature: The Great Brazilian Novel*, Brazzil, 09-30-1998, p. 12.)

(2) novel (in which real people, places or events are portrayed in fictional guise) *n.*: **roman à clef** [French; lit. "novel with a key"]. ∎ [Joe] Klein used the pen name "Anonymous" when he wrote "Primary Colors," the scandalous 1996 **roman à clef** about the '92 presidential campaign. His womanizing Southern governor was widely believed to be based on Bill Clinton. (Author not given, *"Anonymous" Klein Delivers 2nd Novel*, The Cincinnati Post, 01-21-2000.)

(3) novel (which follows the development of its main character over time, as in a coming-of-age story) *n.*: **bildungsroman** [German]. SEE COMING-OF-AGE

(4) novel (style which is dark, gloomy, remote and/or grotesque) *adj.*: **gothic**. SEE DARK

(5) novel (as in of recent origin) *adj.*: **neoteric**. SEE RECENT

novelist (esp. who writes in quantity) *n.*: **fictioneer**. ∎ If you're looking for a critique and celebration of capitalism, for a discussion of ethics or ethnicity, for a distillation of democracy and its discontents, you'd do at least as well to heed [The Simpson's] as you would to ponder similarly prolific prose **fictioneers**, from Norman Mailer to Stephen King. (Ken Tucker, *At 300 Episodes and Counting, The Simpsons — TV's Answer to the Great American Novel — Continues to be a Show About Everything*, Entertainment Weekly, 02-07-2003.)

novelty (love of or enthusiasm for ...) *n.*: **neophilia**. ∎ "Sensation," the present Saatchi exhibition at the Royal Academy, makes the point: the big, flashy, headline gesture is all that counts. These people are inspired by the intrinsic **neophilia** of technology. The technocrat and the machine require no past, only the thin film of the present. The artist similarly bows to the imperative of now. (Bryan Appleyard, *Oasis Are Criticised, Even by Their Heroes the Beatles, for Being Derivative*, New Statesman [1996], 10-10-1997, p. 34.)

novice *n.*: **abecedarian**. SEE BEGINNER

(2) novice *n.*: **catechumen**. SEE BEGINNER

(3) novice *n.*: **dilettante**. SEE AMATEUR

now (for ...) *n.*: **nonce** (used as "for the nonce"). SEE TIME BEING

now and then *adv.*: **betimes**. SEE SOMETIMES

noxious (atmosphere or influence) *n.*: **miasma**. ∎ Air pollution — the gray **miasma** — from coal, industry ash and leaded fuel — that smothers most of China's cities is barely breathable. The World Bank estimates that air pollution causes nearly 300,000 deaths nationwide every year. (Nisid Hajari, *China's*

Environment: A Litany of Ills: China's 10 Top Ecological Problems, Time International, 03-01-1999, p. 21.)

(2) noxious (fumes from waste or decayed matter) *n.*: **effluvium**. SEE ODOR

(3) noxious (smell) *adj.*: **mephitic** (*n.*: **mephitis**). SEE SMELLY

(4) noxious (or harmful) *adj.*: **noisome**. SEE HARMFUL AND SMELLY

nuance (as in a subtle point raised within the context of a philosophical or theological debate; also references such a debate itself) *n.*: **quodlibet**. SEE SUBTLETY

numb *v.t.*: **narcotize**. SEE DEADEN

numbers (having ability with ...) *adj.*: **numerate**. SEE MATHEMATICAL

numbness (as in medication causing inability to feel pain) *n.*: **analgesia**. ∎ Administering pain medication prior to surgery helps patients long after they return home from the hospital. The idea behind preemptive **analgesia** is to head off pain by blocking the central nervous system's response before the surgery occurs. (Author not given, *A Preemptive Strike Before Surgery*, USA Today Magazine, 10-01-1997.)

numbskull *n.*: **jobbernowl** [British]. SEE IDIOT
(2) numbskull *n.*: **mooncalf**. SEE FOOL

numerous (and varied) *adj.*: **manifold**. ∎ For all his **manifold** talents, [Steve] Martin is simply the wrong man for the role [of Sergeant Bilko]. (Author not given, People, 04-15-96, p. 19.)

nuptials (of or relating to ...) *adj.*: **hymeneal**. SEE WEDDING

nurse (or housekeeper in India and Orient, often serving as a wet nurse) *n.*: **amah**. SEE MAID

nuts (as in crazy) *adj.*: **doolally**. SEE CRAZY

O

oaf (habitual ..., as in bumbler) *n.*: **schlemiel** [Yiddish]. SEE BUMBLER

oafish (person) *n.*: **yahoo**. SEE BOOR

obdurate (as in one who clings to an opinion or belief even after being shown that it is wrong) *n.*: **mumpsimus**. SEE STUBBORN

(2) obdurate *adj.*: **pertinacious**. SEE STUBBORN

obedience (as in marked by insistence on rigid conformity to a belief, system or course of action without regard to individual differences) *adj.*: **procrustean** (*n.*: **Procrustean bed**). SEE CONFORMITY

obedient *adj.*: **biddable**. ∎ America likes its neighbours **biddable** and quiet; Cuba, with wars, coups and corrupt governments, has always made a nuisance of itself. (Author not given, *Dances with Wolves* [Cuba's Relations With the US; Survey — Cuba], The Economist, 04-06-1996, p. SC14.)

obese *adj.*: **adipose**. SEE FAT
(2) obese (person, esp. with a large abdomen) *n.*: **endomorph** (*adj.*: **endomorphic**). SEE POT-BELLIED
(3) obese (as in fat) *adj.*: **Pickwickian**. SEE FAT

obesity (branch of medicine dealing with ...) *n.*: **bariatrics**. ∎ As director of a **bariatrics** clinic providing medical treatment of obesity and related conditions, I am often confronted with people who think they can't afford treatment simply because they don't have the proper information. (Author not given, *Mailbag*, People, 05-03-1999, p. 1.)
(2) obesity *n.*: **avoirdupois**. SEE WEIGHT

obey (as in acting subservient as opposed to leading) *adj.*: **sequacious**. SEE SUBSERVIENT

obfuscate (one's vision as if by clouds, fog or vapor) *v.t.*: **obnubilate**. SEE OBSCURE

obituary *n.*: **necrology**. ∎ I was lucky that none of my closest friends perished [on September 11, 2001], but still, I think of those people, and I sometimes think of how they died. And I try to remember to forget. But then I open a newsletter from my college and in a **necrology** there's a startling cluster of three or four names with the date of death: Sept. 11, 2001. (Andy Serwer, *Terrorists Are Ruining My Middle Age*, Fortune, 12-24-2001, p. 135.)

object *v.t.*: **expostulate**. ∎ [When some overweight American Airlines flight attendants were fired], a group of women went to the [Equal Employment Opportunity Commission] claiming discrimination, and the commission turned around and sued American. But wait — [our] readers are **expostulating** in unison — there is no federal ban on weight bias. How could the EEOC launch such a suit? (Daniel Seligman, *Keeping Up: Fat Chances – A Case* *for Putting on Weight, a Weird Job Application, and Other Matters*, Fortune, 05-20-1991, p. 155.)

(2) object (on trivial grounds) *v.t.*: **cavil**. SEE QUIBBLE

(3) object (to, as in oppose, a statement, opinion or action) *v.t.*: **oppugn**. SEE OPPOSE

(4) object (esp. in the form of pleading with) *v.t.*: **remonstrate**. SEE PLEAD

(5) object (as in goal, esp. of life) *n.*: **telos** [Greek]. SEE GOAL

objectionable (in matters of discrimination between groups) *adj.*: **invidious**. SEE DISCRIMINATORY

objective *n.*: **quaesitum**. ∎ [Economist John Maynard] Keynes maintains the vision of an economy moving through time: an economy that is complex and difficult to analyze because organizations change, unexplored opportunities arise, and new choices are made. New factors could come into the picture and the main determinants of analysts' **quaesitum** may change. Furthermore, the **quaesitum** itself may change as new problems develop. (Guiseppe Fontana, *Keynes on the "Nature of Economic Thinking,"* The American Journal of Economics and Sociology, 10-1-2001.)

(2) objective (hidden or ulterior ...) *n.*: **arriere-pensee** (or **arrière-pensée**) [French]. SEE MOTIVE

(3) objective (uncompromisingly ..., as in just) *n.*: **Rhadamanthine**. SEE JUST

(4) objective (directed towards an ...) *adj.*: **telic**. SEE PURPOSEFUL

oblivion *n.*: **Lethe**. ∎ En route to work today, I heard an ad for an alarm clock with soothing sounds to help you sleep. It had the usual sounds to lull you off to **Lethe** — pounding surf, waterfalls, crickets, a C-SPAN hearing. The announcer was pleased to introduce two new sounds: birds and New York Traffic. (James Lileks, *Soothing Sounds — From New York?* Star Tribune, 11-19-2002.)

oblivious (as in ignorant) *adj.*: **nescient** (*n.*: **nescience**). SEE IGNORANT

obscene (compulsive ... behavior) *n.*: **corpopraxia**. ∎ In one painfully hilarious moment, an expert witness for the prosecution, Dr. Rampling, suffers from three neurological conditions, coprolalia, **copropraxia** and echopraxia, which make her shout obscenities [i.e. coprolalia], grab her own breasts and mimic her questioners [i.e. echopraxia] as she testifies, all unconsciously. (Richard Bernstein,

Just a Couple of All-American Orphans on Trial, The New York Times, 08-06-1997.)

(2) obscene *adj.*: **fescennine**. ∎ Nurses minister to people's bodies. Consequently, they invade private and personal territory in ways that other kinds of workers do not. Arguably, **fescennine** comments made by patients to nurses who are doing their jobs may arise from the embarrassment of feeling exposed and vulnerable. (Patricia M. Hanrahan, *"How Do I Know if I'm Being Harassed or if This is Part of My Job?" Nurses and Definitions of Sexual Harassment*, Contemporary Women's Issues Database, 06-01-1997.)

(3) obscene (as in vulgar) *adj.*: **meretricious**. SEE VULGAR

obscenity (excessive use of ..., esp. involuntarily when mentally ill) *n.*: **coprolalia**. SEE CURSING

obscure (vision, as if by clouds, fog or vapor) *v.t.*: **obnubilate**. ∎ The usual, if unarticulated, thinking is that knowing occurs by the mind's getting its version of 20/20 vision — "the view from nowhere," with nothing allowed to **obnubilate** the mental looks. But notice this stark fact: the mind that asks no questions, reaches no answers. In other words, gaping at the Rosetta Stone gets you nowhere. Without asking, "What does this mean?" ... I shall not know. (Patrick Brennan, *The Edge of Meaning* [Book Review], Michigan Law Review, 05-01-2003.)

(2) obscure (as in muddle or confuse) *v.t.*: **befog**. SEE MUDDLE

(3) obscure (as in dark, misty and gloomy) *adj.*: **caliginous**. SEE DARK

(4) obscure (as in cryptic or ambiguous) *adj.*: **Delphic**. SEE AMBIGUOUS

(5) obscure (or cryptic speech or writing, esp. deliberately) *adj.*: **elliptical**. SEE CRYPTIC

(6) obscure (as in difficult to understand) *adj.*: **recondite**. SEE COMPLICATED

obsequious (to behave towards in a ... manner) *v.t.*: **bootlick**. SEE KOWTOW

(2) obsequious (person) *n.*: **lickspittle**. SEE SYCOPHANT

observance (or ceremony which is pretentious) *n.*: **mummery**. SEE CEREMONY

(2) observance (precise ... of formalities or etiquette) *n.*: **punctilio**. SEE ETIQUETTE

observant (person) *n.*: **Argus**. SEE WATCHFUL

observation (as in insight) *n.*: **aperçu** [French]. SEE INSIGHT

(2) observation (or expression or phrase which is

elegant, concise, witty and/or well-put) *n.*: **atticism**. See EXPRESSION

(3) observation (or line which is witty) *n.*: **epigram**. See QUIP

observer *n.*: **scrutator**. ■ Sir — There are no more assiduous or respected **scrutators** of the Northern Ireland security scene than monsignori Faul and Murray. Their latest letter (November 21st) is however sheer nonsense. (Charles Cooke [letter writer], *Reforming the RUC*, The Irish Times, 12-05-1997, p. 15.)

obsession (with an idea or concept) *n.*: **idée fixe** [French]. ■ For those who doubted it before, the book depicts in detail just how completely the company [Volkswagen] was a creature of Nazism. Soon after his rise to power, Hitler began to pester the leaders of Germany's automobile industry with an **idée fixe**. He wanted them to create a mass-produced "people's car" that would be affordable to average Germans. (Christian Caryl, *A Beetle Faces Up To Its Past*, U.S. News & World Report, 12-02-1996, p. 48.)

(2) obsession (with power, wealth, fame, immortality, etc.) *n.*: **megalomania**. ■ In his 60s, [Wilt Chamberlain] was boldly declaring himself the greatest player ever to walk on the hardwood. In a sports world in which we allow our heroes to spend only so much time in the rarefied air before we bring them crashing back to earth, Chamberlain's **megalomania** always begged for its comeuppance. (Jeff Ryan, *Remembering Wilt: A Bum Rap*, The Sporting News, 10-25-1999, p. 12.)

(3) obsession (over one subject or idea) *n.*: **monomania**. ■ [S]tay tuned for a replay of the poisonous psychodrama where race is used as a cynical cover for the real liberal **monomania**, abortion — as if the entire universe revolves around a single issue affecting the private conduct and personal convenience of heterosexual Western women. (Author not given, *Culture, et Cetera*, The Washington Times, 01-19-2001, p. A2.)

(4) obsession (as in focus of emotional energy on an object or idea) *n.*: **cathexis**. See FOCUS

(5) obsession (with shopping) *n.*: **oniomania**. See SHOPPING

obsessive (about work) *n.*: **Stakhanovite**. See WORKAHOLIC

obsolete *adj.*: **antediluvian**. See OUTDATED

obstinate *adj.*: **contumacious**. ■ In a final swipe, the judge derides [President Clinton's] "contuma-cious conduct" [in the Monica Lewinsky matter]. ... All of which raises some interesting questions, given our current state of affairs: Can we really have a **contumacious** commander in chief? Can the leader of the nation's armed forces obstinately resist authority? (And whose authority would he resist, anyway?) (Gloria Borger, *Considering Contempt*, U.S. News & World Report, 04-26-1999, p. 45.)

(2) obstinate (in a contrary or disobedient way) *adj.*: **froward**. See CONTRARY

(3) obstinate (to make or become ...) *v.t.*, *adj.*: **indurate**. See HARDEN

(4) obstinate (as in one who clings to an opinion or belief even after being shown that it is wrong) *n.*: **mumpsimus**. See STUBBORN

(5) obstinate *adj.*: **pertinacious**. See STUBBORN

(6) obstinate (as in resisting constraint or compulsion) *adj.*: **renitent**. See RESISTANT

obstruct *v.t.*: **occlude**. See BLOCK

obtain (by begging or sponging off of) *v.t.*: **cadge**. See BEG

obtuse (as in slow to understand or perceive) *adj.*: **purblind**. ■ Only the naive think [Martin Luther] King's murder begins and ends with [James Earl] Ray. Only the **purblind** ignore FBI Director J. Edgar Hoover's vendetta against King. (Greg Boeck, *Ray Doesn't Need Trial*, USA Today, 02-18-1997, p. 12A.)

(2) obtuse (or dull, ignorant, stupid or uncultured) *adj.*: **Boeotian**. See DULL

occasion (secondary ... which accompanies or results from another) *n.*: **epiphenomenon**. See PHENOMENON

occasionally *adv.*: **betimes**. See SOMETIMES

occupant (of a town) *n.*: **burgher**. See RESIDENT

occupation (requiring little work but paying an income) *n.*: **sinecure**. ■ [After] nearly ten years in government service, where everything is geared to the lowest common denominator, I find it refreshing to have work that rewards initiative and effort. Certainly I would be happy to have a **sinecure** again, but I am no longer brokenhearted that I left one. (Lars Eighner, *Travels With Lizbeth*, St. Martin's Press [1993], p. 124.)

(2) occupation (as in profession) *n.*: **métier** [French]. See PROFESSION

occupy (oneself in a light, frolicsome manner) *v.t.*, *v.i.*: **disport**. See FROLIC

occur *v.t.*: **betide**. See HAPPEN

occurrence (secondary ... which accompanies or results from another) *n.*: **epiphenomenon**. See PHENOMENON

ocean (bottom of the ...) *n.*: **Davy Jones's locker** [origin unknown]. ▪ In the spring of 1990, Pat Kane, a golfer and inventor from San Diego, hopped aboard a cruise ship, eagerly looking forward to sending a few buckets of balls off the practice tee on the fantail and down into **Davy Jones's locker**. But to Kane's disappointment, he discovered that maritime golfing was no longer possible [because it was made illegal]. (Steve Wulf, *Fore and Aft [Golf Balls That Dissolve in Sea Water]*, Sports Illustrated, 04-27-1992.)

(2) ocean (of or pertaining to ... or sea) *adj.*: **pelagic**. See SEA

odd (as in departing from the standard or norm) *adj.*: **heteroclite**. See ABNORMAL

(2) odd (as in unconventional) *adj.*: **outré** [French]. See UNCONVENTIONAL

(3) odd (as in eccentric) *adj.*: **pixilated**. See ECCENTRIC

oddity (as in notion which is odd, stubborn or whimsical) *n.*: **crotchet**. See NOTION

ode (in the form of a song or poem in honor of a bride or bridegroom) *n.*: **epithalamium**. See TOAST

odor (bad ... from waste or decayed matter) *n.*: **effluvium**. ▪ This deathliness generates its own momentum. Nobody in Ladysmith can flee the overpowering stink of enteric and dysentery; the local water becomes fouled by animal waste; the **effluvium** given off by corpses both stings the eyes and causes nausea, bringing more typhus-laden flies into town in a self-renewing cycle of woe. (Peter Wolfe, *The Horrors of Boer War Have the Ring of Truth*, St. Louis Post-Dispatch, 05-21-2000, p. F11.)

(2) odor (bad ... from foul-smelling sweat) *n.*: **bromidrosis**. See SWEAT

(3) odor (foul) *n.*: **fetor**. See STENCH

(4) odor (foul) *n.*: **mephitic** (*n.*: **mephitis**). See SMELLY

(5) odor (foul ...) *adj.*: **noisome**. See SMELLY

offbeat (holding ... opinions or having an ... perspective) *adj.*: **heterodox** (*n.*: **heterodoxy**). See UNCONVENTIONAL

offend (as in insult another's dignity) *n.*: **lese majesty**. See INSULT

offended (easily ...) *adj.*: **umbrageous**. ▪ [In criticizing] the Programme of the Communist Party of the Soviet Union ... we realize full well that they will doubtless think we are just being **umbrageous** over the Programme's view of Western journalism. ("Evermore baleful is the role of the bourgeois mass media which befuddles people in the interests of the ruling class.") (Daniel Seligman, *Keeping Up: Sulfur From Sunkist, Tass Vs. Microsoft, Herblock's Hysterics, and Other Matters*, Fortune, 12-23-1985, p. 131.)

offender (criminal ..., or wrongdoer) *n.*: **malefactor**. See WRONGDOER

(2) offender (as in wrongdoer) *n.*: **miscreant**. See WRONGDOER

offense (surprise ..., as in attack) *n.*: **coup de main** [French; attack by hand]. See ATTACK

(2) offense (small or trifling ...) *n.*: **peccadillo**. See INFRACTION

offensive (to the taste or sensibilities, esp. due to insincere praise) *adj.*: **fulsome**. ▪ Working for a Republican is the "ultimate sacrifice"? Voting for one makes you brave? ... [This strategy of Republicans pandering to conservative blacks] while indisputably brilliant, is laced with equal parts contempt and condescension. How else to interpret such **fulsome** bootlicking except that with blacks there is always danger, even for deviating from the party line? (Debra Dickerson, *The GOP's "Good" Blacks*, The Washington Post, 03-13-2001, p. A21.)

(2) offensive (language) *n.*: **billingsgate**. See LANGUAGE

(3) offensive (in matters of discrimination between groups) *adj.*: **invidious**. See DISCRIMINATORY

(4) offensive (as in vulgar) *adj.*: **meretricious**. See VULGAR

(5) offensive (as in repellent) *adj.*: **rebarbative**. See REPELLENT

offering *n.*: **oblation**. ▪ PGA Tour Inc. (PGA) deserves Scrooge-like infamy for its heartless treatment of disabled golfer Casey Martin [who has a disease which makes it difficult to walk the golf course]. ... Do its petrified forest of nabobs [i.e. the PGA executives] envision Casey Martin as their **oblation** to social Darwinism? (Bruce Fein, *PGA's Heartless Hazard*, The Washington Times, 01-30-2001, p. A14.)

(2) offering (which is all one can afford) *n.*: **widow's mite**. See DONATION

offhandedness (appearance of ...) *n.*: **sprezzatura** [Italian]. See EFFORTLESSNESS

offshoot (as in outgrowth) *n.*: **excrescence**. See OUTGROWTH

offspring (of or relating to) *adj.*: **filial**. ▪ Because families often live with three generations under one roof, parents can find themselves awkwardly positioned between their children and their own parents. Dr. Vo calls them "sandwich parents." If parents side with their Americanized children, she says, they worry that they are not paying "**filial** duty" to the grandparents. (Marilyn Gardner, *New Country, Old Customs*, The Christian Science Monitor, 08-09-2000, p. 11.)

(2) offspring (having had one or more ...) *n.*: **parous**. See BIRTH

oil painting (dealing with evening or night) *n.*: **nocturne**. See PAINTING

oily *adj.*: **lubricious**. See SLIPPERY

(2) oily *adj.*: **oleaginous**. See UNCTUOUS

ointment (esp. used to groom hair) *n.*: **pomade**. See HAIR GEL

old (extremely ...) *adj.*: **hoary**. ▪ [M]any Jews are alarmed by what they see as a worldwide blaze of anti-Semitism: torched synagogues in France, a resurgence of malevolent myths about Jews in the Arab world, sweeping anti-Israel diatribes in European newspapers and a measurable swell in the acceptance of **hoary** stereotypes in the United States. (Justin Davidson, *Bonding In Troubled Times/Fear of a Growing Anti-Semitism and Concerns Over Israel Are Making American Jews Put Aside Their Differences*, Newsday, 07-15-2002, p. B6.)

(2) old (esp. as in outdated) *adj.*: **antediluvian**. See OUTDATED

(3) old (of or relating to ... people, esp. women) *adj.*: **blue-rinse**. See ELDERLY

(4) old (woman who is ugly) *n.*: **crone**. See HAG

(5) old (government by ... people) *adj.*: **gerontocracy**. See GOVERNMENT

(6) old (branch of science dealing with ... people) *adj.*: **gerontology**. See ELDERLY

(7) old (sexual attraction towards ... people) *n.*: **gerontophilia**. See LUST

(8) old (growing ...) *adj.*: **senescent**. See AGING

(9) old (as in decrepit) *adj.*: **spavined**. See DECREPIT

(10) old (and sick person) *n.*: **Struldbrug**. See DECREPIT

old age (often with accompanying senility) *n.*: **caducity**. ▪ Aged care in Australia is teetering on the edge of a crisis, as nurses leave in droves and baby boomers creep closer to **caducity**. (Author not given, *Fed: Nursing Homes Caught in Catch-22 as Crisis Looms*, AAP General News [Australia], 08-08-2003.)

(2) old age (of or relating to ...) *adj.*: **gerontic**. ▪ [In Gertrude Atherton's novel, Agnes's the spinster's] sex-repression results in a middle-aged mania. ... [Mary] urges the spinster to have the "Steinach Treatment" and then have sex. ... Mary is unsympathetic to Agnes's plight, that of a "debauched **gerontic** virgin." (Dale Bauer, *Refusing Middle Age*, ANQ, 01-01-2002.)

(3) old age *n.*: **senectitude**. See ELDERLINESS

old maid (as in prudish) *adj.*: **missish**. See PRUDE

old woman (of or like an ...) *adj.*: **anile**. ▪ But when the camera closed in on [Jane] Fonda ... you could see that she'd let herself go and that the promise of old ladyhood wasn't far off. She was persistently beautiful but the ravages of time were unmistakable, her features having become pointed, sharp, furrowed and **anile**. She'd done nothing to avert the terrible tragedy of age, which pays its cruel visit to us all every minute. (Lloyd Dykk, *Cher and Cher Alike*, The Vancouver Sun, 01-25-1997, p. H3.)

old-fashioned (as in excessive reverence for tradition) *n.*: **filiopietistic**. ▪ The controversy over what should be taught in American history classes reveals a deep fissure between today's dominant school of historians and mainstream public opinion. This is not entirely new. University historians have long disdained the study of great men and what one historian calls the "**filiopietistic**" history of popular imagination. (Robert Lerner, *Gendering American History*, The World & I, 04-01-1996, p. 326.)

(2) old-fashioned (person, spec. a person who is opposed to advancements in technology) *n.*: **Luddite**. See TRADITIONALIST

old-line (person, spec. a person who is opposed to advancements in technology) *n.*: **Luddite**. See TRADITIONALIST

oldest (child) *n.*: **primogeniture**. See FIRSTBORN

ominous *adj.*: **baleful**. See SINISTER

omit (intentionally) *v.t.*: **pretermit**. ▪ [In one case, police included] Davis's name and mug shot in a list of "active shoplifters," even though Davis had been accused but not convicted of that offense. [However] the Supreme Court construed the "life, liberty, or property" protected by due process to exclude reputation. The effect of this ruling was not merely to preclude money damages, but to **pretermit** any federal constitutional scrutiny of official condemnation of identified individuals. (John Jeffries, *Disaggregating Constitutional Torts*, Yale Law Journal, 11-01-2000.)

omitting (or passing over or neglecting) *n.*: **preterition**. ∎ Singer-guitarist Thalia Zedek of Boston used to play in an arty blues-punk band called Come, but she's put all that behind her now. ... Though some of it might be gaining ground. For her first solo [recording] Zedek seems alternately obsessed with and haunted by her past, its lost loves, its missed opportunities and her own tragic **preterition**. (Rommie Johnson, *Spin This*, The Tampa Tribune, 12-14-2001, p. 19.)

omnipotence (one obsessed with one's own greatness, fame or ...) *n.*: **megalomania**. SEE OBSESSION

once (as in former) *adj.*: **quondam**. SEE FORMER

one-time (as in former) *adj.*: **ci-devant** [French]. SEE FORMER

(2) one-time (as in former) *adj.*: **quondam**. SEE FORMER

oneness (as in that quality which makes one thing different from any other) *n.*: **haeccity**. SEE INDIVIDUALITY

onion (characteristic of ... or garlic) *adj.*: **alliaceous**. ∎ Mom was severely allergic to [onions and garlic], and so the onion that was somehow thought essential to the Thanksgiving turkey stuffing was the only **alliaceous** substance that entered her kitchen from year's end to year's end. (Linda Bridges, *Late Discoveries [Food Appreciation]*, National Review, 12-22-1997, p. 72.)

onset (from the ...) *adv.*: **ab initio** [Latin]. SEE BEGINNING

(2) onset (from the ...) *adv.*: **ab ovo** [Latin]. SEE BEGINNING

open (as in guileless) *n.*: **artless**. SEE GUILELESS

(2) open (split ... or crack ...) *v.t., v.i., n.*: **fissure**. SEE CRACK

open spaces (fear of ... or public places) *n.*: **agoraphobia**. SEE FEAR

open-minded *adj.*: **latitudinarian**. ∎ Homosexuals are famously **latitudinarian** on matters sexual. Materials distributed by the Gay Men's Health

Crisis include advice on "fisting," "water sports" and "mutilation." (Mona Charen, *The Two Faces of Gay Activism*, The Baltimore Sun, 6-10-1996, p. 7A.)

opening (narrow ..., as in slit) *n.*: **aperture**. SEE SLIT

(2) opening (as in space or gap) *n.*: **lacuna**. SEE GAP

(3) opening (as in preface) *n.*: **proem**. SEE PREFACE

(4) opening (to a lengthy or complex work) *n.*: **prolegomenon**. SEE INTRODUCTION

opera glasses (with a short handle) *n.*: **lorgnette**. SEE EYEGLASSES

opinion (which is odd, stubborn or whimsical) *n.*: **crotchet**. SEE NOTION

(2) opinion (as in personal preference) *n.*: **de gustibus** [Latin]. SEE TASTE

(3) opinion (preconceived ... on an issue) *n.*: **parti pris** [French]. SEE PRECONCEPTION

(4) opinion (which is controversial or person who holds one) *n.*: **polemic**. SEE CONTROVERSY

(5) opinion (of the world) *n.*: **weltanschauung** [German]. SEE WORLDVIEW

oppose (a statement, opinion or action) *v.t.*: **oppugn**. ∎ Newspaper editors and columnists who **oppugn** the Daily Trust editorial on the grounds that the paper was hawking a military takeover either do not understand the English language or didn't read the said editorial at all. (Author not given, *If This Is Democracy*, Africa News Service, 12-08-2003.)

(2) oppose (as in argue against) *v.t.*: **expostulate**. SEE OBJECT

opposing (esp. majority view) *adj.*: **dissentient**. SEE DISSENTING

(2) opposing *adj.*: **oppugnant**. SEE ANTAGONISTIC

(3) opposing (as in resisting constraint or compulsion) *adj.*: **renitent**. SEE RESISTANT

opposite (having ... ideas or qualities) *adj.*: **bipolar**. ∎ Liquidity. It's at the center of the current debate about [Amazon.com's] viability, a debate that keeps growing sharper. "There are a lot of **bipolar** opinions about this company," Bezos said. (David Streitfeld, *Analysts, Vendors Increasingly Wary About Amazon*, The Washington Post, 02-21-2001, p. E1.)

opposition (between laws, rules, or principles) *n.*: **antinomy**. SEE CONFLICT

(2) opposition (to set in ...) *v.t.*: **counterpose**. SEE CONTRAST

oppression (of a religious, national or racial group) *n.*: **helotism** (*v.t.*: **helotize**). ∎ Since the Germans were **helotizing** the denizens of the [concentration] camp world, they, not surprisingly, took many measures to dehumanize them. (Daniel Goldhagen, *Hitler's Willing Executioners*, Knopf [1996], p. 175.)

(2) oppression (as in burden) *n*.: **incubus**. See BURDEN

oppressive (ruthlessly and violently ...) *adj*.: **jackbooted**. ∎ The bureau [of Alcohol, Tobacco and Firearms] is not the **jackbooted** monolith of N.R.A. lore, however. Far from it: court documents and internal reports uncovered in a two-month TIME investigation reveal ATF as a divided and troubled agency far more likely to abuse the rights of its own employees than those of law-abiding citizens. (Erik Larson, *ATF Under Siege — Demon Agency? Far from It; Torn by Internal Strife, the Bureau Has Lost its Sense of Mission*, Time, 07-24-1995, p. 20.)

optimist (as in one habitually expecting an upturn in one's fortunes, sometimes without justification) *n*.: **Micawber** (*adj*: **Micawberish**) [based on the character Wilkins Micawber from the Charles Dickens novel *David Copperfield*, who always said that "something will turn up"]. ∎ By their nature Americans are optimistic. But none of their leaders, not even FDR, has exhibited the quality like Mr. Reagan. It was **Micawberish** at times, a seemingly blind conviction that even the darkest events had a silver lining; but no other politician could summon that politically priceless "feel-good factor." (Rupert Cornwell, *Ronald Reagan 1911-2004: A President Whose Optimism Earned Him a Place in History*, The Independent [London], 06-07-2004.)

optimistic (esp. blindly or naively ...) *adj*.: **Panglossian** [based on Dr. Pangloss, the optimistic tutor of Candide in the novel of the same name, by Voltaire]. ∎ Although overall holiday-sales forecasts range from **Panglossian** to Scroogesque, analysts agree that online shopping is booming. (Paul Andrews, *Christmas Clicking*, U.S. News & World Report, 12-15-2003.)

(2) optimistic (excessively or unrealistically ... person) *n*.: **Pollyanna**. ∎ "[W]e will win games this year. I'm very confident of that" [said Chicago Bears coach Dave Wannstedt]. ... He is talking Super Bowl — and he insists he is serious. Apparently, he hasn't looked at the schedule. ... It's no wonder Bears fans are confused: Do they have a great coach needing more time to develop or a **Pollyanna**, who is in over his head? (T.J. Simers, *Bullish on Chicago? Bad News, Bears Fans*, The Sporting News, 08-18-1997, p. 15.)

option (of taking what is offered or nothing; i.e. no real option at all) *n*.: **Hobson's choice**. See PREDICAMENT

(2) option (bad ..., as in the situation of having to make a move where any move made will weaken the position) *n*.: **zugzwang** [German]. See PREDICAMENT

opulent (excessively ..., esp. in a sensuous way) *adj*.: **sybaritic**. See LUXURIOUS

oracular *adj*.: **vatic**. See PROPHETIC

oral *adj*.: **nuncupative**. See VERBAL

(2) oral *adj., adv*.: **viva voce** [Latin]. See VERBAL

orate (on a topic, esp. in a long-winded or pompous manner) *v.i*.: **bloviate**. See SPEAK

(2) orate (pompously, loudly, or theatrically) *v.i*.: **declaim**. See PROCLAIM

oration (very enthusiastic or excited ... or writing) *n*.: **dithyramb**. See ENTHUSIASTIC

ordeal (as in painful journey or experience) *n*.: **via dolorosa** [derives from Jesus' route from Pontius Pilate's judgment hall to Calvary to be crucified]. ∎ From the Nazi occupation and the liquidation of Lidice, to the Communist show trials and the persecution of Charter 77, Czech history in the past century has been — apart from two periods of independence under Masaryk and Havel — a **via dolorosa**. (Daniel Johnson, *The Dwarves Who Posture on the Shoulders of Giants*, The Daily Telegraph, 09-28-2000.)

(2) ordeal (a great ..., as in experience of intense suffering) *n*.: **Calvary** [based on hill near Jerusalem where Jesus was crucified]. See SUFFERING

(3) ordeal (as in burden) *n*.: **incubus**. See BURDEN

order *v.t*.: **adjure**. ∎ Ho Chi Minh is a wispy man (100 lbs.), mild and slow-spoken, and disarmingly forthright. ... "You must give the people an example of poverty, misery and denial," he sometimes **adjures** his disciples, and off he plods, ostentatiously, through the villages, with a knapsack on his back. (Author not given, *1946-1960 Independence: A Tidal Wave of Nationalist Fervor Washed Away Centuries of Colonial Rule, Transforming the Physical and Political Map*, Time International, 05-04-1998, p. 70.)

(2) order (as in sequence or progression) *n*.: **consecution**. See SEQUENCE

(3) order (as in decree) *n*.: **diktat**. See DECREE

(4) order *n*.: **ukase**. See DECREE

ordinary (as in routine or mechanical) *adj*.: **banausic**. See ROUTINE

(2) ordinary (people, as in the masses) *n.*: **canaille**. SEE MASSES

(3) ordinary (people, as in the masses) *n.*: **hoi polloi**. SEE COMMONERS

(4) ordinary (in tastes and ideas and culture) *adj.*: **philistine**. SEE UNCULTURED

(5) ordinary (of or relating to the ... people) *adj.*: **plebian**. SEE COMMON

(6) ordinary *adj.*: **quotidian**. SEE MUNDANE

(7) ordinary (as in mundane; everyday) *adj.*: **sublunary**. SEE EARTHLY

orgasm (failure or inability to achieve ...) *adj.*: **anorgasmic**. ▪ This approach is a basic step in treatment programs for sexual dysfunction. For example, a majority of **anorgasmic** women discover that their mother either never talked about sex with her mother, or grew up thinking sex was sinful or dirty and similarly warned her daughter. (Dr Judy, *Fitness File/Sex/Q/A*, Newsday, 07-05-1999, p. B17.)

origin (existing from the ..., as in innate) *adj.*: **connate**. SEE INNATE

(2) origin (as in prime mover) *n.*: **primum mobile** [Latin]. SEE PRIME MOVER

(3) origin (principal ...) *n.*: **wellhead**. SEE SOURCE

original (model or example) *n.*: **archetype**. SEE MODEL

(2) original (in the ... position) *adj., adv.*: **in situ** [Latin]. SEE UNMOVED

(3) original (as in of recent origin) *adj.*: **neoteric**. SEE RECENT

(4) original (as in first) *adj.*: **primordial**. SEE FIRST

origins (study of ..., esp. relating to medical conditions) *n.*: **etiology**. SEE CAUSES

ornament (esp. resembling a tuft of plumes) *n.*: **aigrette**. ▪ But despotic rule can produce great art. That of the Ottomans is now seen in Washington in the Corcoran Gallery of Art's "Palace of Gold & Light: Treasures From the Topkapi, Istanbul." ... Other trappings of power appear in the show. Jeweled **aigrettes** for decorating turbans exuded wealth. They took their name from the egret feathers embellishing them. (Joanna Shaw-Eagle, *Turkish Treasures; "Gold, Light" from Topkapi Palace in Istanbul*, The Washington Times, 03-04-2000, p. D1.)

(2) ornament (in a showy or excessive manner) *v.t.*: **bedeck**. SEE ADORN

(3) ornament (or dress in a showy or excessive manner) *v.t.*: **bedizen**. SEE ADORN

(4) ornament (small ... or trinket) *n.*: **bibelot**. SEE TRINKET

(5) ornament (small ... or trinket) *n.*: **bijou** SEE TRINKET

(6) ornament *n.*: **garniture**. SEE DECORATION

(7) ornament (small ... or trinket) *n.*: **gewgaw**. SEE TRINKET

ornate *adj.*: **baroque**. ▪ The **baroque** style, which originated in Rome during the 1600s, is art in the grandest manner. Florid, ornate and luxurious, baroque art was designed to dazzle the eye and reflect the owner's importance and wealth. (Mary Abbe, *Institute Lends Artifacts to New York Show*, Minneapolis Star Tribune, 04-25-1999, p. 8F.)

(2) ornate *adj.*: **florid**. ▪ Overwriting [is] so common and so ridiculous that a national contest [exists for the worst writing]. ... The contest is named for [the] novelist who first penned the words "It was a dark and stormy night" and whose work was so **florid** that it inspired guffaws. We see ornate and affected prose everywhere, from the modest workplace memo to the ambitious academic report. (Paula LaRocque, *Poor Writing Often Tries Too Hard To Impress*, The Dallas Morning News, 03-13-2000, p. 13A.)

(3) ornate *adj.*: **rococo**. ▪ He grew portly and his mustache evolved in shapes ever more luxurious and **rococo**, for he had become what Pinkerton called a "silk glove man." (Ben Macintyre, *The Napoleon of Crime*, Farrar, Straus & Giroux [1997], p. 158.)

ornery *adj.*: **atrabilious**. SEE SURLY

(2) ornery *adj.*: **bilious**. SEE SURLY

(3) ornery (person) *n.*: **crosspatch**. SEE GROUCH

(4) ornery *adj.*: **liverish**. SEE IRRITABLE

(5) ornery *adj.*: **querulous**. SEE PEEVISH

(6) ornery *adj.*: **shirty**. SEE IRRITABLE

orphan (as in baby who is deserted or abandoned) *n.*: **foundling**. ▪ At ten days old, Dave, now 30, was dumped in a London tube station toilet. He is one of Britain's **foundling** babies — last year there were five — whose mothers are never traced. (Author not given, Daily Mirror, *Anguish of the Foundling Babies*, 02-28-96, p. 6.)

ostentatious (object) *n.*: **frippery**. ▪ The indictment [against Harry and Leona Helmsley] claimed that they listed as business expenses such personal **fripperies** as a $130,000 indoor-outdoor stereo system for their home. (Joyce Wadler, *For the Love of Money — They Have Each Other and More than a Billion Dollars, But, Charges the Government, Harry and Leona Helmsley Wanted More and Broke the Law To Get It,*

People, 05-02-1988, p. 90.)

(2) ostentatious (speech or writing) *adj.*: **fustian**. SEE POMPOUS

(3) ostentatious (but actually superficial knowledge of a subject) *n.*: **sciolism**. SEE SUPERFICIAL

ostrich (as in complacent person who ignores any unpleasant facts) *n.*: **Podsnap** (*adj.*: **Podsnappian**). ∎ Attorney General Edwin Meese's committee ... pushed for a "common sense" rationale for prosecution of pornographers when scientific evidence inconveniently suggested nonintervention. ... Meese is rendered as a modern-day Mr. **Podsnap**, that pathetic character in Dickens's *Our Mutual Friend* who would haughtily dismiss any inconvenient fact, saying, "I don't want to know about it; I don't choose to discuss it; I don't admit it!" (Michael S. Kimmel, *The Secret Museum: Pornography in Modern Culture, [Book Reviews]*, Psychology Today, 02-01-1988.)

(2) ostrich (of, relating to or resembling) *adj.*: **struthious** [a word used figuratively as often as not]. ∎ It rankles me whenever I see a reference to "reluctant allies" or "the opposition of our allies." These **struthious** populations of France and Germany are not our allies [any longer. They] try to ennoble their own dishonest motives by describing war as the ultimate failure of diplomacy, something to be avoided at all costs, claiming the moral high ground by virtue of their having experienced the horrors of war. If they would get their heads out of the sand, they might avoid repeating those experiences. (Author not given, *Another Word for "Allies,"* The Orlando Sentinel, 01-26-2003.)

otherworldly *adj.*: **fey**. ∎ The greatest mystery of [Arthur Conan] Doyle's life is how the creator of Sherlock Holmes — that "perfect reasoning and observing machine" — would eventually champion **fey** phenomena like seances and fairies, so that by his 1930 death at age 71 he was considered "hopelessly crazy." (Kristen Baldwin, *Books/The Week*, Entertainment Weekly, 04-23-1999, p. 58.)

out of sight (as in, in concealment) *adv.*: **doggo** (esp. as in "lying doggo"; slang). SEE CONCEALMENT

out-of-control (and undisciplined person) *n.*: **bashi-bazouk** [Turkish]. SEE UNDISCIPLINED

outbreak (of violence or disorder) *n.*: **émeute** [French]. SEE REBELLION

outburst (of emotion, feeling or action) *n.*: **paroxysm**. ∎ [A]fter the 1970 ouster of Prince Norodom

Sihanouk, Cambodia suffered **paroxysms** of violence that battered the entire populace and the country's infrastructure, including its roads. (Kay Johnson, *From Sapporo To Surabaya/Taheng, Cambodia: The Road To Riches: After Three Decades of Turmoil, Cambodia is Trying to Repave its Way Back to Peace and Prosperity*, Time International, 08-21-2000, p. 80.)

(2) outburst (as in temper tantrum) *n.*: **boutade** [French]. SEE TEMPER TANTRUM

(3) outburst (marked by a sudden or violent ...) *adj.*: **vesuvian** (esp. as in ...temper). SEE TEMPER

outcast *n.*: **Ishmael** [after the son of Abraham in the Old Testament who was conceived in adultery with Sarah's handmaid Hagar and was outcast after Sarah gave birth to Isaac]. ∎ Hardie ... chairman of the Parliamentary Labour Party [viewed] his role within Parliament, as an agitator rather than an administrator or organiser. [His proposals in favor of the working man] had little expectation of success in a Conservative-dominated Parliament but every hope of maximum publicity. Hardie seemed to relish the role of lone rebel and once described himself as "an **Ishmael** in public life." (Roger Spalding, *Keir Hardie: Socializing the World for the Workers: [Hardie is] One of the Key Figures in the History of the Labour Party*, History Review, 12-01-2001.)

outcry (as in plea; lit. cry of the heart) *n.*: **cri de coeur** [French]. SEE PLEA

outdated *adj.*: **antediluvian**. ∎ Take me out to the ball game, Take me out to the Diamond View Suites. Buy me some Dijon-marinated jumbo shrimp and Grgich Hills Chardonnay, I don't care 'cause the company will pay. ... Given the current state of pro sports economics, Take Me Out to the Ball Game needs a little updating. And so does the **antediluvian** notion that fan support is the key to franchise success. (Steve Wulf, *Business: How Suite it Isn't — Cities Are Winning and Losing Teams Based on How Many Luxury Boxes They Can Offer Greedy Owners*, Time, 07-10-1995, p. 52.)

(2) outdated *adj.*: **démodé** [French]. SEE OUTMODED

outdoors *adv., adj.*: **alfresco**. ∎ [The 42-year-old teacher and her 15-year-old student] returned to Hampstead Heath at least 20 times [to carry out their affair.] The **alfresco** aspect of their sexual relations has greatly exercised the press but, contrary to all the reporters' salacious innuendo, [they] did not feel that there was any erotic bonus to their trysting outdoors. (Zoë Heller, *What Was She Thinking?* Henry Holt [2003], p. 122.)

(2) outdoors (fear of being ...) *n.*: **agoraphobia**. SEE FEAR

outfit *v.t.*: **accouter**. ▪ [Dennis] Rodman claims that just as he visits gay bars without caring what people think, so he **accouters** himself regardless of others. So what the hell, when Rodman hits the road, he always packs some women's clothes. (Evan Gahr, *Bad As I Wanna Be [Book Reviews]*, National Review, 07-01-1996, p. 53.)

outfitter (for men's clothing) *n.*: **haberdasher**. SEE CLOTHIER

outgrowth *n.*: **excrescence** [This word is often used literally, such as to describe an abnormal growth on the body or of a bodily part, such as a wart, but just as often is used in the sense of being an offshoot or consequence of a prior event or circumstance]. ▪ [In *Ceasefire!* author Cathy Young's intention] is to unmask the false claims of these "thought police," especially as they concern the supposed continued inequality of women in the United States. [C]ourt cases involving gender violence and sex crimes, child abuse and domestic violence, child custody and school curricula [are] **excrescences** of a cultural agenda that has been put in place to support spurious feminist claims and provide employment for enforcers. (Elizabeth Powers, *What Our Mothers Didn't Tell Us: Why Happiness Eludes the Modern Woman*, Commentary, 03-01-1999.)

outlaw (as in outcast) *n.*: **Ishmael**. SEE OUTCAST

outline (in a sketchy or incomplete way) *v.t.*: **adumbrate**. ▪ Nikolai Gogol was nineteenth-century Russia's greatest writer of prose. Not its greatest prose writer: Dostoyevsky, [Tolstoy] and others, framed complexities that have no counterpart in their odd predecessor, and they wrote on a scale that dwarfed his. They explored ideas; he, at best, **adumbrated** them. (Donald Fanger, *The Unrealist*, The New Republic, 11-02-1998.)

(2) outline (as in summary) *n.*: **conspectus**. SEE SURVEY

(3) outline (as in set the boundaries of) *v.t.*: **delimit**. SEE DEMARCATE

(4) outline (distinctive ..., often of a face) *adj.*: **lineament** (often **lineaments**). SEE CONTOUR

outlying (area) *n.*: **purlieus**. SEE OUTSKIRTS

outmoded *adj.*: **démodé** [French]. ▪ Remember when popular movies had women in them? In 1994's top films, the ladies were lucky if the guys let

them even drive a bus. Affirmative action is **démodé** these days, but Hollywood needs some spur to bring women into full partnership with the Toms [Hanks] and Arnolds [Schwarzenegger] and Simbas [the lion]. (Author not given, *The Best Cinema of 1994*, Time, 12-26-1994, p. 132.)

outmoded *adj.*: **antediluvian**. SEE OUTDATED

outrageous (as in infamous, esp as to a crime or evil deed) *adj.*: **flagitious**. SEE SCANDALOUS

(2) outrageous (and reckless person) *n.*: **rantipole**. SEE WILD

outset (from the) *adv.*: **ab initio** [Latin]. SEE BEGINNING

(2) outset (from the) *adv.*: **ab ovio** [Latin]. SEE BEGINNING

(3) outset (existing from the ..., as in innate) *adj.*: **connate**. SEE INNATE

outside (from the ...) *adv.*: **ab extra** [Latin]. SEE EXTERNALLY

(2) outside (fear of being ...) *n.*: **agoraphobia**. SEE FEAR

(3) outside (as in outdoors) *adv., adj.*: **alfresco**. SEE OUTDOORS

(4) outside (as in originating from elsewhere; not endemic) *adj.*: **ecdemic**. SEE FOREIGN

outsider (as in foreigner) *n.*: **auslander**. SEE FOREIGNER

(2) outsider *n.*: **Ishmael**. SEE OUTCAST

outskirts *n., pl.*: **purlieus**. ▪ Some guys will do anything for a laugh. Michael Smith has donned fake eyeglasses that make him look Japanese — in a room full of Japanese people. In the laid-back **purlieus** of Silicon Valley such idiosyncratic behavior might go unnoticed. But [Smith is] the government's chief trade negotiator, and that makes him a maverick in an unfunny business. (Andrew Kupfer, *The Year's 25 Most Fascinating Business People: Smith to Japan: Here's the Beef*, Fortune, 01-02-1989, p. 53.)

outstanding (as in of the highest quality) *n.*: **first water** (usu. as in "of the first water"). SEE QUALITY

(2) outstanding *adj.*: **frabjous** (often as in "Oh frabjous day!"). SEE WONDERFUL

(3) outstanding *adj.*: **galumptious**. SEE EXCELLENT

(4) outstanding *adj.*: **palmary**. SEE EXCELLENT

(5) outstanding *adj.*: **skookum**. SEE EXCELLENT

over the top (as in excessive) *adj.*: **de trop** [French]. SEE EXCESSIVE

overabundance *n.:* **nimiety**. See EXCESS

overactive *adj.:* **sthenic**. See OVERSTIMULATED

overall (as in predominant) *adj.:* **regnant**. See PREDOMINANT

overambitious *adj.:* **Icarian** [based on the Greek mythological character Icarus who flew so high on man-made wings that the sun melted them]. ■ Edward O. Wilson's book is audacious, prophetic, and bound to become a recurrent touchstone to test intellectual progress in the twenty-first century. ... E. O. Wilson boldly seeks no less than a unification of all knowledge so that we might "know who we are and why we are here." He acknowledges that this **Icarian** reaching for the sun is dangerous but asks to "see how high we can fly before the sun melts the wax in our wings." [Note: The author of this passage is using "Icarian" in the sense of "daring" (as opposed to "overly daring"), and the word is sometimes used in this sense. However, for something to be truly "Icarian," it must be overambitious and not merely ambitious, because the latter implies possible success and the former does not. Moreover, Mr. Wilson aspires to "see how high we can fly *before* the sun melts the wax in our wings," not "until" the sun melts the wax. Thus, in this example, since it is clear that the author feels that Mr. Wilson's venture was ultimately successful, it might have been more precise to call it "potential" Icarian reaching.] (Michael Werner, *Consilience: The Unity of Knowledge [Review]*, The Humanist, 03-01-1999.)

overbearing (as in condescending) *adj., adv.:* **de haut en bas** [French]. See CONDESCENDING
(2) overbearing (woman who is domineering and ...) *n.:* **virago**. See SHREW

overblown (as in pompous) *adj.:* **tumid**. See BOMBASTIC
(2) overblown (as in pompous) *adj.:* **turgid**. See POMPOUS

overcritical *adj.:* **captious**. See FAULTFINDING
(2) overcritical (person) *n.:* **smellfungus**. See FAULTFINDER

overdone (as in gaudy) *adj.:* **meretricious**. See GAUDY
(2) overdone (behavior) *n., adj.:* **operatics**. See MELODRAMATIC

overeat *v.t.:* **gormandize**. See DEVOUR

overeating (or drinking too much) *n.:* **crapulence**. See INDULGENCE

overexcited *adj.:* **sthenic**. See OVERSTIMULATED

overflowing (with) *adj.:* **aswarm**. See TEEMING

overhead *adj.:* **superjacent**. See OVERLYING

overheat (a person or thing, often to create sweat) *v.t.:* **parboil**. See HEAT

overindulgence (esp. from eating or drinking too much) *n.:* **crapulence**. See INDULGENCE
(2) overindulge (on food) *v.t.:* **gormandize**. See DEVOUR

overlap (like roof shingles or fish scales) *v.t.:* **imbricate**. ■ There is almost no English surname, however ancient and dignified, that cannot be instantly improved by the prefix "Spanker." So deeply is the habit and culture of corporal punishment **imbricated** with the national psyche that whole shelves of specialist literature ... are regularly devoted to the subject. (Christopher Hitchens, *Minority Report: Johnson & Johnson*, The Nation, 06-29-1998, p. 8.)

overlying *adj.:* **superjacent**. ■ [L]et me say that under section 44 of the National Land Code 1965, a landowner is guaranteed his right to the use and enjoyment of his land, the **superjacent** air space and the subsoil (Salleh Buang, *Onus on Local Authority to Act Against Illegal Factories*, New Straits Times [Malaysia], 01-20-2001, p. 35.)

overprotect (or overly indulge) *v.t.:* **mollycoddle**. ■ A series of arrests, and the perception [Nebraska coach Tom Osborne] was **mollycoddling** his players, brought torrents of criticism, none creating more than the case of Lawrence Phillips. Phillips ... pleaded no contest to charges of assaulting a former girlfriend. Osborne initially announced he was kicked off the team but reinstated him in time for Nebraska's Fiesta Bowl victory over Florida. (Vahe Gregorian, *Osborne Will Retire; Orange Bowl Game Will Be His Farewell*, St. Louis Post-Dispatch, 12-11-1997, p. B1.)

overreaching (as in overambitious) *adj.:* **Icarian**. See OVERAMBITIOUS

overrun (with) *adj.:* **aswarm**. See TEEMING

oversee (students taking an examination) *v.i.:* **invigilate**. See PROCTOR

overseer *n.:* **gerent**. See MANAGER
(2) overseer (as in boss or owner) *n.:* **padrone**. See BOSS
(3) overseer (brutal ..., as in taskmaster) *n.:* **Simon Legree**. See TASKMASTER

overstate (as in exaggerate) *v.t.*: **aggrandize**. SEE EXAGGERATE

overstatement (abnormal propensity towards ...) *n.*: **mythomania**. SEE EMBELLISHMENT

overstimulated *adj.*: **sthenic**. ∎ [Sexual disease] was conceived as an imbalance in the fundamental life force of the body, taking the form of either overexcitement (**sthenic** illness, as in nymphomania) or underexcitement (aesthenia). (Ann Goldberg, *The Eberbach Asylum and the Practice(s) of Nymphomania in Germany, 1815-1849*, Journal of Women's History, 01-01-1998.)

overthrow (sudden attempt to ... a government) *n.*: **putsch**. SEE COUP

overturning (as in abandonment, from one's religion, principles or causes) *n.*: **apostasy**. SEE ABANDONMENT

(2) overturning (esp. regarding one's beliefs, causes or policies) *n.*: **bouleversement** [French]. SEE CHANGE OF MIND

(3) overturning (an ... regarding one's beliefs, causes or policies) *n.*: **tergiversation** (*v.i.*: **tergiversate**). SEE CHANGE OF MIND

overused (remark or statement) *n.*: **platitude**. SEE CLICHE

overview (of a subject, as in survey) *n.*: **conspectus**. SEE SURVEY

overweight (as in beer-bellied) *adj.*: **abdominous**. SEE BEER-BELLIED

(2) overweight (medical branch concerning ... people) *n.*: **bariatrics**. SEE OBESITY

(3) overweight (and squat) *adj.*: **fubsy**. SEE SQUAT

(4) overweight *adj.*: **Pickwickian**. SEE FAT

owner *n.*: **padrone**. SEE BOSS

ox (of, relating to or resembling) *adj., n.*: **bovine**. ∎ Worldwide, most of the 400,000,000 animals trained for draft are of the **bovine** persuasion, according to Richard Roosenberg, director of Tillers International, an organization that promotes the use of draft animals in general and ox power in particular. (Gail Damerow, *Is There a Draft Animal in Your Future?* Countryside & Small Stock Journal, 11-21-1996, p. 37.)

oxygen (absence or deficiency of ...) *n.*: **anoxia**. ∎ It seems to me that in about one-quarter of twin labors, the area of uterus overlying the second baby's placenta shrinks drastically enough to cut off the oxygen supply to that placenta, and consequently to the baby still in the uterus. When that happens, I believe the baby still has about 30 minutes before it will run into serious **anoxia**. (John Stevenson, *What If Something Goes Wrong?* Contemporary Women's Issues Database, 03-01-1994, p. 6.)

P

pacify (as in appease) *v.t.*: **dulcify**. SEE APPEASE

(2) pacify *v.t.*: **propitiate**. SEE PLACATE

pacifying (as in peacemaking) *adj.*: **irenic**. SEE PEACEMAKING

pack (as in group) *n.*: **gaggle**. SEE GROUP

(2) pack (of riders in a bike race) *n.*: **peloton** [French]. SEE CLUSTER

packed (together, esp. in rows) *adj.*: **serried**. SEE CROWDED

paddle (instrument such as a ... for punishing children) *n.*: **ferule**. ∎ [His] warmth did not affect what I judged the extreme severity of the punishment I was twice sentenced to, for whatever social infraction. The first time it was a single **ferule** stroke, smacked down on my open hand. (William F. Buckley, Jr., *A Spiritual Autobiography [Adapted from "Nearer, My God: An Autobiography of Faith"]*, National Review, 10-13-1997, p. 33.)

pain (medication causing inability to feel) *n.*: **analgesia**. SEE NUMBNESS

(2) pain (in joints) *n.*: **arthralgia**. SEE ARTHRITIS

(3) pain (as in place, condition or society filled with ...; spec., opposite of utopia) *n.*: **dystopia**. SEE HELL

(4) pain (as in place or occasion of great suffering, or hell) *n.*: **Gehenna**. SEE HELL

(5) pain (as in occasion or place of great suffering) *n.*: **Gethsemane**. SEE HELL

(6) pain (as in occasion or place of great suffering) *n.*: **Golgotha**. SEE HELL

pain in the ass *n.*: **proctalgia** [Of course, this is technically a medical term (often used as part of the phrase "proctalgia fugax"), but it can obviously have other uses.]. ∎ I'm predicting that the ass falls out of that whole celebrity-worship thing. It's really been taken to an excruciating level, and I think there has to be some sort of a backlash. It's not like in the

'60s, when [celebrities] were celebrities because they were creating new and original work. Now it's that whole red-carpet celebrity adulation. It's just so **proctalgia** inducing of course, it's a cyclical thing. (Simon Doonan, *Forecast: Culture [Public Not as Enamored of Fame in Future]*, Esquire, 03-01-2001.)

pain-reliever *n.*: **anodyne**. ∎ As a boy, Rick had found in basketball his **anodyne**, his escape from loneliness, and he had spent hours on the courts of Queens, losing himself in the game. (William Nack, *College Basketball [Bonus Piece]: Full-Court Pressure — The Kentucky Wildcats' Relentless Attack Reflects the Ferocious Drive of Their Coach, Rick Pitino*, Sports Illustrated, 02-26-1996, p. 80.)

(2) pain-reliever (as in something which induces forgetfulness or oblivion of pain, suffering or sorrow) *n.*: **nepenthe**. See NARCOTIC

pain-relieving (as in comforting and soothing) *adj.*: **anodyne**. See SOOTHING

painful (journey or experience) *n.*: **via dolorosa**. See ORDEAL

painting (dealing with evening or night) *n.*: **nocturne**. ∎ Making art outdoors on misty autumn evenings and brisk winter nights has its ups and downs for painter Mike Lynch and photographer Chris Faust, whose serene show of poetic nightscapes opens today at the Minneapolis Institute of Arts. [Faust] had admired Lynch's **nocturnes** for nearly 30 years, having first seen them when he was still in high school. (Mary Abbe, *Night Moves / Photographer Chris Faust and Painter Mike Lynch Do Their Best Work on the Third Shift*, Minneapolis Star Tribune, 12-15-2000, p. 12.)

painting (which looks like a photograph or something real) *n.*: **trompe l'oeil** [French]. See ILLUSION

paintings (produced in the artist's youth) *n.*: **juvenilia**. See COMPOSITIONS

pair (two individuals or units regarded as a ...) *n.*: **dyad**. ∎ She also shows how a commitment to the ideal of a mother-child **dyad** has created the conditions in which mother and child can only function as a **dyad**. (Rebecca Abrams, *Mother of All Myths: How Society Molds and Constrains Motherhood [book reviews]*, New Statesman, 07-31-1998, p. 44.)

(2) pair (arranged in or forming a ...) *adj.*: **jugate**. ∎ Political buttons come in all sizes, shapes, and classifications. ... Picture buttons are the most popular, especially the **jugates** that picture both running

mates on the same button. (Jesse Palmer, *Button Up Your Social Studies Classroom*, The Social Studies, 03-13-1996, p. 52.)

(3) pair (of people, as in partnership) *n.*: **duumvirate**. See DUO

pal (faithful ..., as in companion) *n.*: **Achates**. See COMPANION

palatable (as in tasty) *adj.*: **sapid**. See TASTY

pale (as from absence of sunlight) *adj.*: **etiolated**. ∎ I've been re-acquainting myself with parts of my body I have not seen since last summer. Such as my legs. And quite a shock it has been, to wiggle out of my boots and tights and see them in all their **etiolated** glory. They're so pale they're practically luminous. So I start a process of leg rehabilitation: the fake tan goes on, the drying position is assumed. (Hermione Eyr, *Beauty Spot — Hermione Eyre Takes it All Off*, Independent on Sunday [London], 05-09-2004.)

(2) pale (or corpselike) *adj.*: **cadaverous**. See CORPSELIKE

palm-reading *n.*: **chiromancy**. ∎ [A new ordinance] bans "the practice of foretelling events and the prophecy of the future." Since [the ban], business has been slow for the [fortunetellers] with tarot cards unturned and palms unread. ... Certainly, **chiromancy** and tarot readings are no more absurd than the horoscopes published in this and other newspapers that circulate in Terrebonne Parish. (James Gill, *Crystal Ball Says Law Must Go*, Times-Picayune [New Orleans, LA], 10-08-2000.)

paltry *n.*: **exiguous**. See MEAGER
(2) paltry (as in meager) *adj.*: **mingy**. See MEAGER

pamper *v.t.*: **cosset**. ∎ Let's start by defining terms. The "nanny state" is the phrase conservatives have long used to disparage liberal programs that they believe **cosset** the poor with entitlements and nitpick everyone else with meddlesome rules and regulations. (Ronald Brownstein, *When Daddy Is a Nag*, U.S. News & World Report, 06-01-1998, p. 30.)

(2) pamper (in an overprotective way or indulge) *v.t.*: **mollycoddle**. See OVERPROTECT
(3) pamper (as in treat with excessive concern) *n.*, *v.t.*: **wet-nurse**. See CODDLE

panacea *n.*: **catholicon**. See REMEDY
(2) panacea (alleged ... which is untested or unproved) *n.*: **nostrum**. See REMEDY

pandemonium (as in chaos) *n.*: **tohubuhu**. See CHAOS

panhandler *n.*: **mendicant**. See BEGGAR

panic *n.*: **Torschlusspanik** [German. This word means literally "gate-closing panic," as in not wanting to be the last one left before the gate closes, or having the feeling that life's opportunities may be passing one by, and is used in a myriad of figurative ways including: (1) a midlife crisis; (2) for women, the sense that one's biological clock is ticking; (3) at an auction, the sense that one must have one of the last pieces of a collection being sold; and (4) in a financial panic, such as when there is a run on a bank. The example used here is somewhat more literal, but the concept is clear.] ▪ The idea for the [Berlin] Wall is credited to Walter Ulbricht, leader of the GDR, who had told a press conference in June 1961: "No one intends building a wall." No one took the hint. But with so many East Germans gripped with **Torschlusspanik** — the rush to escape before the door was finally shut (30,415 arrived in West Berlin in July 1961) — the authorities had to do something drastic. (Alan Taylor, *The Wall to End All Walls*, Scotland on Sunday, 10-31-1999, p. 14.)

(2) panic (state of ..., as in distress) *n.*: **swivet** (as in "in a swivet") *inf.* See DISTRESS

panting *adj.*: **suspirious** (*v.t.*: **suspire**). ▪ If you missed the first episode [of the TV movie *Anna Karenina*] you've missed most of the excitement, such as it was. Anna and Vronsky ... had at each other after about two chats and three glances — one of those blurry, **suspirious** TV fumbles where both parties seem to go from nought to orgasm in 10 seconds flat, and that's not easy with all those Victorian layers to remove. (James Hall, *Screenwatch — Passion at a Price*, The Australian, 07-06-2000.)

paradise (as in place of extreme luxury and ease where physical comforts and pleasures are always at hand) *n.*: **Cockaigne**. ▪ Imagine a country where whole cooked chickens fall from the sky, rivers of ricotta cheese flow freely, and laziness is rewarded. In fact, working will get you arrested. This is the Land of **Cockaigne**, a fabled place longed for by the overworked, underfed peasants of the Middle Ages. It was their idea of paradise. Each age has had its visions of an ideal society. (Author not given, *From Ancient Eden to the Hippie Era — Searching for Utopia: New York Public Library Launches a New Exhibition on the Perfect Place*, The Christian Science Monitor, 10-19-2000.)

(2) paradise (spec. a place of fabulous wealth or opportunity) *n.*: **El Dorado** [derives from legendary place in South America thought to exist by 16th century explorers]. ▪ If there is an **El Dorado**, it may look like this. ... Outside [of the Boca Raton Resort & Club], conjuring up a modern vision of the legendary city of fabulous wealth, yachts bob at pristine docks, exotic birds flit through manicured tropical foliage, and golfers purr around a lush course in motorized pink carts. (Susan Harrigan, *A White Man's World: Diversity in Management*, Newsday [New York], 04-13-2000, p. A6.)

(3) paradise *n.*: **Xanadu** [after "Xanadu," a place in *Kubla Kahn*, a poem by Samuel Taylor Coleridge]. ▪ [From the plane,] a stunning landscape glides into view: jagged fjords, ice-capped peaks, a green carpet of ancient cedars. [Douglas Tompkins] has spent four years and $15 million quietly buying up this 667,000-acre swath in remote southern Chile. The ... committed environmentalist, wants to turn his pristine **Xanadu** into a national park, protecting this fragile land forever. There is only one problem. The locals think he is crazy. (David Schrieberg, *Firestorm in Paradise* [American Billionaire Douglas Tompkins Buys 667,000 Acres in Chile to Make Into a National Park, Faces Much Opposition From Chileans], Newsweek, 5-22-1995.)

paragon *n.*: **nonesuch**. ▪ Parade magazine asks Priscilla Presley if she believed daughter Lisa Marie Presley was behaving responsibly when she wed pop **nonesuch** Michael Jackson. The reply: "I don't think she thought she was irresponsible. Then she took responsibility and got out of it." (Harry Levins, *People*, St. Louis Post-Dispatch, 02-08-1997, p. 24.)

paralysis (as in the dilemma of being given a choice between two equally appealing alternatives and thus being able to choose neither one) *n.*: **Buridan's ass** [attributed to 4th century French philosopher Jean Buridan, who presented a situation where an ass is given the option of two equally wonderful piles of hay, and starves to death because it cannot choose]. ▪ Sarah Jessica Parker has ... **Buridan's ass**. Poor girl. ... In the issue of Newsweek that commemorates the anniversary of September 11, Little Miss Zeitgeist is asked to choose between "a pair of Manolos and a Kelly bag," and she replies, "Oh, well, that's like 'Sophie's Choice.' That's an impossible situation." This is what passes for smart in Manhattan now. (Leon Wieseltier, *Washington Diarist: Still*, The New Republic, 09-22-2003.)

paraphernalia (esp. trivial or worthless ...) *n.*: **trumpery**. See JUNK

paraphrase *n.*: **oratio obliqua** [Latin for "indirect speech"]. ∎ [H]ow did it come about that Mrs. Thatcher [was never told] the truth about the man at the heart of the Westland leak? ... [T]hat can only be answered by those who were there in the thick of it. Which is why even two and a half hours of Sir Robert Armstrong's courtly **oratio obliqua** were not, in the end, any adequate substitute [for the actual] witnesses it had sent for but been denied. (David McKie, *Parliamentary Commentary: A Little Light Shines Wanly*, The Guardian [London], 02-06-1986.)

parasite (esp. someone who seeks to associate with or flatter persons of high rank or social status) *n.*: **tuft-hunter**. SEE HANGER-ON

pardon (as in place or occasion of humiliation or to seek forgiveness) *n.*: **Canossa**. SEE PENANCE

pardonable *adj.*: **venial**. SEE FORGIVABLE

parent (biological ...) *n.*: **genitor**. ∎ Among the Nayar of India, a woman weds several men. Any one of them can be a **genitor**, a biological father, but only one can be a pater, one who fulfills all the functions and social duties of a father. (David Murray, *Disappearance of Marriage Threatens to Destroy Our Culture*, National Minority Politics, 08-31-1994.)

parents (in place of) *adv.*: **in loco parentis** [Latin]. ∎ Not so long ago, administrators acted **in loco parentis**, trying to protect the welfare of their students by setting down rules of conduct, ethics, even dress. But in the aftermath of the '60s rebellion, all that changed. Students demanded to be treated as autonomous adults, and administrators obliged. (Naomi Schaefer, *Campus Crackdown*, National Review, 04-05-1999.)

pariah (as in outcast) *n.*: **Ishmael**. SEE OUTCAST

parish *n.*: **laity**. ∎ Abbott claims that Episcopal ordination "does not raise priests to some superior status above the **laity**." But it does. The proof is in the practice: No Episcopal lay person can preside at the Lord's Supper because **laity** lack the special grace given in ordination. (Author not given, *Letter From Reader*, Minneapolis Star Tribune, 05-27-2000, p. 6B)
(2) parish (as in church congregation) *n.*: **ecclesia**. SEE CONGREGATION

parochial *adj.*: **parish-pump** [British]. ∎ It is TV ... that gives a voice to smaller communities. Topics for discussion will include not only the national or international issues of the day — but also local **parish pump** issues from that particular town. (Author not given, *Small Towns Hit Big Time*, The Evening Post [Wellington, New Zealand], 06-12-2000, p. 6.)

parody (esp. by ridiculing or making fun of someone) *n.*, *v.t.*: **pasquinade**. SEE SATIRIZE

parrot (of, relating to or resembling) *adj.*: **psittacine**. ∎ [W]hen Polly wants more than a cracker, there's www.parrot.com/birdhealth/-recipes.htm. Among the **psittacine**-friendly recipes: popcorn pizza, sweet potato balls and tropical rice pudding. (Denise Flaim, *Just for Pets*, Newsday, 03-28-2004.)
(2) parrot (as in repeat, mindlessly ideas which have been drilled into the speaker or repeating things which reflect the opinions of the powers-that-be) *v.t.*, *v.i.*, *n.*: **duckspeak**. SEE RECITE

part (as in portion) *n.*: **moiety**. SEE PORTION

partial (to a particular point of view) *adj.*: **tendentious**. SEE BIASED

particular (overly ...) *adj.*: **persnickety**. SEE PICKY

particularity (as in that quality which makes one thing different from any other) *n.*: **haeccity**. SEE INDIVIDUALITY

parting shot *n.*: **Parthian shot** [derives from the custom of horsemen from Parthia, an ancient kingdom in West Asia, of firing arrows back at the enemy while retreating, or pretending to be retreating]. ∎ [F]ormer Bush aide John DiIulio ... complained in his **Parthian shot** that the Bush White House paid far more attention to politics and message management than policy. "In eight months, I heard many, many staff discussions, but not three meaningful, substantive policy discussions," he wrote in a memo published by *Esquire* magazine. (Ron Hutcheson, *Insiders Portray President as Deaf to Outside Voices*, The Miami Herald, 03-28-2004, p. A1.)

partisan (as in fanatic) *n.*: **energumen**. SEE FANATIC
(2) partisan *adj.*: **tendentious**. SEE BIASED

partition (into two parts, esp. by tearing apart or violent separation) *n.*: **diremption**. SEE SEPARATION

partner (as in comrade) *n.*: **tovarich** [Russian]. SEE COMRADE

partnership (of two people) *n.*: **duumvirate**. SEE DUO

party (with boisterous public demonstrations) *v.i.*: **maffick** [British]. SEE CELEBRATE

partyer (female ...) *n.*: **bacchante** (male ... : **bacchant**). See REVELER

partying (riotous ...) *n., adj.*: **bacchanal** (reveler *n.*: **bacchant**). See REVELRY

pass over (intentionally) *v.t.*: **pretermit**. See OMIT

pass out *n.*: **syncope**. See FAINTING

passage (difficult or painful ...) *n.*: **via dolorosa**. See ORDEAL

passé (as in outdated, obsolete) *adj.*: **antediluvian**. See OUTDATED

(2) **passé** *adj.*: **démodé** [French]. See OUTMODED

passing (as in brief or fleeting) *adj.*: **evanescent**. See TRANSIENT

(2) **passing** (away quickly) *adj.*: **fugacious**. See FLEETING

passing comment *n.*: **obiter dictum** [Latin]. ∎ I am in error about "an economic writer" and need to get out of error fast. In a recent **obiter dictum**, I parenthesized: "An 'economic writer' is a writer who uses as few words as possible." ... "Didn't you really mean 'economical writer'?" [correctly] comments George Kelley. (William Safire, *On Language — Let Freedom Love*, The New York Times, 05-16-1982.)

passing gas (of or relating to) *adj.*: **borborygmic**. ∎ Cows, as it turns out, are highly **borborygmic**, though their gas does not pass through the anus but rather through the mouth. Indeed, cows produce 60 million tons of methane gas a year from their ruminative digestive practices and burp it into the atmosphere, producing more than 15% of the world's methane each year. (Adam Bresnick, *Baedeker for the Bowels*, The Los Angeles Times, 11-14-1999.)

(2) **passing gas** (of or relating to reducing ...) *adj.*: **carminative**. See FARTING

passing over (or omitting or neglecting) *n.*: **preterition**. See OMITTING

passion (sexual ... for the elderly) *n.*: **gerontophilia**. See LUST

passionate (as in sexual lovemaking) *adj.*: **amatory**. See LOVEMAKING

passive (as in sluggish or lethargic) *adj.*: **torpid**. See LETHARGIC

passivity (as in lethargy) *n.*: **hebetude**. See LETHARGY

past (as in former) *adj.*: **quondam**. See FORMER

pastime (as in favorite topic or activity) *n.*: **cheval de bataille**. [French for "battle-horse"]. See HOBBY

pastoral (as in a place which is peaceful, rustic and simple) *adj.*: **Arcadian**. ∎ [T]he festival's **Arcadian** home [is] nestled in the foothills of the Green Mountains in southern Vermont, ... far from the stresses of urban life. ... Being at Marlboro, says [a musician], "is like being in a kind of idyllic paradise where your purpose for all this practicing that you've done in your life is realized." (Jeremy Eichler, *The Marlboro Music Festival Celebrates 50 Years of Artistic Freedom and Determination*, Newsday, 11-03-2000.)

paternal (of or relating to name of ... ancestor) *adj.*: **patronymic**. ∎ [B]ecause in the societal shifts of the past 40 years, women have repeatedly won the legal right to give their children their surnames. This has been a change from the **patronymic**, male-dominant norm handed down through several hundred years of European law that formed the basis for U.S. legal codes and social customs. (Neely Tucker, *Alexander's Last Name Is Illegal; Parents Seeking a Birth Certificate Fight D.C. Regulation*, The Washington Post, 05-15-2002, p. A1.)

patience (in the face of adversity) *n.*: **longanimity**. ∎ What my Christian experience teaches me [is that] forgiveness does ideally come first and can, with ... **longanimity**, yield a rich harvest of justice and peace in the way it facilitates the righting of wrongs and the reconciliation of the estranged. (Michael Hurley, *A Sober Truth Must Be Faced About Lack of Forgiveness*, The Irish Times, 10-24-1995, p. 12.)

patron (regular ... of a place, esp. a place of entertainment) *n.*: **habitué** [French]. See REGULAR

(2) **patron** (generous ..., esp. of the arts) *n.*: **Maecenas**. See BENEFACTOR

patronizing (as in condescending) *adj., adv.*: **de haut en bas** [French]. See CONDESCENDING

pause *n.*: **caesura**. ∎ Many of [the best moments in the novel *Battle Creek*] have to do with baseball, a subject Lasser knows his way around; he captures the game's interludes, its breaths and **caesuras**, with subtlety and grace. (David L. Ulin, *Baseball's Sweet Song*, Newsday, 05-02-1999, p. B12.)

(2) **pause** (as in hesitate to act due to indecision) *v.i.*: **dither**. See PROCRASTINATE

(3) **pause** (words such as um, uh, you know, etc.) *n.*:

embolalia (or **embololalia**). SEE STAMMERING

(4) pause (as in procrastinate or hesitate to act) *v.i.*: **shilly-shally**. SEE PROCRASTINATE

payback (in kind) *n.*: **lex talionis** [Latin]. SEE EYE FOR AN EYE

payment (or wages) *n.*: **emolument**. SEE WAGES

peace (Hindu doctrine of ..., as in nonviolence) *n.*: **ahimsa**. SEE NONVIOLENCE

peace of mind *n.*: **heartsease**. ▪ The players ... one by one sought [golfer Greg Norman] out to [tell him] that they were proud of him and thoroughly impressed by the way he handled his defeat at the Masters. Everywhere, the galleries stood and cheered. The goodwill was **heartsease** to Norman, and more than his cynicism could take. On Wednesday he declared himself a changed man. (Robinson Holloway, *Lovable Loser — A Funny Thing Happened to Greg Norman After His Disaster at the Masters*, Sports Illustrated, 04-29-1996, p. G6.)

(2) peace of mind (as in calmness) *n.*: **ataraxy** (or **ataraxia**). SEE CALMNESS

peace offering (such as flowers, to a wife from a guilty husband) *n.*: **drachenfutter** [German; lit. dragon-fodder.] ▪ It used to be common practice for German men working on a katzenjammer (a monumentally severe hangover) to go out carousing with their **drachenfutter** already bought and wrapped in anticipation of the harangue ahead. (Sam Orbaum, *Korinthenkacker*, The Jerusalem Post, 01-20-1989.)

(2) peace offering *n.*: **eirenicon**. ▪ [Martin Luther King's "I have a dream"] speech can be appreciated as an **eirenicon** — a thing of peace — which even today brings disparate people together more than the civil rights leader could ever have dreamed. (Jonathan Keats, *The Power of the Pulpit*, Christian Science Monitor, 07-10-2003.)

peaceful (as in a place which is ..., rustic and simple) *adj.*: **Arcadian**. SEE PASTORAL

peacefulness (as in gentleness) *n.*: **mansuetude**. SEE GENTLENESS

(2) peacefulness (as in tranquility) *n.*: **quietude**. SEE TRANQUILITY

peacemaking *adj.*: **irenic**. ▪ Peace is not exciting. ... It is a rare society that tells exemplary stories of peacemaking — except, say, for the Gospels of Christ, whose **irenic** grace may be admired from a distance, without much effect on daily behavior. (Lance Morrow, *Men of the Year: The Peacemakers to Conquer the Past*, Time, 01-03-1994, p. 32.)

peacock (of or resembling) *adj.*: **pavonine**. ▪ We wish Russia would issue new ruble denominations to bridge the rather expansive gaps between 10 rubles and 50 rubles, or 100 and 500. This lack of "in-betweenies" puts a strain on consumers and retailers alike. ... Russia has shown almost **pavonine** vanity in the past when it comes to revamping its currency — let that spirit rise again, this time in a way that will truly be useful. Give the people their 25-ruble notes! (Author not given, *Best Wishes For Russia In New Year*, The Moscow Times [Russia], 12-23-2000.)

(2) peacock (man who is vain like a ...) *n.*: **fop**. SEE VAIN

(3) peacock (man who is vain like a ...) *n.*: **popinjay**. SEE VAIN

pearly *adj.*: **nacreous**. SEE IRIDESCENT

(2) pearly *adj.*: **opalescent**. SEE IRIDESCENT

peculiar *adj.*: **outré** [French]. SEE UNCONVENTIONAL

(2) peculiar *adj.*: **pixilated**. SEE ECCENTRIC

peculiarity (as in notion which is odd, stubborn or whimsical) *n.*: **crotchet**. SEE NOTION

pedantic (person on issues of grammar) *n.*: **grammaticaster**. ▪ [Peter Prescott, an editor at Newsweek magazine wrote to me to say:] "I shouldn't have used a word ['fulsome'] that is so often misused that its correct use will set the **grammaticasters** to fluttering." (William Safire, *On Language*, The New York Times, 01-30-1983.)

(2) pedantic (of a ... word or term) *adj.*: **inkhorn**. ▪ Mariani adds an academic, contemporary slant to his assessment of Crane's life and poetry. In his Prolegomenon (an **inkhorn** term for an introduction), he says: "It would be difficult to find a serious poet or reader of poetry in the U.S. today who has not been touched by something in Hart Crane's music." (Author not given, *Each Desperate Choice*, The Toronto Star, 05-16-1999.)

(3) pedantic (speaker or writer who is dull and boring) *n.*: **dryasdust**. SEE BORING

(4) pedantic (but actually superficial knowledge of a subject) *n.*: **sciolism**. SEE SUPERFICIAL

pee *v.i.*: **micturate**. SEE URINATE

peek (with a sideways ...) *adv.*: **asquint**. SEE GLANCE

(2) peek (quick ..., as in glance) *n.*: **coup d'oeil** [French]. SEE GLANCE

(3) peek *n.*: **dekko** [British inf.]. SEE GLANCE

peerless (person or thing) *n.*: **nonesuch**. SEE PARAGON

peevish *adj.*: **querulous**. ▪ For now, [Ross] Perot's jousts with the press pay off for him. Each time reporters try to rough him up on television, scores, if not hundreds, of new campaign volunteers step forward. Over time, however, a series of confrontations could make him seem **querulous** and diminish his appeal. (David Gergen, *Riding the Perot Wave*, U.S. News & World Report, 06-15-1992, p. 26.)

(2) peevish *adj.*: **atrabilious**. SEE SURLY

(3) peevish *adj.*: **bilious**. SEE SURLY

(4) peevish (person) *n.*: **crosspatch**. SEE GROUCH

(5) peevish *adj.*: **liverish**. SEE IRRITABLE

(6) peevish *adj.*: **splenetic**. SEE IRRITABLE

(7) peevish *adj.*: **shirty**. SEE IRRITABLE

(8) peevish *adj.*: **tetchy**. SEE GROUCHY

penalize *v.t.*: **mulct**. ▪ [O]ne doesn't have to look [far] to find examples of courts willing to soak foreign companies. ... A North Carolina jury recently **mulcted** the Meineke muffler chain for an estimated $400 million to $600 million, more than the annual profits of its large British parent company, after a lawyer invited jurors to "send a message to foreign companies." (Walter Olson, *Their Own Petard*, [*The New York Times' Columnist Bob Herbert*], Reason, 01-01-1998, p. 42.)

(2) penalize (as in impose a monetary fine) *v.t.*: **amerce**. SEE FINE

penalty *n.*: **mulct**. SEE PENALIZE

penance (place or occasion of ... or humiliation or hoped for forgiveness) *n.*: **Canossa** (often as in "go to Canossa") [derives from town in Italy to which Emperor Henry IV traveled in 1077 to seek penance (and revocation of his excommunication) from Pope Gregory VII for appointing his own bishops]. ▪ This was ... Donald Rumsfeld's **Canossa**. At Munich's annual security policy conference the American defense secretary ... kept his mouth shut ... which was itself so dramatic a change from his abrasive performance last year. ... The reason for his change is that the occupation and democratic reinvention of Iraq is going rather badly, and the United States wants Europe's help, even the help of those European governments that opposed Washington on the war. (William Pfaff, *In Munich, Rumsfeld's Silence Speaks Volumes: Seeking Help for Iraq*, International Herald Tribune, 02-13-2004.)

penetrating (having a ... quality) *adj.*: **gimlet** (esp. as in "gimlet eye") [based on a gimlet tool which is used for boring holes]. ▪ "I'm on a very lucky streak, and I can't believe there's any real reason for it," says [Wayne Knight, who played "Newman" in Seinfeld], who off-camera is smart, funny and quick to turn a **gimlet** eye on the unreality that surrounds his business. ["When people ask me], 'Where's Jerry?' I want to tell to them, 'I don't know, get out of your pitiful fantasy world and come back to Earth.'" (Drew Jubera, *Seinfeld's Wiseguy*, The Atlanta Journal and Constitution, 08-08-1993, p. N1.)

(2) penetrating (as in keen or incisive) *adj.*: **trenchant**. SEE INCISIVE

penetration (esp. of penis into vagina) *n.*: **intromission** (*v.t.*: **intromit**). ▪ One way [that a person with Peyronie's disease can become sexually disabled] is that the penis becomes distorted so that, mechanically, **intromission** cannot be achieved. Some innovative patients manage to remain sexually active, but it is a matter of acrobatics and, for most couples, is not very enjoyable. (Author not given, *Charting Reconstruction's Present, Future*, Urology Times, 01-01-1995, p. 2.)

penis (removal of one's own) *n.*: **autopeotomy**. ▪ It is a brave, foolhardy, and desperate man who will perform an **autopeotomy**, in which one removes one's own organ — the more so when the operation is done in an unsterile environment and with a pen knife. (Simon Winchester, *The Professor and the Madman*, Harper Collins [1998], p. 193.)

(2) penis (having an erect ...) *adj.*: **ithyphallic**. ▪ Min was an **ithyphallic** god, with a very pronounced penis on the early statutes, and the vajra in Tibet had a mystic connection with male power. (Author not given, *The Meaning of the Thunderbolt*, Parabola, 01-01-92.)

(3) penis *n.*: **membrum virile** [Latin]. ▪ [In *The Golden Ass*, written in the 2nd century,] the randy young intellectual finds himself transformed not into the wise owl he had hoped to become, but an ass. He's captured by robbers, turned into a freak show, humiliated and beaten, but there is one bonus. Society ladies find his impressive **membrum virile** irresisitible — and don't seem at all deterred by the fact that it is attached to a donkey. (Charles Spencer, *A Thoroughly Enchanting Ass*, The Daily Telegraph [London], 08-17-2002, p. 21.)

(4) penis (small ...) *n.*: **microphallus**. ▪ In a 1997 *Men's Health* article entitled "An Inch Too Far," I'd stated categorically that the only people who should even think of getting penis extensions were "men cursed with **microphalluses**, victims of car accidents, or editors at *Vanity Fair*. (Joe Queenan, *My Goodness*, Hyperion [2000], p. 158.)

(5) penis (insertion of ... into vagina) *n.*: **intromission** (*v.t.* **intromit**). See PENETRATION

(6) penis (of, relating to or resembling a ...) *adj.*: **priapic**. See PHALLIC

penitence (as in place or occasion to show ... and to seek forgiveness) *n.*: **Canossa**. See PENANCE

penmanship (study of ... esp. to study character) *n.*: **graphology**. See HANDWRITING

pennant (suspended from a crossbar, as opposed to on a flagstaff) *n.*: **gonfalon**. See BANNER

penniless *adj.*: **impecunious**. See POOR
(2) penniless *adj.*: **necessitous**. See POOR

penny pincher (as in miser) *n.*: **lickpenny**. See MISER

perceive (by careful observation or scrutiny) *v.t.*: **descry**. ∎ Dear Oddist: As a lifelong devotee of the weird, outre, and paranormal, I was naturally all aquiver on August 1 when the Dow Jones industrials rose by 33.67, a figure that "eerily matched" the gains of the previous trading day. ... I was wondering if you might conceivably **descry** significance in the fact that it happened soon after those comets started banging into my favorite planet, Jupiter. (Daniel Seligman, *Keeping Up: Strange Days on Wall Street*, Fortune, 09-05-1994, p. 113.)

(2) perceive (based on past experience) *v.t.*: **apperceive**. See COMPREHEND

(3) perceive (through the senses) *adj.*: **sensate**. See FEEL

perceptible (barely ...) *adj.*: **liminal**. See INVISIBLE

perception *adj.*: **ken**. ∎ There are limits, however, to how well the e-noses can be educated. Wine connoisseurs, for example, can distinguish fragrances beyond the **ken** of any chip. (Unmesh Kher, *Science: Electronic Noses Sniff Out a Market or Two: Chemical Sensing Just Got Sexy, Can't You Smell It?* Time, 03-20-2000, p. 64.)

(2) perception (high degree of ...) *adj.*: **acuity**. See KEENNESS

(3) perception *n.*: **aperçu** [French]. See INSIGHT

perceptive *adj.*: **perspicacious**. See ASTUTE
(2) perceptive (as in wise) *adj.*: **sapient**. See WISE
(3) perceptive *adj.*: **trenchant**. See INCISIVE

performer (street ...) *n.*: **busker**. ∎ Separately, around 50 **buskers** urged the City Council to let them work the streets and earn a living amidst a mounting official crackdown aimed at restoring order in the city. "We only want to sing. We don't want to cause trouble," 23-years-old Adji Kusuma, one of the street singers, told Commission E on public welfare. (Author not given, *Mayors Postpone Crackdown on Street Vendors*, The Jakarta Post, 07-18-2000.)

perhaps *adv.*: **perchance**. See POSSIBLY

perilous *adj.*: **parlous**. ∎ [Columbia Pictures' executive David] Begelman made an extremely sweet offer, almost twice as much as Warner's, way more than was prudent, given Columbia's **parlous** financial condition, and given the fact that Begelman hated the script [to the movie *Shampoo*], thought it was cynical and offensive. (Peter Biskind, *Easy Riders, Raging Bulls*, Simon & Schuster [1998], p. 191.)

(2) perilous (journey or passage, with dangers on both sides) *idiom*: **between Scylla and Charybdis**. See PRECARIOUS

period (suppression of or absence of woman's monthly ...) *n.*: **amenorrhea**. See MENSTRUATION

(2) period (of or over the same ...) *adj.*: **coetaneous**. See CONTEMPORANEOUS

(3) period (of the same time ...) *adj.*: **coeval**. See CONTEMPORANEOUS

(4) period (woman's first ...) *n.*: **menarche**. See MENSTRUATION

periodically *adv.*: **betimes**. See SOMETIMES

perk (as in extra or unexpected gift or benefit, sometimes as thanks for a purchase) *n.*: **lagniappe**. See GIFT

permissible (as in legal) *adj.*: **licit**. See LEGAL

permit (as in bestow, by one with higher power) *v.t.*: **vouchsafe**. See BESTOW

pernicious *adj.*: **baleful**. See SINISTER

perquisite (as in extra or unexpected gift or benefit, sometimes as thanks for a purchase) *n.*: **lagniappe**. See GIFT

persecution (of a religious, national or racial group) *n.*: **helotism** (*v.t.*: **helotize**). See OPPRESSION

persevering (in holding to a belief or opinion) *adj.*: **pertinacious**. See STUBBORN

(2) persevering (in effort or application) *adj.*: **sedulous**. SEE DILIGENT

persistent (as in one who clings to an opinion or belief even after being shown that it is wrong) *n.*: **mumpsimus**. SEE STUBBORN

(2) persistent (in holding to a belief or opinion) *adj.*: **pertinacious**. SEE STUBBORN

(3) persistent (in effort or application) *adj.*: **sedulous**. SEE DILIGENT

personification (as in embodiment) *n.*: **avatar**. SEE EMBODIMENT

perspective (centered on male ...) *adj.*: **androcentric**. SEE MALE

(2) perspective (which is controversial or person who holds one) *n.*: **polemic**. SEE CONTROVERSY

perspiration (foul-smelling ...) *n.*: **bromidrosis**. SEE SWEAT

(2) perspiration (an agent which causes ... or having the power to cause ...) *n., adj.*: **diaphoretic**. SEE SWEAT

(3) perspiration (cause ... by subjecting person or thing to intense heat) *v.t.*: **parboil**. SEE HEAT

persuading (as in urging someone to take a course of action) *adj.*: **hortatory**. ■ [Writer Meg Greenfield] loved argument and continued a tradition under which [Washington] Post editorials avoided **hortatory** calls to action in favor of making points by marshaling facts. (J.Y. Smith, *Editorial Editor Meg Greenfield Dies; For More Than 30 Years, Opinion Writer Honed Post's Views*, The Washington Post, 05-14-1999, p. A1.)

persuasion (of another by flattery) *n.*: **blandishment** (*v.t.*: **blandish**). SEE FLATTERY

pertaining *adj.*: **appurtenant**. ■ Not very long ago the path to class glory was clear. You landed in a management-training program at some large company [and] eventually found yourself battling it out with a few others for one of the top positions. ... There was absolutely no confusion about your class status; you were an Executive, with all the perks and status **appurtenant** thereto. (Kenneth Labich, *The Society: Class in America — Old Socioeconomic Rankings Have Given Way to the Increasing Segmentation of the U.S. Population, and More Americans Are Unsure Where They Stand*, Fortune, 02-07-1994, p. 114)

pertinent *n.*: **apposite**. SEE RELEVANT

pervasive *adj.*: **regnant**. SEE PREDOMINANT AND WIDESPREAD

perversion (place of ..., as in corruption) *n.*: **Augean stable**. SEE CORRUPTION

perverted (preference for ... or unusual sexual practices) *n.*: **paraphilia**. SEE DEVIANT

(2) perverted (morally ...) *adj.*: **scrofulous**. SEE DEPRAVED

pessimism (world-weariness or sentimental ... over the world's problems) *adj.*: **Weltschmerz** [German]. ■ [There appears to be] an unprecedented prevalence of pessimism about the future. The nation appears to be trudging gloomily on its daily round burdened with mental sandwich-boards bearing the doomiest of legends. On cursory inspection, there is little unusual in this nationwide outbreak of **Weltschmerz**: it is the business of polls to point up dissatisfactions and the business of political parties to promise to put them right. (Author not given, *A Fearful Look to the Future*, The Scotsman, 06-13-1995, p. 10.)

pessimist (as in one always predicting catastrophe) *n.*: **catastrophist**. ■ Lester Brown ... has been warning since the '60s of a soon-to-emerge food deficit and preaching the gospel of birth suppression. Mr. Peron thinks the **catastrophist** mindset was best illustrated in "The Problem Is Us," a government-sponsored travelling exhibit warning American school children in the 1970s that "the birth rate must decrease and/or the death rate must increase." It showed them a picture of a rat on a dinner plate, and warned that when starvation overtakes the earth their parents might eat them. (Link Byfield, *A Good News Bulletin on the Population Crisis: There Isn't One*, Alberta Report/Western Report, 11-20-1995.)

(2) pessimist *n.*: **crepehanger**. ■ Steve Forbes, Republican Presidential Candidate: America does not have to fear the world, America does not have to fear the future. Unlock the genius of the American people, and we'll once again prove wrong the critics and the skeptics and the **crepehangers** and the doubters and the isolationists and the wall-builders. (Author not given, *Pat Buchanan Narrowly Leads the Pack in New Hampshire*, Morning Edition [NPR], 02-21-1996.)

pester *v.t.*: **chivvy**. ■ Changing patent law is a job for politicians, and they can hardly complain if [private] genomics companies are taking advantage of their inertia. Nor should they be **chivvying** firms to give up hard-won and costly information just because public researchers have not been able to find it first. (Author not given, *Business Forum — In Genomics, the U.S. and British Governments Are Meddling in Things That Do Not Concern Them*, Minneapolis Star Tribune, 04-02-2000, p. 9D.)

(2) pester *v.t.*: **hector**. SEE BULLY

pet (as in caress or fondle) *v.i.*: **canoodle** (often "canoodle with"). SEE CARESS

pet name (as a term of endearment) *n.*: **hypocorism** (*adj.*: **hypocoristic**). SEE NICKNAME

petals (of a flower taken separately or as a whole) *n.*: **corolla**. ∎ Flowers may be as large as a wine cork or smaller than a pencil eraser, slim or chubby, with upturned or down-hanging sepals and tightly cupped or flared **corollas**. These **corollas** may be sublimely single, with only four petals; semidouble, with eight; or double, with heaven knows how many. (Wayne Winterrowd, *A Fancy for Fuchsias*, Horticulture, The Art of American Gardening, 02-01-1998, p. 54.)

petty (person on issues of grammar) *n.*: **grammaticaster**. SEE PEDANATIC

(2) petty *adj.*: **picayune**. SEE TRIVIAL

petulant (as in surly) *adj.*: **atrabilious**. SEE SURLY

(2) petulant (as in surly) *adj.*: **bilious**. SEE SURLY

(3) petulant (as in grouchy, person) *n.*: **crosspatch**. SEE GROUCH

(4) petulant (as in irritable) *adj.*: **liverish**. SEE IRRITABLE

(5) petulant *adj.*: **querulous**. SEE PEEVISH

(6) petulant (as in irritable) *adj.*: **shirty**. SEE IRRITABLE

phallic *adj.*: **priapic**. ∎ To state the obvious first: Crimson Tide is a submarine movie and therefore entirely about penises. The USS Alabama and its Russian counterpart surge through the depths in a way that can only be called **priapic**, discharging manfully streamlined torpedoes at each other. (Jonathan Romney, *Crimson Tide [Movie Reviews]*, New Statesman & Society, 11-03-1995, p. 32.)

phantom *n.*: **wraith**. SEE APPARITION

phenomenon (secondary ... which accompanies or results from another) *n.*: **epiphenomenon** (*adj.*: **epiphenomenal**). ∎ He argued that the study of everyday life shows how normal life was for most Germans, most of whom were absorbed by the routine tasks of daily life. They were uninvolved in, and even unaware of, the regime's crimes. The racist, oppressive, inhuman aspects of Nazism were **epiphenomenal** to the texture of the quotidian in Hitler's Germany. (Daniel Goldhagen, *Pride and Prejudice*, The New Republic, 03-29-1999.)

philanthropic (as in charitable) *adj.*: **caritative**. SEE CHARITABLE

(2) philanthropic *adj.* **eleemosynary**. SEE CHARITABLE

philanthropist (esp. who gives to the arts) *n.*: **Maecenas**. SEE BENEFACTOR

philosopher (bad ..., or one who pretends to be a ...) *n.*: **philosophaster**. ∎ Reagan won the 1980 and 1984 debates and elections because he spoke plain sense to the American people. Simple phrases. Common words. Plainstuff. Broken sentences. So what? That's how normal people speak. ... In contrast, Carter and Mondale spoke more in the highfalutin' lingo our professors and other **philosophasters** love. (Author not given, *Silliness About Senility*, The Orange County Register, 12-27-1987, p. G4.)

phony (as in artificial) *adj.*: **factitious**. SEE ARTIFICIAL

(2) phony (esp. a person who sells quack medicines) *n.*: **mountebank**. SEE HUCKSTER

(3) phony (as in hypocrite, esp. one who affects religious peity) *n.*: **Tartuffe** (or **tartuffe**). SEE HYPOCRITE

(4) phony (as in hypocrite, esp. one who acts humbly) *n.*: **Uriah Heep**. SEE HYPOCRITE

phrase *n.*: **locution**. ∎ "As the child of Holocaust survivors. ..." This is the exemplary **locution** of multicultural America, the highest rank that you can pull in a culture of victimhood. But what special authority, really, do the sons and daughters of the wretched possess? We are not victims. Our parents were victims. We are merely American Jews, the brats of Jewish history. (Author not given, *Washington Diarist: Shrunken*, The New Republic, 11-09-1998.)

(2) phrase (as in saying or adage) *n.*: **apothegm**. SEE SAYING

(3) phrase (or expression or comment which is elegant, concise, witty and/or well-put) *n.*: **atticism**. SEE EXPRESSION

(4) phrase (witty or clever ... or line) *n.*: **bon mot**. SEE LINE

(5) phrase (misuse or strained use of word or ..., sometimes deliberate) *n.*: **catachresis**. SEE MISUSE

(6) phrase (of a ... or word which is pedantic) *adj.*: **inkhorn**. SEE PEDANTIC

(7) phrase (just the right ... or word) *n.*: **mot juste** [French]. SEE WORD

(8) phrase (new ..., expression or word) *n.*: **neologism**. SEE WORD

physician (equipment, including supplies and instruments, used by a ...) *n.*: **armamentarium**. SEE DOCTOR

(2) physician (disease caused by a ...) *adj.*: **iatrogenic**. SEE DISEASE

(3) physician (replacement ...) *n.*: **locum tenens**. SEE TEMPORARY

physique (of a person esp. as relating to tendency to develop disease) *n.*: **habitus**. ∎ Other variables affecting cardiac hypertrophy in athletes include body **habitus**, height, age, and gender. (Gordon Huie, *Cardiomyopathy in Athletes*, Physician Assistant, 05-01-1997, p. 136.)

pickpocket (spec. an adult who instructs children how to be a ...) *n.*: **Fagin**. SEE THIEF

picky (overly ...) *adj.*: **persnickety**. ∎ RU 486, the so-called French abortion pill, would probably sail through the **persnickety** approval process at the Food and Drug Administration — if someone would put in an application. (Author not given, *Rethinking RU 486–With Clinton In, the French Abortion Pill May Finally Make it to the U.S*, Time, 03-08-1993, p. 21.)

(2) picky (as in pedantic person on issues of grammar) *n.*: **grammaticaster**. SEE PEDANTIC

picture (as in to conceive of or form an image of) *v.t.*: **ideate**. SEE VISUALIZE

pieces (as in bits and ...) *n.*: **flinders**. SEE BITS AND PIECES

piercing (having a ... quality) *adj.*: **gimlet** (esp. as in "gimlet eye"). SEE PENETRATING

pig (as in hearty eater) *n.*: **trencherman**. SEE GLUTTON

pig out *v.t.*: **gormandize**. SEE DEVOUR

piggish (as in greedy person) *n.*: **cormorant**. SEE GREEDY

pig-headed (as in one who clings to an opinion or belief even after being shown that it is wrong) *n.*:

mumpsimus. SEE STUBBORN

(2) pig-headed (in holding to a belief or opinion) *adj.*: **pertinacious**. SEE STUBBORN

pigs (give birth to a litter of ...) *v.t.*: **farrow**. ∎ I have always found them to be idle, companionable, greedy and clean. The occasional boar is irritable, and sows, understandably, are wary of strangers visiting them soon after they have **farrowed**. But on the whole, particularly if you spend time with them, pigs are docile and sociable. (Lord Cranborne, *Sunday Review Features: Pig is Beautiful*, The Sunday Telegraph, 04-18-1999, p. 2.)

(2) pigs (of or relating to) *adj.*: **porcine**. ∎ "They're destroying everything, those beasts," grumbled Jeannot Romana, a farmer in Provence. ... "It's a plague of pigs." From the Luberon to the Riviera, in Southern France, homeowners report uninvited **porcine** families happily lounging by their swimming pools. Deep holes like bomb craters mar vegetable patches and flower beds. (Mort Rosenblum, *Pigs Have French Farmers Squealing; Wild Ones Gobble Treasured Truffles*, The Washington Times, 02-23-1999, p. A1.)

pile (confused or jumbled ...) *n.*: **agglomeration**. SEE JUMBLE

(2) pile *n.*: **cumulus**. SEE HEAP

pilgrimage (to a sacred place or shrine, esp. to Mecca) *n.*: **hadj**. ∎ Visiting the [Scrabble] Archives, which I do first on a gloriously early summer's day, becomes a personal **hadj**: Mecca, the Louvre and Cooperstown rolled into one. (Stefan Fatsis, *Word Freak*, Houghton Mifflin [2001], p. 90.)

pillage *v.t., v.i.*: **depredate** (*n.*: **depredation**) SEE PLUNDER

(2) pillage *n.*: **rapine**. SEE LOOTING

pink (as in ruddy) *adj.*: **florid**. SEE RUDDY

pins and needles (as in, in a state of suspense) *idiom*: **on tenterhooks**. SEE SUSPENSE

pious (or hypocritical and/or insincere speech) *n.*: **cant**. ∎ For all their sanctimonious **cant**, I find that [Jerry] Falwell and the "Christian" folk in the athletic department at Liberty University are really no different from their win-at-all-cost brethren at our more established football factories. (Gay Flood, *Letters: Falwell's Team*, Sports Illustrated, 12-11-1989, p. 6.)

(2) pious (hypocritically ...) *adj.*: **Pecksniffian**. SEE SELF-RIGHTEOUS

(3) pious (hypocritically ...) *adj.*: **Pharisaical**. SEE SELF-RIGHTEOUS

pipe dream (as in hope or goal which is not realistically obtainable) *n.*: **will-o'-the-wisp**. ∎ [S]ince the **will-o'-the-wisp** of bipartisanship was likely to evaporate anyway, a fight to the finish could provide the President with an opportunity to charge that it was the Democrats who spoiled the atmosphere first. (Richard Lacayo, *Nation: So Much for Bipartisanship — If the Republicans Cannot Save Tower, They Are Determined to Tar the Democrats*, Time, 03-13-1989, p. 20.)

piss *v.i.*: **micturate**. SEE URINATE

pitchman (esp. a person who sells quack medicines) *n.*: **mountebank**. SEE HUCKSTER

pithy (saying) *n.*: **gnome** (*adj*: **gnomic**). SEE CATCHPHRASE

pity (of an argument appealing to one's sense of ...) *adv., adj.*: **ad misericordium** [Latin]. SEE ARGUMENT

placate *v.t.*: **propitiate**. ∎ [Historian Arthur Schlesinger wrote that "President Clinton] lacks self-discipline. ... His political resilience strikes many as flagrant opportunism. His reactions are instinctively placatory. He rushes to **propitiate** the audience before him, often at his own expense." (Godfrey Sperling, *How Will History Rate Clinton?* The Christian Science Monitor, 05-25-1999, p. 21.)
(2) placate *v.t.*: **dulcify**. SEE APPEASE

place (close together, side-by-side or in proper order) *v.t.*: **collocate**. ∎ East of Los Angeles, the San Andreas fault crosses Cajon Pass where many vital lifelines (highway; railroad; natural gas, water, and petroleum pipelines; fiber optic lines, and electric power transmission lines) are **collocated** in a very narrow pass subject to fault rupture. (Author not given, *Earthquakes*, Congressional Testimony, 10-20-1999.)
(2) place (as in condition of being located in a particular ...) *n.*: **ubiety**. ∎ [T]he global merchant and investor community is defined not by spatial location governed by a spatially located sovereign, but by professional activity, commercial interest, and various social ties. [T]he global merchant and investment community has no "**ubiety**." It does not depend on a particular place. (Marc R. Poirier, *The NAFTA Chapter 11 Expropriation Debate Through the Eyes of a Property Theorist*, Environmental Law, 09-22-2003.)
(3) place (one frequents) *n.*: **purlieu**. SEE HANGOUT

place name *n.*: **toponym**. ∎ Many foreign visitors confuse "Newark" with "New York." To the foreign ear, the two **toponyms** are almost interchangeable. So it's not unusual to find sightseers from other countries wandering the streets of Newark, believing they are actually in New York City. During my last trip ... in Newark's Central Ward, I encountered a group of ... Belgian tourists who were looking for the St. Regis Hotel. (Mark Leyner, *Xmas in Newark, [Perspectives on Little Moments That Make up Life]*, Esquire, 12-01-1997.)

plaintive (often regarding something gone) *adj.*: **elegiac**. SEE SORROWFUL
(2) plaintive (sounds) *adj.*: **plangent**. SEE MOURNFUL

plan (as in course of action) *n.*: **démarche** [French]. SEE COURSE OF ACTION

plane (tail assembly of) *n.*: **empennage** [French]. SEE AIRPLANE

plants (animal that feeds mainly on ...) *n.*: **herbivore** (*adj.*: **herbivorous**). ∎ Consumers like deer can eat plants directly, or consumers such as mountain lions can eat plants indirectly when they eat the deer that ate the plant. **Herbivores** are known as primary consumers. (Ted Kerasote, *Hunters, Gatherers, and the Cycle of Life*, Sports Afield, 05-01-1998, p. 36.)

plausible (as in appearing to be true or accurate) *adj.*: **verisimilar**. ∎ One of the most illuminating, sympathetic passages in his book deals with the Garden of Gethsemane, where Christ lingered and prayed the night he was betrayed and arrested. ... [The author] looks at the actual ground. The result is a strikingly **verisimilar** explanation of the whole night, in very human terms, based on topography that still exists here. (Michael Browning, *Where Jesus Walked*, The Palm Beach Post, 12-08-2000, p. 1E.)

play (as in frolic) *v.t., v.i.*: **disport**. SEE FROLIC
(2) play *v.i.*: **gambol**. SEE FROLIC
(3) play (of, relating to, or connoting) *adj.*: **ludic**. SEE PLAYFUL
(4) play (on words) *n.*: **paronomasia**. SEE WORD PLAY

playboy (as in man who seduces women) *n.*: **Lothario**. ∎ Of Worth's inner circle, Ned Wynert, a **Lothario** to the last, had suffered the traditional adulterer's fate, gunned down [in the act] by an enraged husband. (Ben Macintyre, *The Napoleon of Crime*, Farrar, Straus & Giroux [1997], p. 175.)

(2) playboy *n.*: **roué** [French]. ∎ Though a newly-wed, [Jerry Lewis' father] Danny was still a dashing young man; in his bearing and wardrobe there would always be a hint of the **roué**, and [Jerry Lewis' mother] Rae more than anyone knew he could lay on the charm. (Shawn Levy, *The King of Comedy*, St. Martin's Press [1996], p. 9.)

playful *adj.*: **gamesome**. ∎ The attractive design [in this book of letters of the alphabet] skillfully blends illustrations and type to create many **gamesome** touches, such as a dolphin diving through the letter D and the letter R getting stuck in a reindeer's antlers. (Author not given, *From Albatross to Zoo: An Alphabet Book in Five Languages*, Publishers Weekly, 09-28-1992.)

(2) playful *adj.*: **ludic**. ∎ **Ludic** language ... should be at the heart of any thinking we do about language, for it is closely bound up with our ability to be creative. ... When partners cease to enjoy each other's language play — their Monty Python voices, made-up words, or nonsense noises — they will not be partners for much longer. (David Crystal, *From Scrabble to Drabble via Babble*, Independent, 08-13-1998, p. 7)

(3) playful (girl with ... or impish appeal) *n.*: **gamine** [French]. SEE GIRL

(4) playful (young woman) *n.*: **hoyden**. SEE TOMBOY

(5) playful (as in witty) *adj.*: **waggish**. SEE WITTY

plea *n.*: **cri de coeur** [French; lit. cry of the heart]. ∎ There is indeed a great unhappiness in the land, but the letters suggest the emotion is less of anger than of pain, a **cri de coeur** from people who grew up believing America was special and now see that quality under assault from within. Louis Weinstein of Glenside, PA, lamented a "moral corruption" that is eating away at the nation's innards. (David Gergen, *What Troubles Our Readers*, U.S. News & World Report, 10-23-1995, p. 102.)

(2) plea (of a ... to one's sense of pity or compassion) *adv., adj.*: **ad misericordium** [Latin]. SEE ARGUMENT

plead (with earnestly) *v.t.*: **adjure**. ∎ "This [President Clinton impeachment plan] is turning against the Republicans," a senior House Democrat said last week, **adjuring** members to vote against the G.O.P. impeachment plan. (Romesh Ratnesar, *Clinton's Crisis: Why The Midterms Matter: Impeachment Isn't the Godsend the G.O.P. Hoped For, But the Election Outlook is Still Bleak For Democrats*, Time, 10-19-1998, p. 54.)

(2) plead (in protest or objection) *v.t.*: **remonstrate**.

∎ "Who else hasn't been [vaccinated]?" Amadou asks the gathering mothers, hands on hips as she begins **remonstrating** with one who volunteered only two of her three children. A few mothers push their reluctant children forward. (Simon Robinson, *Letter From Niamey: Two Drops of Salvation*, Time International, 07-03-2000, p. 34.)

pleasant (sounding) *adj.*: **dulcet**. SEE MELODIOUS

(2) pleasant (sound) *adj.*: **euphonious** (*n.*: **euphony**). SEE MELODIOUS

(3) pleasant (voice or sound) *adj.*: **mellifluous**. SEE MELODIOUS

(4) pleasant (as in warm and cozy) *adj.*: **gemütlich** [German]. SEE COZY

pleasantness (as in affability) *n.*: **bonhomie**. SEE AFFABILITY

pleasantries (relating to ..., where the purpose is to establish a mood of sociability rather than to communicate information or ideas, such as "have a nice day") *adj.*: **phatic**. ∎ "Cheers," small, unpretending [word] that it seems, is a strange modern gesture of fellowship, a formal declaration of informality. ... There is no stopping it. ... It is our word for all weathers, our **phatic** egalitarian gesture. (John Mullan, *Word of the Week: Cheers: Let Us Give Thanks*, The Guardian [London], 11-21-2001.)

pleased (very ... often in a boastful way) *adj.*: **cock-a-hoop**. SEE ELATED

pleasing *adj.*: **prepossessing**. ∎ "The appearance of the boy was **prepossessing**," Samuel wrote years later. "His eyes were bright and unclouded, and above them was a massive forehead and a finely shaped head, which might have been chosen as a model for an artist." (Lawrence Striegel, *Long Island: Our Past/A Voice Raised For Freedom*, Newsday, 01-01-2001, p. A35.)

(2) pleasing (to the ear) *adj.*: **dulcet**. SEE MELODIOUS

(3) pleasing (as in wonderful) *adj.*: **frabjous** (often as in "Oh frabjous day!"). SEE WONDERFUL

(4) pleasing (as in wonderful) *adj.*: **galluptious** [slang]. SEE WONDERFUL

(5) pleasing (in appearance, esp. sexually) *adj.*: **toothsome**. SEE SEXY

pleasure *n.*: **delectation**. ∎ Members of the jury, for your **delectation** — sorry, deliberation — we have here Exhibit A, as in awfully attractive: one Benjamin Bratt, a.k.a. suave homicide detective Rey Curtis of NBC's Law & Order. (Author not given,

The 50 Most Beautiful People in the World 1999: Benjamin Bratt, Actor, People, 05-10-1999, p. 96.)

(2) pleasure (causing or tending to produce ...) *adj.*: **felicific**. See HAPPINESS

(3) pleasure (as in happiness) *n.*: **felicity**. See HAPPINESS

(4) pleasure (delusive or illusory ...) *n.*: **fool's paradise**. See ILLUSION

(5) pleasure (sexual ... from rubbing against something or someone) *n.*: **frottage**. See RUBBING

(6) pleasure (from witnessing other's misfortunes) *n.*: **Roman holiday**. See SADISM

(7) pleasure (from other's misfortunes) *n.*: **schadenfreude** [German]. See SADISM

pleasure-seeker (as in lazy person devoted to seeking pleasure and luxury) *n.*: **lotus-eater**. See HEDONIST

pledge (of marriage) *v.t.*: **affiance**. See MARRIAGE

plenty (illusion of ... when in fact there is little) *adj.*: **Barmecidal** (esp. as in "Barmecidal feast"). See ILLUSION

pliable *adj.*: **ductile**. ∎ Steel cars are made of "monocoque" metal shells. Their strength and ability to bear loads resides largely in pressed-steel structures. Key parts of these structures, such as the floor-pan and the door pillars, involve complicated pressings for which steel, a **ductile** alloy, is well suited. But aluminium is not so **ductile**, and cannot easily be pressed into strong monocoques. (Author not given, *Aluminium Cars: Audi-Lite*, The Economist, 04-15-2000.)

plight (as in choice of taking what is offered or nothing; i.e. no real choice at all) *n.*: **Hobson's choice**. See PREDICAMENT

(2) plight (as in the situation of having to make a move where any move made will weaken the position) *n.*: **zugzwang** [German]. See PREDICAMENT

plop (as in light splash) *n.*: **plash**. See SPLASH

plot (secret ... or group of plotters) *n.*: **cabal**. ∎ Founded in 1958, the Birch Society became famous in the 1960s for its crusade against the fluoridation of water and for its elaborate conspiracy theories, which include the notion that President Eisenhower and his brother Milton were agents of the international Communist **cabal**. (Peter Carlson, *Pat Buchanan's Far Right Hand; Ezola Foster Can Make Even the Reform Party Candidate Look Like a Liberal*, The Washington Post, 09-13-2000, p. C1.)

plotters (group of ...) *n.*: **camarilla**. See ADVISORS

plotting (and evil or shameless woman) *n.*: **jezebel** (sometimes cap.). See WOMAN

pluck *n.*: **hardihood**. See COURAGE

plug (up) *v.t.*: **occlude**. See BLOCK

plump (condition of having a ... physique) *n.*: **embonpoint**. ∎ Unlike his fellow moguls, [John D. Rockefeller] was "lean as a greyhound" in a time when the measure of a man's prosperity was his **embonpoint**. (David Walton, *"Titan" Gives Rockefeller His Balance Due*, The Dallas Morning News, 05-31-1998, p. 9J.)

(2) plump (as in beer-bellied) *adj.*: **abdominous**. See BEER-BELLIED

(3) plump (as in fat) *adj.*: **Pickwickian**. See FAT

(4) plump (having a short ... physique) *adj.*: **pyknic**. See STOCKY

(5) plump (woman who is pleasingly ...) *adj.*: **zaftig** [Yiddish]. See FULL-FIGURED

plunder *v.t., v.i.*: **depredate** (*n.*: **depredation**). ∎ In 1766 the Spanish explorer Nicolas de Lafora found the dunes "very troublesome" and ... required moving cautiously, for the Apache Indians "are wont to surprise and kill passers-by." Plodding south with his wagon train in 1839, the American merchant Josiah Gregg found that Apaches "continue to lay waste the ranches in the vicinity, and to **depredate** at will." (Joseph Leach, *The Dunes of Samayaluca*, Americas [English Edition], 05-15-1996, p. 14.)

(2) plunder *n.*: **rapine**. See LOOTING

poem (consisting of one line) *n.*: **monostich**. ∎ These [very short entries in Nabakov's collection of writings] reminded me of the quintessential American **monostich**: "You owe me $64." I read it in Poetry magazine about a quarter of a century ago and am still stumped by it. It's there on the page, but what is it in aid of? (Roy Sergei, *Nabokov's Butterflies*, The Moscow Times, 06-03-2000.)

(2) poem (or song in honor of a bride or bridegroom) *n.*: **epithalamium**. See TOAST

(3) poem (or song of mourning, esp. for a dead person) *n.*: **threnody**. See REQUIEM

poet (bad ...) *n.*: **poetaster**. ∎ And now her first book of poems, Yesterday I Saw the Sun, has become a cause for further hiding. Just before the book's publication last month, a New York Post gossip item ridiculed her as a **poetaster**, contributing to her latest headache. "Ally Sheedy from bad to verse," chortled the headline on the item. (Author not given, *Heartbreak–Ally Sheedy Says She Wrote Her Poems to Heal Her Wounds, But Their Publication Has Only Made Them Another Source of Pain*, Entertainment Weekly, 03-29-1991, p. 28.)

point of view (centered on male ...) *adj.*: **androcentric**. See MALE

(2) point of view (which is controversial or person who holds one) *n.*: **polemic**. See CONTROVERSY

point of no return *n.*: **Rubicon**. See IRREVERSIBILITY

pointless *adj.*: **bootless**. See FUTILE

(2) pointless (mission or project) *n.*: **fool's errand**. See HOPELESS

(3) pointless (relating to the view that all human striving and aspiration is ..., or people who hold such a view) *adj., n.*: **futilitarian**. See FUTILE

(4) pointless (something which is ..., as in useless) *n.*: **vermiform appendix**. See USELESS

poise (and confidence) *n.*: **aplomb**. See CONFIDENCE

(2) poise (esp. under pressure or trying circumstances) *n.*: **sang-froid** [French]. See COMPOSURE

poised *adj.*: **equable**. See SERENE

poisonous (or noxious atmosphere or influence) *n.*: **miasma**. See NOXIOUS

polemic *adj., n.*: **eristic**. See DEBATE

police (member of French ... organization, which is a branch of the armed forces) *n.*: **gendarme**. ▪ Some 300 elite French troops and **gendarmes** had launched an operation to rescue 23 Frenchmen from a cave where they had been held by Melanesian separatists. In the 7 1/2-hour gun battle that ensued, two **gendarmes** and 19 militants died. (Michael S. Serrill, *Hostages–By Negotiation and by the Sword: Controversy Rages After Two Sets of French Captives Are Freed*, Time, 05-16-1988, p. 55.)

policeman (Italian) *n.*: **carabiniere**. ▪ Patrolling the island [of Sardinia for a soccer game] will be 3,200 police and paramilitary commandos, some with dogs, others in camera-equipped helicopters, and all of them armed with pistols and rifles. Says a **carabiniere** commander: "If the hooligans see officers with rifles, they will be a little more afraid than of just a police stick." (Author not given, *Sport: The Last Bit of English Hooliganism on Sardinia*, Time International, 06-11-1990, p. 42.)

polished (and intelligent person) *n.*: **bel esprit**. See CULTIVATED

(2) polished (in an affected manner) *adj.*: **niminy-piminy**. See DAINTY

(3) polished (as in refined or elegant) *adj.*: **raffiné** (or **raffine**) [French]. See REFINED

(4) polished *adj.*: **soigné** [French]. See ELEGANT

politician (who is petty, unstatesmanlike or generally contemptible) *n.*: **politicaster** [The word also has a secondary meaning of one who dabbles in politics and is a kind of political wannabe. The example used here appears to reference the latter definition, insofar as the author uses the phrase "politicians and politicasters," but it is clear from the context that he would consider the subject to be a "politicaster" in the primary sense as well even if he were an actual politician]. ▪ Are there not in all those places, politicians and **politicasters** as demagogic and unscrupulous as the former Soviet pilot Dudayev, capable of stirring up an entire population with nationalist or religious rhetoric, and precipitating it into the most reckless adventures? (Mario Vargas Llosa, *Insights Into the World; Russia Fueling Chechen Nationalism*, The Daily Yomiuri, 04-17-1995.)

(2) politician (inept ...) *n.*: **Throttlebottom** [after Alexander Throttlebottom, the name of a character who is the inept Vice President in the musical comedy *Of Thee I Sing* (1932)]. ▪ Wednesday night's [televised Vice-Presidential debate] Donnybrook between Lloyd Bentsen and Dan Quayle — that might be called The Revenge of the Second Bananas. Bentsen was solid, senatorial and soothingly statesmanlike. Quayle, who often seemed as lost as an actor missing half the pages of his script, struggled to overcome his own **Throttlebottom** image — and lost. (Walter Shapiro, *How it Plays in Toledo; The Debate and the Campaign as Seen Through the Eyes of a Key Rustbelt City* [Presidential Elections 1988], Time, 10-17-1988.)

(3) politician (who is corrupt) *n.*: **highbinder**. See CORRUPT

politicians (as in actions of government officials who are pompous but inefficient) *n.*: **bumbledom**. See BUREAUCRACY

politics (of power ..., as in belief that political power is best achieved through use of force) *n.*: **machtpolitik** [German]. ▪ When the lethal consequences of **machtpolitik** were stopped after two world wars that killed tens of millions of people, international institutions were created to obviate the use of war as an instrument of policy by a state or group of states invoking legal or political "necessity." The pertinent prohibitions are entrenched in the Charter of the United Nations. (Hugh MacDonald, *Playing Fast and Loose*, The Jerusalem Post, 04-05-1999.)

(2) politics (based on political realities as opposed to ethical, moral or theological considerations) *n.*: **realpolitik** [German]. ▮ Chinese Premier Wen Jiabao [and] President George W. Bush [will discuss] Taiwan, trade and the North Korean nuclear impasse. What's encouraging is that both leaders seem willing to be pragmatic and flexible over these issues. It's refreshing Bush has accepted the need for diplomatic ambiguity in dealing with China over Taiwan, a **realpolitik** approach his former-president father would have approved and a welcome shift in his often-moralistic tone. (Author not given, *With Chinese Leader, Bush Shows He Can Be Pragmatic*, Newsday, 12-09-2003.)

polluted (morally ...) *v.t.*: **cankered**. See corrupted

polygamy (as in having more than one wife at a time) *n.*: **polygyny**. ▮ **Polygyny** is everywhere accompanied by the "bride price," a payment by the husband to the wife's family that, in effect, reflects the shortage of eligible brides. (The "dowry," a sum of money to make an eligible daughter more attractive, is strictly the product of monogamy.) (William Tucker, *All in the Family [African American Families]*, National Review, 03-06-1995, p. 36.)

pomp (as in pretentious ceremony) *n.*: **mummery**. See ceremony

pomposity (in speech or writing) *n.*: **grandiloquence**. ▮ The politicians [in the 1868 impeachment trial of Andrew Johnson], untroubled by the absence of televised talk shows, missed no opportunity for **grandiloquence**. "This trial has developed, in the most remarkable manner, the insane love of speaking among public men," complained James Garfield, congressman and future president. (Author not given, *Temper of Times Was Much Nastier in 1868 Impeachment*, Minneapolis Star Tribune, 10-18-1998, p. 10A.)

pompous *adj.*: **flatulent**. ▮ Trudeau was a disaster as a prime minister. This arrogant, **flatulent** pseudo-intellectual is responsible for turning our parliamentary system into an elected dictatorship. (R. H. Nucich, *Letters: The Trudeau Record*, Maclean's, 04-07-1997, p. 9.)

(2) pompous (speech or writing) *adj.*: **fustian**. ▮ [New Yorker Magazine editor Robert Gottlieb was] anxious to rid The New Yorker of its **fustian** ways, including such standard issue New Yorker language as "We betook ourselves." (Mary Vespa, *Picks & Pans: Pages*, People, 10-10-1988, p. 42.)

(3) pompous *adj.*: **hoity-toity**. ▮ When is it socially acceptable for a snob to be snooty? When she has earned the right to be **hoity-toity**, of course. [Actress Patricia Routledge] has, through her portrayal of the embarrassingly haughty "Keeping Up Appearances" housewife ... won the hearts, begrudgingly, of millions of television viewers worldwide. (Author not given, *Fed: Popular British Actress Patricia Routledge in Australia*, AAP General News [Australia], 07-11-2000.)

(4) pompous (esp. regarding speaking or writing style) *adj.*: **magniloquent**. ▮ From the plucking of the piano strings in Hymn to a Celestial Musician and the striking of the strings with percussion sticks in Pastoral, No. 1, to the use of ostinato techniques (not drone-like as the **magniloquent** and pretentious liner notes state) ... Hovhaness has shown an understanding of many styles and a mastery of the vignette. (Michael H. Arshagouni, *Music: "Sacred Art" Remastered*, AIM: Armenian International Magazine, 12-31-1991.)

(5) pompous (esp. regarding speaking or writing style) *adj.*: **orotund**. ▮ Damisch is repetitive, elliptical, pompous. He likes to end segments of argument not with conclusions, but with disinguous and **orotund** questions. (Christopher S. Wood, *Le Jugement de Paris [Book Reviews]*, The Art Bulletin, 12-01-1995, p. 677.)

(6) pompous *adj.*: **turgid**. ▮ By their formidable intellect and persuasiveness as well as their personal charm, Rehnquist and Scalia stand at least a chance of making the [Supreme Court] more cohesive and coherent. Their judicial opinions will be more sprightly and readable than the **turgid** fare churned out by most of their brethren. (Evan Thomas, *Reagan's Mr. Right — Rehnquist is Picked for the Court's Top Job*, Time, 06-30-1986, p. 24.)

(7) pompous (and vain person) *n.*: **coxcomb**. See conceited

(8) pompous (as in vain person) *n.*: **popinjay**. See vain

(9) pompous (but superficial knowledge of a subject) *n.*: **sciolism**. See superficial

(10) pompous *adj.*: **tumid**. See bombastic

pompousness *n.*: **ampollosity**. ▮ By George, we think he's got it. A lot of those GIO shareholders feeling somewhat disenfranchised might say that the "it" was **AMPollosity**, and that George Trumpet had plenty. ... Let's face it, we didn't like the Trumpet; he was too loud, too quickly rich, too disdaining of opposition. He wasn't like us at all. [AMP is a company in Australia which owns another company, GIO. The author was using a play on words.] (Chris Twyman, *T For 2 — It's Our Cuppa*, Sydney Morning Herald, 07-31-1999.)

ponder (as in think about) *v.t.*: **cerebrate**. SEE THINK

(2) ponder (as in think about) *v.t.*: **cogitate**. SEE THINK

(3) ponder (something, often used as a directive, as in "Consider this:") *v.t.*: **perpend**. SEE CONSIDER

ponderous (and clumsy like an elephant) *adj.*: **elephantine**. SEE CLUMSY

ponds (of or occurring in ... or lakes) *adj.*: **limnetic**. SEE WATERS

pontificate (on a topic, esp. in a long-winded or pompous manner) *v.i.*: **bloviate**. SEE SPEAK

pool (esp. indoor swimming ...) *n.*: **natatorium**. ■ Plans for the tide-fed pool in Kapiolani Park remain in limbo, but the city is restoring the **natatorium's** imposing archway and public showers and changing rooms. (Laura Bly, *Constructing a New Image*, USA Today, 05-12-2000, p. 4D.)

poop (obsession with) *n.*: **coprology**. SEE EXCREMENT

(2) poop (feeding on) *n.*: **coprophagous**. SEE EXCREMENT

(3) poop (interest in ..., often sexual) *n.*: **coprophilia**. SEE EXCREMENT

(4) poop *n.*: **egesta**. SEE EXCREMENT

(5) poop (esp. that of sea birds) *n.*: **guano**. SEE BIRD DUNG

(6) poop (study of or obsession with) *n.*: **scatology**. SEE EXCREMENT

(7) poop (eating) *adj.*: **scatophagous**. SEE EXCREMENT

(8) poop (of or relating to) *adj.*: **stercoraceous**. SEE EXCREMENT

poor *adj.*: **impecunious**. ■ Besides the 6.7 million Hong Kong people who are expected to saturate [the Disney park in Hong Kong] during its first year, most of the other visitors would be relatively **impecunious** mainlanders. (Until recently, many top hotels in the city discouraged mainland Chinese from booking rooms, worried they couldn't afford the bill.) (Mahlon Meyer, *Still Waiting for Mickey*, Newsweek International, 07-12-1999, p. 67.)

(2) poor *adj.*: **necessitous**. ■ In [Franklin Roosevelt's] last State of the Union Address in 1944, he said that: "**Necessitous** men are not free men. People who are hungry and out of a job are the stuff of which dictatorships are made." (Author not given, *Human Rights — Comment*, Canada and the World, Backgrounder, 05-01-1997.)

(3) poor (people, as in lowest class of society) *n.*: **lumpenproletariat**. SEE UNDERCLASS

populace (pertaining to the ..., as in the common people) *adj.*: **demotic**. SEE MASSES

(2) populace (suitable for or comprehensible by the ...) *adj.*: **exoteric**. SEE ACCESSIBLE

popular opinion (of an argument designed to appeal to ...) *adj., adv.*: **ad captandum** (or **ad captandum vulgus**) [Latin]. SEE ARGUMENT

populated (by persons from many countries or backgrounds) *n.*: **cosmopolis**. SEE DIVERSITY

(2) populated (heavily ... region OR city) *n.*: **megalopolis**. SEE CROWDED

pornographic (desire to look at ... scenes) *n.*: **scopophilia**. SEE VOYEURISM

portal (spec. the corridor in a stadium which connects the outer concourse to the interior of the stadium itself) *n.*: **vomitory**. SEE CORRIDOR

portend *v.t.*: **betoken**. ■ The relatively high level of uninvested cash that mutual funds are holding **betokens** a ready source of funds to drive up the market when portfolio managers spot some bargains. (John Paul Newport Jr., *Believe it or Not, More Bull — There's a Growing Feeling Among Market Analysts That Stocks Are Headed for a Rally in the Next Few Months*, Fortune, 03-14-1988, p. 155.)

(2) portend *v.t.*: **adumbrate**. SEE FORESHADOW

portion *n.*: **moiety**. ■ The original stand-up-turned-novelist, Ben Elton, had a head start on the pack, thanks to his experience in sitcom writing, and because his stand-up voice was used to balancing mirth with belief, screams with themes, the tension demanded by the conflicting **moieties** of the novel: dialogue and plot on one side, reflection and issues on the other. (Ra Page, *Sit-Down Comics Lose Sight of the Audience [Assessment of Ben Elton as Writer]*, New Statesman [1996], 06-12-1998, p. 49.)

portly (person, esp. with a large abdomen) *n.*: **endomorph** (*adj*: **endomorphic**). SEE POT-BELLIED

(2) portly (condition of having a ... physique) *n.*: **embonpoint**. SEE PLUMP

(3) portly (having a short ... physique) *adj.*: **pyknic**. SEE STOCKY

portray (as in describe, by painting or writing) *v.t.*: **limn**. SEE DESCRIBE

posh *adj.*: **nobby** [British]. SEE ELEGANT

position (preconceived ... on an issue) *n.*: **parti pris** [French]. SEE PRECONCEPTION

(2) position (which is controversial or person who holds one) *n.*: **polemic**. SEE CONTROVERSY

(3) position (as in condition of being located in a particular place) *n.*: **ubiety**. SEE PLACE

possible (as in appearing to be true or accurate) *adj.*: **verisimilar**. SEE PLAUSIBLE

possibly *adv.*: **perchance**. ∎ Those Republicans who will never forgive Mr. McCain for his stand on [campaign finance reform] are already lost to him (unless, **perchance**, he is the nominee, in which case everyone will forgive him). (Tod Lindberg, *Mr. McClean Campaign; McCain Ready, Willing and Available*, The Washington Times, 11-30-1999, p. A19.)

posterior (toward or located near ... or tail) *adj.*: **caudal**. SEE TAIL

postpartum *adj.*: **puerperal**. ∎ An even more severe form of mental disease called **puerperal** psychosis may occur two days to three days after birth — and may last for three months to four months. This condition is associated with hallucinations and paranoid delusions and occurs in up to 1 percent of all pregnancies. (Paul L. Ogburn Jr., *Postpartum Depression Is Very Real*, Newsday, 06-28-2001, p. A43.)

(2) postpartum (woman) *n.*: **puerperium**. ∎ Finally, offer the vaccine to these persons: women who are in the third trimester of pregnancy or early **puerperium** during the influenza season. (Martin M. Stevenson, *It's Just About Time to Start Giving the New Flu Vaccine*, Modern Medicine, 09-01-1995, p. 47.)

postpone (as in avert or ward off) *v.t.*: **forfend**. SEE AVERT

(2) postpone (esp. a session of Parliament) *v.t.*: **prorogue**. SEE DISCONTINUE

postponement (as in procrastination or intentional delay) *n.*: **cunctation**. SEE DELAY

postponing (engaging in ... tactics, esp. as a means to wear out an opponent or avoid confrontation) *adj.*: **Fabian**. SEE DILATORY

posture (of or relating to erect ...) *n.*: **orthostatic**. SEE STANDING

pot-bellied (person) *n.*: **endomorph** (*adj.*: **endomorphic**). ∎ When he showed up on campus weighing 344 pounds, he was, shall we say, roundly hailed. ... Somewhat **endomorphic** — nobody would call him fat, exactly — his distinction was entirely physical. If he was going to terrorize anybody, it would be restaurateurs. (Richard Hoffer, *On the Wall of a University of Washington Hangout Called Shultzy's*, Sports Illustrated, 09-21-1992, p. 40.)

potency (as in power or might) *n.*: **puissance**. SEE POWER

potion (as in magic ... or love ...) *n.*: **philter**. ∎ The herbalist is also the source for amulets, **philters**, and potions intended to further the intentions of the purchaser [such as one] seeking success as a lover. (Irving Kaplan, *South Africa: Indigenous Religions*, Countries of the World, 01-01-1991.)

potpourri (as in assortment) *n.*: **farrago**. SEE ASSORTMENT

(2) potpourri (as in assortment) *n.*: **gallimaufry**. SEE ASSORTMENT

(3) potpourri (as in assortment) *n.*: **olla podrida** [Spanish]. SEE ASSORTMENT

(4) potpourri (as in assortment) *n.*: **omnium-gatherum** [Latin]. SEE ASSORTMENT

(5) potpourri (as in assortment) *n.*: **salmagundi**. SEE ASSORTMENT

pout *n.*: **moue** [French]. ∎ His name was Stevie. She was eight years old. He broke her heart. "He was my brother's best friend," she says. "He was the love of my life, and he never loved me." [Whatever happened to Stevie?] "I don't know," she says, raising her eyebrows briefly, pursing her lips in a mock **moue**. "I think he's dead." And then she smiles, a smile that says, "Isn't it pretty to think so?" (Linda Darling, *Linda Fiorentino's Dirty Little Secret*, Esquire, 11-01-1995, p. 108.)

poverty *n.*: **penury**. ∎ Beggary, **penury**, crime, alcoholism, stress, the horrible novelty of unemployment (now 9%, according to the International Labour Organisation) and a male life expectancy of 58 years all help to keep the anger bubbling [in Russia after Communism]. (Author not given, *Could it Lead to Fascism?* The Economist, 07-11-1998.)

powder (reduce to ..., as in pulverize) *v.t.*: **comminute**. See PULVERIZE

powdery *adj.*: **pulverulent**. ▪ [T]he BMW Tropical Beach Handbook calls the 7 kilometers of Boracay's coast the "world's best stretch of sand." "Every **pulverulent** particle that clings to your sun-drenched body is a speckle of white coral and shell worn down by the powerful currents of the China and Sulu Seas on the southeastern edge of Asia." (Author not given, *Travel Philippines — Philippine Gov't Frantically Woos Tourists*, Kyodo World News Service, 12-28-2001.)

power *n.*: **puissance**. ▪ This summer Tiger [Woods] has disrupted countless weekend itineraries. Last month 28 million Americans, a 32% increase over last year, watched one of the least dramatic final rounds in the history of the British Open. They stayed for a glimpse of golfing **puissance** — and to see a reflection of themselves. (Romesh Ratnesar, *Sport/Tiger/How the Best Got Better: Changing Stripes Just as With His Golf Game*, Time, 08-14-2000, p. 62.)

(2) power (one having a delusional fantasies about ... or omnipotence) *n.*: **megalomania**. See DELUSIONAL AND OBSESSION

(3) power (as in domination of a nation or group over another) *n.*: **suzerainty**. See DOMINATION

power politics (as in belief that political power is best achieved through use of force) *n.*: **machtpolitik** [German]. See POLITICS

powerful (as in influential person, esp. in intellectual or literary circles) *n.*: **mandarin**. See INFLUENTIAL

powerless *adj.*: **impuissant**. ▪ When [the Greater Toronto Authority] flexes its planning muscle, local councils will simply become **impuissant** and impotent. Basic decision-making will be relegated to ... recreational programs, library building, doling out parking and building permits, and maintaining our streets and back roads. Important decisions in the field of urban waste management, transportation, or trunk sanitary sewage lines will be made [by others]. (Frank Threlkeld, Jr., *Municipalities Losing Autonomy*, The Toronto Star, 06-20-1989, p. E4.)

practical (politics, as in decisions based on political realities as opposed to ethical, moral or theological considerations) *n.*: **realpolitik** [German]. See POLITICS

practice (or custom) *n.*: **praxis**. See CUSTOM

pragmatic (politics, as in decisions based on political realities as opposed to ethical, moral or theological considerations) *n.*: **realpolitik** [German]. See POLITICS

praise *n.*: **approbation**. ▪ The series about Long Island judges was a great public service and the extensive research that went into it deserves **approbation**. (John V. Conti, *Letters / Judging the Series on Rating Long Island Judges*, Newsday, 12-29-1999, p. A49.)

(2) praise *n.*: **encomium** (one who delivers ... or tribute *n.*: **encomiast**). ▪ Mayor Richard Riordan jetted off to Asia to drum up business. [I would have liked to have gone with him.] Would that I were a first-class **encomiast** living off the gratuities of someone rich and powerful, traveling by his side, chronicling his every word and deed, scattering flowers at the feet of his entourage, laughing heroically at his witty cultural faux pas, wiping spittle from his chin. (Jane Robison, *Mayor's Costly Jaunt Leaves Asia in Wonder*, Daily News, 03-08-1998.)

(3) praise (one who seeks favor through ..., esp. of one in power) *n.*: **courtier**. See FLATTERY

(4) praise (formal expression of ...) *n.*: **encomium**. See TRIBUTE

(5) praise (as in tribute) *n.*: **panegyric** (one who does so *n.*: **panegyrist**). See TRIBUTE

praiseworthy *adj.*: **palmary**. See EXCELLENT

(2) praiseworthy (as in of the highest quality) *n.*: **first water** (usu. as in "of the first water"). See QUALITY

(3) praiseworthy *adj.*: **skookum**. See EXCELLENT

praising (insincerely...) *adj.*: **fulsome**. See INSINCERE

prance *v.i.*: **curvet**. See DANCE

(2) prance (around) *v.i.*: **gambol**. See FROLIC

(3) prance (about so as to attract attention) *v.i.*: **titt-up**. See STRUT

prank *n.*: **dido**. ▪ The most annoying vehicle is the water scooter. The scooter is noisier than most other craft, and that is annoying, but most concerning is that these things are high-speed, unstable toys, subject to no marine rules of the waterways, operated by youth seeking thrills and spills in erratic **didoes** in areas where sensible boat operators are traveling. (Burt Raughley [letter writer], *Water Scooters Need Controls*, St. Petersburg Times [Florida], 06-22- 1990.)

preaching (relating to or in the nature of ..., esp. on a practical, rather than theological, matter) *adj.*:

homiletic. ∎ [Rockefeller] especially enjoyed the company of ministers whose genial, **homiletic** style matched his own. (Ron Chernow, *Titan*, Random House [1998], p. 121.)

preachy (hypocritically ...) *adj.*: **Pecksniffian**. SEE SELF-RIGHTEOUS

(2) **preachy** (hypocritically ...) *adj.*: **Pharisaical**. SEE SELF-RIGHTEOUS

preamble *n.*: **proem**. SEE PREFACE

(2) **preamble** (to a lengthy or complex work) *n.*: **prolegomenon**. SEE INTRODUCTION

precarious (as in a journey or passage with dangers on both sides) *idiom*: **between Scylla and Charybdis**. [This term derives from a formerly dangerous passage between Scylla, a rock on the Italian coast, which is opposite the whirlpool Charybdis on the Sicilian coast; also represented as two female sea monsters in Greek mythology. It appears in two different ways which are shown in the examples here.] ∎ [Federal Reserve chairman Alan Greenspan] is damned if he does and damned if he doesn't, trapped **between Scylla and Charybdis** [e.g. the risks of cutting or not cutting interest rates]. ... For rate-cut enthusiasts, he allowed that the economy was still in a precarious state. For tax-cut enthusiasts, he averred that the economy's fundamentals were still so strong that the federal budget would likely produce big surpluses for several years. (Jodie T. Allen, *Is the Chairman Painted Into a Corner?* U.S. News & World Report, 03-12-2001.) ∎ No subject needs the exercise of cool and critical intelligence more than that of child sexual abuse. We need to steer **between** the **Scylla** of indifference and denial, **and** the **Charybdis** of hysteria. In the present climate, Charybdis poses the greater danger. (No author given, *Salem in Newcastle: What a Recent Child-Abuse Scare in England Tells Us*, National Review, 09-02-2002.)

(2) **precarious** (as in perilous) *adj.*: **parlous**. SEE PERILOUS

preceding (a meal, esp. dinner) *adj.*: **preprandial**. SEE MEAL

(2) **preceding** *adj.*: **prevenient** (often as in "prevenient grace"). SEE ANTECEDENT

precious stone (which is highly polished and unfaceted) *n.*: **cabochon**. SEE JEWEL

(2) **precious stone** (one who cuts and polishes a ...) *n.*: **lapidary**. SEE JEWELER

precipitous *adj.*: **declivitous** (*n.*: **declivity**). SEE DECLINE

precipitous (as in impetuous) *adj.*: **gadarene**. SEE IMPETUOUS

preconception *n.*: **parti pris** [French]. ∎ I began to follow his work attentively, and I noticed that, unlike some revered modern writers, [Polish poet Zbigniew] Herbert had no **parti pris**, no prior and axiomatic theory of the world. Instead of such dogma, I found in Herbert's work an unforced, flexible search for meaning. (Adam Zagajewski, *Is Literary Greatness Still Possible: The Shabby and the Sublime*, The New Republic, 04-05-1999.)

precursor *n.*: **progenitor**. SEE PREDECESSOR

predatory (person) *n.*: **harpy**. ∎ As chief instigator of [Rockefeller's] misery, he cited George Rice, an independent refiner, who would pursue him with the tenacity of a **harpy** for decades. (Ron Chernow, *Titan*, Random House [1998], p. 213.)

(2) **predatory** *adj.*: **lupine**. ∎ Some fishery biologists speculate that the presence of the predatory pike in the same drainage as brook trout may be responsible for the great size these Labrador trout achieve. ... The brookies have to get big fast to evade the **lupine** jaws of the pitiless pike. (Robert F. Jones, *First Person: A Sojourn in Brobdingnag in Labrador, Brook Trout Grow Big — But Dumb*, Sports Illustrated, 09-10-1990, p. 146.)

predecessor *n.*: **progenitor**. ∎ Despite the size of the deal [the merger between Time Warner and America Online], it remains to be seen whether the new company can embrace the divergent backgrounds of its **progenitors**. The companies operate on different internal clocks, analysts said, and corporate harmony could become a merger casualty. (William Glanz, *Merger Boosts Case Legend; "Positive Spinoffs" Seen from AOL-time Warner Deal*, The Washington Times, 01-13-2000, p. B9.)

predicament (as in choice of taking what is offered or nothing; i.e. no real choice at all) *n.*: **Hobson's choice** [derives from Thomas Hobson (1544-1630), English liveryman, who required his customers to take the horse nearest to the stable door or no horse]. ∎ Most of the land in Sumatra is not legally registered or titled, so the people working it often do not have rights of ownership. If a corporate bigwig can negotiate a land-use permit from the central government in Jakarta, the farmer faces a **Hobson's choice**: sell to the only available buyer, or try to stay and be harassed and forced to sell anyway. (Author not given, *Sumptuous Sumatra: Indonesia*, The Economist, 09-24-1994, p. 33.)

(2) predicament (as in the situation of having to make a move where any move made will weaken the position) *n.*: **zugzwang** [German. This word ordinarily refers to a chess situation where any particular move is disadvantageous to the player. It is occasionally used in a broader context as in the example below.] ∎ Many in the GOP would like to take a pass on the abortion issue. ... Stem cell [research, supported by some Republicans, offers] the hope of a cure for disease, everything from diabetes to Alzheimer's. But to right-to-lifers, each embryo, even if it is just a cluster of cells in a test tube, is an unborn child. ... Bush and the GOP are caught in the middle. ... But in politics, as in chess, **zugzwang** is not an option. (James P. Pinkerton, *Republicans Can't Evade Abortion Issue*, Newsday, 01-22-2001.)

(3) predicament (as in dangers on both sides) *idiom*: **between Scylla and Charybdis**. SEE PRECARIOUS

(4) predicament (resulting from an inopportune occurrence) *n.*: **contretemps**. SEE MISHAP

(5) predicament (which is difficult to solve) *n.*: **Gordian knot**. SEE DILEMMA

predict *v.t.*: **vaticinate**. ∎ Democracy, [the authors] **vaticinate**, will ultimately trump tyranny because most people believe legitimate government pivots on the consent of the governed, and most professional military officers believe in civilian supremacy (for example, in Nigeria, Bosnia, Somalia, or Burma). (Bruce Fein, *Book Reviews*, Perspectives on Political Science, 06-01-1994, p. 149.)

(2) predict *v.t.*: **adumbrate**. SEE FORESHADOW

predictable (as in trained to show a conditioned response) *adj.*: **Pavlovian**. SEE CONDITIONED

prediction (as in acting as if or threatening that a future event [usually unwanted] has already occurred by reference to an event that precedes it, for example "if you look at my diary, you're dead") *n.*: **prolepsis**. ∎ The ragged-looking protestors say the planned highway is a violation of the earth. ... [They] have an apocalyptic air, as if this is all that has been left of urban civilisation after some terrible eco-disaster [as if] the population of Britain has been decimated by an awful laboratory-created virus, leaving everyone still alive in ragged Aran sweaters. ... This is protest as **prolepsis**: an anticipation of what they seek to prevent. (Will Self, *Tree Surgery*, The Observer, 02-04-1996.)

predictive *adj.*: **fatidic**. SEE PROPHETIC

predictor (as in one who makes correct predictions of misfortune which are ignored) *n.*: **Cassandra** [Note: There is some discrepancy among the dictionary definitions for this word as to (1) whether the predictions must prove to be correct, (2) whether the predictions must be of misfortune, doom or disaster and (3) whether the predictions must be ignored. For example, although the OED references all three, *Webster's Third* references only the second condition and neither of the other two. *The American Heritage Fourth* references only the third. However, the original Cassandra had the gift of prophecy bestowed upon her by Appollo, but when she spurned him, he converted the gift to a curse by fating that she would not be believed. Thus her curse was to know of future disasters and yet be powerless to prevent them. Accordingly, it is submitted that all three conditions must be met for a correct use of the word, which is the case in the following example.] ∎ Among the chorus of **Cassandras** prophesying the doom of financial markets if junk bond takeovers were not curbed was SEC Chairman Shad. Said he: "The more leveraged takeovers and buyouts today, the more bankruptcies tomorrow." (Brett Duval Fromson, *Special Report: The Last Days of Drexel Burnham*, Fortune, 05-21-1990, p. 90.)

(2) predictor (by using lightning or animal innards) *n.*: **haruspex**. SEE FORTUNETELLER

predilection (as in personal preference) *n.*: **de gustibus** [Latin]. SEE TASTE

predisposed (to a particular point of view) *adj.*: **tendentious**. SEE BIASED

predisposition *n.*: **parti pris** [French]. SEE PRECONCEPTION

predominant *adj.*: **regnant**. ∎ By the 1996 elections, American politics had come half-circle: Now you don't have to call yourself conservative to be one; it is simply the political air everyone, Democrats and Republicans alike, breathes. Once again an end of ideology has been proclaimed, only this time it disguises the fact that the **regnant** ideology is conservatism. (Rick Perlstein, *Ideas/Left Overtures for the Renewal of Liberalism*, Newsday, 01-26-1997, p. A34.)

preeminence (as in superiority or state of being better) *n.*: **meliority**. SEE SUPERIORITY

preface *n.*: **proem**. ∎ Eugene Jolas's extraordinary memoir (he called it "my novel — autobiography — my fact and fiction book") opens with a rhapsodic **proem**. (Daniel Aaron, *A Child of the Century*, The New Republic, 11-09-1998.)

(2) preface (often to a speech or writing) *n.*: **exordium**. SEE INTRODUCTION

(3) preface (to a lengthy or complex work) *n.*: **prolegomenon**. SEE INTRODUCTION

preference (as in personal ...) *n.*: **de gustibus** [Latin]. SEE TASTE

pregnancies (woman who has had two or more ...) *n.*: **multigravida**. ▌ Ness, et al, evaluated women from the Framingham cohort and found that the rates of coronary heart disease were higher among **multigravida** women than among women who had never been pregnant. (Mary Ann D'elio, *Are Life Stress and Social Support Related to Parity in Women?* Behavioral Medicine, 06-22-1997, p. 87.)

pregnancy (period of ...) *n.*: **antepartum** [Latin]. ▌ **Antepartum** care encompasses the physical and psychosocial care of the family experiencing a pregnancy. (Virginia H. Kemo, *Perinatal Home Care [Issues in Family and Community Health]*, Family and Community Health, 01-01-1996, p. 40.)

(2) pregnancy (just after ...) *adj.*: **puerperal**. SEE POSTPARTUM

(3) pregnancy (woman right after ...) *n.*: **puerperium**. SEE POSTPARTUM

pregnant *adj.*: **enceinte** [French]. ▌ It was probably only a matter of time. A British firm has unveiled what is believed to be the first line of maternity wedding gowns, in white and ivory, for today's **enceinte** bride. "Just because they're pregnant, there's no reason they shouldn't look beautiful," explains Jennie Andrews, designer for Ellis Bridals. (Thom Geier, *Eye on the '90s*, U.S. News & World Report, 09-25-1995, p. 26.)

(2) pregnant *adj.*: **gravid**. ▌ Should we take another look at those heatedly denied rumors about Julia Roberts being pregnant? ... So, **gravid** or not? "Please, she's starting Mary Reilly in early May," says a Roberts spokeswoman, "and she's doing a cameo for Robert Altman's Pret-a-Porter in March, so she can't be pregnant." (Author not given, *News and Notes*, Entertainment Weekly, 11-19-1993, p. 14.)

(3) pregnant (woman who is ... for the first time or has had only one child) *n.*: **primipara**. ▌ With breastfeeding, however, the "condition" does not really exist prior to hospital discharge; the mother's breasts have not yet begun to fill. The **primipara** has no experience of the condition, so it is unlikely that she will know if it becomes better or worse than it should be. (Marie Biancuzzo, *Breastfeeding Education for Early Discharge: A Three-Tiered Approach*

[Breastfeeding], Journal of Perinatal & Neonatal Nursing, 09-01-1997, p. 10.)

(4) pregnant (cause to become ...) *v.t.*: **fecundate**. SEE IMPREGNATE

prehistoric (person, as in neanderthal) *n.*: **troglodyte**. SEE NEANDERTHAL

prejudgment (as in preconception) *n.*: **parti pris** [French]. SEE PRECONCEPTION

prejudice (preconceived ... on an issue) *n.*: **parti pris** [French]. SEE PRECONCEPTION

prejudiced (as in narrow-minded) *adj.*: **hidebound**. SEE NARROW-MINDED

(2) prejudiced (as in advocating a particular point of view) *adj.*: **tendentious**. SEE BIASED

prelude *n.*: **proem**. SEE PREFACE

(2) prelude (to a lengthy or complex work) *n.*: **prolegomenon**. SEE INTRODUCTION

premonition (that something is going to occur) *n.*: **presentiment**. [Usage note: Presentiment often, but not necessarily, refers to a premonition that something bad is going to occur.] ▌ The feeling that something could go very wrong [when the date becomes January 1, 2000] turns out to be hard to shake. ... You can't criticize the decision to stay on the safe side. Who knows what lunatic or team of lunatics might turn a **presentiment** of doom into an active effort to usher it in? Maybe, just maybe, tonight will bring chaos. (Amy Schwartz, *New-Year Fears*, The Washington Post, 12-31-1999.)

preoccupation (with an idea or concept) *n.*: **idée fixe** [French]. SEE OBSESSION

(2) preoccupation (undue ... over one subject or idea) *n.*: **monomania**. SEE OBSESSION

preoccupied (esp. because of worries or fears) *adj.*: **distrait**. SEE DISTRACTED

preposterous *adj.*: **fatuous** SEE DELUSIONAL

presage *v.t.*: **adumbrate**. SEE FORESHADOW

(2) presage *v.t.*: **betoken**. SEE PORTEND

presence (having ... through magnetism or charm) *n.*: **duende**. SEE CHARISMA

(2) presence (as in condition of being located in a particular place) *n.*: **ubiety**. SEE PLACE

present (as in blessing) *n.*: **benison**. SEE BLESSING

(2) present (such as flowers, to a wife from a guilty

husband) *n*.: **drachenfutter** [German; lit. dragon-fodder.]. SEE PEACE-OFFERING

(3) present (extra or unexpected ... often given with customer's purchase) *n*.: **lagniappe**. SEE GIFT

(4) present (for the ...) *n*. **nonce** (used as "for the nonce"). SEE TIME BEING

pressed (together, esp. in rows) *adj*.: **serried**. SEE CROWDED

pressing *adj*.: **clamant**. SEE URGENT

(2) pressing *adj*.: **necessitous**. SEE URGENT

pressure (as in burden) *n*.: **incubus**. SEE BURDEN

pretend (to be sick or incapacitated to avoid work) *v.i*.: **malinger**. SEE SHIRK

pretender (as in hypocrite, esp. one who affects religious peity) *n*.: **Tartuffe** (or **tartuffe**). SEE HYPOCRITE

(2) pretender (as in hypocrite, esp. one who acts humbly) *n*.: **Uriah Heep**. SEE HYPOCRITE

pretense (as in something which is impressive-looking on the outside but which hides or covers up undesirable conditions or facts) *n*.: **Potemkin village**. SEE FACADE

pretentious (as in pompous) *adj*.: **flatulent**. SEE POMPOUS

(2) pretentious (or ostentatious object) *n*.: **frippery**. SEE OSTENTATIOUS

(3) pretentious (speech or writing) *adj*.: **fustian**. SEE POMPOUS

(4) pretentious (person on issues of grammar) *n*.: **grammaticaster**. SEE PEDANATIC

(5) pretentious (or self-important person or official) *n*.: **high muck-a-muck**. SEE BIGWIG

(6) pretentious *adj*.: **hoity-toity**. SEE POMPOUS

(7) pretentious (esp. regarding speaking or writing style) *adj*.: **magniloquent**. SEE POMPOUS

(8) pretentious (esp. regarding speaking or writing style) *adj*.: **orotund**. SEE POMPOUS

(9) pretentious (or self-important person or official) *n*.: **panjandrum**. SEE BIGWIG

(10) pretentious (but superficial knowledge of a subject) *n*.: **sciolism**. SEE SUPERFICIAL

pretty (esp. sexually) *adj*.: **toothsome**. SEE SEXY

prevailing *adj*.: **regnant**. SEE PREDOMINANT

prevalent *adj*.: **pandemic**. SEE WIDESPREAD

(2) prevalent *adj*.: **regnant**. SEE WIDESPREAD

prevent (intended to ... against evil) *adj*.: **apotropaic**. SEE PROTECT

(2) prevent (as in avert or ward off) *v.t*.: **forfend**. SEE AVERT

(3) prevent (a person's movement by holding down his arms) *v.t*.: **pinion**. SEE IMMOBILIZE

previous (as in former) *adj*.: **ci-devant** [French]. SEE FORMER

(2) previous (as in former) *adj*.: **quondam**. SEE FORMER

prickling (of skin sensation) *n*.: **paresthesia**. ▪ [A] touch player with little or no sensation in her hands probably has a limited future, and [golfer Cathy] Gerring gets constant reminders of the odds stacked against her as a result of a burn accident]. ... On cold days, her fingers ache. She also suffers from **paresthesia**, a pain she compares to being stabbed by needles. (Kevin Cook, *Golf Plus/News & Notes*, Sports Illustrated, 05-04-1998, p. G27.)

prickly *adj*.: **echinate**. ▪ Almost any fool should be discerning enough to recognize evil disguised as religion. ... The harder issue is whether there's any eternal difference between and among religions followed by people of good will, [and] by people with a social conscience. ... Joseph C. Hough Jr., president of Union Theological Seminary in New York, has been raising this **echinate** question in recent months. (Bill Tammeus, *Toward Theology in Dialogue*, Kansas City Star, 03-30-2002, p. B7.)

pride (as in self-esteem) *n*.: **amour-propre** [French]. SEE SELF-ESTEEM

(2) pride (which is overbearing, as in arrogance) *adj*.: **hubris**. SEE ARROGANCE

priest (government by a ... or other clergy members) *n*.: **hierocracy**. SEE GOVERNMENT

priestly *adj*.: **sacerdotal**. ▪ After [Cardinal-to-be John O'Connor] was ordained a priest in 1945, he followed the usual **sacerdotal** path, teaching high school and doing parish work. (Hanna Rosin, *Cardinal John J. O'Connor Dies; N.Y. Archbishop, 80, Was Leading U.S. Catholic Prelate*, The Washington Post, 05-04-2000, p. A1.)

prim *adj*.: **governessy**. SEE FASTIDIOUS

(2) prim (and proper like a prude) *adj*.: **missish**. SEE PRUDE

(3) prim (in an affected manner) *adj*.: **niminy-piminy**. SEE DAINTY

primary (as in basic) *adj.*: **abecedarian**. SEE BASIC

prime mover *n.*: **primum mobile** [Latin]. ■ [Randall Robinson who wrote *The Debt: What America Owes to Blacks*] is hardly alone in his basic insistence that the growth of the black middle class is somehow "beside the point." ... This sense of racism as rendering all black success "accidental" is ultimately the **primum mobile** of the reparations movement. ... This belief that there is no path for blacks to the top accounts for Robinson's sour attitude toward blacks making progress. (John McWhorter, *Why African Americans Can Believe in America*, The New Republic, 07-23-2001.)

primitive *n.*: **artless**. SEE CRUDE

(2) primitive (as in crude, or poorly put together, esp. with respect to a writing or speech) *adj.*: **incondite**. SEE CRUDE

(3) primitive (person) *n.*: **troglodyte**. SEE NEANDERTHAL

prince (or other ruler who holds great power or sway) *n.*: **potentate**. SEE RULER

principle *n.*: **shibboleth**. ■ The Democrats had been out of power for 12 years when Clinton came on the scene as a "new Democrat" who defied some Democratic **shibboleths**, supporting welfare reform, free trade and the death penalty. (Susan Page, *GOP's New Face: "W," as in Win: Tired of Losing, Party Hands Bush the Reins; Will it Last?* USA Today, 08-03-2000, p. 1A.)

printing (of secret or government-banned literature, or the literature produced by such a system) *n.*: **samizdat**. SEE UNDERGROUND

prior (as in former) *adj.*: **ci-devant** [French]. SEE FORMER

(2) prior (to a meal, esp. dinner) *adj.*: **preprandial**. SEE MEAL

(3) prior *adj.*: **prevenient** (often as in "prevenient grace"). SEE ANTECEDENT

(4) prior (as in former) *adj.*: **quondam**. SEE FORMER

prison *n.*: **bastille**. ■ He has even lost the timbre of his voice. Facing him behind a sheet of perforated Plexiglas in the narrow visiting room of the prison — a **bastille** built in 1840 to entertain captured pirates — one has to press an ear against the barrier to hear him speak. (William Nack, *The Muscle Murders — When Bertil Fox, a Former Mr. Universe, Was Arrested for Double Homicide Last Year, He Became Only the Latest Accused Murderer Among Hard-Core*

Bodybuilders, Sports Illustrated, 05-18-1998, p. 96.)

(2) prison (where a guard can see all prisoners) *n.*: **panopticon**. ■ Walk through the nearly completed seven-room house in Studio City, Calif, where 10 contestants will spend 89 days being filmed for edited, same-day broadcasts. ... It is Martha Stewart's hell, a cold Bauhaus **panopticon** riddled with cameras. The decor, says creator Romer, is intentional. The hope is that the "houseguests" will decorate their prison themselves. (Benjamin Nugent, *We Like To Watch — Led by the Hit Survivor, Voyeurism Has Become TV's Hottest Genre*, Time, 06-26-2000, p. 56.)

(3) prison (study of ... management) *n.*: **penology**. ■ Formerly smooth-running, [Ottawa's Grande Cache prison] has since seen ceaseless trouble, and last month, a riot. The guards' union and a Reform MP say the incidents prove that Ottawa's liberal **penology** produces prisoners who are bored, irritable — and destructive. (Davis Sheremata, *The Results of Cherishing Prisoner Individuality*, Alberta Report/Western Report, 12-09-1996, p. 30.)

(4) prison *n.*: **durance** (often as in "in durance vile"). SEE JAIL

prisoners (group of ... or slaves chained together) *n.*: **coffle**. ■ On his way to view the opening of a new session of the houses of Congress [in 1815], he was shocked to confront a slave **coffle** in the neighborhood of Capitol Hill. Nothing in his life had prepared him for the sight of men, women, and children being herded in chains through the streets of Washington. (John Davis, *Eastman Johnson's "Negro Life at the South" and Urban Slavery in Washington, D.C.*, The Art Bulletin, 03-01-1998, p. 67.)

prissy (and proper like a prude) *adj.*: **missish**. SEE PRUDE

private (as in, of or relating to a court, legislative body or other group that meets in ..., and often makes decisions which are harsh or arbitrary) *adj.*: **star chamber**. SEE CLOSED-DOOR

(2) private (most ... parts, thoughts or places) *n.*: **penetralia**. SEE SECRET

privately *adj.*: **in petto** [Italian]. ■ When she auditioned with Verdi and he explained to her that she would have no solos, she assured him she didn't mind, she was so honored to have been chosen by the maestro for the Falstaff premiere. Still, Verdi wrote afterward, he could tell that **in petto** she was disappointed, and he added the solo. (Joseph Kerman, *Verdi: A Biography [Book Reviews]*, The New Republic, 01-10-1994, p. 42.)

prize (as in reward) *n.*: **guerdon**. See REWARD

prized (household items) *n.*, *pl.*: **lares and penates**. See TREASURES

probable (as in appearing to be true or accurate) *adj.*: **verisimilar**. See PLAUSIBLE

probe (closely) *v.t.*: **catechize**. See QUESTION
 (2) probe (through formal questioning about governmental policy or action) *v.t.*: **interpellate**. See INTERROGATE
 (3) probe (as in touch, esp. for medical reasons) *v.t.*: **palpate**. See TOUCH

problem (which is difficult to solve) *n.*: **Gordian knot**. See DILEMMA
 (2) problem (which is difficult to solve) *n.*: **nodus**. See COMPLICATION

procedure (mode of ..., as in course of action) *n.*: **démarche** [French]. See COURSE OF ACTION

procession (of attendants, as for an important person) *n.*: **cortege**. ∎ These days one of the flashier **corteges** roaring around Moscow has a BMW out front, bodyguards in Mitsubishi jeeps on either side and a dark-blue, bulletproof Mercedes 600 in the center. It belongs not to Boris Yeltsin but to the other Boris — the most influential new capitalist tycoon in Russia, Boris Berezovsky. (Fred Coleman, *Rich, the Russian Way*, U.S. News & World Report, 01-13-1997, p. 37.)

proclaim (pompously, loudly, or theatrically) *v.i.*: **declaim**. ∎ Sir James Goldsmith's Referendum Party ... loudly opposes a federal Europe. At a recent rally, the tycoon **declaimed**, "If the only choice we have is to be part of a federal Europe, a superstate, then I would definitely get out." (James Walsh, *The Battle of Britain–A Nation Ruled by Conservatives for the past 18 Years Prepares Itself for a New Era of Tony Blair's Gentler, Centrist "New Labour,"* Time International, 04-28-1997, p. 22.)
 (2) proclaim *v.t.*: **annunciate**. See ANNOUNCE

proclamation *n.*: **ukase**. See DECREE

procrastinate (due to indecision) *v.i.*: **dither**. ∎ [BP Amoco head] Browne, 51, is not the kind of chief executive who **dithers**. He ordered up $2 billion of cost-cutting from BP Amoco by the end of 2000. Then, when oil prices tanked last year, he moved the target date up to the end of 1999. Boom. (Toni Mack, *Brass-Ring Time*, Forbes, 05-03-1999, p. 56.)
 (2) procrastinate *v.i.*: **shilly-shally**. ∎ Green had his staff pore over Victoria's Secret catalogs for days on end until they determined that the Secret people did not show enough minority models wearing their underwear. Green didn't **shilly-shally**. He cited them with a violation of city regulations — hell, right on the spot. (Michael Shain, *Inside New York*, Newsday, 06-20-1993, p. 11.)

procrastinating (engaging in ... tactics, esp. as a means to wear out an opponent or avoid confrontation) *adj.*: **Fabian**. See DILATORY

procrastination (or delay) *n.*: **cunctation**. See DELAY

proctor (a school examination) *v.i.*: **invigilate**. ∎ A few weeks into my so-called teaching career, the dreaded four-letter word started appearing more and more often in the students' vocabulary. E-X-A-M. Preparing the question papers for the exam was no easy feat but being only a temporary teacher, I was spared that. Nonetheless, I still had to **invigilate** (which is an extremely tiresome and boring job) and yes, mark the exam papers. (Mark Hoew Han, *Teaching's Not For the Quitter*, New Straits Times, 05-16-2003.)

prod (as in stimulus) *n.*: **fillip**. See STIMULUS

prodding (as in urging someone to take a course of action) *adj.*: **hortatory**. See URGING

produce (as in build cheaply and flimsily) *v.t.*: **jerry-build**. See BUILD

product (as in outgrowth) *n.*: **excrescence**. See OUTGROWTH

productive (esp. as in fertile) *adj.*: **fecund**. See FERTILE
 (2) productive (make ...) *v.i.*: **fructify**. See FRUITFUL
 (3) productive (in producing offspring) *adj.*: **philoprogenitive**. See FERTILE

profess (as in confide, one's thoughts or feelings) *v.t.*, *v.i.*: **unbosom**. See CONFIDE

profession *n.*: **métier** [French]. ∎ [Senator Joseph] McCarthy was in a business that permitted a certain latitude: it was politics, not physics. "McCarthy's record is ... not only much better than his critics allege, but, given his **métier**, extremely good." Thus he "should not be remembered as the man who didn't produce 57 Communist Party cards but as the man who brought public pressure to bear ... to eliminate from responsible positions flagrant security risks." (Elliott Abrams, *McCarthy and His Enemies [Book Reviews]*, National Review, 02-26-1996, p. 57.)

professor (as in teacher) *n.*: **pedagogue**. See TEACHER

proficient *adj.*: **habile**. See SKILLFUL

profile (distinctive ... or outline, often of a face) *adj.*: **lineament** (often **lineaments**). See CONTOUR

profit (as in, "to whose ...?") *n.*: **cui bono** [Latin]. See ADVANTAGE

profligate *n.*: **wastrel**. See SLACKER

progression *n.*: **consecution**. See SEQUENCE

project (which is fruitless or hopeless) *n.*: **fool's errand**. See HOPELESS

proletariat *n.*: **canaille**. See MASSES
 (2) **proliferate** (as in burgeon or expand; lit.: bear fruit) *v.i.*: **fructify**. See BURGEON
 (3) **proletariat** *n.*: **hoi polloi**. See COMMONERS

prolific (esp. as in fertile) *adj.*: **fecund** (*v.t.*: **fecundate**). ∎ The manatee population continues to grow despite the few that are killed in boating accidents, just as our deer populations continue to thrive despite the deer that are struck on the highways. Manatees are not particularly **fecund** animals, but they have no natural predators. (Frank Sargeant, *Manatees Are Not Endangered Species*, The Tampa Tribune, 09-13-2000, p. 3.)
 (2) **prolific** (in producing offspring) *adj.*: **philoprogenitive**. See FERTILE

prominent (and/or wealthy person) *n.*: **nabob**. See BIGWIG

promiscuous *adj., n.*: **libertine**. ∎ This drew on a plebeian morality in which the value placed on chastity was relatively low, and which allowed premarital sex upon promise of marriage and common-law marriage if a first marriage broke down. ... For women the **libertine** ethic was perilous: pregnant sweethearts and abandoned wives and children paid for the freedoms of bachelor culture. (Anna Davin, *Before the Glass Ceiling*, Women's Review of Books, 12-01-1995, p. 13.)

promise (of marriage) *v.t.*: **affiance**. See MARRIAGE

promotion (of military officer without pay increase) *v.t., n.*: **brevet**. ∎ By the end of the year, though still nominally a lieutenant, he was **breveted** with the

rank of captain as a reward for his services. (Simon Winchester, *The Professor and the Madman*, Harper Collins [1998], p. 67.)

pronounce (with hissing sounds) *v.t.*: **assibilate**. See HISSING

pronouncement (made without proof or support) *n.*: **ipse dixit** [Latin]. See ALLEGATION
 (2) **pronouncement** *n.*: **ukase**. See DECREE

pronunciation (words having the same ..., but different meaning) *adj.*: **homophonic**. ∎ For no reason I can think of, the letter "P" provides the thickest file of **homophonic** pests. ... [For example], to peak is to reach a maximum point. To peek is to look furtively or briefly. To pique is to arouse interest. Many writers have a terrible time with "pedal" and "peddle." (James Kilpatrick, *Helping the Homophonically Challenged to Help Themselves*, Denver Rocky Mountain News, 03-30-1997, p. 45A.)

proofread (text or language by removing errors or flaws) *v.t.*: **emend**. See EDIT

propaganda *n.*: **agitprop**. ∎ If foodmakers can no longer count on the public's unquestioning acceptance of their products, it's not just because of activist theatrics and shrill **agitprop**. (Frederic Golden, *Trade Wars/Genetically Modified Food*, Time, 11-29-1999, p. 49.)

proper *adj.*: **comme il faut** [French]. ∎ The French, on the other hand, think U.S. table manners are not **comme il faut**. "I have seen French dinner party hosts recoil in horror when their American guests have helped themselves to wine and gulped it down as if it was Coca Cola," says Platt. "Another shocker would be to leave food on the plate. This is considered very impolite. Of course, the Americans do this all the time." (Barbara Wall, *Americans Still Bedeviled by Image as Yahoos Abroad*, USA Today, 04-12-1996, p. 5A.)
 (2) **proper** (a ... thing to do) *n.*: **bon ton** [French]. See APPROPRIATE

proper name (of, relating to or explaining a ...) *adj.*: **onomastic**. See NAME

properly (as in "by the book") *idiom*: **according to Hoyle**. See BY THE BOOK

prophesier (as in one who makes correct predictions of misfortune which are ignored) *n.*: **Cassandra**. See PREDICTOR

prophesy (spec. acting as if or threatening that a future event [usually unwanted] has already occurred by reference to an event that precedes it, for example "if you look at my diary, you're dead") *n.*: **prolepsis**. SEE PREDICTION

(2) prophesy *v.t.*: **vaticinate**. SEE PREDICT

prophet (as in predictor, by using lightning or animal innards) *n.*: **haruspex**. SEE FORTUNETELLER

prophetic *adj.*: **fatidic**. ▪ [In Revelation, St. John the Devine predicted that Satan will stage] one final epic battle — Armageddon — but will be defeated and "thrown into the lake of fire" where he and all of his servants, including all false prophets, "will be tormented day and night for ever and ever." To some doomsday prophets, this **fatidic** vision will be played out at the end of human history. But how will we know when we are nearing it? (Michael Shermer, *The Fire That Will Cleanse*, Skeptic, 06-22-1999.)

(2) prophetic *adj.*: **vatic**. ▪ It was, arguably, Rockefeller's supreme inspiration that he believed in the Ohio-Indiana [oil] fields — one of those flashes of **vatic** power that made him a business legend. (Ron Chernow, *Titan*, Random House [1998], p. 284.)

proponent (or leader of a cause) *n.*: **paladin**. ▪ In reality, Rockefeller voted for James G. Blaine, a **paladin** of business interests, and predicted the election would be "a great calamity" if [Grover] Cleveland won. (Ron Chernow, *Titan*, Random House [1998], p. 291.)

(2) proponent (strong ... of a cause, religion or activity) *n.*: **votary**. SEE SUPPORTER

proprieties (precise observance of ... or etiquette) *n.*: **punctilio**. SEE ETIQUETTE

proprietor *n.*: **padrone**. SEE BOSS

propriety *n.*: **correctitude**. ▪ The [Church of England] is ... liturgically corrupt, demonstrating in its appointment of women priests its subservience to political **correctitudes**. (Brian Sewell, *What This Country Needs Is ... [Opinions of What the UK Needs]*, New Statesman, 04-11-1997, p. 29.)

prose (which is concise, precise or refined; lit. "as if engraved in a precious stone") *adj.*: **lapidary**. SEE WRITING

prosper (often at another's expense) *v.i.*: **batten**. SEE THRIVE

prosperity *n.*: **weal** (usu. as in *weal or woe* or *weal and woe*). SEE WELL-BEING

prosperous (and/or prominent person) *n.*: **nabob**. SEE BIGWIG

prostitute *n.*: **bawd**. ▪ Outside the Clink, Londoners were frequently entertained by the "cartings" of topless whores being whipped to the prison where they were branded on the forehead with a B for **bawd**. (Alex Berlyne, *Richard the Cubhearted*, Jerusalem Post, 01-08-1999, p. 31.)

(2) prostitute *n.*: **demimondaine**. ▪ In one excerpt cited in the book, Trink describes the [prostitutes] as "meretricious, avaricious, mendacious and bone lazy. Never give your heart to a **demimondaine**: she'll chew it up and spit it out." (Robert Horn, *A Walk on the Wild Side — An Entertaining Biography Examines the Man Who Has Chronicled Bangkok and its Sex Scene for 35 Years*, Time International, 10-16-2000, p. 59.)

(3) prostitute *n.*: **doxy**. ▪ [Historically,] many prostitutes found the wages of sin to be death — dismal and early. The shameful sisterhood took heavy casualties but remained multitudinous. Since days of the republic, Texas was never without **doxies**. (Kent Biffle, *What Were Once Vices Still Are*, The Dallas Morning News, 02-09-2003.)

(4) prostitute *n.*: **trollop**. ▪ From a men's room tucked into the corner of a scabrous press bullpen in a criminal-courts building, out walks a **trollop** and a policeman adjusting his clothes after what has obviously been a brief but close encounter. (William A. Henry III, *Theater: Hello, Sweetheart, Get Me Rethink*, Time, 12-08-1986, p. 83.)

prostitutes (as a group) *n.*: **demimonde**. ▪ The nineties have not been kind to prostitution. Despite the superficial appeal of life as a Heidi Fleiss-style call girl — or even as a Sunset Boulevard streetwalker invited into Hugh Grant's BMW — denizens of the **demimonde** are in decline. (Ted Gup, *What's New with the World's Oldest Profession?* Cosmopolitan, 10-01-1995, p. 236.)

prostitution (house of ...) *n.*: **bagnio**. SEE BROTHEL

protect (intended to ... against evil) *adj.*: **apotropaic**. ▪ [For Vincent Van Gogh], it is as though the calmer color, the growing penchant for structuring his work as a process of sequential research into a given motif — a walled field near the asylum, the olive grove outside it, the pines in the asylum garden — had an **apotropaic** use for him, keeping at bay the demons of the unconscious. (Robert Hughes, *Art: Sanity Defense for a Genius — The Metropolitan Reveals Van Gogh's Shocking Freshness*, Time, 12-01-1986, p. 80.)

(2) protect *v.t.*: **forfend**. ∎ Writes Seton, "Maybe that's one of the things that draws me to farming, the vast plain of unbudgeable routine. ... In farming there is a rigid set of limitations governing one's versatility. Farmers can't move their land to a more desirable climate. They can't manipulate the rhythms of season nor **forfend** against freaky climatic extremes. (Kari Granville, *Read This*, Newsday, 01-31-1995, p. B19.)

(3) protect (in an overprotective way or indulge) *v.t.*: **mollycoddle**. SEE OVERPROTECT

protection (against attack or danger) *n.*: **bulwark**. ∎ Says Bill Martin: ... "There's not great hope that GATT [General Agreement on Tariffs and Trade] can achieve much in the way of further trade liberalization. But GATT is a very important **bulwark** against galloping protectionism." (Barbara Rudolph, *Business: Bitter Standoff in Montreal — Hopes for a GATT Agreement Fade Over Farm Subsidies*, Time, 12-19-1988, p. 58.)

(2) protection (spec. a piece of armor) *n.*: **cuirass**. SEE ARMOR

(3) protection (line of ... which is thought to be effective, but is not in reality) *n.*: **Maginot Line**. SEE DEFENSE

protective (covering like a turtle shell) *n.*: **carapace**. SEE SHELL

protest *v.t.*: **expostulate**. SEE OBJECT

(2) protest (bitter ...) *n.*: **jeremiad**. SEE COMPLAINT

(3) protest (against, as in oppose a statement, opinion or action) *v.t.*: **oppugn**. SEE OPPOSE

(4) protest (esp. in the form of pleading with) *v.t.*: **remonstrate**. SEE PLEAD

protocol (precise observance of ...) *n.*: **punctilio**. SEE ETIQUETTE

prototype (example which serves as a ...) *n.*: **paradigm**. SEE MODEL

(2) prototype (as in original model or example) *n.*: **archetype**. SEE MODEL

protrusion (as in outgrowth) *n.*: **excrescence**. SEE OUTGROWTH

proud *adj.*: **orgulous**. SEE HAUGHTY

(2) proud (like a peacock) *adj.*: **pavonine**. SEE PEACOCK

province (as in area of activity or interest) *n.*: **purlieu**. SEE DOMAIN

provincial (as in parochial) *adj.*: **parish pump** [British]. SEE PAROCHIAL

provocation (as in event which causes or provokes [literally] war or [figuratively] conflict) *n.*: **casus belli** [Latin; occasion of war]. ∎ Time now to suggest a new concept of "fought-over words," words that adversaries in national debate try to capture. ... [N]otice that, for a majority of Americans, "equal opportunity" is in, "preferences" are out, and "affirmative action" is still a **casus belli**. (Daniel Schorr, *Good Words, Bad Words*, The Christian Science Monitor, 12-26-1997, p. 15.)

provocative *adj.*: **piquant**. ∎ [Pauline] Kael was in her 40s before she became a fixture among cinephiles in Berkeley, California, where her criticism appeared in the form of program notes, radio reviews, screeds in the local film magazine. She couldn't have been further out of the [Hollywood] loop ... so she devised a **piquant** strategy for being heard: she would go to a movie and review the audience. (Richard Corliss, *The Arts & Media/Books*, Time International, 11-28-1994, p. 68.)

provoke (as in agitate) *v.t.*: **commove**. SEE AGITATE

proximity (in place, time or relation) *n.*: **propinquity**. SEE CLOSENESS

(2) proximity (physical ..., as in vicinity) *n.*: **vicinage**. SEE VICINITY

prude *n.*: **bluenose**. ∎ [W]henever **bluenoses** demand restraint against the porn and violence that are the staple of popular culture, they are met with "Who appointed you guardians of the public taste? Let the people decide." (Charles Krauthammer, *Essay: Casablanca in Color? I'm Shocked, Shocked!* Time, 01-12-1987, p. 82.)

(2) prude (like a ...) *adj.*: **missish**. ∎ In the ballet *Don Quixote*, Kitri's costumes (by Barry Kay) are outright disasters. What senorita of her mettle would be seen dead in that dreary, long-sleeved raspberry day dress, more suitable for English autumns than Spanish heat? Rojo, like Kitri, is a girl made for dangerous colours, not **missish** ones. (Ismene Brown, *Stretton's Arrival Marred by a Damp Squib*, Daily Telegraph [London], 10-25-2001.)

prudence (as in moderation) *n.*: **sophrosyne**. SEE MODERATION

prudish (and intolerant conventionality) *n.*: **Grundyism**. SEE PURITANICAL

pry (one who would ... into other's affairs) *n.*: **quidnunc**. See busybody

psychic *adj.*: **fey**. See clairvoyant

psychoanalysis (person undergoing ...) *n.*: **analysand**. ∎ Psychoanalysis is the one form of therapy which leaves it to **analysands** to determine for themselves what their specific goals will be. (Jonathan Lear, *The Shrink Is In: A Counterblast in the War on Freud*, The New Republic, 12-25-1995, p. 18.)

psychotic (person) *n.*: **bedlamite**. See lunatic

puberty (onset of ... for a woman, as in her first menstruation) *n.*: **menarche**. See menstruation

public (suitable for or comprehensible by the ... at large) *adj.*: **exoteric**. See accessible

publication (of secret or government-banned literature, or the literature produced by such a system) *n.*: **samizdat**. See underground

publicity *n.*: **réclame** [French]. ∎ At 19, Fernando Bujones was dubbed the "Bad Boy of American Ballet," the result of the young dancer's outspoken views vis-a-vis the Russian defectors who had been given preferential treatment by American Ballet Theater. ... Particularly incensed over the **réclame** attending Mikhail Baryshnikov's defection and subsequent appearances with ABT in 1974, Bujones [said] "Baryshnikov has the publicity but I have the talent!" (John Gruen, *Ballet's 'Bad Boy' Grows Up*, The New York Times, 06-15-1989.)

pudgy (condition of having a ... physique) *n.*: **embonpoint**. See plump
 (2) **pudgy** (having a short ... physique) *adj.*: **pyknic**. See stocky

pugnacious *adj.*: **bellicose**. See belligerent

pull (used to ...) *adj.*: **tractive**. ∎ Content to be just a normal family wagon the rest of the year, confining its **tractive** excellence to occasional pulls of the boat up algae-infested ramps, the Legacy becomes Super-Skimobile mid-year. (Paul Owen, *Subaru's Luxury Ride to Family Fun*, The Evening Post, 06-14-1996, p. 2.)

pullout (desperate ..., as in retreat) *n.*: **Dunkirk**. See retreat

pulverize (or reduce to powder) *v.t.*: **comminute**. ∎ Other raw material animal foods such as **comminuted** foods (chopped, ground, flaked, or minced

foods, such as ground beef, gyros, sausage, and fish) must be cooked to 155 [degrees] for at least 15 seconds. (Jorge Hernandez, *Preparation and Cooking*, Restaurant Hospitality, 05-01-1998, p. 162.)

pun *n.*: **paronomasia**. ∎ [I am writing a novel which is reminiscent of *The Count of Monte Cristo*, but I don't want to make it too close, so I am making a few changes. For example, in my book] Edmond's affianced [who is named Mercedes in *The Count of Monte Cristo*] transforms herself (in an unforgivable example of automobile **paronomasia**) into Portia. (Stephen Fry, *Forget Ideas, Mr. Author; What Kind of Pen Do You Use?* The New York Times, 07-29-2002.) See word play

pungent *adj.*: **acrid**. ∎ The second-best known Mexican beverage might be tequila, the **acrid** and potent distillation of the yeasty home brew pulque, itself fermented from the agave cactus. (Jack Robertiello, *Drinking in the Flavors of Mexico [Recipes]*, Americas, 03-01-1994, p. 58.)
 (2) **pungent** (agreeably ... in taste or flavor) *adj.*: **piquant**. See zesty

punish (as in impose a monetary fine) *v.t.*: **amerce**. See fine
 (2) **punish** (oneself) *v.t.*: **flagellate** (*n.*: **flagellation**). See criticize
 (3) **punish** (by imposing a fine or penalty) *v.t.*: **mulct**. See penalize

punishing (of convicted persons, spec. burning of heretics at the stake) *n.*: **auto-da-fe**. See execution
 (2) **punishing** (journey or experience) *n.*: **via dolorosa**. See ordeal

puny (as in meager) *adj.*: **mingy**. See meager

puppets (or showing or employing ..., as in marionettes) *n., pl.*: **fantoccini** [Italian]. See marionettes

purchasing (compulsion for ... things) *n.*: **onomania**. See shopping

pure (as in chaste) *adj.*: **vestal**. See chaste

purge (spec. criminal prosecution of French and Italian officials considered to have been Nazi collaborators after World War II) *n.*: **epuration**. ∎ As part of the general process of **epuration** undertaken by the French government after the liberation of Paris, a number of collaborationist writers, critics, and political journalists were arrested, tried, and sentenced to death, primarily for the words they wrote.

(David Carroll, *The Collaborator: The Trial and Execution of Robert Brasillach [Book Review]*, American Scholar, 06-22-2000.)

(2) purge (a book or a writing in a prudish manner) *v.t.*: **bowdlerize**. See EDIT

purify (or cleanse) *v.t., v.i.*: **depurate**. See CLEANSE

puritanical (and intolerant conventionality) *n.*: **Grundyism** [derives from Mrs. Grundy, a prudish character in Thomas Morton's 1798 play *Speed the Plow*]. ▪ His sexual investigations were brave and original. His unexpurgated translations of *The Thousand and One Nights* and other Eastern classics, defying all the **Grundyism** of the day, were great works of scholarship. (Jan Morris, *Books: 10,001 Nights of Piety and Pornography*, Independent, 10-31-1998, p. 15.)

(2) puritanical (person who is ...) *n.*: **bluenose**. See PRUDE

(3) puritanical (as in prudish) *adj.*: **missish**. See PRUDE

purpose (hidden or ulterior ...) *n.*: **arriere-pensee** (or **arrière-pensée**) [French]. See MOTIVE

(2) purpose (esp. of life) *n.*: **telos** [Greek]. See GOAL

purposeful *adj.*: **telic**. ▪ As there is a semblance to Orwell's Animal Farm, one might call the work an allegory, but where Orwell designed a **telic** action with specific goals set for well-defined characters, "A Book of Pigs" forces upon its hero too many purposeless meanderings. (Alfred Straumanis, *Cuku Gramata [Book Reviews]*, World Literature Today, 09-01-1996, p. 999.)

purposelessness (of a person or group as a result of lack of standards or values) *n.*: **anomie**. See BREAKDOWN

purse (women's drawstring ...) *n.*: **reticule**. See HANDBAG

pus (to form or discharge ...) *v.i.*: **suppurate**. ▪ Pimples, zits or plain old spots, call them what you will, but you weren't really a proper teenager if you didn't have those angry red plooks. ... [I still have acne at 44.] Friends congratulate me on my wrinkle-free skin, but I am beginning to think that I would prefer crows feet to **suppurating** pimples. And they could be around for a few decades yet. (Jennifer Veitch, *Black Spots on Your Landscape*, Evening News [Edinburgh, Scotland], 02-26-2001.)

pushing (someone to take a course of action) *adj.*: **hortatory**. See URGING

pushy *adj.*: **bumptious**. ▪ When **bumptious** Donald Trump turned up in Palm Beach, Fla, in 1985, stuffy locals greeted him like a bad sunburn. "Too much, too soon, too lavish, too showy," complained one Old Guard resident of The Donald's arrival. (Cynthia Sanz, *Too Close for Comfort — When You've Got a Celebrity Residing Next Door, the Living May be Far From Easy*, People, 08-09-1993, p. 34.)

put (close together, side-by-side or in proper order) *v.t.*: **collocate**. See PLACE

put down (as in insult, delivered while leaving the scene) *n.*: **Parthian shot**. See PARTING SHOT

put off (or discontinue, esp. a session of Parliament) *v.t.*: **prorogue**. See DISCONTINUE

put together (clumsily, roughly or hastily) *v.t.*: **cobble**. See ASSEMBLE

(2) put together (cheaply and flimsily) *v.t.*: **jerry-build**. See BUILD

putrid *adj.*: **fetid**. See SMELLY

(2) putrid *adj.*: **mephitic** (*n.*: **mephitis**). See SMELLY

(3) putrid *adj.*: **noisome**. See SMELLY

putting in (as in insertion, of something between existing things) *n.*: **intercalation**. See INSERTION

(2) putting in (esp. penis into vagina) *n.*: **intromission** (*v.t.*: **intromit**). See PENETRATION

pyrrhic victory (as in a victory obtained only at great cost to the victor) *n.*: **Cadmean victory** [derives from Cadmus, a prince in Greek mythology, who killed a dragon but with only five of his men surviving]. ▪ The obscure poem of Lycophron enumerates many of these dispersed and expatriated heroes, whose conquest of Troy was indeed a **"Cadmean" victory** ..., wherein the sufferings of the victor were little inferior to those of the vanquished. (George Grote, *Fall of Troy*, History of the World, 01-01-1992.)

Q

quack (as in a person who sells quack medicines) *n.*: **mountebank**. See HUCKSTER

quake (rapidly or spasmodically) *v.i.*: **judder**. See SHAKE

quality (as in aura or impalpable emantion) *n.*: **efflu-vium**. See AURA

(2) quality (of outstanding ...) *n.*: **first water** (usu. as in "of the first water"). ▪ [The book] *Dialect of the Southern Counties of Scotland* was to be published in 1873 and it fully confirmed for James Murray a reputation that he had begun to grow as early as the 1860's: that he was a philologist [i.e. linguist] **of the first water**. (Simon Winchester, *The Meaning of Everything*, Oxford [2003], p. 78.)

quandary (which is difficult to solve) *n.*: **Gordian knot**. See DILEMMA

(2) quandary (as in choice of taking what is offered or nothing; i.e. no real choice at all) *n.*: **Hobson's choice**. See PREDICAMENT

(3) quandary (as in dangers on both sides) *idiom*: **between Scylla and Charybdis**. See PRECARIOUS

(4) quandary (as in the situation of having to make a move where any move made will weaken the position) *n.*: **zugzwang** [German]. See PREDICAMENT

quantifying (act or process of ..., as in measuring) *n.*: **mensuration**. See MEASURING

quantitative (having ... ability) *adj.*: **numerate**. See MATHEMATICAL

quantity (illusion of ... when in fact there is little) *adj.*: **Barmecidal** (esp. as in "Barmecidal feast"). See ILLUSION

quarrel (as in brawl, esp. public) *n.*: **affray**. See BRAWL

(2) quarrel (initiate a ..., fighting or violence) *v.i.*: **aggress**. See FIGHT

(3) quarrel (as in heated disagreement or friction between groups) *n.*: **ruction**. See DISSENSION

quarrelsome *adj.*: **querulous**. See PEEVISH

quest (as in crusade, for an idea or principle) *n.*: **jihad**. See CRUSADE

question (closely) *v.t.*: **catechize**. ▪ Uma [Thurman] is beautiful, but if you bring it up, she was mildly cross, as I suppose we all would if we were continually being **catechized** about our appearance, as Uma is. (Mim Udovitch, *An Alternate Umaverse [Actress Uma Thurman]*, Esquire, 03-01-1998, p. 70.)

(2) question (as to one's opinion on an issue, esp. arising from awareness of an opposing viewpoint) *n.*: **aporia**. See DOUBT

(3) question (formally about governmental policy or action) *v.t.*: **interpellate**. See INTERROGATE

(4) question (as in oppose a statement, opinion or action) *v.t.*: **oppugn**. See OPPOSE

(5) question (esp. as in "beyond ...") *n.*: **peradventure**. See DOUBT

questionable (morality or taste) *adj.*: **louche**. ▪ Some gay conservatives even blame the leftists for the enduring image of homosexual men — in the minds of some people — as effeminate, **louche**, odd balls who wear leather jockstraps. (Author not given, *Now for a Queer Question About Gay Culture*, The Economist, 07-12-1997.)

questionableness *n.*: **dubiety**. See DOUBTFULNESS

questioner (of an astrologer) *n.*: **querent**. ▪ A Tarot deck has it all — the secret wisdom, the unexplained powers, the strange coincidences. ... Why not [take a chance]? In one prediction, she [predicts] "I see a lot of travel for you ... [to Europe or South America or Africa or Asia]." Does this rule out Australia? The **querent** doesn't ask. Who can psych out the psychic? (Henry Allen, *The Tarot Psychic*, The Washington Post, 11-24-1980, p. B1.)

(2) questioner *n.*: **querist**. ▪ [Isaac Newton] wanted to know the cause of gravity, not merely how it worked. His laws as stated did not satisfy the inward **querist** in Newton himself and his notes show him at his extended search. (Roger Sworder, *Gravity's Harmony*, Quadrant, 07-01-1999.)

quibble *v.t.*: **cavil**. ▪ QUESTION: Why are drive-through lines so long and service so slow at fast-food restaurants around here? ANSWER: Sir, we really must protest. You, apparently a newcomer, find yourself living in a desert paradise, a metropolitan area bursting with good weather, good health and good cheer, and you **cavil** at how long you must wait for a burger and fries. (Clay Thompson, *Sorry for the Wait, Sir, We're Flipping as Fast as We Can*, The Arizona Republic, 03-19-2000, p. B3.)

(2) quibble *v.i.*: **pettifog**. ▪ In 1994, the United States, having been burned in Somalia, was desperate to stay out of Rwanda. How to manage that? By **pettifogging**. By arguing about semantics: the Clinton way. His Administration, pressed to honor the 1948 Genocide Convention (not to mention human decency) by intervening, quibbled at a furious rate about the meaning of the word genocide. (Lance Morrow, *Essay: Rwandan Tragedy, Lewinsky Farce*, Time, 10-12-1998, p. 126.)

quick (as in hasty) *adj.*: **festinate**. See HASTY

quickly (very ..., as in, in an instant) *n.*: **trice** (as in, in a trice). ∎ We were there [at the car dealership] for the taking. Armed, as we were, with a gratifyingly cheap loan from a nice man at the NatWest, any half-decent salesman would have had our signatures on the dotted line in a **trice**. (Neil Darbyshire, *Motoring: Wheel Life — All I Want Is a New Motor*, The Daily Telegraph, 04-08-2000, p. 5.)

quickness *n.*: **alacrity**. SEE SPEED

(2) quickness (as in speed or haste) *n.*: **celerity**. SEE SPEED

quiet (as in not moving or temporarily inactive) *adj.*: **quiescent**. SEE INACTIVE

(2) quiet (said in ... tones, not to be overheard) *adv., adj.*: **sotto voce**. SEE WHISPERED

quip *n.*: **bon mot** [French]. ∎ But his protestations notwithstanding, [basketball player Shaquille O'Neal] has never passed up an opportunity to deliver a **bon mot** on behalf of a corporate sponsor: ... BROKAW: This is a serious question. What do you want to be when you grow up? SHAQ: I want to be a successful entrepreneur, such as yourself. I want to be happy. I want to always drink Pepsi. (Author not given, *Scorecard*, Sports Illustrated, 04-24-1995, p. 13.)

(2) quip *n.*: **epigram**. ∎ The cafe has a colorful outdoor mural on its north wall and an **epigram** painted over the entrance that reads, "We are itching to get away from Portland, Oregon," a reference to a supposed "flea epidemic" of 1915, according to a cafe flier. (Paul Iorio, *The Howl Tour of San Francisco; For a Fresh View of the City by the Bay, Follow the Beat Path Forged by '50s Poet Allen Ginsberg*, The Washington Post, 05-07-2000, p. E1.)

(3) quip *v.i., n.*: **jape**. SEE JOKE

quit (an office or position) *v.i., v.t.*: **demit** (as in demit office). SEE RESIGN

quiver (from moment of intense excitement) *n.*: **frisson** [French]. SEE SHUDDER

(2) quiver (rapidly or spasmodically) *v.i.*: **judder**. SEE SHAKE

quivering *adj.*: **tremulous**. ∎ Near the end of the show [Cabaret], [Natasha] Richardson-as-Sally [Bowles] walks shakily onto the stage and reveals that she has had an abortion. She paints an unflinching portrait of denial, regret, and despair: the knocking knees, the **tremulous** voice, the vacant stare. (Steve Daly, *Don't Tell Mama*, Entertainment Weekly, 07-31-1998, p. 32.)

quiz (closely) *v.t.*: **catechize**. SEE QUESTION

quotation (at the start of a literary piece setting forth a theme or message) *n.*: **epigraph**. ∎ The title page of E.L. Doctorow's wonderful 1975 novel, "Ragtime," has a warning **epigraph** from rag master Scott Joplin himself: "Do not play this piece fast. It is never right to play Ragtime fast." (Linda Winer, *Literary Notes / Doctorow's "Ragtime,"* Newsday, 12-09-1996.)

R

rabbit (of or relating to a ...) *adj.*: **leporine**. ∎ Peter Rabbit, once a real English pet and now a worldwide licensing megabusiness, celebrates the 100th anniversary of his breaking into print this October. Three sites in England's Lake District can be visited to learn about the writer of the famous **leporine** tales, Beatrix Potter (1866-1943). (Martin Hollander, *Itinerary Ideas*, Newsday, 03-29-2002.)

rabbit fur *n.*: **lapin** [French]. ∎ Most of the play's comic relief comes from two sources. There's Wilson's portrayal of the annoying yet amusing Aunt Girlie who insists her *fur* coat is made of "**Lapin**, not rabbit!" (Noel Gallagher, *Heartfelt Play Done With Loving Care*, The London Free Press, 08-25-2001, p. C4.)

rabble *n.*: **canaille**. SEE MASSES

(2) rabble (as in the common people) *n.*: **hoi polloi**. SEE COMMONERS

racket (as in noise, esp. from simultaneous voices, and confusion) *n.*: **babel**. SEE NOISE

(2) racket (as in din or clamor) *n.*: **bruit**. SEE DIN

racy (as in scandalous) *adj.*: **scabrous**. SEE SCANDALOUS

radiant *adj.*: **effulgent**. SEE BRIGHT

(2) radiant *adj.*: **fulgurant**. SEE BRIGHT

(3) radiant (esp. as to talent, wit or ability) *adj.*: **lambent**. SEE BRILLIANT AND SHIMMERING

(5) radiant *adj.*: **lucent**. SEE GLOWING

(6) radiant *adj.*: **refulgent**. SEE BRIGHT

radical (as in dissenter, orig. Catholics who did not follow Church of England) *n.*: **recusant**. SEE DISSENTER

(2) radical (a political ..., who often believes in violence to attain an end) *n*.: **sans-culotte**. SEE EXTREMIST

radicalism (esp. in political matters) *n*.: **ultraism** SEE EXTREMISM

rage (as in temper tantrum) *n*.: **boutade** [French]. SEE TEMPER TANTRUM
(2) **rage** (marked by a sudden or violent ...) *adj*.: **vesuvian** (esp. as in ... temper). SEE TEMPER

ragged *adj*.: **tatterdemalion**. ▮ These days, [ex-Pittsburgh Steeler Joe] Gilliam roams the streets of Nashville panhandling for food, $12 for the flophouse and for whatever. ... Bob Costas and the rest wanted to know how Gilliam felt about the Steelers' chances and how his life had collapsed to such a **tatterdemalion** state. (Les Payne, *The Benched Man Might Be the Best*, Newsday, 02-04-1996, p. A42.)

raging (woman) *n*.: **maenad**. SEE WOMAN

raid *v.t., v.i.*: **depredate** (*n*.: **depredation***)*. SEE PLUNDER

railing (and supports for) *n*.: **balustrade**. SEE HANDRAIL

rain (of or relating to) *adj*.: **pluvial**; **pluvious**. ▮ Lloyd's of London has always been synonymous with insurance underwriting expertise and the sober assessment of risk. ... Lloyd's also issues what it calls **pluvious** policies to compensate sporting events, such as cricket matches, for losses caused by rain. (Barbara Rudolph, *Business*, Time International, 07-08-1991, p. 32.)

rainstorm *n*.: **cataract**. SEE DOWNPOUR

rake (as in lecherous man or playboy) *n*.: **roué** [French]. SEE PLAYBOY

raling (characterized by loud ... sounds) *adj*.: **stertorous**. SEE SNORING

ramble (aimlessly) *v.i.*: **maunder**. ▮ Gray thinly disguises his **maundering** narrator as "Brewster North," but the book has no fictional texture at all. It's a series of childhood memories, anecdotes, dreams, sexual fantasies, and feelings gotten in touch with. ... [W]e get the aimless wanderings, transient enthusiasms, and permanent adolescent confusion of the narrator. (Author not given, *Print: Boy Talk*, Entertainment Weekly, 07-17-1992, p. 50.)
(2) **ramble** *v.i.*: **divagate**. SEE DIGRESS

rambling *adj*.: **discursive**. ▮ [Poet Henry Wadsworth] Longfellow is **discursive**. He cannot resist adding description, lush and sometimes seemingly endless, to his narratives. (Paul O. Williams, *America's Favorite, Forgotten Poet*, The Christian Science Monitor, 10-26-2000, p. 18.)

ramming (spec. the act of one object ... a stationary object, usually applied to ships) *n*.: **allision**. SEE COLLISION

rampage (in speech) *n*.: **philippic**. SEE TIRADE

rampant *adj*.: **pandemic**. SEE WIDESPREAD
(2) **rampant** *adj*.: **regnant**. SEE WIDESPREAD

rancid *adj*.: **mephitic** (*n*.: **mephitis**). SEE SMELLY
(2) **rancid** *adj*.: **noisome**. SEE SMELLY

rancor *n*.: **asperity**. SEE ACRIMONY

random (as in by chance) *adj*.: **adventitious**. SEE CHANCE
(2) **random** (as in unpredictable outcome) *adj*.: **aleatory**. SEE UNPREDICTABLE

range (as in sphere or realm) *n*.: **ambit**. SEE REALM

rank (odor) *adj*.: **mephitic** (*n*.: **mephitis**). SEE SMELLY
(2) **rank** (odor) *adj*.: **noisome**. SEE SMELLY

ransack *v.t., v.i.*: **depredate** (*n*.: **depredation**). SEE PLUNDER

rant *n*.: **jeremiad**. SEE COMPLAINT
(2) **rant** *n*.: **philippic**. SEE TIRADE

rapacious (as in predatory) *adj*.: **lupine**. SEE PREDATORY

rapidity *n*.: **alacrity**. SEE SPEED
(2) **rapidity** *n*.: **celerity**. SEE SPEED

rapture *n*.: **beatitude**. SEE BLISS
(2) **rapture** *n*.: **felicity**. SEE HAPPINESS

rapturous *adj*.: **beatific** (to make ... *v.t.*: **beatify**). SEE JOYFUL
(2) **rapturous** (as in delightful or blissful) *adj*.: **Elysian**. SEE BLISSFUL

rare *adj*.: **recherché** [French]. ▮ When a city stakes a claim to sophistication and social significance, a few indispensable items had better be in its possession: a major-league sports franchise, a newspaper that has taken a few scalps among local politicians, restaurants offering ethnic cuisines more **recherché** than Italian and Chinese. (William A. Henry III, *Theater:*

Portland Offers a Calling Card in an Elegant Structure, Time, 12-12-1988, p. 88.)

rarity *n.:* **rara avis** [Latin]. ▪ John Feinstein is that **rara avis** of sports literature, a best-selling author. In fact, according to his publishers, his first book ... *A Season on the Brink,* which recounted the sometimes unseemly adventures of coach Bobby Knight and his Indiana University basketball team, is nothing less than the "best-selling sports book of all time." (Ron Fimrite, *Books,* Sports Illustrated, 10-14-1991, p. 6.)

rascal *n.:* **rapscallion.** ▪ In public, Southerners preach a hard gospel against sin and perdition, particularly sexual transgressions. But the South has a rich and storied lineage of silver-tongued political devils — most of them white males. And Southerners secretly celebrate their rogues and **rapscallions.** (Jim Nesbitt, *Bubba Factor — Overblown South's Distaste for Clinton "Isn't About Sex, It's About Ideology,"* The Palm Beach Post, 01-10-1999, p. 1E.)
(2) rascal (or unprincipled person) *n.:* **blackguard.** SEE SCOUNDREL
(3) rascal *n.:* **scapegrace.** SEE SCOUNDREL

rash (as in impetuous) *adj.:* **gadarene.** SEE IMPETUOUS
(2) rash (and irresponsible) *adj.:* **harum-scarum.** SEE RECKLESS
(3) rash (as in overambitious) *adj.:* **Icarian.** SEE OVERAMBITIOUS

rashly (as in, in a disorderly and hasty manner) *adv.:* **pell-mell.** SEE DISORDERLY

rat (as in informer or accuser) *n.:* **delator.** SEE ACCUSER

rat out (as in tattle) *v.i.:* **peach.** SEE TATTLE

rate *v.t.:* **assay.** SEE EVALUATE
(2) rate (under a new standard, esp. one which differs from conventional norms) *v.t.:* **transvaluate.** SEE EVALUATE

rational (as in sane) *adj.:* **compos mentis.** SEE SANE
(2) rational (as in logical) *adj.:* **ratiocinative.** SEE LOGICAL

rationale (formal ..., as in justification, for one's acts or beliefs) *n.:* **apologia.** SEE JUSTIFICATION

rationalize (specious reasoning intended to ... or mislead) *n.:* **casuistry.** SEE FALLACIOUS
(2) rationalize (try to ... an offense with excuses) *v.t.:* **palliate.** SEE DOWNPLAY

rats (of or relating to ... or mice) *adj.:* **murine.** SEE RODENTS

rattle (rapidly or spasmodically) *v.i.:* **judder.** SEE SHAKE

ravage *v.t., v.i.:* **depredate** (*n.:* **depredation***).* SEE PLUNDER

ravenous *adj.:* **edacious.** SEE VORACIOUS
(2) ravenous *adj.:* **esurient.** SEE HUNGRY
(3) ravenous (as in predatory) *adj.:* **lupine.** SEE PREDATORY

raving (woman) *n.:* **maenad.** SEE WOMAN

razz (playfully) *v.t., v.i., n.:* **chaff.** SEE TEASING

reaction (as in reflex) *n.:* **tropism.** SEE REFLEX

reactionary (in beliefs and often stuffy, pompous and or elderly) *adj., n.:* **Colonel Blimp.** SEE CONSERVATIVE
(2) reactionary (as in hatred or fear of anything new or different) *n.:* **misoneism** (person holding this view: **misoneist**). SEE CONSERVATISM
(3) reactionary (a political ..., who often believes in violence to attain an end) *n.:* **sans-culotte.** SEE EXTREMIST

reactivate (as in revive) *v.t.:* **refocillate.** SEE REVIVE

read (people who ... too much) *n.:* **bibliobibuli.** ▪ Thomas Carlyle declared that "in books lies the soul of the whole past time," while Mencken complained about "**bibliobibuli**," those compulsive readers who are "constantly drunk on books, as other men are drunk on whisky or religion." (Michiko Kakutani, *"History of Reading" Rooted in Author's Own Passion for Books,* Seattle Post-Intelligencer, 12-10-1996.)
(2) read (inability to) *adj.:* **analphabetic.** SEE ILLITERATE

real (as in genuine) *adj.:* **pukka.** SEE GENUINE

realistic (as in reflecting reality) *adj.:* **veridical.** ▪ In an important and influential paper, Weinstein & Nicolich (1993) argued that empirical research on the relationship between perceptions of risk and behaviour has often confused two issues. The first is whether people's risk perceptions are **veridical** and accurately reflect their behaviour. (D.R. Rutter, *Perceptions of Risk in Motorcyclists: Unrealistic Optimism, Relative Realism and Predictions of Behaviour,* British Journal of Psychology, 11-01-1998, p. 681.)

(2) realistic (appearing to be ... or accurate) *adj.*: **verisimilar**. ▪ Tables inside his studio hold a variable smorgasbord of **verisimilar** victuals, enough fake baked hams, plum puddings, cookies, cakes, plump walnuts, boiled beef, artichokes and pastry-topped stews to make a hungry reporter weep. (Melissa Stoeltje, *Fee Fi Faux Fare: Herni Gadbois Is a Giant in the Field of Fake Food*, The Houston Chronicle, 12-23-1994, p. 1.)

reality (in ...) *adj., adv.*: **de facto** (as contrasted with de jure: legally or by law) [Latin]. SEE IN FACT

realization (sudden ...) *n.*: **epiphany**. ▪ I have always loved [Christmas's] tacky excesses. ... But a couple of years ago, I had a midnight **epiphany** at Wal-Mart. Weighed down by sporting equipment and plastic toys, I realized that I had bought more gifts than anyone on my list could want or need and that it wasn't good for their spirits — or mine. (Amy Dickinson, *Personal Time/Your Family*, Time, 12-20-1999, p. 115.)

(2) realization (while coming into ...) *adv.*: **aborning**. SEE BORN

(3) realization (moment of ... , often the point in the plot at which the protagonist recognizes his or her or some other character's true identity or discovers the true nature of his or her own situation) *n.*: **anagnorisis**. SEE RECOGNITION

(4) realization (as opposed to potentiality) *n.*: **entelechy**. SEE ACTUALITY

(5) realization (as in perception or awareness) *n.*: **ken**. SEE PERCEPTION

realize (based on past experience) *v.t.*: **apperceive**. SEE COMPREHEND

(2) realize (as in making an abstract concept seem real) *v.t.*: **reify**. SEE MATERIALIZE

realm *n.*: **ambit**. ▪ Mexico is a comparative bright spot in the region, as are other countries directly in the **ambit** of U.S. foreign investment. (James Graff, *Time Finance/World Economic Forum: Of Risks and Rewards*, Time International, 02-14-2000, p. 56.)

(2) realm (as in area of activity or interest) *n.*: **purlieu**. SEE DOMAIN

reappearance (of something after a period of dormancy or inactivity) *n.*: **recrudescence** (*v.i.*: **recrudesce**). ▪ In a country where female liberation posted one of the speediest, most far-reaching success stories of our time, a **recrudescence** of age-old prejudices is eating away the gains like acid rain at a monument's base. Women who grew up with remarkably fair job and schooling opportunities are under pressure to stay at home. (James Walsh, *Women: Born to Be Second Class in China, Old Biases Against Women Have Emerged Once Again*, Time International, 09-11-1995, p. 46.)

rear (in or towards the ...) *adv.*: **astern**. SEE BACK

rear end (having a nicely proportioned ...) *adj.*: **callipygian**. ▪ Are chopped-up celebrities worth more than whole regular people? You betcha. ... **[C]allipygian** singer/actress Jennifer Lopez insured her bodacious back end for a tidy $300,000,000 (and her entire body for $1 billion). (Melissa August, *Notebook: The $400 Million Celebrity*, Time, 12-20-1999, p. 32.)

(2) rear end (having a hairy ...) *adj.*: **dasypygal**. ▪ This current generation [entering college] has emerged into a world with standards of health and wealth [but] do they count their blessings? Probably not. ... [But if they go out and vote for] only those politicians who promise to take education seriously ... and [turn] the volume of their in-car stereos down a bit, and pull their trousers up over their **dasypygal** features, there might be hope, yet. (Revel Barker, *Open Eye*, The Independent [London], 09-05-2000.)

(3) rear end (a fat ...) *n.*: **steatopygia** (having a fat ... *adj.*: **steatopygic**). ▪ The editorial content [of the rap magazine *Vibe* includes] a feminist critique of Sir Mix-a-Lot's salute to **steatopygia**, "Baby Got Back" [which includes the lyric: "I like big butts and I can not lie."] (David Mills, *The Corporate Hip-Hop Hope*, The Washington Post, 09-14-1992, p. D1.)

(4) rear end (as in buttocks) *n., pl.*: **nates**. SEE BUTTOCKS

reason (use the power of ...) *v.t.*: **cerebrate**. SEE THINK

(2) reason (use the power of) *v.t.*: **cogitate**. SEE THINK

(3) reason (against) *v.t.*: **expostulate**. SEE OBJECT

(4) reason (logically) *v.i.*: **ratiocinate**. SEE ANALYZE

reasonable (as in logical) *adj.*: **ratiocinative**. SEE LOGICAL

reasoning (of ... appealing to pity or compassion) *adv., adj.*: **ad misericordium** [Latin]. SEE ARGUMENT

(2) reasoning (as in making an argument suggesting the use of force to settle an issue) *n.*: **argumentum ad baculum** [Latin]. SEE THREAT

(3) reasoning (that silence from an opposing side or absence of evidence is itself indicative that the person making the argument must be correct) *n.*: **argumentum ex silentio** [Latin]. SEE ARGUMENT

(4) reasoning (specious ... intended to mislead or rationalize) *n.*: **casuistry**. SEE FALLACIOUS

(5) reasoning (which is complicated and often illogical) *n.*: **choplogic**. SEE FALLACY

(6) reasoning (given to ... which may be specious or one who is) *adj., n.*: **eristic**. SEE SPECIOUS

(7) reasoning (person who hates ... or enlightenment) *n.*: **misologist**. SEE CLOSED-MINDED

rebel *n.*: **frondeur** [French]. ▪ Inevitably, the political resistance to Hitler and the Nazis within the Reich was fundamentally different from the paramilitary resistance to the Germans in occupied Europe. For the German **frondeurs** did not only confront a totalitarian state: they had also to wrestle with their consciences as German patriots. (Daniel Johnson, *All Delays Are Dangerous in War*, The Times [London], 07-21-1994.)

(2) rebel (orig. Catholics who did not follow Church of England) *n.*: **recusant**. SEE DISSENTER

rebellion *n.*: **émeute** [French]. ▪ [In Les Miserables, Victor] Hugo takes the time to comment upon the great **émeute** which he witnessed — that of 1848, which completely toppled the monarchy in France. (Author not given, *Victor Hugo: Part V: Jean Valjean*, Monarch Notes, 01-01-1963.)

rebellious *adj.*: **contumacious**. SEE OBSTINATE

rebirth *n.*: **palingenesis**. ▪ Chapter 4 very helpfully expounds various conceptions of the end of the world: as successfully endured catastrophes, as cyclical **palingenesis**, as a one-time event, as annihilation and renewal, as destruction of the cosmos, as the decline of the West, as limits to growth, and as a nuclear holocaust. (Peter C. Phan, *The End of the World: A Theological Interpretation*, [book reviews], Theological Studies, 03-01-1997, p. 175.)

reborn (as in revived) *adj.*: **redivivus**. SEE REVIVED

rebuke (sharply) *v.t.*: **keelhaul**. ▪ It would be a mistake for Clintonites to be complacent in the post-election period. While some Republicans sincerely want to work with Clinton, others are ready to **keelhaul** him when an opportunity arises. The press is also poised to turn against him, and the economy could cool off, too. (David Gergen, *Shoring Up a Second Term*, U.S. News & World Report, 11-18-1996.)

(2) rebuke (as in criticism) *n.*: **animadversion** (*v.t.*: **animadvert**). SEE CRITICISM

(3) rebuke (as in criticize) *v.t.*: **flay**. SEE CRITICIZE

(4) rebuke (harshly) *v.t.*: **fustigate**. SEE CRITICIZE

(5) rebuke *v.t.*: **objurgate**. SEE CRITICIZE

rebuttal (as in responding to an anticipated objection to an argument before that objection has been made) *n.*: **prolepsis**. ▪ Stephen Glass' [novel] ... is a **prolepsis**, an extended, creepy one. ... [He] disgraced himself at The New Republic by fabricating interviews. ... [As a result, there was concern that the book wouldn't be reviewed at all or be reviewed poorly.] The problem is that Mr. Glass has pre-empted both [arguments]. ... He brings it up first thing in an author's note: "I was fired in 1998 from my job as a writer at The New Republic." [Presumably, the anticipatory response is not concealing what happened and admitting to it right at the outset.] (Jerome Weeks, *Glass' Repentance Highly Transparent; ex "New Republic" Writer Seeks Forgiveness in "The Fabulist,"* The Dallas Morning News, 06-22-2003, p. 11G.)

recalcitrant (to yield or be swayed) *adj.*: **renitent**. SEE RESISTANT

recall (having detailed ... of visual images) *adj.*: **eidetic**. SEE MEMORY

recant *v.t.*: **abjure**. SEE RENOUNCE

recantation (as in retraction) *n.*: **palinode**. SEE RETRACTION

recap *v.t.*: **precis** [French]. SEE SUMMARIZE

recapitulation *n.*: **precis** [French]. SEE SUMMARY

recent (of ... origin) *adj.*: **neoteric**. ▪ As a final shot at Breyer, Thomas lectures that "ironically, the **neoteric** Eighth Amendment claim proposed by Justice Breyer [i.e. that executing a prisoner after too lengthy a stay on death row is itself "cruel and unusual punishment"] would further prolong collateral review by giving virtually every capital prisoner yet another ground on which to challenge and delay his execution." (David C. Slade, *Decades on Death Row*, The World & I, 04-01-2000, p. 80.)

receptacle (esp. as shrine for displaying relics) *n.*: **reliquary**. ▪ [T]he Constitution is not a delicate artifact. It sits in a helium-filled case over at the National Archives in one of those soundproof, heatproof and humidity-controlled **reliquaries** designed to protect its every word and wrinkle. (Nancy Gibbs, *Nation/Election 2000: Before Honor Comes Humility, Proverbs Says*, Time, 12-18-2000, p. 28.)

receptive (to other views and opinions) *adj.*: **latitudinarian**. SEE OPEN-MINDED

recess (as in gap) *n.*: **lacuna**. SEE GAP

recite (as in mindlessly repeating ideas which have been drilled into the speaker or saying things which reflect the opinions of the powers-that-be) *v.t., v.i., n.*: **duckspeak** [This is a word which is part of "Newspeak," the language of the monster state in George Orwell's "*1984*." In "duckspeak," one repeats the orthodox opinions (thus, quacking like a duck) of the power structure, namely Big Brother]. ▪ The public school system is systematically destroying America by undermining our culture and destroying our understanding of the necessity of liberty, particularly in the minds of the common people and the working class. Though students are graduating from schools unable to read, no student is leaving school not knowing how to **duckspeak** the slogans of the liberal ruling class. (Bill White [letter writer], *9 Hopefuls Striving for Single Seat*, The Washington Post, 03-02-2000, p. M1.)

reckless (and irresponsible) *adj.*: **harum-scarum**. ▪ After [George W. Bush made fun of the phrase "risky tax scheme"], no Democrat is ever again going to be able to utter the phrase "risky tax scheme" without raising more guffaws than fears. ... Next time Mr. Clinton and the Dems want to denounce GOP tax relief, they can call it a ... "**harum-scarum** ... tax contrivance." (Maggie Gallagher, *Lexicon That Taxes the Voting Class*, The Washington Times, 08-14-2000, p. A20.)

(2) reckless (and irresponsible) *adj.*: **feckless**. SEE IRRESPONSIBLE

(3) reckless (as in overambitious) *adj.*: **Icarian**. SEE OVERAMBITIOUS

(4) reckless (and wild person) *n.*: **rantipole**. SEE WILD

reclining *adj.*: **decumbent**. SEE LYING DOWN

recluse (esp. for religious reasons) *n.*: **anchorite**. ▪ A judge is always the subject of public scrutiny. ... That does not necessarily mean judges should live like **anchorites**. But the fact is that the public believes that distancing is a vital criterion in promoting confidence in their impartiality. Mingling with corporate figures, politicians, lawyers and prosecutors involved in cases before them may call their integrity into question. (Author unknown, *Guaranteeing Impartiality*, New Straits Times, 04-30-2003.)

(2) recluse (esp. for religious reasons) *n.*: **eremite** (practice of living in such fashion *n.*: **eremitism**). ▪ "The monks have to learn that everything changes. The world is not what it used to be," [said an Athens city official.] Even the monks would not deny that. Over the past year, the community has thrown **eremitism** to the winds, hooking up with the world through the Internet, computers and mobile phones. (Helena Smith, *Eve Demands Access to Garden of Eden*, The Observer, 04-12-1998, p. 13.)

recognition (moment of ... , often the point in the plot at which the protagonist recognizes his or her or some other character's true identity or discovers the true nature of his or her own situation) *n.*: **anagnorisis**. ▪ [Faced with his own] artistic doubts about [the quality of] his bird drawings ..., it seems that the largely self-taught [John] Audubon experienced a wrenching creative **anagnorisis**, one that triggered a revised approach to the whole artistic ornithological oeuvre that we would come to know as the superb *Birds of America*. (Lee Gaillard, *The Reader Replies*, American Scholar, 09-22-1999.)

(2) recognition *n.*: **ken**. SEE PERCEPTION

recognize (based on past experience) *v.t.*: **apperceive**. SEE COMPREHEND

recoil *v.i.*: **resile**. ▪ Ours is a principled policy based on upholding the rights of the oppressed people of Kashmir, and there can be no bargain or trading on it. We cannot **resile** from our moral and principled support to the Kashmiris, nor should the world. (Karamatullah Khan Ghori, *Trip to Washington Was for a Private Visit*, The Washington Times, 05-11-2000, p. A22.)

(2) recoil (out of fear or shying away from) *v.i.*: **blench**. SEE FLINCH

recollection *n.*: **anamnesis**. SEE REMEMBRANCE

(2) recollection (having detailed ... of visual images) *adj.*: **eidetic**. SEE MEMORY

(3) recollection (having an exact or vivid ...) *n.*: **hypermnesia**. SEE MEMORY

(4) recollection (confusion of ... with actual fact) *n.*: **paramnesia**. SEE MISREMEMBER

recompense (as in reward) *n.*: **guerdon**. SEE REWARD

reconciliation (of conflicting ideas, esp. to make peace) *n.*: **eirenicon**. SEE PEACE-OFFERING

rectify (as in atone for) *v.t., v.i.*: **expiate**. SEE ATONE

recycled (as in warmed over food or old material) *n.*, *adj.*: **rechauffé** [French]. SEE WARMED OVER

red (blood-...) *adj.*: **incarnadine**. SEE CRIMSON

red-handed (as in caught ..., esp. of committing an offense or a sexual act) *adv.*: **in flagrante delicto**. SEE IN THE ACT

reddish *adj.*: **rufous**. ∎ Carex buchananii [is a type of grass which] has a **rufous** quality, a foxy red cast to its twirling leaves that brings out the pumpkin shades hidden in many purple leaves. (Author not given, *Reigning in Fall: There's Garden Glory Still to Behold*, Seattle Post-Intelligencer, 11-07-1996.)
(2) reddish (as in ruddy) *adj.*: **florid**. SEE RUDDY

reddish-brown *adj.*: **ferruginous**. SEE RUST

redressing (as in atoning for) *adj.*: **piacular**. SEE ATONING

reduce (in value, amount or degree) *v.t.*: **attenuate**. SEE LESSEN
(2) reduce (as in condense the flavor or essence of something, as if by boiling down) *v.t.*: **decoct**. SEE BOIL DOWN

redundancy *n.*: **pleonasm**. ∎ It was, after all, public officials who gave us "safe haven" during the Persian Gulf War. Someone apparently grafted the "safe" from "safe harbor" (not all harbors are safe) onto "haven" (by definition, a safe place). The creation of this obnoxious **pleonasm** ... illustrates the bureaucrat's familiar combination of self-importance, pretension, and ignorance. (John E. McIntyre, *Words That Survive the Test of Time*, The Christian Science Monitor, 12-30-1999, p. 11.)
(2) redundancy *n.*: **macrology**. SEE VERBOSITY

reek *n.*: **fetor**. SEE STENCH

reeking *adj.*: **fetid**. SEE SMELLY
(2) reeking *adj.*: **mephitic** (*n.*: **mephitis**). SEE SMELLY
(3) reeking *adj.*: **noisome**. SEE SMELLY

reference book *n.*: **vade mecum**. SEE GUIDEBOOK

refined *adj.*: **raffiné** (or **raffine**) [French]. ∎ The [James Bond] formula remains stirring but not shaken. Bond still astonishes headwaiters with his **raffine** tastes, fondles weapons and women with equal ardor and moves with eerie confidence though a world of constant, cosmic peril. ... The only evil talent his enemies lack is an ability to aim straight when shooting at him. "Do you lose as gracefully as you win?" one archscoundrel asks Bond. "I don't know," Bond shrugs elegantly. "I've never lost." (Frank Lidz, *007 Has Moved Smoothly Through the Last 35 Years*, The Dallas Morning News, 12-30-1997, p. 12 C.)
(2) refined (and intelligent person) *n.*: **bel esprit**. SEE CULTIVATED
(3) refined (in an affected manner) *adj.*: **niminy-piminy**. SEE DAINTY
(4) refined *adj.*: **soigné** [French]. SEE ELEGANT

reflect (as in think about) *v.t.*: **cerebrate**. SEE THINK
(2) reflect (as in think about) *v.t.*: **cogitate**. SEE THINK
(3) reflect (on something, often used as a directive, as in "Consider this:") *v.t.*: **perpend**. SEE CONSIDER

reflection (as in mirror image) *n.*: **enantiomorph**. SEE MIRROR IMAGE
(2) reflection (staring at one's belly-button as an aid to ...) *n.*: **omphaloskepsis**. SEE MEDITATION

reflex *n.*: **tropism**. ∎ Over the year Amando Doronila, a columnist for the *Manila Chronicle*, has mused repeatedly on the unshakable Filipino attraction to basketball, even as that **tropism** always seemed to lead to disappointment [in international competition]. (Alexander Wolff, *Big Game, Small World*, Warner Books [2002], p. 225.)

reflexive (as in trained to show a conditioned response) *adj.*: **Pavlovian**. SEE CONDITIONED

refresh (as in revive) *v.t.*: **refocillate**. SEE REVIVE

refreshing (as in restorative, esp. with respect to effect of certain drugs or medications) *adj.*: **analeptic**. SEE RESTORATIVE

refuse (study of a culture by examining its ...) *n.*: **garbology**. SEE GARBAGE
(2) refuse *n.*: **offal**. SEE TRASH

refutation (as in responding to an anticipated objection to an argument before that objection has been made) *n.*: **prolepsis**. SEE REBUTTAL

regal (of a ... and stately woman, often voluptuous) *adj.*: **Junoesque**. SEE VOLUPTUOUS

regard (pay ... to, as in homage, not necessarily sincere or unforced) *n.*: **obeisance**. SEE HOMAGE

regarding *prep.*: **anent**. ∎ Peter Stone's new version [of *Annie Get Your Gun*] called for vivisection of this fabulous musical, removing such Irving Berlin gems as "I'm a Bad, Bad Man," "I'm an Indian, Too" and "Colonel Buffalo Bill." Done, no doubt, in the name of political correctness **anent** intellectual Indians and liberated women — two groups apparently not around in 1946. (Richard Traubner, *It Was the Worst of Times*, American Record Guide, 07-01-1999, p. 27.)

regardless *adv.*: **withal**. SEE NEVERTHELESS

regimented (strictly ...) *adj.*: **monastic**. SEE STRICT

region (populated by persons from many countries or backgrounds) *n.*: **cosmopolis**. SEE DIVERSITY

(2) region (densely populated ... or city) *n.*: **megalopolis**. SEE CROWDED

regret (as in disappointment) *n.*: **Dead Sea fruit**. SEE DISSAPPOINTMENT

regular (at a place, esp. a place of entertainment) *n.*: **habitué** [French]. ∎ Station Road's skillful manager, Carol Covell, will be familiar to **habitues** of Della Femina, both in East Hampton and New York. (Peter M. Gianotti, *Dining Out/Station Road*, Newsday, 07-07-2000, p. G16.)

(2) regular (people, as in the masses) *n.*: **canaille**. SEE MASSES

(3) regular (people, as in the masses) *n.*: **hoi polloi**. SEE COMMONERS

(4) regular (of or relating to the ... people) *adj.*: **plebian**. SEE COMMON

(5) regular (as in mundane; everyday) *adj.*: **sublunary**. SEE EARTHLY

regurgitation (act of ...) *n.*: **emesis**. SEE VOMITING

(2) regurgitation (an agent which causes ...) *n., adj.*: **emetic**. SEE VOMITING

rehabilitation (study of ... of criminals) *n.*: **penology**. SEE PRISON

rehashed (as in warmed over food or old material) *n., adj.*: **rechauffé** [French]. SEE WARMED OVER

reigning *adj.*: **regnant**. ∎ Conventions for the incumbent are supposed to be ceremonial reaffirmations of the **regnant** leader. (Garry Wills, *U.S. Campaign: Unfriendly Skies: Faced With its Own Explosive Issues, the G.O.P. Heads to Houston on a Wing and a Prayer*, Time, 08-17-1992, p. 34.)

reject (esp. responsibility or duty) *v.t.*: **abnegate**. SEE RENOUNCE

rejection (as in disdain) *n.*: **misprision** (*v.t.*: **misprize**). SEE DISDAIN

rejoice (or boast, esp. about the accomplishments of a relative) *v.t., n.*: **kvell** [Yiddish]. SEE BOAST

(2) rejoice (with boisterous public demonstrations) *v.i.*: **maffick** [British]. SEE CELEBRATE

rejoicing (often in a boastful way) *adj.*: **cock-a-hoop**. SEE ELATED

rejoinder (charging accuser with similar offense) *n.*: **tu quoque** [Latin]. SEE ANSWER

rekindled (as in revived) *adj.*: **redivivus**. SEE REVIVED

related *adj.*: **cognate**. ∎ His great theme is the decline, from its zenith at the turn of the century, of the "Anglo-American-Celtic" world dominance and of its **cognate** social expression, the ideal of the gentleman. (James Bowman, *A Thread of Years [Book Reviews]*, National Review, 05-18-1998, p. 52.)

relating (to) *prep.*: **anent**. SEE REGARDING

(2) relating (to, as in associated with or incident to) *adj.*: **appurtenant**. SEE PERTAINING

relations (as in family ties) *n.*: **propinquity**. SEE KINSHIP

relatives *n., pl.*: **kith and kin**. ∎ Authorities made clear that the testimony of strangers is not enough. It is a citizen's duty to betray his own **kith and kin**. The Zhou clan, willingly or by coercion, did its duty. [The sister of] Zhou Fengsuo ... explained that after seeing the wanted notices for her brother, she contacted security officials. (Jill Smolowe, *China: Deng's Big Lie — The Hard-liners Rewrite History to Justify Arrests and Bury Democracy*, Time, 06-26-1989, p. 32.)

relaxed *adj.*: **dégagé** [French]. SEE EASYGOING

relaxing *adj.*: **calmative**. ∎ Mimieux practices neither [Buddhism or Hinduism], but she says they made their mark on her mind as well as her exercise routine, which combines **calmative**, deep-breathing techniques with stretching and balancing routines. (Leah Rozen, *Picks & Pans: Screen*, People, 12-11-1995, p. 25.)

(2) relaxing (of pain, distress or tension) *adj.*: **anodyne**. SEE SOOTHING

release (from slavery, servitude or bondage) *v.t.*: **manumit**. SEE EMANCIPATE

relevant *n.*: **apposite**. ∎ Oddly enough, H.D. Molesworth, explaining that the monarchy works at a powerful emotional rather than rational level, had once given a particularly **apposite** example. Many people — and this was common to various civilizations — he wrote, are convinced that the Blood Royal is "possessed of something special, like a petrol additive." (Alex Berlyne, *Homing Pidgin*, Jerusalem Post, 12-30-1994.)

reliance (on faith alone rather than reason, esp. in philosophical or religious matters) *n.*: **fideism**. SEE FAITH

relief (medicine which offers ... from pain) *n.*: **anodyne**. SEE PAIN-RELIEVER

relieving (of pain, distress or tension) *adj.*: **anodyne**. SEE SOOTHING

religions (concerned with establishing unity among ...) *adj.*: **ecumenical**. SEE CHURCHES

religious (lacking ... reverence) *n.*: **impiety** (*adj.*: **impious**). SEE IRREVERENCE

relinquish (esp. responsibility or duty) *v.t.*: **abnegate**. SEE RENOUNCE
 (2) relinquish (an office or position) *v.t.*: **demit** (as in demit office). SEE RESIGN

relish (the taste of) *v.t.*: **degust**. SEE SAVOR

reluctance (as in unwillingness) *n.*: **nolition**. SEE UNWILLINGNESS

reluctant (to yield or be swayed) *adj.*: **renitent**. SEE RESISTANT

remains (fascination with or erotic attraction to human ...) *n.*: **necrophilia**. SEE CORPSES

remark (as in insight or observation) *n.*: **aperçu** [French]. SEE INSIGHT
 (2) remark (in which one references an issue by saying that they will not discuss it; e.g. "I'm not even going to get into the character issue.") *n.*: **apophasis**. SEE FIGURE OF SPEECH
 (3) remark (or phrase or comment which is elegant, concise, witty and/or well-put) *n.*: **atticism**. SEE EXPRESSION
 (4) remark (upon, esp. at length) *v.i.*, *n.*: **descant**. SEE TALK
 (5) remark (or line which is witty) *n.*: **epigram**. SEE QUIP

remedy (universal ...) *n.*: **catholicon**. ▪ In the end, even the most intrusive measures [regarding verification of another country's nuclear capability] will not be foolproof: there is no verification **catholicon**.

But perfect verification is as illusory as it is unnecessary. (Bruce Van Voorst, *Arms Control — An Exercise in Trust*, Time, 07-31-1989, p. 24.)
(2) remedy (which is untested or unproved) *n.*: **nostrum**. ▪ Hypochondriacs that so many of us are, Americans are easily persuaded that we can improve our sex lives, avoid cancer and live longer by swallowing pills or nibbling on herbs. To clothe these largely unproved remedies in respectability, the sellers have come up with scientific-sounding terms for their **nostrums**: nutraceuticals or phytonutrients. (Paul Klebnikov, *A Healthy Business*, Forbes Magazine, 09-21-1998, p. 89.)

remembrance *n.*: **anamnesis**. ▪ The finale of the novel is marked ... by **anamnesis**. ... Karnau's renewed listening to the children's voices almost fifty years after the end of the war leads to a repetition and retrieval of his own history. (Ulrich Schonherr, *Topophony of Fascism: On Marcel Beyer's The Karnau Tapes*, The Germanic Review, 09-22-1998, p. 328.)
 (2) remembrance (having detailed ... of visual images) *adj.*: **eidetic**. SEE MEMORY
 (3) remembrance (having an exact or vivid ...) *n.*: **hypermnesia**. SEE MEMORY
 (4) remembrance (confusion of ... with actual fact) *n.*: **paramnesia**. SEE MISREMEMBER

reminiscence (as in memory) *n.*: **anamnesis**. SEE REMEMBRANCE

reminiscent (of, or smelling like) *adj.*: **redolent**. ▪ As the sun rose, a tinny portable radio played and a powerful miasma enveloped the scene, the odor of unwashed bodies and open sewers **redolent** of a teeming, unruly refugee camp. (Warren P. Strobel, *Seeking Shelter*, U.S. News & World Report, 04-19-1999, p. 28.)

remorseless *adj.*: **impenitent**. SEE UNREPENTANT

remote (or most distant destination or goal) *n.*: **ultima Thule**. SEE DISTANT

remuneration (as in wages) *n.*: **emolument**. SEE WAGES

renaissance (as in rebirth) *n.*: **palingenesis**. SEE REBIRTH

rendezvous (esp. for illicit sexual relations) *n.*: **assignation**. SEE APPOINTMENT

renew (as in revive) *v.t.*: **refocillate**. SEE REVIVE

renewal (as in updating of an organization to meet contemporary conditions, esp. as proposed by Pope John XXIII with respect to the Catholic church after Vatican II) *n.*: **aggiornamento** [Italian]. SEE UPDATING

(2) renewal (as in rebirth) *n.*: **palingenesis**. SEE REBIRTH

(3) renewal (of something after a period of dormancy or inactivity) *n.*: **recrudescence** (*v.i.*: **recrudesce**). SEE REAPPEARANCE

renewed (as in revived) *adj.*: **redivivus**. SEE REVIVED

renounce *v.t.*: **abjure**. ∎ Newly married to Henry Stanton, an antislavery pragmatist who had broken with Garrison, [Elizabeth Cady] Stanton refused to **abjure** her own loyalties to the women's rights wing of abolition. (Author not given, *The Feminism of the Mothers, the Feminism of the Daughters*, The New Republic, 08-10-1998.)

(2) renounce (esp. responsibility or duty) *v.t.*: **abnegate**. ∎ And while these Germans may have experienced personally the hatred and slights of others, they have never **abnegated** responsibility or understanding of that history. For these Germans this adopted voice poses the unspoken question: What is the statute of limitations on the Holocaust? (Ken Baron, *Opening and Closing the Wounds: A Young Jew Married to a German*, The Jewish Week, 02-03-1994.)

renown *n.*: **réclame** [French]. SEE PUBLICITY

rent (exorbitant ...) *n., v.i., adj.*: **rackrent** [This word can be used as a noun (referring to the rackrent itself), a verb (referring to charging the rackrent), or an adjective (esp. when referring to a "rackrent landlord" as in this example)]. ∎ The book [Dear Mama ... An African Refugee Writes Home is a tour] of the desperate fringes of the new Europe, a landscape peopled with pimps and prostitutes, **rackrent** landlords and forgers, drug couriers and mules, welfare scammers and bigamists. (Author not given, *The Rules of the Asylum Game*, The Irish Times, 03-11-1999.)

reoccurrence (of something after a period of dormancy or inactivity) *n.*: **recrudescence** (*v.i.*: **recrudesce**). SEE REAPPEARANCE

repartee (light or playful back and forth ...) *n.*: **badinage**. SEE BANTER

(2) repartee *n.*: **persiflage**. SEE CHITCHAT

repeat (often for emphasis) *v.t.*: **ingeminate**. ∎ [The] Bob Woodward book of dubious reportage ... claims to **ingeminate** actual events from behind closed doors and to **ingeminate** verbatim conversations — though no stenographer was present. (R. Emmett Tyrell, Jr., *Artificial Ingemination*, The American Spectator, 01-01-2003.)

(2) repeat (as in to spread news or a rumor about) *v.t.*: **bruit**. SEE RUMOR

(3) repeat (mindlessly ideas which have been drilled into the speaker or which reflect the opinions of the powers-that-be) *v.t., v.i., n.*: **duckspeak**. SEE RECITE

repeating (pathological or uncontrollable or a child's ... of another's words) *n.*: **echolalia**. ∎ Another symptom that "autistic-like" visually impaired children may share with autistic children is **echolalia**. There has been much speculation about what might cause some visually impaired children to echo in parrot-like fashion the words they hear spoken to them. (Charles Gourgey, *Music Therapy in the Treatment of Social Isolation in Visually Impaired Children*, Re:View, 01-15-1998.)

(2) repeating (pathological or uncontrollable ... of another's actions) *n.*: **echopraxia**. ∎ In one painfully hilarious moment, an expert witness for the prosecution, Dr. Rampling, suffers from three neurological conditions, coprolalia, copropraxia and **echopraxia**, which make her shout obscenities [i.e. coprolalia], grab her own breasts [i.e. copropraxia] and mimic her questioners as she testifies, all unconsciously. (Richard Bernstein, *Just a Couple of All-American Orphans on Trial*, The New York Times, 08-06-1997.)

(3) repeating (a particular act over and over, often after initial stimulus has ceased) *n.*: **perseveration** (*v.i.*: **perseverate**). ∎ [A co-worker of the narrator has been falsely accused of sexual harassment in the workplace.] "This is all so degrading and atrocious," said [my wife]. ... My wife has a tremendous ability to be outraged at the common injustices society visits on its members. ... At long last, she simply stopped **perseverating** on this subject and moved on to new ones. (Stanley Bing, *You Look Nice Today*, Bloomsbury [2003], p. 104.)

(4) repeating (of words) *n.*: **macrology**. SEE VERBOSITY

(5) repeating (unnecessary ... of words) *n.*: **pleonasm**. SEE REDUNDANCY

repellent *adj.*: **rebarbative**. ∎ [Rudyard Kipling's] literary gifts were increasingly eclipsed in the public eye by his unpalatable politics. Which is not to deny that his views were often **rebarbative**: anti-feminist, chauvinist, racist, and anti-Semitic. (Martin Rubin, *English Writer Who Lost a Following*, The Washington Times, 04-30-2000, p. B7.)

repetition (of word or phrase at the end of sentences or clauses) *n.* **epistrophe**. ▮ [T]he headline for an Isuzu Trooper ad reads "Cargo Ship." The ad uses a verbal metaphor to equate the Trooper to a cargo ship because it has the most cargo space in its class. ... The headline [two pages later] reads "Kin Ship" and uses a pun to imply that the Rodeo is for families. In effect, the ad on page 17 layers onto the ad on page 15 to create a verbal **epistrophe** in which the word "ship" is repeated at the end of each headline. (Edward F. McQuarrie, *The Development, Change, and Transformation of Rhetorical Style in Magazine Advertisements 1954-1999*, Journal of Advertising, 12-22-2002.)

replacement (esp. of a doctor or clergyman) *n.*: **locum tenens**. SEE TEMPORARY

reply (clever ... that one thinks of after the moment has passed) *n.*: **esprit d'escalier** [French]. SEE RETORT
(2) reply (as in responding to an anticipated objection to an argument before that objection has been made) *n.*: **prolepsis**. SEE REBUTTAL
(3) reply (charging accuser with similar offense) *n.*: **tu quoque** [Latin]. SEE ANSWER

repose (in ..., as in not moving or temporarily inactive) *adj.*: **quiescent**. SEE INACTIVE

repository (for bones or bodies of the dead) *n.*: **charnel**. ▮ [The Nazi commandant] was ordered to open the mass graves and exhume the bodies of the thousands of Jews who were murdered during the liquidation of the ghetto in Krakow in 1943 ... and to burn the bodies in pits. Anybody who has seen photographs or films of these fiery, open-air **charnels** knows that the camera has probably never recorded a sight more obscene. (Leon Wieseltier, *Schindler's List [Movie Reviews]*, The New Republic, 01-24-1994, p. 42.)
(2) repository (esp. as shrine for displaying relics) *n.*: **reliquary**. SEE RECEPTACLE

reprehensible *adj.*: **opprobrious** (*n.*: **opprobrium**). SEE CONTEMPTUOUS

represent (as in describe, by painting or writing) *v.t.*: **limn**. SEE DESCRIBE

representation (or image) *n.*: **simulacrum**. ▮

Disneyland was another bet-the-farm risk, and Disney threw himself obsessively into the park's design, which anticipated many of the best features of modern urban planning, and into the "imagineering" by which the **simulacrums** of exotic, even dangerous creatures, places, fantasies could be unthreateningly reproduced. (Richard Schickel, *Time 100/Ruler of the Magic Kingdom: Walt Disney*, Time, 12-07-1998, p. 124.)

representative (rather than a literal representation, esp. with respect to objects of worship) *adj.*: **aniconic**. SEE SYMBOLIC
(2) representative (or leader esp. for a political cause) *n.*: **fugleman**. SEE LEADER

repress (something that serves to ...) *n.*: **quietus** (esp. as in "put the quietus to"). SEE TERMINATE

reprimand (as in criticism) *n.*: **animadversion** (*v.t.*: **animadvert**). SEE CRITICISM
(2) reprimand (as in criticize) *v.t.*: **flay**. SEE CRITICIZE
(3) reprimand (sharply) *v.t.*: **keelhaul**. SEE REBUKE
(4) reprimand *v.t.*: **objurgate**. SEE CRITICIZE
(5) reprimand (being subject to ..., esp. public) *n.*: **obloquy**. SEE ABUSE

reprisal (esp. to recover lost territory or political standing) *n.*: **revanche** [French]. SEE REVENGE

reproach (as in criticism) *n.*: **animadversion** (*v.t.*: **animadvert**). SEE CRITICISM
(2) reproach *v.t.*: **flay**. SEE CRITICIZE
(3) reproach *v.t.*: **objurgate**. SEE CRITICIZE
(4) reproach (being subject to ..., esp. public) *n.*: **obloquy**. SEE ABUSE

reproval (being subject to ..., esp. public) *n.*: **obloquy**. SEE ABUSE

reprove *v.t.*: **objurgate**. SEE CRITICIZE

reptile (of, relating to or resembling ..., as in lizard) *adj.*: **lacertilian**. SEE LIZARD

repudiate *v.t.*: **abjure**. SEE RENOUNCE

repugnant *adj.*: **rebarbative**. SEE REPELLENT

repulsive (ugly, terrifying or ... woman) *n.*: **gorgon**. SEE UGLY
(2) repulsive *adj.*: **ugsome**. SEE LOATHSOME

reputed (as in supposed) *adj.*: **putative**. SEE SUPPOSED

request (earnestly) *v.t.*: **adjure**. SEE PLEAD

requiem *n.*: **threnody**. ▮ [In] *The Perfect Storm*, Sebastian Junger describes the ominous siren song made by the wind during an apocalyptic ocean deluge: "Force 10 is a shriek. Force 11 is a moan. Over Force 11 is something fishermen don't want to hear ... a deep tonal vibration like a church organ." I went [to see the movie version] hoping to hear, at least once, that otherworldly church-organ **threnody**. (Owen Gleiberman, *Movies: The Wet Look — There's Water, Water Everywhere in the Perfect Storm, But the Book's Dark Drama Gets Lost at Sea*, Entertainment Weekly, 07-14-2000, p. 51.)

require (to act, esp. by violent measures or threats) *v.t.*: **dragoon**. SEE COERCE

(2) require (a person or group to go from one place to another, whether literally or figuratively) *v.t.*: **frogmarch**. SEE MARCH

required (element or condition) *n.*: **sine qua non** [Latin]. SEE INDISPENSABLE

rescind *v.t.*: **abjure**. SEE RENOUNCE

rescission (as in retraction) *n.*: **palinode**. SEE RETRACTION

resemblance (of sounds to each other) *n.*: **assonance**. SEE SIMILARITY

(2) resemblance (as in representation) *n.*: **simulacrum**. SEE REPRESENTATION

resentful (easily made ..., as in offended) *adj.*: **umbrageous**. SEE OFFENDED

resentment (as in bitterness) *n.*: **bile**. SEE BITTERNESS

residence (as in very large house) *n.*: **manse**. SEE MANSION

resident (of a town) *n.*: **burgher**. ▮ "[The Disney-designed town of Celebration, Florida] was full of people who so believed in human interaction that they'd bought closely clustered homes with porches. Still, I wasn't sure whether the **burghers** of Celebration really understood what a national 3-on-3 basketball championship would deliver [to their town]. (Alexander Wolff, *Big Game, Small World*, Warner Books [2002], p. 69.)

resign (from an office or position) *v.i.*: **demit** (as in demit office). ▮ Speaker Occah Seapaul last week rejected a no-confidence motion brought against her by the government. ... In response to this unprece-dented turn of events the government advanced a legislative proposal to change the country's constitution and require the speaker to **demit** office. (Elijah Charles, *Trinidad Military on Coup Alert: Security Has Been Stepped Up*, The Weekly Journal, 07-27-1995.)

resistance (as in unwillingness) *n.*: **nolition**. SEE UNWILLINGNESS

resistant (to yield or be swayed) *adj.*: **renitent**. ▮ It is not that [poet Seamus Heaney] has lost his "gutteral muse." He still, like a farmboy who stoops at the plough to grub out some shiny lump of quartz, picks up those **renitent** words that seem most resilient to language. [The author does not specify which of Heaney's words are "most resilient to language." Nevertheless, if they are in fact resilient, then it follows that "renitent" is being used properly to show that they are also resistant.] (Rachel Campbell-Johnston, *Danger: High Voltage Poetry*, The Times [London], 04-04-2001.)

resolute *adj.*: **doughty**. SEE BRAVE

resolve *n.*: **hardihood**. SEE COURAGE

resonant (as in full and rich sound or voice) *adj.*: **orotund**. SEE SONOROUS

resourceful (person) *n.*: **debrouillard** (or **débrouillard**) [French]. ▮ Adolphe Mulinowa ... hustles to a roadside with a few plastic bottles of pink gasoline, which he hawks alongside dozens of other street vendors. ... In a town of **debrouillards**, Mulinowa has learned to exploit tiny advantages. He has figured out that, because Goma has dozens of gasoline vendors, his chances are better two miles away at the Rwanda-Congo border. There, drivers have to slow down and are more likely to notice him. (Davan Maharaj, *When the Push for Survival is a Full-Time Job; What is it like to Live on Less Than a Dollar a Day? Hundreds of Millions in Sub-Saharan Africa Know*, The Los Angeles Times, 07-11-2004, p. A1.)

respect (with ... to) *prep.*: **anent**. SEE REGARDING

(2) respect (personal ..., as in honor) *n.*: **izzat** [Hindi]. SEE HONOR

(3) respect (not necessarily sincere or unforced) *n.*: **obeisance**. SEE HOMAGE

respectful (to be ... in a servile way) *v.i.*: **genuflect**. SEE KNEEL

resplendent (as in shining brightly) *adj.*: **effulgent**. SEE BRIGHT

(2) resplendent (as in shining brightly) *adj.*: **fulgurant**. SEE BRIGHT

(3) resplendent (as in shining brightly) *adj.*: **refulgent**. SEE BRIGHT

response (clever ... that one thinks of after the moment has passed) *n.*: **esprit d'escalier** [French]. SEE RETORT

(2) response (as in ... to an anticipated objection to an argument before that objection has been made) *n.*: **prolepsis**. SEE REBUTTAL

(3) response (charging accuser with similar offense) *n.*: **tu quoque** [Latin]. SEE ANSWER

rest (as in pause) *n.*: **caesura**. SEE PAUSE

resting (as in not moving or temporarily inactive) *adj.*: **quiescent**. SEE INACTIVE

restlessness (as part of depressed state) *n.*: **dysphoria**. SEE DEPRESSION

(2) restlessness *n.* **inquietude**. SEE ANXIETY

restorative (esp. with respect to effect of certain drugs or medications) *adj.*: **analeptic**. ∎ For since the turn of the century, ... Irn-Bru has peddled a successful myth that the drink is in fact "a refreshing tonic beverage." ... Of course, with the introduction of the all-new alcoholic ... Irn-Bru into the equation, [who knows] whether the **analeptic** properties of the orange stuff are derived from the 32 secret ingredients in the pop or the proof alcohol? (Author not given, *Pop Goes the Elixir*, The Herald [Glasgow], 12-30-1996, p. 13.)

(2) restorative (used often of a medicinal treatment) *adj.*: **balsamic**. SEE SOOTHING

(3) restorative (as in having the power to cure or heal) *adj.*: **sanative**. SEE HEALTHFUL

restored (as in revived) *adj.*: **redivivus**. SEE REVIVED

restrain (a person by holding down his arms) *v.t.*: **pinion**. SEE IMMOBILIZE

restrained (as in not indulgent) *adj.*: **abstemious**. ∎ The Jones work at acquiring fine wines but are relatively **abstemious** in their own consumption. "Today, we are concentrating on acquiring fine wines in the birth years of our children," Dennis said. (Joan Foster Dames, *Wine Collectors — Know How to Put a Little Spirit Into Their Lives*, St. Louis Post-Dispatch, 07-11-1993, p. 4.)

restraint (as in marked by simplicity, frugality, self-discipline and/or ...) *adj.*: **Lacedaemoninan**. SEE SPARTAN

restrict (as in confine) *v.t.*: **immure**. SEE CONFINE

(2) restrict (a person's movement by holding down his arms) *v.t.*: **pinion**. SEE IMMOBILIZE

result (as in outgrowth) *n.*: **excrescence**. SEE OUTGROWTH

resurrection (as in rebirth) *n.*: **palingenesis**. SEE REBIRTH

retaliation (in kind) *n.*: **lex talionis** [Latin]. SEE EYE FOR AN EYE

(2) retaliation (esp. to recover lost territory or political standing) *n.*: **revanche** [French]. SEE REVENGE

retarded (psychiatric diagnosis for one who is ...) *adj.*: **oligophrenic**. ∎ Children [in Russia] who show no signs of illness at birth but fall behind in school are sent off for further tests by child psychiatrists. They risk being found to be feebleminded, or **oligophrenic** — a catchall term for any form of mental problem, borrowed from 18th century French usage. ... Any of these primitive diagnoses condemns the child to life in a home. (Vanora Bennett, *Russia's Forgotten Children; The Mentally Ill — and the Misdiagnosed — are Kept in Bleak State Homes*, The Los Angeles Times, p. A1.)

retch (making an effort to ...) *v.i.*: **keck**. SEE VOMIT

retort (clever ... that one thinks of after the moment has passed) *n.*: **esprit d'escalier** [French; roughly the "wit of the staircase," as in the thought that comes to mind on the staircase as one is leaving]. ∎ Proselytizing for Jehovah's Witnesses during last Sunday's Vikings game wasn't the smoothest call Prince has ever made. [He knocked on the door of a Jewish woman named Rochelle:] "It was so bizarre, you would have just laughed," she said. The perfect **esprit d'escalier** came to Rochelle after Prince left: "If I showed up at Paisley [Park], would you let me in your front door to talk about Judaism?" (Cheryl Johnson, *I-Witness News: Visit From Prince; Proselytizing Pop Star Knocks on Previously Committed Door*, Star Tribune [Minneapolis, MN], 10-12-2003.)

(2) retort (charging accuser with similar offense) *n.*: **tu quoque** [Latin]. SEE ANSWER

retract *v.t.*: **abjure**. SEE DISAVOW

retraction *n.*: **palinode**. ∎ According to this story, told by Plato in the Phaedrus, the poet wrote some verses insulting to Helen, for which she blinded him; to regain his sight, he composed an apologetic **palinode**. (Adam Kirsch, *All Mere Complexities*, The New Republic, 05-18-1998.)

retreat (desperate ...) *n*.: **Dunkirk** [after city in Northern France from which 330,000 Allied troops were evacuated from its beaches in the face of enemy fire in May-June, 1940]. ■ It has become an unwritten law of TV journalism that CBS can't really do anything [right] in the morning. ... Everything seems to fail. The new strategy is to ... let local stations take over what they'd like to take over. ... What we are seeing is really a disguised retreat. This is CBS News' **Dunkirk**. New owner Westinghouse has come in, surveyed the situation and said, "Hit the beaches, men." (Marvin Kitman, *Could "Capt. Kangaroo" Rescue CBS?* Newsday, 04-15-1996.)

(2) retreat (as in recoil) *v.i.*: **resile**. SEE RECOIL

retribution (in kind) *n*.: **lex talionis** [Latin]. SEE EYE FOR AN EYE

return (property or territory) *v.i.*: **retrocede**. ■ All that Americans knew in 1802 were rumors that Napoleon had induced Spain to **retrocede** Louisiana to France, including, as many thought, both East and West Florida. For Americans, and especially for President Jefferson, nothing could have been more alarming. (Gordon Wood, *Sale of the Century*, The New Republic, 05-26-2003.)

(2) return (of something after a period of dormancy or inactivity) *n*.: **recrudescence** (*v.i.*: **recrudesce**). SEE REAPPEARANCE

returns (one who ... after lengthy absence or death) *n*.: **revenant**. ■ [The clothing line] also underscored Versace's debt to the arrowy, tidy chic of André Courreges, another '60s **revenant**. (Martha Duffy, *Classic Acts in the Established Bastions of High Fashion*, Time International, 10-09-1995, p. 54.)

reused (as in warmed over food or old material) *n., adj.*: **rechauffé** [French]. SEE WARMED OVER

reveal *v.t.*: **disinter**. SEE DISCLOSE

(2) reveal (as in confide, one's thoughts or feelings) *v.t., v.i.*: **unbosom**. SEE CONFIDE

revel (noisily) *v.i.*: **roister**. ■ But as [the burlesque] audience dwindled with age, its children — who had no firsthand knowledge of burlesque or the silent-film clowns — came to think of Jerry [Lewis] as merely a **roistering** physical comic. (Shawn Levy, *The King of Comedy*, St. Martin's Press [1996], p. 43.)

(2) revel (in, or boast, esp. about the accomplishments of a relative) *v.t., n*.: **kvell** [Yiddish]. SEE BOAST

(3) revel (with boisterous public demonstrations) *v.i.*: **maffick** [British]. SEE CELEBRATE

revelation (as in creative inspiration) *n*.: **afflatus**. SEE INSPIRATION

(2) revelation (sudden ...) *n*.: **epiphany**. SEE REALIZATION

reveler (female ...) *n*.: **bacchante** (male ...: **bacchant**) [derives from Bacchus, the Roman god of wine]. ■ *Aphrodite: A Memoir of the Senses* [by] Isabel Allende [is] an unabashedly whimsical hodgepodge of memories, [and lore. She] is by turns the sighing romantic ("The only true aphrodisiac is love"), the playful **bacchante** ("When you plan your orgy, you must count on it lasting all night, so a buffet isn't a good idea; after a few hours everything goes limp"). (Margaria Fichtner, *Aphrodite Seduces the Senses With its Phrasing, Imagery*, The Miami Herald, 03-22-1998.)

revelry (riotous ...) *n., adj.*: **bacchanal**. ■ The Oakland Athletics had decided against staging the riotous **bacchanal** that these days almost always accompanies world titles, sensing, quite rightly, that the sight of players pouring champagne over each other would have been inappropriate in the aftermath of the earthquake. (Steve Wulf, *Swept Away*, Sports Illustrated, 11-06-1989, p. 24.)

revenge (esp. to recover lost territory or political standing) *n*.: **revanche** [French]. ■ [Russian President Boris] Yeltsin had to maintain democratic illusions to keep his power, which he did by nurturing the Zyuganov-led "intransigent" opposition to scare Russians with the threat of a Red **revanche**. (Yuri Zarakhovich, *Europe: Viewpoint: Forward Into the Past: Russia Keeps Trading in One Group of Oppressors for Another*, Time International, 10-12-1998, p. 41.)

(2) revenge (in kind) *n*.: **lex talionis** [Latin]. SEE EYE FOR AN EYE

revere (often in a servile manner) *v.i.*: **genuflect**. SEE KNEEL

reverence (not necessarily sincere or unforced) *n*.: **obeisance**. SEE HOMAGE

reversal (as in abandonment, from one's religion, principles or causes) *n*.: **apostasy** SEE ABANDONMENT

(2) reversal (esp. regarding one's beliefs, causes or policies) *n*.: **bouleversement** [French]. SEE CHANGE OF MIND

(3) reversal (sudden ... of events, often in a literary work) *n*.: **peripeteia**. SEE TURNAROUND

(4) reversal (a ... regarding one's beliefs, causes or

policies) *n*.: **tergiversation** (*v.i.*: **tergiversate**). SEE CHANGE OF MIND

(5) reversal (of policy or position) *n*.: **volte-face** [French]. SEE ABOUT-FACE

reverse (as in recoil) *v.i.*: **resile**. SEE RECOIL

review *v.t.*: **assay**. SEE EVALUATE

(2) review (as in summarize) *v.t.*: **precis** [French]. SEE SUMMARY

reviewer (who is inferior or incompetent) *n*.: **criticaster**. SEE CRITIC

(2) reviewer (who is who is given to unjust quibbling) *n*.: **Zoilus**. SEE CRITIC

revise (text or language by removing errors or flaws) *v.t.*: **blue-pencil**. SEE EDIT

(2) revise (a book or writing in a prudish manner) *v.t.*: **bowdlerize**. SEE EDIT

(3) revise (text or language by removing errors or flaws) *v.t.*: **emend**. SEE EDIT

revision (as in correction, esp. in printed material) *n*.: **corrigendum**. SEE CORRECTION

revitalization (as in updating, of an organization to meet contemporary conditions, esp. as proposed by Pope John XXIII with respect to the Catholic church after Vatican II) *n*.: **aggiornamento** [Italian]. SEE UPDATING

revival (as in rebirth) *n*.: **palingenesis**. SEE REBIRTH

revive *v.t.*: **refocillate**. ▮ [The TV show] "The National Lottery — In It to Win It," which returned to BBC1 on Saturday night, [is unoriginal]. The [station's] plan was to **refocillate** its load of old balls by running a full-length quiz show ahead of the main draw, but the result will surely increase public apathy ... because the lazy and derivative format smacks of desperation, not creativity. (Victor Lewis-Smith, *A Load of Old Balls and Dale [Review]*, The Evening Standard [London], 04-28-2003.)

revived *adj.*: **redivivus**. ▮ It's the old hippie dream **redivivus**: "Wouldn't it be great if wars could be fought just by the [assholes] who start them," says Costner's Postman to the General. And, lo, for once it comes to pass! (James Bowman, *The Talkies: There's No Growing Up — If You Film It, They Will Come*, The American Spectator, 02-01-1998.)

revocation (as in abandonment, from one's religion, principles or causes) *n*.: **apostasy**. SEE ABANDONMENT

(2) revocation (esp. regarding one's beliefs, causes or policies) *n*.: **bouleversement** [French]. SEE CHANGE OF MIND

(3) revocation (a ... regarding one's beliefs, causes or policies) *n*.: **tergiversation** (*v.i.*: **tergiversate**). SEE CHANGE OF MIND

revolutionary (as in rebel) *n*.: **frondeur** [French]. SEE REBEL

(2) revolutionary (a political ..., who often believes in violence to attain an end) *n*.: **sans-culotte**. SEE EXTREMIST

revolving (or spiraling motion, often an ocean current) *n*.: **gyre**. SEE SPIRALING

reward *n*.: **guerdon**. ▮ [Everyone] will be stirred by the sheer gotta-dance, gotta-sing energy of Telson's music [in] The Gospel at Colonus and the performances it receives from a stage brimming over with inspired musicians. Virtually everyone in the cast (the largest to appear on a Broadway stage in many years) merits his or her own **guerdon** of praise. (Peter Biskind, *The Manchurian Candidate*, The Nation, 05-14-1988.)

rewarmed (as in warmed over food or old material) *n., adj.*: **rechauffé** [French]. SEE WARMED OVER

reworked (as in warmed over old material) *n., adj.*: **rechauffé** [French]. SEE WARMED OVER

rhetorical (device in which one references an issue by saying that they will not discuss it; e.g. "I'm not even going to get into the character issue.") *n*.: **apophasis**. SEE FIGURE OF SPEECH

(2) rhetorical (device in which one makes only passing mention of something in order to emphasize rhetorically the significance of what is being omitted; often preceded by the phrase "not to mention") *n*.: **paraleipsis**. SEE FIGURE OF SPEECH

rhyme (as in similarity of sounds to each other) *n*.: **assonance**. SEE SIMILARITY

rib (playfully) *v.t., v.i., n.*: **chaff**. SEE TEASING

rich (and/or prominent person) *n*.: **nabob**. SEE BIGWIG

(2) rich (sound or voice) *adj.*: **orotund**. SEE SONOROUS

(3) rich (government by the ...) *n*.: **plutocracy**. SEE GOVERNMENT

(4) rich (study of or focus on the ..., esp. in artistic works) *n*.: **plutography**. SEE WEALTH

(5) rich (government by the ..., i.e. in proportion to wealth or property ownership) *n.*: **timocracy**. SEE GOVERNMENT

riches (source of great ...) *n.*: **Golconda**. SEE WEALTH
(2) riches (devotion to the pursuit of ...) *n.*: **mammonism**. SEE WEALTH
(3) riches *n.*: **pelf**. SEE WEALTH

rid (get ... of) *v.t.*: **extirpate**. SEE ABOLISH

ridicule (esp. through the use of satire) *v.t.*: **pasquinade**. SEE SATIRIZE
(2) ridicule (as in good-natured teasing) *n.*: **raillery**. SEE TEASING

ridiculous (as in absurd or preposterous) *adj.*: **fatuous** SEE FOOLISH
(2) ridiculous (as in laughable) *adj.*: **gelastic**. SEE LAUGHABLE
(3) ridiculous (as in laughable) *adj.*: **risible**. SEE LAUGHABLE

ridiculousness *n.*: **folderol** (or **falderal**). SEE NONSENSE
(2) ridiculousness *n.*: **piffle**. SEE NONSENSE
(3) ridiculousness *n.*: **trumpery**. SEE NONSENSE

riffraff *n.*: **canaille**. SEE MASSES
(2) riffraff (as in the common people) *n.*: **hoi polloi**. SEE COMMONERS

right (necessarily ...) *adj.*: **apodictic**. SEE INCONTROVERTIBLE
(2) right (on the ... side or right-handed) *adj.*: **dextral**. SEE RIGHT-HANDED

right way (do things the ..., as in "by the book") *idiom*: **according to Hoyle**. SEE BY THE BOOK

right-handed *adj.*: **dextral**. ∎ The researchers reckon that a child with two right-handed parents has a 91% probability of being right-handed ... [but] ... even if identical twins have parents who are both **dextral**, factors such as their position in the womb may result in the twins not preferring the same hands. (Author not given, *Sinister Evolution: Population Genetics*, The Economist, 08-26-1995, p. 69.)

right-wing (very ... in beliefs and often stuffy, pompous and/or elderly) *adj., n.*: **Colonel Blimp**. SEE CONSERVATIVE

rigid (as in narrow-minded) *adj.*: **hidebound**. SEE NARROW-MINDED
(2) rigid *adj.*: **monastic**. SEE STRICT

rigidity (condition characterized by muscular ...) *n.*: **catalepsy**. ∎ Cannon proceeds to the next stage, "arm **catalepsy**." Your arm will become like a rod of steel. She lifts Valentyne's arm until it's thrust out at a right angle directly in front of her, tugs on the wrist to lock the elbow straight, then lets go. Valentyne's arm remains rigid. (Lily Nguyen, *Hed Goes Here — Hypnosis*, The Toronto Star, 05-21-2000.)

rile up (as in agitate) *v.t.*: **commove**. SEE AGITATE

rim (as in edge) *n.*: **selvage**. SEE EDGE

ring (as in surround) *v.t.*: **girdle**. SEE SURROUND

ring-shaped *adj.*: **annular**. ∎ In an **annular** eclipse, the Moon's conical umbra, or shadow, doesn't quite reach the Earth — hence we have a broad, bright ring of light rather than a total eclipse, which is characterized by a darkened sky and a dramatic corona. (Cathy Johnson, *Celestial Occurrences*, [*Appreciating Celestial Phenomena*], Country Living, 09-01-1994, p. 74.)

ringing (in one's ears) *n.*: **tinnitus**. ∎ Until six years ago, Dr. Stephen Nagler, 51, was a busy breast- and colon-cancer surgeon in Atlanta. But then he suddenly began suffering from **tinnitus**, which most people describe as a ringing in the ears. (Judy Foreman, *Learning to Tune Out* **Tinnitus**, Minneapolis Star Tribune, 01-09-2000, p. 3E.)
(2) ringing (of bells) *n.*: **tintinnabulation**. ∎ Once again, love will redeem the beast, and Beauty's dancing clocks and singing teacups will blend marvelously with the **tintinnabulation** of bells this holiday season. (Mark Goodman, *Picks & Pans: Screen*, People, 11-18-1991, p. 21.)

riot *n.*: **émeute** [French]. SEE REBELLION

riotous (celebration) *n., adj.*: **bacchanal**. SEE REVELRY
(2) riotous (as in unruly) *adj.*: **indocile**. SEE UNRULY

rip (apart) *v.t.*: **rive** (past sense: **riven**). SEE TEAR

ripping (adapted for ... apart flesh) *adj.*: **carnassial** (*n.*: a tooth so adapted). SEE TOOTH

rise (above) *v.t.*: **bestride**. SEE DOMINATE

rising *adj.*: **assurgent**. ∎ At the time of the Russian revolution, a generation of artists, **assurgent** with hope for the future, liberated their imaginations to turn out a decade's worth of works that were both: a) masterpieces, and b) works in support of the state. It couldn't last; it didn't. Stalin and his apparatchiks took over. (Stephen Hunter, *Films Under Fire, Politicians Talk of a Perfect Past That Never Was*, The Baltimore Sun, 06-18-1995, p. 1J.)

(2) rising (esp. too high for safety) *adj.*: **Icarian**. SEE SOARING

risky (journey or passage, with dangers on both sides) *idiom*: **between Scylla and Charybdis**. SEE PREDICAMENT

(2) risky (and irresponsible) *adj.*: **harum-scarum**. SEE RECKLESS

(3) risky (as in perilous) *adj.*: **parlous**. SEE PERILOUS

risqué *adj.*: **scabrous**. SEE SCANDALOUS

rite (funeral ...) *n.*: **obsequy** (often pl.). SEE FUNERAL

ritual (which is pretentious) *n.*: **mummery**. SEE CEREMONY

ritzy *adj.*: **nobby** [British]. SEE ELEGANT

river (of, relating to or inhabiting) *adj.*: **fluvial**. ▌ "We have high standards for who we consider to be qualified to mess around with people's bodies in medicine," says Dave Montgomery, a **fluvial** geomorphologist at the University of Washington, "but we haven't hit that state of valuing rivers enough to require similar expertise." (Kathleen Wong, *Bringing Back the Logjams*, U.S. News & World Report, 09-06-1999, p. 60.)

(2) river (of, relating to or resembling) *adj.*: **riverine**. ▌ The Rockefellers lived three miles east of town in an area of soft, bucolic meadows and **riverine** groves. (Ron Chernow, *Titan*, Random House [1998], p. 31.)

(3) river (of, relating to or living in a moving water system, such as a stream or ...) *adj.*: **lotic**. SEE WATER

river bank (of or relating to a ...) *adj.*: **riparian**. SEE WATER BANK

roam (aimlessly) *v.i.*: **maunder**. ▌ It's true, the Democrats have hired Terry McAuliffe. But aside from **maundering** around Florida upsetting the old folks with his constant whining, his primary function is as the imperator of importuning, the prince of beggars, the sultan of slush. He performs a coo for cash, not a coup for power. (Tony Blankley, *A Failing Grade; Dems' First 100 Days*, The Washington Times, 04-25-2001, p. A19.)

(2) roam (about, esp. on foot) *v.t., v.i.*: **perambulate**. ▌ Over in the land of saints and scholars this is a notable day. June 16. Bloomsday. The occasion on which, in 1904, Leopold Bloom and Stephen Dedalus **perambulated** around Dublin in James Joyce's Ulysses, expeditions chronicled so exactly that Joyce believed Dublin, if ever razed by catastrophe, could have been reconstructed from his novel. (Author not given, *Tough Areas Get a Chance to Shine*, The Toronto Star, 06-16-1998.)

(3) roam (about, esp. on foot) *v.t., v.i.*: **peregrinate**. ▌ The petty thieveries and lies of later childhood metastasized into a lunatic binge, in which our 17-year-old hero **peregrinated** around England on someone else's credit card. (Rod Dreher, *Moab Is My Washpot*, National Review, 05-31-1999.)

(4) roam (from the subject) *v.i.*: **divagate**. SEE DIGRESS

(5) roam (compulsion to ... or travel) *n.*: **dromomania**. SEE TRAVEL

(6) roam (able to ... freely in a given environment; used of species) *adj.*: **vagile**. SEE MOVE

roamer (as in one who strolls through city streets idly) *n.*: **flâneur** [French]; (strolling *n.*: **flânerie**). SEE IDLER

rob (through swindling) *v.t.*: **bunco**. SEE SWINDLE

(2) rob (as in embezzle) *v.i.*: **defalcate**. SEE EMBEZZLE

(3) rob (as in plunder) *v.t., v.i.*: **depredate** (*n.*: **depredation**). SEE PLUNDER

(4) rob (as in embezzle) *v.t., v.i.*: **peculate**. SEE EMBEZZLE

robbery *n.*: **brigandage** (**robber** *n.*: **brigand**). His getaway was as flawed as his intended **brigandage**. (Tibor Fischer, *The Thought Gang*, The New Press [1994], p. 37.)

robbing (as in pillage or plunder) *n.*: **rapine**. SEE LOOTING

robe (of a priest) *n.*: **alb**. ▌ Davis considered himself a Roman Catholic priest. [He] sometimes donned a long white **alb** and, all by himself outside the boma, performed services beside his Land Rover, chanting the Latin in a rich bass. (Lance Morrow, *Essay: Africa*, Time, 02-23-1987, p. 44.)

robot *n.*: **automaton**. ▌ Reggie, a 4-foot-tall wheeled **automaton**, may be coming to a hospital near you. ... The hospital staff uses the robots, called HelpMates, to carry meal trays and deliver sterile supplies to nurses' stations. (Mark Alpert, *News/Trends: Sorry, No Bedpans*, Fortune, 08-26-1991, p. 18.)

robotic (repetition of ideas which have been drilled

into the speaker or which reflect the opinions of the powers-that-be) *v.t., v.i., n.*: **duckspeak**. SEE RECITE

robust (having a ... and muscular body build) *adj.*: **mesomorphic**. SEE MUSCULAR

rock and a hard place (between a ... , as in dangers on both sides) *idiom*: **between Scylla and Charybdis**. SEE PRECARIOUS

rod (instrument such as a ... for punishing children) *n.*: **ferule**. SEE PADDLE

rodents (of or relating to ..., such as mice or rats) *adj.*: **murine**. ∎ But hormones aside, the stimulating role of motherhood itself would seem to play a role. When the investigators gave ... rats [who had never given birth] another mother's pups to raise, the **murine** foster moms did almost as well in tests as their ... counterparts [who had given birth]. (Author not given, *Does Mothering Make Females Smarter?* Medical Post, 02-09-1999, p. 37.)

rogue (or unprincipled person) *n.*: **blackguard**. SEE SCOUNDREL

(2) rogue *n.*: **rapscallion**. SEE RASCAL

(3) rogue *n.*: **scapegrace**. SEE SCOUNDREL

roll up *v.t.*: **furl**. ∎ The Rev. Jesse Jackson called Georgia's flag an "insult," adding that "the vanquished do not have the right to fly their flag." State Rep. Tyrone Brooks, an Atlanta Democrat, warned of "sanctions, boycotts and international embarrassment" if the General Assembly refuses to **furl** the flag. (Dan Chapman, *Behind the Scenes on the Flag Fight State*, The Atlanta Journal and Constitution, 01-07-2001, p. D1.)

romantic (as in amorous) *adj.*: **amative**. SEE AMOROUS

romanticized (or glamorized conception of oneself, as a result of boredom in one's life) *n.*: **Bovarism**. SEE SELF-DELUSION

Romeo (as in man who seduces women) *n.*: **Lothario**. SEE PLAYBOY

room (adequate ... for living) *n.*: **lebensraum** [German]. SEE BREATHING SPACE

rooster *n.*: **chanticleer**. ∎ Sunrise over the misty Mekong marks the beginning of the day in Vientiane. If not awakened by the crowing of the **chanticleers**, the beat of the drum at the Buddhist wat (monastery) across the street should do it. (Vern Harnapp, *Laos: Now Open for Tourist Business*, Focus, 06-22-1998.)

root (about or through) *v.t.*: **fossick** [Australian]. SEE RUMMAGE

rose-colored (or rosy) *adj.*: **roseate**. SEE ROSY

rosy *adj.*: **roseate**. ∎ Despite Rockefeller's **roseate** memories [of his childhood], early photos of him tell a much more somber tale. (Ron Chernow, *Titan*, Random House [1998], p. 17.)

(2) rosy (esp. as in ... cheeks) *adj.*: **rubicund**. ∎ Passing bills is an awful bore but it has to be done. Mary Mulligan, deputy health minister, is an awful bore about whom something should be done. ... After ten minutes of her sugary, insubstantial voice, I'd made up my mind to swing down from the gallery, pinch her **rubicund** cheeks ..., and shout: "For God's sake, Mary, shut yir gob!" (Robert McNeil, *A Moderately Reflective Day To Be Passing Bills*, The Scotsman [Edinburgh, Scotland], 02-07-2002.)

(3) rosy (as in ruddy) *adj.*: **florid**. SEE RUDDY

rotate (a log by spinning with the feet) *v.t.*: **birl**. SEE LOGROLLING

rotating (or spiraling motion, often an ocean current) *n.*: **gyre**. SEE SPIRALING

rote (repetition of ideas which have been drilled into the speaker or which reflect the opinions of the powers-that-be) *v.t., v.i., n.*: **duckspeak**. SEE RECITE

rotund (condition of having a ... physique) *n.*: **embonpoint**. SEE PLUMP

(2) rotund (person, esp. with a large abdomen) *n.*: **endomorph** (*adj.*: **endomorphic**). SEE POT-BELLIED

(3) rotund (having a short ... physique) *adj.*: **pyknic**. SEE STOCKY

rough *adj.*: **scabrous**. ∎ The paganized, foul-tempered Mickey Sabbath is beyond all that. Some readers will find the material and language too **scabrous** for their taste. (R.Z. Sheppard, *Aging Disgracefully: Philip Roth's Latest Complainer Is Lecherous, Meanspirited, Politically Incorrect — And, After All These Years, Still Funny*, Time, 09-11-1995, p. 82.)

(2) rough (as in crude, or poorly put together, esp. with respect to a writing or speech) *adj.*: **incondite**. SEE CRUDE

roughness (as in acrimony or bitterness) *n.*: **asperity**. SEE ACRIMONY

roundabout (way of speaking or writing) *n.*: **circumlocution**. SEE VERBOSITY

(2) **roundabout** (way of speaking or writing) *n.*: **periphrasis**. SEE VERBOSITY

rounded *adj.*: **bulbous**. SEE BULB-SHAPED

route (difficult or painful ...) *n.*: **via dolorosa**. SEE ORDEAL

routine (or ordinary) *adj.*: **banausic**. ▮ Actually, when the question [of what do you do] comes, I quite often don't say "art critic." I say "commercial illustrator." That was once my living. It sounds a decent, **banausic** sort of trade. It causes no trouble. Whereas "art critic" — well, it's one of the very worst classes of person. (Tom Lubbock, *"I'm No Artist But ...,"* Independent, 12-15-1998, p. 10.)

(2) **routine** (as in habit or custom) *n.*: **praxis**. SEE CUSTOM

(3) **routine** (as in ordinary) *adj.*: **quotidian**. SEE MUNDANE

(4) **routine** (as in mundane; everyday) *adj.*: **sublunary**. SEE EARTHLY

rove (from the subject) *v.i.*: **divagate**. SEE DIGRESS

(2) **rove** (aimlessly) *v.i.*: **maunder**. SEE ROAM

rowdy (as in unruly) *adj.*: **indocile**. SEE UNRULY

rub (away or off by friction or scraping) *v.t.*: **abrade**. SEE CHAFE

rubbing (against another something or someone for sexual pleasure) *n.*: **frottage**. ▮ To get a laugh, Tom Green has eaten human hair, slurped milk straight from a cow's udder and engaged in a bout of **frottage** with a dead moose. (Kendall Hamilton, *A Wild and Crazy Guy*, Newsweek, 04-05-1999, p. 68.)

rubbish *n.*: **detritus**. SEE DEBRIS

(2) **rubbish** *n.*: **dross**. SEE TRASH

(3) **rubbish** (study of a culture by examining its ...) *n.*: **garbology**. SEE GARBAGE

(4) **rubbish** (accumulation of ..., esp. prehistoric) *n.*: **midden**. SEE TRASH

(5) **rubbish** *n.*: **offal**. SEE TRASH

ruddy (complexion) *adj.*: **blowzy**. ▮ While she had none of Christine's almost aristocratic delicacy, she was just as good-looking in a **blowzier** way. Even that young — perhaps twenty-five, twenty-six — her face was ruddy from drink, but the ruddiness became her like a rouge. (Karen Siegel, *The Year of the Glamorous Aunts*, The Antioch Review, 06-22-1994, p. 448.)

(2) **ruddy** *adj.*: **florid**. ▮ A short, plump man in a well-tailored suit approaches. He asks if he may help. ... He is standing behind her. She looks at his smooth skin and prosperous, **florid** cheeks. (Sheila Kohler, *The Bride's Secret, [Short Story]*, Redbook, 08-01-1996, p. 132.)

(3) **ruddy** (esp. as in ... cheeks) *adj.*: **rubicund**. SEE ROSY

rude (towards another, often by being insulting or humiliating) *adj.*: **contumelious**. SEE CONTEMPTUOUS

(2) **rude** (comment which seems to be offering sympathy but instead makes the person feel worse, either intentionally or unintentionally) *n.*: **Job's comforter**. SEE TACTLESS

rudeness (in behavior or speech due to arrogance or contempt) *n.*: **contumely**. SEE CONTEMPT

rudimentary *adj.*: **abecedarian**. SEE BASIC

rugged (having a ... and muscular body build) *adj.*: **mesomorphic**. SEE MUSCULAR

ruin (state of spiritual ...) *n.*: **perdition**. SEE DAMNATION

ruinous (mutually ... to both sides) *adj.*: **internecine**. SEE DESTRUCTIVE

rule (as in tenet) *n.*: **shibboleth**. SEE PRINCIPLE

ruler (esp. hereditary) *n.*: **dynast**. ▮ By the 1950s [Gucci's] expensive bags, shoes, belts, scarves, ties and watches had begun to adorn the svelte and wealthy around the world. [In 1995] its best known **dynast**, Maurizio Gucci, was shot in a Milan street. (Author not given, *The Velvet Revolution*, The Economist, 12-14-1996, p. 70.)

(2) **ruler** (who holds great power or sway) *n.*: **potentate**. ▮ Their own way of ruling has a regal feel. The 55-year-old Pachakhan, Governor of three provinces, is an irascible **potentate** who holds court in the time-honored manner, seated on cushions at the far end of a long audience room. ... In a far corner, his civil servants sit on the floor, leafing through papers. (Paul Quinn, *Standing Their Ground — A Family of Regional Royalist* **Potentates** *May Help Take Out Al-qaeda — But Isn't Too Keen on Ceding Power to Kabul*, Time International, 01-28-2002, p. 25.)

(3) **ruler** (as in dictator, esp. in Spanish-speaking

countries) *n*.: **caudillo**. SEE DICTATOR

(4) ruler *n*.: **duce** (Italian). SEE COMMANDER

(5) ruler *n*.: **gerent**. SEE MANAGER

rules (one who demands rigid adherence to ...) *n*.: **martinet**. SEE DISCIPLINARIAN

ruling (or political dominance of men) *n*.: **androcracy**. SEE GOVERNMENT

(2) ruling (by women) *n*.: **gynarchy**. SEE GOVERNMENT

(3) ruling (or political dominance by women) *n*.: **gynocracy**. SEE GOVERNMENT

(4) ruling (as in reigning) *adj*.: **regnant**. SEE REIGNING

rumination (staring at one's belly-button as an aid to ...) *n*.: **omphaloskepsis**. SEE MEDITATION

rummage (about or through) *v.t*.: **fossick** [Australian]. ∎ In a tale to gladden the hearts of all who **fossick** through local art fairs looking for forgotten gems, a work that Boston businessman Edward Puhl bought more than 30 years ago turned out to be Little Regatta, by Paul Klee. The bad news was that it had been stolen. (Belinda Luscombe, *People*, Time, 06-30-1997, p. 79.)

rumor *v.t*.: **bruit**. ∎ Yet [Rockefeller] remained extremely fussy about his food, taking small, sparing bites in a manner that spawned a thousand myths about his ruined system. For years it was **bruited** that he had a standing million-dollar offer for any doctor who could repair his stomach. (Ron Chernow, *Titan*, Random House [1998], p. 322.)

(2) rumor (false ...) *n*.: **furphy** [Australian]. ∎ [Will the Seven Network] change *Witness's* time slot from 9.30 pm Thursdays[?] There's a rough draft of Seven's post-Winter Olympics schedule doing the rounds which places the program at 7.30 pm Thursdays. However, those who have seen the schedule are sceptical. They wonder if it is a **furphy** to confuse the other networks about Seven's plans after the Winter Games. (Jacqueline Lee Lewis, *Wall-to-Wall Reality*, The Daily Telegraph [Sydney, Australia], 01-29-1998, p. 30.)

(3) rumor (or story which is false, often deliberately) *n*.: **canard**. SEE HOAX

(4) rumor (spec. which is false, defamatory and published for political gain right before an election) *n*.: **roorback**. SEE FALSEHOOD

rumormonger *n*.: **quidnunc**. SEE BUSYBODY

rumors (spread false ...) *v.t*.: **asperse**. SEE DEFAME

run (heavily or clumsily) *v.i*.: **galumph**. SEE TROMP

(2) run (along swiftly and easily, used esp. of clouds) *v.i*.: **scud**. SEE MOVE

run off (as in a departure which is unannounced, abrupt, secret or unceremonious) *n*.: **French Leave**. SEE DEPARTURE

run-of-the-mill (as in routine or mechanical) *adj*.: **banausic**. SEE ROUTINE

rundown (and broken-down) *adj*.: **raddled**. SEE WORN-OUT

(2) rundown (as in decrepit) *adj*.: **spavined**. SEE DECREPIT

(3) rundown *adj*.: **tatterdemalion**. SEE RAGGED

runny (having a ... nose) *adj*.: **rheumy**. SEE WATERY

rural *adj*.: **agrestic**. SEE RUSTIC

(2) rural (as in a place which is ... peaceful and simple) *adj*.: **Arcadian**. SEE PASTORAL

(3) rural *adj*.: **bucolic**. SEE RUSTIC

rush in (as in burst in, suddenly or forcibly) *v.i*.: **irrupt**. SEE BURST IN

rushed (as in hasty) *adj*.: **festinate**. SEE HASTY

rushing (as in at top speed) *adv*.: **tanivy**. SEE TOP SPEED

rust (colored) *adj*.: **ferruginous**. ∎ Crystal-bearing cavities ... with the most **ferruginous** material contain the least amount of topaz, which might indicate that these cavities were breached during early stages of topaz crystallization. ... Reddish-brown crystals are reported to fade upon long exposure to daylight. (Peter J. Modreski, *Colorado Topaz*, Rocks & Minerals, 10-01-1996, p. 306.)

rustic *adj*.: **agrestic**. ∎ [Dubuffet's] attachment to rural images from earlier French art, particularly the earthy fields of Millet, is pervasive and obvious; the funniest and most **agrestic** of all his paintings were, undoubtedly, the cows — a snook cocked at Picasso's heroic Spanish bulls. (Robert Hughes, *Art: An Outlaw Who Loved Laws*, Time, 07-26-1993, p. 62.)

(2) rustic *adj*.: **bucolic**. ∎ The N4 turned out to be an idyllic route to travel ... that winds through quaint villages and **bucolic** farmland. (Sheila Rothenberg, *Irresistible Ireland*, USA Today Magazine, 09-01-1996.)

(3) rustic (as in a place which is ... peaceful and simple) *adj*.: **Arcadian**. SEE PASTORAL

rustling (to make a soft ... sound) *v.i*.: **sough**. ∎ I wake to the **soughing** sound of my neighbour's wife sweeping the pavements of leaves outside our homes because cleanliness was ingrained in her as a small girl in Kashmir. (Maureen Messent, *Straight Talking: Muslims Not Our Enemies*, Birmingham Evening Mail, 09-21-2001.)

(2) rustling (or whispering sound) *n.*: **susurrous**. SEE WHISPERING

S

sacred (as in inviolable) *adj.*: **infrangible**. SEE INVIOLABLE

sacred place *n.*: **adytum**. SEE SANCTUM

sacrifice (to kill as a ...) *v.t.*: **immolate**. ▪ So might some Russian of the 3rd millennium A.D. rhapsodize about the ancient sacrificial rites of Stalinism, **immolating** its millions to the God of the Future. (Robert Hughes, *Art: Onward From Olmec: A Monumental Exhibit of Mexico's Art Redeems the "Image Problem,"* Time, 10-15-1990, p. 80.)

(2) sacrifice (large-scale ... and slaughter) *n.*: **hecatomb**. SEE SLAUGHTER

(3) sacrifice (as in offering) *n.*: **oblation**. SEE OFFERING

sacrificial *adj.*: **piacular**. SEE ATONING

sad *adj.*: **tristful**. ▪ Wilbur wittily denounces the so-called confessional poets in his poem, "Flippancies" (90): If fictive music fails your lyre, confess — Though not, of course, to any happiness. So it be **tristful,** tell us what you choose: Hangover, Nixon on the TV news, God's death, the memory of your rocking-horse, Entropy, housework, Buchenwald, divorce, Those damned flamingoes in your neighbor's yard. (Isabella Wai, *Wilbur's Cottage Street, 1953, [Analysis of a Richard Wilbur Poem]*, The Explicator, 03-01-1996, p. 183.)

(2) sad (as in dejected) *adj.*: **chapfallen**. SEE DEJECTED

(3) sad (chronically ..., as in depressed) *adj., n.*: **dysthymic**. SEE DEPRESSED

(4) sad (often regarding something gone) *adj.*: **elegiac**. SEE SORROWFUL

(5) sad (sounds) *adj.*: **plangent**. SEE MOURNFUL

(6) sad (as in sullen or morose) *adj.*: **saturnine**. SEE SULLEN

sadism (as in pleasure derived from witnessing other's misfortunes or suffering) *n.*: **Roman holiday** [This term does not require one's own infliction of the misfortune, as sadism implies. It derives from gladiatorial combats of the ancient Roman circus staged for the entertainment of the audience. The word is similar to the German word "schadenfreude," except that "Roman holiday" implies that one is actually witnessing the event in question. The word also refers to both one's enjoyment from the event or the event itself (SEE SPECTACLE)]. ▪ [A] videotape of [former Tyco International CEO Dennis Kozlowski's] wife's Sardinian birthday party was screened for jurors in New York. Kozlowski was on trial for allegedly looting Tyco of millions, and the video depicts toga-clad models on a lavish set reeking of indulgence at shareholder expense. [C]olumnist Rachel Beck had a **Roman holiday** with the story: ... "[T]he Tyco video was momentous. It had executives live on tape surrounded by such excess." [One presumes that her Roman holiday refers to watching Kozlowski's reaction to the video in the courtroom and neither to Kozlowski on the video itself, nor to the Tyco shareholders watching the video.] (Author not given, *Fox News, Pentagon, Kozlowski and Michael Jackson on List of 10 Worst 2003 PR Gaffes; Ninth Annual PR Blunders List Unveiled*, PR Newswire, 12-16-2003.)

(2) sadism (as in pleasure derived from other's misfortunes, although it does not require one's own infliction of the misfortune, as ... implies) *n.*: **schadenfreude** [German]. ▪ For **schadenfreude** buffs, 1998 has turned out to be one of the most enjoyable of recent years. ... People who actually like to see the tallest poppies chopped down ... have been beside themselves with joy as Bill Gates, Warren Buffett and hundreds of other billionaires have taken their lumps during the recent stock market collapse. (Joe Queenan, *Don't Worry, Be Happy*, Forbes Magazine, 10-12-1998, p. 42.)

(3) sadism *n.*: **algolagnia**. SEE MASOCHISM

sadness *n.*: **dolor** (*adj.*: **dolorous**) ▪ [NBC President Bob] Wright sounds as if he'd be positively relieved if Letterman would pack up [and leave] just so long as he doesn't have to see an unhappy Dave roaming the halls anymore! But this would be a serious mistake for NBC, because despite Dave's **dolor**, there's still no talk show funnier or more exciting than Late Night. (Ken Tucker, *Blues in the Night — David Letterman's Contempt for His Lot in Life After Being Passed Over for the Tonight Show Seems to Grow With Every Late Night*, Entertainment Weekly, 07-17-1992, p. 42.)

(2) sadness (as in inability to experience pleasure or happiness) *n.*: **anhedonia**. SEE UNHAPPINESS

(3) sadness (express ... over) *v.t.*: **bewail**. SEE LAMENT

(4) sadness (as in depression) *n.*: **cafard** [French]. SEE DEPRESSION

(5) sadness (as part of depressed state) *n.*: **dysphoria**. SEE DEPRESSION

(6) sadness (to fret or complain, including as a result of ...) *v.i.*: **repine**. SEE COMPLAIN

(7) sadness (as in world-weariness or sentimental pessimism over the world's problems) *adj.*: **Weltschmerz** [German]. SEE PESSIMISM

safecracker *n.*: **yegg**. ■ From the Greensboro Daily News, Dec. 15-21, 1949 — **Yeggs** managed to cut through a safe at Belk Department Store in downtown Greensboro but an alert policeman walking a beat at 3 a.m. foiled their getaway plans and saved the store $138,000 in U.S. savings bonds. (Author not given, *100 Years Ago [People & Places]*, The News & Record [Piedmont Triad, NC], 12-15-1999.)

safeguard (intended to ... against evil) *adj.*: **apotropaic**. SEE PROTECT

(2) safeguard (against attack or danger) *n.*: **bulwark**. SEE PROTECTION

(3) safeguard *v.t.*: **forfend**. SEE PROTECT

sage (as in wise) *adj.*: **sapient**. SEE WISE

sail (along swiftly and easily, used esp. of clouds) *v.i.*: **scud**. SEE MOVE

saints (worship of ...) *n.*: **hagiolatry**. ■ The concluding chapter [describes] an unprecedented surge in **hagiolatry** and pilgrimage rites connected to the shrines of venerated "saints." (Susan Einbinder, *Sephardi Religious Responses to Modernity [book reviews]*, The Journal of the American Oriental Society, 01-12-1998, p. 109.)

(2) saints (literature dealing with lives of ...) *n.*: **hagiology**. ■ Reflecting on the day DiMaggio's streak finally ended, [Robert W. Creamer] writes, "I used to wonder why there were so many saints in the Christian **hagiology**. ... But in our own secular times Western civilization, proud of its pragmatic Enlightenment, has created its own saints [like DiMaggio]. (Ron Fimrite, *Books*, Sports Illustrated, 07-01-1991, p. 7.)

salacious (as in lustful) *adj.*: **lickerish**. SEE LUSTFUL

(2) salacious (as in lewd or lustful) *adj.*: **lubricious**. SEE LEWD

(3) salacious (as in scandalous or risqué) *adj.*: **scabrous**. SEE SCANDALOUS

salary *n.*: **emolument**. SEE WAGES

saliva (dribbling from the mouth) *v.t., n.*: **slaver**. SEE DROOL

salty *adj.*: **brackish**. ■ The Apalachicola, Carrabelle and St. Marks Rivers meet the salty gulf to form a **brackish** paradise for oysters, shrimp and fish between the mainland and the barrier islands of St. George, St. Vincent and Dog Island. (Craig Walker, *Florida's "Forgotten Coast" Is Unforgettable Experience*, The Washington Times, 08-19-2000, p. E4.)

(2) salty *adj.*: **briny**. ■ When pro football's lowly Philadelphia Eagles soared over the Dallas Cowboys in their season opener, several Eagles players credited an unlikely factor: pickle juice. Seems that before the game Eagles trainer Rick M. Burkholder said the **briny** stuff would help balance his players' electrolytes and prevent dehydration. ... [The Eagles are] still downing the salty stuff. (Eileen Glanton, *Eagle-ade*, Forbes Magazine, 10-16-2000, p. 62a.)

salutation (relating to a ..., where the purpose is to establish a mood of sociability rather than to communicate information or ideas, such as "have a nice day") *adj.*: **phatic**. SEE PLEASANTRIES

sanctimonious (or hypocritical, pious and/or insincere speech) *n.*: **cant**. SEE PIOUS

(2) sanctimonious *adj.*: **Pecksniffian**. SEE SELF-RIGHTEOUS

(3) sanctimonious (hypocritically ...) *adj.*: **Pharisaical**. SEE SELF-RIGHTEOUS

(4) sanctimonious (person, esp. one who hypocritically affects religious peity) *n.*: **Tartuffe** (or **tartuffe**). SEE HYPOCRITE

sanction (officially) *v.t.*: **approbate**. SEE AUTHORIZE

sanctum *n.*: **adytum**. ■ [Elizabeth Cady Stanton wrote:] There is a solitude which each and every one of us has always carried with him, ... the solitude of self. Our inner being which we call ourself, no eye nor touch of man or angel has ever pierced. It is more hidden than the caves of the gnome; the sacred **adytum** of the oracle. ... Such is individual life. (Alice Leuchtag, *Elizabeth Cady Stanton: Freethinker and Radical Revisionist*, The Humanist, 09-19-1996, p. 29.)

sandal (with woven leather strips) *n.*: **huarache**. ■ By now [Tom] Clancy thrillers have evolved into something of a summer ritual, each hitting the bookstores just in time to be snatched up and tossed in the beach bag along with the **huarache** sandals and the aloe vera. (Andrew Ferguson, *Books & Ideas: Tom Clancy's Star Wars Story: His Latest Thriller Has That Patent Insider Feel*, Fortune, 07-18-1988, p. 101.)

sandstorm (esp. in Arabia and Africa) *n.*: **haboob**. ∎ The mission was under strict radio silence. But Col. Guidry said one of his lingering regrets is that he didn't break that silence to relay a message to the helicopter pilots who were flying off the USS Nimitz in the Persian Gulf that might have warned them of the **haboob**. ... One helicopter crew had instrument failures in the swirling sand clouds and aborted the mission. (Michael Hedges, *Disaster Foiled Rescue in Iran; 20 Years Ago, Crash "Lit up the World,"* The Washington Times, 04-25-2000, p. A11.)

sane *adj.*: **compos mentis**. ∎ The pop star who swore at the Duchess of York in front of a global audience on live television was brought up to be a "well-mannered child who never got into trouble," his mother said yesterday. ... [S]he wondered if he had been plied with too much to drink and "was not really **compos mentis**" when he made his outburst. (Sean O'Neill, *He's a Nice Lad, Says Swearing Star's Mum: Pop Singer Who Insulted the Duchess of York on Live TV*, The Daily Telegraph, 11-14-1998, p. 4.)

sanitize (a book or a writing in a prudish manner) *v.t.*: **bowdlerize**. See EDIT

sap (as in weaken or deprive of strength) *v.t.*: **enervate**. See DEBILITATE

sarcastic (bitingly ...) *adj.*: **mordant**. ∎ Dole's darts have injected about the only amusement there has been in this presidential campaign — but far from being rewarded, he has been castigated. Dole is called sarcastic, sardonic, **mordant** and, most often, mean. People seem to think his biting wit bares too many teeth, prompting even his handlers to debate whether to "let Dole be Dole." (Neal Gabler, *No Fooling — Dole is a Funny Guy*, Newsday, 03-25-1996, p. A29.)

sashay (about so as to attract attention) *v.i.*: **tittup**. See STRUT

Satan *n.*: **Beelzebub**. ∎ But Manson's well-publicized Church of Satan membership has helped fuel rumors of onstage animal and virgin sacrifices ... though he evidently no more believes in a personal

Beelzebub than a personal Jesus. (Chris Willman, *Manson Mmmbad: Out From Under Hanson's Feel-Good Rock Crawls the Blasphemous Marilyn Manson, Mom and Dad's Worst Nightmare*, Entertainment Weekly, 07-25-1997, p. 36.)

satiate (to the point of excess, esp. things sweet) *v.t.*: **cloy**. ∎ If the seasonal sweetness is starting to **cloy**, try a tart taste of "Bah! Humbug!" the holiday family show from the Imaginary Theatre Company. The musical spoof by Jack Herrick upholds Dickens' message of generosity and caring, but it's updated with engaging songs, slapstick humor and contemporary references. (Judith Newmark, *"Bah! Humbug!" Spoofs Dickens, Shares Theme*, St. Louis Post-Dispatch, 12-16-1996, p. 2B.)

satirize (esp. by ridiculing or making fun of someone) *n.*, *v.t.*: **pasquinade**. ∎ Joseph Biden, the Democratic senator from Delaware, lost his credibility during the 1988 presidential race when he was caught plagiarizing a speech. (Both [Gary] Hart and Biden were **pasquinaded** in other jokes: What's the title of Gary Hart's new book? Six Inches From the Presidency. Did you hear Joe Biden was writing his autobiography? It's called Iacocca.) (Alan Dundes, *What's So Funny? [Political Humor]*, Mother Jones, 01-11-1996, p. 18.)

satisfaction *n.*: **eudemonia** (or **eudaemonia**). SEE HAPPINESS

(2) satisfaction (as in happiness) *n.*: **felicity**. SEE HAPPINESS

(3) satisfaction (delusive or illusory) *n.*: **fool's paradise**. SEE ILLUSION

(4) satisfaction (from witnessing other's misfortunes) *n.*: **Roman holiday**. SEE SADISM

(5) satisfaction (from other's misfortunes) *n.*: **schadenfreude** [German]. SEE SADISM

satisfy (as in appease) *v.t.*: **dulcify**. SEE APPEASE

saturate (as in soak) *v.t.*: **imbrue**. SEE SOAK

saucy (girl) *n.*, *adj.*: **hoyden**. SEE TOMBOY

sausage *n.*: **banger** [British]. ∎ The latest notch on the commission's Fair Trading Act enforcement belt is a meaty settlement with the Thorndon New World supermarket after its beef sausages were found to have been made from mutton. Commission chairman John Belgrave is promising to sniff out any more bent **bangers**. (Author not given, *Loose Change*, Sunday Star Times [New Zealand], 09-03-2000, p. 1.)

savage (as in untamed) *adj.*: **ferine**. See UNTAMED

savor (the taste of) *v.t.*: **degust**. ∎ The De Pelikaan tea and coffee room, in Zutphen, is a haven where one can **degust** to one's fill and then amble out with a giftwrapped package for one's love, or merely for the love of fine tea and coffee. (Jonathan Bell, *A. Garsen Coffee/Tea Retailer Opens De Pelikaan Tea Room*, Tea & Coffee Trade Journal, 12-01-1990.)

savory *adj.*: **sapid**. See TASTY

say (as in declare) *v.t.*: **asseverate**. See DECLARE

saying *n.*: **apothegm**. ∎ The old **apothegm** reiterated by those who reject stricter gun-control laws takes on a different resonance if it's paraphrased this way: "Guns don't kill children — children kill children." (Author not given, *The Death of Innocence?* Newsweek, 04-03-2000, p. 18.)

(2) saying (witty or clever ... or line) *n.*: **bon mot**. See LINE

(3) saying (at the start of a literary piece setting forth a theme or message) *n.*: **epigraph**. See QUOTATION

(4) saying (pithy ...) *n.*: **gnome** (*adj:* **gnomic**). See CATCHPHRASE

(5) saying (as in phrase or expression) *n.*: **locution**. See PHRASE

sayings (given to stating ..., esp. in a moralizing way) *adj.*: **sententious**. See APHORISTIC

scan (quick ..., as in glance) *n.*: **coup d'oeil** [French]. See GLANCE

scandal (as in dishonor to one's reputation) *n.*: **blot (or stain) on one's escutcheon** *idiom*. See DISHONOR

scandalmonger *n.*: **quidnunc**. See BUSYBODY

scandalous *adj.*: **flagitious**. ∎ Tories and Liberals vied for the support of the rich, and the more or less discreet sale of honours became the recognised means of securing that support. That happy arrangement came unstuck when Lloyd George sold honours in a particularly **flagitious** way to some exceptionally dubious personages. (Geoffrey Wheatcroft, *Wanted: A Better Way to Fund Our Political Parties*, Independent on Sunday, 07-25-1999, p. 24.)

(2) scandalous *adj.*: **scabrous**. ∎ Last week NBC Nightly News gravely confirmed a Drudge Report item that Clinton and Lewinsky once had sex after he attended Easter services. No big deal. More **scabrous** stuff than that bounces regularly from cyberland to Jay Leno without stopping for the niceties of confirmation. (Richard Lacayo, *Nation: The Politics Of Yuck*, Time, 09-14-1998, p. 40.)

scanty *n.*: **exiguous**. See MEAGER

(2) scanty (as in meager) *adj.*: **mingy**. See MEAGER

scar *n.*: **cicatrix**. ∎ Today Laumann's leg, after seven operations, has a principal scar running from mid-calf to ankle, from which small tributaries of **cicatrix** extend. (Michael Farber, *Battle Scarred Canadian Rower Silken Laumann Has Fought Through Pain — in and Out of Competition*, Sports Illustrated, 07-21-1996, p. 34.)

scare *v.t.*: **affright**. ∎ They erupt like indignant metal jungle birds, and they whoop all night. They make American cities sound like lunatic rain forests, all the wildlife **affrighted**, violated, outraged, shrieking. Like the hungry infant's cry, the car alarm is designed to be unignorable — that is, unendurable. (Lance Morrow, *The Thing That Screams Wolf — What Thief Has Ever Been Deterred by Those Unendurable Car Alarms? They're a Crime in Themselves*, Time, 06-24-1991, p. 46.)

scared (as in cowardly) *adj.*: **pusillanimous**. See COWARDLY

(2) scared *adj.*: **tremulous**. See FEARFUL

scatter (tending to ... or break up) *adj.*: **fissiparous**. See BREAK UP

scatterbrained (person) *n.*: **flibbertigibbet**. See FLIGHTY

scavenge (about or through) *v.t.*: **fossick** [Australian]. See RUMMAGE

scene (as in setting or physical environment) *n.*: **mise en scène** [French; putting on stage]. See SETTING

scheme (secret ... or group of plotters) *n.*: **cabal**. See PLOT

schemers (group of ...) *n.*: **camarilla**. See ADVISORS

scheming (and evil or shameless woman) *n.*: **jezebel** (sometimes cap.). See WOMAN

(2) scheming (esp. underhanded) *n.*: **jiggery-pokery**. See TRICKERY

schizophrenic (as in two-faced) *adj.*: **Janus-faced**. See TWO-FACED

schmaltzy *adj.*: **mawkish**. See SENTIMENTAL

scholar (as in lover of learning) *n.*: **philomath**. ∎ Thirty years earlier, [Benjamin] Franklin's fellow **philomath** Nathaniel Ames had written in his widely read New England almanac for 1758: "The curious have observ'd that the progress of humane literature (like the sun) is from the East to the West; thus it has traveled through Asia and Europe, and now is at the eastern shore of America." ... America's rising sun was then the symbol not only of a new political system but of a new civilization. (Thomas Wendel, *America's Rising Sun; Two Hundred Years Ago*, National Review, 07-13-1984.)

(2) scholar (as in person who is very knowledgeable in many areas) *n.*: **polymath**. [This word and *philomath* are fairly close synonyms and in most instances a person who is one will likely be the other as well. The distinction is that a philomath is one who loves the learning process, while a polymath is one who already is knowledgeable in many areas.] ∎ A self-educated **polymath** endowed with formidable charm and considerable intellect, [Benjamin] Franklin quickly became the leading figure in colonial politics, literature, science, and social reform. (Alan Taylor, *For the Benefit of Mr. Kite*, The New Republic, 03-19-2001.)

scholarly (woman with ... or literary interests) *n.*: **bluestocking**. SEE WOMAN

(2) scholarly (of a ... but pedantic word or term) *adj.*: **inkhorn**. SEE PEDANTIC

(3) scholarly (write or speak in a ... manner, often used in a derogatory fashion) *v.i.*: **lucubrate**. SEE DISCOURSE

(4) scholarly (person, esp. in intellectual or literary circles) *n.*: **mandarin**. SEE INFLUENTIAL

scholarship (excess striving for or preoccupation with ...) *n.*: **epistemophilia**. SEE KNOWLEDGE

(2) scholarship (pretense of ... which is actually superficial) *n.*: **sciolism**. SEE SUPERFICIAL

schoolteacher *n.*: **pedagogue**. SEE TEACHER

scold *v.t.*: **flay**. SEE CRITICIZE

(2) scold *v.t.*: **objurgate**. SEE CRITICIZE

scolding (as in criticism) *n.*: **animadversion** (*v.t.*: **animadvert**). SEE CRITICISM

(2) scolding (woman, as in shrew) *n.*: **harridan**. SEE SHREW

(3) scolding (in speech) *n.*: **philippic**. SEE TIRADE

(4) scolding (woman, as in shrew) *n.*: **termagant**. SEE SHREW

(5) scolding (woman who is domineering and ...) *n.*: **virago**. SEE SHREW

(6) scolding (woman, as in shrew) *n.*: **vixen**. SEE SHREW

(7) scolding (woman) *n.*: **Xanthippe**. SEE SHREW

scorn (treat with ...) *v.t.*: **contemn**. ∎ Schopenhauer defined the arrogance no great man is without — the one that **contemns** the views of his contemporaries and lets him, undisturbed, create what they censure, and despise what they praise. (John Simon, *The Spanish Prisoner [movie reviews]*, National Review, 05-04-1998, p. 59.)

(2) scorn *n.*: **misprision** (*v.t.*: **misprize**). SEE DISDAIN

(3) scorn (being subject to ..., esp. public) *n.*: **obloquy**. SEE ABUSE

scornful (towards another, often by being insulting or humiliating) *adj.*: **contumelious**. SEE CONTEMPTUOUS

(2) scornful *adj.*: **opprobrious** (*n.*: **opprobrium**). SEE CONTEMPTUOUS

scorpion *n.*: **arachnid**. ∎ I was doing 70 when Brian, a decorous and soft-spoken man, politely informed Claudia that a black scorpion was crawling up her bare leg. Aaaaaah! I turned hard and braked on dirt. Brian executed the intruder, garnering new respect from the womenfolk. There was no point speculating how the **arachnid** had joined us. (Alan Behr, *Yucatan Peninsula/A Coastal Warming in Mexico*, Newsday, 10-06-1996, p. D13.)

scoundrel (or rascal) *n.*: **scapegrace**. ∎ Dissolute and profligate, elegant and hypnotically charming, Silas [Ruthvyn] has squandered vast sums of money, married a barmaid, committed the usual unspeakable crimes, possibly even murder. ... [His brother Austin], though a **scapegrace** [himself] in his younger days, could be guilty of such devilry, and he longs to restore the family name. (Michael Dirda, *A Classic of Terror — and Unsettling Ambiguity*, The Washington Post, 02-01-2004.)

(2) scoundrel (or unprincipled person) *n.*: **blackguard**. ∎ It should be obvious what the problem is if you are ever to win an election in a democracy when you think the other party is a crowd of buffoons in thrall to a cabal of **blackguards**. To begin with, it means that your campaign discourse must be designed not to persuade voters, but to deceive them. Worse, it precludes your ever examining your opponents' premises, arguments and conclusions in good faith. (Frank Wilson, *Misunderestimating May Cost You*, The Philadelphia Inquirer, 11-14-04, p. C5.)

(2) scoundrel (or thief) *n*.: **gonif**, **ganef**, or **goniff** [Yiddish]. SEE THIEF

(3) scoundrel *n*.: **rapscallion**. SEE RASCAL

scream (like a cat in heat) *v.i*.: **caterwaul**. SEE SCREECH

screaming (as in shrill, sound made by bagpipes) *n*.: **skirl**. SEE BAGPIPES

screech (like a cat in heat) *v.i*.: **caterwaul**. ▪ [Singer James Brown] doesn't bounce back from those splits quite so fast anymore. He still knows, however, how to **caterwaul** as if someone had just dropped an anvil on his bunion and make it sound not only passionate but musical. (Ralph Novak, *Picks & Pans*, People, 11-10-1986, p. 9.)

screw up (esp. a golf shot) *v.t*., *n*.: **foozle**. SEE BOTCH

sea (of or pertaining to the ocean or ...) *adj*.: **pelagic**. ▪ Aboard the Shogun, a 90-foot mother ship, we would sail southward from San Diego to the rich fishing grounds off the Baja Peninsula and, using only flytackle, attempt to capture **pelagic** beasts that are usually the quarry of big-game fishermen armed with giant reels and trolling rods: striped marlin, yellowfin tuna and, most elusive of all, wahoo. (Philip Caputo, *California Dreamin' — Baja Style, [Flyfishing]*, Sports Afield, 11-01-1994, p. 102.)

sealed (completely ...) *adj*.: **hermetic**. ▪ Today's [college] recruiting showpieces are instead mammoth training complexes, combination indoor practice facilities and weight rooms situated a few steps from the dorms, allowing football players to exist in a sort of **hermetic** theme park. (Alexander Wolff, *Football Dorms*, Sports Illustrated, 10-14-1991, p. 52.)

search (about or through, as in rummage) *v.t*.: **fossick** [Australian]. SEE RUMMAGE

seas (supremacy on the ...) *n*.: **thalassocracy**. SEE SUPREMACY

seashore (of or on a ...) *n*., *adj*.: **littoral**. SEE SHORE

seclusion (social ...) *n*.: **purdah**. ▪ [Hilary Clinton's] wild, subversive earnestness has been put on the back burner. She has been in **purdah**, taken the veil, donned the [robe] of political invisibility, played second string to her husband, and spent her days like a Victorian heroine on some White House couch. (John O'Sullivan, *She's Baaack! [Hillary Rodham Clinton]*, National Review, 11-10-1997, p. 4.)

second (as in, in a ..., as in very shortly) *n*.: **trice** (as in, in a trice). SEE QUICKLY

second fiddle *n*.: **deuteragonist**. SEE SECONDARY

second-class (as in acting subservient as opposed to leading) *adj*.: **sequacious**. SEE SUBSERVIENT

secondary (actor to the protagonist in classical Greek drama) *n*.: **deuteragonist** [now used in the sense of one who plays second fiddle or serves as a foil to another]. ▪ Jennifer Paterson became famous as half of television's most improbable culinary duo [as a star of the British TV show, Two Fat Ladies]. She cut such an extraordinary figure that it was easy to overlook the fact that she was, for most of her life, a **deuteragonist** rather than a main player. Her wit was considerable but it was reactive rather than initiatory. (Jonathan Meades, *Before She Was Fat*, The Times [London], 09-02-2001.)

(2) secondary (phenomenon which accompanies or results from another) *n*.: **epiphenomenon**. SEE PHENOMENON

(3) secondary (rank, esp. in the military) *n*.: **subaltern**. SEE SUBORDINATE

secrecy *n*.: **hugger-mugger**. ▪ [Before George W. Bush could name Richard Cheney as his running mate], a bit of **hugger-mugger** had to be carried out. Cheney, a long-time resident of Texas, had to sneak over to Wyoming, where he once carpetbagged as a congressman, to change his voter registration to dodge Constitutional strictures against two candidates from the same state sharing a ticket. (Author not given, *Read It and Veep*, The St. Petersburg Times [Russia], 08-01-2000.)

(2) secrecy (as in, in concealment) *adv*.: **doggo** (esp. as in "lying doggo"; slang). SEE CONCEALMENT

secret (most ... parts, thoughts or places) *n*.: **penetralia**. ▪ The Elgin marbles rate among the greatest treasures of art history. [They are on traveling display in a museum in huge cardboard boxes.] The installation is also strange because it confounds the experience of cowering through the **penetralia** of some priceless archaeological site with the experience of a dense warehouse full of packed fridges. (Robert Nelson, *Boxes Have Lost Their Marbles*, The Age [Melbourne], 12-14-1994, p. 23.)

(2) secret (as in, of or relating to a court, legislative body or other group that meets in private, and often makes decisions which are harsh or arbitrary) *adj*.: **star chamber**. SEE CLOSED-DOOR

(3) secret (codes hidden in various forms of communication) *n*.: **steganography**. SEE CODES

secret name *n*.: **cryptonym**. SEE CODE NAME

secretary (as in one who takes dictation) *n.*: **amanuensis**. ∎ When it came time to take the bar exam, Bartlett petitioned the New York Board of Law Examiners for special arrangements [due to an alleged reading disability]. She wanted unlimited time for the test, access to food and drink, a private room and the use of an **amanuensis** to record her answers. ... After her third failure [of the bar exam], she sued the board. (Ruth Shalit, *Why Johnny Can't Read, Write or Sit Still*, The New Republic, 08-25-1997.)

secretly (as in privately) *adj.*: **in petto** (Italian). SEE PRIVATELY

section (as in portion) *n.*: **moiety**. SEE PORTION

sedate (as in desensitize) *v.t.*: **hyposensitize**. SEE DESENSITIZE
(2) sedate (as in to dull or deaden) *v.t.*: **narcotize**. SEE DEADEN

sedative (as in something which induces forgetfulness or oblivion of pain, suffering, or sorrow) *n.*: **nepenthe**. SEE NARCOTIC
(2) sedative (as in sleep-inducing) *adj.*: **soporific**. SEE SLEEP-INDUCING

seduce (as in bewitch or enchant) *v.t.*: **ensorcell** (or **ensorcel**). SEE ENCHANT

seducer (man who is a ... of women) *n.*: **Lothario**. SEE PLAYBOY

seduction (as in lure or temptation) *n.*: **Lorelei call**. SEE LURE

seductive (and charming woman) *n.*: **Circe**. SEE ENCHANTRESS
(2) seductive (as in tempting) *adj.*: **siren**. SEE TEMPTING

see (something which may be difficult to discern) *v.t.*: **descry**. SEE PERCEIVE

see-through (as in sheer or transparent) *adj.*: **diaphanous**. SEE TRANSPARENT
(2) see-through (as in sheer or transparent) *adj.*: **gossamer**. SEE TRANSPARENT

seedy (as in unkempt or slovenly) *adj.*: **frowzy**. SEE MESSY

seeing (everything ... in one view) *adj.*: **panoptic**. SEE VISIBLE

segment (as in portion) *n.*: **moiety**. SEE PORTION

segregate (from others, as in isolate) *v.t.*: **enisle**. SEE ISOLATE
(2) segregate (as in consider separately) *v.t.*: **prescind** (generally as in "prescind from"). SEE ISOLATE

segregated (as in against the world) *adv., adj.*: **contra mundum** [Latin]. SEE AGAINST THE WORLD
(2) segregated (as in things which cannot be mixed) *adj.*: **immiscible**. SEE INCOMPATIBLE

seize (for oneself without permission) *v.t.*: **expropriate**. ∎ As Iraq lays claim to Kuwait, so might Syria, Turkey, and Iran decide it's time to **expropriate** Iraqi territory they believe falls more naturally within their borders. (Lee Smith, *War Special Report: What Comes Next?* Fortune, 02-11-1991, p. 36.)
(2) seize (as in usurp) *v.t.*: **accroach**. SEE USURP
(3) seize (for oneself without right) *v.t.*: **arrogate**. SEE CLAIM
(4) seize (property to compel payment of debts) *v.t.*: **distrain**. SEE CONFISCATE

seizing (adapted for ..., esp. a tail) *adj.*: **prehensile**. SEE GRASPING

seizure (forcible ... of another's property) *n.*: **rapine**. SEE LOOTING

select (as in choice or excellent) *adj.*: **eximious**. SEE EXCELLENT

self-assurance (and poise) *n.*: **aplomb**. SEE CONFIDENCE
(2) self-assurance (excess ...) *adj.*: **hubris**. SEE ARROGANCE

self-confidence (and poise) *n.*: **aplomb**. SEE CONFIDENCE
(2) self-confidence (excess ..) *adj.*: **hubris**. SEE ARROGANCE

self-control (as in marked by simplicity, frugality, self-restraint and/or ...) *adj.*: **Lacedaemoninan**. SEE SPARTAN
(2) self-control (as in moderation) *n.*: **sophrosyne**. SEE MODERATION

self-controlled *adj.*: **phlegmatic**. SEE EVEN-TEMPERED

self-delusion (living in a world of ..., with a glorified or romanticized conception of oneself, as a result of boredom in one's life) *n.*: **Bovarism** [derives from principal character in the novel *Madame Bovary* by Gustave Flaubert]. ∎ If she concentrates solely on fantasies and the things she can't have, it's because neurosis has cut her off from reality. More than a melancholic form of affectivity, **Bovarism** is a malady of perception. (Bertrand Poirot-Delpech, *Flaubert's Fool*, Manchester Guardian Weekly, 08-30-1998, p. 13.)

self-denial (as in person who practices extreme ..., esp. for spiritual improvement) *n., adj.*: **ascetic**. SEE AUSTERITY

self-discipline (person who practices extreme ..., esp. for spiritual improvement) *n., adj.*: **ascetic**. SEE AUSTERITY

(2) **self-discipline** (as in marked by simplicity, frugality, self-restraint and/or ...) *adj.*: **Lacedae-moninan**. SEE SPARTAN

self-esteem *n.*: **amour-propre** [French]. ∎ [Actor Michael] Douglas, with Fatal Attraction and Basic Instinct behind him, knows all about playing male victimization without total loss of **amour-propre**. (Richard Schickel, *The Arts & Media/Cinema: Sexual Harassment is a Good Subject for Legal Briefs*, Time International, 02-06-1995, p. 58.)

self-generated *adj.*: **autogenous**. ∎ With the support of the Korea Employer's Federation, the advocates maintain that a leased labor law should be legislated. They claim that leased work has been created by the **autogenous** needs of the labor market — demand and supply. (Kim Young-Ock, *The Unstable Transition of Female Employment and Related Policy Tasks*, Contemporary Women's Issues Database, 01-01-1996, p. 107.)

self-gratification (as in masturbation) *n.*: **auto-erotism**. SEE MASTURBATION

(2) **self-gratification** (as in masturbation) *n.*: **onanism**. SEE MASTURBATION

self-identity *n.*: **ipseity**. ∎ American military exports to World War II Britain included ... the worst attitudes and fatal repercussions of racism. Britain reeled at such prejudice. John Bull, the personification of their **ipseity**, knew precious little of Uncle Sam, our father figure, let alone Jim Crow, his seedy Southern cousin. All that slave stuff in America, it was thought, surely ended with the Civil War. (Paul Dean, *Fighting Racism With a Segregated Army [Book Review]*, Los Angeles Times, 03-13-1988.)

self-important (as in pompous) *adj.*: **flatulent**. SEE POMPOUS

(2) **self-important** (person or official) *n.*: **high**

muck-a-muck. SEE BIGWIG

(3) **self-important** *adj.*: **hoity-toity**. SEE POMPOUS

(4) **self-important** (person or official) *n.*: **panjan-drum**. SEE BIGWIG

self-indulgence (esp. from eating or drinking too much) *n.*: **crapulence**. SEE INDULGENCE

self-interest (making an argument appealing to one's monetary ...): **argumentum ad crume-nam** [Latin]. SEE ARGUMENT

self-opinion (unduly high ..., esp. of a little man) *n.*: **cockalorum**. SEE EGOTISTIC

self-produced *adj.*: **autogenous**. SEE SELF-GENER-ATED

(2) **self-proclaimed** *adj.*: **soi-disant** [French]. SEE SELF-STYLED

self-regard (unduly high ..., esp. of a little man) *n.*: **cockalorum**. SEE EGOTISTIC

self-reliant (country or region) *n.*: **autarky**. SEE SELF-SUFFICIENT

self-respect *n.*: **amour-propre** [French]. SEE SELF-ESTEEM

self-restraint (as in person who practices extreme ..., esp. for spiritual improvement) *n., adj.*: **ascetic**. SEE AUSTERITY

(2) **self-discipline** (as in marked by simplicity, frugality, self-restraint and/or ...) *adj.*: **Lacedae-moninan**. SEE SPARTAN

(3) **self-restraint** (as in moderation) *n.*: **sophro-syne**. SEE MODERATION

self-righteous (hypocritically ...) *adj.*: **Pecksnif-fian** [after Seth Pecksniff, a character in the Charles Dickens novel *Martin Chuzzlewit*]. ∎ George magazine (founded and edited by JFK Jr.) [showed] a picture of Kennedy apparently nude, "artfully seated [showing] only limbs, chest, and face as he ponders a dangling apple," in the words of the AP. ... Moreover, in the same issue of his magazine, Mr. Kennedy was delivering a **Pecksniffian** lecture to assorted cousins for licentious behavior. (William F. Buckley, Jr., *The Honored Guest*, National Review, 06-14-1999.)

(2) **self-righteous** (hypocritically ...) *adj.*: **Phari-saical** [as in characteristic of the Pharisees, an ancient Jewish sect]. ∎ What a dreadful thing, that a mother was so poor that she was inclined to abort one of her children. Couldn't she be helped? The

pro-abortion people [muttered] that it was an outrageous breach of medical confidentiality that the story should come out at all: a somewhat **Pharisaical** comment in the light of skillful media manipulation from the same sources when the case suited them. (Mary Kenny, *Death Before Birth*, National Review, 09-30-1996.)

(3) self-righteous (speech) *n.*: **cant**. SEE PIOUS

(4) self-righteous (person, esp. one who hypocritically affects religious peity) *n.*: **Tartuffe** (or **tartuffe**). SEE HYPOCRITE

self-styled *adj.*: **soi-disant** [French]. ▮ It is such a bloody bore when the weather is so hot and one's **soi-disant** boyfriend refuses to go anywhere nice with you. (Helen Fielding, *Bridget Jones' Diary*, Viking [1998], p. 124.)

self-sufficient (country or region) *n.*: **autarky**. ▮ But in an interdependent world well into the Third Industrial Revolution, as the latest explosive advances in technology and communications are sometimes known, **autarky** and isolation are no longer an option. Just ask the Albanians. (Strobe Talbott, *WORLD: America Abroad: And Now For the Sequels*, Time, 09-09-1991, p. 44.)

self-taught (person) *n.*: **autodidact** (*adj.*: **autodidactic**). ▮ The only way to master anything is **autodidactically**. Lessons are just for the companionship. (Erik Tarloff, *The Man Who Wrote the Book*, Crown [2000], p. 104.)

selfhood (as in self-identity) *n.*: **ipseity**. SEE SELF-IDENTITY

sell (museum items in order to purchase more) *v.t.*: **deaccession**. ▮ In 1990, to pay for the acquisition of a 300-piece collection of minimalist and conceptual art owned by Count Giuseppe Panza di Biumo, Krens **deaccessioned** three works from [the Guggenheim] museum's permanent collection. (Author not given, *Object Lesson on Museums' Future*, The Washington Post, 11-02-2001, p. T54.)

seller (esp. of quack medicines) *n.*: **mountebank**. SEE HUCKSTER

sellout (relating to a ... of one's soul to the devil) *adj.*: **Mephistophelean** [after the devil in the Faust legend to whom Faust sold his soul]. ▮ The unwritten clause [in the contract pursuant to which boxer Sonny Liston obtained a manager], the **Mephistophelean** clause, the only clause that mattered, stipulated silently that Sonny now belonged, body and soul to [the Mob]. (Nick Tosches, *The Devil and Sonny Liston*, Little Brown [2000], p. 108.)

semblance (as in representation) *n.*: **simulacrum**. SEE REPRESENTATION

sendoff (act of giving a ...) *n.*: **valediction**. SEE FAREWELL

senility (that comes with old age) *n.*: **caducity**. SEE OLD AGE

seniors (of or relating to ..., esp. women) *adj.*: **blue-rinse**. SEE ELDERLY

sense of humor (person who has no ...) *n.*: **agelast**. SEE HUMORLESS

(2) sense of humor (having a ..., as in ability or tendency to laugh) *n.:* **risibility**. SEE LAUGH

sense (that something is going to occur) *n.*: **presentiment**. SEE PREMONITION

sensible (as in logical) *adj.*: **ratiocinative**. SEE LOGICAL

sensuous (and luxurious) *adj.*: **sybaritic**. SEE LUXURIOUS

sentencing (of convicted persons, spec. burning of heretics at the stake) *n.*: **auto-da-fe**. SEE EXECUTION

sentimental (in an excessive or contrived way) *adj.*: **bathetic**. ▮ Right now, aside from **bathetic** song tributes and the mastications of the self-loathing news media, no one knows what to do about [Princess] Diana's death; the public, for its part, is mesmerized by its operatic grief. (Bruce Handy, *After Princess Diana: I Can't Laugh Without You: With Comedy and Mourning, Timing Is Everything*, Time, 09-22-1997, p. 34.)

(2) sentimental (overly ...) *adj.*: **mawkish**. ▮ Where great passion leaves off and **mawkishness** begins, I'm not sure. But our tendency to scoff at the possibility of the former and to label genuine and profound feelings as maudlin makes it difficult to enter the realm of gentleness required to understand the story of Francesca Johnson and Robert Kincaid. (Robert James Waller, *The Bridges of Madison County*, Warner Books [1992], p. xii.)

sentimentality (which is excessive or contrived) *n.*: **bathos**. ▮ A weepie, in movie-speak, is a film that relies on a strong dose of sentimentality for its forward momentum. ... But what of a weepie that doesn't work? ... ["Autumn in New York"] manages to pull out all the mawkish stops without prompting in its viewers so much as a half-hearted sniffle. [The movie is], equal parts perversity and **bathos**. (Adina Hoffman, *An Affair to Forget*, Jerusalem Post, 01-12-2001, p. 15.)

separate (into thin layers) *v.i.*: **delaminate**. ▪ With many [paint] strippers, the softened paint finish begins to swell. This swelling produces tension forces that cause the paint layers to **delaminate** from one another and the wood or metal you are refinishing. (Tim Carter, *Paint Strippers Require You to Read Label, Be Patient*, Minneapolis Star Tribune, 05-22-1997, p. 7.)

(2) separate (into component parts) *v.i.*: **disaggregate**. ▪ Torre believes that unless educational programs which are designed for Hispanics are redesigned with Puerto Ricans specifically in mind, the needs of Puerto Ricans students will be ignored every time. ... "We [Puerto Ricans have] been made 'Hispanics.' We need to **disaggregate** the data by subgroup. Otherwise the needs of the subgroups will not be met," she says. (Author not given, *Reaching Out, But In Which Direction? The Future Focus of Academic*, Black Issues In Higher Education, 02-20-1997.)

(3) separate (state or quality of being ... , as in different, from others) *n.*: **alterity**. SEE DIFFERENT

(4) separate (esp. from one's accustomed environment) *v.t.*: **deracinate**. SEE UPROOT

(5) separate (from others, as in isolate) *v.t.*: **enisle**. SEE ISOLATE

(6) separate (tending to ... or disintegrate) *adj.*: **fissiparous**. SEE BREAK UP

(7) separate (out, as in consider separately) *v.t.*: **prescind** (generally as in "prescind from"). SEE ISOLATE

separated *adj.*: **cloven**. SEE SPLIT
(2) separated (from outside influences) *adj.*: **hermetic**. SEE SEALED

separateness (as in that quality which makes one thing different from any other) *n.*: **haeccity**. SEE INDIVIDUALITY

separating *adj.*: **diacritical**. SEE DISTINGUISHING
(2) separating (act of ... into parts) *n.*: **fission**. SEE SPLITTING

separation *n.*: **diremption**. ▪ Sin is a breach in one's relationship to others, to the creation and to God [and evil] makes the re-establishment of the relationship and healing appear impossible. The bond is forever broken. That is why evil is so chilling. Its victory results in complete **diremption**, the loss of all hope of relationship, atonement, or redemption. (Andrew Kimbrell, *Confronting Evil*, Tikkun, 11-01-2001.)

(2) separation (often from as in division, within a group or union) *n.*: **scission**. SEE SPLIT

sequence *n.*: **consecution**. ▪ Subdivide each topic into studies; each study into lessons; each lesson into specific facts and formulae. Let the child proceed step by step to master each one of these separate parts, and at last he will have covered the entire ground. ... Thus emphasis is put upon the logical subdivisions and **consecutions** of subject matter. (Judy W. Kugelmass, *Educating Children With Learning Disabilities in Foxfire Classrooms*, Journal of Learning Disabilities, 11-01-1995, p. 545.)

(2) sequence (as in chain or link) *n.*: **catenation** (*v.t.*: **catenate**). SEE CHAIN

serene *adj.*: **equable**. ▪ But, as the seventh youngest of the nine children born to Jim and Jocelyn Rafter in the bleak copper [Australian] mining town of Mount Isa, [U.S. Open champion Patrick Rafter] was, as he says, "kept level" in the matter of humility, though he acknowledges a temper lurks beneath that **equable** exterior. (Ronald Atkin, *The Interview — Patrick Rafter; Tennis: Straight Down the Line*, Independent on Sunday, 08-29-1999, p. 14.)

(2) serene (as in a place which is ..., rustic and simple) *adj.*: **Arcadian**. SEE PASTORAL

serenity (as in peace of mind) *n.*: **heartsease**. SEE PEACE OF MIND

series (as in chain or link) *n.*: **catenation** (*v.t.*: **catenate**). SEE CHAIN

serious (as in critical, stage or period) *n., adj.*: **climacteric**. SEE CRITICAL

sermonizing (relating to or in the nature of ..., esp. on a practical, rather than theological, matter) *adj.*: **homiletic**. SEE PREACHING

servant (as in aide or assistant) *n.*: **factotum**. SEE ASSISTANT

servile (to behave towards in a ... manner) *v.t.*: **bootlick**. SEE KOWTOW
(2) servile (to act in a ... manner) *v.i.*: **genuflect**. SEE KNEEL
(3) servile (person) *n.*: **lickspittle**. SEE SYCOPHANT
(4) servile (to be ... towards) *v.i.*: **truckle**. SEE KOWTOW

servitude (as in forced work for little or no pay) *n*.: **corvee**. ∎ For what makes a woman is a specific social relation to a man, a relation that we have previously called servitude, a relation which implies personal and physical obligation as well as economic obligation ("forced residence," domestic **corvee**, conjugal duties, unlimited production of children, etc.), a relation which lesbians escape by refusing to become or to stay heterosexual. (Jacob Hale, *Are Lesbians Women?* Hypatia, 03-01-1996, p. 94.)

(2) servitude (free from ...) *v.t*.: **manumit**. SEE EMANCIPATE

(3) servitude *n*.: **thralldom**. SEE BONDAGE

set (close together, side-by-side or in proper order) *v.t*.: **collocate**. SEE PLACE

set aside (as in consider separately) *v.t*.: **prescind** (generally as in "prescind from"). SEE ISOLATE

set apart (from others, as in isolate) *v.t*.: **enisle**. SEE ISOLATE

setting (or physical environment) *n*.: **mise en scène** [French; putting on stage]. ∎ [T]he blighted streets and conveniently vacant buildings way east of Bunker Hill are enjoying a newfound stardom. Directors, production designers and location managers turn to them, drawn by all the built-in glamour and elaborate, decaying detail, for a ready-made, post-apocalyptic **mise en scène**. The run-down area bordering skid row is, on nearly any weekday ... crowded with movie trailers. (Mary Melton, *Movies: We'll Fake Manhattan*, Los Angeles Times, 08-30-1998.)

settlement (temporary ... between opposing parties pending final deal) *n*.: **modus vivendi** [Latin]. SEE TRUCE

seven (group of ..., or a week) *n*.: **hebdomad** (*adj*.: **hebdomadal**). SEE WEEKLY

severe (as in ... remarks) *adj*.: **astringent**. SEE HARSH

severing (often from or within a group or union) *n*.: **scission**. SEE SPLIT

sewer *n*.: **cloaca**. ∎ [The Thames River] was "dirty" in a most literal sense, too, since for many years all the sewers of London ran directly into its water, creating a vast **cloaca** of stench and disease. (Peter Ackroyd, *In Praise of London's "Old Father,"* Newsweek International, 11-22-1999, p. 76.)

sex (boy who has ... with a man) *n*.: **catamite**. ∎ [O]f another uncle [the author writes]: "He was addicted to vice and debauchery. He drank wine continually. He kept a lot of **catamites**, and in his realm wherever there was a comely, beardless youth, he did everything he could to turn him into a **catamite**." (Amitav Ghosh, *Empire and Soul*, The New Republic, 01-06-1997.)

(2) sex (excessively interested in) *adj*.: **hypersexual**. ∎ REM sleep seems to play a central role in regulating sex drive. Animal studies point the way: Cats that are deprived of REM sleep show dramatic increases in drive-oriented behaviors. They become more aggressive, develop a greater appetite, and become **hypersexual**. (Michael Segell, *The Secrets of Sleep*, Esquire, 10-01-1994, p. 123.)

(3) sex (or marriage involving persons of different races) *n*.: **miscegenation**. ∎ Gerald Morgan, Jr., secretary of the Monticello Association of the Descendants of Thomas Jefferson — which currently consists only of white descendants — says it would be a "moral impossibility" for Jefferson to have impregnated slaves, given his vehement opposition to **miscegenation**. (Barbra Murray, *Clearing the Heirs*, U.S. News & World Report, 12-22-1997, p. 54.)

(4) sex (one having characteristics or reproductive organs of each ...) *n*.: **hermaphrodite** SEE BISEXUAL

(5) sex (outside of marriage) *n*.: **hetaerism**. SEE AFFAIR

(6) sex *n*.: **houghmagandy** (Scottish). SEE INTERCOURSE

(7) sex (as in intercourse, spec. insertion of penis into vagina) *n*.: **intromission** (*v.t*.: **intromit**). SEE PENETRATION

(8) sex (man who has ... with a boy) *n*.: **pederast**. SEE SODOMIZER

(9) sex (excessive desire for ... by a man) *n*.: **satyriasis**. SEE HORNINESS

(10) sex (simulated ..., as in intercourse, between two women) *n*.: **tribadism**. SEE INTERCOURSE

(11) sex (as in the act of ...) *n*.: **venery**. SEE INTERCOURSE

sexual (excessive ... desire) *n*.: **erotomania**. ∎ It was quickly revealed that [actor Bob Crane] had a passion for promiscuous sex that was only matched by his passion for documenting that passion. ... Crane was also a pioneer of the now booming phenomenon of do-it-yourself video porn. ... [T]he hours of tapes and stacks of photographs shot by Crane ... amounted to a virtual museum of first-person **erotomania**. (Geoff Pevere, *Addicted to the Wrong Kind* *of Love*, Toronto Star, 09-08-2002.)

(2) sexual (relating to or exhibiting ... behavior in many forms) *adj.*: **pansexual**. ∎ In his persona, meanwhile, [the singer Prince] presented himself as a sort of **pansexual** sprite. Tiny, mascara wearing, lubricious, he gave erotically charged performances and bestowed on his records titles like Lovesexy. (David E. Thigpen, *The Arts & Media/Music: Born Again — Years After Prince Suppressed it, His Fabled Black Album Appears*, Time, 12-12-1994, p. 94.)

(3) sexual (of or relating to illicit ... love) *adj.*: **paphian** (or **Paphian**). ∎ [W]henever [Casanova] is laid low with venereal disease — a not infrequent occurrence in these volumes — he typically reviles the unlucky woman he believes to have infected him: numerous are the outbursts in these memoirs against the "whores," "wretches," and "she-monsters" who have passed on to him the **Paphian** disorder. (Terry Castle, *Boogie Nights*, The New Republic, 11-03-1997.)

(4) sexual (as in ... lovemaking) *adj.*: **amatory** SEE LOVEMAKING

(5) sexual (boy who has ... relations with a man) *n.*: **catamite**. SEE SEX

(6) sexual (having a ...desire) *adj.*: **concupiscent** (*n.*: **concupiscence**). SEE LUSTFUL

(7) sexual (excitement from rubbing against something or someone) *n.*: **frottage**. SEE RUBBING

(8) sexual (attraction towards old people) *n.*: **gerontophilia**. SEE LUST

(9) sexual (preference for unusual ... practices) *n.*: **paraphilia**. SEE DEVIANT

(10) sexual (excessive ... craving by a man) *n.*: **satyriasis**. SEE HORNINESS

(11) sexual (desire to look at ... scenes or images) *n.*: **scopophilia**. SEE VOYEURISM

(12) sexual (intercourse) *n.*: **venery**. SEE INTERCOURSE

(13) sexual (attraction to animals) *n.*: **zoophilia**. SEE BESTIALITY

sexy *adj.*: **toothsome**. ∎ Sexiest leading lady: ... The hottest Welsh import since Richard Burton, Catherine Zeta-Jones turns on not only her intended, Michael Douglas, but 28% of those surveyed. Hot on her heels: **toothsome** Julia Roberts (27%). (Author not given, *What's Sexy Now!* In Style, 09-01-2000, p. 564.)

(2) sexy (as in flirtatious glance) *n.*: **oeillade** [French]. SEE GLANCE

shabby (as in unkempt or slovenly) *adj.*: **frowzy**. SEE MESSY

(2) shabby *adj.*: **tatterdemalion**. SEE RAGGED

shade (giving ...) *adj.*: **umbrageous**. ∎ Masking his steps on the crunchy snow by timing them with the elk's audible footfalls, the hunter moved through the lodgepole pines. Dawn resolved itself into a thin, **umbrageous** light. (Ted Kerasote, *The New Hunter, [Ethics and Ethical Hunters]*, Sports Afield, 11-01-1998, p. 78.)

(2) shade (having only one ... of color) *adj.*: **monochromatic**. SEE COLOR

(3) shade *n.*: **tincture**. SEE HUE

shaded (by trees or bushes, or set in the woods) *adj.*: **bosky**. SEE TREES

shadow-boxing *n.*: **sciamachy**. ∎ [T]he Champ is in full-time training now, jumping rope, sparring with Floyd, doing his **sciamachy**. (Jeffery Ewener, *Yo! Ontario's "Rocky" Steps Into the Ring*, The Toronto Star, 04-11-1994, p. A13.)

shadows (interplay of ... and light, often in a pictorial representation) *n.*: **chiaroscuro**. SEE LIGHT

shady (morality or taste) *adj.*: **louche**. SEE QUESTIONABLE

(2) shady (as in giving shade) *adj.*: **umbrageous**. SEE SHADE

shake (rapidly or spasmodically) *v.i.*: **judder**. ∎ The car was serviced at 12,000 miles in Caithness in March 1994 before I moved to Lincolnshire. Then, noticing severe wheel **judder**, I took the car to a Skegness dealer, who greased the suspension and told me to bring the car back if it got worse. (Answers by Honest John, *Letter to Motoring: When Rust Remains Hidden*, The Daily Telegraph, 09-12-1998.)

Shakespeare (worship of ...) *n.*: **bardolatry**. ∎ [In Germany], in the 18th century, Shakespeare enthralled scholars, actors and directors in such numbers that Goethe was moved to ruminate on the rampant **bardolatry** in an essay titled "Shakespeare ad Infinitum." (Barry Hillenbrand, *The Arts & Media/Theater: Can This Be Shakespeare?* Time International, 12-05-1994, p. 52.)

shaking *adj.*: **tremulous**. SEE QUIVERING

shallow (as in superficial knowledge of a subject) *n.*: **sciolism**. SEE SUPERFICIAL

sham (as in something which is impressive-looking on the outside but which hides or covers up undesirable conditions or facts) *n.:* **Potemkin village**. See facade

shame (to one's reputation) *n.:* **blot (or stain) on one's escutcheon** *idiom.* See dishonor

(2) shame (being subject to ..., esp. public) *n.:* **obloquy**. See abuse

shameful *adj.:* **opprobrious** (*n.:* **opprobrium**). See contemptuous

shameless (and conceited person) *n.:* **jackanapes**. See conceited

(2) shameless (and scheming woman) *n.:* **jezebel** (sometimes cap.). See woman

(3) shameless (and unprincipled person) *n.:* **reprobate**. See unprincipled

shamelessness *n.:* **impudicity**. See brashness

shantytown (esp. in Brazil) *n.:* **favela**. See slum

shape (distinctive ... or outline, often of a face) *adj.:* **lineament** (often **lineaments**). See contour

shaped (capable of being ..., such as with plastic, clay or earth) *adj.:* **fictile**. See molded

shapely (as in busty) *adj.:* **bathycolpian**. See busty

(2) shapely (rear end) *adj.:* **callipygian**. See rear end

share (as in portion) *n.:* **moiety**. See portion

sharp (as in biting or tart) *adj.:* **acidulous**. See tart

(2) sharp (to taste or smell) *adj.:* **acrid**. See pungent

(3) sharp (as in ... remarks) *adj.:* **astringent**. See harsh

(4) sharp (as in having a penetrating quality) *adj.:* **gimlet** (esp. as in "gimlet eye"). See penetrating

(5) sharp (agreeably ... in taste or flavor) *adj.:* **piquant**. See zesty

(6) sharp (as in incisive or perceptive) *adj.:* **trenchant**. See incisive

sharpness (as in incisiveness) *adj.:* **acuity**. See keenness

shave (one's head) *v.t., n.:* **tonsure**. ∎ The pre-Christian Greeks shaved the heads of their slaves, and the tradition survived for as long as slavery did, even into 19th-century America. Imitating slaves, the first Christian monks adopted the monastic **tonsure** as a sign of submission to God. (Colby Cosh, *The Shape of Things to Come*, Alberta Report/Western Report, 10-14-1996, p. 26.)

sheath (for a dagger, sword or knife) *n.:* **scabbard**. ∎ Edmund Burke, lamenting the death of chivalry, once thundered that a thousand swords should have leaped from their **scabbards** to prevent Queen Marie Antoinette from being dragged to the guillotine by a mob of French revolutionaries. (Norman Podhoretz, *"Sexgate," the Sisterhood, and Mr. Bumble*, Commentary, 06-01-1998, p. 23.)

shed *v.i.:* **abscise**. ∎ What is true decline? It often begins only with patches of leaves being smaller than normal and perhaps discolored. These same leaves may drop, or **abscise**, prematurely. (John Ball, *Going, Going, Gone: Diagnosing Tree Decline*, Grounds Maintenance, 09-01-1999.)

(2) shed (with one slope or pitch) *n.:* **lean-to**. ∎ Anchor a tarp over a log or a partially overturned canoe or boat. For more room, lash a cross-pole between two trees to make a **lean-to** out of the tarp. (Anthony Acerrano, *How to Stay Alive!* Sports Afield, 07-01-1995, p. 68.)

sheep (of, relating to or characteristic of) *adj.:* **ovine**. ∎ Hello, Dolly [a cloned sheep], brave new **ovine**; art thou a wolf in sheep's cloning? (Author not given, *Letters*, Time, 03-31-1997, p. 10.)

sheer *adj.:* **diaphanous**. See transparent

(2) sheer *adj.:* **gossamer**. See transparent

shell (of a turtle, like a protective covering) *n.:* **carapace**. ∎ All marriages begin in myth. The myth is the **carapace** under which the real marriage takes shape; the cracking of the **carapace**, like the breakup of the ice on a spring-swollen river, is a deafening thing. (Lynn Darling, *For Better and Worse*, Esquire, 05-01-1996, p. 58.)

shelter (as in surround, often protectively) *v.t.:* **embosom**. See surround

shelve (as in discontinue, esp. a session of Parliament) *v.t.:* **prorogue**. See discontinue

shift (esp. regarding one's beliefs, causes or policies) *n.:* **bouleversement** [French]. See change of mind

(2) shift (sudden ... of events, often in a literary work) *n.:* **peripeteia**. See turnaround

(3) shift (a ... regarding one's beliefs, causes or policies) *n.:* **tergiversation** (*v.i.:* **tergiversate**). See change of mind

shifting (about) *adj.:* **ambulant** (*v.i.:* **ambulate**, *adj.:* **ambulatory**). See moving

shiftless (person) *n*.: **wastrel**. SEE SLACKER

shimmering (lightly over a surface) *adj*.: **lambent**. ∎ An inconstant breeze stirred through the valley, and sometimes the wild grass seemed to roll like ocean waves across the slopes, softly aglimmer with **lambent** lunar light. (Dean Koontz, *Intensity*, Bantam [2000], p. 17.)

(2) shimmering *adj*.: **coruscant**. SEE GLITTERING

shining *adj*.: **effulgent**. SEE BRIGHT

(2) shining *adj*.: **fulgurant**. SEE BRIGHT

(3) shining (softly ...) *adj*.: **lambent**. SEE SHIMMERING

(4) shining *adj*.: **lucent**. SEE GLOWING

(5) shining *adj*.: **refulgent**. SEE BRIGHT

shirk (work by pretending to be sick or incapacitated) *v.i.*: **malinger**. ∎ Players are regarded [by team owners] as overpaid louts who greedily want more than they deserve. ... When a player is injured, he is suspected of **malingering** if he doesn't return to action immediately — unless the bone is sticking through the meat. (Ron Mix, *So Little Gain for the Pain; Striking NFL Players Deserve Much, Much More*, Sports Illustrated, 10-19-1987, p. 54.)

shirker *n., v.i.*: **goldbrick**. ∎ [V]oters rarely have the option of firing [elected officials] until the end of their term. So you can lollygag for a few years — if that's your preference. ... Which brings us to Jefferson County Treasurer Mark Paschall, who managed to drag himself into the office on only 132 days last year, according to county records. A **goldbrick**? Quite possibly. But there's nothing to be done about it until 2006. (Author not given, *On Point*, Denver Rocky Mountain News, 01-15-2004.)

(2) shirker *n*.: **embusque** [French]. SEE SLACKER

shit (obsession with) *n*.: **coprology**. SEE EXCREMENT

(2) shit (feeding on) *n*.: **coprophagous**. SEE EXCREMENT

(3) shit (interest in ..., often sexual) *n*.: **coprophilia**. SEE EXCREMENT

(4) shit *n*.: **egesta**. SEE EXCREMENT

(5) shit (esp. that of sea birds) *n*.: **guano**. SEE BIRD DUNG

(6) shit (study of or obsession with) *n*.: **scatology**. SEE EXCREMENT

(7) shit (eating) *adj*.: **scatophagous**. SEE EXCREMENT

(8) shit (of or relating to) *adj*.: **stercoraceous**. SEE EXCREMENT

shivering (fit of ... with cold alternating with fever) *n*.: **ague**. SEE CHILLS

shoemaker *n*.: **cordwainer**. ∎ Until the capitalist era, that is, for thousands and thousands of years up to only two centuries ago, the history of work was, with certain specialized exceptions, the history of craftsmanship. ... The potter made clay vessels; the cobbler or **cordwainer**, footwear; the weaver, cloth; the tailor, clothing; and so on. (Harry Braverman, *The Making of the U.S. Working Class*, Monthly Review, 11-01-1994, p. 14.)

shopping (compulsion for ...) *n*.: **oniomania**. ∎ About 90 percent of compulsive shoppers are women. ... Most are so overcome by feelings of guilt about their spending that only another trip to the shops can make them feel better. ... Women may have a higher incidence of **oniomania** because of the way they respond to lower-than-normal levels of seratonin. (James Langton, *Cure Being Tested for Shop-till-you-drop Syndrome*, The Washington Times, 06-12-2000, p. A1.)

shore (of or on a ...) *n., adj*.: **littoral**. ∎ His descriptions of poverty-stricken shore life accord most faithfully with contemporary accounts. The world of the seaweed collectors had become, by 1836, something of a stock-in-trade of **littoral** writing. (James Hamilton-Paterson, *Signals of Distress* [book reviews], The New Republic, 05-06-1996, p. 38.)

short (speech or writing being very ..., as in terse) *adj*.: **elliptical**. SEE TERSE

(2) short (and squat) *adj*.: **fubsy**. SEE SQUAT

shortcoming (tragic ..., esp. in a literary character) *n*.: **hamartia**. SEE FLAW

shortened (something ...) *n*.: **bobtail**. SEE ABRIDGED

shorthand *n*.: **tachygraphy**. ∎ [Samuel] Pepys's Cambridge years were formative. While there he learnt Shelton's **Tachygraphy**, a form of shorthand invaluable for lecture notes but which later came in handy for encrypting his fruitier diary entries. (Author not given, *Peterborough: New Peep at Pepys*, The Daily Telegraph, 02-23-1999.)

(2) shorthand (as in code words, spec. words conveying an innocent meaning to an outsider but with a concealed meaning to an informed person, often to avoid censorship or punishment) *n*.: **Aesopian language**. SEE CODE WORDS

(3) shorthand (where a part is used to stand for the whole or vice versa) *n*.: **synecdoche**. SEE FIGURE OF SPEECH

shortly *adv.*: **anon**. SEE MOMENTARILY

(2) shortly (very ..., as in, in an instant) *n.*: **trice** (as in, in a trice). SEE QUICKLY

shout (as in screech, like a cat in heat) *v.i.*: **caterwaul**. SEE SCREECH

show (violent ... in which shame, degradation or harm is inflicted on a person, often for the enjoyment of onlookers) *n.*: **Roman holiday**. SEE SPECTACLE

(2) show (as in send a signal) *v.t., v.i.*: **semaphore**. SEE SIGNAL

showcase (glass ...) *n.*: **vitrine**. ∎ The dining room, paneled in dark oak with leaded-glass windows, is the focal point for her collection of Chinese Export porcelain. She and Wick designed a glass **vitrine** along one wall to showcase the pieces. (Kirsten Rohrs, *A Music-Loving Couple Orchestrates the Holiday*, Colonial Homes, 01-01-1997, p. 44.)

shower (as in downpour) *n.*: **cataract**. SEE DOWNPOUR

showoff (talk or person) *n.*: **cockalorum**. SEE EGOTISTIC

(2) showoff *n.*: **Gascon** (act of being a ... *n.*: **Gasconade**). SEE BRAGGART

showy (but cheap, or such an object) *adj., n.*: **brummagem**. ∎ Robert Altman is American film's chief artisan of costume jewelry. At first glance, the design seems cunning, the gold and the jewels seem rich. Before long, we can see that the design is a mere contraption, the ingredients are gilt and glass. It doesn't take long in Altman's latest, Kansas City (Fine Line), for the **brummagem** to show. (Stanley Kauffmann, *The Fan [movie reviews]*, The New Republic, 09-09-1996, p. 37.)

(2) showy (but cheap or tasteless, or such an object) *adj., n.*: **gimcrack**. ∎ On Tuesday the Absolutely Fabulous star Joanna Lumley will open a giant multiplex cinema at the Great North Leisure Park, just outside Finchley, north London. ... To those who loathe the stench of fried food, hate the tinny beat of endless muzak, and deplore the **gimcrack** architecture topped with a grinning Daffy Duck, it is Absolutely Horrid. (Catherine Pepinster, *In England's Green and Multiplexed Land*, Independent on Sunday, 07-07-1996, p. 7.)

(3) showy *adj.*: **baroque**. SEE ORNATE

(4) showy *adj.*: **florid**. SEE ORNATE

(5) showy (as in pompous, speech or writing) *adj.*: **fustian**. SEE POMPOUS

(6) showy (esp. regarding speaking or writing style) *adj.*: **magniloquent**. SEE POMPOUS

(7) showy (in a gaudy way) *adj.*: **meretricious**. SEE GAUDY

(8) showy (esp. regarding speaking or writing style) *adj.*: **orotund**. SEE POMPOUS

shreds (as in bits and pieces) *n.*: **flinders**. SEE BITS AND PIECES

shreiking (as in shrill, sound made by bagpipes) *n.*: **skirl**. SEE BAGPIPES

shrew *n.*: **harridan**. ∎ Set Up a Job Jar. Sure, grandma has used this tactic for ages. But why should that disqualify it? The beauty of the job jar is that husbands see the demanded tasks as issuing from an unemotional cylinder of glass rather than a finger-wagging **harridan**. (Elizabeth Rapoport, *8 Ways to Get Your Husband to Help*, Redbook, 12-01-1995, p. 53.)

(2) shrew *n.*: **termagant**. ∎ [Arianna Huffington] is the author of six books ..., a friend to the rich and powerful on two continents, the mother of two young daughters, an intellectual advocate of spiritual awakening ..., a conservative chat-show hostess, and a reputed **termagant** with the servants. Whew! (Walter Shaprio, *The $20 Million Man, [California Republican Michael Huggington]*, Esquire, 10-01-1994, p. 60.)

(3) shrew *n.*: **virago**. ∎ Enlarging on themes from his earlier books, Mr. Nagel depicts [John Quincy Adams' mother] Abigail Adams as a driving, ambitious, nagging **virago**, a perfect "calamity" of a parent, especially in contrast to her husband, John Adams. (Catherine Allgor, *John Quincy Adams: Public Success — and Private Pain*, The Washington Times, 10-12-1997, p. 24.)

(4) shrew *n.*: **vixen**. ∎ [Winnie Mandella has] been called a shrew. A **vixen**. ... Baleka Kgotsisile of the ANC Women's League ... admires Winnie's power, energy and dynamism, but says "The problem with Winnie is that if you don't want to play her game by her rules, she walks away; she simply doesn't play. That is not good for building an organization." (Nokwanda Sithole, *Winnie Mandela: Her Story*, Essence, 04-01-1994, p. 76.)

(5) shrew *n.*: **Xanthippe**. ∎ [derives from Socrates' wife, who had such a reputation]. Remember ... when a young man and woman couldn't be left alone in room without a chaperone? ... This hag ... had a sense of moral outrage which moved her to find evil in a caress. Now this modern day **Xanthippe** runs a sexist women's organization which denies the existence of false abuse allegations and expects millions of American fathers to accept supervised visitation with their own children. (Francis King, *Taliban Movement Gains Strength in the United States*, Fathering Magazine, 09-28-2001.)

shrewd *adj.*: **perspicacious**. SEE ASTUTE

shrill (sound made by bagpipes) *n.*: **skirl**. SEE BAGPIPES

shrink (back out of fear or shying away from) *v.i.*: **blench**. SEE FLINCH

(2) shrink (back out of fear or desire to shy away from) *v.i.*: **resile**. SEE RECOIL

shrinkage (as in reduction in size of a swollen object, e.g. loss of erection) *n.*: **detumescence**. ∎ The interesting thing about these lines on impotence is that they were written by a man who died in his 34th year. ... Still, as we all know today, involuntary **detumescence** can strike at any moment, even when the victim is young and wishes only to demonstrate his love for a woman. (Henry Porter, *If You Want a Good Time, Pay For It*, Independent on Sunday, 07-12-1998, p. 5.)

shrivel *v.i.*: **wizen**. ∎ Unfortunately, pumpkins and squashes start to rot after a few months, while most other gourds slowly dry out and turn a pale straw color. Some gourds keep their full, rounded or warty shape, while others **wizen** a little. (Author not given, *The Fertile Mind*, Denver Rocky Mountain News, 10-19-1997, p. 17F.)

shrubs (mass of ...) *n.*: **boscage**. SEE BUSHES

shudder (from moment of intense excitement) *n.*: **frisson** [French]. ∎ The thing about exploring a guy's back while he's lying facedown is that he's at your mercy — and that's a major turn-on for both of you. Plus, there's so much possibility for serious **frissons** along the length of that gorgeous and muscular terrain. "My guy loves it when I slowly travel up his back with my tongue to his neck," says one woman. "It makes him quiver all over." (Pamela Lister, *5,000 Men Reveal: Their Other Hot Spots*, Redbook, 12-01-2000, p. 120.)

(2) shudder (as in flinch) *v.i.*: **blench**. SEE FLINCH
(3) shudder (rapidly or spasmodically) *v.i.*: **judder**. SEE SHAKE

shun (as in treat with contempt) *v.t.*: **contemn**. SEE SCORN

shutter (window ... with adjustable horizontal slats) *n.*: **jalousie**. SEE WINDOW BLIND

shy (esp. from lack of self-confidence) *adj.*: **diffident**. SEE TIMID

(2) shy (and unassertive person) *n.*: **milquetoast**. SEE UNASSERTIVE

(3) shy (as in timid and unassertive person) *n.*: **nebbish** [Yiddish]. SEE TIMID

shy away *v.i.*: **resile**. SEE RECOIL

sickening (as in overly sentimental) *adj.*: **mawkish**. SEE SENTIMENTAL

sickly (and weak person, esp. one morbidly concerned with his own health) *n., adj.*: **valetudinarian**. ∎ At 71, after two heart attacks, he has adopted a distinctly **valetudinarian** demeanor. (Brooke Allen, *Starting Out in the Evening [book reviews]*, The New Leader, 12-29-1997, p. 25.)

(2) sickly (elderly person) *n.*: **Struldbrug**. SEE DECREPIT

sickness (esp. from eating or drinking too much) *n.*: **crapulence**. SEE INDULGENCE

(2) sickness (caused by a physician) *adj.*: **iatrogenic**. SEE DISEASE

(3) sickness (of a ... or disease which has no known cause) *adj.*: **idiopathic** (*n.*: **idiopathy**). SEE ILLNESS

(4) sickness (pretend to have a ... or other incapacity to avoid work) *v.i.*: **malinger**. SEE SHIRK

sickout (esp. by policemen) *n.*: **blue flu**. ∎ When a "**blue flu**" epidemic empties the Seattle police department, Lt. Lou Boldt and the few members still working are stretched to their limits, not unlike the nerves of a reader paging through this engrossing new novel. (Laurie Trimble, *Engrossing Cops-and-Robbers Tale Starts With a Round of "Blue Flu,"* The Dallas Morning News, 07-08-2000, p. 4C.)

side dish *n., pl.*: **entremets**. ∎ According to the food historian Giles MacDonagh, he ingested "a hundred Ostend oysters, 12 Prée-Saléé mutton cutlets, a duckling with turnips, a brace of roast partridges, a sole Normand, without counting hors d'oeuvres, **entremets**, fruits, etc."(Bee Wilson, *La Gastronomie Humaine*, New Statesman, 07-19-1999.)

sidestep (as in avert or ward off) *v.t.*: **forfend**. SEE AVERT

siege (of or relating to being under ...) *adj.*: **obsidional**. SEE BESEIGED

sighing (as in panting) *adj.*: **suspirious** (*v.t.*: **suspire**). SEE PANTING

sight (loss of) *n.*: **amaurosis**. SEE BLINDNESS

(2) sight (having poor ..., as in nearly blind) *adj.*: **purblind**. SEE BLIND

sightseers (person who guides ...) *n.*: **cicerone**. SEE GUIDE

sign (or symbol which gives information nonverbally) *n.*: **glyph** SEE SYMBOL

(2) sign (showing an idea without words; e.g. "$," or Chinese or Japanese symbols) *n.*: **ideogram**. SEE SYMBOL

(3) sign (early ... of disease) *n.*: **prodrome**. SEE SYMPTOM

signal *v.t., v.i.*: **semaphore** (spec. a visual signal such as flags or mechanical arms, but often used in broader sense of taking any action to send a signal). ▪ [Warner Bros. cast of cartoon characters included] Porky Pig [as] the harassed middle-management type [and] Elmer Fudd the chronic, choleric dupe. Bugs Bunny ... became the cartoon Cagney — urban, crafty, pugnacious — and then the blasé underhare who wins every battle without ever mussing his aplomb; one raised eyebrow was enough to **semaphore** his superiority to the carnage around him. (Richard Corliss, *Chuck Reducks: Chuck Jones Just Made Cartoons, But They Were Far More Than Kid Stuff*, Time, 03-04-2002.)

significance (of equal ...) *n.*: **equiponderance**. SEE IMPORTANCE

significant (of an event or period which is ...) *adj.*: **epochal**. SEE MOMENTOUS

(2) significant (person in a field or organization) *n.*: **wallah**. SEE NOTABLE

signify (as in portend) *v.t.*: **betoken**. SEE PORTEND

silly (as in absurd or preposterous) *adj.*: **fatuous**. SEE FOOLISH

(2) silly (as in flighty or scatterbrained person) *n.*: **flibbertigibbet**. SEE FLIGHTY

(3) silly (as in laughable) *adj.*: **gelastic**. SEE LAUGHABLE

(4) silly (as in laughable) *adj.*: **risible**. SEE LAUGHABLE

silver (resembling) *adj.*: **argentine**. ▪ [A] moment ago, we are almost certain, we saw the brief silver flash of a tailing permit. ... The fish makes an initial run of about 150 yards in the direction she came from, and her companion sticks right with her, two fleeing spirits in their **argentine** brilliance. (Dan Gerber, *Permit: The Most Difficult Fish in the World*, Sports Afield, 09-01-1994, p. 92.)

similar (as in related) *adj.*: **cognate**. SEE RELATED

similarity (of sounds) *n.*: **assonance**. ▪ In fact, internal rhyme and **assonance** have long been a trademark of one-hit wonders. A look back suggests that Chumbawamba has just one hit left in them. Scritti Politti 1 [top 10 hit]; Kajagoogoo: 1; Bananarama: 0; Oingo Boingo: 5; Milli Vanilli: 3; Blues Magoos: 1. (Joel Stein, *People*, Time, 12-08-1997, p. 111.)

(2) similarity (as in resemblance) *n.*: **simulacrum**. SEE REPRESENTATION

simple *adj.*: **abecedarian**. SEE BASIC

(2) simple (as in guileless) *n.*: **artless**. SEE GUILELESS

(3) simple (as in understandable) *adj.*: **limpid**. SEE UNDERSTANDABLE

(4) simple (as in clear, in thought or expression) *adj.*: **pellucid**. SEE CLEAR

(5) simple (as in understandable) *adj.*: **perspicuous**. SEE UNDERSTANDABLE

simpleton *n.*: **jobbernowl** [British]. SEE IDIOT

(2) simpleton *n.*: **mooncalf**. SEE FOOL

simplicity (false showing of ...) *adj.*: **faux-naif** [French]. SEE DISINGENUOUS

(2) simplicity (in speech or writing) *n.*: **pablum**. SEE TRITENESS

simultaneous (existence in two places) *n.*: **bilocation**. ▪ One [19th century magician] is renowned for an impossible trick where he seems to be in two places at once; the other is spurred to create a more stunning **bilocation** act using the new technology of electricity. (Gene Lyons, *Books: The Week*, Entertainment Weekly, 11-01-1996, p. 64.)

sin (in public office) *n.*: **malversation**. SEE WRONGDOING

(2) sin (small or trifling ...) *n.*: **peccadillo**. SEE INFRACTION

(3) sin (confession of ...) *n.*: **peccavi**. SEE CONFESSION

sinful *adj.*: **peccant**. ▪ [Otis] did less well by his son, Delmore, whom he hasn't seen since Delmore was eight. ... [But Otis has a] current, lovingly savvy woman (there must be redemption even for a formerly **peccant** father). (John Simon, *Lone Star* [movie reviews], National Review, 07-29-1996, p. 54.)

(2) sinful (as in wicked) *adj.*: **flagitious**. SEE WICKED

(3) sinful *adj.*: **iniquitous**. SEE WICKED

(4) sinful *adj.*: **malefic**. SEE EVIL

(5) sinful *adj.*: **malevolent**. SEE EVIL

singer (female ... who speaks, rather than sings, the lyrics) *n.*: **diseuse** [French] (male singer: **diseur**). ▪ [S]ingers like Frank Sinatra ... learned the value of honoring a lyric [from Mabel Mercer]. To an extent, that was because, in the last decades of her colorful life, she was less chanteuse than **diseuse**. She, of course, knew the melodies of the songs she chose to interpret, but only followed them when so inclined. Rather, she regarded songs as monologues to be acted with passion and insouciance. (David Finkle, *Oh Happy Day! CD's from Mabel to Michael [Bistro Bits]*, Back Stage, 07-19-2002.)

singing (responsive ... or chanting) *n.*: **antiphony**. SEE CHANTING

single (state of being ..., or nonrecognition or nonregulation of marriage) *n.*: **agamy**. SEE UNMARRIED

(2) single (woman, whether divorced, widowed or never married) *n.*: **feme sole**. SEE WOMAN

singular (as in specific to one person or thing; e.g. languages which use symbols or pictures instead of words) *adj.*: **idiographic**. SEE UNIQUE

(2) singular (person or thing) *n.*: **rara avis** [Latin]. SEE RARITY

(3) singular (as in unique) *adj.*: **sui generis** [Latin]. SEE UNIQUE

sinister *adj.*: **baleful**. ▪ The successful mapping of the entire human genetic code is such a stupendous feat — and so full of potential for good — that it seems almost gratuitous to start worrying about downsides. Yet I do worry — and not primarily about the **baleful** uses to which the new information could possibly be put: invasions of privacy, ranking of human beings by insurance risk, that sort of thing. (William Raspberry, *Genetic Side Effects*, The Washington Post, 06-30-2000, p. A31.)

(2) sinister *adj.*: **iniquitous**. SEE WICKED

(3) sinister *adj.*: **malefic**. SEE EVIL

(4) sinister *adj.*: **malevolent**. SEE EVIL

sink (cause to ... into mud) *v.t.*: **bemire**. SEE MUD

(2) sink (to the bottom of the ocean) *v.i.*: **go to Davy Jones's locker**. SEE OCEAN

sinking (as in worsening) *adj.*: **ingravescent**. SEE WORSENING

siren song *n.*: **Lorelei call**. SEE LURE

sissy *n.*: **pantywaist**. ▪ In any event, that Bradley attack — and another on Gore for arriving late to the Democrats' anti-tobacco efforts — was clumsy.

Bradley is no **pantywaist** in debates; he's trying to be combative. But the "sharp elbows" he promised supporters last year are not finding Gore's rib cage. (Jonathan Alter, *Bumps Along the High Road*, Newsweek, 01-24-2000, p. 52.)

(2) sissy (as in coward) *n.*: **poltroon**. SEE COWARD

site (as in condition of being located in a particular place) *n.*: **ubiety**. SEE PLACE

situation (which is difficult or complex) *n.*: **nodus**. SEE COMPLICATION

skeptic (as in one with no faith or religion) *n., adj.*: **nullifidian**. SEE NONBELIEVER

skeptical *adj.*: **Zetetic**. ▪ The ostensible aim of Mr. Randi's hoax [i.e. convincing researchers that two boys had paranormal powers] was to make psychic researchers rely more widely on the advice of magicians. ... [However,] the editor of **Zetetic** Scholar, a journal devoted to the skeptical analysis of paranormal claims, [stated:] "In no way will his project teach psychic researchers a lesson and make them more likely to trust to magicians' advice." (William Broad, *Magician's Effort to Debunk Scientists Raises Ethical Issues*, The New York Times, 02-15-1983, p. C3.)

sketch (out in an incomplete way) *v.t.*: **adumbrate**. SEE OUTLINE

skill (person's area of) *n.*: **bailiwick**. SEE EXPERTISE

(2) skill (area of ...) *n.*: **métier** [French]. SEE FORTE

skillful *adj.*: **habile**. ▪ The first [choice for the West] was to tolerate Slobodan Milosevic's police and military campaign. ... The other choice was a NATO military intervention. ... Thanks to [the dilemma that both choices seemed to lead to disaster], and to the **habile** cunning, combined with ruthlessness, which has made Milosevic the man he is, the West has lost influence over Yugoslav events. (William Pfaff, *NATO Should Halt the Yugoslav Offensive in Kosovo*, The Chicago Tribune, 09-08-1998, p. 19.)

(2) skillful (as in resourceful, person) *n.*: **debrouillard** (or **débrouillard**) [French]. SEE RESOURCEFUL

skimpy *n.*: **exiguous**. SEE MEAGER

(2) skimpy (as in meager) *adj.*: **mingy**. SEE MEAGER

skin (of, relating to or affecting) *adj., n.*: **cutaneous**. ▪ The American Academy of Dermatology urges that [tatoo] artists be trained, regulated and licensed in precautions having to do with "sanitation, sterilization, **cutaneous** anatomy." (Amy Dickinson, *Why Not Tattoo? Kids Love 'Em, But Parents Can Point Out*

That They're One Form of Foolery That Won't Go Away, Time, 11-22-1999, p. 113.)

(2) skin (tingling or prickling sensation with respect to) *n*.: **paresthesia**. SEE PRICKLING

skinflint *n*.: **lickpenny**. SEE MISER

skinny (esp. in a pale or corpselike way) *adj*.: **cadaverous**. SEE CORPSELIKE

skirmish (as in brawl, esp. public) *n*.: **affray**. SEE BRAWL

skull (study of shape of) *n*.: **phrenology**. ∎ Modern **phrenology** was developed in the late 1700s by Austrian physician Franz Joseph Gall, who felt that the form of the head represents the form of the brain, and thus reflects the development of brain organs. (Jim Bernstein, *Vital Signs/Oddity/Head Cases*, Newsday, 09-26-1999, p. G3.)

sky (or or relating to) *adj*.: **empyreal**. SEE LOFTY
(2) sky (as in heavens) *n*.: **welkin**. SEE HEAVENS

sky-blue *adj*.: **cerulean**. SEE BLUE

slacker *n*.: **embusque** [French]. ∎ All along I had been convinced that the United States ought to aid in the struggle against Germany. With that conviction, it was plainly up to me to do more than drive an ambulance. The more I saw the splendour of the fight the French were fighting, the more I felt like an **embusque** — what the British call a "shirker." So I made up my mind to go into aviation. (James R. McConnell, *True Stories Of The Great War: II — Story Of The Personnel Of The Escadrille*, History of the World, 01-01-1992.)
(2) slacker *n*.: **wastrel**. ∎ Hard as he partied, [NBA player Walt "Clyde" Frazier] always worked harder. Not so [son] Walt. Clyde gave Walt a jump rope to quicken his feet. It went unused. He gave him exercises to improve his lateral movement. Nada. ... But don't get the idea that Walt was a **wastrel**. "I always stressed his being a good kid and a good student," says Clyde. From an early age, Walt was both. (Jack Friedman, *Jocks: Belatedly Learning That Father Knows Best, Walt Frazier III Tries to Be a Clyde Off the Old Block*, People, 02-27-1989, p. 73.)
(3) slacker (as in one who avoids work or assigned duties) *n., v.i.*: **goldbrick**. SEE GOLDBRICK
(4) slacker (as in person who stays in bed out of laziness) *n*.: **slugabed**. SEE LAZY

slander *v.t.*: **asperse**. SEE DEFAME
(2) slander *n*.: **calumniate** (*v.t.*: **calumny**). SEE MALIGN

(3) slander (so as to humiliate or disgrace) *v.t.*: **traduce**. SEE MALIGN

slant (as in upward slope) *n*.: **acclivity** (*adj*.: **acclivitous**). SEE INCLINE
(2) slant (as in downward slope) *n*.: **declivity** (*adj*.: **declivitous**). SEE DECLINE
(3) slant (esp. extending down from a fortification) *n*.: **glacis**. SEE DECLINE

slaughter (large-scale ... or sacrifice) *n*.: **hecatomb**. ∎ It is unlikely that even the Serbian "irregulars" in Kosovo have exceeded what they accomplished in that Bosnian "safe haven" in July 1995: the organized killing and interment of perhaps 10,000 male captives. That **hecatomb** was carved out ... as NATO troops stood by and exchanged pleasantries with the overworked executioners. (Christopher Hitchens, *Minority Report: Srebrenica Revisited*, The Nation, 04-19-1999, p. 8.)
(2) slaughter (mass ... of unresisting persons) *n*.: **battue** [French]. SEE KILLING

slaughterhouse *n*.: **abattoir**. ∎ Now it is impossible to find meat of any kind, except chicken, in Delhi. A high court ruled that the city's main Idgah **abattoir** was killing too many animals. More than 12,500 sheep, goats and buffaloes a day were slaughtered there under infernal conditions. (Tim McGirk, *Out of India: Hindu Right-Wing Takes Tough Line in Beef*, Independent, 04-30-1994.)

slave *v.i.*: **moil**. SEE TOIL
(2) slave (female ... in a harem or concubine) *n*.: **odalisque**. SEE CONCUBINE

slave driver (as in strict disciplinarian) *n*.: **martinet**. SEE DISCIPLINARIAN
(2) slave driver (brutal ...) *n*.: **Simon Legree**. SEE TASKMASTER

slave labor (as in forced work for little or no pay) *n*.: **corvee**. SEE SERVITUDE

slavery (free from ...) *v.t.*: **manumit**. SEE EMANCIPATE
(2) slavery *n*.: **thralldom**. SEE BONDAGE

slaves (group of ... or prisoners chained together) *n*.: **coffle**. SEE PRISONERS

slavish (as in very hardworking) *n*.: **Stakhanovite**. SEE WORKAHOLIC

slay (by strangling or cutting the throat) *v.t.*: **garrote**. SEE STRANGLE
(2) slay (by strangling or cutting the throat) *v.t.*: **jugulate**. SEE STRANGLE

slaying (of one's brother or sister) *n.*: **fratricide**. See MURDER

(2) slaying (of one's mother) *n.*: **matricide**. See KILLING

(3) slaying (of one's parent or close relative) *n.*: **parricide**. See KILLING

(4) slaying (of one's father) *n.*: **patricide**. See KILLING

(5) slaying (of a king) *n.*: **regicide**. See KILLING

(6) slaying (of wife by her husband) *adj.*: **uxoricide**. See KILLING

sleek (as in elegant and fashionable) *adj.*: **soigné** [French]. See ELEGANT

sleep (sudden attacks of deep ...) *n.*: **narcolepsy**. ▪ Symptoms of **narcolepsy** include excessive daytime sleepiness (even dropping off to sleep at any time, whether it be watching TV or driving a car). (Kathleen A. Rickard, M.D, *Solving the Mysteries of Sleep*, USA Today Magazine, 07-01-1997.)

sleep-inducing *adj.*: **soporific**. ▪ She [has] been lobbying to have U.S. high schools start later. Some begin classes as early as 7:10 a.m. ... Schoolmates Arthur Law and William Hui, both 15, go to bed around midnight and are up by 7. They often fall asleep in class, lulled, they say, by the **soporific** effect of social studies or French. (Jennifer Hunter, *Are You Getting Enough: Accidents, Mistakes, Forgetfulness, Impaired Judgment — Canadians Pay a Steep Price For Their Restless Nights*, Maclean's, 04-17-2000, p. 42.)

sleepiness (relating to period of ... just before falling asleep) *adj.*: **hypnagogic**. See DROWSINESS

sleepless (night) *n.*: **white night**. ▪ And his coach-house parties, **white nights** in which no one had trouble staying awake, were legendary. (Author not given, *Wild Nights in Movieland: How Toronto's Film Festival Came of Age While Grappling With the Egos and Appetites of Hollywood Stars*, Maclean's, 08-28-2000, p. 30.)

sleepy (as in sluggish or lethargic) *adj.*: **torpid**. See LETHARGIC

sleight-of-hand *n.*: **prestidigitation**. ▪ He tells us that until he saw [Bill] Bradley play [basketball], he'd lost interest in the game because it had, by the sixties, "attracted exhibitionists who seemed to be more intent on amazing a crowd with aimless **prestidigitation** than with advancing their team by giving a sound performance." (Ron Rosenbaum, *The Revolt of the Basketball Liberals, [Criticism of African American Basketball Players by White Sports Writers and Coaches]*, Esquire, 06-01-1995, p. 102.)

(2) sleight of hand (sometimes in a deceitful way) *n.*: **legerdemain**. See TRICKERY

slender (and graceful woman) *n.*: **sylph**. See WOMAN

(2) slender (body type) *adj.*: **ectomorphic**. See LEAN

slick (as in slippery) *adj.*: **lubricious**. See SLIPPERY

slide (a ... down an incline such as a snowy mountain) *n.*: **glissade**. ▪ He perches on the edge of the desk, and a small **glissade** of dislodged documents slides smoothly away into the wastepaper basket. (Michael Frayn, *Headlong*, Metropolitan Books [1999], p. 87.)

(2) slide (downward ...) *n.*: **declension**. See DECLINE

slim (body type) *adj.*: **ectomorphic**. See LEAN

slip (of the tongue) *n.*: **parapraxis**. See BLUNDER

slip of the pen *n.*: **lapsus calami** [Latin]. ▪ How many of you, I wonder, spotted my **lapsus calami** of yesterday? ... Let me quote you the offending passage: "Of the many towns and cities on the rivers Elbe and Oder affected by the catastrophic floods of summer 2002, Prague was perhaps the most severely hit." Oops! As schoolchild knows, Prague lies neither on the Oder nor the Elbe, but on the River Vltava. (Brendan McWilliams, *Kepler a Big Part of Prague's History*, The Irish Times, 06-04-2004.)

slip of the tongue *n.*: **lapsus linguae** [Latin]. ▪ President Bush was smart to choose Spain as his gateway to Europe last week. The Spaniards appreciated the gesture. ... True, Bush mispronounced the name of Spain's Prime Minister Jose Maria Aznar, but not even that **lapsus linguae** could sour the mood in the first meeting between the two conservatives. (Author not given, *Bush's Gateway to Europe*, Los Angeles Times, 06-22-2001.)

slippage (downward ...) *n.*: **declension**. See DECLINE

slippery *adj.*: **lubricious**. ▪ Because of their **lubricious** nature, silicones have been added to both aerosol and pump hair spray formulas to reduce friction (and therefore clogging) during spraying. (M.D. Berthiaume, *Silicones in Hair Fixatives & Finishing Products: A Brief Review*, Drug & Cosmetic Industry, 05-01-1995, p. 60.)

(2) slippery (lit. soapy) *adj.*: **saponaceous**. ▪

Perhaps the most revealing incident is the chapter on the kidnapping of Roger Tamraz. Tamraz, a **saponaceous** Lebanese businessman with US citizenship, became known to the American public in September 1997, when he testified before the Senate Finance Committee on a contribution of $300,000 he had dropped into the Democratic Party coffers. (Walid Harb, *Books & the Arts: "Snake Eat Snake,"* The Nation, 07-19-1999, p. 25.)

slit *n.*: **aperture**. ∎ I'm told the women of Yemen are particularly beautiful but it's impossible to tell since they are all — at least those over the age of 14 — swathed head to toe in swishing black drapery, with the full hijab hiding the face as well as the hair and neck. A few women allow for a narrow **aperture** to reveal their enchanting kohl-painted eyes. (Author not given, *Bare Arms Draw Daggers, Sweet Words Greet Visitor*, The Toronto Star, 07-28-2000.)

slobber *v.i., n.*: **slaver**. SEE DROOL

slogan (pithy ...) *n.*: **gnome** (*adj*: **gnomic**). SEE CATCHPHRASE

(2) slogan *n.*: **shibboleth**. SEE CATCHWORD

slope (upward) *n.*: **acclivity** (*adj.*: **acclivitous**). SEE INCLINE

(2) slope (downward) *n.*: **declivity** (*adj.*: **declivitous**). SEE DECLINE

(3) slope (steep ..., as in cliff) *n.*: **escarpment**. SEE CLIFF

(4) slope (downward ..., esp. extending down from a fortification) *n.*: **glacis**. SEE DECLINE

slothful *adj.*: **fainéant** [French]. SEE LAZY

(2) slothful (person, who stays in bed out of laziness) *n.*: **slugabed**. SEE LAZY

slothfulness (sometimes in matters spiritual, and sometimes leading to depression) *n.*: **acedia**. SEE APATHY

slovenly *adj.*: **frowzy**. SEE MESSY

(2) slovenly (person) *n.*: **grobian**. SEE BOOR

slow (tempo) *adv.*: **andante**. ∎ The message was clear: under new management, the Catskill Mountains could go far. But ... Mac Robbins, a fast man with a one-liner, was playing it **andante** today: "It's a sad, sad time. What can you say? It's the passing of what used to be." (Stefan Kanfer, *American Scene: In New York: Simon Says Condo*, Time, 10-27-1986.)

(2) slow (abnormally ... heart rate) *n.*: **bradycardia**. SEE HEARTBEAT

(3) slow (in understanding or perception) *adj.*: **purblind**. SEE OBTUSE

slow-witted (esp. used of a person, as in ... and confused) *adj.*: **addlepated**. SEE CONFUSED

(2) slow-witted *adj.*: **gormless** [British]. SEE UNINTELLIGENT

slowing (engaging in ... tactics, esp. as a means to wear out an opponent or avoid confrontation) *adj.*: **Fabian**. SEE DILATORY

sluggish *adj.*: **bovine**. ∎ [Boxer Ray] Mercer spent two days in detention before being arraigned before Supreme Court Justice George Roberts yesterday [for trying to fix a fight]. His face had the gentle and almost **bovine** look familiar in old heavyweights who will to the wars no more. (Murray Kempton, *They'll Back You Only If It's Worth It*, Newsday, 06-30-1993, p. 13.)

(2) sluggish *adj.*: **logy**. ∎ The doctors prescribed powerful tranquilizers, Haldol and Clonopin, which helped control the seizures but made him **logy** and incapable of performing at a major league level. (Richard Demak, *Fighting the Enemy Within: Jim Eisenreich's Promising Major League Career Was Derailed by a Mysterious Ailment, But Now He's Working His Way Back*, Sports Illustrated, 06-22-1987, p. 40.)

(3) sluggish (as in weakened) *adj.*: **etiolated**. SEE WEAKENED

(4) sluggish *adj.*: **torpid**. SEE LETHARGIC

sluggishness (sometimes in matters spiritual, and sometimes leading to depression) *n.*: **acedia**. SEE APATHY

(2) sluggishness (as in lethargy) *n.*: **hebetude**. SEE LETHARGY

(3) sluggishness *n.*: **torpor**. SEE LETHARGY

slum (esp. in Brazil) *n.*: **favela**. ∎ Forget Carnival and the girl from Ipanema. The hot new attractions for visitors to Rio de Janeiro are the **favelas** — those infamous, scruffy, often felonious shantytowns that cling to Rio's sheer peaks. (Author not given, *Slumming Is Hot in Rio*, Newsweek, 04-17-2000, p. 74.)

slur (as in insult, delivered while leaving the scene) *n.*: **Parthian shot**. SEE PARTING SHOT

sly (characterized by ... and cunning conduct) *adj.*: **Machiavellian**. SEE DECEITFUL

small (very ...) *adj.*: **bantam**. SEE TINY

(2) small (very ...) *adj.*: **Lilliputian**. SEE TINY

small talk (idle ...) *n.*: **palaver**. ∎ How much sharing of personal information at work should you do? How much is too much? And on the other side, how do you handle personal questions flung your way at the office? ... Of course, we're just talking about everyday random **palaver** here. We're not talking about serious illness or major personal catastrophes. (Amy Joyce, *Too Personal for Professionals? Office Chitchat Can Be Harmless, But Sometimes It Crosses That Blurry Line*, The Washington Post, 04-07-2002, p. H6.)

(2) small talk *n.*: **bavardage**. SEE CHITCHAT

smart aleck *n.*: **wisenheimer**. ∎ Once upon a time, the big thrill for young **wisenheimers** who perched on Santa's lap was to pull off the old guy's fake beard. But these days, according to a new study, 95% of mall Santas are "Natural Santas" — that is, they have their own beard. (Eisenberg, *Notebook*, Time, 12-22-1997, p. 11.)

(2) smart aleck (and conceited person) *n.*: **jackanapes**. SEE CONCEITED

smell (loss of sense of ...) *n.*: **anosmia**. ∎ Why is it difficult to smell a fragrance on yourself? "Because you develop **anosmia**," says Antonia Bellanca, a top perfumer. "Your sense of smell becomes saturated, and your brain turns off to the fragrance." (Lois Joy Johnson, *Scents and Sensability*, Ladies Home Journal, 05-01-1996, p. 148.)

(2) smell (of or relating to sense of ...) *adj.*: **olfactory**. ∎ While we must rely on only three quarters of a square inch of **olfactory** equipment — as opposed to ten square inches on a dog and twenty-four square feet on a shark, which can smell a drop of blood from miles away — the human nose can still be turned into a powerful antenna. (Cal Fussman, *Fee-fi-fo-fum, I Smell ... Orange Peel, Leather, and My Daughter's Diaper*, Esquire, 09-01-1998, p. 168.)

(3) smell (which is fragrant) *n.*: **ambrosia** (*adj.*: **ambrosial***)* SEE FLAVOR

(4) smell (bad ... from body sweat) *n.*: **bromidrosis**. SEE SWEAT

(5) smell (bad ... from waste or decayed matter) *n.*: **effluvium**. SEE ODOR

(6) smell (foul) *n.*: **fetor**. SEE STENCH

smelling (like, or reminiscent of) *adj.*: **redolent**. SEE REMINISCENT

smelly *adj.*: **fetid**. ∎ Ask any economist to name the top 100 appreciating assets, and it is highly unlikely that old sneakers would make anyone's list. Yet the value of those decrepit shoes in the back of your closet — yes, even the ones that reek worse than **fetid** feta — may well have increased by a multiple akin to Amazon.com's stock. (L. Jon Wertheim, *The Smell of Money — There's a Hot Resale Market for Fetid Old Sneakers*, Sports Illustrated, 11-16-1998, p. R1.)

(2) smelly *adj.*: **mephitic** (*n.*: **mephitis**). ∎ An organization called the Human Ecology Action League has declared: "Perfume is going to be the tobacco smoke of tomorrow." To those who want to make America scent-free, perfume vapor, like nicotine smoke, is a **mephitic** poison in the nose, like the smell of a reeky skunk. (Richard Klein, *Get a Whiff of This: Breaking the Smell Barrier [History of Scent]*, The New Republic, 02-06-1995, p. 18.)

(3) smelly *adj.*: **noisome**. ∎ Odor caused by gum or mouth disease or that originates in the gastrointestinal system is impervious to brushing, rinsing and chewing, says [one dentist]. For common bad breath, mints are also a bad idea, says Kliossis. "You're feeding the bacteria with sugar — it's actually making the problem worse." He says regular brushing and flossing ought to take care of most **noisome** aromas. (Bo Emerson, *The Dragon Slayers: Our Minty Obsession With the Monster in Our Mouths*, The Atlanta Journal and Constitution, 11-08-2001.)

(4) smelly (atmosphere of crowded or poorly ventilated area) *n.*: **fug**. SEE MUSTY

smile (in a silly, self-conscious or affected manner, or say something in such a fashion) *v.i.*, *n.*: **simper**. SEE SMIRK

smiling (as in cheerful) *adj.*: **riant**. SEE CHEERFUL

smirk (in a silly, self-conscious or affected manner, or say something in such a fashion) *v.i.*, *n.*: **simper**. ∎ One heinous transgression is making another woman feel like half a woman because she didn't deliver her child "naturally." ... One day, during our mothers' group, [a woman] announced in a **simpering** voice that she had been able to put her daughter on her chest two seconds after birth (as opposed to those of us who'd had cesareans and had to wait several minutes). (Ellen Welty, *My Friend, My Rival*, Redbook, 05-01-1995, p. 116.)

smoky (and sooty) *adj.*: **fuliginous**. SEE SOOTY

smooch *v.t.*: **osculate**. SEE KISS

smooth (sounding) *adj.*: **dulcet**. SEE MELODIOUS

(2) smooth (sound) *adj.*: **euphonious** (*n.*: **euphony**). SEE MELODIOUS

(3) smooth (voice or sound) *adj.*: **mellifluous**. SEE MELODIOUS

smudged (or impure) *adj., v.t.*: **maculate**. SEE IMPURE

smutty *adj.*: **fescennine**. SEE OBSCENE

snake (of, relating to or resembling) *adj.*: **colubrine**. ∎ What do you get when you book one of the biggest house DJs on the planet into one of Cambridge's smallest clubs? We're guessing a serious party. ... Doors open at 8; we advise getting to Central Square early. By the time the music starts throbbing at 9, there will undoubtedly be a **colubrine** line slithering down Mass. Ave. (Christopher Muther, *Go! Wednesday,* The Boston Globe, 03-06-02, p. D2.)

snarl (as in confused or disarrayed mass) *n.*: **welter**. SEE JUMBLE

sneaky (scheming or trickery) *n.*: **jiggery-pokery**. SEE TRICKERY

snitch (or accuser) *n.*: **delator**. SEE ACCUSER
(2) snitch (on) *v.i.*: **peach**. SEE TATTLE

snivel (weakly) *v.i.*: **mewl**. SEE WHIMPER
(2) snivel (in a whiny or whimpering way) *v.i.*: **pule**. SEE WHIMPER

snob (esp. someone who seeks to associate with or flatter persons of rank or high social status) *n.*: **tufthunter**. SEE HANGER-ON

snoop (one who would ... into other's affairs) *n.*: **quidnunc**. SEE BUSYBODY

snoring (characterized by loud ... sounds) *adj.*: **stertorous**. ∎ [B]ut when, three days later, Elvis' condition dramatically worsened and his breathing became noticeably **stertorous**, the worried physician had no choice but to admit him to the hospital. (Peter Guralnick, *Careless Love: The Unmaking of Elvis Presley,* Little Brown [1999], p. 515.)

snowy *adj.*: **niveous**. ∎ Apart from Shakespeare, no other writer is more visible than Mark Twain. No other creature, excluding T. rex, has been returned to life more frequently than the man with the **niveous** hair, roustabout mustache and ivory-and-cream suit. (George Myers, Jr., *Twain's Mark Most American of Writers; Still Has Country's Number,* Columbus Dispatch [Ohio], 02-09-1997.)

snub (as in treat with contempt) *v.t.*: **contemn**. SEE SCORN

snubbing (as in disdain) *n.*: **misprision** (*v.t.*: **misprize**). SEE DISDAIN

so-called (by oneself) *adj.*: **soi-disant** [French]. SEE SELF-STYLED

soak *v.t.*: **imbrue**. ∎ That very night Black Partridge, a friendly chief, delivered to Heald a medal which had been given him by the Americans, saying he could not restrain his young men who were resolved to **imbrue** their hands in the blood of the white people, and he would no longer wear that token of friendship. (Benson J. Lossing, *Our Country: Volume 5: Chapter XCIII,* U.S. History, 09-01-1990.)
(2) soak (flax to separate fibers) *v.t.*: **ret**. SEE MOISTEN

soapy *adj.*: **saponaceous**. ∎ I learned that day that lather and taste buds do not mix, for Mother washed my mouth out with Ivory Soap. ... Yes, she was right to teach me that some words were wrong to utter, but I wish that that **saponaceous** experience had somehow taught me to consider why I would later want to use certain words rather than simply not to use them. (Thomas Nunnally, *Word Up, Word Down,* National Forum, 04-01-1995, p. 36.)

soaring (esp. too high for safety) *adj.*: **Icarian**. ∎ Gyrating exchange rates — led by the dollar's **Icarian** rise and fall — are the worst offenders of global economic order these days. (Sylvia Nasar, *What Governments Should Be Doing [Countries Need to Work Together to Ease Difficulties of International Competition],* Fortune, 03-14-1988.)

sob (in lament for the dead) *v.i.*: **keen**. SEE WAIL
(2) sob (in a whiny or whimpering way) *v.i.*: **pule**. SEE WHIMPER
(3) sob (as in wail) *v.i.*: **ululate**. SEE WAIL

sobbing (of or relating to) *adj.*: **lachrymal**. SEE TEARS
(2) sobbing *adj.*: **lachrymose**. SEE TEARFUL

social (and festive) *adj.*: **Anacreontic**. SEE CONVIVIAL

social climber (esp. having attained a position without effort or merit) *n.*: **arriviste**. SEE UPSTART
(2) social climber *n.*: **parvenu**. SEE UPSTART

social structures (breakdown or collapse of ...) *n.*: **anomie**. SEE BREAKDOWN

society (fashionable ...) *n.*: **beau monde** [French]. SEE HIGH SOCIETY
(2) society (fashionable ...) *n.*: **bon ton** [French]. SEE HIGH SOCIETY

sodomizer (as in man who commits sodomy on or has sex with a boy) *n.*: **pederast**. ∎ Pederasts in particular have lots of help in finding a good time in Asia, Africa or Latin America. ... One of the most notorious guides to world sex spas for homosexuals seeking boys is called the Spartacus International Gay Guide. (Michael S. Serrill, *Defiling the Children — In the Basest Effect of the Burgeoning Sex Trade, the Search for Newer Thrills Has Chained Increasing Numbers of Girls and Boys to Prostitution*, Time, 06-21-1993, p. 52.)

soil *v.t.*: **begrime**. See DIRTY
(2) soil (with mud) *v.t.*: **bemire**. See MUD
(3) soil *v.t.*: **besmirch**. See TARNISH

soiled (or impure) *adj., v.t.*: **maculate**. See IMPURE

soldier (British ...) *n.*: **Tommy Atkins** [based on Thomas Atkins, a fictitious name used in sample blank military forms for the British army]. ∎ It's a sad legacy from the days when Brittania ruled the world with its legions of working-class soldiers doing the dirty work from Canada to Egypt, from India to China. Today the descendants of **Tommy Atkins** find themselves on the dole, with the manufacturing jobs gone off to the colonies Britain once ruled. Their only release, it seems, is to follow their soccer teams, get blind drunk and wreak havoc. (Jack Todd, *English Soccer's Shame*, The Gazette [Montreal, Quebec], 06-18-2004, p. C1.)
(2) soldier (or, relating to or suggesting) *adj.*: **martial**. See WARLIKE

solicitude (treat another with excessive ...) *n., v.t.*: **wet-nurse**. See CODDLE

solid (having a ... and muscular body build) *adj.*: **mesomorphic**. See MUSCULAR

solitary (person, as in recluse, esp. for religious reasons) *n.*: **eremite**. See RECLUSE AND ANCHORITE

solitude (social ...) *n.*: **purdah**. See SECLUSION

somber (as in suggestive of a funeral) *adj.*: **sepulchral**. See FUNEREAL

sometimes *adv.*: **betimes**. ∎ I can't say we had any affection for [our teacher], but we respected him and never gave him any guff. We read Caesar; then we read Cicero; then we read Virgil, and **betimes** we made side trips either in class or in Latin club to look at other writers, even to a couple of Milton's Latin poems. (John Gould, *On the Verge, a Boost from Virgil*, The Christian Science Monitor, 02-18-2000, p. 23.)

son (of or relating to a daughter or ...) *adj.*: **filial**. See OFFSPRING

song (of a gondolier) *n.*: **barcarole**. ∎ 2:49 P.M.: The gondolier is in full-throated **barcarole** when, suddenly, he clutches his chest, grimacing horribly, and lurches backward into the canal, taking his oar with him. I assume a massive coronary. (Mark Leyner, *Gondola! [Stranded in Venice — Humor]*, Esquire, 04-01-1997, p. 54.)
(2) song (or poem in honor of a bride or bridegroom) *n.*: **epithalamium**. See TOAST
(3) song (or poem of mourning esp. for a dead person) *n.*: **threnody**. See REQUIEM

sonorous *adj.*: **orotund**. ∎ The P. A. system carried her Star Spangled Banner over infield dirt, outfield grass and bleacher brick. Annie's operatic soprano drowned everything in its path, rolling in a flood of **orotund** vowels. (Franz Lidz, *Focus: Belting it Out of the Park: Anthem Annie Aims to Sing in Every Baseball Stadium in the Major Leagues*, Sports Illustrated, 09-18-1995, p. R1.)

soon *adv.*: **anon**. See MOMENTARILY
(2) soon (very ..., as in, in an instant) *n.*: **trice** (as in, in a trice). See QUICKLY

soot (abnormal fear of ... and dirt) *n.*: **mysophobia**. See FEAR

soothe (as in placate) *v.t.*: **propitiate**. See PLACATE

soothing (of pain, distress or tension) *adj.*: **anodyne**. ∎ In his ideal America, marijuana would be **anodyne**, better than medicine. More like one of those cheerful balms that help take a rough corner or two off life — like a latte grande with skim, or a Disney theme park. (Hanna Rosin, *California Gears Up For a Long, Strange Trip*, The New Republic, 02-17-1997.)
(2) soothing (used often of a medicinal treatment) *adj.*: **balsamic**. ∎ Torn between Valium and Prozac, she reached instead for her new Stress-Begone Potpourri. According to the label, its lovely flowers and colorful leaves had been perfumed with a mystical combination of floral and **balsamic** notes that the ancient Aztecs had turned to when they needed soothing and comforting after a particularly stressful day of human sacrifices and tortures. (Peter Dichter, *I Smell a Lawsuit*, Drug & Cosmetic Industry, 06-01-1998, p. 71.)
(3) soothing (lotion or balm) *n.*: **demulcent**. ∎ Comfrey is often called knit-bone and healing herb. ... Glycerin is used [as an ingredient in comfrey] because it is a **demulcent** and is so healing. (Joseph

Van Seters, *Comfrey: The Forgotten Herb*, Mother Earth News, 12-01-1994, p. 18.)

(4) soothing (agent) *n.*: **anodyne**. SEE PAIN-RELIEVER

(5) soothing (to the ear) *adj.*: **dulcet**. SEE MELODIOUS

soothsayer (by using lightning or animal innards) *n.*: **haruspex**. SEE FORTUNETELLER

sooty *adj.*: **fuliginous**. ∎ London, by reason of the excessive [cold air hindering] the ascent of the smoke, was ... filled with the **fuliginous** steam. (Author not given, *When Nature Roars*, Earth Explorer, 02-01-1995.)

sophisticated (as in trendy and wealthy young people) *n.*: **jeunesse dorée** [French]. SEE FASHIONABLE

(2) sophisticated (as in refined or elegant) *adj.*: **raffiné** (or **raffine**) [French]. SEE REFINED

sophistry *n.*: **casuistry**. SEE FALLACIOUS

sorcery *n.*: **necromancy**. SEE BLACK MAGIC

sorrow (express ... over) *v.t.*: **bewail**. SEE LAMENT

(2) sorrow (as in depression) *n.*: **cafard** [French]. SEE DEPRESSION

(3) sorrow *n.*: **dolor** (*adj.*: **dolorous**). SEE SADNESS

sorrowful (often regarding something gone) *adj.*: **elegiac**. ∎ [Richard] Danielpour addressed the audience from the stage to explain the genesis of his trio, "A Child's Reliquary," which he composed last year to mark the death of a colleague's 18-month-old son. "I know of nothing more tragic or heartbreaking than the death of a child," he said, and yet the music inspired by the occasion was much more than just **elegiac**. (Jeremy Eichler, *A Glimpse At The Piano Trio Times Three*, Newsday, 05-08-2000, p. B9.)

(2) sorrowful (sounds) *adj.*: **plangent**. SEE MOURNFUL

(3) sorrowful *adj.*: **tristful**. SEE SAD

sort (into separate parts) *v.i.*: **disaggregate**. SEE SEPARATE

sorts (of all ...) *adj.*: **omnifarious**. SEE VARIED

soul *n.*: **anima**. ∎ Dear Dr. Fox: I was having a debate with a friend about whether animals have souls. I said yes, and she said "prove it." What's your answer, Doc? [Answer:] ... The spirit, or animating principle, can be objectively observed but cannot be weighed or measured. Cut off an animal's head and

see what happens. Same for humans. You're left with a body and the **anima** has gone. (Michael Fox, DVM, *Do Animals Have Souls? Tell the Doc*, St. Louis Post-Dispatch, 06-08-1997, p. 12D.)

(2) soul (loss of the ..., as in damnation) *n.*: **perdition**. SEE DAMNATION

sound (which is unpleasant or incongruous) *n.*: **dissonance**. ∎ [After the jockey fell into unconsciousness and slid off the horse during the race,] there was the awful **dissonance** of the lone horse galloping riderless. (Laura Hillenbrand, *Seabiscuit*, Random House [2001], p. 330.)

(2) sound (which is repeating such as a drumbeat, machine-gun fire or hoofs of a galloping horse) *n.*: **rataplan**. ∎ Gore accused Dukakis of being "absurdly timid" in criticizing [Jesse] Jackson, declared that "we're not choosing a preacher, we're choosing a president," and finally, after garnering what he thought was the coveted endorsement of Ed Koch, stood by as the irascible mayor delivered a **rataplan** of one-liners about [Jackson]. (Ellen Nakashima, *13 Ways of Looking at Al Gore and Race*, The Washington Post, 04-23-2000, p. W06.)

(3) sound *n.*: **sonority**. ∎ And perhaps I'm simply a poor bet for her or anybody, since I so like the [ringing bells] of early romance, yet lack the urge to do more than ignore it when that sweet **sonority** threatens to develop into something else. (Richard Ford, *Independence Day*, Knopf [1995], p. 10.)

(4) sound (which is harsh and unpleasant) *n.*: **cacophony**. SEE NOISE

(5) sound (of ... mind) *adj.*: **compos mentis**. SEE SANE

(6) sound (financially ..., esp. with respect to a plan, deal or investment that can be trusted completely because it is supposedly safe and sure to succeed) *adj.*: **copper-bottomed** [British]. SEE SURE-FIRE

(7) sound (which is pleasant) *adj.*: **euphonious** (*n.*: **euphony**). SEE MELODIOUS

(8) sound (words having the same ..., but different meaning) *adj.*: **homophonic**. SEE PRONUNCIATION

(9) sound (which is full and rich) *adj.*: **orotund**. SEE SONOROUS

(10) sound (fear of) *n.*: **phonophobia**. SEE FEAR

sounds (which are pleasing to the ear) *adj.*: **dulcet**. SEE MELODIOUS

sour (as in tangy or tart) *adj.*: **acidulous**. SEE TART

source (principal ...) *n.*: **wellhead**. ∎ In Portland, where your sex life is considered your business unless it affects the air quality, the response was not warm. To a number of locals, the sole consolation was that Lewinsky and Bleiler — unlike Packwood and Harding — were not really local products, but came from the **wellhead** of all dubious outbursts, Southern California. (David Sarasohn, *L'Affaire Lewinsky Rocks the Weirdness Capital*, Newsday, 02-08-1998, p. B4.)

sourpuss (as in person who never laughs) *n*.: **agelast**. SEE HUMORLESS

south (of, pertaining to or coming from the ..., esp. lower southern hemisphere) *adj*.: **austral**. ∎ No aircraft landing has ever been attempted at the South Pole during the **austral** winter due to the severe cold, high winds and total darkness, experts say. (The Associated Press, *Medical Airdrop Over South Pole a Success*, Newsday, 07-14-1999, p. A25.)

space (between teeth) *n*.: **diastema**. SEE GAP

(2) space (esp. between the end of a sovereign's reign and the ascension of a successor) *n*.: **interregnum**. SEE INTERVAL

(3) space (esp. small ... between things or events) *n*.: **interstice**. SEE GAP

(4) space (as in gap) *n*.: **lacuna**. SEE GAP

(5) space (adequate ... for living) *n*.: **lebensraum** [German]. SEE BREATHING SPACE

spacious *adj*.: **capacious**. ∎ The new building was tall and **capacious**, and although today it is filled to bursting with more than a million books, back in 1857 it had only a few thousand volumes and plenty of extra space to spare. (Simon Winchester, *The Professor and the Madman*, Harper Collins [1998], p. 77.)

spacy (person, as in an impractical contemplative person with no clear occupation or income) *n*.: **luftmensch** [lit. "man of air"; German, Yiddish]. SEE DREAMER

Spanish (speaking neighborhood) *n*.: **barrio**. ∎ In the **barrios** of Los Angeles, an Argentine can watch the latest movies from his homeland at any of a dozen theaters, while a Guatemalan can find a soccer league composed entirely of players from the country he left. (George J. Church, *A Melding of Cultures: Latins, The Largest New Group, Are Making Their Presence Felt*, Time, 07-08-1985, p. 36.)

sparing (as in not indulgent) *adj*.: **abstemious**. SEE RESTRAINED

sparkle *v.i*.: **coruscate**. ∎ In the best of this writing

[by Ralph McInerny] — including the Priest (1973), Connolly's Life (1983), Leave of Absence (1986), and the novels featuring his detective protagonist Father Rodger Dowling — are found gems of **coruscating** insight. (Author not given, *Football, Neo-thomism and the Silver Age of Catholic Higher Education*, Christianity Today, 09-10-96.)

sparkling *adj*.: **coruscant**. SEE GLITTERING

spartan (as in marked by simplicity, frugality, self-discipline and/or self-restraint) *adj*.: **Lacedaemoninan** [Derives from Lacedaemon, the ancient Greek city of Sparta.] ∎ [In] *Manhood at Harvard* [author] Kim Townsend [states that at] the end of the 19th century Harvard University fostered ... many of the ideals ... that were to dominate American culture in the first half of the 20th century. ... A real man rose to challenges, didn't whimper, complain or turn tail but rather embodied an almost **Lacedaemonian** self-discipline and a truly Christian generosity. (Author not given, *Hardcovers in Brief*, The Washington Post, 11-03-1996, p. X13.)

spasms (as in convulsions, during or after pregnancy) *n*.: **eclampsia**. SEE CONVULSIONS

spastic *adj*.: **clonic**. ∎ "The two most common forms are **clonic** repetitions like cartoon character Porky Pig with his 'Th-th-th-that's all, folks!'" says Dr. Bernard Landes, an audiologist and speech pathologist in Long Beach, Calif. (Carole Rust, *Stuttering is Common in Toddlers and Usually Curable*, The Dallas Morning News, 06-02-1998, p. 2C.)

speak (esp. in a long-winded or pompous manner) *v.i*.: **bloviate**. ∎ Guess times aren't what they used to be for Harvard Law School. Apparently, the venerable institution feels its professors — aside from a famous handful — aren't being quoted enough in the press. So the news office is sending out word to the media ... that Harvard Law has many experts available to **bloviate** at the drop of a [hat]. (Al Kamen, *Inquiring Minds and Monica*, The Washington Post, 04-03-2001, p. A19.)

(2) speak (inability to ... due to brain injury) *n*.: **aphasia** SEE UNCOMPREHENDING

(3) speak (quickly and excitedly) *v.t*.: **burble** SEE GUSH

(4) speak (pompously, loudly, or theatrically) *v.i*.: **declaim**. SEE PROCLAIM

(5) speak (inability to ... due to hoarseness): **dysphonia**. SEE HOARSENESS

(6) speak (or write at length on a subject) *v.i*.: **expatiate**. SEE EXPOUND

(7) speak (or write in a scholarly manner, often used in a derogatory fashion) *v.i.*: **lucubrate**. SEE DISCOURSE

(8) speak (at length) *v.i.*: **perorate** (*n.*: **peroration**). SEE MONOLOGUE

speaker (or writer who is dull and boring) *n.*: **dryasdust**. SEE BORING

speaking (fear of ... aloud) *n.*: **phonophobia**. SEE FEAR

spear *n.*: **assegai**. ∎ If he had lived in the time of the legendary King Shaka, Sifiso Nkabinde would have been a 19th century Zulu warrior, destined to live and die by the **assegai**. (Peter Hawthorne, *Africa: Bloodlines of the Zulu: The Assassination of a Latter-day Tribal Warlord Reignites One of South Africa's Bitterest Conflicts*, Time International, 02-08-1999, p. 35.)

specialty (area of ...) *n.*: **métier** [French]. SEE FORTE

specific (to one person or thing; e.g. languages which use symbols or pictures instead of words) *adj.*: **idiographic**. SEE UNIQUE

specious (engaging in argument which may be ...) *adj., n.*: **eristic**. ∎ The law, roundly stated, tells us that you may not kill another person except in self-defense. The Menendez brothers had no such excuse, but they were got off by a lawyer who mesmerized the jury into rogue theories of psychological compulsions. Such arguments go to **eristic** legal lengths. (William F. Buckley, Jr., *The Susan Smith Case*, National Review, 08-28-1995, p. 54.)

(2) specious (reasoning intended to ... rationalize or mislead) *n.*: **casuistry**. SEE FALLACIOUS

(3) specious (and/or illogical argument) *n.*: **choplogic**. SEE FALLACY

(4) specious (argument where one proves or disproves a point which is not at issue) *n.*: **ignoratio elenchi** [Latin]. SEE IRRELEVANCY

speckled (with a darker color) *adj.*: **brindled**. SEE SPOTTED

spectacle (violent ... in which shame, degradation or harm is inflicted on a person, often for the enjoyment of onlookers) *n.*: **Roman holiday** [derives from gladiatorial combats of the ancient Roman circus staged for the entertainment of the audience]. ∎ The last time a convict was executed in broad daylight [in 1936], 20,000 people showed up. ... Most of us probably don't want to see someone put to death, but a lot of people do. ... [Reporters] wrote that souvenir hunters rushed the body, and that the sheriff created a "**Roman holiday**." (Kim Ode, *Should We See the Execution [of Timothy McVeigh]? It Might Teach Us a Lesson*, Star Tribune [Minneapolis, MN], 04-28-2001.)

(2) spectacle (or ceremony which is pretentious) *n.*: **mummery**. SEE CEREMONY

specter *n.*: **wraith**. SEE APPARITION

speculation (sometimes in stocks) *n.*: **agiotage**. ∎ The secretary of the Dagestani Security Council said on Monday that there will be no total mobilization in Dagestan. ... According to [the secretary], the **agiotage** around the statement of the Dagestani Security Council issued on Sunday is explained by technical mistakes. (Author not given, *No Total Mobilization in Dagestan — Security Council*, ITAR-TASS, 09-06-1999.)

speech (formal ...) *n.*: **allocution**. ∎ During an **allocution** that left him hoarse, Mr. Craig attacked from every angle the truth and constitutionality of Article I, charging perjury [by President Clinton] before the grand jury. (Frank J. Murray, *President's Defense Team Attacks Seriousness of Charges*, The Washington Times, 01-21-1999, p. A1.)

(2) speech (pattern which is unique to each person) *n.*: **idiolect**. ∎ And you've finally abandoned that flawed notion of Standard English as a superior dialect. Now it's time for a naked look in your linguistic mirror. Take a closer look. See the unique way you put words together? That's your **idiolect**: your personal dialect. That's your language; no one else has it. (Chris Redgate, *The Red Pencil*, The Washington Post, 05-17-2001, p. C9.)

(3) speech (inability to comprehend ... or written words due to brain injury) *n.*: **aphasia**. SEE UNCOMPREHENDING

(4) speech (which is hypocritical, sanctimonious, pious and/or insincere) *n.*: **cant**. SEE PIOUS

(5) speech (very enthusiastic or excited ... or writing) *n.*: **dithyramb**. SEE ENTHUSIASTIC

(6) speech (or writing which is cryptic or obscure, esp. deliberately) *adj.*: **elliptical**. SEE CRYPTIC

(7) speech (unintelligible ..., esp. heard in certain Christian congregations) *n.*: **glossolalia**. SEE UNINTELLIGIBLE

(8) speech (or writing which is pompous or bombastic) *n.*: **grandiloquence**. SEE POMPOSITY

(9) speech (as in common language between people of different languages) *n.*: **lingua franca**. SEE LANGUAGE

(10) speech (which is wordy or repetitive) *n*.: **logorrhea**. SEE VERBOSITY

(11) speech (which is full and rich) *adj*.: **orotund**. SEE SONOROUS

(12) speech (or writing which is trite or simplistic) *n*.: **pablum**. SEE TRITENESS

(13) speech (free ...) *n*.: **parrhesia**. SEE FREE SPEECH

(14) speech (regional ... or dialect) *n*.: **patois**. SEE DIALECT

(15) speech (lengthy) *n*.: **peroration**. SEE MONOLOGUE

(16) speech (relating to ... where the purpose is to establish a mood of sociability rather than to communicate information or ideas, such as "have a nice day") *adj*.: **phatic**. SEE PLEASANTRIES

(17) speech (common ... of the people) *n*.: **vulgate**. SEE VERNACULAR

speechless (lit. loss of voice due to disease, injury or psychological causes) *n*.: **aphonia**. SEE LARYNGITIS

speed *n*.: **alacrity**. ∎ [The Porsche 911 Turbo] also goes around corners. Which is just as well, for it can bridge the gap between them with such **alacrity** that a less than faithful chassis would be a serious oversight. (Dave Moore, *Big Boys' Toy Story — Fast But Silent Porsche 911 Turbo*, The Press [Canterbury, New Zealand], 12-06-2000, p. 50.)

(2) speed *n*.: **celerity**. ∎ Only a coach, or an old offensive lineman, would find a center captivating. The rest of us, hypnotized over the years by television, usually follow the same old path; our eyes go where the football goes. But if you have a chance to watch the Steelers through your lenses instead of a TV camera's, watch Dawson. You will marvel at the **celerity** and dexterity displayed by this 6-2, 290-pound lineman. (Dennis Dillon, *The Best, Hands Down, [Center Dermontti Dawson]*, The Sporting News, 09-02-1996, p. S18.)

(3) speed (at top ...) *adv*.: **tanivy**. SEE TOP SPEED

speedy (as in hasty) *adj*.: **festinate**. SEE HASTY

(2) speedy *adv*.: **tanivy**. SEE TOP SPEED

(3) speedy *adj*.: **velocious**. SEE FAST

spellbind (as in bewitch or enchant) *v.t.*: **ensorcell** (or **ensorcel**). SEE ENCHANT

spelling (expert) *n*.: **orthographer**. ∎ After 10 tense rounds, Jody-Anne Maxwell, 12, of Kingston, Jamaica, correctly spelled chiaroscurist (an artist who emphasizes light and dark), outspelling 248 finalists in the Scripps Howard National Spelling Bee last week. The young **orthographer** — the first from outside the continental U.S. — won $10,000, a trophy, and other prizes. (Author not given, *Phil Hartman; Alice Walton; Lyle and Erik Menendez; Jody-Anne Maxwell*, U.S. News & World Report, 06-08-1998, p. 9.)

(2) spelling (art or study of correct ...) *n*.: **orthography**. ∎ Our educational practices are now so bizarre that they would defy the pen of a Jonathan Swift to satirize them. [Where] I work, for example, the teachers have received instructions that they are not to impart the traditional disciplines of spelling and grammar. Pettifogging attention to details of syntax and **orthography** is said to inhibit children's creativity and powers of self-expression. (Theodore Dalrymple, *Oxford's Lofty Image to the Contrary, Brits Revel In a Cult of Stupidity*, Minneapolis Star Tribune, 01-30-1995, p. 7A.)

spent (as in weakened) *adj*.: **etiolated**. SEE WEAKENED

sphere *n*.: **ambit**. SEE REALM

(2) sphere (as in area of activity or interest) *n*.: **purlieu**. SEE DOMAIN

spicy (agreeably ... in taste or flavor) *adj*.: **piquant**. SEE ZESTY

spider *n*.: **arachnid**. ∎ Spiders often send shivers down our spines, turn dreams into nightmares and clutter our ceilings with discarded webs. They are also beautiful creatures, these **arachnids**, with their soft curves, graceful movements and long, sleek legs, says artist Jack Plummer. (Kathy A. Goolsby, *Artist's Creepy Spiders Capture Art Gallery Spotlight*, The Arlington Morning News, 01-09-2000, p. 1C.)

spiders (fear of ...) *n*.: **arachnophobia**. ∎ According to a recent survey, **arachnophobia** is the UK's second most common phobia (after public speaking). In other words, more people are scared of spiders than are scared of death itself. (Author not given, *Health and Wellbeing: Spiders Are Not Out to Get You*, The Daily Telegraph, 02-18-2000.)

spin (a log by rotating with the feet) *v.t.*: **birl**. SEE LOGROLLING

spine (curvature of the ...) *n*.: **lordosis**. ∎ Recently retired Cowboy defensive tackle Randy White was another swaybacked athlete. For linemen like White, a few extra pounds and pronounced **lordosis** mean more leverage and strength. Besides, who wants to tell White he's paunchy? Heck, I would even be afraid to tell him he has pronounced **lordosis**. (Jack McCallum, *Gut Feelings: Hey Guys, Don't Look Down — Something May Be Gaining on You*, Sports Illustrated, 07-30-1990, p. 56.)

spineless (or a person who is ...) *adj., n.:* **namby-pamby**. ∎ But whether hawk or dove, many strategists still seem to favor only one of the two paths [to picking stocks]. Can that really be the answer? Choose one road for 2001 and stick to it? No way, I say. I don't want to sound **namby-pamby**, but I think you have to own stocks from both the old world and new. (Andy Serwer, *Investor's Guide 2001: Street Life — The Split-Screen Market This Year Has Thrown Many Investors For a Loop*, Fortune, 12-18-2000, p. 226.)

(2) spineless (as in cowardly) *adj.:* **pusillanimous**. See COWARDLY

spinning (or spiraling motion, often an ocean current) *n.:* **gyre**. See SPIRALING

spinning off (act of ... into parts) *n.:* **fission**. See SPLITTING

spiny (as in prickly) *adj.:* **echinate**. See PRICKLY

spiral *adj.:* **helical**. ∎ The spiral staircase leading to Tim Tully's office and laboratory at Cold Spring Harbor Laboratories in New York represents the **helical** structure of DNA. (Judy Silber, *Scientist Probes Beyond "Genes Are Everything" Thesis*, The Christian Science Monitor, 08-27-1998.)

spiraling (motion, often an ocean current) *n.:* **gyre**. ∎ Widening **gyre**. The escalating expenses and tuition costs of the 1980s have led to a dangerous financial spiral in higher education. State and federal aid together rose 50 percent, less than half the rate of increase in college costs. (Betsy Wagner, *The High Cost of Learning*, U.S. News & World Report, 06-21-1993, p. 58.)

spirit (as in vigor, energy and enthusiasm) *n.:* **élan** [French]. ∎ If Ueberroth is an impresario embodying the renewed American spirit, that **élan** has taken up residence most notably among the generation of Americans called yuppies, the young urban professionals (aged roughly from the mid-20s to the late 30s) who are supplying much of the bright entrepreneurial energy driving the American economy. (Lance Morrow, *Man of the Year: Feeling Proud Again Olympic Organizer Peter Ueberroth Puts on an Extraordinary Spectacle, Showing What America's Entrepreneurial Spirit Can do*, Time, 01-07-1985, p. 20.)

(2) spirit (distinctive ... of a place) *n.:* **genius loci** [Latin]. ∎ For more than 30 years Sir Nicholas threw his energy and, when available, his money into renovation of his home, which he once described as "the centre of my existence." As the purchaser will soon discover, he is still the castle's **genius loci**, with almost every corner of the house and grounds reflecting his exuberantly complex personality. (Tom Kidd, *Property: A Tower That Mary Queen of Scots Was Pleased to Sleep in — Fordell Castle, in Fife*, The Daily Telegraph, 08-14-1999, p. 5.)

(3) spirit (of an era) *n.:* **zeitgeist**. ∎ Every decade is remembered for some expression of its **zeitgeist**. By their actions and their deeds, overindulgent Americans have unwittingly branded the last decade of the old millennium The Narcissistic '90s. (Author not given, *Culture, et Cetera*, The Washington Times, 11-30-1999, p. A2.)

(4) spirit (as in aura or impalpable emantion) *n.:* **effluvium**. See AURA

(5) spirit (evil ... who has sex with sleeping women) *n.:* **incubus**. See DEMON

(6) spirit (evil female ... who has sex with sleeping men) *n.:* **succubus**. See DEMON

spirited *adj.:* **mettlesome**. ∎ The $1 billion for housing gives purpose, and the soul is flourishing, a lively urban soul that fulfills the two love letters to New York spelled out uniquely in brass letters on the plaza fence. [One] from Walt Whitman: "City of the sea! ... Proud and passionate city — **mettlesome**, mad, extravagant city!" (Bonnie Angelo, *Living: Where the Skyline Meets the Shore — After a Massive Recycling Effort, a Lively Neighborhood Blooms in the Shadow of Wall Street*, Time, 10-23-1989, p. 82.)

(2) spirited (as in jolly) *adj.:* **Falstaffian**. See JOVIAL

(3) spirited (girl) *n., adj.:* **hoyden**. See TOMBOY

spiritual (pertaining to knowledge of ... or intellectual things) *adj.:* **gnostic**. ∎ Unhappily, the Markhams, out of ignorance and pigheadedness, have failed to intuit the one **gnostic** truth of real estate (a truth impossible to reveal without seeming dishonest and cynical): that people never find or buy the house they say they want. (Richard Ford, *Independence Day*, Knopf [1995], p. 24.)

spit (dribbling from the mouth) *v.t., n.:* **slaver**. See DROOL

splash (light ...) *n.:* **plash**. ∎ They burble, they babble, they **plash**. ... No matter how you describe the calm-down sound of water trickling over polished stones into a serene pool, Zen-inspired tabletop relaxation fountains — now available just about everywhere — are making a big splash this holiday shopping season. (Don Oldenburg, *Focus; A Cash Niagara From Desktop Waterfalls*, The Washington Post, 12-21-1999, p. C4.)

splendid (as in of the highest quality) *n.*: **first water** (usu. as in "of the first water"). SEE QUALITY

(2) splendid *adj.*: **frabjous** (often as in "Oh frabjous day!"). SEE WONDERFUL

(3) splendid *adj.*: **galumptious**. SEE EXCELLENT

(4) splendid *adj.*: **palmary**. SEE EXCELLENT

(5) splendid *adj.*: **skookum**. SEE EXCELLENT

splinters *n.*: **flinders**. SEE BITS AND PIECES

split *adj.*: **cloven**. ∎ A fast-growing population in a region **cloven** by the borders of New Mexico, Texas and Mexico could be facing a crisis not far down the road — where to find enough water to supply the demands of more people and expanding industry. (Author not given, *Water Crisis Threatens Rio Grande Cities*, The Dallas Morning News, 07-12-1999, p. 17A.)

(2) split (often from or within a group or union) *n.*: **scission**. ∎ The Scottish Nationalist Party and the Northern (formerly Lombard) League both pretend that their **scission** from Great Britain or the Italian Republic will pose no problems and may even pass unnoticed within a united Europe. (G.M. Tamas, *A Legacy of Empire*, [The Rise of Europe's Little Nations], The Wilson Quarterly, 01-01-1994, p. 77.)

(3) split (into thin layers) *v.i.*: **delaminate**. SEE SEPARATE

(4) split (open) *v.t., v.i., n.*: **fissure**. SEE CRACK

split apart (tending to break into, ... or disintegrate) *adj.*: **fissiparous**. SEE BREAK UP

splitting (act of ... into parts) *n.*: **fission**. ∎ After an uncharacteristically long wait of nine months, Michael Dingman, 58, is spinning off yet another part of his Henley Group, a conglomerate given to amoeba-like **fission**: This makes the fourth time it has divided itself since it was created three years ago. (Alan Deutschman, *Fortune People: Spin Control*, Fortune, 11-06-1989, p. 195.)

(2) splitting (into two parts, esp. by tearing apart or violent separation) *n.*: **diremption**. SEE SEPARATION

spoil *v.i.*: **cosset**. SEE PAMPER

(2) spoil (or indulge another person in an overprotective way) *v.t.*: **mollycoddle**. SEE OVERPROTECT

(3) spoil (as in treat with excessive concern) *n., v.t.*: **wet-nurse**. SEE CODDLE

spoken (not capable of being ...) *adj.*: **ineffable**. SEE INDESCRIBABLE

(2) spoken *adj.*: **nuncupative**. SEE VERBAL

spokesman (or leader esp. for a political cause) *n.*: **fugleman**. SEE LEADER

(2) spokesman *n.*: **prolocutor**. ∎ To appreciate McCurry's talents [as President Clinton's spokesman], transport yourself back and picture [President Nixon's spokesman] Ronald Ziegler dealing with Watergate. Bland, insipid, wind-him-up-and-listen-to-him-recite. He never gave a substantive answer to a question in six years. ... George Bush's **prolocutor** Marlin Fitzwater was also able, but too stiff. (Joseph Spear, *Mike McCurry: Simply, the Best*, San Jose Mercury News [California], 07-31-1998.)

sponge (off of) *v.t.*: **cadge**. SEE BEG

spooky *adj.*: **eldritch**. SEE EERIE

spot (something which may be difficult to discern) *v.t.*: **descry**. SEE PERCEIVE

spotlight *n.*: **réclame** [French]. SEE PUBLICITY

spotted (with a darker color) *adj.*: **brindled**. ∎ On a summer's day now, mint-green pastures are dotted with the tall, **brindled** cows, their white coats sporting distinctive brown markings. Their black-patched eyes resemble natural sunglasses. (Author not given, *Friend or Foe? Cows Were Both in '44*, St. Louis Post-Dispatch, 09-05-1994, p. 1E.)

(2) spotted *adj.*: **dappled**. ∎ Gateway computers, manufactured at North Sioux City, are packed in boxes printed to look like the black-and-white **dappled** hide of a cow because the company was founded by the son of a Sioux City cattle buyer. (George F. Will, *Meanwhile, in South Dakota*, The Washington Post, 05-13-1999, p. A27.)

(3) spotted (esp. in black and white) *adj.*: **piebald**. ∎ Sarah Jane Hurley [is] a drunken derelict known as Cow Lady because of her black-and-white spotted coat. ... When a fellow street person wearing the trademark **piebald** coat is murdered, Cow Lady realizes ... that once they realize they've killed the wrong woman, she will be next. (Gail Cooke, *Intricate Intrigue Hits Home*, The Dallas Morning News, 07-26-1998, p. 10J.)

(4) spotted (as if by drops) *adj.*: **guttate**. SEE DROPS

spouse *n*.: **helpmeet**. SEE HELPMATE

spray (esp. with holy water) *v.t.*: **asperse**. SEE SPRINKLE

spread (false charges or rumors) *v.t.*: **asperse**. SEE DEFAME

(2) spread (over a surface in a scattered way) *v.t.*: **bestrew**. SEE COVER

(3) spread (news or a rumor about) *v.t.*: **bruit**. SEE RUMOR

sprightly (and magical) *adj*.: **elfin**. ∎ For reasons as difficult to identify as the gradations of excellence that turn silver to gold, sports fans quadrennially [i.e. in every Olympic Games] bestow their affection on an **elfin** gymnast. (Jill Smolowe, *Olympic Special Section: Sprite Fight: Which of the Extraordinary Tumbling Pixies Will Become the Seoul Sweetheart?* Time, 09-19-1988, p. 54.)

spring (back, as in recoil) *v.i.*: **resile**. SEE RECOIL

sprinkle (esp. with holy water) *v.t.*: **asperse**. ∎ Even Sixtus V, who insisted on having his obelisks **aspersed** with holy water to cast out their devils, admired the brilliance of the Egyptians who had been able to carve such great stones. (Anthony Grafton, *The Obelisks' Tale*, The New Republic, 11-24-1997.)

spruce up *v.t.*: **titivate**. ∎ Of all the charges that technophobes level against the computer, one that is undeniably true is that it is ugly. ... Computer firms have attempted to **titivate** their technology by encasing it in svelte, matte-black plastic. (Author not given, *Monitor, Monitor on the Wall*, The Economist, 11-08-1997.)

spunky (girl) *n., adj*.: **hoyden**. SEE TOMBOY

spur (as in stimulus) *n*.: **fillip**. SEE STIMULUS

spurious (and/or illogical argument) *n*.: **choplogic**. SEE FALLACY

squander (something away) *v.t.*: **fribble**. ∎ But it isn't so much this ill-conceived and high-handed notion of billing me for product not delivered [internet access services] that fuels my ire, but the fact that without my permission you will have a full month's use of mine and thousands of others' millions of dollars to fritter and **fribble** and squander. A pox on your house, sir! (Author not given, *Letters*, Denver Rocky Mountain News, 05-30-1999, p. 2G.)

squat (and fat) *adj*.: **fubsy**. ∎ Well, it was another night of The Simpsons for Bill and Hillary. In separate dens, no doubt. The rest of us got Monica [Lewinsky], the **fubsy** Lolita. ... I'm not saying that the [Barbara] Walters interview didn't teach me a lot. I now know that being a fat girl in Beverly Hills is hell on earth. Barbara certainly didn't miss the point, bringing up Monica's weight problem half a dozen times. (Michael Harris, *Temptress Monica Revealed*, The Ottawa Sun, 03-04-1999, p. 14.)

(2) squat (condition of having a ... physique) *n*.: **embonpoint**. SEE PLUMP

(3) squat (having a short ... physique) *adj*.: **pyknic**. SEE STOCKY

squeal (on, as in tattle) *v.i.*: **peach**. SEE TATTLE

squealer (or accuser) *n*.: **delator**. SEE ACCUSER

stability *n*.: **ballast**. ∎ For months, the Smiths have sought in vain to find a four-bedroom house in the North Babylon school district, where all the children are established. With the free-floating uncertainty in their lives, the Smiths want school to be the **ballast** for the kids. (Paul Vitello, *No Home and No Answers*, Newsday, 06-19-1997, p. A8.)

stage setting (or physical environment) *n*.: **mise en scène** [French; putting on stage]. SEE SETTING

stagnant (place or situation) *n*.: **backwater**. ∎ But as Gore tries to tar Bush by portraying Texas as some kind of third-world **backwater**, he'd be wise to recall 1992, the last time a governor ran for president. Because if there's one state that does worse than Texas in the rankings game, it's Arkansas [where Bill Clinton is from]. (Scott S. Greenberger, Staff, *Election 2000: Gore's New Strategy: Attack Texas as Backward*, The Atlanta Journal and Constitution, 04-16-2000, p. A16.)

(2) stagnant (as in not moving or temporarily inactive) *adj*.: **quiescent**. SEE INACTIVE

stain (with blood) *v.t.*: **ensanguine**. ∎ The Reformation, which was to divide and **ensanguine** Europe, and divides western Christendom even now, was irretrievably on its way. (Author not given, *Reform and Rome: Luther on the Stand: 1521*, The Economist, 12-31-1999.)

(2) stain *v.t.*: **begrime**. SEE DIRTY

(3) stain *v.t.*: **besmirch**. SEE TARNISH

(4) stain (as in dishonor to one's reputation) *n*.: **blot (or stain) on one's escutcheon** *idiom*. SEE DISHONOR

stained (or impure) *adj., v.t.*: **maculate**. SEE IMPURE

staining (of or relating to ..., as in dyeing) *adj.*: **tinctorial**. SEE DYEING

stale (as in musty) *adj.*: **fusty**. SEE MUSTY

(2) stale (atmosphere of crowded or poorly ventilated area) *n.*: **fug**. SEE MUSTY

stalling (engaging in ... tactics, esp. as a means to wear out an opponent or avoid confrontation) *adj.*: **Fabian**. SEE DILATORY

stammering (words such as um, uh, you know, etc.) *n.*: **embolalia** (or **embololalia**). ■ My recent column on filler words, such as *you know, well, uh,* and *basically*, has provoked numerous responses [as to the best word for that]. ... **Embololalia** (or **embolalia**) seem to fit, but I suspect that most of us, in trying to say, uh, **embololalia**, would find ourselves resorting to it. (Jack Smith, **Embololalia** *or* **Embolalia**, *It's ... Er ... Static to Our Ears*, Los Angeles Times, 08-19-1991, p. E1.)

standard (as in original model or example) *n.*: **archetype**. SEE MODEL

standing (of or relating to ... upright) *n.*: **orthostatic**. ■ For example, body fluid changes during space flight can cause astronauts to suffer from dizziness and lightheadedness when they return to Earth — a condition called **orthostatic** intolerance. Most space travelers cannot stand quietly for 10 minutes just after landing without feeling faint. (Earl Lane, *Space Aches/Scientists Are Just Beginning to Study the Biological Effects on Astronauts*, Newsday, 10-13-1998, p. C3.)

star (shooting ...) *n.*: **bolide**. SEE FIREBALL

starchy *adj.*: **farinaceous**. ■ But it's the pastas that should turn any conversation away from films, philosophy and the unexplained. Actually, you could revel in pastas here. With two or three diners, all friends of the **farinaceous**, you might end up sampling nine of them — certainly an adventure in small portions. (Peter M. Gianotti, *Dining Out*, Newsday, 05-09-1993, p. 30.)

stars (cluster of ... smaller than a constellation) *n.*: **asterism**. ■ The Winter Circle comprises six named stars. ... The six stars are in an oval-shaped **asterism** easily spotted because all the stars in the large pattern are similar in brightness to the naked eye — except Sirius. But that is the best star to spot to find the rest. (Michael Alicea, *Everyday Phrases Reveal Ignorance of Astronomy*, The Palm Beach Post, 04-23-2000, p. 8D.)

(2) stars (of, relating to or resembling) *adj.*: **astral**. ■ Religious millennialists have yet to be heard from in great numbers, but before the end of this year there will be all kinds of predictions and movements and staged events. Astronomers, too, may get conjunctivitis trying to find new millennium stars, and astrologers may get conjunctionitis trying to give us the meaning of **astral** relations for the new era. (James S. Chesnut, *New Millennium? Bah, Humbug*, The Tampa Tribune, 09-18-1999, p. 19.)

(3) stars (of or relating to ... or constellations) *adj.*: **sidereal**. ■ It's war! In the year 2063, Earth's space colonists are suddenly under attack from a brutal race of extraterrestrial marauders. ... As if they weren't trouble enough for our **sidereal** settlers, there are also packs of robots knocking around the planets who are identical to humans except for their spooky X-pupil eyes. (David Hiltbrand, *Picks & Pans: Tube*, People, 11-06-1995, p. 15.)

start (from the) *adv.*: **ab initio** [Latin]. SEE BEGINNING

(2) start (from the) *adv.*: **ab ovo** [Latin]. SEE BEGINNING

(3) start (existing from the ..., as in innate) *adj.*: **connate**. SEE INNATE

(4) start (often to a speech or writing) *n.*: **exordium**. SEE INTRODUCTION

(5) start (as in establishment, of something) *n.*: **instauration**. SEE ESTABLISHMENT

start and finish *n.*: **alpha and omega**. SEE BEGINNING AND END

starter (as in beginner) *n.*: **abecedarian**. SEE BEGINNER

starting (as in coming into being) *adj.*: **nascent**. SEE EMERGING

starvation (of child leading to progressive wasting away) *n.*: **marasmus**. SEE MALNOURISHMENT

starving (as in hungry) *adj.*: **esurient**. SEE HUNGRY

state (as in announce) *v.t.*: **annunciate**. SEE ANNOUNCE

(2) state *v.t.*: **asseverate**. SEE DECLARE

(3) state (as in condition) *n.*: **fettle**. SEE CONDITION

stately (as befitting a baron) *adj.*: **baronial**. ■ [Cardinal John] O'Connor has often publicly questioned his own abilities and accomplishments. For years, he has said how uncomfortable it felt to him, a painter's son from a south Philadelphia rowhouse, to live in the **baronial** 1880 archbishop's mansion behind St. Patrick's. (Rick Hampson, *Courage Carries*

"*American Pope,*" USA Today, 01-17-2000, p. 1A.)

(2) stately (of a ... woman, often voluptuous) *adj.*: **Junoesque**. SEE VOLUPTUOUS

statement (or expression or phrase which is elegant, concise, witty and/or well-put) *n.*: **atticism**. SEE EXPRESSION

(2) statement (in which one references an issue by saying that they will not discuss it; e.g. "I'm not even going to get into the character issue.") *n.*: **apophasis**. SEE FIGURE OF SPEECH

(3) statement (made without proof or support) *n.*: **ipse dixit** [Latin]. SEE ALLEGATION

stationary (as in not moving or temporarily inactive) *adj.*: **quiescent**. SEE INACTIVE

status (as in condition) *n.*: **fettle**. SEE CONDITION

status quo (person who favors the ..., spec. a person who is opposed to advancements in technology) *n.*: **Luddite**. SEE TRADITIONALIST

(2) status quo (favoring the ... as in hatred or fear of anything new or different) *n.*: **misoneism** (person holding this view: **misoneist**). SEE CONSERVATISM

steadfast (as in one who clings to an opinion or belief even after being shown that it is wrong) *n.*: **mumpsimus**. SEE STUBBORN

(2) steadfast (in holding to a belief or opinion) *adj.*: **pertinacious**. SEE STUBBORN

steadiness *n.*: **ballast**. SEE STABILITY

steady (in rhythm or tempo) *adj.*: **metronomic**. ∎ [T]he next day you delight in the way the light splashes on the snow, or the **metronomic** plop of an icicle melting in the noon glare. Mood swings are built into the Minnesota temperament. (James Lileks, *Want the Tar Pit to Go? Don't Hold Your Breath*, Minneapolis Star Tribune, 11-07-1997, p. 3B.)

(2) steady (as in unvarying) *adj.*: **equable**. SEE UNVARYING

steal (as in embezzle) *v.t., v.i.*: **peculate**. ∎ [The Mazda] Miata gets passersby smiling and talking. ... Other conspicuous cars are costly and imposing and draw hate waves, as they are intended to. Decent householders glare, knowing you couldn't own the thing unless you were a drug dealer or a **peculating** [bureaucrat]. (John Skow, *Living: Miatific Bliss in Five Gears, This Is Definitely Not Your Father's Hupmobile*, Time, 10-02-1989, p. 91.)

(2) steal (as in embezzle) *v.i.*: **defalcate**. SEE EMBEZZLE

steep *adj.*: **declivitous** (*n.*: **declivity**). SEE DECLINE

stench *n.*: **fetor**. ∎ All sorts of processes can create a stink. A major sewage lift station at Cadiz and the river may contribute to the problem downtown. A rendering plant occasionally insults the olfactory nerves of Cadillac Heights residents. But the central plant is the likely culprit for the **fetor** wafting along the river on summer nights. (Author not given, *Stinky Problem: Whatever the Odor is, Dallas Needs to Eliminate it*, The Dallas Morning News, 02-23-1999, p. 10A.)

(2) stench (having a ...) *adj.*: **mephitic** (*n.*: **mephitis**). SEE SMELLY

(3) stench *adj.*: **noisome**. SEE SMELLY

stenography (as in writing in shorthand) *n.*: **tachygraphy**. SEE SHORTHAND

step down (from an office or position) *v.t.*: **demit** (as in demit office). SEE RESIGN

sterile *adj.*: **acarpous**. ∎ But, according to the doomsayers, if a satellite doesn't clobber you into the next millennium, there's always the danger its plutonium payload will turn your neighbourhood area into an **acarpous** wasteland. (Adrian Bradley, *Space Junk Roulette*, The Australian, 11-19-1996, p. 11.)

stern (and unyielding) *adj.*: **flinty**. ∎ For all his passionate concern about injustice across the board, [Supreme Court Justice William] Brennan was not a **flinty** moralist in person. ... Genuinely curious about the interests of people he talked to, he was the most naturally friendly person I have ever known. (Nat Hentoff, *Brennan Believed Constitution Lived*, Denver Rocky Mountain News, 08-04-1997, p. 43A.)

(2) stern (as in ... remarks) *adj.*: **astringent**. SEE HARSH

steward (as in butler) *n.*: **major-domo**. SEE BUTLER

stick (instrument such as a ... for punishing children) *n.*: **ferule**. SEE PADDLE

stickler (rigid ... for rules and procedures) *n.*: **martinet**. SEE DISCIPLINARIAN

sticky *adj.*: **glutinous**. ∎ I remembered the **glutinous** stashes of spearmint gum that the boys at the school run by my parents used to leave under dining room tables, chapel hassocks and behind bedsteads. (Quentin Letts, *Features: By Gum, I'll Blow You Away — Discarded Chewing Gum Is the Plague of the Modern City*, The Daily Telegraph, 10-22-1997, p. 18.)

(2) sticky *adj.*: **mucilaginous**. ∎ Some folks may

assert, tentatively, that [marshmallow] is made from a marsh plant called the mallow or maybe the marsh mallow. Indeed, it used to be based on the **mucilaginous** sap from the root of the marsh mallow, but that was very long ago, and people who offer that explanation are only guessing. (Al Sicherman, *Making Marshmallows; Easy, Fast and Fat-free*, Minneapolis Star Tribune, 12-22-1996, p. 2E.)

(3) sticky *adj.*: **viscid**. ∎ Honey bees are on the buzz. Why? You guessed it. Flowers are blooming. It's time for the bees to get out there, find the nectar, wing it back to the hive and convert it into sweet, **viscid** honey. (Walter Nicholls, *Bees Do It*, The Washington Post, 04-07-1999, p. F7.)

(4) sticky (situation or problem) *n.*: **nodus**. SEE COMPLICATION

stiffen *v.t.*: **anneal**. SEE STRENGTHEN

stiffness (in relations between people) *n.*: **froideur** [French]. SEE CHILLINESS

stigma (as in dishonor to one's reputation) *n.*: **blot (or stain) on one's escutcheon** *idiom*. SEE DISHONOR

still (as in not moving or temporarily inactive) *adj.*: **quiescent**. SEE INACTIVE

(2) still (as in nevertheless) *adv.*: **withal**. SEE NEVERTHELESS

stimulate (as in enliven) *v.t.*: **vivify**. SEE ENLIVEN

stimulating *adj.*: **piquant**. ∎ Examine the following strategies for stimulating babies to learn. ... Sometimes during the day, turn on the tape player and play any music that is **piquant** and engaging. (Author not given, *Parenting For Education: "Babes In Arms" Learning*, Atlanta Inquirer, 08-29-1998, p. 3.)

(2) stimulating (as in restorative, esp. with respect to effect of certain drugs or medications) *adj.*: **analeptic**. SEE RESTORATIVE

stimulation (source of ..., as in inspiration) *n.*: **Pierian spring**. SEE INSPIRATION

stimulus (as in boost, spur or prod) *n.*: **fillip**. ∎ [T]he West has an interest in making Ukraine less dependent on Russian energy. ... But financing these reactors is a curious way to help Ukraine. The purpose seems as much to give a **fillip** to the West's sagging nuclear industry as to avert another potential environmental disaster. (Author not given, *Nuclear Blackmail*, The Economist, 03-01-1997.)

(2) stimulus (as in creative inspiration) *n.*: **afflatus**. SEE INSPIRATION

stingy *adj.*: **costive**. ∎ Yet at the same time there was something **costive** about [artist Jasper] Johns, in sharp contrast to the effusive generosity of Robert Rauschenberg's vision. He didn't want to give anything away. (Robert Hughes, *Behind the Sacred Aura: Jasper Johns Gives Nothing Away, But His Cool, Lovely Mastery of Indirection Finally Becomes Claustrophobic*, Time, 11-11-1996, p. 76.)

(2) stingy *adj.*: **mingy** [This is likely a blended word — also known as a portmanteau word — which combines "mean" and "stingy." However, in actual usage, it is generally used as a synonym for "stingy" or for the less pejorative "meager."] ∎ When I wrote skeptically four years ago about the spread of computerized checkout clerks, I said that it was nothing more than a cost-saving conspiracy by **mingy** merchants who'd devised a way to get the customers to do work they should be paying a clerk to do. That part remains true. Machines work more cheaply than people. And the merchant is getting you, the customer, to do a task that once was part of the service he was being paid to provide. (Dave Addis, *Sometimes, Face-to-screen Is Better Than Face-to-face*, The Virginian Pilot, 11-19-2003.)

(3) stingy *adj.*: **niggardly**. ∎ Postponed or **niggardly** 401(k) contributions are still the easiest routes to a destitute retirement. (Richard S. Teitelbaum, *Retirement Guide/Special Issue: How Your 401(k) Can Make You Rich: You're the Boss of Your Retirement Plan, and the Stakes Are Enormous*, Fortune, 07-24-1995, p. 74.)

(4) stingy *adj.*: **penurious**. ∎ Then there are the whispers that Cincinnati, the most **penurious** franchise in the league, hired [coach] Dave Shula in part because he came cheaply. (Michael Kinsley, *Jaw to Jaw*, The Sporting News, 10-03-1994, p. 12.)

stink (from body sweat) *n.*: **bromidrosis**. SEE SWEAT

(2) stink (as in bad odor from waste or decayed matter) *n.*: **effluvium**. SEE ODOR

(3) stink *n.*: **fetor**. SEE STENCH

stinky *adj.*: **fetid**. SEE SMELLY

(2) stinky *adj.*: **mephitic** (*n.*: **mephitis**). SEE SMELLY

(3) stinky *adj.*: **noisome**. SEE SMELLY

stir (as in fuss, over a trifling matter) *n.*: **foofaraw**. SEE FUSS

(2) stir (as in commotion) *n.*: **maelstrom**. SEE COMMOTION

(3) stir (as in commotion) *n.*: **pother**. SEE COMMOTION

stock certificates (hobby of collecting old ...) *n.*: **scripophily**. ∎ Turns out those tanking tech stocks sometimes are worth the paper they're printed on. On websites like eBay and **Scripophily**.com, there's a lively market for original stock certificates — collectibles that can fetch more than the stock's share value. [Example:] eToys — Share value $0 (defunct) — Sold for $58. (Author not given, *Notebook*, Time International [Spanish Edition], 07-30-2001.)

stocky (having a short ... physique) *adj.*: **pyknic**. ∎ There are three basic types of body builds [one of which is] endomorphic, characterized by predominance of structure developed from endodermal layers of embryo, that is, internal organs. And also characterized by a large abdomen, general roundness, hence of the **pyknic** (wonder if the spelling is a coincidence) type. (Pearl Swiggum, *Falling Wallpaper Creates Major Family Catastrophe*, Wisconsin State Journal, 03-06-1995, p. 2B.)

(2) stocky (condition of having a ... physique) *n.*: **embonpoint**. SEE PLUMP

stockyard (as in slaughterhouse) *n.*: **abattoir**. SEE SLAUGHTERHOUSE

stoic (as in unemotional or even-tempered) *adj.*: **phlegmatic**. SEE EVEN-TEMPERED

stomach (of, relating to or associated with) *n.*: **gastric**. ∎ "My first advice would be moderation in the size of the meal and the amount of alcohol consumed," said Dr. J. Patrick Waring, a specialist in digestive disorders at Emory University School of Medicine in Atlanta. That's because a big meal sets you up for **gastric** distress. (M.A.J. McKenna, *Festive Feasts Can Make Us Bloated Beasts*, The Palm Beach Post, 12-06-1999, p. 1E.)

(2) stomach (surgical excision into ... usually for feeding) *n.*: **gastrotomy**. ∎ Three of the six children in the Bellevue class have been fed through **gastrotomy** tubes, or "G-tubes," in their stomachs because they reject oral feedings. (Mike Lindblom, *Therapy Intended to Help Youngsters Overcome Fear of Food*, The Dallas Morning News, 02-20-2000, p. 9F.)

(3) stomach (or mouth or jaws of a carniverous animal) *n.*: **maw**. SEE MOUTH

stomp (as in move heavily or clumsily) *v.i.*: **galumph**. SEE TROMP

stonewalling (engaging in ... tactics, esp. as a means to wear out an opponent or avoid confrontation) *adj.*: **Fabian**. SEE DILATORY

stool pigeon (or accuser) *n.*: **delator**. SEE ACCUSER

stop (up) *v.t.*: **occlude**. SEE BLOCK

storage place (esp. for hiding valuables or goods) *n.*: **cache**. SEE HIDING PLACE

storm (as in commotion) *n.*: **maelstrom**. SEE COMMOTION

story (as in fable) *n.*: **apologue**. SEE FABLE

(2) story (which is false, often deliberately) *n.*: **canard**. SEE HOAX

stout (condition of having a ... physique) *n.*: **embonpoint**. SEE PLUMP

(2) stout (having a short ... physique) *adj.*: **pyknic**. SEE STOCKY

straight (of or relating to standing ...) *n.*: **orthostatic**. SEE STANDING

strained (use or misuse of words or phrase, sometimes deliberate) *n.*: **catachresis**. SEE MISUSE

straitlaced (and intolerant conventionality) *n.*: **Grundyism**. SEE PURITANICAL

strange (as in eerie) *adj.*: **eldritch**. SEE EERIE

(2) strange (as in otherworldly) *adj.*: **fey**. SEE OTHERWORLDLY

(3) strange (as in unconventional) *adj.*: **outré** [French]. SEE UNCONVENTIONAL

(4) strange (as in eccentric) *adj.*: **pixilated**. SEE ECCENTRIC

stranger *n.*: **inconnu** [French]. ∎ [Five years ago, Penguin Publishers] rejected a manuscript about a boy wizard [Harry Potter] by a penniless, unknown Edinburgh-based author [J.K. Rowling]. Penguin had no intention of being wrong-footed again, so [they paid] Eoin Colfer ... a little-known author, £500,000 [for his children's book]. Colfer isn't quite the impoverished **inconnu** that Rowling was but his story has a similar charm. (Anne Johnstone, *Mixed-up World With a New Spin on the Art of Fantasy*, The Herald [Glasgow], 05-12-2001, p. 12.)

(2) stranger (as in outcast) *n.*: **Ishmael**. SEE OUTCAST

(3) stranger (as in foreigner, from another country or place) *n.*: **outlander**. SEE FOREIGNER

strangle *v.t.*: **garrote**. ∎ 7:00 A.M. I would like to unfold Brian's precious pocket square and **garrote** him with it. I have seen Golf Central four times, and must endure four more replays over the next two hours. I am Bill Murray in Groundhog Day. I am Charlie on the MTA. (Austin Murphy, *Golf Plus: Get Me Outta Here — Watching the Golf Channel for 48 Straight Hours Was Nearly the Undoing of the Author*, Sports Illustrated, 07-10-1995, p. G8.)

(2) strangle *v.t.*: **jugulate**. ▪ As Douglas Hurd, who refused to sign the letter, could see full well, this is not an attempt to change Tory policy on the single European currency. It is an attempt to **jugulate** William Hague; or at least to begin the tightening of the ligature about his youthful neck. (Boris Johnson, *Politics: Savaged by a Dead Sheep*, The Daily Telegraph, 01-07-1998.)

strapping (having a ... body build) *adj.*: **mesomorphic**. See MUSCULAR

stray (from the subject) *v.i.*: **divagate**. See DIGRESS

streaked (with a darker color) *adj.*: **brindled**. See SPOTTED

stream (small) *n.*: **rivulet**. ▪ Neuwiller's language lab lies off Mill Creek, a marshy **rivulet** near his home on Maryland's Eastern Shore. "You've got to listen to a lot of geese to speak goose," he says. "I've listened to them my whole life." (Franz Lidz, *Outdoors*, Sports Illustrated, 02-21-1994, p. 86.)

(2) stream (of, relating to or inhabiting) *adj.*: **fluvial**. See RIVER

streams (of or occurring in ... or lakes) *adj.*: **limnetic**. See WATERS

street show *n.*: **raree show**. ▪ Some things need not be belabored: like, for instance, that the [baseball] players and owners, in an orgy of selfishness right out of Neronian Rome, irretrievably polluted a century-old national myth — the myth that this game, of all games, was not just another **raree show**, but was based on a contract of common passion for the game itself between the players and the spectators. (Frank McConnell, *Baseball*, Commonweal, 11-18-1994, p. 31.)

strength (loss of ... or muscle tone due to extreme emotional stimulus) *n.*: **cataplexy**. See MUSCLE TONE

(2) strength (deprive of ...) *v.t.*: **geld**. See WEAKEN

(3) strength (as in power or might) *n.*: **puissance**. See POWER

strengthen *v.t.*: **anneal**. ▪ Yet these smaller manufacturers and service companies are a vital and vulnerable part of U.S. competitiveness. ... If these companies are not **annealed** by the fire of global competition, they will burn in it. Says Earl Landesman, an A.T. Kearney consultant: "Those just sitting in the U.S. will be blindsided." (Thomas A. Stewart, *Competitiveness: The New American Century — Where We Stand*, Fortune, 06-10-1991, p. 12.)

strenuous (task, esp. of cleaning up or remedying bad situations) *n.*: **Augean task**. See HERCULEAN

(2) strenuous (as in laborious) *adj.*: **operose**. See LABORIOUS

stretching (and yawning) *n.*: **pandiculation**. See YAWNING

strict *adj.*: **monastic**. ▪ Although [the head of the Thai Power of Virtue Party] doesn't set **monastic** standards for party members — many businessmen are on the ticket and his handpicked replacement for governor is a flashy millionaire architect — he runs the party with a military style that may deter potential allies. (Jay Branegan, *He Wears a Simple Morhom, or Farmer's Shirt, and Sandals*, Time International, 03-23-1992, p. 42.)

strife (of or relating to ... within a group or country) *adj.*: **internecine**. See DISSENSION

(2) strife (as in heated disagreement or friction between groups) *n.*: **ruction**. See DISSENSION

(3) strife (or conflict among the gods) *n.*: **theomachy**. See GODS

strike (on basis of alleged sickness, esp. by policemen) *n.*: **blue flu**. See SICKOUT

(2) strike (repeatedly, often used figuratively) *v.t.*: **buffet**. See HIT

striking (spec. the act of one object ... a stationary object, usually applied to ships) *n.*: **allision**. See COLLISION

(2) striking (as in dazzling, in effect) *adj.*: **foudroyant** [French]. See DAZZLING

strip tease (artist) *n.*: **ecdysiast**. ▪ By day a computer consultant at a Wall Street bank, Miller morphs at night into an offbeat writer who adds zip to what he considers the staid form of obituary writing. ... Minneapolis-born stripper Lili St. Cyr, who died early this year, was "one of the finest **ecdysiasts** ever," he raved, then recounted her famed bathtub routine. (Liz Leyden, *On the Web, Special Parting Words; GoodBye! Rewrites Obituaries to Give Fuller Account of the Dead*, The Washington Post, 11-27-1999, p. C2.)

striving (mental process marked by ... to do something) *n*.: **conation**. SEE DETERMINATION

(2) striving (the ... to achieve a particular goal or desire) *n*.: **nisus**. SEE GOAL

stroke (as in caress or fondle) *v.i.*: **canoodle** (often "canoodle with"). SEE CARESS

stroll (a slow, leisurely ...) *n*.: **paseo**. ∎ The brochures, of course, portray glossy twenty somethings, but those thronging the cafes and terraces are mostly over 60, or else families with young children. Snatches of conversation are in Dutch, German, Portuguese and English, interspersed with Spanish. You can spot the northern Europeans because they walk faster than the leisurely art of the **paseo** strictly requires. (Elizabeth Nash, *Beaches*, Independent, 07-12-1997, p. 26.)

(2) stroll (about, esp. as in roam or wander) *v.t.*, *v.i.*: **perambulate**. SEE ROAM

(3) stroll (about, esp. as in roam or wander) *v.t.*, *v.i.*: **peregrinate**. SEE ROAM

stroller (as in one who strolls through city streets idly) *n*.: **flâneur** [French]; (strolling *n*.: **flânerie**). SEE IDLER

strong (as in sharp or bitter to taste or smell) *adj*.: **acrid**. SEE PUNGENT

(2) strong (and courageous woman) *n*.: **virago**. SEE WOMAN

struggle (of or relating to ... within a group or country) *adj*.: **internecine**. SEE DISSENSION

(2) struggle (for an idea or principle) *n*.: **jihad**. SEE CRUSADE

(3) struggle (people who ... , as in fight, as if to the death) *n*.: **Kilkenny cats** (esp. as in "fight like Kilkenny cats"). SEE FIGHT

(4) struggle (in the soul between good vs. evil) *n*.: **psychomachia**. SEE GOOD VS. EVIL

strut (about so as to attract attention) *v.i.*: **tittup**. ∎ It's 9 pm ... and a party at the Rebecca Hossack Gallery is spilling on to the pavement. ... Terry Major-Ball in a sensible overcoat blinks sleepily at the vision of the cocktail babes **tittupping** by on high heels: Amy (17) and Bella (16), the hostess's absurdly tall daughters, two hormonal volcanoes with angel's wings attached to their backs. (John Walsh, *Rebecca, Queen of the Desert*, Independent, 03-28-1998, p. 21.)

strutting (behavior) *n*.: **fanfaronade**. SEE BRAVADO

(2) strutting (person in a vain manner) *n*.: **popinjay**. SEE VAIN

stubborn (person, as in one who clings to an opinion or belief even after being shown that it is wrong) *n*.: **mumpsimus** [This unusual but non-archaic word was invented by a 15th century English priest, who, when corrected for reading a nonsense phrase "quod in ore mumpsimus" (instead of "sumpsimus," which would mean "which we have taken into the mouth") in the mass, replied, "I will not change my old mumpsimus for your new sumpsimus"]. ∎ [Thoroughbred trainer Laura de Seroux] has been training her horses at San Luis Rey Downs and taking them by van to [other tracks] just before they race [which has been a successful approach for her. She said:] "[P]eople who say you can't win training at [one track] and shipping [to another], who say you have to be at the track where you race. They're being **mumpsimus**." [This is not a completely correct use of the word, since it actually is a noun referring either to the person clinging to the erroneous belief, or to the belief itself. It is not an adjective. However, though many articles discuss what a wonderful word it is, there are nevertheless not many examples of it (other than those which discuss the word merely by defining it) so beggars can't be choosers.] (Hank Wesch, *Word Is, De Seroux Has Come Up With Winning Vocabulary*, The San Diego Union-Tribune, 08-10-2002, p. D10.)

(2) stubborn (in holding to a belief or opinion) *adj*.: **pertinaceous**. ∎ Traditionalists clutch for old stereotypes. Men are initiatory, rational, aggressive, ambitious. Woman are receptive, passive, nurturing, intuitive. ... [These stereotypes] appear to represent a deep-seated fear of losing the assurance of differences — a **pertinacious** insistence that, without hard-line definitions, we shall all soon become androgynous clones. (Kathryn Hume, *Why Can't a Woman/Man Be More Like a Man/Woman?* Minneapolis Star Tribune, 03-17-1995, p. 14A.)

(3) stubborn (as in resistant to control or authority) *adj*.: **refractory**. ∎ Intractable debt, stubborn state needs, whimsical and **refractory** legislators, a staggering economy, all stirred in a mix of double binds on the issue of taxation, surely will try even [the] considerable talents and energy [of California governor Arnold Schwarzenegger]. (Herbert Gold, *He Came, He Saw, He Compromised: The Further Adventures of Arnold S., Alpha Male*, The Sacramento Bee, 12-28-2003, p. E1.)

(4) stubborn (as in obstinate) *adj*.: **contumacious**. SEE OBSTINATE

(5) stubborn (in a contrary or disobedient way) *adj*.: **froward**. SEE CONTRARY

(6) stubborn (as in narrow-minded) *adj.*: **hidebound**. SEE NARROW-MINDED

(7) stubborn (to make or become ...) *v.t., adj.*: **indurate**. SEE HARDEN

(8) stubborn (as in resisting constraint or compulsion) *adj.*: **renitent**. SEE RESISTANT

stubby (condition of having a ... physique) *n.*: **embonpoint**. SEE PLUMP

(2) stubby (having a short ... physique) *adj.*: **pyknic**. SEE STOCKY

student (of a subject at a beginning level) *n.*: **catechumen**. SEE BEGINNER

study (as in analyze closely) *v.t.*: **anatomize**. SEE ANALYZE

stuff (as in junk or paraphernalia) *n.*: **trumpery**. SEE JUNK

stuffy (atmosphere of crowded or poorly ventilated area) *n.*: **fug**. SEE MUSTY

(2) stuffy (as in musty) *adj.*: **fusty**. SEE MUSTY

(3) stuffy (and intolerant conventionality) *n.*: **Grundyism**. SEE PURITANICAL

stunning (in effect) *adj.*: **foudroyant** [French]. SEE DAZZLING

stunt (as in prank) *n.*: **dido**. SEE PRANK

stupid (person) *n.*: **dummkopf** [German]. ▋ [Merging the National and American Leagues] is the worst idea in the history of baseball. ... [T]he National and American leagues are priceless brand names built up over a hundred years. Even the biggest corporate **dummkopf** knows that brand names with as much recognition as McDonald's and as much history as Coca-Cola are irreplaceable. (Charles Krauthammer, *A Batty Idea From Barons of Baseball*, Denver Rocky Mountain News, 08-04-1997, p. 43A.)

(2) stupid (esp. used of a person, as in ... and confused) *adj.*: **addlepated**. SEE CONFUSED

(3) stupid (person, as in one mentally deficient from birth) *n.*: **ament**. SEE MORON

(4) stupid (or dull or ignorant or obtuse or uncultured) *adj.*: **Boeotian**. SEE DULL

(5) stupid (class of people regarded as ... or unenlightened) *n.*: **booboisie**. SEE UNSOPHISTICATED

(6) stupid (or foolish, in a smug or complacent manner) *adj.*: **fatuous**. SEE FOOLISH

(7) stupid *adj.*: **gormless** [British]. SEE UNINTELLIGENT

(8) stupid (person) *n.*: **jobbernowl** [British]. SEE IDIOT

(9) stupid (person) *n.*: **mooncalf**. SEE FOOL

(10) stupid (as in slow to understand or perceive) *adj.*: **purblind**. SEE OBTUSE

stupidity *n.*: **betise** [French]. ▋ [T]he Republicans have only themselves to blame for the **betise** of indicting Mr. Clinton on Monica Lewinsky charges. The counts were bound to be mischaracterised as "lying about sex," and bound to serve as a perverse vindication for the President. If that is all his persecutors could find, we keep hearing, there cannot be much else. (Anbrose Evans-Pritchard, *Comment: Republicans Let Clinton Off the Hook*, The Daily Telegraph, 02-10-1999.)

(2) stupidity (as in nonsense) *n.*: **folderol** (or **falderal**). SEE NONSENSE

(3) stupidity (as in nonsense) *n.*: **trumpery**. SEE NONSENSE

sturdy (having a ... and muscular body build) *adj.*: **mesomorphic**. SEE MUSCULAR

style (out of ...) *adj.*: **démodé** [French]. SEE OUTMODED

(2) style (the latest ... or fad) *n.*: **dernier cri** [French]. SEE TREND

stylish (and wealthy young people) *n.*: **jeunesse dorée** [French]. SEE FASHIONABLE

(2) stylish *adj.*: **nobby** [British]. SEE ELEGANT

(3) stylish *adj.*: **raffiné** (or **raffine**) [French]. SEE REFINED

(4) stylish (as in elegant and fashionable) *adj.*: **soigné** [French]. SEE ELEGANT

suave (as in refined or elegant) *adj.*: **raffiné** (or **raffine**) [French]. SEE REFINED

subjective (as in taking place entirely within the mind) *adj.*: **immanent**. ▋ The following remarks ... consider a definite condition in which history appears to be concentrated into a single focal point, like those traditionally found in the utopian images of the thinkers. ... The historical task is to disclose this **immanent** state of perfection and make it absolute, to make it visible and dominant in the present. (Michael Andre Bernstein, *Walter Benjamin's Long, Limited View: One-Way Street*, The New Republic, 12-08-1997.)

subjugation *n.*: **thralldom**. SEE BONDAGE

sublime *adj.*: **empyreal**. SEE LOFTY

submerge (as in soak) *v.t.*: **imbrue**. SEE SOAK

submission (as in marked by insistence on rigid conformity to a belief, system or course of action without regard to individual differences) *adj.*: **procrustean** (*n.*: **Procrustean bed**). SEE CONFORMITY

submissive *adj.*: **biddable**. SEE OBEDIENT

(2) submissive (to be ... towards) *v.i.*: **truckle**. SEE KOWTOW

(3) submissive (overly ... or devoted to one's wife) *adj.*: **uxorious**. SEE DOTING

subordinate (esp. in the military) *n.*: **subaltern**. ∎ The longing for authority and **subaltern** mentality was widespread in those who found appeal in the early Nazi movement. (Ian Kershaw, *Hitler*, Norton [1998], p. 295.)

(2) subordinate (loyal ..., esp. of a political leader) *n.*: **apparatchik**. SEE UNDERLING

(3) subordinate (apt to act ... as opposed to leading) *adj.*: **sequacious**. SEE SUBSERVIENT

subservient (being ... as opposed to leading) *adj.*: **sequacious**. ∎ [In 1945, Janet Kalven] called for "an education that will give young women a vision of the family as the vital cell of the social organism, and that will inspire them with the great ambitions of being queens in the home." By which she did not mean a **sequacious** [wife] to the Man of the House, picking up his dirty underwear and serving him Budweisers during commercials, but rather a partner in the management of a "small, diversified family firm." (Bill Kauffman, *The Way of Love: Dorothy Day and the American Right*, Whole Earth, 06-22-2000.)

(2) subservient (person) *n.*: **lickspittle**. SEE SYCOPHANT

(3) subservient (to be ... towards) *v.i.*: **truckle**. SEE KOWTOW

substitute (esp. of a doctor or clergyman) *n.*: **locum tenens**. SEE TEMPORARY

substitution (as in using one word or phrase in substituion for something with which it is usually associated, such as using "city hall" to refer to city government) *n.*: **metonymy**. SEE FIGURE OF SPEECH

subtlety (raised within the context of a philosophical or theological debate; also references such a debate itself) *n.*: **quodlibet** [This word can be used in a complimentary fashion, as in to praise the subtlety of the argument, or in a pejorative fashion, as in to

suggest that the argument is overly subtle and thus in the nature of a technicality. The example used here shows the latter sense of the word, although, to be sure, the author is being facetious at this point in his article. See also the use of this word under "debate."] ∎ Common confusion about the words *its* and *it's* and of the apostrophe in general are signs of the declining respect for grammar and reading. ... It's? Its? How complicated can this be? How difficult is it to teach a sixth grader how to punctuate correctly? [But] why worry about such **quodlibets**? When was the last time anyone even noticed? (Charles S. Larson, *Its Academic, or Is It? Soon, No One Will Care about Correct Grammar, and the Apostrophe Will Disappear Into Infinity*, Newsweek, 11-06-1995.)

subversive (as in traitors or group of ... working within a country to support an enemy and who may engage in espionage, sabotage or other subversive activities) *n.*: **fifth column**. SEE TRAITORS

succeed (often at another's expense) *v.i.*: **batten**. SEE THRIVE

success (notable or conspicuous ...) *n.*: **éclat**. ∎ The roll call of artists and writers who have suffered attacks from those less fortunate is long and distinguished. ... [Playwrite Neil] Simon should content himself with the great **éclat** he enjoys and stop worrying about what some newspaper twit writes about him. (Jonathan Yardley, *Jonathan Yardley*, The Washington Post, 10-10-1999, p. X02.)

(2) success (with the critics but not the public) *n.*: **succès d'estime** [French]. ∎ Reclusive playwright Sam Shepard has pulled a startling switch. ... Often teased as the "Masked Man of the American Theater," Shepard is suddenly a wide-screen, posterized movie star playing legendary jet jockey Chuck Yeager in the American epic *The Right Stuff*. Sure, Shepard's done other films (*Days of Heaven*, *Resurrection*, *Raggedy Man*), but they fall into the **succès d'estime** category, seen by too few to endanger his cult status. (Author not given, *He Has it All as a Laureate of Stage and Screen: So Now What's He Want? Anonymity*, People Weekly, 01-02-1984.)

succinct (saying) *n.*: **gnome** (*adj*: **gnomic**). SEE CATCHPHRASE

succulent *adj.*: **toothsome**. SEE TASTY

sucker (as in one easily duped) *n.*: **gudgeon**. ∎ "Novocaine" [follows the] tradition of suckers and saps corrupted by the come-ons of a leggy dame. ... Susan Ivy [is a dental] patient who doesn't blink twice when she asks Dr. [Frank] Sangster. ...: "Have you ever done it in the chair?" ... When, after his illicit office clinch with the saucy Susan, a whole cache of prescription painkillers has gone missing, Frank realizes he's been played for a monkey, a patsy, a gull, a **gudgeon**. (Steven Rea, "*Novocaine*" *[Movie Review]*, Knight Ridder/Tribune News Service, 11-14-2001.)

(2) sucker (as in gullible person) *n.*: **gobemouche** [French]. SEE GULLIBLE

sudden (as in impetuous) *adj.*: **gadarene**. SEE IMPETUOUS

sufferance (in the face of adversity) *n.*: **longanimity**. SEE PATIENCE

suffering (experience of intense ...) *n.*: **Calvary** [based on hill near Jerusalem where Jesus was crucified.] ■ In recent weeks the flamboyant [soccer goalie Fabien] Barthez ... has committed a series of spectacularly awful errors. ... [I]f goalkeeping is a treacherous business in which even Popes have to jettison the dogma of infallibility ... few muddied custodians have known the **Calvary** recently being experienced by the once exuberant Barthez. His descent has been nothing less than vertiginous. (James Lawton, *The Goalkeeper's Fear of ... Losing it*, The Independent [London], 11-27-2001.)

(2) suffering (as in place, condition or society filled with ...; spec., opposite of utopia) *n.*: **dystopia**. SEE HELL

(3) suffering (place or occasion of great ...) *n.*: **Gehenna**. SEE HELL

(4) suffering (occasion or place of great ...) *n.*: **Gethsemane**. SEE HELL

(5) suffering (occasion or place of great ...) *n.*: **Golgotha**. SEE HELL

sugar-coat (as in make pleasant or less harsh) *v.t.*: **edulcorate**. SEE SWEETEN

suggesting (as in urging someone to take a course of action) *adj.*: **hortatory**. SEE URGING

suggestion (as in small amount) *n.*: **soupçon** [French]. SEE TRACE

suggestive (rather than a literal representation, esp. with respect to objects of worship) *adj.*: **aniconic**. SEE SYMBOLIC

(2) suggestive (of, or smelling like, used with "of") *adj.*: **redolent**. SEE REMINISCENT

suicide *n.*: **felo-de-se**. ■ One morning, acclaimed

novelist and short story writer AL Kennedy, blocked, a writer no longer a writer, looks out of her study window and internally prepares herself to jump to her death. What stops her are the strains of a particularly irritating song — Mhairi's Wedding — to which it would be absurd to commit a **felo-de-se**. (Nicholas Lezard, *Pick of the Week: Horns of Grace: Nicholas Lezard Gets Into the Ring With a Writer of Uncommon Steel: On Bullfighting, by AL Kennedy*, The Guardian [London], 07-01-2000.)

(2) suicide (commit ... by setting oneself on fire) *v.t.*: **immolate**. ■ When Thic Quang Duc **immolated** himself on a Saigon street in 1963, it was news around the world and helped set the stage for the U.S.-backed assassination of Diem. (William McGurn, *Good Morning, Vietnam: On the Long Road to Freedom and Prosperity, Vietnam Is Taking the First Halting Steps*, National Review, 05-15-1995, p. 51.)

suitable *n.*: **apposite**. SEE RELEVANT

(2) suitable *adj.*: **comme il faut** [French]. SEE PROPER

(3) suitable (as in appropriate) *adj.*: **felicitous**. SEE APPROPRIATE

suitcase (large ..., opening into two compartments) *n.*: **portmanteau**. ■ So a week later the official sent up a leather **portmanteau** by rail: It held a frock coat and three waistcoats. (Simon Winchester, *The Professor and the Madman*, Harper Collins [1998], p. 121.)

suits (as in persistent instigation of lawsuits, esp. groundless ones) *n.*: **barratry**. SEE LAWSUITS

sulk (as in pout) *n.*: **moue** [French]. SEE POUT

sullen *adj.*: **saturnine**. ■ Even a casual inspection of Benjamin's occasional writings over these years reveals the seeds of self-destruction. Not only do many of his chosen topics ... reflect a temperament drawn toward disaster. Several others, such as "Left-Wing Melancholy," echo his **saturnine** disposition, a gnawing sense that life itself — certainly his own — was a disaster waiting to happen. (Haim Chertok, *Benjamin: A Powerhouse Failure*, Jerusalem Post, 10-01-1999, p. 13B.)

sullied (or impure) *adj., v.t.*: **maculate**. SEE IMPURE

sully *v.t.*: **besmirch**. SEE TARNISH

summarize *v.t.*: **précis** [French]. ■ The theatre, which has a strict policy on not admitting latecomers until a suitable break, is to start giving the aforementioned latecomers a synopsis in the foyer of what they have missed. ... Of course, it would have taken a confident female member of staff to **précis** the first 20 minutes of Nicole Kidman in The Blue Room. (David Lister, *Arts Diary*, Independent, 02-06-1999, p. 12.)

(2) summarize (the flavor or essence of something, as if by boiling down) *v.t.*: **decoct**. SEE BOIL DOWN

summer (of, like or relating to) *adj.*: **aestival** (or **estival**). ▪ Four-fifteen of a turquoise afternoon. Cloudless, becalmed, **estival**. Wind bearing east off the ocean, eight knots and ebbing trays of iced tea floating through the Turf Club at Del Mar, two knots and tinkling. Sea gulls circling the infield lake, their flaps and landing gear down, hovering. (William Nack, *Four-fifteen on a Turquoise Afternoon: Cloudless, Becalmed*, Sports Illustrated, 07-15-1991, p. 68.)

(2) summer (spend the ... in a state of relative inactivity) *v.i.*: **aestivate**. SEE LAZE

summit *n.*: **apogee**. SEE HEIGHT

sun (having the ... as the center) *adj.*: **heliocentric**. ▪ [Copernicus'] startling conclusion: the so-called retrograde motion could be best explained by a **heliocentric** universe. "Finally," he wrote in the math-filled argument published shortly before his death, "we shall place the sun himself at the center of the universe." (Johanna McGeary, *Person Of The Century*, Time, 12-31-1999, p. 162.)

sundown *n.*: **gloaming**. SEE TWILIGHT

(2) sundown (of, relating to or occurring in ... or evening) *adj.*: **vespertine**. SEE EVENING

sunrise (of or relating to ...) *adj.*: **matutinal**. SEE MORNING

superb (as in of the highest quality) *n.*: **first water** (usu. as in "of the first water"). SEE QUALITY

(2) superb *adj.*: **palmary**. SEE EXCELLENT

(3) superb (as in first-class) *adj.*: **pukka**. SEE FIRST-CLASS

(4) superb *adj.*: **skookum**. SEE EXCELLENT

superficial (knowledge of a subject while pretending to be learned) *n.*: **sciolism**. ▪ [T]alk-show hosts [sit] on their almighty thrones [with their] fingers on the cut-off buttons ready to spring into action at the slightest hint of statements that could expose the hosts' shallowness. ... I feel that if host stations were, by law, forced to allow time for rebuttals by individuals or groups ... unfairly attacked through this medium, most hosts would rapidly seek work elsewhere, unable to face certain exposure of their **sci-**olism and hypocrisy. (Jean Paquette [letter writer], *Few Mental Giants?* The Gazette [Montreal, Quebec], 10-11-1996.)

(2) superficial (describe in a ... or incomplete way) *v.t.*: **adumbrate**. SEE OUTLINE

superficialiality (speech or writing) *n.*: **pablum**. SEE TRITENESS

superfluous *adj.*: **supererogatory**. ▪ For our purposes, the [Southern California] earthquake of 1971 was **supererogatory**, unnecessary, gilding the lily, as Hollywood has always been wont to do. The real earthquake, the cultural revolution that upended the film industry, began a decade earlier. (Peter Biskind, *Easy Riders, Raging Bulls*, Simon & Schuster [1998], p. 14.)

(2) superfluous (words) *n.*: **macrology**. SEE VERBOSITY

(3) superfluous (word or phrase) *n.*: **pleonasm**. SEE REDUNDANCY

superhuman (as in very hardworking) *n.*: **Stakhanovite**. SEE WORKAHOLIC

superior (... view of one's own ethnic group) *n.*: **ethnocentric**. ▪ Japanese writer Shintaro Ishihara doesn't apologize for what some critics call xenophobia. "I am a nationalist," he said. "I like sumo and I like kabuki, but I don't necessarily have **ethnocentric** ideas that everything Japanese is better." (Tim Larimer, *Asia: Maverick, Patriot ... Governor!* Time International, 04-26-1999, p. 23.)

(2) superior (as in condescending) *adj., adv.*: **de haut en bas** [French]. SEE CONDESCENDING

(3) superior (as in pompous or haughty) *adj.*: **hoity-toity**. SEE POMPOUS

(4) superior (as in first-class) *adj.*: **pukka**. SEE FIRST-CLASS

superiority *n.*: **meliority**. ▪ At first glance, he was nobody special, with no special talent [but he had] a penis the size of a horse's. Yet it was this prodigious endowment that set John Holmes apart. ... He saw, dangling freakishly between his legs, the key to a future of unimaginable wealth and opportunity. Sometimes a physical **meliority** could do that. Think of basketball star Kareem Abdul-Jabbar, a full head taller than his rivals on the court. (Shane Danielsen, *Rise and Fall of a Porn Star*, The Weekend Australian, 02-07-1998, p. R7.)

supernatural *adj.*: **numinous**. ▪ [T]he very best children's books, however fantastical, always seem to have such characters, in the sense that we find them in naturalistic novels, vivid, individual, and, however grotesque, with some element of reality at their base. ... But in North Wind ... MacDonald did create a goddess of authentic **numinous** power, beneficent and destructive, sinking ships and drowning those aboard. (Richard Jenkyns, *Phallus in Wonderland*, The New Republic, 10-26-1998.)

(2) supernatural *adj.*: **preternatural** ∎ Countless odes have been sung to [basketball player Michael] Jordan's uncanny, unearthly, **preternatural** ability to defy gravity. (Richard Stengel, *Sport: Yo, Michael! You're the Best! Jordan Rises — and Rises — to the Occasion, Removing the Last Shadow of Imperfection From His Peerless Career*, Time, 06-24-1991, p. 47.)

supervise (students taking an examination) *v.i.*: **invigilate**. See PROCTOR

supervisor (brutal ..., as in taskmaster) *n.*: **Simon Legree**. See TASKMASTER

supply (to the point of excess, esp. things sweet) *v.t.*: **cloy**. See SATIATE

support (persons hired to yell ... at a performance) *n.*: **claque**. See APPLAUD

(2) support (on which something is built) *n.*: **warp and woof**. See FOUNDATION

supporter (loyal or subservient ... or military person, esp. who supports or protects a political leader) *n.*: **Janissary** [after an elite force of celibate Christians who protected the Ottoman throne in the 15th Century onward]. ∎ [Romanian dictator] Nicolae Ceausescu and his wife Elena are dead [having been executed after an uprising] — victims of a people too frightened of him and the wall of modern **Janissaries** he constructed around himself to wait for a public trial and measured judgment of his crimes against them. (Hannah Pakula, *Under the Eye of "the Big C,"* The Washington Post, 12-27-1989, p. A19.)

(2) supporter (strong ... of a cause, religion or activity) *n.*: **votary**. ∎ As the labor secretary-designate, Mrs. Chavez was the most provocative Bush nominee, and the most inspired. Big Labor feared she might challenge the privileges unions now enjoy — such as immunity from election laws and Supreme Court edicts. She also could have transformed the department into an advocate of the New Economy, not just a **votary** of the old. (Tony Snow, *Resourcefulness Under Fire*, The Washington Times, 01-14-2001, p. B3.)

(3) supporter *adj.*: **acolyte**. See FOLLOWER

(4) supporter (generous ..., esp. of the arts) *n.*: **Maecenas**. See BENEFACTOR

(5) supporter (of a cause) *n.*: **paladin**. See PROPONENT

supposed *adj.*: **putative**. ∎ In one of [Roz Chast's] most famous cartoons, the careless foibles of motherhood are turned into the stuff of legend through a **putative** ad for "Bad Mom Cards (Collect the Entire Set!)." The pictured examples: "... Gloria B. — Promised to take daughter to the mall after school — and then didn't." (Fred Kaplan, *Drawing from Life / Roz Chast Has Been Drawing Cartoons for the New Yorker for 19 Years*, The Boston Globe, 05-21-1995, p. F1.)

(2) supposed (as in invented or substituted with fraudulent intent) *adj.*: **supposititious**. ∎ Not only were [the Russians] submitted to a long and horrifying experience based on a false historical theory; they were also robbed of knowledge of the historical facts. ... First, a **supposititious** "class" scheme was imposed on every public fact: so that, for example, a wholly invented class of [wealthy farmers] was created and real people were assigned to it, and then repressed by the million. (Robert Conquest, *History, Humanity, and Truth*, National Review, 06-07-1993.)

suppress (something that serves to ...) *n.*: **quietus** (esp. as in "put the quietus to"). See TERMINATE

supremacy (naval ...) *n.*: **thalassocracy**. ∎ The real force of the Etruscans, however, was on the seas. ... As early as the 5th century B.C. the Etruscans were exploring the southern coast of what would become the Italian peninsula. This **thalassocracy**, or dominion of the seas, gave the Etruscans tremendous potential for trade as well as piracy. (Greg Burke, *The Arts/Art: Masters of Power and Pleasure — A Display of Etruscan Arts and Crafts Reveals a Civilization That Seemed to Enjoy a Good Fight as Much as a Good Party*, Time International, 02-12-2001, p. 54.)

(2) supremacy (of one political state over others) *n.*: **hegemony**. See DOMINANCE

(3) supremacy (as in superiority or state of being better) *n.*: **meliority**. See SUPERIORITY

(4) supremacy (as in domination, of a nation or group over another) *n.*: **suzerainty**. See DOMINATION

sure (as in unavoidable) *adj.*: **ineluctable**. See UNAVOIDABLE

sure thing (esp. with respect to a plan, deal or investment that can be trusted completely because it is supposedly safe and sure to succeed) *adj.*: **copper-bottomed** [British]. ∎ People laugh when I say there are sometimes bets available which give a **copper-bottomed** guarantee of profit — but that's because I usually say it when I've sucked a helium balloon and my voice sounds all squeaky. (Derek McGovern, *Sports Betting*, The Mirror [London], 08-09-2003.)

surly *adj.*: **atrabilious**. ∎ Maneka's cause was the environment, and she set herself up as a temperamental Green Queen. ... Her most recent public utterances have been richly **atrabilious**. Newspapers reported her anger on returning from an overseas trip to find that her official bungalow had been forcibly occupied by a newly elected member of Parliament. (Author not given, *Gandhi Crest*, New Republic, 09-02-91.)

(2) surly *adj.*: **bilious**. ∎ The old arrogance typified by the **bilious** head of the House Resources Committee, Alaskan Don Young — who once vowed revenge on "the waffle-stomping, intellectual bunch of idiots" known as environmentalists — lost some of its strut, but none of its purposefulness. (B.J. Bergman, *Environmental Impact [Candidates Running for Congress Who Can Effect Environmental Policy]*, Sierra, 09-19-1998, p. 50.)

(3) surly (person) *n.*: **crosspatch**. SEE GROUCH

(4) surly *adj.*: **liverish**. SEE IRRITABLE

(5) surly *adj.*: **querulous**. SEE PEEVISH

(6) surly *adj.*: **shirty**. SEE IRRITABLE

surname *n.*: **cognomen**. ∎ I've got a new favorite site. It's called How Stuff Works and is found easily at (www.howstuffworks.com). ... It's material is written by Marshall Brain (yes, that seems to be his apt **cognomen**) and features superlatively lucid explanations of the mechanics of the world around us for those of us who don't have a clue. (Jay Bailey, *Sign of the Times*, Jerusalem Post, 02-12-1999, p. 7.)

surpass (the limits, resources or capabilities of) *v.t.*: **beggar**. ∎ It somewhat **beggars** belief that the museum turned his job application down. (Simon Winchester, *The Professor and the Madman*, Harper Collins [1998], p. 37.)

surplus *n.*: **nimiety**. SEE EXCESS

surrender (esp. responsibility or duty) *v.t.*: **abnegate**. SEE RENOUNCE

(2) surrender (an office or position) *v.t.*: **demit** (as in demit office). SEE RESIGN

(3) surrender (as in give back, often a territory) *v.t.*: **retrocede**. SEE GIVE BACK

surround (often protectively) *v.t.*: **embosom**. ∎ The community [of Aspen, Colorado] sits along the Roaring Fork River, high in the central Colorado Rockies. Peaks **embosom** the town. (Author not given, *Aspen at 50*, Newsday, 01-12-1997, p. D12.)

(2) surround *v.t.*: **girdle**. ∎ I dressed and left my motel, then turned off the commercial strip along Highway 192, past the white polymerized vinyl picket fence that **girdles** the town [of Celebration, Florida], and the water tower that is no water tower at all, just a stagy billboard. (Alexander Wolff, *Big Game, Small World*, Warner Books [2002], p. 69.)

surrounding *adj.*: **ambient**. ∎ That oxygen-deprived state is called hypoxia, and that's basically the state you're in whenever you're above 24-, 25,000 feet on Everest, with or without supplemental oxygen. ... You're wearing supplemental oxygen, but it's mixed with **ambient** air. (Marty Moss-Coane, *Everest*, Fresh Air [NPR], 11-11-1997.)

(2) surrounding *adj.*: **circumambient**. ∎ But it is Joan Plowright who walks away with top honors [in "Tea With Mussolini"] in a performance that blends warmth and pawkiness, sparkle and gravitas, heart and backbone. So perfect a being could hardly exist, but the actress makes her grittily alive without allowing the occasionally **circumambient** sentimentality to creep into her work. (John Simon, *Notting Hill*, National Review, 06-28-1999.)

surroundings (as in place one frequents) *n.*: **purlieu(s)**. SEE HANGOUT

survey (of a subject) *n.*: **conspectus**. ∎ "America in Black and White" [is a] comprehensive survey of the issues of race in America. ... Out of the hundreds of cogent observations in their historical **conspectus**, let me begin with this one: black anger and white surrender have become a staple of contemporary racial discourse. (Kenneth S. Lynn, *Books in Review: Up From Gunnar Myrdal: America in Black and White: One Nation, Indivisible, by Stephan Thernstrom and Abigail Thernstrom*, The American Spectator, 10-01-1997.)

(2) survey (quick ..., as in glance) *n.*: **coup d'oeil** [French]. SEE GLANCE

suspect (morality or taste) *adj.*: **louche**. SEE QUESTIONABLE

suspend (as in discontinue, esp. a session of Parliament) *v.t.*: **prorogue**. SEE DISCONTINUE

suspenders (for trousers) *n., pl.*: **galluses**. ▪ Bavarians cling as tightly to their traditional dress — Lederhosen (leather pants), knee socks, brightly embroidered **galluses**, hats sporting a white eagle's feather — as Texans do to string ties, cowboy boots, and Stetsons. (Author not given, *Bavarian Farm Vacations*, German Life, 05-31-1997.)

suspense (in a state of ...) *idiom*: **on tenterhooks**. ▪ Russia is **on tenterhooks** waiting to see if its parliament today will confirm President Boris Yeltsin's appointment of Viktor Chernomyrdin as prime minister. (Author not given, *Russians Turn to Barter to Keep Wheels Turning*, The Washington Times, 09-07-1998, p. A1.)

sustenance (as in nourishment) *n.*: **alimentation**. SEE NOURISHMENT

(2) sustenance (esp. insipid, like baby food) *n.*: **pabulum** (also **pablum**). SEE INSIPID

swaggering (behavior) *n.*: **fanfaronade**. SEE BRAVADO

(2) swaggering (person) *n.*: **Gascon** (act of being a ... person *n.*: **Gasconade**). SEE BRAGGART

swallow (greedily) *v.t.*: **englut**. ▪ [T]he current fashion among non-profit companies [is] accepting "enhancement money" to [name] their theaters after corporate sponsors such as American Airlines. [This is] the theatrical version of the hostile takeover. "**Englut** and devour" — the name that Mel Brooks once invented for a Hollywood studio — is becoming the motto of the American stage. (Author not given, *Robert Brustein on Theater*, The New Republic, 09-18-2000.)

(2) swallow (as in guzzle) *v.t., v.i.*: **ingurgitate**. SEE GUZZLE

swallowing (act or process of) *n.*: **deglutition**. ▪ Justice, or more pointedly the judge, in this case should have been more compassionate. "There is a point beyond which even justice becomes unjust," Sophocles said. "Justice untempered by feeling is too bitter and husky a morsel for human **deglutition**," wrote Charlotte Bronte. (Author not given, *Observer: Death of an Abused Wife*, The Filipino Express, 10-18-1998, p. 10.)

swamp *n.*: **fen**. ▪ The process of reworking natural topography to suit the needs of an urbanizing and industrializing society was refined by 1900. ... Draining the **fens** in England is one classic example, and the infilling of Boston's Back Bay and the waterfront expansion of New York are well-known urban instances in this country. (Craig E. Colten, *Industrial Topography, Groundwater, and the Contours of Environmental Knowledge*, The Geographical Review, 04-01-1998, p. 199.)

swampy *adj.*: **paludal**. ▪ Bud DeWitt's Swamp Omelet doesn't take its name from any **paludal** odor, texture, or appearance. The name refers only to its place of birth: a duck-hunting camp, where it's served to hunters when they return from swampy blinds with cold feet and ravening hunger. (Author not given, *His Cowboy Beans Are Assertive, Not Aggressive* [Chefs of the West], Sunset, 05-01-1984.)

swanky *adj.*: **nobby** [British]. SEE ELEGANT

(2) swanky *adj.*: **soigné** [French]. SEE ELEGANT

swarm *v.i.*: **pullulate**. SEE TEEM

swearing (excessive ..., esp. involuntarily when mentally ill) *n.*: **coprolalia**. SEE CURSING

sweat (foul-smelling ...) *n.*: **bromidrosis**. ▪ Q: "I can't take off my shoes because my feet smell horrible. What can I do?" Sara, 18, Salt Lake City, UT. A: "You may have **bromidrosis**, a disorder you can get if your feet sweat a lot. What happens is, bacteria live off your sweat and cause an odor." (Kristen Kemp, *Your Most Intimate Body Questions–Answered!* CosmoGirl! 09-01-2003.)

(2) sweat (an agent which causes ... or having the power to cause ...) *n., adj.*: **diaphoretic**. ▪ Borage tea is another possibility. Apparently it's excellent for soothing sore throats. ... [T]he word "borage" is a Latinised version of the Arabic abu arak, which means "father of sweat" — a term due no doubt to its use as a **diaphoretic**. (Grant Simon, *The Beauty of Borage*, The Evening Post [Wellington, New Zealand], 12-05-1996.)

(3) sweat (inducing) *adj.*: **sudorific**. ▪ [At the Earth Sanctuary Day Spa you] step into a midnight blue bath filled with warm water. ... The heat soon induces you into a **sudorific** stupor and you can either drift off to sleep or try to read the thoughtfully provided book on the benefits of water therapy. Once sufficiently sweaty, you're asked to dry off. (Samuel Ee, *Revenge of the Little White Ball*, The Business Times [Singapore], 04-26-2002.)

(4) sweat (cause ... by subjecting person or thing to intense heat) *v.t.*: **parboil**. SEE HEAT

(5) sweat (in a ..., as in distress) *n.*: **swivet** (as in "in a swivet") *inf.* SEE DISTRESS

sweeping *adj.*: **pandemic**. SEE WIDESPREAD

sweet (sounding) *adj.*: **mellifluous**. SEE MELODIOUS

sweet talk *n.*: **palaver**. ∎ Such success didn't always appear to be in the cards, although at 14 [singer Barry] White had already developed a reputation for smooth **palaver** and made money counseling adults in his Los Angeles neighborhood about their relationships. (Steve Jones, *Barry White's Love Has "Stayin Power,"* USA Today, 09-03-1999, p. 6E.)

sweet-talking (by flattery) *n.*: **blandishment** (*v.t.*: **blandish**). SEE FLATTERY

sweeten (as in make pleasant or less harsh) *v.t.*: **edulcorate**. ∎ [I]ndependently produced movies permit film-makers to tackle themes that the major studios, pressured by the need to attain the widest possible audience, would either **edulcorate** beyond all recognition or reject outright. No major, patently, would ever have financed Trust or Sex, Lies and Videotape or Drugstore Cowboy or Reservoir Dogs or Metropolitan. (Gilbert Adair, *War of Independents*, Sunday Times [London], 11-26-1995.)

sweetheart *n.*: **acushla** [Irish]. SEE DARLING
 (2) sweetheart (female) *n.*: **inamorata**. SEE GIRLFRIEND
 (3) sweetheart (male ...) *n.*: **inamorato**. SEE BOYFRIEND
 (4) sweetheart (my ...) *n.*: **Mavoureen** [Irish]. SEE DARLING

swelling (or inflammation of skin due to exposure to cold) *n.*: **chilblains**. SEE INFLAMMATION
 (2) swelling (reduction of a ... to normal size, e.g. loss of erection) *n.*: **detumescence**. SEE SHRINKAGE

sweltering (as in of or relating to dog days of summer) *adj.*: **canicular**. SEE DOG DAYS

swerve (from a course or intended path) *v.t.*: **yaw**. SEE VEER

swiftness *n.*: **celerity**. SEE SPEED

swimming (of or relating to ...) *adj.*: **natatorial**. ∎ Some golfers might throw up their hands in surrender after a slice or a shanked five-iron, but how many pack up their clubs and become world-class in a fallback sport? Swimmer Ed Moses has done that with only two years of full-time training. So meteoric has his rise through the **natatorial** ranks been that he seems to have answered the commandment of his sign-waving mother, Sissy. (Brian Cazeneuve, *Leaving The Links To Pick Up A Stroke — With Three World Cup Wins, Former Golfer Ed Moses Proved*

Water's No Hazard, Sports Illustrated, 11-29-1999, p. R20.)
 (2) swimming (pool, esp. indoor) *n.*: **natatorium**. SEE POOL

swindle *v.t.*: **bunco**. ∎ Samuel Adams ... belonged to the tradition of the American West, "full of liars and braggarts." He saw profit in recognition by the federal government, and in 1867 **buncoed** a tiny mining town into providing [supplies for his trip]. His boats quickly came apart on the boulders, but that didn't deter Adams from claiming he had accomplished the trip, and lobbying Congress for money. (James Conaway, *Fakers of the Frontier; Great Exploration Hoaxes*, The Washington Post, 12-17-1982, p. F10.)
 (2) swindle *v.t., v.i.*: **cozen**. SEE DEFRAUD
 (3) swindle (as in cheat) *v.t.*: **euchre**. SEE CHEAT
 (4) swindle (as in deceive) *v.t.*: **hornswoggle**. SEE DECEIVE

swine (of or relating to) *adj.*: **porcine**. SEE PIGS

swing (with arms like a monkey) *v.i.*: **brachiate**. ∎ *The Good Seed* [by Mark Leyner] describes a sperm bank on the 71st floor of the Empire State Building: "You can pick a donor with Mensa membership going back to the Mayflower and a breakfront filled with gymnastics trophies, and end up giving birth to a slavering **brachiating** moron." (Elaine Gale, *Successful Offbeat Writer / Mark Leyner's Popularity Fueled by a Unique Style*, Minneapolis Star Tribune, 04-17-1995, p. 1E.)

swirling (or spiraling motion, often an ocean current) *n.*: **gyre**. SEE SPIRALING

swollen (used often of body parts such as a penis) *adj.*: **tumescent**. ∎ For if ... the jury is left to decide on the oral evidence alone [in Paula Jones' lawsuit against President Clinton], then her lawyers may well be able to argue, "OK. So our client has enjoyed numerous sexual liaisons — which means she is all the more qualified to recognise an abnormally **tumescent** penis when she sees one." (John Carlin, *No Moles, No Growths*, Independent on Sunday, 11-16-1997, p. 19.)
 (2) swollen *adj.*: **tumid**. ∎ There are some troubled taters in East Texas. Stunted by drought when young, the sweet potatoes ballooned into misshapen giants when heavy rains fell later in July. Now they are more **tumid** than tuber. They are as big as footballs. (Author not given, *Too-big Tubers: A Sad Fate Awaits Gigantic Sweet Potatoes*, The Dallas Morning

News, 10-31-1996, p. 28A.)

(3) swollen (reduction of a ... object to normal size, e.g. loss of erection) *n.*: **detumescence**. SEE SHRINKAGE

sycophant *n.*: **lickspittle**. ∎ Perhaps [Secretary of Energy Bill] Richardson himself deserves some of the blame for his predicament. Too eager to please, he constantly agrees to run fool's errands for his boss [President Clinton]. A cynic might even call him a **lickspittle**. (Franklin Foer, *Bill Richardson, Masochist*, The New Republic, 07-03-2000.)

(2) sycophant (esp. someone who seeks to associate with or flatter persons of rank or high social status) *n.*: **tuft-hunter**. SEE HANGER-ON

sycophantic (esp. praise or flattery) *adj.*: **fulsome**. ∎ [T]he most salient single technique of all the conventions ... is the use of the crippled, the sick and the lately deceased for political effect. ... At the Reform Party convention, **fulsome** tributes were paid to Ross Perot by a Vietnamese soldier who had aided American prisoners of war (whose agonies were described). (Jonathan Schell, *Jonathan Schell's Campaign '96/Convention Tears Are Cheap*, Newsday, 09-01-1996, p. A43.)

(2) sycophantic *adj.*: **gnathonic**. ∎ Ideally, the new San Francisco fire chief would be selected from a qualified pool of experienced and competent aspirants with acknowledged backgrounds in firefighting and administration. Unfortunately, the next chief will probably be a poster boy (or girl) for diversity or a **gnathonic** ... backer of Mayor Brown. (Edward J. Fitzpatrick [Letter to the Editor], *Picking a Fire Chief*, Chicago Tribune, 05-27-1990.)

(3) sycophantic (to behave towards in a ... manner) *v.t.*: **bootlick**. SEE KOWTOW

sycophants *n.*: **claque**. SEE ADMIRERS

syllables (having more than three ...) *adj.*: **polysyllabic**. ∎ "Firing Line," the eminently civil talk show ... was ending its run after more than 33 years on the air. And William F. Buckley Jr., the spiritual force of America's conservatives and the professor with the famously **polysyllabic** vocabulary, was cementing his record as the longest active host of a TV show. (Paul D. Colford, *A Conversation Comes to an End / On TV's 'Firing Line,' Host William F. Buckley Jr. and Guests Would Talk — at Length. It's the Sort of Talk That's Been Overtaken by the Sound Bite*, Newsday, 12-21-1999, p. B6.)

symbol (or sign which gives information nonverbally) *n.*: **glyph**. ∎ One of the **glyphs** that has been imposed on the American consciousness since illiteracy and immigration made such retrogression necessary is ... a band running diagonally across a circle, a synonym for the word "no." If combined with a drawing of a cigarette it means "no smoking." If combined with a big letter P, it means "no parking." (Bob Wiemer, *NAFTA'S Glyphs Are Sinister Lunacies*, Newsday [New York], 08-26-1996, p. A26.)

(2) symbol (representing an idea without words; e.g."$," or Chinese or Japanese symbols): **ideogram**. ∎ Why have the Japanese latched onto faxing more than electronic mail? It all boils down to this: In Japan, where writing the language requires oodles of **ideograms** and two systems of syllables in hundreds of different combinations, it is easier to hand-write messages than to find the right combination of computer keys. (Karen de Witt, *Floods of Free-flowing Fax a Daily Fact of Life in Japan / Transmissions Just as Common, and Less Expensive, Than Traditional Letters*, Minneapolis Star Tribune, 11-24-1995, p. 34A.)

(3) symbol (an inspiring ..., esp. a flag or banner) *n.*: **oriflamme**. SEE BANNER

(4) symbol (as in figure of speech, where a part is used to stand for the whole or vice versa) *n.*: **synecdoche**. SEE FIGURE OF SPEECH

symbolic (rather than a literal representation, esp. with respect to objects of worship) *adj.*: **aniconic**. ∎ Antiquarian authors of the second century ... described an age before art in which primitive peoples worshiped unformed, **aniconic** images such as rocks and planks. To their way of thinking, this simple age preceded a subsequent "age of art," a period in which worship was transformed by the introduction of images created with aesthetic sense and skill. (Sarah Guberti Bassett, *"Excellent Offerings": The Lausos Collection in Constantinople*, The Art Bulletin, 03-01-2000.)

sympathizers (as in traitors or group of ... working within a country to support an enemy and who may engage in espionage, sabotage or other subversive activities) *n.*: **fifth column**. SEE TRAITORS

symptom (early ... of disease) *n.*: **prodrome**. ∎ Recurrent Herpes Simplex Virus. Recurrent outbreaks are usually much milder than primary outbreaks and rarely cause systemic symptoms. Patients may experience a **prodrome** of burning or stinging in the area of the original outbreak. (Elizabeth Reifsnider, *Common Adult Infectious Skin Conditions*, The Nurse Practitioner, 11-01-1997, p. 17.)

synopsis *n*.: **conspectus**. SEE SURVEY

(2) synopsis *n*.: **precis** [French]. SEE SUMMARY

T

tacky (as in sticky) *adj*.: **mucilaginous**. SEE STICKY

tactile *adj*.: **haptic**. SEE TOUCH

tactless (comment which seems to be offering sympathy but instead makes the person feel worse, either intentionally or unintentionally) *n*.: **Job's comforter** [derives from comments made to Job, whose friends pretended to comfort him but actually found fault with him]. [Last month we asked our readers for humorous] examples of "**Job's comforters**" .... Almost everyone weighed in with some form of "You're much better in bed than your sister." [Others included:] "I can't believe your husband ran off with the nanny. Oh well, at least you know she'll be good with your kids if he marries her." "So that was your daughter in that porn video I saw? Oh, well, let me tell you that she was really good at what she was doing!" (Author not given, *The Style Invitational*, The Washington Post, 02-13-2005.)

tactless (comments) *n*.: **dontopedalogy**. SEE FOOT-IN-MOUTH

tail (toward or located near) *adj*.: **caudal**. ∎ The lower tip of the walleye's **caudal** fin is white-tipped, while the sauger's isn't. (Jerry Davis, *Walleye Wonderland — Anglers on Thin Ice, but Chase Coveted Fish Anyway*, Wisconsin State Journal, 01-21-1996, p. 11D.)

tainted (morally ...) *v.t*.: **cankered**. SEE CORRUPTED

take (for oneself without right) *v.t*.: **arrogate**. SEE CLAIM

(2) **take** (property to compel payment of debts) *v.t*.: **distrain**. SEE CONFISCATE

(3) **take** (for oneself without permission) *v.t*.: **expropriate**. SEE SEIZE

(4) **take** (a person or group from one place to another against their will, whether literally or figuratively) *v.t*.: **frogmarch**. SEE MARCH

take back (as in renounce or disavow) *v.t*.: **abjure**. SEE RENOUNCE

take in (as in ingest) *v.t*.: **incept**. SEE INGEST

take over (as in usurp) *v.t*.: **accroach**. SEE USURP

take place *v.t*.: **betide**. SEE HAPPEN

take-it-or-leave-it (as in choice of taking what is offered or nothing; i.e. no real option at all) *n*.: **Hobson's choice**. SEE CHOICE

takeover (sudden attempt at government ...) *n*.: **putsch**. SEE COUP

taking (forcible ... of another's property) *n*.: **rapine**. SEE LOOTING

tale (as in fable) *n*.: **apologue**. SEE FABLE

(2) **tale** (as in lie) *n*.: **fabulation** (one who does so: **fabulist**). SEE LIE

talent (area of ...) *n*.: **métier** [French]. SEE FORTE

talk (about, esp. at length) *v.i*., *n*.: **descant**. ∎ [Handwriting expert Elias Samas] can **descant** for an hour on the secrets a single letter may conceal. "Take the letter 'T,'" he says. "I can give you 30 interpretations on the way people write that letter." (Drew Fetherston, *City & Co./He's Got Analysis Down to a T/Handwriting Expert Sees Past Alphabet's Letters*, Newsday, 11-26-2000, p. C3.)

(2) **talk** (formal ...) *n*.: **allocution**. SEE SPEECH

(3) **talk** (inability to ... due to brain injury) *n*.: **aphasia**. SEE UNCOMPREHENDING

(4) **talk** (light or playful back and forth ...) *n*.: **badinage**. SEE BANTER

(5) **talk** (small ..., as in chitchat) *n*.: **bavardage**. SEE CHITCHAT

(6) **talk** (on a topic, esp. in a long-winded or pompous manner) *v.i*.: **bloviate**. SEE SPEAK

(7) **talk** (quickly and excitedly) *v.t*.: **burble** SEE GUSH

(8) **talk** (informal ..., as in chat or discussion) *n*.: **causerie**. SEE CHAT

(9) **talk** (casually) *n*.: **chinwag** [slang]. SEE CHAT

(10) **talk** (casually) *v.i*.: **confabulate**. SEE CHAT

(11) **talk** (as in discussion, esp. about art or literature) *n*.: **conversazione** [Italian]. SEE CONVERSATION

(12) **talk** (pompously, loudly or theatrically) *v.i*.: **declaim**. SEE PROCLAIM

(13) **talk** (one skilled at dinner ...) *n*.: **deipnosophist**. SEE CONVERSATION

(14) **talk** (between two people or groups in which neither side hears or understands or pays attention to the other) *n*.: **dialogue des sourds** [French]. SEE DIALOGUE

(15) **talk** (inability to ... due to hoarseness) *n*.: **dysphonia**. SEE HOARSENESS

(16) talk (or write at length on a subject) *v.i.*: **expatiate**. SEE EXPOUND

(17) talk (as in discussion) *n.*: **interlocution**. SEE DISCUSSION

(18) talk (at length) *v.i.*: **perorate** (*n.*: **peroration**). SEE MONOLOGUE

(19) talk (casual ..., as in chitchat) *n.*: **persiflage**. SEE CHITCHAT

(20) talk (in a foolish or inept way, or ... nonsense) *v.i.*, *n.*: **piffle**. SEE NONSENSE

(21) talk (between three people) *n.*: **trialogue**. SEE CONVERSATION

talkative (as in characterized by a ready and easy flow of words) *adj.*: **voluble**. ▪ You have to be very specific about what you ask women. If, for example, you missed a Redskins game, and you know a woman who saw it, never, ever ask, "What happened?" Unless you have nowhere to go until Thursday. ... Left to their own devices, girls go through life **volubly** answering essay questions. (Tony Kornheiser, *Pumping Irony*, Times Books [1995], p. 248.)

(2) talkative (condition of being overly ...) *n.*: **logorrhea**. SEE VERBOSITY

talks (esp. at the start of negotiations) *n.*: **pourparler** [French]. SEE DISCUSSION

tameness (as in gentleness) *n.*: **mansuetude**. SEE GENTLENESS

tangent (as in digression) *n.*: **excursus**. SEE DIGRESSION

(2) tangent (as in passing comment) *n.*: **obiter dictum** [Latin]. SEE PASSING COMMENT

tangible *adj.*: **tactile**. ▪ But like all Olympics, this will be a place where the world's greatest athletes vie for a shot at immortality. For Koons and every other person playing a role, Nagano [Japan] will forever be the place where their dreams, once broad and abstract, take on the **tactile** dimensions of an overstuffed bag, a racing bib, an Olympic uniform, or a gold medal. (Sam Walker, *Testing Olympic Dreams on Ice and Snow ... Among the Palm Trees*, The Christian Science Monitor, 02-06-1998, p. 9.)

tangle (as in confused or disarrayed mass) *n.*: **welter**. SEE JUMBLE

tangy (as in tart) *adj.*: **acidulous**. SEE TART

(2) tangy (agreeably ... in taste or flavor) *adj.*: **piquant**. SEE ZESTY

tantalizing (as in tempting) *adj.*: **siren**. SEE TEMPTING

tantrum *n.*: **boutade** [French]. SEE TEMPER TANTRUM

(2) tantrum (marked by a sudden or violent ...) *adj.*: **vesuvian** (esp. as in ... temper). SEE TEMPER

target (as in objective) *n.*: **quaesitum**. SEE OBJECTIVE

tarnish *v.t.*: **besmirch**. ▪ "Never in all of this four years of activity have I ever said anything to **besmirch** anyone's reputation. I think we owe one another as a part of basic human dignity treating one another with dignity and with respect and basic civility. That's the way I was trained in the law." (Author not given, *The Paula Jones Decision: Excerpts*, The Atlanta Journal and Constitution, 04-03-1998, p. A16.)

tarnished (or impure) *adj.*, *v.t.*: **maculate**. SEE IMPURE

tart *adj.*: **acidulous**. ▪ People seem to think [Senator Robert Dole's] biting wit bares too many teeth, prompting even his handlers debate whether to "let Dole be Dole." Dole's **acidulous** wit underscores how humorless the Bush and Bill Clinton years have been compared with past administrations. (Neal Gabler, *No Fooling — Dole Is a Funny Guy*, Newsday, 03-25-1996, p. A29.)

(2) tart (as in ... remarks) *adj.*: **astringent**. SEE HARSH

(3) tart (agreeably ... in taste or flavor) *adj.*: **piquant**. SEE ZESTY

taskmaster (brutal ...) *n.*: **Simon Legree** [after the cruel slave dealer in Harriet Beecher Stowe's 1852 novel *Uncle Tom's Cabin*]. ▪ Nearly half of the 3rd Infantry's 20,000 still in Iraq have been deployed at least six months, some more than a year. Yesterday, they were told that their departure from Iraq would be delayed a second time. ... [D]oes it make sense, spending what we do to recruit volunteers — and then leave them with an ill-defined mission under conditions that only a **Simon Legree** could think reasonable? (Lionel Van Deerlin, *Our Fighting Forces in a Sour Mood*, The San Diego Union-Tribune, 07-16-2003, p. B7.)

taste (as in personal preference) *n.*: **de gustibus** [Latin, often used as part of the expression "de gustibus non est disputandum," as in "there is no disputing about taste." This phrase is sometimes used pejoratively, as in questioning the taste of others, and sometimes not, as in merely pointing out that everyone has his own opinion.] ■ Two of the most traditional approaches [determining what goes on TV are paternalism, which] derives its authority from the conviction that culture is all about providing the public with what it needs rather than what it wants, [and populism, which] defers meekly to the relativistic assumption that **de gustibus non est disputandum**; it does not so much judge quality as merely rubberstamp the ratings. (Graham McCann, *How to Define the Indefinable: Television*, Financial Times [London], 03-26-2003.)

(2) taste (of or relating to sense of ...) *adj.*: **gustatory**. ■ Among the **gustatory** delights of Cajun country: An alligator sausage and seafood gumbo. (Anne Rochell Konigsmark, *Cajun Spice Marking Three Centuries of French Flavor in Louisiana, a Year's Worth of Festivals Has the Good Times Really Rolling on the Bayou*, The Atlanta Journal and Constitution, 05-30-1999, p. L1.)

(3) taste (savor the ... of) *v.t.*: **degust**. SEE SAVOR

tasteless (or inappropriate comments) *n.*: **dontopedalogy**. SEE FOOT-IN-MOUTH

(2) tasteless (and cheap or showy, or such an object) *adj., n.*: **gimcrack**. SEE SHOWY

tasting (act or faculty of ...) *n.*: **gustation**. ■ Describing the enormous respect she has gained for **gustation**, Allende tells of a lecture in which a Jewish guru gave his students a rosy grape and instructed them to spend no less than 20 minutes eating it. (Jessica Lee, *"Aphrodite" Serves Orgy of Epicurean Delights*, USA Today, 04-02-1998, p. 6D.)

tasty *adj.*: **sapid**. ■ In previous reviews, I've raved about the elegant and earthy lobster-and-truffle sausage, the **sapid** sea bass with coarse salt poached in lobster oil, and the indescribably complex and delectable ballottine of lamb stuffed with ground veal, sweet-breads and truffles. (James Villas, *Why Taillevent Thrives [Three-star Restaurant in Paris, France]*, Town & Country Monthly, 03-01-1998, p. 134.)

(2) tasty *adj.*: **toothsome**. A highly buffed, $1-million stainless steel kitchen opens onto one side of the dining room so diners can watch while a dozen pleated white toques bob and weave. There, chef Philippe Feret and his team assemble their **toothsome** French classics. (Jane Freiman, *Dining Out*, Newsday, 11-11-1994, p. B27.)

tattered *adj.*: **tatterdemalion**. SEE RAGGED

tatters (as in bits and pieces) *n.*: **flinders**. SEE BITS AND PIECES

tattle (on) *v.i.*: **peach**. ■ A few days ago a rumor spread like fire through a straw rick that "Deep Throat," world's most famous news source, was [Alexander Haig]. What made this story far-fetched was not that Haig had been a big shot in the Nixon White House in Watergate days, so wouldn't have **peached** on his boss [but rather] on literacy grounds [since] he is utterly incapable of making anything perfectly clear once he starts to talk. (Russell Baker, *Tiresome News Dept.*, The New York Times, 10-07-1989, p. 23.)

tattler (or accuser) *n.*: **delator**. SEE ACCUSER

tawdry *adj.*: **meretricious**. SEE VULGAR

teach *v.t.*: **catechize**. ■ A tireless army of social workers, nurses, and home visitors targeted poor families in the tenements of New York and Chicago, **catechizing** them in scrubbing, sweeping, dusting, and disinfecting. (Roy Porter, *The Enemy Within*, The New Republic, 04-20-1998.)

teacher *n.*: **pedagogue**. ■ "Truthfully, if someone gave Andre [Agassi] a million dollars to go to Wimbledon, he'd still want to go home," said his coach, tennis **pedagogue** Nick Bollettieri, after Agassi's 4-6, 6-2, 7-5, 5-7, 6-0, sorry-tank's-empty loss to [Mats] Wilander [in the 1988 French Open]. (Alexander Wolff, *Mats Mania it Wasn't*, Sports Illustrated, 06-13-1988, p. 26.)

(2) teacher (of Christianity) *n.*: **catechist**. SEE CHRISTIANITY

teaching (as in tenet) *n.*: **shibboleth**. SEE PRINCIPLE

tear (apart) *v.t.*: **rive** (past tense: **riven**). ■ Her 12-year marriage and her husband's subsequent illness [AIDS] cast Pearson, a poet and Mormon, into a complex drama in which she was not only **riven** with self-doubts but forced to reconcile her deep feelings for her husband and a religion that regards a homosexual life-style as an ex-communicable offense. (Kristin McMurran, *Sequel: Carol Lynn Pearson Pens a Moving Memoir on Her Gay Husband's Death from AIDS*, People, 02-02-1987, p. 91.)

tearful *adj.*: **lachrymose**. ■ This is not to belittle [Senator Robert] Dole's genuine emotion as he battled to hold back the tears on Wednesday. No one in public life is so stoical and yet so **lachrymose**. Dole's eyes mist each time he returns to his hometown of Russell, Kansas. (Walter Shapiro, *"Citizen Bob" Chooses: All or Nothing*, USA Today, 05-17-1996, p. 2A.)

tearing (adapted for ... apart flesh) *adj.*: **carnassial** (*n.*: a tooth so adapted). SEE TOOTH

tears (of or relating to) *adj.*: **lachrymal**. ∎ **Lachrymal** Gender Gap — At the Ramsey Clinic's Dry Eye and Tear Research Center in St. Paul, Minn, William H. Frey II [found that] boys and girls up to age 12 cry with the same frequency, but afterward, girls cry more. After age 18, women cry almost four times as frequently as men. (Mary Ann Hogan, *Just Cry, Cry, Cry*, Newsday, 03-12-1994, p. 31.)

tease (as in joke) *v.i.*, *n.*: **jape**. SEE JOKE

(2) **tease** (esp. through the use of satire) *v.t.*: **pasquinade**. SEE SATIRIZE

teasing (playfully) *n.*, *v.t.*, *v.i.*: **chaff**. ∎ To call someone hideously ugly was capable of being defamatory; whether it was so or not must depend on the circumstances of the case. ... Lord Justice Millett, dissenting, said **chaff** and banter were not defamatory, and even serious imputations were not actionable if no one would take them seriously. (Paul Magrath, *Law Report: "Hideously Ugly" Tag Could Be Defamatory*, Independent, 10-04-1996, p. 16.)

(2) **teasing** (good-natured ...) *n.*: **raillery**. ∎ Some people still joke about British food, but for the last 20 years their **raillery** has been way off the mark. The British have been luxuriating in a food revolution that has stocked their supermarkets with a cornucopia of good things and brought them an array of splendid (if expensive) restaurants. All this has been partly powered by immigrants, many from Asia, who brought new foods with them. (Claire Hopley, *From Marzipan to Pork Pies, Sampling Britain's Cornucopia, [Books]*, The Washington Times, 01-18-2004.)

technicality (as in a subtle point raised within the context of a philosophical or theological debate; also references such a debate itself) *n.*: **quodlibet**. SEE SUBTLETY

tedious (passage or section in a book, speech or work of performing art) *n.*: **longueur**. ∎ [T]he Federation commemoration stumbles on and on with no end in sight. Speech followed dreary speech. ... Birth of democracy .. historic event ... national spirit ... great debt ... supreme sacrifice ... heavy responsibility ... unique values ... challenges that lie ahead, dah-de-dah; you could feel the frontal lobes turning to porridge as the **longueurs** yawned to infinity. (Author not given, *Vaudeville, Boredville, The Bums Were Numb*, Sydney Morning Herald, 05-12-2001, p. 28.)

(2) **tedious** (writer or speaker) *n.*: **dryasdust**. SEE BORING

(3) **tedious** (as in uninteresting or dull) *adj.*: **jejune**. SEE UNINTERESTING

teem *v.i.*: **pullulate**. ∎ And far from rising above anxiety, classical Greek art **pullulated** with horrors: snakes, monsters, decapitated Gorgons, all designed to ward off the terrors of the spirit world. (Robert Hughes, *Art: The Masterpiece Road Show — An Exhibit of Ancient Greek Sculpture Is Used to Advance a Specious Political Argument*, Time, 01-11-1993, p. 48.)

teeming (with) *adj.*: **aswarm**. ∎ As tea, silk and porcelain lured Marco Polo, word of outsized human treasure drew me to China. I'd heard that the country's basketball courts were **aswarm** with big men. (Alexander Wolff, *Olympics 2000/Basketball: The Great Wall — China Has Three Towering NBA Prospects in its Frontcourt — and 100 More 7-footers in Reserve, if You Believe the Rumors*, Sports Illustrated, 09-11-2000, p. 148.)

teeth (arrangement of ...) *n.*: **dentition**. ∎ [Bad fake teeth] fit seamlessly into our obsessions with gross-out comedy, kitsch and "hillbilly" humor. From Mike Myers's snaggled but sexy **dentition** in the "Austin Powers" films to Jim Carrey's antics in the current "Me, Myself & Irene" and 1994's "Dumb & Dumber," fake buckteeth are just another landmark on our endless landscape of crass culture. (Ian Shapira, *Less Taste, More Fillings; The Roots of the Fake Bad Teeth Fad*, The Washington Post, 07-04-2000, p. C1.)

(2) **teeth** (having many ...) *adj.*: **multidentate**. ∎ [In the movie "The Faculty"], a group of student eccentrics — pretty attractive eccentrics, but that's what they tell us — is the last line of defense between total world domination by hideous **multidentate** slithering beasts. (John Anderson, *And You Thought Algebra Was Tough*, Newsday, 12-28-1998, p. B9.)

(3) **teeth** (clenching or grinding of ..., during sleep) *n.*: **bruxism**. SEE GRINDING

(4) **teeth** (decay of ...) *n.*: **caries** (*adj.*: **carious**). SEE DECAY

(5) **teeth** (adapted for tearing flesh) *n.*, *adj.*: **carnassial**. SEE TOOTH

(6) **teeth** (gap or space between ...) *n.*: **diastema**. SEE GAP

(7) **teeth** (having no ...) *adj.*: **edentulous**. SEE TOOTHLESS

tell (on, as in tattle) *v.i.*: **peach**. SEE TATTLE

(2) tell (as in confide, one's thoughts or feelings) *v.t., v.i.*: **unbosom**. SEE CONFIDE

temerity *n.*: **hardihood**. SEE GALL

temper (having a violent or unpredictable ...) *adj.*: **vesuvian** (esp. as in ... temper). ▪ [Philadelphia A's pitcher Lefty] Grove had a **vesuvian** temper that was quite as famous as his fastball, and he left behind him a trail of wrecked water coolers and ruined lockers. There were many days when players, particularly skittish rookies, dared not speak to him as he observed the world from the long shadows of his bony scowl. (William Nack, *Lost in History: From 1929 to 1931, the Philadelphia A's Were the Best Team in Baseball*, Sports Illustrated, 08-19-1996, p. 74.)

(2) temper (as in harden or strengthen) *v.t.*: **anneal**. SEE STRENGTHEN

(3) temper (bad or ill ...) *n.*: **bile**. SEE BITTERNESS

(4) temper (bad or ill ...) *n.*: **choler** (*adj.*: **choleric**). SEE ANGER

temper tantrum *n.*: **boutade** [French]. ▪ Many a rising scholar has sipped [Michael Fleury's] champagne in the baroque disorder of his study, learnt from his wisdom and been alarmed by his outrageous **boutades**. With his towering stature and air of authority, Fleury seemed destined to rule, and his gift for invective ... sustained him in many a controversy. (Author not given, *Michael Fleury*, The Times [London], 04-15-2002.)

temperate (as in not indulgent) *adj.*: **abstemious**. SEE RESTRAINED

temperature (abnormally high body ...) *n.*: **hyperthermia**. ▪ In the last week, 11 deaths have been attributed to the wave of blast-furnace heat. ... The Dallas County medical examiner's office has ruled 16 deaths since June 1 as related at least in part to **hyperthermia**. (Jason Sickles, *Dallas County Declares Emergency as Deaths From Heat Climb to 16*, The Arlington Morning News, 07-15-1998, p. 6A.)

(2) temperature (abnormally low body ...) *n.*: **hypothermia**. ▪ With the holidays over, the big chill has settled in, along with the special gifts that only eight more weeks of winter can bring — frostbite and **hypothermia**. (Kathy Wollard, *Test Yourself*, Newsday, 01-26-1999, p. C5.)

temperence *n.*: **sophrosyne**. SEE MODERATION

temporary (esp. with respect to political office holders) *adj., adv.*: **ad interim**. ▪ [President Andrew Johnson] decided to rid himself of [Secretary of War] Stanton once and for all, this time in defiance of the Tenure of Office Act. In February 1868 he announced the appointment of Lorenzo Thomas as secretary **ad interim**, whereupon the House passed a resolution of impeachment. (Author not given, *Andrew Johnson*, The Reader's Companion to American History, 01-01-1991.)

(2) temporary (esp. a doctor or clergyman) *n.*: **locum tenens**. ▪ Some hospitals use temporary physicians on a regular basis. "A lot of people in the urban areas are looking at **locum tenens** as a ... practice management tool," Mr. Robb said. (Carla D'Nan, *Temporary Doctors Ease Texas' Staffing Shortages in Hospitals*, The Dallas Morning News, 02-27-2000, p. 37L.)

(3) temporary (as in lasting only briefly) *adj.*: **evanescent**. SEE TRANSIENT

(4) temporary (as in fleeting) *adj.*: **fugacious**. SEE FLEETING

tempt (someone to do something by coaxing or flattery) *v.t.*: **inveigle**. SEE LURE

temptation (of another by flattery) *n.*: **blandishment** (*v.t.*: **blandish**). SEE FLATTERY

(2) temptation *n.*: **Lorelei call**. SEE LURE

tempting *adj.*: **siren call**. ▪ [T]o eliminate the **siren call** of the Ben & Jerry's [ice cream] from your freezer at home, bypass the ice cream aisle at the supermarket. (Patricia Kitchen, *Willpower/May the Force Be With You*, Newsday, 08-20-1996, p. B17.)

tenacious (in holding to a belief or opinion) *adj.*: **pertinacious**. SEE STUBBORN

(2) tenacious (in effort or application) *adj.*: **sedulous**. SEE DILIGENT

tendency (as in personal preference) *n.*: **de gustibus** [Latin]. SEE TASTE

tenet *n.*: **shibboleth**. SEE PRINCIPLE

tension (a state of nervous ... often with irritability) *n.*: **fantod** [usu. "fantods," and often as in "gives one the fantods"]. ▪ Faced with [having to take a geography test, I] would be hyperventilating. I get nervous just figuring out that Jefferson is in Jackson County but Louisville is the county seat of Jefferson County in my own home state. If the word "test" gives you the **fantods**, contemplate a test that is simple to take, doesn't reflect on your intelligence and has no wrong answers. Consider performing a soil test on your landscape. (Walter Reeves, *Soil Tests Have All* *the Right Answers*, The Atlanta Journal and Constitution, 01-23-2003.)

tenuous *adj.*: **gossamer**. ∎ In the nether world of prosecutorial logic, a federal investigation of the Monica Lewinsky matter was justified by the **gossamer** connection between the president's alleged efforts to cover up his complicity in the Whitewater bank fraud — a charge that has never been made, much less proven — and his easier-to-prove efforts to conceal his sex life from Paula Jones's lawyers. (Harvey A. Silverglate, *Starr Teachers*, Reason, 05-01-1999.)

term (of a ... or word which is pedantic) *adj.*: **inkhorn**. SEE PEDANTIC
 (2) term (of a ... or name consisting of one word) *adj.*: **monomial**. SEE NAME
 (3) term (or name consisting of one word) *n.*: **mononym**. SEE NAME
 (4) term (relating to or explaining a name or a ...) *adj.*: **onomastic**. SEE NAME

termination (as in put an end to) *n.*: **quietus** (esp. as in "put the quietus to"). ∎ Once you do make it to the entrees, you'll be equally intrigued. A deceptively simple turkey breast is stuffed with Fontina cheese ... and served with a La Famiglia di Robert Mondavi Sangiovese that should put the **quietus** to that only-white-wine-with-poultry nonsense. (Eve Zibart, *Fare Minded; A Toast to Grapeseed*, The Washington Post, 05-19-2000, p. N25.)

terrible (person) *n.*: **caitiff**. SEE DESPICABLE

terrific *adj.*: **frabjous** (often as in "Oh frabjous day!"). SEE WONDERFUL
 (2) terrific *adj.*: **galluptious** [slang]. SEE WONDERFUL

terrify *v.t.*: **affright**. SEE SCARE

terror (as in panic) *n.*: **Torschlusspanik** [German]. SEE PANIC

terse (speech or writing which is ...) *adj.*: **elliptical**. ∎ Amy Hempel ... is a leading exponent of minimalist fiction. ... The idea is to avoid conventional narrative development and dramatic climaxes and achieve your effect in an **elliptical** way — a few terse, oblique details, images, lines of dialogue, yielding a sudden illumination or at least a tangible mood. (Author not given, *Print at the Gates of the Animal Kingdom, by Amy Hempel*, Entertainment Weekly, 03-09-1990, p. 27.)

test out *v.t.*: **assay**. SEE EXPERIMENT

testicle (having only one ...) *adj.*: **monorchid**. ∎ Worse, [Adolf Hitler] had been born **monorchid**, an unfortunate anatomical deficiency. ... The fact was confirmed by an autopsy performed on the Fuhrer's corpse by Red Army pathologists. (Author not given, *Obituary of Robert Waite — Historian Who Explained Hitler's Character and Behaviour by Applying Freudian Theories*, The Daily Telegraph, 10-28-1999, p. 41.)

testicles (surgical removal of one or both ...) *n.*: **orchiectomy**. ∎ Though it has been used in the US as elsewhere — on 397 prisoners in San Diego in the early Fifties, for example — the Supreme Court in 1985 ruled that **orchiectomy** was a cruel and unusual punishment. No one has yet been sentenced to chemical castration under the new laws, but when they are, civil liberties groups are geared up to challenge them as an invasion of bodily privacy. (Tim Cornwell, *Castration by Knife May be the Kindest Cut After All*, Independent on Sunday, 07-20-1997, p. 13.)

testy *adj.*: **querulous**. SEE PEEVISH
 (2) testy *adj.*: **splenetic**. SEE IRRITABLE
 (3) testy *adj.*: **tetchy**. SEE GROUCHY

textbook (as in handbook or manual) *n.*: **enchiridion**. SEE HANDBOOK

theatrical (overly ... behavior) *n., adj.*: **operatics**. SEE MELODRAMATIC

themselves (between or among ...) *adj., adv.*: **inter se** [Latin]. ∎ Consequently, the [Australian] Federal Government took the case to the High Court. One of its duties is to hear **inter se** disputes between the Commonwealth [of Australia] and the states. (Daryl Best, *Australia's Greentime History*, History Today, 10-01-1997, p. 9.)

theory (which is complicated and often illogical) *n.*: **choplogic**. SEE FALLACY

thesaurus *n.*: **synonymicon**. ∎ [The first book which was close to a dictionary was published in 1604, and entitled *A Table Apphabeticall, conteyning and teaching the true writing and understanding of hard usuall English words*. ...] The book was by today's standards more a **synonymicon** than a true dictionary — it offered very brief (often one-word) glosses rather than true definitions. (Simon Winchester, *The Meaning of Everything*, Oxford [2003], p. 22.)

thick-skinned *adj.*: **pachydermatous**. ∎ If [former Governor] Edwin Edwards had stormed out of the room every time his integrity was questioned, we'd never have gotten anything done. [Present Governor] Foster, though he looks **pachydermatous** enough, is evidently not yet used to the slings and arrows of outrageous — or outraged — senators. (James Gill, *The Governor's Temper Tantrum*, The Times-Picayune, 06-12-1996, p. B7.)

thicken *v.t.*, *v.i.*: **inspissate**. ▪ The rangers, one of several patrols combing the frontier to monitor Indian activity, "observed an **inspissate[d]** Juice, like Molasses, distilling from the Tree. They found it sweet and by this Process of Nature learn'd to improve it into Sugar." (Author not given, *1000 Years Of Loudoun; "Crossroads of the Indian World,"* The Washington Post, 12-05-1999, p. V8.)

thicket (of trees or shrubs) *n.*: **copse**. ▪ The summit itself (794 feet above Lake Superior) is cloaked with thick **copses** of sugar maple and birch, but a short hike east or west will lead you to rocky outcroppings with unobstructed views. (Jim Gorman, *Jawdroppers: 21 Wilderness Vistas So Big, So Beautiful That They Inspire Profound Sentiments Like, "Wow!"* Backpacker, 04-01-1997, p. 56.)

(2) thicket *n.*: **boscage**. SEE BUSHES

thief (spec. an adult who instructs children how to steal) *n.*: **Fagin** [based on character in Dickens novel *Oliver Twist*, who teaches children to be pickpockets]. ▪ Young armed robbers would walk into a jewelry store. ... One would hammer a glass display. ... Another would scoop up the spoils. ... But a single clue, a handgun carelessly left behind in a car, turned out to be the thread that led investigators to a modern-day **Fagin** who recruited teens in Flatbush to rob jewelry stores in Baltimore and then found Baltimore teens to pull heists in Brooklyn. (Michele Salcedo, *"Fagin" Gang Busted/Robbery Ring Faces Prison Sentences*, Newsday, 07-14-1997.)

(2) thief *n.*: **gonif** or **ganef** or **goniff** [Yiddish]. ▪ "They're robbing me blind!" she cried. She harangued anyone who would listen with tales accusing her elderly brother of stealing $20,000 and a six-carat diamond that her late husband, the diamond broker, had given her. "He's a **gonif**!" she would spit. (Amy Dickinson, *The Case of the Stolen Stradivarius; The Diva Was On Her Deathbed, The Dastardly Deed Was Done, But Who Done It?* The Washington Post, 05-09-1999, p. F1.)

thievery *n.*: **brigandage** (thief *n.*: **brigand**). SEE ROBBERY

thin (esp. in a pale or corpselike way) *adj.*: **cadaverous**. SEE CORPSELIKE

(2) thin (body type) *adj.*: **ectomorphic**. SEE LEAN

things (as in junk or paraphernalia) *n.*: **trumpery**. SEE JUNK

think *v.t.*: **cerebrate**. ▪ Yet [TV star Tim] Allen is more inclined to **cerebrate** about success than to celebrate it — his antic imagination and rapid-fire mouth are offset by a warily analytical mind. (Author not given, *The Entertainers — Tim Allen — A No. 1 Show, a No. 1 Book, Now That's Horsepower*, Entertainment Weekly, 12-30-1994, p. 20.)

(2) think *v.t.*: **cogitate**. ▪ For a month or so, volunteers spent fourteen hours each day in darkness. As other animals do, the subjects would sleep awhile, wake up out of a dream, think about the dream or **cogitate** casually about some other topic for a couple of hours, then fall back to sleep. (Michael Segell, *The Secrets of Sleep*, Esquire, 10-01-1994, p. 123.)

(3) think (about, as in analyze closely) *v.t.*: **anatomize**. SEE ANALYZE

(4) think (about something, often used as a directive, as in "Consider this:") *v.t.*: **perpend**. SEE CONSIDER

(5) think (logically) *v.i.*: **ratiocinate**. SEE ANALYZE

think up (by full and careful consideration, an idea, plan, theory or explanation) *v.t.*: **excogitate**. SEE DEVISE

thinker (as in one who pretends to be a philosopher) *n.*: **philosophaster**. SEE PHILOSOPHY

thinking *n.*: **mentation**. ▪ Dear Dr. Donohue: My mother and two of her sisters have senile dementia. What is it? How does it start? A: Dementia is a diminished state of **mentation** — trouble remembering, reasoning, learning, etc. "Senile" refers to aging, a term considered passé in this connection today. Old age has little to do with dementia. (Dr. Paul Donohue, *Steroids Aren't Tops in Fighting Arthritis*, St. Louis Post-Dispatch, 09-06-1993, p. 2E.)

(2) thinking (staring at one's belly-button as an aid to ..., as in meditation) *n.*: **omphaloskepsis**. SEE MEDITATION

third (choice, as in middle ground) *n.*: **tertium quid** [Latin for "third thing"]. SEE MIDDLE GROUND

third-person (person who refers to himself or herself in the ...) *n.*: **illeist**. ▪ I've read that some famous sports figures become **illeists** during press conferences: "He (meaning the speaker) has to work more on his free throws." I have but one thing to say about that, "Redgate finds that sort of thing somewhat irritating." (Chris Redgate, *The Red Pencil*, The Washington Post, 03-15-2000.)

thorny (as in prickly) *adj.*: **echinate**. See PRICKLY

thorough (as in total or complete, esp. when used with "nonsense") *adj.*: **arrant**. See TOTAL

thought (as in concept or idea which can be expressed in one word) *n.*: **holophrasis** (*adj.*: **holophrastic**). See IDEA

(2) thought (about which one is obsessed) *n.*: **idée fixe** [French]. See OBSESSION

(3) thought (staring at one's belly-button as an aid to ..., as in meditation) *n.*: **omphaloskepsis**. See MEDITATION

thoughtless (comment which seems to be offering sympathy but instead makes the person feel worse, either intentionally or unintentionally) *n.*: **Job's comforter**. See TACTLESS

thousand (a ... years) *n.*: **chiliad**. See MILLENIUM

thrash (generally used figuratively) *v.t.*: **larrup**. See WHIP

threadbare *adj.*: **tatterdemalion**. See RAGGED

threat (as in suggesting the use of force to settle an issue or argument) *n.*: **argumentum ad baculum** [Latin for "to the stick" or "rod"]. ▪ In *The Godfather*, when the mafioso ... "make[s] him an offer he can't refuse" he is using an **argument[um] ad baculum**, or rod, in rod's modern slang sense of pistol. (Philip Howard, *Rhetoric and All That Rot*, The Times [London], 04-12-1991.)

(2) threat (spec. acting as if or threatening that a future event [usually unwanted] has already occurred by reference to an event that precedes it, for example, "if you look at my diary, you're dead") *n.*: **prolepsis**. See PREDICTION

threaten (someone with divine punishment) *v.i.*: **comminate**. ▪ As a useful corrective [to all the positive publicity surrounding the millennium], this column will, from now until the McMillennium, be chronicling the ... plethora of ... wrong turnings of the past thousand years. ... And what shall we have a go at? What horrors shall we denounce and **comminate**? Well ... could be almost anything. There's an [embarrassment of riches], to be frank. (Michael Bywater, *Fed Up Already With All the Millennium Gush? Read On...* , The Observer Review, 01-31-1999, p. 16.)

threatening (or menacing) *adj.*: **minatory**. See MENACING

thrill (as in moment of intense excitement) *n.*: **frisson** [French]. See SHUDDER

thrive (often at another's expense) *v.i.*: **batten**. ▪ The bureaucracy has effectively run Japan for the past four decades, and it **battens** on its power — not to mention the plum private-sector jobs that go to many senior government officials when they retire. A recent study by Tokyo Shoko Research, for example, discovered that nearly 1 in 5 construction-company board members is a former bureaucrat. (Edward W. Desmond, *Japan: Hosokawa's Way — Abandoning Traditional Politics, the Prime Minister Muscles Through a Political Reform That Points the Way Toward Even More Profound Change*, Time, 11-29-1993, p. 20.)

throng (of people) *n.*: **ruck**. See MULTITUDE

throw (something or someone out of a window) *v.t.*: **defenestrate** (*n.*: **defenestration**). ▪ The first problem for the prosecution, however, came when Kid Twist, while under police guard at the Half Moon Hotel in Coney Island, sailed out his window and down five stories to his death. To this day, Kid Twist's **defenestration** remains a mystery, if only to the New York City Police Department. (David Remnick, *King of the World*, Random House [1998], p. 60.)

throw up (making an effort to ..., by retching) *v.i.*: **keck**. See VOMIT

throwing up (act of ...) *n.*: **emesis**. See VOMITING

(2) throwing up (an agent which causes ...) *n.*: **emetic**. See VOMITING

tie (as in chain or link) *n.*: **catenation** (*v.t.*: **catenate**). See CHAIN

(2) tie (together) *v.t.*: **colligate**. See UNITE

tight-fisted (as in stingy) *adj.*: **mingy**. See STINGY

tightrope (walker, or one who balances on things) *n.*: **equilibrist**. ▪ Among the more bizarre stunts is the "Roller Boller Balancer" number by Pavel and Natasha Lavrik. Pavel is an **equilibrist** who balances himself atop a stack of rolling cylinders. While pivoting from this precarious perch, he and his wife Natasha play catch with a dozen juggling pins. (Steve Parks, *Russia's National Treasure: Moscow Circus*, Newsday, 12-20-1994, p. B7.)

tightwad *n.*: **lickpenny**. SEE MISER

tilt (as in upward slope) *n.*: **acclivity** (*adj.*: **acclivitous**). SEE INCLINE

(2) tilt (as in downward slope) *n.*: **declivity** (*adj.*: **declivitous**). SEE DECLINE

(3) tilt (esp. extending down from a fortification) *n.*: **glacis**. SEE DECLINE

time (measurement of) *n.*: **chronometry**. ▌It is no longer enough, in these complex times, for a college hoopster to have a thorough knowledge of his team's motion offense and a firm grasp of the principles of man-to-man defense. He must also master the **chronometry** of as many as six time zones in order to know when to call his girlfriend. (Austin Murphy, *College Basketball: Basket Case — Our Travel-Weary Correspondent Flew to the Ends of the Earth — Well, O.K, to Hawaii and Alaska — to Find Out That the Best Teams in the Early Going Were Local Rivals*, Sports Illustrated, 12-08-1997, p. 74.)

(2) time (science of measuring ... or making timepieces) *n.*: **horology**. ▌In the early 19th century, the [American] clockmakers practically invented mass production, using interchangeable parts even before the Springfield Artillery Co. did so. By the early 1840s, American producers were able to export $2 clocks to Britain and undercut English manufacturers by $8 and more. Naturally, the English makers, long the leaders in **horology**, accused the Americans of dumping. (Rita Koselka, *Made in the U.S.A. [Howard Clock]*, Forbes, 06-15-1987.)

(3) time (of or over the same ... period) *adj.*: **coetaneous**. SEE CONTEMPORANEOUS

(4) time (of the same ... period) *adj.*: **coeval**. SEE CONTEMPORANEOUS AND CONTEMPORARY

(5) time (esp. short ... between things or events) *n.*: **interstice**. SEE GAP

time being (for the ...) *n.*: **nonce** (used as "for the nonce"). ▌The shacks were shoddy and the university was certain to raze them, but for the **nonce** they were boarded up. (Lars Eighner, *Travels With Lizbeth*, St. Martin's Press [1993], p. 191.)

timeless *adj.*: **atemporal**. [Hermes menswear designer Veronique] Nichanian says she tries to design in an "**atemporal**" style. "There is an evolution, a gradual change. But you can always put my clothes together, even if you buy them two or three seasons apart." (Alix Sharkey, *Fashion: She Has Designs on Men*, Independent, 11-25-1998, p. 10.)

timid (esp. from lack of self-confidence) *adj.*: **diffi-dent**. ▌Weaker women are really strong women in disguise: They need nurturing in order to bring out their self-confidence, but the good stuff is within, waiting to be tapped. (The very same applies to shy, **diffident** men.) (Susan Deitz, *Single File/Not Just Feminists Want Some Respect*, Newsday, 10-04-1998, p. D33.)

(2) timid (person) *n.*: **nebbish** [Yiddish]. ▌The eternal second banana [George Bush], the man thought too timid to sculpt his own political persona ... the bland campaigner who ended one debate by apologizing for his lack of eloquence — this consensus choice as political **nebbish** suddenly transformed himself into the prim reaper who could not be denied. (Laurence I. Barrett., *Nation: Bush by a Shutout After His Southern Sweep, the Vice President Builds Really "Big Mo,"* Time, 03-21-1988, p. 14.)

(3) timid (and unassertive person) *n.*: **milquetoast**. SEE UNASSERTIVE

(4) timid (as in spineless or indecisive, or such a person) *adj., n.*: **namby-pamby**. SEE SPINELESS

(5) timid (as in cowardly) *adj.*: **pusillanimous**. SEE COWARDLY

tinge (as in trace or small amount of) *n.*: **tincture**. SEE TRACE

tingle (from moment of intense excitement) *n.*: **frisson** [French]. SEE SHUDDER

tingling (or prickling of skin sensation) *n.*: **paresthesia**. SEE PRICKLING

tint *n.*: **tincture**. SEE HUE

tiny *adj.*: **bantam**. ▌Furnish your rooms with what Seidman and Cohen call "psychic comforts." These are the small, often affordable touches that inspire you to relax: warm towels, fresh flowers, a CD player in the bath. Replace **bantam** throw pillows with oversized, down-stuffed pillows that practically telegraph their invitation from across the room. (Dylan Landis, *Live in Style and Comfort*, Minneapolis Star Tribune, 09-19-1996, p. 8.)

(2) tiny *adj., n.*: **Lilliputian** [based on the Lilliputians, a people in *Gulliver's Travels*, by Jonathan Swift]. ▌Pister is just one of thousands of scientists and engineers around the world who have immersed themselves in the **Lilliputian** world of micromachines, convinced not only that small is beautiful but that it is also the wave of the technological future. One Japanese firm has assembled tiny parts into a working automobile the size of a grain of rice. (Leon Jaroff, *Global Agenda: Tiny Technology: A New*

Lilliputian World of Micromachines: Scientists Are Creating Wasp-Size Helicopters and Building Mechanical Systems on Slivers of Silicon, Time International, 12-02-1996, p. 58.)

tip (in Near Eastern countries, esp. to expedite service) *n.*: **baksheesh**. See GRATUITY

(2) tip (as in extra or unexpected gift or benefit, sometimes as thanks for a purchase) *n.*: **lagniappe**. See GIFT

(3) tip (as in gratuity) *n.*: **pourboire** [French]. See GRATUITY

tiptoe (as in ballet step on point of toe) *n.*: **pas de bouree** [French]. ∎ I have learned not to ignore this warning from [my dog] Lizbeth, whether I perceive the tiny [fire] ants or not, but to remove ourselves at Lizbeth's first **pas de bouree**. (Lars Eighner, *Travels With Lizbeth*, St. Martin's Press [1993], p. 123.)

tiptop *adj.*: **galumptious**. See EXCELLENT

(2) tiptop (as in excellent) *adj.*: **palmary**. See EXCELLENT

(3) tiptop (as in first-class) *adj.*: **pukka**. See FIRST-CLASS

tirade *n.*: **philippic**. ∎ Cleaves ... launched into a biting tirade directed at his teammates. ... Cleaves's **philippic** wasn't exactly borrowed from the win-one-for-the-Gipper school of oratory; another player summarized the crux of his message as, "Y'all motherf — — -s better get your s — - together!" But it got his point across just the same. (Seth Davis, *NCAA's Midwest Regionals: Following the Leader: The Spartans Paid Heed to a Lively Locker-Room Lecture From Mateen Cleaves and Secured a Return Trip to the Final Four*, Sports Illustrated, 04-12-2000, p. 62.)

(2) tirade *n.*: **jeremiad**. See COMPLAINT

tired (as in weakened) *adj.*: **etiolated**. See WEAKENED

tiring (as in laborious) *adj.*: **operose**. See LABORIOUS

tizzy (in a ..., as in distress) *n.*: **swivet** (as in "in a swivet") *inf.* See DISTRESS

to wit (as in namely) *adv.*: **scilicet**. See NAMELY

(2) to wit (as in namely) *adv.*: **videlicet**. See NAMELY

to-do (over a trifling matter) *n.*: **foofaraw**. See FUSS

toady *n.*: **lickspittle**. See SYCOPHANT

(2) toady *v.i.*: **truckle**. See KOWTOW

(3) toady (esp. someone who seeks to associate with or flatter persons of rank or high social status) *n.*: **tuft-hunter**. See HANGER-ON

toadying (as in sycophantic) *adj.*: **gnathonic**. See SYCOPHANTIC

toast (in the form of a song or poem in honor of a bride or bridegroom) *n.*: **epithalamium** ∎ I shout [over] the phone at her. "Guess what — I'm getting married!" The shocked silence that greets this news goes on forever — at least until my money runs out. "Congratulations, hen," a man says as I come out of the phone box. "I hope you'll be very happy," and I must make do with his whiskey-laced **epithalamium**. (Kate Atkinson, *Behind the Scenes at the Museum*, St. Martins Press [1998], p. 312.)

toddler *n.*: **moppet**. See CHILD

toe (big ...) *n.*: **hallux**. See BIG TOE

toes (having more than normal number of ... or fingers) *adj.*: **polydactyl**. ∎ Often, states have different criteria for diagnosing birth defects. Missouri does not consider **polydactyl** infants, those born with more than five fingers or toes, as having a birth defect, for example. Other states do. (David J. Mitchell, *Tracking Birth Defects Is Goal of Bond's: Bill Proposal Calls for Spending $70 Million Over the Next Two Years*, St. Louis Post-Dispatch, 03-17-1998, p. A6.)

toil *v.i.*: **moil**. ∎ "Deepak Chopra will go down as one of the greatest medical salesmen in history," says Dr. John Renner, a critic who has been following his career. Why **moil** for years in therapy with an over-priced shrink if you can simply transcend the maze of the self? Why accept the narrow, negative definition of reality imposed by parents and society and "realistic" friends if you can have a much more expansive version? (Chip Brown, *Deepak Chopra Has [Sniff] a Cold, [A Medical Doctor and Practitioner of Mind-Body Medicine]*, Esquire, 10-01-1995, p. 118.)

toilet (communal) *n.*: **cloaca**. See LATRINE

tolerance (in the face of adversity or suffering) *n.*: **longaminity**. See PATIENCE

tolerant (of other views and opinions) *adj.*: **latitudinarian**. See OPEN-MINDED

tomboy (as in girl who is high-spirited or boisterous) *n.*: **hoyden**. ∎ Espied by the legionnaires as a potential recruit, she is asked to help out at a catechism class for a gaggle of foulmouthed, streetwise little **hoydens**, whose recitation of the Hail Mary sounds "taunting and lewd, like a jeering chant from an angry crowd at a football game." (John Elson, *Books:*

Dirt From the Old Sod, Time, 08-30-1993, p. 64.)

(2) tomboy (as in girl with playful or impish appeal) *n.*: **gamine** [French]. SEE GIRL

tongue (of, resembling, or relating to) *adj.*: **glossal**. ■ [How do] chameleons capture creatures nearly one-sixth their size — the equivalent of a human bagging a large turkey — using only their **glossal** appendages[?] Granted, the lizards' slingshot tongues are comparatively longer than humans' tongues, but that still doesn't account for chameleons' prodigious snaring abilities. (Author not given, *Slip Of The Tongue*, National Wildlife, 04-01-2001.)

(2) tongue *n.*: **lingua** [Latin]. ■ Contrary to popular belief, Latin is not a dead language. In fact, it's alive and well and riding the best-seller lists in the form of Latin for All Occasions, a **lingua**-in-bucca [tongue-in-cheek] book by Henry Beard on how to spice up your conversation with Latin phrases. (Steve Wulf, *Scorecard: Contrary to Popular Belief, Latin is Not a Dead Language*, Sports Illustrated, 01-14-1991, p. 9.)

(3) tongue (of or relating to) *adj.*: **lingual**. ■ Even if you've already pierced your tongue, you can still come to your senses. The body has an amazing ability to heal itself. ... But if you absolutely must persist in **lingual** lunacy, at the very least keep your tongue jewelry clean, don't wear it at night or while you're eating, and, whatever you do, don't bite down! (Christine Gorman, *Your Health: A Risky Fashion — Piercing Your Tongue Leaves You Vulnerable to Cracked Teeth, Infection and Other Bodily Danger*, Time, 08-31-1998, p. 77.)

tongues (gift of ...) *n.*: **glossolalia**. SEE UNINTELLIGIBLE

too (as in moreover) *adv.*: **withal**. SEE MOREOVER

too much *n.*: **nimiety**. SEE EXCESS

tooth (adapted for tearing flesh) *n., adj.*: **carnassial**. ■ This opening program goes back to the demise of the dinosaurs to discover the roots of the carnivores, and to reveal a vital key to their success: the development of the **carnassial** tooth. (Author not given, *Science Fare*, The Dallas Morning News, 04-22-1996, p. 7D.)

(2) tooth (or bone decay) *n.*: **caries**. SEE DECAY

toothless *adj.*: **edentulous**. ■ Dentists gave Fifty-Year Awards to fluoridating water systems including: seven West Virginia and 5 Kentucky water districts. Yet, 42% of mostly fluoridated West Virginians and Kentuckians are **edentulous**, the country's worst toothless rates. (Author not given, *Dentists Award the Cavity-Prone and Toothless*, PR Newswire, 05-25-2004.)

top (as in "the ... of") *n.*: **apogee**. SEE HEIGHT
top-notch *adj.*: **palmary**. SEE EXCELLENT
(2) top-notch *adj.*: **skookum**. SEE EXCELLENT

top speed (at ...) *adv.*: **tantivy**. ■ This column's first annual Psychic Award goes to [Scott] Sklamba, who admitted before he entered the contest [as to what to name the NBA franchise that was supposedly moving from Minnesota to New Orleans, but did not, as predicted by Sklamba] that he was ready "to place the right side of my brain into warp, **tantivy** over-drive" for the effort [as to what to name the team]. (Angus Lind, *The Columnist Who Cried Wolf*, Times-Picayune [New Orleans, LA], 06-22-1994, p. E1.)

torch (lighted) *n.*: **flambeau**. ■ Though [American Steve] Timons wasn't able to close [Russian Jaroslav] Antonov down, he kept him from setting the Soviets on fire [in the 1988 men's Olympic volleyball tournament]. Meanwhile, the Americans were an emotional **flambeau**. (Bruce Anderson, *Volleyball — West Bests East: The U.S. Men Spiked Their Rivals and Drinking Buddies, the Soviets, For the Gold*, Sports Illustrated, 10-10-1988, p. 104.)

torment (as in place, condition or society filled with ...; spec., opposite of utopia) *n.*: **dystopia**. SEE HELL
(2) torment (as in instance or place of great suffering) *n.*: **Gehenna**. SEE HELL
(3) torment (as in instance or place of great suffering) *n.*: **Gethsemane**. SEE HELL
(4) torment (as in instance or place of great suffering) *n.*: **Golgotha**. SEE HELL

tormented (as if by a witch or by unfounded fears) *adj.*: **hagridden**. ■ [W]e can solve the AIDS scourge only [by] burying the overmastering but quite hollow colour [e.g. race] arrogance that has **hagridden** Europe for so many centuries, causing totally unnecessary misery not only to people of other colours but also to Europeans themselves. (Philip Ochieng, *"Foreign Girls" and AIDS–Stigma From the West*, Africa News Service, 12-06-1998.)

torn (apart) *v.t.* **riven** (present tense: **rive**). SEE TEAR

torpor (sometimes in matters spiritual, and sometimes leading to depression) *n.*: **acedia**. SEE APATHY

tortoise (of or relating to a ... or turtle) *adj.*: **chelonian**. ■ Timmy the Tortoise has put up with some indignities in his time. But heaven knows how the Duke of Devonshire's cabbage-chewing **chelonian** lodger will deal with Powderham Castle's summer guests. For Alice Cooper, the outlandish American singer, is to play a concert there in July, along with a raft of his fellow "monsters of rock." (Simon Davis, *Peterborough: Timmy Eyes Up the Monsters of Rock*, The Daily Telegraph, 03-20-1999.)

(2) tortoise (of or relating to a ... or turtle) *adj.*: **testudinate**. SEE TURTLE

tortuous *adj.*: **anfractuous** (*n.*: **anfractuosity**). ▪ Everything [at Kennebunkport, Maine] looked just as the nation remembers it: that familiar house, with its gray shingled siding and mullioned windows and stone chimney; the surf pounding the **anfractuous** New England coastline; the fresh-clipped lawn, where daily briefings once charted the early escalation of the Persian Gulf War. (David Von Drehle, *Campaign Diary; Father, Son Talk of Their Relationship; For Candidate Bush, a Pause on Dad's 75th Birthday*, The Washington Post, 06-14-1999, p. A3.)

toss (something or someone out of a window) *v.t.*: **defenestrate** (*n.*: **defenestration**). SEE THROW

total (esp. when used with "nonsense") *adj.*: **arrant**. ▪ Some people think there are too many bowl games (three more have applied for certification this year), and I believe this to be **arrant** nonsense. Too many bowl games in America? In the land of the free and the home of the roadside reptile farm? You might as well say we have too many beauty queens. (Charles P. Pierce, *The Naked Guy Wore Clothes and the Beauty Queen Left Early [1997 Independence Bowl Football Game]*, Esquire, 12-01-1998, p. 50.)

(2) total , (esp as in ... power) *adj.*: **plenary**. SEE COMPLETE

touch (of or relating to sense of ...) *adj.*: **haptic**. ▪ There is something extremely tactile about [Jackson Pollock's] art; he's an artist, like Vincent van Gogh, who had to feel the forms, whose responses to the world were more **haptic** than visual. (John Zeaman, *The Shape of Things to Come*, The Record [Bergen County, NJ], 10-25-1997, p. Y1.)

(2) touch (esp. for medical reasons) *v.t.*: **palpate** (*n.*: **palpation**). ▪ Lift the breast and lay it flat in the palm of your hand. Sandwich the breast by placing the other palm down over it. **Palpate** carefully with the top hand all the way along and across the breast, feeling for any thickening or lumps. (Lisa Jones Townsel, *Good Defense: A Monthly Breast Self Exam*, St. Louis Post-Dispatch, 10-31-1998, p. 39.) ▪ My

mother's struggle [with breast cancer], which lasted 21 years, has become part of my medical history, carefully chronicled in manila folders at the doctor's office. It has meant especially diligent **palpations** from my gynecologist. (Joanne Kaufman, *Will I Inherit My Mother's Disease? [Breast Cancer]*, Redbook, 02-01-1997, p. 49.)

(3) touch (as in small amount) *n.*: **soupçon** [French]. SEE TRACE

(4) touch (of, relating to, or perceptible to sense of) *adj.*: **tactile**. SEE TANGIBLE

(5) touch (as in trace or small amount of) *n.*: **tincture**. SEE TRACE

touched (appearing ... as if under a spell) *adj.*: **fey**. SEE CRAZY

(2) touched (as in slightly insane, often used humorously) *adj.*: **tetched**. SEE CRAZY

touchy (as in peevish or grouchy) *adj.*: **tetchy**. SEE GROUCHY

tough (as in thick-skinned) *adj.*: **pachydermatous**. SEE THICK-SKINNED

toughen *v.t.*: **anneal**. SEE STRENGTHEN

tourists (person who guides ...) *n.*: **cicerone**. SEE GUIDE

tower (over, as in dominate) *v.t.*: **bestride**. SEE DOMINATE

trace (as in small amount) *n.*: **soupçon** [French]. ▪ [E]ven as they take their first steps against porno chic, the French aren't likely to stop selling and celebrating sex. But a **soupçon** of moral outrage may do France, and the world, some good. (Stephen Baker, *Commentary: Why "Porno Chic" Is Riling the French*, Business Week, 07-30-2001.)

(2) trace (as in small amount) *n.*: **tincture**. ▪ Gradually, the Democratic party withdrew from the [Kennedy] family, leaving them members only of the Kennedy party. John Jr. escaped all this. He maintained at least a **tincture** of the promise that Ted and the others had leeched out of the Legacy. (Peter Collier, *A Kennedy Apart*, National Review, 08-09-1999.)

track (closely to a line, rule, or principle) *v.i.*: **hew**. SEE CONFORM

trade (as in profession) *n.*: **métier** [French]. SEE PROFESSION

tradition (excessive reverence for ... or forebears) *n.*: **filiopietistic**. SEE OLD-FASHIONED

traditionalism (as in hatred or fear of anything new or different) *n.*: **misoneism** (person holding this view: **misoneist**). SEE CONSERVATISM

traditionalist (spec. a person who is opposed to advancements in technology) *n.*: **Luddite** [The word is based on a group of British workers who destroyed laborsaving textile machinery between 1811 and 1816 for fear that the machinery would reduce employment. It is generally, but not always, used disparagingly.] ∎ [Al Gore's] role as an enemy of medical progress should come as no surprise. When biotech **Luddite** Jeremy Rifkin wrote *Algeny* — a diatribe against gene-based drug development in which he implied that the human life span should revert to that enjoyed before the Bronze Age so that mankind could be closer to nature — it was Al Gore who wrote the glowing blurb that Rifkin has given us "an insightful critique of the changing way in which mankind views nature." (Robert Goldberg, *The Luddite: [Al Gore] Invented the Internet?* National Review, 08-14-2000.)

tragedy (as in episode having the quality of a nightmare) *n.*: **Walpurgis Night**. SEE NIGHTMARE

trail (slowly) *v.i.*: **draggle**. SEE FOLLOW

train *v.t.*: **catechize**. SEE TEACH

trained (to show a conditioned response) *adj.*: **Pavlovian**. SEE CONDITIONED

traitor (esp. who aids an invading enemy) *n.*: **quisling**. ∎ The German-speaking countries aren't alone with this shame. When French President Jacques Chirac was mayor of Paris, his son-in-law lived in a building seized from Jews by French **quislings** during World War II. (Walter Russell Mead, *Long After War, Nazi Taint Lives On In Europe*, Minneapolis Star Tribune, 11-10-1996, p. 23A.)

(2) traitor (esp. who betrays under guise of friendship) *n.*: **Judas**. SEE BETRAYER

traitorous (as in unfaithful or disloyal) *adj.*: **perfidious**. SEE UNFAITHFUL

traitors (or group of sympathizers working within a country to support an enemy and who may engage in espionage, sabotage or other subversive activities) *n.*: **fifth column** [derives from the name given to sympathizers of the four rebel columns who advanced on Madrid during the 1936 Spanish Civil War]. ∎ One thing about Osama [bin Laden] and his flacks, they know how to manipulate our media.

Drop a tape on them and they stand up and salute. He has a built-in propaganda machine working for him. All I can say is that it's a good thing they didn't have American TV at the time of Hitler. TV news, especially cable, seems to be Osama's mindless **fifth column**. (Marvin Kitman, *Enough With Osama Cable*, Newsday [New York], 02-23-2003, p. D35.)

tramp *n.*: **clochard** [French]. SEE VAGRANT

(2) tramp (as in move heavily or clumsily) *v.i.*: **galumph**. SEE TROMP

trance (unintelligible speech given as if in a ..., esp. heard in certain Christian congregations) *n.*: **glossolalia**. SEE UNINTELLIGIBLE

tranquil (as in a place which is ..., rustic and simple) *adj.*: **Arcadian**. SEE PASTORAL

(2) tranquil *adj.*: **equable**. SEE SERENE

tranquility *n.*: **quietude**. ∎ [T]he American people are simply not in a revolutionary mood. And why should they be? This is an era of profound political and social **quietude**. (Charles Krauthammer, *Conservatives: Quit Whining and Enjoy Winning*, Newsday, 10-07-1997, p. A42.)

(2) tranquility *n.*: **ataraxy** (or **ataraxia**). SEE CALMNESS

(3) tranquility (as in peace of mind) *n.*: **heartsease**. SEE PEACE OF MIND

tranquilizer (as in something which induces forgetfulness or oblivion of pain, suffering or sorrow) *n.*: **nepenthe**. SEE NARCOTIC

tranquilizing (as in sleep-inducing) *adj.*: **soporific**. SEE SLEEP-INDUCING

transcend (as in surpass the limits, resources or capabilities of) *v.t.*: **beggar**. SEE SURPASS

transfer (to oneself without permission) *v.t.*: **expropriate**. SEE SEIZE

transform (esp. in a strange, grotesque, or humorous way) *v.t.*: **transmogrify**. ∎ In 1962 Bette [Davis] co-starred with Joan Crawford in Hollywood's camp classic, *Whatever Happened to Baby Jane?* Playing a child star **transmogrified** by time into a demented crone, she pulled off one of Hollywood's grandest grotesques. Yet inside this horror comic sight gag, Bette finds a touching and tragic character. (Brad Darrach, *Grande Dame*, People, 10-23-1989, p. 82.)

transformation (complete ...) *n.*: **permutation**. ∎ As countless observers have pointed out, Madonna has held our fascination these many years by both periodically reinventing herself, and by going out of her way to shock us a little more with every **permutation**. So far, the formula has worked like a charm. (Bill Ervolino, *Oh, No! More About Madonna*, The Record [Bergen County, NJ], 10-18-1992, p. E1.)

transient *adj.*: **evanescent**. ▪ Each political season begins with a prayerful belief that this time the public and the press will get it right — that we will select a president based on substance and stature rather than attack ads, **evanescent** polls and a cockeyed primary calendar. (Author not given, *Candidates Dodging the Issues Convention*, USA Today, 01-05-1996.)

(2) transient *adj.*: **fugacious**. SEE FLEETING

translating (as in interpretative, often of a document or text, such as scripture) *n.*: **hermeneutic**. SEE INTERPRETATION

translator (and guide for travelers, esp. where Arabic, Turkish or Persian is spoken) *n.*: **dragoman**. SEE GUIDE

translucent *adj.*: **diaphanous**. SEE TRANSPARENT

(2) translucent *adj.*: **gossamer**. SEE TRANSPARENT

transmit (as in send a signal) *v.t., v.i.*: **semaphore**. SEE SIGNAL

transparent *adj.*: **diaphanous**. ▪ Webster's defines "glamor," which is fashion's favorite buzzword for spring, as "bewitching charm." But most women would have to be under a pretty potent incantation before donning some of the almost wanton creations that slunk off runways for the upcoming season: teetering high heels, slit-to-there skirts, glove-fitting suits and **diaphanous** blouses leaving nothing to the imagination. (Denise Flaim, *Spring Fashion — Glamor Gets Real*, Newsday, 03-09-1995, p. B35.)

(2) transparent *adj.*: **gossamer**. ▪ During the Mogul empire, the muslin woven in Dacca was so **gossamer** that it was said to be lighter than a cobweb. Legend has it that the 17th century Emperor Aurangzeb rebuked his daughter for being naked when she was actually wearing seven layers of sheer muslin. (Marguerite Johnson, *Fashion, Like So Much in India, Goes Back to Ancient Times*, Time International, 05-17-1993, p. 44.)

(3) transparent (like glass) *adj.*: **hyaline**. SEE GLASSY

trappings *n.*: **habiliment(s)**. ▪ What we would now consider our multicultural diversity was in fact greater at that time than it is today ..., but it was not much in evidence as a phenomenon. Everyone, it seems, had decided to mute differences under the **habiliments** of a common culture. (Nathan Glazer, *Social and Political Stability*, Commentary, 11-01-1995, p. 62.)

(2) trappings (as in finery) *n.*: **caparison**. SEE FINERY

(3) trappings (showy ..., as in finery) *n.*: **frippery**. SEE FINERY

trash *n.*: **dross**. ▪ Why wait around for authors to turn themselves into celebrities when it's possible to sign up people who are already famous or semi-so? Whether such folk could actually write novels mattered hardly at all. Turning unmitigated **dross** into **dross** that will sell is how editors and, sotto voce, ghostwriters earn their keep. (Paul Gray, *Damsel in Distress — Random House Scorned Joan Collins' Manuscripts and the Dispute Wound up in Court. So Whither the Celebrity Novel?* Time, 02-19-1996, p. 75.)

(2) trash (accumulation of ..., esp. prehistoric) *n.*: **midden**. ▪ In some cases the **midden** gives clues to the diets of prehistoric people. Along the shores of the Hudson River at Croton Point, New York, archaeologists found a **midden** of oyster shells several meters deep and four hectares (10 acres) in area. Generations of Indians must have gathered oysters for food and thrown away the shells. (Author not given, *Trashy Treasures*, Earth Explorer, 02-01-1995.)

(3) trash *n.*: **offal**. ▪ A mountain of garbage is to become one of the most romantic vistas on Long Island. Long known as "Merrick Mountain," the Hempstead Town trash heap is about to begin a two-year, $15-million transformation into Overlook Park at Merrick. Perched atop some 3 million tons of **offal**, visitors will be able to see the Robert Moses Causeway to the east and the Manhattan skyline to the west. (Issac Guzman, *In Hempstead/Mound of Muck Fertilizes a Park/"Merrick Mountain" Will Become a Spot for Nature and Exercise Enthusiasts*, Newsday, 05-11-1997, p. E13.)

(4) trash (as in printed material which is trivial) *n.*: **bumf** [British]. SEE JUNK

(5) trash *n.*: **detritus**. SEE DEBRIS

(6) trash (study of a culture by examining its ...) *n.*: **garbology**. SEE GARBAGE

travel (compulsion to ... or wander) *n.*: **dromomania**. ▪ [Edwina Ashley, for a time the richest woman in England] developed a textbook case of **dromomania**, becoming so addicted to compulsive travel that once she forgot her children, leaving them in

Hungary with their governess. (Florence King, *Mountbatten's Wild, Beloved Edwina*, The Washington Times, 10-07-1991, p. E4.)

(2) travel (to a sacred place or shrine, esp. to Mecca) *n.*: **hadj**. See PILGRIMAGE

(3) travel (about, esp. on foot and esp. as in roam or wander) *v.t., v.i.*: **perambulate**. See ROAM

(4) travel (about, esp. on foot and esp. as in roam or wander) *v.t., v.i.*: **peregrinate**. See ROAM

(5) travel (able to ... freely in a given environment; used of species) *adj.*: **vagile**. See MOVE

traveler *n.*: **viator**. ▪ It is a question of caveat **viator**. If you travel to countries which have Draconian penalties [e.g. Saudi Arabia] and commit a crime, you cannot expect to be heard and punished according to Western European norms. (Author not given, *Leading Article: The Saudi Lash*, The Daily Telegraph, 09-24-1997.)

traverse (a body of water, esp. in a shallow part) *v.t.*: **ford**. See CROSS

tray *n.*: **salver**. ▪ By Jeeves, the butler is back. Like a note on a silver **salver**, the decision by Rupert Murdoch's former valet to tell all in the latest edition of Punch has drawn attention to the return of that ultimate status symbol, the gentleman's gentleman. (Cole Moreton, *Focus: What the Butler Saw ... and Told*, Independent on Sunday, 07-05-1998, p. 22.)

treacherous (as in perilous) *adj.*: **parlous**. See PERILOUS

(2) treacherous (as in unfaithful or disloyal) *adj.*: **perfidious**. See UNFAITHFUL

treasonist (esp. who aids an invading enemy) *n.*: **quisling**. See TRAITOR

treasonists (as in traitors or group of ... working within a country to support an enemy and who may engage in espionage, sabotage or other subversive activities) *n.*: **fifth column**. See TRAITORS

treasures (of a household) *n., pl.*: **lares and penates**. ▪ On April 23, an auctioneer at New York's Sotheby's will start the bidding on furniture, jewelry and odds and ends belonging to one of this century's most famous women [Jacqueline Onassis]. She was also one of its most private, a circumstance seemingly at odds with her family's putting up her **lares and penates** for public consumption. (Author not given, *Even at the Auction of Her Effects, Jackie O Will Remain Elusive*, Minneapolis Star Tribune, 03-28-1996, p. 22A.)

treat (as in delicacy or delight) *n.*: **bonne bouche** [French]. See DELICACY

treatment (supposed ... which is untested or unproved) *n.*: **nostrum**. See REMEDY

tree trunk *n.*: **bole**. ▪ Climbing that old fig-tree, though, had been our tactical masterstroke. The buffalo circled the sturdy trunk endlessly and with increasing irascibility, occasionally standing on its hind legs, with forefeet propped against the **bole**, in vain attempts to haul us down out of there. (Donald Macintosh, *Travel — Book Award: Up a Fig-Tree Without a Gun*, The Daily Telegraph, 07-17-1999, p. 10.)

trees (relating to, resembling or living in) *adj.*: **arboreal**. ▪ The tree-saving tendency is part of the wider picture of Nimby [not in my back yard] environmentalism, the distinctive badge of those with time and money to waste. This **arboreal** sentimentality won't die out with the older generation, for even the young are bursting with [tree] lunacy. "Save the rainforests" is the modern version of the Children's Crusade. (Jane Jakeman, *A Nation Obsessed by Large Lumps of Wood*, Independent, 12-30-1994, p. 15.)

(2) trees (having many ..., or set in the woods) *adj.*: **bosky**. ▪ Elbert and Anne Chapman are Greens. They are spiritual siblings of those militant environmentalists who are giving European governments fits. Greens dress in rough-hewn woolens and sneakers and breathe the more liberating air of the '60s. They rail against industrial pollution and ache to dwell in **bosky** bucolia. (Holly Wheelwright, *Retirement Planning: Your Cost of Living: Adding It Up*, Money, 11-08-1989, p. 14.)

(3) trees (having many ...) *adj.*: **arboreous**. See WOODED

(4) trees (mass of ... or bushes) *n.*: **boscage**. See BUSHES

trek (to a sacred place or shrine, esp. to Mecca) *n.*: **hadj**. See PILGRIMAGE

(2) trek (difficult or painful ...) *n.*: **via dolorosa**. See ORDEAL

tremble (rapidly or spasmodically) *v.i.*: **judder**. See SHAKE

trembling *adj.*: **tremulous**. See QUIVERING

trend (the latest ...) *n.*: **dernier cri** [French]. ▪ [I have] a reflexive need to test-drive the newest exercise contraption in the faint hope that it will do what the Stairmaster, treadmill and Nordic Track before it could not: lure me to the gym with any semblance of consistency. So it was hardly a volitional act that led me to experience the cardiovascular **dernier cri**, a spinning class, at my Manhattan gym. (L. Jon Wertheim, *Eyes Shut, Ears Open, Mind Puzzled Spinning May Be the Latest Craze, But One Skeptical Practitioner Finds It Flaky*, Sports Illustrated, 07-13-1998, p. R10.)

trends (one who adopts current ...) *n.*: **weathercock**. SEE FICKLE

trendy (not ...) *adj.*: **démodé** [French]. SEE OUTMODED

(2) **trendy** (and wealthy young people) *n.*: **jeunesse dorée** [French]. SEE FASHIONABLE

tribute (formal expression of ...) *n.*: **encomium** (one who delivers praise or ... *n.*: **encomiast**). ∎ In a memorial service filled with military pageantry, tearful reminiscences and glowing **encomiums**, Goldwater, who was 89 when he died Friday of natural causes, was hailed as a man of honesty and principle to a fault and a politician who did more than any other to set the Republican Party on its current conservative course. (Author not given, *Goldwater Honored as Man of Principle and Blunt Honesty / Politicians Join Citizens in Saying Goodbye*, Minneapolis Star Tribune, 06-04-1998, p. 4A.)

(2) **tribute** *n.*: **panegyric** (one who gives tribute *n.*: **panegyrist**). ∎ Though time, history, and cinema have somewhat passed it by, Sergei Eisenstein's *Alexander Nevsky* is still a great Russian bear of a film, a ritualistic **panegyric** to the beauty of warriors in battle, and to the concept of homeland above all. (Author not given, *Alexander Nevsky*, Magill's Survey of Cinema, 06-15-1995.)

trick (as in swindle) *v.t.*: **bunco**. SEE SWINDLE

(2) **trick** (as in deceive or defraud) *v.t., v.i.*: **cozen**. SEE DEFRAUD

(3) **trick** (as in prank) *n.*: **dido**. SEE PRANK

(4) **trick** (as in cheat) *v.t.*: **euchre**. SEE CHEAT

(5) **trick** (as in deceive) *v.t.*: **humbug**. SEE DECEIVE

(6) **trick** (or force someone into doing something, esp. by fraud or coercion) *v.t.*: **shanghai** (person who does so *n.* **shanghier**). SEE COERCE

trickery *n.*: **jiggery-pokery**. ∎ Conveniently enough, the revisions have made it more likely that the economy will fulfill the pledge made by Keizo Obuchi, the prime minister, of 0.6% growth for this fiscal year. ... But not everyone is happy with all the statistical **jiggery-pokery**. In a recent report, the IMF noted dryly that Japan's statistical methods were "not well understood outside of the Economic Planning Agency." (Author not given, *Japanese Statistics: The Mystery of Numbers*, The Economist, 12-11-1999.)

(2) **trickery** (sometimes in a deceitful way) *n.*: **legerdemain**. ∎ Indeed, the footnotes can be the most important part of an annual report. They provide details of the accounting practices the company used in preparing the report. You can pick up hints from footnotes that the company took unusual measures to enhance its profits. A change in accounting procedures can sometimes signal bookkeeping **legerdemain**. (Robin Micheli, *Investing Basics: A Few Key Items in an Annual Report Can Tell You a Lot*, Money, 03-01-1988, p. 181.)

(3) **trickery** (as in sleight of hand) *n.*: **prestidigitation**. SEE SLEIGHT-OF-HAND

trickle (as in light splash) *n.*: **plash**. SEE SPLASH

tricky (situation or problem) *n.*: **nodus**. SEE COMPLICATION

trifle (as in idle or waste time) *v.i.*: **footle** (usu. as in "footle around"). SEE DAWDLE

trifling (thing or matter) *n.*: **bagatelle**. ∎ Needless to say, [Jeffrey] Katzenberg has everything to prove in the partnership [Dreamworks SKG]; he even mortgaged his house to raise the $33m down payment on his share of the company, a mere **bagatelle** for the immensely more wealthy [Steven] Spielberg and [David] Geffen. (Roger Clarke, *Film: The Great White Shark of Tinseltown*, Independent, 12-10-1998, p. 11.)

(2) **trifling** (a fuss over a ... matter) *n.*: **foofaraw**. SEE FUSS

(3) **trifling** *adj.*: **footling** [chiefly British]. SEE UNIMPORTANT

(4) **trifling** *adj.*: **nugacious**. SEE TRIVIAL

(5) **trifling** (as in vain or worthless) *adj.*: **nugatory**. SEE WORTHLESS AND UNIMPORTANT

(6) **trifling** *adj.*: **picayune**. SEE TRIVIAL

(7) **trifling** *adj.*: **piffling**. SEE TRIVIAL

trinket *n.*: **bibelot**. ∎ We are living in a time of such wealth that people can fritter their money away on useless but scrumptious desirables like ... little silver boxes designed 100 years ago for the safe conveyance, in one's pocket or purse, of a few wooden matches. These **bibelots** were made at the turn of the last century, a period of similar wealth and ostentatious consumption. (Carol R. Richards, *Again, Spending for the Sake of Spending*, Newsday, 02-04-2000, p. B8.)

(2) trinket *n*.: **bijou**. ▪ "Oh, it's beautiful," she says quietly, turning the Neanderthal [fox tooth] pendant in her fingers, peering at it over her glasses. "It's beautiful and it's moving. A 35,000-year-old **bijou** — isn't that moving?" (Robert Kunzig, *Learning to Love Neanderthals*, Discover Magazine, 08-01-1999.)

(3) trinket *n*.: **gewgaw**. ▪ Just turn on the TV. Pick up a catalog. Walk into almost any department store, and there it is — along with mounds of other gimmicky gadgets and garish **gewgaws** that ... the world can live without. (James A. Russell, *What the World Needs Now ... Is Not Another Gimmicky Gadget or Worthless Doohickey*, St. Louis Post-Dispatch, 09-09-1995, p. 1D.)

trip (to a sacred place or shrine, esp. to Mecca) *n*.: **hadj**. SEE PILGRIMAGE

trite (as in excessive or contrived sentimentality) *adj*.: **bathetic**. SEE SENTIMENTAL

(2) trite (remark or statement) *n*.: **platitude**. SEE CLICHE

triteness (speech or writing) *n*.: **pablum**. ▪ But on Israel and the Middle East, the audience wanted mush [from the candidates]. And that's exactly what it got: **pablum** that offered a gloss of reassurance while revealing almost nothing of what these candidates really think about the spectacular changes — and the enormous dangers — in the region. (James D. Besser, *Candidates Dishing Out Cheap Slogans*, Baltimore Jewish Times, 10-21-1994.)

(2) triteness (as in excessive or contrived sentimentality) *n*.: **bathos**. SEE SENTIMENTALITY

triumph (with the critics but not the public) *n*.: **succes d'estime** [French]. SEE SUCCESS

trivial *adj*.: **nugacious**. ▪ Should an appointed bureaucracy award tax funds to anyone it chooses to write, photograph, paint or otherwise depict [pornography?] ... The market is there. ... But it shouldn't be the public's money. What's needed is a wall of separation between crud and state. Let **nugacious** trash be provided not by government but by free enterprise, as it is on television. (A.E.P. Wall, *Separation of Crud and State? No Tax Money for Trash*, Orlando Sentinel, 11-15-1990, p. G3.)

(2) trivial *adj*.: **picayune**. ▪ Some referees, however, took F.I.F.A.'s instructions much too seriously. Their cautionary yellow cards were flashed with abandon, often for infractions as **picayune** as failing to throw a ball into play quickly enough or neglecting to form a proper defensive wall for a free kick. (Barry Hillenbrand, *USA 94: The Defining Moment of the 1994 World Cup Came Early*, Time International, 07-18-1994, p. 36.)

(3) trivial *adj*.: **piffling**. ▪ This depressing development [high unemployment in some former Communist countries] is overshadowed by a much more peculiar one. A few countries have managed to keep unemployment rates remarkably low. The Czech Republic, for one, has a rate of only 3.4%. In Russia a mere 2.4% of the workforce is officially registered unemployed; in Ukraine it is a **piffling** 0.4%. What can explain this? (Author not given, *A Puzzling Job*, [Unemployment Varies Widely Among Former Communist Countries], The Economist, 02-18-1995, p. 70.)

(4) trivial (or worthless matter) *n*.: **dross**. SEE WORTHLESS

(5) trivial (a fuss over a ... matter) *n*.: **foofaraw**. SEE FUSS

(6) trivial *adj*.: **footling** [chiefly British]. SEE UNIMPORTANT

(7) trivial *adj*.: **nugatory**. SEE UNIMPORTANT

(8) trivial (as in fault, offense or sin which is forgivable) *adj*.: **venial**. SEE FORGIVABLE

tromp (as in move heavily or clumsily) *v.i*.: **galumph**. ▪ So they reinvented Godzilla. Instead of barrel legs that **galumph** through the Ginza, Godzilla now has runner's calves to bolt down Broadway. (Howard Chua-Eoan, *The Arts/Cinema: Godzilla Redux — The Monster That Has Made a Meal of Tokyo for Decades Is Back, this Time With an Appetite for New York City*, Time International, 07-06-1998, p. 26.)

trouble *n*.: **tsuris** [Yiddish]. ▪ Against any human [chess] player, [Garry Kasparov] would have moved aggressively and gone for the win. But he wasn't playing against a human. "I still have a chance of making a blunder. ... So with all those facts, it was reduced to a simple decision [agree to a draw]. To lose is a disaster." [The computer] suffered none of this **tsuris**. "I'm calculating publicity factors, scientific factors, psychological factors, while the machine is just taking account of the chess factors," moans Kasparov. (Steven Levy, *Machine vs. Man: Checkmate*, Newsweek, 07-21-2003.)

(2) trouble (as in bother or inconvenience) *v.t*.: **discommode**. SEE INCONVENIENCE

(3) trouble (as in bother or inconvenience) *v.t*.: **incommode**. SEE BOTHER

troublemaker *n*.: **scapegrace**. SEE SCOUNDREL

troublemaking (behavior, as in mischief) *n*.: **doggery** [i.e. doglike behavior]. SEE MISCHIEF

truce (temporary ... between opposing parties pending final deal) *n.*: **modus vivendi** [Latin]. ∎ The Christmas recess signaled a make-or-break time for the [settlement] effort [in Northern Ireland]. ... If the republicans and unionists did not find some grounds for pursuing a **modus vivendi** by this May, conciliators feared, the talks might seem futile to everyone, giving way to summer confrontations and street violence. (James Walsh, *Europe: Out of the Labyrinth — At Last, Northern Ireland Gets a Peace Plan With Light at the End of the Tunnel*, Time International, 01-26-1998, p. 28.)

true (necessarily ..., as in incontrovertible) *adj.*: **apodictic**. SEE INCONTROVERTIBLE

(2) true (as in reflecting reality) *adj.*: **veridical**. SEE REALISTIC

(3) true (appearing to be ... or accurate) *adj.*: **verisimilar**. SEE REALISTIC

truncated (something ...) *n.*: **bobtail**. SEE ABRIDGED

trunk (of a tree) *n.*: **bole**. SEE TREE TRUNK

trust (as in reliance on ... alone rather than reason, esp. in philosophical or religious matters) *n.*: **fideism**. SEE FAITH

truthful *adj.*: **veridical** [see also this word under "realistic" in the sense of "reflecting reality"]. ∎ The concept of a sudden, uncharacteristic adherence to the truth is not new either, Jim Carrey having recently played a lawyer magically condemned to a **veridical** 24 hours in "Liar, Liar." (James Gill, *Beatty Movie Right on the Money*, Times-Picayune [New Orleans, LA], 05-27-1998, p. B7.)

try (the ... to achieve a particular goal or desire) *n.*: **nisus**. SEE GOAL

try out *v.t.*: **assay**. SEE EXPERIMENT

tug (used to ...) *adj.*: **tractive**. SEE PULL

tumble (esp. from a position of strength or condition) *n.*: **dégringolade** [French]. SEE DOWNFALL

tumult *n.*: **maelstrom**. SEE COMMOTION
(2) tumult *n.*: **pother**. SEE COMMOTION
(3) tumult (as in chaos) *n.*: **tohubuhu**. SEE CHAOS

turbulent (situation) *n.*: **maelstrom**. SEE COMMOTION
(2) turbulent (situation) *n.*: **pother**. SEE COMMOTION

turmoil (movement towards or degree of ... in a system or society) *n.*: **entropy**. SEE DISORDER
(2) turmoil (of or relating to ... within a group or country) *adj.*: **internecine**. SEE DISSENSION
(3) turmoil *n.*: **maelstrom**. SEE COMMOTION
(4) turmoil *n.*: **pother**. SEE COMMOTION
(5) turmoil (as in chaos) *n.*: **tohubuhu**. SEE CHAOS

turn (away from a course or intended path) *v.t.*: **yaw**. SEE VEER

turn over (as in give back, often a territory) *v.t.*: **retrocede**. SEE GIVE BACK

turnaround (sudden ... of events, often in a literary work) *n.*: **peripeteia**. ∎ Although scalped in Atlanta, this year's Cleveland Indians, in case you hadn't noticed, posted the best record in baseball. Given their five excruciating decades as patsies of the American league, even for someone who has never sat down in Cleveland to change flights, their **peripeteia** was exhilarating. (Haim Chertok, *Rooting for the Home Team Brings out the Confessions of a Revolving Fan*, Jerusalem Post, 11-17-1995.)

(2) turnaround (regarding one's beliefs, causes or policies) *n.*: **bouleversement** [French]. SEE CHANGE OF MIND

(3) turnaround (a ... regarding one's beliefs, causes or policies) *n.*: **tergiversation** (*v.i.*: **tergiversate**). SEE CHANGE OF MIND

(4) turnaround (as in reversal of policy or position) *n.*: **volte-face** [French]. SEE ABOUT-FACE

turncoat (esp. who betrays under guise of friendship) *n.*: **Judas**. SEE BETRAYER
(2) turncoat (esp. who aids an invading enemy) *n.*: **quisling**. SEE TRAITOR

turncoats (as in traitors or group of ... working within a country to support an enemy and who may engage in espionage, sabotage or other subversive activities) *n.*: **fifth column**. SEE TRAITORS

turned up (esp. a nose) *adj.*: **retroussé** [French]. SEE NOSE

turns (full of ..., as in tortuous) *adj.*: **anfractuous** (*n.*: **anfractuosity**). SEE TORTUOUS

turtle (of or relating to a ... or tortoise) *adj.*: **testudinate**. ∎ [Maryland Terrapin (terrapin being a type of turtle) coach Gary] Williams went to work mending fences [after sanctions were imposed on the basketball program]. And he devised a recruiting strategy that centered on high school underclassmen, who would come in after the worst of the sanctions expired. Fortunately for him, he found a few good ones with **testudinate** instincts. (Jack McCallum, *Back From the Depths — Maryland is an ACC Power Once Again, Ending a Decline That Began With Len Bias's Death*, Sports Illustrated, 02-20-1995, p. 20.)

(2) turtle (shell, like a protective covering) *n.*: **carapace**. SEE SHELL

(3) turtle (of or relating to a ... or tortoise) *adj.*: **chelonian**. SEE TORTOISE

tutor *n.*: **pedagogue**. SEE TEACHER

twilight (of or relating to) *adj.*: **crepuscular**. ∎ My current hate list is made up of three types of people: dog-owners who permit their animals to "foul the public footpath" (actually, "permit" is a very poor word for those **crepuscular** pooch-lovers who take their animals out at twilight or dawn with the express purpose of fouling the footpath). (David Aaronovitch, *Off With His Head, and Other Sweet Revenges*, Independent, 05-29-1997, p. 20.)

(2) twilight *n.*: **gloaming**. ∎ The Duel at Dusk, Part II, featuring the Orioles and the Cleveland Indians, will start at 4:15 ET, just as the sun starts to slip behind the third-base grandstand at Camden Yards. ... The effects of that diminishing light and whether batters will be able to see pitches in the **gloaming** dominated conversations Tuesday afternoon. (Mel Antonen, *Orioles, Indians Fear Shadows Today — Players Agree Pitchers Gain Most in Twilight Starts*, USA Today, 10-15-1997, p. 1C.)

(3) twilight (of or relating to) *adj.*: **vespertine**. SEE EVENING

twin (ghostly ... of a living person) *n.*: **doppelganger**. ∎ Before I left, my sister gave me a card. It shows a hiker, stooped beneath his backpack at a bend in the trail. He wears a startled expression as he encounters a briefcase-toting **doppelganger** of himself in a business suit. The caption: "Stanley was deeply disappointed when, high in the Himalayas, he found his true self." (Mike Klesius, *Everyman's Everest; Any Hearty Hiker Can Climb the Killer Mountain's Smaller Neighbor — Without Disappearing Into Thin Air*, The Washington Post, 06-27-1999, p. E1.)

twinkling (as in emitting flashes of light) *adj.*: **coruscant**. SEE GLITTERING

(2) twinkling (lightly over a surface) *adj.*: **lambent**. SEE SHIMMERING

(3) twinkling (as in, in a ...) *n.*: **trice** (as in, in a trice). SEE QUICKLY

twisted (as in tortuous) *adj.*: **anfractuous** (*n.*: **anfractuosity**). SEE TORTUOUS

twitter (like a bird) *v.i.*: **chitter**. SEE CHIRP

two-faced (as in hypocritical) *adj.*: **Janus-faced** [This word is based on Janus, the god of gates or doorways, depicted with two faces looking in opposite directions. Sometimes it has a non-pejorative meaning, in the sense of merely having two contrasting aspects or sides (as shown in the first example), and sometimes it has a pejorative meaning, such as hypocritical (as shown in the second example)]. ∎ There's something about the sport itself that makes it suited to Georgia. The state's identity has long been **Janus-faced**, part good ol' boy with a gun rack on his truck, part genteel Man in Full, just back from the quail hunt. Football's mix of testosterone-driven violence and elegance and dash accommodates both sensibilities. (L. Jon Wertheim, *Dawg Days: All Is Right Again in Georgia, Where the Beloved Bulldogs Have Reclaimed Their Gridiron Legacy*, Sports Illustrated, 12-23-2002.) ∎ [President Bush's] message to the world has been ... free trade is an unalloyed good that leads to the enrichment of all involved. ... Unfortunately, Bush has weakened his hand by agreeing to exempt large segments of the U.S. economy from the less fortunate short-term outcomes of free trade [through tariffs on foreign countries and subsidies]. If a foreign nation pursued the **Janus-faced** trade policies coming out of his administration, George W. Bush would yell foul. (Avrum D. Lank, *Bush Is Two-faced on Free Trade*, Milwaukee Journal Sentinel, 05-31-2002.)

two-sided *adj.*: **Janus-faced**. SEE TWO-FACED

twosome *n.*: **duumvirate**. SEE DUO

(2) twosome (two individuals or units regarded as a ...) *n.*: **dyad**. SEE PAIR

(3) twosome (arranged in or forming a ...) *adj.*: **jugate**. SEE PAIR

tying (act of ... or binding up or together) *n.*: **ligature**. ∎ Auto-erotic asphyxiation — also known as "scarfing" — aims to increase sensation at orgasm. One psychologist said yesterday that sex involving **ligature** is "said to be among the most powerful orgasmic experiences a man can have." It is also extremely dangerous and doctors warned that anyone indulging in it should seek sexual counselling immediately. (Celia Hall, *Fatal Hazards of a Dangerous Sexual Practice*, Independent, 02-09-1994.)

type (original ... or example) *n.*: **archetype**. SEE MODEL

types (of all ...) *adj*.: **omnifarious**. See varied

typical (as in usual or customary) *adj*.: **wonted**. See customary

tyrannical (ruthlessly and violently ...) *adj*.: **jack-booted**. See oppressive

U

UFOs (study of ...) *n*.: **ufology**. ▪ [The book] *Communion* seems to signal a dramatic new era in **UFOlogy**. This time around an increasing number of everyday folk are claiming not merely to have spotted saucer-shaped spacecraft, but to have had disagreeable encounters with creepy travelers from another Time, Space, or Universe. (Michelle Green, *Making Communion With Another World — America's Fascination With UFOs Booms Again as Three New Books Suggest That Humanoids Are Here*, People, 05-11-1987, p. 34.)

ugly (repulsive or terrifying woman) *n*.: **gorgon**. ▪ [T]he most memorable film noir villainesses were formidable and unmistakably alluring. You search in vain for some of the same charisma in the new killer women of the movies. Instead they are unfeeling, unimaginative, unattractive **gorgons**, and [you wonder what] disturbing cultural malaise that is producing this virulent wave of revulsion toward women who want to take charge. (Stephen Farber, *Movies; Commentary; That's No Lady — That's Our Nightmare*, The Los Angeles Times, 03-18-2001, p. 22.)

(2) ugly (old woman) *n*.: **beldam**. See hag

(3) ugly (woman who is old) *n*.: **crone**. See hag

ultimate (to the ...) *adv*.: **à l'outrance** [French]. See utmost

(2) ultimate (as in decisive remark, blow or factor) *n*.: **sockdolager**. See decisive

(3) ultimate (as in most distant, or remote, destination or goal) *n*.: **ultima Thule**. See distant

ultraconservative (in beliefs and often stuffy, pompous and /or elderly) *adj., n*.: **Colonel Blimp**. See conservative

umbrella *n*.: **bumbershoot**. ▪ Some of the heaviest rain downtown fell during lunch hour. Umbrella-armed pedestrians scurrying for food turned sidewalks into **bumbershoot** battlegrounds. (Jingle Davis, *Georgia Welcomes Needed Rain*, The Atlanta Constitution, 07-28-1998, p. B1.)

unable (as in powerless) *adj*.: **impuissant**. See powerless

unambiguous *adj*.: **univocal**. ▪ David Klinghoffer seeks to defend Mel Gibson's film about the death of Jesus, "The Passion," on the basis of corroborative statements found in the Talmud and medieval writings. However, those sources are neither **univocal** nor reliable. [The] ancient rabbinic writings ... were recorded decades after the fact and represent political, theological and polemic tendencies, not historiography. (Rabbi Dan Shevitz [letter writer], *What Good Can Come of Gibson's "Passion"?* Los Angeles Times, 01-05-2004, p. B10.)

unamusing (as in person who tries to be funny but is not) *n*.: **witling**. See humorless

unanimously *adj., adv*.: **nem con** [short for *nemene contradicente*]. See unopposed

unanticipated (event which may be an act of God) *n*.: **force majeure**. ▪ But if there's a fire, flood, strike, or other mishap classed as an act of God (**force majeure**), the builder can further extend occupancy [of the buyer at the builder's development] without limit and without having to pay compensation or provide accommodation [to the buyer]. (Author not given, *Builders Allowed Some Delays*, The Toronto Star, 07-03-1999.)

unapologetic (as in unrepentant) *adj*.: **impenitent**. See unrepentant

unasked *adj*.: **unbidden**. See uninvited

unassertive (and timid person) *n*.: **milquetoast**. ▪ [Warren Buffet]: "Mergers will be motivated by very good considerations. There truly are synergies in a great many mergers. But whether there are synergies or not, they are going to keep happening. You don't get to be the CEO of a big company by being a **milquetoast**. You are not devoid of animal spirits." (Brent Schlender, *The Bill & Warren Show — What Do You Get When You Put a Billionaire Buddy Act in Front of 350 Students? $84 Billion of Inspiration*, Fortune, 07-20-1998, p. 48.)

(2) unassertive (person) *n*.: **nebbish** [Yiddish]. See timid

unattractive (woman who is old) *n*.: **crone**. See hag

unavailing *adj.*: **bootless**. See FUTILE

(2) unavailing (as in vain or worthless) *adj.*: **nugatory**. See WORTHLESS

(3) unavailing *adj.*: **otiose**. See USELESS

(4) unavailing (efforts which are laborious but ...) *adj.*: **Sisyphean**. See FUTILE

unavoidable *adj.*: **ineluctable**. ▌ [T]he much maligned welfare system seems particularly ripe for experimental reform — and not just because it is universally detested. In fact, the case for experimental reform stems from two **ineluctable** truths. The first is that no one knows for sure how to slash the welfare rolls, short of simply cutting off benefits. The second is that the problem of dependency has now reached epidemic proportions. (David Whitman, *Welfare*, U.S. News & World Report, 10-05-1992, p. 38.)

unaware (as in ignorant) *adj.*: **nescient** (*n.*: **nescience**). See IGNORANT

unbalanced (slightly mentally ..., often used humorously) *adj.*: **tetched**. See CRAZY

unbefitting (as in undignified) *adj.*: **infra dig**. See UNDIGNIFIED

unbeliever (as in one with no faith or religion) *n.*, *adj.*: **nullifidian**. See NONBELIEVER

unbiased (uncompromisingly ..., as in just) *n.*: **Rhadamanthine**. See JUST

unbounded (in exhibiting emotion or celebration) *adj.*: **saturnalian**. See UNINHIBITED

unbreakable *adj.*: **infrangible**. ▌ Concrete, that most common and **infrangible** of surfaces, is accessible to everyone. Yet it is virtually virgin terrain for professional sports. The founders of [Roller Hockey International] have recognized this and are taking full advantage of it. (Kelli Anderson, *Roller Hockey: That Professional Sports Had Entered Uncharted Territory Was Clear*, Sports Illustrated, 08-16-1993, p. 50.)

uncanny (as in eerie) *adj.*: **eldritch**. See EERIE

uncaring (as in thick-skinned) *adj.*: **pachydermatous**. See THICK-SKINNED

uncertain (as in unpredictable outcome) *adj.*: **aleatory**. See UNPREDICTABLE

(2) uncertain (as in indecisive) *adj.*, *v.i.*, *n.*: **shilly-shally**. See VACILLATE

uncertainty (as in indecisiveness) *n.*: **abulia**. See INDECISIVENESS

(2) uncertainty (expression of ... as to one's opinion on an issue, esp. arising from awareness of an opposing viewpoint) *n.*: **aporia**. See DOUBT

(3) uncertainty (as in the dilemma of being given a choice between two equally appealing alternatives and thus being able to choose neither one) *n.*: **Buridan's ass**. See PARALYSIS

(4) uncertainty *n.*: **dubiety**. See DOUBTFULNESS

(5) uncertainty (esp. as in "beyond ...") *n.*: **peradventure**. See DOUBT

unchanging (as in stagnant or backward place or situation) *n.*: **backwater**. See STAGNANT

(2) unchanging *adj.*: **equable**. See UNVARYING

(3) unchanging (in rhythm or tempo) *adj.*: **metronomic**. See STEADY

(4) unchanging (as in everlasting) *adj.*: **sempiternal**. See EVERLASTING

uncivilized *adj.*: **gothic**. See BARBARIC

(2) uncivilized (person, as in neanderthal) *n.*: **troglodyte**. See NEANDERTHAL

unclean (as in unkempt or slovenly) *adj.*: **frowzy**. See MESSY

uncleanliness (abnormal fear of ...) *n.*: **mysophobia**. See FEAR

unclear *adj.*: **Delphic**. See AMBIGUOUS

(2) unclear (as in cryptic or obscure speech or writing, esp. deliberately) *adj.*: **elliptical**. See CRYPTIC

(3) unclear (or cryptic or ambiguous) *adj.*: **sybilline** (or **sibylline**; often cap.). See CRYPTIC

uncomfortable (by not affording enough space) *adj.*: **incommodious**. See CRAMPED

uncommon (as in unconventional) *adj.*: **outré** [French]. See UNCONVENTIONAL

(2) uncommon (very ... person or thing) *n.*: **rara avis** [Latin]. See RARITY

(3) uncommon *adj.*: **recherché** [French]. See RARE

uncomplicated (as in elementary or basic) *adj.*: **abecedarian**. See BASIC

uncomplimentary (as in faultfinding) *adj.*: **captious**. See FAULTFINDING

(2) uncomplimentary (person) *n.*: **smellfungus**. See FAULTFINDER

uncomprehending (spoken or written words due to brain injury) *n.*: **aphasia**. ∎ **Aphasia** is not caused by paralysis but by damage to the parts of the brain that turn our thoughts into words we can say and write, and turn the words we hear and read into thoughts we understand. Talking, listening, reading and writing are all more or less equally impaired in **aphasia**. (Richard C. Katz, *Helping Aphasia Victims Communicate*, The Arizona Republic, 07-15-1999.)

unconcern (esp. on matters or politics or religion) *n.*: **Laodiceanism**. SEE INDIFFERENCE

unconditional (as in complete or unlimited, esp as in ... power) *adj.*: **plenary**. SEE COMPLETE

unconscious *n.*: **insensate**. She wasn't capable of running over him while he lay **insensate**. (Dean Koontz, *Intensity*, Knopf [1995], p. 295.)

uncontrollable (and undisciplined person) *n.*: **bashi-bazouk** [Turkish]. SEE UNDISCIPLINED

(2) uncontrollable (event which may be an act of God) *n.*: **force majeure**. SEE UNANTICIPATED

(3) uncontrollable (as in unruly) *adj.*: **indocile**. SEE UNRULY

(4) uncontrollable (as in resistant to control or authority) *adj.*: **refractory**. SEE STUBBORN

uncontrolled (as in impetuous) *adj.*: **gadarene**. SEE IMPETUOUS

unconventional (holding ... opinions or having an ... perspective) *adj.*: **heterodox** (*n.*: **heterodoxy**). ∎ His growing ... **heterodoxy** could, with hindsight, be seen as the first overt signs of a growing alienation from convention and society that would later evolve into a radical sense of separateness and disconnection. (Sylvia Nasar, *A Beautiful Mind*, Simon & Schuster [1998], p. 143.)

(2) unconventional *adj.*: **outré** [French]. ∎ It's exciting to discover in a new guide, published since the Marriage Act relaxed the rules last year, more than 500 attractively **outré** places to get married. Depending on your personality traits, the Reptile House at London Zoo may strike you as the ideal place to tie the knot. Or perhaps the Bass Museum of Brewing? (Author not given, *The Weasel, An Exquisite New Torture to Inflict on Friends and Relatives*, Independent, 02-24-1996, p. 5.)

(3) unconventional (thinker, esp. on matters of morals and religion) *n.*: **libertine**. SEE FREE-THINKER

uncoordinated (as in clumsy) *adj.*: **lumpish**. SEE CLUMSY

uncouth (person) *n.*: **grobian**. SEE BOOR
uncouth (person) *n.*: **yahoo**. SEE BOOR

uncover *v.t.*: **disinter**. SEE DISCLOSE

unctuous *adj.*: **oleaginous**. ∎ I can say awful things to a president or member of Congress, but for some reason, I tremble before **oleaginous** [car] salesmen. You know the type: They spend half of their time scampering off to confer with unseen managers, only to return with sheaves of paper purporting to show the "true factory invoice." And once we have completed the ugly deal, they stalk us by mailing out desk calendars at Christmas. (Tony Snow, *Minivan Shopping Is Poor Cure for Washington Blahs*, The Dallas Morning News, 06-30-1996, p. 7J.)

(2) unctuous *adj.*: **fulsome**. SEE INSINCERE

uncultivated (person) *n.*: **grobian**. SEE BOOR

uncultured *adj.*: **philistine**. ∎ The intellectual left [in England] hated Thatcherism because it seemed so **philistine**. Yet the Thatcherite indifference to culture, the separation of the cultural classes from power, had the paradoxical effect of allowing a certain eccentric freedom. It was, after all, under Thatcher ... that the Saatchi Collection, the most ambitious private museum of cutting-edge art in the world, got built and prospered. (Adam Gopnik, *Cool Britannia — Tony Blair's Regime Is Transforming the Way Britain Thinks About Itself*, The Sunday Telegraph, 07-13-1997, p. 5.)

(2) uncultured (or dull or stupid or ignorant or stupid) *adj.*: **Boeotian**. SEE DULL

(3) uncultured (class of people regarded as ...) *n.*: **booboisie**. SEE UNSOPHISTICATED

undebatable *adj.*: **irrefragable**. SEE UNQUESTIONABLE

undeniable *adj.*: **irrefragable**. SEE UNQUESTIONABLE

under cover (as in, in concealment) *adv.*: **doggo** (esp. as in "lying doggo"; slang). SEE CONCEALMENT

underbrush *n.*: **boscage**. SEE BUSHES

underclass (of society) *n.*: **lumpenproletariat**. ∎ Americans, male and female, who listen to talk radio (two-thirds of whom say they find it a significant source of information and ideas) are affluent and well-educated. These Americans may not be the "overclass" that so many gabble about these days, but they're not exactly the **lumpenproletariat**. (Frank Gaffney Jr., *Talking a Stereotype to Death*, The Washington Times, 10-09-1995, p. 37.)

underground (publishing system or publication of government-banned literature, or the literature produced by such a system) *n*.: **samizdat** [originally referred to secret publication of government-banned literature in the Soviet Union]. ▪ In 1969 Daniel Ellsberg ... smuggled from his office safe a top-secret government study detailing American involvement in Vietnam. [He] duplicated the so-called Pentagon Papers, a page at a time on a first-generation Xerox machine. Ellsberg leaked the **samizdat** to antiwar leaders and reporters, including the New York Times's Neil Sheehan. (David Greenberg, *The Insider*, The Washington Post, 07-22-2001.)

underhanded (as in unscrupulous) *adj*.: **jackleg**. SEE UNSCRUPULOUS

(2) underhanded (scheming or trickery) *n*.: **jiggery-pokery**. SEE TRICKERY

(3) underhanded (characterized by ... and cunning conduct) *adj*.: **Machiavellian**. SEE DECEITFUL

(4) underhanded (conduct) *n*.: **skullduggery**. SEE DECEITFULNESS

underling (loyal ..., esp. of a political leader) *n*.: **apparatchik**. ▪ To date, [Russian President Vladimir] Putin has carried out the policies of other men, the perfect faceless **apparatchik**. (Bill Powell, *Russia's Mystery Man*, Newsweek International, 01-17-2000, p. 30.)

undermine (as in deprive of strength) *v.t*.: **geld**. SEE WEAKEN

undernourishment (condition of ... of a child) *n*.: **marasmus**. SEE MALNOURISHMENT

underpinning (on which something is built) *n*.: **warp and woof**. SEE FOUNDATION

underprivileged (people, as in lowest class of society) *n*.: **lumpenproletariat**. SEE UNDERCLASS

understand (inability to ... spoken or written words due to brain injury) *n*.: **aphasia**. SEE UNCOMPREHENDING

(2) understand (based on past experience) *v.t*.: **apperceive**. SEE COMPREHEND

(3) understand (difficult to ...) *adj*.: **recondite**. SEE COMPLICATED

understandable *adj*.: **limpid**. ▪ Unlike other recent biographers of Darwin ... Miss Browne does not dwell on the complex social, political and psychological background of his scientific work. ... Instead the reader is given an exceptionally **limpid** and focused description of how Darwin gradually pieced together his theory from his geological, biological and anthropological observations. (Author not given, *Why We Get Sick: The New Science of Darwinian Medicine [book reviews]*, The Economist, 07-29-1995, p. 65.)

(2) understandable *adj*.: **perspicuous**. ▪ One [of the "Principles of Mathematics"] was the "theory of descriptions" which purported to solve a problem that Plato had wrestled with, namely how one can think and speak of non-existent things. The theory showed how various tricky propositions could be translated into something more **perspicuous** and less puzzling; it soon came to be seen as a model of how to philosophise. (Author not given, *The Philosophers That Sophie Skipped*, The Economist, 12-07-1996, p. 79.)

(3) understandable (to the general public) *adj*.: **exoteric**. SEE ACCESSIBLE

(4) understandable (in thought or expression) *adj*.: **pellucid**. SEE CLEAR

understanding (moment of ... , often the point in the plot at which the protagonist recognizes his or her or some other character's true identity or discovers the true nature of his or her own situation) *n*.: **anagnorisis**. SEE RECOGNITION

(2) understanding (sudden ...) *n*.: **epiphany**. SEE REALIZATION

(3) understanding (as in perception or awareness) *n*.: **ken**. SEE PERCEPTION

(4) understanding (of other views and opinions) *adj*.: **latitudinarian**. SEE OPEN-MINDED

understatement (as in "He's not bad.") *n*.: **litotes**. ▪ In another column, I expounded the art of **litotes**, by which we damn with faint praise or praise with faint damns. The usual example is, "She's not a bad soprano," which is subtly different from saying that the lady is a good soprano. (James Kilpatrick, *When Counseling Erring Writers, You Better Have Right Stuff*, Denver Rocky Mountain News, 12-28-1997, p. 63A.)

(2) understatement *n*.: **meiosis**. ▪ Of the two common types of irony, understatement or **meiosis** ("This assignment required more than a minute") generally is better received than overstatement or hyperbole. ("This assignment took forever"). (Stephen Wilbers, *Humor Can Be a Powerful Communications Tool*, Minneapolis Star Tribune, 06-27-1997, p. 2D.)

underworld (relating to gods and spirits of the ...) *adj.*: **chthonic**. ∎ In the phrase "in heaven and on earth and under the earth," Philippians would recognize the areas in which the cosmic and **chthonic** powers were thought to rule. (Edgar Krentz, *Work Out Your Own Salvation*, The Christian Century, 09-11-1996.)

undignified *adj.*: **infra dig**. ∎ Increasingly MBAs must search in the hidden job market (Hello, Uncle Herbert?), a disturbingly **infra dig** undertaking for folks who just paid $70,000 for what they thought was the heights. (Alan Deutschman, *Careers: The Trouble With MBA's*, Fortune, 07-29-1991, p. 67.)

undiplomatic (or tasteless comments) *n.*: **dontopedalogy**. SEE FOOT-IN-MOUTH
 (2) undiplomatic (comment which seems to be offering sympathy but instead makes the person feel worse, either intentionally or unintentionally) *n.*: **Job's comforter**. SEE TACTLESS

undisciplined (and uncontrollable person) *n.*: **bashi-bazouk** [Turkish. Derives from the irregular, undisciplined, mounted mercenary soldiers of the Ottoman army]. ∎ I admit it: I cut through. To get ... to my daughter's school, I drive through residential streets in Homeland. ... This commuter traffic does not please residents of Homeland, to whom apparently, we motorists on our way to school and work are a crowd of **bashi-bazouks** galloping over the hill to plunder their houses and slaughter their cattle. (John McIntyre, *Cruising Through Homeland*, The Baltimore Sun, 01-18-1999, p. 13A.)

unearthly (as in eerie) *adj.*: **eldritch**. SEE EERIE

uneasiness (as in a state of tense and nervous ... often with irritability) *n.* **fantod**. SEE TENSION
 (2) uneasiness *n.*: **inquietude**. SEE ANXIETY
 (3) uneasiness (in a state of ...) *idiom*: **on tenterhooks**. SEE SUSPENSE

uneasy (to make ..., as in disconcert) *v.t.*: **discomfit**. SEE DISCONCERT

uneducated (as in unenlightened) *adj.*: **benighted**. SEE UNENLIGHTENED
 (2) uneducated (class of people regarded as ..., as in unsophisticated) *n.*: **booboisie**. SEE UNSOPHISTICATED
 (3) uneducated (as in ignorant) *adj.*: **nescient** (*n.*: **nescience**). SEE IGNORANT

unemotional (or even-tempered) *adj.*: **phlegmatic**. SEE EVEN-TEMPERED

unending (as in everlasting) *adj.*: **sempiternal**. SEE EVERLASTING

unendingly *adv.*: **in aeternum** [Latin]. SEE FOREVER

unenlightened *adj.*: **benighted**. ∎ We hear an awful lot about teenagers these days. According to the tabloids, they are lazy, feckless and ignorant. According to just about everyone, including the Office of National Statistics, they are having too much sex. According to some experts, we have only ourselves to blame. If teenagers are **benighted**, it's because we have left them in the dark. (Maureen Freely, *They Never Tell Us the Things We Really Want to Know*, Independent, 11-01-1999, p. 8.)
 (2) unenlightened (class of people regarded as ...) *n.*: **booboisie**. SEE UNSOPHISTICATED
 (3) unenlightened (as in ignorant) *adj.*: **nescient** (*n.*: **nescience**). SEE IGNORANT
 (4) unenlightened *adj.*: **philistine**. SEE UNCULTURED

unequalled (person or thing) *n.*: **nonesuch**. SEE PARAGON

unequivocal *adj.*: **univocal**. SEE UNAMBIGUOUS

unethical (person, spec. one who accepts bribes) *n.*: **boodler**. SEE CORRUPT
 (2) unethical (as in unscrupulous) *adj.*: **jackleg**. SEE UNSCRUPULOUS
 (3) unethical (characterized by ... and cunning conduct) *adj.*: **Machiavellian**. SEE DECEITFUL
 (4) unethical (conduct) *n.*: **skullduggery**. SEE DECEITFULNESS

unexpected (event which may be an act of God) *n.*: **force majeure**. SEE UNANTICIPATED

unexplorable (in depth, meaning or significance) *adj.*: **unplumbable**. ∎ Fascinating organization, the U.S. Postal Service. Hard to fathom, though. To take just one question of **unplumbable** depth, how do you suppose the fellows decide which artists will get to do those "love" stamps? (Daniel Seligman, *Keeping Up: Love in the Post Office, and Other Matters*, Fortune, 08-19-1985, p. 219.)

unfair (in matters of discrimination between groups) *adj.*: **invidious**. SEE DISCRIMINATORY

unfaithful *adj.*: **perfidious**. ∎ Tory wives ... are never more themselves than when standing by a faithless husband who has just betrayed them to the flashbulbs of the newshounds and the sniggers of the world. ... [T]hey descend in an unbroken line, brave smiles hiding the heartache. That at least is the tabloid reading: wife's trusting innocence shattered at one leap by **perfidious** male. (Rosalind Miles, *A Necessary Backdrop in the Roadshow of His Life*, Independent, 01-07-1994.)

(2) unfaithful (to a belief, duty or cause) *adj.*: **recreant**. ■ All right, here is the cardinal [John O'Connor] who troubles our comfort with his insistence that a sin is a sin and must be reproved with severity as it is to be absolved with mercy. ... Of course he abrades; he would be **recreant** to duty if he didn't. (Murray Kempton, *The Politics Of Profanity*, Newsday, 10-23-1994, p. A41.)

(3) unfaithful (man married to an ... wife) *n.*: **cuckold** (*v.t.*: to make a ... of). SEE ADULTEROUS

unfashionable *adj.*: **démodé** [French]. SEE OUTMODED

unfathomable (through investigation or scrutiny) *adj.*: **inscrutable**. SEE MYSTERIOUS

unfeeling (as in medication causing inability to feel pain) *n.*: **analgesia**. SEE NUMBNESS

(2) unfeeling (as in inanimate) *adj.*: **insensate**. SEE INANIMATE

(3) unfeeling (as in thick-skinned) *adj.*: **pachydermatous**. SEE THICK-SKINNED

unfit (mentally) *adj.*: **non compos mentis** [Latin]. SEE INSANE

unfitting (as in things which do not mix together) *adj.*: **immiscible**. SEE INCOMPATIBLE

(2) unfitting *adj.*: **malapropos**. SEE INAPPROPRIATE

unflappability *n.*: **ataraxy** (or **ataraxia**). SEE CALMNESS

unflappable *adj.*: **equable**. SEE SERENE

(2) unflappable (as in unemotional or even-tempered) *adj.*: **phlegmatic**. SEE EVEN-TEMPERED

unforgivable (as in unpardonable) *adj.*: **irremissible**. SEE UNPARDONABLE

unforseen (occurrence, leading to an awkward or embarrassing situation) *n.*: **contretemps**. SEE MISHAP

(2) unforseen (event which may be an act of God) *n.*: **force majeure**. SEE UNANTICIPATED

unfortunate *adj.*: **infelicitous**. ■ Ideally, an SI swimsuit shoot should take six weeks or so, with each model brought to the location for about a week. Campbell has found through experience that two

models sharing one photographer can be an **infelicitous** triangle. Often one of the women feels she's playing second fiddle. (Frank Deford, *Lights, Camera, Action! Our Master at Combining Models with Swimsuits and Scenery*, Sports Illustrated, 02-07-1989, p. 51.)

(2) unfortunate (occurrence, leading to an awkward or embarrassing situation) *n.*: **contretemps**. SEE MISHAP

(3) unfortunate *n., adj.*: **hoodoo**. SEE BAD LUCK

(4) unfortunate (perpetually ... person) *n.*: **schlimazel** [Yiddish]. SEE UNLUCKY

unfriendliness (as in chilly relations between people) *n.*: **froideur** [French]. SEE CHILLINESS

unfulfilled (or frustrated in realizing one's goals) *adj.*: **manque** (as in "artist ..."). SEE FRUSTRATED

unfunny (as in person who tries to be funny but is not) *n.*: **witling**. SEE HUMORLESS

ungainly *adj.*: **lumpish**. SEE CLUMSY

ungraceful *adj.*: **lumpish**. SEE CLUMSY

unhappiness (as in inability to experience pleasure or happiness) *n.*: **anhedonia**. ■ The numbers are not good. Clurman says 63 per cent of us wish we could be doing something else with our lives. ... A good friend theorizes that she and I repeatedly mentally return to the republic of **anhedonia** because our families are from Saskatchewan. We don't do fun well. So we went shopping. (Jennifer Wells, *No Fun at Mall These Days*, The Toronto Star, 01-31-2003.)

(2) unhappiness (experience of intense ... , as in suffering) *n.*: **Calvary**. SEE SUFFERING

(3) unhappiness (general feeling of ... as form of depression) *n.*: **dysphoria**. SEE DEPRESSION

(4) unhappiness (as in place, condition or society filled with ...; spec., opposite of utopia) *n.*: **dystopia**. SEE HELL

(5) unhappiness (as in instance or place of ...) *n.*: **Gehenna**. SEE HELL

(6) unhappiness (as in instance or place of ...) *n.*: **Gethsemane**. SEE HELL

(7) unhappiness (as in instance or place of ...) *n.*: **Golgotha**. SEE HELL

(8) unhappiness *n.*: **megrims** (plural of megrim) (also means migraine headache). SEE HEADACHE

(9) unhappiness (to fret or complain, including as a result of ...) *v.i.*: **repine**. SEE COMPLAIN

(10) unhappiness (as in world-weariness or sentimental pessimism over the world's problems) *adj.*: **Weltschmerz** [German]. SEE PESSIMISM

unhappy (as in miserable or wretched, esp. as to poverty) *adj.*: **abject**. See WRETCHED

(2) unhappy (as in dejected) *adj.*: **chapfallen**. See DEJECTED

(3) unhappy (chronically ...) *adj., n.*: **dysthymic**. See DEPRESSED

(4) unhappy (as in unfortunate) *adj.*: **infelicitous**. See UNFORTUNATE

unhealthy (or unwholesome) *adj.*: **insalubrious**. See UNWHOLESOME

(2) unhealthy (atmosphere or influence) *n.*: **miasma**. See NOXIOUS

unhinged (slightly mentally ..., often used humorously) *adj.*: **tetched**. See CRAZY

uniform (as in unvarying) *adj.*: **equable**. See UNVARYING

unimportant *adj.*: **footling** [chiefly British]. ▪ The objection that commentators of the right make about Michael Moore is, generally, that his arguments are facile. ... But the tearing up of the Constitution and Bill of Rights is happening [under President Bush] with surprising speed and reach. ... Moore lists the erosion of liberty with enough precision to make objections to his flippancy seem **footling**. (Nicholas Lezard, *Awkward Questions for the President [Book Review of "Dude, Where's My Country?" by Michael Moore]*, The Guardian [London], 06-12-2004.)

(2) unimportant (or insignificant) *adj.*: **nugatory**. ▪ Immigration is not needed economically; its contribution to the prosperity of native-born Americans is **nugatory**; and along with bilingualism, multiculturalism, and the cultural balkanization promoted by quotas, it helps to undermine the sense of a common American identity. (John O'Sullivan, *Going West?* National Review, 12-11-1995, p. 58.)

(3) unimportant (thing or matter) *n.*: **bagatelle**. See TRIFLING

(4) unimportant (or worthless matter) *n.*: **dross**. See WORTHLESS

(5) unimportant (as in useless) *adj.*: **inutile**. See USELESS

(6) unimportant *adj.*: **nugacious**. See TRIVIAL

(7) unimportant *adj.*: **picayune**. See TRIVIAL

(8) unimportant (as in trivial) *adj.*: **piffling**. See TRIVIAL

(9) unimportant (something which is ..., as in useless) *n.*: **vermiform appendix**. See USELESS

uninformed (as in unenlightened) *adj.*: **benighted**. See UNENLIGHTENED

(2) uninformed (class of people regarded as ... or unenlightened) *n.*: **booboisie**. See UNSOPHISTICATED

(3) uninformed (as in ignorant) *adj.*: **nescient** (*n.*: **nescience**). See IGNORANT

uninhibited (in exhibiting emotion or celebration) *adj.*: **saturnalian**. ▪ The young New Yorker perceived that the Hijra, lower in caste even than the Untouchable dung-cleaners, somehow cut to the heart of the paradox of India. They were clownish and **saturnalian** in spirit: "I thought of them almost like Shakespearian fools, being given permission to comment on society and speak their mind in the way that no one else could." (Author not given, *Caste Aside*, Independent, 07-29-1997, p. 6.)

unintelligent *adj.*: **gormless** [British]. ▪ [I]n the Royal Pioneer Corps in the Fifties, I was frequently involved in preparing paperwork for courts martial. ... They all had three things in common. The prosecuting officer was an intelligent, ambitious captain (he became a brigadier). The defense was conducted by a rather **gormless** National Service second lieutenant. I don't recall anyone being found not guilty. (John Aulton, *Letter: Rough Justice*, Independent, 03-01-1997, p. 19.)

(3) unintelligent (esp. used of a person, as in ... and confused) *adj.*: **addlepated**. See CONFUSED

unintelligible (speech, esp. heard in certain Christian congregations) *n.*: **glossolalia**. ▪ **Glossolalia** happens when people are so filled with the Holy Spirit, with a kind of rapture, that they speak in words and sounds that are not recognizable. It conveys the ecstasy of God's spirit within them. (Martha Sawyer Allen, *Footsteps of Paul / Hunting for the Holy Spirit*, Minneapolis Star Tribune, 09-18-1999, p. 5B.)

uninterested *adj.*: **pococurante**. See APATHETIC

uninteresting *adj.*: **jejune**. ▪ "There's a magnetic field here," explains [actor Peter] O'Toole. "I'm attracted to these larger-than-life roles, and they to me." Offscreen, Peter was living a life that made some of his characters look almost **jejune**. Drinking and carousing, he became a mythic figure at home and abroad. (Andrea Chambers, *Stage: Though He Is Plagued by a Custody Fight Over His Son, Peter O'Toole Is a Triumph in Pygmalion*, People, 06-29-1987, p. 96.)

uninvited *adj.*: **unbidden**. ▪ When my children were very little, they were afraid of the dark. I appointed myself their Guardian Angel, always ready to protect them from the **unbidden** monsters of their dreams. (Peggy Dolgin, *500 Words or Less — Fearful Angel*, Newsday, 06-28-1993, p. 63.)

unique (as in specific to one person or thing; e.g. languages which use symbols or pictures instead of words) *adj.*: **idiographic**. ∎ But what is it that Chinese writers are writing, and Chinese readers are reading? Very little of this huge outpouring of prose is finding its way into translation, and China's **idiographic** script is notoriously difficult to learn. (Steven W. Mosher, *Publishing Without Perishing in China; Writers Juggle New Freedoms, Same Old Limits*, The Washington Times, 07-25-1999, p. B8.)

(2) unique (as in one of a kind) *adj.*: **sui generis** [Latin]. ∎ The Holocaust was a **sui generis** event that has a historically specific explanation. (Daniel Goldhagen, *Hitler's Willing Executioners*, Knopf [1996], p. 419.)

(3) unique (or rare person or thing) *n.*: **rara avis** [Latin]. SEE RARITY

uniqueness (as in that quality which makes one thing different from any other) *n.*: **haeccity**. SEE INDIVIDUALITY

unit (as a ...) *adv.*: **en bloc** [French]. SEE WHOLE

unite *v.t.*: **colligate**. ∎ [The] reconstruction [of the values of Nigerian society] becomes mandatory as a result of the heterogenous ethnic-cultural composition of the Nigerian nation. It also amounts to attempts to discover the binding thread that can **colligate** and guarantee a successful coexistence within this larger political unit. (Onyemaechi Udumukwu, *Ideology and the Dialectics of Action: Achebe and Iyayi [Chinua Achebi and Festus Iyayi]*, Research in African Literatures, 09-01-1996, p. 34.)

(2) unite (as with glue) *v.t.*: **agglutinate**. SEE ADHERE

(3) unite (in a series or chain) *v.t., adj.*: **concatenate** (*n.*: **concatenation**). SEE CONNECT

(4) unite (as in bring together) *v.t.*: **conflate**. SEE COMBINE

(5) unite (as in blend) *v.t., v.i.*: **inosculate**. SEE BLEND

united (by a close relationship) *adj.*: **affined**. SEE CONNECTED

(2) united (closely ...) *adj.*: **coadunate**. SEE JOINED

(3) united (of things that cannot be ...) *adj.*: **immiscible**. SEE INCOMPATIBLE

unity (concerned with establishing ... among churches or religions) *adj.*: **ecumenical**. SEE CHURCHES

universal (in scope or applicability) *adj.*: **ecumenical**. ∎ [N]orthern Ireland's Betty Williams, co-winner of the 1976 Nobel Peace Prize, told graduating seniors at Quinnipiac College in Hamden, Conn., "Men have made enough mess of the world, and it's about time they moved over." At Texas A&M, Democratic Senator Lloyd Bentsen was more **ecumenical** in his exhortation: "You are our best hope for the future," he said. "Don't blow it." (Author not given, *Education: New Prospects, Old Values*, Time, 06-17-1985, p. 68.)

(2) universal (as in widespread) *adj.*: **pandemic**. SEE WIDESPREAD

universe (study of evolution of) *n.*: **cosmogony**. ∎ The mind resists reducing **cosmogony** to cartoons. On the other hand, what could be more in the spirit of Coyote and Road Runner than the Big Bang [theory of evolution]? (Lance Morrow, *Viewpoint: Mars as Divine Cartoon*, Time, 08-19-1996, p. 65.)

unkempt *adj.*: **frowzy**. SEE MESSY

(2) unkempt *adj.*: **blowsy** (or **blowzy**). SEE DISHEVELED

unkind (as in wicked) *adj.*: **flagitious**. SEE WICKED

unknowable (in depth, meaning or significance) *adj.*: **unplumbable**. SEE UNEXPLORABLE

unknown (person) *n.*: **inconnu** [French]. SEE STRANGER

unlikelihood (statement of ..., expressed in the form of an exaggerated comparison with a more obvious impossibility; for example: "the sky will fall before I get married.") *n.*: **adynaton**. ∎ Ten days ago, I was asking Boris Johnson if he was going to be the next editor of the Daily Telegraph and he said: 'I think the possibility is so remote, it's more likely that I would be blinded by a champagne cork, decapitated by a Frisbee or locked in a disused fridge. What [is that] called in ancient poetry, where you list a series of things, the adunata? ... Anyway, it's highly unlikely.' [As the author later discovered, the word that Mr. Johnson had in mind was "**adynaton**" rather than "adunta."] (Lynn Barber, *Charmed, I'm Sure*, The Observer, 10-05-2003.)

unlimited (esp as in ... power) *adj.*: **plenary**. SEE COMPLETE

unlucky (perpetually ... person) *n.*: **schlimazel** [Yiddish. The counterpart to this word is "schlemiel", a habitual bumbler. Thus, the schlemiel will spill his soup and it will land on the schlimazel].

▮ Anderson plays the genial **schlimazel**. ... [H]e spends a great deal of time taking people to the airport, a chore one has to be tricked into. ... When traveling himself, he inevitably gets a plane on which all the overhead compartments are full, even if he's the first passenger to board. And then the flight attendant handing out the peanuts mysteriously passes him by. (John J. O'Connor, *A Comic Who Finds Humor in the Everyday*, The New York Times, 09-14-1998, p. C26.)

unlucky *n., adj.*: **hoodoo**. SEE BAD LUCK

unmanagable (as in uncontrollable and undisciplined person) *n.*: **bashi-bazouk** [Turkish]. SEE UNDISCIPLINED

(2) unmanagable (as in unruly) *adj.*: **indocile**. SEE UNRULY

(3) unmanageable (as in resistant to control or authority) *adj.*: **refractory**. SEE STUBBORN

unmanly *adj.*: **epicene**. SEE EFFEMINATE

(2) unmanly (person) *n.*: **pantywaist**. SEE SISSY

unmarried (state of being ..., or nonrecognition or nonregulation of marriage) *n.* **agamy**. ▮ [T]he low birth-rate [in Europe] is not a function of **agamy** but of low fertility of married couples. (Kingsley Davis, *Kingsley Davis on Reproductive Institutions and the Pressure for Population*, Population and Development Review, 09-01-1997.)

(2) unmarried (woman, whether divorced, widowed or never married) *n.*: **feme sole**. SEE WOMAN

unmatched (person or thing) *n.*: **nonesuch**. SEE PARAGON

unmelodious *adj.*: **scrannel**. SEE CACOPHONOUS

unmitigated (esp. when used with "nonsense") *adj.*: **arrant**. SEE TOTAL

unmoved (as in, in the original position) *adj., adv.*: **in situ** [Latin]. ▮ [O]pening arguments cannot be delivered until tomorrow, precisely because much prosecution evidence is still **in situ** as exhibit material over at the Muhammad trial. It will need to be hauled back and forth, submitted into evidence here but required for jury deliberation in Virginia Beach. (Rosie DiManno, *Doodling Sniper Suspect Keeps Pace With Artists*, The Toronto Star, 11-12-2003.)

unnamed (as in anonymous) *adj.*: **innominate**. SEE ANONYMOUS

unnatural (as in artificial) *adj.*: **factitious**. SEE ARTIFICIAL

unnecessary (words) *n.*: **macrology**. SEE VERBOSITY

(2) unnecessary (word or phrase) *n.*: **pleonasm**. SEE REDUNDANCY

(3) unnecessary (as in superfluous) *adj.*: **supererogatory**. SEE SUPERFLUOUS

unopposed *adj., adv.*: **nem con** [short for *nemene contradicente*]. ▮ Sir: No one who values democracy can regard with equanimity the prospect of [Prime Minister Tony] Blair's re-election virtually **nem con**. ... A long list of Tory policies have richly earned them the epithet of the Stupid Party [in this case for running a candidate who, in the writer's view, had no chance to defeat Blair]. (Tom MacFarlane [writer], *Letters: Tories on the Way Out*, The Independent [London], 06-02-2001.)

unorthodox (holding ... opinions or having an ... perspective) *adj.*: **heterodox** (*n.*: **heterodoxy**). SEE UNCONVENTIONAL

(2) unorthodox *adj.*: **outré** [French]. SEE UNCONVENTIONAL

unpalatable *adj.*: **brackish**. ▮ Coffee Grinders are fanatical? Not if you hate bad coffee. For years, I was convinced I didn't like coffee. Finally it dawned on me: I liked coffee-flavored things. Maybe I'd been drinking bad coffee. I began a near-maniacal program to produce coffee that wasn't sour and **brackish**. In the process, I acquired a coffee grinder, and I haven't been without one since. (Ann Lemons, *It's a Grind*, St. Louis Post-Dispatch, 04-26-1997, p. 22.)

unpardonable *adj.*: **irremissible**. ▮ The Christian code known as the Apostolic Decrees formulated three **irremissible** sins: idolatry, adultery, and [homicide]. (Sarah Currie, *The Killer Within: Christianity and the Invention of Murder in the Roman World*, A Journal of Feminist Cultural Studies, 07-31-1996, p. 153.)

unpolished (or poorly put together, esp. with respect to a writing or speech) *adj.*: **incondite**. SEE CRUDE

unpredictable (or uncertain outcome) *adj.*: **aleatory**. ▮ [Quoting Thomas Dewey] Man finds himself living in an **aleatory** world; his existence involves, to put it baldly, a gamble. The world is a scene of risk; it is uncertain, unstable, uncannily unstable. Its dangers are irregular, inconstant, not to be counted upon as to their times and seasons. (Stephen Holmes, *John Dewey and the High Tide of American Liberalism* [book reviews], The New Republic, 03-11-1996, p. 40.)

unprincipled (person) *n*.: **reprobate**. ∎ When Bill Clinton first ran for president, nobody doubted his devotion to issues or penchant for plunging into the vagaries of public policy. Nor did the public question his political skill. We merely wondered whether he was a **reprobate**. (Now we know.) (Tony Snow, *In Leisurely Pursuit*, The Washington Times, 11-14-1999, p. B3.)

(2) unprincipled (person) *n*.: **blackguard**. SEE SCOUNDREL

(3) unprincipled (government by the most ... people) *n*.: **kakistocracy**. SEE GOVERNMENT

(4) unprincipled (behavior) *n*.: **knavery**. SEE CORRUPTION

(5) unprincipled (characterized by ... and cunning methods) *adj*.: **Machiavellian**. SEE DECEITFUL

(6) unprincipled (conduct) *n*.: **skullduggery**. SEE DECEITFULNESS

unprogressive (person, spec. a person who is opposed to advancements in technology) *n*.: **Luddite**. SEE TRADITIONALIST

unqualified (government by the most ... people) *n*.: **kakistocracy**. SEE GOVERNMENT

(2) unqualified (as in complete or unlimited, esp as in ... power) *adj*.: **plenary**. SEE COMPLETE

unquestionable *adj*.: **irrefragable**. ∎ [T]he California Civil Rights Initiative ... was the model of justice and simplicity: the state cannot discriminate, either for or against individuals or groups, in employment, education, or contracting. But Judge Henderson believes that this prohibition against discrimination is itself discriminatory! By his **irrefragable** logic, the Fourteenth Amendment's command that "No State shall ... deny to any person ... equal protection of the laws" is unconstitutional! (Edward J. Erler, *Popped 209 [California Civil Rights Initiative — Proposition 209]*, National Review, 02-10-1997, p. W1.)

unquestioning (and loyal assistant) *n*.: **myrmidon**. SEE ASSISTANT

unreal (as in artificial) *adj*.: **factitious**. SEE ARTIFICIAL

(2) unreal (as in delusional) *adj*.: **fatuous**. SEE DELUSIONAL

unrealistic *adj*.: **chimerical**. Even if tobacco's opponents could achieve the **chimerical** goal of eliminating smoking by minors, they would not be satisfied. (Jacob Sullum, *[Let's Make a Deal]*, Reason, 10-01-1997, p. 26.)

(2) unrealistic (as in idealistic but likely impractical or ...) *adj*.: **quixotic**. SEE IDEALISTIC

unreasonable (as in fallacious or illogical argument) *n*.: **paralogism** (*adj*.: **paralogical**). SEE FALLACY

unrefined (person) *n*.: **grobian**. SEE BOOR

(2) unrefined (or poorly put together, esp. with respect to a writing or speech) *adj*.: **incondite**. SEE CRUDE

(3) unrefined (as in indifferent or antagonistic to artistic or cultural values) *adj*.: **philistine**. SEE UNCULTURED

(4) unrefined (person) *n*.: **yahoo**. SEE BOOR

unrepentant *adj*.: **impenitent** ∎ Judge William Kelsay on Monday sentenced former Judge William Danser ... to 90 days' house arrest and 400 hours of community service for cutting special, lenient deals for friends and pro athletes. ... Neither has apologized for his behavior. ... And he said, in ridiculing the **impenitent** defendants, "Maybe I was foolish to come to court and think I might hear some kind of public apology." (Dan Reed, *Ex-judge Avoids Jail in Ticket Scheme*, San Jose Mercury News [California], 07-27-2004, p. A1.)

unreserved (and reckless person) *n*.: **rantipole**. SEE WILD

(2) unreserved (in exhibiting emotion or celebration) *adj*.: **saturnalian**. SEE UNINHIBITED

unrest *n*.: **maelstrom**. SEE COMMOTION

(2) unrest *n*.: **pother**. SEE COMMOTION

unrestrained (as in impetuous) *adj*.: **gadarene**. SEE IMPETUOUS

(2) unrestrained (morally or sexually) *adj., n*.: **libertine**. SEE PROMISCUOUS

(3) unrestrained (in exhibiting emotion or celebration) *adj*.: **saturnalian**. SEE UNINHIBITED

unrivaled (person or thing) *n*.: **nonesuch**. SEE PARAGON

unruly *adj*.: **indocile**. ∎ The Guadalupe River rowdies are rearing their ugly heads of dysfunction. For years, this marauding group of **indociles** has swarmed down on the Guadalupe River on Labor Day, leaving a path of destruction along the river similar to that of the Exxon Valdez. How difficult can it be to ban alcohol from these individuals? How much is the ecology of the river worth in dollars? (Steve Ochoa, *Sound Off*, San Antonio Express-News, 09-03-2000, p. 6G.)

(2) unruly (as in uncontrollable and undisciplined, person) *n.*: **bashi-bazouk** [Turkish]. SEE UNDISCIPLINED

(3) unruly (as in resistant to control or authority) *adj.*: **refractory**. SEE STUBBORN

unsafe (as in perilous) *adj.*: **parlous**. SEE PERILOUS

unscrupulous *adj.*: **jackleg**. ▮ Be wary, he said, of offers ... to invest in short-term investments or promissory notes with enticingly high interest rates dangled as a profitable return. Be especially wary, he added, when the pitch includes such phrases as "it really does work" and "fully guaranteed." And **jackleg** investment outfits often have high-sounding words like "global" and "trust" in their titles, he noted. (Larry Wilkerson, *In the Season of Giving, Some Folks Get Taken*, The Atlanta Journal and Constitution, 12-07-2000, p. J1.)

(2) unscrupulous (politician) *n.*: **highbinder**. SEE CORRUPT

(3) unscrupulous (behavior) *n.*: **knavery**. SEE CORRUPTION

(4) unscrupulous (characterized by ... and cunning methods) *adj.*: **Machiavellian**. SEE DECEITFUL

(5) unscrupulous (conduct) *n.*: **skullduggery**. SEE DECEITFULNESS

unseemly (as in undignified) *adj.*: **infra dig**. SEE UNDIGNIFIED

unseen (nearly ...) *adj.*: **liminal**. SEE INVISIBLE

unsophisticated (class of people regarded as ...) *n.*: **booboisie**. ▮ [T]he myth of a heartland filled with **booboisie** — dear to intellectuals and the consultants who claim to control the populace — is etched in stone in this land. The daring thought that citizens are enlightened and knowledgeable, due to profound changes in the economy and in the new multiplicity of information sources, is too daring. (Douglas Davis, *Puritanical Pols Ignore Polls, Other Big "P": Privacy*, The Arizona Republic, 12-27-1998, p. E12.)

(2) unsophisticated *n.*: **artless**. SEE CRUDE

(3) unsophisticated (false showing of ... behavior) *adj.*: **faux-naif** [French]. SEE DISINGENUOUS

unsound (mentally) *adj.*: **non compos mentis** [Latin]. SEE INSANE

(2) unsound (as in fallacious or illogical argument) *n.*: **paralogism** (*adj.*: **paralogical**). SEE FALLACY

unspeakable (as in indescribable) *adj.*: **ineffable**. SEE INDESCRIBABLE

unstable (as in changeable) *adj.*: **labile**. SEE CHANGABLE

unsteady (as in changeable) *adj.*: **labile**. SEE CHANGABLE

unsuccessful *adj.*: **abortive**. ▮ [Saddam Hussein's] first venture into subversive politics came in 1956 when, as a new member of the Baath Party, he participated in an **abortive** coup against King Faisal II. (Jill Smolowe, *Iraq — Sword of the Arabs — Brutal Perhaps, But Only as Crazy as a Desert Fox, Saddam Hussein Mounts a Crude Push for Middle East Supremacy and Worries the World*, Time, 06-11-1990, p. 32.)

unsuitable (as in things which do not mix together) *adj.*: **immiscible**. SEE INCOMPATIBLE

(2) unsuitable *adj.*: **malapropos**. SEE INAPPROPRIATE

unsupported (as in fallacious or illogical argument) *n.*: **paralogism** (*adj.*: **paralogical**). SEE FALLACY

unsure (as to one's opinion on an issue, esp. arising from awareness of an opposing viewpoint) *n.*: **aporia**. SEE DOUBT

(2) unsure (as in indecisive) *adj., v.i., n.*: **shilly-shally**. SEE VACILLATE

untamed *adj.*: **farouche** [French]. ▮ True, in the concerto's finale she discarded the tempo set by her conductor, Emmanuel Krivine, and decided on a more congenial, faster one for herself. But on her new recording of the Chopin concertos with Charles Dutoit — released on EMI last month — she is obedient, less **farouche**. (Dermot Clinch, *Molto Agitato*, New Statesman [1996], 04-02-1999.)

(2) untamed *adj.*: **feral**. ▮ On part of that land they had built a private zoo, to which they charged admission. ... I said it sounded like a good place to start. It would be good to take a look at the animals in confinement before we went thrashing around in the bush after **feral** ones. (Bil Gilbert, *Nasty Little Devil*, Sports Illustrated, 11-21-1994, p. 72.)

unthinking (repetition of ideas which have been drilled into the speaker or which reflect the opinions of the powers-that-be) *v.t., v.i., n.*: **duckspeak**. SEE RECITE

untidy *adj.*: **frowzy**. SEE MESSY

untroubled *adj.*: **dégagé** [French]. SEE EASYGOING

untruthful *adj.*: **mendacious**. SEE DISHONEST

(2) untruthful (abnormal propensity towards being ..., esp. by embellishing) *n.*: **mythomania**. See EMBELLISHMENT

unusable *adj.*: **inutile**. See USELESS

unusual (as in departing from the standard or norm) *adj.*: **heteroclite**. See ABNORMAL

(2) unusual (holding ... opinions or having an ... perspective) *adj.*: **heterodox** (*n.*: **heterodoxy**). See UNCONVENTIONAL

(3) unusual (as in unconventional) *adj.*: **outré** [French]. See UNCONVENTIONAL

(4) unusual (as in supernatural) *adj.*: **preternatural**. See SUPERNATURAL

(5) unusual (as in eccentric) *adj.*: **pixilated**. See ECCENTRIC

(6) unusual (very ... person or thing) *n.*: **rara avis** [Latin]. See RARITY

(7) unusual *adj.*: **recherché** [French]. See RARE

unvarying *adj.*: **equable**. ∎ Its gardens, rich in fuchsias and roses, flourish in the damp, **equable** climate. (Michel Arnaud, *A Great Little Dane [Falsled Kro, Rural Inn Near Millinge, Denmark]*, Town & Country Monthly, 10-01-1995, p. 118.)

(2) unvarying (in rhythm or tempo) *adj.*: **metronomic**. See STEADY

unwavering (as in one who clings to an opinion or belief even after being shown that it is wrong) *n.*: **mumpsimus**. See STUBBORN

(2) unwavering (in holding to a belief or opinion) *adj.*: **pertinacious**. See STUBBORN

unwelcome *adj.*: **persona non grata** [Latin]. ∎ In his newspaper interview, Mr. Wolf revealed that he wanted to immigrate to Israel in 1991, apparently when he was declared **persona non grata** by the Russians, who were under pressure by the German government to send him back. (John O. Koehler, *Israel Welcomes Terrorists' Best Friend*, The Washington Times, 07-28-1996, p. 34.)

(2) unwelcome (as in not asked or invited) *adj.*: **unbidden**. See UNINVITED

unwholesome *adj.*: **insalubrious**. ∎ Next to the garment district — in an even more **insalubrious** part of [Los Angeles], heavily populated with drunks — is Toy-town, home to more than 100 businesses, most of them owned by Chinese immigrants. (Author not given, *How to Remake a City*, The Economist, 05-31-1997.)

(2) unwholesome (or harmful) *adj.*: **noisome**. See HARMFUL

unwillingness *n.*: **nolition**. ∎ We may speculate that after [the many disturbances in European life during the last few decades (the war in Algeria, terrorism, etc.)], these countries may be suffering from a kind of fatigue ... or the weakening of the will, including the will to exist. ... On the other hand, this may only appear to be the case. These countries may only appear to lack the will or volition to continue existing whereas, in reality, there is no such **nolition**. (Victor Perez-Diaz, *The Role of Civil Nations in the Making of Europe*, Social Research, 12-22-2000.)

unyielding (and stern) *adj.*: **flinty**. See STERN

(2) unyielding (as in one who clings to an opinion or belief even after being shown that it is wrong) *n.*: **mumpsimus**. See STUBBORN

(3) unyielding (in holding to a belief or opinion) *adj.*: **pertinacious**. See STUBBORN

upbeat (as in one habitually expecting an upturn in one's fortunes, sometimes without justification) *adj.*: **Micawberish** (*n.*: **Micawber**). See OPTIMISTIC

(2) upbeat (esp. blindly or naively) *adj.*: **Panglossian**. See OPTIMISTIC

(3) upbeat (excessively or unrealistically ... person) *n.*: **Pollyanna**. See OPTIMISTIC

upbraid (as in criticize) *v.t.*: **flay**. See CRITICIZE

(2) upbraid *v.t.*: **objurgate**. See CRITICIZE

upbraiding (being subject to verbal ..., esp. public) *n.*: **obloquy**. See ABUSE

updating (of an organization to meet contemporary conditions, esp. as proposed by Pope John XXIII with respect to the Catholic church after Vatican II) *n.*: **aggiornamento** [Italian]. ∎ [After] World War II, Lavrenty Beria ... counterposed a "reformist" program to the policy of retrenchment. ... He put forward a decidedly liberal program, proposing to loosen some of the strictures of central planning and to allow a measure of "decentralization." In foreign policy, he proposed an **aggiornamento** — no direct confrontation with the West, the neutralization of Germany — in a way a forerunner of the detente of the 1970s. (Laurent Murawiec, *Putin's Precursors*, The National Interest, 06-22-2000.)

upheaval *n.*: **maelstrom**. See COMMOTION

(2) upheaval *n.*: **pother**. See COMMOTION

(3) upheaval (as in chaos) *n.*: **tohubuhu**. See CHAOS

upper class (as in fashionable society) *n.*: **beau monde** [French]. See HIGH SOCIETY

(2) upper class (as in fashionable society) *n.*: **bon ton** [French]. SEE HIGH SOCIETY

(3) upper class (study of or focus on the ..., esp. in artistic works) *n.*: **plutography**. SEE WEALTH

uppercase (letter) *n.*: **majuscule**. SEE CAPITAL LETTER

upright (of or relating to standing ...) *n.*: **orthostatic**. SEE STANDING

uprightness (as in virtue or integrity) *n.*: **probity**. SEE INTEGRITY

uprising *n.*: **émeute** [French]. SEE REBELLION

uproar *n.*: **maelstrom**. SEE COMMOTION

(2) uproar *n.*: **pother**. SEE COMMOTION

uproot *v.t.*: **deracinate**. ■ The "re-potting hypothesis" blames American mobility: Frequent re-potting of plants damages roots, and frequent changes of residence — blame economic dynamism, the automobile, suburbanization, the lure of the Sun Belt — produce a **deracinated** population. (George Will, *Democracy Is Healthy If Bowling Leagues Are*, Newsday, 01-05-1995, p. A36.)

uprooted (of ... people having lost class status) *adj.*: **lumpen**. SEE DISPLACED

upset (extremely) *adj.*: **apoplectic**. SEE ANGRY

(2) upset (as in indignant) *n.*: **dudgeon** (often expressed as "in high dudgeon"). SEE INDIGNANT

(3) upset (as in angry) *adj.*: **wroth**. SEE ANGRY

upstart (social or economic, esp. having attained a position without effort or merit) *n.*: **arriviste**. ■ The real reason [Arianna Huffington] has been so angrily attacked [for writing a biography of Pablo Picasso], she argues, is that the art establishment perceives her as a dilettante and **arriviste**. "It's not a question of having an art degree," she says, "but whether or not you have been certified by the clique." (Dan Chu, *Pages: An Unflattering Portrait of Picasso Leaves Art Critics in a Hanging Frame of Mind*, People, 07-25-1988, p. 50.)

(2) upstart (esp. social or economic) *n.*: **parvenu**. ■ Mocked for his pompous speaking style and his pompadour hair style, his overweening ambition and his underwhelming intellect, he seems to be a stereotype of the social climbing **parvenu** who somehow manages to keep insinuating himself into a better class of society, but can't stop his embarrassed hosts from laughing behind his back. (Mark A. Heller, *David Levy: Not Such a Buffoon*, Jerusalem Post, 12-04-1998, p. 9.)

upward (slope) *n.*: **acclivity** (*adj.*: **acclivitous**). SEE INCLINE

urban (region) *n.*: **conurbation**. SEE METROPOLIS

(2) urban (densely populated ... area) *n.*: **megalopolis**. SEE CROWDED

urbane (and intelligent person) *n.*: **bel esprit**. SEE CULTIVATED

(2) urbane (as in refined or elegant) *adj.*: **raffiné** (or **raffine**) [French]. SEE REFINED

urge *v.t.*: **adjure**. SEE PLEAD

(2) urge (as in irresistible compulsion) *n.*: **cacoëthes**. SEE COMPULSION

(3) urge (mental process marked by ... to do something) *n.*: **conation**. SEE DETERMINATION

urgent *adj.*: **clamant**. ■ [Headline is play on words, as article refers to decline in clam population in Babylon, Long Island] (Joie Tyrrell, *In Babylon/A Clamant Try to Boost Numbers*, Newsday, 11-07-1999, p. G19.)

(2) urgent *adj.*: **necessitous**. ■ A black Fairfax County police officer whose white supervisor asked him to shine the supervisor's shoes was justified in resigning from the police department because working conditions were "just too oppressive," a state examiner has ruled. [The examiner] wrote that Jackson, who said he feared for his safety after complaining that his supervisor's remark was racist, had "compelling and **necessitous**" reasons for resigning. (Patricia Davis, *Treatment Drove Black Officer Out of Fairfax Force, Ruling Says*, The Washington Post, 10-28-1992, p. C6.)

urging (someone to take a course of action) *adj.*: **hortatory**. ■ [Writer Meg Greenfield] loved argument and continued a tradition under which [Washington] Post editorials avoided **hortatory** calls to action in favor of making points by marshaling facts. (J.Y. Smith, *Editorial Editor Meg Greenfield Dies; For More Than 30 Years, Opinion Writer Honed Post's Views*, The Washington Post, 05-14-1999, p. A1.)

urinate *v.i.*: **micturate**. ■ Also, in 1996 Stephen Herek's film [101 Dalmations] can dare show something old Walt [Disney] could never have allowed: a **micturating** puppy. The benefits of such frankness are debatable. Should your kiddies shriek with laughter at the sight of wee-wee, you might want to consider abandoning them. (Kevin Jackson, *101 Dalmatians, One Real Bitch*, Independent on Sunday, 12-15-1996, p. 11.)

urine (uncontrolled or involuntary discharge of) *n.*: **enuresis**. SEE BED-WETTING

usage (new ..., phrase or word) *n.*: **neologism**. SEE WORD

useful *adj.*: **utile**. ∎ Of all of the pickups on the road, the 2003 Chevy Avalanche is certainly one of the most **utile**. That is, not only is there such things as the midgate that allows the vehicle to change from two rows of seats in the cab to a single row and additional cargo space, when it comes to cargo, there are two lockable storage compartments in the cargo box. (Author not given, *Dimensionally Like a Rock*, Automotive Design & Production, 04-01-2003.)

useless *adj.*: **inutile**. ∎ Bush has also considered ending a nascent program under which the United States would pay Russia to render plutonium **inutile** for weapons use by burning it at atomic power plants. (Gregg Easterbrook, *The Real Danger is Nuclear*, The New Republic, 11-05-2001.)

(2) useless *adj.*: **otiose**. ∎ [The] blind infatuation [of the mass media and penal experts] with taxpayer-funded **otiose** rehabilitation programs and crusading against the alleged "root" causes of crime, i.e, poverty, unemployment, malparenting ..., deters their acknowledging the obvious and fuels unconstructive whining against tough but condign punishments. (Bruce Fein, *Treating Criminals With the Contempt They Deserve*, The Washington Times, 01-08-1996, p. 30.)

(3) useless (something which is ...) *n.*: **vermiform appendix** [after the body part which is generally considered unnecessary]. ∎ Many [voters] have strong expectations of Gore. President Clinton regularly introduces Gore as the most active vice president in American history, and few challenge the idea. Contrasted with the image of the vice president as the **vermiform appendix** of American government, Gore has been a close presidential adviser with his own responsibilities in streamlining government, dealing with Russia and environmental themes. (Author not given, *Democrats Should Pick Gore*, The Sunday Oregonian, 02-27-2000, p. G4.)

(4) useless (or futile) *adj.*: **bootless**. SEE FUTILE

(5) useless (mission or project) *n.*: **fool's errand**. SEE HOPELESS

(6) useless (relating to the view that all human striving and aspiration is ..., or people who hold such a view) *adj., n.*: **futilitarian**. SEE FUTILE

(7) useless (as in vain or worthless) *adj.*: **nugatory**. SEE WORTHLESS

(8) useless (efforts which are laborious but ...) *adj.*: **Sisyphean**. SEE FUTILE

usual *adj.*: **wonted**. SEE CUSTOMARY

usurp *v.t.*: **accroach**. ∎ It was an article in the charge of treason, or, as it was then styled, of **accroaching** royal power, against Mortimer, that he intermeddled in the king's household without the assent of this council. (Henry Hallam, *History Of Europe During The Middle Ages: Part XXV*, History of the World, 01-01-1992.)

utmost (to the ...) *adv.*: **à l'outrance** [French]. ∎ Yet the foreign policy events of the White House of Mr. Clinton that will be remembered are more in terms of military power than of durable peacemaking: the twin interventions in Bosnia and Kosovo, the series of small engagements against Iraq, the missile strikes on Sudan and Afghanistan. None of these was the kind of [war] **a l'outrance** threatened and in some cases waged by his predecessors. (Andrew Marshall, *A President in Search of His Legacy*, The Independent, 07-10-2000, p. 5.)

utopia (as in place of extreme luxury and ease where physical comforts and pleasures are always at hand) *n.*: **Cockaigne**. SEE PARADISE

(2) utopia (spec. a place of fabulous wealth or opportunity) *n.*: **El Dorado**. SEE PARADISE

(3) utopia (in which everyone rules equally) *n.*: **pantisocracy**. SEE GOVERNMENT

(4) utopia *n.*: **Xanadu**. SEE PARADISE

utter (as in total or complete, esp. when used with "nonsense") *adj.*: **arrant**. SEE TOTAL

V

vacillate (as in being indecisive) *adj., v.i., n.*: **shilly-shally**. ∎ [In the Truman administration,] there was no **shilly-shallying** over the role of First Lady [as contrasted with the Clinton administration]. (David Ellis, *Up Front: Wild About Harry — The Late President's Daughter and His Biographer Separate Bush and Clinton From the Tried and Truman*, People, 09-21-1992, p. 52.)

vagabond *n.*: **clochard** [French]. SEE VAGRANT

vagina (of or relating to) *adj.*: **yonic**. ∎ [The exhibition by] sculptor Cathy de Monchaux [includes] a collection of sexually explicit photographs of women. ... Natalie Angier writes: "As symbols go, the phallus is a yawn." ... But the vagina, now there's a Rorschach with legs. You can make of it practically anything you want, need or dread. ... This, Cathy de Monchaux knows. Which is not to say that the artist's work is all about the **yonic**. (Michael O'Sullivan, *De Monchaux's Female Form and Function*, The Washington Post, 08-11-2000.)

(2) vagina (insertion of penis into ...) *n.*: **intromission** (*v.t.*: **intromit**). SEE PENETRATION

vagrant *n.*: **clochard** [French]. ■ And then there are the disquieting, all too visible symptoms of what's become known as the economic malaise — metro cars animated by unemployed young men hawking newspapers, passed-out **clochards** sleeping in doorways, train stations crawling with brutish, suspicious cops. (Judith Sullivan, *Letter From Paris/Resisting Change, One Ballot at a Time*, Newsday, 06-01-1997, p. G4.)

vague *adj.*: **Delphic**. SEE AMBIGUOUS

(2) vague (as in cryptic speech or writing, esp. deliberately) *adj.*: **elliptical**. SEE CRYPTIC

(3) vague (or cryptic or ambiguous) *adj.*: **sybilline** (or **sibylline**; often cap.). SEE CRYPTIC

vain (person) *n.*: **fop**. ■ If makeup represents the worst possible cosmetic combo (fake and detectable), muscles represent the best (obvious and real). [W]riter Sam Fussell ... in a 1991 book about his bodybuilding career ... describes the advent of a new male subspecies: the muscle **fop**. (Alan Farnham, *Male Vanity: You're So Vain I Bet You Think This Story's About You*, Fortune, 09-09-1996, p. 66.)

(2) vain (person) *n.*: **popinjay**. ■ The variance between [a vain man's] perception of himself and the public's is simply too wide. Thus one's irritation when senior golfer Jim Colbert cocks his finger and struts like a **popinjay** after sinking a putt vanishes when you see that under his floppy white hat lies the world's lousiest rug. (Tad Friend, *You Look Great [The Truth About Male Vanity]*, Esquire, 03-01-1997, p. 71.)

(3) vain (as in unsuccessful) *adj.*: **abortive**. SEE UNSUCCESSFUL

(4) vain (as in useless or futile) *adj.*: **bootless**. SEE FUTILE

(5) vain (and conceited person) *n.*: **coxcomb**. SEE CONCEITED

(6) vain (mission or project) *n.*: **fool's errand**. SEE HOPELESS

(7) vain (relating to the view that all human striving and aspiration is in ..., or people who hold such a view) *adj., n.*: **futilitarian**. SEE FUTILE

(8) vain (as in without substance or worth) *adj.*: **nugatory**. SEE WORTHLESS

(9) vain (as in useless or ineffective) *adj.*: **otiose**. SEE USELESS

(10) vain (like a peacock) *adj.*: **pavonine**. SEE PEACOCK

(11) vain (efforts which are laborious but in ...) *adj.*: **Sisyphean**. SEE FUTILE

value (under a new standard, esp. one which differs from conventional norms) *v.t.*: **transvaluate**. SEE EVALUATE

valueless (thing or matter) *n.*: **bagatelle**. SEE TRIFLING

(2) valueless (deeming something as ...) *n.*: **floccinaucinihilipilification**. SEE WORTHLESS

(3) valueless (as in useless) *adj.*: **inutile**. SEE USELESS

(4) valueless *adj.*: **nugatory**. SEE WORTHLESS

(5) valueless (something which is ...) *n.*: **vermiform appendix**. SEE USELESS

values (of a person, people or culture) *n.*: **ethos**. SEE CHARACTER

vanish *v.t.*: **evanesce**. SEE DISAPPEAR

vanishing (as in lasting only briefly) *adj.*: **evanescent**. SEE TRANSIENT

vanity (full of ... and boastful) *adj.*: **vainglorious**. SEE BOASTFUL

variable (as in changable) *adj.*: **labile**. SEE CHANGABLE

varied (as in of all varieties) *adj.*: **omnifarious**. ■ Ms. Ono says both the music and art of her late husband [John Lennon] were profoundly influenced by his **omnifarious** interests, including metaphysics and UFOs. (Thomas Rop, *When She's 64 ...: Yoko Ono: Will We Still Need Her? Will We Still Heed Her?* The Dallas Morning News, 01-13-1997, p. 12C.)

(2) varied (composed of a ... of items) *adj.*: **farraginous**. SEE MIXED

(3) varied *adj.*: **multifarious**. SEE VERSATILE

(4) varied (often used of a performer or artist) *adj.*: **protean**. SEE VERSATILE

variety (as in region populated by people from a ... of countries or backgrounds) *n.*: **cosmopolis**. SEE DIVERSITY

(2) variety (as in diversity) *n.*: **heterogeneity** (*adj*: **heterogenous**). SEE DIVERSITY

(3) variety (having great ...) *adj.*: **multifarious**. SEE VERSATILE

(4) variety (as in diversity) *n.*: **variegation** (*v.t.*: **variegate**). SEE DIVERSITY

veer (from a course or intended path) *v.t.*: **yaw**. ▪ At last week's U.S. Open a television camera ... captured — and no doubt added to — the anxiety of the world's best golfers as they teed off on the most traumatic opening hole in tournament golf. [P]anic visited the eyes of third-round leader Ernie Els, who watched his tee shot ... **yaw** left toward terra incognita. (John Garrity, *Golf Plus*, Sports Illustrated, 06-27-1994, p. 44.)

vegetables (mixture of ... and/or fruits) *n.*: **macédoine** [French]. SEE MIXTURE

veil (or disguise) *n., v.t.*: **vizard**. SEE DISGUISE

veiled (as in dark, misty and gloomy) *adj.*: **caliginous**. SEE DARK

venerate (often in a servile manner) *v.i.*: **genuflect**. SEE KNEEL

veneration (of dead people) *n.*: **necrolatry**. SEE WORSHIP

(2) veneration (not necessarily sincere or unforced) *n.*: **obeisance**. SEE HOMAGE

venture (which is fruitless or hopeless) *n.*: **fool's errand**

veracious (as in reflecting reality) *adj.*: **veridical**. SEE REALISTIC

verbal *adj.*: **nuncupative**. ▪ Q: What is a **nuncupative** will? A: It is an oral will made by someone who is in imminent peril of death. (Michael Ferry, *Oral Will Has Strictly Limited Usefulness*, St. Louis Post-Dispatch, 01-09-1997, p. 4.)

(2) verbal *adj., adv.*: **viva voce** [Latin]. ▪ Yesterday I got one from an editor ... who wanted permission to quote something I said to him in a phone conversation last summer. I asked him not to, explaining that **viva voce** quotes are dangerous; they might be picked up and requoted wrong, either by accident or design, and there would be no published version under my byline to prove what I really said. (Florence King, *The Misanthrope's Corner*, National Review, 12-31-1996, p. 60.)

verbose (as in rambling) *adj.*: **discursive**. SEE RAMBLING

(2) verbose (as in characterized by a ready and easy flow of words) *adj.*: **voluble**. SEE TALKATIVE

verbosity *n.*: **circumlocution**. ▪ When Ferdinand Magellan circumnavigated the globe in the early 16th century, he proved the world was round, thus providing a valuable service to humankind. But when we use **circumlocution** in writing — when we use an excessive number of words to arrive at our destination — we do a great disservice to our readers: We waste their time. (Stephen Wilbers, *Get to the Point, So You Don't Waste Readers' Time*, Minneapolis Star Tribune, 09-04-1998, p. 2D.)

(2) verbosity *n.*: **logorrhea**. ▪ Frankly, I would have enjoyed a few moments of silence instead of the **logorrhea**, talkiness and banalities offered by anchors for two hours [during the O.J. Simpson chase]. (Liz Smith, *That O.J. Coverage*, Newsday, 06-21-1994, p. A11.)

(3) verbosity *n.*: **macrology** [This word can be used in a "macro" sense, as in any speech or piece of writing which is unnecessarily long and contains superfluousness, or in a "micro" sense of redundancy of words, for which a synonym would be "pleonasm" (see "redundancy")]. ▪ The term "focusing on core businesses" is often just chief executive **macrology**, something that sounds good in the annual report. (Tim Knapton, *Sharper Focus Has AWA Looking Like A Winner*, Australian Financial Review, 02-07-1998.)

(4) verbosity *n.*: **periphrasis**. ▪ As you will have discerned from my strikingly unadorned, almost Amish- style prose, I'm an earthy, New Age kind of a guy. Honest. Not for me the style-obsessed grandiloquent **periphrasis** of other, more arch columnists. (David Benedict, *Theatre: Reviews*, Independent, 08-30-1997, p. 20.)

(5) verbosity (through use of unnecessary words or phrases) *n.*: **pleonasm**. SEE REDUNDANCY

vernacular (as in speech used by members of the underworld or a particular group) *n.*: **argot**. ▪ Until last week, most stock-market investors were confident that the U.S. economy was not headed for a recession anytime soon. A slowdown, when it came, was expected to be gradual — a soft landing, in the economic **argot**. (Author not given, *The Economy — Headed For a Hard Landing?* Time, 07-10-1989, p. 47.)

(2) vernacular (as in speech used by members of the underworld or a particular group) *n.*: **cant**. ▪ **Cant** is often associated with gangs who wish to keep their activities secret. As Cardozo-Freeman (1984) explains, "Secret languages are a thriving folk tradition constantly used, particularly in segregation and the hole." (Peter M. Wittenberg, *Language and Communication in Prison*, Federal Probation, 12-01-1996, p. 45.)

(3) vernacular *n.*: **vulgate**. ∎ Stretching a cultural point, Eszterhas is a kind of modern-day American Dante, telling us again the true story we have just lived through — the Clinton impeachment — using the coarse and vulgar way people really talk these days (the real "**vulgate**," so to speak.) (Liz Smith, *Red-Hot "Rhapsody,"* Newsday, 07-18-2000, p. A13.)

(4) vernacular (as in vocabulary) *n.*: **lexicon**. SEE VOCABULARY

(5) vernacular (regional ...) *n.*: **patois**. SEE DIALECT

versatile *adj.*: **multifarious**. ∎ Nevertheless, [The Black Album by Prince] is a rich and complex record by one of pop's most talented, **multifarious** performers. (David E. Thigpen, *The Arts & Media/Rock Music*, Time International, 01-09-1995, p. 47.)

(2) versatile (often used of a performer or artist) *adj.*: **protean**. ∎ So now at last one sees the work whole — more than 240 paintings, drawings, prints, sculptures and ceramics, the outpouring of a **protean** talent [Paul Gaughin] who influenced the course of modern painting more than anyone except Cezanne. (Robert Hughes, *Art: Seeing Gauguin Whole — At Last a Masterly Exhibition Corrects Myths and Moonshine About the Pioneering Painter*, Time, 05-09-1988, p. 76.)

vestibule (spec. the passageway in a stadium which connects the outer concourse to the interior of the stadium itself) *n.*: **vomitory**. SEE CORRIDOR

vestige (as in trace or small amount of) *n.*: **tincture**. SEE TRACE

vex *v.t.*: **chivvy**. SEE PESTER

vial *n.*: **ampoule**. ∎ Ayalon police are investigating two incidents at Holon's Wolfson Hospital, in which doctors noticed that the **ampoules** of ephedrine they were about to inject into their patients seemed "strange." (Raine Marcus, *Police Probe Ampoule Case*, Jerusalem Post, 06-25-1995.)

vibrate (rapidly or spasmodically) *v.i.*: **judder**. SEE SHAKE

vice (place of ..., as in corruption) *n.*: **Augean stable**. SEE CORRUPTION

vicinity *n.*: **purlieu**. ∎ Neither does Richler ask an equally obvious question about the missing element in his Arab-Jewish equation: in which cafes in Damascus have Syrian novelists argued for the legitimacy and moral necessity of Israel? In what **purlieu** of Montreal is there a Canadian-Arab writer making the case for the Jews? (Edward Alexander, *This Year in Jerusalem [Book Reviews]*, Commentary, 01-01-1995, p. 82.)

(2) vicinity (physical ...) *n.*: **vicinage**. ∎ We demand a jury trial and overwhelming proof of guilt in criminal cases to prevent government oppression, persecution or harassment. The twin rights of the defendant operate by requiring each element of a crime to be found by a cross-section of his peers in the **vicinage**. (Bruce Fein, *Freestsyle Law When Sentences Are Imposed*, The Washington Times, 12-25-2001.)

victory (obtained only at great cost to the victor) *n.*: **Cadmean victory**. SEE PYRRHIC VICTORY

view (which is odd, stubborn or whimsical) *n.*: **crotchet**. SEE NOTION

(2) view (seeing everything in one ...) *adj.*: **panoptic**. SEE VISIBLE

(3) view (preconceived ... on an issue) *n.*: **parti pris** [French]. SEE PRECONCEPTION

(4) view (as in tenet) *n.*: **shibboleth**. SEE PRINCIPLE

(5) view (of the world) *n.*: **weltanschauung** [German]. SEE WORLDVIEW

viewpoint (centered on male ...) *adj.*: **androcentric**. SEE MALE

(2) viewpoint (which is controversial or person who holds one) *n.*: **polemic**. SEE CONTROVERSY

vigilant (person) *n.*: **Argus**. SEE WATCHFUL

(2) vigilant (as in on the lookout) *v.*: **on the qui vive** *idiom*. SEE LOOKOUT

vigor (lacking ...) *adj.*: **bovine**. SEE SLUGGISH

(2) vigor *n.*: **brio**. SEE ENERGY

(3) vigor *n.*: **élan** [French]. SEE SPIRIT

(4) vigor (lack of ... from having no energy or nourishment) *n.*: **inanition**. SEE EXHAUSTION

(5) vigor (lacking ...) *adj.*: **logy**. SEE SLUGGISH

(6) vigor (as in energy coupled with a will to succeed) *n.*: **spizzerinctum**. SEE ENERGY

vilification (being subject to ..., esp. public) *n.*: **obloquy**. SEE ABUSE

villain (as in scoundrel or unprincipled person) *n.*: **blackguard**. SEE SCOUNDREL

villainous (as in wicked) *adj.*: **flagitious**. SEE WICKED

(2) villainous *adj.*: **malefic**. SEE EVIL

(3) villainous *adj.*: **malevolent**. SEE EVIL

vindication (finding ... through testimony of others) *n.*: **compurgation**. SEE ACQUITTAL

vinegar *n.*: **acetum**. ∎ The other simple pleasure Casanova extols repeatedly is salad. He would add anchovies and hard-boiled eggs to the green leaves and then dress them with olive oil (from Lucca, if possible) and herb-flavoured vinegar (he favoured a brand called **acetum** quattuor latronum — "four thieves vinegar"). (Matthew Sturgis, *Food and Drink: Darling, I Eat Your Hair — Casanova's Voracious Appetite Was Not Confined to the Bedroom*, The Daily Telegraph, 05-30-1998.)

vintage (wine of superior quality) *n.*: **supernaculum**. SEE WINE

violence (initiate ...) *v.i.*: **aggress**. SEE FIGHT

violent (in the manner of an oppressive and despotic organization) *adj.*: **jackbooted**. SEE OPPRESSIVE

(2) violent (spectacle in which shame, degradation or harm is inflicted on a person, often for the enjoyment of onlookers) *n.*: **Roman holiday**. SEE SPECTACLE

VIP (or self-important person or official) *n.*: **panjandrum**. SEE BIGWIG

(2) VIP (or self-important person or official) *n.*: **high muck-a-muck**. SEE BIGWIG

(3) VIP *n.*: **nabob**. SEE BIGWIG

(4) VIP (in a field or organization) *n.*: **wallah**. SEE NOTABLE

Virgin Mary (worship of ...) *n.*: **mariolatry**. ￭ An authoritarian who believed that world Catholicism should be rigidly controlled from the Vatican, [Pope Pius XII] was in the tradition of the despotic popes, whose ranks include Pius IX, Pius X and the present incumbent. All these authoritarians vigorously promoted **mariolatry** in all its forms; the Virgin Mary has always been used as an anti-liberal or anti-communist icon. (Frank McLynn, *Books: A Pontiff Stripped of His Lies*, Independent on Sunday, 09-26-1999, p. 10.)

virginal *adj.*: **vestal**. SEE CHASTE

virile (relating to or concerned with being...) *adj.*: **priapic**. SEE MANLY

virtue (personal ..., as in honor) *n.*: **izzat** [Hindi]. SEE HONOR

(2) virtue (lit. "humanity," often used in the sense of decency) *n.*: **menschlichkeit** [German, Yiddish]. SEE DECENCY

(3) virtue *n.*: **probity**. SEE INTEGRITY

visible (everything ... in one view) *adj.*: **panoptic**. ￭ Now [Jerome, Arizona] is a sun-dappled conglomeration of large wooden homes with sunporches, steep stone stairways, charming restaurants, and **panop-**

tic views of Sycamore Canyon and the Mogollon Rim. (Brad Gooch, *Red Rocks West [Sedona, Arizona]*, Harper's Bazaar, 10-01-1995, p. 159.)

vision (loss of ...) *n.*: **amaurosis**. SEE BLINDNESS

(2) vision (having poor ..., as in nearly blind) *adj.*: **purblind**. SEE BLIND

visionary *n.*: **fantast**. ￭ Stars, Dream Factory a **Fantast** Plot? ... [D]raw near and listen closely as officials in both Nassau and Suffolk hype their vision of Long Island's newest industry. The movie industry is big business, and officials in Nassau and Suffolk Counties want to capture Hollywood's eye with proposals for an outside-the-filmway studio. (Jessica Kowal, *Eye on Long Island: The Industry Scene*, Newsday, 01-22-1995, p. A8.)

(2) visionary *adj.*: **fey**. SEE CLAIRVOYANT

visitor (as in foreigner, from another country or place) *n.*: **outlander**. SEE FOREIGNER

visualize (as in to conceive of or form an image of) *v.t.*: **ideate**. ￭ Because I like reporting better than **ideating** I try as often as I can to let the reporting generate the idea. People frequently ask, "Where do you get your ideas from?" There's no simple answer. (Sydney H. Schanberg, *The Best Ideas Come From Your Bones*, Newsday, 08-20-1993, p. 57.)

vitality (lacking ...) *adj.*: **bovine**. SEE SLUGGISH

(2) vitality *n.*: **brio**. SEE ENERGY

(3) vitality (lack of ... from having no energy or nourishment) *n.*: **inanition**. SEE EXHAUSTION

(4) vitality (lacking ...) *adj.*: **logy**. SEE SLUGGISH

(5) vitality (as in energy coupled with a will to succeed) *n.*: **spizzerinctum**. SEE ENERGY

vocabulary *n.*: **lexicon**. ￭ "The Godfather" did more than hit it big. It became a part of the American **lexicon**, the source of catch-phrases still in use more than a quarter of a century later — for example, "I made him an offer he couldn't refuse." (Harry Levins, *Puzo Hour Equals 35 Minutes*, St. Louis Post-Dispatch, 07-28-1996, p. 4C.)

(2) vocabulary *n.*: **wordhoard**. ￭ Some writers [when giving speeches] conserve their **wordhoard** like squirrels preparing for winter, but [Martin] Amis gives as good value in person as he does on the page. (Allison Pearson, *Martin Amis: Allison Pearson Strips Away the Hype and Finds a Clever, Funny Human*, The Daily Telegraph, 10-04-1997, p. 60.)

(3) vocabulary (specialized ... or speech used by a particular group) *n.*: **argot**. SEE VERNACULAR

(4) vocabulary (used by members of the underworld or a particular group) *n.*: **cant**. SEE VERNACULAR

(5) vocabulary (of or relating to) *adj.*: **lexical**. SEE WORDS

vociferous (and boisterous) *adj.*: **strepitous**. SEE LOUD

vogue (not in ...) *adj.*: **démodé** [French]. SEE OUTMODED

voice (loss of ... due to disease, injury or psychological causes) *n.*: **aphonia**. SEE LARYNGITIS

(2) voice (which is full and rich) *adj.*: **orotund**. SEE SONOROUS

voices (fear of or aversion to ...) *n.*: **phonophobia**. SEE FEAR

volatile (potentially ... place or situation) *n.*: **tinderbox**. SEE EXPLOSIVE

volcanic (eruption) *adj.*: **pelean** (or **Pelean**). ▪ **Pelean** volcanoes are named for Mt. Pelee, which exploded in Martinique in 1902 and killed 36,000 people. Instead of spitting fiery lava, which flows at less than a mile a day, **Pelean** volcanoes explode in deadly avalanches of superheated gas, steam and rocks — called pyroclastic flows, literally "fiery rocks" — that roar down the slopes at speeds up to 100 m.p.h. (Bob Drogin, *Mt. Pinatubo: Scientists' Countdown to Eruption*, The Los Angeles Times, 06-27-1991, p. A4.)

volcano (landslide from ...) *n.*: **lahar**. ▪ Huge **lahar** building on Mt Ruapehu ... A HUGE mudslide that threatens to wipe out bridges, roads and power pylons is building on Mt Ruapehu. (Jon Morgan, *Huge Lahar Building on Mt. Ruapehu*, The Dominion [Wellington, New Zealand], 04-12-2001, p. 3.)

volition (mental process marked by ... to do something) *n.*: **conation**. SEE DETERMINATION

voluptuous (woman, often with stately or regal bearing) *adj.*: **Junoesque** [after ancient Italian goddess Juno, wife of Jupiter]. ▪ After rejections from countless modeling agencies, [Anna Nicole Smith was selected to be in Playboy magazine]. Her **Junoesque** appeal led straight to a three-year contract with Guess? "I always wanted to get back to be smaller than I was," she says. "But I just couldn't. Now I feel very good about it, and I wouldn't change my figure for anything." (Author not given, *Anna Nicole Smith Is Livin' Large and Loving it*, People, 09-20-1993, p. 76.)

(2) voluptuous (as in busty) *adj.*: **bathycolpian**. SEE BUSTY

(3) voluptuous (young woman) *n.*: **houri** [French]. SEE WOMAN

vomit (making an effort to ..., by retching) *v.i.*: **keck**. ▪ [T]hrowing up has been a relief for moviemakers since before *The Exorcist*. ... And while the blueberry pie barf-athon in 1986's *Stand by Me* is memorable, it is the rotund Mr. Creosote ... in Monty Python's 1983 comedy epic *The Meaning of Life* who remains the **kecking** king. [Note that "keck" actually refers to making the effort to vomit as opposed to vomiting itself, but although this example is not technically accurate, the concept is clear.] (Author not given, *Hurls, Hurls, Hurls! [Vomiting in Film Comedies]*, Entertainment Weekly, 07-31-1998.)

vomiting (act of ...) *n.*: **emesis**. ▪ Michigan: Of patients who received marijuana, 71.1 percent reported results ranging from no **emesis** at all to moderate nausea and increased appetite. About 90 percent chose to continue using marijuana as an anti-nausea therapy. (Barbara Yost, *The Straight Dope/ Don't Expect Your Physician to Say "Smoke Two Joints, and Call Me in the Morning,"* The Arizona Republic, 01-07-1999.)

(2) vomiting (an agent which causes ...) *n.*: **emetic**. ▪ Of course, there are people who can and do stick to diets religiously (quite literally, in some cases), but the rest of us will do anything to try to cheat the system. ... Then, if I had a pound for every laxative, **emetic**, diuretic, anorectic or amphetamine swallowed in the cause of weight loss, I shouldn't need to be writing this article. (Rose Shepherd, *Slim Chance*, Independent, 01-11-1997, p. 15.)

voodoo *n.*: **necromancy**. SEE BLACK MAGIC

voracious *adj.*: **edacious**. ▪ [W]e were privy to a bloodbath between two women (the daughters of Muhammad Ali and Joe Frazier) the run-up to which benefitted from a healthy dose of media hype. ... [My friend] thinks it's admirable that Laila Ali and Jacqui Frazier-Lyde went after each other, took loads of punches, earned six figures in prize money apiece and were greeted by an **edacious** and fawning media. (Bonnie Erbe, *Progress For Women Will Not Be Found in the Ring or a Shoe Box*, Ventura County Star, 06-20-2001, p. B4.)

(2) voracious (as in hungry) *adj.*: **esurient**. SEE HUNGRY

vote (direct ... where electorate exercises right of self-determination) *n.*: **plebiscite**. SEE ELECTION

voyage (difficult or painful ...) *n.*: **via dolorosa**. SEE ORDEAL

voyeurism (as in desire to look at erotic scenes or images) *n.*: **scopophilia**. ▪ "In studies of **scopophilia** made in Denmark in the 1970's, twice as many men as women reported experiencing excitement from the visual pleasure of watching heterosexually pornographic materials, 22% of the men as opposed to the 11% of the women." (Author not given, *Shakespeare, Zeffirelli and the Homosexual Gays*, Literature Film Quarterly, 10-01-92.)

vulgar *adj.*: **meretricious**. ▪ "We didn't copyright the X [movie rating]," Valenti says. "So it was pilfered by pornographers. It became so soiled and tainted that the X became synonymous with the most tawdry and **meretricious** kind of work." (Marshall Fine, *My, How the Movies Have Changed: 25 Years after "Midnight Cowboy,"* Gannett News Service, 02-24-1994.)

(2) vulgar (compulsive ... behavior) *n.* **corpropraxia**. SEE OBSCENE

(3) vulgar *adj.*: **fescennine**. SEE OBSCENE

(4) vulgar (and abusive woman) *n.*: **fishwife**. SEE WOMAN

vulnerable (as in a journey or passage, with dangers on both sides) *idiom*: **between Scylla and Charybdis**. SEE PRECARIOUS

W

waffle (as in avoid a straight answer) *v.t.*: **tergiversate**. SEE EVADE

wages *n.*: **emolument**. ▪ [Baseball's umpires] ... backed themselves into a corner [by resigning en masse], and baseball is letting them have exactly what they deserve [by accepting the resignations]. It obviously has taken them completely by surprise, but they have just learned that they are not irreplaceable and that their **emoluments** are not entitlements. (Jonathan Yardley, *Victimization Strikes Out*, The Washington Post, 08-02-1999, p. C2.)

waiflike *adj.* **gamine** [French]. ▪ Everywhere else it may be the year of the woman. But in fashion, this is the year of the waif. Models like Claudia Schiffer, Christy Turlington, Naomi Campbell and Linda Evangelista — the glamour amazons with their hyper hair, teeth and curves — are being edged out by a budding crop of **gamines** — wan, wistful, doe-eyed and as thin as adolescent boys. (Tracy Achor Hayes, *The Waif of the Future*, St. Louis Post-Dispatch, 07-29-1993, p. 1.)

wail (in lament for the dead) *v.i.*: **keen**. ▪ When word spread through the convent, recalls one nun, "Everybody rushed to [the Mother Teresa's] room. They were all around her, wailing and hugging the Mother's body." The sisters' **keening** was heard by the communists, whose party headquarters are next door, and they tipped off journalists that Teresa had died. (Tim McGirk, *Religion: "Our Mother Is Gone!" In a Lavish Ceremony That Mother Teresa Would Have Scorned, Calcutta and the Rest of the World Bid a Touching Farewell to an Angel of Mercy*, Time International, 09-22-1997, p. 54.)

(2) wail *v.i.*: **ululate**. ▪ "They guided and helped Mossad elements in the assassination of my husband," [Fathia Shkaki] told reporters at Damascus Airport soon after her late husband's body arrived on a special Tunisian aircraft. She **ululated** as the coffin, wrapped in a Palestinian flag, was taken off the plane. (Jon Immanuel, *Shkaki to Be Buried Today*, Jerusalem Post, 11-01-1995.)

(3) wail (like a cat in heat) *v.i.*: **caterwaul**. SEE SCREECH

wailing (in Irish folklore, female spirit who predicts death by ...) *n.*: **banshee**. ▪ He came over, did Sean McDonald, in 1976. He came here with his parents and his brother, John, from Dublin, where only once did the **banshee** wail into the night to announce the death of a cop. (Jimmy Breslin, *He Came From Ireland to Hear a Banshee in Bronx*, Newsday, 03-17-1994, p. 4.)

waiting (as in anticipatory) *adj.*: **prevenient**. SEE ANTICIPATORY

walk (around something, esp. as part of a ritual) *v.t.*: **circumambulate**. ▪ On a snowy morning, prayer beads in his hand, the king of Lo is **circumambulating** his walled city, Lo Monthang. (Claudia Glenn Dowling, *Isolated in the Himalayas for Centuries, the Fabled Kingdom of Lo Finally Opens its Gates to the Modern World: The Last Days of Shangri-La*, Life, 02-01-1993, p. 78.)

(2) walk (a slow, leisurely ...) *n.*: **paseo**. SEE STROLL

(3) walk (esp. as in roam or wander) *v.t., v.i.*: **perambulate**. SEE ROAM

(4) walk (esp. as in roam or wander) *v.t., v.i.*: **peregrinate**. SEE ROAM

(5) walk (affectedly to attract attention) *v.i.*: **tittup**. SEE STRUT

walker (as in one who strolls through city streets idly) *n.*: **flâneur** [French]; (wandering *n.*: **flânerie**). SEE IDLER

walking (faster and faster involuntarily) *n.*: **festination**. ■ In **festination**, the person takes short steps, barely clearing the ground. As walking continues, the steps become progressively rapid, almost to the point of a loping gait. **Festination** is one sign of Parkinson's disease. (Dr. Paul Donohue, *Festination: Warning Sign of Parkinson's Disease*, St. Louis Post-Dispatch, 12-15-1995, p. 2G.)

(2) walking (of ... with soles of feet entirely on the ground, as humans and bears do) *adj.*: **plantigrade**. ■ I'm just about to stick my head out [of the tent] to take a peek when Marian blows her nose loudly. The next sound we hear is that of stampeding **plantigrade** feet. Charlie follows the tracks in the dew, and reports that the cubs fled for hundreds of yards out of sight. "Bears don't like to be surprised," Maureen explains. (Paul Rauber, *Running With Bears*, Sierra, 03-01-1999.)

(3) walking (about) *adj.*: **ambulant** (*v.i.*: **ambulate**, *adj.*: **ambulatory**). SEE MOVING

walkout (on basis of alleged sickness, esp. by policemen) *n.*: **blue flu**. SEE SICKOUT

wan (as in pale or corpselike) *adj.*: **cadaverous**. SEE CORPSELIKE

(2) wan (as from absence of sunlight) *adj.*: **etiolated**. SEE PALE

wander (from the subject) *v.i.*: **divagate**. SEE DIGRESS

(2) wander (compulsion to ... or travel) *n.*: **dromomania**. SEE TRAVEL

(3) wander (aimlessly) *v.i.*: **maunder**. SEE ROAM

(4) wander (about, esp. on foot) *v.t., v.i.*: **perambulate**. SEE ROAM

(5) wander (about, esp. on foot) *v.t., v.i.*: **peregrinate**. SEE ROAM

wanderer (as in one who strolls through city streets idly) *n.*: **flâneur** [French]; (wandering *n.*: **flânerie**). SEE IDLER

want (as in need or require) *v.t.*: **desiderate**. ■ Keynes was quite dismissive of governments and government-controlled central banks from this point of view. He argued that "it is natural, after what we have experienced, that prudent people should

desiderate a standard of value which is independent of finance ministers and state banks." (Philip Arestis, *The Independence of Central Banks: A Nonconventional Perspective*, Journal of Economic Issues, 03-01-1995, p. 161.)

(2) want (strong ..., as in craving) *n.*: **appetence**. SEE CRAVING

(3) want (as in strong craving) *n.*: **avidity**. SEE CRAVING

(4) want (slight or faint ...) *n.*: **velleity**. SEE HOPE

wanting *adj.*: **athirst**. SEE EAGER

wanton (as in lewd or lustful) *adj.*: **lickerish**. SEE LUSTFUL

(2) wanton (as in lewd or lustful) *adj.*: **lubricious**. SEE LEWD

war (act or event which causes or provokes ..., literally or figuratively) *n.*: **casus belli** [Latin; occasion of war]. SEE PROVOCATION

(2) war (or relating to or suggesting) *adj.*: **martial**. SEE WARLIKE

ward off *v.t.*: **forfend**. SEE AVERT

warfare (marked by a lack of aggression or progress) *n.*: **sitzkrieg**. ■ One of the draft resolutions Congress considered but did not pass last week called on President Bush to postpone military action against Iraq and give sanctions time to work. ... [However] Saudi Arabia, Egypt and Syria are nervous about keeping so many U.S. troops in the region indefinitely. The entire coalition could come unglued if the **sitzkrieg** continues much longer. (Bruce W. Nelan, *The Gulf: Can Sanctions Still Do the Job? Given Time, the Embargo Would Cripple Iraq, But That Does Not Mean Saddam Would Pull Out of Kuwait*, Time, 01-21-1991, p. 40.)

warlike *adj.*: **martial**. ■ There is a ridiculously **martial** air to all this [turkey hunting]. Guns slung, head nets smashed around our necks, camo boat cushions banging into the backs of our knees, we walk single-file back up along the treeline, away from the forested hill. (Guy Martin, *Operation Turkey*, Sports Afield, 12-01-1995, p. 143.)

(2) warlike *adj.*: **bellicose**. SEE BELLIGERENT

(3) warlike (as in belief that political power is best achieved through use of force) *n.*: **machtpolitik** [German]. SEE POLITICS

warm (as in of or relating to dog days of summer) *adj.*: **canicular**. SEE DOG DAYS

(2) warm (and cozy) *adj.*: **gemütlich** [German]. SEE COZY

warmed over (food or old material) *n., adj.*: **rechauffé** [French]. ▮ John Barton's entertainment by, and about the kings, queens and notables of England has always had a considerable charm in its 40-year history. But this current tour, presented by Duncan C. Weldon and Paul Elliott (men who do much to ensure quality theatre is kept alive in this country) has a kind of **rechauffé** feel to it, as though it has been warmed up from the production scene last year in Stratford. (Richard Edmonds, *Culture: Review: Sinden Is a Storyteller Supreme*, The Birmingham Post [England], 09-10-2003.)

warmth (as in cordiality) *n.*: **empressement** [French]. SEE CORDIALITY

warning *n.*: **alarum**. ▮ Here we go again. No sooner had the Senate, despite the nearly universal predictions to the contrary, passed the campaign finance reform bill than the **alarums** and dirges about its fate recommenced. Tom DeLay would fight it in the House! (Elizabeth Drew, *McCain's Baby; Opposing Campaign Reform Won't Be Easy This Time Around*, The Washington Post, 05-08-2001, p. A23.)

(2) warning (as in suggesting the use of force to settle an issue or argument) *n.*: **argumentum ad baculum** [Latin]. SEE THREAT

(3) warning (as in alarm bell) *n.*: **tocsin**. SEE ALARM

warranted (esp. in reference to a punishment) *adj.*: **condign**. SEE DESERVED

warts (of, relating to or resembling) *adj.*: **verrucous**. ▮ Sometimes the condition [crusted scabies] causes scaly, **verrucous**-like plaques that cover large areas anywhere on the body. (Chet Scerra, *Scabies: Tips for Diagnosing and Cautions About Treatment*, Modern Medicine, 03-01-1996, p. 27.)

wary (as in watchful, person) *n.*: **Argus**. SEE WATCHFUL

wash (as in cleanse) *v.t., v.i.*: **depurate**. SEE CLEANSE

washing (of the body) *n.*: **ablution**. SEE CLEANSING

(2) washing (like detergent) *v.t.*: **detersive**. SEE CLEANSING

wasps (of, relating to or resembling) *adj.*: **vespine**. ▮ August is a truly dreadful month for those who write daily for a living. I have too often written laudatorily of the only citizen whose season it is, the common wasp, to be comfortable doing it yet again. What could I do to ease the unbearable burden of writing through the full month of August, and also spare the world yet another column of winsomely **vespine** musings? (Kevin Myers, *An Irishman's Diary*, The Irish Times, 09-06-2000, p. 17.)

waste time (as in hesitate to act due to indecision) *v.i.*: **dither**. SEE PROCRASTINATE

(2) waste time (as in procrastinate or hesitate to act) *v.i.*: **shilly-shally**. SEE PROCRASTINATE

waste (parts, esp. from an animal) *n.*: **offal**. ▮ This is a preliminary list of European products that the United States is threatening with 100% tariffs in a dispute with the European Union over hormone-treated beef. ... Edible **offal** of bovine animals, swine, sheep, goats, horses, etc., fresh, chilled or frozen. (Author not given, *Preliminary 100% Tariff Targets*, USA Today, 03-23-1999, p. 2B.) SEE TRASH

(2) waste (away) *n., v.i.*: **atrophy**. SEE WITHER

(3) waste (as in printed material which is trivial) *n.*: **bumf** [British]. SEE JUNK

(4) waste (matter) *n.*: **dross**. SEE TRASH

(5) waste (from the body) *n.*: **egesta**. SEE EXCREMENT

(6) waste (or squander something away) *v.t.*: **fribble**. SEE SQUANDER

wasting (of the body resulting from chronic disease) *n.*: **cachexia**. ▮ Despite its legacy of tragic birth defects in newborn infants 30 years ago, thalidomide is showing encouraging signs of being a potent weapon against a variety of ailments, including ... the AIDS-associated wasting disorder, **cachexia**. (Robert Cooke, *Thalidomide: A Nasty Drug Changes its Spots: Once Linked With Tragic Birth Defects, it Now May Help Fight Other Serious Health Problems*, Newsday, 06-14-1994, p. B27.)

(2) wasting (progressive ... away) *adj.*: **tabescent**. ▮ While others were indulging in pre-emptive fumbles behind the Ruddington Methodist Chapel, ... I was inhabiting a sensual desert, refreshed only by the occasional trip up Mickleborough Hill where, beneath the roots of a **tabescent** sycamore tree, I had buried ... a copy of Parade magazine with an interesting artistic feature on Cyd Charisse's legs. (Michael Bywater, *Believe it or Not: I Was a Teenage Toy Boy Too*, Independent on Sunday, 08-10-1997, p. 34.)

(3) wasting (of child's body due to malnourishment) *n.*: **marasmus**. SEE MALNOURISHMENT

watch (over students taking an examination) *v.i.*: **invigilate**. SEE PROCTOR

(2) watch (as in on the ...) *n.*: **on the qui vive** *idiom*. SEE LOOKOUT

watchdog *n*.: **Cerebus** [derives from the 3-headed dog assigned to guard the entrance to Hades in Greek mythology]. ▪ "American Playhouse," the public television dramatic series ... provides PBS with 12 programs a year, which makes it the nation's most prolific independent film outlet, not to mention a sort of cultural watchdog in the hellish world of commercial film making — **Cerberus** at the gates of Hollywood. (Bruce Weber, *Television: Big Movies on Little Budgets*, The New York Times, 05-17-1992.)

watches (science of making ... or clocks) *n*.: **horology**. SEE TIME

watchful (person) *n*.: **Argus** [derives from the giant in Greek mythology who had 100 eyes and was made guardian of the land of Io. It is sometimes used as an adjective as in "Argus-eyed."] ▪ [Actor Gregg Thomas] is often described as a physical actor. Off stage, he strides with a bounding gait. He watches people with **Argus** eyes, keenly observant, vigilant. (Elizabeth Cronin, *Leading Man — This Seattle Actor Has Paid His Dues to Get Starring, Challenging Roles*, The Seattle Times, 09-16-1990, p. 12.)

water (pure ...) *n*.: **aqua pura**. ▪ As the global population expands, putting pressure on the limited supply of clean freshwater, more armed conflict over who gets access to **aqua pura** seems inevitable. (Michael S. Serrill, *Water: Wells Running Dry, Rampant Waste and Pollution of Our Most Vital Resource Create a Crisis That Could Lead to Future Armed Conflicts*, Time International, 11-01-1997, p. 16.)

(2) water (of, like or relating to) *adj*.: **aqueous**. ▪ The largest reservoir in northeastern Colorado at 6.5 miles long, it offers retirees — and unretirees, for that matter — a number of **aqueous** activities, such as boating and swimming. (James B. Mcadow, *End of the Rainbow for Many, the Golden Years Lie in Fort Collins*, Denver Rocky Mountain News, 06-07-1999, p. 3D.)

(3) water (containing ..., esp. crystallized) *adj*.: **hydrous**. ▪ [T]hermodynamic data suggest that ice in contact with anhydrous minerals like those in Apollo and Luna soil samples will eventually react, forming **hydrous** minerals in which the constituents of water are chemically bound into the mineral crystals. (A.B. Binder, *No Ice on the Moon?* Science, 07-23-1999.)

(4) water (of, relating to or living in moving ...) *adj*.: **lotic**. ▪ The ecology of rivers and streams (**lotic** systems) is influenced by flow, and erosion and deposition of sediments. (Masaki Hayashi, *Effects of Ground Water Exchange on the Hydrology and Ecology of Surface Water*, Ground Water, 05-01-2002, p. 309.)

(5) water (of or relating to underground ...) *n*.: **phreatic**. ▪ The first scare occurred on Tuesday, July 18th, when what the volcanologists term a "**phreatic** eruption" — a steam explosion caused by the interaction between molten rock material or very hot solid rock and groundwater — set off fears that a major eruption was imminent. (George John, *In the Shadow of a Volcano*, Caribbean Today, 07-31-1996.)

(6) water (of or relating to hot ...) *adj*.: **hydrothermal**. SEE HOT WATER

(7) water (fear or dread of ...) *n*.: **hydrophobia**. SEE FEAR

(8) water (consisting of ... and land) *adj*.: **terraqueous**. SEE LAND

water bank (of or relating to a ...) *adj*.: **riparian**. ▪ Most states also enforced **riparian** law, which provides that all who have property abutting a waterway or body of water have the right to normal use of the water, but may not reduce its use and enjoyment by others and downstream users. (Roger Meiners, *Get the Government Out of Environmental Control*, USA Today Magazine, 05-01-1996.)

watercolor *n*.: **aquarelle** [French]. ▪ It was Dali's **aquarelle** Sun King, which he painted half a century ago as an expression of his admiration for Louis XIV, that inspired the fragrance of the same name. (Greer Fay Cashman, *The Sweet Smell of Summer*, Jerusalem Post, 08-28-1997, p. 18.)

watered down *adj*.: **anodyne**. SEE BLAND

waterfall (very large or high ...) *n*.: **cataract**. ▪ The roar of the plunging cascade and the fine spray that rises 500 m above Victoria Falls are aptly captured in the great **cataract's** local tribal name, mosioatunya — the smoke that thunders. (Peter Hawthorne, *Environment: Too Many Trips to the Falls — The Battle Is on to Save Africa's Great Scenic Wonder From the Ravages of a Tourist Boom*, Time International, 07-01-1996, p. 40.)

waters (of or occurring in ... such as lakes or ponds) *adj*.: **limnetic**. ▪ In all, [The Nature Conservatory] has about a thousand preserves scattered throughout the country. The smallest, half an acre, is on Scotia Lake Island, near Schenectady, N.Y., and has a good but tiny bit of undisturbed **limnetic** woodland. (Bil Gilbert, *The Nature Conservancy Game*, Sports Illustrated, 10-20-1986, p. 86.)

watery (eyes or runny nose) *adj.*: **rheumy**. ▪ He always had a flamboyantly coloured silk handkerchief tucked into one sleeve so he could make regular dabs at his **rheumy** eyes. (Val McDermid, *A Place of Execution*, St. Martin's Press [2000], p. 221.)

wavelength (on the same ...) *adj.*: **simpatico**. See COMPATIBLE

waver (as in indecisive) *adj.*, *v.i.*, *n.*: **shilly-shally**. See VACILLATE

waves (resembling ... in appearance or motion) *adj.*: **undulant**. ▪ Undoubtedly, doctors and dentists who have aquariums in their offices have instinctively sensed what recent research has shown: Concentrating on the **undulant** motion of fish and seaweed is relaxing and anxiety-reducing for patients. (Catherine Houck, *The 9 Best Ways to De-stress*, Good Housekeeping, 09-01-1995, p. 82.)

way of speaking *n.*: **façon de parler** [French]. ▪ For Mr. Searle, the idea of the brain as computer remains ... just a metaphor that can mistakenly be taken literally. [For example]: "The gastrointestinal tract is a highly intelligent organ. ... [Although this is not of course literally true], the idea that the gut shows intelligent behavior is only a harmless **façon de parler** that is not likely to lead anyone into serious error. (Anthony Gottlieb, *The Lesson of the Drunk and the Streetlight*, The New York Times, 10-11-1992.)

weak (from loss or lack of body strength) *adj.*: **asthenic** (*n.*: **asthenia**). ▪ While it could be argued that [the Nissan Pathfinder is] understressed and thus promises longevity as well as requiring only 87-octane fuel, it looks rather **asthenic** compared to even such a six-cylinder as Jeep (195 hp/225 foot-pounds) or Blazer (190 hp/250 foot-pounds) offers. (Alan Vonderhaar, *When I Received the Nissan Pathfinder*, Gannett News Service, 02-02-1999.)

(2) weak (as in ineffective) *adj.*: **feckless**. See INEFFECTIVE

(3) weak (as in powerless) *adj.*: **impuissant**. See POWERLESS

(4) weak (as in spineless or indecisive, or such a person) *adj.*, *n.*: **namby-pamby**. See SPINELESS

(5) weak (and sickly person, esp. one morbidly concerned with his own health) *n.*, *adj.*: **valetudinarian**. See SICKLY

weak-minded (state of being ..., as in indecisiveness) *n.*: **abulia**. See INDECISIVENESS

weaken (as in deprive of strength) *v.t.*: **geld**. ▪ [T]he great American middle class wants [federal programs left intact, including] its Social Security, its Medicare, its long-term care, its tax credits, [etc.] ... Any unreconstructed conservative who threatens to take them away ... does so at his peril. That is why conservatives have changed the subject. They have given up on the campaign to **geld** the federal government. (Jack Beatty, *How the GOP Went Wrong*, The Washington Post, 09-11-1994, p. 5.)

(2) weaken (in value, amount or degree) *v.t.*: **attenuate**. See LESSEN

(3) weaken (as in deprive of strength) *v.t.*: **enervate**. See DEBILITATE

weakened *adj.*: **etiolated** [The primary sense of this word is the weakened effect on a plant caused by depriving it of exposure to sunlight (which also accounts for this word meaning "pale"). However, it is also more generally used to refer to anything weakened or enfeebled.] ▪ [In 1996, the] gender war turned its attention from female victimhood to male identity crises, and by most accounts the male sperm-count dropped to little more than **etiolated** dribble. Estrogen fall-out was blamed, but it may well have been exacerbated by The Girlie Show. (Oliver Bennett, *1996: The Year That Went Pop*, The Independent [London], 12-29-1996.)

weakening (esp. of moral principles or civil order) *n.*: **labefaction**. ▪ As a black minister in Washington, I know that it is iconoclastic for me to blame the general **labefaction** [of] the present D.C. administration [i.e. Marion Barry] for making a black and white coalition impossible. Washington is divided by race [and] it has become politically advantageous to maintain that division. (Kirk D. Monroe [letter writer], *United, We Can Stand*, The Washington Post, 05-21-1989.)

wealth (source of great ...) *n.*: **Golconda** [based on city in India where diamond mines were once located]. ▪ Harvard provides the Democrats with brainy talent. Hollywood delivers the glamour. But for money, there's no place like New York City's Upper East Side, especially ZIP code 10021, a **Golconda** of campaign cash for Democratic candidates. (W. John Moore, *Lobbying & Law: Mr. Gore's and Mr. Bradley's Neighborhood*, National Journal, 08-14-1999.)

(2) wealth (devotion to the pursuit of ...) *n.*: **mammonism**. ▪ The survey revealed that **mammonism**, or the principle of the almighty dollar, is strong in Korea with 46 percent of those polled agreeing that money can buy happiness. (Author not given, *44 Pct of Koreans Feel More Dejected After IMF*, The Korea Times, 02-21-1999.)

(3) wealth *n.*: **pelf**. ∎ The carrot isn't always monetary. In advertising, show business, and journalism, people work themselves to the nub for glitz and glory more than for **pelf**. (Ford S. Worthy, *Executive Life: You're Probably Working Too Hard*, Fortune, 04-27-1987, p. 133.)

(4) wealth (study of or focus on ..., esp. in artistic works) *n.*: **plutography**. ∎ **Plutography** is to money what pornography is to sex, explains the 56-year-old pioneer of the New Journalism [author Tom Wolfe], emphasizing that "today it is impossible to be too ostentatious." (R.Z. Sheppard, *Books: The Haves and the Have-Mores — The Bonfire of the Vanities by Tom Wolfe*, Time, 11-09-1987, p. 101.)

(5) wealth (of or relating to the gaining of ...) *adj.*: **chrematistic**. SEE MONETARY

wealthy (and/or prominent person) *n.*: **nabob**. SEE BIGWIG

(2) wealthy (government by the ...) *n.*: **plutocracy**. SEE GOVERNMENT

(3) wealthy (government by the ..., i.e. in proportion to wealth or property ownership) *n.*: **timocracy**. SEE GOVERNMENT

wear (away by friction or scraping) *v.t.*: **abrade**. SEE CHAFE

weariness (from lack of energy or nourishment) *n.*: **inanition**. SEE EXHAUSTION

wearing apparel *n.*: **raiment**. SEE CLOTHING

wearying (as in laborious) *adj.*: **operose**. SEE LABORIOUS

wedding (of or relating to a ...) *adj.*: **hymeneal**. ∎ The tasteful [Donald] Trump-[Marla] Maples nuptial ceremony took place last night. The low-key **hymeneal** rites were attended by all of Donald's and Marla's closest friends, with the exception of Mike Tyson, the pugilist, who was detained. (Sydney H. Schanberg, *Donald and Marla — This Is a Love Story?* Newsday, 12-21-1993, p. 85.)

week *n.*: **hebdomad** (**weekly** *adj.*: **hebdomadal**.) ∎ Sadly, the vast majority of humanity, and even a large majority of Jews, do not have the time or the strength to remind themselves that they have a soul, a spirit. Shabbat could be a **hebdomadal** reminder of that, for if we observe it properly, we do not merely feed our bellies with those Shabbat delicacies, but we also feed that soul, that spirit. (Moshe Kohn, *How Judaism Trains Us to Achieve Spirituality*, Jerusalem Post, 10-13-1995.)

weep (in lament for the dead) *v.i.*: **keen**. SEE WAIL

weeping (of or relating to) *adj.*: **lachrymal**. SEE TEARS

weepy *adj.*: **lachrymose**. SEE TEARFUL

weight (or state of being overweight) *n.*: **avoirdupois**. ∎ In the ensuing two years Gibson blew up to more than 400 pounds as he ate an overabundance of fast foods, and he caught the eye of recruiters from Indiana, Purdue and Wisconsin, who detected the soul of an athlete beneath all the **avoirdupois**. (Tim Crothers, *Gibson Pruned His Weight to 371 and Blossomed into a Bulldozer of a Blocker Who Probably Will Be the First Lineman Taken in the NFL Draft*, Sports Illustrated, 02-22-1999, p. 56.)

(2) weight (loss resulting from chronic disease) *n.*: **cachexia**. SEE WASTING

weird (as in eerie) *adj.*: **eldritch**. SEE EERIE

(2) weird (as in eccentric) *adj.*: **pixilated**. SEE ECCENTRIC

welfare (general ... of the community) *n.*: **weal**. SEE WELL-BEING

(2) welfare (general ..., as in well-being) *n.*: **commonweal**. SEE WELL-BEING

well-being (general ...) *n.*: **commonweal**. ∎ It is a four-alarm national embarrassment that here, on the doormat of the 21st century, we're still debating whether and how to teach evolution to schoolchildren. No other developed country finds Darwin a menace to the **commonweal**. None of the major organized religions opposes the theory of evolution. (Curt Suplee, *Facts of Faith*, The Washington Post, 04-11-1999.)

(2) well-being *n.*: **weal** [This word can be used in the sense of prosperity and happiness (often as in *weal or woe* or *weal and woe*), or in the sense of the general well-being of the community. The first example demonstrates the former sense and the second example demonstrates the latter.] ∎ Because we recognize that the **weal and woe** of others is as real as our own, we also recognize that factors bearing on their well-being should enter into our own practical accounting, albeit not with the same weighting that one's own good (and that of one's loved ones) carries. (Loren Lomasky, *Generosity: Virtue in Civil Society* [book reviews], Reason, 05-01-1998, p. 58.) ∎ Clinton campaigned for the presidency stressing themes that lie at the center of the new politics [columnist E.J.] Dionne favors — the intelligent use of government to improve the public **weal**. (Ronald Radosh, *They Only Look Dead: Why Progressives Will Dominate the Next Political Era* [book reviews], Commentary, 06-01-1996, p. 62.)

(3) well-being *n.*: **eudemonia** (or **eudaemonia**). SEE HAPPINESS

well-endowed (woman) *adj.*: **bathycolpian**. SEE BUSTY

well-groomed *adj.*: **soigné** [French]. SEE ELEGANT

welt (on the skin) *n.*: **weal**. ∎ Along with room attendants who burst in at inopportune moments, bed bugs are just one more essential component of these establishments and waking to find itchy red **weals** all over our bottoms is part and parcel of the experience. (Jeremy Atiyah, *Stop Trashing Bedbugs! They Give Hotels a Certain Cache*, Independent on Sunday, 09-14-1997, p. 2.)

werewolf *n.*: **loup-garou** [French]. ∎ Looking for a model for a mythical, wolf-like **loup-garou**, he used a photograph of Tiffany, his black-and-white spaniel-terrier mix, who had died five years earlier. To convey the spirit of the ghostly **loup-garou**, Rodrigue painted Tiffany blue. (Michael J. Neill, *Arts: Howling Success: How Much Is That Doggy? If It's Blue, $150,000*, People, 12-07-1992, p. 131.)

(2) werewolf *n.*: **lycanthrope**. ∎ By the time Michael Landon began attacking classmates in I Was a Teenage Werewolf (1957), the cinematic **lycanthrope** seemed on the verge of extinction. (Author not given, *Werewolves? Everywhere! "Wolf" Joins a Pack of Monster Movies Gone Astray*, Entertainment Weekly, 01-13-1995, p. 68.)

(3) werewolf (ability to assume characteristics of or delusion where one thinks he is a ...) *n.*: **lycanthropy**. ∎ Once upon a time, in the gloriously disreputable days of I Was a Teenage Werewolf (1957) and Werewolves on Wheels (1971) and I Married a Werewolf (aka Werewolf in a Girl's Dormitory, 1961) and Face of the Screaming Werewolf (1959), **lycanthropy** was strictly midnight fodder for the unwashed hordes of gore fans. (Kevin Jackson, *Film / The Werewolf as Social-Climber*, Independent, 08-25-1994.)

wet (from rain) *adj.*: **pluvial** or **pluvious**. SEE RAIN

whim *n.*: **boutade** [French]. ∎ [On his new album,] Tori Kudo and his associates make skewed, strange and gentle music. At times the 41 tracks (many are

mere **boutades**) recall [The Velvet Underground]. [H]alfway through, you're won over by his whimsy. (Luke Bainbridge, *The Next 15*, The Observer, 11-16-2003.)

(2) whim (as in notion which is odd, stubborn or whimsical) *n.*: **crotchet**. SEE NOTION

whimper *v.i.*: **mewl**. ∎ Women are never so macho as when beauty is at stake. Show us a large cockroach and we're **mewling** sissies, but bring out a pan of hot wax that's going right onto our flesh, and suddenly we're as tough and impassive as Arnold Schwarzenegger in The Terminator. (Lynn Snowden, *Beauty Hurts*, Harper's Bazaar, 07-01-1995, p. 124.)

(2) whimper (or whine) *v.i.*: **pule**. ∎ The [President Clinton] impeachment fight had been over for weeks, the outcome clear as day: Senate Democrats would block conviction; House managers would whine and **pule** about how they were prevented from presenting a proper prosecution. (Michelle Cottle, *On The Hill: Played Out*, The New Republic, 03-01-1999.)

whine *v.i.*: **girn** [Scottish]. Alan Cochrane, *Comment: We'll Have Only Ourselves to Blame But, Says Alan Cochrane, That Won't Stop His Fellow Scots "Girning" About the English*, The Daily Telegraph, 05-06-1999.

(2) whine (weakly) *v.i.*: **mewl**. SEE WHIMPER

(3) whine *v.i.*: **pule**. SEE WHIMPER

whining (as in complaining) *adj.*: **querulous**. SEE PEEVISH

whip (generally used figuratively) *v.t.*: **larrup**. ∎ Andy Benes, who was **larruped**, 10-7, by the Giants in St. Louis, will take a 7-7 mark against them into Friday's series opener. (Author not given, *St. Louis Cardinals Team Notes*, The Sports Network, 06-07-1996.)

(2) whip *v.t.*: **flagellate**. SEE CRITICIZE

whirling (or spiraling motion, often an ocean current) *n.*: **gyre**. SEE SPIRALING

whispered (said in ... tones, not to be overheard) *adv.*, *adj.*: **sotto voce**. ∎ On the subject of swings, the world's top golfers can be as gossipy as seventh-graders at a slumber party. So it is said, **sotto voce**, that Leonard doesn't hit the ball that well. (Ivan Maisel, *Golf Plus/U.S. Open Preview*, Sports Illustrated, 06-15-1998, p. G38.)

whispering (or rustling sound) *n.*: **susurrous**. ∎ [When my book "Town Without Rivers" opens, Reka has] just gotten out of prison for killing her lover and has gone back to the town where she grew up. ... She was accustomed to ... porch sitters falling silent as she appeared, their **susurrous** gossip rising faintly like wind through pine needles as she passed into what they considered out of earshot. (Author not given, *Interview: Michael Parker Reads a Portion From His New Novel "Towns Without Rivers,"* All Things Considered (NPR), 07-19-2001.)

whistle *v.i.*: **siffle**. ∎ Since I noticed [that "lower classes" don't whistle a tune anymore], I've checked the places where it used to happen, and it isn't happening. You can hang about under a ladder with a chap up it painting a window [or] peer under a car where another chap is lying on his back on one of those trolley things ... and you won't catch a note, not so much as a canary's bleep, not a single **siffle**. (Hannah Pool, *Jackdaw*, The Guardian [London], 07-25-1997, p. 18.)

whistling (as in to make a soft rustling sound) *v.i.*: **sough**. See RUSTLING

white (of an egg) *n.*: **albumen**. ∎ Medieval Europeans raiding gull colonies marveled at how some eggs contained nutritious yolk and **albumen** while others, apparently identical, held a baby bird, and still others were rotten. (Laura Erickson, *No Yoke: Egg Came Before Chicken*, Minneapolis Star Tribune, 04-17-1995, p. 15.)

(2) white (becoming ...) *adj.*: **albescent**. See WHITISH

(3) white (as in pale, as from absence of sunlight) *adj.*: **etiolated**. See PALE

(4) white (covered with ... or gray hair as if with age) *adj.*: **hoary**. See GRAY

white-hot *adj.*: **candescent**. ∎ Straight ahead and side-to-side, the **candescent** glow [of the street light] offers a measure of safety. (Jim Bencivenga, *Fencing Heaven*, The Christian Science Monitor, 08-02-2001, p. 11.)

whitish *adj.*: **albescent**. ∎ As for [Michael] Jackson, do you think he has a clue just how strange he looks? With his cruelly abridged nose, **albescent** skin, glassy eyes and startled expression — and an outfit that included those metallic shin guards — he looked like he had stepped out of a Peter Max cartoon. (David Hiltbrand, *Picks & Pans: Tube*, People, 07-03-1995, p. 15.)

(2) whitish (or turning white) *adj.*: **canascent**. ∎ The calendar said it was spring, but the weather said different. Boston was being battered by a nasty

nor'easter, and 10 miles north in Lynnfield, the snow swirled out of a **canescent** sky. (Robert Parker, *Robert Parker Brings a Soft Touch to the Hard-Boiled School of Mystery Writing*, People, 05-07-1984, p. 58.)

whole (as a ...) *adv.*: **en bloc** [French]. ∎ But 15 years later, as many had predicted, a majority of French Quebecers voted to split, their will thwarted by non-francophones, including Jews who voted **en bloc** to keep Quebec Canadian. (Ron Csillag, *Jews Consider Bidding Quebec "Adieu,"* Jerusalem Post, 11-30-1995.)

whore *n.*: **bawd**. See PROSTITUTE

(2) whore *n.*: **demimondaine**. See PROSTITUTE

(3) whore *n.*: **trollop**. See PROSTITUTE

whorehouse *n.*: **bagnio**. See BROTHEL

whores (as a group) *n.*: **demimonde**. See PROSTITUTES

who's who (as in a series of short biographical sketches) *n.*: **prosopography**. See BIOGRAPHY

wicked *adj.*: **facinorous**. ∎ U.S. District Judge Garland Burrell said allowing the federal government to return to [confessed Unabomber Theodore Kaczynski] his rambling personal journal, in which he put down his innermost thoughts while living in a rural Montana cabin, would effectively "preserve for posterity some evidence of the evils wrought by his **facinorous** Unabomber actions." (Michael Taylor, *Unabomber Journal Stays Secret*, The San Francisco Chronicle, 03-10-2004, p. A17.)

(2) wicked *adj.*: **flagitious**. ∎ [In Dr. Seuss's "How the Grinch Stole Christmas"] the Grinch [is] a nefarious, **flagitious**, sly, nasty, troublesome, bad-tempered, intolerant and foul-smelling character who, for reasons never fully explained, lives in a cave above the town. (Robin Greer, *Carrey Christmas*, News Letter, [Belfast, Ireland], 12-01-2000, p. 24.)

(3) wicked *adj.*: **iniquitous**. ∎ To begin with, Sir Jeremy suggests ... that mine is a simpleminded version of history [i.e. the Cold War], in which a perfectly virtuous West triumphs over a thoroughly **iniquitous** East. (Author not given, *CNN's "Cold War,"* Commentary, 07-01-1999.)

(4) wicked (person) *n.*: **caitiff**. See DESPICABLE

(5) wicked *adj.*: **malefic**. See EVIL

(6) wicked *adj.*: **malevolent**. See EVIL

widen (in scope) *v.t.*: **aggrandize**. See EXPAND

wideness (as in diversity) *n.*: **variegation** (*v.t.*: **variegate**) See DIVERSITY

widespread *adj.*: **pandemic**. ▮ But with renewed emphasis on a more family-oriented service and the embarrassing legacy of scandals such as Tailhook, the Pentagon appears to be cracking down on adultery and related offenses. But it is not just allegations of **pandemic** sexual misconduct, such as those at the Aberdeen Proving Ground, attracting prosecutors' attention. (Tamara Jones, *One Lieutenant's Adultery,* Newsday, 05-13-1997, p. B4.)

(2) widespread *adj.*: **regnant**. ▮ Consequently the debate seems to have been polarized and stalled by the crosscurrents of white backlash, black rage, and liberal despair. African American scholar Derrick Bell conveys some of the **regnant** frustration: "We have made progress in everything, yet nothing has changed." (Dinesh D'Souza, *Myth of the Racist Cabbie [Rational Discrimination Versus Racism]*, National Review, 10-09-1995, p. 36.)

(3) widespread (in scope or applicability) *adj.*: **ecumenical**. SEE UNIVERSAL

widowhood *n.*: **viduity**. ▮ It's a matter for conjecture how far [Queen Elizabeth II] can discharge her role as mother to the nation, aged 74, while "Mummy" [i.e. the Queen Mother] — or, as her daughter used to style her, "the Problem" — continues to grind out her interminable **viduity**. (Glen Newey, *You're No Better Than a Stuffed Badger, Ma'am; Long Live the Republic — Even Her Daughter Calls Her "The Problem,"* The New Statesman, 08-07-2000.)

wife (having one ... at a time) *n.*: **monogyny**. ▮ In retrospect, I have to say that **monogyny** isn't all that bad. Sure it lacks variety and the thrill of getting caught and telling lies, but it has its subtle compensations. Deception and betrayal aren't everything, after all. (Dick Dougherty, *A Lot of Married Men Like Me Are Consumed by Regret,* Gannett News Service, 08-11-1999.)

(2) wife (of, relating to or having characteristics of) *adj.*: **uxorial**. ▮ Only a few months ago, I had been a struggling reporter, a nice girl from Nebraska who could outsit them on a barstool. Now, I was going to become a society wife, the **uxorial** ornament of a legend, tyrant, and infamous playboy. It was unbelievable, even to me. (Lynn Woodward, *Be Careful What You Wish For ... It Might Come True,* [Woman's Disastrous Marriage to Older Millionaire], Cosmopolitan, 05-01-1994, p. 274.)

(3) wife (esp. when referring to a traditional ... who may, for example, stay at home and raise the children) *n.*: **helpmeet**. SEE HELPMATE

(4) wife (having more than one ... at a time) *n.*: **polygyny**. SEE POLYGAMY

(5) wife (murder of ... by her husband) *adj.*: **uxoricide**. SEE KILLING

(6) wife (overly devoted to or submissive to one's ...) *adj.*: **uxorious**. SEE DOTING

wig (esp. worn by men in 17th and 18th centuries) *n.*: **peruke**. ▮ The old moguls hated movies where people wore powdered wigs and wrote with feathers. So this film's first images should set the old bosses spinning in their mausoleums. A gentleman's **peruke** is affixed, a lady's bosom powdered. (Richard Corliss, *Cinema: Lust Is a Thing With Feathers,* Time, 01-16-1989, p. 64.)

wild (and reckless person) *n.*: **rantipole**. ▮ [The play] could be an extension of Bragg's fascination with self-destructive stars, inspired by his first-rate biography of Richard Burton. [The lead in the play] goes for a Burton, giving us not just the **rantipole** boozer and the insecure star but also implying an educated distaste for the whole business of masquerade. (Michael Billington, *Tragic Hero Who Goes for a Burton,* The Guardian [London], 07-10-1992.)

(2) wild (as in uncontrollable and undisciplined person) *n.*: **bashi-bazouk** [Turkish]. SEE UNDISCIPLINED

(3) wild (as in frenzied) *adj.*: **corybantic**. SEE FRENZIED

(4) wild *adj.*: **farouche** [French]. SEE UNTAMED

(5) wild (as in untamed) *adj.*: **ferine**. SEE UNTAMED

(6) wild (sexually) *adj., n.*: **libertine**. SEE PROMISCUOUS

will (mental process marked by having ... to do something) *n.*: **conation**. SEE DETERMINATION

willpower (pertaining to a lack of ...) *adj.*: **abulia** (or **aboulia**). ▮ Thus when he comes to praise those who recognize poverty as owing as much to circumstances as to **abulia**, his discussion immediately widens to include spiritual truth and the reception of The Word. (Henry Golemba, *"Distant Dinners" in Crane's "Maggie": Representing "The Other Half,"* Essays in Literature, 09-22-1994, p. 235.)

wimp (as in coward) *n.*: **poltroon**. SEE COWARD

(2) wimp *n.*: **pantywaist**. SEE SISSY

wince *v.i.*: **blench**. SEE FLINCH

wind (of, relating to, caused by or carried by) *adj.*: **eolian** (or **aeolian**). ▮ Two formerly peaceful streets in this town of 453 bear the savage mark of a tornado. Houses splintered. Trees stripped. Cars in storefronts. Baby carriages impaled on posts. It's all the work of set decorators bent on reproducing an **eolian** nightmare. (Marco R. Della Cava, *"Apollo 13" Star Plunges Right Into "Twister,"* USA Today, 07-07-1995.)

(2) wind (in and out) *v.i.*: **sinuate**. ▪ They crossed the far stone wall that marked the top of the Seep Square and, cutting left again, began to **sinuate** their way up through the thorn apples. (Robert F. Jones, *Are You Lonesome Tonight?* Sports Afield, 10-01-1994, p. 90.)

(3) wind (sudden violent gust of ...) *n.*: **williwaw**. SEE GUST

(4) wind (gentle ...) *n.*: **zephyr**. SEE BREEZE

wind currents (pertaining to rising ...) *adj.*: **anabatic**. ▪ Winds, such as katabatic (downslope) and **anabatic** (upslope) breezes, are generated thermo-topographically. Land and sea breezes result from thermal circulation systems, which are generated by contrasting thermal responses of land and water. (Paul John Beggs, *An Integrated Environmental Asthma Model*, Archives of Environmental Health, 03-13-1995, p. 87.)

winding (full of ... turns, as in tortuous) *adj.*: **anfractuous** (*n.*: **anfractuosity**). SEE TORTUOUS

window (bay ...) *n.*: **oriel**. ▪ The newer Renaissance section [of the Rothenburg town hall], built in 1572, replaced the portion destroyed in the fire. It's decorated with intricate friezes, an **oriel** extending the building's full height, and a large stone portico opening onto the square. (Author not given, *Germany: 3, The Romantic Road*, Frommer's Europe, 01-01-1998.)

(2) window (throw something or someone out of a ...) *v.t.*: **defenestrate** (*n.*: **defenestration**). SEE THROW

window blind (with adjustable horizontal slats) *n.*: **jalousie**. ▪ Begun lived in a cell measuring about 10 ft. long and 5 ft. wide. It contained two narrow wooden cots and an open toilet. At one end was a small window that let in narrow strips of light. "It had metal **jalousies** to keep out the sun and block the view to the prison yard," Begun said. (James O. Jackson, *Soviet Union — A Day in the Depths of the Gulag*, Time, 03-09-1987, p. 52.)

windows (having ...) *adj.*: **fenestrated** (*n.*: **fenestration**). ▪ Tucked beneath the soaring roof, the Siffs' bedroom is spacious and full of light, but its sloping walls make it cozy as a bear's den. A quartet

of windows frames a panorama of pines and snowy hills. "It's as if you're in a great tree house!" he declares. Luckily, the other end, though less **fenestrated**, is elegant too. (Kenneth Miller, *The Way We Live: Dream House '95*, Life, 05-01-1996, p. 102.) ▪ "If this is some cheap bill-collecting dodge, I'll throw the sonofabitch out the window." "There is no **fenestration** in this building," said Wismer Strook, "only glass walls." (Tom Wolfe, *A Man in Full*, Farrar Straus & Giroux [1998], p. 550.)

(2) windows (one that cuts and fits glass for) *n.*: **glazier**. ▪ Remember that glass pane on the terrace door that cracked last year when your toddler whacked it with his toy hammer? The one you've been meaning to take to the **glazier**? The one you doctored with masking tape? ... Well, replacing a windowpane is not the work of wizards. (Tal Katz, *Installing New Glass in a Window Need Not be a Complete Pane*, Jerusalem Post, 02-23-1995.)

wine (study of) *n.*: **enology**. ▪ Richard Vine (that's right, Vine — and his Ph.D. is in agricultural economics) is one of America's foremost authorities on agriculture's most glamorous product. He has written an authoritative textbook on wine, and teaches **enology** at Purdue University in West Lafayette, IN. (Joseph Scott, *A Good [Cheap] Bottle of Wine*, Good Housekeeping, 08-01-1996, p. 39.)

(2) wine (lover or connoisseur) *n.*: **oenophile**. ▪ This favorite of discriminating Manhattanites is well stocked, so you'll be too. As for gifts, that fussy **oenophile** on your list won't balk at an imperial bottle of 1978 Chateau Lafite-Rothschild ($1,450). (Joshua B. Adams, *T&C's New York Holidays*, Town & Country Monthly, 12-01-1994, p. 125.)

(3) wine (of superior quality) *n.*: **supernaculum**. ▪ There are now more than 400 commercial vineyards in England and Wales, plus countless hobby enterprises, and most of them got through a difficult spring with buds intact. One might even produce the **supernaculum** of 1991. (David Hoppit, *Property; Bibulous Bargain-Hunting*, Financial Times [London], 10-12-1991.)

(4) wine (body, color and taste of) *n.*: **vinosity**. ▪ Most important, add a little grape-juice concentrate. I know it is expensive, I agree it is a cheat, but nothing else gives the wine that round **vinosity** that distinguishes wine from Appellation Controlee Rat's Urine. (Michael Buerk, *Wine: Why Chateau Buerk Is the Stuff For Me*, The Daily Telegraph, 06-06-1998, p. 10.)

(5) wine (of, relating to or made with) *n.*: **vinous**. ▪ Terrible, terrible news! Rich yuppies are lapping up all the great wines. No price is too steep for a Wall Streeter when his palate craves **vinous** delight. A restaurant wine bill can run to thousands of dollars when these conspicuous consumers are in the bibulous vein. (Russell Baker, *When a Bottle Costs $1,975, What's Inside Isn't the Point*, Minneapolis Star Tribune, 02-23-1998, p. 7A.)

(6) wine (person who drinks a lot of ...) *n*.: **winebibber**. ∎ Robert Finigan's Private Guide to Wines newsletter, likes Opus One very much. He suspects, however, that people are buying it to show it off — not drink it — because drinking a $50 wine would be a conspicuous presumption. If you're more **winebibber** than collector, Finigan advises waiting until Opus One is discounted, as he thinks it inevitably will be before too long. (Author not given, *Magnum Opus [Opus One, Wine at $50 Dollars a Bottle]*, Money, 05-01-1984.)

wings (without ...) *adj*.: **apterous**. ∎ To test this notion, they compared genes in flies and crustaceans, which are insects' closest relatives with gills. ... They discovered that two previously discovered insect wing genes, called pdm and **apterous**, were hidden in the DNA of the flightless crustaceans. (Author not given, *The Origin of Insect Flight*, ScienceNOW, 02-12-1997.)

(2) wings (insects which have shed their ... or of or about such insects) *n*., *adj*.: **dealate**. ∎ Dealates: Only 1 percent of the tens of thousands of [termites] survive the process of leaving the colony, landing and looking for a mate. Those that survive will pair off, beat their wings from their bodies, and begin a highly structured mating ritual. (Author not given, *Fortress of Destruction*, The Times-Picayune, 06-29-1998, p. A6.)

wink *v.i.*: **nictitate**. See BLINK

winking (spasmodic ... of one or both eyes) *n*.: **blepharospasm**. See BLINKING

winner (with the critics but not the public) *n*.: **succes d'estime** [French]. See SUCCESS

winter (of, related to or occurring in) *adj*.: **brumal**. ∎ Two days before I was due to arrive at Branford [for a January duck hunt], a **brumal** wind howled down from Canada, the shore areas of the Sound froze over, and we spent our day feeding stale bread to ragged bands of disconsolate mallards standing on the ice in the cove near his house. (Nelson Bryant, *Outdoors; Ducks Elusive in Trip to Sound*, The New York Times, 01-14-1985, p. C11.)

(2) winter (of, relating to or occurring in) *adj*.: **hibernal**. ∎ [W]e made up an entire 156-person field out of threesomes. In each, the golfers have a common bond. Can you guess what it is? ... David Frost, Andy North, Don January. ... [Answer:] **Hibernal**. (Michael Bamberger, *Golf Plus/U.S. Open Preview*, Sports Illustrated, 06-14-1999, p. G12.)

(3) winter (of, relating to or occurring in) *adj*.: **hiemal**. ∎ Attending a Jimmy Buffett concert is like participating in a spring break frat bash for baby boomers. Defying balmy but decidedly **hiemal** temperatures, graying fans of the beach-bum balladeer arrived for his sold-out Madison Square Garden gig in full Parrot Head regalia. (Letta Tayler, *A Baby-Boomer Break/Buffett Gives High-Flying Parrot Heads What They Want*, Newsday, 02-21-1998, p. B7.)

wipe out (as in abolish) *v.t.*: **extirpate**. See ABOLISH

(2) wipe out (as in put an end to) *n*.: **quietus** (esp. as in "put the quietus to"). See TERMINATE

wisdom (universal ...) *n*.: **pansophy** (*adj*: **pansophic**). See KNOWLEDGE

(2) wisdom (pretense of ... on a subject which is actually superficial) *n*.: **sciolism**. See SUPERFICIAL

wise *adj*.: **sapient**. ∎ [S]urprisingly, there has hitherto been no systematic account of [C.S. Lewis's conversion to Christianity]. David C. Downing seeks to fill this [gap.] Coming from a **sapient** Lewis scholar, Downing's narrative is precise and rounded; it also contains many intelligent insights into Lewis's work. ... [I]t is still of considerable worth to Lewis critics and of use to all scholars of modern Christian thought. (Adam Schwartz, *The Most Reluctant Convert: C. S. Lewis's Journey to Faith [Book Review]*, Christianity and Literature, 09-22-2002.)

wise guy (and conceited person) *n*.: **jackanapes**. See CONCEITED

(2) wise guy (as in buffoon, who is sometimes boastful) *n*.: **Scaramouch**. See BUFFOON

(3) wise guy (as in smart aleck) *n*.: **wisenheimer**. See SMART ALECK

wish (as in strong craving) *n*.: **avidity**. See CRAVING

(2) wish (for) *v.t.*: **desiderate**. See WANT

(3) wish (slight or faint ...) *n*.: **velleity**. See HOPE

(4) wish (which is delusive or not realistically obtainable) *n*.: **will-o'-the-wisp**. See PIPE DREAM

wishy-washy (state of being ...) *n*.: **abulia**. See INDECISIVENESS

(2) wishy-washy *adj*., *n*.: **namby-pamby**. See SPINELESS

wistful *adj.*: **tristful**. See SAD

witch (as in ugly old woman) *n.*: **beldam**. See HAG
 (2) witch (as in shrew) *n.*: **harridan**. See SHREW
 (3) witch (as in shrew) *n.*: **termagant**. See SHREW
 (4) witch (as in shrew) *n.*: **virago**. See SHREW
 (5) witch (as in shrew) *n.*: **vixen**. See SHREW
 (6) witch (as in shrew) *n.*: **Xanthippe**. See SHREW

witchcraft *n.*: **necromancy**. See BLACK MAGIC

witches (assembly of ...) *n.*: **coven**. ∎ Now the witches are forced to confront a question their predecessors faced since the dawn of Christianity: Should they retreat back into secret **covens**, or try their luck in the open market of America's scattered spirituality? (Hanna Rosin, *An Army Controversy: Should the Witches Be Welcome? Flap Over Wiccans Tests Military's Religious Tolerance*, The Washington Post, 06-08-1999, p. A1.)

witchlike (old woman) *n.*: **crone**. See HAG

withdraw (from office or membership) *v.i.*: **demit** (as in demit office). See RESIGN
 (2) withdraw (as in recoil) *v.i.*: **resile**. See RECOIL

withdrawal (desperate ..., as in retreat) *n.*: **Dunkirk**. See RETREAT
 (2) withdrawal (social ...) *n.*: **purdah**. See SECLUSION

wither (away) *n., v.i.*: **atrophy**. ∎ The greatest threat to our nation's future is not economic, but moral. "Middle class morality" is under siege — all around we see the results of the **atrophying** of personal responsibility and the breakdown of the family. Leaders like Clinton can only make things worse. (Katherine Kersten, *Why Feminist Crusaders Are Silent on Clinton*, Minneapolis Star Tribune, 02-11-1998, p. 19A.)
 (2) wither *v.i.*: **wizen**. See SHRIVEL

withered (old woman) *n.*: **crone**. See HAG

without (from ...) *adv.*: **ab extra** [Latin]. See EXTERNALLY
 (2) without (anything better) *adv.*: **faute de mieux** [French]. See LACKING

witty *adj.*: **waggish**. ∎ In one of his **waggish** moments, Henry Kissinger once commented, "There cannot be a crisis next week. My schedule is already full." (James Walsh, *Confronting Chaos*, Time, 10-18-1993, p. 20.)
 (2) witty (line) *n.*: **bon mot** [French]. See QUIP
 (3) witty (line) *n.*: **epigram**. See QUIP

(4) witty (person who tries to be ... but is not) *n.*: **witling**. See HUMORLESS

wizardry *n.*: **necromancy**. See MAGIC

wobbly (as in quivering) *adj.*: **tremulous**. See QUIVERING

wolf (characteristic of or resembling) *adj.*: **lupine**. ∎ Few actors are as entertaining as [Jack] Nicholson when he cuts loose (i.e. Batman and The Shining), but such an approach would nosedive [the movie] Wolf. He plays it perfectly, even under Rick Baker's mounds of makeup. He's always had a **lupine** edge to his work, anyway. (Mark Burger, *Nicholson Steals the Show in "Wolf,"* Jewish Journal, 06-23-1994.)
 (2) wolf (ability to assume characteristics of or delusion where one thinks he is a ...) *n.*: **lycanthropy**. See WEREWOLF

woman (with scholarly or literary interests) *n.*: **bluestocking**. ∎ At 59, slender with close-cut hair, [Pauline] Maier appears more outdoorsy than professorial, a self-described "Radcliffe **bluestocking**" who quickly belies that description with an infectious laugh. (Michael Kenney, *A New Look at Exceptional Document / Author: Plain Folk Shaped Declaration of Independence*, Minneapolis Star Tribune, 07-09-1997, p. 8E.)
 (2) woman (single ..., whether divorced, widowed or never married) *n.*: **feme sole**. ∎ Flavia Luisinha De Souza (In her 50s — "Don't print my age. I want to keep them guessing!"). "I made up my mind at 16 that I didn't want to get married," said this petite woman who runs a music studio. ... She didn't quite say "So there!" but it was there alright! So you can guess that she has no qualms about being [a] **feme sole**. (Author not given, *Single, and it Feels So Right!* New Straits Times, 04-15-2002, p. 15.)
 (3) woman (who is coarse and abusive) *n.*: **fishwife**. ∎ The market puts on a good show: huge quantities of fish and a rich running dialogue between the dealers, which tends to go along the lines of: "*@$$! my brother you @/*X!" "Oh yeah? Well, I'll *&%XO you, you ?!OX*$!" It doesn't take long to work out where the phrase "swears like a **fishwife**" comes from. (Tim Dowling, *Features: Welcome to Fishville*, The Sunday Telegraph, 04-19-1998, p. 3.)
 (4) woman (regarded as ugly, repulsive or terrifying) *n.*: **gorgon**. ∎ [T]he most memorable film noir villainesses were formidable and unmistakably alluring. You search in vain for some of the same charisma in the new killer women of the movies. Instead they are unfeeling, unimaginative, unattractive **gor-**

gons, and [you wonder what] disturbing cultural malaise that is producing this virulent wave of revulsion toward women who want to take charge. (Stephen Farber, *Movies; That's No Lady — That's Our Nightmare*, The Los Angeles Times, 03-18-2001, p. 22.)

(5) woman (French working-class young ...) *n.*: **grisette** [French]. ▮ Some [women who eventually became prostitutes] were upper-class girls, down on their luck, who chose to service rich men rather than serve as governesses to their children. ... Many more were born into a life of poverty, earning paltry livings as **grisettes**, or seamstresses, before emerging like glittering butterflies from the grey muslin dresses that gave them their name. (Lucy Moore, *How to Get Ahead in Bed*, The Sunday Times [London], 02-24-2002.)

(6) woman (beautiful and alluring ...) *n.*: **houri** [French]. ▮ Ask any shortstop what it's like trying to turn a double play when the base runner barreling toward him is a suicide bomber who believes that his martyrdom will ensure a place for his family in paradise and unlimited access to hundreds of virginal **houris**. It's intense, baby! (Mark Leyner, *The Most Dangerous Games*, Esquire, 10-01-1997, p. 64 .)

(7) woman (who is scheming and evil) *n.*: **jezebel** (sometimes cap.). ▮ "Bobby, I think I can handle a good-looking girl reporter." Seen it happen again and again. They come in, bat their pretty eyes at you, cross their legs a few times, and before you know, it's "I shouldn't really be telling you this" and "Would you like to see our confidential files?" Beware of **Jezebels** with tape recorders." (Christopher Buckley, *Thank You for Smoking*, Random House [1994], p. 71.)

(8) woman (frenzied or raging ...) *n.*: **maenad**. ▮ While men everywhere winced [when Lorena Bobbitt cut off her husband's penis], a lot of women were gleefully triumphant. ... Now the submissive pinup was suddenly revealed as a screaming **maenad**. "Lorena Bobbitt's a total heroine," says punk singer Maffeo. (Tad Friend, *Yes, [Feminist Women Who Like Sex]*, Esquire, 02-01-1994, p. 48.)

(9) woman (who hates men) *n.*: **misandrist**. ▮ Feminist ideologues have recently falsely accused men of being wildly abusive to woman on Super Bowl Sunday. They have held men responsible for 150,000 anorexia deaths each year. ... My book [Who Stole Feminsim] documents a widespread ongoing campaign of mean-spirited, socially divisive, **misandrist** Ms/information. (Christina Hoff Sommers, *Letters From the People*, St. Louis Post-Dispatch, 08-29-1994, p. 12B.)

(10) woman (who is slender and graceful) *n.*: **sylph**. ▮ The first song [I dance to at the strip club] is "Brick House," an homage to women who butter their potatoes. This is not a song for a **sylph**. A diminutive dancer I know played it one night and was humiliated when a man in the audience shouted out, "But you're flat!" (Lily Burana, *Strip City*, Talk Miramax Books [2001], p. 174.)

(11) woman (who is strong and courageous) *n.*: **virago**. ▮ Feminists don't like strong women because too many **viragos** would put them out of business. To prosper they need a steady supply of women who exemplify the other V-word, "victim." (Florence King, *The Misanthrope's Corner, [Female Misogyny]*, National Review, 03-10-1997, p. 64.)

(12) woman (of or like an old ...) *adj.*: **anile**. SEE OLD WOMAN

(13) woman (who is old and ugly) *n.*: **beldam**. SEE HAG

(14) woman (hired to do cleaning work) *n.*: **charwoman**. SEE MAID

(15) woman (who is charming and seductive) *n.*: **Circe**. SEE ENCHANTRESS

(16) woman (old and ugly) *n.*: **crone**. SEE HAG

(17) woman (who is married) *n.*: **feme covert**. SEE MARRIED

(18) woman (girl or young ... who is impish or playful) *n.*: **gamine** [French]. SEE GIRL

(19) woman (regarded as vicious and scolding) *n.*: **harridan**. SEE SHREW

(20) woman (young ... who is high-spirited or boisterous) *n.*: **hoyden**. SEE TOMBOY

(21) woman (with whom one is in love or has intimate relationship) *n.*: **inamorata**. SEE GIRLFRIEND

(22) woman (of a ... who is stately and regal, esp. tending towards voluptuous) *adj.*: **Junoesque**. SEE VOLUPTUOUS

(23) woman (who is head of a household) *n.*: **materfamilias** [Latin]. SEE HEAD OF HOUSEHOLD

(24) woman (state of being a ...) *n.*: **muliebrity**. SEE FEMININITY

(25) woman (of or relating to a ... who has never given birth) *adj.*: **nulliparous**. SEE CHILDLESS

(26) woman (who is pregnant for the first time or has had only one child) *n.*: **primipara**. SEE PREGNANT

(27) woman (relating to a ... right after childbirth) *adj.*: **puerperal**. SEE POSTPARTUM

(28) woman (right after childbirth) *n.*: **puerperium**. SEE POSTPARTUM

(29) woman (who is a shrew) *n.*: **termagant**. SEE SHREW

(30) woman (condition of a ... having masculine tendencies) *n.*: **viraginity** (*adj.*: **viraginous**). See Masculine

(31) woman (shrewish ...) *n.*: **vixen**. See shrew

(32) woman (who is a shrew) *n.*: **Xanthippe**. See shrew

womanhood *n.*: **muliebrity**. See femininity

womanizer (as in man who seduces women) *n.*: **Lothario**. See playboy

(2) womanizer (as in lecherous man or playboy) *n.*: **roué** [French]. See playboy

women (kept by wealthy lovers or protectors) *n.*: **demimonde**. ▮ Gigi's family is part of the **demimonde**, the class of women in 19th century France who were supported by well-to-do lovers or protectors. (Gerry Kowarsky, *With Help of Act Inc, Humor in "Gigi" Withstands Test of Time*, St. Louis Post-Dispatch, 07-22-1999, p. 4.)

(2) women (as a group) *n.*: **distaff** (often as in "distaff side"). ▮ Womantrek is for women only. Husbands, boyfriends, brothers and sons need not apply. Bordas, 41, hastens to explain that Womantrek is not an exercise in antimale discrimination. Rather, its aim is to create a **distaff** equivalent of male bonding. (Dan Chu, *Adventure: When Bonnie Bordas Leads a Wilderness Tour, There's No Male Call at All*, People, 05-08-1989, p. 135.)

(3) women (fond of ...) *adj.*: **philogynous**. (*n.*: **philogyny**) ▮ [To promote her book Misogynies, feminist writer Joan] Smith gave a reading at the radical Silver Moon bookshop. ... Accompanying her, as representative of the New Man supreme, was husband Francis Wheen, (who is hailed in Misogynies as "living proof of the possibility of a **philogynous** future"). (Author not given, *Diary*, The Sunday Times, 05-06-1990.) ▮ [I]ndustry and commerce will be looking for an extra 1.5 million employees over the next five years but ... fewer than a million new employees will come forward; 83 per cent of these will be women. Not out of **philogyny** then, but out of desperation, employers are rushing to make working practices less prejudicial to those who would like at least the choice of whether to have children. (Elizabeth Heron, *Graduate Careers: Wanted: Women With Skills; Workplace Conditions Are Changing as Employers Gear Up to Meet a Different Job Market*, The Independent [London], 02-15-1990.)

(4) women (government or society or group ruled by) *n.*: **gynarchy**. See government

(5) women (government by or political or social dominance by) *n.*: **gynocracy**. See government

(6) women (person who hates ...) *n.*: **misogynist**. See hatred

wonderful *adj.*: **frabjous** (often as in "Oh frabjous day!") [This derives from the line "O frabjous day! Callooh! Callay!" in Lewis Carroll's *Through the Looking Glass* (1872). The speaker was expressing his pleasure upon discovering that the Jabberwock had been killed, and we know he was pleased because "he chortled in his joy" — "chortled" itself being a more well-known Carroll coinage stemming from the same source.] ▮ Oh, **Frabjous** Day! A real American man would rather miss Thanksgiving Day dinner than Super Bowl Sunday, the true national campfire. ... For those lucky enough to actually be there ... it is the heartiest party of the year, the macho New Year's Eve, especially now that this endless TV day has been reaffirmed by billion-dollar network contracts. (Robert Lipsyte, *Backtalk; On Such a Macho Day, Reality is a Blur*, The New York Times, 01-25-1998.)

(2) wonderful *adj.*: **galluptious** [slang]. ▮ He painted his own little bestiary of self-styled animals and other friends with as much glee and gimlet-eyed subtlety as he used to play a rhinocerous on stage. His creatures are genetic mixtures that are sometimes as ludicrous as a cross between a chihuahua and a peccary. But they are blessed with such personalities and presence that they have their own **galluptious** but unimpeachable reality. (David Shirey, *Art Paintings by Zero Mostel Make the Viewer Chuckle and Think*, The New York Times, 07-27-1980.)

(3) wonderful (as in of the highest quality) *n.*: **first water** (usu. as in "of the first water"). See quality

(4) wonderful *adj.*: **galumptious**. See excellent

(5) wonderful *adj.*: **palmary**. See excellent

(6) wonderful *adj.*: **skookum**. See excellent

wood (of, relating to, or having the texture or appearance of) *adj.*: **ligneous**. ▮ The tree-saving tendency is part of the wider picture of Nimby [not in my back yard] environmentalism, the distinctive badge of those with time and money to waste. This arboreal sentimentality won't die out with the older generation, for even the young are bursting with **ligneous** lunacy. "Save the rainforests" is the modern version of the Children's Crusade. (Jane Jakeman, *A Nation Obsessed by Large Lumps of Wood*, Independent, 12-30-1994, p. 15.)

wooded *adj.*: **arboreous**. ▮ However, Monona is a Tree City, it owes its uniqueness to its **arboreous** nature, and one wonders if a regulation curtailing wholesale removal of greens would not be in order.

(J.T. Carstensen, *Downing of Monona Trees Cries for Regulations*, Wisconsin State Journal, 08-28-1995, p. 7A.)

(2) wooded *adj.*: **sylvan**. ∎ For more than 30 years, Ed and Eva Gumbert's 230-acre farm on the Etowah River in north Cherokee County has been their **sylvan** haven. It was ... a world of soaring hawks, majestic hardwood trees and unspoiled blue-ridged vistas. (Julie B. Hairston, *Asphalt Rumble — Proposed Northern Arc Has Proved a Dividing Highway, From Northside vs. Southside to Neighbor vs. Neighbor*, The Atlanta Journal and Constitution, 02-04-2002, p. B1.)

woods (of or relating to ..., or having many trees) *adj.*: **bosky**. SEE TREES

(2) woods (of or relating to) *adj.*: **sylvan**. SEE WOODED

woody *adj.*: **ligneous**. SEE WOOD

woolly (having a ... appearance) *adj.*: **flocculent**. SEE FLUFFY

word (which derives from the name of a real or fictitious person) *n.*: **eponym** (*adj.*: **eponymous**). ∎ The point to sadomasochistic sex, one assumes, is knowing when to stop. ... The [movie Quills] uses the life of the Marquis de Sade (1740-1814), the French aristocrat turned literary pornographer (whose very name became the **eponym** for the painful sex practices he wrote about), to examine the rights of an artist versus the rights of society. (Leah Rozen, *Screen, [Picks & Pans]*, People Weekly, 12-04-2000.)

(2) word (or form which has only one recorded use) *n.*: **hapax legomenon** [Greek]. ∎ Blimah is a biblical **hapax legomenon**, appearing in Job 26:7, within a paean to God's might as creator: "He it is who stretches out Zaphon over chaos; Who suspended earth over blimah." (Azzan Yadin, *A Web of Chaos: Bialik and Nietzsche on Language, Truth, and the Death of God*, Prooftexts: A Journal of Jewish Literary History, 03-22-2001.)

(3) word (misuse of ..., by confusing a similar one) *n.*: **malapropism**. ∎ When Dent was fired [by New York Yankee owner George Steinbrenner], Peterson, in a neat **malapropism**, said, "George has been languishing long and hard over this decision." (Tim Kurkjian, *The Boss Strikes Again — George Steinbrenner's Yanks Sank, So He Fired the Manager, of Course*, Sports Illustrated, 06-18-1990, p. 48.)

(4) word (just the right ... or phrase) *n.*: **mot juste** [French]. ∎ He is in such a rush to say so many things that he cannot always be bothered to find the **mot juste**: if *guys* is his trademark noun, *helluva* is Iacocca's favorite modifier. (Kurt Andersen, *A Spunky Tycoon Turned Superstar: Straight-Talking Lee Iacocca Becomes America's Hottest New Folk Hero*, Time, 04-01-1985, p. 30.)

(5) word (invented just for a particular occasion) *n.*: **nonce word**. ∎ Lexicographers must beware the dreaded one-time-only "**nonce**" **word**, such as "Disneyitis" or "Borkability" (which means, by the way, the potential for a candidate to be damaged by a media campaign). Coined to live in one article, **nonce words** die like mayflies. (Liesl Schillinger, *NYC What's the Word? The New Three-Volume Random House Slang Dictionary Is Right Up One Lexicographer's Alley*, Newsday, 05-02-1994, p. B4.)

(6) word (new ..., phrase or expression) *n.*: **neologism**. ∎ Back during Watergate, the President's men were always having to announce that he had "misspoke himself," an odd **neologism** that made it sound as though Nixon had just wet his pants. Just once it would be nice to hear a White House press secretary say, "The President made a faux pas." (Christopher Buckley, *Hoof In Mouth*, Forbes FYI, 05-04-1998, p. 31.)

(7) word (long ..., or one given to the use of) *n., adj.*: **sesquipedalian**. ∎ The longest word in the works of Shakespeare (Love's Labour's Lost) is honorificabilitudinitatibus, truly **sesquipedalian** but rarely used. (Laurence McNamee, *Dous-ies*, The Dallas Morning News, 04-27-1997, p. 9J.)

(8) word (or phrase which is being defined in a dictionary or elsewhere) *n.*: **definiendum**. SEE DEFINITION

(9) word (definition of a ... or phrase in a dictionary or elsewhere) *n.*: **definiens**. SEE DEFINITION

(10) word (of a ... which is pedantic) *adj.*: **inkhorn**. SEE PEDANTIC

(11) word (distortion or destruction of sense of ...) *n.*: **verbicide**. SEE DISTORTION

word list *n.*: **onomasticon**. ∎ Bodies are sometimes lost or stolen. He returned them. ... Not only was his profession unrecognized, there was not even a word for what he did. Words such as "brigand," or "pirate," or perhaps "body hunter" give some vague notion of it. Even the ... **onomasticon** was of no help to her. While she was able to find all sorts of names for mythological and religious figures who aided and abetted the human world, there was no name to be found for what he did. So she would call him "the body retriever," an invention of her own. (Manya Steinkoler, *The Body Retriever [Short Story]*, Literature and Psychology, 03-22-2002.)

(2) word list *n.*: **lexicon**. See dictionary

word play *n.*: **paronomasia**. ∎ Rosten's humor depends on comic dialect, the solecism, the pun, the malapropism ... [and] **paronomasia**. (Don Nilsen, *Humorous Contemporary Jewish-American Authors: An Overview of the Criticism [Ethnic Humor]*, Melus, 12-01-1996, p. 71.)

(2) word play (as in pun) *n.*: **paronomasia**. See pun

word of mouth (by ...) *adj., adv.*: **viva voce** [Latin]. See verbal

wordiness *n.*: **circumlocution**. See verbosity

(2) wordiness *n.*: **logorrhea**. See verbosity

(3) wordiness *n.*: **macrology**. See verbosity

(4) wordiness *n.*: **periphrasis**. See verbosity

(5) wordiness (through use of unnecessary words or phrases) *n.*: **pleonasm**. See redundancy

words (pronounced alike, but meaning is different) *n.*: **homophone**. ∎ You warned about body piercing and noted precautions to be taken against infections in those who "can't resist a naval ring." Isn't a naval ring something worn only by Annapolis graduates? Guess you meant navel. Ah, for a spell checker that warns about **homophones**! (Author not given, *Letters*, Time, 07-12-1999, p. 8.)

(2) words (of or relating to) *adj.*: **lexical**. ∎ One good authority suggests that "an educated speaker of English can understand, and potentially use, at least 50,000 words." ... But Chambers Dictionary, the official Scrabble dictionary in Britain, has some 300,000 words, and the Oxford English Dictionary has 500,000. ... What are we to make of such **lexical** waste, such idle riches? (Thomas Sutcliffe, *Glossary/Scrabbling for Linguistic Domination*, Independent, 11-24-1994, p. 23.)

(3) words (study of) *n.*: **logology**. ∎ The essence of **logology** is discovering word patterns, as in palindromes, e.g., deified; tautonyms, e.g., murmur; words dependent on alphabetic order, e.g., almost; and isograms, long words in which no letter appears more than once, e.g., ambidextrously. (Howard Richler, *A Logologist Could Probably Turn Water into Wine*, The Montreal Gazette, 03-28-1998, p. J6.)

(4) words (dispute about or battle of ...) *n.*: **logomachy**. ∎ A **logomachy** about "discrimination" and "equal opportunity" is unlikely to solve a subtle distributive problem encountered in intercollegiate athletics, but colleges can foster harmony if they are allowed to adopt local policies of distributive justice. (Louis M. Guenin, *A Choice of Extent, [Women in Intercollegiate Athletics]*, National Forum, 03-22-1997, p. 22.)

(5) words (love of) *n.*: **logophilia**. ∎ Where most rock music is fueled by booze, drugs and a cranky dissatisfaction, the John Huss Moderate Combo's tunes are propelled by pure **logophilia**. Clever, playful and indefatigable, Huss' wordplay dominates his songs with unexpected rhymes and kaleidoscopic imagery. (Rick Reger, *Music, Concert Line*, The Chicago Tribune, 01-24-1997, p. 19.)

(6) words (aversion to or fear of) *n.*: **logophobia**. ∎ Does using a large vocabulary make you "elitist"? ... The author of A Little Stranger, castigated in many review pages, wonders if her attackers suffer from **logophobia**. (Candia McWilliam, *In My View*, The Times of London, 01-29-1989.)

(7) words (excessive use of or obsession with) *n.*: **verbomania**. ∎ [Today's] lawyers fall victim to the belief that all human experience can be verbalized. ... [But] if one looks back in the history of the law, it appears that the use of demonstrative evidence was much more widespread, ... in 19th century courtrooms than it is today. Perhaps this historical curiosity tends to confirm my hypothesis concerning the source of [today's] lawyers' **verbomania**. (Mark Foster, *Demonstrative Evidence Often Speaks Louder Than Words*, The Legal Times, 07-1982, p. A2.)

(8) words (inability to understand spoken or written ... due to brain injury) *n.*: **aphasia**. See uncomprehending

(9) words (or speech used by members of the underworld or a particular group) *n.*: **argot**. See vernacular

(10) words (or speech used by members of the underworld or a particular group) *n.*: **cant**. See vernacular

(11) words (misuse or strained use of ... or phrases, sometimes deliberate) *n.*: **catachresis**. See misuse

(12) words (excessive use of ...) *n.*: **circumlocution**. See verbosity

(13) words (which are meaningless or deceptive) *n.*: **flummery**. See deceptive

(14) words (excessive use of ...) *n.*: **logorrhea**. See verbosity

(15) words (inability to recall meaning of ... or using them incorrectly) *n.*: **paramnesia**. See amnesia

(16) words (excessive use of ...) *n.*: **periphrasis**. See verbosity

(17) words (one who studies ... and language) *n.*: **philologist**. See linguist

(18) words (having more than three syllables) *adj.*: **polysyllabic**. See syllables

(19) words (given to the use of long ...) *adj.*: **sesquipedalian**. SEE WORD

wordy (as in rambling) *adj.*: **discursive**. SEE RAMBLING

work (doing ... only when the boss is watching) *n.*: **eyeservice** [Although this word may not appear in any dictionaries, its does appear in the Bible. Colossians 3:22 provides: "Servants, obey in all things your masters according to the flesh; not with eyeservice, as menpleasers; but in singleness of heart, fearing God." Thus, while obviously not a common word, it is nevertheless presumably mentioned and discussed in English-speaking churches all over the world every Sunday (as evidenced in part by the example), and in that sense, is not archaic. Plus, it's a useful word.] ∎ Do you work hard or hardly work? My pastor posed this question recently during a sermon. He asked members of the congregation if they engaged in "**eyeservice**." ... In other words, do you work hard only when the boss has his or her eyes on you? (Michelle Singletary, *Working Wonders*, The Washington Post, 01-09-2003.)

(2) work (forced ... for little or no pay) *n.*: **corvee**. SEE SERVITUDE

(3) work (avoider) *n.*: **embusque** [French]. SEE SLACKER

(4) work (as in toil) *v.i.*: **moil**. SEE TOIL

workaholic *n.*: **Stakhanovite** [This word derives from Alexei Stakhanov, a Russian miner who devised a system to award recognition and special privileges to Soviet workers for output beyond production norms. Although a noun, the word is frequently used in the adjectival sense of "hardworking" or "obsessive"]. ∎ The first thing you must understand about [baby-boomers], is how hard they work. Among them a 60-hour week is standard, with many — especially the younger ones, the singles, and the entrepreneurs — reporting 70, 80, even 90 hours on the job each week. Experts confirm the boomers' reports of **Stakhanovite** schedules. (Walter Kiechel, III, *The Workaholic Generation*, Fortune, 04-10-1989.)

worker (Mexican ... allowed to work in U.S.) *n.*: **bracero**. SEE LABORER

workshop (spec. a final effort made by architectural students to complete a solution to a problem within an allotted time, but sometimes is used to refer to any kind of ... or brainstorming session) *n.*: **charette** (or **charrette**). ∎ A six-day design workshop starting tonight will bring together neighborhood residents, business owners and public agencies to brainstorm about the future of the area from Uptown to Lyndale Av. S. and Lake St. Called the West Lake Design **Charette**, the workshop will tackle a range of issues, from parking proposals to a Metro Transit bus layover station. (Linda Mack, *Uptown Workshop Will Seek Solutions For a Neighborhood Swamped With Cars*, Star Tribune [Minneapolis, MN], 04-16-1998.)

worldview *n.*: **weltanschauung** [German]. ∎ [Marlon is an excellent African-American Scrabble player who is having bad luck on his tile draws.] I point out that the problem may not be Marlon's letters but Marlon's **weltanschauung**. "Surely he doesn't think The Man is fixing his tiles," Matt says. He doesn't have to think it's racial, I say. (Stefan Fatsis, *Word Freak*, Houghton Mifflin [2001], p. 279.)

worm-shaped *adj.*: **vermiform**. ∎ Even more eccentric is Eric Roy's *Worm on Quartz*, a fantasy in which a smoky quartz suggests an abstract sea cucumber with an inlaid and colorful **vermiform** shape on its back. (Donald Miller, *Cases of Wonder: Jewel Beauty, Museum Treasures at Carnegie*, Pittsburgh Post-Gazette, 03-201-1999, p. D11.)

worms (of, relating to, resembling or caused by) *adj.*: **vermicular**. ∎ Another artist who mixes media audaciously and goes for complex conceptual effects is Mona Hatoum. ... She is also greatly concerned, in various ways, with the **vermicular**, writhing shapes of intestines and the metamorphosis of domestic items into something strange and nasty. (Martin Gayford, *The Arts: As Majestically Italian as Olive Oil and Garlic Art*, The Sunday Telegraph, 08-30-1998, p. 11.)

worn-out (and broken-down) *adj.*: **raddled**. ∎ Thus you get ... what seems likely to be the most tasteless scene of the year in which Ethan gets to give a **raddled** old hooker (played by 50's sex bomb Mamie Van Doren who really must need the money to endure such degrading treatment) a bed bath and a grope. (Author not given, *Culture: It's Slack by Name and Slack by Nature*, Birmingham Post, 05-10-2002, p. 15.)

(2) worn-out (as in decrepit) *adj.*: **spavined**. SEE DECREPIT

worried (as if by a witch or by unfounded fears) *adj.*: **hagridden**. SEE TORMENTED

worry *v.t., v.i., n.*: **cark**. ∎ I don't remember all our dogs, because they were many and they constantly faced danger and were more expendable than dogs nurtured in the lap of luxury without **cark** or care. (John Gould, *The Life and Times of Farm Dogs*, The Christian Science Monitor, 04-17-1998, p. 13.)

(2) worry (as in a state of nervous tension, often with irritability) *n.*: **fantod**. SEE TENSION

(3) worry (as in anxiety) *n.*: **inquietude**. SEE ANXIETY

(4) worry (or complain) *v.i.*: **repine**. SEE COMPLAIN

(5) worry (state of ...) *n.*: **swivet** (as in "in a swivet") *inf.* SEE DISTRESS

(6) worry (as in trouble) *n.*: **tsuris** [Yiddish]. SEE TROUBLE

worsening *adj.*: **ingravescent**. ❚ To Americans who worry that their country is going the way of ancient Rome, only faster, two of the most alarming trends are the **ingravescent** influence of money in politics and the exponential growth of gambling. As was inevitable, these have merged. ... [T]he gambling industry poured nearly $4 million in "soft money" into the Democratic and Republican parties last year. (Martin Dyckman, *Gambling Interests Invest in Politics*, St. Petersburg Times [Florida], 07-08-1997, p. 11A.)

worship (of dead people) *n.*: **necrolatry**. ❚ While many of the most devout of the Elvis People are concurrently devout Christians — and there are those who think that referring to Elvis as "The King" is blasphemous — there is a strain of Elvis worship that veers close to **necrolatry**. (Philip Martin, *In the Land of Elvis, Death Meant Never Being Obsolete*, The Arkansas Democrat-Gazette, 08-19-2001, p. J2.)

(2) worship (often in a servile manner) *v.i.*: **genuflect**. SEE KNEEL

(3) worship (not necessarily sincere or unforced) *n.*: **obeisance**. SEE HOMAGE

(4) worship (of women) *n.*: **philogyny**. SEE WOMEN

worshipful (biography) *n.*: **hagiography** (*adj*: **hagiographic**). SEE BIOGRAPHY

worst *adj.*: **pessimal**. ❚ Local governments should have complete discretion to use allocated federal reconstruction dollars for maintenance. ... In that way, local governments could choose optimal strategies for the use of all tax dollars available to them, rather than the "**pessimal**" one they now employ. (Lucius J. Riccio, *An Ounce Of Prevention*, Newsday [New York], 08-04-1992, p. 36.)

worthless (matter) *n.*: **dross**. ❚ [The Clinton impeachment trial] was supposed to be a monumental event, a sombre and historical process that either demonstrated America at its best or America at its worst. But most assuredly, it was not expected to tumble immediately into the **dross** of daytime television drudgery, as insignificant and non-compelling as the endlessly scrolling TV listings. (Author not given, *Bill in Reruns But Hillary Eyes New Show*, The Toronto Star, 01-18-1999.)

(2) worthless (deeming something as ...) *n.*: **floccinaucinihilipilification**. ❚ [North Carolina Senator Jesse Helms:] "I note your distress at my **floccinaucinihilipilification** of the Comprehensive Test Ban Treaty." (*Perspectives*, Newsweek, 08-09-1999.)

(3) worthless *adj.*: **nugatory**. ❚ Judge Bork raises yet another argument, which is that the President has the power to pardon anyone accused or convicted of "offenses against the United States" and thus could render any conviction **nugatory** by pardoning himself. (Daniel E. Troy, *The Indictment Option*, National Review, 04-06-1998, p. 26.)

(4) worthless (as in made without regard to quality) *adj.*: **catchpenny**. SEE INFERIOR

(5) worthless (as in useless) *adj.*: **inutile**. SEE USELESS

(6) worthless (something which is ...) *n.*: **vermiform appendix**. SEE USELESS

wrapping (act of ..., tying or binding up or together) *n.*: **ligature**. SEE TYING

wreath (for the head) *n.*: **chaplet**. SEE GARLAND

wretched (esp. as to poverty) *adj.*: **abject**. ❚ Women now make up more than half of the estimated 50 million Chinese living in **abject** poverty, it was reported yesterday amid calls for greater government intervention. (Author not given, *More Than Half of Nation's 50 Million Poor Are Women*, The Washington Times, 04-09-1999, p. A12.)

(2) wretched (as in despicable, person) *n.*: **caitiff**. SEE DESPICABLE

wrinkle *n., v.t.*: **rimple**. ❚ [In the Bush-Gore 2000 election fight,] Bob Dole recommended that both campaigns agree to take a second look at invalidated ballots from military personnel. Noting that a hand recount in South Florida is carefully scrutinizing ballots for "a dimple, a pimple or **rimple**," Dole argued, "If you're going to do that, you ought to look at the intent of the military absentee ballots." (Kathy Kiely, *Bush Fights Rejection of Military Ballots — Officials Mark 1,420 Overseas Votes Invalid*, USA Today, 11-20-2000, p. 4A.)

wrinkled (very ...) *adj.*: **rugose**. ■ A couple of years ago, right before an endometrial biopsy, [the nurse] and the female gynecologist stared suddenly at my [vagina]. Was it shrunken and dry like an old woman's supposedly is? Was it too colorful — more purple than pink? [Was] its inside unusually **rugose**, both characteristics said to be indicative of a woman who enjoys sex and has had a lot of it? (Joanna Frueh, *Vaginal Aesthetics*, Hypatia, 09-22-2003.)

write (irresistible compulsion to ...) *n.*: **cacoëthes scribendi** [Latin]. ■ The diametrically opposite disorder is writer's itch. "Scribble, scribble, scribble, Mr. Gibbon," George III (or, some say, his brother, the Duke of Gloucester) famously buttonholed the historian of the Decline and Fall of the Roman Empire. Linked to the libido sciendi, this **cacoëthes scribendi** had already reached epidemic proportions by the Renaissance. (Roy Porter, *Reading Is Bad For Your Health*, History Today, 03-01-1998, p. 11.)

(2) write (inability to ...) *n.*: **disgraphia**. ■ Some [children] have auditory processing problems; some are dyslexic and don't see words the way other children do; some have **disgraphia**, a writing disorder; and some have attention deficit disorder. (Ellen Sweets, *Lap-Time Lessons: Parents Can Give Children the Gift of an Early Love of Reading*, The Dallas Morning News, 06-02-1998, p. 16A.)

(3) write (or speak at length on a subject) *v.i.*: **expatiate**. SEE EXPOUND

(4) write *v.t.*: **indite**. SEE COMPOSE

(5) write (or speak in a scholarly manner, often used in a derogatory fashion) *v.i.*: **lucubrate**. SEE DISCOURSE

writer (or speaker who is dull and boring) *n.*: **dryasdust**. SEE BORING

(2) writer (of fiction, esp. who writes in quantity) *n.*: **fictioneer**. SEE NOVELIST

(3) writer (professional ...) *n.*: **wordmonger**. SEE AUTHOR

writing (of ... which is clear and elegant) *adj.*: **Addisonian** [after English essayist Joseph Addison (1672-1719)]. ■ And then you met him. You did if you were a working journalist in New York or covered a national political campaign. [Murray Kempton] enjoyed being in a group of reporters; he liked to try out ideas for columns, dropping fully formed **Addisonian** sentences into conversation to see which ones got a nod or a laugh. The winners turned up in the next day's paper. (David Von Drehle, *A Journalist's Singular Voice*, The Washington Post, 05-06-1997, p. D1.)

(2) writing (of ... which is concise, precise or refined; lit. "as if engraved in a precious stone") *adj.*: **lapidary**. ■ [Kennedy Fraser] trusts her keen eye, her subject matter and good writing to tell her stories. ... Fraser has produced a book of exquisite set pieces — compelling stories told in seamless narrative, in **lapidary** prose. (Maureen Dezell, *Book Review*, The Boston Globe, 01-30-1997, p. E8.)

(3) writing (or speech characterized by the affected choice of obscure words) *n.*: **lexiphanicism** (*adj.*: **lexiphanic**). ■ Can a book be both funny and tiresome? It is not the logorrhoea [wordiness] of the narrator, Harry Driscoll, that bothers me, nor his **lexiphanic** prose ... (I love reading with a dictionary to hand). (Debra Adelaide, *In Short*, Sydney Morning Herald, 03-29-2003.)

(4) writing (poor ..., esp. characterized by the affected choice of archaic words) *n.*: **tushery**. ■ This novel, set in the last days of Rome in the Eastern Empire, ... tells the story of [a woman] who discovers that she is a born doctor ..., but soon realises that there is no room for her in a society where medicine is the province of men. As a piece of historical romance it is saved from **tushery** by down-to-earth writing and a quite remarkable amount of information about early medicine which proves fascinating in itself. (Robery Nye, *Review of "The Beacon at Alexandria" by Gillian Bradshaws*, The Guardian [London], 02-06-1987.)

(5) writing (inability to understand ... due to a brain injury) *n.*: **aphasia**. SEE UNCOMPREHENDING

(6) writing (of, by or pertaining to ... by an author) *adj.*: **auctorial**. SEE AUTHOR

(7) writing (very enthusiastic or excited ... or speech) *n.*: **dithyramb**. SEE ENTHUSIASTIC

(8) writing (or speech which is cryptic or obscure, esp. deliberately) *adj.*: **elliptical**. SEE CRYPTIC

(9) writing (table) *n.*: **escritoire**. SEE DESK

(10) writing (or speech which is pompous or bombastic) *n.*: **grandiloquence**. SEE POMPOSITY

(11) writing (study of ..., as in handwriting, esp. to study character) *n.*: **graphology**. SEE HANDWRITING

(12) writing (or speech which is trite or simplistic) *n.*: **pablum** (also **pabulum**). SEE TRITENESS

(13) writing (in shorthand) *n.*: **tachygraphy**. SEE SHORTHAND

writings (collection of ... by an author) *n.*: **chrestomathy**. SEE ANTHOLOGY

(2) writings (or artistic works created in the author's or artist's youth) *n*.: **juvenilia**. See COMPOSITIONS

written material (inability to read or understand) *n*.: **alexia**. ∎ Researchers conducting studies on **alexia** found that damage to certain areas of the left hemisphere resulted in the inability to read and write; individuals could not recognize words and their respective meanings at an automatic level. (Karen J. Rooney, *Dyslexia Revisited: History, Educational Philosophy, and Clinical Assessment Applications*, Intervention in School & Clinic, 09-01-1995, p. 6.)

wrong (reasoning which is intended to mislead or rationalize) *n*.: **casuistry**. See FALLACIOUS

(2) wrong (engaging in argument which may be ..., as in specious) *adj., n*.: **eristic**. See SPECIOUS

wrongdoer *n*.: **malefactor**. ∎ In the crowded western part of New Delhi sits a vast but packed prison surrounded by high yellow walls. Built in 1958 for a few thousand thieves, murderers and other **malefactors**, Tihar Jail is now home to more than 11,500 prisoners. (Meenakshi Ganguly, *Asia: A Place to Call Home — New Delhi's Tihar Jail Has Gone From Being an Unruly Hellhole to a Global Model for Prison Reform*, Time International, 12-11-2000, p. 32.)

(2) wrongdoer *n*.: **miscreant**. ∎ Although the U.S. claims the legal right to try anyone for the murder of an American citizen abroad, prosecutors first have to get their hands on the suspect, and that has proved a major stumbling block even in cases where **miscreants** are firmly identified. (Johanna McGeary, *World: Sifting For Answers — As the Dead Are Buried, the Gritty Work of Finding the Terrorists Proceeds Slowly in Africa*, Time, 08-24-1998, p. 48.)

wrongdoing (in public office) *n*.: **malversation**. ∎ A third charge is that [President Clinton's first-term national security adviser Anthony] Lake is guilty of **malversation**, the evidence being a token $5,000 fine he was assessed by the Justice Department for failing to sell several stock holdings promptly. (Jacob Heilbrunn, *Dr. Maybe Heads for the CIA*, The New Republic, 03-24-1997.)

(2) wrongdoing (confession of ...) *n*.: **peccavi**. See CONFESSION

X

x-rays (not transparent to ...) *adj*.: **radiopaque**. ∎ If you've always wondered how to translate plethysmograph (an electronic device to monitor the amount of blood in the body), head degausser (a demagnetizer on the head of an electronic speaker) and **radiopaque** (insulation against x-rays) into Hebrew, you now have a new source of information. (Judy Siegel-Itzkovich, *Seeds of Hope Beneath Charred Remains*, Jerusalem Post, 11-01-1998, p. 10.)

Y

yawning (and stretching) *n*.: **pandiculation**. ∎ His constantly changing answering-machine message has featured recitations on the pre-sleep state of "**pandiculation**" and sportscast-style accounts of the recent Short-Kasparov chess match. (Peter Goodman, *Piano Forte: The Pianist from Central Casting He's Not; But Awadagin Pratt Goes His Own Way, and It's Paying Off*, Newsday, 01-09-1994, p. 10.)

year (awful ...) *n*.: **annus horribilis** [Latin]. ∎ The Queen famously called 1992 — a year of separations, divorce and scandal — her **annus horribilis**. The emotional low point may have come on Nov. 20, her 45th wedding anniversary, when Windsor Castle caught fire. (James Collins, *Restoring the Windsors [And Windsor Castle, Too]*, Time, 12-01-1997, p. 60.)

(2) year (of wonders) *n*.: **annus mirabalis** [Latin]. ∎ The year 1492 was Spain's **annus mirabilis**, a year of marvels. A Spanish Pope was elected that year, a Borja from Catalonia. (He was called Borgia in Italy, where the Two Sicilies already had Spanish rulers.) King Ferdinand and Queen Isabella, who had just united their kingdoms, drove the Moors from the Spanish peninsula by a military victory at Granada. (Garry Wills, *History: 1492 vs. 1892 vs. 1992: Al Three Imperial Moments, Three Columbuses Reveal Something About Their Different Eras*, Time, 10-07-1991, p. 61.)

(3) year (great ...) *n*.: **annus terrificus** [Latin]. ∎ [The good things that happened in 1992] may not be a solid trend, only a faint glimmering, a tiding. Even so, if the tiding is genuine, then it would be justified, with a suitable bow to the Queen [who called 1992 an "annus horribilis"], to rename 1992: **annus terrificus**! (Author not given, *The Best Of 1992 — Standouts, From Pained Royals to Royal Pains to the Aristocrats of Talent*, Time, 01-04-1993, p. 53.)

yearn (for) *v.t*.: **desiderate**. See WANT

yearning *n*.: **appetence**. See CRAVING

(2) yearning *n.*: **avidity**. SEE CRAVING

yell (as in screech) *v.i.*: **caterwaul**. SEE SCREECH

yellow (strong ...) *adj.*: **gamboge**. ∎ His belly is no longer swollen [having just received a new liver]. His skin is pink, not **gamboge** yellow. He can eat. He can live. (Michael Bywater, *Giving the Greatest Gift of All*, Independent on Sunday, 06-15-1997, p. 42.)

yen (condition involving ... to eat nonfood items) *n.*: **pica**. SEE CRAVING

yes man *n.*: **lickspittle**. SEE SYCOPHANT

yet *adv.*: **withal**. SEE NEVERTHELESS

young *adj.*: **neanic**. ∎ [In 1964,] the world was being made aware of something called the Free Speech Movement. [A graduate student at UC-Berkeley, Jack Weinberg, stated]: "We don't trust anybody over 30." Despite being beyond the deadline set by this whimsical imperative of **neanic** gerontology. ... I managed to write a couple of pieces about the FSM. (Gene Marine, *Geezers of the FSM*, The San Francisco Examiner, 09-25-1994, p. A19.)

(2) young (hatred of ... people) *n.*: **misopedia**. SEE HATRED

youngster (male ... who is awkward and clumsy) *n.*: **hobbledehoy**. SEE CLUMSY

(2) youngster *n.*: **moppet**. SEE CHILD

youth (male ... who is awkward and clumsy) *n.*: **hobbledehoy**. SEE CLUMSY

youthful *adj.*: **neanic**. SEE YOUNG

Z

zeal (as in full of energy) *n.*: **brio**. SEE ENERGY

(2) zeal (undue ... for one subject or idea) *n.*: **monomania**

zealot *n.*: **energumen**. SEE FANATIC

zealous *adj.*: **perfervid**. SEE IMPASSIONED

zesty (agreeably ... in taste or flavor) *adj.*: **piquant**. ∎ In ancient times, Arab traders spread tales that precious Eastern spices grew in lakes guarded by winged animals. Later, explorers risked death searching for a seagoing spice route. ... Indian

"fusion" — the cross-fertilization of traditional Western cuisine with the aromatic and **piquant** flavors of the East — has arrived. (Linda Kulman, *Hotter Than Ginger Spice*, U.S. News & World Report, 03-22-1999, p. 72.)

About the Author

Peter E. Meltzer has had a lifelong interest in lexicology. He started creation of this thesaurus in 1995 when he concluded that traditional thesauruses rarely offered interesting synonym choices and that there was a key flaw inherent in the structure of these thesauruses. In compliling the word list and the examples, he has consulted over 500 dictionaries, word books, periodicals, newspapers and internet sources.

When not plying his avocation, Mr. Meltzer is a practicing attorney in Philadelphia, specializing in the field of creditors' rights, and representing a number of major financial institutions. He has published numerous articles in various legal periodicals and has taught classes as an Adjunct Professor of Law at Rutgers University Law School periodically since 1991. Since 1997, he has been selected to the *Bar Register of Preeminent Lawyers in America*.

His e-mail address is pmeltzer@meltzerlaw.net